THE LINCOLN LIBRARY OF SOCIAL STUDIES

THE LINCOLN LIBRARY OF SOCIAL STUDIES

THE FRONTIER PRESS COMPANY, COLUMBUS, OHIO

FIRST EDITION, 1968
EIGHTH EDITION, 1978

LIBRARY OF CONGRESS CARD NUMBER 68-1285
ISBN: 0-912168-02-1

Geography and Travel

SUBJECT GUIDE

Longs Peak, highest point in the snow-capped Front Range of the Rocky Mountains. Named for explorer Stephen Long, it rises 14,255 feet in Rocky Mountain National Park.

Mt. Rushmore National Memorial was established in 1929 and completed in 1941 in the Black Hills. Sculptor Gutzon Borglum and his son Lincoln carved the colossal busts of Washington, Jefferson, Theodore Roosevelt, and Lincoln.

Spider Rock, Canyon de Chelly, Monument Valley, Arizona. The giant sandstone pinnacle, in an area inhabited by Navajos, rises 800 feet from the canyon floor. The valley became a national monument in 1931.

Bryce Canyon (Utah), covering 56 square miles, was created a national park in 1928. Named for pioneer Ebenezer Bryce, it is noted for magnificent forests and the natural coloring of its eroded rock formations. (*Union Pacific Railroad*)

Above: **Castle Geyser,** Yellowstone National Park, Wyoming. The cone resembles the ruins of an old castle. Established in 1872, Yellowstone is the oldest national park. Left: **Bridalveil Falls** drops 620 feet to the floor of Yosemite Valley in California.

Below: **Grand Canyon,** Arizona, from Bright Angel Point, North rim. The Colorado gorge, 217 miles long and 4–18 miles wide, is a spectacular example of erosion. Discovered in 1540 by Garcia Lopez de Cardeñas, the canyon records vast geologic change.

Canadian Parliament, Ottawa—Winter view of the Parliament through the iron tracery of the central gate. The three Gothic-style buildings stand on a promontory over the Ottawa River. The original center building was designed mainly by Thomas Fuller. Begun in 1860, the group was completed in 1865. In 1916 the center was swept by fire, but rebuilt by 1920. The central Peace Tower, with a carillon of 53 bells, is 291 feet high, patterned after the famous Big Ben clock-tower of Britain's Parliament. The center section contains the Senate Chamber, House of Commons, and government offices. (*Canadian Dominion Bureau of Statistics*)

Canadian Government Scenes: Quebec. The Citadel rises 350 feet above Quebec—the only fortified city in North America. Controlling the St. Lawrence waterway, it was built between 1823 and 1832, and was the site of wartime conferences in 1943 and 1944 between Churchill and Roosevelt. Below: In a colorful ceremony the Guard is changed. Garrisoned by the Royal 22nd Regiment, the fortress is the official Quebec residence of Canada's Governor General. (*Quebec Department of Tourism*)

PHOTOGRAPHY IN EARTH SCIENCE—This panorama of Nevada, Arizona, and California was taken from an aircraft at near-space altitude. Through infrared focusing, the camera defines earth characteristics not evident in normal color or black and white. The results aid in establishing earth resources criteria. The deep reds are reflected from chlorophyll in plant life. In the foreground above is Las Vegas, with scattered lawns and trees. The stream from Las Vegas to Lake Mead (center left) provides moisture for growth along its banks. Flowing from Lake Mead to Lake Mojave, the Colorado River moves through rocky areas without plant life. Right of Lake Mojave lies Needles, Cal., whose irrigated fields provide the large red pattern. At left are mountains tinged with red, indicating forests. For geologists, tonal differences provide a key to earth structure, stratification, and the location of river deltas. Such information is also useful to agronomists and foresters in preserving natural resources. Future applications include determining crop life-cycle states and yields. The data will also assist in locating hidden minerals and oil deposits. Other contributions will lie in expanding air and water pollution controls. (*Courtesy Hycon, Monrovia, Cal.*)

Geography and Travel

INTRODUCTION

The word geography comes from *ge* and *grapho*, two Greek words which, in combination, mean a description of the earth. Geography differs from geology and other sciences of the earth in the fact that geography studies the earth as the abode of mankind. It is closely related, in certain of its aspects, to the sciences of economics, history, astronomy, botany, zoology, and meteorology.

Divisions. Geography is usually classified, on the basis of its subject matter, into mathematical geography, physical geography, or physiography, and biological geography. Mathematical geography concerns the size, shape, and movements of the earth; physical geography deals with the layers of the earth's surface—land, sea, and air; and biological geography studies the life conditions of plants and animals, on the one hand, and of man on the other.

The geography of man discusses the races of mankind and their distribution throughout the earth; it discusses also density of population and the various types of human occupation—fishing, hunting, pasturing, agriculture, mining, manufacture, and commerce. That part of human geography which is concerned with man's industries is classified as economic, or commercial, geography. The study of mankind by countries is known as political geography.

Development of Geography. Nearly all parts of the world have been inhabited by men from very early times and, consequently, have been known in a certain sense. Such knowledge, however, does not constitute geography. The science of geography begins only when people attempt to describe by word or chart the relations of one part of the earth's surface to other parts.

Advance in geographical knowledge has been due mainly to exploration and enterprise. The rate of advance, however, has been highly irregular. Three chief periods of progress may be roughly distinguished: first, that of ancient Greece, when the first serious attempts were made to describe and to explain scientifically the varied conditions of different localities; secondly, the age of discovery, from the 15th to the 19th century, when the main features of the earth were finally learned; and, lastly, the modern scientific period, more or less overlapping the second in time and continuing to the present, when the utmost resources of science have been systematically utilized to chart and to describe every part of the earth's surface.

As a descriptive and systematic science, geography is of comparatively recent origin. Its foundation is due in large part to Alexander von Humboldt, a German scholar who was born in 1769. He developed and supported with observed facts the concept of the earth in evolution, which had been previously set forth in outline by the philosopher Kant. Advancing from this fundamental conception, recent geographers have devoted much of their attention to studies of the effect of geographical environment on human settlement and ways of life.

The Earth and Mankind. The degree of man's dependence on the earth is apt to be obscured in a highly developed society. In point of fact, both in the state of savagery and of civilization, his activities and very life rest solely on the bounty of the earth. A sudden rise or fall of 100° in the mean temperature of the earth's surface would wipe out civilization and probably exterminate the human race.

Climate not only determines what plants and animals can thrive so as to enable any people to subsist, but it exerts decisive effects on their appearance, their stature, their vigor, and their health. The tropics, while bountiful, discourage activity. The polar regions restrict all manner of life. But the seasonal changes of the temperate zones not only predispose populations to activity but force them to make use of their resources to provide against the winters.

Mountains and coasts have served to restrict settlements; rivers and plains, to extend them. Each of these natural features has placed a characteristic imprint on the society which it dominated, largely fashioning its mode of life, its customs, morals, and temperament.

With the growth of inventions, however, the range of the earth's gifts to man has multiplied and has tended to free him from the effects of a restricted environment. Minerals and waterfalls, once useless, now provide shelter, heat, light, power, and transportation in extraordinary abundance. These developments, together with the world-wide exchange of commodities, processes, and ideas, multiply the bonds of man to the earth but also make these bonds much more elastic. To an ever greater degree the earth itself, rather than any particular locality, is becoming the environment of each person. One result is a tendency toward uniformity. Another is an extremely rapid increase of population, the growing pressure of which, in the opinion of many observers, is full of portent for human institutions and customs.

Geography in Schools. The first modern geography in English which was written explicitly for use in schools appeared in 1746. It was called *Introduction to Geography* and was published in England by J. Cowley, "geographer to his Majesty." The first professor of geography in an American university was Arnold Henry Guyot, appointed by Princeton University in 1854.

The study of geography has long held an important place in the public schools of America. The manner of teaching the subject, however, has changed considerably in the past 70 years. The major emphasis was first placed on the facts of political geography. More especially in the years following 1890, physical geography received greater attention. In the past few decades, the study of "home geography" has been favored, chiefly as a means of making pupils familiar with geographical causes operating in their own neighborhood; this familiarity in turn has enabled them to see how larger regions of the earth are affected by the same causes. Finally, with the development of human geography, regional studies are encouraged in order to determine the factors of all kinds which have affected human habitation in a particular region or may be expected to do so in the future.

Value of the Study. A knowledge of geography is necessary for the intelligent reading of newspapers and of books. Such knowledge enables one, as a citizen, to form sounder opinions of the foreign countries with which our government has relations or with which our merchants deal. The study may also impart a new interest to the materials which we handle, enabling us to picture, more or less accurately, the distant scenes from which have come our tin, cork, rubber, tea, chocolate, and other articles of common use.

Geography is, to a large extent, the study of causes. To learn many facts, more or less isolated, about countries, rivers, cities, and peoples has its value. It is more enlightening, however, to understand the *causes* behind the facts; to know, for example, *why* Arizona is dry, *why* northern Europe is warmer than Labrador, and *why* Chicago has grown up where it is. Familiarity with the reasons lying behind such facts gives us a new interest also in the conditions of our own locality.

Travel. Improved means of transportation within the past century have made it possible for hundreds now to travel for each one that did so in earlier times. Travel has become a new form of enjoyment and a new means of instruction. The novelty of unfamiliar scenes, the glamor of places famous in history, the fascination of nature in its most charming or its most desolate aspects, engage the mind and bring home to it the varied panorama of the great world in which we live.

Geography a Substitute for Travel. Many people, however, lack the financial means and the leisure necessary for extensive travel. For such people, geography provides the nearest equivalent of travel. By the printed word and by picture, one may visit the most interesting and the most remote parts of the world. He may see the head-hunters of Borneo, the crowded cities of China, the treeless steppes of central Asia, or the jungles of the Amazon, inhabited by naked savages. Under the guidance of what he reads, he may take a trip to the "land of the midnight sun," and he may enjoy the beauties of Yellowstone park or of Paris.

Plan of Department of Geography. In the following pages, the geography of the world is treated by continents. This plan has at least two distinct advantages over an alphabetic arrangement of geographical topics. In the first place, it is possible in this way to bring into strong relief the contrast between the continents. Secondly, the reader is enabled to obtain a single view of each continent as a whole. There are certain aspects of geography which cannot be classified under continents. Such, for example, are the oceans, the zones, and the movements of the earth. A treatment of these general facts concerning the earth precedes the description of the continents.

Treatment of Countries. Following the general account of each continent, the countries and other political divisions within it are described in more detail. For the United States, the treatment has been made regional, each subdivision consisting of a group of states having a common geographic character. An exception is made of the off-shore states of Hawaii and Alaska, each of which is treated separately. Moreover, information regarding the individual states has been grouped in several tables, carefully prepared with a view to conciseness, easy visualization, and ready comparison.

Cities and Other Points of Interest. The description of countries or other divisions is followed by sections in which, under alphabetic arrangement, the cities, towns, and other places of interest are each accorded a special treatment. In the selection of such places, the guiding principle has been the importance of the place and its interest to the general reader. The lists contain the capitals of all countries as well as those of the American states and of the Canadian provinces. They contain also the important cities in all parts of the world. A very large number of other places are included. Some of these are notable for historic reasons, such as Yorktown or Ypres. Others are chosen because their names have become associated with a particular industry, such as Waltham, Mass., or Limoges, France. Many places are described which are not incorporated settlements. These include such features as Pikes peak, Mammoth cave, and Lincoln highway in America or Belleau woods and the Riviera in Europe. An instructive section has been added also on the meanings of place names.

Scope. In mere extent of text, this department far exceeds the volume of the average school geography, being more thorough in treating each subject and more inclusive in the selection of topics, especially topics that have recently become important. The point of especial distinction, however, is the addition of material having a travel interest. The study of geography is thereby made more entertaining and far more helpful to the student.

Purposes. The department of geography is not intended to be used as a textbook for the schoolroom. It is too complete for that purpose. On the other hand, it does not purport to describe every place, without exception which appears on the map. In other words, it is not an atlas or a gazetteer. Consequently, it is neither dry nor mechanical. It is much more than a textbook or an atlas.

This treatment of geography has three principal purposes. In the first place, it contains a rich store of supplementary material both for the student and for the teacher of geography. Secondly, when used in connection with the test questions, it provides an extremely valuable aid for any person desiring systematically to study geography by himself. Lastly, it is an excellent source of general information for all ages and all classes of people.

Statistics. The figures published in this department have been prepared with unusual care. Those representing factors which constantly change, such as population and trade, are based, in all cases, on the latest official bulletins.

It is a fact that even in statistics representing such constant factors as the length of coast lines and areas of districts adjoining the sea, a considerable divergence often appears among geographical authorities. Such differences are frequently due to methods of measurement. A coast line, for example, may be surveyed from headland to headland, and the result obtained may be much less than the total arrived at by including all the insignificant inlets. Somewhat similar difficulties arise in statistics regarding lengths of rivers, heights of mountains, and many other such measurements.

These difficulties, however, detract nothing from the real value of statistics, which is to enable the reader to make comparisons. For ordinary purposes it is of no significance whether Mount Everest is 29,002 or 29,000 feet high or whether Mount McKinley is exactly 20,300 feet in altitude. The essential value of the figures is in showing that Mount Everest is about 9000 feet higher than Mount McKinley. In spite of such considerations, however, the statistics in this department represent the most painstaking efforts to reconcile authorities where they differ and to attain a degree of accuracy that is not to be found in any similar material in print.

Maps. Geographical position has been indicated throughout the text with a view to enabling the reader, by consulting the pertinent maps, to see at a glance the location of the principal places. The maps have been recently revised and take into account the numerous changes that have occurred during and since World War II.

Spelling of Names. The form of the names in the text has been made, in most instances, to conform with the spelling adopted by the United States Geographic Board. Those names which have not been made the subject of decisions by this board follow the spelling of the National Geographic Society, or, failing authority from either source, they conform to Webster's *Gazetteer*.

GEOGRAPHICAL DISCOVERY

Ancient ideas of the earth were vastly different from those of the present day. One of the earliest concepts of the earth is that revealed by the Homeric poems, written about 1000 B. C. In these poems, the earth is supposed to be a circular disk surrounded by a river, which was called Ocean.

Phœnicians. Such early views were probably based on the reports of the Phœnicians, who were the earliest navigators known to history. From these people, too, in all likelihood, came the information which the Hebrews had regarding such distant points as those called, in Hebrew literature, Gomer, Sinim, Cush, Sheba, Ophir, and Tarshish. Gomer is believed to mean the northern shores of the Black Sea; Sinim is conjectured to be southern Egypt; Cush is identified with Abyssinia; Sheba, with Yemen in southwestern Arabia; Ophir is placed in southeastern Africa; and Tarshish, in southeastern Spain.

Africa was circumnavigated as early as 600 B. C. by a Phœnician expedition. This expedition was dispatched by Necho, king of Egypt, with orders to sail through the Red Sea into the Indian Ocean and around Africa. After three years, the ships returned by way of the Strait of Gibraltar and the Mediterranean Sea.

Greeks. The earlier Greek geographers, Hecatæus and Herodotus, both of the 5th century B. C., did not advance beyond the idea of the earth conceived of as a disk. Hecatæus in his *Periodos*, "Trip around the World," and Herodotus in his *Histories*, added immensely to the available knowledge of different lands and peoples, each writer having traveled over most of the world as then known.

Aristotle, living in the 4th century B. C., has the honor of being the first to demonstrate that the world is a sphere. He based his proof on two facts which could be tested by observation: first, that the shadow of the earth thrown on the moon during an eclipse is always circular; and, secondly, that the horizon always retreats as the observer advances. To Aristotle also is due the division of the earth into a torrid zone bounded by two temperate zones with a frigid zone surrounding each pole.

It was in this period that maps of the world first showed the land surface of the earth surrounded by a wide expanse of sea instead of by a river. The name Ocean, which formerly designated the river, was applied to this sea. The sea was believed to extend around the globe, bathing on every side the great land mass in the eastern hemisphere. Our modern sense of ocean, as one of the major divisions of the water surface of the earth, arose since the 15th century, when it was learned that the universal sea was divided into parts by the continent of America and by other land areas previously unknown.

The inclination of the earth to the plane of its orbit was first measured by Eratosthenes, who lived in the 3d century B. C. His result was correct within 23 minutes of the angle as determined by the most accurate modern instruments. Eratosthenes also calculated the size of the earth and devised a system of indicating geographical position by drawing two lines of reference, one from east to west and the other from north to south. The location of any place could thus be indicated by giving its distance north or south of the one line and east or west of the other line.

The lines of reference drawn on the earth by Eratosthenes suggested to Hipparchus of Nicæa, in the 2d century B. C., the idea of drawing a series of circles of latitude and longitude. One circle was drawn for each degree on the earth's surface. In the 2d century A. D., Ptolemy, a Greek of Alexandria, compiled a work on geography which embraced all that was known of the earth until his day. This work formed the starting point of modern geography.

According to Ptolemy's geography, Africa extended southward and eastward, eventually joining Asia. The two continents thus enclosed the Indian Ocean. The farthest land to the north was called Thule, probably the Shetland islands. Something also was known of the Baltic Sea, western Russia, the great plains of Asia, and even the distant countries of China and Japan.

Romans. The Romans did little in the field of scientific geography. For the purpose of conquest and organization, however, surveys were made of practically all the territory surrounding the Mediterranean Sea, as well as of France, part of Britain, and Asia Minor. Nero dispatched an expedition in search of the source of the Nile river about 60 A. D. In the 6th century A. D., Justinian sent two monks to China, who returned with eggs of the silkworm concealed in a hollow cane. The culture of the silkworm was thus introduced into Europe.

Middle Ages. With the general decline of learning after the downfall of Rome, Ptolemy's work was forgotten in Europe, and people reverted to a primitive conception of the earth, believing it to be flat. Maps of this period frequently show Jerusalem as the center of the terrestrial disk.

The Arabs, however, translated Ptolemy's work into their own language, keeping alive a knowledge of geography as it had been developed. Arab astronomers measured a degree of latitude on the plains of Mesopotamia, deducing from it the approximate size of the earth. Prominent among Arabian books of travel was the *Meadows of Gold*, written by Masudi about 950 A. D. It contained geographical observations collected by its author, who, with this purpose in view, traversed all the countries lying between China and Spain. Ptolemy's geography became known to Europe by translation into Latin from the Arabic and later from the original Greek text.

Earliest Modern Discoveries. Before the period of the Renaissance, a number of notable voyages and discoveries were recorded. Greenland was sighted by Northmen in the 9th century, and, in the following century, men of the same race landed on the coast of North America. Little geographic interest, however, was aroused by these discoveries or by the trips of monks to remote parts of Asia and of Africa in search of a mythical Christian kingdom, ruled over by Prester John. The travels of Marco Polo, however, in the 14th century, did much to stimulate interest in distant lands. He visited the Far East, where he ruled a province of China for three years. A golden statue of him in a great temple at Soochow, China, still bears witness to his former influence in the Orient.

Age of Discovery. The 15th and the 16th century were distinguished by extraordinary activity in exploration. The previous invention of the mariner's compass did much to facilitate the sea voyages of the period.

Portuguese sailors discovered the Madeira islands and, by 1482, had sailed south as far as the Congo river. In 1486, a Portuguese ship sighted the Cape of Good Hope, and, 11 years later, Vasco da Gama doubled the cape and finally reached India.

In 1492, Columbus, sailing west, discovered the New World and thereby revolutionized the prevailing conception of the earth. Within 30 years from his historic landing on San Salvador island, the whole east coast of America from Greenland to Cape Horn had been explored, and the globe had been circumnavigated. Before the middle of the 16th century, America's west coast had been explored as far north as San Francisco bay, and Spanish colonists had settled in various parts of South America. On the other side of the world, progress had been made in knowledge of countries whose coasts were bathed by the Indian Ocean, including

Arabia, East Africa, India, and the great Malay archipelago. Apart from the Portuguese and the Spaniards, the nations most active in discovery at this period were the English, the Dutch, and the French.

The 17th and the 18th century witnessed the discovery of Australia, Tasmania, and New Zealand. Captain Cook, an English navigator, in the last quarter of the 18th century, explored widely in the Pacific Ocean, adding Hawaii and numerous other islands to the known world.

The task of geographical discovery was completed in the 19th and the 20th century. The chief accomplishments in this period were the exploration of Africa; the forcing of a passage by water northwest of America and of a passage through the icebound seas northeast of Asia; and, finally, the discovery of the north and south poles. The exploration of Africa is described in the section devoted to that continent.

Polar Exploration. Repeated efforts were made, from the 16th century on, to sail around North America's northern boundary. It was thought for many years that North America terminated in a northern cape, just as South America tapers to a cape at its southern extremity. As no such cape was found in the north, many later geographers believed that North America extended in an unbroken land mass to the north pole. The overland journeys of Hearne and Mackenzie, however, refuted that error and proved that an ocean washed the northern limits of the western continent.

Among the navigators who tried to effect this northwest passage from the Atlantic to the Pacific Ocean were Davis, Hudson, Baffin, Scoresby, Parry, Ross, and Franklin. Finally, in 1851-53, McClure, entering from Bering Strait, was forced to abandon his ship on Banks Land, but he and his crew were brought out to Baffins Bay by another expedition, thus demonstrating the northwest passage. In 1903-06, Roald Amundsen sailed by a more southern route from Baffins Bay to San Francisco. In 1878-79 Nordenskjöld sailed through the northwest passage from Sweden to Bering Strait.

The quest for the north pole engaged many explorers during the latter half of the 19th century. These include Greely, Nansen, and the duke of Abruzzi. The goal was actually reached, however, by Peary, who, on April 7, 1909, raised the American flag over the north pole.

Land was first found in the south polar region by Pierre Bouvet (French) in 1739. The first explorer known to have crossed the Antarctic Circle was Cook (British) in 1773. Further explorations were made by Bellingshausen, Biscoe, Weddell, Ross, Dumont d'Urville, and Borchgrevink. The pole was finally reached December 14, 1911, by the Norwegian explorer Amundsen. Just five weeks later, Captain Scott, an Englishman, arrived there. While returning, Scott perished a few miles from a relief station.

Recent Geographical Research. With the discovery of the two poles, the age of discovery came to an end. The next and more arduous step remained, to investigate and map regions already known only in outline. Mount Everest, the world's highest mountain, was first scaled in 1953 by Hillary (New Zealand) and Norkay (Nepal). Mapping of inaccessible regions was advanced rapidly by many countries through the use of aerial photography. Many geographical expeditions were sponsored by scientific societies, notably the National Geographic Society of Washington, D.C., which pioneered in reporting its findings in popular form. A spectacular example of Antarctic research was Richard E. Byrd's establishment of a "Little America" in 1929 not far from the south pole.

More systematic researches were undertaken in the so-called Geophysical Year (1957–58), when all the resources of science were brought to bear on the mysteries of the earth. Meanwhile, with an assist from atomic devices, geology and archeology were unlocking many of the secrets of historical geography, aiming to show what the earth was like in earlier ages. *See Antarctica, Geophysical Year.*

DATES OF GEOGRAPHICAL DISCOVERIES*

	B. C.
Phœnicians circumnavigate Africa	600
Himilco, Carthaginian merchant, at Ierne (Ireland)	500
Hanno, Carthaginian navigator, off Sierra Leone, Africa	470
Alexander the Great in the Punjab, India	327
Nearchus, Greek general, in the Indian Ocean	325
Pytheas of Marseilles at Ultima Thule (Shetland Islands)	320
Eudoxus, Greek sailor, crosses the Arabian Sea	118
Julius Cæsar in England	55
	A. D.
Cosmas Indicopleustes, Egyptian merchant, in India	550
Suleiman, Arab trader, voyages to China	850
Ottar, Norwegian explorer, rounds the North Cape, Europe	852
Sindbad the Sailor on the coast of India	9th c.
Al Masudi, Arab traveler, in China	920
Iceland colonized from Norway	930
Eric the Red colonizes Greenland	982
Benjamin of Tudela, Spanish traveler, visits India	1160–73
Friar John of Carpini, visits Karakorum, Asia	1246
Rubruquis, Flemish traveler, explores the Caspian Sea	1247
Marco Polo, the Venetian, at the Court of Kublai Khan, China	1270
Fr. Odoric, of Pordenone, Italian monk, enters Lhasa, Tibet	1320
Ibn Batuta, the Arab traveler, reaches Quiloa, E. Africa	1329
Ibn Batuta visits Timbuktu and the Niger River	1350
Clavijo, a Spanish knight, ambassador at Samarkand	1405
Zarco, Portuguese navigator, sights the Madeira Islands	1418
Conti, Italian traveler, explores southern China	1440
Cintra, Portuguese navigator, at Sierra Leone, Africa	1462
Cão, Portuguese navigator, discovers the Congo River, Africa	1484
Bartholomew Diaz, Portuguese navigator, doubles the Cape of Good Hope, South Africa	1488
Covilhão, Portuguese ambassador, penetrates into Abyssinia	1490
Columbus, Italian navigator, discovers San Salvador Islands, West Indies	1492
Vasco da Gama, Portuguese navigator, voyages to India by the Cape route	1497
John Cabot, Italian navigator in English service, lands on coast of North America	1497
Vespucci, Italian navigator, coasts along North American and South American shores†	1497–1503
Cabral, Portuguese explorer, discovers South America	1500
Pinzon, Spanish navigator, at the mouth of the Amazon, South America	1500
Columbus sights Central America	1502
Varthema, Italian traveler, visits the sacred city of Mecca	1503
Serrão, Portuguese sailor, reaches the Molucca Islands by way of India	1512
Balboa, Spanish explorer, discovers the Pacific Ocean	1513
Ponce de Leon, Spanish explorer, traverses Florida	1513
Solis, Spanish navigator, ascends the La Plata River, South America	1516
Grijalva, Spanish navigator, touches coast of Mexico	1518
Cortés, Spanish adventurer, in central Mexico	1518
Expedition of Magellan circumnavigates the globe	1521–22
Pizarro, Spanish adventurer, in Peru	1532
Cartier, French navigator, in the Gulf of St. Lawrence	1534
Coronado, Spanish explorer, marches from Mexico through Arizona and New Mexico to Kansas	1539–42
Alarcon, Spanish explorer, reaches the Colorado River, U. S.	1540
Cardenas, Spanish explorer, at the Grand Canyon, Arizona	1540

*Dates for ancient and medieval discoveries in various instances are only approximate.

†According to his narratives, the trustworthiness of which is disputed.

	A. D.
De Soto, Spanish explorer, discovers the Mississippi River	1541
Orellana, Spanish explorer, descends the Amazon	1541
Cabrillo, Portuguese navigator, on California coast	1542
St. Francis Xavier, Spanish Jesuit missionary, visits Japan	1549
Chancellor, English navigator, reaches the White Sea, Russia	1553
Willoughby, English navigator, sights Nova Zembla	1553
Gaetano, Spanish navigator, lands on the Hawaiian Islands	1555
Jenkinson, English traveler, reaches Persia	1561
Frobisher English navigator, in Frobisher Bay, Arctic North America	1576
Davis, English navigator, in Davis Strait, Arctic North America	1587
Barentz, Dutch navigator, at Spitzbergen, Arctic Europe	1594
Western Australia sighted by Portuguese sailors	1601
Gosnold, English navigator, at Cape Cod, United States	1602
Göes, a native of the Azores, traverses Central Asia	1603–05
Champlain, French explorer, on Maine coast, United States	1604
Torres, Spanish navigator, in New Guinea	1606
Smith, English colonist, in Chesapeake Bay	1608
Hudson, English navigator, ascends Hudson River to present site of Albany	1609
Champlain, French colonizer, discovers Lake Champlain	1609
Hudson, English navigator, discovers Hudson Bay, Canada	1610
Baffin, English navigator, in Baffin Bay	1616
Hartog, Dutch navigator, on the Australian coast	1616
Schouten, Dutch navigator, discovers Cape Horn, South America	1616
Nicolet, French voyager, reaches Lake Michigan	1634
Tasman, Dutch navigator, at Tasmania	1642
Deshnev, Russian navigator, sights Bering Strait	1648
Fr. Menard, French missionary, reaches Lake Superior	1660
Marquette and Joliet, French explorers, reach the Arkansas River	1673
Fr. Hennepin, Flemish missionary, at Niagara Falls, Canada	1678
Fr. Hennepin, at St. Anthony Falls, U. S.	1680
La Salle, French explorer, descends the Mississippi	1682
Fr. Kino, Spanish Jesuit, discovers the Casa Grande ruins, U. S	1694
Bering, Danish navigator, in Bering Strait	1728
Gwosdef, Russian sailor, lands on the Alaskan coast	1731
Verendrye, French explorer, reaches the Rocky Mountains	1740
Karstens Niebuhr, German traveler, explores Arabia	1761–67
Bruce, Scotch traveler, on the Blue Nile, Abyssinia	1768–73
Hearne, English traveler, discovers Great Slave Lake	1772
Cook, English navigator, first to cross the Antarctic circle	1773
Cook, English navigator, explores the Hawaiian Islands	1774–79
Peter Pond, Canadian explorer, reaches Lake Athabaska	1778
La Perouse, French navigator, explores eastern coast of Asia	1787
Mackenzie, Scotch explorer, discovers the Mackenzie River, Canada	1789
Gray, American navigator, ascends the Columbia River, U. S.	1792
Mungo Park on the Gambia river, West Africa	1795
Humboldt, German scientist, explores South America	1799
Lewis and Clark explore the northwestern United States	1804–06
Colter, American trapper, discovers Yellowstone Park, U. S.	1807
Hutchins, American pioneer hunter, discovers the Mammoth Cave, United States	1809
Bellingshausen, Russian navigator, on the Antarctic continent	1821
Clapperton and Denham, English travelers, cross the Sahara	1822
James Bridger, American explorer, discovers Great Salt Lake, United States	1824
Sturt, English explorer, traverses Australia	1828
Ross, English navigator, in Boothia Felix, Arctic North America	1831
Schoolcraft, American scientist, discovers Lake Itasca	1832
Wilkes, American navigator, on the Antarctic continent	1840
Abbé Huc travels in Tibet	1844
Krapf and Rebmann, German missionaries, at Mt. Kilimanjaro, East Africa	1848
McClure, Irish navigator, achieves the Northwest Passage, Arctic Ocean	1851
Boling, American soldier, visits the Yosemite	1851
Livingstone, Scottish missionary, discovers Zambesi River	1851–56
Kane, American explorer, on Grinnell Land, Arctic North America	1853
Livingstone, Scottish missionary, at Victoria Falls, Africa	1855
Barth, German traveler, explores the Sudan	1856
Burton and Speke, English explorers, discover Lake Tanganyika, Africa	1858
Speke, English explorer, discovers Victoria Nyanza, Africa	1858
Burke and Wills, Irish explorers, cross Australia from south to north	1860–61
Richthofen, German scientist, explores China	1868–72
Przhevalski, Russian traveler, crosses Mongolia	1871–73
Stanley, American explorer, traces the course of the Congo	1876–77
Nordenskjöld, Swedish explorer, accomplishes the Northeast Passage, Arctic Ocean	1878–79
Borchgrevink, Norwegian explorer, at the South Magnetic Pole, Antarctic continent	1899
Hedin, Swedish scientist, explores Central Asia	1890–1908
Peary, American naval officer, proves the insular character of Greenland	1892
Roald Amundsen, Norwegian navigator, sails through Northwest Passage	1903–06
Peary discovers the North Pole	1909
Amundsen discovers the South Pole	1911

GENERAL FACTS ABOUT THE EARTH

The earth, or globe, is an oblate spheroid; that is, a sphere slightly flattened at two opposite points, called the poles. The two poles are the ends of the axis about which the globe rotates. The north pole is in the Arctic Ocean. The south pole is in the continent of Antarctica, which, directly at the pole, reaches an elevation of about 10,000 feet.

In order to make it possible to describe the exact location of any place on the earth, geographers have drawn around the globe certain circles, to which the position of any point may be referred. The equator is such a circle, encompassing the earth equidistant from the poles. Other circles are drawn parallel to the equator, dividing the distance between the equator and each pole into 90 equal parts. These circles are called parallels of latitude, and the distance between successive circles is called a degree. A degree (°) of latitude measures about 69 miles. Parallels of latitude are numbered from the equator north and south. Thus the north pole lies at 90° north latitude, and the south pole is at 90° south latitude. In passing from the north pole to the south pole, a traveler would traverse 180° of latitude and, in completing the circuit of the earth, he would pass through a total of 360° of latitude.

A second series of circles, 180 in number, is drawn about the earth, each circle passing through both poles. That half of each circle which extends from one pole to the other is called a meridian of longitude. Since each circle consists of 2 meridians, the 180 circles comprise a total of 360 meridians. Meridians are distant from each other about 69 miles at the equator. As one approaches the poles, however, the distance between two successive meridians decreases. Thus a degree of longitude is not constant, but varies from about 69 miles at the equator to zero at the poles. Meridians of longitude are numbered east and west from the meridian passing through Greenwich, England. The 180th meridian of east longitude coincides with the 180th meridian of west longitude, this meridian being the meridian in the western hemisphere corresponding to the Greenwich meridian in the eastern hemisphere.

The rotation of the earth takes place from west to east—the direction opposite to that in which the hands of a clock move. This movement of the earth causes the alternation of day and night.

A second movement of the globe is its revolution about the sun. The revolution takes place in an almost circular orbit. The earth's axis is not perpendicular to the plane of this orbit, but is inclined 23½° away from the perpendicular. To this inclination are due the varying lengths of day and night at different latitudes and in different seasons and also most of the seasonal variations in temperature. It provides the basis also for the division of the earth into zones, or "belts."

The boundaries of the zones are determined by the noonday inclination of the sun's rays to the surface of each zone. Thus the Torrid Zone comprises that part of the earth over which, at some time of the year, the sun is directly overhead. This zone extends for 23½° of latitude north and 23½° of latitude south of the equator, so that it has a total width of 47° of latitude. The North Frigid Zone and the South Frigid Zone, each of which extends 23½° of latitude from the poles toward the equator, comprise those parts of the earth in which, at some time in the year, the sun does not rise above the horizon at noon. Of the two remaining zones,—the North Temperate Zone and the South Temperate Zone,—each occupies 43° of latitude. In these zones, the sun never stands directly overhead and never remains for a whole day beneath the horizon. The variations of temperature between the different seasons are least in the Torrid Zone and are greatest in the two frigid zones.

The Torrid Zone is divided from the North Temperate Zone by the circle called the Tropic of Cancer and from the South Temperate Zone by the Tropic of Capricorn. The North Temperate Zone is separated from the North Frigid Zone by the Arctic circle. The corresponding line of division between the South Temperate Zone and the South Frigid Zone is called the Antarctic circle.

The following statistics regarding the earth are based on the latest research and are the nearest available approximations to the actual facts.

Equatorial diameter (miles)	7,926.6
Polar diameter (miles)	7,899.9
Circumference at the equator (miles)	24,901.7
Meridional circumference (miles)	24,859.4
Area of land surface approximately (square miles)	54,000,000
Area of water surface approximately (square miles)	143,000,000
Total area of the earth's surface approximately (square miles)	197,000,000
Volume of the earth (cubic miles)	259,900,000,000
Mean density of the earth	5.53
Density of water	1.00
Density of surface rock	2.72
Density at the earth's center	10.87
Pressure at earth's center (tons per square inch)	22,500
Weight of the earth (tons)	6,592,000,000,000,000,000,000

(Six sextillion five hundred ninety-two quintillion tons)

CONTINENTS, AREA AND POPULATION

The following table gives the area and the population of each of the continents, as estimated by the latest reliable authorities.

In the present state of geographical knowledge, it is impossible to obtain exact and strictly accurate statistics covering such large divisions of land as the continents. Even for North America, Europe, and Australia, all of which are inhabited by civilized peoples, no complete measurement of the area has been made. Only small parts of South America, Asia, and Africa have been surveyed. Consequently, it is impossible to obtain more than a careful estimate of the extent of land surface in each continent.

In arriving at the figures for population, somewhat similar difficulties have been encountered. It still remains impossible to obtain exact statistics for the number of inhabitants in large parts of Asia and of Africa. Official estimates have been utilized for these regions. In all places where regular censuses are taken, the figures here given are based on the latest returns except in a few instances, in which the most recent official estimates are used.

Name	Area Sq. Miles	Population
North America	9,361,767	309,000,000
South America	6,885,321	180,000,000
Europe	1,903,000	455,000,000
U.S.S.R.	8,649,412	238,000,000
Asia	10,630,105	1,946,000,000
Africa	11,703,849	336,000,000
Oceania	3,286,097	18,500,000
Total	52,419,638	3,483,000,000

Source: United Nations, *Statistical Yearbook*, 1969. Land area includes land and inland waters but excludes uninhabited polar regions and some islands.

OCEANS, AREA AND DEPTH

Authorities differ widely in their estimates of the areas of oceans. This is owing in part to the absence of definite boundaries for separating the oceans. It is due also to the fact that, while some authorities include with the oceans various inland seas, such as the Mediterranean or Hudson bay, other exclude them. See *Ocean*.

Name	Estimated Area Sq. Miles	Greatest Depth Feet	Mean Depth Feet
Arctic	4,000,000	13,120	3,840
Atlantic	34,000,000	27,498	12,660
Indian	28,000,000	22,968	12,888
Pacific	71,000,000	36,056	13,440
Southern or Antarctic	6,000,000	13,932	

HIGHEST, LOWEST, AND MEAN ALTITUDES OF THE CONTINENTS

The following table gives the highest and the lowest point in each of the continents. It will be observed from the figures given that the highest part of the land surface of the earth is the peak of Mount Everest, 29,002 feet above the sea, and the lowest point is the shore of the Dead Sea, which is 1290 feet below the level of the ocean. The land elevation of the world, therefore, varies within the limit of 30,431 feet, or about 5.7 miles. The figures for the mean elevations of the continents are approximations, being the latest estimates published by the United States Geological Survey.

Continent	Mean Elevation* (feet)	Highest Point		Lowest Point	
		Name	Above Sea Level (feet)	Name	Below Sea Level (feet)
North America	2,000	Mount McKinley, Alaska	20,270	Death Valley, Cal.	276
South America	1,800	Mt. Aconcagua, Chile-Arg.	22,835	Sea level	....
Europe	980	Mt. Elbrus, Caucasus Mts.	18,481	Caspian Sea, Russia	86
Asia	3,000	Mt. Everest, India	29,002	Dead Sea, Palestine	1,290
Africa	1,900	Kibo Peak, (Kilimanjaro) Tanganyika	19,565	Libyan Desert	440
Australia	1,000	Mt. Kosciusko, N. S. W.	7,305	Lake Eyre, South Aust.	38

* Approximate

NORTH AMERICA

The land mass of the western hemisphere with the adjacent islands is called America. The name was given in honor of Amerigo Vespucci, an Italian navigator who is said to have visited South America in 1499. It is often styled the New World because of its discovery and settlement in modern times by peoples from the eastern hemisphere, now commonly spoken of as the Old World.

Extent of America. The mainland extending from Alaska in the northwest and from Boothia Felix in the northeast to the south end of Patagonia is about 8700 miles long. This immense length is prolonged to about 9600 miles by the vast archipelago north of Hudson bay and by the island of Tierra del Fuego south of Patagonia. Cape Columbia in Grant Land and Cape Morris Jesup in Peary Land are within 450 miles of the north pole. Cape Horn, the southernmost point of Tierra del Fuego, is 2350 miles from the south pole. Greenland belongs to America, but Iceland, though partly in the western hemisphere, is associated with Europe. The area of America, including islands, is about 16 million square miles.

The Two Continents Compared. America comprises the two continents of North America and South America. These are connected by the narrow Isthmus of Panama. Each continent, like Africa, bears some resemblance to a triangle, the base, or shortest line, being along the northern border, and the apex, at the southern end. The climates, however, of the corresponding parts of the two continents are reversed. The northern part of North America is polar in character, while the northern part of South America is tropical. The physical features of America are displayed on a gigantic scale. There are great rivers, fresh-water lakes that are veritable inland seas, long, lofty ranges of mountains, and vast plains.

North America and South America alike have a chain of mountains extending from north to south along their western sides. Moreover, each continent has a broad central plain and a low eastern mountain range, and both continents have magnificent rivers affording access far into the interior. Vast, unbroken plains and immense forests are other characteristic features common to the two continents.

Extent of North America. The name, North America, is assumed by most geographers to mean all the continent, and all the outlying islands, north of the narrowest part of the Isthmus of Panama. Thus defined, North America includes Central America, Mexico, the West Indies, the United States, Canada, Alaska, and Greenland. For convenience of reference, Central America is often regarded as a separate section of the western hemisphere. The area of North America, including islands, is about 8.5 million square miles.

Oceans and Coasts. North America's shores are washed by the waters of three oceans—the Arctic on the north, the Atlantic on the east, and the Pacific on the west. On the south, the Gulf of Mexico and the Caribbean Sea are large bodies of water also associated with North America. Deep indentations mark the Atlantic coast and form many excellent harbors. The Pacific coast, for the most part, is without sheltered bays, and, in consequence, has fewer seaports.

Surface Features. Two mountain systems dominate the surface of the continent. On the east side is the Appalachian system. This is a series of worn-down mountains, very old geologically, which stretch from the coast plain of the Gulf of Mexico northeast to Labrador. On the west side of the continent rise the lofty ranges of the great Cordilleran system. These massive, rugged mountains are of relatively recent geological formation.

Cordilleran System. As a whole, this system extends in a northwest direction from Central America to the northern shores of Alaska. The most important ranges are the Sierra Madre of Mexico and the Rockies of the western United States, Canada, and Alaska. Between the Rocky mountains proper and the Pacific Ocean lie the Sierra Nevada of California, the Cascades of Oregon and Washington, the Selkirks of British Columbia, and the Coast ranges. Each of more than 30 peaks of the Rocky Mountain chain is over 14,000 feet high. Mt. Whitney, with an altitude of 14,495 feet, in California, is the highest peak in the continental United States. Mt. Logan, 19,850 feet high, in Yukon Territory, is the loftiest summit in Canada. Mt. McKinley, with a height of 20,270 feet, in Alaska, is the culminating point of North America.

Between the Appalachian system in the east and the Rocky Mountain system in the west lie the great medial plains. These occupy a central depression extending from the Arctic Ocean to the Gulf of Mexico. In this vast valley are situated Hudson bay, the Great Lakes, and the drainage basins of many large rivers.

Appalachian System. The Appalachian Mountain system, which trends generally northeast and southwest, consists of numerous ranges. Among these are the Great Smoky, the Allegheny, the Blue Ridge, the Catskill, the Adirondack, the Green, and the White mountains in the United States and the Notre Dame mountains in Quebec. The loftiest summit is Mt. Mitchell, 6684 feet high, in North Carolina.

Great Basin. A vast plateau, called the Great Basin, with an elevation of from 5000 to 7000 feet, lies between the lofty Wasatch range of eastern Utah and the still higher Sierra Nevada of eastern California. In this arid region, rivers disappear in sandy wastes or flow into saline marshes and salt lakes. North of the Great Basin is the less elevated and more fertile Columbia River plateau, situated between the Rockies and the Cascades. Between the Rocky mountains and the Coast ranges of Canada, a somewhat lower plateau, called the Northern Interior plateau, extends northwest to Alaska where it joins the Yukon plateau named for the great river which drains it.

Colorado Plateau. South of the Great Basin is an immense elevated tract called the Colorado plateau. This forms a plain that extends far into Mexico but attains its widest development in the southwestern United States. Much of this vast highland is from 7000 to 9000 feet above sea level. In it the Colorado river and its tributaries have carved the most stupendous examples of erosion in the world.

Mexican Plateau. This is the southeastern continuation of the great Colorado plateau. In shape, the Mexican plateau, called also the plain of Anahuac, resembles a broad wedge, with its widest portion adjoining the southwestern United States and with its narrowest portion extending to southern Mexico.

This interior plain is bordered both on the east and on the west by high ranges of the Sierra Madre, those on the west having an average elevation of 10,000 feet. On either side, the mountain slopes which face toward the sea are usually very steep and precipitous, while those which face inland toward the plateau are, for the most part, much more gentle.

The Mexican plateau increases in elevation southward, rising from about 3500 feet above sea level, opposite western Texas, to 9000 feet around the southern border. In the high southern portion lies the famous "valley of Mexico," containing Lake Tezcuco, on the shores of which were built the ancient Aztec capital and the present city of Mexico.

Medial Plains. Because of their immense extent in the northern part of the continent, the medial plains are sometimes called the Arctic valley. The width of this region, measured from the highlands of Labrador to the Rockies of northern Alberta, is fully 2000 miles. Between the Allegheny mountains of Pennsylvania and the Rocky mountains of Colorado, the plains region is about 1400 miles wide. This central depression extends south from the Arctic Ocean to the Gulf of Mexico, a distance of about 3000 miles. In this vast interior portion of the continent lie the drainage basins of large river systems. The most important of these are the Mississippi-Missouri draining into the Gulf of Mexico, the Saint Lawrence flowing into the Atlantic Ocean, the Nelson-Saskatchewan emptying into Hudson bay, and the Mackenzie-Athabaska with outlet to the Arctic Ocean. The total area drained by the four systems is about three million square miles.

Rivers. Numerous navigable rivers afford entrance to the interior of the continent. The Mackenzie and the Yukon, flowing into northern waters, are icebound during the greater part of the year. The Saint Lawrence, which flows into the Gulf of Saint Lawrence, is likewise frozen during the winter months. But portions of the Hudson, the Delaware, the mighty Mississippi with many important tributaries, are open practically all the year, as are also the navigable parts of the Rio Grande, the Colorado, the Sacramento, the Columbia, and numerous lesser streams. These provide transportation for much inland commerce and some furnish water for irrigation purposes.

Lakes. Besides the five Great Lakes in the east central part of the continent, there are several other large lakes. Of these, the most important are Great Bear lake, Great Slave lake, and lakes Winnipeg and Athabaska, situated in central and northwestern Canada. In the western United States is Great Salt lake. This is a relic of a former sea which, in geological times, occupied a large part of the Great Basin.

Glaciers. The most extensive remnants of the ice age on the mainland of North America are found in the coastal mountains of Alaska. Some of the great glaciers in the region bordering on the Gulf of Alaska are hundreds of square miles in extent. These continental glaciers, however, are very small when compared with the immense ice sheet that covers the greater part of Greenland. The higher mountains from Colorado and California northwestward to Alaska contain many glaciers.

Volcanoes. In North America, as in South America, there are extensive volcanic areas in the great mountain system bordering on the Pacific coast. Central America contains many active volcanoes, among the most noted of which are Coseguina, Izalco, Cerro Quemado, Santa Maria, Fuego, and Agua. On the Mexican plateau are situated some of the world's most gigantic volcanic mountains, as, for example, Orizaba, altitude 18,250 feet, and Popocatepetl, with an elevation of 17,876 feet. A short distance west of the plateau is Colima, a very active volcano, which rises to a height of about 13,000 feet. Another noted Mexican volcano is Jorullo.

In the United States, Lassen peak, in California, is the only active volcano. The Cascade range has many volcanic peaks but only a few display signs of volcanic activity. Mt. Saint Helens and Mt. Baker, both in the state of Washington, are said to have been in eruption between 1840 and 1850. Mt. Hood, in Oregon, exhales volcanic vapors. Of volcanic origin also are Mt. Shasta and Mt. Rainier, which rank among the grandest peaks of the continent. In the Rocky mountains, there are but few volcanic peaks, but evidence of volcanic activity is very marked in the geysers and in other wonderful features of Yellowstone national park.

Alaska contains numerous volcanoes, some of which are very active. These are found along the coast ranges of southern Alaska and in the Aleutian islands. Among the more noted of the active or the recently active volcanoes on the mainland are Mt. Fairweather, Mt. Wrangell, and Mt. Katmai. The Aleutian volcanic belt is a narrow chain of islands extending westward from the Alaskan peninsula for a distance of more than 1500 miles. Some 25 of these islands contain one or more volcanoes, either active or only recently extinct. On Unimak island, near the southern mainland, is Mt. Shishaldin, with a symmetrical cone rivaling that of Fuji, Japan, in graceful contour.

Climate. In so vast a continent, extending through 75 degrees of latitude, great variations of climate naturally occur. In the far north, arctic severity rules, while in southern Mexico and Central America the climate is tropical. Most of the central portion of the continent has a temperate climate. However, a marked difference exists between the temperatures of parts of the Atlantic and of the Pacific coast having the same latitude. The climate of Washington or of Oregon, on the Pacific coast, is much milder than the climate of Maine or of Massachusetts, which are Atlantic coast states situated in nearly the same latitudes.

In July, a great inland area in North America becomes much warmer than the waters on the east and west coasts. Compared with the weather then prevailing on the oceans, the summer heat of eastern North America is excessive. Moreover, the winter cold is severer than in European countries of the same latitude. For example, in January, Labrador is 40° F. colder than northern Germany.

As the great interior plain has no mountain ranges crossing it, cold winds from the north sometimes sweep unimpeded far to the south, suddenly causing a fall of many degrees in temperature. Occasionally, these winds destroy early plantings or belated harvests as far south as Texas. In the plains region east of the Rocky mountains, a drop of 110° F. within 48 hours has been recorded. Such great changes of temperature are unknown on the Pacific coast. In the eastern part of the continent, quick changes of temperature occur, especially in winter, but are much less extreme than in the Great Plains region.

Rainfall. Along the Gulf coast from 50 inches to 55 inches of rain fall every year. At some points near the Gulf of Mexico, the annual rainfall exceeds 60 inches. A rainfall of 80 inches in a year is not uncommon in the Puget Sound region, and in some localities on the northern Pacific coast the annual precipitation is more than 100 inches. From Manitoba and central Kansas eastward the annual rainfall averages about 35 inches. On the high plains immediately east of the Rocky mountains, the rainfall seldom exceeds 20 inches annually. In Wyoming west of the Rockies and in Nevada, the rainfall is rarely more than 10 inches. Arizona and southern California contain limited areas which are practically rainless.

Minerals. In mineral wealth, North America leads all the other continents. Gold, silver, iron, copper, lead, zinc, nickel, coal, and other minerals are produced in immense quantities. The continent is the world's chief source of petroleum. Large quantities of natural gas occur in many widely separated regions.

Flora. The flora of the temperate regions of North America is remarkable for the great number of species of trees which it contains. Forests, whose acreage totals hundreds of millions, yield enormous quantities of hard and of soft wood timber. The lowland flora of the North American countries which lie south of the United States is characterized by a profusion of tropical flowers, vines, and trees. Mexican and Central American forests produce mahogany, rosewood, ebony, and other fine cabinet woods. The plant life of the Pacific coast region differs in a marked degree from that of the eastern part of the continent. The pines, spruces, firs, and redwoods of the Pacific slope have no equals in size elsewhere in America. In bulk, the gigantic sequoias or "big trees" of California surpass all other known trees.

Fauna. Many of the animals native to North America closely resemble those found in the temperate parts of Europe and Asia. The bird fauna, for example, is strikingly similar. But the mocking bird, catbird, Baltimore oriole, wild turkey, turkey buzzard, bobolink, sage grouse, and various humming birds represent species found only in America. North America has various other distinctive animals which do not occur in the Old World. Among these are the American bison, popularly called buffalo, the grizzly bear, musk ox, bighorn sheep, Rocky Mountain goat, pronghorn, rattlesnake, Gila monster, and prairie dog.

GREENLAND

The largest island in the world, with the exception of Australia. The island lies northeast of Canada, from which it is separated by Baffin bay and Davis strait. It is almost wholly within the North Frigid Zone and stretches to a point within 450 miles of the north pole. Its estimated area is 840,000 square miles, and it has a maximum length north and south of 1400 miles, with a maximum width of 690 miles.

Physical Features. Greenland is bordered by a rocky shore rising abruptly several hundred feet above the water and cut by numerous deep fiords. The surface is a plateau having an average elevation of about 4500 feet but reaching, at a few points, an altitude of more than 10,000 feet. Spreading over about 85 per cent of the island's area is a covering of perpetual ice. This inland ice buries far below it all but the highest mountains, thereby affording an excellent example of such conditions as prevailed in the ice age. The ice constitutes a huge glacier flowing slowly toward the coasts. Each year it discharges into the ocean icebergs estimated to weigh in the aggregate more than one billion tons. The interior of Greenland contains one of the coldest areas on the globe, in which a temperature of 92° below zero has been recorded.

Area of Habitation. The southwest part of Greenland has a coastal strip which, in the summer, is covered with green lichens, trailing plants, and berries. The musk ox, white bear, wolf, arctic fox, and many varieties of birds subsist there.

This coastal strip was settled by Danes and is an integral part of the Commonwealth of Denmark. A large proportion of the 47,000 inhabitants are Eskimos, who although professing Christianity, still adhere to many of their pagan customs. The main occupations are fishing and hunting; whale oil, seal oil, skins, and eiderdown are exported. Greenland is the only source in the world of the mineral cryolite, or Greenland spar, used in making aluminum; lead, zinc, and wolfram are also mined.

Greenland was so named by Eric the Red, a Norseman who voyaged along the coast about 982 A. D. It was colonized by Scandinavians in the same century. Between 1410 and 1721, however, the island was neglected, and the European settlers disappeared, probably by intermarriage with the Eskimos. The present colony was planted in the 18th century. The capital is Godthaab, with a 1969 population of 3179.

HUDSON BAY

A large inland sea, situated in northeastern North America, and connected with the Atlantic Ocean by Hudson strait. From Fox channel, at the north, to the southern end of James bay, at the south, Hudson bay is about 1300 miles in length. In its main body, it is about 600 miles wide. It lies wholly within the Dominion of Canada, in a region of rigorous climate.

Area and Depth. The area of Hudson bay, estimated at 475,000 square miles, is about three times that of the Baltic Sea, and approximately half that of the Mediterranean. In its main portion, the bay varies in depth from 400 to 600 feet. The southern extension, called James bay, is very shallow except in the center.

Tides and Currents. On the extreme north, Hudson bay communicates with the Arctic Ocean through Fury and Hecla strait and the Gulf of Boothia. From this passage Hudson bay receives much arctic ice. In Fox channel the tide rises 40 feet, producing a strong current by which thick ice floes are driven southward into Hudson strait, where they menace navigation.

Character of Shores. The eastern shore, called the East Main, and the western shore north of Churchill are, for the most part, rocky and fringed with numerous small islands. The western shore is called the West Main. From Churchill southward it is low and flat. A low divide separates the drainage basin of Hudson bay from the two other great drainage basins of Canada, namely, the Mackenzie and the Saint Lawrence.

Tributary Rivers. The most important river system tributary to Hudson bay is the Nelson-Saskatchewan. Within this great drainage system lie the chief wheat producing areas of Manitoba, Saskatchewan, and Alberta. The system includes also the Red River of the North, which drains parts of North Dakota, South Dakota, and Minnesota, in the United States. This river flows north into Lake Winnipeg, the outlet of which is the Nelson river. The Nelson river empties its waters into Hudson bay at Port Nelson on the southwest coast.

Second in importance among tributaries is the Churchill river, which enters the bay at Churchill, about 125 miles northwest of Port Nelson. Its deep, capacious mouth forms the best harbor on the entire coast of Hudson bay. Among other affluents are the Albany river, on the southwest, flowing into James bay, and the Big, the Moose, and the Rupert river entering from the east shore. The total area of the Hudson Bay drainage basin is estimated at 1,486,000 square miles, or about one-half of the entire mainland of Canada.

Fisheries and Fur Trade. Hudson bay contains extensive and valuable fisheries. American whaling vessels often winter at Marble island in the northwest part of the bay, and the cod fisheries extend into Hudson strait. The Hudson's Bay Company has several stations, called factories, at various points on the coast. Of these, York Factory, at the mouth of Hayes river, is the leading trading post. For more than 200 years a cargo of valuable furs has been shipped annually from York Factory to England.

East and west of the northern part of Hudson bay are the Barren Grounds. These are dreary wastes where only stunted forms of vegetable life exist. But this desolate region is the feeding ground of caribou and musk oxen, and of various smaller animals hunted for their fur.

Commercial Importance. From Montreal and from Port Nelson the sailing distance to Liverpool is practically the same. Much of the grain produced in the Canadian Northwest is shipped to Montreal by way of Winnipeg and the Great Lakes. The distance from Winnipeg to Liverpool, by way of Port Nelson or Churchill, is more than 500 miles shorter than by way of Montreal. From Edmonton to Liverpool, by way of Hudson Bay ports, the distance is more than 1000 miles less than by way of Winnipeg and Montreal.

Other conditions being equal, it would be cheaper to export grain to Europe by way of Hudson bay. Wheat exports were begun over this route after the completion in 1929 of a railroad to Churchill. While neither Hudson bay nor Hudson strait is ever entirely frozen over, there is great danger to navigation from floating ice during the greater part of the year. For sailing ships, the season for safe navigation is from about July 15 to October 1.

THE GREAT LAKES

A chain of large fresh-water lakes, situated in the east central part of North America. They include lakes Superior, Huron, Michigan, Erie, and Ontario, and form a part of the boundary between the United States and Canada. None lies entirely within the territory of either country except Lake Michigan, which is situated wholly within the United States.

Area and Drainage Basin. The combined area of these lakes is about 94,600 square miles and constitutes the largest body of fresh water in the world. The land area in their drainage basins exceeds 185,000 square miles. No large river arising in the land flows into any of the Great Lakes; but the Saint Lawrence, the stream through which the system finally drains into the Atlantic, is one of the great rivers of the continent. The depressions occupied by the Great Lakes system are separated by low ridges from two other large drainage systems. One of these, lying on the north, drains into Hudson bay; the other, lying on the south and the west, drains through the Mississippi River system into the Gulf of Mexico.

Outlets and Connections. Lake Superior, situated at the head of the great chain, is the largest and deepest of the series. It empties through the Saint Marys river, 55 miles long, into Lake Huron. At Saint Marys rapids, called also Sault Sainte Marie, and the Soo, the river falls about 20 feet. The Sault Sainte Marie canals and locks, built on both the Canadian and the American side, permit deep-water navigation around these rapids. They form one of the most important artificial waterways in the world.

The outlet of Lake Michigan is the Strait of Mackinac, which empties into Lake Huron at a point near the mouth of the Saint Marys river. Lake Huron drains into Lake Erie through the Saint Clair river, 42 miles long; Saint Clair lake, 29 miles long; and the Detroit river, 28 miles long. Lake Erie empties into Lake Ontario through the Niagara river, 26 miles long. In its course between the two lakes, the Niagara river makes a descent of 326 feet, half of which occurs in one sheer drop at Niagara falls, the most noted of the world's great cataracts.

In order to establish navigation between Lake Erie and Lake Ontario, the Welland canal, 26 miles long, with an elaborate system of locks, was completed in 1833. This connected Port Colborne, on Lake Erie, with Port Dalhousie on Lake Ontario. Enlargements have transformed this early Canadian waterway into an important modern ship canal.

Lake Ontario drains through the Saint Lawrence river, about 750 miles long, into the Atlantic Ocean. In various rapids between the outlet of Lake Ontario and Montreal, the Saint Lawrence river descends nearly to sea level. As Lake Superior, with an altitude of 602 feet, is only 30 feet higher than Lake Erie, it will be seen that most of the descent to sea level is made in the Niagara and Saint Lawrence rivers between Buffalo and Montreal. Despite the rapids, the Saint Lawrence is navigable for downstream boats, including passenger steamers, but a series of canals has been constructed on the Canadian side to permit of upstream navigation.

The total length of the Great Lakes-Saint Lawrence water system is about 2200 miles. From Duluth to Buffalo the sailing distance is 997 miles; from Chicago to Buffalo, 929 miles; from Duluth to Ogdensburg, 1235 miles; and from Duluth to Montreal, 1350 miles.

Commercial Importance. In the industrial and commercial development of the eastern United States and Canada, the Great Lakes have been a factor of immense importance. For the early explorers, these lakes, with their river connections, furnished easy routes to the unknown interior. They also afforded avenues through which settlers reached the productive lands adjoining their waters. Later, these inland waterways provided efficient transportation of farm, forest, and mineral products throughout a vast region rich in natural resources. Thus the Great Lakes have contributed in a marked degree to the industrial supremacy of the United States. For example, the rapid development of the immense iron ore resources of the Lake Superior region was made possible by cheap water transportation.

From the times of the French-Canadian fur traders, with their flotillas of birch-bark canoes, the Great Lakes have been a water highway between eastern and western Canada. Down this waterway float much of Canada's huge surplus of wheat for export and also flour, iron, and lumber in vast quantities. In the opposite direction go coal and those manufactured articles for which the West exchanges its products with the East.

At Buffalo, on Lake Erie, is the western terminus of the New York State Barge canal. This gives the Great Lakes a very important connection with the seaboard by way of the Mohawk and the Hudson river to New York harbor. With no increase in capacity, the barge canal is capable of transporting every year millions of tons of grain and other staple products from the lake region to tidewater.

Magnitude of Lake Traffic. The total population of the eight American states and of the Canadian province bordering on the Great Lakes runs to scores of millions. The three largest inland cities of the New World are situated on their shores. In volume, the lake traffic is enormous. The tonnage passing annually through the Detroit river exceeds that which enters and clears in the foreign trade of both the Atlantic and the Pacific ports of the United States. The yearly traffic through the Sault Sainte Marie canal around Saint Marys falls is greater in point of tonnage than that of any other artificial waterway.

THE GREAT LAKES

Item	Superior	Michigan	Huron	Erie	Ontario
Latitude, north	46° 30′ 49° 00′	41° 37′ 46° 06′	46° 00′ 43° 00′	41° 23′ 42° 53′	43° 10′ 44° 10′
Longitude, west	84° 30′ 92° 06′	84° 45′ 88° 00′	80° 00′ 84° 45′	78° 50′ 83° 30′	76° 10′ 79° 53′
Elevation above sea level in feet	602.3	581.2	581.2	572.5	246.2
Greatest length in miles	360	307	206	241	193
Greatest breadth in miles	160	118	101	57	53
Maximum depth in feet	1,012	870	750	210	738
Area in square miles	32,060	22,336	22,978	9,968	7,243
Length of coast line in miles	1,500	745	1,165	657	540
Drainage basin in square miles	44,074	43,463	49,300	24,605	25,737
United States shore line in miles (approx.)	735	1,200	470	350	230
Boundary line in miles	280	None	220	250	160
Outlet	St. Marys River	Str. of Mackinac	St. Clair River	Niagara River	St. Lawrence River
Discoverers or early explorers	Brulé	Nicolet	Brulé and Le Caron	Chaumonot and Brébeuf	Champlain
Date of exploration or discovery	1622	1634	1615	1640	1615
Largest port	Duluth	Chicago	Bay City	Cleveland	Toronto

THE UNITED STATES

The United States, a Federal republic, occupies the central part of North America, and extends from the Atlantic Ocean to the Pacific and from Canada to Mexico. The area of the continental United States, including Alaska, almost equals the area of Europe. Besides Alaska, the republic possesses various island dependencies. See *Territorial Growth of the United States*.

Character of Coasts. In the northeast, the Atlantic shore is rugged and has numerous inlets, but south of New York bay the coast belt is flat, sandy, and in only a few places rises more than 100 feet above the sea. Numerous lagoons, reefs, keys, and sandbars render the Gulf coast dangerous to navigation. Most of the Pacific shore is bold and rocky, San Francisco bay and Puget sound being the only important indentations. On the northern border are the Great Lakes—Superior, Huron, Michigan, Erie, and Ontario.

U.S. COASTLINE BY CHIEF DIVISIONS

(In Statute Miles)

Division	General Coastline	Tidal Coastline
United States	12,383	88,633
Atlantic Coast	2,069	28,673
Connecticut	0	618
Delaware	28	381
Florida	580	3,331
Georgia	100	2,344
Maine	228	3,478
Maryland	31	3,190
Massachusetts	192	1,519
New Hampshire	13	131
New Jersey	130	1,792
New York	127	1,850
North Carolina	301	3,375
Pennsylvania	0	89
Rhode Island	40	384
South Carolina	187	2,870
Virginia	112	3,315
Gulf Coast	1,631	17,141
Alabama	53	607
Florida	770	5,095
Louisiana	397	7,721
Mississippi	44	349
Texas	367	3,359
Pacific Coast	7,623	40,298
Alaska	5,580	31,383
California	840	3,427
Hawaii	750	1,052
Oregon	296	1,410
Washington	157	3,026
Arctic Coast, Alaska	1,060	2,521

Source: Department of Commerce, *Coastline of the United States.*

Surface Features. Dominant physical features of the republic are the Appalachian Mountain system along the Atlantic side with a lowland between the mountains and the ocean; the great Rocky Mountain system in the west, extending nearly north and south; and the vast valley between these highlands.

Other important physical features are the Sierra Nevada, the Cascade, and the Coast ranges, situated between the Rocky mountains and the Pacific Ocean; the vast desert area, called the Great Basin, lying between the Rockies and the Sierra Nevada; and the narrow fertile valleys, extending north and south, between the Sierra Nevada and the Coast ranges. Flanking the Great Basin on the east and the south are the lofty plateaus of Utah and Arizona. To the north of the Great Basin lies the less elevated Columbia River plateau.

Mountains and Plateaus. The high plateaus and mountain ranges of the western United States are a part of the great Cordilleran system which dominates the whole western side of North America. This system extends entirely across the United States from Mexico to Canada, through New Mexico, Colorado, Wyoming, and Montana, and throughout the region between these states and the Pacific Ocean. Measured from the eastern base of the Rockies, across Colorado, Utah, Nevada, and California, to the western base of the Coast ranges, the Cordilleran system is about 1000 miles in breadth.

The northern section of this western mountain region, particularly the Columbia River plateau, contains more extinct volcanoes than are found in any other equal area in the world. Here lavas, from ancient fissure eruptions, overspread an area of 200,000 square miles.

Scenery. The sublimity of the scenery of the western mountains is celebrated. The Yosemite falls of the Merced river in the Sierra Nevada are the highest in the world. In grandeur the Shoshone falls of the Snake river in southern Idaho rival Niagara. No Alpine lakes surpass Crater lake and Lake Tahoe in scenic beauty. The wonderlands of the globe, Yellowstone national park and Glacier park, are in the Rocky Mountain country. The Grand Canyon, nature's most marvelous example of erosion, traverses the high plateau of northwestern Arizona.

Mississippi Basin. The vast valley between the Rocky mountains and the Appalachians, called the Mississippi basin, is chiefly a grassy plain, mostly treeless, rising gently from the Gulf of Mexico toward Canada and also toward the highlands east and west. Through this basin the great Mississippi river, rising near the Canada border, flows southward into the Gulf of Mexico. In the south-central part of the valley is the only elevated section. This is the Ozark plateau, mostly from 800 feet to 1000 feet above the sea, but with summits in Arkansas which reach an elevation of 2800 feet.

About one-half the total area of the United States lies within the Mississippi basin. This basin, on account of the great fertility of its central and its eastern parts, is the most important agricultural region of the globe. Much of the western part, known as the Great Plains, with an elevation of 6000 feet in some places, has only a light rainfall. This region affords excellent natural pasturage, and, when irrigated, the soil is very productive.

Drainage Systems. The drainage waters of the United States find their way into the adjoining oceans chiefly through streams grouped in four general drainage systems, namely, the Atlantic, the Gulf, the Great Lakes, and the Pacific. Parts of North Dakota, South Dakota, and Minnesota, however, are drained by the Red River of the North, whose waters, joining those of the Nelson-Saskatchewan, flow into Hudson bay. Of the river systems, the Mississippi-Missouri, with numerous tributaries, is by far the largest. Other important large river systems are the Rio Grande, the Colorado and the Columbia.

Climate and Rainfall. Situated within the Temperate Zone, but covering a vast area having lowlands and highlands, the United States has many varieties of climate. In general, however, the climate is that which normally prevails in temperate regions, though subject to greater extremes than those which occur in Europe. Intense heat prevails in the southwest deserts in summer. In the northwest, in winter, the mercury falls below −40° F. But the dryness of the air in these regions renders endurable extremes of both heat and cold. Within the same degrees of latitude, the Pacific coast is much warmer than the Atlantic coast. Over the central and eastern portions of the country, the climate is continental.

HIGHEST AND LOWEST POINTS AND AVERAGE ELEVATION

United States and Possessions

State or Possession	Highest Point			Lowest Point			Mean Elevation (feet)
	Name	County	Elevation (feet)	Name	County	Elevation (feet)	
Alabama	Cheaha Mt.	Clay-Talladega	2,407	Gulf of Mexico		S. l.*	500
Alaska	Mt. McKinley		20,300	Pacific Ocean		S. l.	
Arizona	San Francisco Pk.	Coconino	12,611	Colorado River	Yuma	100	4,100
Arkansas	Blue Mountain	Polk-Scott	2,800	Ouachita River	Ashley-Union	55	650
	Magazine Mt.	Logan	2,800				
California	Mount Whitney	Inyo-Tulare	14,496	Death Valley	Inyo	–276†	2,900
Canal Zone	Cerro Galera	S. W. part of Zone	1,207	Pacific Ocean		S. l.	100
Colorado	Mount Elbert	Lake	14,420	Arkansas River	Prowers	3,350	6,800
Connecticut	Bear Mountain	Litchfield	2,355	Long Is. Sound		S. l.	500
Delaware	Centerville	New Castle	440	Atlantic Ocean		S. l.	60
Dist. Columbia	Tenleytown	Northwest part	420	Potomac River		S. l.	150
Florida	Iron Mountain	Polk	325	Atlantic Ocean		S. l.	100
Georgia	Brasstown Bald	Towns-Union	4,768	Atlantic Ocean		S. l.	600
Guam	Mt. Lamlan		1,334	Pacific Ocean		S. l.	
Hawaii	Mauna Kea	Hawaii	13,784	Pacific Ocean		S. l.	
Idaho	Borah Peak	Custer	12,655	Snake River	Nez Percé	720	5,000
Illinois	Charles Mound	Jo Daviess	1,241	Mississippi R.	Alexander	279	600
Indiana	Greensfork Tp.	Randolph	1,240	Ohio River	Vanderburg	316	700
Iowa	West boundary	Osceola	1,675	Mississippi R.	Lee	477	1,100
Kansas	West boundary	Wallace	4,135	Verdigris R.	Montgomery	700	2,000
Kentucky	Big Black Mt.	Harlan	4,150	Mississippi R.	Fulton	257	750
Louisiana	N. W. part of Co.	Claiborne	400	Gulf of Mexico		S. l.	100
Maine	Mt. Katahdin	Piscataquis	5,267	Atlantic Ocean		S. l.	600
Maryland	Backbone Mt.	Garrett	3,340	Atlantic Ocean		S. l.	350
Massachusetts	Mount Greylock	Berkshire	3,505	Atlantic Ocean		S. l.	500
Michigan	Porcupine Mts.	Ontonagon	2,023	Lake Erie		572	900
Minnesota	Mesabi Range	St. Louis	1,920	Lake Superior		602	1,200
Mississippi	Near Iuka	Tishomingo	780	Gulf of Mexico		S. l.	300
Missouri	Taum Sauk Mt.	Iron	1,800	St. Francis R.	Dunklin	230	800
Montana	Granite Peak	Park	12,850	Kootenai River	Flathead	1,800	3,400
Nebraska	S. W. part of Co.	Banner	5,300	S. E. part of Co.	Richardson	825	2,600
Nevada	Boundary Peak	Esmeralda	13,145	Colorado River	Clark	470	5,500
New Hampshire	Mt. Washington	Coos	6,288	Atlantic Ocean		S. l.	1,000
New Jersey	High Point	Sussex	1,805	Atlantic Ocean		S. l.	250
New Mexico	N. Truchas Peak	Rio Arriba	13,306	Red Bluff	Eddy	2,876	5,700
New York	Mount Marcy	Essex	5,344	Atlantic Ocean		S. l.	1,000
North Carolina	Mount Mitchell	Yancey	6,684	Atlantic Ocean		S. l.	700
North Dakota	Black Butte	Slope	3,468	Pembina	Pembina	790	1,900
Ohio	Campbell Hill	Logan	1,550	Ohio River	Hamilton	425	850
Oklahoma	Black Mesa	Cimarron	4,978	Red River	McCurtain	300	1,300
Oregon	Mount Hood	Clackamas-Hood River	11,253	Pacific Ocean		S. l.	3,300
Pennsylvania	Negro Mountain	Somerset	3,213	Delaware River		S. l.	1,100
Puerto Rico	Luquillo Mts.	Humacao	3,532	Atlantic Ocean		S. l.	
Rhode Island	Durfee Hill	Providence	805	Atlantic Ocean		S. l.	200
Samoa	Lata	Tau Island	3,056	Pacific Ocean		S. l.	
South Carolina	Sassafras Mt.	Pickens	3,548	Atlantic Ocean		S. l.	350
South Dakota	Harney Peak	Pennington	7,242	Big Stone Lake	Roberts	962	2,200
Tennessee	Clingmans Dome	Sevier	6,642	Mississippi R.	Shelby	182	900
Texas	El Capitan	Culberson	8,700	Gulf of Mexico		S. l.	1,700
Utah	Kings Peaks	Duchesne	13,498	Beaverdam Crk.	Washington	2,000	6,100
Vermont	Mt. Mansfield	Lamoille	4,393	Lake Champlain	Franklin	95	1,000
Virginia	Mount Rogers	Grayson-Smyth	5,719	Atlantic Ocean		S. l.	950
Virgin Islands	Crown Hill	Is. of St. Thomas	1,550	Atlantic Ocean		S. l.	
Washington	Mt. Rainier	Pierce	14,408	Pacific Ocean		S. l.	1,700
West Virginia	Spruce Knob	Pendleton	4,860	Potomac River	Jefferson	240	1,500
Wisconsin	Rib Hill	Marathon	1,940	Lake Michigan		581	1,050
Wyoming	Gannett Peak	Fremont	13,785	Belle Fourche R.	Crook	3,100	6,700
United States	Mount McKinley		20,300	Death Valley	Inyo, Cal.	–276†	2,500

* Sea level. † Below sea level.

The rainfall varies greatly in different sections. The northwest Pacific coast and the Gulf coast have a heavy annual rainfall. In the central Mississippi valley the rainfall is ample for crop production. Around the Great Lakes the precipitation is moderate, but sufficient for agriculture. Tornadoes occur from the Great Plains eastward, but are most destructive in the lower Mississippi valley. Tropical hurricanes, sweeping northward from the Gulf of Mexico, sometimes cause serious damage along the coast from Texas to Florida.

Minerals. No other country in the world is so rich in minerals. Coal, iron ores, lead, zinc, silver, tungsten, gold, quicksilver, and copper are mined. Petroleum, natural gas, clays, cement, building stone, sulphur, lime, salt, slate, and other minerals are also produced in the United States. The mineral industry has developed with extraordinary rapidity. In 1870, the value of mineral products was about $200,000,000; in 1900, $1,109,000,000; in 1920, $6,981,000,000; in 1948, $27,830,000,000; in 1962, $18,834,000,000.

Vegetation. A wide range of climatic conditions, many different soils, and a surface diversified with mountains and valleys produce a varied vegetation. Plants characteristic of the North Temperate Zone are well represented, and there are also many species peculiar to the United States. Large forests are found in the extreme northwest and also in the southern, north central, and eastern states. It is estimated that there are at least 150 species of trees of industrial importance.

The central and eastern United States has many forests containing oaks, elms, maples, chestnuts, hickories, ashes, walnuts, and other well-known species. Characteristic trees of the South are palmettoes, magnolias, tulip trees, sour gums, and yellow pines. Cypresses are abundant in the southern swamps. In the Great Lakes region, firs, pines, spruces, and larches abound. Pines, spruces, and junipers are common in the Rocky Mountain region and yuccas and cactuses in the southwestern deserts.

Cone-bearing trees attain their greatest development in the Pacific Coast region. Gigantic sequoias, believed to be the largest and the oldest of living plants, form groves in the Sierra Nevada. These remarkable trees are unknown elsewhere on the globe. Douglas firs, true firs, and various pines, cedars, hemlocks, and spruces also attain immense size, the Douglas fir and the sugar pine ranking with the sequoias among the great trees of the continent. There are many species of native grasses suitable for fattening live stock. Numerous kinds of berries, various species of nut trees, and hundreds of varieties of wild flowers are also found.

The original forests of the United States covered about 820 million acres and contained, it is estimated, over five trillion board feet of lumber. There remain now about 470 million acres of forested land, containing more than two trillion board feet. The annual growth of forest timber is only about one-sixth of the amount removed. The United States Bureau of Forestry is endeavoring to conserve the country's valuable timber resources and to grow new forests in suitable regions.

Animal Life. With the exception of arctic and tropical species, practically all the larger animals native to North America are found in the United States. Among grazing mammals now occurring wild are the moose, the wapiti or American elk, the bighorn, the Rocky Mountain goat, the pronghorn or American antelope, and various species of deer. Among native flesh-eating mammals are the black and the grizzly bear, the timber wolf, coyote, fox, puma, lynx, wolverene, raccoon, and cacomistle. Other interesting mammals are the beaver, porcupine, opossum, muskrat, woodchuck, badger, prairie dog, peccary, armadillo, numerous rabbits, hares, and squirrels, and various small fur-bearers, such as the skunk, mink, and ermine. The manatee or sea cow is found in Florida waters, and sea lions occur on the Pacific coast.

The birds are represented by several hundred species. Among game birds, the more highly prized are the partridge, sage hen, prairie hen, and other species of grouse; the mallard, teal, canvasback, and other kinds of ducks; the wild turkey, bobwhite, plumed quail, woodcock, and various kinds of geese, rails, plover, and snipe. Typical song birds are the robin, mockingbird, brown thrasher, wood thrush, bluebird, cardinal, goldfinch, and catbird; also several species of orioles, grosbeaks, and wrens. The birds of prey include the bald eagle (the American national emblem), the golden eagle, and numerous hawks, buzzards, owls, and vultures. Among birds of prey, the huge California vulture ranks second in size only to the condor of the Andes.

Of the large reptiles, the alligator is the best-known, though a true crocodile occurs in Florida. Numerous sea turtles, fresh-water terrapins, and land tortoises are found. The so-called horned toad, the chuckwalla, and the Gila monster are peculiar kinds of lizards inhabiting southwestern deserts. There are numerous species of snakes, but only the rattlesnakes, the copperhead, the water moccasin, and a few other species are venomous.

Both the coastal and the inland waters abound in fish. Cod, halibut, mackerel, bluefish, tuna and many other valuable food fishes are taken in large quantities by the fisheries. Many inland streams teem with salmon, trout, shad, catfish, and sturgeon. In the larger lakes, various food fishes, such as whitefish, lake trout, ciscoes, bass, pike, and perch, occur in immense numbers. Along the north Atlantic coast, oysters and lobsters abound, the annual catch being one of the most valuable of American fisheries.

Manufacturing. In manufacturing, the United States surpasses all other countries. Immense natural resources—minerals, timber, water power, hydroelectric power—and an ample supply of skilled labor enable the republic to produce, year after year, a vast, varied, and increasing output of manufactures. In 1860, the total value of manufactures was less than 2 billion dollars; in 1963, it exceeded 150 billion dollars.

Commerce. The rapid development of the three great industries, mining, agriculture, and manufacturing, produced an equally rapid increase in railroad construction and also gave rise to an enormous foreign trade. The commerce of the United States is sure to increase to still greater dimensions because, in addition to its immense trade with countries in the temperate zones, the imports from tropical or subtropical countries are increasing. Rubber, tea, coffee, cacao, sugar, raw cotton, raw silk, tin, hides, nitrates, and gums come from countries lying within the Torrid Zone or near it. In 1860, the total foreign commerce of the United States was valued at about 700 million; in 1920, at about 13 billion; in 1960, over 20 billion.

GEOGRAPHICAL FACTS ABOUT THE UNITED STATES

The land area of the United States is 3,548,974 square miles.

The water area, exclusive of the Great Lakes, is 66,237 square miles.

The most northern point of conterminous United States is in Minnesota, latitude 49° 23′ N. and longitude 95° 9′ W.

The most southern point of conterminus United States is Cape Sable, Florida, latitude 25° 7′ N. and longitude 81° 5′ W. Hence Cape Sable is 49 miles farther south than the extreme southern point of Texas.

The most eastern point of the United States is West Quoddy Head, a Maine cape which projects into the Atlantic Ocean. This headland is in longitude 66° 57′ W. and latitude 44° 49′ N.

The most western point in conterminus U.S. is Cape Alava in Washington. This cape, which projects into the Pacific Ocean, is in longitude 124° 44′ W. and latitude 48° 10′ N.

The longest distance in a straight line from north to south is measured from the boundary between Canada and the United States, the 49th parallel of latitude, to the southernmost point of Texas—1598 miles.

The shortest distance from the Atlantic to the Pacific is a straight line drawn from a point near Charleston, South Carolina, to a point near San Diego, California. This distance is 2152 miles.

The longest distance in a straight line from the Atlantic to the Pacific is measured from West Quoddy Head to a point near Yaquina Head, an Oregon cape projecting into the Pacific Ocean. These points are 2807 miles apart.

The length of the boundary of the United States, as given by the United States Coast and Geodetic Survey, is 10,748 miles, divided as follows: Atlantic Ocean, 1883; Gulf of Mexico, 1639; Pacific Ocean, 1316; Mexico, 2013; Canada, 3897.

In the conterminus United States the temperature has fallen as low as 60° below zero in northern Montana and has risen as high as 134° in the shade in Death valley, California.

The annual rainfall on the north shore of the Gulf of Mexico exceeds 60 inches. Around Puget sound it reaches 100 inches. In the vicinity of the Great Lakes it ranges between 30 and 35 inches. At the eastern base of the Rocky mountains it is about 15 inches. In the deserts of the Great Basin it is usually less than 10 inches. At Yuma, in southwestern Arizona, it is only 3 inches.

The average yearly rainfall over all the continental United States equals 1300 cubic miles. This quantity of rain water would weigh six trillion tons.

The geographic center of the United States is a point 17 miles due west of Castle Rock, Butte county, South Dakota, approx. latitude 44° 58′ N., longitude 103° 46′ W.

The center of population in the United States in 1960 was at a point 50 mi. east of St. Louis, Mo., 6½ mi. northwest of Meridian Twp., Clinton Co., Ill. lat. 38° 35′ 58″N., long. 89° 12′ 35″ W., a movement of 57.0 mi. west and 16.5 mi. south since 1950.

The highest peak in the United States, including all territories, is the Alaskan mountain, Mt. McKinley, 20,300 feet.

The state having the lowest average elevation is Delaware. Its surface, if leveled, would be only 60 feet above the sea. Colorado has the highest average elevation, 6800 feet.

NATIONAL PARKS

Name	Location	Area Sq. Mi.	Established	Distinctive Characteristics
Acadia	Maine Coast	65.05	1919	Mountains and coastal area on Mount Desert Island.
Big Bend	West Texas	1106.60	1944	Last great Texas wilderness, in bend of the Rio Grande.
Bryce Canyon	Southwestern Utah	56.26	1928	Massive mountain uplift; magnificent forests; fantastically eroded pinnacles; extraordinary natural coloring.
Canyonlands	S. E. Utah	402.56	1964	Pinnacles, monoliths, deep gorges, rock formations.
Carlsbad Caverns	New Mexico	73.05	1930	Largest and deepest known cavern system.
Crater Lake	Southwestern Oregon	250.45	1902	Lake of extraordinary blue in crater of extinct volcano. No known inlet or outlet. Sidewalls 500 to 2000 feet high.
Everglades	Southern Florida	2188.33	1947	Part of the only subtropical area in the United States; vast forests, prairies, and watercourses; abundant bird life.
Glacier	Northwestern Montana	1582.86	1910	Mountain region, 250 glacier-fed lakes of romantic beauty, 60 glaciers. Precipices thousands of feet high. Trout fishing. With the adjoining Waterton Lakes national park of Canada.
Grand Canyon	North central Arizona	1052.46	1919	Greatest example of erosion and most wonderful scenic spectacle in the world. The stupendous gorge has average depth of about 1 mile and is from 4 to 18 miles wide.
Grand Teton	Wyoming	484.92	1929	Picturesque mountains in a great "dude ranch" district.
Great Smoky Mountains	North Carolina and Tennessee	801.05	1930	Picturesque mountains, including about 40 peaks.
Guadalupe Mountains	Texas	30.68	1968	Diversified and beautiful scenery.
Haleakala	Maui Is., Hawaii	41.25	1961	Huge dormant volcano, 10,023 feet high, has one of the largest and most colorful craters known.
Hawaii Volcanoes	Hawaii Island	344.28	1916	Kilauea, Mauna Loa, largest active volcanoes in the world.
Hot Springs	Arkansas	1.61	1921	Forty-seven hot springs possessing curative properties.
Isle Royale	Lake Superior N. Michigan	842.73	1940	Extensive wilderness; habitat of one of the largest moose herds in America.
Kings Canyon	Middle eastern California	719.26	1940	Two canyons of the Kings River; mountain peaks to 14,000 feet; General Grant tree 40.3 feet in diameter.
Lassen Volcanic	Northern California	167.08	1916	Lassen Peak, 10,453 feet in altitude. Only recently active volcano in conterminous United States. Hot springs; mud geysers; ice caves; majestic canyons.
Mammoth Cave	S. W. Kentucky	80.24	1936	Large cavern including spectacular cave onyx formations.
Mesa Verde	S. W. Colorado	81.36	1906	Best preserved prehistoric cliff dwellings in United States.
Mount McKinley	S. C. Alaska	3030.45	1917	Highest mountain in North America (altitude 20,300 feet).
Mount Rainier	West central Washington	378.09	1899	Forty-eight square miles of glacier, 50 to 500 feet thick. Immense fields of wild flowers.
Olympic	N. W. Washington	1400.94	1938	Finest remnant of the Pacific Northwest rain forest; numerous glaciers; feeding ground for rare Roosevelt elk.
Petrified Forest	Arizona	147.17	1962	Fossil tree trunks; colored rocks of Painted Desert.
Platt	So. Oklahoma	1.42	1906	Numerous well-known medicinal springs.
Rocky Mountain	North middle Colorado	409.88	1915	Heart of the Rockies; snow-topped range; peaks 11,000 to 14,255 feet high; sublime scenery.
Sequoia	California	604.47	1890	The Big Tree National Park; 12,000 sequoia trees ranging from 10 to 36 feet in diameter; towering mountain ranges; startling precipices.
Shenandoah	N. W. Virginia	331.72	1935	Region of scenic grandeur in the Blue Ridge mountains.
Virgin Islands	St. John Island	23.67	1956	White sand beaches and semi-tropical climate. Embraces scenery and plant life totally different from any other national park. Area covers two-thirds of St. John Island.
Wind Cave	South Dakota	43.84	1903	Cavern having miles of galleries and numerous chambers containing many peculiar geological formations.
Yellowstone	Wyoming, Montana, and Idaho	3471.52	1872	More geysers than in all rest of world; boiling springs; mud volcanoes; petrified forests; Grand Canyon of the Yellowstone; waterfalls; vast wilderness inhabited by deer, elk, bison, bear, mountain sheep, and other wild animals.
Yosemite	California	1188.99	1890	Valley of world famed beauty; lofty cliffs; romantic vistas; waterfalls of extraordinary height; many snow-crowned peaks; good trout fishing.
Zion	Southwestern Utah	229.74	1919	Magnificent gorge(Zion canyon), depth from 1500 to 2500 feet, with precipitous walls of great beauty; picturesque scenery.

Parks and Monuments. Modern public parks and monuments have these principal purposes: To provide enjoyment to visitors; to safeguard the property so as to afford like enjoyment to future generations; and to make use of them as illustrations in spreading popular education in geography, science, and history.

In the United States, national parks differ from national monuments in that the parks require acts of Congress for their establishment, while monuments may also be established by executive order pursuant to the Antiquities Act of 1906. In general, the national parks are large areas of scenic magnificence, while the national monuments and related areas are, with a few exceptions, smaller and more often are primarily of historic or prehistoric interest. The states also, as well as many municipalities, have set aside millions of acres in all as parks or monuments.

Of other countries, Canada has the largest system of national and provincial parks. South Africa, Holland, Czechoslovakia, Italy, Kenya, and France also have at least one large area each for the preservation of natural scenery and of certain animals and plants. In fact, though not in name, Italy, France, and most other European countries have numerous public areas administered much like the American parks and monuments for the preservation of historic sites, such as Pompeii in Italy and Stonehenge in England.

The number of areas supervised by the U.S. National Park Service as reported on Jan. 1, 1966, was 214, with a total area of 26,548,693 acres. Of this number, 32 were national parks, 77 were national monuments, 23 were national historic sites or parks, 28 were national military or memorial parks, 12 were national battlefields, battlefield parks, or battlefield sites, and the rest were national seashores, recreation areas, cemeteries, parkways, and other areas.

The table above gives data about the national parks. On the two pages following appears a tabulation of national monuments and related areas, followed by a summary of state parks and related areas showing by states the number and acreage of such areas.

NATIONAL MONUMENTS AND ALLIED AREAS*

Name	Location	Area (Acres)	Established	Distinctive Characteristics
Abraham Lincoln Birthplace (*h*)	Kentucky	117	1916	Contains log cabin where Abraham Lincoln was born.
Andrew Johnson (*h*)	Tennessee	17	1942	Andrew Johnson's home, tailor shop, and grave.
Antietam (*b*)	Maryland	784	1890	Scene of one of the greatest battles of the Civil War.
Appomattox Court House (*h*)	Virginia	972	1940	Scene of the surrender of the Confederate Army, April 9, 1865.
Arches (*m*)	Utah	34,010	1929	Natural arches, windows, and other effects of wind erosion.
Arkansas Post (*m*)	Arkansas	221	1965	Earliest permanent white settlement in region.
Aztec Ruins (*m*)	N. Mex.	27	1923	Pueblo ruins, one containing 500 rooms.
Badlands (*m*)	S. Dakota	111,530	1939	Spectacular exhibit of erosion—fantastic ridges, cliffs.
Bandelier (*m*)	N. Mex.	29,661	1916	Vast ruins of prehistoric cliff dwellings.
Bent's Old Fort (*h*)	Colorado	178	1963	Fort built about 1833, trading post in fur trade.
Big Hole (*b*)	Montana	666	1910	Scene of victory, 1877, over force of Nez Perce Indians.
Black Canyon of the Gunnison (*m*)	Colorado	13,683	1933	10 miles of deepest and most scenic portion of Black Canyon.
Booker T. Washington (*m*)	Virginia	218	1957	Plantation on which Booker T. Washington was born.
Buck Island Reef (*m*)	Virgin Is.	850	1961	Marine garden with coral, grottoes, tropical fish.
Cabrillo (*m*)	California	81	1933	Memorial to discoverer of San Diego Bay in 1542.
Canyon de Chelly (*m*)	Arizona	83,840	1931	Deep canyon; Indian cliff dwellings; very ancient ruins.
Capitol Reef (*m*)	Utah	39,173	1937	Cliff dwellings, fossils, imprints of prehistoric animals.
Capulin Mountain (*m*)	N. Mex.	775	1916	Cinder cone of geologically recent formation.
Casa Grande Ruins (*m*)	Arizona	473	1889	Buildings of a prehistoric race. Ruins discovered in 1694.
Castillo de San Marcos (*m*)	Florida	22	1924	Oldest masonry fort in continental U.S.; built 1672.
Cedar Breaks (*m*)	Utah	6,155	1933	Spectacular canyons and cliffs of vivid coloring.
Chaco Canyon	N. Mex.	21,509	1907	Numerous ruins of cliff dwellings, including communal houses.
Chalmette (*h*)	Louisiana	136	1907	Scene of battle of New Orleans, Jaunary 8, 1815.
Channel Islands (*m*)	S. Calif.	18,167	1938	Parts of Anacapa and Santa Barbara Islands; fossil elephants.
Chesapeake & Ohio Canal (*m*)	Md.-W.Va.	4,475	1961	Old American canal with minimum alterations.
Chickamauga and Chattanooga (*b*)	Ga.-Tenn.	8,190	1890	Beautiful scenic park, embracing battlefields of Chickamauga, Missionary Ridge, and other conflicts of the Civil War, 1863.
Chiricahua (*m*)	Arizona	10,646	1924	Wilderness of unusual rock shapes.
Christiansted (*h*)	Virgin Is.	27	1952	Danish colonial government buildings.
City of Refuge (*h*)	Hawaii	182	1961	Until 1819, sanctuary for individuals fleeing death.
Colonial (*h*)	Virginia	9,430	1936	Jamestown, Williamsburg, Yorktown, connected by parkway.
Colorado (*m*)	Colo.	17,362	1911	Many lofty monoliths; unusual scenic beauty.
Coronado (*p*)	Arizona	2,834	1952	Commemorates Coronado's exploration in 1540–42.
Craters of the Moon (*m*)	Idaho	53,545	1924	Volcanic region with weird landscape effects.
Cumberland Gap (*h*)	Ky.-Tenn.-Va.	20,169	1955	Pass explored by Boone and used by western settlers.
Custer Battlefield (*m*)	Montana	765	1946	Site of Battle of the Little Bighorn River, June 25, 1876.
Death Valley (*m*)	Calif.-Nev.	†2,981	1933	Arid tract containing lowest point in the western hemisphere.
De Soto (*p*)	Florida	30	1949	Commemorates explorer's landing in 1539.
Devils Postpile (*m*)	Calif.	798	1911	Spectacular six-sided aggregation of basaltic columns.
Devils Tower (*m*)	Wyoming	1,347	1906	865-foot rock tower of volcanic origin. First national monument.
Dinosaur (*m*)	Utah-Col.	206,233	1915	Deposits of fossil animal remains of great scientific interest.
Edison (*h*)	N. Jersey	21	1955	Edison's home and laboratory.
Effigy Mounds (*m*)	Iowa	1,468	1949	Indian mounds in shape of animals.
El Morro (*m*)	N. Mex.	1,279	1906	Rock containing inscriptions cut by early Spanish explorers.
Fort Caroline (*p*)	Florida	120	1953	Overlooks site of French colony planted in 1564.
Fort Clatsop (*m*)	Oregon	125	1958	Winter campsite of Lewis and Clark.
Fort Davis (*h*)	Texas	460	1963	Fort to protect frontier and early settlers.
Fort Donelson (*p*)	Tennessee	600	1928	Site of Civil War fort.
Fort Frederica (*m*)	Georgia	250	1945	Built (1736–48) by Gen. James E. Oglethorpe.
Fort Jefferson (*m*)	Florida	47,125	1935	Largest all-masonry fort in Western world, built 1846.
Fort Laramie (*h*)	Wyoming	586	1938	Center for migrants and explorers 1834–90.
Fort Matanzas (*m*)	Florida	258	1924	Early Spanish stronghold.
Fort McHenry (*m*)	Maryland	43	1925	Defense of this fort on Sept. 13–14, 1814 inspired the composition of our national anthem.
Fort Necessity (*b*)	Pa.	500	1931	Scene of opening battle of French and Indian War.
Fort Pulaski (*m*)	Georgia	5,517	1924	Brick fort built 1829–47, bombarded in Civil War.
Fort Raleigh (*h*)	N. C.	160	1941	Site of "Lost Colony" settlement in 1585–87.
Fort Smith (*h*)	Arkansas	14	1964	Early military post in Louisiana Territory.
Fort Union (*m*)	N. Mex.	721	1956	Ruins of key fort in southwestern settlement.
Fort Vancouver (*h*)	Wash.	90	1961	Western Headquarters of Hudson's Bay Co. 1825–49.
Fredericksburg and Spotsylvania (*p*)	Virginia	3,672	1927	Portions of four great battlefields of Civil War.
George Washington Birthplace (*m*)	Virginia	394	1930	Memorial mansion and gardens.
Geo. Washington Carver	Missouri	210	1951	Site of cabin where he was born. Museum with relics and records.
Gettysburg (*p*)	Pa.	3,672	1895	Beautiful natural park. Scene of great Civil War combat, 1863.
Gila Cliff Dwellings (*m*)	N. Mex.	533	1907	Highly interesting remains of cliff dwellings.
Glacier Bay (*m*)	Alaska	†3,554	1925	Tidewater glaciers of first rank.
Grand Canyon (*m*)	Arizona	198,280	1932	Adjoins Grand Canyon Nat. Park.
Grand Portage (*m*)	Minnesota	770	1960	Exploration route, fur trading post of North West Co.
Gran Quivira (*m*)	N. Mex.	611	1909	Important relic of Spanish missions in the United States.
Great Sand Dunes (*m*)	Colorado	36,740	1932	Sand dune 1000 feet high in San Luis Valley.
Guilford Courthouse (*p*)	N. Car.	224	1917	Near Greensboro. Scene of great battle of the Revolution, 1781.
Hampton (*h*)	Maryland	45	1948	Historic 18th century mansion.
Harper's Ferry (*h*)	W.Va.-Md.	1500	1955	Site of John Brown's raid before Civil War.
Home of Franklin D. Roosevelt (*h*)	N. York	188	1945	Roosevelt residence and library at Hyde Park.
Homestead (*m*)	Nebraska	163	1939	Site of first homestead in the United States.
Hopewell Village (*h*)	Pa.	848	1938	17th-century center of iron making, ruins.
Horseshoe Bend (*p*)	Alabama	2,040	1959	Site of Jackson's victory over Indians.
Hovenweep (*m*)	Utah-Col.	505	1923	Groups of prehistoric towers and pueblo ruins.
Independence (*h*)	Penn.	22	1956	Philadelphia's Independence Hall and other structures.

NATIONAL MONUMENTS AND ALLIED AREAS*—Continued

Name	Location	Area (Acres)	Established	Distinctive Characteristics
Jefferson National Expansion Memorial (*h*)	Missouri	85	1935	Commemorating westward expansion of U.S.
Jewel Cave (*m*)	S. Dakota	1,275	1908	Vast limestone cavern of extraordinary beauty.
Joshua Tree (*m*)	Calif.	557,992	1936	The Joshua tree, a spectacular feature of western desert land.
Katmai (*m*)	Alaska	†4,215	1918	Volcanic phenomena; "Valley of Ten Thousand Smokes."
Kennesaw Mountain (*b*)	Georgia	3,683	1947	Scene of battle in Civil War, June 27, 1864.
King's Mountain (*p*)	S. Car.	3,950	1931	Site of American victory, Oct. 7, 1780, in Revolutionary War.
Lava Beds (*m*)	Calif.	46,239	1925	Volcanic formations; battleground Modoc Indian War, 1873.
Lehman Caves (*m*)	Nevada	640	1922	Limestone caverns of much beauty and scientific interest.
Lincoln Boyhood (*m*)	Indiana	200	1963	Farm where Lincoln lived from 8th to 21st year.
Lincoln Memorial (*m*)	D.C.	164	1911	Parthenon-like structure with colossal statue of seated Lincoln.
Manassas (*b*)	Virginia	3,109	1940	Scene of two Civil War battles in 1861 and 1862.
Minute Man (*h*)	Mass.	750	1959	Scene of opening skirmish of Revolutionary War.
Montezuma Castle (*m*)	Arizona	842	1906	Prehistoric cliff-dwelling in the face of a high cliff.
Moores Creek (*b*)	N. Car.	50	1926	Scene of a memorable battle of the Revolutionary War.
Morristown (*h*)	N. Jersey	958	1933	Washington's headquarters in 1779–80.
Mound City Group (*m*)	Ohio	68	1923	Prehistoric mounds in Camp Sheridan military reservation.
Mount Rushmore (*p*)	S. Dakota	1,278	1925	Colossal figures of four presidents carved on cliff.
Muir Woods (*m*)	Calif.	503	1908	Noted redwood grove; located 7 miles from San Francisco.
Natural Bridges (*m*)	Utah	7,600	1908	Three natural bridges, largest 222 feet high; span 261 feet.
Navajo (*m*)	Arizona	360	1909	Numerous ancient pueblos, or ruins of cliff dwellings.
Ocmulgee (*m*)	Georgia	683	1936	Indian mounds in and around Macon.
Oregon Caves (*m*)	Oregon	480	1909	Vast caves of dazzling whiteness called "Marble Halls."
Organ Pipe Cactus (*m*)	Arizona	330,874	1937	Unique forms of native plant and animal life.
Pea Ridge (*b*)	Arkansas	4,283	1960	Scene of Civil War battle in 1862.
Perry's Victory (*m*)	Ohio	21	1936	Commemoration of victory over British fleet in 1813.
Petersburg (*b*)	Virginia	2,731	1926	Scene of Civil War conflicts.
Pinnacles (*m*)	Calif.	14,498	1908	Many spirelike rock formations, 500 to 1200 feet high.
Pipe Spring (*m*)	Arizona	40	1923	Historic fort built by Mormon pioneers.
Pipestone (*m*)	Minnesota	283	1937	Source of material for Indian peace pipes.
Rainbow Bridge (*m*)	Utah	160	1910	Natural bridge 309 feet above water; span is 278 feet.
Richmond (*b*)	Virginia	747	1944	Scene of battles in defense of Richmond during Civil War.
Russell Cave (*m*)	Alabama	310	1961	Archeological record of human habitation from 6000 B.C.
Sagamore Hill (*h*)	New York	85	1963	Theodore Roosevelt's home from 1885 till his death.
Saguaro (*m*)	Arizona	78,644	1933	Giant cacti of unusual scientific interest.
Saint Gaudens (*h*)	N. H.	86	1965	"Aspet," home of sculptor Augustus St. Gaudens.
Salem Maritime (*h*)	Mass.	11	1938	Nathaniel Hawthorne's place in Salem.
San Juan (*h*)	P. Rico	38	1949	16th-century Spanish fortifications.
Saratoga (*h*)	New York	5,500	1948	Scene of American victory over British, 1777.
Scotts Bluff (*m*)	Nebraska	3,084	1919	Landmark on Oregon trail.
Shiloh (*b*)	Tenn.	3,515	1894	Embraces the battlefield of Shiloh, near Pittsburg Landing.
Sitka (*m*)	Alaska	54	1910	Park of great natural beauty, scene of massacre of Russians.
Statue of Liberty (*m*)	N.Y.-N.J.	58	1924	Famous statue on Liberty Island, gift of the French people.
Stones River (*b*)	Tennessee	331	1927	Scene of Civil War battle.
Sunset Crater (*m*)	Arizona	3,040	1930	Volcanic crater with lava flows and ice caves.
Theodore Roosevelt (*p*)	N. Dak.	70,436	1947	Part of Roosevelt's Elkhorn ranch.
Thomas Jefferson (*m*)	D. C.	18	1934	Colonnaded rotunda in style favored by Jefferson.
Timpanogos Cave (*m*)	Utah	250	1922	Limestone cavern almost 600 feet in length.
Tonto (*m*)	Arizona	1,120	1907	Cliff dwellings in an unusually good state of preservation.
Tumacacori (*m*)	Arizona	10	1908	Spanish Mission established in late 17th century.
Tuzigoot (*m*)	Arizona	43	1939	Ruins of ancient pueblo with valuable relics.
Vanderbilt Mansion (*h*)	New York	212	1940	Palatial residence at Hyde Park.
Vicksburg (*p*)	Miss.	1,741	1899	Scene of the siege and surrender of Vicksburg, 1863.
Walnut Canyon (*m*)	Arizona	1,879	1915	Cliff dwellings of much scientific and popular interest.
WashingtonMonument (*m*)	D. C.	106	1848	Obelisk, 555 feet high, commemorating George Washington.
White Sands (*m*)	N. Mex.	146,535	1933	Sands resembling snow; interesting plant and animal life.
Whitman Mission (*h*)	Wash.	98	1940	Site of first mission in Pacific Northwest.
Wilson's Creek (*b*)	Missouri	1730	1965	Civil War battlefield of 1861 for control of Missouri.
Wright Brothers (*p*)	N. Car.	425	1933	Scene of first sustained flight by airplane.
Wupatki (*m*)	Arizona	35,233	1924	Prehistoric dwellings of ancestors of Hopi Indians.
Yucca House (*m*)	Colo.	10	1919	Mounds left by prehistoric people.

* Exclusive of areas less than 5 acres. † Square miles. (*b*) National military parks or national battlefields, battlefield sites, or battlefield parks. (*h*) National historical parks or national historic sites. (*m*) National monuments. (*p*) National memorials or national memorial parks.

STATE PARKS AND RELATED AREAS—1968

State	No.	Acres (1000)	State	No.	Acres (1000)	State	No.	Acres (1000)
Alabama	139	410	Louisiana	47	1,807	Ohio	492	358
Alaska	117	336	Maine	625	241	Oklahoma	88	491
Arizona	691	121	Maryland	99	198	Oregon	267	951
Arkansas	49	178	Massachusetts	574	340	Pennsylvania	495	3,033
California	216	921	Michigan	2,953	4,199	Rhode Island	101	31
Colorado	72	113	Minnesota	735	3,701	South Carolina	56	158
Connecticut	230	160	Mississippi	144	1,262	South Dakota	406	215
Delaware	35	24	Missouri	294	318	Tennessee	1,374	743
Florida	809	2,891	Montana	268	634	Texas	954	388
Georgia	312	773	Nebraska	122	131	Utah	123	241
Hawaii	90	1,302	Nevada	22	319	Vermont	161	152
Idaho	144	593	New Hampshire	285	76	Virginia	126	156
Illinois	129	1,008	New Jersey	134	291	Washington	1,546	4,148
Indiana	246	230	New Mexico	90	346	West Virginia	63	262
Iowa	513	160	New York	304	3,638	Wisconsin	1,075	944
Kansas	226	102	North Carolina	156	282	Wyoming	62	88
Kentucky	135	152	North Dakota	216	84	Total	18,610	39,701

GROWTH OF THE UNITED STATES IN POPULATION, 1900-1970

State	Population 1900	Population 1940	Population 1950	Population 1960	Population 1970	% of inc. 1960–70	Rank	Largest City
Alabama	1,828,697	2,832,961	3,061,743	3,266,740	3,444,165	5.4	21	Birmingham
Alaska	63,592	72,524	128,643	226,167	302,173	33.6	51	Anchorage
Arizona	122,931	499,261	749,587	1,302,161	1,772,482	36.1	33	Phoenix
Arkansas	1,311,564	1,949,387	1,909,511	1,786,272	1,923,295	7.7	32	Little Rock
California	1,485,053	6,907,387	10,586,223	15,717,204	19,953,134	27.0	1	Los Angeles
Colorado	539,700	1,123,296	1,325,089	1,753,947	2,207,259	25.8	30	Denver
Connecticut	908,420	1,709,242	2,007,280	2,535,234	3,032,217	19.6	24	Hartford
Delaware	184,735	266,505	318,085	446,292	548,104	22.8	47	Wilmington
Dist. Columbia	278,718	663,091	802,178	763,956	756,510	−1.0	41	Washington
Florida	528,542	1,897,414	2,771,305	4,951,560	6,789,443	37.1	9	Jacksonville
Georgia	2,216,331	3,123,723	3,444,578	3,943,116	4,589,575	16.4	15	Atlanta
Hawaii	154,001	....	....	632,772	768,561	21.5	40	Honolulu
Idaho	161,772	524,873	588,637	667,191	712,567	6.8	43	Boise
Illinois	4,821,550	7,897,241	8,712,176	10,081,156	11,113,976	10.2	5	Chicago
Indiana	2,516,462	3,427,796	3,934,224	4,662,498	5,193,669	11.4	11	Indianapolis
Iowa	2,231,853	2,538,268	2,621,073	2,757,537	2,825,041	2.4	25	Des Moines
Kansas	1,470,495	1,801,028	1,905,299	2,178,611	2,249,071	3.2	28	Wichita
Kentucky	2,147,174	2,845,627	2,944,806	3,038,156	3,219,311	6.0	23	Louisville
Louisiana	1,381,625	2,363,880	2,683,516	3,257,022	3,643,180	11.9	20	New Orleans
Maine	694,466	847,226	913,774	969,265	992,048	2.4	38	Portland
Maryland	1,188,044	1,821,244	2,343,001	3,100,689	3,922,399	26.5	18	Baltimore
Massachusetts	2,805,346	4,316,721	4,690,514	5,148,578	5,689,170	10.5	10	Boston
Michigan	2,420,982	5,256,106	6,371,766	7,823,194	8,875,083	13.4	7	Detroit
Minnesota	1,751,394	2,792,300	2,982,483	3,413,864	3,805,069	11.5	19	Minneapolis
Mississippi	1,551,270	2,183,796	2,178,914	2,178,141	2,216,912	1.8	29	Jackson
Missouri	3,106,665	3,784,664	3,954,653	4,319,813	4,677,399	8.3	13	St. Louis
Montana	243,329	559,456	591,024	674,767	694,409	2.9	44	Billings
Nebraska	1,066,300	1,315,834	1,325,510	1,411,330	1,483,791	5.1	35	Omaha
Nevada	42,335	110,247	160,083	285,278	488,738	71.3	48	Las Vegas
New Hampshire	411,588	491,524	533,242	606,921	737,681	21.5	42	Manchester
New Jersey	1,883,669	4,160,165	4,835,329	6,066,782	7,168,164	18.2	8	Newark
New Mexico	195,310	531,818	681,187	951,023	1,014,979	6.7	37	Albuquerque
New York	7,268,894	13,479,142	14,830,192	16,782,304	18,190,740	8.4	2	New York
North Carolina	1,893,810	3,571,623	4,061,929	4,556,155	5,082,059	11.5	12	Charlotte
North Dakota	319,146	641,935	619,636	632,446	617,761	−2.3	46	Fargo
Ohio	4,157,545	6,907,612	7,946,627	9,706,397	10,652,017	9.7	6	Cleveland
Oklahoma	790,391	2,336,434	2,233,351	2,328,284	2,559,253	9.9	27	Oklahoma City
Oregon	413,536	1,089,684	1,521,341	1,768,687	2,091,385	18.2	31	Portland
Pennsylvania	6,302,115	9,900,180	10,498,012	11,319,366	11,793,909	4.2	3	Philadelphia
Rhode Island	428,556	713,346	791,896	859,488	949,723	10.5	39	Providence
South Carolina	1,340,316	1,899,804	2,117,027	2,382,594	2,589,891	8.7	26	Columbia
South Dakota	401,570	642,961	652,740	680,514	665,507	−2.2	45	Sioux Falls
Tennessee	2,020,616	2,915,841	3,291,718	3,567,089	3,924,164	10.0	17	Memphis
Texas	3,048,710	6,414,824	7,711,194	9,579,677	11,196,730	16.9	4	Houston
Utah	276,749	550,310	688,862	890,627	1,059,273	18.9	36	Salt Lake City
Vermont	343,641	359,231	377,747	389,881	444,330	14.0	49	Burlington
Virginia	1,854,184	2,677,773	3,318,680	3,966,949	4,648,494	17.2	14	Norfolk
Washington	518,103	1,736,191	2,378,963	2,853,214	3,409,169	19.5	22	Seattle
West Virginia	958,800	1,901,974	2,005,552	1,860,421	1,744,237	−6.2	34	Huntington
Wisconsin	2,069,042	3,137,587	3,434,575	3,951,777	4,417,933	11.8	16	Milwaukee
Wyoming	92,531	250,742	290,529	330,066	332,416	0.7	50	Cheyenne
Total, U.S.	75,212,166	131,669,275	150,697,361	179,323,175	204,765,770	13.4		New York

Source: U.S. Bureau of the Census.

NEW ENGLAND STATES

The New England states, comprising Maine, New Hampshire, Vermont, Massachusetts, Rhode Island, and Connecticut, are situated in the northeastern part of the United States. The total area of these six states, 66,608 square miles, is less than the area of Oklahoma, 69,919 square miles, while the total population, 11,699,726, is more than four times the population of that state, 2,498,378.

Surface. The principal upland regions of New England are the old, worn-down White mountains in New Hampshire, the Green mountains in Vermont, and the Berkshire Hills in Massachusetts. Numerous harbors, formed from submerged valleys, indent the coast. Northern New England has many small lakes noted for scenic beauty. The Rangeley lakes in Maine and lakes Sunapee and Winnepesaukee in New Hampshire are popular resorts.

Rivers. New England is well watered. Many of the rivers are broken by falls or rapids, and some of these furnish hydroelectric power. The Connecticut, Penobscot, Kennebec, Mystic, Charles, and Thames are navigable for steamers.

Climate. The climate is continental. Winter, a very cold season, is rendered more unpleasant by the humidity of the air. Northeast winds passing over the cold Labrador current flowing along the New England shore are chilled and, blowing inland, bring heavy snows in winter and cause fogs and cold rains in summer. The southeast winds are much milder, as they sweep over warm ocean currents from the Gulf of Mexico.

Minerals. New England has but little mineral wealth. Building stones, feldspars, and various clays are found. Granite, basalt, marble, and slate are the chief quarry products, and rank in importance in the order named. Among these states, Vermont stands first in total value of quarry products, with Massachusetts second, and New Hampshire third. Besides leading in the production of granite, Vermont quarries large quantities of slate and much beautiful marble. In each of the New England states, except Connecticut in which basalt leads, granite is the most valuable quarry product.

Fisheries. Fishing early became a prominent industry, the nearness of rich fishing grounds attracting a large class of workers. Cod, halibut, mackerel, swordfish, haddock, hake, herring, and pollock are the principal catches. Oysters, clams, crabs, lobsters, and shrimps form important items in the total annual value of the fisheries. Menhaden are taken in immense quantities for oil and fertilizing material. In amount and value of sea fish taken, Massachusetts leads all other states in the Union.

Forests. Forests still cover large tracts of land in this section, especially in Maine, New Hampshire, and Vermont. The pine is the most common tree

Spruce is cut in Maine for making paper and wood pulp, the principal manufactures of the state. Maine still ships considerable lumber.

Agriculture. Much of New England is stony and difficult to cultivate, and abandoned farms are not uncommon. The Connecticut valley, however, has very fertile soil, and there is also considerable good farm land in the valleys of several smaller rivers. Hay is the chief crop. Potatoes, rye, corn, and oats are also raised. Connecticut Valley tobacco ranks second only to Cuban tobacco. Dairying is an important occupation, especially in Vermont. Market gardening is a profitable industry in recent years. Apples, pears, and cherries are the chief orchard fruits. More than half the world's supply of cranberries is grown in Massachusetts.

Manufacturing. In all these states, manufacturing is the principal occupation. Hundreds of different articles are made. Among the chief products are metal wares, boots and shoes, leather, paper, brass goods, machinery, electrical apparatus, clothing, rubber goods, barbed wire, carpets, and refined sugar. Although many textile mills have moved to the South, textiles are still important to the economy of New England. Every city in this division is a manufacturing center.

Many western states have counties each larger than southern New England. This section lacks coal, iron, copper, lead, zinc, timber, wool, cotton, hides—in short, all the basic materials of industrial work in mill, factory, or machine shop. Yet the intelligence, skill, energy, and inventiveness of its people have made southern New England the greatest center of diversified manufacturing in the Union. Massachusetts is a striking example. Forty-three states exceed it in area. Yet in population it stands ninth among the states, and its enormous manufacturing output gives it still higher rank in commerce.

Commerce. The seaboard states have a large commerce, both domestic and foreign, and the harbors of their important ports are crowded with shipping at all times of the year. Manufactures constitute the bulk of the exports; the imports consist mainly of raw materials from various parts of the globe. Numerous railroads link this section with the rest of the Union. The principal ports are Boston, Mass., Portland, Me., Providence, R. I., Portsmouth, N. H., and New Haven, Conn.

MIDDLE ATLANTIC STATES

Because of their medial position with reference to the seaboard, and on account of a general similarity in surface features, the states of New York, New Jersey, Pennsylvania, Delaware, Maryland, Virginia, and West Virginia are generally grouped together. The first four have been called the "Middle" states and the last three have been placed with "South Atlantic" or "Southern" states. By some, the first three are styled "Middle Atlantic" while all the others are called "South Atlantic" states.

The total area of the states comprising this group is less than one-sixteenth of the entire area of the country. Yet these seven states have about one-fourth of the population, own more than one-third of the manufacturing capital, and contain nearly two-fifths of the wage earners of the United States.

Surface. The Appalachian Mountain system extends across this group of states from northeast to southwest, and the coastal plain gradually widens southward. On the west side of the mountains is the Allegheny plateau. It is a rugged area, sloping toward the Mississippi, and is but thinly populated. Numerous bays and inlets indent the Atlantic Coast and several of them form excellent harbors.

The coastal plain is low and sandy, and much of it is bordered by swamps. Some of the rivers are navigable and add greatly to the transportation facilities of the region. Among the more important tidal streams are the Hudson, the Delaware, the Patapsco, and the James. The Ohio River on the west is a great artery of interstate trade. The shores of Chesapeake Bay are dotted with ports actively engaged in coastwise traffic.

Climate. Between the northern and southern limits of this division the distance is nearly 600 miles. This distance, together with variations in surface features, causes marked differences in the climatic conditions of the northern and southern parts. In northern New York the mean winter temperature is 17° F.; in southern Virginia, 35° F. The summer temperature averages 60° F. along the northern boundary of this group of states and 75° F. along the southern. The fruit belt of western New York owes its favorable climate to the equalizing influence of Lake Erie and Lake Ontario. The Gulf Stream passes near the Virginia coast and moderates the winds blowing from the ocean. In all the states of this division the rainfall is amply sufficient for farming.

Mining. Iron is found in all the states except Delaware. Enormous quantities of coal are mined in Pennsylvania, West Virginia, Maryland, and Virginia. Petroleum, first discovered in Pennsylvania in 1859, is produced in that state, in New York, and in West Virginia. Natural gas, piped from the gas fields, is utilized for heating and lighting in many cities.

Their vast supplies of coal, iron, petroleum, and natural gas, the basic materials of industrial wealth, have enabled these states to lead the nation in various steel and iron manufactures.

Forests. Northern New York is well forested, and much forest land in the Adirondack region is under the protection of the state. In the Appalachians, the United States government has reserved extensive forested tracts. Hemlock is the principal timber cut in New York and Pennsylvania. Spruce for making wood pulp is obtained chiefly in New York and in West Virginia. Oak, maple, poplar, walnut, and other broad-leaved trees are common in all these states. Yellow pine is an important source of lumber in Virginia, and cypress and cedar are found in the coastal swamps. Hardwoods produced in this group come mostly from West Virginia.

Agriculture. In these states, agriculture has always been an important industry. There is much fertile soil, and large crops of grains, potatoes, apples, peaches, pears, grapes, and strawberries are grown. Virginia ranks as one of the leading tobacco states. Peanuts also form an important crop in that state. Buckwheat is grown extensively in Pennsylvania and in New York. Peas, corn, tomatoes, berries, and orchard fruits are canned in enormous quantities. Market gardening is a profitable occupation near the large centers of population. Much attention is paid to dairying, especially in New York. The annual output of butter and cheese is very large. Vast quantities of milk are supplied to the great cities in this section. Besides cattle, the other large farm animals most commonly reared are horses, sheep, and hogs. Poultry raising is an important industry.

Fisheries. Fishing is an occupation of great importance. Oysters form the most valuable single item. Shad, bluefish, and mackerel are taken in the bays and rivers. Lakes Erie and Ontario furnish large quantities of lake trout, pike, ciscoes, and other food fish.

Manufacturing. In this section manufacturing is the foremost industry. New York, called the Empire State, ranks first in the Union in manufacturing as well as in population, wealth, and commerce. Of its long list of diversified manufactures, the most valuable single industrial product is wearing apparel. Other important manufactures of this division of states are iron and steel wares, foundry and machine shop products, chemicals, woolen goods, silk, glass, and leather goods. Oil refining is the leading industry in New Jersey.

Commerce. The commercial supremacy of this group of states arises from favoring geographic conditions and from abundant transportation facili-

CHANGING SKYLINES

Hotels of impressive size and varied architecture give Miami Beach, Florida, a distinctive character.
Miami Beach News Bureau

Expressing its dynamic growth and varied interests is the skyline of the city called "Dazzling Dallas," in Texas.
Photo by Squire Haskins

Dominating a view of Telegraph Hill in San Francisco, Calif. is the white fluted shaft of Coit Tower, a monument to volunteer firemen.
San Francisco Chamber of Commerce

Los Angeles, California, is readily identified by this background of palms and tall buildings.

Tradition and modernity are blended in the impressive water front of Baltimore, Maryland.
Baltimore Ass'n of Commerce

Towering above adjacent slightly Venice-like waterways is an example of latest architectural style at Marina City in Chicago, Ill.
Chicago Ass'n of Commerce & Industry

PROGRESS IN ARCHITECTURE

Modern in spirit is the Tyrone Guthrie Theatre in Minneapolis, Minn., built in 1963 for a repertory company producing classical plays.
Minneapolis Chamber of Commerce

Daring originality characterizes Frank Lloyd Wright's design of the Guggenheim Museum, New York City.
Ezra Stoller

Renewal of Pittsburgh's core area is seen to special advantage in this view of "The Golden Triangle."
Samuel A. Musgrave

"U.N." type structures in the Prudential Center. Boston, Mass.
Greater Boston Chamber of Commerce

Space Needle and Monorail at the Seattle Exposition.

ties. Two-thirds of the foreign commerce of the United States passes through New York, Philadelphia, Baltimore, and other ports of this division. Unsurpassed facilities for collecting raw materials and for distributing manufactured goods account for the growth of the larger industrial cities. Equal facilities for gathering and for distributing exports have made several cities great seaports.

The Great Lakes aid the growth of the Middle Atlantic states by furnishing a waterway for transporting raw materials needed in many industries. Of high value also are the Hudson and Mohawk valleys. These furnish easy routes of rail, river, and canal communication between the Atlantic seaboard and the West. The New York State Barge canal connects the Hudson river with the Great Lakes. The Allegheny and Monongahela rivers, uniting to form the Ohio, afford water transportation between this group of states and the central and southern parts of the United States.

CENTRAL STATES

The large division of the Union called the Central states consists of Kentucky, Ohio, Indiana, Illinois, Michigan, Wisconsin, Missouri, Iowa, Minnesota, North Dakota, South Dakota, Nebraska, and Kansas.

Surface. Prairies occupy a large part of this division. They are level or gently rolling and for the most part are covered with a rich dark soil. On such plains modern farm machinery can be used to great advantage; hence the central and eastern parts have become the chief agricultural regions of the United States.

Along the western border there is considerable highland, including the Black Hills, noted for their gold mines. In the southwest corner of South Dakota are the famous Bad Lands. These consist of a maze of ridges and pinnacles of sandstone; the soil is mostly bare clay of different colors, and the whole region is very difficult of travel.

Rivers. Most of this division is drained by the Mississippi and its affluents. Six of the states, however, border on the Great Lakes and are in part in the Saint Lawrence basin. Some streams in Minnesota, North Dakota, and South Dakota flow into the Red River of the North. Hence the waters of the Central states find their way into the Atlantic through the Gulf of Mexico, the Saint Lawrence gulf, and Hudson bay. Besides the hundreds of streams that water this vast valley, there are thousands of small lakes that dot the surface, especially in Minnesota and in North Dakota. The principal rivers navigable by steamboats are the Mississippi, Missouri, Ohio, Wabash, Illinois, and Red River of the North.

Climate. In the north, the winter is long and extremely cold weather prevails, while the summers are short and hot. Along the southern border, in Kentucky, Missouri, and Kansas, the climate is milder. Snow seldom falls there and never stays on the ground long. The rainfall is sufficient for farming over all this division, except in the extreme western plains.

Minerals. This group of states is very rich in mineral wealth. Coal is mined extensively in Kentucky, Iowa, Indiana, Ohio, Kansas, and Illinois, the last ranking third among the coal producing states of the Union. Petroleum wells are in operation in Kentucky, Indiana, Kansas, and Illinois. Natural gas is produced in several states, notably in Illinois and Indiana. Gold, silver, lead, zinc, potter's clays, building stone, gypsum, asbestos, and graphite are obtained. Michigan has long been noted for its yield of copper and salt. In Minnesota and Michigan there are vast deposits of iron ore. Because of this supply, made available by cheap transportation, great centers of the iron industry have been developed on lakes Michigan and Erie.

Forests. Michigan, Wisconsin, and Minnesota, once leaders in the cutting of timber, are still important producers of lumber and pulp wood. Pine for lumber and spruce and hemlock for pulp wood are the principal items in the annual timber cut. Despite the destruction of the chief forests, large woodlands still exist in several of the states, and forest industries furnish employment for many workers.

Agriculture. Every crop known to the temperate zones can be grown in this division. Hundreds of millions of bushels of corn, oats, barley, rye, and wheat are raised annually. Hay, potatoes, vegetables, and orchard fruits are important crops. Tobacco is cultivated in the eastern part of this division. Kentucky is one of the leading states in the Union in tobacco production. Sugar beets are grown in ten states in this group; Nebraska, Michigan, and Minnesota lead in sugar beet production. Flax is grown in the northwest. No other section of equal area on the globe rivals the central Mississippi valley in agricultural productiveness. Even on the higher western plains, abundant harvests are reaped wherever the land is irrigated.

Live Stock. Cattle, horses, mules, and hogs (fattened on corn) are raised in immense numbers. Sheep are reared in every state, and the annual wool clip totals about one-third of that of the entire United States. Dairy interests, already very large, are becoming increasingly valuable. Butter, cheese, and condensed milk from this division now go to all parts of the civilized world. Poultry farming is a profitable occupation.

Manufacturing. The range in manufacturing is exceedingly extensive. In several states the manufactures surpass in value the farm products. More automobiles are made in this division than in all the rest of the world. Meat packing is so vast an industry that it influences prices in every city in the United States. Much of the world's supply of flour is milled in these states.

The iron and steel interests, concentrated in centers of industry in northern Ohio, Indiana, and Illinois, employ many thousands of workers. The yearly output of refined petroleum represents many millions of dollars. Glass, furniture, wearing apparel, foundry and machine shop products, pottery, lumber, agricultural implements, tobacco goods, chemicals, metal wares, farm machinery, boots and shoes, beet sugar, paints and varnishes are other products whose aggregate output is enormous.

Fisheries. The Great Lakes supply annually over 100 million pounds of fish. Whitefish, ciscoes or lake herring, and lake trout constitute the principal catch. The frozen fish industry has become extensive.

Commerce. The states in this division have excellent railway facilities. Within their borders are operated more than 100,000 miles of railways, or about two-fifths of the entire railway mileage of the United States. The Ohio river and the Mississippi river are important arteries of commerce. Fleets of steamers, handling an enormous tonnage, ply on the Great Lakes. In connection with the lake traffic, the New York State Barge canal is used to transport various raw materials to the Hudson river, which serves as the final link in an all-water connection with the seaboard. But by far the larger part of the foreign shipments reach the great eastern seaports, New York, Boston, Philadelphia, and Baltimore, by railroad.

SOUTHERN STATES

Alabama, Arkansas, Florida, Georgia, Louisiana, Mississippi, North Carolina, Oklahoma, South Carolina, Tennessee, and Texas comprise the Southern states.

This division of the Union is bounded on the north by the Middle Atlantic states and by the Central states; on the east by the Atlantic Ocean; on the south by the Gulf of Mexico and Mexico; and on the west by New Mexico. The shortest distance between the extreme eastern and western limits is about 1700 miles. The width from north to south varies from about 425 to 850 miles. The total area of these eleven states is 781,657 square miles, or more than one-fourth of the area of the continental United States. For convenience of reference this division is treated in two sections—an eastern section and a western.

EASTERN SECTION

North Carolina, South Carolina, Tennessee, Georgia, Florida, Alabama, and Mississippi constitute the eastern section of the Southern states.

Surface. The Appalachian Mountain system, occupying much of this section and broadening out in the north, reaches its highest point in Mt. Mitchell, 6684 feet high, in North Carolina. Southward the mountains diminish in height until, in Alabama, they become low hills. All Florida and Mississippi, and parts of North Carolina, South Carolina, Georgia, and Alabama, are in the coastal plain. The principal rivers, including the Mississippi, Savannah, Saint John's, and Cape Fear, are navigable for steamers.

Climate and Rainfall. Along the Gulf coast, a region of heavy rains, the temperature averages about 85° F. in summer and 50° F. in winter. On the Atlantic shore, the climate is almost as warm, though not so humid. The climate of the upland districts is cool and bracing. Flowers bloom the year round in the more southern section, and the mildness of the climate draws numerous visitors to the winter resorts along both the Atlantic and the Gulf coast. From 40 inches to 60 inches of rain a year falls in the seaboard districts.

Minerals. Coal and iron ore are mined in Tennessee and Alabama, and mica in North Carolina Georgia and Tennessee produce excellent marble. Granite, limestone, and sandstone are abundant. Florida has large deposits of phosphate rock. In all these states there are numerous beds of potter's clay and other minor minerals.

Forests. Forests overspread thousands of square miles, the trees including yellow pine, cypress, hickory, ash, maple, and other hardwoods. In size and variety of species the forest trees of this section exceed those of all other parts of the Union, except the Pacific states. Lumbering is an important industry in many sections.

Agriculture. The chief occupation is farming. All the crops of the Temperate Zone can be grown in these states. Cotton is the most valuable single crop. Sea-island cotton is grown along the Atlantic coast. Millions of acres are devoted to corn and tobacco. Oats, white potatoes, peanuts, sweet potatoes, hay, wheat, and fruits are also widely cultivated. Rice is raised in the coast belt. Apples, plums, pears, watermelons, strawberries, peaches, and grapes grow in abundance. Southern Florida produces pineapples, figs, oranges, grapefruit, avocados, guavas, and other subtropical fruits. Garden vegetables are grown extensively for northern markets. Strawberries are shipped north every spring by fast-freight trains. Similarly, oranges, grapefruit, and various vegetables are sent in winter. Georgia leads in the production of pecans.

Fisheries. Oysters are obtained along the Atlantic shore. Bluefish, mullet, shad, mackerel, kingfish, tarpon, and other sea fish are caught. Valuable fisheries, including sponge fishing, are established on the Florida coast.

Stock Raising. Hogs, horses, mules, sheep, and cattle are raised in every state. Dairying has become an important industry. Milk, butter, and cheese are produced in large quantities.

Manufacturing. Manufacturing is developing rapidly in this section. Among the important industrial products are cotton textiles, cottonseed oil, cottonseed cake, lumber, iron and steel, tobacco goods, and naval stores. Cigars and cigarettes are made in great quantities in North Carolina and in Florida. Cotton goods form the leading industrial product. North Carolina leads all other states of the Union in cotton manufacturing. Flour milling and woodworking are valuable industrial interests. Iron and steel products are made in Tennessee and in Alabama. Aluminum is produced in Tennessee and North Carolina. The canning of fruits and vegetables is a growing industry in all these states. In this group, North Carolina, Georgia, and Tennessee lead in manufactures in the order named. Among important industrial centers are Atlanta, Ga., Birmingham, Ala., Winston-Salem, N. C., Memphis, Tenn., and Nashville, Tenn.

Commerce. Much merchandise for export is shipped down the Mississippi to New Orleans, where it is transferred to seagoing vessels. Portions of other rivers are utilized to some extent as inland waterways. Cotton is the largest export of this section. Pine lumber, phosphate rock, and naval stores are also sent abroad in large quantities. There are ample facilities for transportation by rail to all parts of the Union. The principal seaports serving these states are Wilmington, N. C., Charleston, S. C., Savannah, Ga., Jacksonville, Fla., Tampa, Fla., Pensacola, Fla., Mobile, Ala., and New Orleans, La.

WESTERN SECTION

Arkansas, Louisiana, Texas, and Oklahoma form the western section of the Southern states.

Surface. The northeastern part of this section is included in the Ozark plateau. This upland extends into the northern part of Arkansas and into the eastern part of Oklahoma. Louisiana and southeastern Texas lie in the coastal plain. The elevated western parts of Texas and Oklahoma form the southern extension of the Great Plains. The principal rivers are the Mississippi, Red, Brazos, Sabine, Trinity, and Colorado. All these drain into the Gulf of Mexico.

Climate and Rainfall. An abundant rainfall occurs over the eastern and southern parts of this section, while on the western side, which is mostly an elevated plain, the rainfall seldom exceeds 20 inches annually. The extreme southwest is dry. The summers are long and hot, but the Gulf winds lower the temperature, and winter is a pleasant season.

Agriculture. Agriculture is the chief source of wealth. Rich soil and favorable climate make it possible to grow in this section any crop of the Temperate Zone. Cotton is the principal crop. Other important products are rice, corn, potatoes, sweet potatoes, hay, wheat, tobacco, and numerous fruits. Vegetables are grown in enormous quantities for the northern markets. Louisiana is the leading state in sugar production. Texas is a large producer in several lines of agriculture. It is easily the first state in cotton. Texas also leads all the other states in value of crops produced. These frequently approximate a billion dollars in total value.

Lumbering. There are great forests of pine and cypress in the coastal plain and immense forests of hardwoods in high lands in the interior. This section is one of the chief timber regions of the country. Louisiana is the second state in the Union in lumber production.

Minerals. Sulphur mining is important in Louisiana and Texas. These states now furnish the world's chief supply of sulphur. Bauxite, the most valuable ore of aluminum, is obtained in Arkansas. In Oklahoma, Texas, and Louisiana, immense quantities of petroleum and natural gas are found. The Oklahoma oil field yields a very substantial proportion of the annual output of the petroleum of the United States. Beds of rock salt are worked in both Louisiana and Texas. Oklahoma is one of the leading states of the Union in zinc production and a considerable amount of lead also is obtained there. Manganese, potter's clay, quicksilver, coal, and copper are other valuable minerals obtained in this section. Building stone is abundant in all the states.

Stock Raising. The farm animals reared in this section bring enormous sums annually. Texas is the chief cattle raising state. Mules, horses, hogs, and sheep also are raised in great numbers. Texas ranks as one of the foremost wool producing states. The wool clip of Texas normally exceeds 25 million pounds annually.

Manufacturing. The principal manufactures of this section are petroleum products, lumber, refined sugar, packed meats, flour, cottonseed oil, and cottonseed cake. The manufacture of ice and of textiles are growing industries. Louisiana leads the group in the refining of cane sugar and in rice polishing, rice and sugar cane being distinctive crops of that state. Oklahoma ranks highest in the production of flour. Texas leads in manufactures, and is followed by Louisiana, Oklahoma, and Arkansas in the order named.

Commerce. The eastern part of the section has ample transportation facilities, and the thinly populated western section is crossed by numerous railways. Railroads connect all the commercial centers with the large cities east and north, and the rivers furnish hundreds of miles of waterways navigable for steamboats. The chief seaports are New Orleans, La., and Galveston, Houston, and Port Arthur, Texas. Important inland cities are Little Rock, Ark., Shreveport, La., Oklahoma City and Tulsa, Okla., Dallas, Fort Worth, San Antonio, and El Paso, Texas.

PLATEAU STATES

The Plateau states division of the Union is composed of Arizona, Colorado, Idaho, Montana, Nevada, New Mexico, Utah, and Wyoming. These states cover more than 850,000 square miles, or more than one-fourth of the total area of the United States. Idaho, the smallest state in the group, is larger than all the New England states combined.

Surface. This division embraces most of the region occupied by the Rocky Mountain system in the continental United States. The surface is mainly a series of plateaus surmounted by lofty ranges, which attain their greatest height in Colorado. The mean or average elevation of the Plateau states is approximately 5300 feet, or slightly more than one mile, above sea level. Colorado and Wyoming have the highest average elevation; Montana and Arizona, the lowest. In all of the states there are mountains which rise above 12,000 feet. Peaks more than 13,000 feet high are found in Nevada, New Mexico, Utah, and Wyoming. In Colorado, many summits rise above 14,000 feet.

In geological times this vast upland was a scene of tremendous volcanic action. There are many extinct volcanoes, and ancient lava beds cover many thousand square miles. The great geysers of Yellowstone park are situated in a volcanic region.

Rivers. The Plateau states are drained chiefly by streams belonging to two great drainage systems, the Gulf and the Pacific. Important rivers whose waters reach the Gulf of Mexico are the Rio Grande, the Arkansas, the Platte, the Yellowstone, and the Missouri. The principal rivers whose waters finally flow into the Pacific are the Colorado, Green, Grand, Snake, and Clark Fork. The Green and the Grand are affluents of the Colorado; the Snake and Clark Fork are tributaries of the Columbia.

The streams of the Great Basin, a very dry region comprising much of western Utah and nearly all of Nevada, usually flow only during the brief rainy season. They either disappear in sandy valleys or discharge their scanty waters into alkaline lakes having no outlet. The Humboldt, the largest river in Nevada, flows nearly across the state from east to west. It empties into the Humboldt and the Carson sinks where its waters evaporate, leaving alkaline deposits. Similarly, the Sevier river, the longest stream in western Utah, flows into the salty Sevier lake. The Weber, the Bear, and the Jordan are small rivers which empty into Great Salt lake.

Climate. Because of a wide range in latitude, great variations in altitude, and marked diversity of surface features, the Plateau states have many varieties of climate. On the highest mountains, arctic conditions prevail. In the elevated plains at the base of the mountains there are severe extremes of heat and cold. In the far southwest are some of the hottest desert areas known.

The widest extremes of temperature are observed on the high plains of Montana, flanking the eastern base of the Rockies. Here temperatures ranging from about 60° below zero in winter to 108° above zero in summer have been noted. In southwestern Arizona, near the Mexican border, summer temperatures of 120° have been recorded, but in winter the thermometer rarely falls below freezing. The climate of the various interior parts of the Plateau states is similar, but with less pronounced extremes.

A noteworthy feature of the climate of the plateau region is the great daily variation in temperature which takes place, especially in summer. No matter how warm the days, the nights are almost invariably cool, even in the hottest deserts.

Strong winds, which prevail in many sections, often exercise a marked influence on the climate. A well-known example is the so-called chinook, a warm wind which, sweeping down the eastern slope of the Rockies and far out on the adjacent plains, sometimes melts heavy snowfalls within a few hours.

Notwithstanding severe extremes, the climate of the Plateau states is dry and invigorating, and, on the whole, unusually salubrious.

Rainfall. On one-fifth of the United States the rainfall is so light that agriculture cannot be successfully carried on without irrigation. Most of the dry area is in this division. Because of scanty rainfall, all these states have tracts of true desert. Thousands of square miles also are covered with alkali deposits. These dreary wastes have often no vegetation whatever. In other sections, the traveler may ride for hours over dusty plains, with yuccas, cactuses, greasewoods, or sagebrushes the only conspicuous plants in sight. These require but very little moisture.

Forests. In all of the Plateau states, forests are found on the slopes of the mountains. The trees are generally pines, spruces, firs, and other conifers. About one-sixth of the total area is more or less wooded. In each state there are large forested districts under government protection. These reserves, some 90 in all, are known as national forests. Their total area, about 140,000 square miles, is greater than that of any state in the group except Montana. Among the Plateau states, Idaho, with over 30,000 square miles of protected woodlands, has the greatest area in national forests. Montana ranks second, with Colorado, Arizona, Wyoming, New Mexico, and Utah following in the order named. Nevada, with reserves of 7780 square miles, ranks last. See *Forests, U. S. National.*

Minerals. The Plateau states are exceedingly rich in mineral wealth. Among important mineral productions are gold, silver, copper, coal, petroleum, lead, tungsten, uranium, vanadium, gems, and

RANK OF THE STATES IN POPULATION, 1820-1970

State	1820	1830	1840	1850	1860	1870	1880	1890	1900	1910	1920	1930	1940	1950	1960	1970
Alabama	19	15	12	12	13	16	17	17	18	18	18	15	17	17	19	21
Alaska	..	..	..	..	..	..	..	..	..	..	..	..	..	..	51	51
Arizona	..	..	..	..	..	46	44	47	47	46	46	44	44	38	35	33
Arkansas	26	28	25	26	25	26	25	24	25	25	25	25	24	30	31	32
California	..	..	..	29	26	24	24	22	21	12	8	6	5	2	2	1
Colorado	..	..	..	..	38	41	35	31	32	32	33	33	33	34	33	30
Connecticut	14	16	20	21	24	25	28	29	29	31	29	29	31	29	25	24
Delaware	22	24	26	30	32	35	38	43	45	47	47	47	47	47	47	47
Dist. of Col.	25	25	28	33	35	34	36	40	41	43	42	41	37	36	40	41
Florida	..	26	27	31	31	33	34	32	33	33	32	31	27	20	10	9
Georgia	11	10	9	9	11	12	13	12	11	10	12	14	14	13	16	15
Hawaii	..	..	..	..	..	..	..	..	..	..	..	..	..	..	44	40
Idaho	..	..	..	..	..	44	46	46	46	45	43	43	43	44	43	43
Illinois	24	20	14	11	4	4	4	3	3	3	3	3	3	4	4	5
Indiana	18	13	10	7	6	6	6	8	8	9	11	11	12	12	11	11
Iowa	..	..	29	27	20	11	10	10	10	15	16	19	20	22	24	25
Kansas	..	..	..	..	33	29	20	19	22	22	24	24	29	31	28	28
Kentucky	6	6	6	8	9	8	8	11	12	14	15	17	16	19	22	23
Louisiana	17	19	19	18	17	21	22	25	23	24	22	22	21	21	20	20
Maine	12	12	13	16	22	23	27	30	31	34	35	35	35	35	36	38
Maryland	10	11	15	17	19	20	23	27	26	27	28	28	28	24	21	18
Massachusetts	7	8	8	6	7	7	7	6	7	6	6	8	8	9	9	10
Michigan	27	27	23	20	16	13	9	9	9	8	7	7	7	7	7	7
Minnesota	..	..	..	36	30	28	26	20	19	19	17	18	18	18	18	19
Mississippi	21	22	17	15	14	18	18	21	20	21	23	23	23	26	29	29
Missouri	23	21	16	13	8	5	5	5	5	7	9	10	10	11	13	13
Montana	..	..	..	..	..	43	45	45	43	40	39	39	40	43	42	44
Nebraska	..	..	..	..	39	36	30	26	27	29	31	32	32	33	34	35
Nevada	..	..	..	..	41	40	43	49	49	49	49	49	49	49	50	48
New Hampshire	15	18	22	22	27	31	31	33	37	39	41	42	45	45	46	42
New Jersey	13	14	18	19	21	17	19	18	16	11	10	9	9	8	8	8
New Mexico	..	..	..	32	34	37	41	44	44	44	44	45	42	40	37	37
New York	1	1	1	1	1	1	1	1	1	1	1	1	1	1	1	2
North Carolina	4	5	7	10	12	14	15	16	15	16	14	12	11	10	12	12
North Dakota	..	..	..	..	42	45	40	42	40	37	36	38	39	42	45	46
Ohio	5	4	3	3	3	3	3	4	4	4	4	4	4	5	5	6
Oklahoma	..	..	..	..	..	..	..	39	30	23	21	21	22	25	27	27
Oregon	..	..	..	34	36	38	37	38	36	35	34	34	34	32	32	31
Pennsylvania	3	2	2	2	2	2	2	2	2	2	2	2	2	3	3	3
Rhode Island	20	23	24	28	29	32	33	36	35	38	38	37	36	37	39	39
South Carolina	8	9	11	14	18	22	21	23	24	26	26	26	26	27	26	26
South Dakota	..	..	..	..	..	..	..	35	38	36	37	36	38	41	41	45
Tennessee	9	7	5	5	10	9	12	13	14	17	19	16	15	15	17	17
Texas	..	..	..	25	23	19	11	7	6	5	5	5	6	6	6	4
Utah	..	..	..	35	37	39	39	41	42	41	40	40	41	39	38	36
Vermont	16	17	21	23	28	30	32	37	39	42	45	46	46	46	48	49
Virginia	2	3	4	4	5	10	14	15	17	20	20	20	19	16	14	14
Washington	..	..	..	..	40	42	42	34	34	30	30	30	30	23	23	22
West Virginia	..	..	..	..	..	27	29	28	28	28	27	27	25	28	30	34
Wisconsin	..	..	30	24	15	15	16	14	13	13	13	13	13	14	15	16
Wyoming	..	..	..	..	..	47	47	48	48	48	48	48	48	48	49	50

precious stones. In gold production, Colorado, Utah, and Arizona rank highest in the group. Utah, Montana, and Idaho are the chief producers of silver in the United States. In copper production, Arizona stands first, while Utah and Montana also rank among the most important copper producing states of the Union. Colorado, Wyoming, Utah, and New Mexico have valuable coal deposits. Wyoming contains rich petroleum fields. Colorado is the world's chief source of molybdenum, and Nevada and Colorado stand first in the production of tungsten.

Agriculture. Dry farming is successfully practiced in some districts, but dependence is placed chiefly upon irrigated land. This will grow most of the standard crops of the temperate zones. Wheat, barley, oats, potatoes, and sugar beets are raised. Alfalfa is a highly profitable crop, several harvests being reaped in a year. Truck farm products, as Colorado and Arizona melons, bring high prices in eastern markets. Apple culture has become a valuable pursuit in Montana and Idaho. Peaches are grown in Colorado and Utah. In the southwest, the hot climate fosters the growth of dates, olives, figs, oranges, and other subtropical fruits. Egyptian or long-staple cotton has become a leading crop in Arizona.

Government irrigation work has already reclaimed millions of acres of arid land. Farms of irrigated soil are small, and intensive agriculture is practiced. Improved land in farms comprises about one-twentieth of the total area. Montana has the largest acreage of crop land, Colorado stands second, and Idaho is third.

Stock Raising. For many years, stock raising has been an important industry in this division, and much capital is invested in the rearing of cattle, sheep, and horses. These rank in value in the order named. The annual wool clip of these states amounts to about two-fifths of that of the entire United States. Native grasses afford excellent pasturage, and, in the southern and central parts, farm animals feed in the open all the year round. Large numbers of cattle are sent to Omaha, Kansas City, Chicago, and other meat packing centers, where they are slaughtered, the meat being packed and distributed largely in refrigerator cars.

Manufacturing. Copper, lead, refined ores, flour, beet sugar, butter, condensed milk, dressed meat, canned vegetables, railroad cars, foundry materials, and lumber are the principal industrial products of the Plateau states. Manufacturing to supply local needs is increasing. Immense water power is available for future development. Colorado stands first among these states in value of manufactures; Montana is second, Utah third, and Arizona fourth.

Commerce. Railroads afford ready transportation to all parts of the Union. Several transcontinental lines cross this section, and there are numerous local lines. Mine products, lumber, cattle, cotton, and fruits form the chief items of outgoing shipment. These are sent both to the East and to the West chiefly in exchange for manufactures and other staples which the plateau region does not as yet produce.

PACIFIC STATES—CONTIGUOUS

The Pacific States consist of (1) the three continental States of California, Oregon, and Washington and (2) the off-shore states of Alaska and Hawaii. The geography of the three continental Pacific states will be treated here as a unit, as with the preceding regions of continental United States. But since Alaska and Hawaii are separate geographic areas, each of them will be treated separately.

Surface. No other equal area in the continental United States displays such diversity in surface features as does this division. In its mountain ranges are found the highest peaks, and in its deserts occur the lowest depressions. The rivers plunge down from alpine valleys over the highest known waterfalls. Here also is the only active volcano in the country.

The Sierra Nevada range extends nearly north and south through eastern California and, under the name of the Cascade range, continues northward through Oregon and Washington. Near the Pacific shore, the Coast ranges traverse these states from north to south. Between the Sierra Nevada and the Coast ranges lies the great central valley of California. This is about 50 miles wide and 400 miles long and is remarkably fertile. In the southern part, irrigation is needed for successful farming. Farther north are the Columbia, Willamette, and Puget Sound valleys, all having soil of great fertility.

The extensive region lying east of the Sierra Nevada and the Cascades is mostly a barren desert. An exception is the fertile district situated between the Columbia and Snake rivers. A highland, largely of volcanic origin, known as the Columbia River plateau, occupies much of eastern Oregon and Washington. Parts of California adjacent to Nevada form the western rim of the Great Basin. East of the southernmost extensions of the Sierra Nevada and bordering on Arizona are the Mojave desert and the Colorado desert. On the Pacific side of the Sierra Madre, San Bernardino, and other ranges that form the western borders of these deserts, lies the valley of southern California, a coastal plain of remarkable productiveness under irrigation.

Rivers. The Columbia, which rises in Canada, is the only large navigable river in the Pacific states. Together with its tributaries, the most important of which are the Snake and the Willamette, the Columbia drains the greater part of Oregon and Washington. Next in importance are the Sacramento and the San Joaquin. The lower portions of each of these streams are navigable. These two rivers, with their affluents, drain the great central valley of California. There are numerous smaller streams, many of which are broken by rapids or falls. Some of these furnish hydroelectric power. Numerous streams supply water for mining and for irrigation purposes.

Climate. The great length of this division and its intersection by several mountain ranges result in many varieties of climate. These range from the very wet to the very dry, and from the arctic cold of high mountain tops to the torrid heat of California's southeastern deserts. Owing to the moderating influence of winds from the ocean, a mild climate prevails along the entire Pacific shore. This coastal climate ranges from subtropical and dry in southern California to temperate and moist in the Puget Sound region.

Rainfall. In western Washington, the rainfall over the valleys averages 65 inches a year and, in the mountain districts, reaches 100 inches. Western Oregon also has a heavy rainfall. But in the eastern sections of both states less than 20 inches of rain falls annually. In parts of the Colorado desert near the Arizona boundary, the average yearly rainfall is less than three inches.

Summer is a dry season in this division, and the winters are wet. In summer, trays of fruits are left outdoors, day and night, to dry, the drying period often lasting several weeks. Abundant rain falls in northern California, but, in the southern part of the state, irrigation is essential for crop raising.

Minerals. Gold was discovered in California in 1848, and since then the state has yielded every year millions of dollars worth of this precious metal. Though gold is now mined in several other states, California still leads in gold production.

At least 50 other minerals of high commercial value are found in this division. Among them are silver, lead, copper, bismuth, manganese, quicksilver, tungsten, chromium, zinc, magnesite, lithium, and arsenic. The southeastern deserts of California contain immense deposits of borax. Coal of good quality is mined in Washington. Building stone is quarried in all the states. But the most important product is petroleum. California's output of petroleum exceeds in value the yield of all her mines.

TWENTY-FIVE LARGEST CITIES OF THE UNITED STATES

City and Rank	Population 1900	Population 1910	Population 1920	Population 1930	Population 1940	Population 1950	Population 1960	Population 1970
1. New York, N.Y.†	3,437,202	4,766,833	5,620,048	6,930,446	7,454,995	7,891,957	7,781,984	7,867,760
2. Chicago, Ill.	1,698,575	2,185,283	2,701,705	3,376,438	3,396,808	3,620,962	3,550,404	3,366,957
3. Los Angeles, Calif.	102,489	319,198	576,673	1,238,048	1,504,277	1,970,358	2,479,015	2,816,061
4. Philadelphia, Pa.	1,293,697	1,549,008	1,823,779	1,950,961	1,931,334	2,071,605	2,002,512	1,948,609
5. Detroit, Mich.	285,704	465,766	993,678	1,658,452	1,623,452	1,849,568	1,670,144	1,511,482
6. Houston, Texas	44,633	78,800	138,276	292,342	384,514	596,163	938,219	1,231,394
7. Baltimore, Md.	508,957	558,485	733,826	804,874	859,100	949,708	939,024	905,759
8. Dallas, Texas	42,638	92,104	158,976	260,475	294,734	434,462	679,684	844,401
9. Washington, D.C.	278,817	331,069	437,571	468,869	663,091	802,178	763,956	756,510
10. Cleveland, Ohio	381,768	560,663	796,841	900,429	878,336	914,808	876,050	750,903
11. Indianapolis, Ind.	163,502	233,650	314,194	364,161	386,972	427,173	476,258	743,155
12. Milwaukee, Wisc.	285,315	373,857	457,147	578,249	587,472	637,392	741,324	717,099
13. San Francisco, Calif.	342,782	416,912	506,676	634,394	634,536	775,357	742,855	715,674
14. San Diego, Calif.	17,700	39,578	74,683	147,995	203,341	334,387	573,224	693,931
15. San Antonio, Texas	53,321	96,614	161,379	231,542	253,854	408,442	587,718	654,153
16. Boston, Mass.	560,892	670,585	748,060	781,188	770,816	801,444	697,197	641,071
17. Memphis, Tenn.	102,390	131,105	162,351	253,143	292,942	354,102	497,524	623,497
18. St. Louis, Mo.	575,238	687,029	772,897	821,960	816,960	856,796	750,026	622,236
19. New Orleans, La.	287,104	339,075	387,219	458,762	494,537	570,445	627,525	591,502
20. Phoenix, Ariz.	5,544	11,134	29,053	48,118	65,414	106,818	439,170	581,562
21. Columbus, Ohio	125,560	181,511	237,031	290,564	306,087	375,901	471,316	539,677
22. Seattle, Wash.	80,671	237,194	315,312	365,593	368,302	467,591	557,087	530,831
23. Pittsburgh, Pa.	451,512	533,905	558,343	669,817	671,659	676,806	604,332	520,117
24. Jacksonville, Fla.	28,429	57,699	91,558	129,549	173,065	204,517	201,030	518,131
25. Denver, Colo.	133,859	213,381	256,491	287,861	322,412	415,786	493,887	514,678

† Population of the city as now constituted. Source: U.S. Bureau of the Census.

A CENTURY OF GROWTH

In Area, Population, Wealth, Agriculture, Com-

Item	1870	1880	1890	1900	1910
Area, Population, Wealth, and Debt:					
Area . . . . Sq. mi.	3,026,789	3,026,789	3,026,789	3,026,789	3,026,789
Population	38,558,371	50,155,783	62,947,714	75,994,575	91,972,266
Wealth . . . . $	30,068,518,000	43,642,000,000	65,037,091,000	88,517,307,000	187,739,071,090 (*a*)
Wealth per capita . . . . $	779.83	870.20	1,035.57	1,164.79	1,965.00 (*a*)
Debt, national . . . . $	2,331,169,956	1,919,326,747	890,784,370	1,107,711,257	1,046,449,185
Debt, per capita . . . . $	60.46	38.27	14.13	14.55	11.34
Interest on debt . . . . $	118,784,960	79,633,981	29,417,603	33,545,130	21,275,602
Agriculture:					
Farms, number of	2,659,985	4,008,907	4,564,641	5,737,372	6,361,502
Persons engaged in agriculture . . No.	5,922,471	7,713,875	8,565,926	10,381,765	12,659,203
Value farms and farm property . . . $	8,944,857,749	12,180,501,538	16,082,267,689	20,439,901,164	40,991,449,000
Value farm products . . . . $	1,958,030,927	2,212,540,927	2,460,107,454	4,717,069,973	8,498,311,413
Wheat produced . . . . bu.	235,884,700	498,549,868	399,262,000	522,229,505	635,121,000
Corn produced . . . . bu.	1,094,255,000	1,717,434,543	1,489,970,000	2,105,102,516	2,886,260,000
Cotton produced . . . . . 500 lb. bales	4,024,527	6,356,998	8,562,089	10,123,027	11,608,616
Sugar (cane) produced . . . . . . lbs.	87,043,000	178,872,000	301,284,395	322,549,011	750,400,000
Sugar (beet) produced . . . . . . lbs.	806,000	2,688,000	4,934,720	163,458,075	1,024,938,000
Farm animals, value . . . . $	1,518,465,000	1,576,917,556	2,418,766,028	2,228,123,134	5,138,486,000
Wool produced . . . . lbs.	162,000,000	232,500,000	276,000,000	288,636,621	321,362,750
Mineral Production:					
Gold, value of . . . . $	50,000,000	36,000,000	32,845,000	79,171,000	96,269,100
Silver, value of . . . . $	16,434,000	34,717,000	57,242,100	35,741,100	30,854,500
Coal . . . . tons	29,496,054	63,822,830	140,866,931	240,789,310	447,853,909
Petroleum . . . . gals.	220,951,290	1,104,017,166	1,924,590,024	2,672,062,218	8,801,404,416
Iron ore . . . . tons	3,031,891	7,120,362	16,036,043	27,553,161	56,889,734
Pig iron . . . . tons	1,665,179	3,835,191	9,202,703	13,789,242	27,303,567
Steel . . . . tons	68,750	1,247,335	4,277,071	10,188,329	26,094,919
Copper . . . . tons	12,600	27,000	115,966	270,588	482,214
Total minerals . . . . $	218,598,994	364,928,298	606,476,380	1,107,031,392	1,991,216,220
Manufactures:					
Establishments . . . . No.		253,852	355,405	207,514	268,491
Officials, clerks . . . . No.	. . . . . .	. . . . . .	461,001	364,120	790,267
Salaries paid . . . . $	. . . . . .	. . . . . .	391,984,660	380,771,321	938,574,967
Wage earners . . . . No.	. . . . . .	2,732,595	4,251,535	4,712,763	6,615,046
Wages paid . . . . $	. . . . . .	947,953,795	1,891,209,696	2,008,361,119	3,427,037,884
Cost of materials . . . . $	. . . . . .	3,396,823,549	5,162,013,878	6,575,851,491	12,142,790,878
Products, value of . . . . $	. . . . . .	5,369,579,191	9,372,378,843	11,406,926,701	20,672,051,870
Iron and steel manufactures . . . . $	. . . . . .	296,557,685	478,687,519	803,968,273	1,377,151,817
Cotton manufactures . . . . $	. . . . . .	192,090,110	267,981,724	339,200,320	628,391,813
Wood manufactures . . . . $	. . . . . .	238,085,686	270,527,511	296,990,484	507,166,710
Electricity generated 1000 kwh				4,768,000 (*c*)	17,572,000(*d*)
Radios manufactured, value . . . . . $					
Rayon manufactured, value . . . . $					
Transportation:					
Vessels built . . . . tons	276,953	157,409	294,122	393,790	342,068
Vessels, foreign trade . . . . . . tons	1,516,800	1,352,810	946,695	826,694	791,825
Vessels, coastwise trade . . . . . tons	2,729,707	2,715,224	3,477,802	4,338,145	6,716,257
Vessels, Great Lakes trade . . . . tons	684,704	605,102	1,063,063	1,565,587	2,895,102
Railways . . . . miles	52,922	93,262	163,597	193,346	240,293

* The information herein given has been derived from the Statistical Abstract of the United States and other authoritative sources. For various items satisfactory statistics covering some dates are unavailable. In such cases the spaces are marked with leaders, thus. . . . . In other cases, such as petroleum, the telephone, or beet sugar, in which the subject in question had not yet been discovered, invented, or brought to substantial production or use, the space corresponding to the date is left blank. The statistics of manufactures from 1880 to 1940, inclusive, are those of the Federal census, but, in each case, the figures are those of the preceding year, 1879, 1889, 1899, 1909, 1919, 1929, and 1939. The same applies to agricultural production.

OF THE UNITED STATES

merce, Industry, and Important Productions*

1920	1930	1940	1950	1960	1969 (prel.)
3,026,789	3,026,789	3,022,387	3,022,387	3,615,210	3,615,210
105,710,620	122,775,046	131,669,275	150,689,361	179,323,175	203,184,772 (*u*)
290,000,000,000 (*b*)	320,840,000,000 (*j*)	365,000,000,000 (*o*)	1,054,700,000,000	1,682,100,000,000	2,828,000,000,000 (*r*)
2,689.34 (*b*)	2,919 (*j*)	2,862 (*o*)	6,932	9,391.48	13,854 (*r*)
24,330,889,731	16,185,310,000	42,967,513,037	257,357,352,251	286,330,760,848	353,720,000,000
228.64	131.83	325.19	1,696.61	1,585.60	1,741
1,016,592,219	659,347,613	1,040,935,697	5,749,913,000	9,180,000,000	16,588,000,000
6,448,343	6,288,648	6,096,799	5,382,162	(*p*)3,707,846	2,971,000
10,661,410	10,482,323	9,162,547	10,351,000	6,316,336	4,514,000
77,924,100,338	57,245,544,269	33,641,738,726	75,830,000,000	127,855,000,000	202,600,000,000
21,425,623,614	11,387,396,953	9,583,000,000		30,656,524,000	44,386,000,000 (*s*)
833,027,000	806,648,955	816,698,000	1,026,755,000	1,363,443,000	1,576,000,000
3,208,584,000	2,130,751,782	2,449,200,000	3, 131,009,000	4,353,000,000	4,444,000,000
13,439,603	14,574,405	12,686,000	10,012,000	14,309,000	10,080,000
241,998,400	399,218,000	1,008,000,000	1,128,000,000	3,540,000,000	4,498,000,000
1,452,902,000	2,036,000,000	3,516,000,000	4,018,000,000	4,800,000,000	6,842,000,000
8,165,194,000	6,064,051,430	5,181,951,000	7,481,000,000	16,200,000,000	20,100,000,000
277,905,000	336,007,000	449,800,000	247,000,000	300,163,000	182,900,000
51,186,900	47,247,600	210,108,700	80,100,000	56,133,000	72,000,000
60,801,955	19,538,029	49,483,000	38,291,545	28,233,000	73,000,000
587,331,190	536,911,136	504,729,640	560,377,703	432,677,000	556,706,000 (*s*)
18,622,884,000	37,643,130,000	56,777,574,000	82,890,104,000	108,132,780,000	141,288,000,000
69,558,000	58,408,664	75,198,084	97,151,000	59,164,000	89,242,000
36,925,987	31,752,169	41,927,645	64,586,907	68,566,000	95,017,000
42,132,934	40,699,483	66,983,000	96,836,075	99,282,000	141,262,000
539,759	697,195	909,084	911,352	824,846,000	1,558,000
6,707,000,000	4,764,800,000	5,582,500,000	11,855,000,000	17,241,000,000	26,878,000,000
290,105	210,710	184,230	247,307	286,814	311,754 (*r*)
1,447,227	1,377,760	1,048,607	2,603,691	15,964,000	5,382,000
2,892,371,494	3,579,624,574	2,540,357,370	12,033,313,000	77,983,000,000	50,889,000,000
9,096,372	8,807,536	7,886,567	11,766,056	11,644,000	13,999,000
10,533,600,340	11,649,536,855	9,089,940,916	34,565,698,000	49,504,000,000	81,611,000,000
37,376,380,283	38,293,533,500	32,160,106,681		9,076,451,000	N.A.
62,418,078,773	70,137,459,352	56,843,024,800	89,675,779,000	141,270,297,000	215,383,000,000
3,623,368,934	7,138,007,000	4,779,866,341	N.A.	9,481,200,000	19,568,800,000
2,195,565,881	1,524,177,000	1,168,171,469	3,294,023,000	N.A.	N.A.
1,234,657,092	827,006,000	711,580,350	1,355,209,000	N.A.	N.A.
43,555,900	95,936,000	114,984,565	329,141,343,000	797,354,000	1,334,000,000
	411,637,000	275,870,165	675,000,000	N.A.	217,000,000
	149,546,000 (*l*)	247,065,556		N.A.	N.A.
3,880,639	254,296	449,221	404,617	409,736	418,000
9,928,595	6,303,000	3,047,000	8,352,000	325,670,000	12,268,000
6,395,429	9,765,000	10,654,000	3,924,000	205,535,000	} 13,839,000
3,138,690	2,758,000	1,641,000	1,131,000	131,220,000	
252,845	249,052	233,670	226,101	383,912	208,111 (*t*)

(*a*) 1912. (*b*) Estimate of Prof. David Friday. (*c*) 1902. (*d*) 1912. (*e*) Exclusive of rural delivery routes. (*f*) Includes food animals. (*g*) Includes foodstuffs. (*h*) Includes manufactures ready for consumption and manufactures for further use in manufacturing. (*i*) Ordinary disbursements which include disbursements for war, navy, Indians, pensions, payment for interest, and "civil and miscellaneous," but do not include payments for Panama Canal, public debt, special purposes, or postal service. (*j*) 1926. (*k*) 1927. (*l*) Includes "allied products," such as cellophane. (*n*) 1937. (*o*) 1938; estimate by National Resources Planning Board. (*p*) 1959. (*q*) 1968; 59.3% military. (*r*) 1967p. (*s*) 1968. (*t*) First track; excludes Alaska. (*u*) 1970.

A CENTURY OF GROWTH

In Area, Population, Wealth, Agriculture, Com-

ITEM	1870	1880	1890	1900	1910
TRANSPORTATION—Con.					
Automobiles manufactured . . . . No.				3,700 (c)	127,731 (d)
Automobiles in use . . . . . . No.				5,000	501,000
Aircraft manufactured, value . . . . $					
COMMUNICATIONS:					
Post Offices . . . . No.	28,492	42,989	62,401	76,688	59,580
Post Routes (e) . . . . miles	231,232	343,888	427,990	500,990	447,998
Air Mail Routes . . . . miles					
Telegraphs . . . . miles of line	. . . .	85,645	183,917	192,705	214,360
Telephones . . . . No. stations		47,880	227,857	1,355,911	7,635,367
COMMERCE:					
Imports, merchandise, total . . . . $	435,958,408	667,954,746	789,310,409	849,941,184	1,556,947,430
Imports, free . . . . $	20,140,786	208,301,863	265,668,629	367,236,866	755,311,396
Imports, dutiable . . . . $	415,817,622	459,652,883	523,641,780	482,704,318	801,636,034
Imports, per cent free	4.62	31.19	33.66	43.21	48.51
Imports, per capita . . . . $	11.06	12.51	12.14	10.91	16.52
Imports, agricultural . . . . $	191,559,361	314,617,480	384,100,435	420,139,288	87,509,115
Imports, foodstuffs (rude) (f) . . . . $	54,081,091	100,297,040	128,480,142	97,916,293	144,776,636
Imports, foodstuffs (mfg.) (g) . . . . $	96,081,635	118,125,216	133,332,031	133,027,374	181,566,572
Imports, raw materials for mfg. . . . $	55,615,202	131,861,617	170,637,250	276,241,152	566,270,770
Imports, manufactures (h) . . . . . $	229,183,959	307,366,921	347,609,661	337,348,386	652,861,740
Imports, sugar . . . . lbs.	1,196,773,569	1,829,291,684	2,934,011,560	4,018,086,530	4,094,545,936
Imports, coffee . . . . lbs.	235,256,574	446,850,727	499,159,120	787,991,911	873,983,689
Imports, tea . . . . lbs.	47,408,481	72,162,936	83,886,829	84,845,107	85,626,370
Imports wool (raw) . . . . lbs.	49,230,199	128,131,747	105,431,285	155,928,455	263,928,232
Imports, cotton (raw) . . . . . . lbs.	1,698,133	3,547,792	8,606,049	67,398,521	86,037,691
Imports, raw silk . . . . lbs.	583,589	2,562,236	7,510,440	13,073,718	23,457,223
Imports, rubber (crude) . . . . . lbs.	9,624,098	16,826,099	33,842,374	49,377,138	101,044,681
Exports, domestic, total . . . . . . $	376,616,473	823,946,353	845,293,828	1,370,763,571	1,710,083,998
Exports, agricultural . . . . $	296,962,357	694,315,497	634,855,869	844,616,530	871,158,425
Exports, foodstuffs (crude) (f) . . . $	41,852,630	266,108,950	132,073,183	225,906,246	109,828,320
Exports, foodstuffs (mfg.) (g) . . . . $	50,919,666	193,352,723	224,756,580	319,696,334	259,259,654
Exports, raw materials for mfg. . . . $	213,439,991	238,787,934	304,566,922	325,244,296	565,934,957
Exports, manufactures (h) . . . . . $	70,040,845	121,818,298	178,982,042	485,022,156	766,981,245
Exports, iron and steel mfg. . . . . $	13,483,163	14,716,524	25,542,208	121,913,548	179,133,186
Exports, automobiles . . . . $					
Exports, meat and meat products . . $	21,396,050	113,769,604	123,880,422	175,226,535	128,382,362
Exports, wheat . . . . $	47,171,229	190,546,305	45,275,906	73,237,080	47,806,598
Exports, wheat flour . . . . $	21,169,593	35,333,197	57,036,168	67,760,886	47,621,467
Exports, cotton, quantity . . . lbs.	958,558,523	1,822,061,114	2,471,799,853	3,100,583,188	3,206,708,226
Exports, cotton, value . . . . $	227,027,624	211,535,905	250,968,792	241,832,737	450,447,243
FINANCE:					
Money in circulation . . . . $	676,284,427	973,382,228	1,429,251,270	2,055,150,997	3,102,355,605
Circulation per capita . . . . $	17.51	19.41	22.82	26.93	34.33
Government receipts . . . . $	395,959,834	333,526,501	403,080,983	567,240,852	675,511,715
Receipts per capita . . . . $	10.26	6.65	6.43	7.43	7.48
Customs . . . . $	194,538,374	186,522,065	229,668,585	233,164,871	333,683,445
Internal Revenue . . . . $	184,899,756	124,009,374	142,606,706	295,327,927	289,933,519
Government disbursements (i) . . . $	293,657,005	264,847,637	297,736,487	487,713,792	659,705,391
Disbursements per capita . . . . . $	7.61	5.28	4.75	6.39	7.30
Disbursements, war . . . . $	57,655,675	38,116,916	44,582,838	134,774,768	155,911,706
Disbursements, navy . . . . $	21,780,230	13,536,985	22,006,206	55,953,078	123,173,717
Pensions paid . . . . $	28,340,202	56,777,174	106,936,855	140,877,316	160,696,416
Pensioners . . . . No.	198,686	250,802	537,944	993,529	921,083

* The information herein given has been derived from the Statistical Abstract of the United States and other authoritative sources. For various items satisfactory statistics covering some dates are unavailable. In such cases the spaces are marked with leaders, thus..... In other cases, such as petroleum, the telephone, or beet sugar, in which the subject in question had not yet been discovered, invented, or brought to substantial production or use, the space corresponding to the date is left blank. The statistics of manufactures from 1880 to 1940, inclusive, are those of the Federal census, but, in each case, the figures are those of the preceding year, 1879, 1889, 1899, 1909, 1919, 1929. The same applies to agricultural production.

OF THE UNITED STATES—Con.

merce, Industry, and Important Productions*

1920	1930	1940	1950	1960	1969 (prel.)
1,974,016	4,587,400	3,692,328	8,003,245	6,703,108	8,224,329
9,231,941	23,121,589	32,025,365	49,161,691	71,497,399	78,445,000
	72,019,000	550,000,000	N.A.	6,924,000,000	25,592,000,000
52,638	49,063	44,095	41,464	34,955	32,064
435,342	503,918	541,514	668,265	N.A.	N.A.
3,094	14,907	37,943	158,977	231,604	388,804
246,214	256,809 (*k*)	250,880 (*n*)	1,435,000	1,102,000	N.A.
13,329,379	20,201,576	20,830,950	38,045,000	62,683,000	96,099,000
5,238,352,114	3,060,908,000	2,625,445,000	8,743,000,000	14,562,000,000	35,870,000,000
3,405,233,003	2,051,110,000	1,648,285,000	4,766,786,000	5,780,000,000	13,017,000,000
1,833,119,111	1,009,798,000	892,004,000	3,976,304,000	8,872,000,000	22,853,000,000
65.01	67.0	65	54.5	39.45	36
47.22	24.90	19.93	N.A.	80.06	174.15
3,011,368,157	1,899,521,000	1,285,300,000	5,146,232,000	4,795,000,000	4,958,000,000
577,626,948	400,125,000	285,112,000	1,749,556,000	1,722,000,000	2,141,000,000
1,238,138,941	293,448,000	277,444,000	898,423,000	1,566,000,000	3,043,000,000
1,751,893,014	1,002,161,000	1,010,394,000	2,465,489,000	3,092,000,000	4,121,000,000
1,679,228,466	1,365,175,000	967,339,000	1,503,704	5,258,000,000	26,747,000,000
8,073,759,849	6,989,319,000	5,829,080,000	413,506,000	9,104,000,000	9,528,000,000
1,417,063,513	1,599,317,000	2,055,065,000		3,093,523,000	2,676,000,000
97,826,106	84,926,000	98,963,000	48,869,000	108,233,000	139,961,000
259,617,641	163,734,000	360,637,000	170,787,000	235,000,000	93,523,000
299,994,378	128,373,000	131,780,000		N.A.	21,952,000
30,058,374	81,993,000	47,600,000	22,450,000	4,757,138,000	1,904,000
566,456,136	1,089,830,000	1,824,722,000	742,740,000	1,384,000,000	1,311,000,000
8,080,480,821	3,843,181,000	4,021,564,000	12,584,000,000	20,300,000,000	37,444,000,000
3,466,619,819	1,495,823,000	516,856,000	3,411,000,000	2,271,000,000	5,936,000,000
917,990,828	178,533,000	74,019,000	759,753,000	1,639,000,000	2,086,000,000
1,116,605,173	362,650,000	166,881,000		1,117,000,000	1,782,000,000
1,870,767,054	829,098,000	456,078,000	1,886,042,000	3,522,000,000	3,476,000,000
4,163,354,637	1,898,089,000	3,237,687,000	5,773,238,000	11,435,000,000	30,101,000,000
1,112,835,237	1,186,827,000	515,595,000		858,000,000	940,000,000
	314,536,000	254,322,000	703,000,000	1,216,000,000	1,010,000,000
463,256,758	186,563,000	35,900,000	107,000,000	730,000,000	209,779,000
596,975,396	88,093,000	11,209,000	646,411,000		726,020,000
224,472,448	69,401,000	20,400,000	102,319,000	969,000,000	104,217,000
3,179,313,336	3,492,234,000	2,046,310,000	2,213,500,000	7,532,000	1,192,320,000
1,136,408,916	496,798,000	213,400,000	1,024,000,000	988,000,000	280,408,000
5,467,600,000	4,521,987,962	7,847,500,588	27,156,290,042	32,869,000,000	53,591,000,000
51.32	36.71	59.39	179.03	180.36	267.60
6,704,414,438	4,177,941,702	5,924,836,402	37,044,733,557	77,763,460,220	187,792,000,000 (*o*)
63.00	34.47	44.09	245.82	433.65	937.80
323,536,559	587,000,903	348,590,635	422,650,328	1,083,000,000	2,319,000,000
5,399,149,245	3,039,295,013	5,340,452,346	38,957,131,315	91,774,803,000	143,329,000,000 (*p*)
6,141,745,240	3,994,152,487	9,666,085,539	40,166,835,915	76,539,412,798	184,556,000,000 (*q*)
57.72	32.96	73.16	266.53	426.82	921.75
1,094,834,202	453,524,973	667,100,000	4,147,389,907	9,392,000,000	76,970,000,000
629,893,116	374,165,639	891,600,000	4,125,134,514	11,642,000,000	. . . .
213,344,204	418,433,000	556,700,000	2,009,462,298	3,605,000,000	26,175,600,000 (*s*)
592,190	451,433	600,848	3,026,361	4,173,921	24,877,900 (*s*)

(*a*) 1912. (*b*) Est. of Prof. David Friday. (*c*) 1902. (*d*) 1912. (*e*) Exclusive of rural delivery routes. (*f*) Includes food animals. (*g*) Includes foodstuffs. (*h*) Includes manufactures ready for consumption and manufactures for further use in manufacturing. (*i*) Disbursements for war, navy, Indians, pensions, interest payments, and "civil and miscellaneous," but not payments for Panama Canal, public debt, special purposes, or postal service. (*j*) 1926. (*k*) 1927. (*l*) Includes "allied products," such as cellophane. (*m*) 1937. (*n*) Total receipts, year ending June 30, 1969. (*o*) Federal funds, year ending June 30, 1969. (*p*) Total outlays, year ending June 30, 1969. (*q*) Military defense. (*r*) Social Security (OASDHI) payments and beneficiaries, year ending June 30, 1969.

AIR TRAVEL DISTANCES BETWEEN IMPORTANT CENTERS IN THE UNITED STATES

	Atlanta, Ga.	Boston, Mass.	Chicago, Ill.	Cincinnati, O.	Cleveland, O.	Dal'-Ft. Worth Texas	Denver, Colo.	Detroit, Mich.	Houston, Texas	Indianapolis, Ind.	Jacksonville, Fla.	Kansas City, Kansas	Los Angeles, Calif.	Louisville, Ky.	Memphis, Tenn.	Miami, Fla.	Minneapolis, Minn.	Nashville, Tenn.	New Orleans, La.	New York, N. Y.	Oklahoma City, Okla.	Omaha, Nebr.	Philadelphia, Pa.	Pittsburgh, Pa.	Portland, Ore.	St. Louis, Mo.	Salt Lake City, Utah	San Francisco, Cal.	Seattle, Wash.	Washington, D. C.
Atlanta, Ga.	.....	946	592	377	587	738	1,421	619	730	433	277	745	1,981	324	346	614	942	213	427	762	919	1,016	667	536	2,369	516	1,850	2,308	2,354	547
Boston, Mass.	946	.....	879	814	570	1,565	1,786	632	1,673	821	1,023	1,280	2,739	868	1,161	1,289	1,204	961	1,370	184	1,574	1,301	279	483	2,720	1,118	2,135	2,733	2,831	399
Chicago, Ill.	592	879	.....	255	307	857	909	247	994	162	929	405	1,860	270	508	1,199	350	426	860	724	711	424	671	461	1,804	251	1,258	1,856	1,748	600
Cincinnati, O.	377	814	255	.....	210	870	1,102	242	933	107	714	550	1,910	91	447	1,044	605	247	804	613	518	679	518	285	2,059	550	1,513	2,237	2,003	398
Cleveland, O.	587	570	307	210	.....	1,080	1,216	91	1,405	343	779	712	2,054	301	657	1,109	657	457	1,097	458	1,002	731	363	124	2,150	558	1,565	2,163	2,259	310
Dallas - Ft. Worth	738	1,565	857	870	1,080	.....	683	1,045	241	806	1,075	452	1,243	779	423	1,405	860	623	437	1,381	181	617	1,303	1,318	1,670	547	1,063	1,570	2,199	1,183
Denver, Colo.	1,421	1,786	909	1,102	1,261	683	.....	1,156	924	1,011	1,758	552	838	1,046	1,115	1,911	840	1,084	1,120	1,633	676	485	1,578	1,349	987	781	380	956	1,074	1,519
Detroit, Mich.	619	632	247	242	91	1,045	1,156	.....	1,121	252	870	692	2,052	333	635	1,200	549	489	987	486	942	671	442	214	2,003	463	1,505	2,103	1,947	398
Houston, Tex.	730	673	994	933	1,405	241	924	1,121	.....	869	819	693	1,484	842	486	996	1,101	686	303	1,489	422	858	1,394	1,311	1,911	743	1,304	1,811	1,998	1,274
Indianapolis	433	821	162	107	343	806	1,011	252	869	.....	710	451	1,819	109	383	1,040	512	251	735	658	692	589	580	338	1,966	230	1,420	2,146	1,910	500
Jacksonville	277	1,023	929	714	779	1,075	1,758	870	819	710	.....	1,022	2,196	601	623	330	1,219	490	516	839	1,256	1,348	760	826	2,673	793	2,127	2,523	2,617	640
Kansas City	745	1,280	405	550	712	452	552	692	693	451	1,022	.....	1,360	494	486	1,352	408	532	768	1,117	306	165	1,048	797	1,539	229	931	1,687	1,626	959
Los Angeles	1,981	2,739	1,860	1,910	2,054	1,243	838	2,052	1,484	1,819	2,196	1,360	.....	1,947	1,666	2,611	1,768	1,791	1,680	2,624	1,259	1,323	2,467	2,157	821	1,589	575	327	956	2,426
Louisville, Ky.	324	868	270	91	301	779	1,046	333	842	109	601	494	1,947	.....	356	931	620	156	655	684	727	694	589	376	2,113	265	1,528	2,181	2,032	469
Memphis	346	1,161	508	447	657	423	1,115	635	486	383	623	486	1,666	356	.....	887	858	200	352	971	476	651	876	721	2,055	257	1,448	1,993	2,256	762
Miami, Fla.	614	1,289	1,199	1,044	1,109	1,405	1,911	1,200	996	1,040	330	1,352	2,611	931	887	.....	1,549	820	693	1,106	1,586	1,623	1,042	1,108	3,097	1,123	2,457	3,055	2,947	922
Minneapolis	942	1,204	350	605	657	860	840	549	1,101	512	1,219	408	1,768	620	858	1,549	.....	763	1,176	1,020	714	283	1,021	770	1,454	492	1,122	1,737	1,398	950
Nashville	213	961	426	247	457	623	1,084	489	686	251	490	532	1,791	156	200	820	763	.....	499	771	616	697	676	532	2,217	303	1,671	2,118	2,161	562
New Orleans	427	1,370	860	804	1,097	437	1,120	987	303	735	516	768	1,680	655	352	693	1,176	499	.....	1,186	618	933	1,091	928	2,664	609	1,500	2,007	2,608	971
New York	762	184	724	613	458	1,381	1,633	486	1,489	658	839	1,117	2,624	684	971	1,106	1,020	771	1,186	.....	1,419	1,148	95	320	2,528	888	1,982	2,580	2,418	215
Oklahoma C'y	919	1,574	711	783	1,002	181	676	942	422	692	1,256	306	1,259	727	476	1,586	714	616	618	1,419	.....	471	1,292	1,030	1,663	462	972	1,586	1,666	1,178
Omaha, Nebr.	1,016	1,301	424	679	731	617	485	671	858	586	1,348	165	1,323	694	651	1,623	283	697	933	1,148	471	.....	1,093	844	1,422	394	839	1,434	1,533	1,034
Philadelphia	667	279	671	518	363	1,303	1,578	442	1,394	589	760	1,048	2,467	589	876	1,042	1,021	676	1,091	95	1,292	1,093	.....	251	2,512	841	1,927	2,525	2,647	120
Pittsburgh	536	483	461	285	124	1,318	1,349	214	1,311	338	826	797	2,157	376	721	1,108	770	532	928	320	1,030	844	251	.....	2,217	568	1,678	2,484	2,168	186
Portland, Ore.	2,396	2,720	1,804	2,059	2,150	1,670	987	2,003	1,911	1,966	2,673	1,539	821	2,113	2,055	3,097	1,454	2,217	2,664	2,528	1,663	1,422	2,512	2,217	.....	2,055	637	552	135	2,453
St. Louis, Mo.	516	1,118	251	550	558	547	781	463	743	230	793	229	1,589	265	257	1,123	492	303	606	888	462	394	841	568	2,055	.....	1,161	1,916	1,890	719
Salt Lake City	1,850	2,135	1,258	1,513	1,565	1,063	380	1,505	1,304	1,420	2,127	932	575	1,528	1,448	2,457	1,122	1,671	1,500	1,982	972	839	1,927	1,678	637	1,161	.....	615	694	1,868
San Francisco	2,308	2,733	1,856	2,237	2,163	1,570	956	2,103	1,811	2,146	2,523	1,687	327	2,181	1,993	3,055	1,737	2,118	2,007	2,580	1,586	1,434	2,525	2,484	552	1,916	615	.....	687	2,466
Seattle, Wash.	2,354	2,831	1,748	2,003	2,259	2,199	1,074	1,947	1,998	1,910	2,617	1,626	956	2,032	2,256	2,947	1,398	2,161	2,608	2,418	1,666	1,533	2,647	2,168	135	1,890	694	687	.....	2,562
Washington	547	399	600	348	310	1,183	1,519	398	1,274	505	640	959	2,426	469	762	922	950	562	971	215	1,178	1,034	120	186	2,453	719	1,868	2,466	2,562	.....

Source: Civil Aeronautics Board and U. S. Army Aeronautical Charts.

Forests. The coniferous forests of these states are the noblest in the world. In variety of species, in yield of merchantable timber, and in size, age, and beauty of trees, they are unsurpassed. Oregon and western Washington constitute the most important lumber region in the United States.

The heavy rainfall of the coast districts promotes forest growth. West of the Cascades the Douglas fir attains immense size. In dense, nearly pure forests, this tree covers large areas, and furnishes more than half of the available timber. Large spruces, cedars, and hemlocks also abound. East of the Cascades, western yellow pine and sugar pine are valuable timber trees, the former ranking second in importance to the Douglas fir.

The redwood, a magnificent conifer of the northern California coast, supplies excellent building material. Along the western slopes of the Sierra Nevada there are groves of giant sequoias, the most ancient and massive trees known. Many species of broad-leaved or deciduous trees are found, but native hard woods are of minor importance. In the plains districts of California, various species of eucalyptus provide quick timber and shade.

Agriculture and Horticulture. Farming is the chief industry in these states. Because of wide diversity in soil and climate, a greater variety of agricultural products is grown than in any other equal area in the United States.

In most of the large valleys of Washington, western Oregon, and north central California, sufficient rain falls to insure good harvests. In southern California and in the more arid parts of Oregon and Washington, irrigation is necessary. Among the principal crops are wheat, barley, oats, hay, alfalfa, potatoes, sugar beets, cotton, rice, beans, corn, and numerous fruits and vegetables. In total value the fruits outrank all the other agricultural products of this division. Next to fruits, wheat is the most important single crop, ranking first in value of all crops in Washington, second in Oregon, and third in California. Among hay and fodder crops, alfalfa leads. Although unsuited to the climate, corn, the great staple of the Central states, is grown to a limited extent.

California's great wheat ranches are disappearing, but intensive agriculture, especially fruit growing in connection with irrigation, is making notable progress. All of the Pacific states are famous for their fruits. Apples grown in the Hood River valley in Oregon and in the Yakima district in Washington command high prices in eastern markets Along the Willamette River thousands of acres are planted with apple, peach, pear, and plum trees. In western Oregon, loganberry culture is an extensive industry.

California ranks as the foremost fruit producing state in the Union. Contrary to general opinion in the eastern states, most of this state's great fruit harvest consists of the orchard and vineyard fruits of temperate latitudes,—apples, apricots, cherries, grapes, peaches, pears, plums, and prunes. The best varieties of the European grape flourish, and large quantities of grape juice and raisins are produced. The growing of citrus fruits is a large industry in southern California. From its extensive groves thousands of carloads of oranges, lemons, and grapefruit are shipped to the eastern states every year. Almonds, figs, olives, English walnuts, and melons are grown in large quantities. Among less common fruits whose cultivation has been established in California are the avocado, cherimoya, date, and feijoa.

Irrigation. By irrigation many arid areas in these states have been turned into highly productive lands. A half century ago southern California was mostly a dreary waste. Much that was then desert is now covered with groves of oranges and other fruits, or with fields of grain, alfalfa, melons, or cotton. In no other part of the United States is irrigation so extensively established or devoted to the production of such an immense variety of crops. California leads all the states of the Union in acreage under irrigation and in value of crops produced on irrigated land.

Animal Industry. Large areas in the drier sections are devoted to the raising of cattle and sheep. About one-sixth of the entire wool clip of the United States is produced in the Pacific states. Dairying is a profitable industry. Poultry raising is important, and in some localities, as at Petaluma, California, it has become highly specialized. In the production of honey California usually leads all the other states.

Fisheries. Salmon is the most valuable fish. Puget Sound and the Columbia River are the principal salmon fishing grounds. Millions of pounds of salmon are canned every year and exported to all parts of the world. Fresh salmon are also shipped in refrigerator cars to all the large cities of the Union. Halibut, tuna, herring, and other valuable food fish are taken along the Pacific coast.

Manufacturing. In the contiguous Pacific states, manufacturing ranks second to agriculture in importance. Among the chief manufactures are lumber, canned fruits, refined petroleum, flour, packed meats, and dairy products. Other important products of manufacture are refined sugar, canned fish, and mining machinery.

Manufacturing has been greatly stimulated by the extensive development of hydroelectric power, especially in California and Washington. Particularly since 1910, this factor has been one of rapidly increasing importance in the industry of the Pacific Coast. In southern California many factories use crude petroleum for fuel. Lumber, flour, slaughtering and meat packing, and paper and wood pulp are the leading products of manufacture in Washington; lumber and flour lead in Oregon; and petroleum products, canned fruits, and meat products rank in the order named in California. In total value of manufactures, California stands ninth among the states of the Union.

Commerce. The Pacific contiguous states occupy a position of great commercial advantage. They have fine harbors on the Pacific Ocean and an immense hinterland whose products of farm, forest, and mine are increasing every year. A great trade is carried on through Puget Sound ports. The Panama Canal has brought Europe and the Atlantic states much nearer to this division and thereby stimulated its commerce with those older manufacturing parts of the world. Since 1910 the trade of these states with Japan, the Philippines, Hawaii, New Zealand, Australia, and South America has made a marked gain.

PACIFIC STATES—NONCONTIGUOUS

The noncontiguous, or off-shore, Pacific states of Alaska and Hawaii are treated below in two separate articles. Both admitted into the Union in 1959, they are the only states situated outside of the mainland.

ALASKA

Alaska, the largest state of the United States, situated in the extreme northwestern part of North America. All of it lies to the north and to the west of the United States. Its northernmost point is about 1450 miles farther north than its southernmost point. From its easternmost point to its westernmost point, Alaska extends through a distance greater than that from New York to San Francisco.

Area and Location. Alaska embraces three distinct regions—the main territory, the panhandle, or southeastern Alaska, and the Aleutian Islands.

The main territory comprises all of continental North America lying west of the 141st meridian of west longitude. It is bounded on the east by Canada, on the north by the Arctic Ocean, on the west by the Arctic Ocean, Bering Strait, and Bering Sea, and on the south by the Pacific Ocean and the Gulf of Alaska. The panhandle of southeastern Alaska consists of a narrow fringe of mainland and various islands along the coast, between British Columbia and the Pacific Ocean, extending from Cape Muzon and the Portland Canal, at the extreme south, northward to Mount Saint Elias, where the panhandle joins the main territory.

The Aleutian Islands extend westward from the southwestern part of the main territory, as far as, and including, Attu, off the coast of Asia. Various islands in Bering Sea near the American mainland, including the Pribilof and the Saint Lawrence islands, also belong to Alaska.

The area of Alaska, about 590,000 square miles, is nearly one-fifth that of the "lower 48" states, or more than twice the size of Texas. The coast line of mainland Alaska has a total length of 6542 miles, measured along the tidal shore in units of 3 statute miles. The coast lines of all Alaska's islands measure 8590 miles. These two figures together, 15,132 miles, exceed the general tidal coast line of all the rest of the United States, including Hawaii.

Surface. There are four distinct natural surface divisions in the mainland of Alaska. From south to north, these are the Pacific Mountain system, the Central Plateau region, the Rocky Mountain system, and the Arctic Slope region.

The Pacific Mountain system comprises the Coast, the Mount Saint Elias, the Aleutian, and the Alaska ranges. These form great barrier walls along and near the southern shores. This rugged highland contains the loftiest mountains of the continent, culminating in Mount McKinley, in the Alaska range, the highest peak in North America.

East and north of these majestic ranges is the great central plateau, drained chiefly by the Yukon River. This plateau extends entirely across Alaska from east to west. North of it, the Rocky Mountain system, locally called the Brooks Range, which crosses the international boundary about 100 miles north of the Arctic Circle, extends westerly across Alaska nearly to the Arctic Ocean. North of the Rockies is the Arctic Slope, a barren, featureless, coastal plain.

For about 1000 miles southwestward from the Alaska peninsula extends the Aleutian archipelago which consists of about 70 treeless islands and numerous islets, mostly uninhabited.

Volcanoes. The Aleutian range, in the Alaska peninsula, contains a group of active volcanoes, which, in some respects, are the most remarkable in the world. The eruption of Katmai in this group, in 1912, was one of the most violent volcanic outbursts recorded in modern times. Katmai and its vicinity, including the famous "Valley of Ten Thousand Smokes," have been made a national monument. Aniakchak and Veniamin, with craters 21 and 20 miles in circumference respectively, rank first among active volcanoes in size of their vents.

Glaciers. The mountains bordering on the Gulf of Alaska are covered with perpetual snow. From their slopes, immense glaciers, which increase in size from Glacier Bay northward, extend down to the sea. On the shores between Glacier Bay and Kenai peninsula are found nine-tenths of the permanent ice fields on the mainland of the continent. Here are some 25 active glaciers which discharge their slowly flowing ice into the sea. Among the most noted is the Muir glacier, which has a seaward face 3 miles wide and 300 feet high. The greatest example of all is the Malaspina glacier, 1200 square miles in extent, which rests on the southern slope of Mount Saint Elias and reaches the ocean at Icy cape.

The Muir glacier has recently attracted much scientific attention because of its rapid recession due to melting. This has aroused speculation as to whether the world's climate is gradually becoming warmer.

This great glacier was first visited by John Muir in 1880 and has been named in honor of him. Net recession since then has been almost two miles with parts of the ice mass which melted having been nearly one-half mile thick. The formerly great central ice stream is all melted leaving now 12 separate glacial streams. This is reputed to be the best area in the world for study of glacial phenomena.

Rivers. The chief river in Alaska is the Yukon, the largest American river emptying into the Pacific Ocean. This magnificent river, some 2300 miles long, is formed by the confluence of streams having their headwaters in British Columbia. It flows northward in Yukon territory, and, about midway on the international boundary, enters Alaska. At the northernmost point in its bow-shaped course of about 1500 miles from the Canada boundary to Bering Sea, the Yukon swings slightly north of the Arctic Circle. Its chief tributaries are the Tanana, the Porcupine, and the Koyukuk. Other important Alaskan rivers are the Kuskokwim, the Copper, Matanuska, Kenai, Nushagak, Kobuk, Noatak, Colville, Stikine, Taku, and the Susitna.

Scenery. Alaska, with its great mountains, volcanoes, glaciers, and rivers, is noted for the magnificence of its scenery. The Portland Canal, Chatham strait, and the Lynn Canal, in southeastern Alaska, surrounded by snow-capped mountains rising above immense forests, rank among the finest scenic waterways in the world. Around the Gulf of Alaska, the coast is indented with deep bays resembling the noted fiords of Norway and which likewise include magnificent glaciers. The Taku glacier is only a few miles from the steamer track of the famous inside passage and can be seen from the largest ocean steamers that ply Alaskan waters. Mount McKinley national park, which includes the great mountain, affords some of the grandest mountain views on the continent.

Climate. According to the U. S. Weather Bureau, Alaska is climatically divided into 4 areas—(1) a maritime zone that includes southeastern Alaska, the south coast, and southwestern islands, (2) a transition zone between marine and continental influences (mostly a very narrow band along the southern portion of the Copper River and the northern extreme of the south coast—specifically the Chugach Mountains, Cook Inlet, Bristol Bay, and the coastal regions of west-central Alaska), (3) a continental zone made up of the remainders of the Copper River and west-central Alaska and the interior region, and (4) an arctic zone.

In the maritime zone a coastal mountain range coupled with plentiful moisture produces annual precipitation amounts up to 200 inches in the southeastern panhandle, and up to 150 inches along the northern coast of the Gulf of Alaska. Amounts taper to near 60 inches on the southern side of the Alaska Range in the peninsula and Aleutian Island sections. Precipitation amounts decrease rapidly to the north, with an average of 12 inches in the continental zone and less than 6 inches in the Arctic region.

Snowfall makes up a large portion of the total annual precipitation. For example, Yakutat averages 216 inches of snow annually, and has a total annual precipitation (rain plus water equivalent of snow) of about 130 inches. Along the Arctic slope, Barrow receives an average of 29 inches of snow annually and a total annual precipitation of slightly more than 4 inches. Total snow depths on the ground are controlled by the temperature of an area. Fortunately, most of the areas of heavy snow have relatively mild temperatures which prevent total depths from becoming excessive. The greatest annual precipitation occurred at Little Port Walter (in southeastern Alaska) in 1943, with a total of 269.30 inches. Snowfall extremes are all credited to one station, located at Thompson Pass.

Mean annual temperatures in Alaska range from

the low 40's under the maritime influence in the south to a chilly 10 degrees along the Arctic Slope north of the Brooks Mountain Range. The greatest seasonal temperature contrast between seasons is found in the central and eastern portion of the continental interior. In this area summer heating produces average maximum temperatures in the upper 70's with extreme readings in the 90's. The highest recorded temperature for the state, 100 degrees, occurred at Fort Yukon in June of 1915. In winter the lack of sunshine permits radiation to lower temperatures to the minus 50's and occasionally colder for two or three weeks at a time. Average winter minimums in this area are 20 to 30 degrees below zero. The coldest temperature ever recorded in Alaska was minus 76 degrees at Tanana in January of 1886. In Barrow, Alaska's northernmost town in the frigid arctic region, January temperatures average −18°F. Its minimum, −56°F is higher than at Fairbanks and points inland, due to its open coastal location. The sun circles the sky in Barrow without setting for about 2 months in summer and the Arctic night is also about 2 months in length.

Winter temperatures play a principal role in the flow of most of Alaska's rivers. Several cease to flow completely during the coldest months, generally from late October to early May.

Vegetation. The southern coastal region is heavily forested and contains much valuable timber, chiefly Sitka spruce and hemlock. The Tongass national forest comprises southeastern Alaska, and the Chugatch national forest extends from Controller bay to Cook inlet. Extensive forests of spruce and tamarack, interspersed with poplar, aspen, white birch, and alder, occur along numerous watercourses in the Yukon valley. These forests total nearly 21 million acres with practically all under National Forest Service Administration. In the remaining portions of Alaska, there are but few trees. The Alaska peninsula and the Aleutian islands are grasslands. These grasslands are composed of highly nutritious grasses and are available as pasturage the year round. Cattle and horses released on these areas have grown fat and sleek without attention from man.

The coastal region of Bering Sea and the Arctic Ocean is covered with tundra. The tundra furnishes very desirable pasturage for caribou, reindeer, and musk ox.

Animal Life. Alaska is rich in animal life, especially in game animals, fur bearing animals, and in food fishes. Among the larger land animals are moose, caribou, deer, bighorn, and mountain goat. There are also several species of bear, including the polar bear, the rare glacial bear, and the great Kodiak bear. The reindeer, introduced from Siberia to provide food for the native Indians and Eskimos, now abounds in great herds. It is reared like cattle, and reindeer meat is an article of export to the United States. In the coastal waters are found the walrus, the hair seal, and various whales. The fur bearing animals include the fur seal, sea otter, beaver, ermine, mink, marten, and wolverine. Salmon, cod, halibut, and herring are immensely abundant in Alaskan waters.

Minerals. Alaska possesses vast mineral resources, many of which are undeveloped. The most important mineral products are gold, oil, copper, and coal. Many other valuable metals and minerals are found, among which are silver, lead, antimony, tin, oil, tungsten, platinum, quicksilver, and marble.

Gold has been found chiefly in the Juneau district, the Copper River district, the Yukon valley, and in the Seward peninsula, or Nome region. Gold was first discovered in Alaska in 1861. The gold rush started in 1883, reached its peak about 1887, and experienced a resurgence in 1896. Gold mined in Alaska from 1880 until 1930 is valued at approximately $380 million. Annual production is in the neighborhood of $5 million.

The decline in gold production was accompanied by a rise in the production of other minerals. The mining of copper, found in the coast region from Mount Saint Elias to Cook inlet, began in 1902 and soon surpassed gold in value of output. Copper exceeded all other mineral production until 1962, when it was surpassed by the production of petroleum. Alaska ranks eighth among the states of the Union in the production of oil, with the potential to rank higher. Alaska has sold leases to bidders, giving various companies oil exploratory rights to specified territory, for some $862 million, plus 12½% royalty tax and 4% severance tax on every barrel of oil taken out. The development of the oil industry in Alaska has been slow, with two wells now in operation, one at Prudhoe Bay, and the other at Snag River. The most attractive areas for drilling for oil are adjacent to the Pacific Ocean on the south and the Arctic Ocean on the north. Some of the most desirable areas, however, are not available for drilling or exploratory drilling.

Extensive coal fields are found in widely separated districts from southern Alaska to the Arctic coast. It is estimated that more than 12,000 square miles are underlaid with coal deposits ranging in quality from anthracite to lignite. Silver and lead are also produced in significant quantities. Practically all the tin mined in North America comes from Alaska. Other mineral products include platinum, mercury, and marble. Natural gas, discovered in 1949, is marketed extensively.

ALASKA

Transportation. The development of Alaska's immense resources depends upon the establishment of quick and cheap transportation. The coasts have many good harbors, and the Yukon and other rivers provide some 3000 miles of inland waterways. But the water routes are long, are open only in summer, and do not reach some of the most important districts. Short railways have been built in connection with mining enterprises, but they were not constructed as correlated parts of a railway system designed to serve the needs of the whole territory.

The United States government has, however, completed a railway, some 470 miles long, from Seward, on the Gulf of Alaska, to Fairbanks, at the head of deep water navigation on the Tanana river, chief tributary of the Yukon. This connects the southern coast with the interior valley.

The Alaska Highway, originally called the Alcan Highway, was built by American army engineers for the defense of Alaska in 1942. It extends from Dawson Creek, British Columbia, to Fairbanks, Alaska, a distance of 1523 miles. Open to the public since 1948, tourist services are available along its entire length. Lodging and meal service are good and moderate in cost. Gasoline is available but as yet relatively costly. Autos may now make the round trip overland to Fairbanks; but a tourist seeking variety may drive from Fairbanks to Anchorage or Seward and take a boat over the attractive ocean route to Seattle.

Numerous airports have facilitated rapid transit to otherwise inaccessible points. There are 15 certified carriers and 50 or more irregular carriers. There are also 153 territorial fields. Outposts such as Nome are finding the quick connection by planes much more dependable and desirable than dog teams, which are costly to maintain, requiring constant feed and care.

Alaskans have been referred to as "the flyingest" of all Americans. The description is justified, not only on a per capita mileage basis for citizens of the 49th state, but also for the daring exploits of "bush pilots," who are not daunted by unfavorable weather or difficult terrain. Increasingly, this local use of air transportation is being matched by communication with distant points. Several Federal airports are maintained, and four air lines provide regularly scheduled service between Alaska and the other states.

Commerce and Industry. The industries of Alaska are chiefly in connection with mining, fisheries, and the fur trade, with a limited amount of lumbering. The dominant tree of the commercial timber type is western hemlock, with Sitka spruce a close second. Western red cedar and Alaska yellow cedar are produced to some extent. Local uses of forests are fuel, log cabins, mines, docks, salmon packing cases, etc. During World War II Sitka spruce provided airplane construction material. A more solid basis for Alaska's forest industry is the manufacture of pulp, which is exported mainly to Japan for making of paper and rayon. In value of production, fisheries rank first followed by products of the forests and the mines and oil and gas wells. Apart from pulp, exports include petroleum, canned salmon, copper ore, gold, and furs. Among the most important imports are foodstuffs, clothing, and machinery. As transportation facilities, particularly by air, are continually improving, tourism is becoming an important source of income for Alaska, which has scenic attractions not accessible elsewhere in the United States.

Fisheries. The salmon fisheries were formerly the most valuable in the world, but in the 1940's the catch fell off seriously. Cannery production of salmon reached a high of 8,454,948 cases in the 1930's, fell to an average of 2,797,699 cases for the years 1953–57, and remained in that range thereafter. Next in importance to salmon are herring, halibut, clams, and shrimp.

Furs and Game. Next in value below fishery, forest, and mineral products are furs. The most important land furs include red fox, white fox, blue fox, ermine, lynx, marten, mink, muskrat, and land otter. Fur farming, especially with foxes, is carried on extensively. The fur seal herds, on the Pribilof islands, increased, under government supervision, from 215,000 animals in 1912 to about nine times that number in the 30 years following.

The 1940 seal population of these islands was 2,185,136. Sealskins taken in 1941 were 95,013. The handling of this fur seal herd has been one of the most successful in wildlife administration. The total value of furs shipped from Alaska annually frequently exceeds 4.5 million dollars.

Fine and useful game animals are caribou; reindeer; moose; Dall mountain sheep; mountain goats; brown, grizzly, polar, and black bears; elk; deer; and, at present, a herd of musk oxen are being developed on Nunivak island and a herd of bison near Fairbanks. Immense numbers of ducks, geese, and swans of several species breed abundantly throughout practically the entire territory. Other aquatic fowl form almost continuous coastal rookeries—auklets, murres, guillemots, puffins, cormorants, sheerwaters gulls, and kittiwakes. Eagles, owls, hawks, gyrfalcons are included among the land birds.

Agriculture. Owing chiefly to the shortness of the growing season, agriculture is successful only in limited areas and to a moderate degree. Vegetables are the most important products. These are grown in favored ground in the valleys of the Susitna, the Matanuska, the Kenai, the Koyukuk, the Copper, and the Tanana rivers. Hay, barley, and hardy fruits are also produced. Grazing and dairying are carried on in Kodiak island and other grassland districts. Reindeer thrive in moss covered and lichen covered areas. The government maintains four agricultural experimental stations,—a nursery at Sitka, a grain farm at Rampart, a dairy at Kodiak, and a demonstration farm at Fairbanks.

It is estimated that 65,000 square miles is potential farm land and 35,000 square miles is potential grazing land, not including the reindeer range which is very extensive. The area in farms rose from almost zero in 1900 to a peak of 2774 square miles in 1939 and then declined sharply, standing at 1356 square miles in the 1959 crop year. There were 623 farms in 1939 and 382 in 1964. But, despite this sharp decline in number of farms and area of farm land, the area actually cropped almost doubled—increasing from 12 to 23 square miles—and crops more than quadrupled, while farm animals approximately doubled.

Livestock in 1960 included 750 horses, about 6010 cattle, including 2800 dairy cows, 1200 hogs, and 27,000 sheep and lambs. The number of reindeer reported in herds declined from 712,500 in 1929 to 312,854 in 1939. There are about 38,540 reindeer now in western Alaska, of which 13,200 are located on Nunivak Island and are controlled by the Bureau of Indian Affairs. Individual Eskimo herders own the rest of the reindeer.

Farm production in 1967 was valued at $5,524,000, including $1,931,000 for milk, $1,340,000 for grain crops, $607,000 for potatoes, and $214,000 for vegetables. The chief grains grown are oats and barley; hay is also produced. Fruits and vegetables harvested and sold, like other crops, have increased spectacularly, rising in value from $99,000 in 1949 to $214,000 in 1967. The types grown in quantity include strawberries, raspberries, beans, broccoli, cabbages, lettuce, onions, radishes, rutabagas, and turnips. Despite the fact that Alaska is suitable for farming, it is primarily a food-importing area.

Population. In 1970, the population of the state was 300,382, of whom about half were whites, the remainder Indians, with a few Negroes and Japanese.

The Indians of Alaska belong mainly to four great stocks—the Eskimos, the Aleuts, the Athapascans, and the Tlingits. The Eskimos, 15,576 in number, live near the seashore and on islands, chiefly along Bering Sea and the Arctic Ocean. The Pacific Eskimos live on the south coast around Kodiak island, Controller Bay, and Prince William Sound The Aleutian Eskimos occupy areas about the Alaskan Peninsula and extending along the Aleutian Islands. Asiatic Eskimos live on St. Lawrence Island which is part of the Alaskan Territory. The Bering Sea Eskimos live on Nunivak Island and the opposite mainland including the lower Yukon. The Colville Eskimos occupy the Arctic coast near Wainright Inlet, Cape Smyth, and Point Barrow. The Eskimos have proven good workers and are employed at such summer tasks as longshoremen in loading and unloading supply ships. Able bodied Eskimos were drafted for war service in Alaska in World War II.

Juneau, the capital, has a population of 6050. Other important cities and towns are Anchorage, 48,029; Fairbanks, 14,771; Ketchikan, 6994; and Seward 1587. Alaska has in all 70 incorporated places, among which may be mentioned, in addition to the above, Nome, 2488; Sitka, 3370; and Kodiak, 3798. Population for all of Alaska, 1970, 300,382.

History. In 1741, Vitus Bering, a Danish navigator in the employ of Russia, explored the coast of Alaska. Kodiak island was discovered in 1761 by the Russians, who made a settlement there in 1783. Captain James Cook, in 1778, and Vancouver, in 1793-94, made extensive coastal surveys. Sitka, founded in 1804, became the capital of the Russian territory. The Russians, who were engaged chiefly in fur sealing, did not extensively explore the interior.

In 1867, the United States purchased Alaska from Russia for the sum of $7,200,000—about $12 per square mile, or less than 2 cents an acre.

Preceding the discovery of the gold fields, there was little development, except in connection with the fur trade. Important events in the recent history of Alaska were the fur seal arbitration of 1893, the great gold rush of 1898, the settlement of the Alaska-Canada boundary dispute in 1904, and the construction of the government railway from Seward to Fairbanks, 1916–23.

During World War I, the white population of Alaska declined, but, following the completion of important portions of the government railway and the return of stable conditions, development was again stimulated. Growth of air travel provided an impetus.

In World War II the building up of the defenses of Alaska caused a boom. Numerous military and naval bases were built, especially air bases. Two of Alaska's islands, Attu and Kiska, were occupied by Japanese troops in June 1942. In May 1943, American troops invaded and retook Attu. In the following August, Kiska was bombarded. The landing force found the island had already been evacuated.

The development of atomic weapons and of long range missiles made Alaska a highly strategic point for defense of the United States. Elaborate systems for automatic warning of the presence of airplanes or missiles were constructed as part of lines extending also across Northern Canada, in which the Canadian and American governments pooled their efforts.

The Alaskan flag has a blue field on which gold stars represent the Big Dipper and the North Star. The forget-me-not is the official flower; the willow ptarmigan the official bird. In 1959, Alaska was admitted to the Union as the 49th state.

HAWAII

The state of Hawaii consists of a chain of nine inhabited and several uninhabited islands in the mid-Pacific Ocean. The chief islands are about 2100 miles southwest of San Francisco and approximately 3400 miles southeast of Yokohama, Japan. Their central position in relation to Pacific ports has won for Hawaii the sobriquet "crossroads of the Pacific."

Palmyra Island, 1½ miles in area, lying about 700 miles south of the main group, is officially considered as part of Hawaii. The extreme northwestern islets of the group are called the Midway Islands, being about halfway between Asia and North America. They are inhabited only by the employees of a United States cable station there.

The population of the Hawaiian Islands in 1970 was 768,561. The largest islands of the group are Hawaii, 4030 square miles; Maui, 728; Oahu, 604; Kauai, 555; Molokai, 260; Lanai, 141; Nihau, 72; Kalholawe, 45. The capital, Honolulu, on the island of Oahu, has 324,871 inhabitants.

The islands of Hawaii are of volcanic origin. Their surface is mountainous, reaching, in Mauna Kea, "White Mountain," a maximum altitude of 13,823 feet. If measured from the deep ocean floor, on which it stands, this volcanic giant is several hundred feet higher than Mt. Everest, the world's highest inland mountain. This peak and Mauna Loa (13,675 feet), both in the island of Hawaii, are higher than any other mountain in the islands of the Pacific Ocean. Mauna Loa, "Long Mountain," shares with the near-by mountain of Kilauea the distinction of having active craters which rank among the largest in the world, covering 4.14 square miles. That of Kilauea is about 8 miles in circumference and is the seat of unceasing volcanic activity.

Haleakala, on the island of Maui, has one of the largest of all extinct craters. This crater is 20 miles around and is 2720 feet deep. A 41-square mile area containing it was made a national park in 1961. The island of Molokai is notable for its famous leper settlement. Lanai is owned by a pineapple company which constructed a harbor and a model city. Pearl Harbor, on the island of Oahu, is a United States naval base. It is landlocked, with an area of 10 square miles. The Hawaii Volcanoes National Park includes Kilauea and Mauna Loa on Hawaii Island and Haleakala on Maui.

The climate of the Hawaiian Islands is delightfully equable and invigorating considering its tropical position. Sea level temperatures average between 68.7° F. and 75.8° F. for the Islands. At Honolulu, the maximum recorded temperature is 90° F. and the minimum, 52° F. However, it is a rare summer day in which temperatures rise over 85° F. and a rare winter night when the low is 60° F. Especially noteworthy is the fact that damaging storms, such as hail, tornadoes, hurricanes, and typhoons, are practically nonexistent. Northeast trade winds blow prevailingly for about 10 months in the year. On account of the mountainous character of the islands, much of the moisture in the winds is precipitated, falling mainly on the northeastern side of each island. As a result, the opposite side has insufficient rainfall and frequently suffers from drought. This rainfall variation is one of the largest in the world. Many rain-drenched windward towns officially report well over 200 inches a year. On the leeward side, averages of 20 to 30 inches are common (Honolulu, 25.8 in.) and are often inadequate for crops and water supply. Rain falls every month of the year, but the summer months are markedly drier. The prevailing sunniness of such lee locations as Honolulu is a notable attraction.

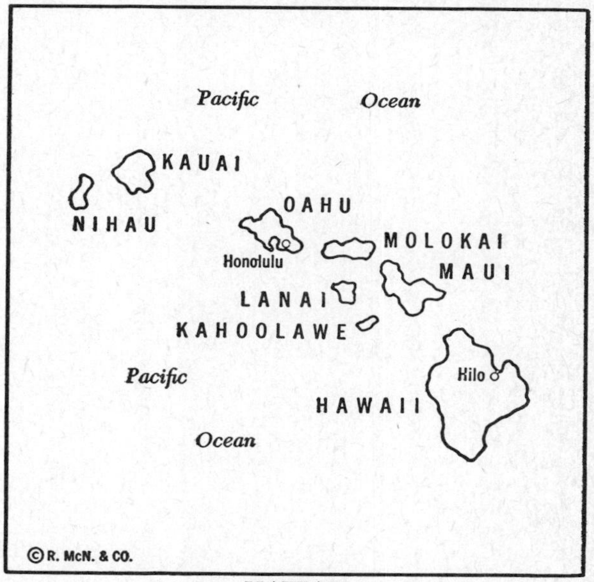

HAWAII

Another significant mountain influence is the change of temperature with altitude. In the land below 2500 feet (Tierra Caliente) frost never occurs and rarely forms even up to 4000 feet. Above 4000 feet (Tierra Templada) frost may occur, and at elevations of 6500 feet snow is occasionally reported.

Above 9000 feet (Tierra Fria) both frost and snow occur regularly and the higher peaks are frequently snow covered. Altogether the Hawaiian Islands are climatically among the most varied in the world.

Plant life is highly varied from tropical jungle to tropical steppe and desert. Only about 10 per cent is grazing land. Approximately four-fifths of the area is unused desert, semidesert, and volcanic waste with dense tropical jungle in favored spots. In the National Park area of the island Hawaii, locally called Big Island, is the world famous "Fern Forest" with some ferns attaining the height of 50 feet. Plant life in the inhabited areas is highly colorful and ornamental providing a major attraction. Among the most noted are royal palms, coconut palms, banyan trees, monkeypod trees, flame trees, bougainvillia, orchid, cacti, hibiscus, poinsettia, plumerias, and ilima. Many of these blooms are made into welcoming leis, a world famous Hawaiian custom with considerable commercial significance.

Although there are many kinds of fish and birds in Hawaii, there is only one mammal that is indigenous to the islands, and that is a species of bat. There are also lizards on the islands.

The soil along the coastal lowlands and in many valleys is very fertile and supports a flourishing agriculture of a tropical type. Since the soils are of volcanic origin they are deep rich clays high in mineral content and capable of sustained yields under cultivation. The staple crops are pineapples and sugar cane. Large quantities of cane sugar and of pineapples are shipped, principally to the United States. Other products exported include coffee, honey, hides, sisal hemp, bananas, rice, wool, tobacco, and cotton. Over half of the total area is in farms and ranches (2.5 million acres), yet only 10 per cent of the total area is cropped.

About 250,000 acres is kept in sugar cane, the major crop, using five times as much land as pineapples. Since the cane is allowed to grow 18 to 20 months before harvesting, the yield per acre is three times that of the annually harvested cane of the United States. Hawaiians annually cut just over half of the acreage in cane. Annual production varies from 700,000 to 1,000,000 tons.

Eighty to ninety per cent of the pineapple products of world trade originate in the Hawaiian Islands, making them world famous. This fame is justly merited, not only in quantity domination over all competitors, but also in leadership in methods of production and processing. Eight corporations dominate the field, led by the Hawaiian Pineapple Corporation founded by James D. Dole, 1922. Confronted by labor shortage, limited water supply, aridity, blowing soil erosion, soil and plant infestations and certain plant food deficiencies, these companies inaugurated far reaching conservation practices. Slopes are contoured; paper covers the soil, conserving moisture, preventing blowing and washing, checking weed growth, thus saving costly weeding. Water supply is obtained by wells, local galvanized roofs, and acres of galvanized sheds on the wetter upper slopes, from which the water can be channeled down as needed; machinery cultivates, plants, harvests, and transports the fruit to the processing factories where all of the pineapple is reduced to valuable products as canned fruit, juice, and citric acid. Cost of services in sanitation, health, and public utilities, formerly provided, must now be borne by the worker. Total sales of pineapples and sugar in 1967 exceeded $324 million, or about 63 per cent of total agricultural income.

Land tenure is a problem, with 60 per cent of the land owned either by the state or by large estates. The famous Bishop Estate owns 10 per cent and endows philanthropic enterprises such as the Kamehameha schools with the million dollar income. The Federal Government owns 429,076 acres, of which 373,384 is in National Parks and 55,559 is under the Navy.

The tourist industry ranks third after sugar and pineapples as an industry. Superior natural attractions are enhanced by luxurious accommodations to make this a world prominent resort. The Pan American Airways and United Air Lines contact the islands from San Francisco in a breakfast-to-dinner run. Several steamship lines connect the island with the United States, Canada, and the Orient. The Moana and Royal Hawaiian hotels on Waikiki beach are widely known.

Honolulu, on Oahu Island, is the capital and chief port of Hawaii. Its name means "quiet harbor." The harbor, which has excellent freight facilities, is almost entirely enclosed by a natural breakwater of coral reefs. The population of the state has a mixed character. More than half are Japanese and Chinese. White inhabitants number less than one-fourth of the total. The aborigines constitute a still smaller proportion. A similar complexity characterizes the language and the religion of the territory. The aborigines are mainly Protestant Christians, although some of their pagan beliefs and customs survive. The Hawaiian natives belong to the Polynesian race. When discovered, they had a well developed political system and a literature. Niihau is still maintained as a pure native asylum by the exclusive Robinson family

The Hawaiian Islands were first made known to the world by Captain James Cook, who discovered them in 1778. He called them Sandwich Islands after the earl of Sandwich. At that time, each island had its king, who exercised authority by a species of feudal organization. In 1790, Kamehameha, one of the kings, extended his sway over the entire group of islands. His successor, being opposed by those who upheld the native worship, abolished the old religion. Christianity was introduced as early as 1820. A system of universal, compulsory education is now established there.

In 1842, the kingdom of Hawaii was recognized by the United States. An internal struggle for constitutional rights arose and lasted, with interruptions, until 1893, when the reigning queen, Liliuokalani, was deposed. An appeal for annexation to the United States was made, but it was rejected by President Cleveland. A second appeal, made to President McKinley, resulted in the approval by Congress, July 7, 1898, of a treaty of annexation. In 1900, the islands were formally organized into the territory of Hawaii, and a territorial governor was appointed by the president. In 1959, Hawaii was admitted to the Union as the 50th state.

On Kealakekua Bay, Hawaii Island, stands an obelisk commemorating Captain Cook, who was slain near that point by natives in 1779. In 1928, a bronze tablet was dedicated in his honor and placed just below the surface of the water to mark the exact spot where he fell. The adjacent region, known as Kaawaloa, was made into a public park.

UNITED STATES DEPENDENCIES

Like the other powerful nations of the 19th century, the United States acquired a number of dependencies. Since America's independence had stemmed from revolt against colonialism, the name colony was never applied to these dependencies. Moreover, the question of their acquisition was the source of bitter political debate, particularly when the Philippines, Puerto Rico, and Guam were ceded to the United States in 1898, American Samoa was acquired by treaty with Britain and Germany in 1899, and Hawaii was annexed in 1900. Alaska had already been purchased from Russia in 1867. The Panama Canal Zone was obtained by treaty with Panama in 1903; the Virgin Islands were purchased from Denmark in 1917.

It has been the official policy of the United States to provide stable government for the possessions and to encourage their economic and educational development with a view to their eventual self-government. Of the above dependencies, the Philippines was granted independence as the Philippine Republic in 1934, and Alaska and Hawaii became states in 1959.

This policy of development has entailed the building of railroads, highways, waterways, and harbor facilities, the introduction of improved methods of agriculture, and the founding of suitable manufacturing industries. Basic to such improvement was provision of free public schools and other educational facilities. The introduction of modern sanitation methods and of methods of preventing and treating diseases led, not only to improved well-being, but to rapid population increases that paced the economic advances.

In this section is treated the geography of American Samoa, Canal Zone, Guam, Puerto Rico, and the Virgin Islands. The small islands of Wake and Midway, and the South Pacific Islands which the United States received in trust under the United Nations for eventual return to Japan, are treated in the Department of Government and Politics.

AMERICAN SAMOA

A group of four inhabited and several uninhabited islands in the south Pacific Ocean, about 4200 miles southwest of San Francisco and about 2000 miles east of Australia. The inhabited islands are Tutuila, Tau, Swain's Island and those of the Manua group—Ofu and Olosega. The total area is 76 square miles.

The islands are largely mountainous in character, but much of the soil is extremely fertile. The moist tropical climate of the islands fosters a luxuriant vegetation. Agriculture is the principal occupation and is carried on mainly by family groups, each of which is directed and ruled by a patriarch, or *matai*. The chief products include copra, taro, breadfruit, yams, pineapples, oranges, and bananas. Copra and canned tuna are exported.

The only large port of American Samoa is Pago Pago. It is a United States naval station under a commandant. The population in 1970, 29,000 (est.). Schools were established in Samoan villages by Christian missionaries as early as 1830. Elementary education in English is available for all in schools supported by the government.

This group of islands came under American sovereignty in 1899 as the result of a treaty with Great Britain and Germany. Since the establishment of American control, the islands have made substantial gains in population and in social welfare.

CANAL ZONE

A strip of land ten miles in width, through the center of which runs the Panama canal. The Canal Zone divides the Republic of Panama into two parts.

The zone was obtained in 1903 from the Republic of Panama for the sum of $10 million with an annual payment of $250,000, changed in 1936 to 430,000 balboas after the American dollar had been devalued in terms of gold. Its affairs are administered by a governor appointed by the United States government. A railroad connects the two terminals of the canal—Balboa, the Pacific port, and Cristobal, on the Caribbean sea. Population 1970, 44,650. See *Panama Canal*.

GUAM

The largest and most southerly of the Mariana Islands, Guam is situated in the Pacific Ocean about 1700 miles east of Manila and some 6000 miles southwest of San Francisco.

The island of Guam is about 30 miles long, and varies in breadth from 4 to 8½ miles, its estimated area being 210 square miles. It is mountainous in the south but plateau-like in the north. Broken coral reefs fringe the shore.

There are only two seasons—a wet season and a dry one. Though the temperature averages 81° F. the year round, the climate is healthful. The soil is fertile, well watered, and yields abundant crops of copra, corn, sweet potatoes, taro, cassava, bananas, citrus fruits, and sugar cane. There are no import duties. Agana, the capital, is the chief city. Apra is the port of entry.

From 1898, when it was acquired from Spain, Guam was administered by the United States navy department, but in 1950 it came under the supervision of the department of the interior.

The natives are of a mixed race, called Chamorros, with the Malayan strain predominating. Chamorro, the native language, and also Spanish and English are spoken.

Guam was discovered in 1521 by Magellan. In 1565, the Spanish took possession of the island. It remained under Spanish rule until 1898, when, as a result of the Spanish American war, it was ceded to the United States. Its location has made it of great strategic importance both as a naval and an air base, and military establishments occupy about one-third of the usable land. During World War II, the Japanese held it from 1941 to 1944. Population, 1968 (est.), 101,000.

PUERTO RICO

A West India island lying about 70 miles east of Haiti and 1425 miles southeast of New York. The island is about 100 miles long and from 30 to 40 miles wide, and has about three times the area of the state of Rhode Island.

The climate of Puerto Rico is regarded as the most healthful in the tropics of the western hemisphere. Through the middle of the island, a broken range of mountains extends from east to west, their altitude varying from about 2000 feet to that of the culminating peak of El Yunque, 3532 feet high. These mountains are clothed to their summits with luxuriant vegetation. The coast belt is a broad, level alluvial plain. The soil is exceedingly fertile and, as the population is dense, most of the arable land is under cultivation.

On the eastern and on the northern slopes of the mountains there is abundant rainfall, the average yearly precipitation being 65 inches. But, in the southern part of the island, irrigation is required in some districts, as the mountains intercept much of the moisture in the trade winds. Puerto Rico is noted for its fine forest trees. Palms, Spanish cedar, ebony, mahogany, ausubo, laurel, sandalwood, and dyewoods abound.

The mineral resources of Puerto Rico, so far as developed, consist chiefly of limestone and volcanic boulders, used in building; various clays, used in making brick and pottery; and gypsum, used for stucco, plaster, and fertilizer. Deposits of marble and lignite occur; along the south coast there are extensive phosphate beds; and on the northern coast there are nearly pure silica sands, used in the manufacture of glass and china. Gold, copper ore, iron ore, and the ores of various other metals have been found in small quantities.

Agriculture is the chief industry, but in recent years manufacturing has rivaled it in value of output. Sugar is the most important crop, followed by tobacco, coffee, pineapples, grapefruit, oranges, and other tropical fruits. After World War II, the government put into effect a policy of purchasing farm land from large corporations and turning it over to individual farmers on a "proportional profit" basis. An aggressive policy of industrialization also was followed, and many United States corporations extended operations to Puerto Rico to take advantage of the tax incentives offered.

Nearly all the exports go to the United States. The chief one is sugar, which was valued at about $92 million in 1968–69. Textile fibers, rum, liquor, and molasses are also exported extensively.

Puerto Rico is densely populated, with about 800 inhabitants to the square mile. To encourage new industries and provide employment, the insular government in 1942 created the Industrial Development Company, which established a number of factories.

THE COMMONWEALTH OF PUERTO RICO

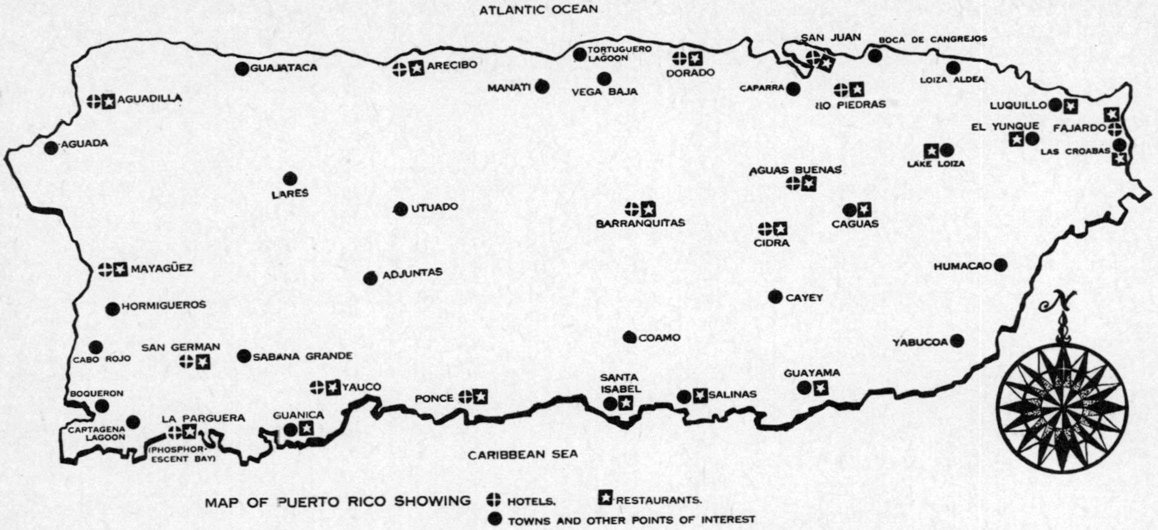

Source: Office of Information, Economic Development Administration, San Juan, Puerto Rico

A bank with a liberal industrial loan policy was also set up, and in 1948 certain industries, old and new, were granted a twelve-year exemption from taxes. That same year the hydroelectric power of the island was increased by the completion of the Caonilas dam.

The principal cities and seaports are San Juan, the capital, on the north coast, with a population of 444,952; Ponce, on the south coast, population 125,926; and Mayaguez, on the west coast, population 69,485. The harbor at San Juan, which has been extensively improved by the United States government, is one of the best in the West Indies. A railroad, built near the coast, almost completely encircles the island, and there are branches into the interior. Surfaced highways, of which more than 3520 miles have been constructed, facilitate transportation in various parts of the island.

Under the school system, education is free and compulsory. In 1968–69, there were 720,313 pupils enrolled in Puerto Rican schools. There is also a well-distributed system of night schools and kindergartens. Colleges include the University of Puerto Rico, at Rio Piedras; the Catholic University of Puerto Rico, at Ponce; the Inter-American University, at San German; and the College of the Sacred Heart, at Santurce. The percentage of illiteracy has declined from 83 per cent in 1889, to 14 percent in 1966.

Puerto Rico was discovered in 1493 by Columbus. The first settlement was made at Pueblo Viejo in 1508 by Ponce de Leon, who, in 1509, was appointed governor by King Ferdinand of Spain. Although attacked at various times by the English and the Dutch, Puerto Rico remained in the possession of Spain until 1898, when, at the close of the Spanish American war, it was ceded to the United States. Since the establishment of American methods of agriculture, American public schools, improved highways and railways, and various civic improvements, Puerto Rico has made remarkable progress. Population. 2,739,000.

VIRGIN ISLANDS

A group of some 50 tropical islands and islets formerly called the Danish West Indies. They lie about 40 miles due east of Puerto Rico. The total area of the group is about 149 square miles, of which 132 is comprised in the three largest islands—Saint Thomas, Saint John, and Saint Croix (Santa Cruz). Almost all the inhabitants are Negroes or mulattoes. Population, 1967, 54,545 (est.).

Saint Thomas is the best known of the islands because its principal town, Charlotte Amalie, population 12,880, is located on one of the finest harbors in the West Indies. The surface of the island is rugged and elevated, and the soil is poor. The exports are principally rum and hides. Most of the imports are foodstuffs and wearing apparel. The College of the Virgin Islands is located on St. Thomas. The area of the island is about 28 square miles. Population, 1967, 28,705 (est.).

Saint Croix, the largest and wealthiest of the islands, lies about 40 miles southeast of Saint Thomas, and has two well-known towns, Frederiksted (Westend) and Christiansted (Bassin). The latter was the capital of the islands under Danish rule. Sugar cane is the chief crop. Longstaple cotton is grown, and cattle are raised. The area of the island is about 84 square miles; population, 1967, 24,295 (est.).

Saint John, the smallest of the three main islands, grows bay leaves for the distillation of bay oil and also has a considerable acreage devoted to cotton, sugar cane, and tobacco. The entire population is considered rural. The area of Saint John is about 20 square miles; population, less than a thousand.

The Virgin islands were discovered in 1493 by Columbus. Saint Thomas was first colonized in 1672 by the Danes. Saint Croix, first occupied in 1625 by Dutch and English settiers, came into the possession of Denmark in 1733. With the exception of two periods—1801-02 and 1807-15—during the Napoleonic wars, when they were seized and held by the English, most of the islands were under the Danish flag for a period of 245 years. In 1917, upon payment of $25 million, they came into the possession of the United States by purchase.

During the days of sailing ships, especially about 1820, Saint Thomas was a supply point of great importance in the West Indian trade. Before the abolition of slavery, in 1848, in the islands, sugar growing was a substantial industry. With the decline of the sugar industry, the population decreased, falling gradually from about 40,000 in 1850 to about 26,000 when the United States took possession in 1917. Tourism has become the chief industry.

The value of the Virgin islands now lies chiefly in their geographic location and their exceptionally fine harbor facilities. Their situation with reference to the Panama canal makes Saint Thomas of great strategic importance as a naval base and as a coaling station.

DICTIONARY OF AMERICAN GEOGRAPHY

In the selection of topics for this section of American geography, the following considerations have governed:

Capital Cities. All capitals of states, territories, and dependencies of the United States are given an item because of their political importance.

Largest Cities. Size in itself would dictate the selection of a large proportion of the cities of United States for special articles. But with size normally go commercial and industrial importance and numerous cultural activities which make their inclusion doubly essential.

Smaller Cities and Places. Various cities and towns with a population of less than 50,000 have been included for specific reasons, such as historical associations like those of Gettysburg, Plymouth, and Ticonderoga, or proximity to features of travel interest, as in the case of Adamana and Grand Junction.

Other cities, such as Butte, Cohoes, Hibbing, Riverside, and Anaconda, are included because they are leading centers in some important economic enterprise. Still others have been selected primarily because they are seats of universities, colleges, or other important educational institutions. Examples of this kind are Ithaca, Oberlin, and Princeton.

The more important Indian towns of the Southwest are given brief treatment. Among these are Isleta, Laguna, and Zuni. Selections of resorts have also been made, including Lake Placid, Palm Beach, and Saratoga Springs. Of the less populous states, the largest and, usually, the second and third largest cities have been included.

Cities of the continental U.S. whose population exceeds a half-million have generally been given special topical treatment. Descriptive matter is divided into topics under separate subheadings. The treatment follows a uniform plan, beginning with a description of the locale, then describing streets, parks, buildings, educational institutions, industries, and other leading features, and ending with important points in the city's history.

Populations figures are based on final U.S. Bureau of the Census reports. At the end of the section appears a tabulation of cities having a population of 30,000 or more in 1970, with populations in that year and in 1960.

Scenic and Travel Interest. Among topics of scenic and travel interest will be found descriptions of some of the most noted features of the continent, including mountains, lakes, deserts, islands, waterfalls, gorges, cliffs, and caves. Examples of the mountains are Mount Rainier, Mount Shasta, Lassen Peak, and Mount Washington. The lakes include Lake Champlain, Lake George, Itasca Lake, and Lake Tahoe. Among the deserts described are Death Valley, the Mojave, the Colorado, and the Painted Desert. Representative of the other scenic features mentioned above are Niagara Falls, Luray Cavern, Mammoth Cave, and the Palisades.

Numerous features, combining both scenic and historic interest, include Harpers Ferry, Lookout Mountain, Stone Mountain, and Starved Rock. Various special regions, such as the Cotton Belt, the Corn Belt, the Wheat Belt, the Citrus Belt, the Blue-Grass Region, and the Inland Empire, are also described. Although the numerous national parks and national monuments are given tabular treatment elsewhere, some of the most noted are described in greater detail in this section; as, for example, Yellowstone Park and the Grand Canyon

Aberdeen. A city of South Dakota, situated in the northern part of the state at the junction of U.S. highways 12 and 281. Aberdeen is the commercial center of a rich agricultural district, producing large crops of wheat, corn, hay, and potatoes. Its industries include meat packing, flour milling, and the manufacture of machinery. The city is the seat of Northern State College, which has a large open-air theater. Population, 1970, 26,476.

Aberdeen. A city of western Washington, on Grays harbor, 50 miles west of Olympia. Aberdeen is a timber, dairy, and agricultural center, with lumber and plywood mills, fish-curing houses, canning establishments, and excellent port facilities. It adjoins Hoquiam on the west and Cosmopolis on the east. Its inhabitants have a large Scandinavian element. Population, 1970, 18,489.

Abilene. This city in Kansas, 100 miles west of Topeka, was established in 1860 as a shipping point at the end of a trail over which cattle were driven from the Southwest. It has become a flourishing trade center for livestock and grain, particularly wheat. The boyhood home and burial site of Dwight D. Eisenhower, Abilene is the seat of the Eisenhower Museum. A part of old Abilene is being restored as it was in pioneer days. Population, 1970, 6,661.

Abilene. A city located in west central Texas. Long known as an agricultural and livestock center, it has added manufacturing (including aerospace components and ladies' garments), and oil production. Nearby is the Dyess Air Force Base. Educational institutions are Hardin-Simmons University, McMurry College, and Abilene Christian College. Population, 1970, 18,563.

Adamana (*ă'dă-mä'nȧ*). A small village on the Santa Fe railway in eastern Arizona. Near it are located the celebrated "petrified forests." Of the three forests which together constitute the Petrified Forest national park, two lie at distances of from 6 to 9 miles south of Adamana. Here some thousands of acres are covered with fragments of petrified wood and with wonderfully preserved fossil tree trunks, many of which are 4 feet in diameter. One of these large mineralized trunks, by spanning a ravine 45 feet wide, forms a natural bridge.

The third forest, usually called "Rainbow Forest," is more readily reached by automobile road from Holbrook, a railway town 20 miles west of Adamana. In this petrified forest there are several hundred whole trees, some of which are more than 200 feet long and 6 feet in diameter, all partially embedded in the ground. These are the remains of great cone-bearing trees that grew in geological times.

Agaña (*ä-gän'ya*). The capital and chief town of Guam, situated on the west coast of the island. Official buildings such as the Governor's Palace, Administration Building, and Post Office are situated here. The people are principally merchants or are in professional trades. Nationalities include Guamanians, Americans, Filipinos, and Japanese. In 1940 Agaña was annexed to Sinajana. Population, 1968, 2400.

Akron. A rubber manufacturing city of Ohio, located 35 miles southeast of Cleveland, with a grain producing region to the south and rich dairy country to the north. Akron has long been noted for its clay products. With the rise of the automobile industry, the city became the center of the world's most extensive manufacture of automobile tires and of rubber goods in general. It produces also synthetic rubber, fishing tackle, zinc oxide, machine shop products, sulphur, salt, and children's books and is the principal center for the manufacture of sheet metal products, defense equipment, and airships. A huge dirigible air dock, The Goodyear Air Dock, adjoining the municipal airport and covering 9 acres, was opened in 1930. Truck transportation is a major activity.

Within the city there are 26 beautiful parks; these cover a total area of 2200 acres. The Portage Lakes, a 2250-acre state park, lies just south of the city. A steel bridge, 190 feet high, spans the Cuyahoga River within the city, and the North Hill viaduct, 135 feet high and 2810 feet in length, provides the main approach from the north and east. Symbolic of Akron's prominence as a rubber center is the Harvey S. Firestone Memorial, created by architect Eric Gugler and sculptor James Earle Fraser, and dedicated in 1950 to commemorate half a century of progress since the founding of the Firestone Company. The chief educational institution is the state University of Akron. "Derby Downs" is the scene each August of the International Soap Box Derby. Population, 1970, 275,425.

Alameda (*ăl'ȧ-mā'dȧ; -mē'dȧ*). A city of California, occupying a narrow island on the east side of San Francisco Bay, opposite San Francisco and directly south of Oakland. An underwater tube and five bridges link the city to the mainland and major highway systems. Alameda is a beautiful residential city, with numerous fine streets and homes. It also maintains substantial industries, among which are potteries, shipbuilding, and the manufacture of motors, pumps, engines, airplanes and lumber. A large naval air station is located there. Alameda's seven miles of municipal beaches, two yacht harbors, and seven parks provide recreational facilities. Population, 1970, 70,968.

Albany. The capital of New York State, situated on the west bank of the Hudson River, near the head of the Tidewater, 145 miles north of New York City.

Albany is the connecting link between the state's barge canal system and ocean navigation via the Hudson River. A feature of its terminal facilities is a grain elevator covering eight acres. Because of its extensive railway connections, the city is one of the leading transfer points in the United States for passenger, express, and mail traffic. Albany is said to have been the first American city to have a municipal airport, having provided one in 1917. The city's manufactures are extensive and varied. Among the chief products are car heaters and other metal wares, clothing, knit goods, paper products, flour, printing, meatpacking products, and felts.

The city occupies a commanding site, affording superb views of the Hudson River valley. Washington Park, the largest of the 27 units in the city's park system, is noted for its natural beauty.

The most imposing building is the State Capitol, which cost over $29 million. The structure, 400 feet long and 300 feet wide, is built of Maine granite in the Renaissance style. The State Office Building, 34 stories high, is the city's tallest structure. Among other noteworthy buildings are the Albany Institute of History and Art; the old Schuyler Mansion, dedicated in 1917 as a historical monument; and Saint Peter's Church.

Albany's educational institutions include the State University of New York at Albany, Albany Law School (Union University), Albany Medical College, and the College of St. Rose.

Established by the Dutch as a trading post in 1614, Albany is said to be the second oldest permanent settlement within the limits of the thirteen Colonies. Its charter, granted in 1686, is said to be the oldest in the United States. The city was Burgoyne's objective before the battle of Saratoga. Population, 1970, 114,873.

Albuquerque (*ăl'bû-kûr'kē*). A city of New Mexico, on the Rio Grande River, slightly northwest of the center of the state. It lies at an elevation of 5000 feet, in a bracing, sunshiny climate, and is a noted health resort. The old town, founded in 1705 by the Spanish, remains as a division of the modern city, which dates from 1879.

Albuquerque is the trade center of a rich timber, livestock, and irrigation farming district. A leading occupation is the entertainment of tourists. The University of New Mexico is located here. The more notable structures include a Federal Building and the Harvey Indian Museum. Features of interest in the vicinity are the ancient church of San Felipe de Neri, built in 1735, and the Isleta Indian pueblo. Population, 1970, 243,751.

Alcatraz. An island in San Francisco Bay, about a mile from the mainland. Its shores rise precipitously from the sea. It had been fortified by the Spaniards. From 1858, it was used by the United States government to intern military prisoners. Beginning in 1933, it was used to incarcerate prisoners convicted of kidnapping, murder, and other serious charges, mostly involving life sentences. It was chosen for the purpose as being practically escape-proof and was designed for punishment rather than reformation. Its use as a prison was discontinued in 1963.

Alexandria. A historic city of northern Virginia on the west bank of the Potomac River, six miles below Washington, D. C. Among its many quaint old buildings are Old Christ Church, which George Washington and Robert E. Lee attended; Carlyle House, where Braddock, in 1775, organized his expedition against Fort Duquesne; and the home of Robert E. Lee. The George Washington National Masonic Memorial, erected at a cost of $5 million, is the most imposing modern building. Alexandria's freight classification yard is one of the largest in the country. Refrigerator cars are made in the city. Population, 1970, 110,938.

Allentown. A manufacturing city of Pennsylvania, 50 miles north of Philadelphia. The products of Allentown's industries include electronic components, trucks, fire engines, communication equipment, textiles, shoes, food and beverages, paints, furniture, and numerous items of metal and paper. Founded in 1762 by William Allen, Chief Justice of Pennsylvania, the city has interesting historical traditions. During the Revolutionary War, the Liberty Bell was concealed here to prevent its capture by the British. The city is the seat of Muhlenberg, Cedar Crest, and Pennsylvania Wesleyan colleges. Population, 1970, 109,527.

Altoona. A railroad city of central Pennsylvania picturesquely situated in a mountainous district about 100 miles east of Pittsburgh. The major industry is railway shop construction and repairs, enormous car shops of the Pennsylvania railroad being located in the city. Other products are textiles and clothing. Population, 1970, 62,900.

Amarillo. This leading commercial and industrial center in the northwestern or "panhandle" section of Texas, is a focal point by rail, air, and highway for one of the richest gas and oil regions in the United States. Helium-bearing sands are found nearby, and the city is the chief producer of this gas for airships. Other industries include oil refining, zinc smelting, meat packing, and flour and cottonseed oil milling. Educational institutions include Amarillo College. Population, 1970, 127,010.

Anaconda. A mining city of southwestern Montana, 26 miles northwest of Butte. Anaconda was founded in 1884 by the Anaconda Copper Mining Company, which has there one of the world's largest non-ferrous reduction plants. It is often called the smelting city and is said to have the tallest smokestack in the world. Population, 1970, 9,771.

Anaheim. A city 28 miles southeast of Los Angeles in the Santa Ana Valley of California. Chief among its diversified industries is the packing and canning of citrus fruits, especially oranges. Population, 1970, 166,701.

Anchorage. A city of Alaska which was founded in 1914 and became construction headquarters for the railroad between Seward and Fairbanks. Reflecting the interests of a growing community, it has expanded to include a land office, an international airport, shipping agencies, oil-producing companies, and varied manufacturing and commercial enterprises. Population, 1970, 48,029.

Anderson. A city in Indiana on the White River, 35 miles northeast of Indianapolis. It is in an agricultural region for which it is a business and industrial center, manufacturing steel products and appliances, among other things. It is the seat of Anderson College. Population, 1970, 70,787.

Annapolis. The capital of Maryland, situated on the right bank of the Severn River, near the center of the western coast of Chesapeake Bay. The city was first settled in 1649, and was called Providence. In 1694, it was named after Queen Anne and was made the capital of the colony of Maryland. The first Federal Constitutional Convention met in Annapolis in 1786. The city is the seat of the United States Naval Academy, on a beautiful site of 200 acres, organized in 1845, and of Saint John's College, founded in 1696. The industries include an oyster packing plant. Population, 1970, 29,592.

Ann Arbor. A city on the Huron River, 36 miles southwest of Detroit. It is an industrial and trading center in the midst of an agricultural region. It is the seat of the University of Michigan. Population, 1970, 99,797.

Appalachian Trail. A wilderness foot trail extending 2050 miles from Mount Katahdin, Maine, to Mount Oglethorpe, Georgia. The longest marked foot path in the world, it follows in general the ridge of the Appalachian Mountains. The project was begun in 1921, largely through the initiative of Benton MacKaye, forester and specialist in regional planning; it was completed in 1938.

Asbury Park. A city of New Jersey, on the Atlantic Ocean, about 40 miles south of New York City. Asbury Park is noted chiefly as a seaside resort and residential city. It has, however, various small industries, including the manufacture of silk, women's apparel, electronic equipment, and leather clothing. Population, 1970, 16,533.

Asheville. A mountain resort and city of North Carolina, picturesquely situated in "The Land of the Sky," a plateau of the southern Appalachian Mountains, 2300 feet above sea level, at the western extremity of the state. It is near Great Smoky Mountains National Park, Mount Mitchell, and numerous other points of scenic interest. Near Biltmore Forest, a suburb, is situated the magnificent estate of George W. Vanderbilt, which is open to the public. Other features of the city include Pack Memorial Library, Grove Arcade, covering an entire block, and the civic center on Pack Square. Craggy Rhododendron gardens, 600 acres of royal purple rhododendrons 15 miles from the city, is one of the finest natural gardens in the world.

Asheville provides a market for nearby producers of fruit and is an important distribution center. Manufactured products include furniture, plastics, mica, rayon, cotton textiles, and blankets. The city was incorporated in 1797. Population, 1970, 57,681.

Astoria. A port of northwestern Oregon, located on the Columbia River, about 10 miles from its mouth. It is noted chiefly for the catching and canning of salmon on an immense scale. Tuna also is caught and packed there. Other industries include lumber mills, and creameries. Astoria has river, rail, and bus transportation to Portland, 105 miles distant, and also considerable ocean commerce, with exports of lumber, grain, fish, and flour. It has also a large tourist traffic. Astoria was named for John Jacob Astor, who founded it in 1811. The first post office and the first customhouse west of the Rockies were located here. Population, 1970, 10,244.

Athens. A city of northern Georgia, on the Oconee River, some 70 miles east of Atlanta. Its industries produce electronic components, non-woven fabrics, textiles, clocks, transformers, baseball bats, and precision parts for the aerospace industry. Athens is a noted educational center and is sometimes styled the "classic city of the South." Its leading institutions include the University of Georgia (the oldest state-chartered university) and the Georgia Center for Continuing Education. The city is known for its ante-bellum homes and memorial gardens. Population, 1970, 44,342.

Atlanta. The capital of Georgia, situated in the north central part of the state, about 300 miles northwest of Savannah.

The ridge on which the city is built is a part of a watershed dividing streams that flow into the Atlantic from those that flow into the Gulf of Mexico. The city lies about 1050 feet above sea level. The Chattahoochee River, flowing within 8 miles of the city, is the source of its water supply.

Atlanta is admirably, though somewhat irregularly, laid out, and contains many beautiful avenues and streets. The city covers about 34 square miles, and includes a park system embracing a total area of more than 1200 acres and containing 75 parks, squares, and open spaces. In Grant Park there is a great cycloramic painting of the battle of Atlanta. About 15 miles to the east of Atlanta is situated Stone Mountain, on the face of which is a huge sculptured memorial to the valor of the Confederate soldiers. The commercial district contains many notable buildings, giving the city a metropolitan aspect. Among these are the State Capitol, the Atlanta Public Library, the Federal Building, the Terminal Station, the Federal Reserve Bank, and numerous imposing office buildings.

Atlanta is a prominent educational center and contains many widely known institutions of learning. Among the leading institutions of higher learning are the Georgia Institute of Technology, Emory University, Oglethorpe University, and Columbia Theological Seminary. The institutions for women include Agnes Scott College, located in the adjoining suburb of Decatur. Among the institutions for Negroes are Atlanta, Clark, and Morris Brown universities, Morehouse College, and Gammon Theological Seminary. There are excellent libraries, and the city is one of the chief centers of printing and publishing in the South.

Because of its advantageous situation and excellent railway facilities, Atlanta has become the chief inland commercial city of the southeastern states. It is the distributing center for a large region and has developed extensive industries, ranking first in the state in manufactures. The leading products include cotton mill products, automobiles, aircraft, confectionery and ice cream, Coca-Cola, furniture, mattresses and bed springs, lumber, clothing, and fertilizers. The city conducts a large merchandising trade.

The growth of Atlanta dates from the building of the first railroads in northern Georgia. The site was settled about 1839. In 1843 it was incorporated as Marthasville. This name was changed to Atlanta in 1845, and in 1847 a city charter was granted. Because of its location, it was one of the most important cities of the Confederacy, and in 1864 was the objective of General Sherman's campaign from Chattanooga. The battle of Atlanta and other severe engagements were fought near the city, which was finally taken by the Union forces and largely destroyed. It was quickly rebuilt after the war and grew rapidly. In 1878, it was made the capital of the state. Population, 1970, 496,973.

Atlantic City. An all-year seaside resort on Absecon Beach, a sandy island five miles off the southeastern mainland of New Jersey, about 55 miles southeast of Philadelphia. There are about 1200 hotels and motels for the accommodation of visitors, the number of which often exceeds 15 million annually. The attractions include many miles of beaches, six large recreation piers, a $28 million convention hall covering 12 acres and seating 41,000 people in its auditorium, and the "Boardwalk," a magnificent promenade, 60 feet wide, extending along the ocean front for a distance of five miles. Permanent population, 1970, 47,859.

Augusta. A commercial and manufacturing city of eastern Georgia, located at the head of navigation on the Savannah river, about 132 miles northwest of Savannah. Augusta is the trade center of a rich agricultural district and one of the leading cotton markets in the United States. Water power and hydroelectric power are extensively used in the city's substantial industries, the chief of which are the manufacture of cotton goods and cottonseed products. Other manufactures include brick, lumber, and fertilizers. A United States arsenal is located there. Augusta was established in 1735, and for a time during and after the Revolutionary War was the capital of Georgia. Educational institutions include Paine College, for Negroes, and the University of Georgia Medical College. Population, 1970, 59,864

Augusta. The capital of Maine, situated on both banks of the Kennebec River, about 40 miles from its mouth. The State Capitol is a handsome structure, built of granite quarried locally. Excellent water and rail transportation facilities have made the city the trade center of a large district. It is also a leading air travel center. Local industries include cotton, paper, and lumber mills. Population, 1970, 21,945.

Aurora. A city of northeastern Illinois, occupying a beautiful site on the Fox River, 38 miles west of Chicago. It is an important manufacturing and railroad center, producing road-building machinery, pumps, drills, and other metal products. Its educational institutions include Aurora College. Aurora was settled in 1834 and chartered as a city in 1857. Population, 1970, 74,182.

Ausable (*ô-sā'b'l*) **Chasm.** A narrow gorge of great scenic attractiveness, situated in northeastern New York, about midway between the Adirondacks and Lake Champlain. The rocks forming the walls are of hard Potsdam sandstone, traversed by numerous fault lines or displacements. Through these the Ausable River has worn a zigzag course about 2 miles long and, in places, 175 feet deep.

Austin. The capital of Texas, located on both sides of the Colorado River, in the south central part of the state. The State Capitol, situated in the ten-acre Capitol Square, is one of the largest in the U.S. Austin is the seat of the University of Texas.

A chain of seven lakes begins within the city limits and winds 150 miles through wooded hills. Called the Highland Lakes, they were created by Colorado River dams as a system for flood control, irrigation, power development, and provision for recreation. The city is the center of a considerable wholesale and shipping business, and carries on an extensive trade in agricultural products, wool, and livestock. Its industries include the manufacture of furniture, electronic instruments, office equipment, food products, finished stone, and fiberglass boats and motor homes. The "association center" of the Southwest, Austin is the headquarters for more than 225 state and national organizations. Austin was incorporated in 1839 and named for S. F. Austin, the "Father of Texas." The site had been selected in 1837 by a state commission instructed to find the most attractive spot for the capitol. Population, 1970, 251,808.

BALTIMORE. The principal city of Maryland, and the largest on the Atlantic seaboard south of Philadelphia. It is situated on the estuary of the Patapsco River, 12.5 miles from Chesapeake Bay and about 170 miles by water from the Virginia capes on the Atlantic. Washington, D. C., lies about 40 miles southwest, and Philadelphia, 97 miles to the northeast. The area of Baltimore is about 79 square miles.

BUILDINGS. Many of the public buildings are noted for size and architectural beauty. Among these are the Peabody Institute, the Roman Catholic Cathedral, said to be the oldest in the United States, the First Presbyterian Church, the Enoch Pratt Free Library, the Walters Art Gallery, the Baltimore Museum of Art, the City Hall, the Federal Building, and the Masonic Temple. The Baltimore Trust Company Building, 509 feet high, affords a landmark of conspicuous beauty.

PARKS AND MONUMENTS. Many fine parks are scattered throughout the city. Of these, Druid Hill Park is the largest and finest. Other noteworthy parks are Clifton, Patterson, Carroll, Herring Run, and Gwynns Falls. A statue of Columbus, unveiled in 1792, the first in any American city to be dedicated to the great discoverer, stands on the grounds of the old Ready school. Mount Vernon Place, the nominal center of the city, is the site of the Washington Monument, a stately column of marble 210 feet high. This monument, the cornerstone of which was laid July 4, 1815, was the first erected by any city in memory of George Washington. Edgar Allen Poe is buried in Westminster Cemetery, one of the oldest and smallest in Baltimore.

EDUCATIONAL INSTITUTIONS. Baltimore is the seat of Johns Hopkins University, a leading institution of higher learning. Connected with it is the widely known Johns Hopkins Hospital. Among other important educational establishments are the University of Maryland, Goucher College for Women, Loyola College, Morgan College, St. Mary's Seminary, and Notre Dame Academy. The Peabody Institute contains a valuable historical library.

TRANSPORTATION AND COMMERCE. In its magnificent system of railroads, its excellent harbor, and its extensive docks, Baltimore has every facility for railway and overseas transportation. Baltimore harbor, one of the largest on the continent with a minimum depth of 35 feet, is capable of accommodating large ocean steamers. Ocean steamers load and unload directly from and into railroad cars at the piers. Baltimore is the chief mercantile and jobbing city of the south Atlantic states and ranks as one of the leading export and import centers of the country. There is an extensive coastwise and intercoastal trade.

MANUFACTURES. Baltimore ranks among the leading cities of the United States in total value of manufactures produced. The principal industries are the making of iron and steel products (the largest single group), shipbuilding, copper, petroleum and sugar refining, and the manufacture of clothing, aircraft, malt and distilled beverages, tin plate, fertilizers, chemicals, and copper products. There are also large establishments for canning fruits and for packing meats and oysters.

Baltimore owes its commanding position as regards manufactures to its easy access to domestic and foreign raw materials and to principal American and world markets.

HISTORY. The first settlement within the present limits of the city was made in 1662. The city was founded in 1729 and was incorporated in 1796. At the time of the American Revolution and especially during the Napoleonic wars, Baltimore attained prominence as a seaport. Its fame was spread throughout the world by its fast-sailing ships called "Baltimore clippers." During an unsuccessful attack by the British on Ft. McHenry, which guarded the city, Francis Scott Key, in 1814, wrote the "Star-spangled Banner."

Baltimore was the first American city to be lighted by gas (1821). The first gas company in America was established there in 1816. The construction of the first important line of railway in the United States, the Baltimore and Ohio railroad, was begun in Baltimore in 1828. Here, also, the first iron steamship was built. In 1844, the first electric telegraph line ever operated was strung between Baltimore and Washington. The first complete, practical electric street railway in the world was installed in Baltimore in 1888. Population, 1970, 905,759.

Bar Harbor. A summer resort in Maine, on the east shore of Mount Desert Island, which lies near the center of the state's coast line. Bar Harbor is partially within Acadia National Park. The scenery in the vicinity is enriched by mountains, by numerous small inlets on the coast, and by many picturesque lakes. Population, 1970, 3,716.

Baton Rouge (*băt'ŭn rōōzh'*). The capital of Louisiana, located on the east bank of the Mississippi River, about 85 miles northwest of New Orleans. The river is spanned at this point by a $10 million bridge. The city occupies a picturesque site on the river bluff, and receives additional charm from its sub-tropical foliage trees and old houses in the Spanish style. The imposing Capitol, dedicated in 1932, has a 33-story tower. South of the city on a 3100-acre campus is the State University. Baton Rouge also is the home of Southern University, said to be the largest and oldest primarily Negro university. By reason of its fine deep-water harbor, Baton Rouge carries on an extensive shipping trade. Its manufacturing interests include sugar and rice mills, wood-working factories, and extensive chemical and petroleum plants. Population, 1970, 165,963.

Battle Creek. A city of south central Michigan, situated about midway between Detroit and Chicago. The city lies in the center of a rich agricultural region and has become noted for its manufacture of cereals. Other manufactures include industrial trucks, valves, cartons, and therapeutic appliances. The Battle Creek Sanitarium is visited by thousands of persons yearly. Population, 1970, 38,931.

Bay City. A city of eastern Michigan, on the Saginaw River, some 4 miles from Saginaw Bay, an arm of Lake Huron, and about 100 miles northwest of Detroit. Bay City has excellent transportation facilities, both by rail and by water, the river being navigable for the largest lake vessels. The surrounding farming district produces large crops of sugar beets. Among the principal industries are automobile parts, electrical and other machinery, fabricated houses, cement, and beet sugar. Recreation facilities include the large Bay County Veterans Memorial Park. First settled in 1837, Bay City received its charter in 1865. Population, 1970, 49,449.

Bayonne (*bā'yōn'*). An industrial city of New Jersey, situated on New York harbor 7 miles southwest of New York City. Bayonne is one of the world's most important centers for the refining of petroleum. It is the terminal of oil pipe lines leading to New York and other eastern cities. The Bayonne Port terminal offers docking facilities among the finest in the New York area. Population, 1970, 72,743.

Beaumont (*bō'mŏnt*). A deep-water port of southeastern Texas, on the Neches River, about 84 miles northeast of Houston. Beaumont is the center of an important rice growing district, and there are great oil fields and large pine and cypress forests in the vicinity. The chief industries are oil refining, lumbering, shipbuilding, and the cleaning and the marketing of rice. Beaumont is the seat of Lamar State College of Technology. Population, 1970, 115,919.

Bellingham. A port of northwestern Washington, located on a natural harbor on Bellingham Bay. It is the commercial center of an extensive agricultural, poultry and lumbering region. Salmon fishing is an important industry. The leading manufacturing establishments include lumber, pulp, and paper mills, salmon and fruit canneries, and cement and sugar beet factories. The city is the seat of the Western Washington State College. Population, 1970, 39,375.

Berkeley (*bûrk'lĭ*). A city of California, situated on San Francisco Bay opposite the Golden Gate and adjoining Oakland, which lies to the south. Berkeley's site overlooking the bay and the equable climate unite to make the city highly attractive from a residential point of view.

Berkeley is the seat of the University of California, the largest university in the world. Excellent transportation facilities and low-priced electrical power have favored the development of various industries. The manufactures include soap, toilet articles, drugs, inks and printing material, pastry products, and chemicals. Berkeley was first settled in 1868, and was incorporated as a town in 1878. Population, 1970, 116,716.

Bethlehem (*bĕth'lē-hĕm*; *-lē-ĕm*). A manufacturing city of eastern Pennsylvania, 52 miles northwest of Philadelphia. It is built on two hills separated by the Lehigh River. The leading industries are steel, foundry and machine products, and silk. Other products include flour, knit goods, radios, electrical equipment, and furniture. Founded in 1741 by Moravians, Bethlehem is the center of the Moravian sect in America. The city celebrates an annual musical festival which is sometimes styled the American Bayreuth. Bethlehem is also the seat of Lehigh University and Moravian College. Population, 1970, 72,686.

Billings. A city in southern Montana on the Yellowstone River, in the heart of an irrigated region noted especially for the raising of sugar beets. Tourist attractions include Beartooth National Forest, the Black Otter Trail, and the Yellowstone Historical Museum. Principal industries are oil refining and diversified manufacturing. Rocky Mountain and Eastern Montana colleges are located in Billings. Population, 1970, 61,581.

Biloxi. A city of Mississippi, about 12 miles east of Gulfport, on a peninsula extending into the Gulf. It is known as a seafood center, with extensive seafood canneries, as well as being a resort area. Biloxi is the site of Keesler Air Force Base and of Beauvoir, the last home of Jefferson Davis. At three times, Biloxi was the capitol of the French province of Louisiana. It was founded by the French in 1699. Population, 1970, 48,486.

Binghamton. A city located in a heavily industrialized area of New York, about 125 miles southwest of Albany. Binghamton is situated at the confluence of the Chenango and Susquehanna rivers. It is the seat of New York State University of Binghamton and Roberson Center for the Arts and Sciences. The birthplace of International Business Machines (IBM), Binghamton is also noted for its manufacture of shoes and photographic equipment and supplies. Binghamton was founded in 1800 by Joshua Whitney, land agent for William Bingham, a wealthy Philadelphia merchant and U.S. Senator from Pennsylvania. It was incorporated as a village in 1834 and became a city in 1867. Population, 1970, 64,123.

Birmingham. A city of Alabama, slightly north of the center of the state. Being situated in the midst of immense coal and iron deposits, Birmingham has risen to high rank among the iron and steel producing centers of the country. Steel and steel products and coke account for a high percentage of the city's extensive output of manufactures, although in recent years the industries of Birmingham have become considerably diversified. The tonnage of its freight is said to be greater than that of all the rest of the South combined. Birmingham is also the trade center of a large and highly productive agricultural district.

The city is substantially and handsomely built, and has many fine streets. beautiful residences, and imposing public buildings, and also numerous commercial structures of the skyscraper type. The municipal park system contains upwards of 39 public parks. Among the most prominent of these are Wilson, North Birmingham, East Lake, Lake View, and Highland parks.

Birmingham is a notable product of the industrial transformation that has taken place in the South since the Civil War. In 1870, the site of the city was a cotton field. In 1871, following the discovery of valuable coal and iron ore deposits in the vicinity, a land company founded Birmingham. Growth at first was slow, but the population rose from about 3000 in 1880 to more than 26,000 in 1890. Population, 1970, 300,910.

Bismark (*bĭz'märk*). The capital of North Dakota, situated on the east bank of the Missouri River, slightly southwest of the center of the state. The most notable buildings include the State Capitol and the Bismarck Civic Arena. The Missouri River is spanned at Bismarck by a bridge. The city's industries include printing, trucking, and the manufacture of farm machinery and concrete products. Population, 1970, 34,703.

Black Hills. A picturesque, mountainous region in South Dakota and northeastern Wyoming. Its 6000 square miles are rich in minerals, particularly gold, and embrace the Black Hills National Forest (970 square miles) and Custer State Park (168 square miles). The highest point is Harney Peak (7216 feet). On Mount Rushmore was begun in 1927 a huge memorial depicting in colossal sculpture the figures of Washington, Jefferson, Lincoln, and Theodore Roosevelt

Black Rock Desert. A dreary waste fully 70 miles long and in some places 20 miles wide, extending northeast from Pyramid Lake in northwestern Nevada. This area, which embraces nearly 1000 square miles, is an alkaline flat or sink, practically devoid of vegetation. During winter, portions are covered with shallow water, whence the name "mud lake," sometimes applied to the region.

Bloomfield. Located 4 miles northwest of Newark, New Jersey, and 11 miles west of New York City, Bloomfield was a part of Newark until 1812. The city is heavily industrialized, with such manufactures as paper and paper products, plastics, rubber goods, textiles, and tile. There is a Revolutionary War soldiers' training ground, now a park, in Bloomfield. Population, 1970, 52,029.

Bloomington. A city about 50 miles southwest of Indianapolis in Indiana. Bloomington is the center of a rich dairy farming region and of the limestone industry, with many quarries in the area. The city has various manufactures. Incorporated in 1876, Bloomington is the seat of Indiana University. Population, 1970, 42,890.

Blue-Grass Region. A district in central Kentucky, lying between the low plains of the west and the mountains on the east. This region is devoted largely to stock raising and is famous for its thoroughbred horses. It is so named because of the prevalence and fine quality of its blue-grass pastures, a common feature of the landscape.

Boise (*boi'sĭ*). The capital of Idaho, located on the Boise River in the southwestern quarter of the state. The surrounding country is rich in minerals and in agricultural products, and the city is an important inland wool market. The varied industries utilize hydroelectric power from the celebrated Arrowrock Dam, constructed 22 miles east of the city and having a height of 349 feet. Boise is unique among cities in possessing a natural supply of hot water from a flowing well. This is used for heating houses and in part for supplying one of the city's outdoor swimming pools. Population, 1970, 74,990.

BOSTON. The capital of Massachusetts, the chief city of New England, is situated on Boston Bay, at the mouth of the Charles and the Mystic rivers, about 230 miles northeast of New York City.

Site. The original site of Boston was a peninsula marked by three historic hills, Beacon hill, Copp's hill, and Fort hill, and contained about 780 acres. By leveling portions of the hills and by filling in various inlets and tidal marshes, this original area was gradually expanded to 1800 acres. The city now contains an area of more than 30,000 acres, or about 50 square miles.

Metropolitan District. Modern Boston consists of the city proper and of the populous metropolitan district of which it is the center. The cities of Somerville and Cambridge extend almost to the heart of Boston, and the fine suburb of Brookline lies almost wholly within the city. These are closely surrounded by other large suburban communities. The center of population in the state of Massachusetts lies within the metropolitan district.

Streets. The narrow, irregular streets, characteristic of the old town, now form but a small section of the North End, mainly an Italian center. The modern city contains about 700 miles of paved streets, which, in the newer districts, are handsomely laid out. Beacon Street, rich in historic associations, and Commonwealth Avenue, one of the finest boulevards in America, are representative of Boston's finest residential avenues.

Parks. Boston ranks high among American cities in the development of parks and playgrounds. This has two distinct phases, municipal and metropolitan. The municipal park system covers 3500 acres, or more than one-tenth of the city's total area. It embraces the historic Common, 48 acres in extent, set aside in 1634, now in the heart of the city, and includes a chain of parks in various other sections, connected by beautiful parkways. These almost encircle the city.

The Metropolitan parks district includes, with Boston, about 40 municipalities. These are administered by a state commission. The Metropolitan parks plan includes such reservations as the Middlesex Fells, 1900 acres; the Blue Hills, 4900 acres; Stony Brook Woods, 460 acres; and Lynn Woods, 2000 acres. The scheme embraces reservations with connecting parkways covering upwards of 10,000 acres.

Monuments. Boston is noted for its monuments and statues, embracing some of the finest sculptural work in America. The most striking is Bunker Hill Monument, a granite obelisk, about 220 feet high, in Charlestown. In the Common is the great Army and Navy Memorial, by Milmore, and the monument commemorating the Boston Massacre, by Kraus. In the Public Gardens is an equestrian statue of Washington, by Ball; and the Ether Monument, commemorating Dr. W. T. G. Morton's experiments, by J. Q. A. Ward. Facing the Capitol is the impressive Shaw Memorial by Saint Gaudens. There are many others.

Buildings. The newer portions of Boston contain some of the finest examples of modern architecture in the United States. Among many notable buildings may be mentioned the Capitol, the Public Library, Federal Building, Prudential Center, Trinity Church, Holy Cross Cathedral, the First Church of Christ Scientist, and the Museum of Fine Arts. The Customhouse, with a tower 505 feet high, is one of the landmarks of the city.

Educational Institutions. Boston is unsurpassed as an educational center. Among its leading institutions are Boston University, Boston College, Simmons College, the New England Conservatory of Music, the Harvard Medical and Dental schools, Northeastern University, and the art school in connection with the Museum of Fine Arts. Harvard University, Radcliffe College, and the Massachusetts Institute of Technology are located across the Charles River in Cambridge. Tufts College, Wellesley College, and other noted institutions are in nearby suburbs. Boston is the home of many important historic, scientific, literary, and musical societies. The Boston Symphony Orchestra is one of the leading organizations of its kind.

Transportation. In large measure, Boston owes its commercial prominence to excellent transportation facilities. It is the chief railway center of New England, and its harbor is one of the finest and best equipped on the continent. It has 8 miles of wharfage, giving 40 miles of berthing space.

Commerce. Boston is the chief seaport of New England and one of the foremost in the United States. The exports are chiefly provisions and manufactures of cotton, wool, leather, iron and steel, and rubber. Among the principal imports are wool, cotton, fibers, sugar, hides, tea, tin, wood products, and chinaware. There is an extensive coastwise trade, and the city has become the leading fish market in the United States. Among the world's wool markets, Boston ranks second only to London. As a chief distributing point for New England, Boston conducts an enormous wholesale trade. The city is also the center of immense mining, railway, and insurance interests.

Manufactures. As a manufacturing center, the Boston area ranks about tenth among the industrial regions of the United States. While no single industry predominates, the city is a leading center for the manufacture of boots and shoes, clothing, confectionery, cocoa products, books, textile and electrical machinery, edge tools, shipbuilding, and numerous specialties.

Points of Interest. Boston, with its environs, offers the traveler an immense number of points of historic and literary interest. Many of the more famous of the earlier buildings have been carefully preserved. Among these are Christ Church (Old North), dating from 1723, Faneuil Hall, the old statehouse, King's Chapel, and the Old South Meetinghouse. Bunker Hill Monument and the navy yard are within the city. In the environs to the northwest are Concord and Lexington, and farther away to the southeast are Plymouth and Plymouth Rock.

Many great writers and scientists lived in or near Boston, including Longfellow, Lowell, Emerson, Holmes, Hawthorne, Thoreau, Dana, Aldrich, Parkman, Prescott, Motley, and Agassiz. Numerous homes and other places of interest connected with the lives of these men are readily accessible.

HISTORY. In a large sense, the history of Boston is the history of New England. Founded in 1630 by Puritans under the leadership of Governor John Winthrop, it was made the capital of the Massachusetts Bay Colony, and has since remained the dominant center of New England. In 1704 the *Boston News Letter*, the first regular newspaper printed in America, began publication. In 1765 began the resistance to the Stamp Act, which culminated in the Revolution. In 1770 occurred the "Boston Massacre," and, in 1773, the famous "Boston Tea Party." At the beginning of the Revolution, Boston was occupied by British troops who defeated the colonists at the battle of Bunker Hill, 1775, but early in 1776 Washington forced the British to evacuate the town Boston received its charter as a city in 1822. During the greater part of the 19th century, Boston was regarded as the literary center of America. Population, 1970, 641,071.

Boulder. A city of northern Colorado, 30 miles northwest of Denver, at the foot of the Rocky Mountains. It is a research and development center, most notably in the area of atmospheric sciences. Manufactures include computer components, technical equipment for satellites, cutlery, and chemicals. The city owns 6000 acres of mountain park land, including Arapahoe Glacier, from which the municipal water supply is obtained. Boulder Canyon nearby possesses great scenic interest. The city is a noted summer and health resort, and is the seat of the University of Colorado. Population, 1970, 66,870.

Bridgeport. The chief manufacturing city of Connecticut, situated in the southwestern part of the state on a natural harbor of Long Island Sound. The city is noted for the diversity of its manufactures, which include electrical machinery, sewing machines, and airplanes. It first attained importance as the seat of the manufacture of sewing machines and as the headquarters of P. T. Barnum's circus. The park system includes Seaside Park, with its two-mile boulevard along the sea wall. The University of Bridgeport has cooperated with the American Shakespeare Festival Theatre to form the Shakespeare Institute, bringing cultural interest to the area. Bridgeport is also the seat of Sacred Heart University. Population, 1970, 156,542.

Brockton. A manufacturing city of eastern Massachusetts, about 20 miles south of Boston. Brockton was one of the largest shoe manufacturing centers in the United States. Other industries include the manufacture of elastic goods, shoe machinery, shoe blacking, nails, and tools. Brockton was settled in 1700, became a town in 1821, and a city in 1881. Population, 1970, 89,040.

Brookline. A town of eastern Massachusetts, on the Charles River, about 3 miles west of Boston. Brookline is chiefly a residential place and ranks among the most beautiful and wealthy suburban towns in America. It produces some manufactures, among which may be mentioned furniture, scientific instruments, and textile products. Brookline is the seat of Cardinal Cushing College and Hebrew Teachers College. Population, 1970, 58,886.

Brooklyn. See *New York*

Brownsville. A city of southern Texas, located on the Rio Grande River. It is an important port of entry, tourist resort, industrial center, shipping point, and agricultural area. It has excellent transportation facilities, manufactures bricks, and cans fruits and vegetables grown in the surrounding area. Founded in 1848 on an old Mexican settlement, Brownsville was an important port during the Civil War. Population, 1970, 52,522.

BUFFALO. A city of New York state, situated at the eastern end of Lake Erie, 22 miles south of Niagara Falls. It occupies a commanding site facing westward on Lake Erie and the Niagara River, and southward to the valley of Buffalo Creek.

STREETS AND BUILDINGS. The city is regularly laid out, with mostly broad streets crossing each other usually at right angles. There are, however, several great diagonal thoroughfares radiating from the commercial center.

Among the many fine edifices are the Federal Building, an impressive granite structure in the French Romanesque style; the County Courthouse; Buffalo and Erie County Public Library; the 32-story City Hall costing $7 million; New York State Building; the William J. Donovan State Office Building; Roswell Park Memorial Institute; the Liberty National Bank, Rand, Marine Midland Trust, Federal Reserve, and Tishman buildings; the 174th Infantry and the 106th Field Artillery armories; the Museum of Natural History and Science, the Buffalo Historical Society Building; the Albright-Knox Art Gallery, an excellent example of refined classical architecture; the modern Kleinhans Music Hall, a $8.7 million Memorial Auditorium; and Saint Joseph's Cathedral. In the adjoining suburb of Lackawanna is the beautiful Basilica of Our Lady of Victory, a national shrine of the Roman Catholic Church.

PARKS AND MONUMENTS. The municipal park system consists of a chain of parks and parkways which nearly encircle the city, covering in all an area of more than 1250 acres. In these are golf links, lakes and ponds, and numerous other facilities for recreation. Delaware Park. 365 acres, with an artistic blending of lake, field, and natural forest, ranks scenically among the leading American parks. The Front and Centennial park, two beautifully landscaped tracts, overlook the outlet of Lake Erie into the Niagara River.

The principal public memorials are the McKinley Monument in Niagara Square and the Soldiers' and Sailors' Monument in Lafayette Square. In Forest Lawn Cemetery, there are monuments in memory of the Indian-chief Red Jacket and of President Fillmore.

EDUCATIONAL INSTITUTIONS. The chief educational institutions are the State University of New York at Buffalo, Canisius College, D'Youville College, the Buffalo Seminary, State University College at Buffalo, Roswell Park Memorial Institute, and the Buffalo Fine Arts Academy which runs the Albright-Knox Art Gallery. In nearby suburbs are Rosary Hill College in Snyder and Erie County Community College in Williamsville.

TRANSPORTATION. Buffalo's unique situation on the Great Lakes, combined with highly developed transportation facilities, gives the city its rank as a world port. The harbor, protected by an immense breakwater, is one of the best on the Great Lakes. The New York State Barge Canal forms a continuous water route to the Hudson River. The Welland Canal, 20 miles northwest of Buffalo, gives water connection with Lake Ontario and the Saint Lawrence Seaway. A railroad bridge and the Peace Bridge for general traffic connect the city with Canada. Moreover, Buffalo is one of the most important railway centers of the nation, being served by 7 major railroads. Thus, by rail as well as by water, Buffalo is on the direct line of communication between the lake ports and the Atlantic seaboard. A segment of the New York State Thruway passes directly through Buffalo.

COMMERCE. In tonnage and in extent of traffic, Buffalo ranks with the leading American and European ports. The water-borne traffic from the West consists principally of grain, iron ore, flour, and general merchandise. Wheat is the chief commodity received, with iron ore second, the two constituting more than half of the total. The water-borne traffic to the West is comprised mostly of manufactured goods, sugar, and anthracite. The total value of goods entering and leaving the port exceeds a billion dollars annually. Besides this large lake and barge canal traffic, immense quantities of merchandise are received and distributed by rail. The city is an important center for the transshipment of grain, its grain elevators having a capacity of about 30 million bushels. Buffalo is also the general trade and wholesale distributing center of a large and highly populous region.

MANUFACTURES. In manufactures, Buffalo usually ranks eighth among the cities of the United States. The city's industries are extensive and varied and their growth has been substantial and enduring. The production of iron and steel and various iron and steel products constitutes one of the chief industries. Storage and milling of grain have always been major activities along Buffalo's busy water front. Among other noteworthy manufactures are automobile parts, rubber tires, chemicals, food preparations, books, linseed oil, and furniture. Buffalo owes its eminence in manufactures to an abundance of electric power, to large supplies of natural gas, and other readily available fuel; and to unexcelled transportation advantages for the distribution of its products.

POINTS OF INTEREST. The pre-eminent feature of scenic interest in the vicinity of Buffalo is Niagara Falls. There are also many points of historical interest in connection with the early settlement of the Niagara frontier and of the conflict with the British and Indians in the War of 1812–14.

HISTORY. La Salle visited the site of Buffalo as early as 1679. The first white settlement was made about 1788 by Indian traders. In 1801–02, a village called New Amsterdam was laid out at the mouth of Buffalo Creek. This village was incorporated and renamed Buffalo in 1810. Three years later it was captured and practically destroyed by the British. It was rebuilt but grew slowly until the completion of the Erie Canal in 1825. Since that date.

Buffalo's progress has been continuous and substantial. In 1832, Buffalo received its charter as a city. The first grain elevator in the world was built in Buffalo in 1843. The city has given to the United States two presidents, Millard Fillmore and Grover Cleveland. In 1901, the Pan-American Exposition was held at Buffalo. Population, 1970, 462,768.

Burbank. A city of southern California, 12 miles north of Los Angeles, noted for its motion-picture and aviation industries. Population, 1970, 88,871.

Burlington. A city of Vermont, located at the approximate center of the east shore of Lake Champlain. Among its manufactures are textiles, armament systems and components, dyes, and apparel. In the vicinity are large quarries of limestone. The city is the seat of the University of Vermont, chartered in 1791, Trinity College for Women, and St. Michael's College. It is headquarters of the Champlain Transportation Company, reputedly the oldest steamship corporation in the world. Greenmount Cemetery contains the grave of Colonel Ethan Allen. Population, 1970, 38,633.

Butte (*būt*). A city of Montana, situated in a mountainous region at an elevation of 5500 feet above sea level. Incorporated in 1879, Butte is the center of an extremely rich copper mining region. Recognition of the city's indebtedness to Marcus Daly, discoverer of the rich copper veins, is expressed in the form of a statue by St. Gaudens. The famous Anaconda mine, said to be the largest copper mine in the world, and many other valuable mining properties are located within a radius of a few miles. Besides copper, the principal product, manganese, gold, silver, lead, and zinc are obtained. The total value of the mineral output to date is approximately $2 billion. The city has an extensive local trade, entertains numerous tourists, and is the seat of the Montana College of Minerals and Technology. Population, 1970, 23,368.

Cambridge. A city of Massachusetts, situated on the Charles River opposite Boston. Cambridge is exceedingly rich in historical, literary, and educational associations.

The Washington elm, under which Washington took command of the American army, stood in Cambridge until 1923, when it was blown down. Elmwood Park commemorates the home of James Russell Lowell Craigie House, once the headquarters of General Washington, became the home of Henry Wadsworth Longfellow. Among the illustrious figures once resident in Cambridge were Oliver Wendell Holmes, Louis Agassiz, and John Fiske. The city is the seat of Harvard University, the oldest university in the United States, of Radcliffe College, of the Massachusetts Institute of Technology, and of the Andover Theological Seminary. A beautiful system of parks includes nearly the entire river front.

The city has numerous important industries, among which are printing and publishing, and the manufacture of electrical machinery, rubber goods, structural ironwork, chemicals, soap, candy, and bakery products.

Cambridge was settled in 1630 by Governor Winthrop and others as Newe Towne. In 1638, Newe Towne was renamed Cambridge; in the same year, Harvard College (founded in 1636) was opened. In 1639, the first printing press in English-speaking North America was set up in Cambridge. The first book printed here was "The Bay Psalm Book," which appeared in 1640. Population, 1970, 100,361.

Camden. A city of southwestern New Jersey, located on the east bank of the Delaware River, opposite Philadelphia. The city occupies a level site, covering an area of about 10 square miles. The park system contains Farnham Park and about 40 other parks or playgrounds. Among the leading industries are shipbuilding and the manufacture of radios, phonographs, canned soups, and worsted goods. Other important manufactures include iron and steel forgings, foundry products, linoleum, chemicals, and pens. In the suburbs are immense market gardens. The city is connected with Philadelphia by steam ferries and by two great bridges: one, the Benjamin Franklin bridge, on its completion in 1926, was the greatest suspension bridge in the world; the other, the Walt Whitman bridge costing $86 million, was opened in 1957.

First settled by Quakers, Camden was organized and named in 1773, and became a city in 1828. Population, 1970, 102,551.

Canaveral, Cape. See *Kennedy, Cape.*

Canton. An industrial city of northeastern Ohio, famed for its manufacture of roller bearings and other iron and steel products, particularly those made from stainless steel. Second only in importance to its metal-working plants are its brick and tile factories. Canton was the home and is the burial place of President McKinley, in whose honor a national memorial has been erected in West Lawn Cemetery. The first home of the National Football League, Canton is now the seat of the Professional Football Hall of Fame. Population, 1970, 110,053.

Carlsbad Caverns National Park. A cavern in southeastern New Mexico, believed to be the largest and deepest in the world. It is entered at the foot of a cliff in the Guadalupe Mountains about 20 miles south of Carlsbad, New Mexico, and 130 miles east of El Paso, Texas.

The cave was formed by water filtering through overlaid rocks and slowly dissolving out beds of rock salt, limestone, and gypsum. The dripping water carrying dissolved minerals has formed stalagmites and stalactites of unrivaled beauty. One of the most impressive portions is the "Big Room," about 4000 feet long with a maximum width of 625 feet. At one point the ceiling is 300 feet high. The "Giant Dome" resembles the leaning tower of Pisa. It is estimated to be 60 million years old. The lowest known point in the cave is some 1350 feet below the earth's surface.

The cave is known to extend at least 25 miles, approximately a third being accessible to the public over carefully marked trails. Artistically concealed electric flood lights emphasize the natural beauty of the cavern. The temperature is constant throughout the year at 56°F.

The most interesting feature of animal life within the cave is a huge colony of bats, estimated to number 3 million, which issues forth from the entrance each evening of summer like a thick cloud. It was this cloud of bats which led to the discovery of the cave in 1901 by Jim White, a cowboy. Milk-white crickets have been found in the cave.

In 1923, an area of about 719 acres surrounding the mouth of the cavern was set aside as a national monument. This was made into a national park in 1930, and its area was subsequently enlarged to about 73 square miles.

Carson City. The capital of Nevada, picturesquely located near the foot of the Sierra Nevada, 14 miles from Lake Tahoe. It contains the Capitol, a Federal building, and a museum containing a series of mastodon skeletons which were discovered nearby. In the vicinity are the State Penitentiary and a government Indian school. Population, 1970, 15,468.

Casa Grande (*kä'sä grän'dā*). The remains of a prehistoric building, situated near the south bank of the Gila River, about 12 miles west of Florence, Arizona. The first white man to visit this impressive structure was Father Kino, a Jesuit missionary. In 1694, he said Mass there. It became a national monument in 1918.

The principal edifice is about 45 by 60 feet in extent. The height of the walls indicates that there were at least three stories, each having various rooms. Above the third story was a smaller room, apparently a watch tower. This structure is only one of many blocks of buildings whose former existence nearby is marked by mounds of debris.

The exterior walls of the Casa Grande building are rough and very much eroded. The interior walls, however, are smoothly plastered. The structure is built of a natural cement, called *caliche* by the Mexicans, composed of lime, earth, and pebbles. This was made into blocks laid in courses.

Casa Grande was probably built about 1350 by the Salado Indians and was occupied by them and the Hohokams for nearly a century before being abandoned.

Casper. A city of Wyoming, in the east central part of the state, on the North Platte River, 150 miles northwest of Cheyenne. It is the site of Fort Caspar, and has extensive commercial interest in the cattle, sheep, wool, and petroleum produced in the surrounding districts. The refinement of petroleum is the chief industry. Casper owns a 440-acre mountain park 5 miles south of the city. Population, 1970, 39,361.

Castle Gate. The entrance to Price River Canyon in central Utah, 115 miles southeast of Salt Lake City. This gatelike passage is formed by two immense pinnacles of sandstone, 450 to 500 feet in height. These pinnacles, strikingly colored, rise like two castles sheer from the narrow canyon bed, barely leaving room for the railway and the river to pass.

Catskill Mountains. A group of mountains in the southeastern portion of New York State about 100 miles north of New York City. The system is about 50 miles long, north and south, and has a breadth of some 30 miles. The highest peak is Slide Mountain, 4204 feet in elevation. In order to supply New York City with water, two creeks on the southern slopes of the Catskills have been impounded: the Esopus by the Ashokan Dam and the Schoharie by the Gilboa Dam. From the resulting reservoirs, which connect by the 18-mile Shandaken tunnel, water is conveyed to New York City by the Catskill aqueduct, which includes a 17-mile tunnel.

Cedar Rapids. A manufacturing city and railway center of east central Iowa, situated on the Cedar River, 220 miles west of Chicago. Its 200 industries include meat packing and the manufacture of cereals, corn products, machinery, and electronic equipment. In total value of manufactures, Cedar Rapids ranks first among the cities of the state. The city is the mercantile center for a rich agricultural region, and enjoys an extensive wholesale trade. The first settlement was made in 1838 at the rapids of the Cedar River. These furnish the water power which has been an important factor in the city's growth. Cedar Rapids is the seat of Coe College. Population, 1970, 110,642.

Champaign. A city in a rich agricultural region of Illinois, about 127 miles southwest of Chicago. It adjoins Urbana, Illinois, Urbana being primarily a residential area, and Champaign, an industrial and commercial area. The University of Illinois is located in Urbana. Champaign manufactures drop forgings, soybean oil, road machinery, deep freezers, air conditioners, and many other items. Population, 1970, 56,532. Population of Urbana and Champaign, 89,332.

Champlain, Lake. An important lake, lying between New York and Vermont, draining through the Richelieu River into the Saint Lawrence. Lake Champlain is about 110 miles long and, at its broadest northern portion, about 13 miles wide. It has a total area of about 600 square miles, two-thirds of which is in Vermont. Its greatest depth is about 300 feet, and it is navigable for the largest vessels.

Lake Champlain is connected with the Hudson River by a canal from Whitehall and serves as a link in New York's extensive system of inland waterways. Among the towns along its shores are Rouses Point, Plattsburg, Port Henry. Crown Point, and Whitehall in New York, and Burlington in Vermont.

Discovered by Champlain in 1609, the lake and its environs became the scene of many stirring events in the French and Indian War and in the Revolutionary War. The decisive naval battle of Lake Champlain was fought off Plattsburg in 1814.

Charleston. The only seaport city of South Carolina, situated 7 miles from the ocean on a peninsula between the Ashley and Cooper rivers. The estuary of these rivers forms a fine landlocked harbor—one of the deepest and most spacious on the Atlantic coast.

The attractive appearance of the city is enhanced by such features as Washington Park, with its pre-Revolutionary statue of William Pitt; Hampton Park; the Customhouse, built of white marble at a cost of $3.4 million; White Point Gardens; and the Esplanade, comprised of the broad, beautiful promenade of the Battery seawall drive.

Manufacturing in Charleston County is widely diversified, including products of wood, metal, tobacco, concrete, paper, asbestos, rubber, chemicals, plastics, and fabrics. An average of more than one hundred ships per month enter and leave the Port of Charleston, and the value of imports and exports is in excess of $200 million annually. Wool is a very important item, with two large wool scouring plants nearby. The port facilities, being fully modernized, handle everything from heavy machinery to tropical fruits. Charleston is one of the country's leading banana ports.

The vicinity of Charleston was the scene of the earliest attempts at colonization in South Carolina. A temporary settlement was made by the French in 1562. The first settlement on the present site of the city was made by English colonists in 1670, who were joined in 1686 by groups of Huguenot refugees. In 1755, a colony of 2000 deported Acadians settled in Charleston.

During the American Revolution, Charleston was captured by the British. The city suffered immense damage in the final campaign of the Civil War in 1865. On August 31, 1886, a heavy earthquake caused great destruction of life and property. After each period of devastation, the city was rebuilt more substantially than before. Charleston has preserved, to a remarkable degree, her interesting historic places and features.

Possessing a well-equipped navy yard, Charleston is an important center of military activity. Located in the immediate vicinity are the Minecraft Base, the Charleston Air Force Base, the U.S. Naval Ammunition Depot, and the U.S. Army Transportation Corps Depot. The system of harbor defenses includes Fort Sumter, whose bombardment in 1861 marked the beginning of the Civil War.

Among the city's leading educational institutions are the College of Charleston, the Medical College of South Carolina, and the Citadel, or State Military College. Population, 1970, 66,945.

Charleston. The capital of West Virginia, situated at the junction of the Kanawha and Elk rivers in a region rich in coal deposits and in petroleum and natural gas. In addition to steel manufactures the city has become noted as a source of nylon, synthetic rubber, resin, and various other chemical products, particularly those having to do with defense. The ready accessibility of silicon, salt brine, and coal-tar products has made this a natural location for such industries. The city's increased activity has been reflected in the completion of the Kanawha County Airport, located on Coonskin Hill. A local educational institution is Morris Harvey College. Charleston was incorporated in 1794, and became the capital of the state in 1870. Population, 1970, 71,505.

Charlotte (*shär'lŏt*). A cotton manufacturing city of North Carolina, located in the rich cotton growing district of the southwestern part of the state. It is at the heart of the hydroelectrical development in the state, and, besides cotton textile mills, has dye and engineering works and automobile assembly plants. The city has a monument erected to the memory of those who, at Charlotte in 1775, signed the Mecklenburg Declaration of Independence. The leading educational institution is Queen's College. Charlotte is the birthplace of President Polk. Population, 1970, 241,178.

Charlotte Amalie. The capital of the Virgin Islands, on the southern side of the island of Saint Thomas, about 40 miles east of Puerto Rico and 1440 miles southeast of New York. Situated on Saint Thomas harbor, one of the finest in the Antilles, it commands strategically the important Virgin Passage.

Charlottesville. A city of central Virginia, built on the Rivanna River, about 70 miles northwest of Richmond. Charlottesville is the seat of the University of Virginia. This was founded by Thomas Jefferson, whose home at Monticello is only 3 miles distant. The city is beautifully located in a rich agricultural and fruit growing region. It was settled in 1744, and the vicinity abounds in historical associations connected with the Revolutionary War. Population, 1970, 38,880. See *Monticello*.

Chattanooga (*chăt'ȧ-nōō'gȧ*). A railroad center and manufacturing city of southeastern Tennessee, situated on the south bank of the Tennessee River. Nearby deposits of coal and iron together with abundant hydroelectric power, marketed at low cost by the Tennessee Valley Authority, facilitate the operation of many industries. Of these, the most important are the manufacture of steel, steel products, and textiles. Near the city stands Lookout Mountain, from whose summit seven states can be seen. Several important battles of the Civil War were fought in the vicinity of Chattanooga. The educational institutions include the University of Tennessee at Chattanooga and the Chattanooga State Technical Institute. Population, 1970, 119,082.

Chautauqua (*shȧ-tô'kwȧ*) **Lake.** A small lake in the extreme southwestern part of New York. It is about 18 miles long and 2 miles wide, and drains through Conewango Creek into the Allegheny River. It lies about 1300 feet above sea level, and 730 feet above Lake Erie, which is only a few miles distant but separated by a range of hills. Chautauqua Lake is noted for its beautiful surroundings and for the widely known Chautauqua summer school located on its banks.

Chelsea (*chĕl'sē*). A city of eastern Massachusetts, situated on the Mystic River, about 3 miles northeast of Boston. Chelsea has substantial industries. These include the manufacture of lithographs, shoes, paper, car wheels, and rubber products. First settled in 1642, as Winnisimmet, Chelsea was incorporated under its present name in 1739. In 1908, a great fire destroyed a large portion of the city. The devastated area, however, was rapidly rebuilt. Population, 1970, 30,625.

Chester. A manufacturing city of southeastern Pennsylvania, located on the Delaware River, about 13 miles southwest of Philadelphia. The chief industrial interests include steel products, munitions, locomotives, automobiles, chemicals, paper, petroleum, machinery, and textiles. It has also one of the largest shipbuilding yards in the country. The city has three parks, also the Deshong Memorial grounds. It is the seat of Pennsylvania Military College. Chester was first settled about 1640 by Swedes. Of historic interest are the City Hall, built in 1724, and the house of William Penn. Population, 1970, 56,331.

Cheyenne (*shī-ĕn'*). The capital of Wyoming, site of America's first ICBM base, is situated in the southeast part of the state, 106 miles north of Denver. The city was founded in 1867 by engineers of the Union Pacific railroad. Because of its central location in an extensive stock-growing section, the city is an important shipping point for beef cattle and for sheep. Among the chief buildings are the State Capitol, the Federal Building, and the governor's mansion. A three-mile boulevard extends from the city to Fort Francis E. Warren, an important government military post. Population, 1970, 40,914.

CHICAGO. The chief city of Illinois, the metropolis of the Middle Western states, and the second most populous city in the United States. It is situated on the southwestern shore of Lake Michigan and on the Indiana boundary, about 185 miles northeast of Springfield, the capital of the state.

SITE. Chicago occupies a remarkably level site, extending along the lake shore for 24½ miles. The city extends inland, at its widest point, for a distance of about 10 miles and embraces a total area of some 212 square miles.

By the Chicago River, a small stream, and by its two branches, the city is divided into three principal districts. The branches of the river unite about a mile west of the lake and approximately midway between the north and the south boundaries of the city. The district lying north of the river and the north branch is called the North Side; that lying south of the river and the south branch is called the South Side; and the much larger district lying west of the two branches is known as the West Side.

STREETS. With few exceptions, Chicago's streets cross at right angles and in east-and-west and in north-and-south directions. Chicago is noted for its exceedingly long and straight streets. Many continue in a direct line for from 5 to 10 or more miles. Some, as, for example, Western Avenue and Halsted Street, extend without deviation for practically the entire length of the city, a distance of 25 miles.

The chief commercial and mercantile center lies south of the river between its south branch and the lake. Here, in an area approximately a mile square, are found most of Chicago's great public edifices, office buildings, and department stores. Many of these are grouped within the so-called "loop," a section surrounded by elevated railroads. On the north it is bounded by the two-level Wacker Drive. State Street contains the great department stores, and, with Wabash and Michigan avenues, constitutes the chief shopping district. LaSalle Street, the center of the financial district, is sometimes styled the "Wall Street" of Chicago. Franklin and Market streets are the principal center of the wholesale trade. The most notable street of the commercial district is Michigan Avenue. For more than a mile this overlooks Grant Park, and its massive buildings, when viewed from Lake Michigan, dominate the city's sky line. Extending northward over the Link Bridge, which spans the Chicago River, it becomes the beautiful Lake Shore drive.

BUILDINGS. Near the center of the business district is the magnificent Civic Center. This is a twin structure of limestone and granite, built in the French Renaissance style. The United States Courthouse, one of the largest structures erected by the United States government outside of Washington, covers an entire city square, about 320 by 400 feet. It is built of granite, 16 stories high, and is surmounted by a massive dome nearly 300 feet high. The Field Museum, on the lake front, erected at a cost of $8 million, ranks among the finest museum buildings of the world. Nearby, on an artificial island, is the Adler Planetarium, the first to be erected in America (1930). Among other notable structures are the Public Library, the great stadium, on West Madison street, the Municipal Pier, the Wrigley Building, the Tribune Tower, the Pure Oil Building, the Board of Trade Building, the Field Building, the Hilton Hotel, the Merchandise Mart, and a $21 million Post Office.

PARKS AND MONUMENTS. Chicago has a magnificent park system embracing about 486 large and small parks, with a total area of more than 7300 acres. The major parks are connected by a system of boulevards and parkways, aggregating 162 miles in length. The circuit through the park system affords one of the finest drives in America. The larger units of the system are Lincoln, Humboldt, Garfield, Douglas, Marquette, Washington, Jackson, Burnham and Grant parks. Among the parkways and drives which link these units into one organic whole are Lake Shore Drive, Sheridan Road, the Outer Drive, and Diversey Avenue on the North Side; Humboldt, Jackson, and Washington boulevards on the West Side; and Eriksen Drive, Michigan Avenue, Grand, Drexel, South Shore Drive, and Garfield Boulevard on the South Side.

Grant Park, on the lake, in front of the business district, contains the Art Institute and the beautiful Buckingham Fountain. Lincoln Park contains a large conservatory and zoological garden and notable statues of Grant and Lincoln, the latter an impressive work by Saint Gaudens.

Jackson Park, the largest of all, overlooks the lake on the South Side. Along the Midway plaisance, connecting Jackson and Washington parks, are the buildings of the University of Chicago. In this plaisance is the impressive sculptural group "Fountain of Time," by Lorado Taft.

Besides the extensive recreation grounds within the city, a metropolitan park district has been created outside of the city. For the purpose of establishing an outer ring of parks, several large forested areas, aggregating more than 37,800 acres, have been purchased.

EDUCATIONAL INSTITUTIONS. Chicago is one of the important educational centers of the country. It is the seat of the University of Chicago, noted for its large post-graduate school. Northwestern University, in the adjoining suburb of Evanston, has most of its professional departments in the city. Other important institutions are Loyola University, De Paul University, the Illinois Institute of Technology, the Lewis Institute, and the art school in connection with the Art Institute.

TRANSPORTATION. Chicago is the chief railway center of America, being the terminus of railway systems embracing about half the total railway mileage of the country. No railroad runs through Chicago, for all of the 22 trunk lines, radiating to all parts of the United States, have terminals in the city. The business district is surrounded by a ring of great passenger stations. A series of belt lines around the city connects the different railroads, forming a complete transfer system. Chicago's 640-acre O'Hare airport is the terminus of numerous converging airplane routes. Meigs and Midway airports are also located in Chicago.

Chicago has also the advantage of inland water transportation, and ranks as one of the chief ports on the Great Lakes. There is a well protected harbor, with docking facilities furnished by the Municipal pier, which extends 3000 feet into the lake. The river and its branches have been deepened so that an immense tonnage, greater than that passing through the Panama Canal, is handled at wharves within the city. By the construction of the Chicago drainage canal, whereby the waters of the river are made to flow outward from the lake into the Des Plaines river, an all-water route to the Mississippi and to the Gulf of Mexico has been made possible.

Local transportation is served by an extensive system of elevated electric railway. The elevated railways radiate from the central loop in the commercial district to all sides of the city. In addition, there is an extensive system of motor bus transportation. Chicago is served also by a large number of suburban electric lines.

COMMERCE. Chicago owes its supreme position in American inland commerce to superior advantages of location and to marvelously developed facilities for transportation. It is situated at the crossroads between the populous industrial sections of the northeastern states and the rich agricultural districts of the Mississippi valley and the great Northwest. The city is the center of shipment of western produce to the East and of eastern manufactures to the West. It is the greatest distributing point in the United States for dry goods, foodstuffs, clothing, household articles, and general merchandise. In Chicago was developed the now extensive business of mail order merchandising.

MANUFACTURERS. Chicago is the industrial as well as the commercial metropolis of the Mississippi Valley region. Among American cities, it stands second only to New York in value of manufactures. Chicago's manufactures normally exceed $3.5 billion in value, or more than two-thirds that of New York's manufactures. Chicago is the world's greatest meat packing center, and leads the country in the manufacture of farm implements, farm machinery, and railroad cars. Its other industries are extensive and exceedingly varied.

HISTORY. In 1803, John Kinzie, the first American settler, built a house on the north bank of the river. In 1804, Fort Dearborn was erected. During the War of 1812, this fort was captured and the settlers massacred by the Indians. Fort Dearborn was reconstructed in 1816, but the village around it grew very slowly until the building of the Illinois and Michigan canal in 1830.

Made a town in 1833, Chicago was incorporated as a city in 1837 with a population of 4170. In 1852, the first railway from the East reached Chicago. Following this event the city's growth was rapid, rising from 28,000 in 1850 to 109,000 in 1860, and to 298,000 in 1870. Since 1870, Chicago has increased in population at the rate of more than a half million in each decade.

In 1871 occurred the "great fire," the most appalling disaster that as yet had befallen an American city. Within a few years the devasted areas were rebuilt and made more substantial than before. In 1893 was held the World's Columbian Exposition, erected at a cost of about $43 million. The centennial of Chicago's incorporation as a town was celebrated by the Century of Progress Exposition in 1933. Population, 1970, 3,366,957.

Chicopee. A manufacturing city of southwestern Massachusetts, located on the Connecticut River, at the mouth of the Chicopee, about 4 miles north of Springfield. Abundant water power is furnished by the Chicopee River for the city's varied and extensive industries. These include the manufacture of firearms, cotton and knit goods, bronze statuary, knitting machines, rubber goods, athletic goods, regalia, swords, and many other articles. Westover Air Base is located nearby. Population, 1970, 66,676.

Chillicothe (*chĭl′ĭ-kŏth′ē*). Capital of the former Northwest Territory and once capital of Ohio, Chillicothe is situated on the Scioto River 45 miles south of Columbus, in the middle of a rich agricultural region. It is also in the center of the Mound City group of prehistoric earthworks which have yielded many artifacts revealing some early American civilization. Chillicothe's manufactures include aluminumware, paper and paper products, shoes, and floor tiling. Camp Sherman was built here during World War I. The city is the site of the Chillicothe Correctional Institute and a U.S. Veterans' hospital. Population, 1970, 24,842.

Cicero. A town of Illinois, partially surrounded by Chicago, of which it is an industrial suburb, being about 7 miles west of Chicago's "loop." Manufactures comprise chiefly electrical equipment, pumps, engines, iron castings, and enamel ware. Population, 1970, 67,058.

CINCINNATI (*sĭn′sĭ-năt′ĭ*). A city in Ohio, situated on the north bank of the Ohio River, 120 miles southwest of Columbus.

Site. Cincinnati is environed by a semicircular range of high hills. From the river bank, it rises in two great terraces or steps, finally reaching a height of 450 feet above the river. Several fine bridges connect the city with Covington, Newport, Ludlow, and other towns on the Kentucky side. Through the center of the city passes Central parkway, a 4½-mile boulevard on the site of the old Miami and Erie canal. The picturesque residential sections of Mount Auburn, Mount Adams, Fairview, Avondale, Hyde Park, College Hill, and Clifton are reached by motor bus lines and by splendid highways.

Buildings and Institutions. Among the more notable buildings are the Post Office, the Public Library, the Music Hall, the County Courthouse, Carew Tower (48 stories, 574 feet high), the Union Central Life building (34 stories, 495 feet high), Saint Peter's Cathedral, and a magnificent terminal station costing about $42 million. Of public monuments, the most artistic are the Tyler-Davidson Fountain, in Fountain Square, and the Barnard Lincoln statue, in Lytle Park. The extensive park system, embracing over 2800 acres, includes Mount Airy Forest, Eden Park, Burnet Woods, Ault, Mount Echo, and various smaller parks.

The city has been long known as an educational, art, and musical center. Among the principal institutions are the University of Cincinnati, a state university; the Ohio Mechanics' Institute; the Art Academy and Art Museum, in Eden Park; Saint Xavier University; Hebrew Union College, Our Lady of Cincinnati College; and the Cincinnati College Conservatory of Music. For many years the May Musical Festivals, held annually, and the annual season of summer opera at the municipally owned Zoological Gardens, have been an indispensable feature of the city's cultural life. The widely known Cincinnati Symphony Orchestra is a well-endowed, permanent organization.

Manufactures. Cincinnati ranks high as a manufacturing city, and owes much of its success as such to its advantageous location midway on the great Ohio River. In addition, the city has the service of eight trunk lines of railway, one of which, the Cincinnati Southern, 338 miles long, is owned by the municipality itself. It is an important air-route center and is an outlet for the bituminous coal fields of Kentucky and West Virginia and for fruits and vegetables grown in the South. Cincinnati's most important manufactures include machine tools, playing cards, soap, building materials, cans, chemicals, clothing, coffins and burial cases, conveyors, cosmetics, electric motors, food products, jet engines, malt and distilled liquors, mattresses, motor vehicles and parts, paper, pianos and organs, plastics, inks, meat products, printing, metal products, shoes, and ceramic products, including the famous Rockwood pottery.

History. In 1788, a village called Losantiville was laid out on the present site of the city. The name of this village was changed in 1790 to Cincinnati, which, in 1802, became incorporated as a town. Its steady growth dates from 1816, when steam navigation was inaugurated on the Ohio River. Cincinnati was incorporated as a city in 1819. Few large cities in the United States have a larger proportion of native-born inhabitants. Population, 1970, 452,524.

Citrus (*sĭt′rŭs*) **Belt.** The name applied to those parts of the states of California and Florida in which the leading citrus fruits—oranges, lemons, and grapefruit—are chiefly produced. Many counties in various parts of California grow oranges on a small scale, but by far the largest part of the state's commercial crop of all citrus fruits is grown in seven counties in the southern part of the state. These are Los Angeles, San Bernardino, Orange, Tulare, Riverside, Ventura, and San Diego counties. Santa Barbara County is an important producer of lemons, and, farther north, Fresno, Sacramento, Butte, Tehama, and Glenn counties produce and market substantial quantities of oranges.

The citrus belt of Florida comprises about 15 counties in the central part of the peninsular portion. It extends across the state from the Gulf of Mexico to the Atlantic Ocean, its center lying a short distance north of Tampa. In this belt the chief citrus fruits produced are oranges and grapefruit. The leading counties in the production of oranges are Polk, Orange, DeSoto, Brevard, Lake, Hillsborough, Volusia, and Pinellas. These counties produce about two-thirds of the total orange crop of the state. The counties leading in grapefruit are Polk, Manatee, Pinellas, Lee, DeSoto, and Saint Lucie. These counties produce about two-thirds of Florida's total yield of grapefruit.

California produces practically all of the lemons, about 70 per cent of the oranges, and some 13 per cent of the grapefruit grown in the United States. Florida grows about 60 per cent of the grapefruit and about 28 per cent of the oranges produced in the country. Texas and Arizona also rank high in grapefruit production, each growing between 10 and 20 per cent of the nation's crop.

Clarksburg. A trade center in the north central part of West Virginia. Among various manufactured products it is noted for articles made of glass, particularly glass tumblers. Clarksburg was founded in 1782. It is the birthplace of "Stonewall" Jackson, after whom one of its leading hotels is named. A Veterans' hospital was opened in 1951. Population, 1970, 24,864.

CLEVELAND. The chief city of Ohio, situated on Lake Erie at the mouth of the Cuyahoga River. It is located in the northeastern part of the state, about 625 miles by rail northwest of New York, and some 360 miles east of Chicago.

Site. Cleveland occupies a beautiful site on elevated ground sloping gently toward the lake, along which it has a frontage of 14 miles. The city is divided unequally by the windings of the Cuyahoga River into a larger portion on the east side and a smaller portion on the west side. The highest point reaches an elevation of about 300 feet above the level of the lake; the lowest points are in the valley of the river and along the lake shore. Immense viaducts, spanning the deep valley of the river, connect the eastern and the western sections. Among the most notable of these are the High Level and Main Avenue bridges and the Abbey Street, Clark Avenue, Lorain-Central, and Harvard-Denison viaducts.

Streets and Buildings. Cleveland is well laid out with many broad, well shaded streets and handsome boulevards. At the intersection of Superior Avenue and Ontario Street, in the heart of the city, is the Public Square. There are also streets connecting with the great viaducts leading to the west side of the city. The chief business section extends from the lower part of the river eastward. The manufacturing districts are mostly along the lake front, in the low flat valley of the river, and along various lines of railway.

A notable architectural feature in the heart of the city is the array of buildings forming the "Municipal Group," or civic center. The project, designed by leading American architects, includes the erection of structures of beautiful and harmonious architecture on a T-shaped tract of land, known as the Mall. The buildings include the County Courthouse, the City Hall, the Federal Building, the Auditorium, the Board of Education Building, and the Public Library. The city is noted for its superb office buildings. Among noteworthy structures are the Museum of Art, the Auditorium, the Keith Building, Federal Reserve Bank, the Union Station with its associated buildings, including the 708-foot Terminal Tower building, the Medical Arts Building, and the Builders Exchange.

Parks. Cleveland's public park system covers a total area of about 3000 acres and includes upwards of 40 miles of connecting boulevards. Important units in the park system are Gordon, Edgewater, Brookside, Garfield, Monumental, Washington, Rockefeller, Wade, and Woodland Hills parks. Among attractive drives are Euclid Avenue, Fairmont and Shaker boulevards on the east side and, on the west side, Lake Avenue and Clifton Boulevard. About the three landward sides of the city extends a belt of boulevards and natural park lands, known as Metropolitan Park.

Educational Institutions. Prominent among Cleveland's cultural institutions are Case-Western Reserve University, John Carroll University, Cleveland State University, Fenn College, the Museum of Art, and the Museum of Natural History. Unique as a means of public education is Cleveland's "Health Museum." In 1949, two new theaters were constructed in the city by nonprofit groups. The Cleveland Orchestra is nationally known.

TRANSPORTATION. The harbor, which is protected by an immense breakwater nearly 6 miles long, is one of the most spacious on the Great Lakes. There is a total lake dock frontage of more than 13 miles, and the Cuyahoga River is also lined with docks. These are equipped with unexcelled facilities for handling iron ore, coal, and lumber, and there is ample dockage at special piers for the extensive passenger service. Cleveland is also one of the great railway centers of the country, with direct lines to most of the leading cities of the United States. It is also an important point of transcontinental air routes. To its already commodious airport facilities for large commercial craft, the city has added a lake-front landing field for light planes.

COMMERCE. Cleveland owes its commanding position in commerce and industry to superior advantages of location. It is situated at the economic focus for the assembly of the raw materials of iron and steel. It is said to be the largest ore market in the world. Within a short distance to the southeast lie iron mines, limestone quarries, and immense coal fields. From the northwest, by cheap all-water transportation, are received enormous supplies of Lake Superior iron ore. In consequence, the city's railways and lake steamer lines handle an immense tonnage of raw materials and distribute manufactured products valued at hundreds of millions of dollars. It is estimated that the total shipments handled at Cleveland aggregate in value more than a billion dollars annually.

MANUFACTURES. Cleveland is one of the great manufacturing centers of America. It ranks fifth among the cities of the United States, being surpassed only by New York, Chicago, Philadelphia, and Detroit. While there is an immense diversity of manufactures, the chief industries are concerned with the manufacture of iron and steel and their products. Other important manufactures are automobile parts, machine tools, household appliances, packed meats, clothing, electrical machinery, and refined petroleum. The Standard Oil Company, which began its operations in Cleveland, has immense refineries in the city. Cleveland is one of the greatest wire and bolt manufacturing centers in the world.

HISTORY. Cleveland was laid out in 1796 and was incorporated in 1814. In 1818, the first newspaper began publication. The Ohio Canal was opened to Akron in 1827, and in 1832 was completed to the Ohio River. This stimulated the growth of Cleveland, which received its city charter in 1836. Since the discovery of iron ore in the Lake Superior region and the construction of the first railroads, 1850–60, Cleveland's growth has been rapid and continuous. The centennial of its status as a city was celebrated by the Great Lakes Exposition in 1936. Population, 1970, 750,903.

Cleveland Heights. A city of northeastern Ohio, being a residential suburb of Cleveland, which it adjoins at Cleveland's eastern boundary. Between 1920 and 1930 it increased in population from 15,236 to 50,945. Population, 1970, 60,767.

Cohoes (*kô-hōz'*). A manufacturing city of eastern New York, located on the Hudson River and the State barge canal, at the mouth of the Mohawk River, about 9 miles north of Albany. Abundant water power and hydroelectric power have led to the development of extensive industries. Cohoes leads all other cities of the United States in the manufacture of knit underwear. Other industries include the manufacture of paper products, shirts and collars, machinery, and building materials. Population, 1970, 18,613.

Colorado Desert. An arid region in southeastern California. It is separated from the Mojave Desert, which lies to the north, by the San Bernardino and the Chocolate ranges, and is bounded on the south by the San Jacinto, the Santa Rosa, and the Superstition mountains.

From the eastern entrance of San Gorgonio pass, the desert extends to the Colorado River, from which it takes its name. It is more than 100 miles long, in some places more than 20 miles wide, and covers an area of about 2000 square miles. Much of this region lies below the sea level. The lowest portion is known as the Salton Sink. In this lies the salt lake, called the Salton Sea, the surface of which is about 280 feet lower than that of the Gulf of California. Parts of the desert show traces of volcanic activity, and there are mud volcanoes and numerous thermal springs.

As in the case of the Mojave Desert and Death Valley, lofty mountain ranges on the west cut off the vapor-laden breezes from the Pacific. Consequently, the Colorado desert is a region of extreme aridity,—in fact, one of the driest and hottest in the world. The normal rainfall ranges from 3 to 4 inches, and summer temperatures as high as 130° have been recorded.

The scanty vegetation is typical of southwestern deserts. it includes the creosote bush, mesquite, cat's-claw, smoke tree, paloverde, and numerous kinds of cactus. In a few canyons at the western end of this desert are the only known groves of the native American fan palm, or Washington palm. Among characteristic desert animals are the chuckwalla lizard and the sidewinder, or horned rattlesnake.

Wherever irrigation is practicable, much of this seemingly worthless desert will produce immense crops of fruits, alfalfa, cotton, and grains. In consequence, prosperous towns and agricultural communities grew up in various parts, notably the rich and populous Imperial valley. In many points this California desert resembles Arabia or Egypt. Here, as in those ancient countries, the date palm, long-fibre cotton, and alfalfa flourish. The desert is traversed from end to end by the Southern Pacific railway, and by the Los Angeles-Yuma and other highways. See *Mojave Desert, Palm Canyon, Salton Sea.*

Colorado Springs. A city of central Colorado, situated near the eastern base of Pikes Peak at an elevation of 6000 feet above the sea. The city is a noted health and pleasure resort and has a beautiful system of parks, covering some 3000 acres. Among places of historic and scenic interest in the vicinity are Pikes Peak, Ute Pass highway, the Garden of the Gods, Cave of the Winds, Manitou Springs, Phantom Cliff Canyon, and Will Rogers shrine, half way up Cheyenne Mountain. The city is the seat of Colorado College, the Colorado Springs Art Center, and the United States Air Force Academy. Population, 1970, 135,060.

Columbia. A city of Missouri, located about 125 miles northwest of St. Louis. Columbia is primarily an educational center, the seat of the University of Missouri and Stephens College for women. The city is in an agricultural area and has light manufacturing. Columbia was incorporated in 1826. Population, 1970, 58,804.

Columbia. The capital of South Carolina, situated near the center of the state on the high eastern bank of the Congaree River. The State capitol, built of granite at a cost of $6 million, is modeled after the national Capitol. Radiating from the capitol are four wide, well shaded avenues. The most important industry is the manufacture of cotton. Electricity is provided by large hydroelectric developments in the vicinity, including the huge Saluda dam. The city is the seat of the University of South Carolina and five colleges. The site of Columbia was settled about 1700; it was chosen for the capital, and the town was laid out in 1786. The legislature first met there in 1790. Population, 1970, 113,542.

Columbia River Highway. An important scenic highway constructed along the south side of the Columbia River in Oregon. It extends west from Portland through Astoria to Seaside on the Pacific Ocean, and east from Portland to Hood River, northeast of Mount Hood, a total distance of about 150 miles. This skirts the Columbia River by running around mountains, over hills, through tunnels, across viaducts, and along embankments.

At some points the highway reaches a height of 700 feet above the river, affording magnificent views. The highway passes near many beautiful cataracts, running immediately beside the celebrated Multnomah Falls, 607 feet high, and so close to Horse Tail Falls that the spray keeps the roadway moist.

Columbus. A city of southern Georgia, about 95 miles southwest of Atlanta, situated at the head of navigation of the Chattahoochee. The falls of this river provide power for the city's industries, and a channel connects the river with the Gulf of Mexico. Columbus played an important role in manufacturing army supplies for the Confederate Army during the Civil War, and is still an important industrial city, producing chiefly cotton textiles among its many manufactures. Fort Benning, the largest infantry post in the United States is located nearby. Population, 1970, 154,168.

Columbus. The capital of Ohio, located in the central part of the state, about 135 miles southwest of Cleveland and 120 miles northeast of Cincinnati. Surrounded by a productive agricultural region and by rich coal, iron, and natural gas fields, the city has developed into an important industrial and commercial center. The leading manufactures include agricultural, electrical, mill, and mining machinery, steel and steel products, boots and shoes, drugs, caskets, meat and other food products. The city is served by four trunk line railroads.

Columbus is laid out in a form somewhat resembling a Maltese cross. Parks and public grounds cover more than 9300 acres. Columbus is the seat of Ohio State University, which has an exceptionally beautiful campus and a stadium capable of seating nearly 100,000 persons. Other educational institutions are the Capital University, Ohio Dominican College, the Josephinum College, and the Columbus College of Art and Design. On spacious grounds in the center of the city is the massive Doric capitol. Bordering the beautiful civic center is the Le Veque Lincoln Tower, an imposing office building 555 feet in height. Civic center buildings also include the City Hall and state and federal government buildings. An important junction point of the nation's airways, Columbus is the site of Port Columbus and the Lockbourne Base Hospital for the U.S. Air Force.

Comparable to the growth of its educational institutions is the development of related activities which have made Columbus a center of scientific research. The internationally known journal *Chemical Abstracts* is published at the Ohio State University. The Battelle Memorial Institute, a foundation with affiliated laboratories in Frankfurt and Geneva, conducts basic research in chemistry, metallurgy, physics, fuels and combustion, and ceramic technology.

The first permanent settlement on the present site of the city was made in 1797. Columbus was laid out and was made the capital of the state in 1812. In 1816, the legislature first met in Columbus. Population, 1970, 539,677.

Concord. A town of Massachusetts, rich in historical and literary interest, situated some 20 miles northwest of Boston. Concord was founded in 1635. It was the British objective in the fighting at Lexington and Concord, which was the first armed conflict of the Revolution. The battle of Concord began at the Old North bridge. Here, April 19, 1775, the "embattled farmers fired the shot heard round the world." The town contains various memorials of the struggle, the most notable of which is the statue of "The Minute Man." Concord is celebrated also as the home of a number of distinguished figures in American literature, including Emerson, Hawthorne, Thoreau, and Louisa M. Alcott. Antiquarian House contains many mementos of the city's rich history. Population, 1970, 16,148.

Concord. The capital of New Hampshire, located in the Merrimack River Valley on a rolling and varied terrain. Industries include printing, electronics, research and development, and the manufacture of paper carton machinery. The famous Concord stagecoaches were made here during the days of Westward expansion in the United States. The impressive State Capitol is built of fine white native granite. Settled in 1725, the village, first called Pennacook and then Rumford, later changed its name to Concord. It became a city in 1853. It was the home of Mary Baker Eddy, founder of Christian Science. Population, 1970, 30,022.

Coney Island. A narrow island five miles in length, situated at the southwestern point of Long Island, near the entrance to New York harbor. The island is the most popular seashore resort in the United States. Coney Island is divided into four well-defined districts: West Brighton, which is provided with numerous popular means of amusement; Brighton Beach, containing a race track; Manhattan Beach, which is partly residential; and Sea Gate, the home station of the Atlantic Yacht Club.

Continental Divide. The crest or height of land in the United States which separates the waters draining into the Atlantic Ocean from those draining into the Pacific. This extends from the Mexican boundary northward across western New Mexico and then somewhat eastward to Rocky Mountain National Park in north central Colorado, its easternmost point. Thence the "great divide" trends northwest through northern Colorado and western Wyoming to Yellowstone National Park. Continuing westward and northward across Montana, it passes through Glacier National Park to the Canadian boundary. In some parts of its course, the Continental Divide is at the crest of the loftiest ranges; in others, it is on gently rolling uplands at the summit of high plateaus, usually 7000 feet or more above sea level.

Corn Belt. The fertile region in the east central United States which is largely devoted to the growing of corn. The most productive area embraces western Ohio, Indiana, Illinois, Iowa, Missouri, eastern Nebraska, eastern Kansas, and southeastern South Dakota. Adjoining parts of Kentucky, northern Oklahoma, and southern Minnesota, which produce large yields of corn, are usually considered as belonging to the Corn Belt. More than half of the corn crop of the United States is grown in this central zone.

Corpus Christi. A city and seaport of southern Texas, situated at the mouth of the Neuces River on Corpus Christi Bay. A deep-water channel to the Gulf of Mexico gives access for ocean ships to the city's well-equipped port facilities, opened in 1926. Corpus Christi Harbor Bridge spans the channel and is the highest bridge in Texas. Corpus Christi's industries and its exports, which include cotton, aluminum, petroleum, and seafoods, are based largely on the resources of the surrounding territory. Corpus Christi was chartered as a city in 1876. After the opening of the port, it grew rapidly, almost doubling its inhabitants in the decade of 1930–40. The University of Corpus Christi is located here. Population, 1970, 204,525.

Cotton Belt. The extensive region in the southern United States in which the immense cotton crop is produced. The zone of grestest productivity embraces eastern North Carolina, most of South Carolina, Georgia, Alabama, and Mississippi, parts of Arkansas, western Tennessee, northern Louisiana, and southern Oklahoma, and much of the northeastern half of Texas. Texas, Mississippi, and Arkansas are the leading states. The Cotton Belt produces about three-fifths of the world's supply of cotton.

Council Bluffs. A railroad, manufacturing, and commercial city of southwestern Iowa, located on the Missouri River opposite Omaha, Nebraska. For the most part, the city, which is well laid out, lies upon a plain largely surrounded by lofty bluffs. There are several parks, of which the chief one is Fairmount. Railroads, and vehicle bridges over the Missouri River, and also electric lines, connect the city with Omaha. Served by 8 major railroads, the city is a leading grain marketing center and has varied industrial interests, including the manufacture of truck bodies, farm implements, freight car wheels, bee supplies and cereals. The name Council Bluffs is said to have been given because of the council held at this point in 1804 between the Indians and the explorers Lewis and Clark. Population, 1970, 60,348.

Covington. A city of Kentucky, situated on the Ohio River, opposite Cincinnati. Covington occupies a beautiful site, partly surrounded by lofty hills, and contains many fine streets and homes. It has excellent transportation facilities by rail and by river, and is connected with Cincinnati by three bridges. While largely residential, Covington has substantial industries, including meat packing and the manufacture of machine tools, canvas goods, hardware, and structural iron. Devon Park, 550 acres, on the outskirts, has a large natural amphitheater. St. Mary's Cathedral, patterned after Notre Dame in Paris, has one of the largest stained-glass windows in the world. Covington, the seat of Thomas More College, was settled in 1812, and became a city in 1834. Population, 1970, 52,535.

Crater Mound (now **Meteor Crater**). A remarkable geological formation in central Arizona, about 40 miles southeast of Flagstaff. First known as Coon Butte and later as Meteorite Mountain, Crater Mound ranks as one of the most remarkable geological features of the West.

Viewed from the Santa Fe railway, which passes some miles to the north, it appears as a low ridge. Upon close approach, this ridge is found to be circular in form and to enclose an immense crater-like hole or depression 4000 feet in diameter and 600 feet deep. The encircling ridge, 100 to 150 feet in height, is composed of fragments of rock and sand blown up from the hole. The beds of rocks in the walls of the hole are limestone above and sandstone below, both more or less upturned near the hole and in part considerably shattered.

The cause of this great hole was long a mystery. The occurrence of many small masses of meteoric iron in the vicinity suggested that it was made by the impact of a meteorite. All efforts to locate the main body of such a meteorite failed until 1932, when with the aid of electrical instruments, geophysicists located the metallic mass at a depth of 680 feet.

Crawford Notch. A picturesque gorge between Mount Webster and Mount Willey, in the White Mountains of New Hampshire. In a narrow passage, at an elevation of about 1900 feet, the Saco River traverses the Notch, which is notable for its fine rock scenery.

Cumberland. A city of western Maryland, situated on the Potomac River, about 155 miles northwest of Baltimore. Cumberland is located in a mountainous region near important coal fields. It ships immense quantities of semi-bituminous coal, highly valued for steaming purposes, and has other extensive industries. The principal manufacturing establishments are railway repair shops, rubber tire, cellulose and glass factories, and silk, flour, and lumber mills. Population, 1970, 29,724.

Cumberland Road, or the National Road or Great National Pike. Originally envisioned by George Washington, the project to connect the East and the central West was initiated by Thomas Jefferson in 1806. Beginning as a federal government project, it was completed as such only from Cumberland, Md., to Wheeling, W. Va. It was then connected with older pikes in the East and with newer ones in the West, with individual states assuming responsibility for maintenance of the road. The Cumberland Road is still a means of travel from Chesapeake Bay, its easternmost point, to St. Louis, Mo., its western limit.

Currecanti Needle. One of the striking scenic features of the Black Canyon of the Gunnison River, in southwestern Colorado. It is a massive pinnacle of highly colored rock, hundreds of feet in height, and tapering at the top to a somewhat pointed spire, whence the name "needle."

Dallas. The second largest city of Texas, located on Trinity River, in the northeastern part of the state, about 185 miles northeast of Austin. Dallas is located in an exceedingly fertile agricultural region, the chief cotton growing district of the state. The city is in the center of the world's largest oil field. It is the largest inland cotton market in the United States, and the leading wholesale and jobbing center southwest of Saint Louis. Dallas is the chief distributing point in the Southwest for farm implements and automobiles. In manufactures, Dallas ranks first among the cities of the state. The principal industries include oil refining, meat packing, printing and publishing, the manufacture of oil well and cotton ginning machinery, airplanes, automobiles, cottonseed oil, saddlery, harnesses, and cotton goods. Its fine commercial structures include the 42-story Southland Tower and the 36-story Republic National Bank Building.

The city's parks embrace an area of more than 15,500 acres, and there are extensive boulevards and drives. The state fair, held annually in the city, attracts more than three million visitors. The city is the seat of the Southern Methodist University, University of Dallas, Baylor Dental School, Dallas Art Institute, and museums of fine arts and natural history. Dallas was settled in 1841 and chartered as a city in 1856. Population, 1970, 844,401.

Danbury. A city of Connecticut, about 13 miles northwest of Bridgeport. Danbury is noted for manufacturing hats, especially felt ones. It was the site of several significant incidents during the Revolutionary War. Danbury was chartered as a city in 1889. Population, 1970, 50,781.

Davenport. A commercial and manufacturing city of eastern Iowa, situated on the slope of a steep bluff of the Mississippi River, opposite Rock Island, Illinois. The chief manufactures include aluminum products, meat products, and farm implements. An extensive business is carried on in flour and grain by river as well as by rail transportation. The city has a municipal art gallery, a public museum, and an excellent park system. Educational institutions include St. Ambrose College, Marycrest College, and Palmer College of Chiropractic. Founded in 1835, Davenport was incorporated as a town in 1838 and received its charter as a city in 1851. Population, 1970, 98,469.

Dayton. A manufacturing city of southwestern Ohio, situated on both banks of the Miami River, about 50 miles northeast of Cincinnati. Among the leading manufactured products are cash registers, envelopes, electric motors, electrical refrigeration machinery, and automobile accessories. A great contribution to the city's prestige has been made by the airplane industry, founded by the Wright brothers, to whose memory a beautiful monument has been erected in the city. Other structures of note include the Art Institute and Museum and the Deeds' Carillon Tower with 32 bells. Wright field accommodates the experimental laboratories of the U. S. Air Corps. Patterson Field and the Fairfield Air Depot are also located here.

First settled in 1796, Dayton became a city in 1841. In 1913 a disastrous flood caused great destruction of property and loss of life. The devasted sections were rebuilt, and a system of five reservoirs, costing $32,000,000, was constructed to prevent a repetition of the disaster. Population, 1970, 243,601.

Daytona Beach. A year-round resort city of Florida, situated on the Halifax River, 53 miles south of St. Augustine. Well-known automobile speed trials are held on the city's 23-mile, hard-packed, white sand beach. Tourism is the chief industry. Population, 1970, 45,327.

Dearborn. A city of southeastern Michigan, ten miles west of Detroit, of which it is a residential suburb. Henry Ford had his home there, his birthplace being on a farm in the vicinity. This farm he restored to its early appearance and he built there a village museum, "Greenfield village," consisting of old buildings collected from all parts of the United States and from England. An outstanding example of modern architecture is the Ford Rotunda exhibit hall. Population, 1970, 104,199.

Death Valley. An extremely arid desert in eastern California, near the Nevada boundary, containing the lowest point of dry land in the Western Hemisphere. The name was given by a survivor of a party of 30 "forty-niners," most of whom perished of thirst in its sands. It lies in a north-and-south direction, is about 150 miles long, and varies in width from 4 miles to 16 miles. On the west it is bordered by the high Panamint Range; on the east it is flanked by the Funeral, the Black, and the Grapevine mountains. The lowest point in Death Valley is 282 feet below sea level. In a direct line, this lowest point is about 86 miles east of Mt. Whitney, 14,496 feet high, the loftiest peak in the United States outside Alaska.

The valley is in the sink of the Amargosa River, a stream that is dry for the greater part of the year throughout much of its course. The eastern side of the valley was formerly the bed of a salt lake. In the entire area, drinkable water can be obtained in only a few places. The salty bottom of the valley is destitute of vegetation, but the bordering slopes have a sparse growth of desert shrubs. The annual rainfall averages 1.66 inches; the average humidity is very low—no dew ever forming, and the summer temperatures, reaching 134°, being the hottest authentically recorded in America. See *Colorado Desert, Mojave Desert.*

Decatur (*dē-kā'tŭr*). Located on the Sangamon River, almost in the center of Illinois, Decatur lies in the corn and soy bean belt. The city's chief industrial establishments include railway shops, metal and wood-working plants, soy bean processing plants, and factories for the making of tractors, graders, air conditioners, window glass, and gas and water systems. Decatur is the seat of Millikin University. Recreation is afforded by a 160-acre park system and by a lake 12 miles long formed by a dam across the Sangamon River. The city was named for Stephen Decatur, naval hero. Population, 1970, 90,397.

Delaware Water Gap. A picturesque gap and narrow gorge in the Kittatinny Range, near Stroudsburg, Pa., on the borders of Pennsylvania and New Jersey. The steep sides of the mountain here rise to an elevation of 1400 feet above the Delaware River, which flows through the gap.

Denver. The capital of Colorado. It is situated at the junction of Cherry Creek and South Platte River. The site, which has an altitude of one mile above the level of the sea, slopes back from both banks of the river and commands a magnificent view of the Rocky Mountains. Denver is the largest city between the Missouri River and the Pacific coast. It is also one of the most important railway centers of the West, to which fact, in great measure, it owes its growth and prosperity.

The city is handsomely planned and contains many fine public buildings and substantial private residences. Among the former may be noted the State Capitol, the Auditorium, the United States Mint, and the Civic Center, whose 5 million-dollar City and County building is said to have the largest bronze doors in the world. The Fitzsimons General Hospital for army tubercular patients is one of the largest buildings in Colorado. Some of the principal educational institutions are the University of Denver, Regis College, Westminister College, and Colorado Woman's College. The City Park, which covers 408 acres, has a zoological garden, a lake, a museum, aviary, and speedway. The park system, including about 40 parks in all, is one of the finest in the United States and is supplemented by a system of 38 municipal mountain parks in the vicinity.

Denver is the principal center of mercantile supply for the agricultural, stock raising, and mining districts of Colorado and New Mexico. The chief industries include meat packing, flour milling, railway car construction, printing and publishing, and the manufacture of iron and steel products, structural iron, clothing, paints, automobile accessories, and chemicals. Population, 1970, 514,678.

Des Moines (*dĕ moin'*). The capital of Iowa, built on both banks of the Des Moines River, in the central part of the state. Des Moines is the commercial center of an exceedingly fertile farming region, with which it carries on an extensive marketing and wholesale trade. Surrounded by rich farm lands, the city has developed numerous and varied industries, prominent among which is the production of machinery, food products, and clothing. Many important farm journals and other publications are printed in Des Moines, which is also the center of large insurance interests.

Chief among many imposing public buildings is the Capitol, built on a slight eminence, and approached by Capitol Extension park. Adjoining this park is the fine State Historical Building. The city's park system includes 58 parks and covers 1500 acres. To this total may be added the 600 acres comprising the State fairgrounds. Des Moines is the seat of Drake University and of the Des Moines College of Osteopathy and Surgery.

By reason of its central location, together with ample hotel and auditorium facilities, Des Moines is a favorite meeting place for conventions. The city's unique civic center consists of a landscaped area taking in the opposite banks of the river. In the group of buildings are the Post Office and Library, the City Hall, the Federal Court Building, the Y.M.C.A., and the municipal armory.

Around Fort Des Moines, which was established in 1843, settlers, in 1846, built a village. This village was incorporated in 1851 as the town of Fort Des Moines. In 1856, the town was made the capital of the state. In the following year, it was chartered as the city of Des Moines. Population, 1970, 200,587.

DETROIT. The chief city of Michigan and the fifth most populous in the United States, situated on the Detroit River, 18 miles from Lake Erie. It lies some 90 miles southeast of Lansing, the capital of the state, and is about 250 miles west of Buffalo and 285 miles east of Chicago. The city occupies a nearly level but gently rising site, extending some 12 miles along the river front, and containing an area of about 138 square miles.

Streets and Buildings. The city is regularly laid out, with wide streets, most of which cross at right angles on the checkerboard plan. There are, however, several broad avenues, 100 to 200 feet wide, which radiate from the Campus Martius and the Grand Circus in the heart of the city.

The commercial district is located mainly around and near the Grand Circus and the Campus Martius. The former is a small, semicircular park, and the latter is a large plaza. These are situated near each other and give an air of openness and spaciousness to the business center of the city. Griswold Street, lined with great office buildings and banking houses is the "Wall Street" of Detroit.

The chief public buildings are located on or near the Campus Martius. Within it is the Michigan Soldiers' and Sailors' monument, facing the City Hall. Nearby is the skyscraper City-County Building. Numerous great office buildings, of the finest modern type, are built around portions of the Grand Circus. Among many notable buildings may be mentioned the General Motors Building, the Veterans Memorial Building, the Ford Auditorium, the Fisher Building, the Federal Building, the Board of Commerce, the Michigan Central Station, the Masonic Temple, the Ford, Penobscot, Stroh, First National Bank, and Majestic buildings, the Public Library, Bank of the Commonwealth, and the Detroit Institute of Art.

Parks and Boulevards. The municipal system contains upwards of 242 parks, embracing an area of about 3600 acres. The most notable of these is the island park, Belle Isle, with an area of 1000 acres, where is situated one of the country's best zoological gardens. This lies opposite the eastern part of the city, with which it is connected by a bridge. River Rouge Park is the largest, 1204 acres in area. In addition to the numerous small parks, many triangles at diagonal street intersections have been improved and ornamented, and there are numerous boulevards.

Educational Institutions. Detroit is the seat of Detroit University, Wayne State University, the Detroit College of Law, the Michigan College of Medicine, the Michigan State Auto School, and various other educational institutions.

Transportation. The city owes its greatness, in a large part, to unique advantages in transportation both by lake and by rail. It is situated midway on the inland waterway system of the Great Lakes. The deep Detroit River, sometimes called the "Dardanelles of America," affords a spacious harbor, accommodating the largest lake vessels. There is a numerous passenger fleet, and the city is a port of call for all steamers from Buffalo to the upper lakes. The tonnage passing through the Detroit River is more than double that passing through the Suez Canal, and is immensely greater than the tonnage arriving at and leaving any other inland seaport in the world.

Local transportation is effected by a comprehensive system of municipally owned street railways and bus lines. The city is connected with Windsor, Canada, by a tunnel and the great Ambassador suspension bridge.

Commerce. Enormous quantities of iron ore, copper products, grain, and coal are handled by the lake traffic. There is a large export trade to Canada and Europe, chiefly foodstuffs, automobiles, and steel products. The city is the commercial center of a great interior district with which it carries on an immense distributing trade. In addition, it ships the products of its vast industries to all parts of the country.

Manufactures. Detroit is the greatest automobile manufacturing center in the world. Its phenomenal growth in the early 20th century corresponded with the vast development of the automobile industry. In value of manufactures, Detroit stands fourth among the cities of the United States. The greater part of this production is automobiles and automobile accessories and parts. There are numerous other substantial industries. Detroit is a leading center for the manufacture of aircraft, brass and bronze products, adding machines, stoves and furnaces, malleable iron, and aluminum castings. Other important manufactures include railway cars, machine tools, electrical apparatus, drugs, chemicals, engines, paint, tobacco, and rubber goods.

History. The first settlement at Detroit was made in 1701 by Cadillac, the French governor of Michillimackinac, who built Fort Pontchartrain. During the French and Indian War, this was captured, 1760, by the British. The first act of Pontiac's conspiracy, 1763, was an unsuccessful attempt to seize this important fort. Detroit was incorporated in 1802 and became the capital of Michigan territory in 1805. In 1812, William Hull surrendered the town to the British, who evacuated it the following year.

Detroit was chartered as a city in 1824, continued as the capital of the territory until 1835, and was the capital of the state, 1835–47. Its growth until 1910 was continuous and substantial. In the decade 1910-20, the city more than doubled in population and more than quadrupled in value of manufactures. Population, 1970, 1,511,482.

Diablo (*dê-ä'blō; dĭ-ăb'lō*), **Mount.** A mountain of west central California, situated on the edge of the great interior valley, about 30 miles air-line distance nearly due east of San Francisco. Its general domelike outline and isolated position have given the erroneous impression that Mount Diablo is an old volcano. It is, in fact, the higher portion of a great overturned arch of sedimentary rocks.

Because of its visibility for long distances in many directions, Mount Diablo has been a noted landmark since the days of the "forty-niners." Through it run the meridian and the base line from which the land surveys of a large part of California are reckoned. While of moderate height, the elevation being 3849 feet, its unique situation makes it one of the finest scenic viewpoints in the state.

Dismal Swamp, Great. A tract of marshy land in southeastern Virginia and northeastern North Carolina. It begins a short distance south of Norfolk, Virginia, extends southward for about 30 miles, and embraces a total area of some 750 square miles. Near its center is Lake Drummond, about 2 miles in diameter and very shallow. The remainder of the swamp is covered, for the most part, with heavy timber and a thick tangled undergrowth. The swamp originally contained an area of about 2200 square miles, but much of it has been reclaimed and placed under cultivation.

Dobbs Ferry. A village of New York State, on the Hudson River 20 miles north of New York City. Here are located two schools for girls—the Masters School and the Sacred Heart Academy. In the Livingston Manor here Washington and Rochambeau planned the Yorktown campaign. Opposite this village the American flag was saluted for the first time by a British sloop of war. Population, 1970, 10,353.

Dover. The capital of Delaware, located slightly north of the center of the state. Dover is surrounded by a rich fruit growing country, the chief crops being apples, grapes, melons, and peaches. The principal industry is the canning of plum pudding, poultry, and other foods. There is an impressive State Capitol and a handsome monument erected to the memory of Cæsar Rodney, one of the signers of the Declaration of Independence. The Archives Building houses Delaware's earliest records. Silver Lake Park and Dover Green are other features of interest. Dover was laid out in 1717 and became the capital of Delaware in 1777. It became a town in 1829; a city in 1925. It is the seat of Delaware State College. Population, 1970, 17,488.

Dubuque (*dōō-būk'*). A city of northeastern Iowa, built on the west bank of the Mississippi River, about 200 miles northeast of Des Moines. Dubuque lies in a fertile farming district and the surrounding region is rich in lead and zinc deposits. Dubuque has substantial manufacturing industries, and is the center of a large marketing and distributing trade by river and by rail. The city is situated partly on a terrace 20 feet above the river and partly on a hill, which rises to a height of 200 feet.

Among the notable features are Eagle Point park which has a very large ledge garden. There is also a monument to Julien Dubuque, who settled on the site of the city in 1788. The first permanent settlement dates from 1833. The village was incorporated as a town in 1837, and, in 1840, was chartered as a city. The educational institutions include Loras and Clarke colleges and the University of Dubuque. Population, 1970, 62,309.

Duluth. An important lake port and the third largest city of Minnesota. It is built on steep and picturesque slopes overlooking a fine natural harbor at the western end of Lake Superior. Enjoying the advantages of exceptional railroad and port facilities, Duluth handles an annual tonnage of grain and iron ore of stupendous proportions. Impetus to its further expansion has come from the newly-developed Taconite industry and the completion of the St. Lawrence Seaway. Hydroelectric power, available in abundance, contributes to a large industrial activity, which includes the manufacture of steel, wood products, clothing, cement, and food products.

The city's natural beauty is enhanced by 106 miles of scenic drives, by 3216 acres of parks, 74 in all, including Minnesota Point, which extends 7 miles into the lake, and by facilities for summer and winter sports. The chief public buildings cluster about the attractively designed civic center. Population, 1970, 100,578.

Durham. A city of central North Carolina, 25 miles northwest of Raleigh. It is one of the leading tobacco centers of the country, both for marketing and manufacturing. Cotton and hosiery mills constitute a second industry of large proportions. Durham is the seat of Duke University, developed from Trinity College and richly endowed by James B. Duke, a large tobacco manufacturer and developer of hydroelectric power. The city contains also North Carolina College at Durham and is the headquarters of the country's leading life insurance company for Negroes. General Johnston surrendered to Sherman at Durham in 1865. Population, 1970, 95,438.

East Chicago. A city of northwestern Indiana on Lake Michigan. It adjoins Hammond, Gary, and Whiting and is 20 miles southeast of the center of Chicago, of which it is an industrial suburb. The part of the city along the lake is known as Indiana Harbor, and handles a large traffic of incoming coal, iron ore, and limestone with shipments of gasoline and steel products. The chief industries are steel manufacture and oil refining. Population, 1970, 46,982.

East Orange. A city of northeastern New Jersey, adjoining Newark, and about 11 miles west of New York City. East Orange is mainly residential, being populated largely by persons doing business in New York and Newark. The city has wide, well shaded streets, and contains many attractive homes and public buildings. There are substantial industries and the chief manufactures include electrical machinery, valves, tools, sewer pipe, and knit goods. East Orange was separated from Orange in 1863 and became a city in 1899. It is the seat of Upsala College. Population, 1970, 75,471.

East St. Louis (*lo͞o'ĭs; lo͞o'ĭ*). A city of southwestern Illinois, built on the east bank of the Mississippi River, opposite Saint Louis. The city is an important railway and manufacturing center. It is also a leading market and distributing point for live stock, especially horses, mules, and hogs. The leading industries include meat packing, flour milling, and the manufacture of iron and steel products, aluminum, baking powder, glass, paints, chemicals, and refined petroleum. Population, 1970, 69,996.

Edison. A rapidly growing residential and industrial suburb in Middlesex County, New Jersey, 27 miles southwest of New York City. Here are located the Menlo Park Museum and the Edison Tower, erected on the site of Thomas A. Edison's laboratories, where the incandescent lamp, the phonograph, and other inventions were developed. Industries include an automobile assembly plant and factories for the fabrication of electronic equipment and plastic and ceramic products. Population, 68,000 (est.).

Elizabeth. A manufacturing and suburban residential city of New Jersey, lying 12 miles southwest of New York City. It is connected with Staten Island by Goethals Bridge, opened in 1928. Among important industries are oil refining and the manufacture of sewing machines, chemicals, and electrical machinery. Elizabeth was settled in 1664 and still preserves many examples of colonial architecture. From 1755 to 1757 the city was the capital of New Jersey. Population, 1970, 112,654.

Elmira (N.Y.). From the village originally called Newtown, which was established in 1790, Elmira grew into a flourishing center of commerce, with water shipping connections by way of the Chemung and Susquehanna rivers and the Chemung Canal. The Erie Railroad was built here in 1849. Elmira's most famous citizen, by marriage and adoption, was Mark Twain, whose wife, Olivia Langdon, lived here. During many summers which they spent at Quarry Farm, the home of Mrs. Theodore Crane, Olivia's sister, Mark used a study that was built for him in the shape of a pilot house on a Mississippi River steamboat. The study is now on the campus of Elmira College. In Woodlawn Cemetery is a monument to Mark Twain, erected at his burial site.

Elmira has extensive manufacturing industries. The more important products include steel bridges, prefabricated houses, television tubes, milk containers, coaster brakes, and aviation equipment. A glider contest is held annually on Harris Hill nearby. Population, 1970, 39,945.

El Monte. A city in California, located 13 miles east of Los Angeles Civic Center, settled by pioneers who found water here at the end of the Sante Fé Trail. There are many hop fields and walnut groves in the area. Although El Monte is primarily residential, nearby South El Monte is heavily industrialized. Population, 1970, 69,837.

El Paso (*ĕl păs'ō*). An important railway center and manufacturing and commercial city of western Texas, about 1200 miles by rail from New Orleans and 800 miles from Los Angeles. El Paso is situated on the Rio Grande River opposite Ciudad Juarez, and is the largest city on the Mexican border.

The chief industries include smelting, flour milling, railway car repairing, box making, meat packing, cotton milling, and the manufacture of cement and garments. The city has extensive wholesale and jobbing establishments, and carries on a substantial trade in copper, silver, lead, wool, hides, and live stock. Trade with Mexico amounts to many millions of dollars annually.

Located at an elevation of about 3800 feet in a region of almost perennial sunshine, El Paso has become a noted health resort. Buildings show a pronounced Mexican influence. Much of the surrounding district is irrigated by the great Elephant Butte Dam, and produces large crops of grains, fruits, vegetables, and cotton, which are marketed chiefly through El Paso. El Paso is the seat of The University of Texas at El Paso.

The first settlement was made in 1829, the town was incorporated in 1869. Population, 1970, 322,261.

Enchanted Mesa (*mā'sā*). A remarkable castle-like rock or, more accurately speaking, a butte, situated near the Indian pueblo of Acoma in west central New Mexico. It is an immense mass of buff sandstone, with perpendicular sides, rising boldly from an arid plain. In shape it is elongated, the length measuring about 2000 feet and the width from 100 to 350 feet. At the base there is a sloping heap of rock debris, 100 to 200 feet high, above which towers the vertical wall to an elevation of 430 feet above the plain.

Evidence of former human occupation is slight, but Acoma Indians believe that their remote ancestors inhabited a pueblo built on the flat-topped summit.

Endless Caverns. A large cave two miles south of New Market, Virginia. Its name indicates that its farthest reaches are unknown.

The cave was discovered by two boys on October 1, 1879. Among the marvelous formations within the cave are "Skyland," recalling by its coloring the play of sun and cloud in the sky, "Alpine Pass," the "Arctic Circle," "Diamond Lake," and "Oriental Palace."

Erie. A manufacturing city of northwestern Pennsylvania, situated on a large natural harbor on Lake Erie. The harbor is protected by Presque Isle, a peninsula about 11 miles long and a mile wide, on which there is a 3100-acre forested state park. There is considerable lake commerce; the leading articles of shipment include pulpwood, sand and gravel, petroleum, and manufactured goods. Among the city's varied manufactures are foundry and machine shop products, engines, excavating machinery, and paper. Erie has 19 parks, one of which, Presque Isle State Park, near the harbor entrance, is the site of an old French fort, erected in 1753. The original site is now occupied by a blockhouse, built by the state in order to commemorate Anthony Wayne, who died at the old fort in 1796. In the War of 1812, Erie was Commodore Perry's headquarters. Population, 1970, 129,231.

Eugene (*ū-jēn'*). A city of western Oregon, located at the head of navigation on the Willamette River, 110 miles south of Portland. It is the commercial center of an extensive farming and stock raising region, and its industrial products include lumber products and canned fruit and vegetables. Eugene was first settled in 1864 and is the seat of the University of Oregon. It is at the head of the Willamette flood control basin. Population, 1970, 76,346.

Evanston. A city of northeastern Illinois, situated on Lake Michigan at the northern boundary of Chicago, of which it is a residential suburb. Evanston is the seat of Northwestern University, including a large technological institute. It is also the national headquarters of the Women's Christian Temperance Union. Manufactures include steel tubing, toys, chemicals, and paper. Population, 1970, 79,808.

Evansville. A manufacturing and commercial city of southwestern Indiana on the Ohio River, about 180 miles southwest of Indianapolis. The city is situated on a high bank of the river and has many fine parks, streets, and drives. It is surrounded by a rich agricultural district, and within the vicinity of the city are numerous coal mines. The chief industries include the manufacture of agricultural equipment, refrigerators, steam shovels, and grain products. Founded in 1816, Evansville became a city in 1847. Population, 1970, 138,746.

Everett. A city of eastern Massachusetts, located on the Mystic River, about 3 miles north of Boston. While mainly a residential suburb, containing many fine streets and homes, Everett is also the seat of important industries. Among these are the manufacture of coke and petroleum products. Everett was settled in 1643, but until 1873 was known as South Malden. In 1892, it was chartered as a city. Population, 1970, 42,485.

Everett. A city of northwestern Washington, with a good harbor on Puget Sound, about 28 miles north of Seattle. The surrounding region is heavily timbered, and there are extensive agricultural, mining, sporting and fishing interests. With these, the various enterprises of the city are chiefly connected. Among leading industrial products are the manufacture of lumber, pulpwood, paper, aircraft, stoves, and machinery. Population, 1970, 53,622.

Everglades. An immense marshy tract in southern Florida, covering an area about 140 miles by 50 miles. Drainage canals have been cut through various parts of the swamp, and some of the higher portions have been rendered suitable for agriculture. It is estimated that some 5000 square miles may eventually be reclaimed. Over 2000 square miles of it was made a national park in 1947.

Fairbanks. A city of Alaska lying in the Tanana River valley, on the banks of the Chena River. It is the terminus of the government railway from the coast, has a large airport, and was once the center of an extensive gold-mining district. It is also the seat of the University of Alaska. Population, 1970, 14,771.

Fall River. A manufacturing city and seaport of southeastern Massachusetts. It is built on the shore of Mount Hope Bay, at the mouth of Taunton River, about 50 miles south of Boston. Fall River is a leading center for dyeing and finishing textiles and for the manufacture of garments, curtains, lighting fixtures, and latex and aluminum products. The city is well laid out and substantially built. Many of the buildings are constructed of fine granite quarried in the vicinity. There are several parks with beautiful drives. The population in 1970 was 96,898.

Fargo. A city of North Dakota, situated on the Red River, somewhat south of the center of the state near the Minnesota boundary. Fargo is the commercial center of a large wheat growing and mixed farming region, and is a leading distributing point for farm implements. Industries include meat packing and manufacture of steel products. It is the seat of North Dakota State University and other educational institutions. There are a number of fine parks totaling 480 acres in area and several beautiful drives. Population, 1970, 53,365.

Finger Lakes. The name given to a group of beautiful lakes in west central New York. These lakes, which are long, narrow, and somewhat finger-like in shape, were formed by the blocking up of deep river valleys with glacial materials. They lie somewhat parallel to each other, extend in a general north and south direction, and give a distinctive character to a fine scenic region.

The largest are lakes Seneca and Cayuga, each of which is about 40 miles long and from 2 to 3 miles wide. Others of the group are lakes Canandaigua, Owasco, Skaneateles, and Otisco. Oneida lake, northeast of Syracuse, and Lake George, in eastern New York, are of similar formation.

Fitchburg. A manufacturing city of northeastern Massachusetts, built on a branch of the Nashua River, about 48 miles northwest of Boston. Fitchburg is attractively located and has many fine homes, public buildings, and parks. The city's extensive manufactures include cotton and woolen goods, turbines, plastics, furniture, paper, saws, bicycles, hardware, and shoes. The city is the seat of Fitchburg State College. Fitchburg was settled in 1719, was incorporated in 1764, and became a city in 1872. Population, 1970, 43,343.

Flagstaff. A city of north central Arizona, located at an altitude of 6907 feet, near the southern base of the San Francisco Mountains. It is the commercial center of a lumbering, mining, and stock-raising district, has large lumber mills, and carries on a trade in Indian curios and blankets. Lowell Observatory is situated on a high mesa near the city.

By reason of its fine climate and varied scenic attractions, Flagstaff is also a tourist resort. Ten miles north are the San Francisco Peaks, of which Humphrey's Peak is the highest, 12,670 feet. The mountains are remnants of an extinct volcano. The region contains ancient lavas and is interspersed with numerous cinder cones. One of the most conspicuous is Sunset Crater, a large cone tipped with bright red cinders, giving it the appearance of being illumined by the setting sun.

About 8 miles east of Flagstaff are the remarkable sink holes in the Kaibab limestone, known as the "Bottomless Pits." In the near vicinity also is the Walnut Canyon national monument containing prehistoric cliff dwellings. Population, 1970, 26,117.

Flint. A manufacturing city of southeastern Michigan, situated on the river of the same name, about 70 miles northwest of Detroit. Flint is, after Detroit, the world's largest center of automobile manufacture. Its industries center around various subsidiaries of the General Motors Corporation, including the Chevrolet, Buick, and Fisher Body divisions. The 42 public parks of the city have a total area of 1275 acres. Population, 1970, 193,317.

Fort Knox. A United States fort in eastern Kentucky directly south of Louisville and 600 miles west of New York City. It is noted as the repository of the greater part of the monetary gold stock of the United States, its location west of the Allegheny Mountains making it comparatively secure from a hypothetical invader from the East. The gold storage building is constructed with walls of solid granite two feet thick, behind which are fabricated coils of steel set in concrete. The building, having a floor area of 10,000 square feet, is two stories high, the second set back so as to leave a parapet at each corner of which machine guns are mounted. The gold vault is 90 feet long, 50 feet wide, and two stories high. All parts of the vault's exterior are visible to guards from all angles by means of mirrors. Microphones and automatic alarms communicate with the guard room, from which messages may be sent to a motorized unit of the army in the adjacent fort. The first shipment of gold was taken to Fort Knox in 1937. Population, 1970, 37,608.

Fort Lauderdale. A flourishing commercial, industrial, tourist, and residential center in the lower east coast area of the Florida peninsula. Its business district is between two and three miles of the Atlantic Ocean. The city's transportation needs are served by two railroads and by major bus and truck lines. Adjacent are the Ft. Lauderdale-Hollywood International Airport and the steamship terminal, Port of Everglades. Because of its favorable climate and excellent visitor accommodations and the transportation facilities, Ft. Lauderdale has become a favorite convention center. Population, 1970, 139,590.

Fort Wayne. A railroad center and manufacturing city of northeastern Indiana. It is built at the confluence of the St. Joseph and the St. Mary's rivers which here join to form the Maumee River. Car shops, car wheel works, foundries, hosiery mills, clothing, motor truck, copper and enamelled wire factories, electrical machinery works, and oil tank shops are among the chief industrial interests. Among the largest buildings is the office of the Lincoln National Life Insurance Company, occupying an entire block. The city encloses the site of a fort built in 1794 by Anthony Wayne, to whom a monument has been erected. Population, 1970, 177,671.

Fort Worth. An important commercial city and railway center of northeastern Texas, situated in the midst of a rich agricultural and oil producing territory. The city is one of the great cattle and grain markets of the United States and one of the world's greatest petroleum pipe-line centers. Seventeen railways enter the city. Industries include oil refining, meat packing and the manufacture of flour, textiles, cement, and cottonseed products.

Of unique distinction is the Casa Manana Theatre, a structure of geodesic design built of aluminum and supported by steel struts. Educational institutions include the Texas Christian University and the Texas Wesleyan College. The city has 101 parks, covering 10,116 acres. Population, 1970, 393,476.

Franconia Notch. A narrow picturesque passage in the Franconia range of the White Mountains in New Hampshire, through which the Pemigewasset River flows. Entering the notch from the east is a narrow passage excavated in the rock, called the "flume." Nearby is the "great stone face" celebrated by Hawthorne. The territory is embraced in a 6000-acre state park.

Frankfort. The capital of Kentucky, situated on the Kentucky River, in the rich "Blue-Grass" and limestone region, somewhat northwest of the center of the state. Its manufactures include lumber, shoes, brooms, twine, tobacco, and concrete pipe. Many thoroughbred trotting horses are raised in the vicinity. In a setting of rare beauty is the State Capitol, behind which is the large Capitol Annex Building.

Frankfort was founded in 1786, and, in 1792, when it had a population of less than 500, was made the capital of the state. The city contains the grave of Daniel Boone and is rich in historical associations. Population, 1970, 21,356.

Fresno (*frĕz'nō*). Commercial center of a noted fruit growing district, Fresno is located in the irrigated portion of the fertile San Joaquin Valley, about 200 miles southeast of San Francisco. In addition to peach growing, in which it excels, the country surrounding Fresno has a high yield of grapes and raisins. Other important crops are alfalfa, flax, cotton, sugar beets, grain, vegetables, and some tropical fruits.

The industrial and commercial activities of the city are centered chiefly upon handling and marketing the county's staple productions. Places of interest in the vicinity are King's River Canyon, Roeding Park, and Kearney Park, the last an irrigated experimental farm belonging to the University of California. Population, 1970, 165,972.

Gadsden. A city of northern Alabama, on the Coose River, 58 miles northeast of Birmingham, to which Gadsden is second in importance in Alabama in industry, manufacturing iron and steel products, rubber products, and many other items. The city has good transportation facilities and is in the midst of an agricultural and mining region. Population, 1970, 53,928.

Gainesville. A city of Florida, located about midway between the Atlantic Ocean and the Gulf of Mexico. It is noted for manufacture of tung oil, used in paints, and as a shipping center for many of the products (such as tobacco, citrus fruits, and pecans) grown in the area. Located in Gainesville are the Florida State Museum and the University of Florida. Population, 1970, 64,510.

Galveston. The world's largest cotton and sulphur port, situated in southeastern Texas. It is built on the east end of Galveston Island between Galveston Bay on the north and the Gulf of Mexico on the south.

The excellent natural harbor facilities have been further improved at vast expense, and the port has been fortified by modern coast defensive works. Manufactures include flour, ships, and steel wire. Since a disastrous flood, caused by a hurricane in 1900, the level of the city has been raised, a sea wall has been built along the shore facing the Gulf, and two 2-mile causeways have been constructed joining the city with the mainland. The Medical School of the University of Texas is situated in the city. In 1901, Galveston adopted the commission form of government, which has since been widely adopted by other American cities. Population, 1970, 61,809.

Garden of the Gods. A small region of about 500 acres, near Colorado Springs, Colorado, noted for its curiously shaped rock formations and for its magnificent views of Pikes Peak. By the action of wind and water, the red and the white sandstone strata have here been worn into many grotesque shapes. To these, various fanciful names have been given, such as "Cathedral Spires," "Balanced Rock," "Siamese Twins," and the "Seal and the Bear." The gateway to these interesting examples of erosion consists of two massive pinnacles of red rock, 300 feet high, which, at their bases, leave barely room for a vehicle to pass between them.

Gary. A steel manufacturing city of northwestern Indiana, at the southern end of Lake Michigan, about 30 miles southeast of Chicago. The city was founded in 1906 and is virtually the creation of the United States Steel Corporation. It contains immense steel works, tin and rail mills, and a cement plant, each of which is among the largest of its kind. The city is well planned with broad boulevards, giving an air of spaciousness. Its 18 parks cover 700 acres, Marquette Park being particularly attractive. A civic gateway, flanked by twin-designed Courthouse and City Hall, leads to the great steel mills over an area traversed by trunk-line railroads. Nearby is the Indiana Dunes State Park. The so-called Gary plan of elementary education originated in the public schools of the city. Population, 1970, 175,415.

Gettysburg. A town of southern Pennsylvania, located about 35 miles southwest of Harrisburg. Gettysburg occupies a picturesque site in a hilly but fertile farming country. President Eisenhower, bought a farm here shortly after his election.

In the vicinity was fought, July 1-3, 1863, one of the most decisive battles of the Civil War. Here the Union army under General Meade defeated the Confederate forces under General Lee. The entire battlefield, comprising 3409 acres, has been converted into a national military park, in which are marked the sites where particular actions took place; a cyclorama painting within a circular building depicts the battle. On Cemetery Hill is the National Cemetery, dedicated by Lincoln in his famous Gettysburg Address. An eternal light peace memorial was dedicated on the battlefield by President Roosevelt in 1938. Population, 1970, 7275.

Glendale. A city of southern California, adjoining Los Angeles on the north. Its elevation varies from 400 feet to 2400 feet. It is a popular residential suburb, but has rapidly expanding industrial interests which include pottery, electronic equipment, and drugs. A feature of particular interest in Forest Lawn Memorial Park, the court of which has a stained glass window design copied from Da Vinci's "Last Supper." Glendale was incorporated in 1906. Population, 1970, 132,752.

Gloucester (*glŏs'tẽr*). A seaport of northeastern Massachusetts, built on the south side of the Cape Ann peninsula, about 30 miles northeast of Boston. The city is an important fishing port, with a large fleet engaged in taking cod, haddock, halibut, redfish, and mackerel. There are various other industries, largely connected with the fisheries. By reason of its picturesque location, quaint, old-fashioned streets, and interesting historic associations, the city is a favorite travel and summer resort, especially for artists. A well-known piece of sculpture there is the famous Fisherman's Memorial. Gloucester was founded in 1623, incorporated in 1642, and became a city in 1874. Population, 1970, 27,941.

Gloversville. A city of east central New York, noted as the chief glove manufacturing center in the United States. Its factories, together with those of the neighboring town of Johnstown, produce a substantial percentage of the gloves made in the country. The leather glove industry is said to have been first introduced into the United States by Sir William Johnson, who, in 1760, settled several families of Scotch glove makers on his lands near the site of Gloversville. Other manufactured products include silk and knitted goods, phonograph records, leather, and lumber. Population, 1970 19,677.

Grand Canyon of the Colorado. The most magnificent scenic spectacle of its kind in the world. This immense gorge, the greatest example of stream erosion known, has been cut by the Colorado River in the high plateau of northern Arizona. The deeper portion is 217 miles long; its vast chasms range from 4000 to 6000 feet in depth from the uppermost rim to the river; and its width from rim to rim varies from 4 to 18 miles.

The canyon consists of two distinct parts: the broad, outer, upper portion, which has been eroded through stratified rocks; and the narrow, inner, lower portion, which has been worn down through unstratified rocks. The outer or upper walls are carved in alternating layers of limestones, sandstones, and shales. These descend in successive benches or escarpments, displaying a multitude of beautifully castellated, temple-like forms, banded in splendid colors, and finally reach the top of the gloomy inner gorge. This is irregularly cut in tough dark granite, and, at its bottom, extending usually from wall to wall flows the foaming, torrential river.

The descent throughout the entire length of the canyon is so great that the river is broken into many rapids and semirapids. These, rushing between almost vertical walls of rock, make navigation, even for the staunchest boats, exceedingly dangerous. The current rolls great boulders along the bottom of the narrow channel, and, at some points, the noise of their grinding in the rocky river bed can be heard above the roaring of the waters.

The most impressive portion of the canyon is included in Grand Canyon National Park. Its area, 1052 square miles, embraces 105 miles of the Grand Canyon, stretching from east to west from its beginning at the mouth of the Little Colorado River. From rim to rim this part of the canyon is from 8 to 15 miles wide; it is more than a mile deep measured from the north rim, which averages nearly 1000 feet higher than the south rim. The eastern boundary includes the lofty, richly colored walls east of which lies the Painted Desert. The western boundary of the park includes the broad Cataract canyon, entering from the south. In this tributary canyon is the Havasupai Indian reservation and a group of five waterfalls.

The first white man to see the Grand Canyon was Cardenas, a member of Coronado's party, who, in 1540, visited the south rim. The first successful passage of the Grand Canyon by boat was made in 1869 by Major John Wesley Powell. An isolated plateau known as Shiva's Temple, believed to have been cut off in the glacial age 12,000 to 35,000 years ago, was explored for the first time in 1937 by Dr. Harold E. Anthony who conducted an investigation into the effects produced on animal life there by its long separation from outside influences.

Grand Coulee Dam. One of the largest dams in the world, backing up the Columbia River in Washington into a lake that extends 151 miles to the Canadian border. The height of the dam is 553 feet and its length is 4200 feet. Into its construction went 11.5 million cubic yards of concrete, an amount of construction unmatched by any other engineering work. The dam is designed to produce 1,974,000 kilowatts of electricity and to irrigate 1,250,000 acres of land. The cost of the dam and power plant, opened in 1941, was 181 million dollars. An additional 209 million dollars was allocated to irrigation canals.

A peculiarity of the dam is that, to be useful for irrigation, a reservoir of water must be created 280 feet above the level to which the dam raises the river. Power developed at the dam is used to pump water into such a reservoir, which, when full, is 23 miles long and covers 2300 acres.

Grand Junction. A city of southwestern Colorado, 255 miles southwest of Denver, at the junction of the Colorado and the Gunnison rivers. Located in the midst of uranium-producing industries, it is also the commercial center of a fertile farming and fruit growing district, watered by a large irrigation canal. The city lies 4600 feet above sea level, and is surrounded by some of the most noted scenic points in Colorado, notably Colorado National Monument and Grand Mesa. Population, 1970, 20,170.

Grand Rapids. A city of Michigan, built on both banks of the Grand River, about 150 miles west of Detroit. The city takes its name from the rapids of the river, which here descends 18 feet in about a mile. While maintaining numerous important industries, Grand Rapids is noted chiefly as a center for the manufacture of furniture. Although exceeded in volume by New York and Chicago, Grand Rapids is distinguished for the design, quality, and finish of its product. In the heart of the city there are large exposition buildings for displaying furniture samples for wholesale buyers.

Among other leading manufactures are automobile parts, carpet sweepers, house furnishings, chemicals, textiles, and gypsum plasters. Public parks cover 1245 acres.

Grand Rapids was settled in 1833, became a village in 1838, and a city in 1850. Educational institutions include Aquinas and Calvin colleges. Population, 1970, 197,649.

Great Falls. The leading manufacturing city of Montana, picturesquely situated at the Great Falls of the Missouri River, about 100 miles north of Helena. The development of immense hydroelectric power in the center of a rich mining and agricultural region has been the chief factor in the growth of the city's manufactures.

Among the leading industrial establishments are copper reduction works, smelting and refining works, and flour and cereal mills. The city is also an important market for wool, shipping several million pounds annually. The municipal park system embraces 48 parks with a total area of 952 acres. Great Falls is a "jumping off" point for motorists driving north to connect with the Alaska Highway. Population, 1970, 60,091.

Great Salt Lake. A salt-water lake in northwestern Utah. Situated at an altitude of 4218 feet above sea level, it has an area of about 1750 square miles with a maximum length of 75 miles and a width of from 30 to 50 miles. Its mean depth is about 20 feet with a maximum of 40 feet. The lake has no outlet, but is fed by the Jordan, Weber, and Bear rivers. Variations in rainfall have a very pronounced effect on its size and on its salinity, the latter fluctuating from 12 to 27 per cent accordingly as the water is high or low. Since the salinity of the ocean is about 3.44 per cent, Great Salt Lake is from four to six times as salty as the ocean. Common salt is the chief mineral constituent of the water, and its recovery is the basis of an active industry. Sodium sulphate and gypsum are also obtained. It is impossible for a bather to sink in the water of the lake.

Great Salt Lake was first accurately described by John C. Frémont in 1845. Geological observations indicate that the lake is the shrunken remnant of an inland sea, Lake Bonneville, which, centuries ago, covered some 20,000 square miles. Great Salt Lake contains nine islands, the longest being 16 miles in length. It is crossed by the Southern Pacific railroad over the Lucin cutoff, a trestle and gravel fill about 27 miles long.

Greeley. A city of northern Colorado, 50 miles north of Denver, on the Cache la Poudre River. It is situated in a fertile agricultural district, and its industries are chiefly based on agriculture. They include sugar refining, flour milling, cold storage warehousing, and canning. Named for Horace Greeley, the place was settled in 1870 by the "Union Colony," composed mainly of New England people. By establishing irrigation, these pioneers transformed an almost barren wilderness into a highly productive region. Greeley is the seat of the University of Northern Colorado. Population, 1970, 38,902.

Green Bay. A city of eastern Wisconsin on high level ground on both sides of the Fox River where it empties into Green Bay, an arm of Lake Michigan. Dating from 1745, it is the oldest settlement in Wisconsin, and Tank Cottage, in Washington Park, is said to be the oldest house in the state. Paper manufacture is prominent among the varied industries. The city is a busy port, shipping chiefly cheese, grain, and fish, and receiving coal, sulphur, steel, and motor cars. Green Bay became a city in 1854. Population, 1970, 87,809.

Greensboro. A manufacturing city in the north central part of North Carolina. The chief products are textiles, cigarettes, machinery, furniture, and hosiery. The city is spacious and open, with 425 acres of parks. It is the seat of Guilford College and two colleges for women—Greensboro and North Carolina. Greensboro was founded in 1809 and named for General Nathanael Greene, hero of the battle of Guilford Court House, which is memorialized by a national military park six miles to the northwest. Population, 1970, 144,076.

Greenville. A city of northwestern South Carolina, built on the banks of the Reedy River, about 110 miles northwest of Columbia. Greenville is an important textile manufacturing center and contains many large cotton mills. Other industrial establishments include foundries, dye works, and garment, textile machinery, and furniture factories. Greenville is the seat of Furman University. Population, 1970, 61,208.

Greylock, Mount. The highest summit in Massachusetts, situated in the Berkshire Hills, on the western border of the state, about 5 miles southwest of North Adams. The broad, flat top, which rises to an elevation of 3500 feet, is accessible by highway and by many beautiful trails. A tract of about 8600 acres on the upper part of the mountain has been purchased by the state for a permanent park.

Gulfport. A port, city, and resort of southeastern Mississippi, on Mississippi sound, an arm of the Gulf of Mexico. It is about midway between New Orleans and Mobile. The shore is protected by a 26-mile concrete sea wall surmounted by a four-lane scenic highway. Gulfport is the second largest banana terminal in the world and also receives sugar, hemp, and other products. It ships locally produced chemicals and fertilizer. Population, 1970, 40,791.

Hagerstown. A city of western Maryland, built on Antietam Creek, 72 miles northwest of Baltimore. It is the trade center for a large agricultural district and has extensive and varied industries. The city's industrial products include silk and knit goods, shoes, pipe organs, aircraft, cement, fertilizers, and sheet metal. In the vicinity are Fort Frederick and the battlefields of Antietam and Gettysburg. Population, 1970, 35,862.

Hamilton. A manufacturing city of southwestern Ohio, on the Miami River, 25 miles north of Cincinnati. Its principal manufactures are machinery, machine tools, paper, stoves, office fixtures, safes and bank vaults, engines, and woolen goods. The city is said to have been the first in the country to own its waterworks, gas plant, and electric light plant. Hamilton was the boyhood home of novelist William Dean Howells. Population, 1970, 67,865.

Hammond. A city of northwestern Indiana, on Lake Michigan, 18 miles southeast of the center of Chicago, of which it is an industrial suburb. Hammond arose as a packing center, George Hammond having established a plant there in 1868. After 1900, steel and railroad car manufacture became of chief importance, and immense oil refineries were built. Other industries include printing, bookbinding, and the making of railroad equipment and chemicals. Population, 1970, 107,790.

Hamtramck (*hăm-trăm'ĭk*). A city of southeastern Michigan, existing as an island municipality within the city of Detroit. Hamtramck owes its rapid growth to the immense development of automobile industries. The city has extensive manufactures of automobile accessories, iron and aluminum castings, wheels, radiators, brass goods, and paints. Population, 1970, 27,245.

Hannibal. A city of northeastern Missouri, situated on the Mississippi River, about 120 miles above Saint Louis. It is the trade center of an agricultural district, and there are coal mines in the vicinity. The chief manufactures include Portland cement, lime, structural steel, lawn mowers, and food products. Hannibal was settled in 1819 and became incorporated in 1839. During boyhood, Mark Twain lived in Hannibal, and his early home is the property of the city. A statue of him stands in the 200-acre Riverview park. The Mark Twain memorial bridge spans the Mississippi at Hannibal. Population, 1970, 18,609.

Harpers Ferry. A historic town 60 miles northwest of Washington in the extreme eastern part of West Virginia, where the state line borders Virginia and Maryland. It occupies a site of remarkable scenic beauty at the junction of the Shenandoah and Potomac rivers, at the point where the latter stream flows through a gap in the Blue Ridge Mountains. Here, in 1859, John Brown attempted his famous raid. During the Civil War, the town was alternately in the possession of the Union and of the Confederate forces. In 1944, it was authorized as a National Monument, and in 1963, made a National Park. Population, 1970, 423.

Harrisburg. The capital of Pennsylvania, situated on the Susquehanna River, in the southeastern part of the state. The city is noted for its diversified manufactures, chiefly of steel and of steel products, and for the extensive railway roundhouses, repair shops, and freight yards, which have made Harrisburg a great distribution center.

The most beautiful of the city's fine buildings is the State Capitol. This impressive edifice, constructed of steel and faced with granite and marble, and decorated with elaborate sculptures, was erected at a cost of $13,000,000. East of it lies Memorial Park, where there are four monumental-type office buildings and a half-mile viaduct in memory of Pennsylvanians who served in the World Wars. Since 1900, extensive civic improvements have won for Harrisburg the sobriquet of the "Model City." The park system covers 1100 acres, of which 666 acres are included in the picturesque Wildwood Park. A beautiful riverside park and boulevard borders on the Susquehanna.

Harrisburg was named for John Harris, an English trader, who settled on its site in 1719. It was incorporated in 1791, and in 1812 became the capital of the state. Population, 1970, 68,061.

Hartford. The capital of Connecticut, built on the west bank of the Connecticut River, in the north central part of the state. The city occupies a commanding site on rolling ground, affording fine views of the Connecticut valley.

Hartford is laid out with wide, well shaded streets and beautiful boulevards. The city is noted for its artistic homes and for its excellent public buildings. In the old State House, designed by Bulfinch, the Hartford Convention of 1814 met. The State Capitol adjoins Bushnell Park, and nearby are the State Library and Supreme Court Building, the State Office Building, the State Armory, Bushnell Memorial Hall, and the Soldiers' and Sailors' memorial arch. Five highway bridges span the Connecticut River.

Its important industries include the manufacture of firearms, typewriters, brushes, precision tools, oil burners, and counting devices. For a long period, Hartford has been one of the leading insurance centers of the country, containing the home offices of nearly 50 companies. The Travelers Insurance Company tower is 527 feet in height. Hartford is the seat of Trinity College and the Wadsworth Atheneum, said to be the oldest free public art museum in America. It has a famous municipal rose garden and celebrates a rose festival annually.

Prior to the settlement of the town in 1635–36 by English colonists from Massachusetts Bay under the leadership of Reverend Thomas Hooker, the Dutch had a trading post and fort at Hartford. Here, in 1639, were drawn up and adopted the "Fundamental Orders of Connecticut," said to be the first written constitution of modern times. In 1687 occurred the attempt of Governor Andros to seize the charter of the colony, and its alleged concealment in the famous "Charter Oak." Hartford was the capital of Connecticut colony until 1701, when it was made joint capital with New Haven. In 1873, Hartford became the sole capital of the state. Population, 1970, 155,868.

Haverhill (*hā'vẽr-ĭl*). A manufacturing city of northeastern Massachusetts, built on both banks of the Merrimack River, about 30 miles north of Boston. Haverhill is one of the chief centers in the United States for the manufacture of boots and shoes. The city was settled in 1640–41 and almost since its founding has been noted for the manufacture of shoes. It now makes about one-sixth of all the women's shoes produced in the United States. The city contains many fine parks, lakes, and drives; also many handsome residences and public buildings. It is the birthplace of John Greenleaf Whittier. Population, 1970, 46,120.

Helena (*hĕl'ē-nȧ*). The capital of Montana, situated in the west central part of the state. The city overlooks an arable valley, the scene of extensive cattle raising, and is surrounded by a mountainous region, rich in gold and other valuable metals. Helena was founded by mining prospectors in 1864 on Last Chance gulch and was incorporated in 1881. From this gulch gold was extracted to the value of $40 million. The industries include lead and zinc smelting.

The per capita wealth of the inhabitants is very high and is reflected in the many fine residences of the city. Among the chief buildings are the State Capitol, the Federal Building, Consistory Temple, Civic Center and Saint Helena Cathedral. Especially noteworthy are the Veterans' and Pioneers' Memorial Building and the Russell Art Gallery. Many points of scenic interest exist in the neighborhood, notably the "Gates of the Mountains," named by Lewis and Clark in 1805. The educational institutions include Carroll College. Population, 1970, 22,730.

Hibbing. A mining village of northeastern Minnesota, in the center of the state's Mesabi Iron Range, 75 miles north of Duluth. It is the site of the world's largest open-pit iron-ore mine and the nation's only "triple divide" watershed. The Greyhound Bus Company originated here in 1914. Population, 1970, 16,104.

Highland Park. A city of southeastern Michigan completely within Detroit, of which it is an industrial suburb. Highland Park was at one time the headquarters of the Ford Motor Company and owes its growth largely to the automobile industry. In 1900, it was a village of 427 inhabitants. Population, 1970, 35,444.

High Point. A manufacturing city of central North Carolina, 99 miles northwest of Raleigh. It is the chief southern center for the manufacture of furniture. The Southern furniture exposition, held there four times annually, is visited by buyers from all parts of the United States. Other important industrial products include textiles, tile, and tobacco. Population, 1970, 63,204.

Hoboken (hō'bō-kĕn'. A manufacturing city of northeastern New Jersey. It is situated on the Hudson River opposite New York, with which it is connected by ferries, and the Holland and Lincoln vehicular tunnels. Hoboken is a large seaport, and is the terminus of several important transatlantic steamship lines. Its industrial output includes coffee, marine equipment, furniture, and pencils. The city is the seat of the Stevens Institute of Technology. The first steam-propelled ferry-boat was invented and put in operation at Hoboken. Population, 1970, 45,380.

Hodgenville. A town of central Kentucky, situated about 50 miles almost due south of Louisville in a fertile region devoted to growing grain, tobacco, and live stock. Three miles distant from the town is the national historic site, Abraham Lincoln Birthplace. Here a beautiful memorial building preserves the log cabin in which President Lincoln was born. Population, 1970, 2562.

Hollywood. A residential and winter resort community in southeastern Florida, 18 miles north of Miami, and 7 miles south of Fort Lauderdale. It has two yacht basins and Port Everglades, a port of entry for southern Florida. Industry is growing in the city, and there are numerous citrus groves in the area. Hollywood was founded in 1921 and incorporated as a city in 1925. Population, 1970, 106,873.

Holy Cross, Mountain of the. A high peak of the Rockies, 30 miles northwest of Leadville, Colorado. The emblem from which this mountain takes its name appears about midsummer. At that time the snow has melted from the higher slopes and ridges and is retained only in two deep canyons, which, by their intersection, form an immense cross high up on the side of the mountain. This white cross remains in view until late autumn, when the entire crest is again covered with snow.

Holyoke (*hol'yok*). A planned industrial city of southwestern Massachusetts, built on the west bank of the Connecticut River, 97 miles southwest of Boston. Immense water power, derived from falls in the river, promoted the rise of extensive industries. These are concerned chiefly with the manufacture of paper, paper products, and textiles. Holyoke is one of the largest producers of fine writing papers and envelopes in the United States. Because of the number and size of its mills, it has long been styled the "Paper City."

The total value of the city's paper products is, however, exceeded by that of its textile products. These include cotton and woolen goods, thread, knit goods, alpaca, and silk. Among other important manufactures are machinery, blank books, and school supplies. Mount Tom and Mount Holyoke are among the many points of interest in the vicinity. Population, 1970, 50,112.

Homestead. A manufacturing city of western Pennsylvania, located on the Monongahela River, about 7 miles southeast of Pittsburgh. Its chief manufacture is steel, and its vast steel plants rank among the largest in the country. Among the "Homestead steel mills," in and around Homestead, is the Carnegie-Illinois strip steel mill, costing 60 million dollars, one of the largest of its kind in the world. Homestead was settled in 1871 and in 1880 was incorporated. Population, 1970, 6309.

Honolulu (*hō'nō-lōō'lōō*). The capital and chief commercial center of Hawaii, situated on a good harbor on the south coast of Oahu. Honolulu is noted for its delightful climate and for its luxuriant tropical gardens. It possesses fine clean streets, spacious open squares, and many handsome public buildings. The University of Hawaii, a state institution, is located in Honolulu.

Representative of the city's industries are pineapple canneries, sugar factories, iron foundries, and artificial ice plants. The native population is industrious and self-supporting. Honolulu occupies a vantage ground of immense importance on the trade routes of the Pacific, and, from a strategic point of view, is of great value as a naval station of the United States. Honolulu harbor was discovered in 1794. The modern town was founded in 1816, and in 1820 it was made the capital of the islands. The population is composed of a mixture of various races, among which predominate Hawaiians, Japanese, Chinese, and Portuguese. Population, 1970, 324,871.

Hood, Mount. A peak of the Cascade range in northern Oregon, about 50 miles east of Portland. It is of volcanic origin and rises symmetrically to a height of 11,225 feet, the loftiest elevation in the state. The lower slopes are forested but the peak is snow capped and there are glaciers on the upper slopes. The summit, which may be ascended without serious difficulty, commands magnificent views of the Columbia River valley and also of many great peaks of the Cascades, including mounts Rainier, Adams, and Jefferson.

Hood River. A town of northern Oregon on the Columbia River, 67 miles east of Portland. It is the trade center and shipping point of the Hood River valley, which extends southward 25 miles to Mt. Hood. This valley, protected by Cascade ranges and provided with a constant flow of gravity-irrigation water, is excellently adapted to fruit growing. Hood River apples and pears are famed throughout the continent and command maximum prices. The Bonneville Dam, 24 miles down the Columbia River, backs the water up to Hood River, thus forming a pool for water sports and recreation. Population, 1970, 3991.

Hoquiam (*hō'kwĭ-ȧm*). A city of western Washington, situated on Gray's Harbor, about 90 miles by rail southwest of Tacoma. It adjoins Aberdeen, with which it shares the distinction of being one of the greatest seaports of the world for shipment of forest products. The industries include lumber mills. wood product factories, and fisheries. Population, 1970, 10,466.

Hot Springs. A health and travel resort, located in central Arkansas 53 miles southwest of Little Rock. The city is picturesquely situated in a narrow valley sheltered by two ridges of the Ouachita Mountains. It surrounds Hot Springs National Park, celebrated for its numerous hot springs having valuable medicinal properties. There are numerous large hotels, sanitariums, and sumptuous bathhouses. Hot Springs Medical Center is one of the tallest buildings in Arkansas. The resort is nearly surrounded by Lakes Catherine and Hamilton, created by power dams in the Ouachita River. Population, 1970, 35,631.

Houston (*hūs'tŭn*). A city of Texas, situated in the southeastern part of the state. It is about 50 miles northwest of Galveston, on a sluggish stream formerly known as Buffalo bayou. This has been widened and deepened into a canal called the Houston ship channel, which permits large ocean steamers to reach the city's wharves.

Houston is the commercial center of a rich agricultural and lumbering region and is one of the world's richest oil producing territories. The city is one of the greatest cotton markets and ports in the United States. In manufactures Houston ranks first among the cities of the state. Its varied industries include petroleum refining, sugar, rice and flour milling, and the manufacture of fertilizers, cement, and chemicals.

The city is laid out with wide, shaded streets, beautiful parks, handsome residences, and imposing public and commercial buildings. The Humble Oil and Gulf buildings are among the tallest in the south. Houston is the seat of Rice University, the University of Houston, and the University of St. Thomas, and has a magnificent Museum of Fine Arts. Houston's Astrodome, built at a cost of $31.6 million, was the world's first air-conditioned all-weather stadium. Its plastic dome is 208 feet high. Houston was settled after the battle of San Jacinto, which was fought near its site in 1836. Incorporated in 1837, it became the capital of the former republic of Texas in 1840. Population, 1970, 1,231,394.

Huntington. A city in West Virginia, located on the Ohio River in the western part of the state. It lies in a rich coal and oil producing region and is an important trade and manufacturing center. It has extensive railroad shops and manufactures nickel, clay products, textiles, optical goods, and mining cars. Huntington is the seat of Marshall College. Population, 1970, 74,315.

Huntsville. An historically interesting city in northern Alabama. In 1811, its earlier name of Twickenham was changed to honor John Hunt, early settler and Revolutionary soldier. At present Huntsville's typical industrial activities are overshadowed by its contribution to America's space program through the Redstone Arsenal. Population, 1970, 137,802.

Imperial Valley. A former desert area in southeastern California, which has been made remarkably productive by irrigation. It lies east and south of the Salton Sea and extends southward to the Mexican border. The improved district is about 40 miles long, with a maximum breadth of 30 miles, and embraces a total area of approximately 500,000 acres.

Water for irrigation is taken from the Colorado River near Yuma, and conducted to the south end of the valley. Thence it is distributed in a network of waterways covering the district. The soil is largely composed of the silts of an ancient delta of the Colorado river. It is of unmatched and seemingly of inexhaustible fertility. Owing to the warm climate and almost continuous sunshine, the growing season is not only very long but also very rapid. By rotation, two or more crops a year are often produced from the same field.

The Imperial Valley has become widely noted for the production of long-staple cotton of unexcelled quality. The district produces also immense quantities of melons, lettuce, asparagus, onions, grapes, oranges, and various other vegetables and fruits. Date culture on a commercial scale is becoming established.

Independence. A city in the western part of Missouri, located in an agricultural district adjacent to Kansas City. Recently, it has become well known as the home of President Harry S. Truman and the site of the Harry S. Truman Library. In an earlier period it was important as a supply point for caravans of pioneers who were going west over the Oregon Trail or the Santa Fe Trail. Population, 1970, 111,662.

Indianapolis. The capital of Indiana, situated on the White River, near the center of the state, about 185 miles southeast of Chicago. In population, transportation facilities, and volume of business transacted, Indianapolis is a major wholesale and retail trade center.

The city occupies a nearly level site, is regularly laid out, for the most part with broad streets, and is substantially and handsomely built. Indianapolis, preeminently a city of homes, is widely noted for its advantages as a residential city.

The park system, which embraces a total area of more than 4564 acres, contains 90 parks. Of these, Eagle Creek, is the largest, covering some 2600 acres. The soldiers' and Sailors' Monument, in Monument Place, a lofty shaft of stone and bronze, 285 feet high and richly decorated with sculptures, is one of the notable military memorials in America. Among numerous fine buildings are the Capitol, the Federal Building, the Riley Public Library, Christ Church, the Indianapolis Art Museum, the Scottish Rite Cathedral, and Indiana State Library. A 15-million dollar World War Memorial Plaza occupies five blocks in the downtown district of the city. The principal structure is the magnificent Shrine Building. A cenotaph stands in the north square at the head of a mall two blocks long. In the northeast corner is a four-story building of Greek architecture which houses the national headquarters of the American Legion. The city's educational institutions include Butler University, Indiana Central College, several professional schools of Indiana University, and several schools of Purdue University.

Indianapolis owes its prominence largely to three important advantages. First, it is the center of a large and highly productive agricultural region; second, it lies near immense supplies of coal, insuring cheap fuel, and third, it possesses unusually excellent transportation facilities. The city is served by numerous railway and air lines radiating in all directions and by very extensive truck and bus systems. A feature for which the city is widely noted is the Indianapolis Motor Speedway. Among the chief industries are meat packing and the manufacture of drugs, motor vehicle engines and parts, aircraft engines, refrigerators, electrical and telephone equipment, television and radio sets, apparel, furniture, and inner tubes for tires.

The site on which the city is located was selected for the state capital and named Indianapolis in 1821. The legislature first met there in 1825. Population, 1970, 743,155.

Inland Empire. A name popularly given to a rich agricultural, stock raising, and mining region of the northwestern United States, lying between the Rocky and the Cascade mountains. It embraces a considerable part of the Columbia River plateau, including eastern Washington, northeastern Oregon, the northern part or "panhandle" of Idaho, and the extreme western part of Montana. The chief railway and commercial center in this large region is Spokane.

Iowa City. A city of eastern Iowa, on the Iowa River, about 120 miles east of Des Moines. The city is primarily a college community (the seat of the State University of Iowa) in the midst of a rich farming and cattle-raising region. The university has excellent medical-research departments cooperating with local hospitals to provide medical service for the state. This city was once the capital of the Territory of Iowa, and from 1846 to 1857 was capital of the state of Iowa. Population, 1970, 46,850.

Irvington. A town of northeastern New Jersey. It is a residential suburb of New York and Newark, which it adjoins on the southwest. It has various industries, including foundries and facilities for the manufacture of chemicals, tools, plastics, and electronic equipment. Settled in 1692, it was called Camptown until 1852, and was then renamed in honor of Washington Irving. Its incorporation as a village dates from 1835, and, as a town, from 1898. Population, 1970, 59,743.

Isleta (*ēs-lā'tä*). An Indian town situated on the west bank of the Rio Grande River, about 10 miles south of Albuquerque, New Mexico. The present town was founded early in the 18th century.The inhabitants, who are of Tanoan Indian stock, retain much of their aboriginal social organization. By primitive means of irrigation, they produce from an arid soil excellent crops of corn, fruits, and vegetables. Population, 1970, 1080.

Itasca (*ī-tăs'kȧ*), **Lake.** A small lake in north central Minnesota. It consists of three long narrow arms, from the northern one of which emerges the Mississippi River. The region immediately surrounding the lake, embracing an area of about 35,000 acres, has been made a state park. Its waters abound in many kinds of fish, beavers are abundant, and a band of elks has been established in the park.

Ithaca. A city of west central New York, located at the south end of Cayuga Lake, about 40 miles south of Syracuse. While the city conducts a substantial trade and maintains various local industries, it is noted chiefly as the seat of Cornell University, with which is connected the New York State Agricultural College. This important educational institution occupies a magnificent campus on East Hill, an eminence rising about 400 feet above the lake and lower city, and commanding unexcelled views of a highly picturesque region. Ithaca was founded in 1789, and was chartered as a city in 1888. Population, 1970, 26,226.

Jackson. A city of southern Michigan, built on both banks of the Grand River, about 70 miles west of Detroit. Jackson is an important railway center, and is situated in the midst of a rich agricultural region. It carries on an extensive trade in grain, fruit, and vegetables, and has substantial industries. The city's manufactures include automobile parts, tires, machine tools, machinery, airplane wheels, and food products. Nearby is a cascade 500 feet long and 64 feet high which is illuminated each night in summer. Jackson was settled in 1829, became a village in 1843, and a city in 1857. The Republican party was organized and named at Jackson in 1854. Population, 1970, 45,484.

Jackson. The capital of Mississippi, located on the Pearl River, about 40 miles east of Vicksburg. Possessing both railway and water transportation, Jackson has become a commercial center for agricultural and manufactured products, with an extensive trade in cotton. The chief local industries include cottonseed oil mills, foundries, lumber mills, and woodworking shops. Among the prominent public buildings are the Capitol and the Carnegie Library. Jackson is the seat of Millsaps College, Belhaven College, and the James Observatory.

The site of Jackson was chosen for the state capital in 1821. During the Civil War, Jackson was the scene of many conflicts, and in 1864 was largely destroyed by General Sherman. Population, 1970, 153,968.

Jackson. A city of western Tennessee, about 80 miles northeast of Memphis. Jackson is the trade center of a rich farming and fruit growing district, is an important cotton and fruit market, and has substantial local industries. Among the city's manufactures are cotton goods, cottonseed oil, lumber, aluminum products, and furniture. Jackson is the seat of Union University and of Lambuth and Lane colleges. Population, 1970, 39,996.

Jacksonville. A city and commercial center of Florida, situated on Saint Johns River, about 27 miles from its mouth. It has an excellent harbor, with a 30-foot channel to the ocean, and carries on an extensive coastwise and foreign trade in lumber, cotton, phosphates, fruits, and vegetables. The leading industries include shipbuilding and the manufacture of fertilizers, lumber, cigars, chemicals, and naval stores; also fruit packing, crab meat packing, and spice milling.

The city's streets, parks, and private residences are rendered attractive by the luxuriance of semi-tropical vegetation. By reason of its mild climate and nearby ocean beaches, Jacksonville is a favorite winter resort. Population, 1970, 518,131.

Jamestown. A manufacturing city of western New York, about 75 miles southwest of Buffalo. Jamestown occupies a hilly site on the outlet of Chautauqua Lake, with abundant water power. It is a leading center for the manufacture of furniture. Other important industries make bearings, automatic voting machines, metal office furniture, and automobile parts. The city is also an important dairy center. Population, 1970, 39,795.

Jamestown. The first permanent English settlement in the United States. It was founded in 1607 on the banks of the James River, in Virginia, about 32 miles above its mouth, and nearly opposite the present town of Williamsburg. The first legislative assembly held in America met at Jamestown in 1619, and here, in the same year, slaves were first introduced into the colonial territory.

During Bacon's Rebellion, 1676, Jamestown was burned to the ground. It was rebuilt and remained the capital of Virginia until 1698, when it was again destroyed by fire and was never reconstructed. The site of the settlement, originally a peninsula, later became an island. Of the former town, there remain only the ruins of the tower of the church of 1639, but the old church has been reconstructed, the foundations of many early structures have been exposed and marked, lot lines and streets have been re-defined, and a modern Visitor Center containing exhibits and an orientation film has been added.

Jefferson City. The capital of Missouri, situated on the south bank of the Missouri River, about 110 miles west of Saint Louis. The city is a trade and commercial center of a rich farming district and contains large railway shops. The chief manufacturing interests include shoe factories, flour mills, machine shops, and foundries. A fine steel bridge spans the Missouri at Jefferson City. Among prominent buildings are the State Capitol, erected at a cost of $4,215,000, the State Supreme Courthouse, and the State Office Building. The site was chosen for the state capital in 1821, the town was laid out in 1822, and the legislature first met here in 1826. Population, 1970, 32,407.

Jersey City. A city of New Jersey, built on the west bank of the Hudson River. It occupies 20.2 square miles directly opposite lower New York City, with which it is connected by four tubes under the Hudson and by the Holland vehicular tunnel.

Jersey City is the terminus of a large number of railroads, which link it with the South and West. As a shipping and receiving port, it is probably second in importance to New York. Among its numerous manufactures are electrical and scientific apparatus, jewelry, musical instruments, soap, radios, and drugs.

The city has many notable public buildings and several parks. John F. Kennedy Boulevard, 19 miles long and 100 feet wide, follows the crest of Bergen Hill, extends past West Side Park, and gives a splendid view of the river and upper New York. Population, 1970, 260,545.

Johnstown. A manufacturing city in southwestern Pennsylvania, about 75 miles east of Pittsburgh. Johnstown is located in a picturesque valley at the foot of the Allegheny Mountains, in a rich coal mining and iron producing region.

The city is one of the leading centers in the state for the manufacture of steel and steel products. Other manufactures include silk, radios, radiators, and paint. Johnstown has 230 acres in 14 public parks. On May 31, 1889, as a result of a flood caused by the bursting of a dam on the south fork of the Conemaugh River, Johnstown was largely destroyed and 2000 lives were lost. A reminder of this tragic occurrence is the Unknown Plot in Grandview Cemetery, where 777 unidentified victims of the flood are buried. Prompt outside aid was extended, and the city was soon rebuilt and its industries re-established. Population, 1970, 42,476.

Joliet (*jō'lĭ-ĕt*). A manufacturing city of northeastern Illinois, situated on the Des Plaines River, about 40 miles southwest of Chicago. The manufacture of steel products, chiefly rods and wire, and of wall paper are major industries. Other products include refined oil, chemicals, and stoves. The American Institute of Laundering is located there. Joliet is also noted for its quarries of fine building stone, known as Joliet limestone. Population, 1970, 80,378.

Juneau (*jōō'nō*). The capital of Alaska, and the supply center of mining, fishing, and lumbering camps. It is situated on a good harbor on the Gastineau Channel, in the "panhandle" portion of southeastern Alaska. Huge quantities of salmon, halibut, and other fish are shipped, mainly within the United States. A decline in gold mining has been accompanied by a growth of the pulp and lumber industry and fur farming. Population, 1970, 6050.

Kalamazoo. A manufacturing center of southwestern Michigan, in a rich agricultural district. Principal industries include metal working and the manufacture of pharmaceuticals, paper, printing machinery, and paper boxes. The city is the seat of Western Michigan University and Kalamazoo and Nazareth colleges. Population, 1970, 85,555.

Kansas City. A city of Kansas, built on both banks of the Kansas River at its junction with the Missouri. It lies adjacent to Kansas City, Missouri, with which communication is facilitated by a two-mile intercity viaduct connecting the higher levels of the cities. It is the second greatest live stock market and meat packing center in the United States. Flour milling is second in importance among the city's extensive industries, which include petroleum refining, soap making, car repairing, and the manufacture of structural ironwork, boxes, chemicals, cooperage, and fertilizers. Parks cover 330 acres, and nearby is Wyandotte County Park of 1400 acres with a 333-acre lake created by an earthen dam. First settled as a trapping post in the 1820's, it became a gateway to the West and was incorporated as a city in 1889. Population, 1970, 168,213.

Kansas City. A city of Missouri on the western border of the state, some 230 miles west of Saint Louis. It occupies a commanding site on the south bank of the Missouri River, at its junction with the Kansas River. The city is built on three levels, in a landscape of high bluffs. Kansas, City, Mo., and Kansas City, Kans., though separate in government, form a continuous settlement at the center of a six-county metropolitan area. Because of its location near the geographical center of the United States and its excellent transportation facilities, including an international airport, Kansas City is one of the most important warehousing and distribution centers in the United States.

Known for its leadership in agricultural enterprise, the city also has a strong and diversified industrial base and ranks high as a center for consulting engineering firms. Also important are its wheat market, cold storage facilities, production of vending equipment, distribution of vending machinery, and automotive assembly plants. Chief industrial products are refined oil, iron and steel products, paints, and chemicals.

Among prominent buildings are the municipal auditorium, city hall, the federal building, and the Nelson Gallery of Art. Here also are the Kansas City Philharmonic Orchestra, the Museum of History and Science, the Midwest Research Institute (operating in 20 fields of science), the Hall Library of Science and Technology, and the University of Kansas City. Population, 1970, 501,859.

Katahdin (*kȧ-tä'dĭn*), **Mount.** The highest mountain in Maine, located in Piscataquis county, slightly northeast of the center of the state. It rises to an elevation of 5267 feet, with precipitous slopes and massive cliffs of richly colored granite. The bare summit furnishes a grand view of forests, rivers, lakes, and mountains.

Kennedy, Cape. A cape on Florida's east coast midway between Jacksonville and Miami where the U.S. government maintains a launching site for space explorations. Its name was changed from Cape Canaveral in honor of President Kennedy after his assassination in 1963. In 1973 the cape was renamed Cape Canaveral. The space launching facility will still be known as the John F. Kennedy Space Center.

Kenosha (*ke-no'sha*). A city of fine homes and choice industrial sites in southeastern Wisconsin, overlooking a fine harbor on Lake Michigan, 34 miles south of Milwaukee. The city's extensive industries include the manufacture of automobiles, brass and copper products, tools, stainless steel fittings, wire rope, hosiery, and knit goods. Population, 1970, 78,805.

Key West. The southernmost city of continental United States, situated on Key West Island, one of the Florida Keys. This small coral island lies in the Gulf of Mexico, about 50 miles southwest of Cape Sable, Florida. It is connected with the mainland by an overseas highway built, in part, upon the chain of low islands, of which Key West is the terminal, and, in part, upon huge concrete causeways connecting the islands. There are large shipping interests and important fisheries. Population, 1970, 27,563.

Kings Mountain. A ridge 100 feet high and a mile long in South Carolina, about 30 miles southwest of Charlotte, N. C. Here on October 7, 1780, a British force of 1100 troops was defeated and captured by less than 1000 mountaineers, who thereby spoiled the strategy of Cornwallis and prepared the way for victory at Yorktown.

Knoxville. An industrial and educational center in eastern Tennessee, built on the north bank of the Tennessee River, about 160 miles east of Nashville. It lies between the Cumberland and Great Smoky mountain ranges in a rich coal mining, iron producing, and marble quarrying region, with which it conducts an extensive trade. Knoxville's industrial products include textiles and clothing, iron and steel products, furniture, plastics, and marble. The city is the seat of the University of Tennessee and Knoxville College. It is headquarters of the Tennessee Valley Authority. Population, 1970, 174,587.

La Crosse. A city of western Wisconsin, on the Mississippi River at the mouth of the La Crosse and Black rivers. Its site is on level ground extending about 2½ miles back from the Mississippi to bluffs which command fine views. Lumber manufacture, formerly the leading industry, has been replaced by a great variety of new industries including the manufacture of motor car instruments and farm machinery. It is the trade center for a rich dairying district. The numerous lakes, picturesque crags, and winding valleys nearby make La Crosse a popular center for tourist travel. Population, 1970, 51,153.

Laguna (*lä-goo'nä*). The second largest Indian pueblo in New Mexico, located near the San Jose River, in an arid desert, 67 miles west of Albuquerque. The inhabitants, who are of Keresan stock, are industrious and self-supporting. By primitive methods of irrigation, they produce crops sufficient for their needs. Wool also is grown.

Lake Charles. A city of southwestern Louisiana, situated on the lake of the same name, about midway between New Orleans and Houston. It is an important seaport, connected with the Gulf of Mexico by a 33-mile deep-water channel. Principal industries are oil refining and chemical manufacturing. McNeese State College is located here, and just north of the city is the 1220-acre Sam Houston Park. Population, 1970, 77,998.

Lake Geneva. A summer resort town of southern Wisconsin, situated on a lake of the same name, about 40 miles southwest of Milwaukee. The lake is a fine body of water, 9 miles long and from 1 to 3 miles wide. Many residents of Chicago have villas on its shores. The town is the seat of a large sanitarium and a military school. Nearby is Yerkes Observatory, containing the great Yerkes 40-inch refracting telescope. Population, 1970, 4890.

Lake George. A small lake in eastern New York, one of the most picturesquely beautiful in America. It is fed chiefly by cold springs, and its waters flow into Lake Champlain through a series of cascades, with one abrupt fall of 30 feet at Ticonderoga.

Lake Mohonk (*mô-hŏngk'*). A popular summer resort, charmingly situated on a small lake of the same name in the Catskill Mountains, of Ulster County, about 75 miles north of New York City. Lake Mohonk is noted also as the seat of a long series of annual conferences on international arbitration. the first of which was held in 1895

Lake Placid. A beautiful small lake in the Adirondacks of northeastern New York. It is situated at the foot of Whiteface Mountain, some 10 miles northeast of Mount Marcy. The lake lies at an altitude of about 2000 feet.

Lakewood. A city of northern Ohio on Lake Erie and adjoining the western limits of Cleveland, of which it is a residential suburb. Lakewood was incorporated in 1911. Population, 1970, 70,173.

Lancaster. A city of southeastern Pennsylvania, about 65 miles west of Philadelphia. Lancaster is the trade center of one of the most productive tobacco and grain growing counties in the United States, and has varied and extensive industries. It is noted for its output of watches, umbrellas, locks, linoleum, cork, silk goods, cotton goods, and leather. Franklin and Marshall College and the Theological Seminary of the Reformed Church are located here. First settled in 1718, Lancaster became the center of a progressive community whose important historic contributions include the Pennsylvania rifle and the Conestoga wagon. It was the home of James Buchanan, 15th president of the United States. Population, 1970, 57,690.

Lansing. The capital of Michigan, built at the junction of the Grand and Cedar rivers, about 85 miles northwest of Detroit. Power developed from these streams is utilized in the city's extensive industries. In value of manufactures, Lansing stands fourth among the cities of the state. Of its industries, the manufacture of automobiles is the most important. Other manufactures are machine shop products and chemicals. Among important public buildings are the new capitol and the Lansing Public Library. Parks cover 1802 acres. East Lansing is the seat of Michigan State University. Lansing was settled in 1837, was laid out for the capital in 1847, and became a city in 1859. Population, 1970, 131,546.

Laredo (*le,ra'do*). A city of southern Texas, on the Rio Grande River, opposite Nuevo Laredo, Mexico, and connected with it by two international bridges. It is the largest port of entry on the U.S.-Mexico border, the distribution center for an area rich in petroleum production, cattle raising, and truck crops. Laredo is a tourist attraction with historical interest. It was founded in 1755 by the Spanish. Population, 1970, 69,024.

Lassen Peak. A volcanic mountain in northern California, situated at the north end of the Sierra Nevada range, about 135 miles north of Sacramento It stands at the extreme southwestern border of the great ancient lava beds which cover more than 200,000 square miles in the Columbia River plateau.

Long inactive and regarded as extinct, Lassen Peak in 1914 began to emit immense clouds of steam and smoke. An area of 167 square miles surrounding and including Lassen Peak has been created a national park. In this are smaller volcanoes, lava fields, cinder cones, fumaroles, hot springs, solfataras, boiling lakes, and other features characteristic of a volcanic region.

Las Vegas. A city in Nevada, located in the southeastern tip of the state. Having advantages of climate and nearness to points of scenic interest, such as Hoover Dam, it has become known as a residential, tourist, and convention city, specializing in entertainment for visitors. Its industries serve the AEC Nevada Test Site and other U.S. bases. Population, 1970, 125,787.

Lawrence. A city in eastern Kansas, on both banks of the Kansas River, about 40 miles west of Kansas City. Lawrence is the trade center of a rich agricultural region and has various local industries, including flour mills, pipe organ and box factories, nurseries, and canning works. It is the seat of the University of Kansas, and the Haskell Institute for Indians is also located here. Founded in 1854 by settlers from New England, Lawrence was the first of the Kansas Free State towns, and became an anti-slavery stronghold. It was sacked by a band of bush rangers from Missouri in 1856. In 1863, Quantrell, the Confederate raider, attacked the town, killing more than 100 of its citizens. Population, 1970, 45,698.

Lawrence. A manufacturing city of northeastern Massachusetts, built on both sides of the Merrimack River, about 26 miles north of Boston. The Merrimack Falls of the river at this point originally played an important part in building up the city's industries. In the production of worsted cloth, Lawrence leads all other cities of the United States. Here are located the huge mills of the American Woolen Company as well as the Pacific and Arlington mills Other manufactures include foundry and machine shop products, shoes, and paper. Population, 1970, 66,915.

Leadville. A mining city of central Colorado, located near the Continental Divide, at an elevation of 10,200 feet. First settled by gold prospectors in 1860, it was a prosperous gold mining center for a few years until the deposits at that time known were exhausted. Thereupon the place was practically abandoned. In 1877, exceedingly rich lead and silver ore bodies were discovered. As a result, the population, which had declined to about 300, increased to more than 6000 in 1878, and to about 35,000 in 1879. For a time thereafter, Leadville held first place in the United States in lead and silver production. During the period

1879–1940, the total value of its mineral output exceeded $550 million. Mineral production has declined to a small fraction of its former value. Nearby is a mine producing most of the world's molybdenum. Population, 1970, 4314.

Lewiston. A leading manufacturing city of Maine, built on the east bank of the Androscoggin River opposite the city of Auburn, about 35 miles north of Portland. The river here falls 60 feet; at the five million dollar Gulf Island dam it furnishes immense hydroelectric power which is utilized in the city's extensive industries. The chief manufacturing establishments are cotton and woolen mills, shoe factories, dye works, and bleacheries. The city is the seat of Bates College. Population, 1970, 41,779.

Lexington. The chief city of the "Blue-Grass region," situated about 80 miles southeast of Louisville. It is located in a highly productive agricultural and stock-raising district and is an important market for grain, tobacco, and livestock, especially thoroughbred horses. Lexington, named for the first battle of the Revolutionary War, is surrounded by beautiful countryside. It is the seat of Kentucky University, Transylvania University, and other educational institutions. It is also the site of a U.S. Veterans' Hospital and a U.S. hospital and farm for the treatment of drug addicts. Lexington was the home of Henry Clay, Mary Todd Lincoln, and General John Hunt Morgan. Population, 1970, 108,137.

Lexington. A town of northeastern Massachusetts, situated about 12 miles northwest of Boston. Lexington village, now chiefly residential, is noted as the scene of the first conflict between the colonists and the British in the Revolutionary War. In the village and its vicinity are many points of great historic interest. Among these are the first battleground of the Revolution; numerous houses, taverns, and other buildings associated with the conflict; and various monuments in commemoration of the men and of the events that made Lexington famous. Lexington was settled about 1642 and for some 50 years was known as Cambridge Farms. In 1839, the first normal school in the United States was opened in Lexington. Population, 1970, 31,886.

Lima. A city of western Ohio and center of oil pipe lines, located on the Ottawa River, 79 miles south of Toledo. Among its chief industrial products are cigars, locomotives, power shovels, electric motors, diesel engines, bus bodies, and steel castings. Population, 1970, 53,734.

Lincoln. The capital and second largest city of Nebraska, situated on a gently sloping site, about 55 miles southwest of Omaha. It is the center of a productive agricultural and stock-raising section, with which it carries on an extensive trade. The industrial products include food products, chemicals, brick, cement, and machinery. The city is regularly laid out, with wide streets. The Capitol is among the great architectural achievements of America. Parks, numbering 42, cover 4028 acres.

Lincoln is the seat of the University of Nebraska, Wesleyan University, and Union College. Fairview, the estate of William Jennings Bryan, is used as a hospital. The first permanent settlement on the site of the city was made in 1856, and in 1864 a village was laid out, called Lancaster. This, in 1867, was selected for the state capital and renamed Lincoln. Population, 1970, 149,518.

Lincoln Highway. A road extending entirely across the northern United States and named in honor of Abraham Lincoln. It was laid out in 1913 with the purpose of establishing a modern vehicular highway, national in character and free to the public at all points, connecting New York and San Francisco. For most of its length, the road is now known as U.S. 30 (Philadelphia to Salt Lake City). From Utah across Nevada into California, it is replaced by U.S. 50.

Little Rock. The capital and largest city of Arkansas, on the Arkansas River, near the center of the state. The name has reference to a bold cliff rising 50 feet above the river at this point. The city is the commercial center of a rich lumbering and cotton-growing district. It became an inland port in 1968 as part of the $1.2 billion Arkansas River Navigation Project. Two new navigation locks and dams are located only a short distance from the city. There are many fine public buildings, among which is the Capitol, built of native Arkansas marble. The park system covers 400 acres. Because of its profusion of roses, Little Rock is often called the "City of Roses." The city is the seat of Little Rock University and the University of Arkansas schools of medicine, nursing, pharmacy, and law. Population, 1970, 132,483.

Lockport. A city of western New York, situated on the State Barge canal, 26 miles northeast of Buffalo and in the center of the highly productive Niagara fruit belt. It occupies a commanding though somewhat uneven site, part of the city being built on a sloping terrace known as "Mountain Ridge." At this point the canal drops some 66 feet, from the level of Lake Erie to that of the Genesee River, by massive locks of masonry, and is crossed by one of the widest bridges in the world. The varied industries include numerous manufactures, notably automobile parts and pulpwood products, chemicals, and high-grade steel. There is a large trade in fruit and grain. The Niagara County Historical Center is located here. Population, 1970, 25,399.

Logan. A city of northern Utah, on Logan River, about 70 miles north of Salt Lake City. Logan is the commercial center of the Cache valley, a rich agricultural district, with some mineral deposits. Its industrial establishments include flour mills, cheese plants, and beet sugar and knitting factories. Utah State University is located there, and a Mormon temple with grounds of great beauty overlooks the city from a hilltop. Population, 1970, 22,333.

Long Beach. An industrial and tourist center on the coast of California, 22 miles south of Los Angeles. It is beautifully located, looking out on the harbor of San Pedro, while the beach from which it takes its name is one of the finest along the Pacific coast. Its harbor, elaborately improved, is the base of the Pacific battle fleet. It accommodates a large trade in fruit, canned fish, petroleum, and lumber, the last two being the chief products of the city's industry. Petroleum is extensively produced within the city limits and is used as fuel for an electric generating plant, one of the largest on the continent. Population, 1970, 358,633.

Lookout Mountain. A steep ridge which rises to an elevation of 2100 feet, overlooking the city of Chattanooga, Tennessee. This rocky height was the scene of the famous battle of the Civil War, sometimes called the "Battle above the Clouds." The summit commands a superb view of the Tennessee River and its valley, the city of Chattanooga, and the surrounding mountainous region.

LOS ANGELES (*lŏs ăng' gĕl-ĕs; lŏs ăn'jĕl-ĕs*). The chief commercial center of southern California and the third most populous city in the United States, Los Angeles is situated on the Pacific coast, about 475 miles southeast of San Francisco and about 10 miles south of the Sierra Madre mountains. Through it passes the Los Angeles River, a dry bed in summer but a considerable stream in winter.

Site. The city lies, for the most part, in a gently sloping plain, with an average elevation of about 270 feet. The site is fairly level, though there are a few steep eminences, and the northern suburbs extend into the foothills. Including extensions to the ocean and taking in San Pedro harbor, the total area of the city exceeds 457 square miles.

Streets and Buildings. The city is regularly laid out, with wide, straight streets, and an extensive system of boulevards and drives. About the old Plaza is the civic center, which includes the $10 million City Hall with a 464-foot tower surmounted by the Lindbergh beacon. Near the plaza is the union station, an $11 million structure. The railway terminals and manufacturing districts lie chiefly to the east and south of the business center, while the large and handsomely built residence sections flank it on the west and north. Los Angeles is preeminently a city of beautiful homes, with the Mission style of architecture, adopted from the Spanish, and the bungalow as characteristic types. The broad avenues and spacious grounds are luxuriant with evergreen foliage and a profusion of flowers which bloom throughout the year.

Parks and Boulevards. There are 112 public parks embracing a total area of more than 9600 acres. Among the more noteworthy of these are Griffith, Elysian, Westlake, Lincoln, Echo, Hollenbeck, Exposition, Central, and Plaza parks. Griffith park, a hilly, wooded tract of 4109 acres, is one of the largest municipally-owned parks in the United States. Many handsome boulevards and driveways connect the parks with various parts of the city and with fine scenic roads to the ocean, fruitful valleys, and mountain wildernesses.

Educational Institutions. Los Angeles is the seat of the University of Southern California, the University of

California at Los Angeles, Occidental College, Loyola University, and Los Angeles City College. The Museum of History and Science in Exposition Park, has a large display of skeletons of extinct animals. The County Museum of Art and the Music Center of the Performing Arts are recent additions to Los Angeles' cultural attractions.

TRANSPORTATION. Los Angeles owes its great growth in part to unusually complete transportation facilities. The city contains terminals of three transcontinental railways which enter the magnificent Union Station, completed in 1939 at a cost of $11 million. There is also a capacious harbor for coastwise and foreign shipping in its municipally-owned wharves at San Pedro. It is connected with the surrounding country by a system of bus lines, some of which reach towns 60 miles distant. Well paved public freeways form a huge network over country districts in all directions. One of the finest is the Arroyo Seco Parkway. These serve as thoroughfares for extensive regularly operated systems of autobuses and autotrucks.

COMMERCE. Los Angeles is the commercial center of the far Southwest and has extensive fruit growing, petroleum producing, manufacturing, and shipping interests. Its foreign and intercoastal shipping vies with that of New York City. The chief imports are lumber and raw materials such as rubber, silk, coffee, and cacao. Exports are largely petroleum and other minerals, food products, and factory goods. The city is a general market for one of the most productive horticultural and agricultural sections of the country. Among leading products handled are oranges, lemons, walnuts, olives, vegetables, beet sugar, beans, cereals, and cotton. Citrus fruits and petroleum are the chief products of the immediate district.

MANUFACTURES. By reason of cheap fuel, in the form of crude petroleum, and abundant hydroelectric power derived from the Hoover Dam, Los Angeles has grown at a prodigious rate as a manufacturing city. The motion picture industry is the best known. Hollywood, the chief center of this industry, is famous throughout the world. The Los Angeles area leads the country in aircraft manufacture. Other important manufactures include petroleum and metal products, lumber, packed meats and other food products, and furniture. The outdoor life and the importance of the motion picture industry have made Los Angeles a style center for sports and other clothes, and the manufacture of women's clothing has become a large industry.

FEATURES OF INTEREST. With its picturesque setting between the mountains and the sea, its numerous historic associations, and its many attractive suburbs, Los Angeles presents an immense number of points of interest. Among those within the city are the Old Plaza Church, China City and Chinatown, Griffith Observatory and Planetarium, Memorial Coliseum, with a seating capacity of 105,000, and the Hollywood Bowl, seating 18,000, Dodger Stadium, the Pilgrimage play, Radio Center, and La Brea pits in Hancock Park. In the near vicinity are San Gabriel Mission with its Mission Play theater, Mount Lowe, and Mount Wilson Observatory, Huntington Library and Art Gallery, and Palos Verdes hills. Attractive beach resorts include Santa Monica, Venice, Redondo Beach, Long Beach, and Santa Catalina Island. Interesting suburban cities include Pasadena, Riverside, Alhambra, Universal City, Glendale, Orange, Pomona, and San Bernardino.

HISTORY. In 1781, Los Angeles was settled by Spanish colonists from Mexico who named it *El Pueblo de Nuestra Senora la Reina de Los Angeles* (the City of Our Lady the Queen of the Angels). Until its final capture in 1847 by United States troops under General Stephan W. Kearny, it served alternately with Monterey as capital of the Mexican province of California.

Los Angeles was chartered as a city in 1850, and attained its first railway connection with San Francisco in 1876. Following the completion, in 1885, of the Santa Fe railway, giving direct access to the East, the growth of Los Angeles was rapid.

The genial climate, the great fertility of the surrounding region under irrigation, and large local supplies of natural gas and petroleum have been influential factors in this development. Two important municipal achievements have also contributed substantially to its rise as a great city. The first was the extension, in 1909, of the city to the ocean at San Pedro, making possible the establishment of a commodious, municipally controlled harbor. The second was the completion, in 1913, at a cost of $25 million, of a great aqueduct from the slopes of Mount Whitney in the Sierra Nevada, across the Mojave desert, and through the Sierra Madre range, by tunnel, to the city. In the 1930's, water from the Colorado River was made available through a 250-mile aqueduct, 108 miles of which was tunneled through the rock, the total cost being $220 million. A third source of supply was secured with the completion of the Mono Basin project in 1940 at a cost of $20 million. Population, 1970, 2,816,061.

Louisville (*loo'ĭ-vĭl*). The chief city of Kentucky, located on the south bank of the Ohio River, 110 miles south of Cincinnati. Louisville occupies a commanding site opposite the rapids or "falls" of the river, at which point is an enormous fossil reef containing what is said to be the world's only exposed relic of the Devonian era, dating from 300 million years ago. A system of locks and dams has recently been added in the falls area.

The city's park system covers some 2177 acres. Cherokee Park, 409 acres, is cut into ravines by Beargrass Creek. Iroquois Park, the largest, 676 acres, rises to eminences of nearly 300 feet, affording views of the city and of the river.

Louisville has excellent transportation facilities by air, expressway, rail, and the Ohio River. It is the commercial center of a large agricultural region. Its leading manufactures include tobacco products, electrical appliances, farm implements, packed meats, whiskey, railroad cars, sanitary plumbing supplies, and gasoline. It leads the U.S. in the production of bathtubs, baseball bats, hickory handles, and wagons. The city is the seat of the University of Louisville and other educational institutions. It is widely known as the site of the Kentucky Derby and the Kentucky State Fair.

The town of Louisville was laid out and named in 1779 and became a city in 1828. Its growth, favored by river traffic, was greatly stimulated by the completion, in 1830, of the Louisville and Portland canal around the rapids. Near the city is the home and the grave of Zachary Taylor. Population, 1970, 361,472.

Lowe, Mount. A peak of the Sierra Madre in southern California. It is situated some 15 miles in direct line northeast of Los Angeles and rises to an elevation of 5650 feet above sea level. An electric scenic railway ascends almost to the summit, which affords superb views of the surrounding region.

Lowell. A manufacturing city of northeastern Massachusetts, situated at the junction of the Merrimack and Concord rivers, about 30 miles northwest of Boston. While electronics has replaced textiles as the main industrial base (many of the textile mills having moved south), manufactures are diversified, including food products, shoes, medicine, clothing, plastics, and paper products. Various civic improvements have recently been made within the city. Lowell is the seat of Lowell Technological Institute and Lowell State College. It is the birthplace of the artist James McNeill Whistler, whose home is now a museum. Population, 1970, 94,239.

Lubbock. A city in the Great Plains area of Texas, 295 miles northwest of Fort Worth. Located in a rich oil region, it is also in the center of an agricultural section whose major products are cotton, cottonseed, and sorghum. Principal educational institution, Texas Technological University. Population, 1970, 149,101.

Luray Cavern. A remarkable cave, situated near the town of Luray, Virginia, in the foothills of the Blue Ridge mountains. There are numerous galleries, rising above one another in tiers to a height of nearly 300 feet. Some contain stalactites and stalagmites of great size and unusual beauty of coloration. The cavern was discovered in 1878.

Lynchburg. A city of central Virginia, on the James River, 112 miles west of Richmond. The city is picturesquely located, sloping in steep terraces upward from the river, with the Blue Ridge and the Peaks of Otter as background. It is situated in a tobacco producing district, of which it is the trade center. Power developed from the river is utilized in various local industries, chiefly in the manufacture of shoes and clothing. Educational institutions include Randolph-Macon Woman's College and Lynchburg College. Population, 1970, 54,083.

Lynn. A manufacturing city of eastern Massachusetts, located about 10 miles northeast of Boston. The city is beautifully situated and admirably laid out. The commercial and industrial districts extend for about 3 miles along Massachusetts Bay, on which the city has a well-developed harbor, while the residential sections occupy the higher portions overlooking the harbor.

Lynn is one of the chief centers in the United States for the manufacture of women's and children's shoes. The city has other important industries, chiefly the manufacture of electrical machinery, jet engines, measurement devices, adhesives, boxes, and proprietary medicines. Lynn was settled in 1629 but was known as Saugus until 1637, when it was given its present name. Its great shoe industry had its beginnings about 1750. Population, 1970, 90,294.

McKeesport. A manufacturing city of Pennsylvania, on the Monongahela River, 14 miles southeast of Pittsburgh. Advantageously situated in a region rich in bituminous coal, iron, and natural gas, the city has become a leading center for the manufacture of iron and steel. It possesses one of the greatest steel tube and iron pipe works in the world, which has earned for it the name of the "Tube City." Among other industrial products are chromium sheet, tools, and other steel products. Population, 1970, 37,977.

Macon (*mā'kŏn*). A city of central Georgia, built at the head of navigation on the Ocmulgee River, about 80 miles southeast of Atlanta. Macon is the commercial center of a highly productive farming and fruit district, and is a leading market for peanuts, pecans, and peaches. Hydroelectric power, derived from the river, is utilized in the city's extensive industries, which include the manufacture of cotton and knit goods, cottonseed oil and cottonseed cake, brick, tile, lumber, flour, fertilizers, foundry and machine shop products, and packed meats. Macon has a municipal auditorium with a huge copper dome.

The city is the seat of Mercer University and Wesleyan College. Macon was first settled in 1822 and was incorporated as a city in 1832. It was the home of the poet Sidney Lanier. Population, 1970, 122,423.

Madison. The capital of Wisconsin, situated in the south central part of the state. The city occupies a picturesque site between lakes Mendota and Monona, in the so-called "Four-Lakes region." It is surrounded by a rich agricultural district, of which it is the trade and industrial center. Madison is noted for its beautiful parks, wide, heavily shaded streets, and scenic lake shore drives. Its industrial output includes meat and dairy products, dry cell batteries, and machine tools. There are many fine public buildings, the most imposing of which is the capitol, built of granite in the Renaissance style.

The city is the seat of the University of Wisconsin, which occupies a magnificent campus, more than a mile in length, bordering on Lake Mendota. Madison has a United States forest products laboratory, opened in 1910, the first in the world. The site of Madison was chosen for the state capital in 1836. Population, 1970, 173,258.

Malden. A city of eastern Massachusetts, built on the Malden River, 5 miles north of Boston. Malden is noted for its extensive manufactures of rubber boots and shoes, and contains some of the largest rubber shoe factories in the United States. Among numerous other manufactures may be mentioned knitted goods, soap, paints, chinaware, and precision instruments. Malden was first settled in 1641, was incorporated in 1649, and was chartered as a city in 1881. Population, 1970, 56,127.

Mammoth Cave. The second largest known cavern in the world, being exceeded in size only by Carlsbad Cave in New Mexico. Situated near the Green River, about 100 miles south of Louisville, Kentucky, it is located in a region which abounds in large caverns and whose surface is marked by thousands of sink holes. Through these depressions, drainage waters find their way to underground streams whose solvent and erosive action has largely produced the caves.

To the geologist, the cave is a laboratory and museum inexhaustibly rich in materials for the study of rock formations and the effects of erosion. For the tourist, the processes of geologic change have created a picturesque setting unlimited in interest and variety. In the St. Louis limestone, a layer of soluble rock capped by sandstone and sometimes reaching a thickness of 300 feet, underground waters have carved a series of pools and streams that are bordered by cathedral-like rooms and ornamental passageways. The walls are lined, not only with the usual rows of stalactites and stalagmites, but also with a panorama of symmetrical statues and grotesque gargoyles.

In more matter-of-fact terms, Mammoth Cave may be described as a complex series of caverns, including more than 200 so-called rooms, chambers, domes, pits, abysses, grottoes, avenues, and galleries, which extend for 9 miles underground. In the lower portions, there are rivers, waterfalls, and small lakes. Among the most interesting features are the vast pits or domes, which are caverns of unusual height. The largest of these, called the Chief City, is 450 feet long and 130 feet wide.

Cleveland Avenue, which extends for fully 2 miles, presents wonderful displays of crystals and incrustations. Stalactites and stalagmites in a great variety of grotesque shapes, many of which resemble architectural forms. When the incrustations are covered with crystals, as in Star Chamber, their sparkling effect when the cavern is lighted is impressive. Among the larger bodies of water within the cavern are the so-called Dead Sea, the Styx, Lethe Lake, Roaring River, and Echo River.

In the waters of the cave are 2 species of blind fish. These, together with crayfish and a few insects, make up the animal life. The temperature remains almost constant at about 54°. The cavern was discovered in 1809 by a hunter named Hutchins. In 1936, a tract including the site of the cave was created Mammoth Cave National Park, covering over 80 square miles.

Manchester. A city of New Hampshire, built on the Merrimack River, 18 miles south of Concord. A fall of some 50 feet in the river, formerly used as direct water power, now provides one of the units in a superpower system. The city's extensive industrial output includes cotton textiles, worsted dress goods, rayon mixtures, shoes, brushes, and cigars. The city has many fine parks, municipal buildings, and educational institutions, including the Manchester Institute of Arts and Sciences and the Currier Art Gallery. Recreation is provided by 35 parks. Population, 1970, 87,754.

Manitou (*măn'ĭ-too͞*) **Springs.** A health and pleasure resort, located at the foot of Pikes Peak, 6 miles northwest of Colorado Springs, Colorado. The town lies at an elevation of about 6300 feet in a region noted for picturesque scenery. The numerous features of interest in the locality include Pikes Peak, the Cave of the Winds, Soda Springs Park, the Garden of the Gods, and various canyons, Cliff Dwellers' ruins, waterfalls, and scenic drives. The famous radioactive mineral springs flow at the rate of a quarter million gallons daily. The summer population is estimated at 25,000. Resident population, 1970, 4278.

Mansfield. A city of north central Ohio, situated in an agricultural region, about 65 miles northeast of Columbus. Its manufactures include appliances, brass products, tires, and plumbing products. Of interest in and around Mansfield are two winter ski resorts; a monument to Johnny (Chapman) Appleseed, who is said to have used his influence to save the settlement from Indians; the Richland County Museum; Malabar Farm, a successful experiment of novelist Louis Bromfield's from the 1930's in farming on ecological principles; and Kingswood Center, a beautiful exhibit of flora and fauna. Population, 1970, 55,047.

Marcy, Mount. The loftiest summit of the Adirondack mountains and the highest peak in the state of New York. It is situated about 10 miles south of Lake Placid, and 30 miles southwest of Lake Champlain. It is a dome-shaped mountain rising to an elevation of 5344 feet. The slopes, except near the summit, are generally wooded. The summit and a portion of the upper northern slope are above timber line. The vegetation above the zone of trees consists of dwarfed and stunted heaths and willows and other plants peculiar to an arctic-alpine vegetation.

Marietta. The oldest town in Ohio, was founded, 1788, by General Rufus Putnam, acting for the Ohio Company. Located at the junction of the Ohio and Muskingum rivers, the city has enjoyed a flourishing river trade and a substantial industrial development. Its chief manufactures are furniture and metal products. It is the site of Marietta College. Population, 1970, 16,861.

Marion. A city of central Ohio, situated 44 miles north of Columbus, in a rich agricultural and limestone quarrying region. The city's extensive industries include the manufacture of power shovels, steel products, road rollers, farm implements, conveying machinery, cereal products, and electric refrigerators. Marion has many fine streets and buildings. The city was the home of President Harding. His tomb stands near the city within a circular colonnade surrounded by a beautifully landscaped tract of 100 acres. Population, 1970, 38,646.

Medford. A city of eastern Massachusetts, 5 miles northwest of Boston, of which it is a residential and manufacturing suburb. Medford was founded in 1630. It has some of the oldest examples of colonial architecture, including Wellington House, dating from 1657, and the Cradock House, built 1677–80. Medford is the seat of Tufts University, which has a campus of 80 acres. Population, 1970, 64,397.

Memphis. The chief city of Tennessee, built on the east bank of the Mississippi River, about 210 miles southwest of Nashville. The city occupies an undulating site, on Chickasaw bluff, about 450 miles by river south of Saint Louis and 740 miles by river north of New Orleans.

At Memphis, the river is spanned by three immense cantilever bridges, and railways radiate from the city in all directions. Because of its advantageous situation on the Mississippi River, in a rich agricultural and lumbering region, Memphis has become an important marketing, manufacturing, and distributing center. It is the chief center of hardwood lumber production in the United States, and is the principal inland cotton market of the South. The city's varied and extensive industries include the manufacture of cottonseed oil and cake, food preparations, lumber, cooperage, window screens, flavoring extracts, television sets, drugs, and automobile tires. The city owns its electric generating and distribution system.

Memphis is regularly laid out, with wide, well shaded streets and handsome residences, and contains many excellent public and commercial buildings. The city's park system, connected by a boulevard 11 miles long, is one of the finest in the South. This system covers a total area of 2500 acres. Important units are Riverside Park, 349 acres, and Overton Park, 357 acres, the latter containing an art gallery and a large zoological garden.

The city is the seat of Memphis State University and of the medical and law schools of the University of Tennessee. Memphis was laid out in 1818 by General Andrew Jackson and associates. It was incorporated in 1826, and, in 1849, received its charter as a city. Population, 1970, 623,497.

Meriden. A heavily industrialized city of Connecticut, 18 miles from Hartford, surrounded by a truck-farming region. It is the home of the International Silver Company, largest manufacturer of sterling and plated silverware in the world. Other manufactures include aircraft products, electronics, plastics, and printing presses. Population, 1970, 55,959.

Meridian. The second largest city of Mississippi, in the east central part of the state. It is the market center of a rich cotton, vegetable, and cattle district. The principal industries include the manufacture of cottonseed oil, cotton gins, lumber, bricks, knitted goods, and airplane tail assemblies. Population, 1970, 45,083.

Miami (*mī-ăm'ĭ*). A commercial and year-round resort city on the lower east coast of Florida on the shores of Biscayne Bay, an inlet of the Atlantic Ocean.

The second largest city in Florida, Miami is in a subtropical region of luxuriant vegetation, producing grapefruit, oranges, limes, guava, pineapples, avocados, mangoes, and coconuts. It is an important center for shipping fruit and winter vegetables to northern markets. Light industry has become increasingly important to Miami's development in recent years, with products ranging from novelties to garments, metal products, and furniture.

Miami, a terminus for two rail lines, has steamer connections with Nassau and other Caribbean ports. The Miami International Airport is said to handle more foreign cargo than any other airport in the United States. Its $26 million terminal was dedicated in 1958, and the $30 million Port of Miami, in 1967.

In adjacent Coral Gables is the University of Miami. Politically, Miami is the hub of a rapidly growing metropolitan center comprised of 27 municipalities, whose activities are co-ordinated by a central county government housed in the 27-story Dade County Court House. Population, 1970, 334,859.

MILWAUKEE. The chief city of Wisconsin. It is situated on Lake Michigan 93 miles north of Chicago. Its area is 96 square miles.

Site. Milwaukee occupies a commanding site overlooking Lake Michigan. Within the city three small rivers join before emptying into the lake—the Milwaukee from the north, the Kinnickinnic from the south, and the Menomonee from the west.

Streets and Buildings. Noteworthy streets include Lincoln Memorial Drive on the shore of Lake Michigan and Wisconsin Avenue, the leading business thoroughfare. MacArthur Square is the civic center plaza around which various public buildings are grouped.

Prominent among the city's imposing edifices is the Municipal Auditorium and Arena, comprising eight halls and covering an entire city block. Other impressive buildings include the City Hall, the Courthouse, the Federal Building, the Public Library, the Art Gallery, the Public Museum, and Northwestern Mutual Life Insurance Building.

Parks. The park system of Milwaukee covers about 1300 acres. Among its 100 units are Mitchell Park, noted for its floral displays; Washington Park, containing a fine zoological garden; and Gordon Park, with recreational facilities.

Commerce. The city's harbor is protected by a long breakwater. Its facilities are well suited to the handling of increased commerce resulting from the opening of the St. Lawrence Seaway. Shipping trade is very extensive and embraces an immense tonnage of coal, grain, and manufactured products. The transportation facilities include several railroad, steamship, bus, and airplane lines, and also a daily car ferry service which transports railroad trains to the east shore of Lake Michigan.

Industry. Milwaukee is one of the leading industrial centers of the country, ranking among the first ten cities of the United States in value of manufactures. These include hosiery, electrical control apparatus, power shovels, electric generators, automobile frames, packed meats, railway cars, engines, beer, shoes, and knit goods.

Educational Institutions. Milwaukee has many educational institutions, including Marquette University; University of Wisconsin, Milwaukee; Mount Mary College; and Cardinal Stritch College.

History. The site of Milwaukee was visited in 1673 by Fathers Marquette and Joliet. The first permanent settlement dates from 1818. The village was organized in 1837, and, in 1845, it became a city. Population 1970, 717,099.

MINNEAPOLIS. The chief city of Minnesota, built on both banks of the Mississippi River, at the Falls of Saint Anthony. Immediately below lies Saint Paul, which adjoins Minneapolis.

Site. Minneapolis attained industrial and commercial importance primarily by reason of the immense water power derived from the falls. This was first utilized principally in sawmills and flour mills. Until about 1870, lumber was the leading product, but since that date the milling of grain has become a pre-eminent industry. One of the great mills situated around the Falls of Saint Anthony is the largest single flour mill in the world. Other important manufactures are linseed oil, cereal foods, agricultural implements, machinery, knit goods, and dairy products. Over recent years, Minneapolis is being recognized as one of the leading centers of electronics equipment manufacturing.

The city is served by 29 railroads, 10 of which are trunk lines, and stands at the head of navigation on the Mississippi River. By reason of its extensive transportation facilities, Minneapolis has become the wholesale distributing center for the Northwest. It is also one of the chief wheat markets of the country.

Minneapolis is predominantly a city of homes, with wide, well shaded streets, handsome residences, charming parks, and beautiful drives. The park system, containing 153 parks, covers 5897 acres. It includes Lake Calhoun, Lake Harriet, Lake of the Isles, Lake Nokomis, Cedar Lake, and 17 smaller lakes and lagoons. By means of canals connecting several lakes, a scenic waterway 9 miles long has been made available for canoes and launches. Minnehaha Park contains the beautiful Minnehaha ("falling water") Falls, immortalized by Longfellow. Here Minnehaha Creek, the outlet of Lake Minnetonka, plunges over a 50-foot cliff just before joining the Mississippi.

Buildings. There are many notable buildings, among them the Public Library, the City Hall, the Art Institute, the Pro-cathedral, Saint Mark's Church, Hennepin Avenue Methodist Church, the Federal Reserve Bank, the 32-story Foshay Tower, the $4 million Post Office, and the Minneapolis Auditorium. Another feature of the city is the large number of handsome bridges across the Mississippi River. The city is the seat of the University of Minnesota, De La Salle Institute, Dunwoody Institute, Augsburg Seminary, the MacPhail and Minneapolis schools of music, and the Minnesota Symphony Orchestra.

History. Father Hennepin, a French missionary, discovered and named the Falls of Saint Anthony in 1680. In 1766, the site of the city was visited by Jonathan Carver, an American traveler, and, in 1805, by Lieutenant Z. M. Pike, who purchased the site of Fort Pike from the Indians. Fort Saint Anthony, later called Fort Snelling, was established in 1819. The first sawmill at the falls was erected in 1822 to provide lumber for the fort. The village of Saint Anthony, on the east side of the river, was incorporated in 1855, and Minneapolis, on the west side, in 1856. In 1872, the two places were united. Population, 1970, 434,400.

Missoula (*mĭ-zōō'lȧ*). A city of western Montana, on the Clark Fork River, about 125 miles by rail northwest of Helena. It is the distributing center for a large farming and fruit growing, lumbering, and mining region, and is the seat of the University of Montana. The National Bison range and the extensive Flathead Indian reservation lie to the north of the city. Population, 1970, 29,497.

Mitchell, Mount. The highest point in the state of North Carolina, and the loftiest summit of the eastern United States. It is a massive, dome-shaped mountain, sometimes called Black Dome, rising to an elevation of 6684 feet, with many high cliffs and precipitous slopes. It is named for Elisha Mitchell, a distinguished scientist who lost his life while attempting, in 1857, to scale the mountain. A large tract of land, including the summit and surrounding spruce forests, has been created a state park, which provides accommodations for travelers.

Mobile. The second largest city and only seaport in Alabama, located on Mobile Bay, 26 miles north of the Gulf of Mexico. It is a leading cotton market and has varied industries, among them shipbuilding, cotton, lumber, and paper mills, chemical and steel factories, oil refineries, and seafood canneries. The harbor has been elaborately improved, and the bay is spanned by the Cochrane bridge. The Bankhead tunnel beneath the Mobile River accommodates vehicular traffic. The chief exports include logs, hewn timber, pine lumber, rosin, cotton, paper, metals, machinery, and coal; the leading

FAMOUS STREETS

Below Looking south on Biscayne Boulevard from N. E. 5th Street in Miami, Florida. Modern Hotel Biscayne and Hotel Everglades at the center. Stately palm trees run nearly the entire length of this famous Florida thoroughfare.

Above The well-known Hollywood Boulevard in Los Angeles, California. Grauman's Chinese Theatre at the left where the footprints of numerous Hollywood picture stars are seen in the cement sidewalk. At the far end of the Boulevard are the large radio and television studios.

Left The crossroads of the world, Times Square, New York. Famous Broadway on the right and, at the left, Seventh Avenue. Hotel Astor marquee on the left, and in the center are the recruiting stations for the Armed Forces.

Below The upper end of the Michigan Avenue Bridge is known as Chicago's Magnificent Mile. At the left is the Wrigley Building. On the right the Tribune and behind it the Sheraton Hotel. The Palmolive Building is in the distance on the right and beyond that the famous swank Gold Coast apartments.

Above Canal Street in New Orleans, America's widest business street, measures 171 feet. It includes two 21-foot sidewalks and 58-foot neutral ground in the center on which there are four street car tracks. Canal Street was named from a projected waterway, which was intended to join the Mississippi River and Lake Pontchartrain.

HISTORIC AMERICA

Mount Vernon, on the Potomac River in Virginia, was George Washington's home from 1752 to 1799. In 1859, on the death of John A. Washington, it was purchased by the Mount Vernon Ladies Association of the Union for preservation in the public interest. The buildings and much of their original furniture have been faithfully restored.

Utah was settled by the Mormons in 1847 and became a state in 1896. It contains many points of historic interest. Pictured is the Mormon Temple in Salt Lake City. The Tabernacle, on the same grounds, seats 8,000 people.

Rosemont, the boyhood home of Jefferson Davis, is about one mile east of Woodville, Mississippi. Many of the Davis family are buried here. The beauty of the home has been preserved by its owner, Mrs. Henry Johnson.

Within this white concrete Visitor Center on the Civil War battleground of Gettysburg is a cyclorama of Pickett's charge, a realistic painting covering the wall of a circular hall. The painting, finished in Paris in 1884, is 356 feet long and 26 feet high. Near Gettysburg, Pa., the battlefield itself is well marked. *NPS Photo*

The Old North Church, in Boston, Mass., is historically connected with Paul Revere's famous ride. The colonial steeple was blown down during a hurricane in 1954, but has since been restored.

imports are bananas, ores, sugar, and chemicals. There is also an extensive local trade in vegetables, fish, and oysters.

The city has broad, regular streets, shaded with live oaks and magnolias and lined with beautiful residences. Important structures are the Mobile County Court House and the Ladd Memorial Stadium. Mobile was founded in 1702 by the French. Later, it was in the possession of the English, the Spanish, and again of the French. It became a part of the United States by the Louisiana Purchase in 1803. Population, 1970, 190,026.

Modesto. A processing, shipping, and marketing center for a rich agricultural region, located 93 miles southeast of San Francisco. Nearby Don Pedro Dam provides the irrigation power that waters the area, which abundantly produces peaches, melons, and other fruits and vegetables. Modesto is a gateway to Yosemite National Park. Population, 1970, 61,712.

Mojave (*mô-hä'vä*) **Desert.** A desert of southeastern California, situated chiefly within the boundaries of San Bernardino county and embracing an area of about 15,000 square miles. It lies south and east of the Tehachapi mountains and north of the Sierra Madre and the San Bernardino mountains. These high ranges intercept the moisture-laden winds from the Pacific, and, in consequence, the Mojave is an exceedingly arid region. The average annual rainfall is only 5 or 6 inches, and the temperature in summer sometimes reaches 120°.

The surface is that of a more or less elevated plateau, broken by numerous small mountains, with intervening valleys and plains. From an elevation of about 4000 feet on the west, this plateau slopes down to 1500 feet elevation or less toward its eastern border. Much of the southwestern portion drains into the Mojave River, which, after flowing in a definite channel for some 50 miles, entirely disappears in valley sands to the eastward.

For the most part, the Mojave Desert presents an aspect of extreme barrenness and desolation. The smaller mountains are mostly jagged masses of naked rock. Many plains are interspersed with saline sinks and dried-up lakes. Some of the valleys are covered with dark-colored sheets of anciently erupted lavas. These volcanic areas also contain numerous cinder cones and small craters.

There are valuable mineral deposits, and, where water for irrigation is available, a few small areas yield good crops. The Santa Fe and the Salt Lake railway cross this desert, as do several well constructed automobile highways. See *Colorado Desert.*

Moline. A city of western Illinois, situated at the junction of the Rock and Mississippi rivers, about 180 miles southwest of Chicago. The city of Rock Island adjoins Moline on the west, and across the Mississippi River from Rock Island is Davenport, Iowa. Moline has one of the largest steel plow plants in the country. Manufacture of agricultural implements is Moline's chief industry. A feature of interest in the vicinity is the United States arsenal on Rock Island. Between this island and Moline is a large roller dam for flood control. Nearby are the Quad-City Airport and the Black Hawk State Park. Population, 1970, 46,237.

Monadnock, Mount. A noted mountain of southwestern New Hampshire, situated about 10 miles southeast of Keene. It is a bold granitic peak with precipitous walls and extremely rugged contour, rising to an elevation of 3186 feet. Because of its isolated position and unusual form, it is one of the most impressive mountains in New England.

Monroe. Originally called Fort Miro, and later renamed for President Monroe, Monroe is situated in northeastern Louisiana, midway between Memphis and New Orleans. It is styled the "Crossroads of Pipelines," being the point where more major pipelines converge than at any other spot in the U.S. Monroe produces chemicals, paper, furniture, and strawberries. It is the seat of Northeastern Louisiana State University. Population, 1970, 56,374.

Monterey (*mŏn'tĕ-rā'*). Second-oldest city in the state, Monterey is a famous tourist attraction situated on the bay side of a peninsula on the California coast, 125 miles south of San Francisco. Fringing the Bay of Monterey is a landscape of great scenic beauty. Among many notable buildings visited by tourists are the old Custom House, built in the Mexican period, the Royal Presidio Chapel, and the home of Robert Louis Stevenson. Nearby are the artist colony of Carmel-by-the-Sea and a grove of ancient cypress trees not known to occur native anywhere else in the world and confined to a small area on Cypress Point. The chief industries are fishing and sardine packing.

Six miles from the city, in 1770, Father Junipero Serra, Spanish missionary to the Indians, established the mission of San Carlos Borromeo. After more than 75 years of Spanish and Mexican occupation, the American flag was run up at Monterey in 1846 and, in 1847, it became the capital of the military government of California. Population, 1970, 26,302.

Montgomery. The capital of Alabama, located on the Alabama River slightly southeast of the center of the state, is the hub of a highly productive grain, fruit, vegetable, cotton, and livestock region, for which it is the central market. A balanced industrial growth has resulted from the combination of favorable climate, excellent water supply, abundant electric power, and an ample labor force. Industries include cotton mills, car shops, foundries, fertilizer plants, machine works, and plywood fabricators.

Montgomery was founded in 1817 and became the state capital in 1846. The Confederate government was organized here in 1861, and this city was the seat of government until the capital was moved to Richmond, Virginia. Historic landmarks are numerous, including spacious antebellum homes and churches and the Confederate White House, occupied by Jefferson Davis, which is now a museum. Montgomery's educational institutions include Huntingdon College and Alabama State University. Population, 1970, 133,386.

Monticello. The residence and estate of Thomas Jefferson, situated in Albemarle County, Virginia, about 3 miles east of Charlottesville. Standing on the summit of a hill (whence the name Monticello, "little mountain"), it commands an extensive view of the surrounding country and has long been regarded as one of the most elegant and picturesque residences in the South. It was constructed from designs made by Jefferson himself, was first occupied in 1770, and remained his home for 56 years. In 1926, it was purchased by patriotic admirers of Jefferson for $500,000 and presented to the nation.

Montpelier (*mŏnt-pēl'yĕr*). The capital of Vermont, located in the north central part of the state. It is the center of an agricultural district and there are many valuable granite quarries in the vicinity. The finest building is the capitol, a granite structure surmounted by a handsome dome. Among its notable institutions are the State Library and the Wood Art Gallery. The town was first settled in 1787, and, in 1805, was selected as the capital of the state. It was made a city in 1895. Population, 1970, 8609.

Moundsville. A city of West Virginia, on the Ohio River 12 miles south of Wheeling. It is in the center of an important agricultural, coal mining, and oil producing district and has varied local industries, including the manufacture of glass. Moundsville is noted for a huge, prehistoric mound, a famous relic of the Mound Builders, after which the city is named. Population, 1970, 13,560.

Mount Clemens. A city and health resort on the Clinton River, about 20 miles northeast of Detroit, Michigan. It has numerous medicinal springs, which attract thousands of persons suffering from chronic ailments, especially rheumatism. Its commercial interests include the growing of roses and the manufacture of tools and dies, metal products, paint, and pottery. Population, 1970, 20,476.

Mount Rubidoux. A bold rocky summit rising abruptly from the Santa Ana valley at Riverside, California. At its crest is a cross dedicated to the memory of Father Junipero Serra, the heroic Franciscan missionary to the Indians. An impressive sunrise service is held on its summit each Easter Sunday.

Mount Tom. A small mountain in Massachusetts which rises precipitously in the Connecticut Valley, opposite Mount Holyoke and about 4 miles south of Northampton. The summit, 1200 feet high, is reached by highway and an incline railroad and affords exceptionally fine views of the surrounding region. A tract of 1700 acres on the mountain has been created a state park.

Mount Vernon. A residential city bordering on the Bronx River and adjoining the northeast section of New York City. Mount Vernon occupies an attractive site, and has wide, well shaded streets and handsome lawns and gardens. While a large portion of the city is restricted to residential purposes, there are several important industrial establishments and a considerable local trade. St. Paul's, the oldest Episcopal Church in America, established in 1665, is located here. Population, 1970, 72,778.

Mount Vernon. The home and burial place of George Washington, situated on the right bank of the Potomac River, in Fairfax county, Virginia, 15 miles south of the National capital. Located on an eminence 200 feet high, the mansion house commands a beautiful view of the river. It is constructed of wood, 2 stories high, 96 feet long, and 30 feet deep, with a high piazza along the front, and is painted white to resemble stone. The main part was built in 1743 by Lawrence Washington, Washington's elder brother, who named it in honor of Admiral Vernon of the British navy. In 1754, soon after the death of his brother Lawrence, the estate came into the hands of George Washington, who added the wings to the house.

In 1858, a tract of 200 acres of the original estate, including the mansion and the brick tomb containing the remains of George and Martha Washington, came into the possession of an association of Southern women which holds it in trust as a shrine of national interest. The six rooms on the ground floor contain many objects of historic value, including the key to the French Bastille, and various pieces of furniture used by the family.

Muncie. A city of eastern Indiana, trading center of an agricultural region, with meat packing and dairying plants. Its manufactures include foundry and machine-shop products, glass, auto parts, and electrical equipment. It is the seat of Ball State University. Population 1970, 69,080.

Muscle Shoals. A series of shallow rapids in the Tennessee River where the stream has a fall of about 134 feet within 37 miles, forming the one interruption to navigation of the river within Alabama.

A canal around the rapids was opened in 1890. In 1918, further development was undertaken by the Federal government for the purpose of improving navigation, generating electric power, and manufacturing a part of the nitrates needed for explosives during World War I. In 1925, Wilson Dam, one of the largest in volume in the world, was completed. Except for sale of current from this dam, the costly property remained idle until 1933. By that time the process for which the nitrate factories had been equipped had become obsolete.

The Tennessee Valley Authority was established in 1933 to take over the properties and to use them in a demonstration of regional planning for the Tennessee River watershed. Other dams were built, making possible a regulated flow the year round, and the nitrate factories were adapted to development of phosphate fertilizers of a superior type. The former home of Helen Keller is in nearby Tuscumbia.

Muskogee (*mŭs-kō'gê*). A city of eastern Oklahoma, situated in the valley of the Arkansas River, about 130 miles east of Oklahoma City. Muskogee is the trade center of a rich agricultural region devoted to the production of cotton, wheat, fruits, and vegetables, and to cattle raising. It has, in addition, large supplies of petroleum and natural gas. Its manufactured products include cottonseed oil, oil well supplies, and refined petroleum. There are several educational institutions. Population, 1970, 37,331.

Nashville. The capital of Tennessee, built on both banks of the Cumberland River, in the north central part of the state. Nashville is situated in a productive agricultural region, near extensive coal fields. These advantages have contributed to make it an important commercial and manufacturing city. It carries on an extensive wholesaling trade. Its leading industries include printing and publishing, meat packing, and the manufacture of glass, aero structures, shoes and boots, food products, clothing, stoves, and furniture. The city is well known for its recording studios (ranking second in the U.S. as a recording center).

Nashville occupies a hilly site, with eminences commanding fine views. On the most lofty hill, stands, like the Acropolis at Athens, the imposing State Capitol. The city has 42 parks and playgrounds covering 5500 acres. They include Centennial Park, where there is an exact replica of the Parthenon in Athens, Greece.

The city is one of the most important educational centers in the South. It is the seat of Vanderbilt University, Belmont College, Peabody College for Teachers, Fisk University, Meharry Medical School, and other public and private institutions.

The first settlement on the site of Nashville was made in 1780, and, in 1806, the city received its municipal charter. From 1812 to 1815 it was the seat of the state legislature. In 1843, it was made the permanent capital of the state. In the park surrounding the State Capitol is the tomb of James K. Polk. The Hermitage, the former home of Andrew Jackson, is about 10 miles east of the city. In 1864, one of the great battles of the Civil War was fought in the environs of Nashville. Population, 1970, 436,044.

Natural Bridge. A bridge of natural rock spanning Cedar Creek 13 miles southeast of Lexington, Va. It is 90 feet long, 50 to 150 feet wide, and about 215 feet above the creek bed. It consists of horizontal limestone strata, which are the remains of the roof of an underground tunnel or a cave through which the creek once flowed. The bridge is crossed by a public road.

Newark (*nū'ĕrk*). A city of New Jersey, situated on the Passaic River and Newark Bay, about 8 miles west of New York City, with which it is connected by several railways, an electric high speed line, and the Holland and Lincoln vehicular tunnels.

The city extends some 3 miles along the west shore of Newark Bay and about 7 miles up the west bank of the Passaic River, from its mouth in Newark Bay to the suburb of Belleville. The site of the city occupies an area of about 24 square miles. For a mile inland from the water front, the surface is fairly level and it then rises gently in a series of plateaus.

Immediately adjoining the city on the north, west, and southwest is a group of smaller municipalities, including Belleville, Bloomfield, East Orange, Orange, West Orange, South Orange, and Irvington. Opposite Newark, on the east bank of the Passaic, are East Newark, Harrison, and Kearny. These and other suburbs are intimately connected with the city and, with it, form a greater Newark whose total population exceeds 1,000,000.

The port of Newark is a deep water harbor 700 feet wide, extending 7000 feet inland. Because of favorable location and fine transportation facilities, including a subway, Newark has become a great manufacturing center, sometimes styled the "Birmingham of America." Its industries are numerous and varied. Among important products are jewelry, electrical machinery, chemicals, paints, varnishes, malt liquors, ships, and meat products. The city is the headquarters of some of the largest life insurance and fire insurance companies.

Newark is a city of fine buildings, wide streets, and spacious parks. Military Park contains Borglum's colossal sculptural group in bronze known as "The Wars of America." Among Newark's most noted buildings are the Public Library, the County Courthouse, City Hall, Federal Building, Newark College of Rutgers University, and the Roman Catholic Sacred Heart Cathedral. Newark was settled in 1666 by Puritans from Connecticut. It was first called Milford but was soon after given its present name. In 1836, it was chartered as a city. Population, 1970, 382,417.

New Bedford. A seaport and manufacturing city of Massachusetts, situated on the Acushnet River, at its mouth in Buzzards Bay, about 55 miles south of Boston. New Bedford was formerly the principal whaling port in the world. This stage of its history is memorialized by the Bourne Whaling Museum and by a rich collection of whaling material in the public library, one of the first free libraries established in the country. After the decline of the whaling industry, it became the leading city in the United States in the manufacture of cotton yarn and cotton cloth. Less important industries include the manufacture of silk goods, fine tools, sperm and whale oil, rayon, shoes, rope cordage, toys, and rubber and paper goods. Educational institutions include Southeastern Massachusetts University and the Swain School of Design. New Bedford was settled in 1652, on land purchased from Massasoit by a company from Plymouth. Population, 1970, 101,777.

New Britain. A manufacturing city of Connecticut, situated in the central part of the state, about 10 miles southwest of Hartford. Because of its extensive production of cutlery, edged tools, and other kinds of hardware, New Britain is sometimes styled the "Hardware City." Other important manufactures include electrical appliances, knit goods, and machine shop products. The city is the seat of Central Connecticut State College and has a unique World War Memorial. New Britain was settled in 1687 but remained a part of Berlin until 1850, when it was incorporated as a town. In 1871, New Britain received its charter as a city. Population, 1970, 83,441.

New Castle. A manufacturing city of western Pennsylvania, built at the junction of the Shenango and the Neshannock rivers, about 50 miles northeast of Pittsburgh. The city's industrial products include chinaware, bronze bearings, strip steel, tin plate, and clothing. New Castle is situated in a fertile agricultural district, rich in coal, limestone, and other mineral deposits. Population, 1970, 38,559.

New Haven. A city of Connecticut, on an inlet of Long Island Sound, some 70 miles northeast of New York City. It occupies a level site partly enclosed by a range of precipitous hills, from 300 to 400 feet high. While a commercial city with extensive shipping interests, the leading industry is manufacturing. In its exceedingly varied industries, there are more than 600 separate manufacturing establishments. Among important manufactures are firearms, clocks, rubber goods, electrical machinery, and an immense variety of iron and steel goods.

The city is well laid out with many imposing public buildings, beautiful parks, and broad, shaded streets. Because of the great number of elms formerly planted in the older sections, New Haven has been called the "City of Elms." It is the seat of Yale University, founded at Saybrook in 1701 and removed to New Haven in 1716. The Harkness Memorial Tower at Yale is one of the finest Gothic towers erected in modern times. The Yale Bowl seats 70,896 people. The first settlement, made by a company of Puritans in 1638, was known as Quinnipiac, but in 1640 it was renamed New Haven. The city is the burial place of S. F. B. Morse, Eli Whitney, Noah Webster, and other noted men. Population, 1970, 137,707.

NEW ORLEANS (*ôr'lē-ănz*). The chief city of Louisiana, the commercial metropolis of the Gulf states, and, after New York City, one of the greatest centers of domestic and foreign trade in the United States. It is situated on the Mississippi River 107 miles above its mouth in the Gulf of Mexico.

The city originally was built along the bend of the river in a semicircular curve and became known as the "Crescent City"; later, its growth up the river followed a backward curve toward Lake Borgne and Lake Pontchartrain, which is spanned by two concrete highway bridges, each about 5 miles in length. Lake Pontchartrain is also spanned by a 24-mile causeway, the world's longest overwater highway bridge.

New Orleans is connected with nearly all the important ports of the world by direct steamship lines, the markets of Asia and western South America being accessible through the Panama Canal. The city forms the gateway to the Mississippi Valley, the greatest agricultural region in the world. It has one of the safest harbors in existence, with a deep water canal from the river through the city to Lake Pontchartrain. More than 100 steamers from 400 to 500 feet in length can be berthed along seven miles of steel docks. Besides public wharves, grain elevators, and coal tipples, the port facilities include also a municipally owned and operated belt line railway.

New Orleans is a leading market for cotton, sugar, molasses, coffee, rice, burlaps, cigars, nitrate, sulphur, timber, and cereals, these products being among its principal exports. It is, moreover, one of the principal manufacturing cities in the South. It makes over three-fourths of the men's wash clothing worn in the United States.

The park system of New Orleans includes the 280-acre Audubon Park, City Park, covering 1500 acres, and a 1400-acre "made" area of boulevards, parks, and bathing beaches on the southeast shore of Lake Pontchartrain. The parks are ornamented with palms, live oaks, magnolias, and a profusion of subtropical shrubs and flowers. The newer residential districts have broad streets, spacious grounds, handsome gardens, and pretentious houses. The old French quarter is a city by itself, with narrow streets lined with rows of quaint old dwellings, built over a hundred years ago in the style of the houses of southern Europe. The Mardi Gras carnival, held yearly, is another heritage of the Latin Old World. New Orleans is often styled the "birthplace of jazz."

Among the buildings of historic interest are the Cabildo, the old archbishop's palace, and the Saint Louis Cathedral, one of the best-known churches in the United States. The principal educational institutions are Tulane and Loyola universities and Newcomb Memorial College for Women.

History. New Orleans was founded by the French in 1718, and came into the possession of the United States with the Louisiana Purchase of 1803, of which territory it was the capital. It remained the capital of the state of Louisiana until 1849. Population, 1970, 591,502.

Newport. A city and seaside resort of Rhode Island. It has a fine harbor which serves as a naval base for the United States Atlantic fleet. Its palatial private residences, public buildings, parks, fountains, and old-time historic structures render it one of the most attractive cities in the country. In Touro Park is the old Stone Mill, or "Round Tower," mentioned by Longfellow in his "Skeleton in Armor." Other features of interest include a Jewish Synagogue dating from 1763. There are various local industries, including manufactures of furniture and brass goods, and extensive fisheries. Population, 1970, 34,562.

Newport News. A city in Virginia, situated on the north side of Hampton Roads near the mouth of the James River, about 12 miles northwest of Norfolk. Newport News is one of the leading ports of the Southern states and an important coaling station. It has enormous shipbuilding yards, drydocks, and ironworks, and is the center of much agricultural and fishing trade. Points of interest include Fort Monroe, Langley Air Field, one of the greatest in the United States, and the Huntington Mariners Museum. Hampton Roads off Newport News was the scene of the battle between the *Monitor* and the *Merrimac* in 1862. Population, 1970, 138,177.

New Rochelle. A city of southern New York on Long Island Sound 16 miles northeast of Grand Central Station in New York City, of which it is a residential suburb. The city consists characteristically of modern residential districts of beautiful parklike contour. Besides several parks and bathing beaches, the city contains 153 "parklets," or open spaces. New Rochelle is named for the French city of La Rochelle, the home of Huguenots who settled on the site in 1688. Iona College is in New Rochelle. Population, 1970, 75,385.

Newton (*nū'tŭn*). A city of eastern Massachusetts, built on the Charles River, 8 miles west of Boston. Newton is chiefly a residential city but maintains substantial industries. The city is admirably laid out, with fine streets, parks, and drives, and contains many beautiful homes. Among the city's manufacturing establishments are silk mills, printing works, worsted mills, curtain factories, and rubber works. The city is the seat of Boston College, Newton Theological Seminary, and other educational institutions. Newton was settled in 1630 as a part of Cambridge. In 1688, it was made a separate town, called New Cambridge, but, in 1692, it received its present name. In 1873, Newton became a city. Population, 1970, 91,066.

NEW YORK. The chief city of the state of New York, the commercial metropolis of the United States, and the most populous city in the western hemisphere. It is situated on New York Bay at the mouth of the Hudson River, about 205 miles in direct line northeast of the National capital at Washington.

Site. No metropolis in the world is more strikingly or more beautifully situated than is the city of New York. It is built on three islands, Manhattan, Staten, and Long Island, with a portion on the adjacent mainland, the Bronx.

The Hudson River, here nearly a mile wide, sweeps majestically down the western side of Manhattan and pours its vast waters into the landlocked harbor of New York Bay at the south end of the island. The bay is connected with the ocean by a mile-wide channel running between Long Island on the east and Staten on the west. Between the Bronx and Manhattan is the Harlem River which is connected with the Hudson by Spuyten Duyvil Creek. Separating Manhattan and the Bronx from Long Island is East River, properly an arm of Long Island Sound.

On the west bank of the Hudson, opposite the upper part of the city, the picturesque Palisades tower to a height of from 300 to 400 feet. The surface of the various divisions of the city is fairly level but rises in some parts, as in upper Manhattan, to commanding elevations affording magnificent views of the city and the harbor.

Main Divisions. Originally, the city was confined to Manhattan Island. This is 13½ miles long, with a maximum width of 2¼ miles and an area of about 22 square miles. In addition to Manhattan, Greater New York, by consolidation, has since come to embrace Staten Island, called Richmond, with an area of about 60 square miles; the western end of Long Island, known as Brooklyn, 80 square miles; an adjoining part of Long Island, known as Queens, 120 square miles; and the portion of the mainland known as the Bronx, 40 square miles. Each of these divisions includes several small adjacent islands. Officially, New York consists of five boroughs, Manhattan, Brooklyn, Queens, Richmond, and the Bronx, and contains a total area of some 325 square miles.

Manhattan is the heart of New York and contains its great commercial, financial, and mercantile institutions, and also its famous museums, libraries, cathedrals, railway stations, and imposing residences. Brooklyn is a residential district with a large number of industrial establishments. Staten Island is mainly residential, with an increasing number of industries; the Bronx is also chiefly residential, while Queens, containing more than a third of the total area of Greater New York, is the "home" borough. Long Island City, in Queens borough, is its industrial center, while the remainder of the borough is principally a district of suburban homes.

Streets and Avenues. In the older portions of various divisions of the city there are narrow, short, irregular streets. The newer sections, however, have been admirably planned, and contain many magnificent thoroughfares.

At the south end of Manhattan, the streets are cramped and irregular, but, north of Washington Square, they cross at right angles. The great, long north-and-south streets, usually 100 feet wide, running lengthwise of the island, are called avenues. The shorter east-and-west thoroughfares, mostly 60 feet wide, are called streets. Differing from the plan of most American cities, the blocks are solid, having practically no alleys.

An exception to this regular street plan is Broadway, the "greatest street in the world." This noted thoroughfare runs diagonally through the city, in a northwesterly direction, from the Battery, at the sea front, to the extreme northern boundary, a distance of about 16 miles. It traverses the entire length of Manhattan Island and continues through the Bronx into Yonkers, completely changing its character in the different portions of the city through which it passes.

Equally famous with Broadway is Fifth Avenue, the most beautiful thoroughfare in the city, and one of the finest streets in the world. It begins at Washington Arch, about a quarter of a mile west of Broadway, and extends northward for 6 miles, crossing to the east of Broadway at 23d street. It is lined with fashionable shops, beautiful churches, elegant clubs, immense hotels, and palatial residences. Above 59th street, it is restricted to residences by a zoning ordinance.

Other beautiful streets are Morningside Drive, which passes Saint John's Cathedral; and Riverside Drive along the Hudson, passing Grant's Tomb and commanding excellent views of the Palisades. A considerable portion of this drive accommodates two levels of traffic.

Beginning at Trinity Church on Broadway and extending eastward to East River is Wall Street, long the money center of America and, since World War I, the chief financial center of the world. In Brooklyn, Ocean Parkway and Flatbush Avenue are magnificent drives; Northern Boulevard, Queens Boulevard, and Hillside Avenue, in Queens, are noteworthy thoroughfares.

Parks. Lying in the center of Manhattan Island is Central Park, one of the most beautiful pleasure grounds in the world. On its eastern border is the magnificent Metropolitan Museum of Art, and on the west side is the great American Museum of Natural History. This park embraces 840 acres, is largely forested, and contains a reservoir, small lakes, and scores of miles of charming drives, roadways, and footpaths. In it are located the Obelisk, or Cleopatra's Needle, and many fine works of sculpture.

Other important parks are Prospect Park, Brooklyn, with an area of 526 acres, noted for the natural beauty of its wooded hills and broad meadows; Bronx Park, 719 acres, containing superb zoological and botanical gardens; Van Cortlandt Park, embracing 1132 acres and containing immense recreation grounds; Pelham Bay Park, containing 1788 acres, with a shoreline of 9 miles; and Marine Park, covering 1522 acres.

Monuments. In New York are many of the most noted monuments, memorials, and other fine sculptural works of America. The famous Statue of Liberty, designed by Bartholdi and presented to the American people by the French nation, stands on Bedloe's or Liberty Island in New York Bay. Grant's Tomb, a mausoleum of great dignity, overlooks the Hudson from Riverside Park, as does the beautiful Soldiers' and Sailors' Monument from Riverside drive. At the entrance to Prospect Park, Brooklyn, there is an imposing memorial arch, surmounted by a large quadriga by Macmonnies, erected in honor of the soldiers and sailors of the Civil War.

On the Plaza, at the southeast corner of Central Park, stands an impressive equestrian statue of General Sherman by Saint-Gaudens. By the same noted sculptor is the fine statue of Peter Cooper, at Cooper Union, and the noble monument to David Farragut, in Madison Square.

Buildings. New York excels all other cities in the size, height, elegance, and costliness of its buildings. These include immense commercial structures, towering temples of finance, imposing public edifices, monumental railway stations, beautiful cathedrals and churches, magnificent apartment houses, and palatial residences. There is a greater number of large and costly buildings on Manhattan Island than upon any other equal area on the globe. For miles, the buildings contain from 12 to 30 or more stories, rising from 200 to 500 feet in height, with some towering higher than the pyramids or the loftiest cathedrals.

Among the large number of great commercial structures may be mentioned the Metropolitan Building, 50 stories and 700 feet high; the Woolworth Building, 55 stories, more than 792 feet high; R. C. A. Building at Rockefeller Center, the largest office building in the world, 69 stories, 853 feet high; Bank of the Manhattan Building, 70 stories, 927 feet high; Sixty Wall Tower (Cities Service Building), 67 stories, 950 feet high; the Chrysler Building, 77 stories, 1046 feet high; and the Empire State Building, 102 stories, 1248 feet high.

Prominent among public edifices is the Municipal Building 41 stories high, covering two city blocks and surmounted by a tower and statue which rise to a height of 580 feet. Among structures noted for their architecture are the marble Stock Exchange, the New York Clearing House, the Chamber of Commerce, the Hall of Records, the Tiffany building, the United Nations Secretariat Building, and the New York Public Library.

The Grand Central Station and the Pennsylvania Station were each great achievements of architectural and engineering skill. Other notable buildings include the Metropolitan Museum of Art, the American Museum of Natural History, the Columbia University Library, and the Eighth Regiment Armory. A unique architectural unit is Rockefeller Center, or "Radio City," covering three city blocks. Its ten building units, ornamented with hanging gardens and artificial waterfalls, house elaborate broadcasting and theatrical facilities and magnificent stores and offices.

Among hundreds of beautiful churches may be mentioned Saint Patrick's Cathedral built of white marble with spires rising 332 feet. This ranks among the finest Gothic structures in America. Other noteworthy churches are the cathedral of Saint John the Divine, Saint Thomas's Church, Saint Bartholomew's Church, the Temple Emanu-El, the great church of Saint Paul the Apostle, and the Riverside Church, containing one of the finest carillons of bells in the western hemisphere.

Intercommunication. East River is spanned by 6 bridges, ranking among the largest in the world. Four of these—Brooklyn Bridge, Manhattan Bridge, Williamsburgh Bridge (connecting New York and Brooklyn), and the Triborough Bridge, joining Queens with the Bronx—are suspension bridges. The Queensboro Bridge, connecting New York and Queens, is a cantilever structure. Hell Gate Bridge, an immense steel arch, connects the Bronx with Queens. Staten Island is connected with New Jersey by three bridges, Kill van Kull at Bayonne, Goethals at Elizabeth, and Outerbridge Crossing at Perth Amboy. Washington Memorial Bridge crosses the Hudson and connects 178th Street with the New Jersey shore. The Verrazano-Narrows Bridge stretches across the entrance to New York's harbor from Staten Island to Brooklyn. The world's longest single-span bridge, it was opened in 1964.

An extensive ferry service and two pairs of subway tunnels for electric cars connect Manhattan with Brooklyn, as does also the Brooklyn-Battery vehicular tunnel, and two pairs also connect Manhattan with Queens. The Holland and Lincoln vehicular tunnels, under the Hudson River, connect New York City with Jersey City, and a 3½-mile viaduct connects it with Elizabeth, New Jersey.

Most of New York's local transportation system is municipally owned. The city operates 250 route miles of rapid transit subway lines and 80 miles of bus routes. Running north and south in the narrow island of Manhattan, there are two 4-track subway lines, both of which continue under the East River to Brooklyn where they connect with steam and electric rapid transit to all parts of Long Island. The Long Island railroad transports more commuting passengers than any other railroad in the world.

Educational Institutions. New York is the seat of two great universities, Columbia University, on Cathedral Heights, and New York University in the Bronx, overlooking the Harlem River. With the former is affiliated Barnard College, the Teachers' College, and the Horace Mann School. Connected with New York University is the Hall of Fame for noted Americans.

Among many other prominent educational institutions are the College of the City of New York, Hunter College, Manhattan College, Brooklyn College, Fordham University, the College of Saint Francis Xavier, Cooper Union, the College of Physicians and Surgeons, and the Rockefeller Institute for Medical Research. Of great influence in the educational life of the city are the Public Library, with more than 40 branches, the Metropolitan Museum of Art, the Guggenheim Museum, the American Museum of Natural History, the Planetarium and the Brooklyn Institute of Arts and Sciences. The Medical Center on Washington Heights, overlooking the Hudson River, takes the first place among institutions of the kind throughout the world.

Transportation. New York Bay, nearly enclosed by islands, forms one of the finest harbors in the world. The city of New York, built around it, has a total water front of some 771 miles, of which more than 345 miles are developed with port facilities. About 100 ocean steamship lines, affording service to all parts of the world, have headquarters in New York. Some 40 lines of river and coastwise steamers likewise operate from the port. New York has water connections to the Great Lakes through the Hudson River and the State Barge Canal. The great railway systems of the New England and the Middle Atlantic states, and also various western railroads, have terminals, either within the city or across the Hudson on the New Jersey shore. The Pennsylvania Railway is connected with New York City by tunnels under the Hudson River.

Commerce. New York's commercial supremacy is owing to its magnificent harbor facilities and to its geographical location. The largest ships are accommodated at its wharves, and railway and inland water routes afford quick collection and distribution of goods throughout the richest and most populous region in America. The commerce of New York is several times greater than that of any other port in the New World, and, in value, usually embraces about one-half the total imports and exports of the United States. The volume of the coastwise trade usually greatly exceeds that of the foreign trade. The wholesale and jobbing trade is enormous, as is also the distribution of the city's immense manufactures. In 1936, a zone in Staten Island was made a free port.

Finance. During the present century, New York has become the dominant money center of the world, with annual banking transactions aggregating more than $300 billion. Here are located the greatest financial institutions of the country, including powerful banks, trust companies, and insurance companies, the New York clearing house, the stock exchange, the cotton exchange, and casualty, credit, fidelity, and surety companies.

Manufactures. In value, the manufactures of the metropolis exceed those of any other manufacturing center in America. Usually about one-tenth of the total manufactures of the United States is produced in New York City. This supremacy is owing to an immense volume of light manufacturing, for the most part carried on in small factories. The industries are exceedingly diversified, including some 30,000 establishments and representing about 90 per cent of all the industries listed in the country. The largest single product is clothing; more than half of the clothing worn in the United States is made in the city. The second largest industry is the printing and publishing of newspapers, magazines, periodicals, and books. Other important industries are meat packing, sugar refining, petroleum refining, and the manufacture of millinery, lace, fur goods, jewelry, tobacco, drugs, shoes, and machinery.

HISTORY. In 1609, Henry Hudson, employed by the Dutch, sailed up the river which bears his name. Dutch fur traders began operations along the Hudson in 1613 and soon after built a fort, near which the first white settlement developed. The first permanent colonists, mostly Walloons, arrived in 1624. Peter Minuit, in 1626, bought Manhattan Island from its Indian owners for $24, and named the settlement New Amsterdam. There were difficulties with the Indians, but, under the rule of Peter Stuyvesant, 1647-64, the settlement grew to a village of 1000 inhabitants.

In 1664, New Amsterdam was captured by the English, who renamed it New York. Despite political conflicts, the town in 1700 had increased to 5000 inhabitants, about half Dutch and half English. During the Revolutionary War, British armies occupied the town for 7 years, 1776–83. In this unfortunate period, New York lost about half its inhabitants and was largely destroyed by fire. Within 8 years, however, the population trebled, commerce revived, and for a year and a half, 1789–90, New York was the capital of the Federal government. Washington, the first president of the United States, was inaugurated, April 30, 1789, in Federal Hall on Wall Street.

The completion of the Erie Canal in 1825, furnishing a waterway from the Hudson to the Great Lakes, made New York the gateway for the commerce of the rapidly developing nation. This so accelerated the city's growth that, in 1835, New York numbered 200,000 inhabitants. The first railway to the Great Lakes was completed in 1851, and thenceforward the history of New York is a record of continuous and monumental growth.

More recent achievements were the consolidation of the five boroughs into Greater New York, the construction of the subway system with tunnels under East River and the Hudson, and the completion of the gigantic Catskill aqueduct, insuring an adequate water supply to the expanding metropolis. Population, 1970, 7,867,760.

Niagara Falls. The grandest cataract in America and the second largest in the world, being exceeded in combined height and volume only by Victoria Falls in South Africa. It is situated about 22 miles north of Buffalo, New York. The Niagara River in its northerly course of over 26 miles descends 326 feet from the level of Lake Erie to that of Lake Ontario. By far the greater part of this descent occurs at the falls and at the rapids immediately above and below them. For the first 2 miles after leaving Lake Erie the river is troubled and rapid. It then expands into a broad, placid stream, from 1 to 2 miles wide, and encircles several islands.

After flowing nearly 20 miles and descending only about 20 feet, the river suddenly narrows and enters a series of beautiful rapids. In about a half mile the river descends 52 feet, in seething, boiling torrents and eddies in which the whole surface is torn and tossed into white spray. The waters then reach the edge of an abrupt declivity, the Niagara escarpment, and make a sudden plunge to the bottom of an immense gorge. A short distance above the brink of the falls, Goat Island separates the river into two unequal streams. The narrow, shallower one, on the American side, discharges over the American Fall, 167 feet in height and 1060 feet wide. The main part of the river swings to the west of Goat Island and discharges over the Canadian or Horseshoe Fall, 158 feet high, with a deep retreating curve in the center and measuring about 2500 feet along the crest. A feature of interest is the illumination of the cataract each evening by shifting lights of rich and varied color.

The water flowing over the American Fall is from 1 to 4 feet deep, but that plunging over the Horseshoe Fall is estimated at about 20 feet in depth. The main cataract carries over fully 90 per cent of the water, while the American Fall discharges less than 10 per cent. The volume of flow is normally about 500,000 tons of water a minute.

The edge of the American Fall is receding at a rate estimated at from 2 to 7 inches a year. In 1954 hundreds of tons of rock, loosened by the seepage of river water, fell into the gorge from the point of land adjoining the falls. Measurements by the U.S. Geological Survey indicate that the Horseshoe Falls has been receding at the rate of about 5 feet a year for nearly a century. In 1969 the water flowing over the American Fall was temporarily diverted with a cofferdam so that the recession could be studied with the intention of "repairing" the fall to prevent its rapid erosion.

For about 7 miles below the foot of the falls, the river descends between nearly perpendicular cliffs, 200 to 300 feet high, through a series of magnificent rapids, the famous Niagara Gorge. In width, the gorge varies from 1700 feet, opposite the American Falls, to 700 feet, opposite the Whirlpool. The river at the bottom of the gorge is considerably narrower, with depths believed to range from 100 to 500 feet, and with a speed in some places estimated at 30 miles an hour.

About 3 miles below the falls the river rushes into the Whirlpool. This is a huge circular indentation worn into the Canadian side of the river and surrounded by walls 300 feet high. The river plunges into this great excavation in a northwesterly direction and is forced to leave it in a northeasterly direction, forming one of the most impressive maelstroms in the world. At the end of the gorge, near Lewiston, the river again widens and flows tranquilly for about 7 miles to its mouth in Lake Ontario.

Niagara Falls is the most accessible to the traveler of any of the great cataracts. Fine parks, with many conveniences for the public, have been established on both sides of the river. There is a bridge to Goat Island. An aerial cable tramway spans the chasm over the Whirlpool, giving a unique view of this natural wonder.

While several early French missionaries, visiting the Niagara region, wrote accounts of the falls received from the Indians, the first white man to describe and depict the great cataract was Father Hennepin, who accompanied La Salle to the Niagara frontier in 1678. French domination of the region continued until 1759, when Fort Niagara was surrendered to the British. The region was controlled by the British until 1796 and was the scene of many conflicts during the War of 1812.

Niagara Falls. A manufacturing city of western New York, situated on the Niagara River at the falls from which it takes its name. By utilizing immense power generated at the cataract, the city has developed extensive manufactories and has become an important center of electrochemical industry. Among the leading manufactures are chemicals, electrical machinery, aluminum ware, carborundum, paper and wood pulp, flour, shredded wheat biscuit, roofing materials, and metallurgical products.

The hydroelectric power is developed by the Power Authority of the State of New York as an agent under the St. Lawrence Waterway Treaty of 1950 with Canada. In order to take maximum advantage of the fall, two intakes were constructed 2½ miles above the falls to convey the water about four miles to one of the world's largest power plants, where nearly 2 million kilowatts of power is developed. Only half of the diversionary flow is taken during the day in the tourist season so as to interfere as little as possible with the scenic attraction of the falls. When demand for current is low, the surplus current is used to pump water into an 1800-acre reservoir above the power plant, and this water in turn, in falling back, develops additional current at times of peak demand.

Because of the falls, which rank among the world's greatest scenic wonders, the city is visited yearly by tens of thousands of travelers. Niagara Falls and Suspension Bridge, formerly two villages, were, in 1892, united as the city of Niagara Falls. Population, 1970, 85,615.

Nogales (*nô-gä'lĕs*). A city on the southern boundary of Arizona, 65 miles south of Tucson. A fence, with gates always open, separates it from the Mexican city of the same name. Nogales is the trade center of a mining and grazing district and is an inland gateway to the western coast of Mexico. A feature of historical interest in the vicinity is the ruin of the Tumacacori Mission. This was founded in 1691 by Father Kino, a Jesuit missionary, was taken charge of by Franciscan fathers in 1769, and is now a national monument. Population, 1970, 8946.

Norfolk. A city and the principal seaport of Virginia, with about 50 miles of waterfront on the Elizabeth River, Hampton Roads, and Chesapeake Bay.

Norfolk, together with Portsmouth, forms the largest naval station in the Union. It is the base for the Atlantic fleet. The harbor is capable of giving anchorage to the largest class of vessels.

A little to the east of the city is a terminus of the Chesapeake Bay bridge-tunnel, completed in 1964 at a cost of $200 million. It provides a 17.6 mile roadway crossing to Cape Charles, the roadway descending from the bridge into tunnels at two points so as to permit passage of ships at these points.

The port carries an extensive shipping trade in cotton, tobacco, lumber, corn, cattle, horses, fish, oysters, fruits, vegetables, and peanuts. The principal manufactures include ships, airplane parts, fertilizers, agricultural implements, lumber, cotton goods, flour, and roasted peanuts.

Among the public buildings may be noted the Custom house, the City Hall, and the Cotton Exchange. The educational establishments include old Dominion University and

Virginia Wesleyan College. Popular seaside resorts nearby include Virginia and Ocean View beaches. Norfolk was first settled in 1682, incorporated as a borough in 1736, and chartered as a city in 1835. Population, 1970, 307,951.

Norwalk. A city of Connecticut, 14 miles southwest of Bridgeport, on Long Island Sound. An industrial center since before the Revolutionary War, Norwalk now manufactures hats, pumps, leather goods, electronic equipment and other items. Norwalk is also a research center and a summer resort. The area is rich in colonial history. Population, 1970, 79,113.

Oakland. The fifth largest city of California, situated on the mainland shore of San Francisco Bay and connected with San Francisco by the 8¼-mile San Francisco-Oakland Bay Bridge. Oakland's metropolitan area extends for 23 miles along the San Francisco Bay eastward to the San Joaquin Valley, consisting of an almost unbroken chain of factories, waterfront industries, commercial trading centers, and residences. Mild year-round temperatures are an outstanding feature of the area.

Oakland is the terminus for three major railroads. Inland waterways and ocean-freight service is provided by the Port of Oakland. The freeway system has also helped to make Oakland a distribution center. Manufactures include processed foods, passenger cars and trucks, office equipment, tin and glass containers, metal products, floor coverings, chemicals, and paints.

Oakland has 65 parks covering 1600 acres. Lake Merritt, a 155-acre body of salt water, is located in the center of the city, surrounded by Lakeside Park. A recent addition to the city is the new $9 million Oakland Museum, featuring a design developed by a competition of the world's leading architects. Among Oakland's educational institutions are Mills College for women, the College of the Holy Names, and the California College of Arts and Crafts. Oakland was founded on a Spanish grant in 1850, was incorporated as a town in 1852, and as a city in 1854. Population, 1970, 361,561.

Oak Park. A village of northeastern Illinois, about nine miles west of the center of Chicago, of which it is a residential suburb. Oak Park was incorporated in 1901. Population, 1970, 62,511.

Oak Ridge. A community in eastern Tennessee, one of the three so-called "atomic cities," which mushroomed during World War II, when it became a center for the development of materials for the atomic bomb. At that time it had an estimated population of 75,000. Oak Ridge sprang from practically nothing, as did also the other two places, Richland, Washington, and Los Alamos, New Mexico. Population, 1970, 28,319.

Oberlin. A town of northeastern Ohio, situated about 35 miles southwest of Cleveland. While it conducts a substantial trade with the surrounding agricultural districts and has local industries, it is chiefly noted as the seat of Oberlin College, the first American college to adopt coeducation. The town is well laid out, with broad, shady streets and fine residences. Population, 1970, 8761.

Ogden. The second largest city of Utah, situated at the junction of the Ogden and Weber rivers, at the foot of the Wasatch Mountains, about 35 miles north of Salt Lake City. It is noted for its picturesque scenery. A boulevard passes through the scenic Ogden Canyon a distance of 8 miles to Ogden Valley and Pine View Dam, which afford various recreational opportunities. Ogden is the distributing center of a productive agricultural, fruit growing, and stock raising district. Electricity for light, heat, and industrial purposes is supplied to the city by the waterfalls from surrounding canyons. Meat packing, fruit and vegetable canning, oil refining, and the manufacture of beet sugar and flour are among the chief industries. Ogden was founded in 1848 and in 1850, under the direction of Brigham Young, was laid out as a city. Population, 1970 69,478.

Oklahoma City. The capital of Oklahoma, situated on the north branch of the Canadian River in the central part of the state. Lying in the midst of a rich oil producing, agricultural, and stock raising country, the city has grown into a community of diverse industry, aviation, manufacturing, distribution, petroleum, utilities, transportation, science and medicine, wholesale and retail trade, finance and various commercial enterprises, and business services. The city's 83 parks and playgrounds cover 9924 acres. An architecturally outstanding addition to the capitol, in Ionic style, and to many large business buildings, is the National Cowboy Hall of Fame and Museum. Oklahoma City was granted its charter in 1891 and was made capital of the state in 1910. Population, 1970, 356,661.

Old Point Comfort. A favorite watering place in Virginia, situated on a neck of land where Hampton Roads at the mouth of the James River joins Chesapeake Bay. Fort Monroe is situated here.

Olympia. The capital of the state of Washington, situated on the southernmost inlet of Puget Sound. The city is the port for a district rich in lumber and in agricultural products. Industries include boat building, the manufacture of plywood, the brewing of beer, and the oyster industry. Manufacturing interests are promoted by the abundant hydroelectric power available, the chief industry being the production of lumber. The noteworthy buildings include the Capitol, the Federal Building, and four other governmental buildings costing in all $15 million. The first settlement was made at Olympia in 1845. The town was laid out in 1851, and became the territorial capital in 1853. Population, 1970, 23,111.

Omaha. The chief city of Nebraska, situated on a commanding site on the west bank of the Missouri River, opposite Council Bluffs, Iowa.

Omaha owes its position as the commercial and manufacturing metropolis of the state to the fact that it is one of the greatest gateways of the West, having the facilities afforded by several great railroad systems and the deepened channel of the Missouri River. The industries of the city, especially those based on agricultural products, are enormous. Its live stock market is the second in the world, while its creameries and macaroni factories are among the largest in the country. It is one of the greatest meat packing centers in the United States. Other industries and manufactures include ore smelting and refining, railway car repairing, flour, steam engines, machinery, and dairy equipment. It is also an insurance center.

Omaha has 3646 acres of parks and many fine public buildings. Among the city's numerous educational institutions may be mentioned the University of Nebraska at Omaha, Creighton University, and the Joslyn Memorial Art Museum. From 1854, the date of the first permanent settlement, to 1867, Omaha was the capital of Nebraska. Population, 1970, 347,328.

Oraibi (*ō-rī'bĭ*). A village of the Hopi Indians in northeastern Arizona, believed to be the oldest continuously inhabited community in the United States. It lies about 100 miles north of Winslow. The community existed as early as 1370, this fact being inferred from a study of the annual growth rings of timbers in the ruins. Population about 100.

Orlando. A city and winter resort of Florida, situated amidst numerous small lakes, some 2000 in all, about 40 miles inland from the approximate center of the state's Atlantic coastline. There are 33 lakes within the corporate limits. Palms, magnolias, and laurels impart a subtropical beauty which joins with the mild climate in attracting winter visitors.

Orlando lies in the center of a rich citrus fruit country, which also produces truck crops and raises cattle. Its primary industries are processing citrus fruits and the manufacture of electronic and defense equipment. Educational institutions include Rollins College and Florida Technological University. Population, 1970, 99,006.

Oshkosh. A city of eastern Wisconsin, situated on the western shore of Lake Winnebago at Fox River, about 75 miles north of Milwaukee. It is located in a once densely wooded region, and the woodworking industry is still a leading commercial interest of the city. Other industries include the manufacture of furniture, travel goods, overalls, and trucks. Oshkosh is a well-known pleasure resort. Lake Winnebago is noted for its game fishing; yachting in the summer and ice boating in the winter are favorite sports. Population, 1970, 53,221.

Pago Pago (*pang'ō-pang'ō*). A fine natural harbor on the south coast of Tutuila, principal island of the American Samoa group. On the shores of this bay are the village of Pago Pago, government offices in the villages of Fagatogo (the constitutional seat of government), business districts, and key industries. Chief exports are copra and canned tuna. Population 1970, 3800 in the bay area—more than 29,000 for all of American Samoa.

Painted Desert. An area of plateaus and low mesas in north central Arizona. It extends from the top of the Marble Canyon of the Colorado River southeastward along the east side of the valley of the Little Colorado for about 100 miles, varying in width from 15 to 40 miles. At the south, it ends near the Santa Fe railway, which crosses it between Holbrook and Winslow. This desert lies at an altitude of about 5000 feet and has an exceedingly arid climate. In consequence, vegetation is so scant that vast areas of rocks are bare or very nearly so. These rocks, mostly Triassic shales and sandstones, exhibit a great variety of colors, whence the name "painted."

Situated on the margin of this desert, about 60 miles north of Winslow, are the seven villages of the Hopi Indians, the best known of which are Walpi and Oraibi. See *Walpi*.

Palisades, The. The name given to a series of massive cliffs on the west bank of the Hudson River. From near Haverstraw, New York, these extend south to Weehawken, New Jersey, a distance of about 30 miles. For the most part, these precipitous cliffs rise almost directly from the water's edge, varying in height from 200 to 550 feet. They consist of basaltic trap rock or diabase, which exhibits marked columnar effects, forming a striking feature in the beautiful scenery of the lower Hudson. The Palisades Interstate Park in New York and New Jersey embraces some of the finest portions of the Palisades.

Palm Beach. A noted winter resort on the southeast coast of Florida, about 64 miles north of Miami. It is situated on Lake Worth, opposite West Palm Beach, the nearest railway town. Its delightful climate, together with its bathing, boating, and fishing facilities, makes Palm Beach one of the most desirable of pleasure haunts. Palatial hotels, spacious parks, and golf links attract thousands of visitors. Population, 1970, 9086.

Palm Canyon. A narrow, rocky gorge opening upon the extreme western end of the Colorado Desert, at the southeastern base of San Jacinto Mountain, about 7 miles south of Palm Springs, California. Near the mouth of this canyon, growing along the small watercourse at its bottom, is one of the largest existing groves of the stately Washington palm, many trees being from 40 to 60 feet high. Their brilliant green foliage makes a striking contrast with the arid, barren rocks forming the canyon walls.

Palo Alto (*păl'ō ăl'tō*). A city 32 miles south of San Francisco, California. Favored by location and climate as a residential site, it is noted as a center of education and research. Large areas of the city are occupied by Stanford University, with its Hoover library of history, its medical center, its art gallery, and its research laboratories, particularly in electronics and biophysics. Some local industries are related to the research in high-energy physics. Population, 1970, 55,768.

Parkersburg. A city of West Virginia, located on the Ohio River, at the mouth of the Little Kanawha, in a region rich in oil, coal, natural gas, and fire-clay. Its manufactures include glass, petroleum products, chemicals, viscose, rayon, lumber, steel products, earthenware, and electrical porcelain. Besides having river and rail transportation, it is an important highway center, being situated at the junction of U.S. routes 50 and 21. Parkersburg was founded in 1789. Population, 1970, 44,208.

Pasadena. A residential city and widely known winter resort of southern California, northeast of Los Angeles and touching its boundaries at several points. It occupies a beautiful site in the foothills of the Sierra Madre, in a region luxuriant with palms, orange groves, eucalyptus, and other subtropical vegetation. The city is noted for its spacious avenues, fine public buildings, and handsome residences, and is the seat of many educational institutions, including the California Institute of Technology.

Among the many features of interest within or near the city are the Huntington Library and Art Gallery, the Rose Bowl, Mount Wilson Observatory, a beautiful public library with outdoor reading rooms, Mount Lowe, San Gabriel Mission, and a mile-long avenue of deodars known as "Christmas Tree Lane." Its 13 parks cover 500 acres, the largest, Brookside, being within a great natural gorge, the Arroyo Seco, which is spanned at Colorado Street by one of the country's most beautiful bridges. The city is widely known for its annual festival, called the "Tournament of Roses," celebrated on New Year's Day. In 1874, a colony from Indianapolis, Ind. settled on the site of Pasadena and began raising fruit; in 1886, Pasadena received its charter as a city. Population, 1970, 113,327.

Pasadena. A large residential suburb of Houston, Texas, Pasadena was the site of the capture of the Mexican General Santa Anna after the Battle of San Jacinto. Population, 1970, 89,277.

Passaic (*pă-sā'ĭk*). A manufacturing city of New Jersey, situated on the Passaic River, about 12 miles northwest of New York City. The chief industry is the manufacture of woolen and worsted goods. Passaic is said to make one-third of the handkerchiefs produced in the United States. Other important industrial establishments include cigar factories, rubber, metal, and dye works. Population, 1970, 55,124.

Paterson. A city of New Jersey, located on the Passaic River, about 16 miles northwest of New York City. Immense power, developed from Passaic Falls, 50 feet in height, is utilized in the city's numerous industries. Paterson is the leading producer of silk fabrics in the United States. It has also cotton and woolen mills, dyeing and finishing establishments, airplane engine factories, and machine shops.

Paterson owes the beginnings of its great industrial growth to the "Society for Establishing Useful Manufactures," promoted largely through the efforts of Alexander Hamilton, in 1791, when he was secretary of the treasury. In 1792, the site, "by the Great Falls of the Passaic," was chosen for the location of the mills which were to be used in bringing about the commercial independence of the United States from Europe. Population, 1970, 144,824.

Pawtucket. A city of Rhode Island, built on both banks of the Pawtucket River, about 4 miles northeast of Providence. The city was the birthplace of the cotton goods industry of the United States. The original mill, founded by Samuel Slater in 1790, is now a museum. Pawtucket produces wire and cable, textiles, toys, and electronic components. Its fine parks, public squares, and imposing bridges across the river serve to make Pawtucket an attractive city. Population, 1970, 76,984.

Pendleton. A city of northeastern Oregon, on the Umatilla River, 225 miles east of Portland. Pendleton is the supply center for the Umatilla irrigation district and has an extensive trade in grain, fruit, and live stock. Pendleton has become widely known through its annual exhibition festival "The Round-Up." Population, 1970, 13,197.

Pensacola. A seaport of Florida, situated on Pensacola Bay, 10 miles north of the Gulf of Mexico. It has a fine landlocked harbor and conducts an extensive domestic trade. Industrial products include paper, fertilizers, wood products, cottonseed oil, and naval stores. A huge navy aviation school is located there. The city was settled by Spaniards in 1559. Points of interest include forts Barrancas, San Carlos, and Pickens, and numerous recreational facilities. Population, 1970, 59,507.

Peoria (*pē-ō'rĭ-ȧ*). A manufacturing city of Illinois, built on the west bank of the Illinois River, 160 miles southwest of Chicago. Peoria is the commercial center of a rich agricultural district, in close proximity to large coal fields. The manufactures include agricultural implements, packed meats, paper goods, stoves, barrels, woven wire fence, cordage, stock foods, and chemicals. Peoria has one of the largest truck-in stockyards in the country. Parks cover about 6810 acres. Lake Peoria and other natural features of the city's environment provide beautiful scenery within and around it. The city is the seat of Bradley University. Population, 1970, 126,963.

Pepin (*pē'pĭn*), **Lake.** An expansion of the upper Mississippi River, situated in a fine scenic region, about 30 miles south of Saint Paul, Minnesota. The lake is about 30 miles long and from 1 to 2 miles wide. It is surrounded by imposing bluffs of limestone, rising about 400 feet above the water and carved by erosion into many remarkable shapes. The town of Red Wing with a population, 1970, of 10,441 is situated at its northern end.

Perth Amboy. A city of eastern New Jersey, located on Raritan Bay, about 20 miles southwest of New York City. Perth Amboy, by reason of its good harbor, has extensive shipping interests, and is an important commercial and industrial center. Among the chief industries are chemical works, copper and silver refineries, and the manufacture of clothing and hats. The city is connected with South Amboy by the Victory Bridge, and with Staten Island by a bridge completed in 1928 at a cost of $16 million. Perth Amboy was settled in 1683, and, for a long period, was the capital of New Jersey province. It became a city in 1718. Population, 1970, 38,793.

Petersburg. A city of southeastern Virginia, situated on the south bank of the Appomattox River, 23 miles south of Richmond. Its chief industries consist of the manufacture of tobacco products, trunks, optical lenses, and cotton clothing. The city is located in an extensive tobacco growing region at the northern end of the peanut belt, and carries on a substantial trade in these products. Historic reminders of the Civil War are found in the Battlefield National Park and the Lee Memorial Park. Population, 1970, 36,103.

Petrified Forests. See *Adamana*.

PHILADELPHIA. The chief city of Pennsylvania, and the fourth most populous in the United States. It is situated at the junction of the Schuylkill and the Delaware River, some 50 miles from the mouth of the Delaware in Delaware Bay and 85 miles by water from the Atlantic Ocean.

SITE. From the confluence of the rivers, Philadelphia extends northerly along the Schuylkill for more than 20 miles and northeasterly along the Delaware for nearly the same distance, and has an irregular northern boundary. The site embraces a total area of about 130 square miles. At the south, between the two rivers, the surface is level. The old city was laid out on this peninsula. This section is now the principal business center.

To the north, the surface rises, culminating in Chestnut hill, 430 feet high, and other similar eminences. The manufacturing districts were developed in this northern area, with Germantown, now within the city limits, occupying the heights above them. That section west of the Schuylkill river is called West Philadelphia and is largely residential.

STREETS. Philadelphia was the first modern city to be

laid out, with broad, long, straight streets, intersecting at right angles, and with small parks and squares located at suitable intervals.

Broad Street, one of the greatest streets of America, bisects the city from north to south. The Benjamin Franklin Parkway extends northwest from the City Hall at Broad and Market streets. Fountains, shade trees, and flower beds make this drive one of the most beautiful in the world.

Parks and Monuments. The city park system, including 140 parks, squares, and parkways, embraces an area of about 8000 acres. The finest unit is Fairmount Park, the largest municipal park in the nation, containing some 3600 acres along the Schuylkill River, and connected with the City Hall by the magnificent Benjamin Franklin Parkway. Wissahickon Drive, 6 miles in length, along Wissahickon Creek in Fairmount Park is regarded as one of the finest scenic drives within the limits of an American city. Among other important parks are League Island, 300 acres; Pennypack, 726 acres; Tacony, 250 acres; Cobb's Creek, 288 acres; Hunting, 86 acres; Burkolme, 69 acres; Whitehall Commons, 35 acres; Bartram's Garden, 27 acres; and the Cope Arboretum, 22 acres. Roosevelt Boulevard, 300 feet wide, is a part of the Lincoln Highway.

Important monuments are the Soldiers' and Sailors' Memorial in Fairmount Park, the imposing Washington Monument at the main entrance to the park, and the World War Memorial on the Parkway. Noted statues within the commercial district are: of Washington, in front of Independence Hall; of Franklin, at the Post Office; and of Girard, Muhlenberg, Leidy, and McClellan, on the city hall plaza. On the plaza stands also Saint-Gaudens's statue of "The Pilgrim." Other noteworthy sculptural works in various parts of the city are Wolff's "Wounded Lioness," Remington's "Cowboy," and statues of Lincoln, Grant, Meade, Garfield, Columbus, Goethe, Schiller, Humboldt, and Joan of Arc.

Buildings. The monumental City Hall, an immense marble structure, is about 470 feet square, and covers 4½ acres. The tower, some 548 feet high, is surmounted by a colossal statue of William Penn.

Among the older buildings, Christ Church and Independence Hall exemplify the Colonial style of architecture, the buildings of Girard College illustrate the Neo-Greek style, and Saint Mark's Church is an example of the Gothic.

United States government buildings include the Federal Building; the United States Mint, one of the greatest in the world; the Post Office; and the Customhouse. Other noteworthy structures include the Reading depot, the immense Pennsylvania railroad station, costing over $100 million, the $16 million Museum of Art on an eminence at the end of the Parkway, and Convention Hall. Among numerous fine commercial buildings may be mentioned the Philadelphia Savings Fund, new Penn Center Plaza buildings, the Girard Trust, the Curtis, the Bell Telephone, the Arcade, the Atlantic, the Morris, and the 35-story Lewis tower, and the Wanamaker, the Gimbel Brothers, the Strawbridge and Clothier, and the Lit Brothers stores. A stadium seating 100,000 people, is a legacy of the Sesquicentennial Exposition, held in 1926 in south Philadelphia.

Historic Structures. No city in the United States, except Boston, has preserved a larger number of important buildings associated with the early history of the nation. Chief among these is Independence Hall, built 1729–34, America's most famous landmark. In this notable building, the second and the third Continental Congress met; here Washington was chosen commander in chief; in it the Declaration of Independence was signed; and from its tower the Liberty bell, still preserved in the building, pealed forth its message of freedom.

To the west of Independence Hall is Congress Hall, where the United States Congress met from 1790 to 1800, and where George Washington, in 1793, and John Adams, in 1797, were inaugurated. East of Independence Hall is the old City Hall, first occupied in 1791, now used as a historical museum. The three buildings—Independence Hall, Congress Hall, and the old City Hall—form what is known as the State House group in Independence Square. A mall around the group is a national monument.

In the same vicinity is Carpenters Hall, where, in 1774, the first Continental Congress met, and where, in 1787, the Constitutional convention framed the Constitution of the United States. On Arch Street stands the home of Betsy Ross, who is said to have made the first American flag.

Among historic churches are Old Swedes' Church, built 1698–1700; Christ Church, begun in 1727; Old Saint Joseph's Church, dating from 1729; and Saint Mary's Church, built in 1762.

The Penn Mansion, built in 1682, was the first brick house erected in Philadelphia. It originally stood between Market and Chestnut streets, in the heart of the city. With the encroachment of great business structures, it was taken down and carefully re-erected in Fairmount Park.

Educational Institutions. Philadelphia is the seat of Temple University, the University of Pennsylvania, and Drexel Institute. It is also a noted center of medical and dental education. Among its prominent medical schools are the Jefferson, the Hahnemann, the Woman's Medical College, and the medical departments of Temple and Pennsylvania universities, which also have important dental schools. Other noteworthy institutions are the planetarium, the schools of the Pennsylvania Academy of Fine Arts, the Franklin Institute, the Curtis Institute of Music, the Spring Garden Institute, the Public Library, Rodin Musuem, the Franklin Memorial Museum of Graphic Arts, Girard College, La Salle College, Saint Joseph's College, and the William Penn Charter School, founded in 1701. In the suburbs are Bryn Mawr, Haverford, Villanova and Swarthmore colleges, Ogontz School, and Overbrook Seminary.

Transportation. Although ships from its wharves sail nearly 85 miles before entering the ocean, Philadelphia is an important seaport. It is the largest fresh water port in the world and America's second busiest. It has more than 35 miles of water front on the Delaware River, which admits the passage of ocean-going ships. The Schuylkill is also navigable.

Philadelphia is also a great railroad center, with a huge network of lines extending, not only into the nearby coal and iron districts, but also into the Ohio and the Mississippi valley and into the South. The city is served chiefly by the Pennsylvania, the Reading, and the Baltimore and Ohio systems, and has the most direct connections with the Middle West of any great Atlantic port. Two municipal airports, including International Airport, rank Philadelphia as a leading aviation center for foreign and domestic flights. Eleven major airlines, including a number of jet lines, provide the city with nearly 400 flights daily.

Local transportation consists of an immense system of surface electric railways, supplemented by both subway and elevated high-speed lines, together with an extensive electric suburban service. Subways beneath Broad Street, Ridge Avenue, Eighth and Locust streets were constructed at a cost in excess of $140 million.

Of numerous fine bridges, the most noteworthy are the Fairmount Avenue bridge, a double-deck truss structure completed in 1895, the great Benjamin Franklin Bridge across the Delaware River, which was completed in 1926 at a cost of nearly $25 million, and the Walt Whitman Bridge over the same river, completed in 1957 and costing $86 million.

Commerce. Philadelphia's high rank as a commercial city is primarily owing to its importance as a port; and its favorable location near vast supplies of raw materials has led to the development of immense industries. The city ranks first among the leading ports of the United States in the value of its foreign import commerce, and conducts a large coastwise trade, especially in oil and coal. Hog Island was purchased from the Federal government by the city in 1930 to be made into a huge sea, rail, and air terminal.

Manufactures. Three factors have made Philadelphia a great manufacturing center—nearness to the sources of raw materials, its advantageous situation as the natural outlet of great coal and iron fields, and excellent transportation facilities.

The city has the largest shipbuilding plant in the United States. The city leads in the quantity of rolling mill, foundry, and machine shop products, and in the manufacture of hats, carpets, and hosiery. In production of woolen and worsted goods, leather goods, and chemicals, in printing and publishing of books, newspapers, and periodicals, and in sugar refining, Philadelphia ranks among the chief manufacturing centers of the country. The League Island navy yard plant includes one of the country's largest aircraft factories.

History. The earliest settlement within the limits of Philadelphia was made in 1636 by a company of Swedes. Late in 1681, William Markham, deputy governor for William Penn, organized an English settlement, and, in 1682, under Penn's supervision, the city was laid out and named. In 1683, a colony of Germans, invited by Penn, settled at Germantown, now a part of the city. In 1723, Benjamin Franklin came to Philadelphia, and in 1729 began the publication of the *Pennsylvania Gazette*. Philadelphia took a leading part in resisting British aggression, and the most important official events of the Revolutionary War occurred in the city. The battle of Germantown was fought in 1777. Philadelphia was occupied by British armies, 1777–78, while Washington's army was at Valley Forge.

Philadelphia was the capital of Pennsylvania from 1683 to 1799, was the seat of the Federal government, 1790–1800, and was the financial center of the country until 1836. The first daily newspaper in the United States, the *Pennsylvania Packet*, appeared in Philadelphia in 1784. The Centennial Exposition, celebrating the centenary of American independence, was held in Fairmount Park in 1876. Philadelphia is called the "Quaker City" and also the "City of Brotherly Love," the latter being the meaning of its name, which is Greek. A popular New Year festivity in Philadelphia is the Mummers parade, a survival from an Old-World custom with modifications coming from American pioneer life. Population, 1970, 1,948,609.

Phoenix. The capital of Arizona, in the south central part of the state, about 400 miles east of Los Angeles. Phoenix is the commercial center of the Salt River Valley, the most productive agricultural region in the state. After the immense extension of irrigation following the construction of the Roosevelt Dam in 1911, the city grew rapidly. Among the crops are Egyptian cotton, alfalfa, cereals, oranges, grapefruit, figs, olives, cantaloupes, strawberries, and winter vegetables. The total value of the crops produced in Maricopa County, of which Phoenix is the county seat, far exceeds that of all the remainder of the state.

The city lies in a wide, irrigated plain surrounded by mountains. It has a mountain park of 14,000 acres 6 miles to the south. Its broad streets are ornamented with palms and other subtropical plants. Prominent public buildings are the Capitol and the City Library. By reason of its dry, salubrious climate, Phoenix is an important winter resort. In the vicinity are numerous points of interest, including Cactus Park, petroglyphics, and the ruins of Aztec community houses. Phoenix was settled in 1870 and became the capital of the territory in 1889. Population, 1970, 581,562.

Piedmont. The name used in the United States to designate that part of the Atlantic plain which lies between the low, flat coastal plain and the true Appalachian highland. It consists chiefly of rolling, rugged lands with deeply eroded valleys. The rocks are a harder formation than those underlying the coastal plain. In consequence, there is a definite line of escarpments, over which most of the rivers descend in rapids or cataracts. This is known as the "fall line." The piedmont plain reaches its greatest extent in Virginia, South Carolina, and North Carolina, being about 300 miles wide in the latter state.

Pierre (*pēr*). The capital of South Dakota, situated on the Missouri River in the central part of the state. It is located in an agricultural and stock raising district and is an important cattle shipping center. Besides the Capitol, Pierre has the State Library, a Federal school for Indians, and a fine Federal Building. The city's parks include the 1500-acre Farm Island in the Missouri River. Four miles upstream is Oahe Dam, the world's largest earth-rolled dam. Fort Pierre, established in 1832, was for many years the chief fur trading post of the Upper Missouri River country. Pierre was laid out in 1880 and was incorporated in 1883. Population, 1970, 9699.

Pikes Peak. A mountain in Colorado, 14,108 feet high, situated in the easternmost range of the Rockies immediately west of Colorado Springs. It was discovered in 1806 by General Zebulon M. Pike of the United States army, and was first successfully ascended in 1819 by Major S. H. Long. In 1891, a cogwheel railway was completed to the summit, which is now reached also by a well constructed automobile road.

While not the highest mountain in Colorado, Pikes Peak is one of the most majestic and imposing. Pine and spruce forests cover the slopes to an elevation of about 11,700 feet, above which there is a fringe of beautiful alpine flowering plants bordering the snow. The summit consists of bare granite rocks. The view from the top is one of unusual magnificence, including rugged mountains, vast plains, and numerous lakes and rivers in a landscape which extends 100 miles in all directions.

Pine Bluff. A distribution center for an agricultural region that produces cotton, livestock, and lumber, situated about 45 miles southeast of Little Rock, Arkansas. Most of the industry within the city is related to the products grown in the area. Pine Bluff is the seat of Arkansas Agricultural, Mechanical, and Normal College. Local residents claim the Civil War actually began in Pine Bluff. Population, 1970, 57,389.

Pinehurst. A noted winter resort of southern North Carolina, about 60 miles southwest of Raleigh. It is 125 miles from the seacoast and 13½ hours ride by rail from New York City, and possesses a mild and equable climate. It was founded as a winter resort in 1895 by James W. Tufts, of Boston, and is famous for the beauty and excellence of its parks, bridle paths, polo grounds, golf links, tennis courts, and other facilities for recreation. The permanent residential population is about 1500, but the winter visitors number 10,000 or more annually.

Piqua (*pĭk'wä*). A city in Miami County, Ohio, about 70 miles west of Columbus, in the center of a rich agricultural district. Its manufactures include knit underwear, walnut veneer, industrial fans and heating equipment, and other wood products. The first settlement was made in 1797. The outpost known as Fort Piqua, at this point, was an important supply base during the War of 1812. Population, 1970, 20,714.

PITTSBURGH. A city of Pennsylvania, situated at the junction of the Monongahela and Allegheny rivers, which here unite to form the Ohio. Pittsburgh lies in southwestern Pennsylvania, about 340 miles west of Philadelphia.

Site. Pittsburgh occupies the most irregular and uneven site of any on which a great American city is built. The three rivers flow through deep narrow valleys and the highlands bordering upon them are broken into a large number of hills. These rise to heights of from 500 to 740 feet above the rivers and are separated by great ravines.

The Monongahela River, from the southeast, is joined by the Allegheny, from the northeast; and the Ohio River, formed by their union, flows northwesterly to the city limits. The chief business district and the greater part of the city lies between the Monongahela and the Allegheny.

By annexation, there have been absorbed into the city more than 40 boroughs and townships. The names of many of these are still in common use locally, as, for example, Esplen, Beltzhoover, Sheraden, and Spring Garden.

Streets and Buildings. After World War II, Pittsburgh began a rebuilding program which converted the older downtown section into a "golden triangle." A 35-acre Point Park was created, and a civic arena was built with a retractable stainless-steel dome 415 feet in diameter and 136 feet high. The Boulevard of the Allies, a magnificent roadway overlooking the Monongahela, sweeps along the precipitous face of a cliff eastward from the business district to Forbes Avenue, which leads to Schenley Park.

By reason of its extremely hilly site, Pittsburgh has perhaps more bridges and viaducts than any other city in the world. The city owns and maintains over 125, including the Liberty bridge, which connects the business section with the South Hills district via the Liberty tubes. These are twin tubes 5714 feet long and cost nearly $6 million to construct. The Bloomfield bridge, spanning a deep valley between Herron Hill and the Bloomfield district, is nearly a mile long. The Larimer Avenue viaduct and the George Westinghouse bridge in East Pittsburgh have concrete arches ranking among the longest in America.

The commercial district, largely concentrated in "The Point," where the Monongahela and Allegheny rivers converge, is noted for its many fine office buildings of the skyscraper type, including the Grant, Koppers, Gulf, and Gateway Center buildings. Other imposing structures are the Courthouse, the Federal Building, Saint Paul's Cathedral, and Trinity Church.

Parks. The municipal park system includes 24 parks, covering a total area of more than 6000 acres. Of these, the finest is Schenley Park containing, within its 422 acres, the Carnegie Institute and Library, and the Phipps Conservatory. Highland Park, covering 366 acres, commands a superb panoramic view of the Allegheny valley. In this park, which contains a large zoological garden, there is a memorial building to Stephen C. Foster, author of "Old Folks at Home," who was born and lived in Pittsburgh. At the entrance of Riverview Park is the Allegheny Observatory. Other noteworthy parks are McKinley, Grandview, and Allegheny.

Public Institutions. Foremost among the public institutions of Pittsburgh are the magnificent buildings of the Carnegie Institute, which includes library, museum, art gallery, and music hall. This beautiful structure, which covers nearly 6 acres, is built in the Italian Renaissance style. Memorial Hall, containing a war museum and a large auditorium, is a notable structure. The Cathedral of Learning, a 40-story building 523 feet high and costing $6 million, houses the University of Pittsburgh. The Phipps Conservatory is one of the largest in America. All the above and many other buildings constitute a civic educational and social center at the entrance to Schenley Park.

Education. The chief educational institutions of the city are the University of Pittsburgh. Carnegie-Mellon University, Duquesne University, Chatham College, the Allegheny Observatory, and the Buhl Planetarium and Institute of Popular Science.

Transportation. Transportation, provided by the rivers and by railroads, and abundant fuel, in the form of coal, petroleum, and natural gas from nearby fields, are some of the factors which have made the city of Pittsburgh one of the great "workshops of the world." The rivers afford connections with an immense system of inland waterways, including not only those of the state, but also those of the Midwest and the South. There is extensive river traffic between Pittsburgh and Cincinnati, Saint Louis, and New Orleans. The city is served by three passenger and five freight railway carriers. Because of the character of the commodities handled, largely coal, ores, and iron and steel products, the tonnage handled at Pittsburgh greatly exceeds that of any other inland river port.

MANUFACTURES. Pittsburgh, long known as "Steel City," is one of the leading centers of the world for the manufacture of iron and steel. About one-fifth of the steel made in the Western hemisphere is made in the Pittsburgh district. Pittsburgh leads all other cities in the manufacture of steel rails, aluminum, pressed steel cars, iron pipe and tubing, and pressed steel plates for shipbuilding. The city is also the chief center in the U.S. for the manufacture of coke, plate glass, window glass, and bottles, and produces a high quality of optical glass. Other important manufactures include aluminum wares, bronze and copper wares, refined petroleum, and aerospace materials. Adjacent to Pittsburgh is the world's first full-scale nuclear plant.

HISTORY. In colonial times, the vicinity of Pittsburgh was the scene of many struggles with the French and Indians. In 1753, the site of Pittsburgh was visited by George Washington who regarded it "extremely well situated for a fort." The French and Indians, however, drove off the Virginians, and built Fort Duquesne. Endeavoring, in 1755, to capture it, Braddock, with a strong British force, met disastrous defeat. In 1758, General Forbes, marching from Philadelphia, took the fort, and, at Washington's suggestion, renamed it in honor of William Pitt. The Block House, built in 1759, the oldest building in the city, is preserved as a relic of colonial days. Pittsburgh was laid out in 1784, was incorporated in 1794, and became a city in 1816. Population, 1970, 520,117.

Pittsfield. A city of western Massachusetts, situated in the Berkshire valley, near Pontoosuc Lake, with a background of fine mountain scenery. It is the largest city in the Berkshire Hills region, and is particularly noted for its wide, shaded streets, fine public buildings, and historic tradition. Its Museum of Natural History and Fine Arts contains the "one hoss shay," made famous by Oliver Wendell Holmes's poem. Holmes, Melville, and Longfellow resided for a time at Pittsfield, and H. W. Shaw ("Josh Billings") lived nearby. The city's industries produce plastics, transformers, bank note paper, textiles, machine tools, and silk. Population, 1970, 57,020.

Plymouth. A town on Plymouth harbor, Massachusetts, about 37 miles southeast of Boston. Founded by the Pilgrim Fathers in 1620, it is the oldest town in New England. Plymouth Rock, on which the Pilgrims are said to have landed, is preserved under a beautiful portico. Pilgrim Hall contains many interesting relics and historical paintings. A full-sized replica of the *Mayflower* has been moored at State Pier. The city is a port of entry, has varied local manufactures, and ships large quantities of cranberries grown in the vicinity. Population, 1970, 18,606.

Pocatello (*pō'kȧ-tĕl'ō*). A city of southeastern Idaho, about 170 miles north of Salt Lake City, Utah. Pocatello is situated in a region largely arid and volcanic, but highly productive by reason of irrigation. The city's industries consist largely of processing farm and dairy products.

Pocatello is the seat of Idaho State University. Population, 1970, 40,036.

Pomona. A city in California, about 30 miles east of Los Angeles. Pomona ships the citrus fruits, walnuts, and various agricultural products grown in the area. Oil refineries are among its industrial establishments. Population, 1970, 87,384.

Ponce. The second largest city in Puerto Rico, located on the dry, southern coast of the island, about 8 miles southwest of San Juan. Its manufactures include clothing, textiles, paper, shoes, and canned tuna, fruits, and vegetables. It is a seaport and the seat of the Catholic University of Puerto Rico. Population, 1970, 125,926.

Pontiac. A city of southeastern Michigan, on the Clinton River, about 25 miles northwest of Detroit. Pontiac is the trade center of a rich farming and dairying region, and has developed extensive industries. The chief manufactures include automobiles, automobile accessories and parts, trucks, buses, paints and varnishes, tools, and machine shop products. Pontiac was settled in 1818, was incorporated in 1837, and, in 1861, was chartered as a city. It was named after the Indian chief. Population, 1970, 85,279.

Port Arthur. A seaport of southeastern Texas, situated on Sabine Lake, 12 miles from the Gulf of Mexico. Port Arthur is one of the largest oil refining centers in the United States. Since the completion of the Port Arthur ship canal, affording passage for large ocean vessels to its fine landlocked harbor, Port Arthur has become a leading port. The Neches River is spanned there by Rainbow Bridge (said to be the tallest bridge in the South over a navigable waterway), connecting Port Arthur and Orange. The city is the seat of Port Arthur College. Population, 1970, 57,371.

Portland. The commercial metropolis of Maine, located on Casco Bay, 108 miles northeast of Boston. It is built on two peninsulas, some encircling territory on the mainland, and islands totaling 2585 acres. Portland is an important seaport and possesses one of the finest harbors on the Atlantic coast. It occupies a picturesque site, with handsome buildings and streets closely bordered with trees. Its industries are extensive and varied, including iron forging, shoe manufacturing, cod and mackerel fishing, the canning of fish and vegetables. and lumber milling. Longfellow was born here. Population, 1970, 65,116.

Portland. The chief city of Oregon, situated on the Willamette River, about 12 miles from its junction with the Columbia, and approximately 100 miles by water from the Pacific Ocean. It occupies a commanding site on the sloping banks of the river, with the snow-capped peaks of Mount Hood, Saint Helens, and Mount Adams in the eastward background.

Portland owes its growth and importance to great natural advantages of situation. It is surrounded by highly fertile valleys and heavily timbered mountains, and has an excellent fresh-water harbor with 27 miles of deep water frontage. The exports consist mainly of grain, flour, lumber, and salmon.

In manufactures, Portland ranks among the leading cities of the Pacific states, its favorable situation enabling it to utilize vast resources of hydroelectric power, as well as natural gas. Among important manufactures are lumber, pulp, paper, clothing, automobile tires, and flour. The city's industries include also fruit canning and meat packing.

The city contains many imposing public buildings and is noted for its fine residences. It is the seat of Reed College and several schools of the University of Oregon besides various other educational institutions. Among features of interest are Council Crest, affording a panoramic view of the city and its surroundings; Terwilliger Boulevard on the west side of the city; Willamette Boulevard on the east side; and Washington Park, containing famous rose gardens and a fine statue of Sacagawea, a Shoshone Indian woman who guided the Lewis and Clark expedition. The environs of the city are reached by numerous scenic roads, including the famous Columbia River Highway, which extends 120 miles east, and 110 miles west to the sea. Portland is called the "Rose City." Its Rose Festival is a beautiful annual pageant.

Settlers from New England founded the city in 1844, naming it after Portland, Maine. Population, 1970, 382,619.

Portsmouth (*pōrts'mŭth*). The only seaport of New Hampshire, built near the mouth of the Piscataqua River, opposite the Maine boundary, about 60 miles north of Boston. The city carries on a substantial coastwise trade especially in coal, and has various local manufactures. Portsmouth was settled in 1623, and incorporated in 1849. It is a quiet city with a quaint, old-fashioned appearance, and contains many fine colonial houses rich in historic and literary interest. The Portsmouth navy yard, on an island in the river, is situated within the boundaries of Maine. In 1905, the Treaty of Portsmouth, ending the Russo-Japanese War, was signed in the "Peace Building" on Seavy's Island. Population, 1970, 25,717.

Portsmouth. A city of southern Ohio, built on the north bank of the Ohio River, at the mouth of the Scioto River, about 90 miles south of Columbus. It is protected from floods by a concrete wall 77 feet above normal water stage. The city is located in an agricultural and industrial region, of which it is the commercial center. Other important manufactures are steel and lumber products, shoes, paper boxes, and furniture. Portsmouth is near the Shawnee state forest, the Goodyear atomic plant, and the Roosevelt game preserve. In the Scioto valley, north of the city, are interesting remains of the ancient Mound Builders. Population, 1970, 27,633.

Portsmouth. A seaport of southeastern Virginia, occupying the mainland side of the important harbor of Norfolk-Portsmouth Here the larger railway systems of the South have deep-water terminals and are connected with Norfolk, just across the harbor, by passenger and railroad car ferries. An immense tonnage, both foreign and domestic, passes through the port of Norfolk-Portsmouth. This consists chiefly of cotton, coal, lumber, fruits, vegetables, oysters, fertilizers, grain, coffee, and peanuts. This port is the greatest peanut market in the world. There are extensive industries, including railroad shops, fertilizer works, barrel factories, cottonseed oil mills, and lumber mills.

A few blocks south of the center of Portsmouth is the navy yard, officially known as the Norfolk navy yard. This occupies 350 acres, contains immense dry docks, and is the most important naval establishment in the United States. Population, 1970, 109,827.

Poughkeepsie (*pô-kĭp'sĭ*). A city in New York State on the east bank of the Hudson River, about 75 miles north of New York City. It is picturesquely situated on high ground commanding a fine view of the Hudson River, which is here crossed by two magnificent bridges. The city conducts an extensive local trade. The chief manufactures include farm machinery, ball bearings, cough drops, cigars, and electronic data-processing machines. Poughkeepsie is the seat of Vassar College. Population, 1970, 32,029.

Princeton. A university town of central New Jersey, about 50 miles southwest of New York City. Founded in 1696, Princeton remained a straggling village until the College of New Jersey, now Princeton University, was removed, in 1756, from Newark to Princeton. It soon became a center of higher education and has remained distinctly a university town. Early in 1777, the battle of Princeton was fought in the vicinity. From June to November, 1783, Congress sat in Princeton. The town is built on an elevated site, commanding fine views of the surrounding country. It has broad, well shaded streets, and the architecture of its colonial period has been largely preserved. Besides the university, Princeton is also the seat of Princeton Theological Seminary, the Institute for Advanced Study, and the Westminster Choir College. Population, 1970, 12,311.

Providence. The capital of Rhode Island, and the second largest city of New England. It is situated on Narragansett Bay, about 45 miles southwest of Boston. The city has excellent railway facilities and a fine harbor.

While maintaining a substantial coastwise shipping trade, Providence is pre-eminently an industrial city, with extensive and varied manufactures. It is a leading center for the manufacture of jewelry, and for similar articles requiring a high degree of artistic skill. Among other important industrial products are abrasives, chemicals, precision tools, plastics, knit goods, pens, pencils, and rubber products.

The city is substantially built, and contains many fine parks and public buildings, including an imposing State Capitol and the beautiful Roger Williams Park. Brown University, chartered in 1764, and other important institutions are located in the city. Providence was founded and named in 1636 by Roger Williams, and here, in 1639, he organized the first Baptist Church in America. Population, 1970, 179,213.

Provincetown. A small town in Massachusetts, at the extreme outer edge of Cape Cod Bay, known to history as the first landing point to which the Pilgrims came in November of 1620, and the place where the Mayflower Compact was signed before the settlers sailed on to Plymouth. Once a thriving center of the whaling trade, the town is still engaged mainly in fishing industries, particularly in the marketing of cod and mackerel. In recent years, Provincetown has become well known as a gathering place for various artist groups, who make up a considerable part of its summer population. Some years ago, through the Provincetown Players, it gained fame as a proving ground for budding playwrights, of whom probably the best known were Susan Glaspell and Eugene O'Neill. Population, 1970, 2911.

Provo. A city of north central Utah, picturesquely situated in a fertile valley at the foot of the Wasatch Mountains, 44 miles south of Salt Lake City. Provo is the trade center of a rich irrigated district devoted to agriculture, fruit growing, and stock raising, and is the seat of Brigham Young University. Population, 1970, 53,131.

Pueblo (*pwĕb'lō*). The second largest commercial and industrial city in Colorado, located on the Arkansas River, about 120 miles south of Denver. Pueblo has immense iron and steel works, and is near a region rich in coal and oil. The city has also various other manufactories and extensive stockyards. There are many fine public buildings, including the State Historical Museum. Population, 1970, 97,453.

Quincy (*kwĭn'sĭ*). A manufacturing city of western Illinois, on the Mississippi River, about 110 miles northwest of Saint Louis. Built on the top of a limestone bluff, Quincy overlooks an enchanting panorama of river, valley, and surrounding hills. The city is the commercial center of a rich agricultural region. Its manufactures include electronic equipment, air compressors, pumps, ranges, truck and trailer bodies, poultry equipment, pulp-board, shoes, containers, and various dairy products. There are numerous fine parks, boulevards, and public buildings. The Mississippi is spanned here by a great bridge. Population, 1970, 45,288.

Quincy (*kwĭn'zĭ*). A city of eastern Massachusetts, situated on Quincy Bay, about 8 miles south of Boston. While essentially a residential suburb of Boston, Quincy has a large granite quarrying industry, and also huge shipyards, engine works, brass and iron works, rivet mills, and soap and aluminum factories. The city contains many fine streets and homes, and the park system covers 2614 acres.

Settled in 1625 as Mount Wollaston, Quincy ranks among the oldest permanent settlements in New England. Until 1792, when the community was incorporated under its present name, it was a part of Braintree. The first commercial railway in America was constructed here 1826–27 to transport granite used in building Bunker Hill Monument. Quincy enjoys the distinction of being the birthplace of two presidents, John Adams and John Quincy Adams, and also of John Hancock. Population, 1970, 87,966.

Racine. A manufacturing city of southeastern Wisconsin, located on a fine harbor on Lake Michigan, 65 miles north of Chicago. In value of its manufactures, Racine ranks second only to Milwaukee among the cities of the state, and is noted especially for the manufacture of threshing machines and farm implements. Other important manufactures include automobiles, machine shop products, furniture, hardware, and electrical equipment. Noted for its beautiful residential sections, Racine also has a park system covering 635 acres. More than one-third of the inhabitants are of Danish descent. Population, 1970, 95,162.

Rainier (*rā-nēr'*), **Mount.** The loftiest peak in the Cascade range, situated in southwestern Washington about 50 miles southeast of Tacoma. It rises to an elevation of 14,408 feet, overtopping all other summits in the Pacific states except Mount Whitney in California.

Like Fuji in Japan, Mount Rainier rises majestically in graceful lines that proclaim its volcanic origin. Its summit lies in perpetual snow and on its upper slopes there are numerous glaciers. These are from 50 to 500 feet thick and cover a total area of about 50 square miles. Some of these glaciers are from 4 to 6 miles long, and in size and beauty rival those of the Alps.

The lower slopes of the mountain are clothed with luxuriant forests, containing trees of unusual size. Above the forests, which extend to an elevation of about 7000 feet, are many picturesque mountain meadows. In summer, these bear a profusion of beautiful alpine flowers that follow the retreating snow banks almost up to the line of perpetual frost. The summit rises about 8000 feet above the general level of the Cascades and affords excellent views of the Puget Sound region. Mount Rainier, in 1899, was created a national park.

Raleigh (*rô'lĭ*). The capital of North Carolina, situated in the central part of the state. Raleigh is a large cotton and tobacco market and has varied industries, the manufacture of textiles, fertilizers, and cottonseed oil being among the more important. The city contains some 13 park areas, including Pullen Park, a 74-acre semiforest tract of exceptional beauty. Nearby is the house in which Andrew Johnson was born. The city's streets are wide and, for the most part, lined with beautiful shade trees. Among the more notable buildings are the State Capitol on grounds covering four acres, the Federal Post Office and Court Building, the State Agricultural Building, Sir Walter Hotel, Christ Church, and the Municipal Auditorium. Raleigh is the seat of North Carolina State University. The site of the city was selected for the state capital in 1792, and the city was founded in that year. Population, 1970, 121,577.

Reading (*red'ĭng*). A city of southeastern Pennsylvania, on the Schuylkill River, 58 miles northwest of Philadelphia. Situated in a rich agricultural region and near large fields of anthracite coal and iron ore, Reading possesses unusual commercial advantages. The chief industries are the manufacture of machine products, auto frames, and electric components. Other industries include railway maintenance and the manufacture of iron and steel, hosiery, castings, copper products, caskets, sweaters, paints, optical products, and building and fire brick.

Reading occupies a site between the base of Mount Penn and the Schuylkill River. The summits of Mount Penn, to the east, and Neversink Mountain, to the south, both rise to elevations of about 800 feet and command magnificent views. The city was laid out in 1748 in accordance with the plans of Thomas and Richard Penn, sons of William Penn. Daniel Boone was born near here. The early inhabitants were mostly German. Population, 1970, 87,643.

Redlands. A city of southern California, picturesquely situated in the foothills of the San Bernardino Mountains, about 60 miles east of Los Angeles. Redlands is a noted residential city, health resort, and educational center, in the heart of an immensely productive orange growing district. Smiley Heights, one of the city's numerous parks, affords a magnificent view of the surrounding region, embracing orange and lemon groves, grain fields, forests, and snow-capped mountains. The city is the seat of the University of Redlands. Population, 1970, 36,355.

Reno. The chief commercial and industrial city of Nevada, located near the western boundary of the state, about 30 miles northwest of Carson City. Reno lies in a sheltered valley near the eastern base of the Sierra Nevada mountains at an elevation of 4500 feet. It is on the Truckee River, which feeds the Truckee-Carson Canal, a government irrigation project that waters more than 100,000 acres. The city is the distributing center of an extensive region devoted to mining, farming, and stock raising. Reno's biggest single industry is tourism, with its related gaming and entertainment operations. The University of Nevada at Reno is located here. Population, 1970, 72,863.

Richmond. An important deep-water Pacific coast port across the bay from San Francisco. Settled on the coming of the railroad in 1899, its industries have shown remarkable development. These include oil-refining, food-processing, and metal fabrication. The Santa Fe railroad's western terminal shops are located here. Many persons are employed in research agencies and distributive industries. Large shipyards were constructed at Richmond during World War II. Population, 1970, 79,043.

Richmond. The capital of Virginia, located at the head of navigation on the James River, about 100 miles almost directly south of Washington. Richmond is an important railway center and has excellent air transportation facilities and a new deep-water river terminal. It is a leading tobacco market and one of the chief manufacturing centers of the South. Industries include packaging of many kinds, and the manufacture of tobacco in various forms, synthetic fibers, chemicals, drugs, paints, food, metals, and men's clothing.

The city occupies a commanding site, covering seven hills, and is sometimes styled the "Modern Rome." It is regularly laid out, rising in terraces from the river. There are many beautiful parks and imposing public buildings. Among the most noteworthy of the latter is the Capitol, designed after the Maison Carrée at Nimes, France, and built 1785–92. The city possesses many fine monumental and sculptural works, including the equestrian statue of Washington at Capitol Square.

Richmond is exceedingly rich in historic associations, and in colonial days, like Boston in New England, it played a prominent part in shaping the destinies of the country. In Saint John's Episcopal Church, in March 1775, Patrick Henry made his noted speech containing the famous exclamation, "Give me liberty or give me death!" From May 8, 1861, to April 2, 1865, it was the capital of the Confederate states. The executive mansion, occupied by Jefferson Davis, 1862–65, has been transformed into a Confederate Museum. The former residence of John Marshall, built in 1795, still stands; also the Lee mansion, occupied by General R. E. Lee's family during the Civil War. Richmond was established as a town in 1733, and chartered as a city in 1782. Population, 1970, 249,621.

Riverside. An important orange-growing center of southern California, situated on the Santa Ana River, 53 miles east of Los Angeles. Much of Riverside's beauty lies in thousands of acres of orange groves and in its 130,000 street trees. The city is noted for its distinctive "Indian rain cross" street lights, patterned after an ancient heathen symbol, prayed to for rain by the Navajo and Central American Indians. The "Parent" Naval Orange tree, from which all navel oranges in California's multimillion dollar citrus industry descended, still flourishes in a park in the center of the city.

Riverside conducts a substantial local trade, has large Portland cement works, and ships annually from its warehouses thousands of carloads of oranges. Riverside is widely known for the Mission Inn, containing numerous exhibits connected with the early Mission days of California. Riverside is the seat of the University of California at Riverside, California Baptist College, and Sherman Indian High School, among other educational institutions. Population, 1970, 140,089.

Roanoke. The chief industrial and mercantile city of southwestern Virginia is situated on the Roanoke River, 150 miles west of Richmond, in a picturesque valley between the Blue Ridge and the Allegheny mountains. As an electric power and transportation center, it affords ample facilities for the development of extensive industries which are diversified in character and number more than 250. Roanoke is a tourist mecca and is the headquarters of the Blue Ridge Parkway. Both Roanoke College and Hollins College are located here. Population, 1970, 92,115.

Rochester. A city of southeastern Minnesota, on the Zumbro River, about 80 miles southeast of Saint Paul. It is the trade center of a rich agricultural district and has substantial industries. The city is the seat of Saint Mary's Hospital and of the Mayo Clinic, founded by the surgeons Charles and William Mayo. The 19-story Plummer Building, which houses part of this clinic, has, in its tower, a 23-bell carillon as a soldiers' memorial. Population, 1970, 53,766.

Rochester. A city of west central New York, built on both banks of the Genesee River, at the Genesee Falls, and extending to Lake Ontario. Rochester ranks second in population and third in manufactures among the cities of the state. Factors which have contributed to its eminence as an industrial center are abundant power, derived from the falls of the river, and excellent transportation facilities afforded by Lake Ontario, the State Barge Canal, numerous rail and bus lines. It has a port on Lake Ontario.

The city's extensive manufactures embrace more than 350 different commodities. These are produced in upwards of 1700 factories and consist largely of articles requiring the employment of a high degree of mechanical skill. Rochester leads the world in the manufacture of photographic, optical, dental, check-protecting, industrial fluid-mixing, and gear-cutting equipment; process-control and recording instruments; enameled steel tanks; mail chutes; and thermometers.

Rochester occupies a nearly level site and is divided into two almost equal parts by the Genesee River, which is spanned by 12 bridges, some of which are 200 feet high. In the center of the city is the Upper Falls, 96 feet in height; below them the river flows in a deep gorge to the Lower Falls, 80 feet high. The park system, covering nearly 2000 acres in 12 units, is one of the most beautiful in America. Highland Park is world-famous for its displays of over 1500 lilac bushes of more than 500 varieties.

The city is the seat of the University of Rochester, Saint Bernard's Seminary, Rochester Institute of Technology, Colgate Rochester Divinity School, St. John Fisher College, Nazareth College, and other important educational institutions, and affords exceptional advantages for the study and enjoyment of art and music, particularly at the Eastman School of Music.

First permanently settled in 1812, Rochester was incorporated as a village in 1817 and chartered as a city in 1834. The completion, in 1825, of the Erie Canal greatly stimulated the city's growth. During the early period, when the Genesee valley was the chief wheat belt of the country, Rochester was known as the "Flour City." With the decline of milling and the rise of the nursery industry this sobriquet was changed to the "Flower City." Since the development of its great camera and photographic supply business, it has been styled the "Kodak City." Population, 1970, 296,233.

Rockford. A manufacturing city of Illinois, on the Rock River, about 90 miles northwest of Chicago. Abundant power, furnished by a great dam in the river, is utilized in its large and varied industries. Among these are the manufacture of machine tools, farm implements, furniture, and hardware. The city is the seat of Rockford College. A park in the center of the city contains the Turtle Indian mound. First settled in 1834, Rockford was chartered as a city in 1852. Population, 1970, 147,370.

Rock Island. A city of western Illinois, on the Mississippi River, adjoining Moline, and opposite Davenport, Iowa, with which it is connected by bridges including the four-lane Centennial bridge. These three cities with East Moline are called the Quad-City area. The city takes its name from an island in the river opposite the upper section of the town. Abundant hydroelectric power, provided by a government dam, has aided in the development of the city's substantial industries, which include the manufacture of agricultural implements, rubber footwear, food products, wood products, clothing, and concrete products. An immense government arsenal is located on the island. Rock Island was chartered as a city in 1841. Population, 1970, 50,166.

ROCKY MOUNTAIN NATIONAL PARK. An area of about 410 square miles in the heart of the Rocky Mountains, reserved as a national park in 1915. It is in north central Colorado about 50 miles northwest of Denver. It is traversed by the Continental Divide, which here rises to a height of over 14,000 feet and provides scenery of unsurpassed grandeur.

SIZE AND SURFACE. The park extends about 25 miles north and south, and from 12 to 20 miles from east to west. Altitudes within it range from 8000 to 14,256 feet above sea level, the highest point being Longs Peak, in the southeastern portion of the park, a mountain of the Snowy range. This range follows a general north and south direction. On its west side this mountain chain slopes gently down in a lovely region diversified by streams and charming lakes, the largest and deepest being Grand Lake. The eastern slope, however, is precipitous and awe-inspiring, bold summits standing out in daring relief separated by gorges with walls often 1000 to 2000 feet high. In the northern portion of the park are several peaks over 13,000 feet in height, including Hagues Peak and Mummy and Ypsilon mountains. Mount Copeland at the extreme south also exceeds 13,000 feet.

Glaciers. There are few places on the earth where the effects of glacial erosion can be seen and understood so easily as in Rocky Mountain Park. Andrews glacier is the largest of those which still exist, but numerous huge moraines attest the stupendous force of these mountain-carving agents in past ages, when they were vastly more extensive. At Moraine Park is a ridge 800 feet high marking the lower edge of an ice-age glacier which crept down from Forest Canyon. The Mills moraine, at the foot of Longs Peak precipice, is 1000 feet high and four miles long. Glaciers still active seldom extend below an altitude of 12,000 feet. The timber line is reached at about 11,000 feet.

Travel Facilities. There are four principal approaches to Rocky Mountain Park, three from the east converging at the hotel village of Estes Park, and one western approach known as the Grand Lake route. Motor highways also give access to the park from Denver, Boulder, and Grand Junction over these same approaches.

The park has over 300 miles of trails, but the principal scenic road is the Trail Ridge Road, which connects the western approach via Grand Lake with Estes Park. Following the crest of the Continental Divide for about three miles at an altitude of 11,800 feet, it is one of the highest roads in North America. It commands superb views of mountain peaks, chasms, waterfalls, glaciers, and mountain lakes.

Animals. Rocky Mountain Park contains many bighorns, which particularly frequent Bighorn mountain, descending daily to drink from Sheep Lake in Horseshoe Park. Beavers are numerous, and much land on valley floors is marshy by reason of dams built by these animals. Deer abound and there are elk herds and some bears. The streams and lakes are stocked with fish from a hatchery in Estes Park.

Rome. A manufacturing city on the Mohawk River in New York, about 90 miles northwest of Albany. Its industrial output includes many items, but Rome is particularly noted for its copper and brass products, and has the largest fish hatchery in New York. Located in or near the city are the Rome State School for Mental Defectives; Griffiss Air Force Base; Fort Stanwix, claimed to be the place where, during the Revolutionary War, the Stars and Stripes were first flown in battle; and the grave of Francis Bellamy, author of the "Pledge of Allegiance to the Flag." Population, 1970, 47,655.

Roswell. This city in the Pecos valley in southeastern New Mexico owes its origin chiefly to its abundant water supply, having been known as an oasis even before the discovery of artesian wells there. A city of homes, with tributary cattle raising and oil industries, it is also prominent as a tourist center, one of its attractions being Bottomless Lake State Park. Educational institutions include Eastern New Mexico University at Roswell and New Mexico Military Institute. Population, 1970, 33,908.

Royal Gorge. The deepest part of the Grand Canyon of the Arkansas River. It is situated in central Colorado, 45 miles west of Pueblo. The entire canyon, about 8 miles long, has precipitous walls of eroded granite which rise to an immense height. In the portion a mile and a half long called the Royal Gorge, these titanic walls tower almost perpendicularly 2600 feet above the foaming torrent of the river. At the narrowest part, the stream fills the canyon nearly from wall to wall, and the railway passes through it over a bridge hung from transverse girders mortised into the rocks of both sides of the canyon.

Sacramento. The capital of California, located on the Sacramento River 90 miles northeast of San Francisco. Sacramento lies in the midst of a very rich farming and fruit growing region, and the most important of the city's varied industries is the canning of fruit. Among the other establishments are large railroad shops; factories making missile engines; flour, rice, and lumber mills; meat packing houses; and a huge air corps supply depot of the army. The city is built on the site of Sutter's Fort, the first settlement in California reached by the gold seekers of 1849 and 1850. The fort, rebuilt, houses relics of the pioneer days.

The handsome Capitol and a number of other state buildings form a multi-million dollar group in a beautiful 38-acre park in the center of the city. The park system covers about 1200 acres, the largest unit being Del Paso Park of 828 acres. Sacramento was incorporated in 1849 and became the state capital in 1854. A state college is located here. Population, 1970, 254,413.

Sagamore Hill. The country estate and residence of Theodore Roosevelt, situated near the town of Oyster Bay, on the northern shore of Long Island, about 30 miles northeast of New York City. In 1963, it was established as a national historic site. Young's Memorial Cemetery, which contains the grave of the former president, is also situated at Oyster Bay.

Saginaw. A city of southeastern Michigan, built at the head of navigation on the Saginaw River, 85 miles northwest of Detroit. The city lies in rich coal and oil fields and has immense supplies of hydroelectric power. There are many salt wells in the vicinity. Its industries produce, among other commodities, automobiles and parts, foundry and machine shop products, furniture, coal, beet sugar, and oil. Saginaw has extensive car shops. There are fine parks and public buildings, including hospitals and educational institutions. Population, 1970, 91,849.

Saint Augustine (*ô'gŭs-tēn'*). The oldest city in the United States, situated on the east coast of Florida, about 30 miles southeast of Jacksonville. Saint Augustine was founded in 1565 by the Spanish under Pedro Menendez de Aviles, sent by Philip II of Spain. With the exception of 20 years, 1763–83, when it was in the hands of the British, Saint Augustine remained a Spanish city until 1821, when the United States acquired Florida. In the old part of the town, the quaint, narrow streets are lined with ancient houses built of the shell material known as coquina. Many of these houses have overhanging balconies and are set amid gardens luxuriant with semitropical vegetation.

Among the many historic buildings are Fort Marion, the oldest fort in the United States, begun in 1656; the remodeled governor's palace; the Old Spanish Treasury; and the famous city gates. Saint Augustine is a noted winter resort and contains many fine hotels. Among these are the Alcazar and the palatial Ponce de Leon hotel, built in the Spanish Renaissance style. Population, 1970, 12,352.

Saint Joseph. A city of Missouri, built on the east bank of the Missouri River, about 60 miles north of Kansas City. The city lies picturesquely along the bluffs of the river. It is the center of a rich agricultural region with which it carries on a large merchandising and marketing trade. Saint Joseph is one of the leading live stock markets of the country, and contains several meat packing establishments. Its chief manufactures are packing-house products and flour products, including pancake flour. Other important manufactures include chemicals, malt beverages, paper products, and cans. Parks occupy about 1350 acres. A park about the Civic Center has a pony express monument, commemorating this service which began in 1860 between St. Joseph and Sacramento, Cal. Saint Joseph was first settled in 1826 by Joseph Robidoux, a French fur trader; it was incorporated in 1845 and became a city in 1851. Population, 1970, 72,691.

SAINT LOUIS (*lo͞o'ĭs*). The chief city of Missouri, situated on the Mississippi River, about 20 miles below the mouth of the Missouri.

Site. Saint Louis occupies a commanding site, rising in a succession of gently sloping hills and depressions, each ridge toward the west ascending higher and finally reaching, at the western limits, an elevation of some 300 feet above the river. The boundaries are two curved lines, the crescent-like bend of the Mississippi on the east and an arbitrary boundary on the west. The total frontage on the river is more than 19 miles, the length of the western boundary is about 21 miles, and the maximum width is nearly 7 miles. The total area slightly exceeds 61 square miles.

Streets and Buildings. In the small, older portion of the city, the streets are narrow and more or less irregular. The modern parts of the city have been laid out, wherever possible, with wide streets, crossing at right angles, and in north-and-south and east-and-west directions.

The Old Cathedral on Walnut Street is the most noteworthy example of the French period in the history of Saint Louis. Among the many notable modern buildings are the City Hall, which resembles an old French hotel de ville; the Union Station, in Renaissance style; the buildings of Washington University, in Tudor Gothic style; the Public Library, built of Maine granite in the early Italian Renaissance style, and the Art Museum and the Jefferson Memorial, in the classic style. Other noteworthy structures are the immense Saint Louis Cathedral, distinctly Romanesque; the Protestant Episcopal Cathedral, in modified Gothic; and the impressive Shaare Emeth Synagogue. A group of imposing buildings on Lindell Boulevard includes the Masonic Temple, the Shriners' Moolah Temple, and the Scottish Rite Cathedral. The tallest buildings include the Civil Courts Building and the 31-story Southwestern Bell Telephone Building.

No city in America excels Saint Louis in the beauty of its exclusive residential districts, called "places." In these are magnificent homes with spacious grounds reflecting the highest skill of the architect and the landscape gardener. Washington Terrace, Westmoreland, Kingsbury, and Portland rank among the most noted of the places. Other fine residential sections are found in Compton Heights, Hortense Place, Parkview, and in Hillcrest, and also along Forsyth and Lindell boulevards.

Saint Louis is distinctively a city of brick, and, with few exceptions, even the most elaborate mansions are built of this material. Owing to comparative cheapness of local building materials, especially brick and limestone, a large percentage of the inhabitants live in separate homes.

Civic Improvements. A unique recreation facility is the Open Air Municipal theater located in Forest Park. A civic center on a memorial plaza, occupying 9 downtown blocks, accommodates an auditorium and other city buildings. A 37-block river-front area constitutes the Jefferson National Expansion Memorial, which commemorates the Louisiana Purchase and Westward expansion in the U.S., with a Gateway Arch, 630 feet high and from base to base, and a rich underground historical museum. Completed in 1966, the steel and concrete arch weighs 16,678 tons. Visitors may ride to the top of the arch in transit gondolas and from there view the city.

Parks. The city has 68 parks, covering an area of more than 3000 acres. Forest Park, the largest, containing 1381 acres, lies almost directly west of the business center. Other important recreation grounds are the Missouri Botanical Garden, Tower Grove, O'Fallon, Carondelet, and Lafayette parks. Forest Park has one of America's finest zoos and a $1.5 million planetarium. Several of the parks are ornamented with noteworthy works of sculpture, including statues of Shakespeare, Columbus, Jefferson, and St. Louis, the crusader king of France, for whom the city was named.

Educational Institutions. Among the leading educational institutions are the University of Missouri at St. Louis, Washington University, Saint Louis University, and Concordia and Eden seminaries. The Missouri Botanical Garden, founded by Henry Shaw and usually called Shaw's Garden, is now maintained for the public. It contains a fine arboretum and a collection of native and foreign plants, especially orchids, rivaling those of Kew Gardens in London.

Transportation. Two great advantages make Saint Louis pre-eminent as a commercial and industrial center. The first is its location in the heart of the great Mississippi valley, the most fertile agricultural region in the world. The second lies in its unsurpassed facilities for transportation. Barge lines handle an immense tonnage between Saint Paul and Minneapolis on the north and New Orleans on the south. Additional facilities include 16 trunk-line railroads, 9 scheduled airlines, and 5 major highways having access to 7 steel bridges across the Mississippi River.

Commerce. Saint Louis is the most important distributing center of the Mississippi valley, handling products representing the entire country. It is a great grain, live stock, horse, tobacco, and wool market and conducts an immense wholesaling trade.

Manufactures. In value of manufactures, Saint Louis ranks among the nine leading cities of the United States. Its extensive industries embrace the manufacture of an exceedingly wide range of products. It is one of the greatest shoe and tobacco manufacturing centers of the United States and has one of the world's largest breweries. Other important manufactures include packed meats, coke, blast furnace, foundry, machine shop, and rolling mill products, refined petroleum, clothing, chemicals, medicinal compounds, locomotive parts, aircraft, railway and rapid transit cars, jute goods, hot-air furnaces, stoves, clay products, automobiles, furs, and furniture.

History. Saint Louis was established in 1764 as a fur trading station by Pierre Laclède Liguest, assisted by Auguste Chouteau. Though under the control of Spain from 1770 to 1804, the place remained essentially French. In 1804, Saint Louis came into the possession of the United States by the Louisiana Purchase. The first newspaper was published in 1808, and, with the arrival of the first steamboat in 1815, a new era in the history of Saint Louis was opened. From 1840 to 1880, it passed 38 other American cities in population, and was passed by only one—Chicago. In 1904, the Louisiana Purchase exposition was held in the city. A feature of interest is the annual festival of the Veiled Prophet, somewhat similar to the Mardi Gras of New Orleans. Population, 1970, 622,236.

Saint Paul. The capital of Minnesota, built on both banks of the Mississippi River, immediately below Minneapolis. A part of the western boundary of Saint Paul is contiguous with the eastern limits of Minneapolis, but the commercial centers of these "Twin Cities" are about 10 miles apart.

The city is built chiefly on the left or east bank of the Mississippi, and occupies three terraces, rising in all from 100 to 200 feet above the river. The lowest section contains railway yards, stock yards, wholesale houses, and factories. Lying above this, on the middle terrace, is the commercial district and a part of the residential section. On the uppermost terrace, crowning the highest bluffs, is the fine residence section.

Saint Paul is admirably laid out, with many handsome streets, among the most scenic of which are Kellogg Boulevard and Summit Drive. The various parks, playgrounds, and connecting boulevards cover a total area of more than 2240 acres. In Como and Phalen parks there are picturesque lakes. Indian Mound Park affords unsurpassed views of the Mississippi River.

Foremost among the city's notable buildings is the beautiful State Capitol, constructed of marble and granite and containing many fine sculptural and mural decorations. Other fine structures are the Roman Catholic Cathedral, the Hill Memorial Library, the Minnesota Historical Building, and the Union railway station, completed in 1926 at a cost of $15 million. The beautiful buildings and grounds of the Minnesota Horticultural Society are at the northern end of the city. The annual state fair held here is one of the largest in the United States. Within the city are several important educational institutions, including Hamline University, Macalester College, Concordia College, Saint Thomas College, and the Saint Paul College of Law.

Saint Paul enjoys exceptional transportation facilities, both by rail and by river. On the completion of extensive canalization work in the Mississippi River, a barge service was opened in 1928. For a long period prior to this the river had scarcely been used for freight transfer although it had earlier been the main artery of commerce.

The St. Paul area is one of the great wholesale and jobbing centers of the country, with a total annual trade exceeding $500 million. The city is also an important market for live stock and, in manufactures, ranks second among the cities of the state. Prominent among the city's manufactures are railway cars, boots and shoes, fur goods, refrigerators, cordage and twine, law books, automobiles, glass, butter, and packed meats.

Settled in 1839, Saint Paul was made the territorial capital in 1849, and, upon the admission of Minnesota into the Union in 1858, was made the capital of the state. From about 1870, following the extensive building of railways and the settlement of the Northwest, the city grew rapidly. Population, 1970, 309,980.

Saint Petersburg. A summer and winter resort of western Florida, about 20 miles southwest of Tampa. The city is charmingly situated on Pinellas Peninsula with the Gulf of Mexico on the west and, on the south and east, Tampa Bay, which is here spanned by the 6-mile Gandy highway bridge. Extending 2400 feet into the bay is a million-dollar recreation pier. The city has 65 parks and 33 miles of water front. The post office is an open-air building, appropriate for the equable, sunny, subtropical climate which attracts an immense number of winter residents. Thousands of green benches on Central Avenue are a feature of the city. Population, 1970, 216,232.

Salem. A city of eastern Massachusetts, built on a peninsula between two inlets of the Atlantic Ocean, 16 miles northeast of Boston. Though irregularly laid out, Salem occupies an attractive site, with a fine drive along the north shore, and contains several beautiful parks. There are several very early colonial houses, numerous old mansions, dating from the period of the city's commercial supremacy, and many fine modern homes.

From early colonial years until about 1860, Salem was an important trading port. With the advent of steam navigation, its foreign commerce was largely transferred to Boston. The city still maintains an extensive coastwise trade, especially in coal. The substantial manufactures include cotton goods, games, radio tubes, leather, and shoes.

Salem is the seat of the Essex Institute, Peabody Museum, and Salem State College. Founded in 1626, Salem is one of the oldest cities of New England, and is rich in historical associations. In 1692, it was the scene of the Salem witchcraft delusion. Many early dwellings are well preserved, as, for example, Hawthorne's birthplace, the House of Seven Gables, and the witch jail, built in 1684. Population, 1970, 40,556.

Salem. The capital of Oregon, situated on the Willamette River in the northwestern portion of the state. Salem is the trade center of a fertile agricultural region; the industrial interests center about hop products, peppermint oil, linen, fruit and meat packing, mobile homes, and wood products. Wide streets and two public parks enhance the appearance of the city. Among the principal buildings are the Capitol, the Federal Building, and the Supreme Court Building. The city is the seat of Willamette University and of various state institutions. Salem was settled in 1840, was incorporated in 1853, and became the state capital in 1860. Population, 1970, 68,296.

Salt Lake City. The capital of Utah, the chief commercial city between Denver and San Francisco. The city is magnificently situated at the western base of the Wasatch Mountains, at an elevation of about 4300 feet above the sea, some 12 miles southeast of Great Salt Lake. It occupies a gently sloping site at the edge of a wide plain made highly fertile by irrigation. A noteworthy feature of the city is its unusually wide streets, at the sides of many of which run conduits bringing water from the mountains for freshening the vegetation of parks, lawns, and gardens. It has 7000 acres set aside as public parks.

Salt Lake City is the distributing center for a vast and rich region devoted to mining, stock raising, and agriculture. There are important mining interests, with large smelters and mineral mills in the city and vicinity. The city's industrial output includes petroleum and steel products, woolens, beet sugar, candy, salt.

In the heart of the city is Temple Square, containing the famous Mormon Tabernacle, a huge oval building capable of seating 8000 people; the impressive granite temple which took 40 years to erect (1853–93); and the large assembly hall built to accommodate 3000 persons. Among other fine buildings are the State Capitol and City and County building. Memory Park, east of the Capitol, commemorates local veterans of World War I. The city is the seat of the University of Utah, a State Normal school, and several other educational institutions.

Approximately 28 miles southwest of Salt Lake City at Bingham Canyon is the Bingham Copper Mine, the largest surface copper mine in North America.

Salt Lake City was founded by Brigham Young, the leader of a party of Mormons who arrived in the valley in 1847, and it has since been the headquarters of the Church of Jesus Christ of Latter-Day Saints. About 40 per cent of the people are Latter-Day Saints, who have more than 54 places of worship in the city. Population, 1970, 175,885.

Salton Sea. A brackish lake in the central depression of the Colorado Desert in southeastern California. Prior to 1905, this was a salt marsh interspersed with shallow saline ponds and lakes, covering an area about 30 miles long and 12 miles wide, with the surface lying about 280 feet below sea level. During the spring rains, however, the lake usually expanded into a body of water occupying an area of some 60 or 70 square miles, which, with the coming of the dry season, rapidly receded.

In 1905 and 1906, by an accidental inflow of water from the Colorado River, through defective irrigation canals, this watery marsh expanded into a lake 40 miles long, from 10 to 16 miles wide, and 90 feet deep, covering in all some 515 square miles. At its greatest height, the surface of the lake was only 194 feet below sea level.

After the inflow of water from the Colorado River was stopped in 1907, the lake receded as a result of evaporation until, by 1920, it covered only 265 square miles. Its surface was then approximately 250 feet below sea level. Since that time it has remained fairly stable, due to the inflow of natural drainage and a large volume of seepage and waste water from the irrigated lands in the Imperial Valley.

San Angelo. A city built near old Fort Concho on the river of that name in western Texas. It is a wool and mohair market and a distributing and shipping center for cattle, agricultural products, and oil. Manufactures include cottonseed oil, petroleum, surgical sutures, ceramic tile, skins and hides, and dairy products. Angelo State University is located here. An outstanding educational institution is the campus-type Central High School. Population, 1970, 63,884.

San Antonio. Next to San Augustine, the oldest city of Texas, situated on a river of the same name, 80 miles southwest of Austin. San Antonio is noted for its delightful and healthful climate and is the pleasure resort of thousands of visitors. On all sides are spacious grounds, luxuriant gardens, and an abundance of subtropical foliage and flowers. The 56 public parks and plazas cover 2200 acres. San Pedro Park, with its picturesque live oaks and its famous springs, is the original site of the Indian settlement of San Antonio. Many of the old buildings, especially the Alamo and San Fernando Cathedral, are full of historical interest. Fort Sam Houston is now the headquarters of the U.S. Fourth Army. Nearby are four important Air Force centers including Randolph Field and Kelly Air Force Base.

San Antonio is the commercial center of a large oil producing, agricultural and stock raising region, and is an important cattle, horse, and mule market. Its industrial establishments include oil refineries, flour mills, foundries, packing houses, cement works, and garment manufacturing.

The first permanent settlement was established in 1718 with the founding of the mission of San Antonio de Valero and the presidio of San Antonio de Bexar. In 1809 this settlement became a city. San Antonio was the scene of stirring events in the early history of Texas. Population, 1970, 654,153.

San Bernardino (*săn bûr'när-dē'nō*). A commercial and industrial city of southern California, about 60 miles east of Los Angeles. San Bernardino is situated in a beautiful valley surrounded by snow-capped mountains, near the entrance of the Cajon pass into the Mojave Desert. It is the trade center of a rich, irrigated district devoted chiefly to growing citrus fruits, grapes, and orchard crops. Its industrial establishments include large railroad shops, foundries, machine shops, and planing mills. First settled by Mormons in 1852, San Bernardino was incorporated as a town in 1868 and, in 1886, was chartered as a city. Population, 1970, 104,251.

San Diego (*dē-ā'gō*). Third largest city of California, with an excellent harbor on San Diego Bay, about 125 miles southeast of Los Angeles. The climate is mild and equable. Subtropical fruits flourish in the area. Among the leading industries are fish canning, the handling of fruits and fruit products, shipbuilding, and the growing of flowers, tomatoes, avocados, and citrus fruits. The manufactures include aircraft. The chief exports are fruits, honey, and citrus products.

San Diego is a United States naval base and one of the greatest naval aviation bases in America. It is also an important commercial aeronautical center, the airport, Lindbergh Field, being within five minutes' drive of the central business district. San Diego possesses many fine parks, Balboa Park alone having an area of 1400 acres. San Diego State College is located here. By reason of its climate and location, San Diego is a prominent health and travel resort. Among local points of interest are Coronado Beach, Fort Rosecrans, Point Loma, and Palomar Observatory. Population, 1970, 693,931.

SAN FRANCISCO. The principal seaport and manufacturing city of the Pacific coast of America, and second only to Los Angeles in population among the cities of the Pacific states. San Francisco is situated about 600 miles northwest of San Diego and about 900 miles south of Seattle.

Site. San Francisco occupies a magnificent site overlooking one of the finest natural harbors in the world. The city is built on the northern end of a semimountainous peninsula lying between the ocean on the west and San Francisco Bay on the east. The site, though generally sloping toward the east, is irregular, and embraces many bold hills, of which the highest, Twin Peaks, 925 feet high, separate the business district from the newer residential sections. The entrance from the ocean to the bay is through the Golden Gate, a narrow, rock-bound waterway whose attractive setting recalls Istanbul and Gibraltar. The city is connected with the north and east shores of the bay by two of the greatest suspension bridges in the world—Golden Gate and San Francisco-Oakland Bay.

Streets and Buildings. In general, the streets of the city are broad and straight, in some cases leading directly up steep hills. The district bounded approximately by Kearney and Stockton streets and by California and Pacific avenues, in the heart of the commercial section, is Chinatown, long a picturesque feature of the city. The level section south of Market Street contains the manufacturing district.

Of many imposing public buildings, the most important are those of the group forming the Civic Center, including the City Hall, the Public Library, and the Auditorium. Other notable buildings are the Post Office, the United States Mint, and the Union Ferry Building. Among the larger office buildings are the Southern Pacific Building, the Federal Reserve Bank, the Russ Building, 30 stories high, the Standard Oil Building, 22 stories high, the Hobart Building, 21 stories high, and the Claus Spreckles Building, 19 stories high, which withstood the ravages of the great fire of 1906.

Parks and Boulevards. The municipal park system includes 127 public recreation and park units covering 4043 acres. The chief of these, Golden Gate Park, covering 1013 acres, extends from near the center of the city west to the ocean. The principal points of scenic and historic interest are reached by an extensive system of boulevards and driveways. Those passing through the Presidio and Lincoln Park give fine views of the Golden Gate. These lead also past Sutro Baths and the Cliff House to the Great highway which runs close to the ocean for 3 miles. The historic Mission Road, the city's oldest thoroughfare, has been modernized. A boulevard extends to the top of Twin Peaks, whose lofty crest affords a splendid view.

Educational Institutions. Among the important educational and scientific institutions are the Memorial Museum, the California School of Fine Arts, the Mechanics Institute, the School of Mechanical Arts, the Cogswell Polytechnic Institute, and the San Francisco State College. The University of California is at Berkeley, across the bay; in San Francisco are located the affiliated colleges, which include the departments of medicine, dentistry, and pharmacy. Leland Stanford University is at Palo Alto, 33 miles distant.

Transportation. The harbor of San Francisco, completely sheltered from the sea by coastal hills, is one of the largest and safest on the globe. It has extensive docks, and is equipped with dry docks and other facilities for the care of vessels. The city is connected, by regular lines of steamships, with all ports on the Pacific coast of North and South America, with Atlantic seaports by way of the Panama Canal, and with Hawaii, the Philippines, Australia, China, and Japan.

San Francisco is the terminus of the Southern Pacific railway from New Orleans. Oakland, on the eastern side of the bay, is the terminus of three transcontinental systems, and connection with San Francisco across the bay is afforded by ferry and bridge services. Two systems of street railways and buses, one municipally owned and operated, provide local transportation.

COMMERCE. In foreign commerce, San Francisco ranks among the chief seaports of the country. The leading articles of export usually include canned fruits, canned salmon, raw cotton, iron and steel manufactures, grain, and oils. Among the principal imports are sugar, coffee, copra, burlap, tea, rubber, silk, and tin. The city also conducts an extensive coastwise commerce with other ports of the United States, and much Western produce is collected at San Francisco for distribution by rail.

FINANCE. San Francisco is the financial center of the Pacific coast. It is noted for the size and strength of its banking institutions, and is the headquarters of two of the largest banking organizations in America.

MANUFACTURES. San Francisco is, after Los Angeles, the leading city of the western United States in the total value of manufactured products. Crude petroleum, piped from vast oil fields, is extensively used for fuel. Among important industries are printing and publishing, meat packing, shipbuilding, coffee roasting, fruit canning, and the manufacture of paper products, furniture, confectionery, and paint.

FEATURES OF INTEREST. Among many noteworthy places of interest within the city and its environs are the Presidio, a large military reservation; the Cow Palace, Telegraph hill, Russian hill, and Twin Peaks, affording excellent views; Chinatown, with its Oriental character and aspect; the ocean shore at Cliff House; the celebrated Seal rocks, Mission Dolores, Mount Tamalpais and Muir Woods north of the Golden Gate; and Angel and Alcatraz islands the latter formerly a Federal prison island.

HISTORY. The site of San Francisco was visited in 1769 by Spaniards who called the place Yerba Buena. The first settlement began in 1776 with the establishment of Mission Dolores. In 1846, the United States took possession of California, and, in 1847, the name of the town was changed to San Francisco. Following the discovery of gold in California in 1848, the development of the town was spectacular, and, in 1850, it became a city. In 1862, telegraphic communication with the East was established, and, in 1869, the first transcontinental railway was completed. The most momentous event in the history of San Francisco was the earthquake of April 18, 1906, followed by a tremendous conflagration which almost totally destroyed the buildings on an area of more than 4 square miles, including the chief commercial and residential districts. Notwithstanding this enormous loss, the devastated area was rapidly rebuilt, and the city reconstructed on a grander and more substantial scale. Population, 1970, 715,674.

San Jose (*săn hô-sā'*). A city of west central California, situated in the beautiful and fertile Santa Clara valley, 50 miles southeast of San Francisco. It is in the midst of an important fruit growing region, and its principal commercial and industrial interests are connected with the cultivation of deciduous fruits. San Jose is noted for its salubrious climate and delightful gardens. Alum Rock Park, 776 acres in area, has 22 mineral springs, each with a grotto. San Jose possesses many fine buildings, including the San Jose State College. Lick Observatory, situated on Mount Hamilton, about 25 miles east of the city, attracts many visitors. The Ames Aeronautical and Space Research Laboratory is 9 miles north of the city. Population, 1970, 443,950.

San Juan (*săn hwăn'*). The capital city and chief seaport of Puerto Rico. It is built on two small islands, San Juan and Santurce, connected by five modern bridges. It possesses an excellent harbor and several fine plazas and gardens. The Capitol is a beautiful building of white marble in the classic style. The chief industry is the manufacture of tobacco and the handling of sugar, grapefruit, pineapples, and other fruits. Various industries have sprung up and flourished under favorable leigslation known as The Industrial Incentives Act.

San Juan was founded about 1519 by Ponce de Leon. The main part of the city is surrounded by medieval ramparts. Morro Castle, built in 1584, stands on a promontory to the west. San Juan came into the possession of the United States by cession at the close of the Spanish American War. Population, 1970, 444,952.

Santa Ana. A city of California located about 80 miles northwest of San Diego. Once a citrus center, Santa Ana now has diversified industry, including electronics and beet sugar refining. Population, 1970, 156,601.

Santa Barbara (*săn'tȧ bär'bȧ-rȧ*). A city of southern California, situated on Santa Barbara channel, about 90 miles northwest of Los Angeles. Santa Barbara lies in a beautiful valley opening southward to the sea, but encircled on the north and east by the Santa Ynez Mountains. Closely paralleling the shore, the high coast range extends for many miles in an east-and-west direction, resulting in a remarkably mild and salubrious climate. The city is in the midst of an important farming, lemon growing, walnut growing, and stock raising region. A large proportion of the lima beans grown for market in the United States are produced in this district. The city is zoned to prohibit industries that are not "smokeless."

The Santa Barbara Mission, founded in 1786, stands in the northern part of the city, and is still occupied by Franciscan monks. Santa Barbara is widely known for its attractive buildings in Spanish architecture. An "Old Spanish Days" fiesta is held each August at the full of the moon. Santa Barbara is a noted all-year resort. Population, 1970, 70,215.

Santa Catalina (*kăt'ȧ-lē'nȧ*). An island of southern California, separated from the mainland of Los Angeles county by San Pedro channel, some 20 miles wide. Santa Catalina is about 25 miles long and the average width is about 4 miles. The surface is semimountainous. Many interesting trees, shrubs, and other plants grow on the island, some of which do not occur elsewhere. The clear waters, remarkable for the beauty and variety of their marine life, are famous game-fishing grounds. Sea lions inhabit the south coast; flying fish are numerous in the channel, and whales are sometimes seen. The only town, Avalon, is a noted resort.

Santa Clara. A town in California, 47 miles southeast of San Francisco. Santa Clara was known for its fruits in the early mission days of California, and is still an important fruit-growing and packing center. It is the seat of the University of Santa Clara. Population, 1970, 87,717.

Santa Fe (*săn'tȧ fā'*). The capital of New Mexico, situated in the north central part of the state. First established in 1610, Santa Fe has ever since been the capital of New Mexico. The city was taken from Mexico by the United States in 1846. Stock raising is the main industry of the surrounding district. Indian pottery in large quantities is made by the Pueblo Indians.

The older part of the city has narrow, crooked streets with houses made of adobe or sun-dried brick. There are many buildings of historic interest: the Palace, beside a central plaza, where the Mexican governors resided; San Miguel Church; Cristo Rey Church; Scottish Rite Temple; and the State Art Museum, built in a mission style of architecture. The new capitol is round and styled as an Indian kiva. Population, 1970, 41,167.

Santa Monica. A city of southern California, on the Pacific Ocean, 16 miles west of downtown Los Angeles. By reason of its climate, bathing beaches, and boating facilities, Santa Monica is a popular year-round resort. Distinctive features include the Palisades Park and many fishing piers. Leading industries are electronics, aerospace research and development, missile production, plastics, ceramics, furniture making, and cosmetics manufacture. Population, 1970, 88,289.

Saratoga Springs. A city and famous watering place of eastern New York, about 30 miles almost directly north of Albany. It is noted for its numerous medicinal springs, which have made it one of the most attractive health resorts in America. The waters are bottled and shipped to various parts of the world. There are many recreational facilities.

Saratoga Springs was founded in 1789 and is the seat of Skidmore College for women. In a 30-acre park is the curious geological display known as the Petrified Sea Garden. The Saratoga battlefield, scene of Burgoyne's surrender and now a national historical park, is located 12 miles east of the city. Population, 1970, 18,845.

Sault Sainte Marie (*sōō sânt mȧ-rē'*). A city of northern Michigan, on the Saint Mary's River, and opposite a town of the same name in Ontario. At this point are the famous rapids (the *Sault* or "rapids" of Saint Mary), which make navigation impossible for lake vessels. However, between Lake Superior and Lake Huron, navigation has been made possible for ships of the heaviest tonnage by an extensive system of canals and locks. Some 25,000 ships, carrying about 100 million tons of freight, pass through this waterway every year. Immense hydroelectric power, generated at the rapids, is utilized in the city's growing industries, the chief of which is the manufacture of calcium carbide. Other manufactories include planing, paper, and machine shops. Sault Sainte Marie is the oldest settlement in Michigan. Population, 1970, 15,136.

Savannah. The second largest city of Georgia, situated on the Savannah River, about 18 miles from the sea. It occupies a fine level site and has an excellent harbor. Savannah is the leading port on the southern Atlantic coast of the United States, and has also large exports of lumber, fertilizers, tobacco, and naval stores. It has extensive industries, which include the manufacture of cottonseed oils, fertilizers, resin, turpentine, refined sugar, foundry and machine shop products, paper, cloth and paper bags, and aircraft.

Savannah is noted for its well shaded streets and for its beautiful parks and gardens luxuriant with subtropical vegetation. The city was founded in 1733 and received its municipal charter in 1789. During the Revolutionary War it was captured by the British, and in the Civil War it was the objective of Sherman's march to the sea. Population, 1970, 114,155.

Schenectady. A city of eastern New York, located on the Mohawk River and the State Barge Canal, 16 miles northwest of Albany. The older parts of the city are built along the river, but the more modern sections occupy the surrounding hills. Schenectady is unique among American cities of its size in that about 90 per cent of its industry grew up through the building of locomotives and the manufacture of electrical machinery, apparatus, and supplies. It contains the laboratories and headquarters of the General Electric Company.

Schenectady was settled in 1661 and chartered as a town in 1798. In 1690, an attacking force of French and Indians massacred most of the inhabitants. The city is the seat of Union College, the second college incorporated in the state. Population, 1970, 77,859.

Scottsdale. A prosperous, residential suburb of Phoenix, Arizona. It is primarily a resort city, part of which has been reconstructed as an old Western town. Population, 1970, 66,852.

Scranton. A city of Pennsylvania, situated on the Lackawanna River, about 100 miles northwest of Philadelphia. Scranton occupies an undulating site surrounded by low mountains. It is the richest coal mining city in the world, being the center of the chief anthracite producing region of the United States.

Scranton is also a leading silk manufacturing center, and its other noteworthy industries include the manufacture of locomotives, iron and steel goods, knit goods, cotton lace, women's clothing, and tobacco products. The fine parks and the lake resorts in the nearby mountains make the city and its environs attractive. Scranton was founded in 1840, incorporated as a borough in 1854, and was chartered as a city in 1866. Population, 1970, 103,564.

Seattle. The chief city of Washington, and the second largest seaport of the Pacific states. It is built on the hilly eastern shore of Puget Sound, 933 miles by water north of San Francisco. The city occupies a commanding site between the Cascade and the Olympic range, with Puget Sound forming its western front, and Lake Washington lying on its eastern border. Evergreen Point floating bridge, 7518 feet long, connects Seattle with Bellevue.

Surrounded by a tributary region rich in timber, fisheries, minerals, and agricultural resources, and possessing exceptional facilities for transportation, Seattle has become one of the foremost commercial centers of the Pacific coast. It is the terminal point of several transcontinental railroads and has regular steamship connections with all parts of the world by way of the Panama Canal and the transpacific routes. In addition to other fine harbor facilities, a ship canal, 8½ miles long, situated wholly within the city, connects Puget Sound with Lake Union and Lake Washington. The leading exports of the port are wheat, flour, lumber, refined copper, automobiles, machinery, and fish; the imports are chiefly silk, rice, tea, coffee, sugar, copper ore, furs, and various Oriental products.

Seattle has one of the largest municipally owned hydroelectric power systems in the world. Industries include flour milling, food processing, shipbuilding, meat packing, lumber and wood products, airplanes, iron and steel products, and machinery. The fishery interests of Alaska and Puget Sound are largely centralized in Seattle which handles enormous quantities of canned salmon and other preserved fish.

Seattle contains many noteworthy buildings, among which are the Cathedral of Saint James, the Public Library, Art Museum, Northern Life Tower, and the Smith Tower, 42 stories high. The park and boulevard system embraces more than 1800 acres and includes upwards of 25 miles of scenic boulevards. The latter afford magnificent views of Mount Rainier and other snow-capped peaks of the Cascades. The campus of the University of Washington, covering 582 acres and situated between lakes Union and Washington, lies entirely within the city. Other educational institutions are Seattle University and Seattle Pacific College.

Seattle, named for a local Indian chief, was first settled in 1851. It was incorporated in 1865, and, in 1869, was chartered as a city. It was the site of the World's Fair in 1962. Population, 1970, 530,831.

Shasta, Mount. A majestic peak in the Sierra Nevada of northern California, situated about 40 miles south of the Oregon boundary. This great mountain, one of the most imposing on the continent, is an extinct volcanic cone which rises to an elevation of 14,380 feet. The summit is continuously covered with snow, and on the north slope there are several glaciers. About 1400 feet below the summit there is a crater nearly 4000 feet in diameter and 2500 feet deep.

Although regarded as extinct, Mount Shasta still shows vestiges of volcanic activity. At the summit there is a sulphurous fumarole which emits hot gases, and on the north slope there is another similar opening. During one of the prehistoric eruptions of Mount Shasta, a stream of lava flowed down its southern slope, entered the channel of the Sacramento River, and followed the bed of that stream for a distance of 50 miles.

The influence of temperature and moisture upon the distribution of plant life is well illustrated in the strong contrast between the vegetation of Mount Shasta and that of Shasta valley. The summit of the mountain is devoid of vegetation because of cold; the Shasta valley, 10 miles distant, is treeless because of a lack of moisture. Between these extremes lies the great forest belt of Mount Shasta. In this heavily forested area the different species of trees are arranged in zones, according to the requirements of each species as regards temperature and moisture. For example, yellow pine and sugar pine predominate in the Transition zone at the foot of the mountain; Shasta fir in the Canadian zone midway on the slope; and whitebark pine in the Hudsonian zone, immediately below the upper limit of trees, at about 9500 feet altitude. Small alpine plants are found as high as 13,000 feet.

Mount Shasta may be ascended with little difficulty. From the city of Mount Shasta, a good trail, about 6 miles in length, leads to Timberline camp. From this camp, the summit may be reached and the return journey made to Mount Shasta city in a single day. The view from the summit of Mount Shasta is unsurpassed by that from any peak in the Cascade range.

Sheboygan (*shê-boi'găn*). A city of eastern Wisconsin, situated on Lake Michigan, 52 miles north of Milwaukee. The city is the trade center of a dairy and farming region and has diversified industries which include stainless steel and enameled kitchen ware, leather, knitted clothing, furniture, toys, molded plastics, shoes, electric sprayers, and hydraulic machinery. Fishing interests process large quantities for national distribution. Population, 1970, 48,484.

Sheridan. A mining and trade center of northern Wyoming. It is an important shipping point for farm products and livestock, and also for coal, which is mined extensively in the neighborhood. Industries include flour mills, sugar refineries, brick and tile works, and concrete plants. The Indian battles of Wolf Creek, Massacre Hill, and Great Wagon Box were fought in the vicinity, 1865–67. population, 1970, 10,856.

Shoshone (*shô-shō'nê*) **Falls.** A great cataract of the Snake River, in southern Idaho, about 120 miles southeast of Boise. This magnificent waterfall is exceeded in grandeur, in the United States, only by Niagara and by the falls in the Yosemite Valley. After coursing through a rocky canyon, some 1200 feet in depth, the deep river, here nearly 800 feet wide, first descends about 30 feet through several rocky channels. The waters then unite and the full volume of the river, in a single sheet, plunges over a precipice about 200 feet high, into the bottom of a narrow gorge. The cataract is easily reached from Twin Falls, about 5 miles distant.

Shreveport. The second largest city of Louisiana, on the Red River, in the northwestern part of the state, about 300 miles from New Orleans. The city has excellent railway facilities and is the commercial center of a large region, rich in oil, gas, lumber, and agricultural products. There is an extensive trade in cotton, corn, peanuts, pecans, fruit, truck crops, and live stock. The local industries include oil refineries, lumber, cotton, and cottonseed oil mills, glassworks, foundries, and machine shops. Industrial output includes also sulphur, salt, and glass. The Caddo Parish Court House is an 8-story building of unusual beauty, having a jail on the two top stories. Population, 1970, 182,064.

Sioux (*sōō*) **City.** A city of Iowa, located on the Missouri River, 200 miles northwest of Des Moines. Sioux City occupies a commanding site embracing parts of the river valley and the encircling bluffs. It is the commercial center of a highly productive agricultural region and has extensive wholesaling and shipping interests. It stands at the head of navigation in the Missouri River. The city is one of the important livestock markets of the country and has large meat packing establishments, creameries, and numerous other substantial industries. In total value of manufactured products, Sioux City ranks first among the cities of the state. There are many fine streets and public buildings, and the municipal park system covers an area of 1519 acres. The largest unit is Stone Park, a 915-acre natural wooded tract on the northwestern edge of the city. Grand View Park contains a music pavilion in a natural amphitheater.

Sioux City was founded in 1849 as an outfitting station for expeditions to the Black Hills, and received its municipal charter in 1857. It is the seat of Morningside College and of Briar Cliff College. Population, 1970, 85,925.

Sioux Falls. A city of South Dakota, on the Big Sioux River, about 320 miles southwest of Minneapolis. The river here falls nearly 100 feet. In the vicinity are extensive beds of quartzite, usually called jasper or red granite. Many buildings, both public and private, are built of this native pink stone. Meat packing, stone quarrying, and the manufacture of plastics and farm equipment are among the chief industries. Augustana College and Sioux Falls College are located here. Population, 1970, 72,488.

Sitka. A city on the west coast of Baranof Island, of southeastern Alaska. The chief industry is the processing and packing of salmon. Though located in a high northern latitude, the winters are not severe, and the general climate is healthful. Across the channel is a large naval air base. Nearby is the Sitka National Monument, a 54-acre park of great natural beauty and the scene of a massacre of Russians by Indians in 1802. Sitka was founded by the Russians in 1799 and later became the capital of the Russian territory of Alaska. From 1867 until 1906, Sitka was the capital of the United States territory of Alaska. Population, 1970, 3370.

Somerville. A residential city of eastern Massachusetts, on the Mystic River, two miles northwest of Boston. It is built on a series of hills and has many historic associations connected with the War of Independence. Paul Revere on his memorable ride passed through Somerville along a road now known as Broadway. Prospect Hill is said to be the scene of the first unfurling of the American flag. Meat packing, food processing, and the manufacture of paper bags are among the city's leading industries. Population, 1970, 88,779.

South Bend. A city of northern Indiana, built at the south bend of the Saint Joseph River, about 85 miles east of Chicago. South Bend has excellent railway facilities, is the commercial center of a rich agricultural and peppermint growing district, and has developed extensive manufacturing industries. The city contains large factories making airplanes and agricultural implements. Other important manufactures include lathes, knit goods, roofing, men's clothing, sewing machine parts, stoves, watches, and washing machines. There are 34 parks covering 623 acres. South Bend was founded in 1823 and was incorporated in 1865. The University of Notre Dame is situated in the environs of the city. Population, 1970, 125,580.

Southern Pines. A noted winter resort of North Carolina, situated some 70 miles south of Raleigh. It is located in a fruit growing region, producing berries, peaches, and grapes. By reason of its mild and equable climate, it is a favorite place of winter residence for people from the Northern states. Population, 1970, 5937.

Spartanburg. An industrial city of South Carolina, about 100 miles northwest of Columbia. It is located in a rich cotton-growing section, and has large cotton and textile mills. Other manufactures include machinery, office furniture, food products, ceramics, and apparel. Peaches and other fruit are grown nearby in large quantities and account for much of the income of the area. Spartanburg is the seat of Wofford College for men and Converse College for women. Population, 1970, 44,546.

Spokane (*spō'kăn'*). A city of Washington, located near the eastern border of the state. It occupies a site at the falls of the Spokane River, which, with other falls in the district, provide immense hydroelectric power for manufacturing. Served by three transcontinental railroads, Spokane has become the chief industrial city of the rich mining, lumbering, stock-raising, and agricultural region known as the "Inland Empire." Among important manufactures are aluminum, lumber products, dairy and meat products, apparel, metal products, flour, and cereals. The city has a system of parks embracing an area of more than 3000 acres, and is the seat of several educational institutions, including Whitworth College and Gonzaga University. The first settlement at Spokane was made in 1872 and, in 1881, the city was incorporated as Spokane Falls, becoming simply Spokane in 1890. Population, 1970, 170,516.

Springfield. The capital of Illinois, situated in the south central part of the state, 185 miles south of Chicago. The city is the center of a highly productive agricultural and coal mining district and has extensive manufacturing interests. Its industries include flour milling and textiles and the manufacture of electrical apparatus, agricultural implements, shoes, tractors, garage equipment, and road grading machinery. The Capitol, erected at a cost of $4.5 million, is built in the neoclassic style of architecture and surmounted by a lofty dome.

Among the points of historic interest are the former residence of President Lincoln and the Lincoln National Monument. The mausoleum in the latter contains the remains of the president. Springfield was first settled in 1818 and was made the capital of Illinois in 1837. Population, 1970, 91,753.

Springfield. A city of southwestern Massachusetts, built on the Connecticut River, about 100 miles southwest of Boston. Springfield occupies a site of great natural beauty on the east bank of the river, and possesses many fine public buildings. Among the most impressive of these is the municipal group, including the Administration Building, the Auditorium, and the Campanile. The top of the Campanile, 300 feet high, affords a magnificent view of the Connecticut valley. Other noteworthy structures are the Public Library, the Art Museum, the Science Museum, the United States Armory, and Trinity Church with a carillon of 61 bells.

Of the city's park system, embracing 1268 acres, the largest unit is the 757-acre Forest Park with a zoological garden. In Merrick Park stands the famous statue of "The Puritan" by Saint Gaudens. Springfield is the seat of the American International College, the Springfield Y. M. C. A. Training College, Springfield College, and Western New England College. Springfield's Naismith Basketball Hall of Fame enshrines many memorabilia of basketball.

The industries of the city are extensive and varied. Among the principal manufactures are firearms, chemicals, envelopes, electrical machinery, toys, and automobile tires.

Springfield was first settled in 1636 and was called Agawam. It assumed its present name in 1640 and, in 1852, was chartered as a city. The city was the center of hostilities in King Philip's War, 1675, and was the scene of various conflicts which took place during Shays's Rebellion, 1786–87. Population, 1970, 163,905.

Springfield. A city of southwestern Missouri, located on a plateau in the Ozark Mountains, about 230 miles southwest of Saint Louis. The city is the commercial center of a large farming, fruit-growing, dairy, and poultry region.

The city is the seat of Drury College, Southwest Missouri State College, Evangel College, and Central Bible College. Springfield was laid out in 1843 and, in 1847, was chartered as a city. In 1956, Springfield was designated as an "All America" city by the National Municipal League. Population, 1970, 120,096.

Springfield. A city of southwestern Ohio, 45 miles west of Columbus. It carries the trade of a rich agricultural region but is primarily an industrial center. Among its chief manufactures are farm implements, metallic caskets, motor trucks, gas engines, automobile parts, and electrical machinery. Here are located the state home of the Masons, the Knights of Pythias, and the Odd Fellows. Springfield is the seat of Wittenberg University. The first settlement was made here in 1799, when a fort was built on the site by Simon Kenton. Population, 1970, 81,926.

Stamford. A manufacturing and residential city of southwestern Connecticut, situated on Long Island Sound, 33 miles from New York City. Stamford is noted especially for the manufacture of mailing machines. Other important products are automobile parts, electric motors, furniture, oil burners, engines, and chemicals. The city was first settled in 1641 by a colony from New Haven, became a borough in 1830, and, in 1894, was chartered as a city. Population, 1970, 108,798.

Starved Rock. A perpendicular cliff of white sandstone, on the south bank of the Illinois River, near the town of Utica, about 90 miles southwest of Chicago. This cliff overhangs the water's edge and rises sheer to a height of about 160 feet. The walls of the fortress-like rock slope precipitously in all directions, and the top is reached by a single narrow rocky stairway. The flat summit, about half an acre, commands an excellent view of the fertile river valley, bordered by wooded hills and grassy slopes.

This almost inaccessible rock was the scene of many interesting events in the early history of Illinois. In 1673, Father Marquette and Joliet spent many weeks at Kaskaskia, the great village of the Illini Indians, in the valley near the rock. In 1681, La Salle and Tonti built a palisaded stronghold on the top of the rock, which they named Fort Saint Louis.

About 1770 occurred the tragic events which gave the cliff its present name. Here perished by starvation the last remnant of the once powerful Illini tribe. At a council at Cahokia, Pontiac, the famous chief of the Ottawas, was stabbed to death by an Illini warrior. Pontiac's followers swore a war of extinction against the Illini, finally entrapping the last survivors of the tribe in this natural fortress. An area of more than 800 acres, including Starved Rock and other historic points, is a state park.

Stockton. An industrial and commercial city of central California, situated 78 miles east of San Francisco on the San Joaquin River, which is deepened so as to be accessible to ocean-going ships. Stockton has important fruit, grain, and livestock interests. Leading manufactures include canned and frozen foods, agricultural implements, and paper products. Stockton is the seat of the University of the Pacific. The settlement which became Stockton was founded in 1847 and was an outfitting point for miners during the gold rush. Population, 1970, 107,644.

Stone Mountain. A huge, cone-shaped hill of granite, located near the town of the same name, about 15 miles east of Atlanta, Georgia. It rises about 1000 feet above the surrounding country and covers an area of some 2 square miles. The surface is almost wholly naked rock. At the base of the northern slope there is an almost vertical cliff, about 800 feet high and 5000 feet long. In 1916, work was begun on a project for transformation of this cliff into a Confederate memorial by chiseling in bold relief figures of Confederate soldiers, centered on colossal figures of Lee, Davis, and Jackson. After many delays, the three central figures were completed and dedicated in 1970, although work remained to be done. The composition as it stands is 190 feet high and 305 feet long.

Superior. A city of northwestern Wisconsin, situated on Lake Superior and lying adjacent to Duluth, Minnesota. Possessing a fine harbor and excellent railway facilities, Superior shares with Duluth the advantages of location at the head of navigation on the Great Lakes. The city ships large quantities of iron ore and grain by water and receives coal to be distributed by rail to inland districts. Among the chief industries are planing and flour mills, iron and steel works, and shipyards. Superior is the seat of Wisconsin State University, Superior.

The early explorers, Radisson and Groseilliers, are supposed to have made their headquarters on the site of Superior in 1661. The explorer Du L'Hut, after whom Duluth was named, established a trading post here about 1680. Superior was laid out as a town in 1853, and, in 1889, was chartered as a city. Population, 1970, 32,237.

Syracuse. A city of New York State, located in the central part of the state, almost exactly midway between Albany and Buffalo, being about 150 miles from each of these cities. It occupies a fine, gently undulating site on Onondaga Lake, 35 miles south of Lake Ontario.

Syracuse owes its prominence as a commercial and industrial city to its central location in a highly productive region and to its superior transportation facilities. It is served by numerous railways which radiate in all directions and by the State Barge Canal system, which affords water transportation north to Lake Ontario, west to Lake Erie, and east to the Hudson River. The city has extensive shipping interests and conducts a large wholesale trade.

Syracuse has upwards of 750 industrial establishments, producing a great variety of articles. Among important manufactures are typewriters, air conditioning equipment, soda ash, tool steel, candles, agricultural implements, chemicals, ceramics, and washing machines.

The commercial district is substantially built, largely of brick and of the native Onondaga limestone, and contains many imposing buildings. The residential sections are noted for their broad, well-shaded streets, and handsome residences and grounds. There are about 60 public parks, ranging in size from small plots at street intersections to spacious tracts such as Burnet Park, on the west, covering 120 acres. Lincoln Park on the east, affords a beautiful view of the city and its environs.

The city is the seat of Syracuse University, with which is connected the State College of Forestry. Le Moyne College also is located here. Another institution, located permanently at Syracuse, is the State Fair.

The site of Syracuse originally belonged to the Onondaga Indians, whose survivors occupy a small reservation south of the city. The salt springs, long known to the Indians, became known to white settlers in 1789. The first settlement on the present site of the city was made about 1805. This was named Syracuse in 1819 and was chartered as a city in 1847. Population, 1970, 197,208.

Tacoma (*tȧ-kō'mȧ*). A city and port of western Washington, built on a fine harbor on Puget Sound, about 30 miles south of Seattle. It occupies a commanding site, rising to an elevation of several hundred feet overlooking the sound, in a beautiful scenic region between the Olympic and the Cascade mountains. Mount Rainier lies about 56 miles southeast.

The city has a substantial wholesale trade, large manufacturing industries, and an extensive coastwise and foreign commerce. The leading manufactures include lumber, furniture, pulp and paper, and machine shop products. Tacoma contains many fine public buildings, has several picturesque parks, in all covering 1200 acres. It is the seat of University of Puget Sound and Pacific Lutheran University. Old Tacoma, founded in 1868, and New Tacoma, founded in 1873, united in 1883 to form Tacoma. Population, 1970, 154,581.

Tahoe (*tä'hō; tä'hō*), **Lake.** A beautiful lake, situated at the eastern base of the Sierra Nevada mountains, at an elevation of 6275 feet above sea level. The boundary line between California and Nevada passes through the lake, which lies about 85 miles (direct) northeast of Sacramento and 12 miles west of Carson City. It is about 20 miles long and from 8 to 12 miles wide, with an extreme depth exceeding 1650 feet. Its remarkably clear waters are discharged through the Truckee River, eastward into Pyramid Lake, Nevada. Lake Tahoe is a favorite summer resort.

Tallahassee. The capital of Florida and seat of Florida State University and Florida Agricultural and Mechanical University. It is the trade center of a rich dairying and poultry region, which also grows corn, tobacco, cotton, vegetables, pecans, figs, grapes, and blueberries. Tallahassee is located 20 miles from the Gulf of Mexico, on rolling hills. Among the principal buildings are the State Capitol, the Governor's Mansion, and the Federal Building. Tallahassee became the state capital in 1824. It was the only capital not captured by Union troops during the Civil War. Population, 1970, 71,897.

Tamalpais (*tăm'ăl-pīs'*), **Mount.** A mountain in the Coast range of California, situated on the Marin Peninsula, about 15 miles in direct line northwest of San Francisco. The triple summit, about 2600 feet high, affords unsurpassed views of tbe surrounding region.

To the south are the Golden Gate, the city of San Francisco, and, far beyond them, Mount Hamilton, 4444 feet high, on which the Lick Observatory is situated. To the east is San Francisco Bay, with Oakland, Berkeley, and other cities on its eastern shore. Beyond these are the Contra Costa Hills and Mount Diablo, the latter rising nearly 4000 feet high. Close by to the north is the reservoir called Lake Lagunitos, and in the distance are ridge after ridge of the Coast range. On the west is the ocean and the rocky Farallon Islands, lying far out at sea. Within walking distance from West Peak is Muir Woods, with its superb forest of sequoias, many of which are 300 feet high. Muir Woods is a national monument.

Tampa. A manufacturing city and winter resort of west central Florida, located at the head of Tampa Bay, an inlet of the Gulf of Mexico. The city has a good harbor and is served by various steamer lines. A large part of the world's supply of Havana cigars is manufactured at Tampa. Other products include cement, phosphate fertilizer, canned citrus fruit, and beer. Among the city's features are the semitropical Plant Park, where Tampa University is situated; and the Tampa Greyhound Track. Davis Island, a fine residential district, is a result of an extensive reclamation project. Two universities are located in Tampa. Population, 1970, 277,767.

Taos (*tä'ôs*). An Indian pueblo and village of northern New Mexico, built near the Rio Grande River, about 50 miles north of Santa Fe. The inhabitants are of Taonan Indian stock. Like all pueblo dwellers, the people of Taos are industrious and self-supporting. Population, 1970, 1030.

Tarrytown. A village of New York State on the Hudson River 25 miles north of New York City. It is noted as the scene of numerous skirmishes in the Revolutionary War. Major John André was captured in the vicinity. The village contains "Sunnyside," the home of Washington Irving, who made famous the neighboring valley, Sleepy Hollow. Its factories include an automobile assembly plant. Nearby is the Tappan Zee Bridge, connecting with the New York Thruway. Population, 1970, 11,115.

Terre Haute (*tĕr'ē hōt'*). A railroad center and manufacturing city of west central Indiana, situated on a high bank of the Wabash River, 73 miles southwest of Indianapolis. The city is the commercial center of a rich agricultural and manufacturing district. Among the chief industries are paper mills, foundries, and the manufacture of plastics, chemicals, and phonograph records. Parks, 20 in number, cover 717 acres. The city is the seat of the Rose Polytechnic Institute, Indiana State University, and, just west of the city, St. Mary-of-the-Woods College. Population, 1970, 70,286.

Thousand Islands. A numerous group of islands in the Saint Lawrence River, located immediately northeast of Lake Ontario. They are situated in an expansion of the river, 40 miles long and from 3 to 7 miles wide. Some of the islands are many acres in extent, but many are mere rocky islets. A large number belong to Canada, 14 of them forming part of the Saint Lawrence Islands National Park, and others are a part of the State of New York. Their attractive scenic setting, together with their cool climate, make the Thousand Islands an ideal place for summer recreation.

Ticonderoga. A village of northeastern New York situated on the creek connecting Lake George with Lake

Champlain, about 95 miles north of Albany. Paper and lumber are its chief industrial products. Because of its many associations with the French and Indian War and the Revolutionary War, Ticonderoga and its environs possess great historic interest. At this point, the French erected, in 1755, a fort which they called Fort Carillon. In 1757, this was heavily garrisoned by Montcalm, but, in 1759, it was taken by the English under General Amherst.

In the Revolutionary War, this stronghold, renamed Fort Ticonderoga, was captured from the English by Ethan Allen and his "Green Mountain Boys." Later, it was retaken by Burgoyne and held until his surrender. The fort fell into disuse but has since been restored and contains a valuable museum. Population, 1970, 3268.

Toledo. A city of Ohio, located about 95 miles directly west of Cleveland and abutting Michigan. It occupies both banks of the Maumee River at its mouth in an inlet of Lake Erie, which provides a seven-mile commercial channel.

Toledo owes its commercial and industrial prominence to its advantageous location at the head of direct water transportation to the East and to its good railway facilities. It is surrounded by a rich agricultural region, with which it maintains an extensive trade, particularly of wheat and soybeans. Toledo is one of the largest distributing points of the Great Lakes for soft coal and is an important oil-refining center.

Toledo has more than 1000 industrial establishments, whose chief products include refined petroleum, auto parts, glass, tools, electrical machinery, ships, and scales.

There are many notable public buildings, among which are the Museum of Art and Our Lady of the Holy Rosary Cathedral, an outstanding example of Spanish architectural design. The park system, covering more than 1500 acres, includes several large parks and some 45 smaller ones. Among noteworthy educational institutions is the University of Toledo, maintained by the state. Toledo was founded in 1837 by the consolidation of two earlier settlements. Population, 1970, 383,818.

Topeka. The capital of Kansas, situated on Kansas River about 70 miles west of Kansas City. It is an important railroad center, being served by four railroad systems and having the extensive car shops of the Santa Fe railroad. An outstanding industry is the publication of farm journals which circulate widely throughout the Middle West. Meat packing, flour milling, and the manufacture of butter are other important industrial interests. The Capitol stands in the center of a beautiful park area. Among other features of the city are a 9-acre rose and rock garden and the 572-acre Lake Shawnee Park. Educational institutions include Washburn University and the Mulvane Art Museum.

Topeka was laid out in 1854 as one of the "free state" towns. In 1856 an antislavery convention there adopted the Topeka constitution, establishing a Topeka government, which was broken up by Federal troops. It became a city in 1857 and capital of the state in 1861. Population, 1970, 125,011.

Trenton. The capital of New Jersey, built on the eastern bank of the Delaware River, at the head of tidewater navigation, about 30 miles northeast of Philadelphia. Proximity to the coal fields of Pennsylvania and to the markets of New York and Philadelphia has contributed to its growth as an industrial center. Among its extensive and varied manufactures, the most noted is that of pottery, which ranks among the finest produced in the United States. Other important industries include the manufacture of wire cables, bridge sections, engines, electric lamps, rubber products, and linoleum.

The city is regularly laid out with many fine public buildings and residences. Among the more notable public buildings are the State Capitol, the Federal Building, the Courthouse, the new State Cultural Center, and Trenton State College. A landmark of historic interest is Battle Monument surmounted by a colossal statue of Washington, which commemorates his command on the battlefield of Trenton. Trenton became a city in 1792. Population, 1970, 104,638.

Troy. A manufacturing city of east central New York. It is situated six miles north of Albany at the head of tidewater navigation on the Hudson River. Once famous as a center for the manufacture of collars and shirts, Troy's manufactures now include ordnance, abrasives, shirts, springs, radiators, brake linings, silicone products, and steel. The chief educational institutions are Rensselaer Polytechnic Institute and Russell Sage College for women. The beautiful Hart-Cluett mansion is maintained as a museum.

The vicinity of Troy was the scene of internecine struggles between the Mohawk and the Mohican Indians, and during the Revolutionary War was the theater of stirring American activities in resisting Burgoyne's invasion. Henry Burden founded his famous ironworks here in the early nineteenth century. Population, 1970, 62,918.

Tucson (*tōō-sŏn'*). A city of Arizona, situated in the southern part of the state, about 65 miles north of the Mexican border. It is the commercial center of a large district devoted to stock raising, mining, and farming. Many new companies engaged in research and engineering science have located in Tucson recently. Tucson is the seat of the University of Arizona and other educational institutions. The warm, dry climate makes it a tourist and health center. A replica of the walled city of Tucson as it looked in 1859 stands 13 miles away, having been erected in making the motion picture *Arizona*, and still being used for similar purposes. Population, 1970, 262,933.

Tulsa. A city of Oklahoma, on the Arkansas River, about 100 miles northeast of Oklahoma City. Tulsa is situated in one of the richest oil and natural gas fields in America. To the immense development of these resources, the city owes its remarkably rapid growth. More than 500 operating and refining oil companies are located in the city. The surrounding district also contains valuable deposits of coal.

The city is the trade center of a large outlying region devoted to farming, stock raising, and dairying, and, by reason of cheap and abundant fuel, has developed substantial industries. Among the chief of these are oil refining, flour and lumber milling, and the manufacture of aircraft, boilers, tools, stoves, and glass.

Tulsa occupies a fine, gently rolling site, and is well laid out, with many beautiful parks, boulevards, and handsome homes built by fortunes made in the oil fields. Mohawk Park covers 2400 acres. The business district is noted for its impressive array of modern office buildings, including the 21-story Philtower Building and the 27-story tower of the Exchange National Bank Building. The city is the seat of Tulsa University and the Philbrook Art Center and Indian Museum. Tulsa was founded in 1887 and was first chartered as a city in 1902. Population, 1970, 330,409.

Tuscaloosa. Located on the Black Warrior River in Alabama, 58 miles southwest of Birmingham, Tuscaloosa is the seat of the University of Alabama and Stillman College. Manufactures, such as paper, lumber, iron, chemicals, building materials, and food products, have become more important to the area than the cotton crop that once made it prosper. Population, 1970, 65,773.

Union City. A city of eastern New Jersey, adjoining Hoboken and Jersey City. It was formed in 1925 by a consolidation of the old towns of West Hoboken and Union. Weehawken, adjoining Union City on the east and fronting on the Hudson River, is the railroad terminal and port. Union City is a residential place for persons employed in New York City and Jersey City. It has also many local industries, their output including embroidery, silk, cement products, and rubber goods. Population, 1970, 58,537.

Utica. A city of central New York, situated on the Mohawk River and the State Barge Canal, about 95 miles west of Albany. Utica is the commercial center of a rich dairy-farming district. Important manufactures include fabricated metal products, men's clothing, textiles, heating and ventilating apparatus, and iron and steel forgings. Utica is an important railway center and transfer point, and is often called the "Gateway to the Adirondacks." Its $4 million Munson-Williams-Proctor Institute has brought new cultural opportunities to Utica. Population, 1970, 91,611.

Vallejo (*văl-yä'hō; vă-lā'ō*). A city of western California, located on an arm of San Pablo Bay, opposite Mare Island, about 25 miles northeast of San Francisco. Mare Island Navy Yard contributes substantially to the commerce of the city. The city's industrial products include flour, lumber, and dairy products. Vallejo was founded in 1851 and was planned as the capital of the state. The legislature held sessions in Vallejo, 1851–53. Population, 1970, 66,733.

Valley Forge. A village on the Schuylkill River, in eastern Pennsylvania, about 20 miles west of Philadelphia. Valley Forge is famous as the place where Washington and the Colonial army of about 11,000 men endured terrible privations during the severe winter of 1777–78. The area with the trenches thrown up by the "ragged Continentals" remains substantially unchanged, and the old stone house where Washington made his headquarters still stands. An area of 2048 acres, including the old camp site, comprises Valley Forge State Park. The site is occupied by replicas of soldiers' huts and by monuments to generals Washington, Wayne, and von Steuben.

Vancouver. A city of southwestern Washington, on the Columbia River, about 8 miles north of Portland, Oregon. The chief manufactures include lumber, aluminum pulp and paper, canned fruit, metal castings, and machine shop products. A long interstate bridge over the Columbia River

SCENIC AMERICAN LAKES

Lake Winona, 1240 acre lake in Ouachita National Forest, Arkansas. This body of water is the source of the Little Rock municipal water supply.

Picturesque Auke Lake located in the heart of Tongass National Forest, Alaska. Mendenhall Glacier in the background.

Beautiful forest lakes in New York State's Saratoga-Lake George region are typical of the state's vacationlands.

Mirror-like Baker Lake reflects Mt. Baker's beauty in Baker National Forest, Washington.

Lake Blue Ridge in Chattahoochee National Forest, Georgia. Blue Ridge mountains in the distance whose streams supply water power for the TVA system.

WASHINGTON AREA BUILDINGS

The Supreme Court building, built when William H. Taft was chief justice, houses our highest court of justice. Of classic architecture, it was designed by Cass Gilbert.

The White House retains its familiar exterior, despite recent reconstruction of its interior. The first occupants were John and Abigail Adams.

Bethesda Naval Hospital, famous landmark for visitors approaching Washington from the north.
Official U.S. Navy Photograph

The Capitol building houses both branches of our Congress and has a floor area of 14 acres. Wings on either side for Senate and House were completed in 1859.

In this new Headquarters Building in Washington are concentrated the activities of the N.E.A., representing all aspects of the country's educational interests.

The colorful Shrine of the Immaculate Conception, the U.S.'s largest Catholic church. Its gilded sapphire dome recalls Byzantium; its bell tower, Venice.

connects Vancouver with Oregon. Vancouver was established in 1825 by the Hudson's Bay Company and was incorporated in 1858. Population, 1970, 42,588.

Vicksburg. Located on high bluffs overlooking the Mississippi River, Vicksburg is an important tourist, industrial, and river port city 45 miles west of Jackson, Miss. The U.S. Army Corps, with three major agencies, is the city's largest employer. The chief industries, most of which depend on the river for cheap transportation or processing water, produce lighting fixtures, earth-moving equipment, chemicals, hardwood lumber and flooring, feeds, house trailers, and boats.

Incorporated in 1825, Vicksburg gained special prominence during the Civil War. Its capture by the Union forces after a prolonged campaign was one of the decisive events of the great struggle between the North and the South. The Vicksburg National Military Park, of 1648 acres, with 30 miles of driveways and many monuments, restores the battleground as it was in 1863. Population, 1970, 25,478.

Vincennes (*vĭn-sĕnz'*). A city of southwestern Indiana, on the Wabash River. It is the oldest settlement in the state, dating from 1727, when Sieur de Vincennes built a fortification there. A French trading post had been erected on the site as early as 1702. The city is in a rich agricultural region and has varied industrial interests, including structural steel, storage batteries, paper products, glass, shoes, and flour.

Vincennes was under the French flag until 1777, was held by the British until 1779, and was taken by American troops in 1779 under George Rogers Clark, to whom is erected a $2 million memorial on the river front. The house still stands where the first territorial legislature met in 1805, Vincennes having been capital of Indian Territory from 1800 to 1813. Crossing of the Wabash River at this point by the Lincoln family in 1830 while migrating to Illinois is memorialized by a bridge, a marble shrine, and life-size bronze statue of Abraham Lincoln. Population, 1970, 19,867.

Waco. A city of east central Texas, on the Brazos River, 100 miles south of Dallas. Waco is the trade and shipping center of a rich agricultural region. The city is a leading cotton market for the interior of the state and has substantial industries. The principal manufactures are textiles, twine, woodwork, tents, awnings, camp furniture, clothing, and cement. Waco is the seat of Baylor University. The city was laid out in 1849 and was named for the Huaco Indians. Population, 1970, 95,326.

Walla Walla. A city of southeastern Washington, situated near the Oregon boundary. Walla Walla is the trade center of a fertile agricultural district. The manufactures include farm machinery, flour, and lumber. The city is the seat of Whitman College and Walla Walla College. At Waiilatpu, seven miles west, is a national monument park commemorating the first white family settling in the Pacific Northwest, that of Dr. Marcus Whitman, who founded a mission there in 1836. The original Fort Walla Walla is now a veterans' hospital. Population, 1970, 23,619.

Walpi. A Hopi Indian village built on a lofty mesa, several hundred feet high, overlooking an arid desert in north central Arizona. The inhabitants are among the most interesting of the Pueblo tribes. These peaceful village dwellers steadfastly adhere to their aboriginal culture and ancient customs. Their houses are constructed of adobe or of stone set in clay mortar, with square rooms and flat roofs, through which trap doors provide entrances.

The elaborate ceremonials of the Hopi people include the celebrated snake dance, in which the performers carry living rattlesnakes. The Hopi are industrious farmers, and maintain abundant stores of corn, beans, and vegetables. They also weave excellent blankets and baskets and display great skill as potters and wood carvers. The village contains about 150 inhabitants.

Waltham (*wŏl'thăm*). A city of eastern Massachusetts, situated on the Charles River, about 10 miles west of Boston. Here in 1854 was made the first successful attempt to manufacture watch movements, on an extensive scale, by machinery. Industries in Waltham are engaged in the manufacture of watches, clocks, knit goods, precision machinery, radar equipment, batteries, and jewel bearings. Other manufactures include emery wheels and furniture.

A point of interest is Norumbega Tower, named in allusion to a fabulous city said by early explorers to be located in New England. Waltham was incorporated in 1738 and was chartered as a city in 1884. A mill established there in 1814 is said to have been the first complete power mill for the making of cotton cloth in America. Population, 1970, 61,582.

Warren. An industrial city in northern Ohio, situated on the Mahoning River, 14 miles northwest of Youngstown. It has good transportation facilities and manufactures steel, automobile parts, tires, electrical products, fire protection equipment, drinking fountains, and many other items. Population, 1970, 63,494.

Warwick. This city is a residential suburb of Providence, Rhode Island, and is situated on the Pawtuxet and Providence rivers in a region of quiet towns and villages. It has some industry, including the manufacture of textiles and the shipping of clams, oysters, and scallops. It was the birthplace of General Nathanael Greene, a hero of the American Revolutionary War. Population, 1970, 83,694.

WASHINGTON. The capital of the United States, situated on the left bank of the Potomac River, about 100 miles from its mouth. Washington is coextensive with the District of Columbia. It is the administrative, legislative, and judicial center of the nation.

Site and Plan. The site was chosen by a commission headed by George Washington, and the city was planned by L'Enfant, a noted French engineer. Congress transferred its sittings from Philadelphia to the new capital in 1800. The city was captured and burned in 1814 by the British. At the time of the Civil War, it was fortified and made the headquarters of the Northern army. Following 1871, important improvements were made in the city, mainly in accordance with the original plan drawn up by L'Enfant. In the 1930's still greater improvements were made particularly the construction of monumental government offices occupying a triangle south of Pennsylvania Avenue. In 1962, President Kennedy appointed a commission to draw up plans for a much more radical improvement. One aspect of the plans called for a second triangle of buildings north of Pennsylvania Avenue, some governmental and others privately owned but architecturally suitable. In addition, an immense National Square would be created at the White House end. The plans envisaged several levels of construction, including underground parking areas, arcades for shopping facilities, and large areas accessible only to pedestrians. To President Kennedy is due also initiation of the Kennedy Cultural Center to the west on the Potomac River.

From 1802 until 1871, Washington's affairs were managed, under a charter, by its own citizens. In 1871 the charter was revoked, and the city was placed directly under the management of the Federal government. In 1961, the XXIII amendment gave residents of the District of Columbia the right to vote in presidential elections.

Area and Surface. The District of Columbia is about 70 square miles in area, including 8 square miles of water surface. The surface, on the whole, is gently undulating and the elevation of the land in the District varies within a range of approximately 400 feet.

Streets. The streets are laid out on a rectangular plan modified by a system of 26 avenues, which intersect the streets at different angles. A number of avenues converge on the two focal points of the city, namely, the Capitol and the executive mansion, or White House, the line of Pennsylvania Avenue passing through both points of intersection. The streets and avenues are from 80 to 160 feet in width, many of them adorned on each side with a double row of trees.

Parks and Malls. In a central square stands a lofty monument erected to the memory of George Washington. Extending north, east, and west from this square are long, parklike areas, or malls. The north mall leads to the White House; the area to the east is the approach to the Capitol; and to the west of the monument along a reflecting pool stretches a vista terminating in the Lincoln Memorial. Small parks and open squares or circles are found in various parts of the city. Potomac Park consists of about 723 acres of land which has been largely reclaimed from the Potomac River. The "tidal basin" is partially surrounded by Japanese cherry trees. Rock Creek Park, covering approximately 1600 acres, is a hilly tract of great natural beauty extending along both sides of the creek, which flows south, and widening at one point to form the picturesque National Zoological Park, covering 170 acres.

Monuments. The monuments and buildings of Washington befit the dignity of the national capital. The Washington Monument, already mentioned, is a majestic obelisk 555 feet in height. The stately Lincoln Memorial takes the form of a Greek temple of the Doric order. It is surrounded by a peristyle of 36 columns, one for each of the states of the Union at the time of Lincoln's presidency. In the interior is a statue, heroic in size, of the martyred president. On the shore of the tidal basin rises the circular, dome-crowned memorial to Thomas Jefferson. A striking monument in the Washington area is the U. S. Marine Corps War Memorial showing the flag-raising on Iwo Jima. Most of the numerous circles throughout the city where avenues cross are adorned with colossal statues of national heroes.

Buildings. The buildings of Washington, which are among the most beautiful in America, are characterized in general by the neoclassical type of architecture. The Capitol, a magnificent structure of the Corinthian order, having two immense wings and surmounted by a beautiful dome, occupies a commanding position on an eminence east of the Mall. The White House exhibits a pleasing and noble simplicity. The Library of Congress, containing one of the world's largest collections of books, is an imposing structure in the Renaissance style, near which stands the annex, modernistic in design. The Treasury, like the Supreme Court building, is an example of pure Greek architecture. One of the city's most exquisite structures is the Folger Shakespearean library.

The diverging lines of Constitution and Pennsylvania avenues form a triangular wedge of monumental buildings extending from the Apex Building, nearest the Capitol, to the Department of Commerce Building and the Treasury Building, near the White House. This group includes the Archives and Internal Revenue buildings and structures housing the justice, post-office, labor and interior departments. South of this group are the Department of Agriculture building, the Smithsonian Institution, and the Natural History and History and Technology museums. Nearer to the Capitol is the National Gallery of Art. West of the triangle are the Federal Reserve and Interior Department buildings.

Other notable structures include the Pentagon, the Corcoran Art Gallery, Constitution Hall, the State, War and Navy Building, the State Department Building, National Academy of Sciences, Pan-American, Red Cross, and Bureau of Engraving and Printing Buildings. The Health, Education and Welfare building and the National Aeronautic and Space Administration building are on Independence Avenue facing the Mall. Notable too are the National Geographic building with its fine exhibits and numerous high-rise office and apartment buildings in newer architectural styles. Ford's Theater, where President Lincoln was assassinated has been completely restored.

The Naval Observatory is the source from which the official time is telegraphed to all parts of the country. Among Washington's many fine churches are the National Cathedral of Saint Peter and Saint Paul, Gothic in architecture, where President Wilson is buried, and the Franciscan Monastery, which contains a replica of part of the catacombs at Rome. In the northeastern part of the city is the Catholic Shrine of the Immaculate Conception, crowned with a colored tile dome, which is offset by a bell tower 329 feet high with a carillon of 56 bells.

Commerce. The industries of Washington are devoted largely to the service of the government and to the supplying of local needs. The city's mercantile business, however, is very extensive. Scientific research plays a large role. Local travel is facilitated by a high-speed belt highway. As a national and international center of travel, it is served by three airports, of which Dulles airport is one of the world's finest.

Educational Institutions The institutions of learning and research are numerous. They include George Washington University, Catholic University of America, American University, the Smithsonian Institution, the Carnegie Institution of Washington, Georgetown University, and Howard University. The Washington Academy of Sciences serves as "federal head" for many learned societies.

Points of Interest. The city and its environs are rich in historical associations. Mount Vernon, the home of Washington, lies on the right bank of the river, about 15 miles below the city. Across the Potomac from the Lincoln Memorial, in Virginia, is Arlington National Cemetery, containing a beautiful memorial amphitheater and the grave of three of the nation's Unknown Soldiers. This cemetery is connected with Washington by the beautiful Arlington Memorial Bridge. To the north of the city lie the Naval Hospital with its conspicuous tower, the widespreading National Health Institutes, the impressive Bureau of Standards building, and the headquarters of the Atomic Energy Commission.

During the Civil War, Washington was surrounded by a ring of 68 forts. Of these, only Fort Myer on Arlington Heights opposite the city is occupied, being used as a training center. Population, 1970, 756,189.

Washington, Mount. The highest peak in the White Mountains of New Hampshire, and the loftiest summit in the northeastern United States. It rises from the massive Presidential range, in the central part of the White Mountain group, and reaches an elevation of 6288 feet. It lies east of Crawford Notch and is about 140 miles almost directly north of Boston.

The mountain is composed chiefly of granite. The east and north sides are gashed with deep gorges and the west slope is precipitous. The rocky summit, which rises many hundred feet above timber line, has a scant covering of alpine vegetation; the lower slopes are extensively forested. Trails, highways, and a rack-and-pinion railroad make it easy for travelers to reach the summit, on which are a government meteorological station and a commodious hotel.

Waterbury. A city of southwestern Connecticut, on the Naugatuck River, 32 miles southwest of Hartford. Abundant water power has contributed largely to the city's industrial prominence. Waterbury is the leading center for the manufacture of brass ware in the United States, and is often styled the "Brass City." It is noted also for the production of clocks and watches. In value of manufactures, Waterbury ranks among the first two or three cities of the state. The city occupies a hilly site and contains parks of great natural beauty. Population, 1970, 108,033.

Waterloo. A city in Iowa on the Cedar River about 110 miles northeast of Des Moines. The surrounding country produces grain, hogs, cattle, and dairy products in great abundance. It is one of the largest manufacturing centers in the state, being noted especially for the manufacture of tractors and other agricultural implements. Waterloo is served by four railroads, one air line, and 32 trucking lines, and is on three federal highways. It is the home of the National Dairy Cattle Congress. Population, 1970, 75,533.

Watkins Glen. A narrow gorge of unusual scenic beauty, situated near the village of Watkins Glen, New York, not far from the head of Seneca Lake, and about 20 miles north of Elmira. Through this chasm, which, in places, is 300 feet deep, a narrow stream flows over a series of charming cascades and rapids. The rocks, which are Devonian shales, were worn into deep gorges by glacial ice.

Waukegan. A lake port and industrial city in the northeast corner of Illinois. Although it has distinct individuality and local pride in educational and other civic enterprises, Waukegan is closely associated with North Chicago in matters of commerce, industry, and transportation. Population, 1970, 65,269.

West Point. A strong military post and noted military educational center in New York State. It occupies a picturesque site on the west bank of the Hudson River, about 50 miles north of New York City. The government reservation, including Constitution Island, covers 3574 acres and is the seat of the United States Military Academy. It has a great repository for the storing of monetary silver. Among many fine buildings and monuments are Memorial Hall, containing trophies of war, and a handsome equestrian statue of George Washington. West Point was a position of great strategic importance in the Revolutionary War. Benedict Arnold plotted, while in command here, to betray it to the British, but this result was prevented by the timely discovery of the plot.

Wheat Belt. The name applied to the section of the United States in which more than three-fourths of the nation's wheat crop is grown. In reality, there are two wheat belts, the winter wheat belt and the spring wheat belt.

The winter wheat belt has two parts. One stretches from Ohio to eastern Colorado, and the other consists of north central Montana and the Pacific Northwest. The chief producing area for winter wheat includes southern Nebraska, Kansas, western Oklahoma, northern Texas, eastern Colorado, north central Montana, Idaho, eastern Washington, Missouri, Illinois, Indiana, and Ohio. The spring wheat belt consists chiefly of North Dakota, South Dakota, Minnesota, and eastern Montana.

Wheeling. A city of West Virginia, on the Ohio River, in the northern "panhandle," about 65 miles southwest of Pittsburgh, Pennsylvania. Wheeling owes its industrial and commercial importance to large supplies of natural gas, to extensive nearby coal fields, and to abundant raw materials, made available by excellent facilities for transportation, both by rail and by water. There are more than 200 manufacturing establishments in Wheeling, and the total value of its products is greater than that of any other city in the state. The leading manufactures include iron and steel products, plastics, glass, tobacco, tin plate, and aluminum ware. There are also print works, packing houses, and large proprietary remedy works.

The city occupies an excellent site, rising gradually from the river, and contains many fine streets and public buildings. Oglebay Park, of 1200 acres, is a country recreational center. Wheeling Island is connected with the main part of the city by a historic suspension bridge.

The first settlement on the site of Wheeling was made in 1769 by Ebenezer Zane. Fort Henry, named for Patrick Henry, was built in 1774 and, during the Revolutionary War, was repeatedly, but unsuccessfully, attacked by the Indians and the British. Wheeling was incorporated in 1795 and was chartered as a city in 1836. From 1863 to 1870, and again from 1875 to 1885, Wheeling was the capital of the state. Population, 1970, 48,188.

White Plains. A city of southern New York about 25 miles north of midtown New York. Here in 1776, Washington's army was attacked by a superior force of British and succeeded in withdrawing across the Hudson River. Population, 1970, 50,220

White Sands National Monument. Located in south central New Mexico, in the vicinity of White Sands Proving Ground (a rocket test site) and about 15 miles from Alamogordo (the site of the explosion of the first atomic bomb in 1945). This national monument is 140,247 acres of dazzling white dunes, which extend far beyond the boundaries appropriated for the monument itself. The dunes range from 5 to 50 feet high and consist of 95% pure gypsum, grading into quartz sand in the north. The dunes are not continuous, but occur in waves, with bare ground showing between them. They move constantly, always in a northeasterly direction and very slowly, shifting a few feet a year. There is a strange, boggy lake bed, Lake Lucero, in the southwest corner of the monument area. It is said that no life can exist in it. Mice, insects, and beetles, which are numerous in the White Sands area, are white or nearly white, apparently a protective coloration. Plant life is confined to the outer stretches of the sands and differs from similar species elsewhere.

White Sulphur Springs. A health and pleasure resort of southeastern West Virginia, located in picturesque Greenbrier County. Famed for its numerous mineral springs, this historic spa and fashion center, dating back to Revolutionary War times, is visited annually by thousands of tourists. Japanese diplomats in Washington at the time of the attack on Pearl Harbor were interned here during World War II. Population, 1970, 2396.

Whitney, Mount. The highest peak in the United States, excluding Alaska. It is situated in the main range of the Sierra Nevada, in eastern California, and is surrounded by a region of unusual scenic magnificence. Its eastern slope rises precipitously nearly 11,000 feet above Owens Valley, and the peak itself towers to an elevation of 14,495 feet above sea level. The lowest land in North America, Death Valley, much of which is below sea level, lies only 86 miles east of this gigantic mountain.

Whittier. A city of California, situated about 12 miles southeast of Los Angeles. It was founded by Quakers and named for the poet John Greenleaf Whittier. It is a residential city, once a citrus empire, now a hub of industry and a packing and shipping point for agricultural products grown in the area. It is the seat of Whittier College and the world's largest Quaker church. Population, 1970, 72,863.

Wichita. A city of Kansas where 64% of the world's private aircraft are manufactured. Beech Aircraft Corporation, the Boeing Company—Wichita Division, Cessna Aircraft Company, and Gates Learjet Corporation are major aircraft plants located in the city. Wichita is also a milling and meat-packing center. Wichita's industry is varied, with manufactures of farm machinery, heating equipment, amusement park equipment, hotel and motel equipment, and camping equipment. The city occupies an excellent site on the banks of the Arkansas River in central Kansas. Three institutions of higher learning are located here—Friends University, Sacred Heart College, and Wichita State University. The city's name was derived from the Wichita tribe of Indians. Settled in 1870, Wichita was incorporated in 1871. A living historical monument recalls the city's origin in a section called "Cowtown," which contains many of the original structures of early Wichita. Population, 1970, 276,554.

Wichita Falls. A city of northern Texas, on the Wichita River, about 100 miles northwest of Fort Worth. Wichita Falls is the distributing point for a large agricultural and stock raising region, and is the center of a rich petroleum oil and gas field. Its principal manufactures are window glass, auto trucks, flour, and oil well machinery. The refining of petroleum is one of the most important industries. Wichita Falls was settled in 1882 and was chartered as a city in 1884. It is the seat of Midwestern University. Population, 1970, 97,564.

Wilkes-Barre (*wĭlks' băr'i*). A city of northeastern Pennsylvania, on the Susquehanna River, about 100 miles northwest of Philadelphia. It is situated in the picturesque Wyoming Valley and is the center of one of the richest anthracite coal fields in the world. Its manufactures include electronic components, furniture, cigars, pencils and writing supplies, aircraft and missle parts, perfumes, malt beverages, clothing, fiber glass, shoes, wire rope, and boilers.

Wilkes-Barre is the seat of Wilkes and King's colleges. Two major annual events include the Fine Arts Fiesta and the Cherry Blossom Time festival, both held in May.

Wilkes-Barre was settled in 1769 by New Englanders, and named in honor of John Wilkes and Isaac Barre, members of the British Parliament. It was the scene of desperate struggles with the British and Indians during the Revolutionary War; the Wyoming massacre took place four miles from its site. The city is noted as the birthplace of the anthracite coal industry. Here "stone coal," as it was called, was first used for domestic purposes. Population, 1970, 58,856.

Williamsburg. A historic city of eastern Virginia, 48 miles east by south of Richmond, in a peninsula between the James and York rivers. It was settled in 1632 and was known as Middle Plantation until 1699. From 1699 to 1780 it was the capital of Virginia. It is the seat of William and Mary College, opened in 1693, which, after Harvard, is the oldest college in the United States.

In 1927, under the active interest of John D. Rockefeller, Jr., the restoration of the colonial area of Williamsburg was undertaken. Among the many restored structures are the original college building, designed by Sir Christopher Wren, and the Raleigh Tavern, where the Virginia assembly met when dissolved by royal governors. Recently erected business structures are made to conform with the earlier architectural style. Here in 1776 the Phi Beta Kappa society was organized. Population, 1970, 9069.

Willimantic. A city of Connecticut, located 28 miles east of Hartford, at the junction of the Willimantic and Natchaug rivers. It has been styled the "Thread City," having produced thread extensively since 1822. The city has other industry and is in the midst of a fertile farm area. It is the seat of Eastern Connecticut State College. Population, 1970, 14,402.

Wilmington. The chief city of Delaware, located on the Delaware River, at its junction with Christina River, about 27 miles southwest of Philadelphia.

The favorable location, excellent transportation facilities, nearness to the great coal fields and the sources of raw material, together with water power furnished by the Christina, have combined to make the city an important manufacturing center. The Du Pont chemical industries center in Wilmington, the city of their origin. They began as a powder mill, established in 1802, the first in America. Other important manufactures are braided rubber hose, leather belting, castings, cork products, iron and steel articles, hosiery, machinery, paper, and petroleum products. Immense powder and dye mills, across the river in New Jersey, contribute substantially to the city's trade.

The town was founded in 1638 by Swedes and was known by various names. Nearby Winterthur Museum, formerly the residence of Henry Francis du Pont, contains a collection of American decorative arts from the seventeenth century through the early nineteenth century. Population 1970, 80,386.

Wilmington. The chief port of North Carolina, situated on the Cape Fear River, 20 miles from the Atlantic Ocean. Wilmington has an excellent harbor, accommodating large seagoing vessels, and is an important commercial city with an extensive shipping trade. The city is located in a highly productive agricultural district, of which it is the mercantile center. Wilmington has a number of textile mills for the manufacture of cotton goods, pile fabrics, hosiery, and wearing apparel. The city is the home of the U.S.S. North Carolina Battleship Memorial and the annual North Carolina Azalea Festival.

Wilmington was first settled in 1730 and incorporated in 1739. Here, in 1765, was the first armed resistance to the British Stamp Act. During the Civil War, the port was the chief gateway between the South and foreign nations. It was the principal resort of the blockade runners. It is the seat of Wilmington College. Population, 1970, 46,169.

Wilson, Mount. A peak in the Sierra Madre range of southern California, about 10 miles northeast of Pasadena. On its summit, which rises to an elevation of 5750 feet, is the Mount Wilson Observatory, containing the famous Hooker 100-inch reflecting telescope and other powerful instruments for astronomical research. An automobile road leads from Pasadena to the summit, which affords excellent views of the surrounding region.

Wind Cave National Park. Tom Bingham discovered Wind Cave in 1881 when he thought he felt wind blowing up from the ground and stopped to determine the source. The narrow entrance to the cave lets wind in when the outside pressure rises, and expels air when the pressure drops, creating a strong current of air and the illusion that the wind is blowing out of the ground. The cave was made a national park in 1903, and is located 12 miles northwest of Hot Springs in South Dakota. Its extensive galleries with many beautiful crystal formations are unusual because there are relatively few stalactites and stalagmites. There is a 44-square-mile game preserve surrounding the cave, with herds of bison, antelope, elk, and deer.

Winona. A city of southeastern Minnesota, situated on the Mississippi River, about 110 miles southeast of Minneapolis. A shipping point for agricultural products grown in the area, Winona is also important for limestone quarrying. Manufactures include sheet metal, glue, automotive equipment, and medicines. It is the seat of Winona State College, College of St. Teresa, and St. Mary's College. Population, 1970, 26,438.

Winston-Salem. A city of North Carolina, situated 108 miles west of Raleigh. It is located in a region noted for tobacco growing, and has become the most important center for the manufacture of tobacco in the United States. Its immense factories are said to turn out more manufactured tobacco products than those of any other city in the world. In value of manufactures, Winston-Salem outranks practically all other cities of the South. Other products include hosiery, underwear, air conditioning machinery, and furniture.

The business and industrial establishments are, for the most part, centered in Winston, while Salem is chiefly residential. The city is the seat of Wake Forest University, Salem College for young women and Winston-Salem State College. Salem was founded in 1766 by Moravians and long remained under the direct control of the Moravian Church. Winston was founded in 1849 and received its municipal charter in 1899. The two communities were consolidated in 1913. Population, 1970, 132,913.

Woodbridge. A large town of New Jersey, located 14 miles south of Newark, on the Arthur Kill, a channel separating New Jersey from Staten Island, New York. Rich clay deposits in the area supply the pottery, tile, and brick industry. Other industries include oil refining and the manufacture of chemicals, tools, and radio tubes. In the vicinity are the Bible Gardens, an outdoor museum of small replicas of the Holy Land's gardens and orchards as they were in Biblical times. Puritans from Massachusetts and New Hampshire settled the town in 1665. Woodbridge was incorporated in 1669. Population, 1970, 98,000 (est.).

Woods Hole. A village in Massachusetts within the town of Falmouth on Cape Cod. Formerly a whaling and shipbuilding center, the village is now widely known as the location of the Woods Hole Oceanographic Institution and Marine Biological Laboratories, which study tides, currents, and marine life.

Woonsocket. A city of Rhode Island, on the Blackstone River, about 16 miles northwest of Providence. The great waterfalls that gave Woonsocket its Indian name have been replaced by a huge dam with hydraulically operated gates as part of a $15 million flood-control system along the entire course of the Blackstone River. Textiles are the city's dominant industry, but other manufactures include plastics, rubber gear, canvas footwear, machine tools, and garments. Woonsocket is a consolidation of several factory villages, was chartered as a village in 1837, and incorporated as a city in 1888. Population, 1970, 46,820

Wooster. A city of northern Ohio, about 30 miles southwest of Akron. It is the trade center for a productive farm country, and is also important industrially, with manufactures ranging from paint brushes to truck bodies. It is the seat of the College of Wooster and the Ohio Agricultural Research and Development Center, which has 1900 acres used in experiments to improve and increase the world's plant and animal production. The city claims to have had the nation's first Christmas tree. Population, 1970, 18,703.

Worcester (*wŏŏs'tẽr*). A city of Massachusetts, built on both banks of the Blackstone River, about 40 miles west of Boston. The city occupies a picturesque site covering the river valley and a number of the surrounding hills.

Worcester is preeminently a manufacturing city and is one of the greatest machine tool centers in the world. Among noteworthy manufacturing establishments are immense rolling mills, wire factories, envelope factories, and loom works. Other manufactures include aviation pressure suits, firearms, abrasives, paper products, athletic shoes, pharmaceuticals, and steam turbines.

The city ranks high among the cities of the state in general civic improvements. There are 17 public parks and many other recreation sites. Lake Quinsigamond forms part of the eastern boundary of the city.

Worcester is the seat of Clark University, College of the Holy Cross, Assumption College, Worcester Polytechnic Institute, and Massachusetts State College, Worcester. There is an excellent art museum; the library of the American Antiquarian Society, founded in 1812, is rich in historical material.

First settled in 1673, Worcester was twice abandoned because of the hostility of the Indians, especially during King Philip's War. It was incorporated in 1722 and was chartered as a city in 1848. Within the vicinity of Worcester were born Eli Whitney, inventor of the cotton gin; Erastus Bigelow, inventor of the carpet-weaving machine; Elias Howe, inventor of the sewing machine; Lucius Knowles, who perfected the modern power loom; and George Bancroft, the historian. Population, 1970, 176,572.

Wyandotte. A city of Michigan, 12 miles southwest of Detroit, of which it is a residential suburb. It is noted for its important chemical industry, which is largely based on the extensive salt beds that underlie the city. It was also important in the development of the steel industry in the U.S., having established the first steel analysis laboratory in 1862, and producing the first commercial Bessemer steel in the U.S. as early as 1864. Population, 1970, 41,061.

Wyandotte Cave. A natural formation in Crawford County, southern Indiana, five miles northeast of Leavenworth. Wyandotte Cave is the third largest cave in the U.S. after Carlsbad Cavern and Mammoth Cave and has a greater number and variety of stalactites and stalagmites than any other known cave in the U.S. Besides the numerous chambers and galleries, the 23 miles of the cave that have been explored contain Monument "mountain," rising 175 feet from the floor, and the Pillar of the Constitution, a large stalagmite 30 feet high and 75 feet in circumference.

Yakima (*yăk'ĭ-mȧ*). A city of central Washington, situated 142 miles southeast of Seattle. Yakima, formerly called North Yakima, is the commercial center of the Yakima Valley. This valley contains one of the largest areas of irrigated land in the western United States and is widely noted for the excellent apples and other fine fruits which it produces. The city's chief industrial establishments include fruit canneries, fruit packing houses, sugar, and lumber mills. Fort Simcoe is a nearby historical attraction. Population, 1970, 45,588.

Yellow Springs. A village of Ohio about 18 miles east of Dayton. It is noted as the seat of Antioch College, which operates on a cooperative plan of work and study. The Fels Research Institute and the Kettering Research Laboratory in Yellow Springs study human development. The village is also the seat of the national headquarters for the American Humanist Association. Population, 1970, 4624.

YELLOWSTONE NATIONAL PARK. The largest national park in the United States, situated mainly in northwestern Wyoming but encroaching slightly upon adjoining portions of Montana and Idaho. It is approximately 62 miles long and 54 miles wide, and covers an area of 3472 square miles. Of this area, 3200 square miles are in Wyoming, 236 square miles are in Montana, and 36 square miles are in Idaho.

Rivers and Lakes. Within the limits of the park are the headwaters of several large rivers, including the Yellowstone, the Snake, the Lewis, the Madison, and the Shoshone. The Continental Divide, passing through the park from southeast to northwest, marks the line of separation of the waters draining into the Atlantic from those flowing into the Pacific. There are also numerous lakes, the largest of which is Yellowstone Lake, some 20 miles long and from about 5 to 15 miles wide. Below timber line, the less precipitous mountains, as well as the more level portions of the park, are beautifully forested with pine, spruce, and other evergreen trees.

Surface and Origin. The central part of the park is essentially a high plateau, lying at an average elevation of about 8000 feet above sea level. Except on its southwestern border, this plateau is surrounded by massive, snowcapped mountains, whose culminating peaks and ridges rise from 2000 to 4000 feet above the enclosed tableland.

In its origin, the whole region is volcanic. Not only the encircling mountains but also the interior plains are made up of volcanic ash and lava, ejected in some former geologic age from far below the surface. Striking evidences of this are seen in the black glass of Obsidian cliff, in the contorted lavas along the road near the summit of Mount Washburn, and in the fused, highly colored sands composing the walls of Yellowstone Canyon.

Scenic Features. The entire park is a scenic wonderland. Its chief features are the geysers, which are the greatest in the world; the Grand Canyon of the Yellowstone, which, in beauty though not in size, rivals the Grand Canyon of the Colorado; Yellowstone Falls, ranking among the finest of American cataracts; and the remarkable fossil forests along the Lamar River.

Geysers. There are five active geyser basins—the Norris, the Upper, the Lower, the Heart Lake, and the Shoshone—all lying in the west and south central parts of the park. The numerous geysers in these various fields differ greatly in size, character, and action. Some, as, for example, Old Faithful, spout at nearly regular intervals, longer or shorter, while others are exceedingly irregular. Some burst upward to a great height, displaying immense power; others shoot tiny streams or bubble and foam while in eruption.

Hot Springs. Besides the geysers, there are marvelously colored hot springs, mud volcanoes, and other strange formations. At Mammoth Hot Springs, and also at Norris and at Thumb, the hot water has brought to the surface immense quantities of white mineral deposits. These have built up high terraces containing beautifully incrusted basins, over the edges of which the hot water pours. Microscopic plants, growing on the edges and on the sides of these basins, color them with brilliant hues of pink, red, and bluish gray. The surface of many hot springs appears brilliantly colored, and the deeper pools in the terraces are often intensely green.

Grand Canyon and Falls. Because of the vivid coloration of its walls, in some places 2000 feet high, the Grand Canyon of the Yellowstone is a scenic feature of the first order. The colors vary from pearly white and pale lemon to orange, pink, and crimson. With the deep green of the forest above, these give a beautiful setting to the Yellowstone Falls, which are twice as high as Niagara. The view of the canyon and of the cataract is one of the most impressive in America.

Fossil Forests. The fossil forests along the Lamar River contain many petrified tree trunks which stand upright in the faces of nearly vertical cliffs that rise to a height of nearly 2000 feet above the valley floor. These petrified trunks are found at different depths, indicating a succession of forests, which, from time to time, have been overwhelmed, like Pompeii, with volcanic materials.

Animal Life. The park is a great wild-animal refuge or natural zoological garden. It contains protected herds of elk, moose, deer, antelope, and American bison. There are also numerous groups of brown, cinnamon, and grizzly bears, some of which have become remarkably tame and friendly. Yellowstone Lake and the other waters of the park abound in trout.

History. In 1806 John Colter, a member of the Lewis and Clark expedition, struck out on his own and in 1807 entered what is now Yellowstone National Park, thus becoming in all probability the first white man to see the region. The area was occasionally visited by hunters and trappers, and their reports of the fantastic sights, along with Colter's accounts, were regarded as pure imagination. Myth and legend grew around the bona fide reports, and the area was often derisively labeled "Colter's Hell." In 1870 the State of Montana organized an expedition, headed by Surveyor-General H. D. Washburn, to explore the area. His associate, N. P. Langford, wrote glowing descriptions of what they saw, confirming what had been regarded as fiction. In 1872 the American geologist Ferdinand Vandeveer Hayden surveyed the area and was influential in its establishment as a national park to guard against private exploitation of the area. In 1872 it became the world's first national park. Even after it became a national park, however, Yellowstone was unsafe for tourists. Indians raided and murdered visitors, hunters, trappers, and explorers. From 1886 to 1916 it was administered by the Army, with headquarters at Fort Yellowstone.

Accessibility. Yellowstone Park is reached by bus at Gardiner, Montana, on the north, and also at West Yellowstone, Montana, on the west. The eastern entrance to the park is reached by auto stage from Cody, Wyoming, 55 miles distant. The southern or Snake River entrance is reached by an auto road from the main north-and-south highway in Idaho. The southern entrance may be reached also by various auto routes.

Travel Facilities. Automobile roads and trails reach all the important features of the park. There are hotels, camps, stores, auto-transportation lines, and various other facilities and accommodations for travelers. The various park utilities are operated during the tourist season, which extends usually from June 20 to September 20.

Yonkers. A residential and manufacturing city of southeastern New York, on the Hudson River, 14 miles north of the center of New York City. It is situated along the east bank of the Hudson River, its site rising in a gradual slope to an elevation of 400 feet, from which may be obtained splendid views of the river and of the towering Palisades.

Of the many industries of Yonkers, the principal are the manufacture of machine shop products, elevators, drugs, clothing, wire and cable, and chemicals.

Yonkers was chartered as a city in 1872. Points of interest include the Philipse Manor House and Andrus Planetarium. Population, 1970, 204,370.

York. A town on the Atlantic coast of Maine, at the mouth of the York River, 40 miles southwest of Portland, in an area of cliffs, beaches, and pine groves. It is composed of several villages, including the well-known summer resorts of York Beach and York Harbor. One of the oldest communities in Maine, it was settled in 1624 under a grant from the Plymouth Company. It became the first English municipal corporation in America when it was chartered as a city in 1642 and named Gorgeana, after a member of the Plymouth Company, Sir Ferdinando Gorges. The city's name was changed to York in 1652. Frequently attacked by Indians, the community was almost annihilated in 1692. There are several buildings of historical note in the town, including the Old Gaol, one of the oldest in the U.S., and now a museum. Population, 1970, 5690.

York. A manufacturing and commercial center of southeastern Pennsylvania, 25 miles southeast of Harrisburg. York is situated in the midst of a highly productive agricultural district with which it conducts an extensive trade. Its chief industries are the manufacture of foundry and machine products and of bakers' machinery. Other manufactures include agricultural implements, safes and vaults, refrigeration machinery, silk goods, and hosiery.

York was first permanently settled in 1735 by a German colony. It was laid out in 1741 by the sons of William Penn, was incorporated in 1787, and received its city charter in 1887. In 1777–78, the Continental Congress held sessions in York while the British were occupying Philadelphia. Population, 1970, 50,335.

Yorktown. A village of southeastern Virginia, situated on an arm of Chesapeake Bay, about 70 miles southeast of Richmond. Yorktown is famous as the scene of the surrender, October 19, 1781, of the British army, by Lord Cornwallis. This virtually ended the Revolutionary War, and there is an impressive monument commemorating the event. The Yorktown battlefield area, reconstructed with fortifications and marked with explanatory signs, forms part of the Colonial national historical park. In 1862, General G. B. McClellan, with a large Union army, besieged the place and compelled its evacuation by the Confederate forces under General J. E. Johnston. On the principal street of the village stands the oldest customhouse in the United States. Population, 1960, 311.

YOSEMITE (*yô-sĕm'ĭ-tê*) **NATIONAL PARK.** A national park, containing some of the most magnificent scenery in America. It lies immediately west of the summit of the Sierra Nevada, in central California, about 160 miles east of San Francisco.

Area and Surface. The park occupies a mountainous tract, some 50 miles long, north and south, with an extreme width, east and west, of about 35 miles, the whole embracing an area of 1189 square miles. This region, in general, slopes to the west, and is traversed by two main rivers, the Merced and the Tuolumne, and by their numerous tributaries.

The surface varies from deep valley floors on the west, which lie at an elevation of less than 4000 feet above the sea, to snow-capped peaks which tower to heights of 13,000 feet, along the eastern boundary. Extensive areas are covered with noble forests of immense evergreen trees. These are interspersed with charming mountain meadows and many beautiful lakes. There are innumerable canyons, gorges, and narrow valleys, with rushing streams, cascades, and cataracts, fed, in large part, from the glaciers and snow fields on the higher mountains.

The surface features that give to the park its most striking character were mainly formed by glacial action and by river erosion. These natural agencies, working through long periods of geological time, have produced the deepest valleys and the highest waterfalls on the continent.

Scenic Features. Like Yellowstone Park, the Yosemite region presents a long succession of scenic wonders. The chief of these are included in the celebrated Yosemite Valley, in the Tuolumne Canyon with the Hetch Hetchy, and in the famous Mariposa grove of "big trees."

Yosemite Valley. This incomparable valley is about 7 miles long, with an average width of about a mile. Through the bottom of this valley, the Merced River flows. On either side, the valley is bordered with a succession of vast cliffs and lofty granite domes which rise almost vertically to immense heights. Among the most noted of these massive rock formations, with the heights of their summits above the valley floor, are: Cathedral Rocks, 2591 feet; El Capitan, 3604 feet; Sentinel Dome, 4157 feet; Half Dome, 4892 feet; and Clouds Rest, 5964 feet.

Waterfalls. Over the edges of towering precipices in the rock walls that enclose the Yosemite Valley plunge some of the most remarkable cataracts known. The Upper Yosemite Falls drop 1430 feet in one sheer descent. Immediately below, the stream cascades through a drop of 620 feet, known as the Middle Yosemite Falls, and then takes a drop of 320 feet over the Lower Yosemite Falls. These three falls, which are parts of one great cataract, make a drop of 2370 feet, equal to 14 Niagaras, before their waters reach the Merced River. Bridal Veil Falls has a drop of 620 feet; Vernal Falls, 320 feet; Illouette Falls, 370 feet; and Nevada Falls, 594 feet. The Ribbon Falls, the highest of all, drops 1612 feet sheer, a straight fall about ten times as great as that of Niagara. Nowhere else in the world is there such an array of stupendous waterfalls.

Tuolumne Valley. With the opening of roads and trails, making this region of the park accessible, the fine scenic features of the Tuolumne basin are also becoming celebrated. These include the beautiful Hetch Hetchy Valley, the Grand Canyon of the Tuolumne, and the remarkable Waterwheel Falls, in which enormous arcs of water are flung from 50 to 80 feet into the air.

Big Trees. The greatest grove of giant sequoias outside of Sequoia National Park is the Mariposa grove in the southern area of Yosemite Park. The monster tree of this grove is the Grizzly Giant, whose girth is 93 feet, whose diameter is 29½ feet, and whose height is 204 feet. In massiveness, this immense tree is exceeded only by the General Sherman tree, 36½ feet in diameter and 280 feet high, in Sequoia National Park, and by the General Grant tree, 35 feet in diameter and 264 feet high, in General Grant National Park. Other noted trees in the Mariposa grove are the Washington tree, slightly smaller than the Grizzly Giant; the Columbia tree, 294 feet high; and the Wawona tree, through whose trunk ran an automobile road 26 feet wide until the tree fell in 1968. There are two minor sequoia groves in the park—the Merced and the Tuolumne.

History. The Yosemite National Park region was once the stronghold of the Awani, or Yosemite (Grizzly Bear), Indians. The first white men to see it were probably Captain Joseph R. Walker's party, who came to the area in 1833. In 1851 a band of militia, the Mariposa Battalion, led by James D. Savage, entered Yosemite seeking retribution for Indian raids, and tried to drive out Chief Tenaya. James Hutchings led the first tourist party through Yosemite and later used his publication, the *California Magazine*, to encourage others to come to see the beautiful Yosemite valley. In 1864 an act of Congress set aside the valley and Mariposa Grove of Big Trees to be administered by California. John Muir, noted American naturalist, lived here in 1868–74 and helped to establish it as a national park. In 1890 a national park was created around the Yosemite Grant, as the section ceded to California in 1864 was called, and in 1906, California returned this grant to the Federal Government as a part of Yosemite National Park.

Accessibility. Yosemite Park is reached by bus and car through El Portal, near the western boundary of the park, and thence into Yosemite Valley. The park is reached also from Merced by auto stage to Mariposa and Wawona, thence to the Mariposa grove of "big trees," and into Yosemite Valley. It may be reached by auto roads from various other points.

Travel Facilities. Automobile roads and trails have been built to the chief places of interest. There are hotels, camps, stores, auto-transportation lines, saddle horses, camping and hiking equipment, and various other facilities and accommodations for travelers. Yosemite Valley is always open. The higher mountain roads usually are not open until early June.

Youngstown. A city of northeastern Ohio, on the Mahoning River, about 65 miles southeast of Cleveland. Youngstown owes its importance as a steel manufacturing center to its advantageous situation near necessary raw materials and to excellent transportation facilities. In the vicinity are coal mines and limestone quarries. Iron ore from Minnesota is available with a short haul from lake ports.

The city's chief industrial establishments are its immense blast furnaces, steel works, and rolling mills. Other manufactures include many subsidiary steel products, such as sheets, pipes, and engine boilers; also tin plate, coke, fireproofing, rubber goods, and electrical machinery. The Youngstown district produces about one-sixth of the pig iron and about one-eighth of all the steel made in the United States. The city has 2633 acres in public parks, including the beautiful Mill Creek Park, covering 2383 acres. Among the public buildings of especial note are the Stambaugh Memorial Auditorium and the Butler Art Institute.

Youngstown was settled in 1796, was incorporated in 1848, and received its city charter in 1867. A blast furnace was built in 1805 and a rolling mill was erected in 1845. Population, 1970, 139,788.

Ypsilanti. A city of Michigan, situated on the Huron River, 28 miles west of Detroit. It is the commercial center of a fertile agricultural region. Primary among its manufactures are automobiles and automobile parts. The site was established as a French fur-trading post in 1809, and as a permanent settlement in 1823. It was named for Alexander and Demetrios Ypsilanti, leaders of the Greek war for independence, which was raging at the time. Ypsilanti is the seat of Eastern Michigan University and Cleary College. Population, 1970, 29,538.

Yuma. A city of southwestern Arizona, built on the east bank of the Colorado River, at the mouth of the Gila, about 7 miles from the Mexican boundary. The surrounding region is remarkable for its almost continuous sunshine and for the extreme dryness of its climate. The annual rainfall of 3.13 inches at Yuma is the lowest recorded at any station of the United States weather bureau. Summer temperatures of 110° to 120° in the shade are recorded. Yet, owing to the low humidity, sunstroke is practically unknown. Yuma was established in 1700 by Spanish missionaries. It is the trade center of a district in which large quantities of alfalfa seed and other irrigated field crops and fruits are produced the year round because of the uniformly warm climate. Yuma is a popular winter resort and the site of the Yuma Indian Reservation and Vincent Air Force Base. Population, 1970, 29,007.

Zanesville. A city in Ohio, located on the Muskingum River at the mouth of the Licking, 58 miles east of Columbus. The Muskingum River is here spanned by a "Y" bridge, branches going to both sides of the Licking River. Zanesville occupies an attractive site, surrounded by lofty hills. Its varied industries include the manufacture of pottery, glass, tiles, electrical transformers, steel, cement, and barrels.

Zanesville was founded in 1797 by Ebenezer Zane and others, and, during 1810–12, it was the capital of the state. It was incorporated in 1814 and was chartered as a city in 1850. Population, 1970, 33,045.

ZION NATIONAL PARK. A national park, 230 square miles in area, containing picturesque mountains, bizarre rock formations, and a long, narrow canyon three-fourths of a mile deep.

History. It is evident from the remains of cliff dwellings in and near Zion National Park that it was inhabited long before the white man arrived. Nephi Johnson, a young Mormon missionary and interpreter for the Paiute Indians, the native inhabitants of the area, was probably the first white man to view the area extensively. The reports of Captain John C. Fremont, who explored the Southwest in 1843–44, influenced some Mormon pioneers to come to the area in 1847. They settled around the Virgin River and named the region Zion, "the heavenly city of God."

The park area, located in southwestern Utah, was set aside in 1909 as Mukuntuweap National Monument. It was enlarged and renamed Zion in 1918, and became a national park in 1919. It was enlarged in 1956 by the addition of the adjoining Kolob Canyon area. The name Zion was first given to the canyon by Mormon settlers in 1850, and many natural features of the area bear names reminiscent of the Mormon faith.

Features. The North Fork of the Virgin River, flowing from north to south, has cut through mountains a narrow gorge eight miles long whose sides rise 2500 to 3500 feet above the bed. The rocky walls are vermilion at the bottom and white at the top, exhibiting a geological history of the rise and fall of the land over a period of 15 million years. A road runs along the bed to a northern observation point 6508 feet high, from which one may see mountains called the Temple of Sinawava, Cathedral, and Majestic, among others. Other high mountains in the park are the Sentinel (7157 feet) and East Temple (7110 feet). The highest point is West Temple (7795 feet). Utah Route 15 passes east and west through the park beside Clear Creek, passing through a mile-long tunnel. To the north of this road is the Great Arch, carved out by millennia of erosion by water and wind.

The park is open throughout the year, and the highways are kept free of snow. There are some 155 miles of trails.

Zuñi (*zōō'nyê; sōō'-*). The largest of the Pueblo Indian villages, situated near the western boundary of New Mexico, about 40 miles south of Gallup. The inhabitants, who possess a distinct language, call themselves Ashiwi. They are descendants of the people of "Cibola," mentioned by the earliest Spanish explorers.

Like Pueblo Indians generally, the Zuni people are peace-loving, devoted chiefly to agriculture, and adhere with great tenacity to their ancient culture and customs. In the construction of their adobe and stone houses, in their methods of irrigation and agriculture, in weaving, in jewelry, in pottery making, and in other arts, as well as in their elaborate ceremonials, they closely resemble the other village-dwelling Indians of the Southwest.

The Zuñi people were first visited by the Spaniards under Coronado in 1540. Later, Spanish missionaries gained considerable influence with them. Population, 1970, 3958.

POPULATION OF URBAN PLACES OF OVER 30,000 IN THE U.S.

City	Pop. 1970	Pop. 1960
Alabama		
Anniston	31,533	33,657
Bessemer	33,428	33,054
Birmingham	300,910	340,887
Decatur	38,044	29,217
Dothan	36,733	31,440
Florence	34,031	31,649
Gadsden	53,928	58,088
Huntsville	137,802	72,365
Mobile	190,026	194,856
Montgomery	133,386	134,393
Prichard	41,578	47,371
Tuscaloosa	65,773	63,370
Alaska		
Anchorage	48,029	44,237
Arizona		
Glendale	36,228	15,893
Mesa	62,853	33,772
Phoenix	581,562	439,170
Scottsdale	67,621	10,026
Tempe	62,907	24,897
Tucson	262,933	212,892
Arkansas		
Fayetteville	30,729	20,274
Fort Smith	62,802	52,991
Hot Springs	35,631	28,337
Little Rock	132,483	107,813
North Little Rock	60,040	58,032
Pine Bluff	57,389	44,037
California		
Alameda	70,968	63,855
Alhambra	62,125	54,807
Altadena†	42,380	40,568
Anaheim	166,701	104,184
Arcadia	42,868	41,005
Arden-Arcade†	82,492	73,352
Bakersfield	69,515	56,848
Baldwin Park	47,285	33,951
Bellflower	51,454	45,909
Berkeley	116,716	111,268
Beverly Hills	33,416	30,817
Buena Park	63,646	46,401
Burbank	88,871	90,155
Carmichael†	37,625	28,075
Carson	71,150	38,059
Castro Valley†	44,760	37,120
Chula Vista	67,901	42,034
Compton	78,611	71,812
Concord	85,164	36,208
Costa Mesa	72,660	37,550
Covina	30,380	20,124
Culver City	31,035	32,163
Cypress	31,026	1,753
Daly City	66,922	44,791
Downey	88,445	82,505
East Los Angeles†	105,033	104,270
El Cajon	52,273	37,618
El Monte	69,837	13,163
Escondido	36,792	16,377
Fairfield	44,146	14,968
Florence-Graham†	42,895	38,164
Fountain Valley	31,826	2,068
Fremont	99,665	43,790
Fresno	165,972	133,929
Fullerton	85,826	56,180
Gardena	41,021	35,943
Garden Grove	122,524	84,238
Glendale	132,752	119,442
Glendora	31,349	20,752
Hacienda Heights†	35,969	15,600
Hawthorne	53,304	33,035
Hayward	93,004	72,700
Huntington Beach	115,960	11,492
Huntington Park	33,744	29,920
Inglewood	89,985	63,390
La Habra	41,350	25,136
Lakewood	82,973	67,126
La Mesa	39,178	30,441
La Mirada	30,808	22,444
Lancaster†	30,948	26,012
La Puente	31,092	24,723
Livermore	37,703	16,058
Long Beach	358,633	344,168
Los Angeles	2,816,061	2,479,015
Lynwood	43,353	31,614
Manhattan Beach	35,352	33,934
Modesto	61,712	36,585
Monrovia	30,015	27,079
Montebello	42,807	32,097
Monterey Park	49,166	37,821
Mountain View	51,092	30,889
Napa	35,978	22,170
National City	43,184	32,771
Newport Beach	49,422	26,564
North Highlands†	31,854	21,271
Norwalk	91,827	88,739
Novato	31,006	17,881
Oakland	361,561	367,548
Oceanside	40,494	24,971
Ontario	64,118	46,617
Orange	77,374	26,444
Oxnard	71,225	40,265
Pacifica	36,020	20,995
Palo Alto	55,768	52,287
Palos Verdes Peninsula†	39,616	....
Paramount	34,734	27,249
Pasadena	113,327	116,407
Pico Rivera	54,170	49,150
Pomona	87,384	67,157
Rancho Cordova†	30,451	7,429
Redlands	36,355	26,829
Redondo Beach	56,075	46,986
Redwood City	55,686	46,290
Richmond	79,043	71,854
Riverside	140,089	84,332
Rosemead	40,972	15,476
Sacramento	254,413	191,667
Salinas	58,896	28,957
San Bernardino	104,251	91,922
San Bruno	36,254	29,063
San Diego	693,931	573,224
San Francisco	715,674	740,316
San Jose	443,950	204,196
San Leandro	68,698	65,962
San Mateo	78,991	69,870
San Rafael	38,977	20,460
Santa Ana	156,601	100,350
Santa Barbara	70,215	58,768
Santa Clara	87,717	58,880
Santa Cruz	32,076	25,596
Santa Maria	32,749	20,027
Santa Monica	88,289	83,249
Santa Rosa	50,006	31,027
Seaside	35,935	19,353
Simi Valley	56,464	....
South Gate	56,909	53,831
S. San Francisco	46,646	39,418
South Whittier†	46,641	....
Stockton	107,644	86,321
Sunnyvale	95,408	52,898
Thousand Oaks	36,334	22,000
Torrance	134,584	100,991
Upland	32,551	15,918
Vallejo	66,773	60,877
Ventura (San Buenaventura)	55,797	29,114
Walnut Creek	39,844	9,903
West Covina	68,034	50,645
Westminster	59,865	25,750
Whittier	72,863	33,663
Colorado		
Arvada	46,814	19,242
Aurora	74,974	48,548
Boulder	66,870	37,718
Colorado Springs	135,060	70,194
Denver	514,678	493,887
Englewood	33,695	33,398
Fort Collins	43,337	25,027
Greeley	38,902	26,314
Lakewood	92,787	19,338
Pueblo	97,453	91,181
Connecticut		
Bridgeport	156,542	159,748
Bristol	55,487	45,499
Danbury	50,781	22,928
East Hartford	57,583	43,977
Enfield	46,189	31,464
Fairfield	56,487	46,183
Greenwich	59,755	53,793
Groton	38,523	29,937
Hamden	49,357	41,056
Hartford	158,017	162,178
Manchester	47,994	42,102
Meriden	55,959	51,850
Middletown	36,924	33,250
Milford	50,858	41,662
New Britain	83,441	82,201
New Haven	137,707	152,048
New London	31,630	34,182
Norwalk	79,113	67,775
Norwich	41,433	38,506
Southington	30,946	22,797
Stamford	108,798	92,713
Stratford	49,775	45,012
Torrington	31,952	30,045
Trumbull	31,394	20,379
Wallingford	35,714	29,920
Waterbury	108,033	107,130
West Hartford	68,031	62,382
West Haven	52,851	43,002
Delaware		
Wilmington	80,386	95,827
District of Columbia		
Washington	756,189	763,956
Florida		
Clearwater	52,074	34,653
Coral Gables	42,494	34,793
Daytona Beach	45,327	37,395
Fort Lauderdale	139,590	83,648
Gainesville	64,510	29,701
Hialeah	102,297	66,972
Hollywood	106,873	35,237
Jacksonville	518,131	201,030
Kendall†	35,497	....
Lakeland	41,550	41,350
Melbourne	40,236	11,982
Miami	334,859	291,688
Miami Beach	87,072	63,145
North Miami	34,767	28,708
North Miami Beach	30,723	21,405
Orlando	99,006	88,135
Panama City	32,096	33,275
Pensacola	59,507	56,752
Pompano Beach	37,724	15,992
St. Petersburg	216,232	181,298
Sarasota	40,237	34,083
Tallahassee	71,897	48,174
Tampa	277,767	274,970
Titusville	30,515	....
West Palm Beach	57,290	56,208

† Unincorporated places. Source: U.S. Bureau of the Census.

POPULATION OF URBAN PLACES OF OVER 30,000 IN THE U.S.

City	Pop. 1970	Pop. 1960
Georgia		
Albany	72,623	55,890
Athens	44,342	31,355
Atlanta	496,973	487,455
Augusta	59,864	70,626
Columbus	154,168	116,779
East Point	39,315	35,633
Macon	122,423	69,764
Rome	30,759	32,226
Savannah	118,349	149,245
Valdosta	32,303	30,652
Warner Robins	33,491	18,633
Hawaii		
Honolulu	324,871	294,194
Kailua	33,783	25,622
Idaho		
Boise City	74,990	34,481
Idaho Falls	35,776	33,161
Pocatello	40,036	28,534
Illinois		
Alton	39,700	43,047
Arlington Heights	64,884	27,878
Aurora	74,182	63,715
Belleville	41,699	37,264
Berwyn	52,502	54,224
Bloomington	39,992	36,271
Calumet City	32,956	25,000
Champaign	56,532	49,583
Chicago	3,366,957	3,550,404
Chicago Heights	40,900	34,331
Cicero	67,058	69,130
Danville	42,570	41,856
Decatur	90,397	78,004
De Kalb	32,949	18,486
Des Plaines	57,239	34,886
Downers Grove	32,751	21,154
East St. Louis	69,996	81,712
Elgin	55,691	49,447
Elmhurst	50,547	36,991
Evanston	79,808	79,283
Galesburg	36,290	37,243
Granite City	40,440	40,073
Harvey	34,636	29,071
Highland Park	32,263	25,532
Joliet	80,378	66,780
Kankakee	30,944	27,666
Lombard	35,977	22,561
Maywood	30,036	27,330
Moline	46,237	42,705
Mount Prospect	34,995	18,906
Niles	31,432	20,393
North Chicago	47,275	22,938
Oak Lawn	60,305	27,471
Oak Park	62,511	61,093
Park Forest	30,638	29,993
Park Ridge	42,466	32,659
Pekin	31,375	28,146
Peoria	126,963	103,162
Quincy	45,288	43,793
Rockford	147,370	126,706
Rock Island	50,166	51,863
Skokie	68,627	59,364
Springfield	91,753	83,271
Urbana	32,800	27,294
Waukegan	65,269	55,719
Wheaton	31,138	24,312
Wilmette	32,134	28,268
Indiana		
Anderson	70,787	49,061
Bloomington	42,890	31,357
East Chicago	46,982	57,669
Elkhart	43,152	40,274
Evansville	138,764	141,543
Fort Wayne	177,671	161,776
Gary	175,415	178,320
Hammond	107,790	111,698
Indianapolis	743,155	476,258
Kokomo	44,042	47,197
Lafayette	44,955	42,330
Marion	39,607	37,854
Michigan City	39,369	36,653
Mishawaka	35,517	33,361
Muncie	69,080	68,603
New Albany	38,402	37,812
Richmond	43,999	44,149
South Bend	125,580	132,445
Terre Haute	70,286	72,500
Iowa		
Ames	39,505	27,003
Burlington	32,366	32,430
Cedar Rapids	110,642	92,035
Clinton	34,719	33,589
Council Bluffs	60,348	55,641
Davenport	98,469	88,981
Des Moines	200,587	208,982
Dubuque	62,309	56,606
Fort Dodge	31,263	28,399
Iowa City	46,850	33,443
Mason City	30,491	30,642
Sioux City	85,925	89,159
Waterloo	75,533	71,755
Kansas		
Hutchinson	36,885	37,574
Kansas City	168,213	121,901
Lawrence	45,698	32,858
Overland Park	76,623	21,110
Salina	37,714	43,202
Topeka	125,011	119,484
Wichita	276,554	254,698
Kentucky		
Bowling Green	36,253	28,338
Covington	52,535	60,376
Fort Knox†	37,608	....
Lexington	108,137	62,810
Louisville	361,472	390,639
Owensboro	50,329	42,471
Paducah	31,627	34,479
Louisiana		
Alexandria	41,557	40,279
Baton Rouge	165,963	152,419
Bossier City	41,595	32,776
Houma	30,922	22,561
Lafayette	68,908	40,400
Lake Charles	77,998	63,392
Metairie†	135,816	....
Monroe	56,374	52,219
New Iberia	30,147	29,062
New Orleans	591,502	627,525
Shreveport	182,064	164,372
Maine		
Bangor	33,168	38,912
Lewiston	41,779	40,804
Portland	65,116	72,566
Maryland		
Baltimore	905,759	939,024
Bethesda†	71,621	56,527
Bowie	35,028	1,072
Catonsville†	54,812	37,372
Chillum†	35,656	....
Dundalk†	85,377	82,428
Essex†	38,193	35,205
Glen Burnie†	38,608	....
Hagerstown	35,862	36,660
Parkville†	33,897	44,800
Randallstown†	33,683	....
Rockville	41,564	26,090
Silver Spring†	77,496	66,348
Suitland-Silver Hill†	30,355	10,300
Towson†	77,809	46,000
Wheaton†	66,247	54,635
Massachusetts		
Arlington	53,524	49,953
Attleboro	32,907	27,118
Beverly	38,348	36,108
Billerica	31,648	17,867
Boston	641,071	697,197
Braintree	35,050	31,069
Brockton	89,040	72,813
Brookline	58,886	54,044
Cambridge	100,361	107,716
Chelmsford	31,432	15,130
Chelsea	30,625	33,749
Chicopee	66,676	61,553
Everett	42,485	43,544
Fall River	96,898	99,942
Fitchburg	43,343	43,021
Framingham	64,048	44,526
Haverhill	46,120	46,346
Holyoke	50,112	52,689
Lawrence	66,915	70,933
Leominster	32,939	27,929
Lexington	31,886	27,691
Lowell	94,239	92,107
Lynn	90,294	94,478
Malden	56,127	57,676
Medford	64,397	64,971
Melrose	33,180	29,619
Methuen	35,456	28,114
Natick	31,057	28,831
New Bedford	101,777	102,477
Newton	91,066	92,384
Norwood	30,815	24,898
Peabody	48,080	32,202
Pittsfield	57,020	57,879
Quincy	87,966	87,409
Revere	43,159	40,080
Salem	40,556	39,211
Somerville	88,779	94,697
Springfield	163,905	174,463
Taunton	43,756	41,132
Waltham	61,582	55,413
Watertown	39,307	39,092
Westfield	31,433	26,302
Weymouth	54,610	48,177
Woburn	37,406	31,214
Worcester	176,572	186,587
Michigan		
Allen Park	40,747	37,494
Ann Arbor	99,797	67,340
Battle Creek	38,931	44,169
Bay City	49,449	53,604
Dearborn	104,199	112,007
Dearborn Heights	80,069	71,551
Detroit	1,511,482	1,670,144
East Detroit	45,920	45,756
East Lansing	47,540	30,198
Ferndale	30,850	31,347
Flint	193,317	196,940
Garden City	41,864	38,017
Grand Rapids	197,649	177,313
Highland Park	35,444	38,063
Inkster	38,595	39,097
Jackson	45,484	50,720
Kalamazoo	85,555	82,089
Lansing	131,546	107,807
Lincoln Park	52,984	53,933
Livonia	110,109	66,702
Madison Heights	38,599	33,343

† Unincorporated places.

POPULATION OF URBAN PLACES OF OVER 30,000 IN THE U.S.

City	Pop. 1970	Pop. 1960
Midland	35,176	27,779
Muskegon	44,631	46,485
Oak Park	36,762	36,632
Pontiac	85,279	82,233
Portage	33,590	27,642
Port Huron	35,794	36,084
Roseville	60,529	50,195
Royal Oak	85,499	80,612
Saginaw	91,849	98,265
St. Clair Shores	88,093	76,657
Southfield	69,285	31,501
Southgate	33,909	29,404
Sterling Heights	61,365	....
Taylor	70,020	49,658
Troy	39,419	19,402
Warren	179,260	89,246
Westland	86,749	....
Wyandotte	41,061	43,519
Wyoming	56,560	45,829
Minnesota		
Bloomington	81,970	50,498
Brooklyn Center	35,173	24,356
Coon Rapids	30,505	14,931
Crystal	30,925	24,283
Duluth	100,578	106,884
Edina	44,046	28,501
Mankato	30,895	23,797
Minneapolis	434,400	482,872
Minnetonka	35,776	25,037
Richfield	47,231	42,523
Rochester	53,766	40,663
Roseville	34,518	23,997
St. Cloud	39,691	33,815
St. Louis Park	48,883	43,310
St. Paul	309,980	313,411
Mississippi		
Biloxi	48,486	44,053
Greenville	39,648	41,502
Gulfport	40,791	30,204
Hattiesburg	38,277	34,989
Jackson	153,968	144,422
Meridian	45,083	49,374
Missouri		
Cape Girardeau	31,282	24,947
Columbia	58,804	36,650
Florissant	65,908	38,166
Fort Leonard Wood†	33,799	....
Independence	111,662	62,328
Jefferson City	32,407	28,228
Joplin	39,256	38,958
Kansas City	501,859	475,539
Kirkwood	31,890	29,421
Lemay†	40,115	....
Raytown	33,632	17,083
St. Charles	31,834	21,189
St. Joseph	72,691	79,673
St. Louis	622,236	750,026
Springfield	120,096	95,865
University City	46,309	51,249
Montana		
Billings	61,581	52,851
Great Falls	60,091	55,244
Nebraska		
Grand Island	31,269	25,742
Lincoln	149,518	128,521
Omaha	347,328	301,598
Nevada		
Las Vegas	125,787	64,405
North Las Vegas	36,216	18,422
Reno	72,863	51,470
New Hampshire		
Concord	30,022	28,991
Manchester	87,754	88,282
Nashua	55,820	39,096
New Jersey		
Atlantic City	47,859	59,544
Bayonne	72,743	74,215
Belleville	34,643	35,005
Bergenfield	33,131	27,203
Bloomfield	52,029	51,867
Camden	102,551	117,159
Clifton	82,437	82,084
East Orange	75,471	77,259
Elizabeth	112,654	107,698
Fair Lawn	37,975	36,421
Fort Lee	30,631	21,815
Garfield	30,722	29,253
Hackensack	35,911	30,521
Hoboken	45,380	48,441
Irvington	59,743	59,379
Jersey City	260,545	276,101
Kearny	37,585	37,472
Linden	41,409	39,931
Long Branch	31,774	26,228
Montclair	44,043	43,129
Newark	382,417	405,220
New Brunswick	41,885	40,139
Nutley	32,099	29,513
Orange	32,566	35,789
Passaic	55,124	53,963
Paterson	144,824	143,663
Perth Amboy	38,793	38,007
Plainfield	46,862	45,330
Sayreville	32,508	22,553
Trenton	104,638	114,167
Union City	58,537	52,180
Vineland	47,399	37,685
Westfield	33,720	31,447
West New York	40,627	35,547
West Orange	43,715	39,895
New Mexico		
Albuquerque	243,751	201,189
Las Cruces	37,857	29,367
Roswell	33,908	39,593
Santa Fe	41,167	33,394
New York		
Albany	114,873	129,726
Auburn	34,599	35,249
Baldwin†	34,525	30,204
Binghamton	64,123	75,941
Buffalo	462,768	532,759
Central Islip†	36,369	....
Deer Park†	31,120	16,726
East Meadow†	46,252	46,036
Elmira	39,945	46,517
Franklin Square†	32,156	32,483
Freeport	40,374	34,419
Hempstead	39,411	34,641
Hicksville†	48,075	50,405
Jamestown	39,795	41,818
Levittown†	65,440	65,276
Long Beach	33,127	26,473
Mount Vernon	72,778	76,010
New Rochelle	75,385	76,812
New York City	7,867,760	7,781,984
Niagara Falls	85,615	102,394
North Babylon†	39,556	....
North Tonawanda	36,012	34,757
Oceanside†	35,028	30,448
Plainview†	32,195	27,914
Poughkeepsie	32,029	38,330
Rochester	296,233	318,661
Rome	47,655	51,646
Schenectady	77,859	81,682
Syracuse	197,208	216,038
Troy	62,918	67,492
Utica	91,611	100,410
Valley Stream	40,413	38,629
Watertown	30,787	33,306
White Plains	50,220	50,485
Yonkers	204,370	190,634
North Carolina		
Asheville	57,681	60,192
Burlington	35,930	33,199
Camp Lejune Central†	34,549	....
Charlotte	241,178	201,564
Durham	95,438	78,302
Fayetteville	53,510	47,106
Fort Bragg†	46,995	....
Gastonia	47,142	37,276
Greensboro	144,076	119,574
High Point	63,204	62,063
Kannapolis†	36,293	28,448
Raleigh	121,577	93,931
Rocky Mount	34,284	32,147
Wilmington	46,169	44,013
Winston-Salem	132,913	111,135
North Dakota		
Bismarck	34,703	27,670
Fargo	53,365	46,662
Grand Forks	39,008	34,451
Minot	32,290	30,604
Ohio		
Akron	275,425	290,351
Barberton	33,052	33,805
Boardman†	30,852	....
Brook Park	30,774	12,856
Canton	110,053	113,631
Cincinnati	452,524	502,550
Cleveland	750,903	876,050
Cleveland Heights	60,767	61,813
Columbus	539,677	471,316
Cuyahoga Falls	49,678	47,922
Dayton	243,601	262,332
East Cleveland	39,600	37,991
Elyria	53,427	43,782
Euclid	71,552	62,998
Fairborn	32,267	19,453
Findlay	35,800	30,344
Garfield Heights	41,417	38,455
Hamilton	67,865	72,354
Kettering	69,599	54,462
Lakewood	70,173	66,154
Lancaster	32,911	29,916

† Unincorporated places.

POPULATION OF URBAN PLACES OF OVER 30,000 IN THE U.S.

City	Pop. 1970	Pop. 1960
Lima	53,734	51,037
Lorain	78,185	68,932
Mansfield	55,047	47,325
Maple Heights	34,093	31,667
Marion	38,646	37,079
Massillon	32,539	31,236
Mentor	36,912	4,354
Middletown	48,767	42,115
Newark	41,836	41,790
North Olmsted	34,861	16,290
Norwood	30,420	34,580
Parma	100,216	82,845
Sandusky	32,674	31,989
Shaker Heights	36,306	36,460
Springfield	81,926	82,723
Steubenville	30,771	32,495
Toledo	383,818	318,003
Upper Arlington	38,630	28,486
Warren	63,494	59,648
Youngstown	139,788	166,689
Zanesville	33,045	39,077
Oklahoma		
Enid	44,008	38,859
Lawton	74,470	61,697
Midwest City	48,114	36,058
Muskogee	37,331	38,059
Norman	52,117	33,412
Oklahoma City	356,661	324,253
Stillwater	31,126	23,965
Tulsa	330,409	261,685
Oregon		
Corvallis	35,153	20,669
Eugene	76,346	50,977
Portland	382,619	372,676
Salem	68,296	49,142
Pennsylvania		
Allentown	109,527	108,347
Altoona	62,900	69,407
Bethel Park	34,791	23,605
Bethlehem	72,686	75,408
Chester	56,331	63,658
Easton	30,256	31,955
Erie	129,231	138,440
Harrisburg	68,061	79,697
Hazleton	30,426	32,056
Johnstown	42,476	53,949
Lancaster	57,690	61,055
McKeesport	37,977	45,489
New Castle	38,559	44,790
Norristown	38,169	38,925
Philadelphia	1,948,609	2,002,512
Pittsburgh	520,117	604,332
Reading	87,643	98,177
Scranton	103,564	111,443
State College	33,778	22,409
Wilkes-Barre	58,856	63,551
Williamsport	37,918	41,967
York	50,335	54,504
Rhode Island		
Cranston	73,037	66,766
East Providence	48,151	41,955
Newport	34,562	47,049
Pawtucket	76,984	81,001
Providence	179,213	207,498
Warwick	83,694	68,504
Woonsocket	46,820	47,080
South Carolina		
Charleston	66,945	65,925
Columbia	113,542	97,433
Greenville	61,208	66,188
Rock Hill	33,846	29,404
Spartanburg	44,546	44,352
South Dakota		
Rapid City	43,836	42,399
Sioux Falls	72,488	65,466
Tennessee		
Chattanooga	119,082	130,009
Clarksville	31,719	22,021
Jackson	39,996	34,376
Johnson City	33,770	31,187
Kingsport	31,938	26,314
Knoxville	174,587	111,827
Memphis	623,497	497,524
Nashville	436,044	170,874
Texas		
Abilene	89,653	90,368
Amarillo	127,010	137,969
Arlington	90,643	44,775
Austin	251,808	186,545
Baytown	43,980	28,159
Beaumont	115,919	119,175
Brownsville	52,522	48,040
Bryan	33,719	27,542
Corpus Christi	204,525	167,690
Dallas	844,401	679,684
Denton	39,874	26,844
El Paso	322,261	276,687
Fort Hood†	32,597	....
Fort Worth	393,476	356,268
Galveston	61,809	67,175
Garland	81,437	38,504
Grand Prairie	50,904	30,386
Harlingen	33,503	41,207
Houston	1,231,394	938,219
Irving	97,260	45,985
Killeen	35,507	23,377
Laredo	69,024	60,678
Longview	45,547	40,050
Lubbock	149,101	128,691
McAllen	37,636	32,728
Mesquite	55,131	27,526
Midland	59,463	62,625
Odessa	78,380	80,338
Pasadena	89,277	58,737
Port Arthur	57,371	66,676
Richardson	48,582	16,810
San Angelo	63,884	58,815
San Antonio	654,153	587,718
Temple	33,431	30,419
Texarkana	30,497	30,218
Texas City	38,500	32,065
Tyler	57,770	51,230
Victoria	41,349	33,047
Waco	95,326	97,808
Wichita Falls	97,564	101,724
Utah		
Ogden	69,478	70,197
Provo	53,131	36,047
Salt Lake City	175,885	189,454
Vermont		
Burlington	38,633	35,531
Virginia		
Alexandria	110,938	91,023
Arlington†	174,284	....
Charlottesville	38,880	29,427
Chesapeake	82,616	73,577
Danville	46,391	46,577
Hampton	120,779	89,258
Lynchburg	54,083	54,790
Newport News	138,177	113,662
Norfolk	307,951	304,869
Petersburg	36,103	36,750
Portsmouth	110,963	114,773
Richmond	249,621	219,958
Roanoke	92,115	97,110
Virginia Beach	166,729	8,091
Washington		
Bellevue	61,102	12,809
Bellingham	39,375	34,688
Bremerton	35,307	28,922
Everett	53,622	40,304
Fort Lewis†	38,054	....
Lakes District†	48,195	....
Seattle	530,831	557,087
Spokane	170,516	181,608
Tacoma	154,518	147,979
Vancouver	42,493	32,464
Yakima	45,588	3,284
West Virginia		
Charleston	71,505	85,796
Huntington	74,315	83,627
Parkersburg	44,208	44,797
Wheeling	48,188	53,400
Wisconsin		
Appleton	57,143	48,411
Beloit	35,729	32,846
Brookfield	32,140	19,812
Eau Claire	44,619	37,987
Fond du Lac	35,515	32,719
Green Bay	87,809	62,888
Janesville	46,426	35,164
Kenosha	78,805	67,899
La Crosse	51,153	47,575
Madison	173,258	126,706
Manitowoc	33,430	32,275
Menomonee Falls	31,697	18,276
Milwaukee	717,099	741,324
Oshkosh	53,221	45,110
Racine	95,162	89,144
Sheboygan	48,484	45,747
Superior	32,237	33,563
Waukesha	40,258	30,004
Wausau	32,806	31,943
Wauwatosa	58,676	56,923
West Allis	71,723	68,157
Wyoming		
Casper	39,361	38,930
Cheyenne	40,914	43,505

† Unincorporated places.

CANADA

Canada is a completely sovereign or independent state and member nation of the Commonwealth of Nations.

Size. Canada, having an area of 3,852,000 square miles, covers a surface nearly as large as Europe and larger than the United States, excluding Alaska. The country measures from east to west at its widest extent more than 3000 miles and from north to south about 1600 miles. A number of islands, which are territory of the Dominion, lie off the northeastern coast. The most northerly island extends to a latitude of 85° N. A large inland sea, connected with the north Atlantic Ocean by Hudson strait, extends into the country from the northeast a distance of about 600 miles. Canada's southern boundary follows the 49th parallel of latitude from the western coast eastward to the Lake of the Woods. Inclining slightly southward to Lake Superior, it passes through the Great Lakes and part of the Saint Lawrence river, which it leaves at the 45th parallel. It then runs with an irregular course eastward to the Atlantic Ocean.

Topography. Canada may be divided into five natural divisions, based on the character of the land surface. These divisions are commonly called (1) the Acadian or Appalachian region, (2) the Canadian shield or Laurentian plateau, (3) the Saint Lawrence lowlands, (4) the great plains, and (5) the Cordilleran region.

1. The Acadian or Appalachian region embraces southeastern Quebec and the maritime provinces. This region is the extension into Canada of the Appalachian mountains of the United States.

2. The Canadian shield or Laurentian plateau is a huge V-shaped area of 2½ million square miles, which encloses Hudson bay at its center. It forms practically all of northern Canada, and comprises the area lying northeast of a line drawn from the Mackenzie River delta to the Lake of the Woods and northwest of a line which passes thence north of the Saint Lawrence River basin. Its southern and Atlantic borders are elevated and outwardly steep, forming the Laurentian mountains. From this outer rim its surface slopes gradually to its low center, Hudson bay. The western portion inclines similarly from an elevated rim toward Hudson bay and the Arctic Ocean. In detail, the surface of the plateau is often broken and rocky with innumerable lakes.

3. The Saint Lawrence lowlands, which run from Lake Huron down the Saint Lawrence valley between the Laurentian plateau and the Acadian highlands, are a northeasterly extension of the central plain of North America drained by the Mississippi valley.

4. The great plains form a northern extension of the topographical division which occupies all North America within the limits of the Appalachian mountains, the Canadian shield, and the Rocky mountains. At the international boundary line, this division has a width of 800 miles, but becomes narrower farther north. For 300 miles north of the boundary the region is prairie, but beyond this latitude it is forested. In the southern portion, traversed by the railway lines, three prairie steppes are clearly marked: an eastern steppe, the basin of the Red river, lying between the Canadian shield and the Manitoba escarpment and having an elevation of 800 feet above the sea; a central steppe, between this escarpment and the Missouri coteau, with an elevation of from 1600 feet in the east to about 2500 feet in the west; and a western steppe, rising to a height of 3000 or 4000 feet, which extends from the Missouri coteau to the Rockies.

5. The Cordilleran region, about 500 miles broad, is made up of a succession of mountain ranges running parallel to the Pacific coast and of the well marked longitudinal valleys which separate the ranges. In the south, where the mountains have been adequately explored, the district falls into three subdivisions: (1) an eastern group of mountain systems, consisting of the Rocky mountains, the Selkirk system, and the Columbian mountains, or Gold ranges; (2) the interior plateaus; (3) the coastal mountains, consisting of the Coast range and the Vancouver range, the latter being in places submerged. In the south the Rocky mountains are the highest, but in the north the coastal mountains far exceed them. Mount Logan, in the St. Elias range, Yukon, 19,850 feet elevation, is the highest point in Canada.

Climate. Canada covers so many degrees of latitude and possesses such vast areas of highland and lowland that it has many varieties of climate.

PRINCIPAL PRODUCTIONS OF CANADA*

Provinces	Field Crops 1966	Livestock & Poultry 1966	Dairy Products 1966	Fisheries 1966	Mineral Products 1967	Lumber** 1966	Manufactures 1966
Alberta	726,488,000	565,115,700	50,065,000	1,383,000	973,327,000	18,188,000	1,429,020,000
Rank	2	2	3	10	2	5	4
British Columbia	45,372,000	97,688,400	42,850,000	123,715,000	379,986,000	521,196,000	3,063,675,000
Rank	6	6	4	1	4	1	3
Manitoba	310,905,000	198,839,100	27,570,000	7,082,000	184,679,000	2,042,000	1,019,000,000
Rank	4	5	5	7	7	8	5
New Brunswick	26,860,000	22,325,500	12,961,000	45,268,000	90,419,000	25,850,000	547,197,000
Rank	7	8	8	4	9	4	7
Newfoundland	....	2,868,400	....	58,473,000	266,365,000	1,181,000	194,102,000
Rank		10		3	6	9	9
Nova Scotia	12,017,000	26,492,000	14,705,000	97,807,000	77,226,000	14,912,000	612,466,000
Rank	9	7	7	2	10	6	6
Ontario	477,924,000	674,586,200	245,046,000	6,744,000	1,194,545,000	72,289,000	19,452,570,000
Rank	3	1	1	8	1	3	1
Prince Edward Is.	24,830,000	20,282,700	6,677,000	9,164,000	2,606,000	139,000	46,781,000
Rank	8	9	9	6	11	11	10
Quebec	198,237,000	350,868,900	220,408,000	13,345,000	734,142,000	105,589,000	10,464,530,000
Rank	5	4	2	5	3	2	2
Saskatchewan	1,216,586,000	389,851,900	27,536,000	4,858,000	362,194,000	6,064,000	470,381,000
Rank	1	3	6	9	5	7	8
Yukon and Northwest Territories	....	26,200	....	1,225,000†	133,182,000	325,000	3,734,000
Rank		11		11	8	10	11
	3,037,219,000	2,348,945,000	647,818,000	355,590,000‡	4,398,671,000	767,773,000	37,303,455,000

* Showing value in dollars for provinces, with rank.
** Includes other sawmill products, but not manufactured products.
† Yukon Territory included with British Columbia rather than with Northwest Territories here.
‡ Lower than sum of provincial totals because duplications resulting from intershipments between provinces are removed..
Source: Dominion Bureau of Statistics

GROWTH OF CANADA, 1911-1966

ITEM		1911	1931	1941	1951	1961	1966
POPULATION . . .		7,206,643	10,353,778	11,506,655	14,009,429	18,238,247	20,014,880
IMMIGRATION . . .		311,084	88,223	11,496	194,391	71,689	194,743
AGRICULTURE:							
Wheat	bu.	215,841,300	298,000,000	540,190,000	562,395,000	283,394,000	827,338,000
Oats	bu.	348,187,600	331,243,000	346,154,000	492,683,000	283,965,000	374,678,000
Barley	bu.	40,641,000	67,972,000	116,659,000	252,795,000	112,640,000	301,235,000
Corn	bu.	18,772,700	5,643,000(5)	12,036,000(5)	15,662,000	33,262,000	72,971,000
Potatoes	bu.	66,023,000	91,815,000	65,206,000	66,647,000	55,436,700	91,131,000
Tame Hay . . .	tons	12,694,000	113,961,000	12,245,000	17,316,000	20,812,000	26,049,000
Horses	no.	2,266,400	3,129,058	2,881,400	1,306,634	512,021	380,000
Cattle	no.	7,086,600	7,990,947	8,797,800	8,370,991	10,900,000	9,747,000
Sheep	no.	2,389,300	3,608,340	3,550,500	1,478,737	1,563,534	1,094,000
Swine	no.	2,792,200	4,716,761	5,994,000	4,915,987	5,332,736	5,443,000
Cheese	lbs.	199,904,205	113,956,639	148,913,300	90,615,000	131,408,000	193,863,000
Butter	lbs.	64,489,398	225,955,246	286,109,500	246,400,000	364,286,000	342,423,000
FISHERIES:							
Total value. . .	$	29,965,433	30,517,306	62,258,997	204,912,000	222,800,000	355,953,000
MINERALS:							
Total production	$	103,220,994	230,434,726	560,241,290	1,245,483,595	2,582,300,000	3,972,480,919
Gold	oz.	473,159	2,693,892	5,345,179	4,392,751	4,474,000	3,319,474
Silver	oz.	32,559,044	20,562,247	21,757,408	161,872,873	31,382,000	33,417,874
Copper	lbs.	55,648,011	292,304,390	608,825,570(6)	539,941,589	878,175,000	1,012,152,458
Lead	lbs.	23,784,969	267,342,482	388,569,550(6)	316,462,751	460,860,000	599,244,120
Nickel	lbs.	34,098,744	65,666,320	226,105,865(6)	275,806,272	465,983,000	447,219,823
Pig Iron	tons	917,535	420,038	1,364,336	2,552,696	4,946,000	7,212,000
Coal	tons	11,323,388	12,243,211	18,225,961	18,586,823	10,398,000	11,391,569
Cement	bbl.	5,692,915	10,161,658	8,368,711	17,007,812	32,800,000	47,740,000
MANUFACTURES:							
Capital	$	1,247,583,609	3,705,701,893	4,095,716,836(7)	4,921,500,000(4)	8,172,000,000†	15,090,000,000†
Employees . . .	no.	515,203	528,640	762,244(7)	1,258,375	1,352,605(1)	1,646,024(1)
Salaries and Wages	$	241,008,416	587,566,990	920,872,865(7)	3,276,281,000	5,701,651,000	8,695,890,000
Products . . .	$	1,165,975,639	2,555,126,448	4,529,173,316(7)	16,392,187,000	25,895,611,000	37,303,455,000
Electric power .	kwh.	793,162,316	16,330,867,000	33,445,000,000	54,851,844,000	113,713,318,000(3)	158,135,232,000(3)
COMMERCE:							
Exports	$	297,196,365	599,560,460	1,640,454,541	3,914,460,376	5,895,215,000(4)	10,325,320,000(4)
Imports	$	472,247,540	628,098,386	1,448,791,650	4,084,856,478	5,768,578,000	9,866,439,000
Exports, Domestic—							
Wheat	bu.	45,802,115	217,243,037	177,967,532	237,060,505	358,000,000(8)	515,300,000(8)
Wheat flour . .	bbl.	3,049,046	7,218,188	10,288,327	12,078,671	. . . . . .	. . . . . .
Oats	bu.	5,431,662	3,258,501	14,396,287(7)	59,272,650	3,500,000	4,800,000
Hay	tons	326,132	156,722	74,598(7)	100,429	78,771	54,106
Bacon	lbs.	56,068,607	12,177,000	345,604,200(7)	61,325	3,896,000	4,142,600
Butter	lbs.	3,142,682	1,162,900	1,337,600(7)	543,700	27,252,000(12)	35,949,000
Cheese	lbs.	181,895,724	79,590,400	106,631,100(7)	30,653,200	19,508,000	35,947,000
Fisheries	$	15,675,544	28,894,983	31,650,889(7)	117,464,445	144,215,000(9)	221,719,000
Forest products .	$	45,439,057	97,369,461	348,006,396(7)	1,399,076,131	1,639,300,000	*
Manufactures. .	$	35,283,118	494,562,000	580,963,000(7)	1,497,235,000	3,622,900,000	6,672,100,000
Mineral products	$	42,787,561	155,697,504	374,120,171(7)	684,535,336(2)	2,235,200,000(10)	3,100,000,000(10)
Newsprint . . .	tons	. . . . .	2,098,241	3,242,789(6)	5,112,061	6,216,000	7,821,481
Imports(4)—							
Agricultural . .	$	35,304,683	177,628,778	157,249,495(7)	411,260,000	754,749,000(12)	*
Animal products	$	23,258,364	45,995,705	35,365,835(7)	278,983,000	136,898,000(12)	*
Fisheries	$	1,995,091	2,885,203	3,503,450(7)	6,425,108	19,156,000(12)	*
Forest products .	$	12,873,875	46,042,029	40,688,785(7)	140,007,000	291,475,000(12)	*
Manufactures. .	$	310,514,144	690,106,000	723,690,140(7)	2,774,766,000	4,344,645,000(12)	*
Mineral products	$	44,020,074	408,090,364	560,156,309(7)	2,383,173,000	710,851,000(12)	*
TRANSPORTATION:							
Steam Railways.	mi.	25,400	42,075	42,441	42,956	43,689	43,003
Electric Railways	mi.	1,224	1,386	1,040(7)	595	. . . . . .	. . . . . .
Urban Transit System, Passengers	no.	. . . . . .	. . . .	. . . .	. . . .	987,319,165	1,036,423,243
Shipping, sea going, cleared	tons	22,297,186	26,535,387	34,865,229(7)	52,750,461	77,140,524	99,852,760
COMMUNICATION:							
Telephones . .	no.	302,759	1,402,861	1,397,272	3,108,437	6,014,015	7,882,628
Telegraphs . . .	mi.	42,351	53,228	52,246	53,580	48,675	50,538
Postal revenue .	$	9,146,952	30,416,106	40,383,366	90,454,678	173,645,658	237,538,585
Postal expenditure	$	7,954,223	36,292,603	38,699,674	91,781,466	178,371,716	240,206,458
Postal money orders issued . .	$	70,614,862	167,749,651	173,565,550	511,915,621	886,976,976	965,095,390
FINANCE:							
Revenue	$	117,780,410	349,587,299	872,169,654	3,112,535,948	6,249,358,000	9,425,407,000(11)
Expenditures . .	$	87,774,198	440,057,336	1,249,641,446	2,901,241,698	7,022,623,000	9,732,839,000(11)
Gross debt . . .	$	474,941,487	2,610,265,698	5,011,399,120	16,923,307,028	22,907,814,464	30,340,137,314(11)
Net debt . . .	$	340,042,052	2,261,611,936	3,648,691,449	11,433,314,949	13,228,127,045	15,964,950,478(11)
Bank deposits .	$	1,073,298,505	2,568,683,245	3,464,781,844	8,464,510,837	15,163,000,000	21,497,000,000

(1) Based on the revised standard industrial classification and new establishment of total activity concepts. Using earlier classification, figures would be 6–7% lower. (2) Nonmetallic minerals. (3) Based on new series; includes power produced by industrial establishments for their own use. (4) Includes re-exports of 140 million for 1961 and 255 million for 1966. (5) Exclusive of fodder corn. (6) 1939; military restrictions prevented publication of detailed figures for copper, lead, and nickel after 1939. (7) 1940. (8) Includes bushel equivalent of wheat flour. (9) 1959. (10) Minerals and metals. (11) Year ended March 31, 1967, DDB statistics. (12) 1962. *Not available; new classifications were instituted in January 1961 for exports and in Jan. 1964 for imports. †Expenditure for new stock. Source (main): *Canada Year Book* (annual editions).

Hoover Dam, at 726 feet, is the highest dam in the U.S. Situated in the Black Canyon of the Colorado River on the Arizona-Nevada boundary line, Hoover Dam was completed in 1936 and required over 4 million cubic yards of concrete. Lake Mead, formed by the dam, is 115 miles in length. The area located 25 miles southeast of Las Vegas attracts thousands of visitors each year.

The Daniel-Johnson Dam in Canada is the world's largest multiple-arch dam. Built by Hydro-Quebec on the Manicouagan River, it created the largest man-made reservoir in North America. The arch dam uses the same engineering principles as the arch bridge and can be built with less concrete than other types of dams. *(Photo courtesy Hydro-Quebec, Montreal, Canada)*

Over the larger part of the Dominion, especially over the great interior plain, a continental climate prevails, the temperature in Fort Simpson, for example, varying from a recorded minimum of 73° below zero to 101° above. In other sections, however, the extremes of heat and cold are modified by the presence of vast bodies of water, as the Atlantic Ocean, the Pacific Ocean, the Great Lakes, and Hudson Bay.

In the maritime provinces, spring is retarded by the presence of the cold arctic current on the Atlantic Coast. The summer climate, however, is equable and the autumn is long and open. British Columbia has one of the finest climates in North America. At New Westminster the mean temperature of the coldest month is 36° F. and that of the hottest is 58° F. The lowest recorded temperature of Vancouver is only 2° lower than that of San Antonio, Texas. The recorded rainfall reaches a higher figure on the Pacific Coast than in any other part of Canada. The region of the Great Lakes has a temperate climate with a fairly high precipitation. The interior plains have a comparatively dry climate, but fortunately the precipitation occurs mainly in the summer, when it can be of value for agriculture.

Waterways. The rivers of Canada are of exceptional magnitude and number. They belong to four large drainage basins: (1) the Atlantic, including the Saint John, the Saint Lawrence and its tributaries, and the Hamilton; (2) the Hudson Bay, including the Moose, the Albany, the Nelson and its tributary,—the Saskatchewan,—the Churchill, and many others; (3) the Arctic, including the Banks, the Coppermine, and the Mackenzie with its tributaries—the Liard, the Peace, and the Athabaska; (4) the Pacific, including the Columbia, the Fraser, the Skeena, the Stikine, and the Yukon, the last emptying into Bering Sea.

Rimming the outer border of the Laurentian plateau are the greatest lakes of the world, the lakes of the Saint Lawrence system—Lake Ontario, Lake Erie, Lake Huron, and Lake Superior. Other large lakes of Canada are Lake Winnipeg, Lake Athabaska, Great Slave Lake, and Great Bear Lake.

The Great Lakes system is the waterway of the most importance for transportation, although the Nelson-Saskatchewan river, flowing into Hudson Bay, and the Mackenzie-Athabaska river, flowing into the Arctic Ocean, were well traveled water highways known to fur traders long before settlements had advanced as far west as Lake Ontario.

By means of enlarging the channel of the Saint Lawrence River, the Dominion government has made it possible for ocean steamers to reach Montreal, which is situated at a distance of 700 miles from the Atlantic Ocean. By the further construction of 117.2 miles of canals, an uninterrupted communication by water has been established from the head of Lake Superior to the Atlantic Ocean, an aggregate distance of 1594 miles.

Minerals. Canada is the world's chief source of nickel, platinum and the platinum metals, and asbestos; it ranks second in gold, aluminum, and zinc, and fourth in copper and lead.

The chief minerals of the maritime provinces are coal and iron, mined mostly in Nova Scotia. These provinces also produce gypsum in large amounts.

Canada's nickel, gold, and cobalt come mainly from northern Ontario, where platinum, copper, and silver also represent a large proportion of Ontario's annual output of minerals. Oil, natural gas, and salt are produced in southern Ontario. Quebec is one of the world's chief sources of asbestos. Other minerals produced in Quebec are mica, copper, gold, building stone, and clay for bricks.

The prairie provinces, particularly Alberta, have large coal deposits. Alberta also produces oil and natural gas in important quantities. From Manitoba come gold and copper.

The mineral output of British Columbia comprises chiefly copper, coal, gold, silver, lead, and zinc. Yukon territory has long been famous for its gold and silver mines. Important discoveries of silver, cobalt, and radium ore deposits were made in 1931 in the Northwest Territories, northeast of Great Bear Lake, and the first shipments of radium ore were made in 1932 for reduction in Port Hope, Ont.

Flora. In Ontario and Quebec, south of a line running from Georgian Bay to Montreal, the flora is of a southern forest type. North of this line to latitude 50°, from the Gulf of Saint Lawrence to Manitoba, a Temperate Zone forest type prevails. In Manitoba the forest disappears, giving place to the prairie grasses and herbage. Prairie vegetation spreads west as far as the foothills of the Rockies. Farther north, along a line drawn from latitude 55° on the Athabaska river to the south end of Lake Winnipeg, the prairie gradually gives place to the northern forest.

This northern forest belt extends from the Atlantic Ocean and the Gulf of Saint Lawrence to the Rockies. It covers all the country, extending from the temperate forest and the prairies northward as far as the Barren Grounds. In its southern half, this area is densely forested, but in the northern half the forest gradually becomes more open and the trees become smaller. The line between the forest and the Barren Grounds runs from Richards Island in the Arctic Ocean to the general region of Churchill on Hudson Bay, and from Richmond Gulf on the east side of the bay to Ungava Bay. In the Barren Grounds, the subsoil is permanently frozen.

In the Cordilleran belt, the flora varies according to climatic conditions. It is characterized by a tropical luxuriance on the coast and on the western slopes of the high ranges, but, in the dry areas east of the ranges, it takes on forms typical of the American desert.

Forests and Lumbering. Canada's forests cover 1,151,454 square miles, nearly one-third of the country's total surface. They are included more or less roughly in three areas: (1) the giant fir forest of the Rocky Mountains and the Pacific Coast; (2) the northern coniferous forest, lying between the prairies and the Barren Grounds; and (3) the deciduous, hardwood forest, extending from Lake Huron through southern Ontario and southern Quebec to New Brunswick and the Atlantic Coast.

The chief timber trees of the Pacific Coast area are Douglas fir, red cedar, Alaska pine, Sitka spruce, and Engelmann spruce. The dominant types of the northern forest include white spruce, balsam fir, tamarack, and black spruce. The more valuable trees of the southeastern forest area are yellow birch, white pine, red pine, eastern cedar, maple, elm, ash, oak, and hickory.

The forests of Canada are owned mainly by the provincial governments. Leases are extended to lumber or pulp companies to cut the timber, usually with the condition that the logs be sawed or manufactured into pulp in Canada.

The products of the forest which represent the largest value are pulp wood, lumber, and firewood. A large part of the lumber and pulp wood or paper manufactured from pulp wood is exported to the United States.

Fauna. The fauna of Canada resembles that of northern Europe. The carnivora are represented by several species of the weasel family, such as the ermine, the marten, and the mink. The lynx, bear, fox, wolf, and skunk are common at a distance from the settled districts. In the prairie provinces, small rodents, called gophers, are so numerous as to constitute a pest. The beaver is a characteristic Canadian animal and has been adopted, along with the maple leaf, as a national emblem. Otters and muskrats are numerous. Caribou range over the northern plains, which are also the habitat of the unique musk ox, an animal almost as large as the domesticated ox but having a close resemblance to the sheep. Moose and deer are found in the forested areas, and goats, sheep, and grizzly bears make the mountains their habitat. White bears, seals, and walruses are common along the northern coasts. Snakes are rare except in the extreme south.

Fur-bearing Animals. The animals which provide the largest aggregate value in pelts are the fox, muskrat, beaver, mink, ermine, and marten. Approximately one-fifth of all Canadian furs come from fur farms. The silver fox is the animal most successfully raised in captivity, but many fur farms are stocked with minks, raccoons, skunks, martens, coyotes, and badgers.

The fur trade constituted Canada's earliest commercial interest. It was formerly a monopoly of the Hudson's Bay Company, which controlled most of the northwest region until 1859. The company still has the largest share of Canada's fur trade, maintaining posts throughout the vast territory of the north.

Fisheries. Canada's sea fishing waters, including bays and inlets, total over 200,000 square miles. Conservation methods to protect the country's immensely valuable fishing industry have been adopted both by the Federal government and by provincial governments. It is officially estimated that the government hatcheries plant annually in suitable waters about two billion fish fry.

Salmon are taken on the Pacific coast; lobsters are obtained from the shore waters of the maritime provinces and of Quebec. Herrings are caught both on the Atlantic coast and on the Pacific coast. Hake, pollock, mackerel, and paddock are products of Atlantic deep-sea fishing. Halibut were formerly plentiful in Atlantic waters, but they now come mostly from the Pacific coast. British Columbia and New Brunswick have developed sardine canning industries. In the Pacific Coast waters, are found the eulachon, or candlefish. Smelts are also abundant there as well as along the shores of the maritime provinces. Alaska black cod is highly prized but is not plentiful.

Prince Edward Island Malpeque oysters were formerly famous for size and quality, but the beds have been greatly depleted as a result of overfishing and of disease. Clams are found on the coasts of both oceans. Large quantities of fresh-water fishes are taken, such as perch, bass, pickerel, pike, tullibee, and whitefish, the last constituting the most valuable food fish obtained from the Great Lakes.

Agriculture. Agricultural land in Canada lies directly north of the American border in a strip extending east and west across the country with a width of several hundred miles. The fertile portion of this strip is interrupted by a large rocky territory in northern Ontario and by the mountains of British Columbia, where cultivation is confined mainly to the valleys. The total area of land under field crops is about 62,000,000 acres, although approximately six times this area is said to be of value for agriculture.

In the maritime provinces, fruit and potatoes are the most important cash crops, although hay, clover, and oats command the largest acreage. Farming in Quebec is mixed and largely self-contained; potatoes and buckwheat are the leading cash crops. Ontario supports dairy farming chiefly in the east; wheat, apples, tobacco, and sugar beets are the principal cash crops in the south; and the Niagara region specializes in the cultivation of peaches, grapes, cherries, and other fruits. The prairie provinces raise the bulk of Canada's wheat crop, which reached a high point of 567 million bushels in 1928. Canada leads the world in wheat exports, and its wheat production is exceeded only by those of Russia and the United States. British Columbia cultivates fruits intensively and raises poultry and cattle.

Livestock. Stock raising is still an exclusive occupation in some parts of Alberta, Saskatchewan, and British Columbia, but elsewhere it is made a part of mixed farming. Specialization in stock raising, just as in grain growing, is being superseded by mixed farming. This change, however, has resulted in an increase rather than in a decrease of the number of live stock raised.

Dairying is an important industry, Canada being one of the largest exporters of cheese in the world. The factory system has been adopted in all the provinces. Experimental farms distributed across the continent are maintained by the government.

Manufacturing. Industrial development has proceeded rapidly in Canada during recent years, partly as a result of the increased availability of cheap hydroelectric power. This expansion has been largely confined to the older provinces. Ontario ranks highest in manufacturing, Quebec comes next, and British Columbia takes the third place. Montreal heads the list of industrial cities with Toronto a close second, Hamilton, Windsor, and Vancouver following in the order named. The industrial output exhibits a wide variety of products, the most important of which is newsprint paper, in the production of which Canada leads the world. Flour manufacture, meat packing, sawmill operations, and automobile and textile manufacture follow. Canada is one of the largest manufacturers of rubber products in the world.

Water Power. The water power available in Canada is enormously extensive, the total available for electric generation being estimated at 33,113,200 horse power at ordinary 6 months flow. Over 80 per cent of all power used in Canada is in the form of electricity, and of this over 98 per cent is generated by water power. This situation is due chiefly to the fact that water power is available close to the centers of population. In the use of electricity Canada is exceeded only by the United States; in its use per capita, Canada leads the world.

Transportation. There are in Canada over 40,000 miles of railroad in operation, of which the government owns more than 20,000 miles. Two transcontinental systems span the country from east to west.

Roads and highways in Canada open to traffic in 1953 had a total mileage of 512,795, of which 181,306 miles were classified as improved highways. They include the Trans-Canada highway, 4860 miles in length, said to be the longest highway in the world. Opened in 1962, it connects all ten provinces of Canada. From its eastern terminus at St. John's, it traverses 500 miles in Newfoundland, utilizes a ferry to Cape Breton Is., N.S., crosses the world's deepest causeway at the Canso Strait into Nova Scotia, and is joined by a ferry-served feeder section from Prince Edward Island. It proceeds through Ottawa, Winnipeg, Calgary, Rogers pass in the Rocky Mountains, and, via ferry to Vancouver island, finds its western terminus at Victoria, B.C.

Shipping. The principal seaports of Canada include Montreal, Vancouver, Victoria, Halifax, Saint John, Sydney, and Quebec. The countries with which Canada has the heaviest sea-borne commerce are the United States, Australia, and Great Britain. The shipping on the Great Lakes is heavy, traffic being mainly of grain, lumber, and ores passing east and of coal and manufactures going west. See *St. Lawrence Seaway*.

Population and Language. More than one-half of the population of Canada is of British descent; about one-third is composed of the descendants of French colonists. In the prairie provinces large numbers of Americans have settled as well as a certain proportion of people from continental Europe. The majority of the latter, however, live in the industrial centers. There are more than 100,000 American Indians, mostly on reserves. The population in 1971 was estimated at 21,681,000.

French shares with English the status of an official language in Canada. Its use is confined mainly to

CANADA, GROWTH OF PROVINCES IN POPULATION, 1901-1971

Province	1901	1911	1921	1931	1941	1951	1961	1966	1971
Alberta	73,022	374,295	588,454	731,605	796,169	939,501	1,331,944	1,463,203	1,628,000
British Columbia	178,657	392,480	524,582	694,263	817,861	1,165,210	1,629,082	1,873,674	2,190,000
Manitoba	255,211	461,394	610,118	700,139	729,744	776,541	921,686	963,066	985,000
New Brunswick	331,120	351,889	387,876	408,219	457,401	515,697	597,936	616,788	629,000
Newfoundland	......	......	......	289,588	321,819	361,416	457,853	493,396	523,000
Northwest Terr.	20,129	6,507	7,988	7,133	12,028	16,004	22,998	28,738	36,000
Nova Scotia	459,574	492,338	523,837	512,846	577,962	642,584	737,007	756,039	770,000
Ontario	2,182,947	2,527,292	2,933,662	3,431,683	3,787,655	4,597,542	6,236,092	6,960,870	7,795,000
Prince Edward Island	103,259	93,728	88,615	88,038	95,047	98,429	104,629	108,535	111,000
Quebec	1,648,898	2,005,776	2,361,199	2,874,255	3,331,882	4,055,681	5,259,211	5,780,845	6,030,000
Saskatchewan	91,279	492,432	757,510	921,785	895,992	831,728	925,181	955,344	927,000
Yukon Territory	27,219	8,512	4,157	4,230	4,914	9,096	14,628	14,382	17,000
Total	5,371,315	7,206,643	8,788,483	10,374,196	11,506,655	14,009,429	18,238,247	20,014,880	21,641,000

Quebec and to a few French settlements in other provinces.

Education. The education of Indian and Eskimo children of school age is a responsibility of the Federal government; the provincial governments are responsible for exercising all other education. Elementary and secondary education is free and compulsory to age 14. As the need for qualified tradesmen, technicians, and professionals has increased, numerous vocational schools and community colleges have come into existence, making nearly 400 institutions of higher education in Canada in 1968. In the same year, more than 3,000,000 adults were enrolled in the large adult education program.

PROVINCES

Canada is divided into ten organized provinces, Yukon Territory, and the Northwest Territories comprising the districts of Franklin, Keewatin, and Mackenzie. The provinces, enumerated from east to west, are Newfoundland, Nova Scotia, Prince Edward Island, New Brunswick, Quebec, Ontario, Manitoba, Saskatchewan, Alberta, and British Columbia.

Alberta. A province of Canada, situated between British Columbia on the west and Saskatchewan on the east and stretching from the American border about 750 miles north to the 60th parallel of north latitude. The southwestern border follows the summit of the Rocky mountains, thereby leaving in Alberta the western mountain slope and the foothills. From the foothills in the southern portion of the province, a plain slopes eastward, forming a part of the Saskatchewan River basin. The northern part of the province consists of a plain of northern drainage, belonging to the Mackenzie-Athabaska basin. A fringe on the extreme south drains into the Missouri river. The elevation varies from 12,294 feet on the top of Mount Columbia in the Rocky mountains to 568 feet at Slave river in the north. Except in the south, Alberta is well watered by numerous rivers, large and small. Lakes abound in the central and northern parts. The area of the province is 255,285 square miles.

The climate of Alberta is continental, involving great extremes of temperature. The air is dry and healthful. In southern Alberta the chinook winds, descending from the ridge of the Rocky mountains, often clear the ground rapidly of snow in the early spring, thus reviving the grasses which serve as sustenance for large herds of cattle.

A dark mold, mostly humus, overlying a clay subsoil, covers the surface of Alberta from six inches to several feet in depth. Such a soil, being exceedingly fertile and at the same time capable of retaining a large amount of moisture, supports a highly developed agricultural industry. Wheat and oats are the principal crops. Mixed farming has tended in recent years to replace specialized grain growing, with the result that potatoes, dairy products, flax, sheep, hogs, and poultry contribute a considerable amount to the total of the agricultural production.

In the southwest of the province, there is an area which requires irrigation in order to insure crops. Over 5400 miles of irrigation canals and ditches have been constructed.

The mineral resources of Alberta are of considerable importance. Immense areas of lignite and of a high grade bituminous coal have been discovered. Anthracite coal is also mined. The output of all kinds of coal amounts normally to over six million tons, a total exceeded by none of the other provinces. Petroleum and natural gas have been found both in the northern and in the southern part.

The capital and largest city of Alberta is Edmonton, in which is located the University of Alberta, supported by the province. The chief industries are those related to agriculture, such as meat packing. Population, 1971, 1,628,000.

British Columbia. The most western province of Canada, extending from the international boundary line to latitude 60°. The province is bounded on the east by Alberta; the western boundary is the Pacific Ocean, for a distance of 500 miles, and, for an additional 600 miles, the province borders on the coast strip of Alaska. British Columbia includes Vancouver island, the Queen Charlotte islands, and numerous other islands off the Pacific coast. The area is 366,255 square miles.

With the exception of a portion of the Peace River country in the northeast, the whole of British Columbia lies within the Cordilleran mountainous belt. The highest point is Mount Fairweather, 15,300 feet. Between the ranges, and occasionally cutting through them, are deep fertile valleys. Between the coastal mountains and the next important range to the east is an interior plateau having much agricultural or grazing land.

A submergence of the coast has resulted in an archipelago of innumerable islands, deep sounds, and fiords, many of them excellent harbors. As a result, the province has a coast line of 7000 miles. Of the rivers, the Fraser, 800 miles long, is the largest. The Columbia river rises in British Columbia and has a course of 500 miles before crossing the boundary line. Beautiful fiordlike lakes are a feature of many of the valleys. The islands and the coast region have a mild climate, rainy in winter but dry in summer. The interior plateaus are dry and subject to greater extremes of temperature.

British Columbia has one of the greatest forests of merchantable timber in North America, besides

CANADIAN NATIONAL PARKS AND RESERVES

Name	Location	Area Sq. Miles	Established	Distinctive Characteristics
Scenic and Recreational Parks:				
Banff	Alberta	2,564	1885	Ideal mountain playground containing the two famous resorts, Banff and Lake Louise.
Cape Breton Highlands	Nova Scotia	390	1936	Northern part of Cape Breton island; rugged coast line with mountain background.
Fundy	New Brunswick	80	1948	Recreational area. Forested region, wildlife sanctuary, rugged terrain.
Georgian Bay Islands	Ontario	5.37	1929	Thirty islands in Georgian bay, scene of bloody inter-tribal Indian war in 1649; includes Flowerpot Island reserve.
Glacier	British Columbia	521	1886	Summit of the Selkirks; Illecillewaet and Asulkan glaciers; Nakimu caves; Marion lake; Rogers and Baloo passes.
Jasper	Northern Alberta	4,200	1907	Immense mountain wilderness; unclimbed peaks, glaciers, snow fields, canyons, lakes; Mt. Edith Cavell, Miette Hot Springs, Mt. Robson.
Kootenay	British Columbia	543	1920	Mountain scenery, Briscoe range, Ice lake, Sinclair canyon, and Radium Hot Springs.
Mount Revelstoke	British Columbia	100	1914	Panoramic views of Columbia and Illecillewaet valleys, Clach-na-Coodin ice field.
Point Pelee	Lake Erie, Ontario	6	1918	Most southerly point in Canada; resting place of many migratory birds; recreational area; unique flora.
Prince Albert	Saskatchewan	1,496	1927	Recreational reserve and wild life sanctuary.
Prince Edward Island Shore	North Shore, P.E.I.	7	1937	Twenty-five mile strip of bathing beaches.
Riding Mountain	Western Manitoba	1,148	1929	Rolling wooded hills. Abundance of large game.
Saint Lawrence Islands	Ontario	189.4*	1914	Thirteen islands and one mainland reservation among the Thousand Islands.
Tar Sands Reservation	N. Alberta	3.2	1926	Four areas reserved for National Parks Branch to supply materials for road building.
Waterton Lakes	Southern Alberta	204	1895	With adjoining U. S. Glacier park forms international park. Mountains noted for beauty of coloring; lovely lakes, waterfalls, and snow peaks; excellent trout fishing; favorite camping resort.
Yoho	British Columbia	507	1886	Rugged scenery of west slope of Rockies; Yoho valley with falls over 1200 feet in height; natural bridge; Emerald lake.
Animal Parks and Reserves:				
Buffalo	Near Wainwright, Alberta	197.5	1908	Government's buffalo herd—over 3000 buffalo also moose, elk, deer, yak, and catalo.
Elk Island	Near Lamont, Alberta	75	1913	Smaller fenced enclosure, containing about 2000 buffalo; also moose, elk, and deer.
Nemiskam antelope Reserve	Southern Alberta	8.5	1922	Fenced reserve containing about 300 pronghorned antelope.
Wood Buffalo	Alberta and N. W. T.	17,300	1922	Home of the wood buffalo.
Historic Parks:				
Fort Anne	Nova Scotia	31*	1917	Fort Annapolis Royal was the center of the struggle between France and England for the possession of the continent.
Fort Beauséjour	New Brunswick	81*	1926	Site of a fort built by the French in 1750-51.

* Acres.

millions of acres of pulp wood yet untouched. Douglas fir, cedar, spruce, western hemlock, larch, and pine attain an unusual diameter and height. Logs 30 feet in girth are not uncommon. In value of output lumbering ranks highest among the industries of the province, providing support for two-fifths of the population and entitling British Columbia to the first place among the lumber producing provinces of the Dominion.

In the fishing industry, British Columbia likewise ranks first among the provinces, supplying 47 per cent of the Canadian production. The salmon fisheries are the most important, and have given rise to a large salmon canning industry. Halibut, herring, and black cod form a considerable part of the annual catch.

The discovery of gold in 1858 in the Fraser River district was the occasion for the earliest settlements in British Columbia. The mineral production since that time has continued to be important, copper, gold, coal, and silver being among the more valuable products of the industry. Nearly all the lead produced in Canada comes from British Columbia, which has one of the greatest lead-zinc deposits in the world. The province mines about one-fourth of the Dominion's mineral output by value.

In recent years agriculture, fruit growing, stock raising, dairying, and poultry raising have made rapid advances. The chief fruits include apples, grapes, peaches, apricots, plums, strawberries, and cherries.

British Columbia has a native supply of coal and of iron, and the province is favorably situated for shipping goods to the markets of Australia, of South America, and of Asia. Mainly as a result of these facts, manufacturing has become important, entitling British Columbia to the third place in regard to industrial output among the provinces of the Dominion.

The public school system is nonsectarian. Instruction must be given in English. The provincial university, called the University of British Columbia, is situated at Vancouver, which is the largest city of the province. The capital is Victoria, on Vancouver Island. Population, 1971, 2,190,000.

Keewatin (*kē-wä'tĭn*), **Mackenzie, Franklin.** Three divisions, each known as a provisional district, formed on January 1, 1920, out of the vast Northwest Territories. The total area of these districts is 1,309,682 square miles, of which 1,258,217 square miles are land and 51,465 square miles are water. In 1966, the population numbered 28,738.

The land is a rolling plain. The principal lakes are Great Bear lake and Great Slave lake, both in Mackenzie; the largest river, the Mackenzie, flows for most of its course through that district, emptying into Mackenzie bay, an arm of the Arctic Ocean. Furs are obtained in all the districts, and minerals—radium, gold, copper, lead, zinc, petroleum, and coal—have been found.

Manitoba (*măn'ĭ-tō'bȧ*). A province of Canada, situated in the south central part of the country between Ontario and Saskatchewan, stretching about 750 miles northward from the American border to 60° north latitude. The eastern boundary follows the 95th meridian about 275 miles northward, then cuts across at an angle of about 45° to Hudson Bay, so that the northeastern part of the province has a coast line on the bay. In the southern part, the drainage is from the southeast and the west to Lake Manitoba and Lake Winnipeg and thence northeast by the Nelson River to Hudson Bay. In the north, the Churchill River basin drains eastward into Hudson Bay. Duck mountain, 2727 feet in altitude, is the highest point. The area of the province is 251,832 square miles.

A large part of the soil is alluvial, a vast lake having occupied the southern part of the province in geological times. This alluvium, a black loam of great fertility, has a very high content of potash, nitrogen, and phosphoric acid, and is, therefore, peculiarly well adapted to the growth of cereals. The southeastern part of the province is rocky and slopes rapidly from the highlands of northern Ontario. This fact has made possible the development, on the Winnipeg River, of extensive hydroelectric power.

The chief primary industry of Manitoba is agriculture. The growing season has a duration of from 85 to 105 days. This period, however, by reason of the long, bright summer days, is sufficient to ripen a hard type of spring wheat which holds a position in the world's markets second to none. Oats, barley, and potatoes are grown also in considerable quantities. The dairy products of Manitoba are important and a great deal of butter and cheese are shipped. Cattle and swine are raised.

Manufacturing in Manitoba has been promoted by the availability of cheap hydroelectric power. In the value of industrial output, the province normally ranks fourth.

The capital and largest city of Manitoba is Winnipeg, which is also the seat of the University of Manitoba. The first permanent settlement was made in 1812 in the Red River district by a company of Scotch colonists. A unique feature of Manitoba's winter life is the annual dog derby, a race in which various dog teams compete on a course some 200 miles in length. Population, 1971, 985,000.

New Brunswick. A maritime province in the southeastern part of Canada, having an eastern coast line on the Gulf of Saint Lawrence and a southeastern coast line on the Bay of Fundy. Maine lies to the southwest of the province, and Quebec, to the northwest. The total coast line is 500 miles long and is indented with many fine harbors. Most of the surface is a rolling plain, lying between the low hills which, in the south, skirt the Bay of Fundy and the subdued mountains of the northwest. The highest point is Carleton mountain, which reaches an altitude of 2716 feet. The area is 27,985 square miles.

A number of navigable rivers traverse the province: the Saint John flows southward into the Bay of Fundy; the Mirimichi and Restigouche follow an eastward course into the Gulf of Saint Lawrence. At Grand Falls on the Saint John River is the spectacular 225-foot cataract which, now harnessed, supplies power for a large hydroelectric plant. At the river's mouth in Saint John Harbor is the famous 'reversing falls'' which, lighted at night, is an impressive sight.

New Brunswick's climate is subject to extremes. The thermometer has ranged from 95° F. in summer to −30° F. in winter.

Agriculture is the leading industry. The principal crops are hay, potatoes, oats, and turnips. Orcharding is important, apples forming the most valuable item. There are numerous cheese factories and creameries. Most of their products are exported to England. The province has much fertile land which has not yet been occupied.

Forests cover a large part of New Brunswick. Lumbering is an important industry, entitling the province to the fourth place in the nation in regard to lumber production. Spruce, pine, fir, maple, hemlock, birch, beech, ash, and elm are among the principal timber trees. At present, spruce is the principal commercial wood and is exported in large quantities.

New Brunswick ranks third among the provinces in the fishing industry. Oysters, lobsters, herring, codfish, haddock, and smelts are caught. The canning of lobsters and oysters and the curing of codfish add greatly to its economy.

The principal manufactured products include lumber, woodenware, wood pulp, boots and shoes, paper, cottons and woolens, nails, mill machinery, and leather. Fredericton is the capital. Saint John, the largest city, is an ice-free harbor at which two transcontinental railways reach tidewater. Population, 1971, 629,000.

Newfoundland. A former British dominion, consisting of the island of Newfoundland, lying across the mouth of the Gulf of Saint Lawrence, and a portion of the Labrador peninsula. Being situated 1640 miles west of Ireland, Newfoundland commands the shortest route from North America to Europe.

The island has an area of 42,734 square miles. In form it resembles a triangle with approximately equal sides of about 325 miles in length. The coasts are, in general, high and rocky, indented by innumerable fiords. Newfoundland's Labrador territory covers about 232,400 square miles, covering the land draining into the Atlantic. Of this, 112,400 square miles came to Newfoundland in 1927 through the favorable outcome of a boundary dispute. Its value lies in the coast fisheries, in pulpwood, and in potential hydroelectric development.

The interior of Newfoundland is a rolling plain, interrupted by a few isolated peaks and rising on the northwest to a ridge of hills, called Long range. From this ridge eastward flows Exploits River, the country's longest stream. The Humber River has cut its way westward through Long range and flows into the Gulf of Saint Lawrence. The rivers are not navigable.

The climate is subject to less extreme variations of temperature than those occurring in any part of the interior of Canada. The mean temperature is lowered by the proximity of the arctic current, which brings melting icebergs from the north and occasions dense fogs along the coasts.

Large portions of the island consist of marshes and of rocky soil supporting lichens and low shrubs of pine and of larch. The river valleys, however, contain large tracts of arable land and extensive areas heavily forested with conifers, birch, and red maple. The wild animals include the black bear, the wolf, the beaver, the deer, and the fox. The Newfoundland dog was developed by a cross between European species and a woolly-coated dog used by the Indians of Labrador.

GROWTH OF CITIES AND TOWNS IN CANADA 1951-71

City or Town	1951	1971
Alma, Que.	22,195[1]	22,353
Anjou, Que.	22,477[1]	33,842
Barrie, Ont.	12,514	26,985
Belleville, Ont.	19,519	34,498
Boucherville, Que.	15,338[1]	20,000
Brampton, Ont.	36,264[1]	41,238
Brandon, Man.	20,598	30,832
Brantford, Ont.	36,727	62,853
Brockville, Ont.	12,301	19,707
Burlington, Ont.	65,941[1]	86,125
Calgary, Alta.	129,060	400,154
Cap de la Madeleine, Que.	18,667	31,120
Charlottetown, P. E. I.	15,887	18.631
Chatham, Ont.	21,218	34,601
Chicoutimi, Que.	23,111	32,900
Cornwall, Ont.	16,899	46,429
Dartmouth, N. S.	15,037	64,002
Dollard-des-Ormeaux, Que.	12,297[1]	25,284
Drummondville, Que.	14,341	31,537
East Kildonan	28,796[1]	29,722
Edmonton, Alta.	159,631	434,116
Fredericton, N. B.	16,018	23,612
Galt, Ont.	19,207	38,134
Gatineau, Que.	17,727[1]	22,356
Glace Bay, N.S.	25,586	22,276
Granby, Que.	21,989	33,958
Grand' Mere, Que.	11,089	17,144
Greenfield Park, Que.	12,288[1]	15,277
Guelph, Ont.	27,386	58,364
Halifax, N. S.	85,589	121,086
Hamilton, Ont.	208,321	307,473
Hull, Que.	43,483	62,842
Joliette, Que.	16,064	19,497
Jonquière, Que.	21,618	28,080
Kingston, Ont.	33,459	61,870
Kitchener, Ont.	44,867	109,954
Lachine, Que.	27,773	44,345
LaSalle, Que.	48,322[1]	72,916
Laval, Que.	196,088[1]	228,101
Lethbridge, Alta.	22,947	40,706
Levis, Que.	13,162	16,566

City or Town	1951	1971
Lindsay, Ont.	9,603	12,090
London, Ont.	95,343	221,430
Longeuil, Que.	25,593[1]	97,483
Magog, Que.	12,423	13,280
Medicine Hat, Alta.	16,364	26,058
Mississauga, Ont.	.....	155,667
Moncton, N. B.	27,334	47,781
Montreal, Que.	1,021,520	1,197,753
Mont-Royal, Que.	21,845[1]	21,470
Moose Jaw, Sask.	24,355	31,284
Nanaimo, B. C.	15,188[1]	14,762
New Glasgow, N. S.	9,933	10,792
New Waterford, N. S.	10,423	9,549
New Westminster, B. C.	28,639	42,083
Niagara Falls, Ont.	22,874	65,271
North Bay, Ont.	17,944	49,063
Oakville, Ont.	52,793[1]	61,365
Orillia, Ont.	12,110	24,016
Oshawa, Ont.	41,545	91,113
Ottawa, Ont.	202,045	298,087
Outremont, Que.	30,057	28,402
Owen Sound, Ont.	16,423	18,281
Pembroke, Ont.	12,704	16,130
Peterborough, Ont.	38,272	57,498
Pierrefonds, Que.	27,924[1]	33,046
Pointe aux Trembles, Que.	29,888[1]	35,521
Pointe Claire, Que.	26,784[1]	27,310
Port Arthur, Ont.	31,161	.....
Prince Albert, Sask.	17,149	27,613
Quebec, Que.	164,016	182,418
Red Deer, Alta.	26,171[1]	27,428
Regina, Sask.	71,319	137,759
Richmond Hill, Ont.	19,773[1]	32,399
Rimouski, Que.	20,330[1]	26,546
Rivière du Loup, Que.	9,425	12,423
Rouyn, Que.	14,633	17,804
St. Boniface, Man.	26,342	46,661
St. Catherines, Ont.	37,984	109,636
Ste. Foy, Que.	48,298[1]	67,834

City or Town	1951	1971
St. Hubert, Que.	17,215[1]	21,753
St. Hyacinthe, Que.	20,236	24,192
St. James, Man.	.....	70,768
St. Jean, Que.	19,305	32,484
St. Jérôme, Que.	17,685	26,131
St. John, N. B.	50,779	87,910
St. John's, Nfld.	52,873	86,290
St. Laurent, Que.	59,479[1]	63,067
St. Léonard, Que.	25,328[1]	52,013
St. Thérèse, Que.	15,628[1]	17,161
St. Thomas, Ont.	18,173	25,062
St. Vital, Man.	29,528[1]	32,613
Sarnia, Ont.	34,697	56,727
Saskatoon, Sask.	53,268	125,079
Sault Ste. Marie, Ont.	32,452	78,175
Sept Iles, Que.	18,950[1]	24,289
Shawinigan, Que.	26,903	27,502
Sherbrooke, Que.	50,543	80,457
Sorel, Que.	14,961	19,317
Stratford, Ont.	18,785	23,863
Sudbury, Ont.	42,410	153,959
Sydney, N. S.	31,317	32,459
Sydney Mines, N. S.	8,410	8,957
Thetford Mines, Que.	15,095	21,662
Three Rivers, Que.	46,074	55,240
Thunder Bay, Ont.	.....	107,805
Timmins, Ont.	27,743	28,252
Toronto, Ont.	675,754	698,634
Transcona, Man.	19,761[1]	22,085
Trenton, Ont.	10,085	14,405
Truro, N. S.	10,750	12,968
Valleyfield, Que.	22,414	29,776
Vancouver, B. C.	360,520	419,433
Verdun, Que.	77,391	74,520
Victoria, B. C.	51,331	60,897
Victoriaville, Que.	13,124	22,088
Waterloo, Ont.	11,991	37,245
Welland, Ont.	15,382	44,222
West Kildonan, Man.	22,240[1]	23,728
Westmount, Que.	25,222	23,570
Whitby, Ont.	17,273[1]	25,291
Windsor, Ont.	120,049	199,784
Winnipeg, Man.	235,710	243,208
Woodstock, Ont.	15,544	25,559

Source: Statistics Canada, preliminary 1971. [1] 1966.

Approximately one-fifth of Newfoundland's population is engaged in fishing and curing codfish. Nearly half the exports are codfish products.

The most important manufactures are pulp and paper. A very small fraction of the arable land is cultivated, in spite of the steps taken by the government to encourage agriculture. The chief crops are potatoes and turnips. Iron, zinc, and copper are mined.

The population of Newfoundland in the 1971 census was 523,000, concentrated mainly in the coast region of the southeast. This figure excludes 5,000 inhabitants of Labrador, mostly Indians. Nearly all the inhabitants are of British descent and Protestants. The schools are denominational.

The government has been undergoing changes since 1934, when the British government suspended the constitution and took over on account of internal financial difficulties. Union with Canada as a tenth province was carried by a small majority in a referendum conducted in Newfoundland July 1948, and was mutually agreed to in December of that year. Canadian and British parliaments and the Newfoundland government ratified this agreement, which came into force March 31, 1949. The population of St. John's, the capital, fishing, industrial, and educational center, in 1971 was 86,290.

Nova Scotia. A maritime province in the extreme southeast of Canada, consisting of a narrow peninsula and of the Island of Cape Breton, which was connected with the mainland by a large rail-highway causeway completed in 1955. The greatest length is 350 miles and the greatest breadth, 100 miles. The maximum elevation of 1500 feet is reached at North Cape plateau, Victoria County. The area of the province is 21,428 square miles.

The main peninsula is a long highland cut by transverse valleys. An important longitudinal valley, the Annapolis valley, runs parallel to the Bay of Fundy, being separated from it by a narrow ridge known as North mountain. The seacoast line is 1500 miles in length, and is indented by several inlets which form excellent harbors.

Bras d'Or lake in Cape Breton is a magnificent landlocked body of salt water. It has become a popular resort for wealthy summer residents. Minas basin, the east arm of the Bay of Fundy, penetrates 60 miles inland. Here the tides, rising some 50 feet, rush in with great force, forming "bores."

Nova Scotia has a healthful climate, with a mean summer temperature of 65° F. and a mean winter temperature of 25° F. Winter weather is variable, and spring is late.

Agriculture is the chief occupation, hay, potatoes, turnips, and oats constituting the principal crops. Fruit growing, dairying, and stock raising are important.

Coal is mined extensively in Cape Breton island and in the northern part of the mainland. Copper tungsten, lead, gold, and manganese are found, and there are enormous beds of iron ore. Gypsum occurs in immense masses. Nova Scotia normally ranks fourth among the provinces in mineral output.

The fisheries of Nova Scotia are among the most productive in the world. The annual value is second only to that of British Columbia, among the Canadian provinces. Mackerel, cod, herring, haddock, and lobsters abound in the coast waters. Lobster canning has become a large industry.

Products manufactured in the province include iron and steel products, cotton and woolen goods, boots and shoes, machinery, farm implements, furniture, paper, sugar, condensed milk, and vehicles. Wood pulp is exported. Lumbering, formerly the chief industry, is still important.

The province is well supplied with railroads, chiefly lines of the Canadian National Railway. Shipping is important, especially in winter, when navigation on the Saint Lawrence is closed. There are three universities. The capital and largest city is Halifax. Population, 1971, 770,000.

Ontario. The most populous and most wealthy province of Canada. It is situated in the southeast of Canada, between Quebec and Manitoba and between the international boundary and Hudson Bay. The province consists of a large northern area joined to a smaller but populous southern area by a narrow neck between Georgian Bay and the Quebec border. The southern portion is part of the Saint Lawrence lowlands, belonging to the Saint Lawrence River basin. This basin is separated by a flat and ill-marked watershed, called the height of land, from the Laurentian plateau, which is an area of southern drainage sloping toward Hudson Bay. The bulk of the population is to be found in the lowlands, where the soil is adapted to agriculture. The northern country is rocky. Tiptop Hill, 2120 feet high, in Thunder Bay district, is the highest point in Ontario. The province is well watered by lakes and rivers. The area is 412,582 square miles.

Since Ontario extends from Hudson Bay to Lake Erie, a distance of about 1000 miles, there is considerable climatic variation. Extreme cold in winter is experienced about the watershed. The southern part, however, has a much milder climate, while the climatic severity of the northern section is tempered by the lowness of its altitude.

In value of mineral production, Ontario leads all the other provinces. The chief products mined are gold, silver, nickel, copper, cobalt, platinum, lead, iron, and arsenic. Nickel and cobalt are distinctive of Ontario's mineral output. Nickel is produced in no other part of the world in similar quantities.

Farming is the most important primary industry. In value of field crops, Ontario usually ranks second among the provinces. The land under cultivation is almost entirely in the lowlands, although agriculture is practicable in parts of the Laurentian plateau, including the clay belt in northern Ontario, through which the Canadian National railway has been constructed. Oats, wheat, barley, and corn are the chief grains. Minor crops are peas, rye, sugar beets, tobacco, potatoes, and turnips. About half the fruit raised in Canada is produced by Ontario. Approximately one million barrels of apples of the high grade are annually shipped to Europe. Similarly, in the output of dairy products and in the number of live stock owned, the province holds the leading position.

In lumbering, Ontario yields the first place to British Columbia, and, in the production of pulp wood, the province ranks third to Quebec. Immense forests cover almost one-fourth of the area of the province. Spruce, pine, and poplar are the principal woods cut, although maple, birch, and elm are also found over considerable areas. Oak and hickory occur in the more southern parts.

The Great Lakes fisheries employ hundreds of vessels. Trout, whitefish, pickerel, and fresh-water herring form most of the catch, a part of which is canned for market.

Ontario is Canada's most highly developed industrial section, manufacturing industries supporting nearly one-half the population. Hydroelectric power is available in large quantities due mainly to the development of the water power of Niagara Falls. The manufactures of the province include machinery, electrical equipment, automobiles, rubber products, farm implements, ironware, railroad rolling stock, metals and alloys, leather, furniture, paper, soap, boots and shoes, sewing machines, woodenware, and textiles. Milling, fruit canning, and meat packing employ many thousands of hands.

Ontario has seven universities, besides a number of church and technical colleges and agricultural schools. The province was formerly called Upper Canada. Its population was considerably augmented by the United Empire Loyalists. The capital and largest city is Toronto. The province also contains Ottawa, the capital of the country. Population, 1971, 7,795,000.

Prince Edward Island. An island province of Canada, situated in the southern part of the Gulf of Saint Lawrence. Prince Edward Island is the smallest and most densely populated province of the nation. The island is about 145 miles long and varies in width from 5 miles to 34 miles. The coast line is a succession of bays and headlands. The surface is gently rolling, the greatest height being 306 feet, at Fredericton Station, Queens County. The area is 2184 square miles.

Due to the influence of the surrounding sea, the province is singularly free from extremes of heat and cold. Fogs are less frequent than on the mainland. The soil is fertile and produces, besides other crops, hay, potatoes, oats, and turnips.

The fisheries provide employment for a large part of the population. Lobsters and oysters of superior quality are canned for market. Cod, herring, hake, and mackerel are also taken.

Dairying receives much attention, and the island's creameries and cheese factories export large quantities of their products. Rivaling it in importance is the production of poultry and eggs. In recent years, silver fox farming has developed into a highly important industry.

Prince Edward Island attracts many summer residents by its pleasant summer climate and its facilities for surf bathing. Higher education is furnished by two colleges. Charlottetown, the capital, is the largest city. Population, 1971, 111,000.

Quebec. A province in eastern Canada, lying between the Gulf of Saint Lawrence on the east and Hudson Bay and Ontario on the west and extending north about 1200 miles from the international boundary to Hudson strait and the Atlantic coastal strip known as Labrador. Quebec is the oldest as well as the largest province in the country and was formerly known as Lower Canada. Its area is 594,434 square miles.

Except for a narrow strip along the Saint Lawrence River, the whole northern part of the province belongs to the Canadian shield with a drainage toward Hudson Bay. To the south of the river rise the Notre Dame Mountains, a continuation of the Appalachian system. Mount Jacques Cartier, on the Gaspe Peninsula, is the highest point in Quebec, with an altitude of 4230 feet.

The climate of Quebec is continental in severity, partly on account of the influence of cold arctic currents and of winds blowing above them and passing over the land. The air is dry, clear, and bracing.

The mining industry of Quebec is confined mainly to the eastern townships and to the district along the Ottawa River. Asbestos is a distinctive product, Quebec supplying over half of the world's market. Other products are copper, gold, chromic iron, cement, magnesite, mica, graphite, apatite, marble, serpentine, roofing slates, and building stone.

The lumber industry has always been of great importance in Quebec, which contains millions of acres covered with commercial timber. The lumber and the pulp industry yield approximately the same returns as in Ontario.

Agriculture and dairying form the chief occupations. The principal crops are hay, oats, and potatoes. Quebec is a close second to Ontario in the production of creamery butter and of factory cheese. Cattle are exported to Europe. The making of maple sirup and of maple sugar centers in this province.

The seacoast fisheries yield cod, mackerel, and lobsters as the principal items of the catch. Large amounts of salt fish are exported.

Quebec ranks second to Ontario as a manufacturing province. Wood pulp, timber products, machinery, cottons and woolens, aluminum, refined sugar, leather, and boots and shoes are included among the principal manufactures. Hydroelectric power installations exceed in horsepower those of any other province. Among the largest plants and ranking among the greatest in the world are those at Arvida near Lake St. John, at Gouin Dam on the St. Maurice River, near Quebec, and at the Beauharnois Dam, near Montreal.

Elementary instruction is free. Catholics and Protestants have separate schools. There are four universities in the province and several agricultural, technical, and trade schools. The capital is Quebec. The largest city is Montreal, which is also one of the largest wheat shipping ports of the world, in spite of the fact that it is icebound during the winter.

Most of the people are descendants of early French settlers, and in most of the rural districts French is the language in common use. Roman Catholicism is the predominant religion. Population, 1971, 6,030,000.

Saskatchewan (*săs-kăch'ĕ-wŏn*). A province of Canada, situated in the south central part of the country between Manitoba and Alberta and extending from the international boundary about 750 miles north to latitude 60° N. The southern half belongs to the great central plains region; the northern portion is part of the Laurentian plateau. South of the North Saskatchewan and of the Saskatchewan River, the surface is prairie, but north of these rivers the province is heavily forested with spruce, pine, tamarack, poplar, and birch. The eastern portion of the prairie belongs to the second prairie steppe; the western section forms a part of the third steppe, which angles across the province and stretches in rolling plains through Alberta to the Rocky Mountains. On the plains, the soil is a rich loam. Excepting for the southwestern section, the province is well watered with rivers and lakes, which are especially numerous in the Laurentian area, in the northern and central parts. The surface covers 251,700 square miles.

On account of Saskatchewan's great length, there is a considerable diversity of climate and of temperature. The southern third has a moderate and changeable climate. The western portion of this section is dry, being subject to the warm chinook winds, and requires irrigation; the eastern part has more moisture and a steadier winter. The central third has a steady winter and a greater precipitation. The climate of the northern region is of a continental severity.

Agriculture is the great, almost the exclusive, industry of Saskatchewan. In point of wheat production in Canada, the province holds the first place. Its fields are free from rust and from insect pests which attack wheat. In the production of oats, Saskatchewan normally ranks first or near the first among the provinces. Mixed farming is increasing in the south. In the north, too, cattle raising is gradually giving place to mixed farming. Dairying is encouraged by the government, especially through the improvement of breeds of stock. Agricultural products are marketed by means of more than 6000 miles of railway, which have been constructed in the province. A government experimental farm, with headquarters at Indian Head, has performed valuable services in the agricultural development of Saskatchewan.

The capital and largest city is Regina. Other important cities are Moosejaw, Prince Albert, and Saskatoon, the last-mentioned city being the seat of the University of Saskatchewan. Population, 1971, 927,000.

Yukon. A territory in the northwest of Canada between British Columbia and the Arctic Ocean. Ranges of the Rocky Mountain system traverse the northeastern portion of the territory, and are separated by the Yukon River basin from the Coast range and the Saint Elias range in the southwest. The Yukon River basin is a plateau country with a general slope toward the northwest. In the extreme southwest, Mt. Logan, the highest peak in Canada, reaches an elevation of 19,850 feet. The area of the territory is 207,076 square miles.

Mining is the principal occupation, gold and silver being the chief products. From 1895 to 1931 the value of the gold output was $211 million. The annual yield has greatly diminished, causing a decline in population from 27,219 in 1901 to 4157 in 1921. The development of a rich silver district later caused a fresh influx of settlers, but the inhabitants numbered only 17,000 in 1971.

A railroad connects Whitehorse, the capital of the territory, on the upper Yukon with Skagway in Alaska. Some of the hardier crops, as barley, oats, rye, potatoes, and turnips, are grown, and, in sheltered valleys, peas, cabbages, lettuce, and other garden vegetables thrive. Dawson, in the west central section, is the center of the Klondike gold region.

TWENTY LARGE CITIES OF CANADA

Showing Growth 1891-1971

City	Population									
	1891	1901	1911	1921	1931	1941	1951	1961	1966	1971
Montreal, Que.	254,278	325,653	490,504	618,506	818,577	903,007	1,021,520	1,191,062	1,222,255	1,197,753
Toronto, Ont.	181,215	218,504	381,833	521,893	631,207	667,457	675,754	672,407	664,584	698,634
Edmonton, Alta.	......	4,176	31,064	58,821	79,197	93,817	159,631	281,027	376,925	434,116
Vancouver, B.C.	13,709	29,432	120,847	163,220	246,593	275,353	344,833	384,522	410,375	419,433
Calgary, Alta.	3,876	4,392	43,704	63,305	83,761	88,761	129,060	249,641	330,575	400,154
Hamilton, Ont.	48,959	52,634	81,969	114,151	155,547	166,337	208,321	273,991	298,121	307,473
Ottawa, Ont.	44,154	64,226	87,062	107,843	126,872	154,951	202,045	268,206	290,741	298,087
Winnipeg, Man.	25,639	42,340	136,035	179,087	218,785	221,960	235,710	265,429	257,005	243,208
London, Ont.	31,977	37,976	46,300	60,959	71,148	78,264	95,343	169,569	194,416	221,430
Windsor, Ont.	12,607	15,198	23,433	55,935	98,179	105,311	120,049	114,367	192,544	199,784
Quebec, Que.	63,090	78,118	78,710	95,193	103,594	150,757	164,016	171,979	166,984	182,418
Regina, Sask.	......	2,249	30,213	34,432	53,209	58,245	71,319	112,141	131,127	137,759
Saskatoon, Sask.	......	113	12,004	25,739	43,291	43,027	53,268	95,526	115,892	125,079
Halifax, N.S.	38,437	40,832	46,619	58,372	59,275	70,488	85,589	92,511	86,792	121,086
St. John, N.B.	39,179	40,711	42,511	47,166	47,514	51,741	50,779	55,153	51,567	87,910
St. John's, Newf'd.	......	......	......	......	......	44,603	52,873	63,633	79,884	86,290
Sherbrooke, Que.	10,097	11,765	16,405	23,515	28,933	35,965	50,543	66,554	75,690	80,457
Verdun, Que.	296	1,898	11,629	25,001	60,745	67,349	77,391	78,317	76,832	74,520
Victoria, B.C.	16,841	20,919	31,660	38,727	39,082	44,068	51,331	54,941	57,453	60,897
Three Rivers, Que.	8,334	9,981	13,691	22,367	35,450	42,007	46,074	53,477	57,540	55,240

Source: Statistics Canada, preliminary 1971.

CITIES, TOWNS, AND OTHER POINTS OF INTEREST

The following section contains articles on some cities of Canada having a population in excess of 25,000. It includes also descriptions of the capital cities of the country and of all the provinces. Since Canada is scenically one of the most attractive countries of the world and draws annually many hundreds of thousands of travelers, many of the places especially worth visiting are described. These include Banff in the Rocky Mountains and Muskoka in Ontario. A number of other places are included for special interest attaching to them, such as the famous shrine center at Sainte Anne de Beaupré and Churchill, the sub-arctic port.

Banff. A health and pleasure resort of southwestern Alberta, picturesquely situated in Banff National Park on the eastern mountain slope. It has a boiling sulphur spring and is the point of departure for numerous scenic features in the vicinity, including Bow Falls, many rocks of unusual formation, and glacier fed lakes. The most beautiful of the lakes is Lake Louise, enclosed by gigantic pine-clad mountains. Lying about a thousand feet above Lake Louise are Lake Agnes and Mirror Lake. Banff itself was the first national park in America, an area of five square miles dedicated in 1885 but since enlarged to over 250 square miles. The town's permanent population is engaged almost exclusively in the tourist trade, the summer visitors numbering over 15,000 a day. Local attractions include the Canadian wax gallery and an annual four-day celebration of "Banff Indian days." The town is governed by a federal park superintendent, but a locally elected council serves in an advisory capacity. Population, 1971, 3,608.

Brandon. A commercial and railway city of southwestern Manitoba, the second largest city in the province. Industries are based primarily on agriculture, including meat and vegetable packing and manufacture of dairy products and fertilizers. Situated 130 miles west of Winnipeg, it is the trade center for Western Manitoba and part of Saskatchewan. Other industries include oil refining and the manufacture of electrical equipment. Brandon College is affiliated with McMaster University in Hamilton, Ont. A Dominion experimental farm and an Indian residential school are located in the vicinity. Population, 1971, 30,832.

Brantford. A manufacturing city on the Grand River in southern Ontario. Its leading manufactures are agricultural implements, binder twine, refrigeration units, and truck bodies. The city is named for the Mohawk chief, Joseph Brant, for whom a beautiful monument has been erected. His body is buried beside Queen Anne's Chapel of the Mohawks, built in 1785. Alexander Graham Bell resided at Brantford when he first demonstrated his telephone in 1874. A handsome monument to his memory stands in Victoria Park, and his homestead is preserved as a public museum. Population, 1971, 62,853.

Calgary. A commercial and manufacturing city of southern Alberta at the junction of the Bow and Elbow rivers. It is the gateway to Banff and the Canadian Rockies, 77 miles distant.

Calgary, incorporated as a town in 1884 and as a city in 1893, owed its early growth to cattle marketing and meat packing. Irrigation of the farm lands to the east brought other industries based on agriculture. The discovery of oil in 1914 and of rich gas fields in 1948 made it a magnet for a wide variety of industries and accelerated its growth. Situated along the east side of the city, these include oil refining and the manufacture of petrochemicals, fertilizers, farm machinery, rubber products, and oil-well equipment. Shops of the Canadian Pacific Railway are located in the city.

Calgary's leading educational institution is the University of Alberta, Calgary. Its 110-acre exhibition ground features an annual stampede and provides sporting and art facilities. There is a 400-acre recreation area known as Happy Valley. Among the more imposing buildings is the Provincial Jubilee Auditorium, a center for concerts and art exhibitions. Population, 1971, 400,154.

Charlottetown. The capital of Prince Edward Island, occupying a high site at the head of Hillsborough Bay at the junction of three tidal rivers. The city has an excellent harbor. The fisheries are extensive. Manufacturing interests include frozen-food processing, meat and poultry packing, iron and brass founding, metal fabricating, and manufacture of industrial and special machinery, concrete and stone products, and chemical fertilizers. Charlottetown has two colleges and several fine public buildings, including the Fathers of Confederation Memorial Centre.

The city was founded in 1756 by French settlers but passed to Great Britain with the cession of Canada in 1763. Two American privateers raided the town in 1775; but the property seized was returned, and the prisoners were restored to their homes by order of General Washington. Charlottetown was incorporated in 1855. Population, 1971, 18,631.

Churchill. A port of northern Manitoba on Hudson Bay. The first commercial shipments of wheat were made through this port in 1932. A railroad connects this point with Winnipeg, and large grain elevators and port facilities have been constructed. By using the route through Hudson Bay during its open season of three or four months, shippers between Western Canadian points and Liverpool same 600 miles over the route via Montreal. Population, 1971, 1,612.

Cobalt. A mining town of Ontario, situated near Lake Timiskaming on the upper Ottawa River. Cobalt was the center of one of the richest silver producing regions in the world. The deposit was discovered in 1903, and production reached its peak in 1911, with shipment of 31,507,791 ounces of silver. In the 1930's the town went into a sharp decline although the district continued to produce a large proportion of the world's cobalt, with nickel and arsenic as by-products. Population, 1971, 2,191.

Dawson. Former capital of Yukon Territory, located in the west central part of the territory on the Yukon River just below the Klondike. At the height of the Klondike's gold-mining prosperity, Dawson had a population of over 20,000; but, when the rich claims in the district were worked out, the number of inhabitants decreased greatly. The name commemorates Dr. G. M. Dawson, the geologist, who first reported on the gold prospects of the district. Population, 1971, 745.

Edmonton. The capital of Alberta, a trading, manufacturing, and oil production center. It occupies a picturesque site on the North Saskatchewan River, which is here spanned by six bridges, one of them 200 feet above the river.

A fur trading station and fort was founded on the site in 1795. In 1891, when a railroad line reached it from Calgary, the population was 400, which was temporarily swollen to 3000 as the starting point of the Klondike gold rush. It became Alberta's capital in 1906, and settlers poured in as the surrounding rich agricultural lands were occupied. Coal mines attracted industries, chiefly those related to agriculture and lumbering.

The discovery of oil nearby in 1947 brought a period of spectacular growth. Edmonton found itself the center of the richest oil and gas field in Canada, and gas was piped to points as far away as Ontario. A mushrooming chemical industry grew up, followed by satellite secondary industries.

The city is regularly laid out with wide streets crossing at right angles. In the early 1960's work was begun on a civic center, its focal point being the strikingly modern city hall. Other structures include the ultra modern Centennial public library, an art gallery, and the Chateau Lacombe hotel. In one of the city's 86 parks is a planetarium, the first to be constructed in Canada. Other imposing buildings are the Parliament Buildings and the buildings on the 300-acre campus of the University of Alberta. Population, 1971, 434,116.

Fort William. A transshipping point and flour milling city of northwestern Ontario, situated on Thunder Bay in Lake Superior at the head of Canadian navigation in the Great Lakes. It is the Great Lakes terminal of Canada's Lake Superior, Canada's western terminus of the St. Lawrence Seaway. It is contiguous with its sister city, Port Arthur, the two being popularly known as the Canadian Lakehead Cities. The economy of both is based on their location, the point where the grain from the prairie provinces is loaded on ships. Although ice-bound for six months a year, the port's tonnage ranks with the largest in Canada. It has a grain storage capacity of 110 million bushels. Its industries include pulp and paper milling and shipbuilding.

The cities' water supply comes from Loch Lomond, a nearby lake 320 feet above the city situated behind Mt. McKay. Eighteen miles to the west is the magnificent Kakabeka Falls, where the water of the Kaministikwia River falls 128 feet into a rocky gorge. In 1966, the population of Fort William was 48,208; that of Port Arthur was 48,340.

Fredericton. The capital of New Brunswick, situated in the southwest part of the province at the head of navigation for large ships in the Saint John River, about 84 miles from its mouth. The leading industries include the manufacture of lumber, machine shop products, and shoes.

Fredericton is the seat of the University of New Brunswick, in whose organization the first step was taken in 1785 on petition of the first settlers, United Empire Loyalists driven from the United States. Several of its buildings were erected through the benefaction of Lord Beaverbrook, whose earliest years were spent in New Brunswick and who became a publisher and peer in England. He donated also the Beaverbrook Art Gallery and the Playhouse, the latter opened in 1964.

Fredericton was incorporated in 1845. Its Parliament buildings, old and impressive, are supplemented by the Centennial Building of ultra-modern construction in the downtown area, which houses most government departments. Population, 1971, 23,612.

Halifax. The capital of Nova Scotia, located on a natural harbor at the center of the southeast coast of the province. Halifax is an important naval base, an ice-free port, and the winter terminus of several steamship lines. The Canadian National railways also use the city as their eastern terminus. The steamship and railway terminal facilities are among the finest on the continent.

The chief interests of Halifax include transportation and shipping, fisheries, and manufacturing. The foreign trade of the port normally approximates $140 million in value. Fish cured in the city are extensively exported to the West Indies and to South America. The leading industries are car shop production, sugar refining, and the manufacture of textiles, furniture, cordage, and foundry products.

The northwest arm of the harbor is used as a pleasure resort by citizens of Halifax. The educational institutions include Dalhousie University, King's College, Technical College, Mt. St. Vincent University, and St. Mary's University. The city was founded by Lord Cornwallis in 1749 under orders to create a bastion to offset France's Port Royal. In 1917, a collision of two ships in the harbor, one loaded with ammunition, caused an explosion that destroyed the north part of the city, killing 1158 persons and injuring 4000 others. Population, 1971, 121,086.

Hamilton. A manufacturing and railroad city and lake port of southern Ontario, the fifth largest city of Canada. It is situated on Burlington Bay, a land locked harbor at the extreme western end of Lake Ontario. The Niagara escarpment, a height of land passing through the south of the city, imparts a picturesque effect which is further enhanced by the presence of numerous shade trees. The greater part of the city lies in the plain between the waterfront and the escarpment, known locally as the mountain.

Numerous railroads and highways enable the city to profit by its central location in the most populous region of Canada with electric power abundant and cheap. The St. Lawrence Seaway makes it an ocean port, whose tonnage places it among Canada's largest shipping centers. It is the center of Canada's steel industry. Other important industrial products include electrical equipment, farm implements, glass, and textiles. Canning is also an important industry.

The city has numerous parks, the finest being Dundurn, which contains a historic castle and is equipped for "sound and light" productions. Other parks include Victoria, with its famed Royal Botanical Garden; Confederation park with beach areas on Lake Ontario; and Cherokee Winter Sports park. The educational institutions include McMaster University, Ontario Teachers College, and Institute of Technology. There is also a fine art gallery. Hamilton was incorporated as a city in 1846. Population, 1971, 307,473.

Hull. A lumber and manufacturing city of southwestern Quebec, on the Ottawa River opposite the city of Ottawa, with which Hull is connected by three bridges. Pulp wood, matches, paper, lumber, cement, and knitted goods are the chief items of manufacture. The city was incorporated in 1875. Population, 1971, 62,842.

Kingston. A city of Ontario, situated at the northeastern extremity of Lake Ontario, where the waters of the lake enter the Saint Lawrence river. The city's manufactures include locomotives, textiles, and leather goods. A natural harbor and excellent railway facilities make Kingston an important point for the transshipping of grain. The Rideau canal connects the city with Ottawa.

Kingston is the seat of Queen's University and of the Royal Military College. The university buildings on a beautiful campus, the Roman Catholic and the Anglican cathedral, the streets adorned with numerous shade trees, and several parks make Kingston an attractive city. Numerous limestone buildings give a distinctive character to the architecture. The historic associations of the city are emphasized by the elaborate fortifications, including the fort and martello towers, which command the harbor.

Kingston was founded in 1673 by Frontenac and La Salle and formed one of the chief French centers of authority and trade with the West. It became the center of loyalist settlements in the West after the Revolutionary War. It was a British naval and military base, until the treaty by which the United States and Great Britain abolished naval establishments on the lakes. From 1841 to 1844 Kingston was the capital of the United Provinces of Upper and Lower Canada. Population, 1971, 61,870.

Kitchener. A prosperous manufacturing city in Waterloo County, southern Ontario. The chief manufactures include automobile tires, shoes, and meat products. Kitchener was incorporated as the village of Berlin in 1854. Its earliest inhabitants were Mennonites who left Pennsylvania shortly after the Revolutionary War. Their German origin and frugal, industrious habits left a lasting impression on the population. Made a city in 1912, it changed its name to Kitchener in 1916.

Among the city's features are the Memorial Auditorium, used for exhibitions, sports, and theatrical productions; Doon, a pioneer village; and the Homer Watson Memorial Park. Adjacent to Kitchener on the north is the city of Waterloo, an insurance center and the seat of Waterloo University. The population of Kitchener in 1971 was 109,954; that of Waterloo was 37,245.

Klondike. A gold mining district in the Yukon Territory near the center of the Alaskan boundary. It covers an area of about 800 square miles. The principal settlement became notable for the discovery of gold there in 1896, since which time it has yielded about $211 million worth of the metal.

London. A commercial, manufacturing, educational, and ecclesiastical center of southwestern Ontario. London is situated midway between Toronto and Detroit in a rich agricultural district. The chief industrial interests include printing, electrical apparatus, hosiery, sheet metal products, machinery, chemicals, and cereals. London is also a financial center. It is the seat of the University of Western Ontario and has two cathedrals, Anglican and Catholic. London was founded in 1826 and was incorporated as a city in 1855. Population, 1971, 221,430.

Moncton. A manufacturing, railroad, and lumbering city of southeastern New Brunswick, standing at the head of navigation on the Petitcodiac River. Moncton is the headquarters for the Atlantic division of the Canadian National railways. It has a large lumber trade and manufactures stoves, engines, and boilers. Moncton has three parks, from one of which, Bore View Park, may be obtained an excellent view of the famous tidal bore from the Bay of Fundy. The University of Moncton is located here. Population, 1971, 47,781.

Montreal. The largest city of Canada, situated in south central Quebec on Montreal Island at the confluence of the Saint Lawrence and Ottawa rivers. The city lies mainly on the east and southern parts of the island and extends north and west to encircle Mount Royal, a magnificent park which commands a panoramic view of the area.

Montreal's harbor is the eastern terminus of the St. Lawrence Seaway, providing access for ocean ships to the head of the Great Lakes. The port, with 131 berths along its 12-mile waterfront is the world's second largest inland port, after Rotterdam. The island city is also a train and truck transportation center and is served by 17 airlines. The Metro, a 16-mile subway system, was first opened in 1966.

Montreal has progressed faster in redevelopment than any other city. While a few narrow streets still exist in the old part, restoration of them is under way to retain the atmosphere dating back to its early days. Other parts of the city are modern in all respects. Chief industries are oil and sugar refining, meat packing, brewing, and the manufacture of aircraft, iron and steel products, tobacco and leather goods, textiles, cement, and flour. The financial center of the nation's economy depends on the Montreal and Canadian Stock Exchanges at Place Victoria in the heart of the city. Place Ville Marie comprises a 42-story office complex and underground city of 40 acres filled with shops, restaurants, and theaters, where some 80,000 people shop and browse daily in a climate-controlled atmosphere. Place d'Armes has an imposing monument to Maisonneuve, founder of Montreal. It is surrounded by several noted buildings, one being Notre Dame Church, the most famous of the city's 300 churches and one of the largest in America. Rising in midtown Montreal is Mary Queen of the World Cathedral, a half-size replica of St. Peter's in Rome.

Place des Arts, with two theaters and a 3000-seat concert hall, is the home of the Montreal Symphony Orchestra. Other cultural centers are the Montreal Museum of Fine Arts, Redpath Museum of McGill University, Contemporary Arts Museum, the Institute of Applied Arts, and the Mount Royal Art Center.

Two man-made islands in the St. Lawrence were the scene of the world's fair Expo '67. At the close of the fair, a large permanent exhibit, Man and His World, and a 135-acre amusement park, La Ronde, became enormously popular as tourist attractions.

Montreal is the seat of McGill University, Montreal University, and a number of colleges. A majority of the population is bilingual. About one-half the inhabitants are of French descent. The prevailing religion is Catholicism.

Montreal was founded in 1642 by Maisonneuve as a religious colony; but, as the outpost of civilization at the door of the Iroquois country, it became a military post, fur trading center, and base for explorations. It was taken by the British in 1760 and was held by the American Continental army in 1775–76. Population, 1971, 1,197,753.

Moose Jaw. A commercial and manufacturing city of south central Saskatchewan, the center of a rich mixed farming district. The city has large stockyards. The industrial products include flour and cereals, oil refining, brick, clothing, millwork, steel products, roofing materials, and insecticides. A potash mine operates nearby. Population, 1971, 31,284.

Muskoka. A lake region of Ontario. It embraces about 4000 square miles lying east of Georgian bay and about 100 miles north of Toronto. Of its 800 to 1000 lakes, the chief are Muskoka, 19 miles long, Rosseau, 12 miles long, and Joseph, 14 miles long. These three lakes are connected and have regular steamship service in summer. The region has extensive forests. Its numerous rivers, lakes, and islands make it an extremely popular playground for summer residents and visitors. The eastern part of the territory is sometimes called the Lake of Bays region, after the largest lake in it. Farther to the northeast lies the Algonquin provincial park, an untamed region of over 2000 square miles.

New Westminster. A port and lumbering center of southwestern British Columbia, situated on the Fraser River 17 miles from its mouth. With an excellent harbor and retail facilities, it is a thriving port, particularly for lumber, which is the city's leading manufacture. Others include paper, fish products, and canned goods. Population, 1971, 42,083.

Niagara Falls. A city of Ontario on the Niagara River beside the cataract. Hydroelectric power developed at and near the city on the Canadian side totals about 3,000,000 horsepower. As in similar developments on the American side, water is pumped electrically by night to a huge reservoir, from which the water is used during the day to develop additional power. The reservoirs are used also in drawing off additional water from the river above the falls at night and in the winter for power purposes. Thus the drain on the cataract's volume of water is kept at a minimum for sightseeing purposes, while at the same time the erosion at the brink of the falls is reduced.

In June 1969 the waters of the Niagara were diverted to the Horseshoe Falls to allow geologists to study how best to curb rock falls on the American side before the waters resumed their normal flow in December 1969.

The city commands a magnificent view of the entire falls from Victoria Park, color illumination being provided for 2½ hours nightly. A panoramic view may be had from three observation towers; a close-up view of the Horseshoe (Canadian) Falls from Table Rock House. At Rainbow Bridge, leading to Niagara Falls, N.Y., is Carillon Tower, containing a 55-bell carillon. The Oakes Garden Theatre has gardens and an open-air amphitheater.

The city's chief manufactures include abrasives, cereals, insulators, and metal products. Incorporated as the village of Elgin in 1853 and the town of Clifton in 1856, Niagara Falls was given this name in 1881 and became a city in 1904. Population, 1971, 65,271.

Oshawa. A manufacturing city of Ontario, situated on Lake Ontario about 30 miles east of Toronto. It is the chief center in Canada for the manufacture of automobiles, particularly of those made by Canadian subsidiaries of the General Motors Corporation. Other industrial products include leather, foundry products, canned goods, glass, and bathing suits. In a large block near the center of the city is the Canadian Automotive Museum, which visually reconstructs the history and prospects of this type of transportation. Oshawa has a huge shopping center laid out in the form of a landscaped mall, with an underground trucking concourse. Population, 1971, 91,113.

Ottawa. The capital and one of the largest cities of Canada, lying in southeastern Ontario and picturesquely situated on the high southern bank of the Ottawa River about 120 miles above its mouth at Montreal. The river, following a winding course between wooded banks and dropping 40 feet at the magnificent Chaudière Falls, presents a beautiful view from Parliament Hill, upon which stands the Parliament Building. Rideau Canal separates Ottawa into west and east parts, known as Upper Town and Lower Town, and inhabited by French and English people respectively.

The Parliament Buildings, Gothic in style, front and flank Confederation Square. The central tower, 291 feet high and known as the "Peace Tower," houses a carillon of 53 bells, one of the finest on the continent. The old, impressive Governor-General's house, Rideau Hall, contrasts with the modern city hall. Among the numerous churches are the Catholic Basilica of Notre Dame and the Anglican Christ Church Cathedral. The famous hotel Chateau Laurier evokes the lines of a castle in old France. Notable also are the National Gallery of Canada, the Dominion Observatory, the Supreme Court of Canada, and the University of Ottawa. The National Arts Center, a 2300-seat concert hall and a theater, was opened in 1969. Winter and summer sports are held at the $9 million Civic Center arena-stadium.

A National Capital Commission was created in 1958 to develop the city and its environs. Among its most impressive achievements was the development of the 100-square-mile Gatineau Park immediately across the Ottawa River from the city. This includes the estate of the former prime minister Mackenzie King, who had re-erected there a number of historic buildings. The commission supervises the tulip festival with its million plants from Holland and provides the many parks and connecting driveways with flowers blooming from spring to late fall. The manufacture of paper products is the city's only sizable industry.

Ottawa was formerly called Bytown in honor of its founder, the engineer in charge of the construction of Rideau Canal, which provides direct communication by water between the Ottawa River and Lake Ontario. The settlement was chartered as a city under the name of Ottawa in 1854 and was selected as the capital of Canada in 1858. Population, 1971, 298,087.

Outremont (*o͞o'tr'-môɴ'*). A city of Quebec on Montreal Island, surrounded by the city of Montreal. It is almost entirely residential in character, having very few industries. Population, 1971, 28,402.

Prince Rupert. A seaport of west central British Columbia, situated on an island connected with the mainland by a steel bridge. It has a natural harbor formed by an inlet of the Pacific Ocean. Prince Rupert forms a western terminus of the Canadian National railways. It is the southern terminus of the Alaska Marine Ferry System and the northern terminus of the ferry system from Vancouver Island. It ships large quantities of grain as well as the output of its halibut processing and its lumber and pulp mills. Its Centennial Museum has a famous collection of carved totem poles. Population, 1971, 15,355.

Quebec. Capital of the province of Quebec and one of the largest cities of Canada. It is picturesquely situated on a bold promontory at the head of the Saint Lawrence estuary. The city was founded by Champlain in 1608 and was long the center of exploration and of government by the French in the northern part of the continent. In 1759, as a result of the battle of the Plains of Abraham, the city, along with the rest of French Canada, fell into the hands of the British. It was unsuccessfully attacked in 1775 by an American force under Montgomery.

The city's importance was due partly to its strong natural defenses and partly to its strategical position, which commanded the entrance to the river leading to the interior of the continent. Quebec is still the point of entry for immigrants from Europe and is the terminus of larger ocean liners. It has one of the largest dry docks in the world. The chief industrial interests include iron castings, pulp and paper, machinery, cutlery, steel, woolens, lumber, tobacco, and rope. Hydroelectric power is available from the Montmorency and Shawinigan falls. The Saint Lawrence River is crossed at Quebec by a bridge which has one of the longest cantilever spans in the world.

The appearance of Quebec reflects the history of the city. The highest point, Cape Diamond, is 333 feet above the river and is crowned by a citadel within a walled enclosure covering 40 acres. On these defensive works over $30 million were spent in the early decades of the 19th century. The upper town, containing the citadel, is used as a residential district and has many of the finer churches and public buildings. Dufferin Terrace, a magnificent promenade, a half mile long, overlooks the Saint Lawrence, which lies 200 feet below. The upper town is reached from the other division of the city, called the lower town, by roads cut in the rock, by flights of steps, and by an elevator. The streets of the lower town are narrow and winding, and they recall the appearance of certain provincial towns of France.

The city's most noteworthy edifices include the Parliament buildings; Château Frontenac; the church of Notre Dame des Victoires, built in 1688; the handsome Franciscan convent; the Ursuline convent, which contains the remains of Montcalm; the Anglican Cathedral; and the Notre Dame de Quebec built in 1647, which contained many valuable pictures and relics. The last-named building was burned in 1922 but has since been rebuilt on the original model. There are numerous statues and monuments of historic interest. In the governor's garden, stands a plain granite column erected to the memory of Wolfe and of Montcalm, both generals having fallen in action at the battle which decided the city's fate.

Quebec is the seat of Laval University, which was chartered by Queen Victoria and Pope Pius IX and is an outgrowth of the Grand Seminary founded in 1663. In the immediate vicinity are Battlefields Park, Wolfe's Cove, the Shrine of Sainte Anne de Beaupré, and many other points of interest. The city is reputed for a famous winter carnival. It has a literary and historical society founded in 1824. The great majority of the population are of French descent, and the prevailing religion is Catholicism. Population, 1971, 182,418.

Regina. The capital and largest city of Saskatchewan, lying in the south central part of the province. Regina was formerly the capital of the Northwest Territories, and is still the western headquarters and training center for the Royal Canadian Mounted Police.

The Regina Campus of the University of Saskatchewan is the city's leading educational institution. Other impressive buildings are the Legislative Building, the curvilinear Saskatchewan Power Corp. Building, the Museum of Natural History, and the Mackenzie Art Gallery.

Founded in 1883, Regina is a service and distribution center for a rich wheat-farming, potash-mining, and oil-producing district. Its chief industries include steel, steel pipes, cement, meat packing, farm machinery, and petroleum products. Population 1971, 137,759.

Sainte Anne de Beaupré (*sănt ăn dĕ bō'prā'*). A village and famous Catholic pilgrim resort 20 miles east of Quebec. A chapel was built there in 1658, on which occasion a devout inhabitant of Beaupré who suffered from rheumatism, after laying three stones on the foundation, found himself free from his affliction. This occurrence was the first of many instances of miraculous healing credited to the saint at the shrine. In 1676 the chapel was superseded by a church, which was replaced by a much larger one in 1876. In 1922 the building was destroyed by fire, but was replaced by a new church, which is one of the finest in Canada. The shrine is annually visited by pilgrims numbering upward of one million. Population, 1971, 1474.

Saint Catharines. A trading and manufacturing city of south central Ontario in the Niagara peninsula on the south shore of Lake Ontario and 12 miles west of Niagara River. It is set in a rich fruit-growing district and celebrates each September as Grape and Wine Festival Time. St. Catharines owes its early growth to the Welland Canal, which was opened in 1829 and was subsequently reconstructed and enlarged to become a key canal in the St. Lawrence Seaway. The Garden City Skyway carries traffic above the canal to avoid delays due to the lift bridge spanning the busy waterways. Manufactures include paper, automobile parts, and a wide variety of other products. It is the seat of Brock University. The Lakeside Amusement Park fronts on Lake Ontario. Population, 971, 109,636.

Saint John. The largest city of New Brunswick, situated at the mouth of the Saint John River on the Bay of Fundy. In the vicinity is the noted "reversing falls," spanned by a steel arch bridge.

St. John is the geographical hub of three Canadian provinces. It is the rail and highway link between east and west besides being an ocean port with a year-round ice-free harbor which handles large shipments of grain and miscellaneous commerce. It has one of the world's largest dry docks and shipbuilding yards. Manufactures include sugar, brushes and brush making machinery, pulp and newsprint, brass goods, petroleum products, lumber, wire and cable, and large thermal electric installations. Parks and public gardens cover more than 500 acres.

St. John was a village of a few hundred people in 1783, when some 9000 refugees from the United States arrived after the Revolutionary War. The coming of these United Empire Loyalists is commemorated in the Loyalist House, built in 1810 and restored a century and a half later. The city was incorporated in 1785 under royal charter—the first city in Canada. Population, 1971, 87,910.

Saint John's. Provincial capital of the island province of Newfoundland. Situated on the coast near the easternmost point of land in North America, Saint John's has a superb harbor capable of accommodating the largest ships. It is the trading center of the province, but its main business is the fishing industry. The Roman Catholic and Anglican cathedrals are both named for St. John the Baptist, on whose feast day, June 24, John Cabot is traditionally believed to have discovered the harbor in 1497, and honored it with the saint's name. Sir Humphrey Gilbert established an English settlement here in 1583. Captured and destroyed twice by the French, Saint John's was finally taken by the English in 1702. Here Marconi received the first wireless message sent across the ocean, 1901. Also the English aviators Alcock and Brown took off from here in 1919 for the first nonstop trans-Atlantic flight. It is the eastern terminus of the Trans-Canada Highway. Population, 1971, 86,290.

Sarnia. An oil refining and petrochemical manufacturing city in southern Ontario situated at the southern tip of Lake Huron. It is connected with Port Huron, Mich., by a tunnel under the St. Claire River, opened in 1891, and by the high-level Blue Water Bridge. Extensive salt deposits and oil wells in the vicinity gave Sarnia its start, but its importance as an industrial center began with the establishment of a synthetic rubber plant and large oil refineries after World War I. Other manufactures include a wide variety of chemicals, foundry products, fiber glass, and plastics. The opening of the St. Lawrence Seaway made it an ocean port.

Among the city's features are Canatara Park on the lake shore and its city hall of strikingly modern construction. Population, 1971, 56,727.

Saskatoon (*săs'kȧ-tōōn'*). The second largest city of Saskatchewan, situated on both sides of the South Saskatchewan River, which is here spanned by six bridges. It lies about 150 miles northwest of Regina. The city is the center of rich farming lands, for irrigation of which a 210-foot-high earth dam on the South Saskatchewan River was constructed in the 1960's. The largest known potash mines anywhere contribute to the city's industrial interests, which include oil refining and the manufacture of machinery, cement, chemicals, and flour. The University of Saskatchewan, Saskatoon, occupies a 3200-acre campus. Other features include the 18-story CN Towers, the Jubilee Auditorium, and the Western Development Museum. Saskatoon was incorporated as a city in 1906. Population, 1971, 125,079.

Sault Sainte Marie (*sōō' sânt mä-rē'*). A manufacturing city of Ontario, situated on the Saint Mary's River, which is here crossed by a bridge one mile in length. Navigation in the river, which connects lakes Superior, Michigan, and Huron, depends on a ship canal. The first one was first opened in 1895; after frequent enlargements it finally became a key link in the St. Lawrence Seaway. The city's largest industry is steel manufacturing. Other industrial products include paper, chemicals, lumber, and beer. The city owns the 75-acre Point des Chenes Park, 12 miles to the west. Population, 1971, 78,175.

Sherbrooke. A manufacturing city of southeastern Quebec about 85 miles east of Montreal. Among its varied manufactures are textiles, machinery, pulp and paper, and machinery. It has two universities—the University of Sherbrooke (French) and Bishop's University (English). Population, 1971, 80,457.

Stratford. A city of southern Ontario, about 90 miles west of Toronto. Stratford arose as a trade center for the surrounding agricultural region. The principal industrial products are furniture and automotive supplies. The city is best known for its Festival Theater, where Shakespearean and other dramas are given during four months each summer, attracting visitors from many countries. The beautiful circular theater is located in Queen's Park, part of a 750-acre system of parks on both sides of the river Avon throughout its course traversing the city. Population, 1971, 23,863.

Sudbury. A mining city of Ontario about 60 miles north of the northern shore of Georgian Bay. Here is mined the greater part of the world's output of nickel; also most of the copper produced in Ontario. The city is the seat of Laurentian University and has an art gallery and a government school of mines. Population, 1971, 153,959.

Sydney. A city in northeastern Nova Scotia, situated on a natural harbor on the east coast of Cape Breton Island. Sydney is noted as a center for coal mining and for the manufacture of steel. It is also a well-known summer resort. Population, 1971, 32,459.

Thetford Mines. A mining town about 75 miles south of Quebec City, noted, along with Black Lake in the vicinity, as a center of the district which produces a large proportion of the world's supply of commercial asbestos. Population, 1971, 21,662.

Three Rivers (Trois Rivières). A manufacturing city of Quebec, situated on the north bank of the Saint Lawrence River where the two mouths of the Saint Maurice River enter it. It is 78 miles southwest of the city of Quebec. Long the center of a large lumber, cattle, and grain trade, it began to grow rapidly with the development of hydroelectric power from nearby waterfalls. Paper and pulp manufacture became the leading industry. With its three large paper mills, it is said to be the world's largest center of newsprint production. Other manufactures include electric lamps, chemicals, cement, and structural steel. Three Rivers was founded in 1634 by Samuel de Champlain. Population, 1971, 55,240.

Toronto. The capital and largest city of Ontario and the second largest city in Canada, situated on the northwest shore of Lake Ontario. Its natural harbor in recent years has been greatly enlarged and improved. About 2000 acres at the waterfront, largely reclaimed land, is municipally owned and used for industrial establishments, railroad sidings, waterways, and parks. The offshore Toronto Island accommodates the city's airport.

As an industrial, railroad, financial, and commercial center, Toronto ranks second only to Montreal. *Turbo*, the new turbine-train runs between these two cities. Toronto's leading manufactures are lumber, farm implements, automobiles, car shop products, packed meats, rubber goods, food products, clothing, hosiery and knit goods, soap, iron castings, and musical instruments. The Toronto hydroelectric system is one of the largest municipal supply undertakings on the continent.

The city rises from the shore to an elevation of about 300 feet. This variation in level lends itself to the construction of many beautiful driveways and boulevards, connecting a large number of parks, the largest being High Park, near which is an elaborate pleasure resort.

The Parliament buildings, in Queen's Park, are the government headquarters of Ontario's more than seven million people. This massive complex is constructed of red stone in the Romanesque style of architecture. Opposite these buildings is the Sigmund Samuel Canadiana building of the Royal Ontario Museum, which houses a fine collection of Canada's historic treasures. Nearby are the many colleges and professional schools of the University of Toronto. Other buildings are the O'Keefe Centre for the performing arts; the main branch of the Public Library, where the Robertson Historical Collection is displayed; and the Art Gallery of Toronto, containing masterpieces by Rembrandt, Gainsborough, Picasso, and several French Impressionists. Riverdale Zoo is notable for its exotic animals and jungle birds. Maple Leaf Gardens is one of Canada's largest auditoriums.

The modern city hall was the first project in Toronto's comprehensive redevelopment program. Dominating the 11½-acre civic center, Nathan Phillips Square, it is in the form of two tall, marble-veneer buildings facing each other in a concave outline embracing a low-lying cupola—the council chamber and auditorium set between them. The square has reflecting pools embellished with fountains, ornamental trees, and an imposing sculpture by Henry Moore. One of Canada's tallest buildings, a 56-story structure, is the headquarters of the Toronto-Dominion bank. By mid-1969, a still higher office building, to be the nation's tallest, was well under way for the Canadian Imperial Bank of Commerce. Many international business firms have headquarters in the city.

The Canadian National Exhibition, an annual fair, is normally visited by more than three million people. On the Exhibition grounds, the Hockey Hall of Fame honors outstanding figures of the country's national sport.

While Toronto owns its own surface transportation system and subway, it does so subject to a larger metropolitan municipality which takes in also 12 suburban areas, the whole covering 240 square miles. The latter has legislative power over finances, roads, education, parks, police, housing, welfare, and pollution control.

Toronto was founded in 1749 as York, and became the capital of Upper Canada in 1793. York was captured by the Americans in 1813. In 1834 it was incorporated under the name of Toronto. Population, 1971, 698,634.

Vancouver. The largest city of British Columbia and one of the largest in Canada, situated at the southwest extremity of the mainland on Burrard inlet, a deep arm of the Strait of Georgia. The harbor is one of the finest on the globe and has helped to place Vancouver among the leading ports of the continent. The area of the harbor is 48 square miles, of which 28 are landlocked. Here Canada's two transcontinental railroads meet the transoceanic shipping lines. Wheat is the chief export. Shipbuilding, lumbering, and salmon-canning are major industries. Vancouver is the commercial metropolis of British Columbia. It has launched an extensive redevelopment program.

The city has several parks and recreation areas. Stanley Park is a partly cleared forest area of 1000 acres, situated on a cape and surrounded by a 9-mile drive along the shore. The city's highest point is the 410-foot Little Mountain in Queen Elizabeth Park, which affords a panoramic view of the city, harbor, and North Shore Mountains. The B.C. Hydroelectric Building (all glass and perpetually lighted), the courthouse, the general hospital, and numerous high-rise office and apartment buildings give the city a striking skyline.

The University of British Columbia and the Simon Fraser University are located here. There are also two community colleges and several art galleries and museums. The Queen Elizabeth Theatre complex affords a variety of year-round entertainment. The Pacific National Exhibition, similar to Toronto's is an annual event for western Canada. Ferry service links Vancouver Island, across the Strait of Georgia, with the mainland.

Incorporated in 1886 with 600 inhabitants, the city, named for Capt. George Vancouver, a British naval officer, grew rapidly when it was connected by railroad with eastern Canada in 1887. Population, 1971, 419,433.

Verdun. A city of Quebec on Montreal Island. It is a residential suburb of Montreal, the southern border of which it adjoins. Population, 1971, 74,520.

Victoria. The capital of British Columbia, occupying the extreme southeastern point of Vancouver Island on the Strait of Juan de Fuca. Possessing a commodious harbor, and being advantageously located from a commercial standpoint, Victoria ranks as one of the four largest ports of Canada. It is the western terminus of the Trans-Canada Highway. Victoria's economy is supported mainly by service industries, including government, trade, and entertainment of tourists. The other industries include manufacture of wood products, fishing, and market and flower gardening. There are three large shipbuilding yards. An extensive trade is carried on in coal, timber, and canned salmon.

The city has fine streets with many beautiful residences, and its delightful climate and beautiful environment attract numerous summer visitors. Beacon Hill Park is the city's chief recreation ground. The provincial Parliament buildings of gray stone are of high architectural merit. The Dominion Astrophysical Laboratory in the city has one of the world's largest telescopes. Adjoining Victoria is Esquimalt, the naval base and dockyard.

Fort Victoria was erected on the present site of the city in 1843 as a trading post of the Hudson's Bay Company. The place was incorporated as Victoria in 1862 and became the capital of British Columbia in 1868. The inhabitants are predominantly of British birth or descent. Population, 1971, 60,897.

Whitehorse, capital and chief city of the Yukon, is in the southern part of the territory. It has an airport and is connected by rail with Skagway, Alaska, and by the Alaska Highway with Dawson Creek, B. C. Population, 1971, 11,084.

Windsor. The most southerly city of Canada, lying in southern Ontario on the Detroit River, opposite Detroit, Mich., with which it is connected by a vehicular tunnel and by the Ambassador suspension bridge, which has a central span of 1850 feet. Windsor is the chief center of automobile production in Canada. Other industrial products are iron and steel, paints and varnishes, salt, drugs, and prepared foods. It is the seat of the University of Windsor and has also the Willistead Art Gallery and Hiram Walker Historical Museum. Windsor became a town in 1858 and was incorporated as a city in 1892. Population, 1971, 199,784.

Winnipeg. The capital of Manitoba and one of the largest cities of Canada. It is located in the southern part of the province at the junction of the Red and Assiniboine rivers. In commerce, Winnipeg occupies a strategic position, comparable to that of Chicago. All traffic between eastern and western Canada is routed through Winnipeg. The city is served by the two Canadian transcontinental railways, with western headquarters here; by several American lines; and by many railroads radiating throughout the rich agricultural district in which it is situated. It is the largest cash grain market in the world, the Winnipeg Grain Exchange having one of the busiest "trading pits" anywhere. Besides being a valuable livestock market, it is the base of the Canadian Wheat Board, which handles the sale of the country's vast wheat crop.

Winnipeg ranks among the leading manufacturing cities of Canada, partly by reason of the availability of cheap hydroelectric power, which is developed from the Winnipeg River rapids. Among the chief industrial products are flour, farm machinery, processed foods, lumber, pulp, and paper. Printing and publishing are also important.

Winnipeg has grown rapidly, its economy being based on its rich agricultural and mineral resources. The modern city hall complex is indicative of its long-range renewal schedule. In 1968 a new concert hall was opened, and completion of a new 6-story museum was scheduled before 1971. The city has one of the most modern air terminals on the continent.

Of the several parks, Fort Garry Park has the greatest historical interest, while the 362-acre Assiniboine Park, containing a zoo and a horticultural conservatory, is the largest. Outstanding in another park is the provincial Legislative Building, built in classic Greek style with a 255-foot dome.

The suburb of Saint Boniface is the Roman Catholic headquarters of the West. It has a magnificent cathedral, the archbishop's palace, and the Catholic College of Saint Boniface. It is the birthplace and burial place of Louis Riel, leader of the Red River rebellion in 1869–70.

The University of Manitoba (1877) and the University of Winnipeg (1871) are the oldest institutions of higher education in western Canada.

In 1733, on the site now occupied by Winnipeg, the French explorer, La Verendrye, built Fort Rouge, a name now used to designate a favorite residential section of the city. In 1821, the Hudson's Bay Company built Fort Garry. The population in 1870 was 250. In 1873 the place was incorporated and the name was changed from Fort Garry to Winnipeg. Population, exclusive of suburbs, 1971, 243,208.

MEXICO

A federal republic of North America, lying south of the United States and extending southeast to Guatemala. The outline of the country resembles a cornucopia modified by two irregularities,—the peninsula of Yucatan in the southeast and the peninsula of Baha California in the northwest. Its area is 760,375 square miles, about half of which is in the Torrid Zone. Its maximum length is over 1900 miles, and its width varies from 1833 miles, along the northern boundary, to 134 miles, at the Isthmus of Tehuantepec. The coast line on the Gulf of Mexico and the Caribbean Sea measures 1727 miles, while the coast line on the Pacific Ocean and on the Gulf of California has a total length of 4574 miles.

Surface and Drainage. The greater part of Mexico consists of a central plateau, called the *tierras templadas*, having an elevation of from 3000 to 8000 feet. It is flanked on the east by a high range of mountains called the Sierra Madre Oriental. At the Isthmus of Tehuantepec, this range converges with the Sierra Madre Occidental, which flanks the central plateau on the west. The mountains of the Isthmus of Tehuantepec belong to the Central American system. The lofty areas above an altitude of 8000 feet are known as the *tierras frias*. On each side of the country, lowlands, or *tierras calientes*, form a fringe between the coast and the mountain range. The peninsula of Yucatan is, for the most part, a low, sandy plain. Baja California is mountainous and consists of a southern extension of the Sierra Nevada range.

The central plateau is of volcanic origin and the sierras contain a large number of volcanoes. The highest, Citaltepetl (Orizaba), has not been active since the 16th century. Its elevation is 18,700 feet. Popocatepetl, "Smoky Mountain," and Iztaccihuatl, "White Woman," are extinct. Violent earthquakes are frequent. In 1920, in the Orizaba Volcano district, about 3000 people were killed by seismic disturbances and ten towns were partially or wholly destroyed.

The drainage system of Mexico is simple. The central plateau has a number of lakes but no large rivers. Several short streams flow from the mountain ranges into the sea. The Rio Grande, on the northern border, receives little water from the Mexican side. No river of Mexico is navigable throughout the year.

Climate and Flora. The *tierras calientes*, on the east, are subject to great heat and a heavy rainfall. They support a luxuriant vegetation and valuable food plants. The banana, coconut, pineapple, pomegranate, vanilla, cacao, and ginger are produced in abundance. Sisal hemp is grown in Yucatan and is exported in large quantities to the United States to be used in the manufacture of rope. Mexico's forest areas, which are estimated to cover 95 million acres, are mainly in the lowlands. Mahogany, ebony, rosewood, and rubber are among the more valuable products of the tropical forests. The Pacific lowlands are arid in the north but have a more copious rainfall in the south.

The plateau has a temperate climate and is well adapted for the cultivation of cotton, tobacco, coffee, rice, sugar cane, corn, wheat, and potatoes. The rainfall in general is light but varies considerably in different parts. The north portion is dry; the cactus appears as a characteristic plant, and irrigation is necessary for successful agriculture. In some parts. however, two or three crops a year may be raised. The forest areas of the plateau contain oak, myrtle, fir, spruce, and pine. The higher mountain regions support an alpine flora.

Animal Life. The lowlands are the habitat of monkeys, pumas, jaguars, ocelots, sloths, armadillos, parrots, parakeets, humming birds, alligators, venomous snakes, and many other animals characteristic of a tropical fauna. The wolf, coyote, otter, and deer are found in the central plateau.

Minerals and Mining. The mineral resources of Mexico make her potentially one of the richest countries in the world. Mining is the chief industry, and petroleum is the chief product. It is estimated that Mexican mines have yielded over $3 billion worth of silver. Mexico is also one of the world's greatest copper and lead producing countries. Gold, zinc, antimony, tungsten, molybdenum, mercury, and opals are also exported. Near the city of Durango is a large hill, the Cerro de Mercado, composed almost entirely of pure iron ore. Improved transportation facilities and development of the vast mineral deposits have been possible with capital from increased tourism.

Other Industries. The production of coffee exceeds a value of $100 million each year. Other large crops are corn, rice, sugar cane, wheat, beans, tomatoes, oranges, and bananas. Irrigation is essential for much of the production and a number of large dams have been constructed for this purpose and to develop electric power. The area employed for grazing purposes is about four times that devoted to agriculture. The chief manufactures are cotton and wool textiles, tobacco and rubber products, iron and steel, cement, shoes, glass, silver and leather handicraft, and pottery.

Inhabitants. The population of Mexico in 1970 was 48,313,438. The language is Spanish, and the prevailing religion is Roman Catholicism. Elementary education is free and compulsory. The largest and oldest university, the University of Mexico, was founded in 1552. The chief cities, in addition to those described below include Monterrey (1,177,361), Ciudad Juarez (436,054), Leon (453,976), Torreon, (257,045), Tijuana (335,125), and Mexicali (390,411).

Ruins in Yucatan. In Yucatan, the extreme eastern state of Mexico, are to be found the most impressive of the monuments left by the civilizations which flourished in America prior to its discovery by Europeans. Here was centered the New Mayan Empire, which was established by the Mayas after the fall of the Old Empire, the territory now known as Guatemala. The Old Empire flourished from the beginning of the Christian era until the 6th century A. D.

The causes of its fall form one of the fascinating enigmas of early American history. Mayan settlers entered Yucatan as early as the 4th century A. D., but the New Mayan Empire was not definitely established until about 1100 A. D. It continued until the coming of the Spaniards in the early 16th century. The chief centers were the capital, Uxmal, and the cities of Mayapan and Chichen-Itza.

The buildings are of one story in height, but in nearly all cases are situated on terraces or pyramids constructed of earth. They are faced with stone and have masonry steps for ascent and descent. The Temple of the Magician at Uxmal crowns a majestic pyramid 80 feet high and 240 by 180 feet at the base. The exterior is richly ornamented with carvings and relief work. Such carving was executed by stone tools, the only metals known to the builders being gold, silver, and copper. Since the true arch was unknown, roofs of Mayan buildings were either flat or, more often, vaulted. The buildings are very narrow, and the walls are usually from three to nine feet thick.

In central Mexico also are numerous pyramids surmounted by stone temples or palaces built by the Toltecs and Aztecs.

It was in what is now Mexico that corn was first cultivated and improved some 4000 to 2000 years before our era. It is believed that this provided a first basis for the civilizations that arose there.

MEXICAN VISTAS

Picturesque Taxco, sometimes called "the silver city."
Courtesy of Mexican Gov't Tourism Dept.

Temple of the Magician in Uxmal, ruined city that ruled Mexico 1000 years ago.
Barbachano Travel Service

The new Maria Isabel hotel on the Reforma Boulevard, Mexico City.
Courtesy of Mexican Gov't Tourism Dept.

Aztec calendar stone, now in Mexico City. An amazing time reckoner.
Pan American Union

Remains of the "Atlantes" Toltec civilization, Hidalgo.
Courtesy of Mexican Gov't Tourism Dept.

Palace of Fine Arts and Latin American Tower, Mexico City.
Courtesy of Mexican Gov't Tourism Dept.

SCENES IN ALASKA AND HAWAII

Above Iolani Palace in Honolulu, residence of the monarchs who once ruled the island.
Right First Chinese Christian Church, a reminder of Hawaii's cosmopolitan population and architecture.
Photos by Hawaii Visitors Bureau

Alaska's Margery Glacier is busy dropping icebergs into the ocean. *Steve McCutcheon*

Shrimp fishing in Alaska—a lucrative occupation. *Steve McCutcheon*

Above Punch Bowl Crater, above an extinct volcano near Honolulu, contains a memorial cemetery.
Hawaii Visitors Bureau

Right Giant Oyster, a totem pole at outskirts of Ketchikan, Alaska.

Guadalajara (*gwä'thä-lä-hä'rä*). The second largest city of Mexico, situated about 150 miles inland from the center of the country's Pacific Coast. The climate is agreeable, the range of the temperature being limited to a few degrees. Guadalajara is an important mining center. The large waterfall of Juanacatlan near by furnishes electric power for street railroads, city lighting, and manufacturing. Among the manufactures are cotton goods, art pottery, tiles, leather articles, and cordage.

The city is well built and has spacious streets and several large parks embellished with fountains and statues. The principal building, the cathedral, noted for its ornamentation and magnificent interior, contains one of Murillo's masterpieces. Aqueducts, eight miles long, bring water to the city. Population, 1970, 1,196,218.

Mexico City. The capital and largest city of Mexico, situated somewhat southeast of the geographic center of the country at an elevation of 7415 feet. Majestic, snow-crowned mountains encircle the city, presenting a scene of surpassing grandeur. The climate is delightful; the air is dry, and the range of temperature seldom exceeds 15°.

Mexico City is the social, literary, financial, and industrial center of the country. Manufactures include textiles, chemicals, paper, boots and shoes, and foundry and tobacco products.

The city, founded by Cortez in 1521 on the site of the Aztec town Tenochtitlan, is regularly laid out with wide, well-paved streets, shaded boulevards, numerous parks and driveways embellished with statues and monuments, and several ornate squares. Mexico City abounds in churches. Fronting Plaza Mayor Square is the great cathedral, a magnificent structure in Spanish Renaissance style, the foundations of which were laid in 1573 on the site of an Aztec temple.

Tourism has greatly increased as a result of much improved roads and highways and the convenience of air travel. The visitor will find in Mexico City numerous buildings (with elaborate façades) and places noted for their beauty and historical associations. A few of these are the National Palace, which has several murals by Diego Rivera; the Palace of Fine Arts; the National Museum of Anthropology; Chapultepec castle, the executive mansion; Xochimilco and its "floating gardens"; the National University, founded in 1551; and the famous 22-ton Aztec calendar stone, noted for its remarkable accuracy.

The modern city has many tall buildings, some with entire walls of glass, others with colorful mosaics, which present an interesting contrast to the older buildings most of which are only one story high. The city, once the hub of Aztec civilization, has become a mecca for thousands of visitors each year. In less than forty years, it has grown from less than one million inhabitants to an estimated population of 3,025,564 in 1970.

Puebla (*pwä'blä*). An important city of Mexico, situated in the vicinity of several of the highest mountains in the country about 60 miles southeast of Mexico City. The manufactures include textiles, soap, glass, straw hats, pottery, and leather goods. Onyx articles, made from the stone quarried nearby, form an important article of export.

The city is well built and has all modern improvements. Besides several professional schools, there are three libraries, an imposing cathedral of Spanish architecture, an art gallery, a museum, an observatory, and many other institutions of note. A short distance from the city are the famous mineral springs of Tehuacan and the prehistoric pyramid of Cholula, 177 feet high and covering nearly 45 acres. The city was founded by the Franciscans in 1532. It was captured by the Americans in 1847 and was taken by the French in 1863. Population, est. 360,576.

Tampico (*täm-pē'kō*). The best equipped port of Mexico, on the Panuco River near its mouth in the Gulf of Mexico. Petroleum is produced in large quantities in the vicinity and forms the chief article of export. Ores, hides, wood, wool, and hemp are also exported; manufactured goods, mainly from the United States, are imported. Modern warehouses, offices, and municipal improvements give Tampico a thoroughly up-to-date appearance. Population, 1970, 196,147.

Vera Cruz. An important seaport of Mexico, situated on the Bay of Campeche, an arm of the Gulf of Mexico. An enervating climate and the prevalence of yellow fever once gave Vera Cruz the name of the City of the Dead. Modern sanitation measures, however, have completely transformed living conditions.

Twenty-five million dollars have been spent on the improvement of the harbor. On a reef near its entrance stands the fortress of San Juan de Ulua. The exports consist chiefly of ore, chicle, dyewoods, and hides, and the imports include textiles, hardware, and other manufactured goods. Fishing is carried on extensively, and there is a considerable manufacturing industry. Population, 1970, 242,351.

CENTRAL AMERICA

A geographical term used to designate the neck of land which connects North America and South America. It stretches in a southeast and northwest direction, lies entirely within the Torrid Zone, and comprises the area between the Isthmus of Tehuantepec, in southern Mexico, on the north, and the Isthmus of Panama, immediately north of Colombia, on the south. Its area is approximately 200,000 square miles. Its width varies from about 30 miles at the Isthmus of Panama to 450 miles in southern Mexico.

Surface. The southwestern coast of Central America is skirted by a broken chain of mountains, which reach a maximum elevation of 13,000 feet. Their formation is distinct from that of the Rocky Mountains and of the Andes range. Volcanic eruptions and violent earthquakes are very frequent. The largest interruption of the mountainous highlands is the basin of Lake Nicaragua, which has a water area in excess of 3500 square miles. The northeastern side of the isthmus slopes gradually toward the sea and has a fertile and well watered soil.

Climate and Flora. The climate varies, according to elevation, from a tropical heat to an arctic rigor. The lava areas are extremely fertile and, where the climate is favorable, produce coffee, sugar, corn, pineapple, bananas, and other products of tropical agriculture. The forests of the lowland are rich in dyewoods and valuable cabinet woods. The higher districts have a characteristic temperate-zone and alpine flora.

Inhabitants. The total population is estimated at more than 15,000,000, mostly of Indian and Spanish blood. The majority live on the southwestern coastal area. Agriculture is the chief occupation, although vast mineral and forest resources await development. Textiles and other manufactured goods are imported. More than 80 per cent of the trade is with the United States.

Politically, Central America comprises the countries lying between Mexico on the north and Colombia on the south. Apart from the Panama Canal Zone and Belize, a member of the British Commonwealth, they consist of six independent republics—Guatemala, Honduras, El Salvador, Nicaragua, Costa Rica, and Panama. Roman Catholicism is the prevailing religion and Spanish is the common language.

Belize (**British Honduras**). Bordering on the Caribbean Sea, Mexico, and Guatemala, the area of Belize is 8598 square miles. Most of the surface is covered with tropical forests yielding mahogany, chicle, and logwood. Bananas and coconuts are also exported in considerable quantities. The coastal area is low, marshy, but not unhealthful. The estimated population in 1970 was 130,000, of whom about 98 per cent were of Negro and Indian origin. The capital is Belmopan. Control of the region was long disputed by the Spanish and it was not secured by Britain until 1836. The settlement was proclaimed a British colony in 1862. In 1884 it became an independent colony of Britain and was made self-governing in 1964.

Canal Zone. A strip of land ten miles wide, from the Atlantic Ocean to the Pacific. Through the zone runs the Panama Canal, finished by the U.S. in 1914. The Canal Zone divides the Republic of Panama into two parts. See *United States Dependencies* and *Panama Canal*.

Costa Rica (*kŏs'tȧ rē'kȧ*). A country occupying the section of Central America between Nicaragua and Panama. The area is about 20,000 square miles, a large part of which is an irregular tableland in which some mountain peaks attain an altitude of more than 10,000 feet. Many mountains are volcanic and have caused a considerable loss of life.

Coffee is the staple product of the subtropical plateau, but cacao, tobacco, and sugar are also grown and exported. Costa Rica is one of the chief banana producing countries of the world. The fruit is grown extensively in the hot, tropical lowlands. Other important industries include lumbering, gold and silver mining, and cattle raising. The manufacture of fiber glass products, textiles, and fertilizers are among the newer industries.

The estimated population in 1970 was 1,800,000, a large number being of Spanish origin. San José is the capital. *Costa Rica* means "rich coast" and was given the name by Christopher Columbus in 1502.

El Salvador. The smallest, but next to Guatemala, the most populous republic of Central America, and the only one without an Atlantic coastline. It is southwest of Honduras, with a coastline of about 160 miles on the Pacific Ocean. Its area is about 8000 square miles. San Salvador is the capital.

There is a level coastal strip that rises, farther inland, to a mountainous plateau containing a number of active volcanoes. One of these, called the Izalco, or "lighthouse," began to rise from the plateau about a century ago and, by means of its own lava, has reached the height of a mile.

The volcanic area is extremely fertile and produces large crops of coffee, sugar, cotton, tobacco, and cacao. Coffee is the chief export, with cotton making great gains. Balsam and hardwoods are the principal forest products sent abroad. Cattle raising and gold and silver mining are carried on extensively. U.S. aid has helped the economic growth of the country considerably. The 1970 population estimate was 3,534,000.

Guatemala (*gwä'tȧ-mä'lȧ*). The second largest and the most populous country of Central America, lying between Mexico and the republic of Honduras. Its area is 45,452 square miles. A mountain ridge, which includes a number of volcanoes, divides the long eastern slope from the narrower but more thickly populated Pacific drainage area. Lake Peten, in the northern part of the country, is noted for being the habitat of 30 species of fish not found elsewhere.

The hot lowlands in the north and east are unhealthful but produce large crops of cacao, sugar cane, and bananas. The dense forests of the valleys yield valuable hardwoods, chicle, and rubber. The staple export of the country, however, is coffee, grown principally on the rich, volcanic soil of the plateau and the western slope. Two annual crops of wheat and three of corn are raised in this district. Cotton is a crop of more recent importance, and by 1961 had become the second largest export, after coffee. At the higher altitudes, apples and potatoes are grown and many cattle are raised. Beginning in 1952, a program of agrarian reform was put into operation, under which land not under cultivation might be expropriated, with eventual compensation, and divided into small holdings.

The population of Guatemala, 1970 est., was 5,188,981, more than half of whom are pure Indians. Guatemala is the capital and lies on the interoceanic railway which connects Puerto Barrios, the port on the Gulf of Honduras, with San José and other ports on the Pacific coast.

Honduras. A country of Central America, lying between Guatemala and Nicaragua, with a coast line of 400 miles on the Caribbean Sea. The southwestern boundary is El Salvador and the Gulf of Fonseca, an inlet of the Pacific Ocean. The surface covers 44,275 square miles, the greater part of which is a plateau ranging in elevation from 5000 to 10,000 feet.

The hot, malarial coastal region produces the bulk of the country's staple export—bananas. Coconuts are grown there also, and, farther inland, large crops of sugar, tobacco, and coffee are produced. Corn is cultivated as the chief article of domestic consumption. Stock raising is one of the principal industries. The dense forests of the coast area and of the valleys yield rubber, dyewoods, and medicinal plants. Cigars and Panama hats are manufactured for export.

The mineral resources of the country are extensive but production is confined to silver, lead, and zinc. Foreign concessionaires must employ Hondurans up to at least half of their labor force. Railroads, totaling about 850 miles, are used mainly to transport bananas. The normal means of transport for both passengers and freight is by airplanes, which are treated as casually as buses. There is one large international airport, at Tegucigalpa, which is the capital and largest city.

The population of the country in 1970 (est.) was 2,582,000. While Spanish is the official language, a number of aboriginal tribes speak languages of their own.

Nicaragua (*nĭk'ȧ-rä'gwȧ*). The largest country of Central America, situated at the center of the intercontinental neck. Its surface is mountainous in the northern and western part, where there are several volcanoes. The eastern section is low, and, in the south, there is a depression forming the basin of Lake Nicaragua, Central America's largest inland body of water. The area of the country is 57,143 square miles.

Most of the population is found in the fertile, volcanic valleys of the uplands on the western side of the country, of which the chief agricultural products are coffee, cacao, sugar cane, and corn. Cattle are raised and the export of hides is important. Bananas are grown in large quantities in the eastern lowlands. Forest industries rank second in importance, timber, dyewoods, gums, oils, fibers, and rubber being obtained on both coasts of the country. Gold and silver are mined. The chief manufactures are Panama hats and cigars.

The estimated population of Nicaragua in 1970 was 1,984,000. The two principal cities are Managua and Leon, the former being the seat of the national government. The Pacific Coast ports of Corinto and San Juan del Sur handle most of the foreign trade. In 1916 the U. S. purchased from Nicaragua the right to build an interoceanic canal through the country. The treaty ended in 1970.

Panama (*păn'ȧ-mä'*). The most eastern country of Central America, stretching from Costa Rica about 480 miles east to Colombia. It occupies the narrowest part of the intercontinental neck and is divided into two parts by the Canal Zone, ten miles in width, controlled by the United States. The area of the country is 28,576 square miles.

Panama is traversed by two broken mountain chains, which are overgrown with dense forests containing rubber trees and valuable hardwoods. Bananas and coconuts are produced in the hot lowlands, and sugar cane, coffee, cacao, and tobacco are grown at higher altitudes. A considerable number of cattle are raised, and hides form a valuable article of export.

The population of Panama, exclusive of the Canal Zone, was estimated to be 1,463,500 in 1970. The city of Panama is the seat of government.

Belize City (*bĕ-lē'z*). The chief seaport of Belize is situated at the mouth of the Belize river near the center of the country's seacoast. The climate is hot but not unhealthful. The exports go mainly to the United States and consist chiefly of mahogany, logwood, coconuts, and bananas. Population, 1965, 45,055.

Guatemala City. The capital of the country of the same name. Guatemala is an inland commercial city, situated in the southern part of the country about 85 miles from the Pacific coast on a plateau 5000 feet above the sea. A large part of its trade is in coffee. The city has various professional schools, a university, and a cathedral, which is the seat of the archbishop. Guatemala has been destroyed four times by earthquakes, most recently in 1976. Pop. 1970, 730,991.

Leon (*lā-ōn'*). A metropolis of Nicaragua and formerly its capital, situated about 15 miles from the coast in the western portion of the country. It has a cathedral built in the Renaissance style, and is the seat of a university. Population, about 47,000.

Managua (*mä-nä'gwä*). The capital of Nicaragua, situated about 25 miles inland from the center of the state Pacific coast line. It is a commercial center for the marketing of coffee grown in the region. The city is the seat of the Central University of Nicaragua. Managua was almost entirely destroyed by earthquake in 1972, but rebuilding was begun at once. Population 262,047.

Panama City. The capital of the Republic of Panama, situated at the head of Panama Bay near the southern terminus of the Panama Canal.

Panama, founded by Pedro Arias in 1519, was one of the first European settlements in the western hemisphere. It was long the capital and Pacific metropolis of Spain's vast possessions in America. Population, 1970, 418,013.

San José (*sän hô-sā'*). The capital of Costa Rica situated in a rich coffee growing region. The city is regularly built and has broad streets, fronted for the most part by one-story brick houses. The principal buildings include the national palace, the university, and the national theater. Population, 1970, 203,148.

San Salvador. The capital and largest city of El Salvador, situated in a fertile valley about 25 miles from the coast. It is about three miles from the volcano of San Salvador, which destroyed most of the city three times. The houses are surrounded by open ground and built low in order to minimize the danger during possible earthquakes. The city carries on an active trade in tobacco, and other products of the region. It has a university, a national library, and a fine botanical garden. Salvador is one of the oldest settlements of the western hemisphere, being founded in 1528 by Alvarado. Pop. 1970, 349,333.

Tegucigalpa (*tâ-gōō sê-gäl'pä*). The capital of Honduras, situated in the southern part of the country about 50 miles from San Lorenzo, its port on the Gulf of Fonseca. The agricultural and mining interests of the surrounding region center in the city, which is also the seat of a national university and of several colleges. Tegucigalpa was formerly an Aztec city. It was made the capital of Honduras in 1880. Population, 1970, 232,276.

THE WEST INDIES

A large group of islands lying between North America and South America and forming the barrier between the Atlantic Ocean and the Caribbean Sea. They stretch in a great curve from Florida east and south to the mouth of the Orinoco river in Venezuela. Their total area is about 92,000 square miles; their population, more than 25,000,000. Most of the islands are rocky. They receive copious rain, brought principally in the summer by the northeast trade winds, which at times develop into destructive hurricanes.

The largest island is Cuba, which, like the two republics on the island of Hispaniola, is an independent country. Puerto Rico belongs to the United States.

Cuba, Hispaniola, Jamaica, and Puerto Rico are sometimes referred to as the Greater Antilles, and the other West India islands, except the Bahamas, as the Lesser Antilles. Antilles is an Anglicized plural of Antilia, a name given on early maps to a mythical island in the Atlantic Ocean.

British West Indies. Islands of the West Indies which are dependencies in, or members of, the British Commonwealth of Nations. They may be divided into the following five groups: The Bahamas, Barbados, Jamaica and its dependencies, the Leeward Islands, and the Windward Islands. Trinidad and Tobago are sometimes added as a sixth group, but their proximity to South America makes it more natural to count them as insular parts of that continent. The total area of the islands is estimated at 12,000 square miles.

The chief occupation of the inhabitants is agriculture, although valuable hardwoods are to be found in the forested areas. English is the common language. The population, 1970, est., was 4,221,000.

Bahama Islands. A group of low islands in the British West Indies, extending from a point near the east coast of Florida, in a general direction parallel with the Cuban coast, to within 100 miles of the island of Hispaniola. While the group includes several hundred islands, only twenty have permanent settlements. These twenty cover an area of 4404 square miles. The population, in 1970, was estimated at 161,000. The islands are an independent nation within the commonwealth, with a capital at Nassau in New Providence island. The staple products are sponges and sisal hemp. Pineapples, both fresh and canned, oranges, and tomatoes are also exported.

Barbados. (*bär-bā'dōz*). The most easterly of the West India islands. The climate is healthful, fever being almost unknown. About two-thirds of its area of 166 square miles is under cultivation. The crop of paramount importance is sugar, exported chiefly to Canada and the United States.

The population in 1970 was 256,000. Washington's visit to Barbados in 1751 was the only foreign journey he ever made. It became an independent member of the British Commonwealth in 1966.

The capital and seaport is Bridgetown Its houses are built of coral rock and of wood. Pop., 1970 est., 238,000.

Jamaica. The largest island of the British West Indies, lying about 100 miles south of the eastern end of Cuba. Its area is 4411 square miles. Jamaica, including some smaller islands with a total area of 224 square miles, is an independent country within the British Commonwealth.

Jamaica is traversed by low hills, which, at the eastern end, culminate in the Blue Mountains with a maximum altitude of 7362 feet. The island is one of the world's largest sources of bauxite, some of which is processed locally into aluminum. Other exports include sugar, bananas, fruit juice, and rum.

The tourist trade is large. The population estimate in 1968 was 1,913,000.

The capital and chief port is Kingston, situated on a landlocked harbor on the southeast coast of the island. The city is well built. It has modern improvements and attractive suburbs. In one of its old parish churches stands the tomb of Admiral Benbow, an English seaman who distinguished himself in a battle with a French fleet in 1702. In 1907, Kingston was almost entirely destroyed by an earthquake. Pop., 1969 est., 1,972,130.

Leeward Islands. A group of West India islands forming a chain which begins to the east of Puerto Rico and curves southeast to the island of Saint Lucia. The majority of the islands are British. France, however, controls Guadeloupe, Martinique, Saint Bartholomew, and part of Saint Martin. The remainder of Saint Martin and the islands of Saint Eustatius and Saba belong to the Netherlands. The British dependencies are Antigua, Dominica, British Virgin islands, Saint Kitts, Montserrat, Barduda, Redonda, Sombrero, Nevis, and Anguilla. The British islands form one colony, having its seat of government at Saint John in the island of Antigua. The islands of the colony cover an approximate area of 428 square miles and support a population, principally Negroes, of more than 145,000. The chief articles of export are cotton, sugar, molasses, cocoa, limes, and coconuts. The name was given in allusion to the fact that the islands are not swept by the northeast trade winds as much as are the Windward Islands to the south.

Windward Islands. A group of British West India islands forming the eastern barrier of the Caribbean Sea, with a total area of 811 square miles. Population, 1970 est., 389,759. The four chief islands are Grenada, Saint Vincent, Saint Lucia, and Dominica. These islands have separate administrative bodies. The products include excellent grades of cotton and of arrowroot; also sugar, cocoa, lime juice, and spices. Most of the trade is with Great Britain.

Bermuda Islands. A group of low coral islands belonging to Great Britain, about 880 miles due east of Charleston, South Carolina, and 699 miles from New York. Twenty of the 150 islands are inhabited. They supported in 1970, on an area of 21 square miles, a population of 54,000. The chief exports are lilies and onions, sent almost entirely to the

United States. Hamilton, situated on Bermuda island, is the capital. During World War II the United States built a naval and air base at Bermuda under a 99-year lease. The climate is genial and attracts numerous visitors from the United States and from Great Britain. The islands are named after the Spaniard, Bermudez, who discovered them in 1515. They were first settled in the 17th century by Somers, an Englishman.

Cuba. The largest island of the West Indies, which, with the Isle of Pines and smaller adjacent islands, constitutes the independent republic of Cuba. Cuba is in the Torrid Zone and lies 92 miles south of Key West in Florida, the most southern town of the United States. The island has an average width of 50 miles and stretches about 730 miles in a general east and west direction. Its area is 44,206 square miles.

The surface of Cuba is in general low and undulating. Hills border the northern coast and in the southeast a short range of mountains, the Sierra Maestra, skirts the sea and reaches at one point an elevation of 8320 feet. The rivers are short. Many of them, however, are noted for disappearing throughout part of their courses. The Moa cascade in eastern Cuba is formed by a river which drops 300 feet into a cave. A number of springs of fresh water are found in the sea rising through the salt water. These are believed to be emerging rivers which disappeared inland.

The climate of Cuba is hot and moist. Improvements in sanitation have virtually banished yellow fever, which formerly afflicted the inhabitants as a yearly epidemic. The soil is rich and supports a luxuriant vegetation. Palms and valuable hardwood trees flourish in forests covering nearly half the island. Bananas and other tropical fruits provide food for the inhabitants and are exported in great quantities. The fauna includes the tarantula, chameleon, scorpion, vulture, scavenger buzzard, and, among the numerous species of snakes, a boa, which often attains a length of 18 feet. The rare insectivore, the almiqui, is indigenous to the island. Alligators infest the waters. Coral insects have produced coral reefs about the coasts in such number as to endanger navigation in many parts.

The chief industry of Cuba is the cultivation of sugar cane and of tobacco. Cuba leads the world in the production of sugar cane. After a Communist-type government was set up in 1959, all land and industries were nationalized. Sugar and other exports, which had gone chiefly to the United States, were taken under barter arrangements by Russia, China, and other Communist countries. Since that time, crops of rice, corn, and beans have increased markedly. Coffee also is an important crop. Rayon and cement are among recent manufactures. Sugar refining remains the leading industry; cigars and cigarettes rank second.

The population of Cuba, 1970 est., was 8,553,395. Spanish is the prevailing language, and the Roman Catholic religion predominates. In 1961, when education was nationalized, many Catholic schools were seized. Elementary education is free and obligatory from ages 6 to 14. There are many vocational schools and a national university. The capital is Havana.

Havana. The capital of Cuba, situated on an excellent natural harbor on the northern coast. The city lies directly south of Florida. Havana is the chief commercial city of the West Indies. It is the focus of Cuba's enormous trade in sugar and in tobacco, and has tobacco factories which are among the largest in the world.

The older section of the city, lying between the harbor and the sea, has narrow, irregular streets. The newer parts have wide, asphalt-paved streets and contain picturesque parks and promenades adorned with shade trees. The most attractive street is the Prado, which has in the center a parkway shaded by laurels and palms. Most of the public buildings are of limestone. They include the costly presidential palace, on the Prado; the Tacon theater, which is one of the largest playhouses in the western hemisphere; and the cathedral, said to have contained the remains of Columbus from 1796 to 1898. The city is a popular winter resort. The chief educational institutions include the University of Havana and the Jesuit College of Belen.

The harbor is equipped with three forts of obsolete construction. In 1898 the American battleship, the *Maine*, was blown up in the harbor. After the expulsion of the Spaniards in 1899, a program of improvements in sanitation was carried out which freed the city from the pestilential scourges to which it was formerly subject. Havana was founded in 1519. Population, 1970, 1,565,700.

Camagüey (*kä'mä-gwā'*). The largest inland city of Cuba, situated in the midst of rich savannas somewhat east of the center of the island. Its port, Nuevitas, located about 50 miles northeast on the Atlantic coast, is the outlet for the products of the live stock industry centering in the city. The sugar interests of Camagüey are also considerable.

Founded in 1516, the city retains an antiquated appearance with narrow, winding streets and poor houses. During the American occupation of Cuba, good water was provided by means of artesian wells and a drainage system was introduced. The city is sometimes known as Puerto Principe. Population, 1970, 170,500.

Cienfuegos (*syĕn-fwā'gōs*). A seaport of Cuba, situated on a landlocked harbor near the center of the island's southern coast. The commerce consists largely of sugar exports. Population, 99,530.

Matanzas (*mȧ-tăn'zȧs*). A city on the northern coast of Cuba, 55 miles east of Havana. It has tobacco factories, distilleries, and iron foundries, and ranks next to Havana in the export of sugar and tobacco. Population, 82,619.

Santiago de Cuba (*săn'tē-ä'gō dā kōō'bä*). A city of southeastern Cuba, situated on a deep, landlocked harbor on the Caribbean Sea. The port is the outlet for the tobacco raised in the district, for forest products, and for iron, manganese, and copper ores. The city was founded in 1514 by Diego Velasquez. In the Spanish-American War, Spain's fleet under Cervera took refuge in Santiago harbor and was destroyed while attempting to escape. San Juan hill nearby is a national park memorializing Theodore Roosevelt's assault in 1898. Population, 1970, 249,600.

Hispaniola. The second largest island of the West Indies, a short distance southeast of Cuba. It is divided between two republics, Haiti and the Dominican Republic, which have a total population of more than 9,000,000. It was discovered on December 6, 1492, by Christopher Columbus, who named it La Española. It was later known as Haiti.

The island, about 405 miles long and 165 miles wide, has an area of about 29,400 square miles. The surface is rugged and has three mountain ranges running east and west. In the Dominican Republic is Hispaniola's highest peak, Pico Duarte, altitude 10,417 feet; a large salt lake, called Enriquillo; and a number of hot mineral springs. The mountains are rich in undeveloped mineral deposits. Abundant rainfall fosters luxuriant vegetation—valuable hardwood trees in the tropical forests, and, in the cultivated areas, large crops of coffee, cacao, cotton, tobacco, and sugar. Coffee is the chief export.

Haiti. A republic occupying the western third of the island of Hispaniola. Its area is 10,700 square miles. Most of the inhabitants live in the hot, unhealthful lowlands, and the death rate is high. The chief industry is the cultivation of coffee and other products of tropical agriculture. The mineral and forest wealth is little developed.

The population, 1970 estimate, was 4,867,000, of whom about 90 per cent have no admixture of white blood. The spoken language is a corrupt dialect of French known as Creole French. The official religion is Roman Catholicism.

The capital and largest city is Port au Prince, situated at the head of the Bay of Haiti. It has a population of about 250,000. It has a university, created in 1921. Port au Prince is sometimes called Port Républicain.

Dominican Republic. A republic of the West Indies, occupying the eastern two-thirds of the island of Hispaniola. Its 18,700 square miles have a subtropical climate.

The chief industry is agriculture. Sugar, cocoa, coffee, livestock products, and tobacco are exported, mainly to the U.S. Forest and mineral resources are extensive, but undeveloped. In 1968 several U.S., Japanese, and European companies formed a trust with the Dominican government to aid in technical training and industrial development.

The common language is Spanish, and Roman Catholicism is the prevailing religion. Customs collections from 1907 and the general administration of the country from 1916 were in the hands of the United States until 1934. The American receivership was abolished in 1941. Population, 1970, 4,325,000.

The capital is Santo Domingo (formerly Ciudad Trujillo) and is situated near the center of the republic's southern coast. The city had a cathedral, in which the bones of Christopher Columbus were entombed from 1542 to 1796, and a statue of him stands in the public square. The settlement was founded in 1496 by the brother of the great discoverer, and, after Isabela on the northern coast, it is the oldest European settlement in the western hemisphere. Population, 822,862.

Curaçao (*kōō'rä-sä'ō*). A political name applied to a Dutch colony which comprises two groups of islands in the West Indies. Curaçao, the largest island, and two others lie about 40 miles off the northwestern coast of Venezuela, while the remaining three form part of the Leeward Islands southeast of Puerto Rico. The total area of the colony is 403 square miles. Population, 1970 est., exceeded 220,000. The chief industry is oil refining. These islands, along with Surinam (formerly Dutch Guiana) were sometimes referred to as the Dutch West Indies.

SOUTH AMERICA

THE southern continent of the western hemisphere, situated, for the most part, south of the equator. It lies east of a line drawn directly south from Florida and extends east to a point about 1000 miles west of Africa's most western meridian. South America is joined to North America by a narrow isthmus, called Central America. The continent extends north and south a distance of about 4550 miles and has a maximum width of approximately 3200 miles. The area is slightly less than that of North America, being commonly estimated at 7,500,000 square miles.

Contour. In outline, the continent has a general resemblance to a triangle. It is widest in the north and tapers in the south to a point several hundred miles farther south than any other large body of habitable land in the world. The coast line is simple, having no major indentations, such as Hudson Bay in North America. There are, however, many small inlets, especially on the southwest coast of Chile, two large estuaries, that of the Amazon river and of the Plata river, and a number of bays and gulfs, of which the principal ones are: the Gulf of Guayaquil, Golfo Corcovado, and Golfo de Penas on the west; Bahia Grande, Gulf of Saint George, Golfo de San Matias, and Bahia Blanca, on the southeast; and on the north the Gulf of Paria and the Gulf of Venezuela, the latter being connected with the inland sea, Lake Maracaibo.

Surface and Drainage. Along the western side of the continent extends a continuous mountain system, known as the Cordillera of the Andes. This system differs from the Rocky Mountain system of North America in being higher and in containing a large number of volcanoes. Numerous short rivers flow down the narrow west incline of the Andes into the Pacific Ocean. On the east, the mountains slope rapidly down to three great plains drained by three of the greatest rivers of the world. The most northerly plain is the basin of the Orinoco River, a level, grass-covered stretch called the llanos. Separated from it by the plateau of Guiana are the silvas, the vast forested plain of the Amazon Valley. The llanos and the silvas drain to the east. The third great plain drains to the south. It is the basin of the Plata-Parana, consisting of undulating tracts, called pampas, adapted to pasturage.

The pampas are separated from the Amazon Valley by a low plateau, which, extending westward branches into a subdued mountain range skirting the Atlantic coast northeast almost to the Amazon and southwest to the mouth of the Plata. This range is cut in the north by a valley through which flows the Francisco river. South of the Plata-Parana River several streams drain into the Atlantic from the eastern slope of the Andes mountains. The largest of these are the Colorado River, the Rio Negro, and the Chubut River.

Islands. A number of islands are reckoned with the continent. In the southwest, numerous small islands are formed by the partially submerged Andes range. The group of islands at the extreme south is called the Archipelago of Tierra del Fuego and is separated from the continent by Magellan strait. Cape Horn is the most southerly of these islands and forms the most southerly point of the continent. The Galapagos islands lie about 600 miles off the Ecuador coast. The island of Trinidad is close to the delta of the Orinoco river. The Falkland Islands are situated about 350 miles east of the continent at its southern extremity.

Climate. The greater part of South America lies within the tropics. Over this region the moist trade winds blow westward from the Atlantic, providing the country with a copious rainfall as far west as the Andes range. Impinging on the mountains, the winds rise and become cooled, thereby losing their moisture, which is precipitated as rain. They descend as hot, dry winds on the Pacific Coast region, in which, consequently, desert conditions prevail. The Atacama desert in northern Chile is said to be the driest area in the world. Farther south, moist winds blow from the Pacific, giving the western slope of the Andes Mountains a heavy rainfall and rendering the pampas to the east a semi-desert country.

South America does not experience such extremes of temperature as does North America, except on the mountains. The temperature in the moist Amazon valley is consistently high, varying little from about 80° F. The southwestern coast similarly has a fairly constant temperature, but the dry region of the western coast and that of the pampas show greater variation. The mean winter temperature in parts of the south falls to 35° F. The hottest mean midsummer temperature is 85° F. and is found in northern Argentina. The higher mountain peaks, however, are snow-capped even under an equatorial sun.

Flora. The hot, moist region at the extreme north of the continent has a characteristic tropical vegetation. Palms, bamboos, and tree ferns are predominant, giving place to conifers on the mountains and to tall grass in the Orinoco River basin. The silvas of the Amazon valley form the largest heavily forested area in the world. The pampas are luxuriantly grassed in their northern portions, but in the south the aridity occasions a stunted vegetable growth. The potato is indigenous to the continent, which is also the world's chief source of coffee. Rubber and quinine come from the tropical forests, and the Temperate Zone region is one of the world's principal wheat growing and stock raising areas.

Fauna. The animal life of South America includes a number of characteristic species. Among them are alpacas, vicuñas, llamas, condors, tapirs, and a number of toothless quadrupeds—sloths, anteaters, armadillos, and bloodsucking bats. Llamas are used as beasts of burden in the mountains, and alpacas provide a superior quality of wool. Birds of brilliant plumage abound in the tropical regions; many monkeys and reptiles and innumerable species of insects and of fish are found, especially in the Amazon basin. The electric eel and the caribe, a savage fish, are among the more noteworthy.

Minerals. The mineral resources of the continent, although great, have been very imperfectly developed, largely on account of difficulties of transportation and of climate. The Cordillera of the Andes contains the bulk of such minerals, although many are found in the Brazilian plateau. Silver and gold were produced extensively before Europeans came to South America. Brazil was long the chief source of diamonds, and Chile exports nitrates to all parts of the world. South America is also the chief source of monazite and of vanadium. Immense quantities of oil come from Venezuela, copper from Chile, and tin from Bolivia. Aluminum ore comes from the Guianas, and platinum and emeralds from Colombia.

Inhabitants. The population of South America in 1969 exceeded 180 million. The largest city is Sao Paulo, with a population of 5,900,000. The majority of the continent's inhabitants are a mixture of white races with native Indians. Possibly one-fifth are pure Indians. Those of unmixed European origin are comparatively few, although they predominate in Argentina and comprise almost the whole of the population in Uruguay. Pure Indians predominate in Paraguay and Bolivia.

Most of the inhabitants speak Spanish, being descended from Spaniards, except in Brazil, where the European strain in the population is Portuguese and the Portuguese language is spoken. The Catholic religion prevails throughout the continent.

The Andes Mountains. The system of mountains running north and south on South America's western border. This system, wide and high in the northern and central part, where it divides into three chains, becomes narrower toward the south and gradually sinks to the level of the sea at the continent's southern extremity. The highest peak is Aconcagua, in west central Argentina, which reaches a height of 22,835 feet. Mt. Huascaran in Peru has an elevation of 22,205 feet. Several of the world's gigantic volcanoes belong to the Andes mountains, such as Chimborazo, Cotopaxi, Antisana, and Misti. Glaciers are found on the tall peaks, even those within the equatorial regions.

The continent's largest lake and one of the highest in the world, Lake Titicaca, lies among the Andes mountains at a level of about 12,500 feet above the sea. The lake, which has no outlet, has an area of 3200 square miles and a maximum depth of about 900 feet. Near its shores, there are many ruins of temples and other relics of a former civilization.

The Amazon River. The largest and one of the longest rivers of the world, draining a tropical basin in South America eastward from the Andes Mountains and emptying into the Atlantic Ocean through an estuary which expands to a width of 150 miles.

The river has several tributaries which are themselves among the major rivers of the world. The Rio Negro is the largest affluent on the north; on the south the chief tributaries are the Purus, the Tapajoz, the Xingu, the Araguaia, and the Madeira, the last of which has an affluent explored by Theodore Roosevelt and named, after him, the Roosevelt River.

The Amazon River is navigable for ocean steamers over a distance of 2300 miles, and 486 miles farther for smaller vessels. The river system affords navigable waterways of 27,000 miles.

Rising tides produce large tidal waves, or bores, which rush up the river with a loud roar and often endanger shipping. The effect of the river's current can be detected 200 miles out at sea. In the flood season the river rises 30 to 40 feet in some parts, inundating the banks for several months of the year.

Plata-Parana. The second largest river system of South America, consisting of the Parana River and the Uruguay River, which unite their streams in the Rio de la Plata, "Silver river," an estuary conducting the water of the system to the Atlantic Ocean, about 20° of latitude north of Cape Horn.

The basin has a southern drainage, sloping from the Brazil plateau in the north. The estuary is 135 miles wide at its outlet. The Plata-Parana stream measures altogether about 2500 miles, of which about 1200 miles are navigable. The chief tributary is the Paraguay river, which flows into the Parana.

Orinoco River. One of the three large rivers of South America, draining a tropical territory in the northern part of the continent. The river rises in the Parima Mountains between Venezuela and Brazil. After traversing immense flat, treeless plains in a course running first west, then north, and finally east, the river winds through a dense tropical forest area and empties into the Atlantic Ocean through several mouths forming a delta south of the island of Trinidad. About 150 miles from its source the river discharges part of its water into the Rio Negro, an affluent of the Amazon River. The Orinoco River is navigable to a cataract 870 miles from its mouth. Its tributaries are very numerous, the chief navigable ones being the Guaviare, the Meta, and the Apure. The system has 4300 miles of navigable streams. See *Venezuela*.

POLITICAL DIVISIONS

Located on the mainland of South America are the nations of Argentina, Bolivia, Brazil, Chile, Columbia, Ecuador, Guyana (formerly the colony of British Guiana and now an independent member of the Commonwealth), Paraguay, Peru, Surinam (formerly the colony of Dutch Guiana), Uruguay, and Venezuela—and the colony of French Guiana. Brazil has the largest land area and Surinam the smallest. Among the islands, Trinidad and Tobago are an independent member of the British Commonwealth, while the Falkland Islands are dependencies of Britain. The Galapagos Islands belong to Ecuador.

Argentina. The most highly developed country of South America and second largest in area, occupying the greater part of the southern portion of the continent. The country has an Atlantic seaboard of 1565 miles and a western land boundary of about 3000 miles, following the continental watershed formed by the Andes. Argentina measures about 2285 miles from north to south and has a maximum width of 930 miles, with an area of 1,084,120 square miles.

The country is drained in the north by the Plata-Parana River. In the south the surface slopes from the ridge of the Andes toward the Atlantic Ocean. The climate varies from the tropical warmth in the low plains of the north, where 120° F. has been recorded, to the more moderate conditions existing in the south, where 3° F. is the lowest temperature officially noted. The rainfall decreases from the eastern coast to the base of the Andes Mountains.

The flora of Argentina shows variations following the differences in climate. In the partly unexplored tropical forests of the north, algaroba trees are especially numerous, and many medicinal shrubs and other plants abound, including the *yerba maté*, or Paraguay tea plant. The mountains are wooded, those around the Strait of Magellan and Tierra del Fuego being covered with immense forests of beech. The most valuable product of the forest is quebracho extract, a dye. The pampas are treeless but are covered with grass. Such tropical and subtropical fruits as oranges, lemons, grapes, and peaches are grown. The animals characteristic of Argentina include the viscacha and the hare of Patagonia.

The chief industries of Argentina are grazing and agriculture, for which the extensive pampas are admirably suited. Wheat and corn are the most valuable crops. Grain and meat form more than 75 per cent of the exports. Argentina is the world's largest exporter of beef, corn, and flaxseed. Lumbering and mining are carried on to some extent. Oil fields yielded 123,076,000 barrels of petroleum in 1968. There are 27,301 miles of railway, all of which are now state property, a greater mileage than that of any other South American country.

Argentina is divided into 22 provinces and 1 federal district. The capital is Buenos Aires. The country has received a great many European immigrants, principally from Italy, Spain, and Germany. The Indian strain in the population is comparatively slight. The population, according to the 1970 estimate, was 24,352,000.

Bolivia. An inland country in the west central part of South America. The southwestern border follows the ridge of the western range of the Andean Cordillera, which in this section spreads out into the Bolivian plateau and occupies nearly half the surface of Bolivia. The average elevation of the plateau is 12,000 feet, but it contains some of the highest peaks of the continent, such as Ancohuma, Sajama, Illampu, and Illimani. In this plateau lies the lofty Lake Titicaca, with which is connected Lake Aullagas. East of the plateau, the surface slopes down in vast undulating plains toward the Amazon River valley in the north and, in the south, toward the llanos of the Parana River basin. The area of the country is estimated at 424,162 square miles.

LATIN AMERICA I

Buenos Aires, capital of Argentina, is the largest city in South America. This obelisk is a copy of that on the Rue de la Concorde, Paris.

This view of Juarez Avenue in Mexico City illustrates the typical broad avenues in the city's regular layout. Shaded boulevards, ornate squares, and numerous parks embellished with sculpture characterize this great city built more than a mile above sea level.

Right Machu Picchu, the "Lost City of the Incas," near Cuzco, Peru, where it is believed that survivors of the Spanish conquest took refuge and eluded the victors in this inaccessible fastness.

Braniff Airways

This is the Equator Monument at zero latitude in Ecuador. The northern hemisphere on the left, southern hemisphere is on the right.

Many of the newer buildings in South America are daringly modern in design. This striking apartment house is in Montevideo, Uruguay.

Italian Museum, Lima, Peru, a gift of Lima's Italian citizens on the occasion of the centenary of Peru's independence in 1921.

Pan American Union

LATIN AMERICA II

Christ of the Andes, a colossal statue on the Chile-Argentina border, celebrating settlement of an old dispute.

Pan American Airways

Altamira Plaza, in Caracas, reflects the spirit of progress in Venezuela and the increase in national wealth that has made possible many modern improvements.

Courtesy—Ministry of Development, Tourist Dept., Caracas, Venezuela

Modern and progressive, Sao Paulo, largest city in Brazil, is a leading manufacturing and business center.

Brazilian Gov't. Trade Bureau

South American Indians still use primitive methods. This fishing boat on a high Andean lake is made of balsa wood, including the sail.

This shadowy, ancient street in La Paz, Bolivia, is typical of many old South American cities, where buildings hundreds of years old rub shoulders with modern architecture.

Bolivia is entirely in the Torrid Zone, but the climate of the upland is of an almost arctic severity. Parts of this plateau support grazing flocks of sheep, llamas, and alpacas, but it is for the most part arid and of value only for its minerals. The fertile eastern slope of the Cordillera, being warmer and well watered, produces wheat, corn, barley, peaches, grapes, and figs. The lowlands support a tropical vegetation. Coffee, cacao, rice, sugar cane, and medicinal plants are cultivated, and vast forests yield rosewood, mahogany, ebony, cedar, and rubber, the last being produced in quantities which entitle Bolivia to rank next to Brazil as a rubber exporting country.

Bolivia's principal industry is mining, and the principal mineral product is tin, in the export of which Bolivia ranks second among the countries of the world. Silver, gold, and copper are also mined in large quantities, and wolfram, vanadium, bismuth, lead, zinc, salt, and antimony are obtained in smaller amounts. Potosi, where the tin and silver mining interests center, is the highest city in the world, having an elevation of 14,350 feet. At such an altitude, operations can be carried on only by the natives. Population, 1970 est. at more than 98,000.

Railroad transportation is limited by the natural obstacles in the way of construction. Some 2200 miles of track, however, are in operation. There is communication by airplane between the principal cities. Llamas are used for carrying light loads over mountainous districts.

The majority of the inhabitants live on the eastern slopes of the mountains. About one-half are pure Indians, and the white race forms about 12 per cent of the population of 5,600,000 (1975 est.). La Paz is the largest city and the seat of Congress, and Sucre is the statutory capital and seat of the supreme court. The country possesses many impressive remains of a vanished civilization. Bolivia was deprived of access to the sea by a disastrous war with Chile which ended in 1883.

Brazil. The largest country of South America, occupying the entire east central part of the continent and having a westward extension which reaches almost to the Andes Mountains. The country's maximum extent north and south is 2660 miles and east and west it measures about 2700 miles, with a total area of 3,289,000 square miles, exceeding that of continental United States.

In the north the climate is moist and tropical in character, while toward the south it becomes more temperate and the rainfall is lighter. The northern region is drained by the Amazon River, south of which lies one of the world's largest unexplored forest areas. The eastern part of the country is a highland through which the river Francisco flows, and the southern district is drained by the Uruguay River and by the upper reaches of the Parana River system.

The mineral resources of Brazil are very great but are largely undeveloped. The production of gold and of diamonds was formerly of great importance. The Morro Velho gold mine, having a depth of 7000 feet, is one of the deepest mines in the world. The deposits of iron are very extensive. Brazil provides the greater part of the world's supply of monazite.

The tropical flora of Brazil includes trees producing an extraordinary variety of useful and of ornamental woods, 200 different kinds of timber having been shown at the national exhibition in Rio de Janeiro in 1922. These woods include mahogany, rosewood, brazilwood, and logwood. The rubber tree and the pine are among those of the greatest commercial value. The rank forests of the Amazon basin abound in brilliantly colored flowers and in countless monkeys, lizards, fish, gaudy butterflies, and other tropical animals. The portions of the country farther south are suitable for agriculture, and produce a large amount of coffee, sugar, cocoa, tobacco, and cotton. About three-fourths of the world's supply of coffee comes from Brazil. The country continues to supply substantial quantities of rubber to world trade. Large areas provide fertile pasture land for raising livestock, notably Brahman cattle.

Brazil exports mainly the products of the forest and farm, and imports some manufactured goods. The textile industry includes the manufacture of silk, woolen, cotton, and jute goods. Other industries rapidly developing are ceramics, glass, electrical appliances, plastics, and cement. There are many tobacco factories and sugar refineries. Carnauba wax, produced only in Brazil, insures a high hard polish and long-wearing protection on furniture and floors.

The population of Brazil, according to the 1970 estimate, was 95,305,000, making the country the most populous in the western hemisphere after the United States. Many Negroes and about 100,000 Indians live in the Amazon valley. In the south there are a number of settlements of Germans, Spaniards, and Italians. The majority of the inhabitants, however, are of Portuguese origin, and the language of the country is Portuguese.

Politically, the country consists of 21 federated states, one federal district, and four territories. The most populous and most prosperous states are Bahia, Minas Gerais, and Sao Paulo, all bordering on the central part of the southeastern coast. These states produce the bulk of the minerals, coffee, sugar, cotton, and live stock. The most extensive state is Amazonas, occupying the upper Amazon valley. From it come most of the valuable woods. The largest city of the country is Sao Paulo and the capital is Brasilia. The port Pernambuco, on the eastern coast, is nearer to Lisbon than to New York.

Chile (*chĭl'ē*). A country of South America, lying on the western coast and extending, with an average width of about 87 miles, from the southern extremity of the continent northward about 2700 miles to Peru. The area is estimated at 286,397 square miles. The eastern boundary follows in general the ridge of the Andes mountains.

A high plateau rises abruptly from the sea along the greater part of the coast, leaving a lofty plain between the sea and the foot of the Andes. There is a gentle slope from the north to the south. The rivers are short and drain into the Pacific Ocean. A number of natural harbors are found among the fiordlike indentations and the numerous islands of the southern coast. The country is subject to severe earthquakes followed usually by destructive tidal waves. One of the most disastrous occurred in 1922. In 1751, the former city of Concepcion was sunk in the Pacific Ocean.

The climate of Chile is hot and extremely arid in the north, where a whole year often passes without rain. The central region, having a more moderate temperature and a greater precipitation, supports a flourishing agricultural industry and contains most of the population. In the south the increased rainfall permits the growth of forests of beech, cypress, and oak, the last of which has been introduced from abroad. In the extreme south the growth of the trees is stunted by the prevailing low temperatures.

The northern third of Chile is the world's chief source of natural nitrate of soda, which is used as a mineral fertilizer and in the production of explosives and of most of the world's supply of iodine. Chile is also one of the leading producers of copper. Other minerals mined in important quantities include iron ore, gold, silver, sulphur, borate, and salt. A large portion of the government's revenue is derived from the export of nitrate.

Agriculture provides employment for about half the population. The principal crops are grapes and wheat. Stock raising also is important. Most of the textiles and other manufactured goods consumed are imported. The United States and Great Britain receive most of the foreign trade.

Chile has a longitudinal railway system of some 6000 miles in length. The Trans-Andean railroad connects Valparaiso, on Chile's Pacific coast, with the Atlantic seaboard at Buenos Aires. Parts of it climb grades of a steepness nowhere else attempted by railroad engineers. The total length is nearly 6000 miles. Air transportation is well developed.

The population of Chile in 1972 was 10,044,940, of whom about one fourth were of Spanish descent. The influence of the Church is greater than in most other countries of the continent. Chile has a powerful fleet and is politically one of the three strongest countries of South America. The capital and largest city is Santiago. Valparaiso is the chief port.

Colombia. A country of South America, occupying the extreme northwestern part of the continent. Colombia borders on the Pacific Ocean for a distance of about 500 miles and on the Caribbean Sea for 700 miles. Its area is 439,520 square miles.

The country is traversed from northeast to southwest by the Cordillera of the Andes, which here consists of a western, a central, and an eastern range separated by fertile plateaus. The eastern slope of the Cordillera drains in the north into the basin of the Orinoco river and, farther south, into the basin of the Amazon river. The central plateaus drain northward by the Magdalena River system into the Caribbean Sea. The western slope of the Cordillera has a number of short rivers emptying into the Pacific Ocean. The Magdalena river is navigable for steamers to La Dorada, a point about 560 miles above its mouth.

The climate of Colombia varies from the intense tropical heat of the coast regions, the valleys, and the llanos, to the temperate conditions of the plateaus and the mountains. There are two wet seasons and two dry seasons over most of the country. The llanos, however, have two seasons only. The rainfall there is deficient and does not permit the growth of trees. The west coast, however, has a large rainfall. The mountain sides are covered with forests of a tropical character, containing, among many other varieties of plants, the wax palm, the rubber tree, and several species of cinchonas.

The mineral wealth of Colombia is great. Gold, platinum, copper, petroleum, and emeralds are exported, the last being produced in Colombia in greater quantities than in the rest of the world. The salt mines are a government monopoly and provide a considerable part of the national revenue.

The chief industries are agriculture and stock raising. Temperate zone cereals are grown on the plateaus, and coffee, sugar, bananas, and cocoa are produced in the valleys and the lower regions. Colombia provides most of the world's supply of mild coffee. Panama hats are produced extensively, although the industry is not centralized in factories. In addition to coffee, the chief exports are petroleum, bananas, gold, and platinum. The bulk of the foreign trade is with the United States. The mountainous surface of the country and the prevalence of tropical forests make transportation difficult except on the rivers and by air. Overhead ropeways are also a feature of Colombia's transportation facilities.

Colombia is divided into 23 departments, 3 intendancies, and 5 commissaries. The capital and largest city is Bogota. The population of the country, 1972 estimate, was 23,210,000.

Ecuador. A country in the northwest portion of South America, bordering on the Pacific Ocean and stretching south from Colombia to Peru. Its area is estimated at 104,516 square miles. Ecuador's coast line is broken by the Gulf of Guayaquil, the only large inlet on the south side of the continent.

The country is traversed from north to south by two ranges of the Andean Cordillera. Between the ranges lies a plateau, which has an average elevation of 9000 feet but in the south falls to a level of about 2000 feet. This plateau contains most of the cultivated land and has a delightful climate. The mountain ranges have many peaks of exceptional height, including Cotopaxi, the world's loftiest active volcano.

The coastal strip in Ecuador is not an arid waste, as in Peru and northern Chile, but is a stretch of tropical jungle with an excessive rainfall. Dense forests are found on the mountain slopes both on the west and on the east of the Cordillera. The east slope gives rise to several navigable rivers of the Amazon basin. One of the largest is the Napo, down which the explorer Orellana sailed in 1541 to the mouth of the Amazon River.

The immense virgin forests of Ecuador yield rubber, ivory nuts, dyewoods, cinchona bark, and many valuable kinds of cabinet wood. The distinctive products of the country, however, are cocoa and toquilla. The latter is the fabric from which Panama hats are made. It is shipped extensively to Colombia where the actual weaving is an important industry. Other products of the tropical agriculture pursued on the coastal strip are coffee, tobacco, and sugar. In the plateau, hay, cereal crops, and fruits and vegetables of a temperate zone character are cultivated, and cattle are raised in large numbers. Alligator skins are exported. Gold and petroleum are produced and silver, copper, iron, lead, coal, and sulphur are found. The production of salt is a government monopoly.

The population, 1974 census, was 6,500,845, the great majority of whom are of Indian origin. The coinage of the country is minted in England and the United States. The country owns the Galapagos, or "turtle", islands, lying 600 miles to the west. The capital of Ecuador is Quito and the principal seaport and largest city is Guayaquil. The name of the country is the Spanish word for equator.

French Guiana. An overseas department in the French Community with an area of about 34,740 square miles in northeastern South America. It is bounded by the Atlantic Ocean, Brazil, and Surinam, and consists of two districts—Cayenne and Inini. Cayenne (the coastal strip 25 miles deep), along with Devil's Island and other islands, was used by France as a penal settlement from 1931 until 1944, when it was closed. Inini, the hinterland district, is rich in valuable hardwoods and has much mineral wealth, including gold, silver, iron, and phosphates. Corn, rice, bananas, and sugar cane are among the principal crops. The population of French Guiana was estimated to be about 44,200 in 1971, most of the people living in the coastal strip, Cayenne. The capital and chief port is also called Cayenne.

Guyana. A former British colony of continental South America, lying between Venezuela and Surinam near the center of the continent's northeastern coast line. Its area is 83,000 square miles. The interior is covered with dense forests as far as the highlands in the southwest. The rivers are not navigable, except for short distances, because of rapids and falls. In the Potaro River are the famous Kaieteur Falls, having a drop of about 800 feet. The coast district, about 40 miles wide, is low, and part of it is protected by dikes. It is very fertile and produces large crops of sugar cane, rice, and coconuts. Gold and diamonds are mined in the highlands. Bauxite, the ore of aluminum, is exported.

The climate of the country is generally hot and moist. It was estimated that the population in 1975 was more than 794,348, about one-half of whom are East Indians, who were brought in to work on the plantations. The capital is Georgetown. England's sovereignty over the colony was disputed by the Dutch and the French until 1815, when the territory finally passed into her possession. The Venezuelan boundary was fixed after a dispute arbitrated in 1899 by jurists of Great Britain and of the United States. Guyana became independent in May, 1966.

Paraguay. An inland country of central South America, bounded by Brazil, Argentina, and Bolivia.

Paraguay is a low-lying country situated between the Parana River and the Paraguay River, with the exception of a district to the northwest, the Gran Chaco. By arbitration with Bolivia in 1930, Paraguay received 91,800 square miles of the Gran Chaco, making her total area about 157,000 square miles.

Apart from the disputed territory, which is subject to alternate floods and droughts, the climate is delightful for the greater part of the year. During the three hottest months, however, the temperature not infrequently rises above 100° F. The rainfall is moderate, but sufficient to foster the growth of dense forests, and rich groves of tropical fruit, particularly oranges, bananas, and lemons. Fine cabinet timbers, dyewoods, drugs, gums, and oils are obtainable from the forests on the hills and in the valleys of the northeast part of the country. Occasional stretches of savannas afford rich pasturage, and flat marshes in the south are adapted to rice culture.

The chief cultivated plants are orange and other tropical fruit trees, corn, sugar cane, rice, tobacco, and cotton. Agricultural methods, however, are still primitive. *Yerba maté*, or Paraguay tea, found wild in great abundance and also cultivated to some extent, is exported. Stock raising is the second industry of the country. Iron, copper, manganese, and marble are to be found in the northeast of the country, but they are not mined extensively.

Transportation facilities for this land-locked country improved noticeably in 1968–69. A new highway to Brazil was completed, new roads were built, and a large hydroelectric project was begun. Access to the sea is by river navigation through Argentina and by a railroad service to Buenos Aires. Chief exports are oranges, tobacco, beef hides, quebracho logs and extract, and vegetable oil. Increased tourism has helped raise the country economically.

The population of Paraguay was estimated in 1972 to be 2,354,071, a very small proportion of whom are white, these being mainly Italian and German immigrants. The settlements are largely confined to the vicinity of the Paraguay River. About one-seventh of the inhabitants are pure Indians, and the native Guarani language is more widely used than Spanish. The percentage of illiteracy is high. The capital, chief port, and the largest city is Asuncion.

Peru. A country of west central South America, bordering on the Pacific Ocean and stretching northward from Chile to Ecuador. Its area is 496,223 square miles.

Peru is traversed from north to south by the Cordillera of the Andes, which, under the name of the Sierra or uplands, constitutes one of the three physiographical divisions of the country. The uplands consist of three ranges, ill defined in parts, and of the intervening plateaus. There are several large volcanoes in this region and violent earthquakes are not uncommon. The rainfall is unevenly distributed. Between the foothills of the Andes and the Pacific Ocean is a dry coastal strip averaging about 30 miles in width. This strip is cut by several rivers, which foster vegetation along their banks and afford means of irrigation. The civilization of the country centers about these rivers. Sloping eastward from the uplands is the Montana, a forest area with a heavy rainfall, in which the Amazon River system takes its rise.

Peru lies wholly within the Torrid Zone. The climate is not oppressively hot, however, except in the eastern valleys and lowlands. The greater part of the Sierra enjoys an equable temperature, and the heat of the coastal strip is moderated by the antarctic currents. Dense fogs frequently hang over the coast.

The eastern part of the Montana, being hot and well watered, supports a tropical vegetation. The cinchona tree is native to Peru and rubber trees grow in abundance but are comparatively inaccessible. Peru is the chief source of the coca shrub, from which cocaine is obtained.

The watered sections of the Sierra and of the coastal area produce sugar and cotton. Other agricultural products include coffee, grapes, palms, cocoa, corn, and wheat. A large number of sheep are raised in the Sierra, and wool, taken in part from sheep but to a great extent from llamas and alpacas, is exported in large quantities. The llama is the principal beast of burden. Mules are used extensively for traveling, the railway mileage being small on account of the mountainous character of the country. The various lines embrace about 2800 miles of track.

Mining ranks second to agriculture among the industries. The chief minerals are petroleum, copper, and silver, but over four-fifths of the world's supply of vanadium comes from Peru. The chief manufactures are sugar and cocaine, other necessary industrial products, such as textiles, lumber, wheat, and coal being imported. Peru has an important fishing industry, the main catch being anchovies, most of which are made into fish meal for cattle and poultry feed. This makes fish meal the leading export, with copper second.

Peru is the seat of the vanished civilization of the Incas, by whom Cuzco is said to have been founded in the 10th century. The population, according to the latest estimate, was 15,400,000, about 53 per cent being white and mestizos, and 46 per cent Indian.

The capital and largest city is Lima. The chief port is Callao on the Pacific Ocean. The steamship service between Peruvian and Bolivian ports on Lake Titicaca is unique in operating at an altitude unequalled on any other navigable body of water. Iquitos, on the upper reaches of the Amazon river, has steamer connections with the Atlantic Ocean, 2500 miles distant.

Surinam. This former Dutch colony became fully independent in 1975. It is situated at the center of the continent's northeast coast between Guyana and French Guiana. Its area—54,291 square miles—makes it the smallest South American nation.

The cultivated area is confined to a coastal strip about 20 miles in width, the interior region being covered with a dense tropical forest as far as the highlands of the southeast. The chief agricultural products are bananas, sugar, cacao, coffee, and rice. Gold is exported also, much of it obtained from alluvium.

The estimated population in 1971 was 384,900, and consists largely of Negroes and people of East Indian origin, who were brought in to work on the plantations. The capital is Paramaribo. The name Surinam is a corruption of Surreyham, which was the original designation given in honor of the Earl of Surrey.

Uruguay. A country south of Brazil between the Atlantic Ocean and the Uruguay River. Its southern coastline is on the Rio de la Plata. The total area is 72,172 square miles.

The surface is rolling and has several chains of hills reaching a maximum elevation of 2000 feet. The climate is equable in the south, but in the north it becomes continental, admitting of greater heat in the summer and of occasional frosts in the winter. The northern hills and valleys are covered with a subtropical forest, while the south and east form extensive fertile plains suited for agriculture and for stock raising. Deer, otters, wild hogs, and wildcats are indigenous. Rheas, or American ostriches, are found; and fur seals, protected by the government, inhabit Lobas island and Castillos island near the coast. There are also storks, swans, cranes, and wild turkeys.

Stock raising is the principal industry of Uruguay, animal products forming nearly nine-tenths of the exports. Wheat, oats, flaxseed, and grapes are also grown and exported. Less than 10 per cent of the country's area, however, is devoted to agriculture, in spite of the fact that the government encourages the industry by supporting agricultural schools. Hailstorms, destructive hurricanes, and occasional droughts occur as factors unfavorable to the raising of crops.

Gold mines are worked, and there are deposits of copper, iron, manganese, and lignite. Manufactures are very slightly developed, the population relying on importation for such industrial products as textiles and hardware. Transportation in Uruguay is facilitated by several hundred miles of navigable river streams and by more than 1700 miles of railway.

The population of Uruguay, according to the latest official estimate, was 2,763,964, of whom about nine-tenths are of European descent, mainly Spaniards and Italians. The earliest settlements were made by Spaniards in 1624 on the Rio Negro, a tributary of the Uruguay River. The capital, foreign port, and largest city is Montevideo.

Venezuela. The most northern country of South America, having a northern coast line of about 1700 miles on the Caribbean Sea and a land boundary separating the country from Guyana, Brazil, and Colombia. Its area, including the islands off the north coast, is 352,143 square miles.

Apart from the small basin of Lake Maracaibo in the northwest, Venezuela is drained by the Orinoco River system. This system flows eastward from the Andes mountains between the Guiana highlands to the south and a northeastern extension of the Andes mountains on the north, and enters the sea through a large estuary overgrown with a mangrove swamp. The upper portion of the river system traverses the llanos. A major irrigation project became a reality with the completion in 1968 of the Guri Dam, 512 feet high, located near the confluence of the Caroni and Orinoco rivers. The tributaries of the Orinoco are numerous and, with the main stream, provide the country with about 4000 miles of navigable waterways.

The climate in the lower levels of Venezuela is tropical but becomes temperate in the highlands and frigid on the higher mountain peaks. The rainfall is copious in the east and in the northwestern parts near the mountains. On the llanos the comparative dryness during one season of the year prevents the growth of trees.

The flora of the eastern lowlands and of the better watered territory in the northwest consists of tropical forests similar to those of the Amazon valley. The forests include many plants from which are available such products as rubber, vanilla, brazil nuts, dyewoods, and drugs. Grasses form the characteristic vegetation of the llanos. The fauna of Venezuela is tropical and rich, and includes such species as the howling monkey, the spectacled bear, the vampire bat, the flamingo and other brilliantly colored but usually songless birds, the anaconda and other snakes, a frog with a voice resembling a human shout, the electric eel, and the caribe.

Venezuela is rich in minerals. It ranks among the world's largest producers of petroleum. Also produced in quantity are gold, salt, and asphalt, the last being found in lakes containing extensive remains of prehistoric animals. Pearl fishing is an industry on a number of islands off the north coast.

In the northern and western parts of Venezuela, where most of the population is concentrated, agriculture is carried on, the chief products being coffee, sugar, and cocoa. Grazing is the chief industry on the llanos. Most of the foreign trade is with the United States.

The name Venezuela is Italian, meaning Little Venice. It was given by early Italian explorers who found, on Lake Maracaibo, an Indian tribe inhabiting huts which were supported by piles driven into the bed of the lake. Reminded of Venice, they gave the region its name.

Venezuela is divided into 20 states, 2 territories, and a federal district. The capital and largest city is Caracas. The 1971 estimated population was 10,721,522, excluding 31,800 Indians.

CHIEF CITIES AND OTHER PLACES OF INTEREST IN SOUTH AMERICA

The preceding articles on South America deal with the larger features of the continent. Other points of interest, including the principal cities, the national capitals, the trade centers, certain islands, and regions of especial note are covered below.

Asuncion (*ä-sōōn'syōn'*). The capital and metropolis of Paraguay, situated on the east bank of the Paraguay River in the west central part of the country. The city is the port and trading center of Paraguay, and is connected by railroad with Buenos Aires. It has foundries, shipyards, and distilleries. The exports include Paraguay tea and lace, the latter a beautiful product of the industry of Indian women. Population, 392,753.

Bahia (*bä-ē'ä*). A city of east central Brazil, picturesquely situated on a high peninsula which partly encloses an excellent natural harbor. Bahia, also called Salvador, is a notable port, shipping coffee, sugar, rubber, cotton, and other products raised in the state. The manufactures are varied, the principal one being cotton cloth. Bahia was formerly the center of the world's largest diamond trade.

The lower part of the city, devoted to commerce, has narrow streets. The upper, or residential, part is accessible by elevators and is attractively built. The churches are very numerous. The cathedral of the archbishop of Brazil is situated in Bahia and is one of the finest basilicas in Brazil. The city has a university, a medical college, and a museum. The culture of seedless oranges was introduced into the United States from Bahia. Founded in 1510 by Correa, a Portuguese navigator, the city was the capital of Brazil until 1763. Population, 863,000.

Barranquilla (*bär'rän-kēl'yä*). The chief port of Colombia, situated on the Magdalena River about 7½ miles from its mouth. The mouth of the river is not navigable. Traffic borne down the river to Barranquilla for export, therefore, is sent by rail to Puerto Colombia, a seaport on the Caribbean Sea. Population, 721,000.

Belem. A seaport of northeastern Brazil, situated on the Rio Para about 85 miles from the Atlantic Ocean. On the land side, it is flanked by dense forests. Belem is the headquarters for the navigation on the Amazon. Exports include cocoa, rice, cotton, rubber, and various forest products of the Amazon valley. Population, 633,000.

Bogota (*bō'gō-tä'*). The capital and largest city of Colombia, situated near the geographical center of the country on a fertile table-land at an elevation of about 8700 feet above the sea. There are many mountains in the vicinity and the mining interests of the city are considerable, the government's salt mines being a short distance north of the city. Coal, iron, and manganese mines lie to the north and east.

The more important edifices of Bogota include the government buildings and the cathedral, the latter being a structure in the Corinthian style of architecture. The city is the seat of the national university, of three endowed colleges, and of a museum containing many relics of the civilization of the Incas. The streets are narrow but well paved. Population, 2,978,000.

Brasilia (*brä-sĭl'ĭ-ä*). Brazil's new capital, located in the Central Plateau in the state of Goias, is designed to integrate 6 million square kilometers of the interior into the general progress of the country. The city's daringly modern buildings are the work of sixty Brazilian architects. Population, 537,000.

Buenos Aires (*bwā'nōs ī'rās; bō'nŭs ā'rĭz*). The capital of Argentina and one of the largest cities in South America, situated on the south shore of the estuary of the Rio de la Plata about 170 miles from the Atlantic Ocean.

Buenos Aires handles the bulk of Argentina's foreign commerce and is one of the largest ports of the world, the harbor having been improved at a cost of about 50 million dollars. Near the wharves is the central fruit market, one of the largest warehouses in the world. The manufacturing industries produce mainly for home consumption.

The oldest part of Buenos Aires has narrow streets. The city is divided from east to west by the magnificent Avenida de Mayo, which is 100 feet wide and connects two beautiful squares. At the eastern end lies the Plaza de Mayo, having an area of more than four acres and fronted by several imposing buildings, including the executive palace and the cathedral. At the western end, the view terminates in the House of Congress, erected at a cost of $6 million. The office of the newspaper *La Prensa* is one of the most handsome buildings of the city.

Buenos Aires has a system of more than 100 parks which cover a total area of over 3000 acres. Numerous monuments have been erected in the city, including a statue of George Washington set up in Palmero park by American residents of the city. The chief educational institution is the University of Buenos Aires.

Buenos Aires was founded by Pedro de Mendoza in 1535. It was destroyed by the Indians and was re-established in 1580 by Juan de Garay, the governor of Paraguay. The city has grown very rapidly in the past half century. Population, 2,966,816.

Callao (*käl-yä'ō*). The principal seaport of Peru, situated on an island-sheltered bay near the center of the country's Pacific coast line. The city is connected by steam and electric railroads with Lima, distant seven miles inland. The chief exports are sugar, cotton, cocaine, minerals, and wool. In 1746 the former city of Callao was submerged with all its inhabitants, and on calm days the ruins are still distinguishable under water. Population, 335,000.

Cape Horn. The most southerly point of South America. The name is applied to a small, rocky island and to the most southerly point of the island, a headland having a height of 600 feet. The cape was discovered by the Dutch navigator, Schouten, who named it after Hoorn, his native town in the Netherlands.

Caracas (*kä-rä'käs*). The capital and largest city of Venezuela, occupying a mountainous site 7 miles from La Guaira, a port near the center of the country's northern coast. The city is an important exporting center for cocoa, coffee, tobacco, and other products of the country. Its principal square contains a large statue of Bolivar. The capitol building covers an area of two acres. The city has all modern improvements. An earthquake in 1812 killed more than 12,000 inhabitants. Population, 1,764,274.

Cayenne (*kā-ĕn'*; *kī-ĕn'*). A fortified seaport, the capital of the colony of French Guiana. The town is built on a low island between the Cayenne River and the Mahury River. The harbor is insecure and shallow. Sugar, gold, hides, woods, spices, and cacao are the principal exports. Thirty miles northwest is the Isle du Diable, "Devil's island," where Captain Dreyfus was imprisoned from 1894 to 1899. Population, 24,000.

Christ of the Andes. A bronze statue of Christ, by Mateo Alonzo, on the border of Chile and Argentina erected to commemorate the peaceful settlement in 1902 of a boundary dispute between the two countries. The statue, more than twice life-size, stands on a pedestal roughhewn from the natural rock near the summit of Uspallata Pass in the Andes at an altitude of 12,796 feet. It was cast from bronze obtained by melting cannon.

Cordoba (*kôr'dō-bä*). A commercial city of central Argentina, situated on the Rio Primero, about 400 miles northwest of Buenos Aires. Live stock, wool, and hides are shipped from this city. Cordoba has a cathedral, a massive Jesuit Church, a National Observatory, two national colleges, and a university, the last founded in 1613. The city dates back to the year 1573. It was formerly the head of the Jesuit missions in South America. Population, 589,153.

Easter Island. An island possession of Chile, lying about 2000 miles to the west in the Pacific Ocean. It contains many colossal stone images, which, according to archaeological evidence, were carved during several centuries after 1100 A.D. Masonry remains go back to about 300 A.D. When Easter Island was discovered by the Dutch captain Roggeveen on Easter Sunday, 1722, it had a population of about 4000, probably of Polynesian origin. Present inhabitants number about 1135. Its area is 45 square miles.

Falkland Islands. A group of about 100 small islands, forming a British crown colony situated in the south Atlantic Ocean, about 300 miles east of the Strait of Magellan. Only two of the islands are inhabited—East Falkland, with an area of 2610 square miles, and West Falkland, having 2090 square miles of surface.

The surface of the larger islands is treeless. Sheep farming was formerly the chief industry, but in recent years whaling has become more important. The climate is equable but cool and damp. South Georgia, the South Orkneys, the South Shetlands, the Sandwich group, and Graham's Land, all lying some hundreds of miles to the southeast, are regarded as dependencies of the Falkland Islands. In 1967 the population of the islands was about 2122. The capital is Stanley, East Falkland. During World War I, a British fleet defeated a German fleet near these islands.

Galapagos (*gä-lä'pä-gōs*) **Islands.** A group of small volcanic islands, sometimes called the Colon Archipelago, lying about 600 miles west of the coast of Ecuador. They have an estimated area of 2868 square miles and a population of about 2412. Politically, they are a dependency of Ecuador. The United States has a naval base there.

The name means turtle islands, and was given because of the prevalence of large turtles described in 1858 by Darwin as capable of carrying several men on their backs. The flora and fauna are distinctive, about one-half of the species of plants being found nowhere else.

Georgetown. The capital and seaport of Guyana, situated near the center of the nation's coast line. The city lies at the mouth of the Demarara river, which can be entered, however, by boats of light draft only. The chief exports are sugar, rice, coconuts, bauxite, gold, and diamonds. The streets cross each other at right angles. Some are 100 feet wide and have, in the center canals leading to the roadways. Most of the better residences are surrounded by private groves of palms and other forest trees. Population, 167,000.

Guayaquil (*gwī'ä-kēl'*). The largest city and chief port of Ecuador, situated on the Guayas River about 30 miles from its mouth in the Gulf of Guayaquil. The principal export is cocoa. The climate is hot and unhealthful. Manufactures, including lumber, machine shop products, and artificial ice, are mainly for local consumption. Population, 814,000.

Juan Fernandez Islands. A group of islands belonging to Chile in the Pacific Ocean, lying 400 miles west of Valparaiso. Alexander Selkirk lived here in solitude for four years. This fact is said to have suggested to Defoe the theme of *Robinson Crusoe.*

La Paz (*lä päs'*). The largest city of Bolivia and the seat of Congress, situated in the west central part of the country about 40 miles southeast of Lake Titicaca. The city has an elevation of 12,470 feet and is flanked by ranges of the Andes mountains. It is connected with the sea by two railroads, terminating at ports in Chile. The streets are narrow and irregular. There are, however, fine public promenades, a university, and a museum containing a valuable collection of Inca antiquities. Population, 697,000.

Lima (*lē'mä*). The capital of Peru. It is situated in the west central part of the country on the Rimac River seven miles from Callao, its port, with which it is connected by two railroads, one on each side of the river. Lima is the western terminus of a transcontinental railroad which, at one point, is 15,000 feet above the sea. Earthquakes have destroyed large parts of the city a number of times.

There are several beautiful squares and promenades lined with trees and flowering plants and ornamented with statues and fountains. The University of San Marcos, founded here in 1551, is the oldest university in the western hemisphere. Of the numerous churches, the largest and finest one is the cathedral. It contains the tomb of Pizarro, the founder of the city. The manufactures include textiles, leather, furniture, cement, chemicals, and rubber, aluminum, tobacco, and petroleum products.

During the war between Chile and Peru, the Chileans held Lima from 1881 to 1883 and in that time destroyed the national library and many monuments, statues, and other works of art. This city was the home of Saint Rose of Lima, the first native inhabitant of the Americas to be canonized. Population, 3,318,000.

Manaus (*mä-nä'ŭs*). A city of Brazil on the Rio Negro, 12 miles above its junction with the Amazon and about 1000 miles from the Atlantic. Manaus is the trading metropolis of the upper Amazon valley, upon which it draws for such articles of export as rubber, brazil nuts, and dyewoods. Manaus became the capital of the city of Amazonas in 1852. Population, 312,000.

Montevideo (*mŏn'tē-vĭd'ē-ō*). The capital and chief city of Uruguay, situated on a chain of hills overlooking a harbor on the north side of the Rio de la Plata.

The principal streets are wide and straight, and the city bears, in general, a European appearance, having all the modern municipal improvements and many fine residences. The Cagancha Plaza and the Solis Theater are among its more notable features. An equable climate makes possible an extensive cultivation of roses.

The city is cosmopolitan and handles all the foreign trade of the country. The chief industries are those connected with stock raising—the drying and packing of meats, and creamery and tannery operations. Montevideo is the seat of a military college and of the University of Uruguay. The name is a corruption of *montem video*, "I see the mountain," said in allusion to the Cerro, a picturesque mountain on the opposite side of the city's harbor. Population, 1,230,000.

Paramaribo (*păr'ȧ-măr'ĭ-bō*). The capital of Surinam, situated at the head of navigation on the Surinam River 16 miles from its mouth in the Atlantic Ocean. The climate is very hot, the mean yearly temperature being over 80° F. The town has regularly laid out streets, shaded by tamarind and orange trees and bordered by well built houses. A commodious harbor lined with wharves enables the handling of international commerce, most of which is with the Netherlands, Great Britain, and the United States. The chief exports are rice, sugar, rum, coffee, bananas, and gold. Population, about 102,000.

Patagonia. A name formerly applied to the portion of South America stretching from the Strait of Magellan about 1200 miles north to the latitude of the Rio Negro. It was claimed both by Argentina and by Chile, and was divided between them in 1881 by a line of demarcation following the ridge of the Andes mountains. From that time the name has been restricted to southern Argentina, the part of the disputed territory sloping in terraces eastward from the mountains to the Atlantic Ocean.

Port of Spain. The capital of Trinidad and Tobago, situated in the northwest extremity of Trinidad. It has a fine harbor, and a large part of the products of the Orinoco basin are shipped from the port. The streets are wide and there are a number of fine residences and public buildings; also a university and a botanical garden. Population, 62,680.

Punta Arenas (*pōōn'tä ä-rā'näs*). The most southerly city in the world, a port in southern Chile on the Strait of Magellan. Surrounded by plains affording excellent grazing, it was the point where sheep-raising was first introduced into South America from the Falkland Islands and it is still an important center of sheep raising. It serves also as a fueling harbor for ships. Population, 67,600.

Quito (*kē'tō*). The capital of Ecuador, situated in a mountainous plateau somewhat north of the country's geographical center and about 114 miles from the Pacific Ocean. The city is less than ten miles south of the equator, but its climate is rendered equable by its elevation of 9000 feet. It is built at the foot of a volcano and is traversed by two deep ravines.

Quito was very difficult of access until the completion in 1903 of a railroad connecting the city with tidewater near Guayaquil. There is a university, an astronomical observatory, and a botanical garden which has the distinction of being the highest in the world. Quito was the central town of an ancient Indian nation until it was taken by the Incas in 1470. It was captured from the Incas by the Spaniards in 1534. Population, 557,000.

Recife (*rā-sē'fĕ*) (**Pernambuco**). A commercial city and port of Brazil situated on the Atlantic Coast at the extreme eastern point of the continent. The harbor is protected from the sea by a long reef and by a breakwater constructed at a cost of about 28 million dollars. Its distance from Lisbon is less than that between New York and Lisbon. The chief exports are sugar and cotton. The imports are mainly foodstuffs, textiles, and iron products.

The city consists of three parts, one built on a peninsula, one on an island, and a third, a pleasant residential section on the continent. Recife is therefore often called the Venice of South America. The climate is tropical.

The city has many fine churches and a celebrated law school. The name Recife means "reef." The first settlement on the site was made in 1535 by Pereira, a Portuguese adventurer. Population, 1,056,000.

Rio de Janeiro (*rē'ō dā zhā-nā'rō*). The second largest city of Brazil, situated on a natural harbor near the center of the country's southeastern coast. Spurs from nearby mountains penetrate into the heart of the city, which spreads into the valleys and up the hillsides. Sugarloaf peak rises abruptly above the city.

The interests of Rio de Janeiro are chiefly commercial. The leading export is coffee and the principal imports include cereals, coal, textiles, and machinery. Manufactures are confined mainly to textiles and flour.

Many of the streets in the older section of Rio de Janeiro are too narrow for wheeled vehicles. The newer portions, however, have wide, well paved avenues adorned with tall palm trees. Avenida Beira-Mar, a beautiful 20-mile boulevard, skirts the edge of the harbor. On the Avenida Presidente Wilson stands a colossal bronze figure representing Amicitia, "friendship," which was presented by the government of the United States. At the base of the pedestal are four statues representing Washington, Lincoln, Bonifacio, and Branco. On Corcovado Mountain, above the city, stands a statue of Christ, 130 feet in height.

There are several fine parks and squares. The Praça 15 de Novembro is surrounded by imposing buildings, among which are the Senate house and the city hall. In the neighborhood is the former Imperial Palace, occupied from 1808 to 1821 by the court of Portugal and now used as a national museum. Other institutions of education and research include the national library, the botanical garden, the historical and geographic institute, the observatory, and the University of Rio de Janeiro. The city was founded by Portuguese colonists in 1567 and from 1762 to 1960 it was the capital of Brazil. Population, 4,252,000.

Rosario (*rō-sä'rē-ō*). A commercial city of Argentina, situated on the left bank of the Parana River, about 230 miles above Buenos Aires. Rosario is the trade center for northern Argentina, being served by six railroads which connect at the city with ocean steamers. The chief exports are wheat and animal products, and the imports consist mainly of manufactured goods, mostly textiles. The city has modern improvements and attractive residential districts. Population, 807,000.

Santiago (*sän'tē-ä'gō*). The capital and largest city of Chile, situated near the center of the country about 50 miles from the Pacific Coast. The city lies at the northern edge of a rich agricultural district for which it is a distributing point and market.

Santiago's location is highly picturesque by reason of the surrounding mountains. A rock within the city, over 200 feet in height, once used as a citadel and a refuge from attacking Indians, is now a park, irrigated and supporting a luxuriant growth of vegetation. The city is traversed by a wide, ornate boulevard, the Avenida de las Delicias, which has a width of more than 300 feet.

Among the city's more impressive buildings are the exposition palace, the hall of Congress, the municipal theater, the cathedral, and the university building. At the head of the institutions of education and research stand the University of Chile and the agricultural school farm, an institution which embraces a zoological garden, a museum of natural history, and various schools for teaching different branches of rural industry. The city was founded in 1541 by Pedro de Valdivia. Population, 3,700,000.

Santos (*säɴ'tōōsh*). A large seaport of Brazil, situated on Santos Bay on the Atlantic Coast about 200 miles southwest of Rio de Janeiro. Santos is the world's largest coffee shipping port, being the outlet for the coffee collected at Sao Paulo. Population, 300,000.

Sao Paulo (*souɴm pou'lōō*). The capital of the state of Sao Paulo and largest city in Brazil, situated in the southeastern part of the state 25 miles inland from Santos, its port on the Atlantic Ocean. The city is the headquarters of the country's vast coffee industry. The coffee is transported from the plantations by a network of railroads leading to Sao Paulo, whence it is sent on by rail to Santos.

Among the more imposing buildings are the cathedral, the government building, and the Ypiranga palace, erected to commemorate Brazil's declaration of independence. The city has a modern appearance, having grown very rapidly in the decades following 1900, when numerous immigrants were attracted to it. Population, 5,900,000.

Sucre (*sōō'krā*). The statutory capital of Bolivia and the seat of the supreme court, picturesquely situated on a wide plateau about 150 miles south of the country's geographical center. The city is a trade center for a rich agricultural and mining region and has rail connection with La Paz, and with Mollendo and Antofagasta on the Pacific Coast. Sucre is the seat of an archbishop and has a normal school and an ancient university. Since 1898 Congress has met at La Paz. The city is 9328 feet above the level of the sea. Population, 88,000.

Trinidad and Tobago. Two islands constituting a member state of the British Commonwealth of Nations. Trinidad is about ten miles off the northeast coast of Venezuela near the delta of the Orinoco River, and the small island of Tobago is 22 miles northwest of Trinidad.

Trinidad has an area of 1864 square miles; that of Tobago is 116 square miles. The interior of Trinidad is a series of rolling, fertile, well watered plains, partly covered by forests of palms, breadfruits, tamarinds, and bamboo trees. Low mountain ranges parallel the north and the south coast. Tobago is a single mountain mass rising to a height of 1800 feet and covered with dense forest.

The most valuable products include petroleum, asphalt, sugar, cocoa, coconuts, and lumber. The asphalt comes mainly from a 114-acre reservoir known as Pitch Lake. The trade is principally with Great Britain and the United States.

Negroes and people of East Indian origin make up the majority of the population, which in 1973 was 1,061,000. Columbus discovered Trinidad in 1496 and Tobago in 1498. They passed from Spanish into British possession early in the 19th century, were colonies, later consolidated, and, in 1962, became an independent member of the British Commonwealth.

Valparaiso (*văl'pä-rī'sō*). The chief seaport of Chile, situated on a bay at the approximate center of Chile's coast line. The port is strongly fortified. The chief imports are textiles and other manufactured goods. The leading articles of export include agricultural products and Chile saltpeter. Its trade increased considerably as a result of the opening of the Panama Canal.

The city was one of the first in South America to introduce the use of street cars, of gas, and of aqueducts for the water supply. There are a number of wide streets and a fine square adorned with many statues. Population, 296,000.

EUROPE

The continent consisting of the northwestern portion of the vast land surface in the eastern hemisphere. Europe may be regarded as a western peninsula of Asia, from which it is divided, more or less arbitrarily, by the Ural mountains, the Caspian Sea, the Caucasus mountains, the Black Sea, the Bosporus strait, the Sea of Marmora, the Dardanelles strait, and the Ægean Sea. To the south of Europe lies the Mediterranean Sea, which separates the continent from Africa. This inland sea communicates with the Atlantic Ocean by the Strait of Gibraltar, where Europe's most southern point, Cape Tarifa, is no more than nine miles from Africa's northern extremity. The continent is bounded by the Atlantic Ocean on the west and by the Arctic Ocean on the north. The continental part of Europe, as distinct from the islands, is often referred to as "the continent" by people in the British Isles and in America.

Size. With the exception of Australia, Europe is the smallest of the continents, covering about 3,900,000 square miles, or very little more than the area of the United States and Alaska. It includes, with all its outlying islands, little more than 7 per cent of the total land surface of the globe. Its greatest length from east to west is 3300 miles, and its maximum extent north and south is about 2400 miles.

Outline and Islands. Europe has a contour diversified by so many irregularities, great and small, that the coast line, winding about all the indentations of the mainland and of the chief islands, has a length of nearly 48,000 miles. The islands and peninsulas, occupying about one-third of the total area of the continent, partially enclose a number of large gulfs and inland seas. Thus, while the small inlets provide numerous harbors, the inland seas make all parts of the continent comparatively easy of access from the sea.

In the extreme northeast, the islands of Nova Zembla separate the Kara Sea from Barents Sea, the latter being shut off from the Arctic Ocean by the islands of Spitsbergen. From the southwest corner of Barents Sea, a strait, called the Gorlo, leads into the White Sea, a three-pronged gulf sheltered behind the Kola peninsula. The Kola peninsula is, itself, part of the huge Scandinavian peninsula, which encloses the Baltic Sea and its three major inlets, the Gulf of Bothnia, the Gulf of Finland, and the Gulf of Riga. The Scandinavian peninsula trends in a general southwestern direction and terminates in two diverging extensions, which open like jaws above the peninsula of Jutland and are separated from it by two straits, the Kattegat and the Skagerrack. The Jutland peninsula and part of the Scandinavian peninsula form the eastern shore of the North Sea, which, stretching westward to the British Isles, has a southwestern outlet through the English channel to the Atlantic Ocean. The British Isles consist of two principal islands, Great Britain and Ireland, separated by the Irish Sea. Dunmore Head on the southwestern coast of Ireland is the most westerly point of Europe. The Bay of Biscay is the only large western inlet.

The southern coast has three major peninsulas—the Iberian peninsula, Italy, and the Balkan peninsula. Between the Iberian peninsula and Italy, in the Mediterranean Sea, lie the Balearic islands, and the three islands—Corsica, Sardinia, and Sicily—which, with Italy, enclose the Tyrrhenian Sea. The Gulf of Taranto stretches inland between the toe and the heel of the bootlike peninsula of Italy, and the whole peninsula is separated by the Adriatic Sea from the Balkan peninsula, which, on its eastern side, is washed by the Ægean Sea, the Black Sea, and the smaller bodies of water connecting the two. The Ægean Sea is dotted with small islands, most of which cluster in archipelagoes known as the Cyclades and the Sporades.

At a distance from the continent, about 700 miles northwest of the Scandinavian peninsula, lies the large mountainous island of Iceland.

Surface. The average elevation of Europe is less than that of any other continent. The highest point is Mount Elbrus, in the Caucasus range, the peak of which reaches a height of 18,481 feet. Marked changes in land level at the coast have been observed within historical times. The land about the Gulf of Bothnia has risen, and the southern shore of the North Sea has subsided. On the eastern side of the Adriatic Sea near modern Rovigno, the island town of Cissa, which was flourishing in the 7th century, is now 85 feet below the sea.

Apart from the Ural and the Caucasus range, there are two chief systems of mountains in Europe—the Kiolen range, forming a longitudinal ridge in the Scandinavian peninsula, and an irregular group of ranges trending in a general east and west direction across southern Europe. This latter group consists of the Pyrenees range, which cuts across the neck of the peninsula of Spain; the Alps, forming a central highland north of Italy; the Apennines, extending to the southern extremity of Italy and finding a continuation in the mountainous regions of Sicily; the Carpathian mountains, extending northeast of the Alps for some distance and then turning southeast toward the Black Sea; the Pindus range, which forms the backbone of Greece; and the Balkan mountains passing eastward north of the Ægean Sea. Other mountainous regions are Iceland, Scotland, and Spain.

Volcanic activity is confined to Iceland and to the Mediterranean region and is most marked in southern Italy, Sicily, and the adjacent islands. Here are situated Mount Stromboli, Mount Etna, and Mount Vesuvius, the last being notable for the eruption which, in 79 A. D., buried the cities of Herculaneum and Pompeii. No part of the continent, however, is free of earthquakes except the great plains of Russia.

A large part of Europe's area consists of fertile plains. Western and northern France, northern Germany, and almost the whole of European Russia constitute what is sometimes called the Great Lowland Plain. Other plains are the Central Plain, occupying Ireland and England; the Plain of Lombardy, south of the Alps; the Hungarian Plain, hemmed in by the Carpathian mountains and by the highland extending from the Alps southeastward into Greece; and the Wallachian Plain, between the southern Carpathians and the Black Sea.

Drainage. Of the many rivers of Europe, only one, the Volga, is more than 2000 miles in length, and, of the others, only the Danube, the Dnieper, and the Don exceed a length of 1000 miles. With few exceptions, however, the rivers admit of navigation and contribute toward making the interior of the continent readily accessible from the coasts.

The chief rivers draining northward, named in order from east to west, are the Pechora, the Dvina, the Duna, the Vistula, the Oder, the Elbe, the Rhine, and the Seine. The Loire and the Gironde River system flow westward into the Bay of Biscay. The plateau of Spain is drained toward the Atlantic Ocean by the Douro, the Tagus, the Guadiana, and the Guadalquivir and, toward the Mediterranean Sea, by the Jucar and the Ebro river. Of the rivers of southern drainage, the Rhone flows into the Golfe du Lion, an inlet of the Mediterranean Sea; the Po, into the Adriatic Sea; the Danube, the Dniester, and the Dnieper, into the Black Sea; the Don, into the Sea of Azof, a northern inlet of the Black Sea; and the Volga, into the Caspian Sea.

Fresh-water lakes are particularly numerous in three regions—the highlands of the Alps, the British Isles, and the territory east and northwest of the Baltic Sea. The last-mentioned region contains by far the most lakes, including the two largest of the continent—Ladoga and Onega.

Climate. Europe lies almost entirely in the temperate zone, a small portion only projecting into the arctic region. The northern part, however, has a warmer climate than other regions of the same latitude on account of warm ocean currents which wash its shores. The southern limit of drift ice from the polar regions nowhere approaches within 50 miles of the Scandinavian peninsula. The northern interior plains, however, suffer much greater extremes of temperature than those occurring near the coast. The southern part of Europe has a subtropical climate.

Europe is the only continent which has no desert region. Warm, moisture-laden winds blow prevailingly from the southwest. In the absence of a mountain wall running north and south, these winds carry their moisture far inland, instead of being intercepted and losing it by precipitation near the coast.

Plant and Animal Life. There are three chief plant regions in Europe—the arctic, possessing scanty vegetation; the intermediate, comprising forest areas,—largely coniferous,—and level steppes which resemble the North American plains; and, lastly, the Mediterranean region in the south. The last is noted for the great variety and economic importance of its flora.

Next to Asia, Europe has contributed to the human race more cultivated plants than any other continent. The more important include, among the grains, oats and rye; among the vegetables, asparagus, beet, cabbage, carrot, endive, horseradish, lettuce, pea, and turnip; the forage plants, clover and timothy; and such fruits as the currant, gooseberry, and fig.

The fauna likewise is rich. It has a general similarity to that of North America. The characteristic mammals include the bear, lynx, badger, wolf, fox, otter, marten, ermine, polecat, squirrel, hedgehog, and rabbit. The desman and chamois are peculiar to the continent. In the south, the fallow deer, ibex, alpine marmot, and civet are found. Of the domesticated animals, Europe is the original home of the goose, pigeon, rabbit, reindeer, and swan.

Minerals. The geology of Europe reveals an immense wealth of mineral resources. Coal and iron are produced in the greatest aggregate value. The chief coal fields are those in Great Britain, in Upper Silesia, in the Ruhr district in Germany, in northeastern France, and in Russia. The Lorraine district in France, the Saar valley in Germany, and northern and central England are the most important iron producing regions. Spain and Upper Silesia produce the world's chief supply of zinc, as Russia does of platinum. Spain and Italy supply a large part of the world's market for quicksilver. Gold and asbestos are obtained from the Ural Mountain region in large quantities. Other mineral products of the continent include salt, sulphur, silver, lead, aluminum tin, copper, and marble.

Industry. The industrial output of Europe exceeds that of any other continent. Industrial development, however, is concentrated largely in a few regions, chiefly those where coal and iron are found in close proximity. Among the principal industries are those making steel, fertilizers and other chemicals, glass, pottery, perfumes, and scientific instruments. There are also many highly specialized products exported, such as art objects, specially designed clothing, and time pieces.

Inhabitants. Human habitation in Europe is very ancient. In various districts, remains of prehistoric men have been found, the earliest going back probably 250,000 years to the second interglacial period. The population of Europe, now numbers over 500 million. With few exceptions, the languages of Europe belong to one family, called by philologists Indo-European. Peoples of Asia speaking related languages are believed to have migrated from Europe to Asia. Counter migrations from Asia brought some Oriental types into Europe, such as the Magyars and Huns.

POLITICAL DIVISIONS

Europe has more old established countries than any other continent. The countries are: Albania, Andorra, Austria, Belgium, Bulgaria, Denmark, Finland, France, Germany, Great Britain and Northern Ireland, Greece, Hungary, Iceland, Eire, Italy, Liechtenstein, Luxembourg, Monaco, the Netherlands, Norway, Poland, Portugal, Rumania, Russia, San Marino, Spain, Sweden, Switzerland, Vatican City, and Yugoslavia.

Of these divisions, Eire is a part of the island of Ireland, and its geography, along with that of Northern Ireland, is treated under the head of Ireland. Vatican City is 109 acres of papal territory within the city of Rome. Andorra is a mountainous, pastoral country between France and Spain; Luxembourg is surrounded by France, Germany, and Belgium; and Liechtenstein is a small principality hemmed in by Austria and Switzerland. These countries, as well as San Marino, an ancient state surrounded by Italian territory in the northeastern part of the peninsula, will be found described from a geographical point of view in the departments of history and government.

In addition to the independent states, there is a territory north of the Sea of Marmora forming part of Turkey. Gibraltar, a bold promontory at the south of the Iberian peninsula is a dependency of Great Britain.

Albania. A mountainous republic on the west of the Balkan peninsula with a coast line on the Adriatic Sea. It has an area of 10,629 square miles and a population, 1974 estimate, of 2,400,000. The people support themselves mainly through agriculture devoted chiefly to livestock. There are vast tracts of undeveloped forests and considerable unexploited mineral wealth, consisting largely of copper, salt, coal, and oil.

Tirana is the capital and largest city. Durrës, the chief port is equipped with modern facilities.

Austria. An inland republic of central Europe, bounded on the north by Germany and Czechoslovakia and on the remaining sides by Hungary, Yugoslavia, Italy, and Switzerland. The western part, known as the Tyrol, is a mountainous region, widely celebrated for its bold, picturesque scenery. In the north, Austria is traversed by the Danube River, which provides a navigable waterway several hundred miles in length.

On an area of 32,366 square miles, Austria supports a population numbering, in 1971, 7,456,403. Agricultural products comprise chiefly wheat, rye, barley, oats, potatoes, and sugar beets. Dairying is a thriving industry. Austria is one of the world's chief sources of graphite. Petroleum also is produced. Manufactures include lumber, textiles, glass, sugar, paper, furniture, pianos, and chemicals. Most of the industry is nationalized. Tourism is a leading source of income. German is the language of Austria.

Most of the inhabitants are Roman Catholic. There is a system of compulsory elementary education. The largest of the three state universities is situated in the capital, Vienna, a city which has for centuries been a center of learning and of art.

Belgium. A small kingdom of Europe with a coast line on the North Sea. The country is bounded by France, Luxembourg, Germany, and the Netherlands. Its area is 11,750 square miles, its latest population figure 9,651,000.

Nearly all of the surface of Belgium is arable and is intensively cultivated. The country is also industrially one of the most highly developed in the world, being favored in this respect by the occurrence of coal and of iron deposits in close proximity to each other. The recovery of Belgium since its liberation in 1944 is extraordinary. Increases in the output of grains, potatoes, beet sugar, milk, meat, coal, chemicals, machinery, glass, paper, beer, textiles, and zinc are outstanding. Diamond cutting is an important industry.

Two languages are spoken in Belgium—French in the south by the Walloons, a people of Celtic origin, and Flemish in the north by the Flemings, who are of the Teutonic race. The majority of the inhabitants professing a religion are Roman Catholics. Of the country's four universities, Louvain is the most celebrated. The capital and largest city is Brussels. Other cities of note are Antwerp, Ghent, Liège, and Ostend.

Bulgaria. A mountainous republic of southeastern Europe, with an eastern coast line on the Black Sea. Bulgaria lies between Rumania on the north and Greece on the south and stretches westward to the borders of Yugoslavia. Its area is 43,000 square miles.

The Balkan mountains divide southern Bulgaria from the northern zone, in which a cool climate and a fertile soil foster agriculture of a temperate zone type. The perfume attar of roses is a distinctively Bulgarian product. Apart from it the chief products are grains, tobacco, livestock, cotton, hemp, flax, silk, beans, sugar beets, fruits, rice, and various flowers. The manufacturing of textiles is the chief industry. The Danube River, which constitutes the northern border of Bulgaria, provides, with its affluents, important water highways for trade.

Agriculture of various kinds engages the activities of about one-fifth of Bulgaria's population, which the latest census listed as 8,706,000. The prevailing religion is Greek Catholicism. Elementary instruction is free and obligatory. Sofia is the capital and largest city of the country.

Czechoslovakia (*chĕk'ō-slō-vä'kĭ-à*). An inland republic of central Europe, closely allied with the Soviet Union. The country is narrow and elongated, lying in a general east and west direction. It is bordered by Poland, Germany, Austria, Hungary, and Russia. The area, 49,359 square miles, is about the size of the state of New York. The population, in 1974, was estimated to be 14,738,377. Approximately three-fourths of the people are Czechs and Slovaks.

About one-third of its area is covered with valuable forests and by 1946 the pulp and paper industry had reached 80 per cent of prewar output. The soil is fertile and supports extensive and intensive agriculture; the chief crops are potatoes, sugar beets, wheat, barley, rye, oats, hops, tobacco, and various fruits and vegetables. The coal deposits are extensive and provide a surplus for export. Gold, silver, copper, lead, and rock salt are also found. The textile, porcelain, glass, furniture, sugar, chemical, and metal factories place Czechoslovakia among the more important manufacturing countries of Europe. By decrees of October 1945 all national resources, public utilities, and other important branches of industry and trade were nationalized. Transportation is provided by the Elbe and Danube rivers, and by more than 13,241 km. of railway and about 73,538 km. of highway.

Approximately seventy-five per cent of the inhabitants are Roman Catholics in spite of the fact that the provinces of Bohemia and Moravia constituted one of the earliest centers of Protestantism. The Moravian Church in America was founded by emigrants from this region. In 1975, universities had a total attendance of 144,325. The capital and largest city is Prague, with a population in 1975 of 1,161,000.

Denmark. A small kingdom of northern Europe, consisting of the greater part of the Jutland peninsula and of several adjacent islands, the largest of which are Zealand and Funen. The Faroe Islands, lying nearly midway between Scotland and Iceland, are administratively a part of Denmark. The total area of the country is 16,619 square miles. Greenland is an integral part of Denmark.

The surface of continental Denmark is a low rolling plain nowhere exceeding 570 feet in altitude. Sand dunes fringe much of the coast line, often extending five or six miles inland. Considerable areas of peat bog provide fuel for the inhabitants. Forests, mainly of beech trees, cover about 750 square miles. Apart from lumbering, the principal industries are agriculture, dairying, and fishing. The value of the annual catch of fish is considerable. The farm produce is marketed largely by co-operative societies. Copenhagen porcelain is a distinctive product of the country's manufacturing industry.

The population of Denmark is 5,054,410, most of whom are Lutheran Protestants in religion. Illiteracy is virtually nonexistent, elementary education having been obligatory since 1814. The University of Copenhagen stands at the head of the educational system, which is of the most enlightened type and is well adapted to the interests of the people. The capital, Copenhagen, is situated on the island of Zealand. With a population of 1,380,204, it contains nearly one-fifth of the inhabitants of the country.

A territory known as Northern Schleswig was added to Denmark in 1920 as a result of the Treaty of Versailles. This territory had been wrested from the Danes by Germany in 1864.

Finland. One of the most northern countries of Europe, lying between the Gulf of Finland and the Gulf of Bothnia and extending northward almost entirely across the neck of the Scandinavian peninsula. The Aland islands off the southern coast are governed as part of Finland. About one-fourth of the country's 130,127 square miles of surface is within the Arctic circle. In the north, mountains rise to a height of 4000 feet, but the remainder of the country is, for the most part, a plateau having an average elevation of about 500 feet. The numerous lakes of glacial formation, which occupy 11 per cent of the area of the country, have won for Finland the name of "the land of the thousand lakes."

Although agriculture employs more workers, forest products, chiefly timber, pulp, and paper, account for a large part of the country's export trade. Nearly two-thirds of the country is covered with pine forests.

The population of Finland in 1974 was 4,691,556. Lutheran Protestantism is the prevailing religion. The country has a well developed system of elementary, secondary, technical, and higher education. The capital and largest city is Helsingfors (Helsinki), a city of 502,383 inhabitants, situated in the southern extremity of the country. Other important towns are Turku (Abo) and Tampere (Tammerfors).

The inhabitants of Finland are mostly of the Finnic race, which is believed to have occupied formerly the whole of northern Asia and northeastern Europe.

France. A republic of western Europe, bounded on the north by the English channel and on the west by the Bay of Biscay. On the south, France is separated from Spain by the Pyrenees mountains and has a southern coast line on the Mediterranean Sea. On the east and northeast, France adjoins Italy, Switzerland, Germany, Luxembourg, and

Belgium. The island of Corsica in the Mediterranean Sea is politically a part of France. The coast line of the country is nearly 2000 miles in length, but, being either sandy or high and rocky, it affords few good harbors. The total area of the republic is 212,919 square miles.

Since World War II France has been successful in securing certain boundary changes. On the Italian border they acquired the pass and enclave of Tenda and Briga in 1947. France also secured minor border rectifications in the areas of Little St. Bernard Pass, Mt. Cenis Pass, and Mt. Thabor and Chaberton. Other eastern continental boundaries reflect the great zone of transition between western and central Europe. After both wars of this century the French were eager to have the Saar with its coal mines under their political, or at least economic, control. In the Rhineland the French have wanted to see an independent unit separate from Germany, and in the industrial Ruhr they have favored international control.

The most elevated part of France is in the southeast, where the Jura mountains and the Alps divide the country from Switzerland and Italy. Mont Blanc, an Alpine mountain within the French border, is the second highest peak in Europe, having an altitude of 15,781 feet. The lower, forest-clad Vosges ridge farther north separates Alsace from the rest of France. These mountain groups form the eastern side of the Rhone-Saone River valley, which is flanked on the west by the Cevennes mountains. The Rhone, rising in Switzerland and being augmented by the Saone river, flows southward into the Mediterranean Sea. The Saone River is connected by a canal with the upper reaches of the Seine river, which, with its tributaries,—the Marne and the Oise,—drains northward into the English channel. The other chief rivers of France flow westward and empty into the Bay of Biscay. They are the Loire, to the north, and, farther south, the Garonne and the Dordogne, which mingle their waters in the broad estuary called the Gironde River.

The principal rivers are all more or less navigable and afford shelter for such seaports as Havre and Rouen on the Seine, Saint Nazaire and Nantes on the Loire, and Bordeaux on the Garonne. The rivers as highways of inland commerce are supplemented by numerous canals.

France has considerable deposits of coal centering around Valenciennes near the northeastern border. The mines of this region were wrecked by the Germans during World War I, and from 1920 to 1935 the French operated the German coal mines in the Saar basin. France controls more iron than does any other European country, the mines being located in Lorraine, from which about one-tenth of the world's supply of iron ore is obtained. Other minerals produced in important quantities include gold, antimony, salt, potash, manganese, and bauxite, the ore of aluminum.

Of the surface of France, about one-fifth is forested, and approximately three-quarters is devoted to agriculture and grazing. Wheat, oats, potatoes, rye, barley, corn, and sugar beets are the leading crops. In the south, the climate is subtropical and fosters the cultivation of olives, peaches, apricots, oranges, mandarins, lemons, walnuts, and almonds. Apples, pears, cherries, plums, and berries are also produced in important quantities. The abundance of grapes grown in France enables her to rank as the leading wine producing country of the world. The cultivation of silkworms is an important industry in the south.

The fisheries of France are among the more important in the world. Large fleets are sent each year to catch cod about Newfoundland and about Saint Pierre and Miquelon, which lie off the south shore of Newfoundland. These two small islands constitute the sole remaining part of France's former empire in North America. Sardines are caught on France's northwestern coast and anchovies and tunny fish are obtained from the Mediterranean Sea.

The textile industries of France are famous the world over. The city of Lyon is the greatest silk center in Europe. Rayon also is manufactured there in large quantities. Rouen, on the Seine River, is noted for its cotton cloth made mainly from cotton grown in the United States. A large wool industry flourishes in the northeast. Paris is the seat of manufacture for the most costly products, including tapestries, shawls, jewelry, watches, and scientific instruments. Other manufactured products include chemicals, iron and steel, automobiles, electrical equipment, fine leather goods, the exquisite porcelains of Sèvres and of Limoges, cut glass, pottery, perfumes, and similar articles requiring skill and taste for their production.

After World War II, the French government stimulated agricultural and industrial production by means of agricultural price supports and tax incentives for industry. Chemical, fertilizer, tractor, shipbuilding, electricity, and automobile industries were greatly expanded. New industries included oil refining and atomic energy. Social welfare measures included old-age pensions, unemployment and medical benefits, and family allowances.

The population of France in 1968 was 49,795,000. The great majority of those professing a religion are Roman Catholics. Illiteracy is almost unknown. At the head of the educational system stand 23 universities, of which the University of Paris is the most notable. Apart from Paris, the capital, the great emporiums of trade include Lyon, Lille, Saint Etienne, Toulouse, Strasbourg, and Reims. The more attractive maritime ports are Marseille, Bordeaux, Le Havre, and Cette.

City	Population	City	Population
Paris	2,590,771	Le Havre	199,509
Marseille	889,029	Lille	190,546
Lyon	527,800	Rennes	180,943
Toulouse	370,796	Toulon	174,746
Nice	322,442	Montpellier	161,910
Bordeaux	266,662	Grenoble	161,616
Nantes	259 208	Brest	154,023
Strasbourg	249,396	Reims	152,967
St. Etienne	213,468	Clermont-Ferrand	148,896

Source: UN *Demographic Yearbook*, 1968.

French Community. Until the beginning of World War II France controlled a colonial empire second only to that of Great Britain. The combined area of French dependencies was more than twenty-one times that of European France. In geographical range, the colonies, mandates, or protectorates administered by France extended from neighboring North Africa to America, to Southeast Asia, to Oceania, and to huge sections south of the Sahara desert, some of them in West Africa along the Atlantic coast, and some in the interior, particularly in Equatorial Africa. Added to these was the large island of Madagascar in the Indian Ocean.

From the war France emerged weakened but determined to retain her empire. However, the tide of the future was against her until she learned from two costly wars how to ride it. The wave of the future was the spirit of racial equality which inspired the peoples of Africa and Asia to throw off colonial status and to seek by their own efforts to obtain the higher standards of living which modern science had made possible.

France initially surrendered control of Morocco and Tunisia, but held tenaciously to Algeria, where a century of colonization and settlement had resulted in a French population of over ten per cent of the total. Algeria was regarded as administratively a part of France. Independence was refused, and for many years the resistance of the rebels tied down a large portion of the French army. When it became apparent to the French government that it could not win the war, negotiations began looking to Algerian independence. Immediately the French settlers and many of the leaders of the Army opposed the French policy, and civil war was averted only by turning control of the government over to Charles de Gaulle and granting him almost dictatorial power for a limited period.

Meanwhile a similar struggle had gone on in French Indo-China, where the forces seeking independence were assisted by the Chinese Communists. The French were defeated and withdrew before the crisis in Algeria had come to a head.

De Gaulle, having subdued the army insurrection, proposed to France and to all French dependencies a new political formula modeled after the British Commonwealth of Nations. As part of the new constitution adopted by popular vote in 1958 by France and most French territories overseas, each of the latter might choose either to retain its status, to become a department of France, or to be an independent member of the French Community.

Most of the territories elected membership in the Community. Guinea alone rejected the constitution and was cut off from France. Algeria was given complete independence in 1962. Much of the French population in Algeria returned to France to live.

The French Community is organized as follows:

Member States—France (including Corsica), Central African Republic, Congo, Gabon, Malagasy, Senegal, Chad.

Overseas Departments—Martinique, Guadeloupe, Reunion, French Guiana, Saint-Pierre and Miquelon.

Overseas French Territories—French Polynesia, New Caledonia, the Territory of Afars and Issas, Comoro Islands, Southern and Antarctic Territories, Wallis and Futuna Islands.

Independent Countries with Special Agreements—Algeria, Benin, Cameroun, Ivory Coast, Mali, Mauritania, Niger, Togo, Upper Volta.

Germany. A historic and heavily populated commercial and agricultural area in north central Europe. Following the surrender of Nazi Germany in 1945, the country was divided into four zones. The United States occupied the southwest, Great Britain the northwest, France the west, and Russia the east. When the four Allied Powers of World War II were unable to reach a postwar agreement as to the future administration of Germany, the country became permanently split. The three zones occupied by the United States, Britain, and France became the Federal Republic of Germany (West Germany) on May 23, 1949. The Soviet-occupied zone became the German Democratic Republic (East Germany) on October 4, 1949. Former German territories east of the Oder and Reisser rivers—Silesia, East Prussia, and most of Pomerania—were given to Poland by the U.S.S.R. at the close of World War II.

East Germany. The German Democratic Republic covers 41,648 square miles and had a 1973 estimated population of 17,562,068. The country is bordered by the Baltic Sea on the north, on the east by Poland, on the southeast by Czechoslovakia, and on the southwest and west by the Federal Republic of Germany. The northern part of the land is characterized by lakes and low hills. Most of the country's farming is done on the fertile plain of the central region. The heavily forested middle range mountains in the southern area are one of the most scenic parts of Germany. There are five major rivers in East Germany. They are the Elbe, Oder, Saale, Havel, and Spree.

East Germany is largely dependent on industry although there are few natural resources and a great deal of raw material must be imported. The chief industries are iron and steel products, chemicals, fertilizers, synthetic rubber, drugs, and plastics. The East Germans are large food producers and rank in the top ten nations of the world in the production of rye, barley, and oats. Other major crops include potatoes, sugar beets, and wheat. The major trading partners of East Germany are the U.S.S.R. and Czechoslovakia.

The capital city of the German Democratic Republic is East Berlin, with a 1973 population of 1,088,828. Other major cities with their 1973 populations are: Leipzig (574,432), Dresden (506,067), Karl-Marx-Stadt (302,409), and Magdeburg (274,146).

West Germany. The Federal Republic of Germany is bordered by the North Sea and Denmark on the north, East Germany and Czechoslovakia on the east, Austria and Switzerland on the south, and by France, Luxembourg, Belgium, and the Netherlands on the west.

The country covers an area of 95,959 square miles; its estimated 1974 population was 61,991,500. The land is generally flat in the north and hilly in the central and western regions. The Bavarian Alps and the Black Forest make the southern part of the country a major tourist attraction. The principal rivers of West Germany are the Rhine, Danube, Ems, Weser, and the Elbe.

West Germany is one of the most highly industrialized countries in the world. It is rich in natural resources—including coal, iron ore, lead, and zinc. The chief industries are manufacture of iron and steel products, chemicals, electricity, machinery, and aluminum products. Advanced farming techniques have made West Germany a leader in food production and its farms produce a high yield of rye, wheat, oats, barley, and potatoes. West Germany also has major forestry and fishing industries. Its main trading partners are France, Belgium, the Netherlands, and the United States.

The historic capital and largest city of Germany is Berlin. Bonn is the seat of the West German government. The leading cities in West Germany, with their estimated 1974 populations are as follows:

City	Population	City	Population
Berlin (West)	2,023,987	Stuttgart	613,263
Hamburg	1,733,802	Duisburg	599,799
Munich	1,323,434	Bremen	579,430
Cologne	1,022,075	Hanover	562,951
Essen	684,147	Nuremberg	509,813
Dusseldorf	675,437	Bochum	417,336
Frankfort	652,037	Wuppertal	412,403
Dortmund	636,954	Gelsenkirchen	327,591

Gibraltar (*jĭ-brôl′tẽr*). A rocky promontory near the southern point of the Iberian peninsula and commanding the western entrance to the Mediterranean Sea. It is a possession of Great Britain. It covers about two square miles and consists mainly of a fortified rock, 1439 feet high, at the foot of which is the town of Gibraltar with a population in 1967 of 25,281. The fortress was obtained by Great Britain from Spain in 1713. From 1779 to 1783, it withstood a siege of 3 years, 7 months, and 12 days at the hands of a Spanish fleet.

Great Britain. An island kingdom lying north and slightly west of France and separated from it by the English channel, which narrows from a maximum width of 150 miles near the west end to a neck in the east, 21 miles wide, called the Strait of Dover. Geographically, the term Great Britain has reference to the one large island divided, for historical reasons, into England and Wales in the south and Scotland in the north. As a political division, however, Great Britain, officially known as the Kingdom of Great Britain and Northern Ireland, includes also Northern Ireland, the Orkney islands, the Shetland islands, and the Hebrides,—three groups lying north of Scotland,—the Scilly islands and the Isle of Wight in the south, and nearly 800 smaller islands. The Isle of Man in the Irish Sea and the Channel islands,—Guernsey, Jersey, and their dependency, Sark island,—are not subject to British legislation unless specifically designated in particular enactments. The area and the population of Great Britain and of its principal divisions are given in the table of *The British Commonwealth*.

The island of Great Britain is about 700 miles long from north to south, and its width varies from 280 miles in the extreme south to 30 miles in northern Scotland, where Dornoch Firth and Loch Broom penetrate deeply into the land from opposite sides of the island. The coast line is well in excess of 4000 miles, being deeply indented by the estuaries of tidal rivers and, especially in northern and western Scotland, by deep, rocky fiords. The chief of these inlets on the eastern side, named from south to north, are the estuary of the Thames, the Wash, the Humber River estuary, the Firth of Forth, the Firth of Tay, Moray firth, and Dornoch firth. On the western side, the principal inlets are Bristol channel, Cardigan bay, the Dee River and the Mersey River estuary, Morecambe bay, Solway firth, the Firth of Clyde, and the Firth of Lorne with its continuation known as Loch Linnhe.

The seas surrounding Great Britain are shallow, rarely exceeding 300 feet in depth. This circumstance has the effect of protecting the island from the cold arctic currents, so that the country enjoys a climate much milder than that in corresponding latitudes of America. The shallow waters provide a feeding ground for fish, thereby supporting fisheries of great value.

Great Britain has been the most active colonizing nation in Europe. As islanders, the British turned readily to seafaring and were among the first to explore the Americas, Australia, the Orient, Africa, and other regions. The settlers succeeded in carrying their institutions to many distant parts of the world and thus laid the foundation for the present British Commonwealth of Nations and the system of dependencies which are found in every continent. The English language and English basic institutions were transplanted to North America, Australia, and New Zealand. Through the rapid growth of these settlements, in population and power, and particularly of the United States, the influence of the English heritage is widely spread throughout the world.

The worldwide demand of underdeveloped countries throughout the world for political independence had a sharper impact on Great Britain than on any other country for the reason that her commitments among them were the greatest. Drawing on prior experience and modifying old formulas of association, she succeeded in transforming her empire into a commonwealth with a minimum of conflict and political unsettlement. Nearly all such territories after attaining independence requested Great Britain to sponsor their admittance to the British Commonwealth of Nations, and the body consisting of the heads of member states acted favorably on their application.

England. A division of Great Britain comprising most of the southern part of the island and divided from Scotland on the north by a low ridge, called the Cheviot hills. The maximum length of England is 425 miles, and the width varies from 280 miles to 62 miles. The surface is, in general, a rolling plain, rising in the north to the low mountains in Derbyshire, Yorkshire, Westmoreland, and Cumberland. In the northwest is the "lake district," where occur the largest lake and the highest mountain in England—Lake Windermere, 10½ miles long, and Sca Fell, 3210 feet high. The chief rivers flowing into the North Sea on the east are the Thames, the Humber, the Tees, and the Tyne. Those flowing west include the Severn, Dee, and Mersey.

England is one of the leading exporting countries in the world. The richest coal fields are located in the region of Newcastle in northeastern England and in an area 100 to 150 miles farther south, where the proximity of large iron deposits has resulted in the growth of such huge manufacturing cities as Sheffield and Birmingham. In production of iron, England ranks among the world's leading producers. Her manufactures, however, require the importation of additional ore, which comes mainly from Spain and Sweden. The southwestern extremity of England has been the chief European source of tin since the days of the Phœnicians. Lead, silver, and zinc are mined in the northeast.

About 5 per cent of England is covered with forests, of which certain tracts, such as Epping forest near London, were formerly set aside as royal deer forests. Epping forest is now open to the public as a park. The greater part of the country's surface is fertile, and, being tilled according to the most advanced methods, it is highly productive. The live stock of England and of Great Britain generally is of a superior quality. No country has produced more standard breeds of domestic animals.

England was the first country in the world to become industrialized and still remains one of the greatest manufacturing nations. In the making of cutlery and other steel products and of cotton, woolen, and linen textiles, England is excelled by no other country. The shipbuilding industry of Great Britain, favored by the numerous harbors of the island, is likewise unsurpassed. British ships do a large part of the carrying trade of the world. The foreign trade of the country exceeds that of any other country of the world. The total length of canals is about 2,500 miles, and of railways, nearly 20,000 miles.

World War II and the political and economic developments which followed had the effect of weakening England's relative position in the world. But the people accepted years of austerity to safeguard the country's position in commerce and trade, many of the most attractive manufactured products being kept from the home market and reserved for export.

At the same time, welfare measures such as old-age pensions, unemployment compensation, and family allowances were enlarged by a system of health insurance. The educational system was modified to make advanced training more available to persons of all classes of society.

The population of England is about 95 per cent Protestant, the majority belonging to the Anglican, or Protestant Episcopal, Church, which is the "established church" of the country. No civil disabilities, however, attach to any British subject on account of religion. The outstanding universities of England are Oxford, Cambridge, and the University of London. Illiteracy is almost unknown. By an act passed in 1918, part time attendance at free continuation schools is required of all people up to 16 years of age, and, when the necessary facilities are provided, the age limit is extended to 18 years.

London, the capital of Great Britain, is one of the largest cities in the world. The chief cities with estimated populations are as follows:

City	Population	City	Population
London	7,880,760	Wolverhampton	266,890
Birmingham	1,101,990	Enfield	266,640
Liverpool	705,310	Westminster	258,930
Manchester	616,520	Newham	257,350
Sheffield	534,100	Islington	254,580
Bristol	518,640	Haringey	254,120
Leeds	507,780	Newcastle upon Trent	251,650
Lambeth	338,130	Havering	251,160
Coventry	333,830	Hackney	249,140
Wandsworth	330,470	Plymouth	247,400
Croydon	328,290	Redbridge	245,300
Barnet	315,210	Camden	238,020
Nottingham	309,740	Waltham Forest	237,910
Bromley	302,660	Hillingdon	234,470
Ealing	302,570	Greenwich	231,150
Southwark	300,720	Sunderland	219,270
Bradford	296,860	Portsmouth	219,110
Kingston upon Hull	295,900	Bexley	215,330
Brent	293,370	Kensington & Chelsea	213,310
Lewisham	289,700	Hammersmith	211,720
Cardiff	289,320	Southampton	209,790
Leicester	282,800	Harrow	208,200
Stoke on Trent	275,703	Hounslow	206,870

Wales. The roughly rectangular land projection west of England, which lies between the Irish Sea on the north and Bristol channel on the south. Its surface is more mountainous than that of England, the highest peak being Mount Snowdon, 3560 feet in altitude. Wales contains some of the most valuable coal beds in Great Britain, and its largest city, Cardiff, exports more coal than any other city of the world. The inhabitants are of Celtic origin rather than Germanic, and about 40 per cent of them can still speak the native Welsh language. In religion, most of the Welsh are nonconformists, principally Methodists and Presbyterians.

Scotland. The portion of Great Britain north of the Cheviot hills. It is, in general, a more mountainous country than England. The chief rivers flowing to the east are the Tweed, the Forth, and the Tay. The Clyde is the only important river draining westward. Scotland has many beautiful lakes, of which Loch Lomond, 24 miles long, is the largest. The country is divisible, by the nature of its surface, into the highlands of the north, the central lowlands, and the southern uplands.

The highlands of Scotland occupy nearly half the country. They are remarkable for their mountainous masses, which are especially rugged along the western coast. The region is cut into two parts by the Great Glen of Scotland, a depression in which lie the elongated lakes, Loch Ness and Loch Lochy. These have been connected and made part of the Caledonian canal, which provides a waterway from Moray firth in the east to the Firth of Lorne in the west. Southwest of the Great Glen are the Grampian hills, which culminate in Ben Nevis near the center of the western coast. This mountain, having an altitude of 4406 feet, is the highest peak in Great Britain.

The southern uplands constitute a region of low mountains, none exceeding 3000 feet in height. Between them and the highlands of the north lies a fertile plain, which supports a dense population and flourishing industries.

The minerals of Scotland include coal, iron, and oil shale. Of the last named, Scotland has about 80 per cent of the amount in the world known to be available. Agriculture in Scotland is often handicapped by an excessive rainfall. Of the chief crops,—oats, barley, turnips, and potatoes,—oats are grown in the most important quantities. The southern uplands are excellently adapted to grazing, and sheep are raised in large numbers. Cheviot sheep and the Ayrshire, Galloway, Polled Angus, and Jersey cattle were first bred in Scotland, while the Shetland breed of ponies originated in the Shetland islands lying to the northeast.

The industries of Scotland are similar to those of England, consisting chiefly of textiles steel products, and shipbuilding. At Glasgow on the Clyde are located the world's largest shipbuilding yards. Most of the Cunard liners have been built in these yards. The country is noted also for its production of whisky and of preserved fruits.

Scotland is the original home of Presbyterianism, the form of Protestantism professed by the established church of Scotland. The Roman Catholic Church is relatively stronger than in England. There are four universities in the country—Edinburgh, Glasgow, Aberdeen, and Saint Andrews. Scotland enjoys the same system of continuation schools as that described under *England.* The county authorities are empowered to provide educational books for the use of the adult population. The Gaelic language is still spoken in parts of Scotland.

Three-quarters of Scotland's 5,188,000 inhabitants live in towns or cities. The largest urban center is Glasgow, population 960,527. Edinburgh, population 467,986, is the seat of the supreme court, Scotland having courts and a system of law differing from those of England and based on French models

Greece. A maritime country occupying the southern part of the Balkan peninsula and including about 500 near-by islands, of which Crete is the largest. The shores of the mainland are bold, rocky, and deeply indented. The Gulf of Ægina, stretching inland from the east, is connected by a canal with the Gulf of Corinth, which is an inland continuation of the Gulf of Patras on the west coast. The resulting peninsula, called the Peloponnese in ancient times, is now known as Peloponnisos. The total area of the country is about 51,180 square miles.

About four-fifths of the surface of the mainland is crumpled by a complex system of mountains, which divide the surface into a number of small plains. The chief range, running north and south, is called the Pindus. The highest peak is Mount Olympus, in northern Greece, which has an altitude of 9570 feet. Mount Parnassus, celebrated in literature as the home of the Muses, is 8062 feet high. It is situated just north of the Gulf of Corinth and is sometimes known as Mt. Liakura. The progressive deforestation which has taken place in Greece is believed to have made the country drier than it formerly was. The climate is otherwise marked by intensity of heat in the summers and occasionally by severe cold in the winters.

The small plains of Greece provide the major part of the arable land. Agriculture, though practicable on only one-third of the country's surface, is the leading industry of the country. By the draining of Lake Copais in central Greece, about 53,000 acres were reclaimed in 1894. The chief crops are olives, wheat, grapes, corn, currants, figs, tobacco, oranges, lemons, barley, and oats. Currants constitute a distinctive product. The English word currant is a corruption of Corinth, the name of a Greek city from which the fruit is exported. Other industries are the raising of sheep and of goats. Lignite, magnesite, iron, salt, lead, emery, and zinc are mined. Slag from the silver mines at Laurium is being worked over for lead that the ancient Athenians failed to extract.

The Greeks are a commercial people. Along with the manufacture of textiles, leather, and soap, shipbuilding ranks high among the industries. The Greek trader has for more than 2500 years been found everywhere throughout the Levant, as the countries washed by the eastern Mediterranean Sea are sometimes called. Seventy-five per cent of the Greek ocean-going ships were lost during World War II, the coastal fleet was ruined, and Greek ports were severely damaged. Railways and highways suffered similar losses.

Most of Greece's 8,803,000 (1968 est.) inhabitants profess the Greek Catholic faith. The spoken language, known as Romaic, is related to ancient Greek much as Italian is related to Latin; the literary language, however, is much closer to classical Greek. Athens is the capital and largest city of Greece, with a population of 1,852,709. Other notable cities are Salonika, Piræus, which is the port of Athens, and Patrai. Elementary education is nominally obligatory, but the percentage of illiteracy is high. There are government commercial schools and two universities at Athens, where also schools of archeology are maintained by American, British, French, Italian, and German learned societies. The Greek ministry of education is charged with the duty of conserving, repairing, and excavating ancient monuments.

The most notable architectural monuments of Greece date back more than 2000 years. Many of the finest buildings have been seriously mutilated, but some remain almost complete and still retain the dignity of their former state. Apart from Athens, the places containing the more interesting ruins are Olympia, Delphi, and Mycenæ.

Hungary. An inland agricultural republic in the eastern part of central Europe, bounded by Austria, Czechoslovakia, Russia, Rumania, and Yugoslavia. Hungary was defeated in both world wars and as a result, her territory has been reduced from over 60,000 square miles to 35,912, and her population has declined from more than 13,000,000 to 10,510,000.

The chief crops raised in Hungary are corn, wheat, sugar beets, barley, rye, oats, grapes, and tobacco. Most of the industries are those based on agriculture, such as flour milling and sugar refining. There are also iron and steel works. Hard and soft coal and bauxite are mined. Forests cover about 6 per cent of the surface. Important quantities of fish are obtained from Lake Balaton, the largest lake in central Europe, and from the rivers.

The majority of the people are Roman Catholics. There is a well developed educational system with compulsory attendance between the ages of 6 and 14. There are many fine universities and colleges. Budapest is the capital and largest city.

Iceland. An island state situated in the north Atlantic Ocean about 500 miles northwest of Scotland and 150 miles southeast of Greenland. The Arctic circle touches the most northern point of the island. The cold is not extreme, however, being moderated by the proximity of the ocean.

Almost the whole of Iceland's 39,758 square miles of surface is of volcanic origin, magnificent as scenery but unproductive. The ice-strewn plateaus, of which the island consists, average more than 2000 feet in altitude. The most celebrated of the island's 100 volcanoes is the Hekla, 4707 feet in height. The Great Geyser is 60 feet in diameter and, at intervals of several hours, projects immense quantities of hot water about 150 feet into the air. Boiling water from geysers is piped to the capital to heat buildings. About one-eighth of the island is covered by glaciers.

Nearly all the inhabitants of Iceland are dependent for their living on agriculture, stock raising, or fishing. Less than 1 per cent of the island is cultivated. The chief crops are hay, potatoes, and turnips. The exports consist almost entirely of live stock, mainly sheep and horses, and of fish and fish products. Trade is mainly with Great Britain, Russia, and the United States.

The population of Iceland in 1974 was 216,628. The national church is Lutheran. There is a complete system of education culminating in a university situated at Reykjavik, the capital of the republic.

Ireland. The large island lying immediately west of Great Britain and separated from it by the Irish Sea, which is connected with the Atlantic Ocean by Saint George's channel and by North channel. In the narrowest part of North channel, Ireland is separated from Great Britain by 14 miles. The area of the island is about 32,000 square miles. It has a maximum length of 300 miles and a maximum width of 180 miles. Politically, the island is divided into two parts. Eire occupies the whole island except a comparatively small district in the north. This district, under the name of Northern Ireland, constitutes a division of the Kingdom of Great Britain and Northern Ireland. For the area and the population of Northern Ireland, see the table of *The British Commonwealth.* Since 1850 nearly 4,500,000 Irish have emigrated to other countries, by far the greatest number having settled in the United States. The Irish are Celtic in origin. The Irish language was spoken by about 13 per cent of the population in 1920, and since then its use has been actively fostered by the government. Along with English, it is the official language of that state.

About two-fifths of Ireland's surface consists of bog. Most of the remainder is fertile. The humidity of the climate and the equability of the temperature foster a verdant clothing of vegetation, which has earned for Ireland the name of the "emerald isle." The island is drained by the Shannon river, which, having a course of 250 miles, is the longest river in the British Isles. The enchanting and romantic scenery of the lakes of Killarney in the south attracts visitors from all parts of the world.

Eire. This portion of Ireland is predominantly agricultural in its interests, being Great Britain's most important single source of foodstuffs. Marketing is accomplished largely through co-operative societies. The chief crops are potatoes, oats, turnips, barley, and wheat. Dairying and stock raising form an important part of the farm operations. There are also valuable sea and fresh-water fisheries, the catches including salmon, mackerel, cod, and herring. The chief manufactures are food products, beer, ale, and tractors.

The population of Eire, estimated in 1971 at 2,978,000, is predominantly Roman Catholic. At the head of the educational system stand two universities, both situated in Dublin, the capital and largest city of the country. Other cities of note include Cork and Limerick.

Northern Ireland. In addition to agriculture and fishing, the northern division of Ireland has a large manufacturing industry. This industry, which has been developed in spite of the lack of coal and of iron in the island, consists chiefly of shipbuilding, distilling, and the manufacture of linen and of other textiles.

The prevailing religion of Northern Ireland is Protestantism. The educational system is distinct from that of the other divisions of the United Kingdom. Belfast, the largest city, is the seat of a university and of the legislature and the judiciary of Northern Ireland. Londonderry is another important center of manufacture and of trade.

Italy. A republic occupying the large bootshaped peninsula of southern Europe. Italy includes also the islands of Sicily, Sardinia, Elba, and about 70 smaller islands in the surrounding seas. The land boundary at the north follows, in a roughly semicircular course, a mountain wall, which separates Italy from France, Switzerland, Austria, and Yugoslavia. To the east of the mainland lies the Adriatic Sea, at the head of which is the Gulf of Venice. The sea narrows toward the south to the Strait of Otranto, 45 miles wide at its narrowest point. Italy's western coast is washed by the Tyrrhenian Sea and by the Ligurian Sea, the latter having a broad northern inlet called the Gulf of Genoa. On the south, Italy is bounded by the Ionian Sea with its inlet, the Gulf of Taranto. The "toe" of Italy is separated from Sicily by the Strait of Messina, which has a minimum width of two miles. The mainland of Italy has an average width of about 100 miles and a maximum length of 780 miles. The total area of the country is 116,304 square miles.

Italy is mountainous and includes the only part of the European mainland which contains active volcanoes. Spurs of the Alps mountains, extending into Italy from the northern mountain wall, form the beautiful scenery of the celebrated Italian Tyrol. The range of the Apennines passes from the Gulf of Genoa to the southern extremity of the mainland. Vesuvius, a mountain of the latter range, Etna on Sicily, and Stromboli on one of the Lipari islands, north of Sicily, are volcanoes which are seldom quiescent. An earthquake at Calabria, southern Italy, in 1783, destroyed 100,000 lives, and another, about the Strait of Messina in 1908, resulted in the death of some 96,000 people.

The most important river of Italy is the Po, which drains the fertile, well watered plain of Lombardy in the north and discharges near the head of the Adriatic Sea. The Tiber, which empties into the sea near the center of the western coast, is richer in historical associations.

The mineral resources of Italy are comparatively small and insufficient for domestic use except for mercury and sulphur, which are exported. Petroleum, however, is found in quantity in Sicily, where there is one of Europe's largest oil fields. The output, however, is not sufficient to meet Italian demand, and imports are extensive, usually processed in Italian refineries. Other mineral products include marble, copper, zinc, iron, and manganese. The fisheries employ more than 150,000 workers.

The leading industry of Italy is agriculture. The climate, ranging from subarctic in the Alps to subtropical in the south, permits the cultivation of such varied crops as wheat, corn, potatoes, sugar beets, oats, grapes, olives, rice, beans, barley, and rye. Northern Italy is the most productive region, being cultivated by the most improved methods. Over 400,000 acres were reclaimed for agriculture in central Italy in the decade 1920–30. Silk culture is also a considerable industry. Wine, olive oil, and cheese are important exports of Italy.

Italian agriculture consists typically of small farms intensively cultivated but with a minimum of farm machinery, the farmers living in villages or even cities and traveling each day to their outlying farms. Under land reform laws of 1950, the government acquired and made available to farmers about one and a half million acres in lots of less than 12 acres each. A large number of Italian farm laborers have migrated in recent years to France and other members of the Common Market.

The chief manufacturing centers are in the north, where abundant hydroelectric power is available. The principal products include cotton and silk textiles, lace, straw hats, metal products, chemicals, sugar, rayon, leather goods, glass, pottery, perfumes, and paper. Shipbuilding is also an important industry. Among the distinctive products of Italian craftsmanship are cameos and marble statuettes. From Murano, near Venice, comes glass whose unrivalled beauty gives it a secure market throughout the world. The secret processes of manufacture go back at least to the 1200's. To protect them the Venetian rulers made it a capital offense for an artisan to emigrate.

The population of Italy in 1971 was 53,744,737 (est.). The prevailing religion is Roman Catholicism. Elementary instruction is compulsory. Italy has over 40 universities, many of them among the oldest in Europe. In addition, there are many technical colleges, art schools and learned societies. Everywhere throughout Italy are to be found monuments, more or less ruined, which bear witness to the fact that Italy was the chief center of European civilization from the 2d century B. C. to the 16th century A.D. The Italian government has capitalized on this fact by protecting the historical sites and prescribing for guides licenses granted only after rigorous training, thereby attracting tourists who normally exceed 18 million each year. Apart from the government's care for the more obvious historical attractions such as Pompeii, the ancient Roman structures in Rome, and still earlier Greek structures in Sicily, it assists in the archeological study and preservation of hundreds of underground Tuscan tombs which only in recent years have been known to exist.

Rome is the capital and largest city of Italy. The chief cities with their populations are given in the following table:

City	Population	City	Population
Rome	2,856,309	Cagliari	235,892
Milan	1,732,451	Brescia	215,317
Naples	1,224,274	Leghorn	177,526
Turin	1,202,846	Modena	176,796
Genoa	807,138	Parma	176,617
Palermo	661,235	Reggio di Calabria	174,462
Bologna	492,700	Salerno	159,302
Florence	464,897	Ferrara	155,478
Catania	399,635	Foggia	150,725
Bari	374,521	Prato	150,580
Venice	365,431	Ravenna	137,020
Trieste	271,536	Perugia	134,288
Verona	270,815	Reggio nell 'Emilia	129,787
Messina	259,858	La Spezia	122,754
Padua	239,250		
Tarento	238,749		

By the peace treaty signed at Paris February 10, 1947, Italy ceded four of her frontier districts to France, and most of the province of Venezia Giulia to Yugoslavia. She also gave up her former colonies, all in Africa, where her possessions were second in extent only to those of Great Britain and France. The United Nations supervised the reorganization of this colonial empire. Ethiopia, which Italy had conquered in 1936, was restored to independence, and the former Italian colony of Eritrea was joined to it. The former Italian colony of Libya was erected into an independent kingdom in 1951. Italian Somaliland was joined with British Somaliland to form the Somali Republic.

Monaco (*mŏn'à-kō*). One of the smallest states in Europe. Monaco is a constitutional monarchy, lying in southeastern France and bordering on the Mediterranean Sea. The surface, about 2 miles long and half a mile wide, is mountainous and highly picturesque. The chief occupation of the 23,000 (1968 est.) inhabitants is to provide accommodation and entertainment for the visitors who, in numbers exceeding 1,500,000 each year, are attracted by this famous winter resort and gambling center. Despite popular misconception, the famous Monte Carlo gambling casino now furnishes less than 10 per cent of revenues. While tourist trade remains of chief importance, local industries include making electrical appliances, radios, pharmaceuticals, and cosmetics.

Netherlands, The. A kingdom of northwestern Europe, roughly triangular in shape, with a northwestern coast line on the North Sea. The country, sometimes called Holland after the name of two of its provinces, borders on Belgium to the south and Germany on the east. No point in it is more than 120 miles from the sea, which forms more than one-half the total of its boundary. Its seacoast is 465 miles in length.

The surface of the Netherlands, 12,529 square miles in area, is, in large part, too low for natural drainage, portions of it being from 16 to 20 feet below the level of the sea. The population of 13, 269,563 averages about 1,059 persons to the square mile, which makes the Netherlands the most densely populated country on the earth.

The former Zuider Zee, a large shallow gulf, formed by an inundation from the sea in the 13th century, was cut off from the sea by dikes in 1932, in order to be drained to one-third its former size, leaving a lake, Ijsselmeer. This reclamation project is the largest ever undertaken anywhere in the world. It adds 523,000 acres of arable land to the Netherlands, an increase of nearly one-tenth.

Part of the coast is bordered by sand dunes, which keep out the sea from the lowlands. In other parts, artificial embankments, or dikes, are erected for that purpose. In the interior of the country, also, such dikes are used to enclose swampy land, from which the water is pumped by windmills, leaving the soil of these so-called "polders" available for cultivation.

The Netherlands has a network of river mouths through which the Rhine, the Meuse, and the Scheldt rivers discharge their waters. These rivers are supplemented as trade highways by some 2000 miles of canals, which, both in mileage and in utility, vie in importance with the railroads. More than 50,000 people live on barges which ply along the waterways.

The distinctive products of the Netherlands are cheese, butter, margarine, and flower bulbs. More than one-half of the land is arable. It produces among other crops, rye, oats, potatoes, sugar beets, flax, and barley. Dairying is one of the leading occupations of the country. The Holstein breed of cattle, developed first in Holland, is one of the best milk producing varieties in the world. Herring and oysters are the chief products of the deep-sea fisheries, which formerly constituted the foundation of the country's wealth. The industries include shipbuilding, tobacco products, and pottery, and the refining of sugar, cocoa, and chocolate.

Until after World War II, the Netherlands had colonial possessions more than 50 times the area of the country itself, but practically all of them became independent. The Dutch merchant marine is among the world's largest.

The majority of the inhabitants are Protestants, but there is a strong Catholic minority. Both Churches, as well as the Jewish religious bodies, receive grants from the government. Illiteracy is virtually unknown. The educational system provides widely different kinds of training. There are four state universities. Amsterdam was formerly the capital and is still the scene of the royal coronation. The seat of government, however, is The Hague. The following table gives the chief cities with their population in 1968:

City	Population	City	Population
Amsterdam . .	862,085	Utrecht	274,324
Rotterdam . .	719,186	Eindhoven . .	184,202
The Hague . .	582,711	Haarlem . . .	172,955

Source: UN *Demographic Yearbook*, 1968.

Norway. A kingdom of northern Europe, occupying that portion of the Scandinavian peninsula which lies west and north of the ridge of the Kiolen Mountains. The country extends 300 miles within the Arctic circle to a latitude farther north than that of any other part of the European mainland. Norway possesses as a dependency the Spitsbergen Islands, a coal producing archipelago which is situated some 600 miles north of the country's northern extremity and stretches to a point about 650 miles from the north pole. The area of the archipelago is estimated at 25,000 square miles.

The surface of Norway, 125,065 square miles in area, is mountainous and, for the most part, barren. About one-fifth is covered with forests, mainly of pine and fir. The arable portion comprises a scant 4 per cent of the total area. The coast line is cut by deep, picturesque fiords, and is fringed by some 150,000 islands, the larger ones being in the north.

The climate is moderated by the warm ocean currents which flow past the coast. The Arctic coast settlement, Hammerfest, which is the most northern town in the world, has a mean winter temperature higher than that of New York. Numerous summer tourists visit the country, attracted by Norway's scenic beauty and by the spectacle of the "midnight sun." In the north, the sun never sets between the middle of May and the last of July.

The chief occupations of Norway's inhabitants are lumbering and fishing. Herring, cod, mackerel, salmon, whale, walrus, seal, and lobsters form the most valuable part of the catch. Ships from Norway carry on most of the whaling in the Antarctic. The merchant marine of Norway ranks, in tonnage, among the great commercial fleets of the world. The manufacturing industries of the country are largely dependent on water power, which is available in great abundance. The most important industrial products are pulp, paper, and chemicals.

The population of Norway, (3,917,770, 1972 est.) is almost entirely Protestant in religion. The Lutheran Church is endowed by the state. Education is obligatory and illiteracy is almost unknown. The one university is situated in Oslo (475,563), the capital and largest city. Other cities include Bergen (211,970), Trondheim, and Stavanger.

Poland. A nation of eastern Europe, the Polish People's republic was established after World War II. Poland covers an area of 120,665 square miles between Russia on the east and East Germany on the west. Poland borders on Czechoslovakia on the south and the Baltic Sea on the north. Apart from the Carpathian foothills in the south, with a maximum elevation of 2000 feet, the surface is a gently rolling plain, most of it drained northward by the Vistula River and its tributaries.

Since World War II Poland has become highly industrialized, using its abundance of coal, lignite, sulphur, copper ore, and zinc to produce manufactured goods. The major Polish industries are mining, machine manufacture, chemicals, power production, and food production. Poland is also the world's ninth largest producer of ships.

The people of Poland have exerted great effort to restore agricultural production since the war. Collective farming is being phased out by the government and a majority of the land is being turned over to private owners. The major crops of Poland are wheat, rye, potatoes, oats, barley, and sugar beets. The country's main trade partners are the U.S.S.R., Czechoslovakia, East and West Germany, and Britain.

Poland's 1973 estimated population was 33,868, 800, 95 per cent of whom are Roman Catholic.

Education is free and compulsory between the ages of 7 and 15, and there are 89 institutions of higher education. Warsaw is the capital and largest city, with a 1973 estimated population of 1,388,000. Other major cities include Lodz (781,000), Krakow (657, 000), Wroclaw (560,000), and Poznan (499,000).

Portugal. A republic occupying the most western part of the Iberian peninsula and washed on the south and on the west by the Atlantic Ocean. On the land side, to the north and the east, Portugal adjoins Spain. The area of Portugal is given as 34,500 square miles, little more than half of which is productive.

The country is traversed from east to west near its center by the Tagus River, the estuary of which forms one of the best harbors in the world. North of the river, the surface is a mountainous plateau, which is crossed by the deep, gorgelike bed of the Douro River. On the left of the Tagus River, a plain stretches southward to an irregular group of mountains in the southwestern extremity of the country. Between this group and a mountain ridge on the eastern border, the Guadiana River, rising in Spain, flows south to the Atlantic Ocean.

About 26 per cent of Portugal's surface is forested, mainly with pines, chestnuts, oaks, and cork trees. Cork is one of the chief sources of the national wealth. The acorns of the oak forests serve to fatten large herds of swine. The central part of the country produces enormous amounts of grapes, from which is made port wine, so called from Oporto, its point of export. In the south, olives, figs, oranges, lemons, and other tropical fruits are grown. Products of the fisheries—sardines and tuna fish—form, next to wines, the principal article of export. The mineral wealth is considerable. Wolfram, iron, copper, manganese, antimony, lead, tin, and gold are found. A characteristic industry is the manufacture of porcelain tiles. The chief manufactures are textile products.

The population of Portugal is 9,505,000. There is freedom of worship, but Roman Catholicism prevails almost to the exclusion of any other religion. Elementary education is compulsory and, since Portugal became a republic in 1910, has been rigorously enforced. There are three universities and several schools of technology and of art. The two principal cities are Lisbon—the capital—and Oporto.

Rumania. A republic of southeastern Europe with an eastern coast line on the Black Sea. Russia is its immediate neighbor to the north; Hungary and Yugoslavia, to the west; and Bulgaria, to the south. The area of the country is 91,671 square miles.

Rumania is divided into an eastern and a western part by the Carpathian mountains, which, in Rumania, trend south and southwest. This ridge is often known as the Transylvanian Alps, and the western part of the country is known as Transylvania. The remainder of the country is a plain drained by the Danube. This river has 595 miles of its course in Rumania and along the southern border.

After being joined by the Pruth, its great tributary from the north, the Danube empties through several mouths into the Black Sea. Navigation on the Danube according to the peace treaty of 1947 is free and open to all countries on an equal footing.

About four-fifths of the inhabitants of Rumania support themselves by stock raising and by agriculture of the usual temperate zone type, corn and wheat being the leading crops. Rumania is, next to Russia, the most important oil producing country of Europe. Other minerals obtained are lignite, coal, iron, copper, and salt, the mining of the last being a government monopoly. Flour milling, brewing, and distilling are the chief industrial interests. Apart from oil, the leading exports are grain, salt, coal, timber, and hides. In 1947 Rumania's transport services, oil, industry, and entire export-import trade were taken over by Soviet-controlled agencies.

The predominant religion of Rumania's 19,721,000 people is Greek Catholic. There are six universities in the country. Bucuresti (Bucharest) (1,372,937) is the capital and largest city of Rumania. Other cities of importance include Iasi (Jassy), Galati (Galatz), and Cluj.

Russia. The largest country in the world, occupying nearly half the total area of Europe and the whole northern portion of Asia. Including its Asiatic territory, Russia covers an area of 8,599,776 square miles, of which about 2,500,000 are in Europe. Officially known as the Union of Soviet Socialist Republics (U.S.S.R.), it is divided into the Russian Socialist Federated Soviet Republic (R.S.F.S.R.), which occupies about 78 per cent of the entire country, and fifteen other republics, of which seven are in Europe and eight in Asia.

The areas and population of the constituent republics, as estimated in 1969, were as follows:

Republic	Area in sq. miles	Population
RSFSR*	6,593,391	128,526,000
Ukrainian	232,046	46,752,000
Byelorussia (White Russia)	80,154	8,897,000
Moldavia	13,012	3,531,000
Estonia	17,413	1,316,000
Latvia	24,695	2,323,000
Lithuania	26,173	3,103,000
Azerbaijan	33,436	5,042,000
Georgia	26,911	4,710,000
Armenia	11,306	2,363,000
Turkomen	188,417	2,085,000
Uzbek	158,069	11,669,000
Tadzhik	54,019	2,823,000
Kazakh	1,064,092	12,877,000
Kirghiz	76,642	2,926,000
Total	8,599,776	238,943,000

*The first republic listed, the RSFSR, includes territory in Europe and Asia. The next 6 listed are in Europe. The last 8 are in Asia.

The surface of European Russia is a vast rolling plain, which rises, in the Ural mountains on the east, to an altitude of about 8000 feet and, at Mount Elbruz in the Caucasus range, to a maximum height of 18,465 feet. Almost the whole surface, however, is less than 600 feet above the sea.

Extreme cold in winter and extreme heat in summer constitute a general characteristic of Russia's climate. The Valdai hills in the west central part of the country form the chief watershed and give rise to the Don, the Dnieper, and the Volga, all flowing southward. The Dvina, the Neva, and the Volkhof are the most important rivers of northern drainage. The Volga river is navigable for 1800 miles. Canals join the principal rivers, making a system of navigable waterways having a total length of about 90,000 miles. The northern region abounds in lakes of glacial formation. Lake Ladoga near the border of Finland, with an area of 7000 square miles, is the largest lake in Europe.

Prior to the revolution of 1917, Russia was predominantly an agricultural country. In the next 40 years, it became also one of the world's leading industrial nations with over 80 per cent of the output nonagricultural, although the farm and nonfarm population were about evenly divided. But this industrial emphasis led to trouble, and Russia was compelled to import grain on a large scale in 1964. Farm land is partly owned and operated by the state, but most is operated by co-operatives with state-appointed managers. Individual workers are allowed small tracts to raise their own produce.

The official explanation for disappointing returns was that manufacture of fertilizers had been neglected; others attributed them also to inadequate investment and lack of incentive to produce.

Russia is one of the world's largest producers of wheat, barley, rye, flax, and oats. Other important crops are hemp, sugar beets, rice, cotton, tea, and tobacco. The richest soil lies in the so-called black earth belt, which extends from the Carpathian Mountains through the Ukraine in southern Russia to the borders of China. This is by far the greatest single wheat growing land on the face of the globe. In production of farm animals, Russia vies with the United States for the first place.

Industrialization in Russia was carried out by means of governmental planning and control, which extends to every aspect of its economic life. Frequently entirely new cities were created in the process, such as Magnitogorsk for the manufacture of steel. Dneprostroy, where Europe's largest hydroelectric station was erected, became a center for aluminum, ferroalloy, coke, and cement plants. Production of tractors was centralized in Volgograd (formerly Stalingrad) and Chelyabinsk. Russia is one of the world's largest producers of petroleum. Among the older centers of industry are Leningrad, which produces chemicals, matches, and rubber products, and Moscow, where the textiles and publishing industries are centered. Kharkov is a leading center of heavy industry. Centers of the atomic energy industry are scattered and unpublicized.

From the forests of the north come lumber, pulp, tar, turpentine, resin, and fur. Russia is the world's largest exporter of lumber. There are important fisheries in the Arctic Ocean and in the seas. The fisheries of the Volga River and of the Caspian Sea supply most of the sturgeon, whose eggs are salted and made into Russian caviar. From the Ural Mountains come asbestos and platinum. Here, too, is produced gold, making Russia a rival of South Africa as the world's chief source of the yellow metal. One of the chief sources of manganese is southern Russia, where there are also very rich deposits of coal and of iron. Copper is mined in the north.

The population of Russia, 1969 est., was 239,000,000. All forms of religion are permitted in Russia, but atheism is officially encouraged. Following the revolution in 1917, an ambitious and comprehensive system of education was inaugurated. Education is compulsory and even advanced education is free. Medical care and many other social services are provided by the government. The role of women in all phases of Russian life is greater than in any other large country.

The capital and largest city in Russia is Moscow. Other large cities of European Russia are Leningrad, Kiev, Odessa, Kharkov, Dnepropetrovsk, Saratov, and Gorkiy.

See also *Russia in Asia*.

Spain. A country in southwestern Europe, occupying about four-fifths of the Iberian peninsula. It is separated from France on the northeast by the Pyrenees Mountains and, in the southwestern part of the peninsula, surrounds Portugal on the land side. Spain is otherwise bounded by the Atlantic Ocean and the Mediterranean Sea, which are connected, at the southern extremity of the country, by the Strait of Gibraltar. Spain has an area of 194,945 square miles. It extends north and south 540 miles and, east and west, about 620 miles.

Next to Switzerland, Spain has the most elevated surface in continental Europe. Most of the interior is a table-land varying from 2000 to 3000 feet above the sea level. It is divided irregularly by low mountain ranges, of which the Cantabrian Mountains parallel the northern seacoast, the Sierra Nevada range skirts the Mediterranean coast, and the Sierra Morena trend east and west in the interior. Of Spain's rivers, the Douro, the Tagus, and the Guadiana have their mouths in Portugal. The Guadalquivir flows east and south into the Atlantic Ocean, while the Jucar and the Ebro empty into the Mediterranean Sea. The Guadalquivir and the Ebro are the only navigable rivers.

In the interior, the rainfall is light, and the climate is harsh, with cold winters and hot summers. The northern coast has the heaviest rainfall in Europe, and the southern coast has the warmest winter climate of any part of the continent. About one-sixth of the acreage is under forest, the more characteristic trees being the Spanish chestnut and the cork oak.

The leading occupations of the people are agriculture, grazing, fruit culture, mining, fishing, and manufacturing. Cereal crops are raised especially in the north and include, in order of importance, wheat, barley, rye, corn, and oats. Huge flocks of sheep and of goats graze on the dry, treeless plateau, where esparto grass is a characteristic type of vegetation. From this plant, rope and paper are made. In the southern part, which is known as Andalusia, grapes, oranges, olives, figs, peaches, dates, almonds, and other fruits and nuts are grown in abundance.

Spain is one of the chief wine producing countries of Europe. Mulberries are cultivated as a food for silkworms. Valencia in the south is the chief center of the Spanish silk industry. Raisins form a considerable item of export. Saffron and licorice are distinctive products of the region.

The mineral resources of Spain are among the richest in Europe. Iron ore is extensively exported. Spain is the chief European source of lead. Coal, copper, mercury, salt, zinc, tin, and potash are produced in important quantities. With the exception of steel and textiles, there are no important manufacturing industries. The country is deficient in petroleum. One of the chief products is cork, made from the bark of the cork oaks. The fisheries employ over 100,000, the chief catches being sardines, tunny fish, and cod. Oranges, olive oil, wines and cognacs, preserved fruits and fish, and almonds are among the chief exports.

The population of Spain is 33,823,918, practically all of whom are adherents of the Roman Catholic Church. The Basques, living near the head of the Bay of Biscay and numbering about 400,000, are believed to be descendants of a pre-Aryan people known to the Romans under the name of Iberians. Spain has also some 50,000 gypsies. Elementary education is compulsory. There are 13 universities. The capital and largest city is Madrid. Other important urban centers are Barcelona, Valencia, Seville, Malaga, Saragossa, Murcia, Bilbao, and Granada.

Spain was formerly one of the chief centers of Roman civilization. Bullfighting, the most popular national sport, is a survival of the ancient Roman wild beast shows.

Sweden. A republic of northern Europe, occupying the eastern and larger part of the Scandinavian peninsula. The country is 950 miles long and tapers to a blunt point at the north and at the south. It is bounded on the west by Norway and the Kattegat, and, on the east, by the Baltic Sea, the Gulf of Bothnia, and Finland. Its average width is about 190 miles, and its surface covers 173,436 square miles. The country includes many adjacent islands, the largest being Gottland and Oland.

Sweden is mountainous in the west, but the remainder of the country is flat. Most of the rivers are fed by lakes at the base of the Kiolen Mountains, which form the greater part of the Norwegian boundary. Toward the south, four large lakes occur, — Väner, Vätter, Mälar, and Hjälmar, — of which Lake Väner is the third largest in Europe. The first two are part of the Göta Canal system, which, giving access between the Baltic Sea and the Kattegat forms one of the chief arteries of Swedish commerce. The climate of Sweden is cold in winter and hot in summer; other seasons are short.

The most southern part of the country, known as Götaland, is the richest agricultural and industrial region and is the center of the shipping interests. North of Götaland lies Svealand, the center of the political and intellectual life of the country. Norrbotten, stretching to the northern extremity of Sweden, furnishes minerals and timber.

About one-half of the population of Sweden is supported by agriculture. Hay, oats, and rye are the leading crops. Timber is one of the chief sources of Sweden's wealth, and the lumber and pulp wood manufactures hold the leading place among the industries. The iron of Sweden is of a particularly high grade. Rich gold mines in northern Sweden, began production about 1930. Manganese, lead, silver, copper, and zinc are also mined. The industries suffer from lack of coal, being compelled to utilize charcoal or hydroelectric power. The largest hydroelectric plant in Western Europe on the Ume river has helped to increase the output of numerous manufactured goods.

The population of Sweden (1970 cen.) was 8,076,903. Lutheran Protestantism is the established form of religion. There is an excellent system of education, at the head of which are six state universities. Illiteracy is almost unknown. The capital and largest city is Stockholm. Other cities of note are Göteborg and Malmö.

Switzerland. A mountainous inland republic of south central Europe, bounded on the north and east by Germany and Austria, on the west by France, and on the south by Italy. The surface of Switzerland, 15,941 square miles in area, has a greater average elevation than any other European country and contains the headwaters of four great European river systems,—the Rhine, the Rhone, the Po, and the Danube.

The northwestern half of the country is a rolling plateau hedged, near the northwestern border, by the Jura mountains. It drains northward toward the Rhine river and contains the lakes of Neuchatel, Bienne, Zurich, Lucerne, Thun, and Constance. The southeastern half is a region of picturesque mountains that has long been famous for its scenic beauty. The Southern Alps form much of the southern border of the country. Here are found the highest mountains, including Monte Rosa, 12,203 feet in height; Matterhorn, a towering pyramid of solid rock 14,701 feet high; Simplon, with an elevation of 11,117; Saint Bernard, 8110 feet high, near which the Saint Bernard breed of dogs was developed, the animals being used to help in the rescue of travelers lost in the snow. This range descends on the north to the valley in which the Rhone river rises and, flowing westward, broadens into Switzerland's largest body of water, the Lake of Geneva. At the southeastern border lies Lake Maggiore, which has a southern drainage into the Po river.

South of the Rhone valley rise the irregular Burnese Alps, the highest peak of which is the Jungfrau, "The Maiden," so called from the blush which suffuses its snowy peak at sundown. Its height is 13,653 feet.

The mountains of Switzerland are cut by some 40 passes, and over 1000 glaciers furrow the rocky slopes. The mountains are burrowed by several railroad tunnels, that at Mount Simplon, 12½ miles in length, being one of the longest in the world. A warm wind, known as the foehn, often, by rapidly melting the snow and ice, causes avalanches.

Partly as a protection against avalanches, the forests of the country, covering about one-sixth of the republic's area, are carefully guarded by the government. Maples, oaks, and chestnuts flourish at the lower levels. Higher up occur birches, and still higher, firs, pines, and larches. In this region, the characteristic alpine animals, the chamois and the ibex, may be seen. The edelweiss and certain other flowering plants grow almost as far up the mountain side as the summer snow line.

Switzerland is one of the most highly industrialized countries in Europe. Agriculture and dairying rank next as occupations of the inhabitants. Grapes, rye, barley, potatoes, oats, flax, hemp, and tobacco are grown in the valleys and on the plains, while the mountain sides provide abundant pasturage for cattle, goats, horses, and sheep. Swiss cheese, Swiss clocks, watches, and Swiss chocolate form some of the more distinctive products of the country. Machinery, textiles, clothing, chemicals, metals, and watches are the industries that employ the greatest number of people. The entertainment of tourists is one of the major industries.

The inhabitants of Switzerland, 6,269,783 in 1970, are a unit neither in race, language, nor religion. German, French, and Italian are spoken. Illiteracy, however, is virtually nonexistent. The Protestants are slightly more numerous than the Catholics. Higher education is cared for by seven universities, that at Zurich dating from 1460. A distinctive type of dwelling is used in Switzerland, known as the chalet. It has a projecting roof under which are placed balconies and staircases.

Berne is the capital and Zurich is the largest city. Geneva is headquarters of many international organizations.

Turkey. The European territory of Turkey consists of the territory north of the Sea of Marmora extending to the borders of Bulgaria and of Greece. It includes Adrianople and Istanbul, formerly Constantinople. Istanbul is treated among the cities of Europe, but the geography of Turkey is dealt with under *Asia*.

Yugoslavia (*yōō'gō-slăv'ĭ-ȧ*). A republic of southern Europe with a southwestern coast line on the Adriatic Sea. On the land side, the country adjoins Italy, Austria, Hungary, Rumania, Bulgaria, Greece, and Albania. Its area is 98,725 square miles. In the peace treaty of 1947, Yugoslavia gained the state of Venezia Giulia plus the enclave of Zara and the islands of Cherso (Cres), Lussino (Losinj), Pelagosa (Pelagruz), and Pag at the expense of Italy.

Much of the coast is rocky and precipitous, rising inland to a mountainous plateau covering the western and southern part of the country. The eastern portion of the country contains a southern spur from the Carpathian mountains. The greater part of the surface is drained toward the east and the north by the Drava, Sava, and Morava rivers, which empty into the Danube. The Danube River, traversing the northern part of Yugoslavia and forming part of the country's Rumanian boundary, cuts through the eastern mountain barrier at the Iron Gate. The Iron Gate is a mountain pass through which the river formerly rushed over a plateau of rock 1400 feet wide. This point has been made navigable by extensive blasting at a cost of more than $10 million. The river valleys provide most of the country's arable land. Nearly one-half of the surface of Yugoslavia is covered with forest. Lumber leads the exports. The chief minerals are coal, lignite, iron, copper, lead, zinc, gold, salt, chromium, and antimony.

The most important industry is agriculture. The chief crops are wheat, corn, potatoes, barley, oats, sugar beets, tobacco, and temperate zone fruits. Silk culture employs many people. Large numbers of swine are fattened on the beechnuts and the acorns of the wooded land, while cattle and sheep graze on the higher mountain slopes. Flour milling, sugar refining, carpet weaving, tanning, and pottery are important industries. State ownership and control characterize the nation's postwar economic and agricultural systems. Tourism contributes immeasurably to the economy.

The inhabitants of Yugoslavia, estimated at 20,523,000 in 1971, are divided among three chief forms of religion, Greek Catholic, Roman Catholic, and Moslem. There are three universities. Belgrade is the capital and largest city.

CITIES AND OTHER POINTS OF TRAVEL INTEREST

The cities of Europe are distinguished by the richness of their historic associations, and, in many cases, by the wealth of their artistic adornment. Some of them, such as Athens and Rome, still preserve the visible evidences of the brilliant civilization which flourished in the southern part of the continent as early as 600 B. C. In others, the remains of outstanding interest are medieval structures—sublime cathedrals, or castles and dungeons of more sinister memories. Cities of southern Spain tell of Mohammedan enterprise; those of Italy remind us of the flowering of art known as the Renaissance; while the industrial cities of northern Europe often afford a curious blending of old interests and of new.

In World War II many European cities were largely destroyed or suffered extensive damage. In some places the historic buildings and monuments have been rebuilt or repaired, though many which were familiar to generations of American tourists have vanished forever.

The scenic beauties of Europe are not only grand in themselves but have the prestige that comes from centuries of description by travelers. The Alps have given us the term alpine, applicable to mountainous scenery of impressive beauty. The natural charm of the pleasure resorts is supplemented by all the attractions that can be suggested by ingenuity aiming to please vast numbers of tourists. The more noteworthy of these resorts are described in the following section, along with the cities and other places of especial interest on the continent.

In many instances, a city is known in English by a name different from that used by the inhabitants of the country in which it is located. In all such cases, the native name is given in bold-face type in parenthesis after the name commonly used by English-speaking people.

Alps. An irregular mountain system of south central Europe, occupying most of Switzerland and parts of France, Italy, Austria, and Germany. The system is 600 miles in length and has a width varying from 75 to 150 miles. It covers an area of about 85,000 square miles. The highest point is reached by Mont Blanc, 15,781 feet high. Other notable peaks with their heights are Monte Rosa, 15,203; Mischabel, 14,935; Lyskamm, 14,889; Weisshorn, 14,804; Matterhorn, 14,701; Dent Blanche, 14,318; Grand Combin, 14,164; Finsteraarhorn, 14,026; Aletschhorn, 13,803; and Jungfrau, 13,653.

The glaciers of the Alps number about 1200 and cover an area of 1600 square miles. The largest, called the Aletsch, has an area of 50 square miles. Other well-known Alpine glaciers are the Unteraar, the Gorner, the Viesch, the Mer de Glace, and the Miage, the last two being on Mont Blanc. The glaciers give rise to a number of mountain lakes, several of which have become proverbial for their beauty. The chief ones are Lucerne, Geneva, Como, Garda, and Maggiore. Water is often drawn from the bottoms of Alpine lakes to secure an all-year flow to develop electric power.

The Alps are cut by many passes, of which the principal ones have been pierced by tunnels for railroads or vehicular traffic. Under Saint Bernard pass, a two-lane tunnel 3.6 miles through the rock provides a roadway supported for an additional ten miles by concrete pylons. Railroad tunnels pierce the Brenner and Simplon passes and the Saint Gotthard and Mont Cenis mountains. A vehicular tunnel through 7.25 miles of rock under Mont Blanc was completed in 1964 to connect Italy and France. In 1976 a 10-mile, 120-yard vehicular tunnel, the world's longest, was completed in Switzerland. It runs from Goschenen on the northern side of the Alps beneath the St. Gottard range to Airolo in the Ticino area.

There are also numerous scenic railroads in the Alps and automobile roads which are marvels of engineering skill. These supplemented by cable cars giving access to mountain peaks make the Alps the most accessible region of superb mountain scenery in the world. The Swiss Alps and the Tyrol, in Italy and Austria, are among the most popular regions.

Amiens (F. *ä'myăɴ'*; E. *ăm'ĭ-ĕnz*). A cathedral city of northern France, lying about 80 miles north of Paris. The Cathedral of Amiens, for magnificence and for richness of decoration, is not surpassed by any other Gothic building of the world. The city has important textile manufacturing interests and is widely known by tourists for its macaroons. During World War I, Amiens was made the headquarters of the British armies in France. Population, 101,677.

Amsterdam. The largest city and the statutory capital of the Netherlands, although the actual seat of government is The Hague. Amsterdam occupies a low site at the southwestern extremity of the Ijsselmeer and is connected with tidewater by the North Sea canal. The numerous canals, which divide the city into some 90 islands connected by almost 300 bridges, have given rise to the city's characterization as "the Venice of the North." Amsterdam's defenses consist of dikes, by the opening of which the whole district may be flooded.

The city is named after a dam built in 1240 across the river Amstel. Part of the site originally occupied by this dam is now the central square of the city and is called the Dam. From it the principal streets radiate in a semicircle. Nearby stand the New Church and the Royal Palace. In the former, a Gothic structure dating from 1408, the sovereigns of the Netherlands are crowned. The Royal Palace, belonging to the city, is the residence of the country's sovereigns when they are guests of Amsterdam. The Ryks, or State Museum, contains a number of paintings by Rembrandt, who, with the philosopher Spinoza, was among Amsterdam's most famous citizens. The city maintains a municipal abattoir, theater, pawnshop, and museum.

Amsterdam is the chief center of Dutch industry, commerce, and finance. Its diamond-cutting factories are the largest in the world. There are also shipbuilding yards, sugar, and oil refineries, and factories for making dyes, chemicals, glass, liquor, tobacco and steel products. The Bank of the Netherlands, situated in Amsterdam, is one of the leading financial institutions of Europe. The city is the seat of the University of Amsterdam and is the headquarters of the National Academy of Arts, the Royal Academy of Sciences, and the Royal Dutch Geographic Society. Amsterdam's botanical gardens are among the foremost in Europe. Population, 861,034. Greater Amsterdam, 911,248.

Antwerp (Antwerpen). A large city of Belgium, situated on the Scheldt River about 50 miles from its mouth in the North Sea. The river, 2200 feet wide at this point, provides Antwerp with one of the best harbors in the world. By means of 28 miles of quays, 3½ miles being granite and equipped with all modern appliances, the port handles merchandise often exceeding an annual total of one billion dollars. Besides its commerce, Antwerp is important for diamond cutting, sugar refining, and the manufacture of liquors, textiles, and cigars. Urban traffic is facilitated by two tunnels under the Scheldt River.

The most conspicuous building in the city is the Cathedral of Notre Dame, the construction of which was begun in the 14th century. It has a tower 400 feet high and contains three celebrated paintings by Rubens, whose tomb is contained in the splendid Church of Saint James. The richly decorated town hall was built in the 16th century. The art gallery contains a priceless collection of masterpieces by Rubens and Van Dyck, the latter having been born in the city. The Steen, part of an old castle dating from the 10th century, was formerly the seat of the Inquisition, but is now used as an archeological museum. Fine boulevards follow the line of the old city walls.

The city has had a stormy history. Founded in the 8th century, it had become, by the 16th century, the financial center of Europe and one of the chief commercial cities of the world. It was destroyed by the Spaniards in 1576. Napoleon revived the city. By improving its harbor, he hoped eventually to make Antwerp a rival of London. Population, 661,697.

Appian (*ăp'ĭ-ăn*) **Way.** A Roman road running from Rome to Brindisi in southern Italy, 446 miles. Begun in 312 B. C. by Appius Claudius as a public work, it is still in use over a considerable portion of its course. For several miles from Rome it is bordered by ancient tombs and the ruins of monumental buildings.

Arcadia. An inland district of the peninsula of Morea in Greece. Its ancient inhabitants long retained their primitive customs, unaffected by the Dorians who invaded the peninsula in the 12th century B. C. A pastoral poetry arose there in the last centuries of the pre-Christian era and gave support to a literary tradition, which represented Arcadia as a land of primitive simplicity and idyllic happiness.

Argonne Forest. A rocky wooded area northwest of Verdun in northeastern France. It was the scene, in September and October 1918, of one of the bloodiest battles ever waged by American troops. The capture of this forest by the Americans threatened the line of retreat of the German army.

ATHENS (Athēnai). The capital and largest city of Greece, situated in the southeastern portion of the country about five miles from the port of Piræus on the eastern shore of the Gulf of Ægina. The city stands in a plain surrounded on three sides by mountains. Athens is a financial, railroad, and commercial city of importance, but its industrial interests center chiefly in Piræus, where there are establishments for manufacturing cotton, flour, leather, chemicals, and rugs. Near Piræus lies Phalerum, the sea resort of Athens. Athens is named after Athena, the ancient Greek goddess of wisdom.

THE MODERN CITY. For several centuries following 500 B. C., Athens was the intellectual and artistic center of the civilized world and, architecturally, was one of the most beautiful cities on the earth. After many centuries of misfortunes, it was finally reduced to a Turkish village. When, in 1832, Greece became independent, Athens was chosen its capital and was rebuilt as a modern city.

The Square of Harmony forms a center from which radiate wide boulevards, two of them ending in Constitution square—the site of the royal palace and gardens. Between the two squares stand the government offices, the buildings of the Academy of Sciences, the National university, the National library, and the archeological colleges. Other notable modern structures include the Parliament buildings, the Palace of Justice, and the National Archeological Museum, the last housing a priceless collection of Greek antiquities. The city contains also the University of Athens, a beautiful library known as the Gennadeion, and the impressive Temple of Youth, headquarters of the Greek Y.M.C.A. There is a large stadium, in which the Olympic games were held in 1896.

The white marble, which is used in most of the public edifices, imparts to the city's architecture a distinctive and impressive brilliancy. The marble used in the ancient buildings has, through age, become tinged with a russet hue.

ANCIENT BUILDINGS. The ancient city centered about a flat-topped hill, called the Acropolis. This hill is surrounded by a wall and contains four beautiful structures: the Propylæa, a building of mixed Doric and Ionic style, which serves as a stately entrance to the enclosure; the Temple of Victory, a small Ionic edifice beside the Propylæa; the Parthenon, which is the classic example of a pure Doric temple and is justly famed as one of the world's most beautiful buildings; and, finally, the Erechtheum, known best for its Porch of the Maidens, in which the columns take the form of Greek maidens, often called Caryatids. These four buildings were all erected in the 5th century B. C., but they still preserve much of their original impressiveness. The Parthenon was partially restored in 1930.

The chief of the ancient buildings outside the Acropolis are the arch of Hadrian, the Theseum, the open-air theater of Dionysus, the Temple of Zeus, the Tower of the Winds, and the monument of Lysicrates, the last being the earliest extant example of the Corinthian style. The Theseum is the best preserved of the ancient Greek structures. Of the 104 Corinthian columns of the Temple of Zeus, each of them 56 feet in height, only 15 remain erect today.

These ruined structures are the original models for the Greek style of architecture as it has been revived in recent times and employed in the erection of many modern buildings. Excavations are going forward continuously, the most stupendous project being that for unearthing the ancient Agora. Population, 1,852,709.

Athos (*ăth'ŏs*). A mountain of northern Greece, 6670 feet high, occupying the extremity of a peninsula in the northern part of the Ægean Sea. In ancient times it was noted as the scene of the shipwreck of Xerxes' fleet, which sailed to attack Greece in 492 B. C. Since the 9th century A. D., the mountain has been occupied by a group of fortified monasteries, now 20 in number. The control of the mountain was handed over by the Byzantine emperors to the monasteries, which have continued to exercise their rights of self-government to the present day. Under a constitution dated in 1045 A. D., women and female animals are excluded from the holy mountain. The monks, numbering 4800, support themselves by agriculture, fishing, and various handicrafts.

Avignon (*ȧ'vē'nyôɴ'*). A town of southeastern France, situated on the Rhone River about 30 miles from the Mediterranean Sea. Avignon is notable as the former residence of the popes, who made it their seat from 1309 to 1376. The city is built on a wall-girdled height, from the summit of which rise the cathedral and the impressive mass of the old papal palace. Population, 64,581.

Barcelona. The chief manufacturing center and, with the exception of Madrid, the largest city of Spain, located near the northeastern extremity of the country on the Mediterranean Sea. The city has a fine harbor and ranks as the second seaport in Spain. It is the commercial center of a rich fruit growing district. The chief manufactures are cotton, silk, and woolen goods, lace, leather, machinery, furniture, dyes, soaps, and drugs. Fruit, wine, olive oil, as well as manufactured goods, are among its exports.

The city dates from the 3d century B. C., when it was founded by the Carthaginian Hamilcar Barca, after whom it was called Barcino. From the 2d century A. D., the city has, in spite of varying fortunes, remained one of the chief commercial cities of southern Europe.

The older part of the city was formerly surrounded by walls, which have since been replaced by promenades. This section has, in general, narrow, irregular streets. Its chief thoroughfare, however, the Ramblas, which connects it with the "new town," has a handsome promenade on which are situated many of the principal buildings of the city, including one of the finest theaters in Spain. At the highest point of the Ramblas stands a famous 13th century cathedral in Spanish Gothic style. The "new town" is regularly laid out and has all modern improvements. Among the more recent buildings is the terminal station, one of the finest in Europe. The chief educational institution is the University of Barcelona. Population, 1,696,750.

Belfast. The capital and metropolis of Northern Ireland, situated on a small inlet in the northeastern part of the island. The city has an excellent harbor and contains immense shipyards, in which most of the White Star liners have been built. In addition to the linen textile industry, manufactures include the making of rope, liquors, tobacco goods, machine shop products, flour, and chemicals.

Belfast was incorporated as a city in 1888. It is the seat of Queen's university and Campbell college and has several fine churches, an art gallery, and a museum. Population, 399,270.

Belgrade (*bĕl'grād'*) (**Beograd**). The capital and largest city of Yugoslavia, situated near the center of the country's northeastern boundary at the confluence of the Save and the Danube rivers. Belgrade is an important railway junction and is the chief trade center of the country. The city is modern in appearance and has several institutions for higher education, including a university, a national library, a museum, and an academy of sciences. There are several fine Greek Catholic churches. Prior to its capture by the Austrians on Oct. 9, 1915, Belgrade was the capital of Serbia. Population, 585,234.

Belleau (*bĕl'ō'*) **Woods.** A forest of northeastern France, 5 miles northwest of Chateau Thierry and about 42 miles east of Paris. It is celebrated for a bitterly contested battle waged there in June 1918, when American marines and regulars dislodged a strongly entrenched German force and captured the village of Bouresches, 2 miles south of the woods. The battle ground was dedicated in 1923 as a permanent memorial to the Americans who fell there. It was named Bois de la Brigade de Marine.

Bergen (*bûr'gĕn*). A seaport and codfish market on the southwestern coast of Norway. Bergen's fish exports are nearly half those of all Norway. The chief manufactures are ships, paper, and ropes. The buildings include a naval academy, an observatory, and a fishery museum. The city maintains a noted marine biological station and is annually the scene of an international fishermen's fair. Edvard Grieg, the composer, was born there. Population, 117,353.

BERLIN. The capital of prewar Germany. After World War II, it became a divided city, 188 of its 342 square miles being an enclave of West Germany and the remaining 154 square miles being the capital of East Germany. It lies about 50 miles from the Polish border to the east and nearly 100 miles from West Germany, which has access to it by railroad, by a principal highway from Helmstedt, by waterway from Hamburg, and by an air corridor. In 1961 the East Germany government built a concrete wall separating the sectors and mounted armed guards on it to prevent escape to the West.

COMMERCE AND INDUSTRY. The old Berlin was the distributing point for a vast inland trade, being served by 12 trunk railroads and several waterways. Since the war, manufacturing has been concentrated chiefly in West Berlin, whose industries produce mainly clothing, electrical apparatus, locomotives, machinery and other steel products, pharmaceuticals, dyestuffs, porcelain, railroad cars, toys, and liquors.

Three-quarters of the old Berlin was destroyed by bombing and artillery fire in World War II. In 1948-49 the western sector was blockaded by the Russian military government, but the blockade was broken by a massive airlift from the west. Thereafter, restoration went forward rapidly, and manufacturing, commerce, and other civic activities grew apace.

STREETS, BUILDINGS, AND MONUMENTS. Streets are regularly laid out and flanked by handsome residences combined with numerous squares, parks, playgrounds, monuments, fashionable promenades, and splendid public buildings.

Berlin's most famous boulevard is Unter den Linden, so called from the double rows of lime, or linden, trees with which it is planted. The street is 196 feet wide and leads from the former imperial palace, with its 600 rooms, to the Brandenburg Gate, which is the official point of passage between the East and West sectors. This gate is a triumphal arch, modeled on the Propylea in Athens and surmounted by a colossal bronze car of victory. On the boulevard is situated, among other impressive buildings, the palace of William I.

The Brandenburg Gate leads west into the Tiergarten, a magnificent park of 600 acres, which contains one of the largest zoological gardens in the world. The continuation of Unter den Linden into East Berlin is Liebknechtstrasse, formerly Wilhelmstrasse. It passes the Chancellery, once administrative center of Germany and scene of Hitler's suicide. The Reichstag building, erected in the Italian Renaissance style, remains as when gutted by fire in 1933.

Educational Institutions. Berlin is the chief intellectual center of Germany. The University of Berlin, founded in 1810, has numbered among its teachers Hegel, Fichte, Grimm, Niebuhr, Lipsius, Mommsen, and Einstein. Besides numerous technical institutions, there are free astronomical observatories, academies of art and of music, public libraries, botanical gardens, and many learned societies. Population of West Berlin, 2,190,577.

Berne. The capital and fourth largest city of Switzerland. The city is in the northwestern part of the republic and is picturesquely situated on a rocky bluff surrounded on three sides by the river Aar, a tributary of the Rhine. The name Berne is a corruption of the German word for bears, a number of the animals having been slain on the site when Berne was founded in 1191. A den of tame bears is maintained by the city, which has adopted the bear as its emblem.

Berne is noted for its manufacture of toys, engines, scientific instruments, and chocolate. It is the center of the international postal, telegraphic, railroad and copyright associations. The chief edifices are the magnificent Parliament building and a Gothic cathedral begun in 1421 but not completed until 1894. Population, 166,000.

Bingen (*bĭng'ĕn*). A town on the west bank of the Rhine River in Germany, 17 miles west of Mainz. Like many other towns on the Rhine, it has several picturesque ruins of feudal castles, the most notable of which is the Mouse Tower. In this tower, Archbishop Hatto is said to have been devoured by mice in 969 A. D. The Bingenloch, a famous whirlpool, is found a short distance down the river. Population, 20,210.

Birmingham. The second largest city of England, situated near the geographic center of the country. Being in close proximity to rich coal fields and large iron deposits, it was known for its iron products as early as the 16th century, and it has since become famous for its steel manufactures. Other industrial products include glass, jewelry, chemicals, automobiles, railroad cars, plated articles, pins, and hydraulic presses.

Birmingham has led the cities of England in municipal improvements. There are 17 parks and recreation grounds. An excellent school system provides elementary education, while museums, libraries, art galleries, botanical gardens, technical colleges, and an amply endowed university afford means for higher study. James Watt, John Bright, and Joseph Chamberlain are some of the distinguished names connected with the city. Population, 1,102,570.

Bologna (*bō-lōn'yä*). A city of northern Italy, located in a fertile plain at the foot of the Apennine mountains, almost midway between the Gulf of Genoa and the Gulf of Venice. It is an important railroad junction and has a large trade and extensive manufactures. The products for which the city is especially noted are macaroni, Bologna sausages, liquors, and canned fruit. Other industrial establishments include sugar refineries, rice mills, and railroad shops.

Bologna is believed to have been founded in the 8th century B. C. It figures in the career of Hannibal, Alaric, Charlemagne, and Napoleon. The city uses an aqueduct built by Augustus Cæsar. By a popular vote in 1860, Bologna became a part of the kingdom of Italy.

There are some 130 churches, several dating from the 11th century. One of the most noted is the San Domenico, where lies the body of Saint Dominic, the founder of the Dominican order. Bologna's art treasures include Raphael's portrait of Saint Cecilia. Two leaning towers survive from among 180 which Bologna possessed in the Middle Ages. One of the two is 163 feet high and inclines 10 feet from the perpendicular. The University of Bologna is the oldest existing university in Europe. Founded in the 11th century, it became famous as a law school and in 1262 had about 10,000 students, among whom were Dante and Petrarch. Galvani, one of the earliest investigators of electricity, was born in Bologna and lectured in the university. Population, 481,527.

Bonn (*bŏn*). A university city of central Germany, beautifully situated on the Rhine River, now the seat of government of the Federal Republic of West Germany. Establishment of the capital here has led to great expansion of departmental buildings. The University of Bonn, second only to that of Berlin among German universities, occupies the former palace of the electors of Cologne. The city also has a venerable cathedral and a Beethoven museum, the latter containing relics of the famous musician, who was born in the city. The principal manufactures are porcelain, office furniture, and stoneware. Population, 140,482.

Bordeaux (*bôr'dō'*). A commercial city of southwestern France, situated on the Garonne River at the point where it widens to form the Gironde River. It is connected by canal with the Mediterranean Sea. The chief article of export is wine, besides which hides, sugar, rice, cotton and woolen cloth, salt fish, and fruit are shipped abroad, mainly to South America. The city's industries include shipbuilding, canning, sugar refining, and the manufacture of casks, liquors, chemicals, leather, machinery, and pottery. Bordeaux is an important center for fishing fleets which annually visit the shores of Newfoundland and of Iceland.

The University of Bordeaux was founded in 1441. Among the more notable buildings of the city are the Grand Theater, the Church of Saint Croix, Saint Michael's Church, and the Cathedral of Saint André, the last dating from the 11th century. Montesquieu, Montaigne, and Rosa Bonheur were residents of Bordeaux.

Bordeaux was used as a port of disembarkation by the American forces during World War I. For a short period in 1914, it became the seat of the French government when Paris was menaced. Population, 249,688.

Boulogne (F. *bōō'lôn'y'*; E. *bōō-lōn'*). A fortified seaport of northern France, situated at the eastern extremity of the English channel. The city is the chief French station of the North Sea fisheries. It consists of a lower town,—the business part close to the harbor,—and an upper town built on a hill, from which, on clear days, the English coast may be seen. As a center for passenger traffic with England, Boulogne rivals Calais. During World War I, many American troopships landed their passengers in Boulogne. Population, 49,036.

Bradford. A manufacturing city in the north central part of England, the chief center in England for the manufacture of woolen textiles, and the leading wool market of the world. Silks, velvets, and foundry products are also manufactured. Bradford is substantially built, mainly of stone. Among the public buildings are Saint Peter's Church, the Mechanics Institute, the large, covered markets, and the Cartwright Memorial Hall, erected in memory of the inventor of the power loom. Population, 298,220.

Bremen (E. *brĕm'ĕn*; G. *brā'mĕn*). The second largest seaport of Germany. It lies in West Germany about 38 miles from the North Sea on both banks of the Weser River. The "old town" on the right bank is the business district, while the "new town" on the left is a well built residential section. The chief industrial products include ships, iron castings, machinery, refined sugar, tobacco, and cordage. It is the leading German fishing port.

Bremen is the capital of a small state of the same name, which retained its rights of self-government when it entered the German Empire. Population, 598,957.

Breslau (*brĕs'lou*) (**Wroclaw**). An important commercial and manufacturing city of Poland, situated on both banks of the Oder River. It has a large trade in raw materials and holds three annual fairs. The chief manufactures are textiles, steel products, railway cars, paper, and furniture. Breslau consists of an old town surrounded by five modern suburbs. One of the most notable buildings is the Protestant church, with a 300-foot steeple, founded in 1250 and dedicated to Saint Elizabeth. Population 477,300.

Brest. A strongly fortified seaport and one of the chief naval stations of France, located on a wide rock-bound harbor at the northwestern extremity of France. Most of the working population are engaged in industries related to naval maintenance. Between the town and the harbor mouth, the Cours d'Ajot, one of the finest promenades in Europe, skirts the shore. Brest was one of the principal ports used by the American Expeditionary Forces in World War I. A telegraph cable connects the city with Duxbury, Mass. Population, 130,867.

Brighton. The most celebrated seaside resort in England, situated on the English channel, 51 miles due south of London. A magnificent 4-mile promenade and driveway with two fine piers borders the coast. The most noteworthy building is the Royal Pavilion, in Oriental style, occupied by George IV and succeeding British sovereigns. Population, 162,650.

Bristol. A maritime city of southwestern England, situated seven miles south of the estuary of the Severn, with which it is connected by the navigable river Avon. The city has long been noted for its extensive commerce and for its glassworks, potteries, sugar refineries, soap works, tanneries, tobacco, chocolate, shoe, and chemical factories, and shipyards. In the shipyards of Bristol was built, in 1838, the early steamship *Great Western*.

The city is the seat of Bristol university and two colleges. Besides libraries, museums, and art galleries, there are several churches of which the finest architecturally is that of Saint Mary Redcliffe, dating from the 14th century. From Bristol came the first settlers of Newfoundland as well as the island's discoverer, John Cabot. The city was at one time the residence of Southey and of Coleridge. Population, 429,370.

Bruges (E. *brōō'jĕz*; F. *brüzh*). A decadent commercial city of western Belgium. Prior to the 16th century, Bruges was a flourishing center of woolen manufacturing. Among the many medieval structures which the city has preserved from its more prosperous days are the Church of Notre Dame and les Halles, the Market Hall, whose tower, 352 feet in height, contains a chime of 48 bells. This tower was celebrated by Longfellow in his poem "The Belfry of Bruges." The port of Bruges is Zeebrugge, 8 miles distant, which was a German submarine base during World War I. The name of the city means bridges and was applied in allusion to the 54 bridges constructed across the numerous canals which intersect the city. Population, 52,220.

Brünn (*brün*) (**Brno**). An important commercial city of south central Czechoslovakia. Its manufactures include woolen goods, hardware, flour, refined sugar, and machinery. Brünn has several churches of attractive medieval architecture and a beautiful synagogue built in the Saracenic style. The city is a trading center for a thickly populated district. Population, 328,316.

Brussels (**Bruxelles,** or **Brussel**). The capital and largest city of Belgium, situated in the central part of the kingdom. It consists of an upper town,—the new and fashionable quarter,—and the lower, or old, town, devoted to commerce and industry.

Its magnificent boulevards, beautiful squares and parks, and imposing buildings make Brussels one of the most beautiful cities of Europe. The more notable buildings include the Hôtel de Ville, with its open-stonework spire, 374 feet high, and the sumptuous Greco-Roman Palais de Justice. The Church of Sainte Gudule, begun in 1220, is celebrated for its marvelous stained-glass windows. The royal library, the museums, and the art galleries contain many masterpieces of Flemish painters. The University of Brussels is one of the very few European universities which have been founded without the co-operation of church or state. The city has numerous schools and scientific societies.

Brussels suffered severely from the German occupation during World War I. Since that time, however, its industries have resumed their production of Brussels lace, carpets, furniture, steam engines, and other articles manufactured before the war. The city is also the railroad center of the country. Population, 1,074,586.

Bucharest (*bōō'kȧ-rĕst'*; *bū'-*) (**Bucaresti**). The capital and largest city of Rumania, located in the central southern part of the country. Since 1948 it has been the seat of the Cominform (Communist Information Bureau). Bucharest has an extensive commerce in petroleum, cereals, and timber. The industries include oil refining and the manufacture of flour, liquors, chemicals, and brick.

The city's chief attractions are the splendid public gardens and the bright cupolas of the numerous Greek Catholic churches. Among the more imposing structures are the Royal Palace, the National university, the Palace of Justice, and several fine monuments. The customs of the inhabitants exhibit a blending of Oriental and Western influences. The name Bucharest is a corruption of a Rumanian word meaning city of joy. Population, 1,372,937.

Budapest (*bōō'dȧ-pĕst'*). The capital and largest city of Hungary, situated in the central northern part of the country on the banks of the Danube river. Budapest comprises the former city of Buda on the right bank and of Pest on the left bank. The two are connected by six bridges, including two suspension bridges which are among the longest in Europe. These bridges were bombed by the U. S. Air Force in 1944–45.

Buda, the older section, which was founded by the Romans in the 2d century A. D., is built on two hills and contains the royal castle, the government offices, and the former residences of the aristocracy. The newer town, Pest, founded by the Huns under Attila in the 5th century A. D., is built on a low plain. Pest is the commercial, industrial, and intellectual center of the city. The city was largely in ruins in 1945 when the Russians expelled the occupying Germans.

The city's commercial interests are of great importance. Budapest is the railroad center of Hungary and is further served by the Danube, the chief waterway of the country. Population, 1,960,000; with suburbs, 1,970,000.

Cadiz (*kā'dĭz*). An Atlantic port on the south coast of Spain. Cadiz is one of the most ancient cities in Europe. Founded by the Phœnicians, 1100 B. C., Cadiz was captured in turn by the Carthaginians, Romans, Goths, Moors, and Spaniards. The town is still protected by walls and fortresses. When Spain was mistress of most of the New World, Cadiz was the emporium of American commerce and was a city of vast wealth and importance. Today its trade is small, the exports being principally salt, wines, olive oil, and fruits. Population, 117,871.

Calais (*kăl'ā*; *kăl'ĭs*). A fortified port of northeastern France, situated on the Strait of Dover near its narrowest part. Calais is the chief point of disembarkation for travelers from England, being only 21 miles from the English coast. It has considerable commercial, manufacturing, and shipbuilding interests and is the chief center in France for the making of lace.

Calais was held by England from 1347 to 1558. During World War I, it was used by England as the principal point of disembarking troops for France. Population, 70,707.

Cambrai (*käɴ'brĕ'*). An industrial town of northern France, noted for its manufacture of linen and of cotton textiles. The city has given its name to the fabric known as cambric.

In the vicinity of Cambrai, on Nov. 20, 1917, was fought the battle in which tanks were first used on a large scale. Population, 32,601.

Canterbury. A cathedral city in the southeast of England, lying south of the Thames and about 56 miles east of London. Christchurch Cathedral is the crowning architectural feature of the city. Although the cathedral was a target for German bombers during World War II, it was not directly hit. Nearby buildings, however, were destroyed. The Archbishop of Canterbury is, next to the king, the highest official of the Anglican Church. Among the distinguished Catholic archbishops who, prior to the Reformation, presided over the see, were Saint Augustine, Lanfranc, Anselm, and Thomas à Becket, the one last mentioned having been murdered in the cathedral. The building contains, among other tombs, that of Henry IV and of the Black Prince. The city has many interesting ruins, including those of Canterbury castle, a fortress of Norman construction. A public drinking fountain commemorates Marlowe, who was a native of Canterbury. Population, 32,020.

Cantigny (*kän'tēɴ'y'*). A village of northern France, 18 miles south of Amiens. On May 28, 1918, it was the scene of the first American offensive in World War I.

Capri (*kä'prē*). A beautiful, rocky island at the entrance of the gulf of Naples, Italy, visited annually by more than 60,000 tourists. Its area is nearly 6 square miles, and its highest point is about 2000 feet above the sea. One of its most remarkable features is the Blue grotto, the roof and sides of which are composed mostly of stalactites. The grotto is on the coast and is called blue because the light, refracted in passing through the water at the cave's mouth, causes the interior of the grotto to appear blue. Capri is the scene of Norman Douglas's famous modern novel, *South Wind* (1917).

Capri was anciently famous for the palace there to which the Roman emperor Tiberius retired in order to spend his last years in pleasures. It had also a large Roman lighthouse, the remains of which are still visible. A more recent ruin is that of Barbarossa, a castle named after a pirate who partially destroyed it in 1544. Population, about 7000.

Cardiff. The principal seaport and largest city of Wales, situated at the southeastern extremity of the principality near the northern coast of Bristol channel. The city is the largest coal exporting port in Europe and ranks among the largest ports of England in its total shipping tonnage. Besides coal, its chief exports are iron and steel products, machinery, railroad cars, and vehicles. Its docks cover more than 200 acres, and there are 7 miles of wharves. In Cathays park, at the center of the city, is one of the finest groups of public buildings in Great Britain. Near by is Cardiff castle, which embraces structures dating from Roman and medieval times. Cardiff is also the seat of University College of South Wales. Population, 259,700.

Carrara (*kär-rä'rä*). A city of northern Italy celebrated for its marble quarries. It is situated 3 miles inland from the eastern extremity of the Gulf of Genoa in a valley surrounded by marble hills. Most of the city's buildings are of marble, and there is a museum containing numerous statues and Roman antiquities discovered in the vicinity. Population, 37,386.

Cartagena. A Mediterranean port and strong naval station in the southeastern part of Spain. The chief industries are tunny fishing, shipbuilding, lead smelting, glass blowing, ironworking, and the manufacture of cordage and of other esparto grass products. The city is well built and is still surrounded by walls.

Cartagena was named after the city of Carthage. The city was founded about 243 B. C. by Hasdrubal, a Carthaginian general, who called the city *Carthago Nova*, "New Carthage." It was captured by the Romans in 210 B. C. and afterward was occupied successively by the Vandals, Moors, Spaniards, English, and French. Population, 42,424.

Catania (*kä-tä'nyä*). An Italian city on the eastern coast of Sicily, situated at the southeastern base of Mount Etna. The city has broad, well kept streets and many fine public buildings. A large trade in agricultural products is carried on in Catania, and there are important manufactures of linen, cotton, silk goods, and art objects of lava, wood, and marble. The chief attraction is Mount Etna. The city contains the remains of an ancient theater.

Catania was founded by Greeks in 729 B. C. and was held successively by the Carthaginians, Romans, Goths, Saracens, Normans, and the rulers of Aragon, from whom it passed to Italy. Population, 391,709.

Channel Islands. A cluster of islands lying in the English Channel near the northwestern coast of France, of which the principal ones are Jersey, Guernsey, Alderney, and Sark. Originally a part of the Duchy of Normandy, they have belonged to Great Britain since the Norman Conquest. Although rocky, about half of their 75 square miles is arable.

The Channel Islands are much frequented by tourists. Jersey contains a gorge more than 1000 feet deep in the cliffs at Crabbe. Other features of the islands include a picturesque natural archway of rock on Dixcart bay; a feudal manor house at Samares, dating from the 11th or 12th century; and Mousterian caves which, when explored recently, exhibited the remains of Neanderthal men, of the woolly rhinoceros, the cave hyena, and other animals now extinct. The state of New Jersey was named after the island of Jersey. Population, 113,416.

Chateau Thierry (*shä'tō' tyĕ'rē'*). A town in the northern part of France, on the Marne River 47 miles east and slightly north of Paris. At this point, in June 1918, American troops engaged German forces advancing toward Paris and effectively checked their progress. Several weeks later, a general counter attack swept the Germans back a distance of many miles. The town is named after a castle in the neighborhood, which was built by Charles Martel for the Frankish king Thierry IV. On July 15, 1923, a monument commemorating the American victory was erected in a square of the town, renamed United States place. Population, 9356.

Chemnitz (*kĕm'nĭts*) (**Karl-Marx-Stadt**). An industrial city of East Germany situated at the base of the Erzgebirge Mountains. The principal manufactures include locomotives and engines, textiles, hosiery, carpets, chemicals, and dyestuffs. Founded as a market town in 1143, Chemnitz has a varied but unbroken history as an industrial city extending from the 13th century until the present. Population, 294,973.

Cherbourg (*shĕr'bōōr'*). A strongly fortified French naval station near the center of the country's northern coast on the English channel. Its ocean railroad station, opened in 1933, is one of the largest buildings in France. It was from this port that the Confederate cruiser, the *Alabama*, was forced by the French authorities to put out to sea before it was sunk by the United States vessel, the *Kearsarge*. Population 37,096.

Coblenz (**Koblenz**). A commercial and manufacturing city of West Germany, beautifully situated at the confluence of the Moselle and the Rhine River. It was rich in old churches and art monuments until World War II, when most of the city was destroyed.

Coblenz has an active trade in grain. Its manufactures consist mainly of Moselle wine, ships, hats, machinery, pianos, and lacquered wares. The finest edifice is the government building, in which are centered the administrative activities of the province of Rhenish Prussia. Saint Castor's church, founded in 836, ranks among the oldest in Germany. Population, 99,240.

Cologne (*kô-lōn'*) (**Köln**). A large commercial and manufacturing city of central West Germany, beautifully located on the left bank of the Rhine river. *Eau de Cologne* is a distinctive product. The chief manufactures are leather goods, chemicals, starch, textiles, rubber goods, machinery, metal wares, beet sugar, tobacco products, and chocolate.

The outstanding feature of Cologne's architecture is the Gothic cathedral, begun in 1248 and completed in 1880. Two of its towers rise to a height of 512 feet. The cathedral, though damaged, survived World War II, in which most of the other Romanesque and Gothic buildings perished. The Church of Saint Ursula is reported to contain the bones of 11,000 British virgins who were massacred near Cologne on their way to Rome. The Virgin islands in the West Indies owes its name to this tradition.

Cologne was founded in the 1st century A. D. under the name of Colonia Agrippina, of which its modern name is a corruption. Rubens, the painter, lived in the city, and one of the local churches contains the tomb of John Duns Scotus. Population, 861,027.

Copenhagen (*kō'pĕn-hā'gĕn*) (**Köbenhavn**). The capital and largest city of Denmark, situated on a deep, safe, and capacious harbor on the northeast shore of the island of Zealand. Across the harbor, on the island of Amager, is the modern suburb of Christianshavn. Copenhagen commands the sea highway from the Baltic to the North Sea and was at one time the chief distributing mart of the Baltic trade. To offset the advantages given by the Kiel canal to Germany's seaports, Copenhagen, in 1894, made part of its harbor a free port. Shipbuilding is the chief industry. Among the manufactures are agricultural machines, porcelains, textiles, sugar, watches, and chemicals.

A characteristic feature of Copenhagen is the large number of spires, which occur on many public buildings as well as on the churches. The Church of Our Redeemer has a winding staircase built outside the spire 295 feet to its top. Copenhagen is the seat of the University of Copenhagen and is the headquarters of many learned societies. The Thorvaldsen Museum contains over 300 works executed by Thorvaldsen, Denmark's greatest sculptor. Hans Christian Andersen was one of the city's most distinguished residents. Population, 1,377,605.

Cordoba (*kôr'dô-vä*). An inland city of southern Spain, located on the Guadalquivir River. The city was founded by the Phœnicians and attained to considerable importance under the Romans. It later became the metropolis of the Moors in Spain and, from the 9th to the 12th century, was one of the greatest centers of commerce in the world. The Mosque of Cordoba, now used as a Catholic cathedral, is the most magnificent example of Mohammedan architecture in Europe. The city is now in decline, its manufactures being confined largely to textiles, gold and silver filigree work, and cordovan leather. The last named article obtained its name from Cordoba. Cordoba was the birthplace of the Roman poet Lucan, of the two Senecas, and of the Arab philosopher Averroës. Population, 214,296.

Cork. A port of central southern Eire, situated on a capacious natural harbor formed by the estuary of the River Lee. It has a lower harbor, Cobh, formerly Queenstown, located at the river's mouth, an important Irish port of call for trans-Atlantic liners. A heavy trade in foodstuffs is carried on with England. The city's chief manufactures are leather, liquors, gloves, fertilizers, and textiles.

Among the finest buildings are the Anglican and the Catholic cathedral, both dedicated to Saint Finn Barr, who founded the city in 622 A. D. The Church of Saint Anne Shandon has a notable peal of bells. Other features of the city are University college, a school of science and of agriculture, and a public park, 240 acres in extent. Population, 122,146.

Coventry. An industrial city of central England, noted for its manufacture of automobiles, ribbons, artificial silk, telephone equipment, and electric motors. Coventry is a very old town and was for centuries the scene of an annual pageant commemorating the ride of Lady Godiva. According to tradition, she agreed to ride naked through the streets in order to save the citizens from certain exactions, her husband, Earl Leofric, having demanded this action as a condition of relieving the townspeople. The pageant was last celebrated in 1887. Saint Mary's Hall, built in 1450, is one of the finest examples of ornamental architecture in England. Much of the city, including a 14th century cathedral, was destroyed by bombing in World War II. The latter was replaced by a magnificent cathedral in modern architectural style. Population, 331,950.

Dardanelles. A narrow channel, 42 miles long and 1 to 5 miles wide, joining the Sea of Marmora and the Ægean Sea. The territory about the strait, affording an excellent defense of Istanbul from the West, was the scene of a costly offensive against Turkey during World War I. After the war, it was placed under the control of an Allied commission, but Turkey resumed control in 1936.

The ancient name of the Dardanelles was Hellespont, across which, in spite of its strong current, the mythical Leander is said to have swum each evening to visit Hero. Lord Byron swam the Hellespont at the point where Xerxes crossed it in 480 B. C.

Dnepropetrovsk. A large and rapidly developing industrial city of the Russian Ukraine located at the junction of the Dnieper and Donets rivers. Its major industries are iron and steel, machine construction, chemicals, and food products. The city shared in the hydroelectric development of the vast Dnepr dam, destroyed in 1941, but since restored. Its population is 738,000, more than double that of 1926.

Dortmund (*dôrt'mŏŏnt*). A railway center and manufacturing city of central West Germany in the northern part of the Ruhr district. Located in the midst of rich coal mines, the city has become an important point for the manufacture of steel products, including machinery, wire ropes, rails, mining equipment, and safes. Among other products are flour, lumber, and liquors. Since 1900, its population has more than tripled, standing, according to the latest reports, at 657,087. Largely devastated in World War II, it was promptly rebuilt.

Dover. A heavily fortified port and favorite summer resort of England, situated at the southeastern extremity of the country. White chalk cliffs tower nearly 400 feet above the harbor, and, on clear days, afford a view of the opposite coast of France, 21 miles distant. The chief industrial products are ships, sails, rope, and flour. Towering 375 feet above the sea is Dover Castle, covering 35 acres, which includes within its ancient walls a Roman lighthouse. Population, 36,080.

Dragoman. Picturesque Bulgarian town at the easterly end of the Dragoman Pass, near the Yugoslavian frontier. Bernard Shaw made it the scene of his play, *Arms and the Man*, which was later turned into the opera, *The Chocolate Soldier*. The famous international train, the Orient Express, stops at Dragoman for customs inspection.

Dresden. An industrial city of East Germany. It is situated on the Elbe River and is an important railway center. The chief manufactures include pianos, confectionery, silverware, jewelry, chemicals, glassware, and metal goods. Dresden china is made at Meissen, a suburb.

In World War II about 60 per cent of the city, with most of the art and architectural monuments, was destroyed. Since then many art treasures, including Raphael's "Sistine Madonna," which were safely stored outside the city during the war, have been transferred to Russia Population, 507,470.

Dublin. The capital and largest city of Eire, situated on an inlet near the center of Ireland's eastern coast. A large part of the country's exported foodstuffs are handled through the port of Dublin. Liquors are made in considerable quantity.

Dublin as a whole, with its fine bay, wide streets, spacious squares, magnificent 2000-acre park, massive public buildings, and beautiful suburbs, is one of the handsomest capitals in Europe. Christ Church, in Early English Gothic style, was begun in 1038 by a Danish king of Dublin. Saint Patrick's Cathedral is about 700 years old. The city has statues of O'Connell, Burke, Goldsmith, and many other famous Irishmen. The University of Dublin is the chief educational institution. Population, 568,772.

Duisburg (*düs'bŏŏrκ*). A manufacturing city of central West Germany, in the Ruhr district. Its quays, built along canals and on the Rhine and the Ruhr rivers, are said to constitute the largest river harbor in the world. The chief commodities handled are coal and the products of the city's industries—iron and steel products, chemicals, liquors, asphalt, varnish, furniture, and tobacco. The former cities of Duisburg and Hamborn were combined in 1929. Population, 483,993.

Düsseldorf (*düs'ĕl-dôrf*). A manufacturing city of West Germany, situated on the right bank of the Rhine at the influx of the Düssel River. The harbor is spacious and well equipped, and there is a large export trade. The city has great iron and steel industries and textile manufactures. Chemicals, tobacco goods, chocolate, beer, paper, glass, and musical instruments are also made.

Destruction of Düsseldorf in World War II was widespread and drastic. In a situation between the Ruhr coal and steel area and the Federal capital at Bonn, Düsseldorf is becoming more and more the industrial and banking center of West Germany. It is also tending to lead in German commercial development of women's fashions. Population, 698,421.

Edinburgh (*ĕd''n-bŭr-ô*). The second largest city of Scotland. It is built near the south shore of the Firth of Forth, which is here spanned by a bridge 1½ miles in length. Edinburgh is the seat of the supreme court of Scotland and was the seat of government before the country united politically with England. The chief industries include printing and publishing, and the manufacture of liquors, leather, flour, and rubber goods.

Edinburgh consists of an old and a new section. Through the latter runs the magnificent Princes street, one of the finest thoroughfares in Europe. Near it stands the beautiful Scottish American war memorial. Among the city's points of interest are Holyrood Palace; Saint Giles Church, which has a memorial tablet to R. L. Stevenson designed by Saint-Gaudens; a magnificent monument to Sir Walter Scott; a small Greek temple erected to the memory of Robert Burns; and Calton cemetery, which contains a statue of Abraham Lincoln with a freed slave kneeling at his feet. Edinburgh has a handsome library donated by Andrew Carnegie. There are numerous educational institutions, the most famous of which is the University of Edinburgh. The predominance of literary elements in the city's population, combined with its picturesque location, has won for it the name of "modern Athens."

The city was named after Edwin, king of Northumbria, who seized it in the 7th century A. D. and built a fortress on Castle rock, a precipitous height which dominates the city. The Royal Castle now stands on the site of Edwin's fortress. Population, 467,986.

Essen. A steel manufacturing city of West Germany, situated in the Ruhr district and surrounded by rich coal and iron deposits. The recent industrial growth of the city is due mainly to the activities of the Krupp corporation. The town, however, traces its origin to 873 A. D., when construction began on the cathedral, which is one of the oldest churches in Germany. Population, 721,182.

Etna. The largest active volcano in Europe. It is an isolated mountain, 10,705 feet high, in northeastern Sicily near Catania and has a base 90 miles in circumference. On its eastern side is a former crater, now a vast amphitheater with nearly precipitous sides 3000 feet in height.

The first recorded eruption of Etna was in the 8th century B. C. Another, occurring in 477 B. C., is graphically described in Æschylus' *Prometheus Bound*. Later eruptions of a violent character took place in 1169, 1527, 1669, 1693, 1852, 1864, 1879, 1911, 1923, and 1928. In that of 1669 more than 20,000 people were killed. An observatory and a house for the convenience of travelers have been erected near the chief crater. A large part of the world's supply of sulphur came formerly from Mount Etna.

Fingal's Cave. A remarkable cave of basalt formation, on Staffa, a small island off the central western coast of Scotland. The cave extends from the shore a distance of 227 feet within a rocky height and has an arch 66 feet high. Its maximum width is 42 feet. The color effects of the columnar basalt formation are no less striking than the weird sounds produced by the action of wind and wave as they play upon the opening of the huge cave.

Florence (Firenze). A city of north central Italy, lying in a fertile valley near the Apennine mountains. Florence is, next to Rome, the most celebrated Italian city, being noted for its illustrious history and for its art treasures.

The Cathedral of Florence is the city's outstanding structure. Founded in 1296, it occupied about 200 years in construction. Its dome was planned by Brunelleschi. The bell tower of the cathedral was built by Giotto. This tower and the bronze doors of the baptistery, designed by Ghiberti, have enjoyed renown for centuries. The Franciscan church Santa Croce contains the tombs of Galileo, Michelangelo, Machiavelli, and many other distinguished men. The picture galleries contain some of the best works of Titian, Andrea del Sarto, Botticelli, Rubens, Raphael, and other great painters. Among the notable statues are the "Venus de' Medici," "Dancing Faun," and "Knife Grinder."

The city has famous academies of art, a museum of natural history, a university, a botanical garden, a large astronomical observatory, and a number of libraries, chief of which is the Laurentian library founded by Lorenzo de Medici. Florence was the birthplace of Dante and of Florence Nightingale.

The industries of the city include the manufacture of silks, glassware, porcelain, and objects of art, especially mosaics, wood carvings, majolica chinaware, stained glass, and jewelry. Florence was founded in the 2d century B. C., but the period of its greatest prosperity was in the 13th century A. D., when it was an independent city-state. Population, 454,858.

Flushing. A strongly fortified Dutch seaport, built on an island at the western extremity of the Netherlands. There is a large passenger traffic between Flushing and English ports. The city was the birthplace of Admiral de Ruyter, one of Holland's greatest naval heroes. Population, 29,141.

Folkestone. An ancient town and seaport of southeastern England, situated on the Strait of Dover. Folkestone has daily steamer communication with Boulogne in France and is also popular as a summer resort. Harvey, the discoverer of the circulation of the blood, was born in this city. Population, 43,470.

Frankfurt (Frankfort). Important commercial, in-industrial, and transportation center in central West Germany, on both sides of the lower Main River, an eastern tributary of the Rhine. It is the headquarters of the American armed forces in Europe, and of the U. S. zone high commissioner. The city has important literary and historical associations.

About 55 per cent of Frankfort was destroyed in World War II, but some of the most famous buildings, including Goethe's birthplace, have been rebuilt. It has a university, and other colleges and institutes. There is a monument to Gutenberg, the inventor of movable type. Frankfort was formerly the electoral city of the Holy Roman Empire, and, after 1816, the German Parliament held its sessions there. Population, 684,798.

Freiburg (*frī'bo͝ork*). A city in the southwestern extremity of Germany, noted for its magnificent Gothic cathedral. This edifice, built of red sandstone, was begun in 1122 and was completed in 1513. It is admired for the delicate symmetry shown in its design as well as for its splendid tower, which is 386 feet high. Population, 150,437.

Geneva (Genève). A beautiful city of western Switzerland, situated at the lower end of Lake Geneva where its waters flow into the Rhone River. The city covers two islands in the river, one of which, called Rousseau's island, is a public pleasure ground commemorating the revolutionary writer, who was a native of the city. The left bank of the river is occupied by the old city and the business section, while, on the right bank, is the quarter called Saint Gervais, mainly residential in character. The latter district contains numerous hotels for the accommodation of the many tourists who enter Switzerland by way of Geneva.

The University of Geneva was originally founded as an academy in 1559 by Calvin, who made Geneva the chief center of Protestantism in the 16th century. Swiss heroes of the Reformation are further commemorated in Geneva by a recently erected monument entitled the "Wall of the Reformers." The manufactures of the city consist principally of clocks, watches, jewelry, enameled ware, and scientific instruments. Geneva, formerly the headquarters of the League of Nations, is now the European headquarters of the United Nations, and of many other international organizations, including the Red Cross. The city is predominantly French in language and culture. Population, 169,700.

Genoa (*jĕn'ô-ȧ*) **(Genova).** A commercial city of northeastern Italy, picturesquely situated at the head of the Gulf of Genoa. The city is strongly fortified against attacks by sea or land. Rail connections render it the sea outlet for much of the foreign trade of northern Italy, Switzerland, and southern Germany. The manufactures include foundry and other metal products, leather, cotton, cement, motor cars, crystallized fruits, and hats, and the city is also noted for its production of works of art in gold, silver, ivory, alabaster, and coral. It has large shipbuilding facilities and the largest dry dock in the Mediterranean Sea.

Among the notable examples of Genoa's many fine edifices are the ducal palaces, the residences of the doges in the days of the city's independence; the Cathedral of San Lorenzo, containing what is said to be the Holy Grail; the Church of Santissima Annunziata; and the Teatro Carlo Felice. The last named edifice was built in 1828 and ranks among the largest theaters in Italy. Genoa has an imposing sculptural group in honor of Columbus. Population, 845,427.

Ghent (Gent or Gand). A city of western Belgium, located on the Scheldt River and connected with the North Sea by a ship canal. The city is divided into islands by smaller canals, which are spanned by numerous bridges. The older part of Ghent has narrow, gloomy streets, but the newer part is laid out with wide avenues, flanked by fine houses.

Ghent contains the Cathedral of Saint Bavon, in which is the celebrated "Adoration of the Magi" by Van Eyck. There is also a great walled and moated nunnery, which, since its foundation in the 13th century, has been known for the production of exquisite lace. Ghent's principal manufactures are cotton and linen textiles, leather, and refined sugar, and the city has an active export trade in flowers. The emperor Charles V was born in Ghent, where, also, was signed the treaty which closed the War of 1812. Population, 232,736.

Giant's Causeway. A line of three perpendicular cliffs on the northeastern coast of Ireland. According to a legend, they were the beginning of a causeway to be built by giants across the channel to Scotland. They are formed of vertical basalt columns, mainly hexagonal in form and fitting closely together. The three cliffs are called the Little Causeway, the Middle Causeway, and the Grand Causeway. The last has a width of 60 to 120 feet and extends about 500 feet into the sea. On the Middle Causeway is the famous "wishing chair." The vicinity abounds in special points of interest, such as an amphitheater of natural formation and ruined castles perched on the top of isolated crags.

Glasgow. The third largest city in Great Britain situated on the Clyde River somewhat southwest of the geographical center of Scotland. Its harbor has been elaborately improved at the cost of 40 million dollars and has some 8 miles of quays. Glasgow's shipyards are the largest in the world. The industrial development is due partly to the city's location in the midst of extensive deposits of coal and of iron. The chief manufactures, apart from ships, comprise iron and steel products, textiles, coal, paper, chemicals, and whisky.

Glasgow is conspicuous for its successful management of civic operations and improvements, which include the erection of large numbers of modern apartment houses. There are many institutions for technical and higher education, of which the most important is the University of Glasgow. The municipal art gallery contains the finest collection of paintings in Great Britain outside of London, including Whistler's portrait of Carlyle. Saint Mungo's Cathedral, built between 1197 and 1446, is a beautiful example of Early English architecture. It stands on the site of a church erected in the 6th century by Saint Mungo, the patron saint of Glasgow. Population, 960,527.

Gorkiy, formerly **Nizhni Novgorod.** A city of Russia, on the Volga River about 270 miles east of Moscow. From remote antiquity, the city has been famous for its annual fair, one of the greatest of the entire world. Prices of many important commodities throughout Russia depended on those prevailing on this market. Merchandise totaling in some years over 20 million tons changed hands between August 1 and September 15.

The Soviet government chose this city as its chief center for the manufacture of automobiles. About fourteen miles from the old town, an enormous automobile factory, the largest in Europe, was placed in operation in 1931. About it was built a model soviet city designed for 60,000 inhabitants. One-third its area was devoted to parks. Residential units were built to accommodate 200 people per unit, each being equipped for communal meals and provided with facilities for amusement and instruction. The name Nizhni Novgorod was changed in 1932 to Gorki in honor of the famous writer, who was born there in 1868. Population, 1,120,000.

Göteborg (*yû'tĕ-bŏr'y'*). The second largest city of Sweden, situated in the southwestern part of the country at the mouth of the Göta River, which discharges into the Kattegat. The town was founded in 1618 by Gustavus Adolphus, but, in consequence of numerous fires, it has been largely rebuilt in recent times. It has numerous fine buildings and broad, well shaded streets, those near the river having canals running through their centers. Favored by an excellent harbor open all the year round, Göteborg conducts much of the country's foreign commerce. The industries comprise shipbuilding, textile weaving, dyeing, iron-working, brewing, and the manufacture of tobacco, furniture, paper, and leather. Population, 443,292.

Granada. An inland city of southeastern Spain, lying at the base of the Sierra Nevada about 40 miles from the Mediterranean coast. The city, having been formerly one of the chief centers of Moorish civilization in Spain, has a partially Oriental appearance. The residential section of the Moorish nobility is now in ruins and is occupied largely by gypsies. Granada's outstanding edifice is the Alhambra, a magnificent Moorish palace celebrated in America by Washington Irving's book *The Alhambra*. The cathedral, begun in 1529, commemorates the reconquest of Spain by the Christian powers. Granada has a university founded in 1531 by the emperor Charles V.

The city is in a fertile district containing groves of orange, lemon, and fig trees. Its manufactures include textiles, paper, leather, flour, macaroni, chocolate, and soap. Population, 150,186.

Graz (*gräts*). A commercial and industrial city of Austria, situated in a beautiful valley at the eastern extremity of the Alps Mountains. The principal architectural attractions include a Gothic cathedral dedicated to Saint Ogidius and noted for its exquisite stained-glass windows, a mausoleum containing the remains of Emperor Ferdinand II, and the parish church, which, built in 1520, is adorned with an altarpiece by Tintoretto. Graz has a university, founded in 1573.

A rich coal district is near the city. The manufactures comprise iron and steel goods, optical instruments, chemicals, paper, and lithographs. Graz is an important railroad and trade center. Population, 237,080.

Hague, The ('s Gravenhage). The capital of the Netherlands, situated in the southwestern part of the kingdom about two miles from the North Sea. The city is chiefly occupied with the business of governing, although there are manufactures of gold and silver lace, jewelry, and articles of iron, brass, and copper.

The Hague has broad, shaded streets, intersected by picturesque canals and lined by many fine edifices. One of the most noted buildings is the Mauritshuis, which contains masterpieces by Rembrandt, Rubens, Van Dyck, and others. The city is the headquarters of the Permanent Court of International Justice and of the International Court of Arbitration. These courts sit in the Carnegie Peace Palace, which was erected in 1913, partly through the generosity of Andrew Carnegie. Other features of the city are the royal library, the various government buildings, Willem's park, and the royal villa Huis-ten-Bosch, "House in the Woods," which stands in the suburbs amid the magnificent forests separating the city from its seaside resort, Scheveningen. Population, 589,862.

Hamburg. The largest city of West Germany, excluding Berlin, and one of the largest seaports in the world. In northwestern Germany south of the Baltic peninsula, it is connected with Cuxhaven on the North Sea, 75 miles distant, by the Elbe River. Hamburg's two harbors are on two small lakes made by damming the Alster, a stream flowing through the city. The docks are 20 miles in length and are among the best equipped in the world. Hamburg is one of the chief coffee markets of the world and handles immense quantities of wool, grain, cotton, ironware, tobacco, coal, and paper. It is also the headquarters of the Hamburg-American steamship line. The manufactures include ships, tobacco products, liquors, flour, chocolate, rubber, chemicals, electrical goods, motor cars, and steel products. Workingmens' sections were devastated in World War II.

Hamburg was one of the principal cities of the Hanseatic League in the 13th century. In 1842, a large part of the city was destroyed by fire and was since rebuilt in a modern fashion. As a memorial of the fire, the Church of Saint Nicholas was erected, with a spire rising 482 feet above the ground. Hagenbeck's private zoological gardens contain one of the largest collections of wild animals in captivity. The city is the capital of the state of Hamburg, some 160 square miles in area, which has self-governing rights within the German republic. It is also the seat of the University of Hamburg. Population of city, 1,851,327.

Hammerfest. The most northerly incorporated town in the world, situated on an island off the northern coast of Norway 300 miles north of the Arctic circle. The inhabitants support themselves by fishing, raising reindeer, and entertaining tourists, large numbers of whom annually visit the town in order to view the spectacle of the midnight sun. The sun does not set on Hammerfest from May 13 to July 29. Population, 3470.

Hanover (Hannover). An industrial city of northern West Germany, about 150 miles west of Berlin. The leading manufactures are iron and steel products, musical instruments, machinery, rubber, cotton, cork, chocolate, tobacco, furniture, chemicals, and leather. Among the features of Hanover are the city forest, lying in the suburbs and containing a zoological garden; the Grosse Garten, a pleasure ground richly adorned with statuary; Herrenhausen Castle; the Marktkirche, a 14th century church with a tower 300 feet high; and a veterinary school founded by George III of England. It is now capital of the state of Lower Saxony. Hanover was formerly the capital of the Kingdom of Hanover, a state which, from 1714 until 1837, had the same rulers as England. Population, 547,767.

Havre, Le (E. *hä'vẽr*; F. *lẽ ȧv'r'*). One of the largest seaports of France, situated at the mouth of the Seine river near the center of the country's northern coast. Its exports are mainly silk and cotton goods. The manufactures include chemicals, rope, machinery, flour, dyes, textiles, toys, and refined oil.

The importance of Havre dates from 1517, when the improvement of its harbor was begun. During World War I, the city was temporarily made the seat of the Belgian government. Population, 183,776.

Heidelberg. A university town of Baden in southern West Germany. The university was founded in 1385 and numbers among its graduates Melanchthon, Gervinus, Kuno Fischer, and Bunsen. The town has an ancient castle, which contains in its cellar a cask with a capacity of 46,732 gallons. Near Heidelberg, in 1907, the lower jawbone of a prehistoric man was found, and the city has given its name to the racial type which, on the basis of this bone, is believed to have existed many hundreds of thousands of years ago. Population, 124,401.

Helsingfors (*hĕl'sĭng-fôrs'*) **(Helsinki).** The capital and largest city of Finland, located in the south part of the country on a peninsula projecting into the Gulf of Finland. The city is strongly fortified. It is regularly laid out and has many fine buildings and handsome parks adorned with monuments. The University of Helsingfors was originally founded at Abo in 1640 and was moved to Helsingfors in 1827. Helsingfors is the chief industrial city of Finland, manufacturing tobacco, liquors, and carpets. It has a considerable commerce in timber, paper, and dairy products. In 1952, the Olympic Games were held here. Population, 501,474.

Hull. A large seaport of central eastern England, situated at the mouth of the Hull River in the estuary of the Humber. It is the chief outlet for most of England's exports to Denmark, Norway, and Sweden. Its docks cover 200 acres. The city has extensive fishing interests, and its manufactures comprise iron goods, engines, ships, chemicals, soap, cement, paper, cotton goods, and leather. William Wilberforce was a native of Hull. Population, 300,320.

Istanbul, formerly **Constantinople.** The largest city of Turkey. It is built on a peninsula on the northern side of the Bosporus Strait at its outlet into the Sea of Marmara. Istanbul occupies a key position, commanding a vast commerce between the East and the West. It has an excellent natural harbor in the Golden Horn, a northwestern inlet of Bosporus Strait.

Stamboul, or the Turkish section, has a typically Asiatic character, being surrounded by walls, now partly ruined, and having unimproved, crooked streets, picturesque mosques, and extensive, colorful bazaars. There are two suburbs—Galata, the foreign business quarter, built mainly of stone; and Pera, a modern residential section of the foreign inhabitants, which is separated from Stamboul by the Golden Horn. The finest street in the city is the Grande Rue, in Pera, which is lined with fashionable shops and large hotels. Educational institutions include Stamboul university and Roberts college.

The most notable buildings of Istanbul are the mosques. Saint Sophia, originally built by Justinian as a church, and later converted by the Turks into a mosque, is being restored to its original beauty and is to be used as a museum. The Suleymanieh Mosque is the city's outstanding example of genuine Turkish architecture.

Secular buildings of historic interest include the Castle of the Seven Towers, once used as a state prison; the hippodrome completed by Constantine; and the old seraglio, now transformed into a museum, in which is stored an extremely valuable collection of Greek antiquities. Water for the city's use is conveyed long distances by aqueducts, some of which date from the 3d century A. D., and is held in reservoirs until required. One of these reservoirs is covered with a roof supported by 420 marble columns and is said to be the largest work of its kind in the world.

Large manufacturing establishments in Istanbul are few in number, producing mainly ironwares, leather articles, and tobacco goods. The handmade products, however, are important both in variety and in quantity. The chief exports of the city are carpets and rugs, lambskins and wool, attar of roses, embroidery, and filigree work.

Istanbul was often referred to formerly as the Sublime Porte. This is a French term meaning the lofty gate and referred to an elaborate entrance into the enclosure containing the government buildings. This name was used to designate the city as a political capital.

The city was founded in the 6th century B. C. by Greek colonists, who gave it the name Byzantium. In 330 A. D., Constantine the Great made it the capital of the Roman Empire, changing its name to Constantinople. Taken by the Turks in 1453, the city became the capital of the Ottoman empire and the residence of the head of the Moslem religion. In 1920, however, the Turkish Nationalists revolted, choosing as their capital Ankara, in Asia Minor. The name Constantinople was then changed officially to Istanbul. It is now Turkey's chief link with the Western world. Population, 1,750,642.

Jena (*yā'nä*). A university town within East Germany. The university, founded in 1558, has numbered among its professors Humboldt, Hegel, Fichte, Schiller, Haeckel, and Eucken. Goethe resided here at one time. The city is also noted for its production of lenses. Jena was the scene of a disastrous German defeat in the Napoleonic wars. Population, 82,113.

Karlovy Vary. Formerly known as Karlsbad, this is one of the most celebrated fashionable watering places of Europe, situated in Czechoslovakia. It is famous for its hot mineral springs, the daily flow of which is estimated at 2 million gallons. The name means Charle's Bath, Charles IV of France having bathed there.

The principal buildings of Karlovy Vary are an iron and glass structure, called the Sprudel colonnade, and an edifice in the Greek style, called the Muhlbrunnen colonnade. The city is noted also for porcelain manufacture. The resort is visited annually by upwards of 65,000 guests. The permanent population of the town is about 43,091.

Kharkov. An industrial city of southern Russia and the administrative center of the Ukraine soviet republic. Being near to the Donetz coal field and to important iron ore deposits, it has become one of the chief Russian centers of heavy industry. The manufactures include iron and steel, machinery, agricultural implements, tractors, elevators, dynamos and electric motors, rope, coal tar products, and airplanes. Kharkov has an Institute of People's Education, an agricultural and economic institute, and museums for the demonstration of improved agricultural methods. Population, 1,125,000.

Kiev (*kē'yĕf*). One of the oldest cities in Russia, attractively situated amid wooded hills on the Dnieper River in the southwestern part of the country. The Dnieper is here spanned by a suspension bridge, 3510 feet long. In the upper town is the famous Petchersk monastery. The city has numerous churches, whose gilded cupolas, seen at a distance, impart to it an almost Oriental effect. It suffered severely from civil war and famine in 1917-20, during which period it changed hands six times.

Christianity was first preached in Russia at Kiev, which has long been the chief eastern center of the Greek Catholic religion. There is a large trade in flax, wool, wine, cattle, timber, grain, and fruits. The manufactures include sugar, hardware, tobacco goods, machinery, glass, leather, and yeast. Population, 1,413,000.

Königsberg (*kû'nĭks-bĕrk*), **Kaliningrad.** A city located in Western Russia near the border of Poland, lying on the river Pregel, about 4 miles from its mouth in the Frisches bay, a southern inlet of the Baltic Sea. It was almost entirely destroyed in 1945. Its manufactures include locomotives, chemicals, cork, tobacco, sugar, malt liquors, and pianos. Amber articles constitute a distinctive product. The University of Königsberg was founded in 1544. Kant, who was born in Königsberg in 1724, was a member of the university's professional staff. Population, 238,000.

Krakow (*krä'kō*). A city of southwestern Poland, situated at the head of navigation on the Vistula River. It was annexed by Germany in 1939. Krakow was the capital of Poland from 1320 to 1609. Favored by its position as a river port and railroad terminal, Krakow has become the trade center of a large territory. The city was founded in 700 A. D. by the Polish Duke of Krak. Population, 525,000.

Lapland. An area of indefinite extent at the northern extremity of Europe. The region has no separate political existence, but includes parts of Norway, Sweden, Finland, and Russia. Reindeer provide sustenance, clothing, and transportation. The people are called Lapps. They belong to an Asiatic race and average about 5 feet in height.

Lausanne (*lō'zän'*). A city of western Switzerland, built on five hills rising from the north shore of Lake Geneva. The city is a railroad and educational center and has a large tourist trade. The manufactures include chocolate, machinery, tobacco goods, and sugar.

The Protestant Cathedral of Notre Dame is the city's most notable church. It dates from the 13th century and was intimately associated with the rise of Protestantism. The University of Lausanne, founded as an academy in 1537, was one of the first schools established for the training of Protestant ministers. The city has been the scene of many important international conferences of statesmen. The language of the citizens is French. Gibbon wrote most of his *Decline and Fall of the Roman Empire* while a resident of Lausanne. Population, 132,500.

Leeds. A woolen and steel manufacturing city of north central England. The woolen industries especially have been famous for centuries. The chief products of the city, apart from textiles and steel, include machinery, agricultural implements, leather, furniture, artificial silk, and ready-made clothing.

In the midst of the factory district stand the celebrated ruins of Kirkstall Abbey, founded in the 12th century. The city also has a fine university and is noted for a great music festival held every three years Population, 508,000.

Leghorn (Livorno). A seaport and commercial city of northwestern Italy, situated on a spacious, improved harbor on the northeastern coast of the Tyrrhenian Sea. The industries include shipbuilding and the manufacture of copper and brass products, coral ornaments, glass, porcelain, chemicals, electrical apparatus, and flour. The city is noted also as a summer resort. The architectural monuments are comparatively few, the most notable being the cathedral, dating from the 17th century. There is a handsome synagogue founded in 1581. Population, 152,517.

Leicester (*lĕs'tẽr*). A manufacturing city of central England, about 100 miles northwest of London. The chief industrial products are woolen hosiery, boots and shoes, bricks, and dyes. The city lies in a rich coal mining and sheep raising district.

Leicester is a progressive municipality, providing adequately for the health, education, and recreation of its inhabitants. Saint Nicholas church was constructed partly of bricks taken from a Roman wall in the vicinity. The assize court of Leicester is held in a building which was formerly the banquet hall of a Norman castle. Population, 283,540.

Leiden. A city of the Netherlands about 10 miles east of The Hague and 6 miles inland from the North Sea. It has a famous university founded in 1575 by William of Orange. Leiden is also known as the birthplace of Rembrandt and as the city which received the persecuted English emigrants, some of whom sailed later in the *Mayflower* to Plymouth, Massachusetts. Population, 95,964.

Leipzig (E. *līp'sĭk;* G. *līp'tsĭk*). A city of East Germany, noted as the chief center of the country's publishing industry. There are about 1000 establishments engaged in the business. The city is also a world market for furs, which, along with glass, cloth, and leather, are sold in great quantities at fairs, three of which are held each year.

It was the birthplace of Richard Wagner, and Bach is buried in the church of St. John. Many old buildings were damaged or destroyed by bombs in World War II, but one interesting survival is Auerbach's cellar, represented by Goethe as the scene of part of his *Faust*. The city was captured by American forces in April 1945, but is now in the Russian zone. Near Leipzig, in 1813, was fought the battle in which Napoleon was defeated prior to his banishment to Elba. Population, 595,712.

Lemberg (Lvov). A city of the Ukraine, almost surrounded by strongly fortified hills. Formerly known as Lemberg, it is the seat of three archbishops and has three cathedrals—a Roman Catholic, an Armenian, and a Greek Catholic. There are many educational institutions, chief of which is a university founded in 1784, when the city was a part of Austria. Lvov was annexed by Russia in 1939.

Lvov has numerous manufactures, including ironwares, musical instruments, bricks, flour, and spirits, and conducts a large trade in linen, flax, hemp, and wool. The Fair of the Three Kings is held here each January. Population, 469,000.

Leningrad (E. *lĕn'ĭn-grăd*) (R. *lyĕ'nĭn-grät*). One of the largest cities of Russia, situated at the head of the Gulf of Finland on the delta of the Svir River. The port and fortress of the city is Kronstadt, on a near-by island. Canals connect the city with the White and Black seas.

Leningrad, formerly called Saint Petersburg, and, after 1914, Petrograd, was the creation of Peter the Great of Russia, who built it at enormous cost of labor and of life, in order to obtain communication with Western Europe. He populated it, in part, by compelling his wealthier subjects to spend a portion of each year in the city. Its name was changed to Leningrad in 1924.

From the Admiralty, in the center of Leningrad, radiate three great avenues, one of which—Prospekt of the 25th of October—ranks among the finest streets in Europe. Near the Admiralty stands the Winter Palace. It is connected by a gallery with the Hermitage, which houses an art collection of rare value. Across the Neva river from the palace is situated the prison of Saint Peter and Saint Paul, infamous for the many political prisoners formerly confined within its walls. The city has one of the finest subways in the world.

Leningrad was formerly the capital and the greatest commercial and industrial city of Russia, being the outlet for enormous exports of wheat. The Revolution of 1917 broke out there. In 1918, the national government was removed to Moscow. After a period of industrial paralysis, during which the city's population fell from over 2,300,000 to 722,000 it recovered rapidly as an industrial center. Its chief products are metal and machinery, chemicals, textiles, rubber, leather, tobacco, paper, furniture, matches, and foodstuffs. Population, 3,296,000.

Liége (*lē-ĕzh'*) or **Luik.** The chief manufacturing city of Belgium, situated amid rich coal mines in the eastern part of the country and built on both banks of the Meuse river. The chief industrial products are guns, steam engines, machinery, motor cars, and textiles. The city has numerous educational institutions, including Liége university, the museum of which contains the skeletons of many prehistoric animals found in the vicinity.

Liége is the center of the Walloon culture, akin to the French. A chapel built in the 6th century furnished the nucleus about which the city began to grow. The German attack on the surrounding fortresses was one of the first battles in World War I. Population, 450,387.

Lille (*lēl*). An industrial city in northern France, connected by a canal with the North Sea. 30 miles distant. The chief manufactures are linen and cotton textiles. locomotives, structural steel, sugar, chemicals, tobacco, and soap. Lisle thread derives its name from the city.

The city is modern in appearance and well built. Its features include the Church of Saint Maurice, the Palais des Beaux Arts with its extremely valuable collection of paintings, and Lille university, at which Pasteur was a professor. Lille suffered severely during World War I, part of the laboring population having been deported to work in German factories. Population, 193,096.

Limerick. A port of Eire in southwestern Ireland, at the head of the Shannon estuary. Butter and condensed milk are the most important exports. The industries include flour milling, the curing of bacon, and the manufacture of lace, fishhooks, leather, and clothing. Limerick is an ancient city, known to Greek geographers as Regia. It has given its name to the type of nonsense verse known as a limerick. Population, 50,786.

Limoges (*lē'mōzh'*). An old city of France, situated somewhat southwest of the geographical center of the country. It is famous for its porcelain industry, Limoges china being known in all parts of the world. Other important industries are printing and the manufacture of liquors, leather goods, hats, and gloves. The city has a museum of ancient pottery. Every seventh year, the Fête d'Ostension is celebrated to commemorate a plague, which, in the 10th century, destroyed 40,000 people. Limoges was the ancient capital of Limousin, a former French province, which gave its name to the limousine. Population, 113,378.

Lisbon. The capital and largest city of Portugal, beautifully situated at the head of the Tagus estuary about seven miles from its mouth in the Atlantic Ocean. Its harbor has few superiors and facilitates a large commerce. The city has manufactures of cork, textiles, pottery, paper, chemicals, sugar, iron castings, and machine-shop products.

Although founded by the Phœnicians, Lisbon has a modern appearance, having been almost entirely rebuilt after the earthquake and tidal wave which, in 1755, destroyed most of the city and took nearly 40,000 lives. Between the terraced levels of the city, elevators carry people up and down. The Avenue of Liberty, 300 feet wide with a double row of shade trees down the middle, commemorates the freeing of Portugal from Spain in 1640. Other features of the city include the Botanical Garden, the Estrella Garden, the Estrella Church, a university, and numerous other educational and scientific institutions. Camoëns and Vasco da Gama were born in Lisbon. Population, 825,800.

Liverpool. The third largest city of England, situated near the center of the country's western coast on the northeastern side of the Mersey River estuary. Among British cities, its total commerce is second only to that of London, while its foreign trade exceeds London's by a considerable margin, giving it the distinction of having the largest foreign commerce of any city in the world. The harbor has been elaborately improved. By a system of locks, the water level of the inner harbor is rendered independent of the tides. Docks cover an area of 660 acres, and there are about 40 miles of quays. The storage facilities include a 13-story tobacco warehouse with 36 acres of floor space. There are also installations for storing over 100,000 tons of oil and spirits in bulk.

Liverpool is connected with Birkenhead on the opposite side of the Mersey River by a railway tunnel nearly a mile long and a vehicular tunnel which ranks with the greatest in the world. Beneath the city, also, there are five tunnels used by railroads. Liverpool university is widely known for its school of tropical medicine. One of the most noteworthy of the city's buildings is Saint George's Hall, a structure of the Corinthian order, erected with the proceeds of dock profits. The Anglican cathedral, begun in 1904, is designed to be the largest in England. Also under construction is a Catholic cathedral of Christ the King, to be surmounted by a dome 168 feet in diameter, the largest in the world. Liverpool was the first city in England to provide municipal baths, having maintained such establishments since 1794. Population, 712,040.

Lodz. The second largest city of Poland, located in the west central part of the country on a site which, in 1800, was covered with impenetrable forest. It has grown with remarkable rapidity, having become, since 1870, largely through the activity of Germans, the chief center of the textile industry in Poland. Other manufactures include chemicals, beer, machinery, and silk. Population, 745,400.

LONDON. The capital of Great Britain and Northern Ireland, the commercial, financial, artistic, and intellectual center of the kingdom, and the second largest city in the world. It is situated in southeastern England on both banks of the Thames River about 60 miles from its mouth. London consists of three parts: "the City," a space one square mile in area; the County of London; and the "Outer Ring," or metropolitan district. The whole constitutes Greater London, which covers an area of 693 square miles lying within a radius of 15 miles from Charing Cross, a central point in the heart of London.

Commerce. London handles one-third of Great Britain's commerce. The docks cover about 650 acres, and the quays have a total length of 28 miles. Each dock is an interior basin accessible by means of a lock. The port officials and their staffs are accommodated in a domed edifice completed in 1922 at a cost of ten million dollars. London's foreign commerce amounts to nearly four billion dollars annually. Products handled by the port come from all parts of the world and exhibit an extraordinary variety. Wool represents the greatest bulk.

Industry. London easily leads all other cities of Great Britain in the aggregate value of manufactures. The clothing industries engage the greatest number of workers. Other important manufactures are furniture, machinery, silks, and leather products. Printing and bookbinding employ nearly 50,000 persons. The industrial establishments are mainly confined to the eastern and southern parts of the city.

Transportation. All the trunk railway lines of England converge in London, which is, also, connected with European points by airplane service. Electric railways operate subways, or "tubes," and cross beneath the river by means of tunnels. The river is spanned by numerous bridges, of which London bridge, Tower bridge, Blackfriars, Waterloo, and Westminster are among the more noteworthy.

Streets. The thoroughfares of London are not laid out on straight lines but parallel the winding of the Thames river. The more famous streets include a popular promenade along the Thames embankment; Lombard street, the financial center of the city; Fleet street and Paternoster row, both devoted to printing and bookselling; Whitehall street and Downing street, where the government offices are located; Haymarket, a street of theaters and cafes; the Strand, an avenue of retail stores, hotels, and places of amusement; Regent street, with handsome shops; Piccadilly, lined with shops and hotels; and Bond street, also noted for its shops. Large sections of London were devastated during World War II.

Squares, Parks, and Monuments. Charing Cross, standing in the center of Greater London, is named after a memorial cross erected in 1290 by Edward I in the former village of Charing. The cross has disappeared, and its place has, since 1675, been occupied by a statue of Charles I. Popularly, the name is associated with a near-by railroad station, in the courtyard of which stands a modern reproduction of the cross.

Trafalgar square contains a lofty column in memory of Nelson and a statue of Washington, the latter a gift from the state of Virginia in 1922. Hyde park with the adjoining Kensington gardens covers 630 acres and contains a large statue of the duke of Wellington and the national monument to Queen Victoria. Whitehall has a magnificent cenotaph erected "To the Glorious Dead," a memorial to the English soldiers who fell in World War I. In Regent park is located one of the greatest zoological gardens in the world. Other pleasure grounds include Saint James park and Epping forest, the latter being a tract of 5600 acres northeast of London purchased by the city and thrown open to the citizens.

Buildings. The Tower of London, erected by William the Conqueror, stands guard over the eastern entrance of "the City." Formerly used as a prison, it serves now chiefly as a museum and contains the crown jewels of the British sovereigns. The Houses of Parliament, known as Westminster Palace, cover 8 acres on the bank of the Thames river. The building has 1100 rooms and two towers, one with an altitude of 340 feet. The other is 318 feet high and contains a clock which rings "Big Ben," a famous bell weighing 13 tons. Saint Paul's Cathedral, planned by Sir Christopher Wren, is surmounted by a dome which reaches a point 364 feet above the street. Buckingham palace is the residence of the royal family when in London.

Westminster Abbey, dating from 1220, is the coronation church of the British sovereigns. It has a length of 531 feet, a width of 203 feet, and a tower rising 225 feet above the ground. The building is the burial place of many of the country's rulers, and has monuments to famous British warriors and statesmen. The "Poets' Corner," in the south transept, contains the tombs of most of England's great writers from Chaucer to John Ruskin.

Among the other notable buildings and institutions of the city are the British Museum, which contains three million volumes and priceless treasures of ancient art and antiquities; London university, adjoining the British Museum: the Bank of England building, covering four acres of ground; the South Kensington Museum, where classes are conducted in art and in industrial sciences; the Temple, a group of buildings long known as the residences of law students; and the People's Palace, used for recreation and for education of the poorer classes. London university comprises upwards of 30 different colleges located in various parts of the city.

London has many reminders of America. A statue of Lincoln faces Westminster Abbey, and within the famous edifice is a bust of Longfellow and a window and tablet to Lowell. John Harvard, the founder of Harvard university, was baptized in Southwark's cathedral. John Quincy Adams was married in All Hallows church, where, too, William Penn was baptized. Theodore Roosevelt's second marriage was solemnized in Saint George's church, Hanover square. In Saint Margaret's church, Americans have installed a beautiful window to the memory of Phillips Brooks, Episcopal bishop of Massachusetts. Pocahontas is commemorated by a window in a small Gravesend church, where she was buried in 1617. Christ church has a Lincoln tower with the Stars and Stripes cut in the stone. In Westminster Abbey, a tablet was erected in 1923 commemorating Walter Hines Page, American ambassador to Great Britain during World War I. In 1950, a statue of Franklin D. Roosevelt was erected in St. James's Square.

Government. Greater London has no mayor, but, in most matters, is directly under the control of Parliament. "The City," however, is nominally independent even of the sovereign, who may not enter until he receives the key of admission from the lord mayor. London county consists of a large number of boroughs, each having its mayor and alderman.

History. London is first mentioned in history by the Romans, who built walls about the city. It was later burned by the British queen Boadicea, sacked by the Danes, and later was taken by William the Conqueror, who granted the city its charter. In 1666, the Great Fire destroyed four-fifths of the buildings. In 1851, the first international industrial exhibition took place in London. Population, 7,880,760.

Lourdes (*lo͞ord*). A town of southwestern France, situated at the foot of the Pyrenees mountains and about 80 miles from the head of the Bay of Biscay. It is one of the chief places of Catholic pilgrimage in Europe, being visited annually by upward of 600,000 people.

The fame of Lourdes dates from 1858, when the Virgin appeared to a young girl, Bernadette Soubirous. The grotto near which the apparition took place is now surmounted by the magnificent Church of the Rosary, containing a shrine dedicated to the Virgin, "Our Lady of Lourdes." The church contains numerous crutches, tablets, and gifts, which memorialize cures credited to the Virgin. A near-by spring, which appeared at the time of the apparition, is diverted into several basins, in which the pilgrims bathe. On August 20 each year, a national pilgrimage is conducted to Lourdes.

The inhabitants of Lourdes are economically dependent on the pilgrims. The chief products are souvenirs. Population, 15,691.

Louvain. A city of central Belgium, formerly the center of a thriving textile industry. In recent times, the city has been chiefly noted for the University of Louvain, founded in 1425-26, and for several fine buildings, a number of which were burned while the city was under German occupation during World War I. A new library building, erected mainly by American generosity, was dedicated in 1928. Population, 32,524.

Lucerne (Luzern). A city of north central Switzerland, having a location of rare beauty at the northwestern extremity of the Lake of Lucerne. The inhabitants are occupied chiefly in providing accommodation and services for tourists, who throng the city's 70 hotels in numbers exceeding an annual total of 140,000. The most noted memorial of the town is the famous "Lion of Lucerne." It is in a nearby grotto and consists of a colossal figure of a lion transfixed by a spear but still defending the lilies of France. The figure is carved from the solid rock and was executed in memory of the 781 Swiss guards of Louis XVI, who were slain in 1792 during the attack on the Tuileries in Paris. Population, 72,400.

Lyon. A commercial and manufacturing city of France, situated southeast of the country's geographical center at the junction of the Rhône and the Saône rivers. The rivers are crossed by 24 bridges, one of which, opened in 1918, is called President Wilson bridge.

Industrially, Lyon is second only to Paris among the cities of France and is the foremost silk manufacturing city of the world. Other important products include rayon and cellophane, chemicals, machinery, macaroni, hats, chocolate, leather, jewelry, and tobacco goods.

Lyon's importance dates from the period of the Roman republic. The ruins of a Roman bath and of a Roman theater still remain. The city's oldest edifice, the Church of Saint Martin d'Ainay, utilizes several columns of a Roman temple which formerly occupied the site. The Cathedral of Saint Jean, begun in 1110, is one of the finest examples of early Gothic in France. Other notable structures are the Hôtel de Ville, the Bourse, and the Palais des Arts. The University of Lyon ranks next to that of Paris among French universities in number of students. The Roman emperors Claudius and Caracalla were born in Lugdunum, as Lyon was called by the Romans. Population, 528,535.

Lvov. See *Lemberg*.

Madrid. The capital and largest city of Spain, situated 2100 feet above sea level on a plateau near the center of the country. In this city are centered most of Spain's governmental, educational, and artistic activities. Since 1890, manufactures have increased greatly and now include leather, chemicals, pottery and porcelain, matches, cork, paper, glass, foundry products, furniture, and carpet.

Madrid centers about a plaza lined with impressive buildings. The ten most important streets radiate from this plaza. The magnificent Liberty Avenue, traversing the city in a north and south direction and ornamented with four to six rows of trees and with numerous monuments, is one of the finest promenades in the world. The Royal Palace, built of granite and white marble, stands on a hill which overlooks the city from the west. The adjoining armories contain the armor of Columbus and that of Cortés. Other features of the city are the National library, the University of Madrid, the Press Palace of skyscraper-like construction, a magnificent bull ring seating over 13,000 persons, and the National art gallery, the last containing, next to the Louvre, the world's most valuable collection of paintings. Population, 2,599,330.

Maelstrom (*māl'strŏm*). The literary and former name of Moskenstrom, a celebrated tidal eddy, occurring between two small islands at the western end of the Lofoten group off Norway's northwestern coast. The eddy is caused by the tidewaters passing through a narrow channel between the ocean and Vestfiord. The Maelstrom was memorialized by Schiller in his poem "The Diver." When the current flows fastest and the wind blows directly against it, the sea for miles around becomes so agitated that small vessels cannot survive in it. Ordinarily it may be traversed without danger The name is often used as a synonym for whirlpool.

Magdeburg (G. *mäg'dĕ-bo͝ork*; E. *măg'dĕ-bûrg*). A commercial city of East Germany, situated on the Elbe River 88 miles southwest of Berlin. The chief manufactures include steel products, sugar, chemicals, tobacco goods, gloves, fertilizers, cement, glass, and rubber. The old royal palace is now used as a museum. Magdeburg was the birthplace of Otto von Guericke, the inventor of the air pump. The city sided with the Protestant powers during the Thirty Years' war and, in 1631, was sacked and burned, 30,000 of the inhabitants being put to the sword. Population, 268,048.

Malaga (S. *mä'lä-gä;* E. *măl'ȧ-gȧ*). An ancient city of southern Spain, picturesquely located on a fine harbor opening into the Mediterranean Sea. A mountain range surrounds the town on three sides. The principal architectural feature is the vast cathedral dominating the whole view of the city from the sea. Malaga is known for Malaga wine, grapes, and raisins. The site was first settled by Phœnicians. Population, 312,018.

Malmö (*mälm'û'*). A seaport of southern Sweden, situated on The Sound opposite Copenhagen. Malmö is an important railroad terminal and manufacturing center and has grown rapidly in recent years. Among its industrial products are iron castings, railroad cars, and textiles. The city has a large artificial harbor and exports much farm produce. Population, 253,502.

Manchester. A manufacturing city and third largest port of England, lying about 200 miles northwest of London and 35 miles inland from the western seaboard. It is connected with the sea by the Manchester ship canal, which was the first ship canal to be built in England.

Manchester is the largest cotton manufacturing city in the world and the center of one of the world's greatest industrial areas. Besides cotton, the manufactures include structural steel, electrical machinery, chemicals, glass, paper, rubber, and silk. The city has 1600 acres devoted to parks. Victoria University of Manchester is the city's leading educational institution.

The more important buildings include the town hall, a Gothic structure costing over $5 million; the Royal Exchange; The Royal Institution, an art gallery in the Doric style; Free Trade Hall; and Ship Canal House, the tallest commercial building, constructed on American design. Population, 625,250.

Mannheim (*măn'hīm*). A manufacturing city of West Germany, situated at the confluence of the Rhine and the Neckar River, 43 miles south of Frankfort. Mannheim is said to be the most regularly built city on the continent of Europe. It consists of 136 square sections, the whole surrounded by a semicircular boulevard, known as the Ring Strasse. Outside the semicircle are numerous suburbs. Nearly all historic buildings were destroyed in World War II.

Mannheim's commerce consists chiefly of grain, coal, petroleum, tobacco, sugar, and ironware. The manufactures include machinery, celluloid, carpets, chemicals, furniture, glass, and leather goods. Population, 329,911.

Marseille (*mȧr'sâ'y'*). The second largest city of France and the republic's principal seaport, located in the southeastern part of the country on an inlet of the Mediterranean Sea. Southwest of the harbor lies the islet Chateau d'If, celebrated in Dumas's *Count of Monte Cristo*.

Marseille's trade is largely with eastern countries and with the French Community in northern Africa. It consists mainly of woolen goods, ribbons, sugar, and wines. The city has large shipyards and factories for making soap, vegetable oils, and numerous other products.

The national anthem of France, "The Marseillaise," received its name in Paris when a battalion of Marseillais, or citizens of Marseille, sang the song at the storming of the Tuileries. Massilia was the name given to the city by the Romans when the settlement was already many centuries old, having been founded by Phœnicians prior to 600 B. C. It was the home of Pytheas, a Greek explorer who visited Britain in the 4th century B. C. The city's importance in modern times dates from 1848, when the surrounding region was irrigated by a canal from the Durance River about 100 miles distant. Marseille has the finest modern cathedral in France. Population, 778,071.

Milan (*mĭl'ăn; mĭ-lăn'*) **(Milano).** The second largest city of Italy. It lies in the northwestern part of the country about 40 miles from the border of Switzerland. Milan is the chief financial center of Italy and ranks high as an industrial community and as a seat of art and learning. The more important manufactures include locomotives, automobiles, electrical supplies, and rubber articles. The silk, printing, and furniture making trades of Italy are centered in the city,

The Cathedral of Milan, dating from 1386, is the third largest in Europe. Built of white marble, it is 486 feet long and 356 feet high. It contains 3000 statues, and its stained-glass windows are said to be the largest in the world. The edifice has a capacity for 40,000 people. Other features of the city are the Church of Sant' Ambrogio, dating from the 4th century A. D.; the former convent of Santa Maria delle Grazie, which contains Leonardo da Vinci's "Last Supper"; the Brera Palace, one of the finest picture galleries in Italy; the Teatro della Scala, the second largest opera house in Europe; and a celebrated archeological museum.

Milan was captured from the Gauls by the Romans in 222 B. C. It has frequently been sacked and burned, but its position at the northern entrance to Italy has insured its continued importance as a commercial city. Population, 1,228,092.

Monte Carlo. A city in the principality of Monaco, beautifully situated on a sheltered bay in the Mediterranean coast. Monte Carlo is best known for its Casino, a palatial building on a promontory in the east of the city. It is the chief fashionable gambling resort of Europe. The principal games played are roulette and *trente et quarante*, "thirty and forty." In the latter game, the minimum stake is 20 francs and the maximum is 12,000, while, for roulette, the stakes may range from 5 francs to 6000. Tickets are obtained free, and playing takes place between 11:30 A. M. and 11:30 P. M. The inhabitants of Monaco are not allowed to participate.

Adjoining the Casino is the *tir aux pigeons*, "pigeon shooting range," where expert marksmen compete in shooting pigeons released for the purpose. A prize of 20,000 francs is offered for a competition held each January. Population, 9516.

MOSCOW (*mŏs'kō*) (**Moskva**). The capital and largest city of Russia, situated somewhat north of the geographical center of the country's European territory. Built at the intersection of six important highways, the city has long been an important market for grain, hemp, oil, tea, sugar, hides, wool, timber, metal, drugs, and silk. Its leading manufactures are textiles, chemicals, metal and food products, glass, and leather.

Moscow is a city of striking contrasts, with its old wooden houses of the suburbs, the many-storied apartment buildings for workmen recently erected, the low dwellings of the former aristocracy with their pillared porticoes, huge factories, gilded domes of Oriental-like cathedrals, and magnificent palaces of old Russian or ultra-modern design.

THE KREMLIN. This is the old citadel of Moscow, and is the city's outstanding feature. It is a triangular enclosure surrounded by walls about 1½ miles in length. Its walls are surmounted by 18 towers and pierced by 5 gates. The main entrance opens on the Red square, and is fronted by the massive mausoleum of Lenin, within which lies his embalmed body in a glass case. Within the Kremlin stand the government offices and a number of palaces and cathedrals. In the Great Kremlin Palace, built of white stone with a gilded cupola, are held the congresses of the Communist, or Third, International.

Other points of interest in the Kremlin are the Tower of Ivan the Great, which is 322 feet high and contains 34 bells with a total weight of 290 tons; several monasteries of considerable antiquity; and the Czar Bell, cast in 1733, which is the largest bell in the world. It weighs 220 tons and measures 22 feet in diameter and 19 feet 3 inches in height. The bell was never hung, having been cracked by a fire before it left the foundry.

RECONSTRUCTION. Beginning in 1935, a reconstruction of Moscow was begun, with plans calling for its expansion from 68 to 234 square miles and accommodation for five million inhabitants. Eleven miles of a new subway had already been completed in that year.

Under this plan, the Kremlin, preserved and restored, will remain the central feature of the city. Along one side the magnificent Lenin boulevard will be constructed, flanked by many of the finest new buildings in Russia. At one end is the site of the Palace of the International Soviets, planned to be the world's tallest building. Residential and industrial sections form a circular band about the central portion and the entire city will be ringed with parks and forests. One feature of the city as it is being rebuilt is the manner in which large factories dominate districts, each factory, workers' residences, and facilities for living being planned as a unit. Cultural institutions include the Moscow Art theater, the University of Moscow, and the Lenin institute and library.

HISTORY. The earliest reference to Moscow dates from 1147. It was made the capital of Russia, and, in spite of many sieges, conflagrations, and pestilences, it remained the seat of government until 1712, when Saint Petersburg, now called Leningrad, became the capital. In 1812, the Russians burned the city in order to deprive Napoleon of a winter base. In 1918, Moscow was again made the capital of Russia. Population, 6,422,000.

Munich (*mū'nĭk*) (**München**). One of the largest cities of West Germany and the capital of the state of Bavaria, situated near the southern extremity of the country on the Isar river, a tributary of the Danube.

Largely through the effort of King Ludwig I of Bavaria, Munich became, in the 19th century, one of the best built cities of Europe and, architecturally, one of the most beautiful. It is lavishly adorned by numerous squares and pleasure gardens and by buildings constructed in the leading styles. The English Garden, a park of 500 acres adorned with small temples and towers, was designed by Count Rumford, a native of Massachusetts. Other features of the city are the former Royal Palace, the National Theater, the Art Union, numerous museums, and the Old Castle, the last dating from 1253. The art collections in Munich are among the richest on the continent. The University of Munich is one of the leading educational institutions of Germany. Many buildings were destroyed in World War II.

Apart from art and education, the great industry of Munich is the brewing of beer. Other products of the city's workmanship are bronze founding, glass staining, silversmiths' work, wood carving, and lithographing. Railway machinery, wallpaper, gloves, and artificial flowers are also made. Population, 1,231,458.

Nantes (E. *nănts*; F. *näɴt*). A seaport of northwestern France, located at the head of the Loire River estuary and about 50 miles from the sea. The industries include the canning of sardines, sugar refining, shipbuilding, and the manufacture of iron products and of tobacco goods. In history, the city is known for the Edict of Nantes, by which, in 1598, Henry IV granted toleration to the Huguenots. Population, 240,028.

Naples (**Napoli**). The third largest city of Italy, situated near the central part of the kingdom on the Bay of Naples, which opens into the Tyrrhenian Sea. On one side of the bay rises Mt. Vesuvius, and on the other side is the picturesque height of Posilipo. The city has a safe and deep harbor. It is an important naval station and commercial emporium and possesses numerous industrial establishments. The manufactures include steel products, textiles, glass, macaroni, and chemicals. The port is a noted embarkation point for emigrants.

Naples is visited yearly by upwards of 30,000 tourists. Its features include the cathedral, built in 1272; the National museum, containing a priceless collection of antiquities, most notably those obtained from the excavated site of Pompeii and of Herculaneum; the San Carlo opera house, one of the largest in Europe; the most complete marine aquarium in the world; and the University of Naples, founded in 1224. Naples was originally a Greek colony, established about 450 B. C. under the name of Neapolis, "New City." Population, 1,228,092.

Newcastle. One of the largest coal exporting cities of Great Britain, situated in northeastern England on the Tyne river 8 miles from its mouth in the North Sea. Quays and factories line both banks of the river for a distance of 10 miles. There are also large shipbuilding yards and locomotive, engineering, and ordnance works. Other industrial products include Portland cement, chemicals, grindstones, and refined lead. The city's pre-eminence as a coal exporting center is reflected in the popular expression, "carrying coals to Newcastle," indicating superfluous activity.

Newcastle was the site of a Roman fort built to defend the eastern end of the wall that Hadrian constructed across Britain. The city was named from a castle built here in the 11th century by Robert, the son of William the Conqueror. Population, 253,780.

Nice. A city and tourist resort of southeastern France on the Mediterranean coast and at the foot of the Alps Mountains. Its industries produce perfume, liquors, soap, silk, straw hats, and rubber, metal, and tobacco goods. An 8-acre harbor accommodates an active coastal shipping trade. An equable climate, varying from a winter mean of 49°F. to a summer mean of 72°F., lends Nice an attractiveness which is further enhanced by the meeting of sea and mountain scenery in a subtropical setting. The city is famous for its carnivals, especially the battle of flowers.

Nice is about 2000 years old, having been founded by Greek colonists. The name is Greek for Victory. It was subject at various times to Saracen, German, French, Italian, and Spanish power, but was confirmed in French possession in 1860. Population, 292,958.

Nottingham. A manufacturing city of central England, 125 miles northwest of London. It is built on the slope and at the foot of a rocky eminence, which is crowned by an ancient castle, now used as a museum. Nottingham college is on a fine 220-acre campus, called Highfields. The chief manufactures include lace, hosiery, clothing, machinery, tobacco, and bicycles. Population, 310,280.

Nuremberg (Nürnberg). A city of southwestern Germany, noted especially for its manufacture of toys, electrical machinery, and lead pencils.

Because it was an important center for the manufacture of tank, airplane, and marine engines, a majority of this picturesque medieval city was destroyed in World War II, including most of the architectural monuments. Hans Sachs and the artist Dürer were born in the city. Watches were first made here, being known as "Nuremberg eggs." Air guns and geographical globes are also claimed as Nuremberg inventions. Population, 470,778.

Oberammergau (*ō'bĕr-äm'ĕr-gou'*). A village in the extreme south of Germany, celebrated for the Passion play, which takes place there once in each ten years, the most recent performance having been given in 1970. The play represents the crucifixion and the ascension of Jesus. It takes place each Sunday during the summer on a large wooden stage open to the sky, and it usually lasts eight hours. The performance was originally undertaken in fulfillment of a vow made in 1633 by the villagers, who thereby expressed their gratitude for the cessation of an epidemic of the plague. Oberammergau is also famous for wood-carving crafts.

Odessa. A city of southwestern Russia, situated on the north shore of the Black Sea. Its commodious harbor is divided by moles into six ports. Odessa became great as the point of export for vast quantities of grain, wool, sugar, and lumber. Its industrial products include salt, glass, motion picture apparatus, and canned goods.

Odessa was founded in 1794 by Catherine the Great as a stepping-stone to Constantinople. The city is well built and is adorned by many pleasure grounds and fine buildings. The Victims of the Revolution square contains tombs of the fallen, the city having changed hands eight times in 1917-20. Population, 892,000.

Olympia. A plain in the western part of the Morea peninsula, Greece. It contains many ruins, including those of a temple of Zeus and of a stadium in which the Olympic games were originally held. In ancient times, the temple of Zeus contained a colossal statue of this god, the work of Phidias. Carved in ivory and embellished with gold, this statue was one of the seven wonders of the world.

Oporto (Porto). A city of northwestern Portugal, beautifully situated on both banks of the Douro River about 3 miles from its mouth in the Atlantic Ocean. The river is spanned by several bridges, one of which, having an arch of 560 feet, is counted among the great bridges of the world. Manufacturing is the most prominent industry. The city's products include leather, woolens, pottery, corks, hats, and tobacco. Prominent among the exports is port wine, which received its name from Oporto. Population, 324,400.

Oslo. The capital and largest city of Norway, situated at the head of Oslo fiord in the southeastern extremity of the country. The city is the trade center for southern Norway and has large shipyards and important manufactures of woolens, matches, pulp, and nails. Hydroelectric power is abundant and cheap.

Oslo is surrounded on the land side by picturesque hills. The chief edifices are the Parliament buildings, the National Theater, the University of Oslo, the Museum of Art, and a historical museum. Oslo was founded in 1048. Having been destroyed by fire, it was rebuilt in 1624 and named Christiania. The original name was restored in 1925. Population, 487,600.

Ostend (*ŏst-ĕnd'*) **(Ostende).** A fashionable summer resort of northern Belgium, on the North Sea. The city is also a well-known gateway to continental Europe for travelers from England. During World War I, Germany used Ostend as a naval base. Population, 57,230.

Oxford. A university city of England, with a population, in 1969, of 109,720. It is situated about 50 miles northwest of London. The city is the seat of Oxford university, which was founded as early as the 12th century. This university is of especial interest to the English-speaking world on account of the Rhodes scholarships tenable at Oxford and open to students from the British dominions and the United States. The Bodleian library, connected with the university, is one of the world's richest collections of early printed books and of ancient manuscripts.

The university consists of a federation of 31 colleges, each with its own government and teaching staff. Degrees are granted by the university, not by the colleges. Shown below are the names of the colleges and the dates of their founding:

University	1249	All Souls	1438
Balliol	1263	Magdalen	1458
Merton	1264	Brasenose	1509
St. Edmund Hall	1278	Corpus Christi	1517
Exeter	1314	Christ Church	1546
Oriel	1326	Trinity	1554
Queen's	1340	St. John's	1555
New	1379	Jesus	1571
Lincoln	1427	Wadham	1612
Pembroke	1624	St. Catherine's	1962
Worcester	1714	WOMEN'S COLLEGES	
Keble	1868	Lady Margaret Hall	1878
Hertford	1874	Somerville	1879
St. Peter's	1929	St. Hugh's	1886
Nuffield (coed)	1937	St. Anne's	1893
St. Antony's	1950	St. Hilda's	1893

Palermo. An Italian seaport, located on the northwest coast of Sicily. The exports are mainly oranges, lemons, dried fruits, oils, sulphur, and wines. Tuna fishing and shipbuilding are the chief industries. The city ranks third among the seaports of Italy. Palermo has many architectural monuments dating from the periods when Sicily was held successively by the Saracens, the Normans, and the Spaniards. The city was founded by the Phoenicians and was captured in 254 B.C. by the Romans, who called it Panormus. Population, 653,533.

PARIS. The capital of France and the third largest city in Europe, situated on both banks of the Seine River about 110 miles from its mouth in the English channel. Paris is the commercial, artistic, and intellectual center of France and is generally acknowledged to be the most beautiful city in the world.

STREETS AND BOULEVARDS. The streets of Paris do not follow any unified plan. There are, however, several systems of magnificent boulevards. Boulevard is a French word originally meaning bulwark. As the old walls encircling Paris were from time to time torn down to be replaced by others embracing a larger circle, the site of the demolished walls was converted into beautiful driveways, to which the term boulevard was still applied. The boulevards of Paris consist of several concentric systems of roughly circular courses, having their common center in the Ile de la Cité, an island in the Seine river. The longest and most recent of these boulevards owes its origin to the leveling of the 22-mile wall which, until 1919, encircled the city.

Paris is traversed from north to south by an irregular thoroughfare, which, like all the longer streets and boulevards of Paris, is known by different names in different sections of its course. The more important portions of the thoroughfare are called the Boulevard de Sebastopol and the Rue Saint Michel. The latter section passes through the so-called Latin quarter, a district south of the Seine inhabited mainly by students and given its name when university lectures were delivered in Latin.

A straighter thoroughfare crosses the city from east to west on the north side of the Seine river. This thoroughfare, which passes many of the most famous squares, gardens, and buildings of Paris, is known, in different sections, under six different names. The more noteworthy sections are the Rue de Rivoli, the Avenue des Champs Elysées, and the Avenue de la Grande Armée. Other famous streets of Paris are Saint Germain, Rue Royal, and Rue du Faubourg Saint Honoré.

SQUARES, PARKS, AND MONUMENTS. On the north bank of the Seine, near the center of the city, lie the famous gardens of the Tuileries, a 75-acre park with numerous statues. It adjoins the Place de la Concorde, adorned by sculptured fountains and by a huge obelisk brought by Napoleon from Luxor, Egypt. The adjacent Champs Elysées. "Elysian Fields," contain the Grand Palais, built in 1718. Farther west lies the Place de Charles de Gaulle, formerly the Place de l'Etoile, which contains the world's largest triumphal arch. From this square radiate 12 avenues, including the Rue Foch, which leads to the beautiful 2100-acre park in the suburbs called the Bois de Boulogne. A southeastern suburb contains the Bois de Vincennes, an ornamental park with an area of 2300 acres.

Other notable squares and parks of Paris are the Luxembourg gardens, laid out in the 17th century; the Jardin des Plantes, 58 acres in area, where the principal scientific museums of the city are located; the Place de Rivoli, with an equestrian statue of Joan of Arc; the Place de la République; the Place d'Iena, containing a large statue of George Washington; the Place de la Bastille, near the site of the historic prison of the same name; the Place Vendôme, which has a brazen column made by melting 1200 cannon captured by Napoleon; the Square des Innocents, where stands the famous sculptured Fontaine des Innocents; the Place des Etats-Unis, in which stands a bronze monument erected in 1923 to the memory of American volunteers who fought in French armies during World War I; and the Champ de Mars, in which the Eiffel Tower rises to a height of 984 feet. It is named for Alexandre Eiffel, the engineer who constructed it as a feature of the Paris International exposition in 1889. One of France's most beautiful war memorials is a white marble temple in the Parc de Villeneuve-l'Etang, commemorating 67 American aviators who died in French service during World War I.

BUILDINGS. The Ile de la Cité in the Seine contains three remarkable buildings: the Hôtel Dieu, which, founded in A. D. 600, is said to be one of the oldest hospitals in Europe; the Palais de Justice, architecturally one of the finest structures in Paris; and the Cathedral of Notre Dame, the

SCENES IN EUROPE I

The Lorelei rock (to the left) on the Rhine, where legend has it that a siren sat "combing her golden hair" and singing a melody with power to captivate sailors below. Their boats, unguided by the enraptured masters, carried them to their doom on the treacherous rocks.
Germ. Tourist Inf. Off.

Left The cathedral of Notre Dame in Strasbourg, Alsace, built in 1017 of red sandstone along Gothic lines and Romanesque features. The North Tower, designed by Johann Hulyz, was completed in 1439.

Upper right Porta Nigra ("Black Gate") and Roman wall that Constantine the Great built around Trier, Germany, about 300 A.D. With massive stones black with grime of the centuries, it is the best preserved Roman portal in existence. Trier was the military headquarters for the region from Spain to Britain. Saint Simeon immured himself in the tower to the right about 1040.
Germ. Tourist Inf. Off.

One of the more striking features of Venice is the Campanile of San Marco. An earthquake caused its collapse in 1902 and the reconstruction was completed in 1912. The function of a campanile is the housing of a bell, and at one time they were quite numerous throughout Italy, but earthquakes and subsidence of foundations have caused many to fall. In the background is Saint Mark's Cathedral.

SCENES IN EUROPE II

Left New 26-story skyscraper at Dusseldorf, Germany, called by local residents "The Frozen Towel."
Wide World

A new view of London looking down the Thames from the top of the South Bank Power Station.

A monument in honor of Pedro IV situated in Rocio Plaza, Lisbon, Portugal.

Located in the southeastern part of France, the town of Grenoble is one of the most strongly fortified cities on the continent.

The new section of Barcelona, second largest city in Spain.

The South Harbor of Helsinki, the capital of Finland, with a population of over four million. Helsinki is a modern city by European standards and a great deal of the country's income is derived from commerce.

construction of which was begun in 1163. A few of the other great edifices of Paris are the Louvre, which houses the richest collection of art in the world; the palace of the Luxembourg, which contains the world's greatest collection of contemporary art, the American exhibits ranking second in number after the French; the Grand Opéra, one of the most beautiful theaters in the world; the government buildings, fronting the Seine embankment and known as the Quai d'Orsay; the Palais de l'Elysée, where the president of France resides; the Bibliothèque Nationale, one of the world's greatest libraries; the Pantheon, where many of France's most notable citizens have been buried; the Church of the Madeleine, built by Napoleon in the Greek style as a "temple of glory;" and the Hôtel des Invalides, which contains Napoleon's tomb. The railway car in which the armistice was signed on November 11, 1918, was housed in the Hôtel des Invalides until 1927, when it was transferred to a special shelter in Compiégne woods.

Other Features. Paris was spared the fate of many European cities during World War II, suffering scarcely any damage. No other city of the world makes a feature of its sewers. Those of Paris, 9 to 20 feet in diameter and nearly 700 miles in length, are kept so clean and are so well ventilated that there is a regular tourist route through the system by boat and electric car. The University of Paris, which includes the Sorbonne, is one of the oldest and most famous educational institutions in Europe.

Commerce and Industry. Paris is the largest industrial and commercial center in France, and has a worldwide reputation for the manufacture of articles of taste and elegance, such as gold and silver ornaments, furniture, scientific instruments, toys, and perfumes. These industries, as well as the clothing industry of Paris, which largely sets the standard for the Western world in women's apparel, are carried on mainly in small establishments. The manufacture of machinery, railroad supplies, chemicals, beer, porcelain, and leather is centralized in larger factories.

Paris was one of the first cities of the world to establish large departmental stores, the better known ones being Galeries Lafayette and the Bon Marché. The banks of the Seine are lined with docks over which passes a volume of trade exceeding annually one billion dollars in value. There are more than 65 public markets in the city, the largest of which is the Halles Centrales, soon to be replaced by a modern complex and subway. The stock exchange of Paris is called the Bourse.

History. Paris was known to Julius Cæsar, about 50 B. C., as Lutetia. It was then the chief city of the tribe of the Parisii, from whom the city, in the 4th century A. D., adopted the name Paris. In the 10th century, it became the capital of the French monarchy. Paris suffered from an English conquest during the Hundred Years' war and endured several disastrous sieges, the last at the hands of the Germans in 1871. Henry of Navarre, Louis XIV, Napoleon Bonaparte, and Napoleon III contributed most toward the improvement and adornment of the city, thereby making Paris not only a symbol for light-hearted enjoyment, but entitling it also to the claim of being the chief focus of European civilization. Population, 2,790,091.

Pisa (*pē'sä; pē'zä*). A town of northern Italy, 11 miles northeast of Leghorn. Pisa is noted for a leaning tower, 179 feet in height, which inclines 16½ feet from the perpendicular. The tower is built entirely of white marble with walls 13 feet thick at the base. Its construction was begun in 1174, and it was originally intended as a bell tower for the white marble cathedral near by. Within the past century, the inclination of the tower has increased one foot.

Pisa was formerly notable for the victory which its citizens won over the invading Saracens in the 11th century. In the 13th century, it controlled an extensive territory and had a population of 150,000. In recent centuries it has declined in importance, but its walls and its citadel still stand. The only large industry is the manufacture of cotton textiles. Pisa was the birthplace of Galileo, who used the tower in experiments to determine the velocity of falling bodies. Population, 76,846.

Plymouth. A naval station and seaport of southwestern England. Situated on a commodious harbor, Plymouth has a large commerce. Apart from naval equipment, the chief manufactures are chemicals. Sir Francis Drake set out from Plymouth for his voyage around the world. The town has a *Mayflower* commemoration stone, which records the fact that Plymouth was the last point touched by the Pilgrim Fathers on their way to America. Facing the waterfront is the Hoe, one of the finest pleasure grounds in Europe. Population, 213,800.

Portsmouth (*pōrts'mŭth*). A seaport and the chief naval arsenal of Great Britain, situated on Portsea, a small island separated by a creek from the south coast of England. Portsmouth has the most complete fortifications in Britain Its harbor lies close to Spithead, a capacious naval anchorage in the shelter of the Isle of Wight. The government dockyard covers about 500 acres.

The principal industries of the city are connected with the naval establishment. There is considerable traffic in timber, coal, cattle, and agricultural produce. Portchester castle, a ruined Norman fortress to the north of the harbor, occupies the site of the Roman Portus Magnus, "Great Port." Charles Dickens and George Meredith were natives of the city. Population, 221,470.

Prague (*präg*) **(Praha).** The capital and largest city of Czechoslovakia, situated on both banks of the Moldau River, a tributary of the Elbe. It belonged to Germany from 1938 to 1945. Its manufacturing establishments, located mostly in the suburbs, produce railway cars, machinery, flour, chemicals, leather goods, sugar, and furniture. Prague is the focus for the rail and river trade of southern Germany.

The most impressive edifice of Prague is the ancient palace of Hradcany, adjoining which is the Cathedral of Saint Vitus, where the Bohemian kings used to be crowned. The University of Prague, founded in 1348, had, as one of its earliest graduates, John Huss, famous as a martyr to Protestantism. Prominent features of the city are the Charles bridge, 546 yards long, spanning the Moldau and ornamented with two medieval towers and with many statues of saints; the 14th century Tyn church; and a famous clock, one of the oldest in Europe, having, for figures, representations of Jesus and his apostles. Population, 1,022,621.

Ravenna. An ancient city of northern Italy, lying 45 miles east of Bologna and 6 miles inland from the northwestern extremity of the Adriatic Sea. In the 1st century B. C., Ravenna was a naval base and seaport. Subsequent changes in the coast line, which left Ravenna an inland city, diminished its importance. A canal gives it access to the sea. Wine, silk, sugar, and lace are its chief products.

Reminiscences of Ravenna's former greatness are the Church of Sant' Orso, which, although largely rebuilt since, dates back to Roman times; twelve basilicas used as churches and erected between the 5th and the 8th century; a two-storied mausoleum of Theodoric, the Ostrogothic king who subjected Ravenna to a 3-year siege; and the tomb of Dante. Population, 56,815.

Reims (E. *rēmz*; F. *räns*). A cathedral city of northeastern France, lying about 80 miles east of Paris. The Cathedral of Reims, in which the French kings used to be crowned, was built between 1212 and 1430 and is considered to be the finest example of Gothic architecture in the world. During World War I, the structure suffered much damage, which has been largely repaired. Reims is also noted for its wines. Population, 133,142.

Reykjavik (*rā'kyȧ-vēk'*). The capital and largest city of Iceland, located on the island's southwest coast. The city has a university and a cathedral; also a museum containing a collection of Icelandic antiquities. Population, 90,792.

Riga. A city of Russia situated on the Duna River about 10 miles above its mouth at the head of the Gulf of Riga in the Baltic Sea. It was capital of Latvia when the latter was an independent country from 1919 to 1940. By means of canals connecting the Duna with the Volga and Dnieper rivers, Riga has access to Russia's vast regions producing timber, grain, and flax.

The principal manufactures are paper and wood pulp, matches, paints, textiles, shoes, rubber goods, cement, and tobacco. Saint Peter's church is notable for its lofty spire, which rises 440 feet above the street. Riga was founded in 1201 and became important as a member of the Hanseatic League. Nearly half the inhabitants are German. Population, 680,000.

Riviera (*rē-vyâ'rä*). A popular name for the narrow but beautiful coast line of Italy and France, mainly about the Gulf of Genoa. Its mild climate, charming subtropical vegetation, and vistas of rare attractiveness make it one of the most popular parts of Europe for winter tourists. The chief resorts along the Riviera are Cannes, Nice, Mentone, Monte Carlo, and San Remo.

ROME (Roma). The capital and largest city of Italy, and, historically, the most famous city in the world. Rome is situated on both banks of the Tiber River about 15 miles above its mouth in the Tyrrhenian Sea near the center of Italy's western coast. The traditional date of the founding of Rome is April 21, 753 B. C. April 21 is still celebrated annually in Rome as the anniversary of the city's origin. Rome was successively the head of the Roman Republic, the Roman Empire, and the western branch of the Catholic Church. In 1871, it became the capital of the Kingdom of Italy. This long career of uninterrupted greatness has earned for Rome the title of "the eternal city." In 1929, a tract of 109 acres within the city was granted the status of an independent state under papal rule. It is known as Vatican City. This area is in the northwestern section of Rome and includes the former site of Nero's gardens.

THE MODERN CITY. The Tiber, meandering through the city, divides the more populous eastern part from the western section. The eastern part comprises the Campus Martius, "Field of Mars," and the seven hills of ancient Rome—the Capitoline, Palatine, Aventine, Quirinal, Viminal, Esquiline, and Cælian. The western section consists of the hill anciently known as the Janiculum and of the eminence on which the Vatican is situated. The river is spanned by ten bridges, three being of ancient construction. Rome is 15 miles in circumference and is surrounded by a brick wall 55 feet high, constructed mainly by Aurelian about 275 A. D. The wall is pierced by 12 gates. The Porta del Popolo in the north opens upon a road anciently called the Flaminian way, while the famous Appian way leaves the city through a southern gate.

STREETS AND MONUMENTS. The streets are irregular in plan. From the Plaza del Popolo in the north of the city three important thoroughfares diverge—the Corso, the Ripetta, and the Babuino. The Corso terminates at the Piazza di Venezia at the Capitoline hill, which has a colossal monument to Victor Emmanuel II. The Piazza del Campidoglio is adorned by a large statue of Marcus Aurelius, the Roman emperor who erected the so-called Antonine column, which stands in the Piazza Colonna on the Corso. An obelisk, 104 feet high, brought from Heliopolis, Egypt, has been placed in the Piazza di San Giovanni. Garibaldi, the liberator of modern Italy, is memorialized by a huge equestrian statue on the Janiculum hill. An equestrian statue of Victor Emmanuel II in a magnificent setting towers above the Piazza Venetia. Most conspicuous of all is a 180-foot bronze statue of Mussolini. The Fontana Trevi is among the grandest of the city's many sculptured fountains.

MODERN BUILDINGS. The most famous structures associated with modern Rome are those within Vatican City, notably the Vatican and Saint Peter's Church. The Vatican, or papal residence, consists of a group of palaces, covering 13½ acres and containing about 1100 rooms. It houses a library, museum, and picture gallery, each of inestimable value. The decorations of the Vatican were executed by the best artists of the Renaissance, including Raphael and Michelangelo. Saint Peter's Church is generally admitted to be the world's largest and grandest church. Its construction occupied 126 years. The building is 727 feet in length and is surmounted by a huge dome, which rises to a height of 405 feet above the level of the beautiful colonnaded court before the church's entrance.

Other notable buildings of modern Rome include the Quirinal palace, where the Italian sovereigns reside; the Villa Medici, housing the French Academy of Art; the Santa Pudenziana, the oldest church in Rome; and the palaces called Doria, Ruspoli, Corsini, Orsini, Giustiniani, Altieri, Cicciaporci, Farnese, Berberini, and Colonna. On the Capitoline hill are three palaces appropriated for the assemblies of the magistrates, for the observatory, and for the fine arts collection. There are several palaces, which, being surrounded by extensive gardens, are called villas. The most notable of these is the Villa Borghese, the gardens of which form the most fashionable promenade in the city.

EDUCATIONAL INSTITUTIONS. Rome is the seat of the University of Rome, founded in 1244. In addition to the Vatican library and the 10 public libraries, there are the libraries called Nazionale Centrale, Casanatense, and Angelica, and the libraries of the Barberini and of the Corsini palace. No city of the world has richer collections of Roman antiquities and of Renaissance art. The United States and several European countries maintain archeological schools in the city.

ANCIENT BUILDINGS The level of the ancient city of Rome is, except where excavated, from 20 to 60 feet below the level of the present city. Within the past century, a considerable portion of the ruins have been uncovered. These ruins include temples, palaces, public halls, theaters, baths, porticoes, and monuments and indicate that, in the first centuries of the Christian era, Rome was a still more impressive city than it is today.

The best preserved ancient building is the Pantheon, now used as a church, which has a dome larger than that of Saint Peter's Church. The Colosseum had a seating capacity of 45,000. The outer wall alone is said to have cost the equivalent of 50 million dollars to construct. The Forum has been despoiled of most of the palatial buildings, the 1200 marble columns, and the 1000 colossal statues which once adorned its 25 acres of surface. Other impressive ruins are the Mausoleum of Hadrian, used for 15 centuries as the fortress of medieval Rome; the triumphal arches of Titus, Severus, and Constantine; and the baths of Caracalla and of Diocletian, those of the latter having originally covered nearly 9 acres. The outlines of the Circus Maximus are still traceable—a building capable of seating 260,000 spectators.

One of the stateliest buildings of ancient Rome was the residence of the emperors on the Palatine hill. It was called the Palatium, a name from which the word palace is derived. The great drains of ancient Rome are still in use today. Dating from early Christian times are the catacombs, underground passages used as places of burial and of refuge by the persecuted Christians. About 75 groups have been found, having a total length of about 750 miles.

INDUSTRIES. Rome, noted for its fine silks and knit goods, has become a leading center for both men's and women's fashions, with many outstanding designers. Other manufactures are gloves, jewelry, mosaics, cameos, and artificial flowers. The city is also the chief railroad center of Italy and, since World War II, has experienced a vigorous economic growth. Population, 2,484,737.

Rotterdam. The chief commercial port of the Netherlands, situated in the western part of the country, about 10 miles southeast of The Hague. It is on the Meuse River 15 miles above its mouth in the North Sea. The leading articles of commerce are coffee, tea, tobacco, flour, sugar, spices, coal, oil, and foodstuffs. The most important manufactures are ships, refined sugar, margarine, paint, ropes, and leather.

A labyrinth of tree-bordered canals runs through the city, and most houses are built on piles on account of the city's low site. Rotterdam was the birthplace of Erasmus. The central part of the city was completely destroyed by German bombs in 1940. The city was reconstructed according to the most advanced principles of city planning. The port also was reconstructed and soon became one of the world's busiest, being a gateway to the "common market" of Europe, as symbolized by its landmark "Euromast"—a high tower in the form of a mast and forecastle, which houses a restaurant. Population, 727,207.

Rouen (*rwän*). A commercial and manufacturing city of northern France on the Seine River, about 70 miles northwest of Paris. Ocean-going ships ascend the river to Rouen. The industrial products include textiles, machinery, and refined oil. The Cathedral of Rouen has a spire 487 feet in altitude, said to be the highest in France. The Place du Vieux Marché is adorned by a statue of Joan of Arc, who, in 1431, was burned there at the stake. Population, 118,775.

Ruhr (*rōōr*), **The.** An irregularly oval strip of land in the northern part of West Germany, extending eastward from the Rhine for about 40 miles along both sides of the Ruhr River. The district includes the great industrial centers of Essen, Dortmund, Bochum, Gelsenkirchen, Mülheim, Oberhausen and Duisburg. It is the largest single industrial area in Europe and the most thickly populated. The reason for this great concentration of industry in the Ruhr is to be found in the rich coal mines, and the excellent transportation facilities by rail and water. The center of Germany's mining, steel, power, and chemical industries, it suffered serious damage during World War II, and afterwards many of the heavy industrial plants were dismantled. Light industries, however, sprang up, such as coal-tar derivatives, pharmaceuticals, textiles, ceramics. In 1949 France, England, the United States, and the Benelux countries established an international authority over the Ruhr, in which later the West German republic participated. German trustees supervised production, which soon approached the pre-war output.

Saint Gallen (*sânt gäl'ěn*). A city of northeastern Switzerland, situated 12 miles from the south shore of the Lake of Constance. The city is the highest in Europe, having an elevation of 2196 feet above the sea. Its ancient Benedictine monastery, an architectural masterpiece which is now used for government offices, was founded by the Irish missionary Saint Gall, who settled here in 614. Population, 78,300.

Saint-Mihiel (*săN' mē'yěl'*). A town of northeastern France, situated on the Meuse River 23 miles southeast of Verdun. The capture of Saint-Mihiel and the annihilation of the German salient about the town in September 1918 constituted the first military operation carried out independently by the American army in France during World War I. Population, 5,203.

Salzburg. A resort city in western Austria, beautifully situated on the Salzach River. It is one of the most attractive cities of central Europe and the scene of the famous music and theatrical festival held in honor of Mozart, who was born here. There are a Renaissance cathedral, two archiepiscopal palaces, and a castle, which overlooks the city. Salzburg is a manufacturing center for musical instruments. Population, 117,400.

Salonika (E. *sä'lô-nē'kä*); (**Thessalonikē**). A city of northern Greece, the second largest in the country, situated at the head of Salonika Bay, a northern inlet of the Ægean Sea. Salonika, having a capacious, improved harbor, is the sea outlet for Bulgarian and Yugoslavian products. Among the squalid houses which fill most of the city arise lofty spires and minarets, and numerous ruins dating from Greek, Roman, and Byzantine times.

Salonika was founded in 315 B. C. and has been held successively by Macedonia, Rome, the Byzantine Empire, Turkey, and Greece. It was the seat of an early church, to which Saint Paul addressed two epistles. Population, 378,444.

Sarajevo (*sär'ä-yä-vô*). A city of Yugoslavia, 122 miles southwest of Belgrade. It is partially Oriental in appearance, having an extensive bazaar, but, in recent decades, many modern improvements have been introduced. The chief industries are the manufacture of metal ware, silk weaving, and the making of pottery. At Sarajevo in 1914 occurred the incident which precipitated World War I, and thereby brought independence to Yugoslavia. This was the assassination of Franz Ferdinand, heir to the throne of Austria-Hungary, by F. Princip. A statue of Princip was erected in 1930. Population, 143,117.

Seville (*sĕv'ĭl; sē-vĭl'*) (**Sevilla**). A city and port of south western Spain, situated on the Guadalquivir River, about 50 miles above its mouth in the Atlantic Ocean. Seville was an important center of the Moorish civilization in Spain. The Alcazar, now partly in ruins, was a Moorish royal palace. The Cathedral of Seville, one of the largest Gothic churches in the world, retained, as a belfry, the Giralda tower, erected by the Moors. Other notable structures include the Moorish Renaissance palace of the duke of Medinaceli; the Museum of Painting, which houses the largest collection of the masterpieces of Murillo, a native of Seville; the buildings of the University of Seville, founded in 1502; a tobacco factory covering 6 acres; and a bull ring with a seating capacity of 12,000.

Seville was a prosperous seaport in Roman times. It had a monopoly of trade with America for a considerable period. The chief articles of trade at the present time are metals, fruits, cork, grain, and glazed tiles, the last being manufactured in a suburb, Triana. Population, 474,082.

Sheffield. An industrial city of north central England about 30 miles east of Manchester. It is noted for its manufacture of cutlery, armor plate, artillery, scientific instruments, and other steel products. The famous silver Sheffield plate is no longer made, the process being a lost art, but a high quality of silverware is made by a new process. Other industrial products include leather, bicycles, paper, brass goods, brushes, chemicals, and paints. Sheffield university was founded in 1905. The city was a target for German bombs in 1940. Population, 486,490.

Sofia (*sô'fē-yȧ; sô-fē'ȧ*) (**Sofiya**). The capital and largest city of Bulgaria, situated at an altitude of 1800 feet in the western part of the country. Sofia is the commercial and industrial center of Bulgaria and is connected by rail with Vienna, Salonika, and Istanbul. It has an important export trade in agricultural products and attar of roses. The city has been largely rebuilt since 1878. Its principal features include famous baths with hot springs; the ruined Sofia Mosque; and the University of Sofia, founded in 1888. Population, 810,300.

Southampton. A city and port of southern England, 79 miles southwest of London. It was a royal borough before 1086, its fine natural harbor making it at one time a rival of London. After a decline of trade in the 16th century, it was improved in the 1800's and, in 1914, was the chief port of embarkation for British armies. In 1940 it suffered severe damage from repeated German air raids. From this port, in 1620, the *Mayflower* began its voyage for America. Population, 208,710.

Spa (*spä; spô*). A famous watering place and town in central eastern Belgium. Its mineral springs are said to be the oldest in Europe, having been discovered in 1326. The town has been a fashionable resort for centuries. The principal buildings are the Casino and the Pouhon. Population, 9,055.

Stettin (*shtĕ-tēn'*) (**Szczecin**). A seaport and manufacturing city of northwestern Poland, built on both banks of the Oder river, 17 miles from its mouth in an inlet of the Baltic Sea. Tne largest industries are shipbuilding and the manufacture of clothing. Other products are cement, locomotives, sewing machines, and glass. The chief exports are grain, spirits, lumber, sugar, and cement. Population, 299,200.

Stockholm. The capital and largest city of Sweden, situated on a group of hilly islands and peninsulas at Lake Mälar's outlet into the Baltic Sea. Surrounding forests advance almost to the city's confines. On account of the varied levels prevailing in different parts of the city, tunnels and elevators are utilized by the citizens in passing from one part to another. Stockholm's capacious harbor facilitates a large commerce. The chief manufactures are ships, iron and steel products, leather, textiles, and pottery.

The features of the city include the Royal Palace; Saint Nicholas Church, where the Swedish sovereigns are crowned; the city hall, one of the finest modern structures in Europe; Skansen, a 70-acre park illustrating the fauna, flora, and peasant customs of various parts of Sweden; an equestrian statue of Gustavus Adolphus; and a colossal bronze figure of Linnæus. Population, 777,115.

Stoke. A manufacturing city of central England, about 30 miles south of Manchester, noted chiefly for its porcelain and pottery industry. Other industrial products are iron, machinery, electrical and rubber goods, and bricks. The chief public buildings are the town hall, New Market hall and Minton Memorial building. Population, 263,910.

Stonehenge. The most famous prehistoric monument in Great Britain. It is in Wiltshire county, England, about 32 miles inland from the center of the southern coast. It consisted originally of upright stones in two concentric circles surrounding two elliptical groups. The height above ground of the largest stone is 22 feet. The outer, or Sarsen, circle is 97 feet in diameter and consisted of 30 stones, 16 of which are standing, some weighing as much as 40 tons. They were joined by superimposed lintel stones attached by mortise and tenon, of which 6 are in their original position. The inner circle, 76 feet in diameter, had 60 stones, of which 20 remain and 8 are standing. The origin of most of the stones has been identified at two sites, 23 and 240 miles distant. From the center of the circles at a distance of 256 feet is set a stone whose tip is aligned with the rising sun at the summer solstice.

Stonehenge was built over a period from 1800 to 1400 B. C., probably in part by the so-called Beaker people, who distributed the first bronze beakers from Spain and are believed to have erected the thousands of stone menhirs in Brittany, similarly aligned with the sunrise at the summer solstice. It is surmised that an architect of Stonehenge came from Mycenae, Greece, since traces have been observed on a stone of an incised dagger ornament found elsewhere only in Mycenae around 1400 B. C.

Stratford. A town of south central England on the river Avon, chiefly noted as the birthplace and burial place of William Shakespeare. Located here is the Royal Shakespeare Theatre, endowed by popular subscription from people in many countries. In the vicinity are the cottages where Mary Arden, Shakespeare's mother, and Anne Hathaway, his wife, were born. Population, 17,400.

Stuttgart. A well built and beautiful city of southwestern Germany. Stuttgart is the capital of the German state of Württemberg. The city's finest structures center about a large square, called the Schlossplatz. There are exceptionally valuable collections of paintings and of antiquities in the city.

Stuttgart is the chief printing and book publishing city of South Germany. The industrial products include automobiles, furniture, machinery, paper, leather, chemicals, tobacco goods, and textiles. Population, 630,494.

Turin (*tū'rĭn; tū-rĭn'*) (**Torino**). A commercial and manufacturing city of northwestern Italy, situated on the Po River within view of the Alps. It is about 70 miles inland from the Gulf of Genoa and 40 miles from the French border. Turin is the center of the automobile industry in Italy. Other manufactures are machinery, cotton, silk, rayon, leather, and chemicals. Hydroelectric power for the industries is generated from near-by mountain torrents.

Turin is the only large Italian city having streets laid out on a rectangular plan. Among the features of the city are the Piazza Castello, the chief square of Turin; the palace and park once occupied by the rulers of Piedmont; the Palazzo Carignano, in which the Italian Parliament met from 1860 to 1864; and an imposing monument of Cavour, one of the liberators of Italy. The University of Turin was founded in 1405. Population, 1,111,659.

Valencia (*vȧ-lĕn'shĭ-ȧ; -shȧ*). A Mediterranean seaport of Spain near the center of the country's eastern coast. The older part of the city has narrow, winding streets, while the new portion is laid out with wide thoroughfares and well shaded squares. Its features include the cathedral La Seo, with a splendid octagonal tower; the University of Valencia, founded in 1411; the Silk Exchange, a beautiful Gothic structure; the Plaza de Toros, a richly ornamented bull ring, said to be the best in Spain.

The commerce of Valencia consists principally of rice, fruits, silk, wine, and olive oil. The manufactures include tobacco, metal and leather products, glazed tiles, and textiles of silk and of linen. Population, 501,795.

Venice (**Venezia**). A seaport of northeastern Italy, situated on 120 small islands at the head of the Adriatic Sea. Some 177 canals serve as streets, spanned by 400 bridges. Houses are built on piles. The Grand canal divides the city into two equal parts. A bridge, about 2½ miles long, connects Venice with the mainland and, passing as a viaduct over the city, slopes downward to a large open square.

Venice's greatest building, the Cathedral of Saint Mark, dating from 1047 A. D., resembles the Church, now the Mosque, of Saint Sophia in Istanbul. It is surmounted by five Oriental domes and contains four gilded, bronze horses, taken originally from Nero's triumphal arch in Rome. The bell tower of the church, standing separate from the main structure, is 322 feet high. Its construction was begun in 874 A. D. The tower collapsed in 1902 but has since been restored. The Doge's Palace, the building of which occupied the two centuries following 1301, is one of the most picturesque buildings in the world.

Among the many other features of this unique and beautiful city are the Royal Palace; a curious clock tower, built in 1496, upon which two colossal bronze figures strike the hours on a large bell; the Bridge of Sighs, connecting the Doge's Palace with a prison; the Rialto, a marble bridge, on which are situated many busy shops; numerous churches and art galleries containing rich collections of paintings by Italian masters, including many by Titian, a native of Venice; and the museum of the city's arsenal, which exhibits a model of the *Bucentaur*. This was the ship from which, each year, the doge of Venice cast a ring into the Adriatic, thereby representing symbolically the marriage of Venice with the sea.

Venice manufactures heavy machinery, clocks, cotton and woolen goods, glassware, lace, brocades, tapestry, wood carvings, and jewelry. The city is a first-class naval station and has an excellent harbor.

Venice is said to have been founded in 452 A. D. by refugees in flight before Attila the Hun. It became prosperous by trading with the East and with the crusaders. The city's importance declined with the fall of Istanbul, but was revived when the Suez canal opened up a Mediterranean route to Asia. Population, 361,980.

Verdun (*vĕr'dŭɴ'*). A strongly fortified town of northeastern France, about 140 miles east of Paris. It was the objective of desperate German attacks in 1916 and 1917, which, for bitterness and carnage, were unequaled by any other conflict of World War I. The French army retained its hold on the town. Population, 21,406.

Verona (*vē-rō'nä*). A fortified city of northern Italy, lying 71 miles west of Venice. It has an important trade with Switzerland, Austria, and Germany in wines, fruits, rice, and marble. The chief manufactures are cotton, paper, flour, and nails.

Verona was a Gallic town before it passed into the hands of the Romans in 89 B. C. From the Roman period dates the amphitheater, still in use, which the emperor Diocletian built. It is about 500 feet long and 160 feet high with accommodation for 20,000 people. Numerous weather-stained palaces of white marble, mostly built in the period of the Renaissance, give to certain parts of the city an air of sumptuous decay. Population, 175,581.

Versailles (F. *vĕr'sä'y'*; E. *vĕr-sālz'*). A city of north central France, situated about 12 miles southwest of Paris. Versailles is chiefly noted for its palace and park of unparalleled magnificence.

The palace dates mainly from 1661, being mostly the work of Louis XIV. It consists of a central block, surrounding three sides of a large court, and of two immense wings, each enclosing two or more courts. The total length of the building with its dependencies is nearly one-half mile. It houses a picture gallery upon which alone Louis XIV spent 5 million dollars. The play of colored lights in the evening upon the waters of the sculptured fountains within the gardens constitutes a spectacle of rare beauty. An apartment of the palace, called the Hall of Mirrors, was the scene, in 1871, of the coronation of William I as emperor of Germany. In the same hall, in 1919, the representatives of Germany subscribed to the Treaty of Versailles. Population of city, 84,860.

Vesuvius (Vesuvio). An active volcano of Italy, 3891 feet high, near the Bay of Naples and about 10 miles from the city of that name. Prior to 79 A. D., it was not known that the mountain was volcanic. In that year, however, the top of the mountain blew off and ashes, stones, and mud were ejected, burying the Roman cities of Pompeii and Herculaneum in 20 feet of débris. The elder Pliny perished in this eruption, of which the younger Pliny left a detailed description. Other notable eruptions occurred in the years 203, 472, 512, 685, 983, 1631, 1822, 1855, 1865, 1872, 1878, 1880, 1895, 1906, 1929, 1944.

Vichy (*vē'shē*). Health resort and formerly temporary capital of France. Situated 72 miles northwest of Lyon and about 180 miles south of Paris. It owes its location to a group of about 40 springs of warm water having medicinal properties. Heavily charged with sodium bicarbonate and minerals, the water from some of the springs has a temperature as high as 120°F. About 2½ million gallons are bottled and exported annually. The 11 largest springs are state owned and supply public hospitals for treatment of soldiers and of civilians unable to pay for private treatments. The Romans built baths at Vichy, but the modern development, dating from the 17th century, owes much to Napoleon Bonaparte and Napoleon III. When the Germans in 1940 overran France and occupied Paris, the new chief of state, Marshal Pétain, then 84 years old, chose Vichy as the seat of his government. Population, 30,610.

VIENNA (Wien). The capital and largest city of Austria, built on the south bank of the Danube River. Vienna was the capital of the former empire of Austria-Hungary and, from 1938 to 1945, was a part of Germany. Since the 13th century, Vienna has been the chief artistic and cultural center of east central Europe.

Boulevards and Parks. The most notable driveway of Vienna is the Ringstrasse, which follows the line of old fortifications, demolished in 1858. It separates the old, inner city from the more modern portions. The Prater, a 2000-acre park, is the largest of the many ornamented open spaces which, in the aggregate, cover more than 50 per cent of Vienna's surface.

Buildings. The Cathedral of Saint Stephen is the most famous structure in Austria. It was founded in 1144 and has great catacombs beneath it. The cross on its steeple attains a height of 441 feet. Other great buildings are the Imperial opera house, one of the most superb art temples of Europe; the stately Grecian Houses of Parliament; the lavishly decorated Gothic city hall; the Imperial Palace; and the Votivkirche. Most of the inhabitants live in apartment houses, some of which are built on a magnificent scale, adorned with painting and sculpture.

Institutions of Art and Education. The University of Vienna, founded in 1365, enjoys a world-wide reputation. The most notable of the many public and private museums of Vienna is the Imperial Art-History museum, which contains an extraordinarily rich collection of ancient and medieval antiquities and numerous masterpieces of art, embracing nearly every school in the world.

Industries. The manufactures of Vienna include jewelry, ornaments of gold and silver, musical and optical instruments, leather goods, furniture, machinery, textiles, and chemicals. A large commerce in corn, flour, cattle, wine, and sugar is facilitated by a network of railways centering in the city and by the navigable Danube river.

History. Under the name of Vindobona, Vienna was a city of strategical importance to the Romans. It was taken successively by the Huns, the Avars, and the Franks; attained to prosperity in supplying the needs of the crusaders; and, in 1296, became the residence of the Habsburg emperors. Vienna was besieged by the Turks in 1529 and, again, in 1683, but on neither occasion was the city taken. The treaty of peace following the Napoleonic wars was drawn up in Vienna. Population, 1,638,100.

Vimy Ridge. An elevated region of northeastern France, 100 miles north of Paris and about 4 miles northeast of Arras. In May 1917, it was the scene of one of the most bitterly contested struggles in which Canadian troops were engaged during World War I. The ridge had been fortified by the Germans but was relinquished as a result of the battle, which is commemorated by an impressive monument erected by the Canadian government in 1936.

Warsaw (Warszawa). The largest city of Poland, situated on the left bank of the Vistula River. It was the capital of Poland prior to its seizure by Germany in 1939. The old part of Warsaw has many dark, narrow, and squalid lanes, but the new section is quite modern, with wide streets flanked by rows of fine buildings. There are numerous squares, parks, and public gardens. The city has over 30 Catholic and 7 Russian churches, the Catholic Cathedral of Saint John being the largest. Iron bridges connect the city with the prosperous suburb of Praga on the opposite bank of the Vistula.

Among the manufactures are textiles, metal wares, tobacco articles, malt liquors, chemicals, and furniture. Small factories and home industries give employment to many thousands. Population, 1,261,300.

Windsor. A town of southeastern England, on the Thames River about 21 miles west of London Its interest lies chiefly in its parks and its castle, which, since before the time of William the Conqueror, have been a favorite retreat of the English monarchs.

Windsor Castle covers 12 acres of ground in the Home park, which is about 4 miles in circumference. A tree-lined avenue connects this park with the Great park, which has a circuit of 18 miles. The castle, consisting of numerous chapels, cloisters, and apartments, is dominated by the Round Tower, built by Edward III. Population, 29,030.

Ypres (*ē'pr'*). A town of western Belgium about 20 miles from the North Sea. It was the scene of a large number of battles in World War I, being held by the British armies in the face of the most desperate German attacks, made over a period of four years. One of the chief squares contains a monument erected by the Canadian government as a memorial to Canadian soldiers who perished in the sanguinary conflicts near Ypres. The town, almost obliterated as a result of military operations, has a population of 18,121.

Zurich (*zōō'rĭk*) **(Zürich).** The largest city of Switzerland, beautifully situated in the northern part of the country on both banks of the Limmat River as it issues from Lake Zurich. In the older quarter, the streets are narrow, but the newer section is very attractively laid out, its main thoroughfare being a broad boulevard lined with shops comparing well with those of Paris. Zurich is the seat of the Swiss National museum, of the University of Zurich, and of several splendid medieval churches and monasteries. The cathedral known as the Grosse Münster, founded in the 11th century, had Zwingli as one of its pastors.

Zurich is the financial center of Switzerland. Its manufactures include silks, cottons, machinery, paper, and musical instruments. Population, 433,200.

SCENES IN EUROPE III

A peaceful valley near Lucerne, Switzerland
European Travel Commission

Istanbul, in Europe at Bosphorus Strait —as viewed from Asia
European Travel Commission

Lenin State Library, Moscow, USSR
SOVFOTO

The Medicis Fountains in the Luxembourg Gardens in Paris, noted for its art, architecture, and works of sculpture.

This modern cathedral at Coventry, Eng. incorporates ruins of its predecessor bombed in World War II.

French Radio Center, Paris, France
French Gov't. Tourist Office

Moselle Wine Country, Burg Kochem, Germany
European Travel Commission

VIEWS IN ASIA

A street scene in Tokyo, now the largest city in the world (pop. 8,302,565; Greater Tokyo 9,311,774).

The modern administration building at the Hufuf Airport in Saudi Arabia.

Museum of Jade in Singapore, former home of late millionaire ointment king Aw Boon Haw.
Keystone Press

The luxurious Keren Theater, Beersheba, Israel
Israel Gov't. Tourist Office

International Airport at Manila, Philippines

ASIA

THE largest and the most populous of the continents. It lies entirely in the northern hemisphere and, beginning near the equator, stretches 5270 miles northward to a point within 800 miles of the north pole. Its maximum extent east and west is 6820 miles. Having an area of 17,200,000 square miles, it occupies nearly one-third of the land surface of the globe and is larger than North America and South America combined.

With the exception of Europe on the northwest and of the narrow Isthmus of Suez, Asia is entirely surrounded by water. It has the Arctic Ocean on the north, the Pacific Ocean on the east, and the Indian Ocean on the south. In the southwest, the continent is divided from Africa by a line passing through the Isthmus of Suez, the Red Sea, and the Gulf of Aden. At the northeast extremity, Asia is separated from North America by Bering strait, a neck of water less than 40 miles in width at its narrowest point. The coast line of the continent aggregates about 33,000 miles.

Outline and Islands. The line of demarcation on land between Asia and Europe follows roughly the Ural Mountains and the Caucasus Mountains. The remainder of the western boundary passes through the Caspian Sea and through the three seas which wash the shores of Asia Minor, the continent's farthest westward extension. These three seas are the Black Sea, the Ægean Sea, and the Mediterranean Sea. The Black Sea and the Ægean Sea are connected by the small Sea of Marmora, which communicates with the Black Sea by the Bosporus strait and with the Ægean Sea by the Dardanelles strait.

The coast line has many irregularities. Those on the north are mainly the enlarged mouths of rivers, the only major inlet being Nordenskjöld Sea. On the south, however, there are three large peninsulas separated by two deep indentations. Between Arabia, the most western peninsula, and India, in the center, lies the Arabian Sea, which has two important inlets, each connected by a strait with an inland sea. The Gulf of Aden in the west is joined to the Red Sea by the strait of Bab-el-Mandeb, and the Gulf of Oman at the north of the Arabian Sea communicates by the strait of Ormuz with the Persian gulf. The third great peninsula is Indo-China with its southern extension known as the Malay peninsula. It is separated from India by the Bay of Bengal.

The eastern coast is notable for a series of deep inlets and for an irregular chain of islands stretching from the north to the south. This configuration results in a number of island-bound seas. Bering Sea at the north is confined by the Aleutian islands, which are geographically a part of Alaska. South of Kamchatka peninsula lies the Sea of Okhotsk. The Sea of Japan is enclosed by Sakhalin island and by the islands of Japan, which stretch southwestward toward the southern end of the peninsula of Chosen. The Yellow Sea and the China Sea extend southward to the Taiwan strait, as the channel is called which lies between the island of Formosa and the mainland. The South China Sea, bounded on the east and south by the Philippine Islands and by Borneo, has two large inlets, the Gulf of Tonkin and the Gulf of Siam.

South and east of the continent lies, in an elongated cluster, the largest group of islands in the world. This group, known as the Malay archipelago, extends as far as Australia. This archipelago, together with the numerous smaller islands which continue to dot the Pacific for more than 2000 miles still farther east, is sometimes embraced under the term Oceania. The only other large island off the southern coast is Ceylon, near the southern tip of India. The New Siberian islands and Wrangell island lie well within the Arctic circle to the north.

Surface. Asia has the greatest mean elevation of any of the continents except Antarctica, its surface being, on the average, more than 3000 feet above the sea. Moreover, the continent contains the highest mountain, the highest plateau, the most extensive lowland, the lowest lake, and the deepest lake, in the world.

About 2000 miles north of the southern tip of India lies the plateau of Pamir, often called the roof of the world. This plateau, 11,000 feet in height, forms a central point from which mountain chains radiate, most of them trending in a general east and west direction.

The highest range is that of the Himalaya Mountains, curving from the Pamir plateau to the south and east, where it forms a northern wall of India. Mount Everest, in this range, is the highest peak in the world, having a height of 29,002 feet.

North of the Himalaya Mountains lies the world's highest plateau, Tibet, which has an elevation ranging from 9000 to 17,000 feet. The region is volcanic. To the north of the plateau of Tibet lies, at a lower level, the plateau of Mongolia, largely occupied by the Gobi desert. This plateau is separated from Tibet by the Kunlun mountains. The plateau of Mongolia is confined on the northwest side by an irregular group of mountain ranges stretching northeast from the Pamir plateau. Among these mountains lies the deepest body of fresh water in the world, Lake Baikal, in which soundings of 5306 feet have been taken. Both the plateau of Tibet and the plateau of Mongolia widen toward the east and eventually slope downward to the plains of China in the south and, farther north, to the plains of Manchuria.

Westward from the Pamir plateau, a broad mountainous highland stretches to the extreme western part of the continent in Asia Minor. This region contains the lofty Hindu Kush range and, farther west, Mount Ararat, on which Noah's ark is said to have landed. The highland slopes, on the south, down to the plains of Iraq, which drain toward the Persian gulf. South and west of this drainage basin rises the plateau which occupies the greater part of the Arabian peninsula. The northwestern extremity of the plateau falls rapidly to a basin of inland drainage, which constitutes the most remarkable depression on the face of the earth. The lowest point is occupied by the Dead Sea, the surface of which is almost 1300 feet below the level of the sea.

To the north of Asia's great central highland lies the world's vastest plain. Occupying the whole northern part of the continent, it is sometimes called the Great Northern Lowland. Most of it inclines in steppes very gently toward the north, but in the southwest there is an area of inland drainage, part of which slopes toward the Caspian Sea and part toward the Aral Sea.

To the south of the Himalaya Mountains lie the plains of India. These plains rise on the southern side to a table-land of moderate height, sometimes called the Deccan. On the east, the plains are confined by a number of mountain ridges, which constitute a southern spur from the plateau of Tibet. These mountains lose themselves in the plains of Indo-China and in the Malay peninsula.

The plateau of Mongolia sends a similar spur to the northeast, known as the Stanovoi Mountains, which stretch as far as Bering strait. From this extreme northern point, a partly submerged mountain chain passes south through the ocean, emerging in various places to form the numerous islands off the east coast. Many of these mountains, particularly those in Japan, are actively volcanic.

Drainage. The great central highlands of Asia feed six rivers which exceed 2000 miles in length. Two of them, the Yangtze and the Yenisei, rank among the six longest rivers of the world.

The Ob River, the Yenisei River, and the Lena River are the largest of the streams which take their rise in these highlands and wind slowly through the immense steppes down to broad estuaries at the Arctic Ocean. Their lower courses are icebound eight months in the year. For 100 miles above the mouth of the Lena lies a stretch of frozen silt in which are embedded the remains of numerous mammoths and of other animals which were engulfed in quagmire thousands of years ago.

The three greatest rivers flowing to the east are the Amur, the Hwang, and the Yangtze. Each follows a long, meandering course in the central plateau before descending to the plains and emptying into the waters of the Pacific Ocean. Destructive annual floods frequently follow the melting of the upland snows, particularly in the Hwang river in China, which for that reason is often called "China's sorrow."

The southeastern spur of the plateau of Tibet gives rise to three rivers of southern drainage. Named in order from east to west, they are the Mekong River, the Salwin River, and the Irrawaddy River. The Ganges River and the Brahmaputra River both rise in the Himalaya Mountains and mingle their waters in a common delta at the head of the Bay of Bengal. The Brahmaputra River flows eastward along the northern edge of the Himalayas in the plateau of Tibet and, bending southward and westward, passes through a plain which has a heavier rainfall than any other region of the world. The Ganges throughout most of its course flows eastward. The Indus River rises to the north of the Himalaya Mountains and, passing around the western end of the range, empties into the Arabian Sea.

The plains of Iraq are drained toward the Persian Gulf by the Tigris River, which is joined about 100 miles above its mouth by the celebrated Euphrates River. The Ural River flows into the northern end of the Caspian Sea. The Caspian Sea has no outlet but is itself 86 feet below the level of the ocean. The Aral Sea is the center of another basin of interior drainage. Such basins cover, in Asia, a larger area than in any other continent.

Climate. On account of its range of latitude and of altitude, Asia is subject to a great variety of climate. In the interior of Siberia, temperatures of 92° below zero have been recorded, although in summer on the Arctic coast the thermometer sometimes registers 100°. The hottest part of the continent is in Arabia, where the temperature has reached 120° F. and the average for the year is 93°.

While parts of Assam, in the basin of the Brahmaputra River, have a rainfall of about 500 inches, the rainfall of Asia as a whole is scanty. An arid desert, in which the annual precipitation is less than 10 inches, extends in a broad sweep through the center of the continent from east to west. Beginning with the desert of Gobi in the plateau of Mongolia, it passes through central Asia, Iran, and Arabia. Siberia also has a light rainfall. Japan, the plains of China and of the Indo-China peninsula, the Malay peninsula, and eastern and southern India have a copious and, in parts, an excessive precipitation.

Vegetation. Asia is the original source of more of our important economic plants than all other parts of the world combined. From it come wheat, barley, sugar cane, alfalfa, cotton, flax, jute, hemp, tea; such fruits as the apple, cherry, peach, prune, apricot, banana, olive, orange, lemon, grapefruit, date, and pomegranate; and, in the list of vegetables, the radish, cucumber, muskmelon, onion, parsnip, rhubarb, spinach, and eggplant.

Northern Siberia from east to west contains a strip of tundra, or frozen desert, stretching 150 to 500 miles southward from the Arctic Ocean. In this tundra, a permanently frozen subsoil permits the growth of few plants other than mosses and lichens. Coniferous forests and, farther south, forests of deciduous trees cover the steppes. South of the forests lies an immense belt of treeless plains covered with grass. The grass is replaced by a desert flora toward the arid zone of central Asia.

In the regions of copious rainfall, the plant life is extraordinarily rich, India having more species than any other region of equal area in the world. The sacred peepul and the banyan tree, plants producing ginger, members of the pea family, medicinal plants, orchids, gourds, figs, timber trees, gum producing trees, sago palms, bamboos, and teak are representative of the rich flora south of the Himalaya Mountains. On these mountains grow magnolias and large rhododendrons; higher up, pines are found, and also the deodar, a species of cedar similar to that growing on Mount Lebanon in southwestern Asia. The better watered parts of Arabia still produce, in limited amounts, the spices and fragrant plants which, in earlier days, won for the peninsula the poetic characterization of "Araby the blest."

Animal Life. Asia is the original home of most of the world's domesticated animals, including the horse, ox, sheep, pig, goat, camel, chicken, and goose. The humped ox, the water buffalo, and the yak are used as draft animals by the inhabitants of the continent. The elephant of Asia, unlike the African elephant, is easily domesticated.

The Himalaya Mountains form a barrier north of which the climate is unfavorable to animal life. In the north, however, bears, foxes, and wolves are found, as well as other wild animals which inhabit the corresponding latitudes of Europe. South of the barrier, the fauna is extremely rich. Nearly all the families of tropical birds are represented. India is the home of the tiger. There are several species of the rhinoceros. The deadly cobra takes a yearly toll of many thousands of human lives.

Minerals. The natural resources of Asia have been very inadequately explored. There is reason to believe, however, that the continent is extremely rich in minerals. Coal and iron exist in large quantities in China, and the world's richest source of petroleum is in southwest Asia. Most of the world's supply of tin comes from the Malay peninsula and the islands lying near it.

Inhabitants. It is generally acknowledged that it was in Asia that man first turned to agriculture and built cities. From Asia have come all the most wide-spread religions of the world. It justifiably claims the earliest use of writing. Today it supports a larger population than any other continent, its estimated 1900 million inhabitants being about 60 per cent of the human race.

Asiatic peoples comprise about seven-tenths of the total population of the continent. About one-tenth of the population, however, consists of Caucasians, living in Siberia, India, and southwest Asia. From these regions, the Caucasians emigrated at an early period, spreading over northern Africa and Europe, whence they came later to America. The aborigines of America are believed to have reached the western hemisphere by way of northeastern Asia.

Religion. The most widely embraced religions of Asia today are Buddhism, Confucianism, Mohammedanism, Hinduism, Taoism, and Shintoism. Buddhism, Confucianism, and Taoism center principally in China. Shintoism is the chief religion of Japan. In India, Hinduism competes with Mohammedanism, which is the dominant religion of southwestern Asia. Christianity is strongest in northwestern Asia, chiefly Siberia, and in the islands of the Malay archipelago, in many of which it dominates to the virtual exclusion of others. It has also been introduced by missionaries into China, Japan, and India.

POLITICAL DIVISIONS

Asia is a continent most of whose nations have only recently come into existence. This was due to the conquest of most of Asia by European nations in early modern times and the liquidation of those conquests after World War II.

The following are the chief national states of the continent: Afghanistan, Burma, Cambodia, Ceylon (Sri Lanka), China, Cyprus, India, Indonesia, Iran, Iraq, Israel, Japan, Jordan, Korea, Kuwait, Laos, Lebanon, Malaysia, Maldive Islands, Pakistan, Philippines, Saudi Arabia, Singapore, Syria, Thailand (Siam), Turkey, Vietnam, and Yemen.

In addition, a large section of Asia is part of Russia, whose Asiatic territory is about three times the area of European Russia.

Afghanistan. A republic of south Asia, hemmed in by India, Iran, and Turkestan. Its area is about 250,000 square miles. The surface is, for the most part, a dry, mountainous plateau. It is traversed by the Hindu Kush and by other ranges, which in some places attain a height in excess of 17,000 feet.

The mountainsides have forests of cedar, pine, walnut, and other trees; the valleys support crops of cereals and a variety of fruits. Wheat, rice, and mutton are staple foods. Sheep raising is one of the chief occupations.

The population of Afghanistan is about 16,113,000. The capital is Kabul, a city of about 300,000, which is a center of caravan trade with India and central Asia. There are no railroads in Afghanistan. Herat, in the northwest, contains ruins of many buildings erected by Timur, the Mogul warrior who overran Asia in the 14th century.

Bangladesh. Formerly the East Bengal province of Pakistan, the People's Republic of Bangladesh became independent in December 1971. Bangladesh covers 55,126 square miles and has a population of 71,300,000. The country is bordered by India on the north, east, and west, and by the Bay of Bengal on the south.

Bangladesh is largely a subtropical alluvial plain with many river valleys, deltas, and swamps. The chief rivers are the Ganges and Brahamputra. In November 1970 the southern Ganges Delta region was destroyed by a cyclonic tidal wave. More than 220,000 people were reported dead and an estimated 350,000 dwellings were either damaged or destroyed.

The country is agricultural, with some 80 to 90 per cent of the population engaged in agriculture. The major crops are rice, jute, sugar cane, tea, tobacco, and oilseeds. Large reserves of natural gas and some coal deposits are being developed by the government through loans from India.

The capital and largest city of Bangladesh is Dacca (1,310,972). Other major cities are Chittagong (416,733) and Chalna (436,000).

Burma. A republic of southeast Asia on the Bay of Bengal adjoining India and Pakistan on the west and China, Laos, and Thailand on the north and east. Its area is 261,789 square miles.

Burma consists of a central basin with the Arakan Yoma mountains to the west on the India border and the Shan plateau in the east. The central basin is watered by the Irrawaddy River running south through a fertile delta and emptying by nine mouths into the Bay of Bengal. Minerals include lead, silver, zinc, nickel, copper, tin, gold, rubies, sapphires, and jade. The forests produce teak and other valuable hardwoods.

Agriculture is the leading occupation, and Burma normally is a heavy exporter of rice. Sugar cane and groundnuts are also produced in quantity. Industries include silk weaving, rice husking, oil refining, and wood carving. The Baluchaung hydroelectric plant, completed in 1960, is one of the largest in southeast Asia. Buddhism is the established religion. The leading cities are Rangoon, the capital and chief port, and Mandalay, a river port of Upper Burma.

Burma was given independence in 1948 by Great Britain and dissociated itself from the Commonwealth. Population, 26,389,000.

Cambodia. A republic of southeast Asia bounded north by Thailand and Laos, east by Vietnam, and southwest by the Gulf of Siam. Its 69,884 square miles consist chiefly of an alluvial plain watered by the Mekong River.

Agriculture of a subsistence type is the chief occupation, and rice is the principal crop. Other products include rubber, cotton, tobacco, kapok, and corn. Cattle breeding is an important activity.

From the 9th to the 13th century A.D., Cambodia was ruled by the Khmers, whose monarchs constructed at Angkor magnificent shrines and temples. Their ruins, among the most impressive in southeast Asia, were threatened in 1970 during the Vietnam conflict. Angkor Wat is the best known.

Cambodia was part of French Indochina until 1953 and was a constitutional monarchy for several years thereafter. In 1970 it became a republic. The capital and largest city (pop. 393,995) is Phnom Penh. Population, 6,557,000.

Ceylon (Sri Lanka). An island member of the British Commonwealth in the Indian Ocean near the southern extremity of India. The surface, 25,332 square miles in area, is mainly an undulating plain, about one-fifth being mountainous and covered with forests. The island is famous for gems, although the exports of tea, rubber, and coconuts exceed in value any other article shipped abroad. Other products are cocoa, cinnamon, and plumbago. The capital and largest city is Colombo. About 70 per cent of the inhabitants are Buddhists and of Singhalese origin, while 21 per cent are Hindus of Tamil extraction, coming originally from India. Population, 11,964,000.

China. The immense, roughly triangular country in eastern Asia lying between Asiatic Russia on the northwest and India, Pakistan, Burma, Laos, and Vietnam on the southwest. It is about 3,000 miles from east to west, and its maximum extent from north to south is 2400 miles. The area of continental China is 3,754,210 square miles. Known as the People's Republic of China (Communist China), it claims but does not control Taiwan (Formosa), which is ruled by the National Republic of China.

People's Republic. Communist China consists of six regions, which include 23 provinces, 4 autonomous regions (including Tibet, conquered in 1950, and Inner Mongolia), and the 2 administrative areas of Peking, the capital, and Shanghai, the largest city.

Three-fifths of the territory of China is inhabited by about 1 per cent of the population. This sparsely settled part, occupied mainly by nomadic tribes, consists of the lofty, mountainous plateau of Tibet, the desert plateau of Mongolia, and the arid depression of inland drainage known as Sinkiang. The remainder of the country embraces the extremely fertile eastern plains, watered by three great rivers, the Hwang, the Yangtze, and the West river. In China proper as well as in the outlying territories, the surface of China is mainly mountainous. While practically all of the level lands are fertile flood plains, they are subject to disastrous floods.

The climate of China proper, where practically all of the Chinese live, is divided into two main regions, northern and southern. The northern region extends from the crest of the Tsingling and Haiyang mountains to the northern border. It is a temperate region supporting wheat as a major cereal as compared to rice in the southern region. The southern region includes the great Yangtze basin and southward area, with rice as the major climatic adjustment. Northern China is temperate with hot summers, cold winters, and moderate rainfall, while southern China differs by having mild winters and heavy rainfall. China's rainfall is sharply seasonal, falling mainly in summer.

All of China suffers greatly from droughts and floods which are caused by variations in the Monsoon winds which control China's weather. A 1911 flood of the Yangtze affected 50,000,000 people, directly causing the death of upwards of 100,000 and destroying vast properties. Typhoons, earthquakes, and locusts also plague China.

The deposits of coal, of iron, and of copper in China are among the richest in the world. More than one-half of the world's supply of antimony and tungsten comes from China. The proximity of the coal and the iron deposits in the northeastern district of Shan-si has resulted in a large steel industry. The manufacture of porcelain, centering since 220 A. D. in Kingtehchen, a city of about 266,000 inhabitants, is still a distinctive industry of the country. Lacquered ware and textiles of silk and of cotton are other native manufactures for which China has long been noted. In the north are vast deposits of oil shale which are being processed. This region also has a large share of China's coal and iron reserves plus considerable industrial development.

The chief occupation of the Chinese, however, is agriculture, which is carried on more intensively than anywhere else in the world. The soil is very fertile, and irrigation by canals and by irrigation wheels or even by hand is employed where necessary. Rotation of crops has been practiced for centuries. The chief crops include rice, corn, tobacco, soy beans, tea, cotton, and sugar cane, the last three being grown in the southern part of the country. The mulberry tree is cultivated largely for the silkworms which feed on it and from which silk is obtained. Soy beans and silk are the most valuable articles of export. Other important exports are textiles, tea, coal, and cotton. Chickens and pigs are raised everywhere in China, and pig's bristles have become an important article of export. China's farm problems are complex also because 80 per cent of the people live on farms and must depend on farming for their existence. Farm land per capita is only a fraction of an acre (0.45) or 1485 people for each square mile of agricultural land. While her total production of such important crops as wheat and rice are among the largest in the world, probably totaling upwards of 3 billion bushels, it scarcely suffices to feed her huge population who depend upon cereals for 90 per cent of their diet. The Communist government attacked the problem by nationalizing land and trying, in the 1960's, to industrialize farm work by so-called communes.

By 1960, about 20,000 miles of railroad had been constructed in China. The so-called Grand Canal, running from the city of Hangchow a distance of 600 miles north to the Gulf of Chihli, was built 2500 years ago. Parts of it are choked with silt. In 1960, there were more than 250,000 miles of highways. A large part of the country's transportation is provided by the rivers, along which ply numerous "junks" and other boats. Thousands of people live on the rivers in house boats, which are often equipped with gardens made in soil laid on the floors of the boats.

Chinese civilization is ancient and distinctive. For thousands of years, the veneration of parents remained a cardinal principle of Chinese religion, law, and social customs. These cardinal principles of Chinese religion and philosophy were tremendously impressed upon the Chinese people by the zealous teaching of the great philosopher Confucius and his disciple Mencius. This principle encouraged a high birth rate, which, despite recurrent famines, has kept the population of China well above the limits which the country could readily support. The chief religions are Buddhism, Confucianism, and Taoism. About 4 per cent are Mohammedans, and less than 1 per cent are Christians.

As a people, the Chinese have adapted themselves to both cold and hot countries, having settled in large numbers both in the northern remote border regions and in the countries of southeast Asia. In several of the latter countries, they form the principal class of traders. A 30-letter alphabet of the Latin type is gradually replacing the 30,000 characters of the Chinese script.

The impact of western civilization plunged China into social and political chaos. Industrialization, beginning with the manufacture of textiles, flour, and steel, tended to break up the authority of the family. Western ideas of freedom were followed by Communism as a means of catching up with the western economy. But none of the desperate expedients was as effective as, for example, the parallel modernization of Japan's economy.

Apart from the capital, Peking, and Shanghai, the largest city, Communist China's leading cities are Tientsen, Shenyang (formerly Mukden), Wuhan (including former Hankow), Chungking, Canton, and Nanking, which was the capital before the Communist regime. Population, 1968 UN est., 730,000,000.

National Republic. The government of the Chinese National Republic, taking refuge from the Communists, retreated in 1950 to Taiwan (Formosa), an island 13,890 square miles in area, 110 miles off the east coast of the mainland. Lying in a generally north-and-south position, it is 225 miles long and 80 miles across at its widest point. It is traversed axially by a mountain range, steep on the eastern side but sloping gradually on the west to a fertile plain, which is intensively cultivated and produces exportable surpluses of rice and sugar cane. Its extensive forests are the world's chief source of camphor. Mineral output includes gold, silver, copper, and coal. Taiwan's rapidly growing industry produces steel, aluminum, lumber, flour, cement, paper, fertilizers, and refined oil.

Taiwan was held by Japan from 1895 until 1945. After the Nationalist Chinese government took refuge there, the economy of the island was rapidly expanded, partly with aid from the United States, which guaranteed the island's independence and strengthened its armed forces. The capital is Taipei, with a population of 1,155,191. Population of Taiwan, 13,466,000.

Cyprus. An island republic in the northeastern part of the Mediterranean Sea, 3572 square miles in area, with a length of 140 miles east and west and a maximum width of 60 miles. Agriculture is the predominant industry, which provides exports of tropical fruits, wine, potatoes, and tobacco. The most valuable export is copper concentrate, as it was in ancient times, the name of the island being the Greek word for *copper*. The inhabitants are partly Greek and partly Turks. The capital is Nicosia. Population, 622,000.

India. A republic occupying the large southern Asiatic peninsula separating the Indian Ocean on the east and the Arabian Sea on the west. Its northern boundary lies against China and Nepal; the land boundary to the west is Pakistan and to the east are Bangladesh and Burma. India has an area of 1,262,275 square miles.

India has a northern mountain wall, south of which the surface falls to a great plain arid in the extreme west but well watered in the central and eastern regions. Through this plain, which is shared by Pakistan, pass the Indus River and the Ganges River, the latter being joined at its delta by the Brahmaputra River. From the head of the Bay of Bengal, a mountain barrier runs north to the Himalaya Mountains and divides India from Pakistan.

On India's side of the Himalayas are two nominally independent mountain kingdoms, Nepal to the west and Bhutan to the east, with a feudal form of organization. Nepal, with an area of about 56,400 square miles, supports a population estimated at 10,700,000. Livestock is the basis of its economy, which includes manufacture of cement and chemicals. Bhutan has an area of 18,000 square miles and about 800,000 inhabitants. It barters rice, cloth, elephants, and swords.

The central plains of India are the hottest part of the country. The year is divided into three seasons, the hot season, the monsoon rains, and the cold season. The hot season is from late March to early June. In central India temperatures rise daily to over 100° F. in the shade and at times 120° F. Day and night the temperature stands between 95° F. and 115° F. and little outside work can be accomplished during midday.

With the coming of the rainy season, June to mid-September, the temperatures fall appreciably and daily rains prevail. A secondary heat period follows the rainy season, from mid-September to November, when the cold season sets in. This "cold" season is about like summer in northern United States except that no rain falls in India.

Over most of India frost and snow are unknown. Only in the far northwest and in high altitudes do temperatures descend below freezing.

India is a land of great climatic extremes. The droughts caused by failure of the monsoon rains cause famines when literally millions have starved to death. Typhoons bring havoc to both coasts of the Deccan. During the rainy season the heaviest rainfall known in the world falls on the windward side of the Khasi Hills. Over 38 feet (457.8 in.) of rain falls here annually between late March and early October. During a particularly wet year 905 inches (75 feet) of rain fell at the station of Cherrapunji and on one day 41 inches, the equal of a year of rainfall in central United States. A great climatic variation is provided by the towering Himalayas which provide important summer resorts, as at Simla. The eastern regions and a strip along the western coast have a heavy rainfall, confined mainly to the rainy season—June to November. The northwestern section is dry, but the land is productive under irrigation. Irrigation works in India dwarf those of any other country except China. Over 50 million acres of crop land is thus served, mainly by means of canals.

The vegetable and animal life of India is extremely rich, comprising nearly all the tropical species of the continent. Venomous snakes are numerous, and every year their human victims are numbered by the thousand. Man-eating tigers have been known to cause whole villages to be deserted. Crocodiles infest the malarial swamps at the mouths of the large rivers. A species of loud-voiced lizard abounds in all the moister regions.

More than two-thirds of the population of India supports itself by agriculture and stock raising. India is the world's chief producer of jute and one of the largest producers of cotton and tea, the latter being the leading export. The other chief crops are wheat, rice, sugar cane, lac, wool, opium, and nuts. The livestock consists mainly of humped oxen, buffaloes, sheep, and goats. Buffaloes are far more numerous as beasts of burden than are horses, donkeys, or camels. India possesses more cattle than any other country in the world, but, by reason of low quality, their value is not comparable.

Mineral production includes gold, petroleum, manganese, salt, chromium, copper, titanium, china clay, gypsum, and iron. Steel, cement, and fertilizers are among the significant manufactures but textiles form the leading industrial product. Traditionally, India has absorbed enormous amounts of gold and silver for ornaments and treasure.

The population of India is 523,893,000, of whom about 50 per cent are Hindu, 10 per cent Mohammedan, and 2 per cent Christian. Some 220 different languages are spoken, but the prevailing one is Hindi, and English is known to several million people, a legacy of 200 years of British rule. About 90 per cent of the population is illiterate. Religion plays a large role in Indian life, a feature of which is the prevalence of pilgrimages to the holy city of Benares and bathing in the sacred waters of the Ganges to remove physical and spiritual ills. Agra has a world-famed mausoleum, the Taj Mahal, built in 1629–50 by Emperor Shah Jehan as the burial place for his favorite wife, Mumtaz Mahal.

India became a sovereign republic in 1950 after a long period of struggle, in the course of which the former British India was divided into India which was predominantly Hindu, and Pakistan, which was predominately Mohammedan. Extensive population changes took place after the boundaries were agreed upon. India was the first republic to adhere to the British Commonwealth of Nations.

The capital of India is New Delhi, and Bombay is the largest city. Other important cities include Calcutta, Madras, Bangalore, and Kanpur.

Indonesia. A republic of southeastern Asia consisting of seven principal islands and 3000 islets of the Malay Archipelago. It stretches 3000 miles from the Malay Peninsula eastward toward Australia and lies across the equator between the Indian and Pacific oceans. The republic's area is 575,450 square miles. The island of New Guinea is divided between Indonesia and Malaysia.

The western islands of the archipelago, Sumatra, Java, Bali, and Borneo, lie in a shallow sea. This fact and their common flora and fauna indicate that the islands were once a part of the continent of Asia. The eastern islands of the Indonesian Republic offer a striking contrast to the western group. The eastern islands comprise Celebes, the Moluccas, and the lesser Sunda chain from Lombok to the Tanimbar group. These rise abruptly from deep sea basins. They have steep, rugged mountains, short rivers, and narrow coastal plains.

The islands are fertile, warm, and well watered. They show an extraordinary degree of productivity, the exports in some years exceeding $500 million in value. Rice, corn, cassava, tea, sugar, quinine, coffee, rubber, tobacco, indigo, copra, petroleum, and tin are the chief products. Coal is mined also, the annual production exceeding one million tons. Among the more noteworthy forest trees are the teak and the upas.

The island of Java, with 60 million inhabitants, is one of the three most populous islands of the world. Its beauty and tropical luxuriance have won for it the characterization of the "pearl of the East Indies." At Boro Budor in Java stands one of the architectural marvels of the world, the largest and one of the most elaborate Buddhist temples in existence. The island of Bali, east of Java, is a mecca for tourists because of its beauty and picturesque inhabitants.

The capital of Indonesia is Jakarta. Until after World War II, Indonesia was a dependency of the Netherlands. Population, 112,825,000.

Iran (*ē-rän'*). A constitutional monarchy of southwest Asia, formerly known as Persia, with a southern coast line on the Persian Gulf and Arabian Sea. Its northern border, interrupted by the Caspian Sea, adjoins Russia. It is bounded west by Turkey and Iraq and east by Afghanistan and Pakistan. Its surface, covering 627,000 square miles, is a plateau rimmed by mountains on every side except the east. Mount Demavend is 18,500 feet high.

A narrow plain on the southern coast of the Caspian Sea has a heavy rainfall and supports a luxuriant vegetation. Nearly all the remainder of the country is dry and barren. The former name, Persia, gave its name to the peach, the English word being a corruption of the Latin word for Persian. The chief products of the country include petroleum, cotton, tobacco, rice, silk, wool, gums, fruits, opium, cereals, and the famous Persian rugs, the last being made entirely on looms operated by hand. Petroleum accounts for about half the total value of the exports.

The population of Iran is 26,985,000. Of this number, about one-third lead a nomadic life. Most of the inhabitants are Mohammedans, although there is a group of about 10,000 Parsis, or Ghebers, adherents of the ancient Persian religion that flourished as early as the 6th century B.C. Tehran is the capital and largest city of Iran.

Iraq. Formerly known as Mesopotamia, this country of 172,000 square miles stretches northwest from the Persian Gulf to Turkey and Syria. It lies between Iran and Arabia, and occupies the Tigris-Euphrates valley, where 19th-century excavations uncovered very complete records of an ancient civilization. The rich soil yields crops of dates, cotton, and wheat. Petroleum, the chief mineral product, provides most of the national income. The population, mainly Arabs and Kurds, is about 8,634,000. The capital is Baghdad.

Israel. A republic situated on the southeastern coast of the Mediterranean Sea and occupying most of the territory historically designated as Palestine. It is bounded north by Syria and Jordan and south by Saudi Arabia and Egypt. Israel, with a 7993-square-mile area, was established by its founders in 1948 as a national home for the Jews. In the 6-day Israeli-Arab war, June 1967, Israel successfully occupied the Sinai Peninsula, the Gaza Strip, the western bank of the Jordan, and a small area in Syria. Israel still held these areas in 1970, pending direct Arab negotiations and assurance from Egypt of the same shipping rights to the Suez Canal as other nations.

Agriculture in Israel consists of mixed farming under irrigation, dry farming, and grazing of farm animals, most of its area giving returns if properly irrigated. The industry is carried on in several ways—by communal settlements, cooperative settlements, and villages where each settler owns his own land. Products include grain, cotton, grapes, bananas, and especially citrus fruits, which form the chief item of export.

Manufactures include chemicals, building materials, textiles, glass and ceramics, tobacco products, leather goods, precision instruments, and electrical goods. Electric power is distributed from Tiberias, Haifa, and Tel Aviv.

The capital is Jerusalem. A Hebrew university there was founded in 1925. Military service is required of both men and women. Nearly 90 per cent of the inhabitants are Jews, and about half of the remainder are Arabs. Population, 2,745,000.

Japan. An ancient empire, consisting of a chain of mountainous islands off the eastern coast of Asia. The largest island is called Honshu. To the north lies Hokkaido, or Yezo; to the south, Shikoku and Kyushu. Its area is 142,726 square miles.

The islands of Japan, being the projecting portions of an immense submarine mountain range, have a mountainous surface, traversed from end to end by a high ridge. Numerous spurs from the mountains, descending to the coasts, result in a highly irregular coast line. There is, consequently, an abundance of good harbors, most of which are on the Pacific side.

The highest mountain in Honshu is Fuji, 12,388 feet in altitude. There is probably no region of its size in the world which has so many active volcanoes and is subject to such violent earthquakes as Japan. The largest active volcanic peak is Asama in central Honshu, which has a crater 600 to 800 feet deep with absolutely perpendicular sides.

The climate of Japan varies from subarctic to subtropical conditions. The cold northwestern winds from Siberia bring heavy snows in winter on the western side of the northern islands. Farther south, and more especially on the eastern side, the ocean exerts a moderating influence on the temperature and provides a copious rainfall. Violent and destructive windstorms, known as typhoons, usually mark the end of the hot, moist summers.

Japan has a very rich flora. The forests contain such trees as bamboos, camphor trees, oaks, maples, walnuts, laurels, and willows. The cultivation of flowering plants is very extensive, the Japanese being noted for their appreciation of floral beauty. Their national emblem is the chrysanthemum.

The animals include bears, monkeys, hares, wild boars, deer, foxes, wildcats, and pheasants. The buffalo is used for food and for plowing. The crane is considered sacred, being regarded as a symbol of longevity. The silkworm and numerous kinds of fish are of great economic importance.

Japan's mineral resources are gold, silver, copper, and petroleum. The chief occupations are agriculture—rice, fish, wheat, barley, rye, and poultry being the staple foods; fishing, which supports almost a million workers; and manufacturing. Export products are textiles, machinery, motor vehicles, electronic equipment, optical and other precision instruments, sewing machines, pianos, and organs. Japan leads the world in shipbuilding, and ranks second in auto production. Despite the lack of iron ore, it is also a leading producer of steel.

There is complete freedom of religion. The chief forms are Shintoism and Buddhism. Nine years of education are compulsory. There are 37 universities in the empire.

The capital and largest city is Tokyo. Osaka, the principal port, was the site of Expo '70. Other important cities are Kobe, Kyoto, Nagoya, Yokohama, and Nagasaki. The government is a constitutional monarchy under an emperor. Population, 101,090,000.

Jordan. A semi-desert Arab kingdom in Palestine east of Israel. It is bounded north by Syria and south and east by Saudi Arabia and Iraq. More than half the country's 37,301 square miles is desert. Crops of citrus fruits, vegetables, olives, barley, and wheat are grown in the fertile western part of Jordan. Industrial products are tobacco, olive oil, flour, textiles, plastics, and cement. Its only minerals are potash from the Dead Sea, and phosphate, a valuable export. Aqaba is the only port. The capital is Amman.

Education is progressing slowly. Arabic, the official language, and English are taught in the schools. Population, 2,039,000.

Korea. The peninsula of Korea in eastern Asia extending southeast about 600 miles from China and separating the Sea of Japan from the Yellow Sea is occupied by a nation divided as an aftermath of World War II. The dividing line is the 38th parallel of latitude, which separates South Korea from North Korea. The peninsula, 85,266 square miles in area with a maximum width of 350 miles, is a beautiful land of sparkling streams and high mountains. The northern part has cold winters and short summers, but the southern part has a warm, moist, rich climate. The Korean people have a history going back before Christ. China seized Korea in 1667; Japan annexed it in 1910.

South Korea. The Republic of Korea, 38,452 square miles in area, is predominantly agricultural in character, with rice the leading product, but other cereal grains are raised as well as cotton and tobacco. The country is one of the world's chief suppliers of tungsten and graphite. Manufacturing is concentrated in light consumer goods. Fishing is a leading industry.

The capital of South Korea is Seoul, with a population of 3,800,000. Pusan is the leading port. The population of South Korea is 30,470,000.

North Korea. The Democratic People's Republic of Korea, covering 46,814 square miles, is a Communist regime. It is richer in minerals than South Korea, the leading products being iron, coal, tungsten, gold, silver, and petroleum. Agriculture, largely mechanized since the war, produces temperate zone crops. Manufacturing, powered partly by several large hydroelectric projects, turns out steel, chemicals, cement, textiles, and fertilizers. As with South Korea, fishing is a leading occupation.
The capital is Pyongyang, with 653,100 inhabitants. Population, 13,000,000.

Kuwait. A small, oil-rich sheikdom on the northeast corner of the Persian Gulf and adjoining Saudi Arabia and Iraq. Its 9375 square miles are waterless and barren except for their petroleum. Constitutional government on the British model was established in 1963. Population, 540,000.

Laos. A kingdom of southeastern Asia bounded north and east by China and Vietnam, south by Cambodia, and west by Thailand and Burma. Its area of 88,780 square miles is covered in the north by tropical forests and, in the south, by agricultural land producing rice, corn, tobacco, citrus fruits, and opium. About 90 per cent of the inhabitants are engaged in agriculture. There are rich iron ore deposits, but they are not mined. The forests produce teak and other valuable hardwoods.
Laos was part of French Indochina until after World War II, when it declared its independence and was a cockpit of strife between Communists and their foes. French is still one of the official languages. The capital is Vientiane. Population, 2,825,000.

Lebanon. A country on the eastern end of the Mediterranean Sea immediately north of Israel. It is bounded north and east by Syria. North to south it measures about 135 miles with a width of 20 to 35 miles. Most of its area of 3400 square miles is mountainous. About one-fourth is cultivated, the principal crops being oranges, apples, grapes, olives, wheat, and potatoes. Tripoli and Sidon are the terminals of oil pipe lines from Iraq and Saudi Arabia, respectively.
The capital is Beirut. Lebanon has a population of 2,580,000, and was a French dependency until after World War II.

Malaysia. A constitutional monarchy of southeastern Asia comprising most of the southern portion of the Malay Peninsula. It included also Singapore at the southern tip of the peninsula prior to 1965, when Singapore separated. Malaysia's area is estimated at 128,338 square miles.
The wealth of Malaysia is based in considerable part on rubber and tin. Agricultural products comprise chiefly rice, coconuts, and tea. Exports pass mainly through the port of Singapore.

The population is predominantly Malay, whereas in Singapore the Chinese were in the majority and controlled trade there and in Sarawak and North Borneo. This divergence underlay the separation. The capital is Kuala Lumpur in the State of Malaya. Malaysia's population is estimated at 10,384,000.

Maldive Islands. A republic occupying a coral island in the Indian Ocean 300 miles southwest of India. It was a British dependency until 1965. The area is 115 square miles. Population, 106,000.

Pakistan. A civil war in 1971 caused the separation of East and West Pakistan. West Pakistan became the Islamic Republic of Pakistan; East Pakistan became Bangladesh. Pakistan covers 310,403 square miles and is bounded on the south by the Arabian Sea, on the east by India, on the north by China and Afghanistan, and on the west by Iran. The country's landscape varies greatly. The northern part of the country is dominated by the Karakoram and Himalaya mountain ranges; from the foothills of these mountains stretches a barren plain. The fertile Indus plain of the southern and central region is watered by the country's only major river—the Indus.
Pakistan is largely agricultural, much of its exports are grains. The major crops are wheat, cotton, maize, sugar cane, rice, fruits, and dates.

The development of reserves of crude oil and large reserves of natural gas supplies the expanding industries of Pakistan. Principal industries include woolen and cotton products, cement, and refined sugar. Fishing is also a major source of income. Pakistan's chief trade partners are the U.S., Japan, West Germany, and Britain.

Pakistan's 1972 population was 64,890,000, with 235,000 living in the capital city of Islamabad. Other major cities include Karachi (3,469,000), Lahore (2,148,000), Lyallpur (820,000), and Rawalpindi (615,000).

Philippines. An island republic forming the most northern division of the great Malay archipelago. The Philippines lie southeast of China, about 500 miles from its coast, and are bounded on the north and the east by the Pacific Ocean, on the south by the Celebes Sea, and on the west by the South China Sea. The island group is situated north of the equator but entirely within the tropics. It extends north and south for a distance of 1150 miles and east and west for a distance of 650 miles.

There are upwards of 7000 islands and islets, of which only 466 have areas of one square mile or over. Luzon, 40,420 square miles, and Mindanao, 36,537 square miles, rank among the large islands of the world.

Besides the two largest islands, there are 9 others of importance. Their names and approximate areas in square miles are as follows: Samar, 5100; Negros, 4900; Palawan, 4500; Panay, 4450; Mindoro, 3800; Leyte, 2800; Cebu, 1700; Bohol, 1550; and Masbate, 1250. The total area of the entire Philippine group is approximately 115,507 square miles. The population of the islands, 35,993,000.

The islands of the Philippine Archipelago are largely volcanic. There are 12 volcanoes which have been more or less active in modern times, and slight earthquakes are of frequent occurrence. The islands are traversed by irregular mountain ranges, the main ridges of which extend usually in a north-and-south direction. In Luzon, the mountains rise to heights of from 3500 to 4500 feet. Mount Apo, in southern Mindanao, with an elevation of 9690 feet, is the highest peak in the Philippines.

In the larger islands, there are extensive drainage systems. The Cagayan River, in Luzon, 220 miles in length, with a drainage basin of some 10,000 square miles, is the largest river in the Philippines.

The principal minerals are gold, silver, lead, zinc, copper manganese, chromite, iron, mercury, coal, and salt, though none is extensively exploited.
The plant life is distinctly tropical in character and is especially rich in trees. Primeval forests cover about half the area, abounding in dyewoods, cedars, ebonies, wild rubber, and many other valuable trees. The most valuable native plant is the abaca, which yields the fiber called manila hemp. Other products of the Philippine flora include coconuts, cinnamon, pepper, cloves, rattan, and gums.

The islands, while poor in native mammals, are rich in birds, about half of their 700 species being found only in the Philippines. Bright hued tropical birds include parakeets, cockatoos, firebirds, fairy bluebirds, and sunbirds. Among the larger mammals are the timariu (related to the water buffalo), monkeys, deer, wild hogs, civet cats, and fruit bats.

The commonest domestic animal is the water buffalo. Agriculture employs about 60 per cent of the inhabitants. The chief products are rice, manila hemp, copra, sugar cane, corn, tobacco, sweet potatoes, and bananas.

Manufacture is carried on chiefly in homes, although there is factory production of coconut-oil mills, polished rice, cigars, cigarettes, shoes, sugar, and cement. The home industries turn out embroidery, hats, woven cloth, baskets, and pottery.

About 90 per cent of the 35,993,000 inhabitants are of the Malay race and profess Christianity, the Filipinos being the only Asiatic people who, in modern times, have in large part embraced Christianity. The other inhabitants are largely Mohammedans and pagan wild tribes living in the mountains. The original inhabitants were Negritos, a low-statured race of whom about 25,000 remain. Mohammedan Malays are called Moros. The official language is based on Tagalog, although English is the main language of instruction.

The Philippine Islands were discovered in 1521 by Magellan. A Spanish expedition in 1542 named them in honor of Prince Philip, later Philip II of Spain. Spain began their conquest in 1565 and founded Manila in 1571. They were ceded to the United States in 1899 as a result of the Spanish-American War. In 1934, the United States granted a semi-independent status, effective in 1935, intended to lead ten years later to complete independence. On July 4, 1946, the islands became fully independent as the Republic of the Philippines.

In 1970, several powerful typhoons roared across the islands with an estimated 300 deaths and property loss in the millions. Manila, hardest hit, is the largest city, population about 3,100,000. The capital is Quezon City, population 501,800.

Russia in Asia. Russian territory in Asia covers 5,816,000 square miles, which is nearly three times the area of European Russia. The larger part is comprised in the Russian Socialist Federal Soviet Republic (R.S.F.S.R.), subdivided into the Far Eastern area, the Yakutsk autonomous republic, the Siberian area, and many smaller units. In addition, Asiatic Russia comprises eight states which are federated with the R.S.F.S.R. in the Soviet Union. These are the three Transcaucasian republics of Armenia, Georgia, and Azerbaidzhan, between the Caspian and Black seas: and the Turkmen, Uzbek, Tadzhik, Kazakh, and Kirghiz republics, situated north of India, Afghanistan, and Iran (Persia).

Geographically, this huge territory may be divided into three parts—the Great Northern Lowland, over four million square miles in area, which has mainly a northern drainage into the Arctic Ocean; the semi-arid region of Central Asia, some 1,700,000 square miles in area, with an interior drainage into the Caspian and Aral seas; and Transcaucasia, a dry, mountainous, subtropical region of about 75,000 square miles.

The Great Northern Lowland, formerly comprised largely under the name of Siberia, has on the whole a severe winter climate. The northern belt is barren tundra. An intermediate belt of forested land, stretching east and west, is suitable for dairying and flax culture and has enormous lumber resources. The southernmost belt is an immense grassland plain, potentially one of the great wheat areas of the world. The two latter belts, until recently very sparsely inhabited, are in the process of rapid settlement. They are served by the Trans-Siberian railroad. The Ural area, in the west, contains great mineral wealth, including one of the richest iron deposits of the world. For its exploitation one of the world's largest steel plants was erected in 1932 at the city of Magnitogorsk.

The region of Central Asia was from time immemorial the abode of nomadic tribes, with grazing and a primitive type of agriculture carried on in the oases. The Mongolian conqueror Timur had his capital in Samarkand, now an important city of the Uzbek soviet republic. Irrigation on a large scale is carried on with cotton as the principal crop.

Transcaucasia has a subtropical climate. Its principal industry is the production and refining of petroleum, which centers about Baku.

The principal cities of Transcaucasia include Baku, Tiflis, and Batumi; those of Central Asia, Tashkent, Bukhara, and Samarkand; and those of the Great Northern Lowland, Omsk, Sverdlovsk, Novosibirsk, Vladivostok, and Irkutsk.

Saudi Arabia. A desert kingdom occupying four-fifths of the Arabian peninsula in southwestern Asia. Having an area of about 870,000 square miles, it is bounded west by the Red Sea and Egypt, north by Jordan and Iraq, east by Kuwait and the Persian Gulf, and south by Yemen, Southern Yemen, and Oman, which border on the Arabian Sea.

The highlands of the west, 9000 feet high, slope down to 2000 feet at the Persian Gulf. This plateau is an arid, barren desert, inhabited by wandering tribes of Bedouins. Camels are the chief form of wealth among the tribesmen, who maintain themselves at oases. Mainly from the oases also come agricultural products, including dates, honey, hides, wool, barley, and clarified butter known as ghi.

Saudi Arabia is one of the richest oil-producing regions of the world, and oil royalties provide most of the income of the country, paying expenses of government and providing free medical service to the inhabitants.

The capital is Riyadh. Mecca and Medina are the two sacred cities of the Mohammedan world, and pilgrims and tourists visit them in great numbers. The country is an earlier amalgamation of two kingdoms, Hejaz and Nejd. Several other shiekdoms are associated with Saudi Arabia, including Oman at the southeastern extremity of the peninsula. Population of Saudi Arabia, about 7,100,000.

Singapore. See *Malaysia* and article on the city of Singapore.

Syria. A republic of western Asia bounded west by the Mediterranean Sea and Lebanon, north by Turkey, east by Iraq, and south by Jordan and Israel. It has an area of 71,210 square miles and a population of 5,738,000. Although most of the people are Sunni Moslems, some 500,000 are nomadic Bedouins. It is traversed by the Orontes and Euphrates rivers. Damascus, the capital, with a population of 618,457, is the oldest inhabited city in the world. Syria was under French rule before World War II. In 1958, it joined Egypt to form the United Arab Republic, but a revolt in 1961 broke the tie.

Only about half of the area is suitable for farming. Sandy deserts are common. Tobacco, wheat, fruits, cotton, barley, corn, sorghums, hemp, and silk are produced. Besides foodstuffs, manufactures include matches, alcohol, soap, cotton cloth, and cement. There are agricultural, engineering and teachers training colleges as well as universities in Damascus and Aleppo.

Thailand (*tī'lănd*) **(Siam).** An independent kingdom of southeastern Asia, bounded west by Burma, north and east by Laos, and south by Cambodia. It has a southern coast line on the Gulf of Siam. The area of the country is 200,148 square miles.

The richest part of Thailand is the wet, tropical valley of the Menam River. This river valley lies between a western mountain wall and a central plateau that divides the Menam River basin from the western reaches of the Mekong River system. The valley produces valuable timber and dyewoods. Agriculture is carried on intensively. Rice is the national food and is the staple article of export. The live stock of the country consists mainly of oxen and buffaloes but includes several thousand elephants. The white elephant, really a light ashy gray in color, is considered sacred by the inhabitants. Tin is the chief mineral produced on a commercial scale. Most of the trade is in the hands of foreigners, more especially of Chinese.

The population of Thailand is 33,693,000 (1968 est.). Buddhism is the prevailing religion. Thailand has, in recent years, introduced many of the methods of Western civilization, having employed the services of European and American advisers in finance, education, drainage, and many other departments. The capital is Bangkok.

Turkey. A republic of west Asia occupying the whole of Asia Minor and extending eastward to Transcaucasia and Iran. It includes also a number of islands off the coast and a small district of Europe, in which the city of Istanbul is situated. Asiatic Turkey is sometimes called Anatolia.

The area of Turkey is 296,108 square miles, including 9257 square miles in Europe. It consists mainly of a plateau which, except in the mountainous eastern region, sinks on all sides to wooded foothills cut by valleys leading to the sea. The northern coast district is most heavily wooded; the chief region of cultivation is on the west. The interior, particularly the eastern part, is hot and dry.

The principal occupation of the Turks is agriculture. Tobacco, cereals, cotton, figs, grapes, olives, and sugar beets are the chief products of the soil. Rugs, gums, and opium are among the exports. Mineral wealth is considerable but is undeveloped. Meerschaum is a distinctive product. Manufactures are confined mostly to handmade articles, including rugs and copper utensils, although lumber mills, cement works, and an automobile assembly plant have been opened in recent years.

The population of Turkey is 33,539,000. The seat of government is Ankara.

Vietnam. A country of southeast Asia fronting eastward and southward on the South China Sea and extending from China on the north along the borders of Laos and Cambodia on the west. Formerly a part of French Indochina, it was occupied by the Japanese in World War II, and French efforts to reassume their control ended in defeat, after eight years, by local Communist forces aided by the Chinese. A role of neutrality was agreed on in 1954 by interested powers, including the United States, and a commission was set up to establish a government. The northern part refused to cooperate and set up a Communist government on the Chinese model. The southern part set up a republic in 1954, and hostilities continued between the two parts.

After more than two decades of warfare, U.S. troops were withdrawn from the North-South conflict in 1973. In 1975 South Vietnam was defeated and the country was united under the Socialist Republic of the North.

South Vietnam. The former republic of Vietnam has an area of 66,263 square miles. Predominantly agricultural, it exports rice, rubber, tea, coffee, quinine, tobacco, cinnamon, and silk. There is no heavy industry, but light industry includes weaving and the manufacture of textiles, pens, bicycles, radios, sewing machines, and many other articles. The capital was Saigon. The inhabitants are concentrated in the fertile delta of the Mekong River. Population, 17,414,000.

North Vietnam. The Democratic Republic of Vietnam, 63,344 square miles in area, contained the richer part of the former French dependency. Its mineral output includes coal and phosphates. Rice is the chief agricultural product and practically all is grown by peasants grouped in agricultural cooperatives. All business is state-owned. Manufactured products include cement, cotton, and silk textiles, chemicals, and plywood. Hanoi is the capital, and Haiphong is the chief port. Population, 20,700,000.

Yemen. A mountainous republic at the tip of the Arabian peninsula, bounded north by Saudi Arabia, east by Southern Yemen, and west by the Red Sea. Grown in the most fertile part of its 75,000-square-mile area are coffee and grain. Hides, dates, herbs, and fruit are exported. Hodeida, on the Red Sea, is the chief port. Sana, its capital, is an archeological site. Population, 5,000,000.

CITIES AND OTHER POINTS OF TRAVEL INTEREST

The following articles describe the principal cities of Asia. Most of these cities present an appearance in which the marks of ancient civilizations contrast strikingly with the changes introduced by a rapidly penetrating industrialization. In addition to cities, a number of other notable features of Asia are described, such as the Dead Sea, the world's lowest and saltiest body of water; Tai Shan, the sacred mountain of Chinese Confucianists; and the Malay archipelago, the largest group of islands in the world.

Agra (*ä'grä*). A walled city of northern central India. The Mogul emperors left in Agra several monuments of striking magnificence, including the Taj Mahal, "Gem of Buildings," a white marble mausoleum, the construction of which is said to have engaged 20,000 workmen for 22 years. The city has a large trade. Its industries include gem setting and inlaid mosaic work. Population, 543,397.

Amernath. A cave in the Himalaya mountains near the extreme northern border of India. In the cave stands the sacred symbol of the god Siva, which is the object of pilgrimages from all parts of India.

Ankara. The capital of Turkey, officially chosen as such in 1923, replacing Istanbul. It was rapidly transformed from an oriental hamlet in a malarial plain to a modern city with sanitary improvements and well laid out streets. Railroads connecting with other parts of the country were constructed, electric power was provided, and manufacturing industries arose, notably for producing tiles and cotton and linen textiles. A park was laid out, and attractive government buildings were erected. Population, 971,069.

Baghdad. The capital of Iraq, situated on the Tigris River near the geographic center of the country. Like many other Oriental cities, Baghdad has a striking appearance at a distance. There are many ruined mosques, monuments of the city's former splendor. It was, in the 8th century, the capital of the caliphate of Haroun-al-Raschid, a hero of the *Arabian Nights*. Population, 745,328.

Bangkok. The capital and chief seaport of Thailand, on the Menam River 25 miles from the Gulf of Siam. It is noted for many elaborate temples and palaces. The streets, intersected by small canals, are made attractive with gardens and tall palm trees. The city's location on a far-reaching waterway system enables it to carry on an extensive foreign trade in rice, sugar, silk, peanuts, and cotton. Its modern airport, Don Muang, one of the largest in Southeast Asia, is served by 24 international airlines. Population, 3,967,081.

Beirut. Capital and principal seaport of Lebanon, also the seat of the American University and the Lebanese National Museum. Beirut has rail connections with Damascus and with Haifa and Tripoli. Population, about 700,000.

Benares (*bĕn-ä'rĕz*). A city of north central India on the Ganges River. It is sacred to the Hindus, who come there from all parts of India to wash away their sins in the Ganges. There are over 1500 Hindu temples in the city, which abounds in beggars living on the alms of wealthy pilgrims. The river banks are lined with stone and have many landing places, often highly ornamented. The city is a busy trading center. Gold brocade, gold and silver thread, embossed brass vessels, and lacquered toys are manufactured. The Benares Hindu university is situated there. Population, 540,239.

Bethlehem. A town of Jordan about five miles southwest of Jerusalem. Its chief center of interest is the basilica of Constantine, built in the 4th century at the spot where Jesus was believed to have been born. A chapel near by commemorates Jerome, the author of the Vulgate edition of the Bible, who resided and died in Bethlehem. Population, 22,453.

Bombay. The second largest city of India, situated on a small island near the center of the empire's southwest coast. By reason of its industrial development and of its modern improvements, Bombay is the most European in appearance of the cities of India. It has one of the six federal universities of the country. The characteristic Oriental features remain, however, in much of the city, where decorated houses, tea shops, bazaars, and temples bear witness to the more ancient civilization of the Hindus. Bombay was the birthplace of Rudyard Kipling. Population 5,970,575.

Calcutta. The largest city and, until 1911, the capital of India, about 85 miles from the sea at the west of the enormous delta of the Ganges river. Calcutta is the terminus of many railroads and canals and handles about one-third of the entire foreign trade of India. The European section has numerous splendid buildings. Cotton mills, sugar refineries, sawmills, silk mills, flour mills, and shipbuilding yards are among the more important industrial establishments.

The city is the seat of the University of Calcutta, founded in 1857. Victoria Memorial, one of the finest buildings in Calcutta, contains documents and pictures illustrating Indian history. Thackeray, the novelist, was born in Calcutta. Population, 7,031,382.

Canton (**Kwangchow**). A commercial city of southeastern China, situated about 70 miles northwest of the island of Hong Kong. The city is one of the chief centers of the Chinese silk trade. The industries include the manufacture of paper, lacquered wares, textiles, and glass, and the painting of porcelain.

The city is surrounded by a brick wall and partitioned by a cross wall into the old town and the new town. The latter has many wide, paved streets, Canton being one of the most progressive cities of China. Among the pagodas is one covering an area of seven acres. There is a Mohammedan mosque dating from the 9th century. Population, 1,840,000.

Chinese Wall. The most gigantic defensive work in existence, consisting of a wall more than 1500 miles in length, which was begun by the rulers of China in the 3d century B. C. and received its last addition in the 16th century A. D. A part, now destroyed, began near the Gulf of Liaotung in northeast China. The wall follows a general western direction along the southern border of Mongolia. The average height is about 22 feet. The base is from 15 to 25 feet wide, narrowing to 12 feet at the top. Its course passes through valleys and over mountains irrespective of the difficulties of construction.

Colombo. The capital of Sri Lanka (Ceylon), situated on the eastern coast of the island. The city was founded by the Portuguese in 1517 and was named in honor of Columbus. The European section is well built and modern in appearance. Population, 510,947.

Damascus. The capital of the republic of Syria. It is one of the few very ancient cities of the Mediterranean region which have survived until the present day. It is situated in a fertile region 53 miles southeast of its port, Beirut, on the Mediterranean coast. At the time of the Crusades, Damascus produced a famous type of ornamented steel, which has given the name damascening to modern steel etching.

The city has been often destroyed and rebuilt. The Ommiad, the largest of the city's 200 mosques, was formerly a church, which had earlier replaced a temple said to have contained the head of John the Baptist. Damascus, on account of its beautiful surroundings, is believed to have been the model for the paradise described in the *Koran*. The city contains the burial place of Fatima, the only child of Mohammed. Population, 618,457

Dead Sea. A salt-water lake in Palestine. It is 47 miles long and 10 miles wide. Its area is 340 square miles and it has a maximum depth of 1280 feet. Lying 1290 feet below sea level, it is the lowest body of water on the surface of the earth. Its principal affluent is the Jordan river. It has no outlet, its excess water being taken off by evaporation, estimated at about 6,000,000 tons daily. The salinity of the Dead Sea is 23 to 27%, which is about 5 times that of the ocean. The economic value of the various salts in solution is very great.

Delhi (*dĕl'ē*). The capital of India, situated in the north central part of the country. Delhi was formerly the largest city of India. The Mogul emperors made it their capital, and erected many fine buildings, the ruins of which still attest their original grandeur. The Great Mosque, built in 1650, still stands, and is regarded by Mohammedans as one of the wonders of the world. In the vicinity of the city is the Kutb Minar, a tower 238 feet high built of stone, ranging in color from red at the bottom to orange at the top.

The transfer of the seat of government from Calcutta to Delhi in 1911 was the occasion for building a new division of the city, known as New Delhi. This centers about Raisina, a hill six miles south of the walls of old Delhi, with which it is connected by broad, tree-lined avenues. Over $150 million was spent on this city building project, which is the most magnificent the Orient has witnessed in modern times. Population, 3,647,023.

Hangchow (*häng'chō'*). A city of mainland China near the center of the country's eastern coast and standing at the head of Hangchow bay, an inlet of the China Sea. The city is near the southern terminus of the Grand canal, which serves as an artery of the commerce centering in the city. The chief manufactures are silk and fans.

Hangchow is one of the best-built cities of China. The city is surrounded by a massive wall, 12 miles in circuit. The western part of this wall is washed by West lake, a beautiful sheet of water 8 miles in circumference dotted with islands on which are built monasteries, memorial halls, and shrines. To the west of the lake are numerous Buddhist temples. Population, about 784,000.

Hankow (*hăn'kō'*). See *Wuhan*.

Hiroshima. A large city near the southern end of the island of Honshu, Japan. It was an important political and commercial center having rail, air, and ocean connections. As a victim of the first atomic bomb, it was almost completely demolished but has been rebuilt. Population, 515,000.

Irkutsk (*ĭr-kōōtsk'*). A commercial city of south central Siberia, situated near the south end of Lake Baikal. It has a large caravan trade from Mongolia and is one of the three important points on the Asiatic section of the Trans-Siberian railroad. Articles of commerce include tea, silk, porcelain, dried fruit, fur, and fossil ivory. Population, 420,000.

Islamabad. The capital of Pakistan, situated in the north of West Pakistan 15 miles north of Rawalpindi. The latter was provisional capital until 1966 while the new governmental city of Islamabȧd was being built. Population, 235,000.

Izmir. See *Smyrna*.

Jakarta (**Raya**). The capital of the Republic of Indonesia, situated on the north coast of Java Island. It forms the chief outlet for the numerous products of the former Netherlands East Indies. The European section, in the higher, more healthful part, contains the Museum of the Batavian Society of Arts and Sciences, a beautiful structure in the Greek style which houses the largest collection of Javanese art in existence. The University of Indonesia is located here. Population, 4,600,000.

Jerusalem. The capital of Israel, as it had been of the ancient Israelites from about 1000 B.C. It is on an elevation of 2500 feet between the Mediterranean and Dead seas. About it has centered the devotion of Jews, Christians, and Mohammedans. It is the seat of Hebrew University.

The city is surrounded by ravines on three sides. The water and drainage facilities were greatly improved after the city was occupied by the British in 1918. The most prominent building of the city is the Mosque of Omar, standing on the site of Solomon's temple. The Church of the Holy Sepulchre and the Via Dolorosa are of interest for their connection with the crucifixion of Jesus. The "wailing wall," said to be a vestige of Solomon's temple, is sacred to Jews as a place for prayer and lamentation. Population, 344,200.

Kabul. The capital and largest city of Afghanistan It is near the center of the eastern frontier. Surrounded on three sides by mountains, it commands passes leading to India and Russia. Well built roads connect the city with these countries. The city itself is unattractive but it has a fine palace in a magnificent setting overlooking fruitful plains. It has also a small arms factory. Population, 289,703.

Karachi. A seaport in Pakistan, formerly the capital of the country. It is the chief outlet for wheat and raw cotton. Population, 2,721,200.

Keijo (**Seoul**). The capital and chief port of South Korea, situated near the center of the west coast of Chosen, of which it is the chief port and the capital. It is connected with the Trans-Siberian railroad. Silk, tobacco, mats, paper, and fans are made in the city. During the Korean war, it was the scene of bitter fighting and was partly ruined. Population, 3,800,000.

Kobe (*kō'bĕ*). A seaport of Japan, situated on the southern coast of Honshu Island. It is the chief center of Japan's silk export trade. Prominent among the industrial establishments is an imperial ship-building yard. Population, 1,228,000.

Kyoto (*kyō'tō*). An inland commercial and industrial city of Japan, situated near the southern coast of Honshu Island. Kyoto was formerly the capital of Japan and bears evidence of the fact in the regularity of its plan and in its magnificent monuments and temples. Its industries include the manufacture of porcelain, brocade, toys, metal products, and silk fabrics. The city is the seat of an imperial university. Population, 1,379,000.

Lhasa (*läs'ä*). The sacred city of the Lamaists, members of a widespread, ascetic sect of Buddhism. The city is situated in south central Tibet on a plateau having an altitude of 11,830 feet. Being forbidden to the uninitiated, Lhasa was seen by no more than three Europeans before 1904, when the British forced an entrance. Just outside the city stands the imposing former residence of the head of the religious sect, the Dalai Lama. The Chinese took over the city in 1958, destroying the monastic institutions, and the Dalai Lama escaped to India the next year.

Madras. One of the largest cities of India, situated on the southeastern coast of the country. The industrial output includes textiles, cigars, iron, cement, and dyes. The city contains an ornamental park, many fine buildings and monuments, an observatory, museums, a university, and a number of colleges. Population, 3,169,930.

Malay Archipelago. The largest group of islands in the world, lying at the extreme southeastern corner of Asia. The principal islands are Sumatra, Java, Borneo, Celebes, and the Philippine group. Of these, Sumatra, Java, and Borneo are on a continental shelf less than 600 feet deep, which connects with the Philippines by two submarine banks; the others are surrounded by water of great depth. Nearly all the islands present bold profiles and have mountains which are actively volcanic.

The equator passes through the center of the group. A rich soil and the warm, moist climate combine to make these islands extraordinarily fertile. They abound in tropical fruits of many kinds. Among the cultivated crops are rubber, rice, tea, sugar, coffee, kapok, cinchona bark, and coconuts. The mineral wealth of the islands is important, including tin in Banka and other islands near Sumatra, petroleum in Sumatra, coal in Borneo and Sumatra, and lead in all the larger islands. The inhabitants are largely Malaysians. Chinese tradesmen are numerous. The total area of the archipelago is estimated at 1,094,857 square miles, supporting a population of over 60 million.

Mandalay. A city of central Burma, standing on the Irrawaddy River. There are a number of Buddhistic shrines, the most remarkable of which is the Kuthodaw, a square surrounded by 450 pagodas. Within each pagoda is inscribed a part of the Buddhist scriptures, the aggregate of the inscriptions constituting the whole of the sacred writings. A walled section of the city encloses Fort Dufferin, formerly a royal palace. Population, 1968 est., 195,348.

Manila. The former capital and chief city of the Philippines, on the west coast of the island of Luzon. It is built on both banks of the Pasig River at its entrance to Manila Bay. On the south side of the river is the ancient Spanish town, surrounded by a wall, with the cathedral, monastic buildings, and numerous quaint Spanish houses; also the principal residential section, hospitals, and government buildings. On the north side is Binondo, containing the principal shopping and financial district. Manila is important for its foreign and coastwise commerce. It is the world's greatest shipping market for hemp. The Spanish city of Manila was founded in 1571. In 1898, Admiral Dewey destroyed a Spanish fleet in Manila Bay. Population, 1,402,000; Greater Manila, 3,100,000.

Mecca. The most sacred city of the Mohammedans, situated in a barren valley in the southern part of the Saudi Arabia, of which kingdom it is one of the two capitals. It is about 50 miles inland from Jidda, its port on the Red Sea. Most of the inhabitants find support from lodging the pilgrims who, in numbers exceeding 100,000 annually, flock here from all parts of the Mohammedan world to visit the Sacred Mosque, which marks the birthplace of Mohammed. Population, about 185,000.

Medina. An inland city of central Hejaz, sacred to the adherents of Mohammedanism. Mohammed's flight there from Mecca in 622 A. D. marks the year in which the Mohammedan calendar begins. The prophet died in Medina, and a large mausoleum, said to contain his undecayed body, attracts numerous pilgrims. Population, about 72,000.

Mukden. See *Shenyang.*

Nagasaki. An old and large Japanese port of just over 420,000 people. It is important in both trade and industry with steel work and shipbuilding predominant. It is located on the extreme west of the southernmost Japanese island of Kyushi and was the second target of the atomic bomb.

Nagoya. The fourth largest city of Japan, 235 miles southwest of Tokyo. It is one of the greatest centers of Japanese pottery manufacture. Other industries include cotton and silk mills. Many people are engaged in the embroidering of handkerchiefs. Nagoya has a very fine Buddhist temple and a castle dating back to 1610. Population, 1,954,000.

Nanking. The former capital of China. It is about midway between Peking in the north and Canton in the south and lies on the south bank of the Yangtze River 235 miles from the sea. The first sovereign of the Ming dynasty chose it as his capital in 1368. From 1403 until 1928, the Chinese government had its seat at Peking, but returned in the latter year to Nanking. Most of the magnificent buildings of earlier days were destroyed in the Taiping rebellion in 1853. The Republican government in 1928 proceeded to modernize the city. A boulevard has replaced the ancient city wall. On Purple mountain near by, a magnificent monument was erected to Sun Yat Sen, founder of the Chinese republic. Population 1,419,000.

Nazareth. A town of northwestern Israel, about 20 miles from the Mediterranean seacoast. It is memorable among Christians as the early residence of Jesus. A richly decorated basilica, the Church of the Annunciation, stands on what is said to be the site of the residence of Mary, the mother of Jesus, her house allegedly having been miraculously transported to Loreto, Italy. The town was captured from the Turks by Australians in 1918. Population, 26,400.

New Delhi. See *Delhi.*

Omsk. A city of southwestern Siberia on the Trans-Siberian railroad. It is a noted trading center for wheat and for dairy products. Manufactures include agricultural machinery, cloth, and sausages. Population, 774,000.

Osaka (ō'zä'kä). The second largest city of Japan, situated on Osaka Bay in the southern part of the island of Honshu. Being intersected by the Yodo River and by numerous canals spanned by hundreds of bridges, the city has been styled the Venice of the East. Ironworks, cotton and sugar mills, shipyards, and a large government mint are among the more important industries. The city is regularly laid out and contains many notable temples. Population, 3,133,000.

Pacific Islands or **Oceania.** Under these terms are included the numerous islands of the Pacific Ocean east of the Malay archipelago and north and east of Australia. On racial grounds they are frequently divided into three groups —Polynesia, Melanesia, and Micronesia. Melanesia lies directly north and east of Australia and west of the international date line. It includes the Solomon, Santa Cruz, New Hebrides, New Caledonia, and Fiji islands. North of this group lies Micronesia, comprising the Caroline, Marshall, Gilbert, Guam, Nauru, and neighboring islands. Polynesia includes most other islands of the Pacific Ocean east of the groups described above. Among the more important are the Hawaiian, New Zealand, Friendly (Tonga), Society, Cook, Samoan, Marquesas, Manahiki, and Union islands.

Peking. The capital of Communist China. It is located about 80 miles west of the Gulf of Chihli, an inlet of the Yellow Sea. Peking consists of an old city and a new city, usually called the outer city and the inner city. Each is surrounded by a wall, which, in one section, separates the two cities. The new city is larger and more populous. The old city contains a walled imperial city, within which lies the "purple forbidden city," the former palace and court of the emperor. These divisions are now traversed by a broad thoroughfare which passes through Peking from north to south. The finest building in the old city is the famous Temple of Heaven. To the west of the city, on the so-called Mountain of Ten Thousand Ancients, stands the emperor's summer palace, near which, upon a lagoon, floats a marble boat, built as a pleasure house. The grounds contain the celebrated camel back bridge, and near by is a pagoda built of porcelain.

Peking is a great educational center. It is the seat of Yenching University, established by American philanthropy, a number of technical and professional schools, and the oldest observatory in the world. Population, 4,010,000.

Pichola. A small lake near Udaipur in central west India. Each of two small islands in the lake is enclosed by marble walls, within which is erected a marble palace. These marble palaces were built by rulers of Rajputana and exhibit a grace and elegance which are equaled in very few of the great buildings of the world.

Rangoon. The capital and leading port of Burma, located on the southern coast near the Gulf of Martaban. The chief industrial establishments include lumber, rice, and oil mills, the products of which are exported in large quantities. Rangoon has a Buddhist pagoda, 370 feet high and covered with gold leaf, the foundation of which is said to have been laid in 588 B. C. This pagoda, called the Shoay Dagon, contains objects sacred to Buddhists and is annually visited by thousands of pilgrims. A university is situated in the city. Population, 3,662,312.

Rawalpindi. See *Islamabad.*

Samarkand. A historic city in the former Uzbek Republic, USSR. Its ancient name was Maracanda. It was destroyed by Alexander the Great in 329 B.C. After its capture by the Moslems in 911-12 A.D., it became a brilliant seat of Arabic civilization. Jenghis Khan destroyed it in 1221. Timur made it his capital in 1369. The palace and tomb of Timur are among the finest of the city's buildings. The Rigistan square is surrounded by four ancient structures, formerly Moslem colleges. The modern part of the city has broad, shaded streets. Its industries include cotton ginning and the manufacture of leather, flour, brick, pencils, and liquor. Population, 233,000.

Seoul. See *Keijo.*

Shanghai. The largest city, principal port, and chief industrial center of Communist China. It lies at the junction of the Huang River and Soochow creek 12 miles from their mouth in the estuary of the Yangtze River. It is the sea gate for the trade of the richest portion of China and is the spear point of its advancing industrialization. Flour and rice milling, shipbuilding, publishing, and the manufacture of engines, machinery, cotton and silk textiles, paper, cigarettes, leather, and food products are the leading industries.

A portion of the city is modern and well built, having grown up entirely since 1854. In 1932 Japan captured a part of the city and held it for a short time. Population, 6,900,000.

Shenyang (Mukden). A city of Communist China, located about 150 miles north of the Yellow Sea. It is a railroad junction and a point of convergence of several caravan routes. Near the city are the tombs of the Manchu emperors, who, in the 17th century, made Mukden their capital. Huge stone elephants stand on guard over the tombs. In the vicinity of Shenyang was fought the decisive battle of the Russio-Japanese war. Population, 2,411,000.

Singapore. City and member country of the British Commonwealth, situated on an island at the southern tip of the Malay Peninsula. It is the smelting point for the immense amount of tin mined in adjoining Malaysia and ships a major part of the world's block tin. A strong British naval station is maintained there by agreement with the Singapore government. About two-thirds of the 1,820,000 inhabitants are Chinese. See *Malaysia*.

Smyrna (Izmir). A seaport and commercial city of west central Turkey, standing at the head of the Gulf of Izmir, an inlet of the Ægean Sea. The rugs for which Smyrna is famous are made, for the most part, in the surrounding towns. Other articles of trade are silks, cottons, opium, olive oil, gums, and figs. Smyrna is one of the oldest continuously inhabited cities in the world. It was assigned to the Greeks as a mandate in 1920. In 1922 the Greeks were driven out, and the city was put to flames. Population, 417,411.

Srinagar (*srē'nȧ-gŭr'*). The capital of the native kingdoms of Jammu and Kashmir in the northern extremity of India. In the picturesque scenery of the surrounding country was located the "Vale of Cashmere," celebrated in Moore's poem entitled *Lalla Rookh*. Population, 285,257.

Tai Shan. A sacred mountain about 120 miles southwest of the Gulf of Chihli, an inlet of the Yellow Sea. On its summit are several temples, beneath one of which Confucius is said to have been buried. Each year during February and March as many as 10,000 pilgrims in a single day ascend to the summit, 4700 feet in height. The ascent is facilitated by a six-mile mountain road, paved and provided with steps in the more precipitous stages.

Tashkent. A city of southern Russia, capital of the Uzbek republic. It is situated in a vast surrounding plain of arid land on which cotton is grown with the aid of irrigation. Its industrial interests include cotton ginning and lumber mills and tobacco, leather, machinery, and rayon factories. The city has up-to-date water, electric, and street railway systems. Population, 1,239,000.

Tbilisi (Tiflis). The capital and largest city of the Georgian Republic, in the Soviet Union, situated midway between the Black Sea and the Caspian Sea. It is the distributing center for the country and has manufactures of bricks, tobacco, leather, soap, flour, cotton, and furniture. In picturesque contrast to its many wide streets and modern water, electric, and transport services are the Oriental bazaars and markets, where merchants from the East display their silverware, swords, rugs, dried fruits, and silk goods. It was founded as Tiflis in 379 A.D. Russia obtained it in 1799. Population, 842,000.

Tehran (*tĕ-h'rän'*). The capital of Iran, lying on an elevated plain in the north central part of the country about 66 miles south of the Caspian Sea. Manufactures include rugs, silks, cotton goods, and ironware. It has a citadel, called the Ark, within which is the handsome palace of the shah. The principal street is the Boulevard des Ambassadeurs, running through the foreign section. Tehran was founded in the 12th century and became capital of Persia (now Iran) in 1788. Population, 2,695,283.

Tel Aviv. Mediterranean port of Israel, forming, with Jaffa, a joint municipality having a combined population of 389,700. It grew rapidly after World War II with the influx of displaced European Jews, the inhabitants numbering about half a million in the late 1960's.

Tientsin. A commercial city and port of Communist China on the Pei River about 70 miles from its mouth in the Gulf of Chihli. It is 70 miles southeast of Peiping. The waterfront, which is under foreign jurisdiction, has buildings resembling the commercial structures of Western cities. The remainder of the city, which lies on a low plain, has small buildings and narrow, ill-kept streets, although municipal services have been much improved since 1900, when the city walls were destroyed in the Boxer uprising. Tientsin has an immense trade in salt, rice, and tea. Within recent years cotton factories have been established. Population, 3,220,000.

Tokyo. The capital of Japan and largest city in Asia. It stands at the head of Tokyo Bay near the center of the eastern coast of Honshu Island.

The city was largely destroyed in 1923 by earthquake and fire, which laid waste 25 square miles. This catastrophe provided the opportunity for rebuilding according to modern plans. The streets were widened, at the cost of moving some 200,000 houses; sewers were installed; public school playgrounds were enlarged; and a subway for rapid transit was constructed. Buildings in general are low or made of reinforced concrete to minimize danger of damage from earthquakes. The Hall of the Nameless Dead commemorates 33,000 victims of the great fire of 1923.

The chief of the city's many parks is called Tukiage, which contains the palace of the emperor built in a mixed Japanese and European style of architecture. The University of Tokyo is an institution of higher learning of the most advanced type. The eastern portion of the city contains regions known to visitors for their display of flowers. Here, too, is the temple of E-ko-in, where matches are held in jujutsu, the type of wrestling for which Japan is known.

Industries in Tokyo are carried on largely in the lowlands and suburbs, where there are numerous textile mills of a typically Japanese type. They are operated chiefly by girls, who live in huge dormitories owned by the mills.

The site of the city was a fishing village in the 13th century. It first became important in 1457 as the residence of the feudal lord. The name was changed in 1868 from Yedo to Tokyo, meaning Eastern Capital. Population, 8,302,565; Greater Tokyo, 11,005,000.

Trans-Siberian Railroad. A railroad which traverses Russia in an east-west direction, connecting Leningrad in Europe with Vladivostok on the extreme edge of Asiatic Russia. Over 5,500 miles in length, it occupied 11 years for initial construction, which cost $172 million. It was practically completed by 1902.

At a point east of Lake Baykal the road was divided, finally meeting at a point near Vladivostok. One line passed east of Lake Baykal entirely in Russian territory. The other line, passing through Manchuria (now part of Inner Mongolia), was known as the Chinese Eastern Railway and was owned jointly with China. In 1931 it was seized by Manchuria, and a small indemnity was paid to Russia.

The railroad is now double tracked. With feeders and connections running to southern Russia, it has been the central factor in one of the greatest migrations of people in history—settlement of the Siberian plains. Strategically, it makes eastern and western Russia a unit.

Victoria. The capital of the British island of Hong Kong by which name it is usually called. Victoria is a free port and the center of British commerce with China and Japan. The British fleet used the island as a naval base in the first Opium war, 1839-42. Then practically uninhabited, it was ceded to Great Britain in 1841.

It rapidly developed into an important commercial center. Its numerous industries include the manufacture of ships, cement, paper, rope, glass, soap, cigars, and knitted goods. Population of Victoria, 633,138; of Hong Kong island and adjacent leased territory, 3,927,000.

Vladivostok (*vlȧ'dyĭ-vŏs-tôk'*). The chief Pacific Ocean port of Russia and the eastern terminus of the Trans-Siberian railroad. The city is situated in the extreme southeastern part of Asiatic Russia, in the vicinity of valuable iron deposits. The chief products handled are the numerous derivatives of the soy bean. Vladivostok was settled in 1860, two years after its site was acquired by Russia. Population, 397,000.

Wuhan. A city of China, standing at the head of ocean navigation on the Yangtze River about 680 miles from its mouth in the East China Sea. Under the Communist government, this city was formed by the amalgamation of the former Hankow with the neighboring cities of Wuchang and Hanyang. The city contains large iron and steel works, which utilize the extensive iron and coal deposits in the vicinity. Cotton goods, flour, and leather are also manufactured. The chief exports of the city are normally black tea, wood oil, and sesame seed. Population, 2,146,000.

Yokohama. A leading seaport of Japan, situated on Tokyo Bay near the center of the western coast of Honshu Island. The harbor is elaborately improved. The city is of recent growth, having sprung up in the past 60 years as a result of foreign commerce. The chief exports are silk and tea. Yokohama was the first Japanese port open to foreigners and it is still the headquarters for most tourists who visit Japan. The city was almost totally destroyed in 1923 by earthquake and fire. It was reconstructed with wide streets, handsome concrete buildings, and bridges. Population, 2,513,000.

AFRICA

The second largest continent of the world, situated in the eastern hemisphere south of Europe and southwest of Asia, with which it is connected by the Isthmus of Suez. It is separated from Europe by the Mediterranean Sea, an inland body of water which narrows to a width of nine miles at the Strait of Gibraltar. Between Africa and Asia, lie the Red Sea and the Gulf of Aden. The Atlantic Ocean on the west and the Indian Ocean on the east meet at the southern point of the continent.

Africa lies farther to the north than South America. In length, the continent is almost equally divided between the northern and the southern hemisphere. On account of its shape, however, about two-thirds of Africa's surface lies north of the equator. Its most northern point is in the latitude of Washington, D. C., and it extends nearly 5000 miles south to the approximate latitude of Buenos Aires. It has an area of about 11,500,000 square miles, being about 1⅓ times as large as North America and second only to Asia in extent.

Outline. As in the case of South America, the maximum width of the continent is in the north. By reason of a huge western extension, Africa attains a width of 4600 miles, just 400 miles less than its length. Between the western extension and the southern portion of the continent, lies the Gulf of Guinea. The only other major indentation is the Gulf of Sidra near the center of the northern coast. On the eastern coast, the Somali Republic projects as a cape, separating the Gulf of Aden from the Indian Ocean. The coast line is remarkably regular and, consequently, affords very few good harbors.

Surface. Africa is, for the most part, a plateau surrounded by a very narrow strip of coastal lowlands. The southern and the eastern parts of the plateau are higher than the western and the northern parts. The latter contain certain sections, in the interior of the Sahara desert, where the elevation is that of the sea level or even less.

In the extreme southern part of the continent, a ridge rims the plateau, rising, on the eastern side, to a height of nearly 9000 feet. The east central part of the continent consists of a wide, irregular highland cut longitudinally by the so-called Great Rift valley, which contains lakes rivaling in size the Great Lakes of North America. Lake Victoria is the largest, being second only to Lake Superior in area. Lake Tanganyika, farther south, is the longest lake in the world, having a length of 400 miles. Lake Nyasa, the most southern of the group, has the extraordinary depth of 2580 feet. In this region are to be found also the highest mountains of the continent, usually rising abruptly from the surface of the plateau. Mount Kilimanjaro, situated about 200 miles south of the equator and 200 miles from the east coast, reaches an altitude of 19,710 feet. Mount Kenya and Margherita mountain are other notable peaks of the district. Continuing northward, the highland narrows to form the lofty, mountainous region of Ethiopia. An elevated ridge skirts the Red Sea as far as the Isthmus of Suez.

The mean level of the northern and the western parts of Africa is below 2000 feet. Isolated mountain ridges, however, occur in various parts. The highest is the Atlas range at the extreme northwest, running parallel with the coast and attaining to an altitude of 14,000 feet.

Drainage. The absence in Africa of a pronounced continental divide has had the effect of producing two kinds of rivers. Those on the outer slopes of the continental plateau are short and rapid, while those rising in the interior follow a long, winding, inland course. Then, penetrating the mountain rim, they make their way over cataracts and through narrow channels to the sea, where a sand bar is often formed by sediment carried down the stream.

The four largest rivers of Africa are the Nile, the Congo, the Niger, and the Zambezi. The basins of inland drainage, which occupy more than three million square miles in northern Africa, are usually too arid to give rise to large bodies of water. There is a notable exception, however, in the case of Lake Chad.

The Nile is, next to the Mississippi-Missouri, the longest river of the world. Rising in a stream that flows into Lake Victoria, it wends its way northward, and, after passing over six cataracts and traversing a distance of 4000 miles, it empties through a large delta by seven mouths into the Mediterranean Sea. Its lower course lies through the desert region of Egypt, a strip of which it renders productive by means of its annual flood. The river is navigable about 590 miles above its delta to the foot of the first cataract at Aswan and, with interruptions, for a distance of 1550 miles farther toward the source.

The Congo River is the second river of the world in volume of water discharged and in the area of its basin. By means of numerous tributaries, of which the Ubangi is the largest, the Congo drains a tropical basin of central Africa in a general westward direction and discharges its waters into the Atlantic Ocean through a mouth ten miles in width. The river admits of navigation, with some interruptions, for a distance of 2000 miles above its mouth.

The Niger River offers greater facilities for navigation than any other river of Africa. It drains a comparatively low plain in Africa's westward extension. Rising within a few hundred miles of the Atlantic coast, it flows inland toward the northeast, then, bending southeast, it follows a meandering course to an immense delta on the Gulf of Guinea.

The Zambezi River rises on a ridge near the west coast of southern Africa, and flows eastward across the continent to Mozambique channel. Near the middle of its course, it plunges over Victoria Falls, the greatest cataract in the world. Here, over a width of a mile, the river drops 343 feet.

Lake Chad, situated about 850 miles northeast of the head of the Gulf of Guinea, has no outlet. During the rainy season, it occupies an area of about 40,000 square miles, but it diminishes during the dry season to one-sixth of this area.

Climate. Africa extends almost equal distances north and south of the equator. It is, therefore, subject to a smaller variation in temperature than any other large division of land. At the extreme north and at the extreme south, there are belts of temperate or subtropical climate. Between these limits the heat is greater.

The rainfall is greatest in the basin of the Congo. On each side of this equatorial belt of abundant and well distributed rainfall, stretches a zone in which the rainfall is seasonal, a short, wet season being followed by a long, dry one. These two zones pass gradually into the two great desert areas of the continent, Kalahari desert in southern Africa and the Sahara desert in the north. Beyond these arid regions, in the extreme north and in the extreme south of Africa, there are narrow coastal lowlands having a moderate, or even a copious, rainfall.

The Sahara Desert is the largest continuous arid region of the world. Its area, about 3,500,000 square miles, is larger than that of the United States. It occupies all that part of northern Africa from the Atlas mountains on the northwest to the mid-course of the Nile river on the southeast. The small amount of rain which does fall occurs in one season only and, as a rule, sinks immediately into the sand to issue here and there as springs. These springs foster islets of vegetation, known as oases, which are estimated to cover one-fortieth of the desert's surface.

Vegetation. The plant life of Africa varies in a manner determined mainly by the rainfall. The extreme northern section has a flora resembling that of Europe. The forests in this part consist largely of oaks, while the olive, vine, fig, and the cereals of Europe thrive. The extreme southern region, being comparatively isolated, has a characteristic vegetation marked by the prevalence of heaths and of other plants producing brilliant flowers. Forests are scarce, but there is abundant pasturage for sheep.

The equatorial belt, except in the eastern highlands, is covered with dense tropical forests. These forests contain an immense variety of trees, including the wine palm, the oil palm, the silk-cotton tree, and the camwood, besides ebony, mahogany, and many other valuable cabinet wood trees.

Animals. Africa is the home of many distinctive types of animals, including a number of large mammals. The giraffe, okapi, hippopotamus, gorilla, and chimpanzee are among the more notable of African mammals which occur nowhere else. Lions, leopards, two-horned rhinoceroses, zebras, antelopes, and African buffaloes are representative of the large animals which attract hunters. The conservation of such animals was, in 1900, made the subject of an international conference, as a result of which game preserve areas were established in British Africa, Somaliland, and other countries. The African elephant is hunted for its ivory tusks, which for centuries have been brought from the interior of Africa by caravans.

The ostrich is found in the drier regions. Other birds are the maribou stork, the secretary bird, and the parrot. Crocodiles are found in the large rivers and tropical lakes. Insects include the formidable white ant and the deadly tsetse fly.

A European type of fauna characterizes the extreme north, where the bear, the jackal, and the fox are found. The wild ass of east central Africa is said to be the ancestor of the domesticated ass. Camels were introduced very early into the northern desert regions from Asia. In Egypt, the inhabitants anciently regarded as sacred the ibis, the crocodile, and the cat.

Minerals. Africa produces nearly all of the world's supply of diamonds and more than one-third of the world's yearly output of gold. South Africa is the region most productive of both minerals, although gold is also obtained from the Gulf of Guinea region and elsewhere. Some of the richest copper deposits in the world exist west of the great interior lakes, and iron has from the earliest times been worked by the natives. Salt is abundant. Oil is found in the Sahara and elsewhere.

Inhabitants. Although the city civilization of northeastern Africa is probably the world's earliest, the rest of the continent continued as a pastoral and agricultural society organized on a tribal basis until the 20th century. The aborigines of most of the continent are negroid and are believed to have remained relatively immune from foreign conquest because Africa's rivers did not afford ready navigation into the interior. Arabs established themselves on the northern and northeastern regions in the 7th century; the Dutch settled in the south in the 17th century; and the French infiltrated the Mediterranean coast in the 19th century, followed by colonization of most of the continent by Britain, Belgium, Italy, and other European nations. By the middle of the 20th century the colonial empires were almost entirely liquidated.

The Pygmies of the equatorial forests and the Bushmen of the southern arid districts are believed to represent the earliest African races extant. They live by hunting; their dwellings are of the most primitive type. The Hottentots stand, in culture, as in location, between the Bushmen and the Bantus. The Bantus constitute the southern half of a negroid race which inhabits most of Africa from the region of the great lakes northward to the Sahara Desert.

The native Africans speak a language belonging to a family known as Bantu. One branch, spoken chiefly in the east, is Swahili. It has obtained a wide currency as a trade language.

The total population of the continent is estimated at 336 million. It is estimated that less than half the population has been affected by religions of foreign origin. Of this proportion by far the most are Mohammedans.

Discovery. The valley of the Nile river was the seat of what is perhaps the world's earliest civilization. The interior of the continent, however, remained unknown until the 19th century.

As early as the 7th or 6th century B. C. a Phœnician ship sailed around Africa. The possibility of circumnavigation, however, was forgotten until 1486, when the Cape of Good Hope was rounded by Diaz.

Numerous early attempts were made to penetrate the interior of Africa. The first European to cross Africa from ocean to ocean was David Livingstone, who completed the journey in 1856.

POLITICAL DIVISIONS

The last quarter of the 19th century witnessed the partition of Africa into protectorates and colonies of various nations of Europe. By 1976, practically all these colonies had become independent nations, leaving a small residue as dependencies.

Algeria. A republic of northern Africa stretching 640 miles east and west along the Mediterranean Sea between Libya and Tunisia on the east and Morocco on the west and extending south about 340 miles. Its area is 113,883 square miles.

Algeria is divided longitudinally by the Atlas mountains, north of which lies a fertile well-watered plain 50 to 100 miles wide. The rest of the arable land is dry and is productive only with the aid of irrigation. Crops raised include wheat, barley, oats, corn, tobacco, dates, oranges, figs, and grapes, from which wine is made in large quantities. Wool is a leading product of Algeria's agriculture, which is particularly rich in farm animals, including camels.

The population in 1968 was 12,934,000. The capital is Algiers. Other leading cities are Oran, Constantine, and Bone.

Angola. Formerly Portuguese West Africa, Angola has a 1000-mile coastline along the Atlantic and is bounded by Zaire on the north and east, by Zambia on the east, and South West Africa (Namibia) on the south. Its area is 481,351 square miles. Most of Angola's land is desert and plains, although in the northeast there are heavily forested valleys that provide the main exports—diamonds and hardwoods. Along the coast palm trees are grown for their oil and kernels. Angola's population is 5,673,046 (1970)—of whom 475,328 live in Luanda, the capital and largest city.

Benin (Dahomey). A republic of central western Africa, Benin consists of a narrow strip 77 miles wide and 415 miles long. With its southern boundary on the Gulf of Guinea, it is bounded on the west by Togo, on the north by Niger and Upper Volta, and on the east by Nigeria. Benin's 44,290 square miles are devoted mainly to animal industry and agriculture; the chief products are corn, manioc, and yams. Benin's capital is Porto Novo (population: 2,571,000). The nation is a member of the French Community.

Botswana. A land-locked republic of southern Africa. Botswana is bounded by South West Africa (Namibia) on the north and west, Zambia and Rhodesia on the east, and South Africa on the south and southeast. Its area is 222,000 square miles. Most of the country is a tableland with the Kalahari desert in the southwest. In the northwest the Okavango river forms a great inland delta and the swamplands of the river cover 6500 square miles. The Orapa diamond mine in the south contains one of the largest gem deposits ever found. Agriculture and animal raising account for almost half of the national income, but there are also rich deposits of manganese, copper, nickel, coal, and salt. The population was 656,737 in 1973. Gaborone is the nation's capital. Botswana is a member of the British Commonwealth.

Burundi. A republic of east central Africa, 10,744 square miles in area, bounded north by Rwanda, east and south by Tanzania, and west by Congo. Coffee is the principal crop. The capital is Bujumbura. Population, about 3,406,000.

Cameroon. A republic of West Africa, whose west coast lies on the Gulf of Guinea. It is bounded north by Nigeria and Chad, east by the Central African Republic, and south by Congo (Brazzaville), Gabon, and Equatorial Guinea. The republic, 181,476 square miles in area, is a federation of a former French dependency, which was given independence in 1960, and the southern part of a former British dependency, which voted in 1961 to join the Cameroon republic.

The population is made up of about 200 tribes, which support themselves by agriculture and husbandry. There is normally an exportable surplus of cocoa, coffee, rubber, bananas, cotton, palm oil, and timber. Most of the trade is with France and Britain. The capital is Yaounde. Population, about 5,562,000.

Central African Republic. A land-locked country at approximately the geographical center of Africa, bounded north by Chad, east by Sudan, south by Congo and Zaire, and west by Cameroon. Its 238,000 square miles form a rolling plain about 2000 feet in altitude draining southward toward the Congo basin and thence into the Atlantic Ocean. It lies about 300 miles inland from the Gulf of Guinea.

The population of about 1,488,000 is organized on a tribal basis. Cotton, coffee, and peanuts are raised in exportable quantities, and meat is imported. The capital is Bangui. It was formerly part of a French dependency.

Chad. A land-locked republic of north central Africa, 495,000 square miles in area, bounded north by Libya, east by Sudan, south by Central African Republic, and west by Cameroon and Niger. The northern part of the country is a sandy desert, but agriculture, featured by cotton raising and animal husbandry, is carried on in the central steppe land and a southern grassland with scattered trees. The population of about 4,000,000 has a large element professing the Moslem faith. The capital is N'djamena. It is a member of the French Community.

Comoro Islands. A former French dependency, the islands lie off the eastern coast of Africa about 300 miles northwest of Malagasy. The nation is an archipelago of four islands—Mayotte, Anjouan, Grande Comore, and Moheli. The total area is 838 square miles. The islands are of volcanic origin and are extremely mountainous. The highest peak is Mt. Karatab at 7900 feet. Grande Comore island is heavily forested and the timber is used for building. Although there is fishing and animal raising, the country is largely agricultural. The main crops are vanilla, copra, cacao, sisal, coffee, and cloves. The capital is Moroni, on Grande Comore island, and the population of the Comoro Islands is about 300,000.

Congo. The country has about 60 miles of coast on the Atlantic Ocean and stretches some 800 miles northeast with a maximum width of about 400 miles. It is bounded west by Gabon and Cameroon, north by Central African Republic, and east by Zaire, from which it is separated in part by the Congo River.

More than half its 139,000 square miles is covered by forest, from which considerable timber is exported. Other products are palm oil and peanuts. Gold and lead are mined. The chief port, Pointe Noire, as well as the capital, Brazzaville, have modern airports. Population, about 870,000.

Egypt. An Arab republic, situated in the extreme northeast of Africa. Its area is about 386,198 square miles, most of which is arid and unproductive. The population, numbering 31,680,000 in 1968, is almost entirely concentrated in the fertile valley of the Nile River, and is devoted principally to agriculture. The area of the cultivated region is about 13,600 square miles, which includes not only the Nile valley but the delta and oases in the desert. Much of this area has been reclaimed by irrigation.

The chief crop is cotton. The papyrus plant of Egypt was used in the making of paper more than 4000 years ago. Today, however, Egypt imports practically all her paper.

The productivity of the Nile River valley is due to the annual flooding of the river banks in September and October. The area of cultivation has been greatly extended by the construction of irrigation works, consisting of canals, of several barrages, and of the great Aswan and Sennar dams, each over a mile in length, which now regulate the flow of water.

The Nile proper which flows through Egypt is formed by the junction of the Blue Nile and the White Nile at Khartoum in the Sudan. The Blue Nile rises in the mountains of Ethiopia, the White Nile in Uganda. It descends by a series of six cataracts or rapids, and, after flowing through the Nile delta, empties into the Mediterranean by two main channels, one near Alexandria, the other near Port Said. The Nile is one of the world's longest rivers.

Southern Egypt has a dry, healthful climate, which makes it desirable as a resort for tourists. A further attraction is found in the pyramids, the sphinx, various tombs, and other remains of the ancient civilization of the Nile. The northeastern extremity of the country has one of the world's two most celebrated ship canals, the Suez, which connects the Mediterranean Sea with the Red Sea.

Equatorial Guinea. This former Spanish dependency of western Africa consists of Rio Muni on the mainland. It is bounded by Cameroon on the north, Gabon on the east and south, and the Atlantic Ocean on the west. The offshore islands of Marcias Nguema and Pigalu in the Gulf of Guinea are added territories of Equatorial Guinea. The total area is 9,828 square miles. Rio Muni is characterized by a coastal plain and further inland the foothills of the Crystal Mountains. There are 2 volcanos on Marcias Nguema. The country depends greatly on agriculture as there are few industries. The main crops are cocoa, coffee, and wood. Uranium deposits have been found but they have not yet been developed. The capital is Malabo and the population is about 307,500.

Ethiopia. A country of northeast Africa with a northeast coast line on the Red Sea. It is bounded east by French Somaliland and Somali Republic, south by Somali Republic and Kenya, and west by Sudan.

Its area is about 350,000 square miles and is the most mountainous country of Africa. Most of the surface is covered by the Highlands of Ethiopia which reached their greatest height in Ras Dashan, 15,160 feet. The country is naturally rich with fertile soil and abundant rainfall. The climate is cool and bracing because of the high elevation. The chief rivers of Ethiopia, the Blue Nile and Atbara are tributary to the Nile and mainly responsible for its floods. The population is estimated at nearly 24 million.

The commercial products include hides, cattle, and coffee. Musk from the civet is used in perfumes. Gold is washed in the beds of the Atbara and its tributaries. Addis Ababa is the capital.

French Africa. Of France's former immense colonial empire in Africa, all parts were granted independence after World War II except the former French Somaliland in east Africa at the southern end of the Red Sea.

In 1967 French Somaliland officially changed its name to the Territory of the Afars and the Issas. Its 8500 square miles support about 125,000 inhabitants, who engage mainly in cattle raising and fishing. The capital and chief port is Djibouti.

Gabon. A republic of equatorial Africa with 500 miles of western coast line on the Gulf of Guinea. It is bounded north by Cameroon, and east and south by Congo (Brazzaville). Most of its 102,290 square miles are covered with forest. Its products include timber, plywood, and veneer. Exploitation of its rich mineral resources has raised the economy of Gabon. Gabon, with a population of about 480,000, is a member of the French Community. The capital is Libreville.

Gambia. A republic of west Africa on the Atlantic Ocean and otherwise surrounded by Senegal. Its area is 4005 square miles; its population 494,279. Peanuts, rice, and palm kernels are the chief products. Banjul is the capital.

Ghana. A republic of western Africa with a southern coast line on the Gulf of Guinea. It is bounded west by Ivory Coast and Upper Volta, north by Upper Volta, and east by Togo.

About one-third of Ghana's 92,100 square miles is forested, from which comes such valuable timber as mahogany and other tropical woods. The rest of the country is devoted to agriculture. Ghana is the world's largest exporter of cocoa, the production of which is Ghana's major industry. Diamonds, bauxite, and manganese are Ghana's most important mineral exports. The Volta Dam, 370 feet high, was completed in 1966. It backs up the Volta River 300 miles to form Lake Volta, 3500 square miles in area. The hydroelectric plant generates nearly a million kilowatts of electricity.

The capital, Accra, is the seat of a research institute supported by Ghana and some of its neighboring republics, whose purpose is to discover the best methods of land use and disease control. Ghana is a member of the British Commonwealth. Population, 8,545,561.

Guinea. A republic of Africa with a western coast line on the Atlantic Ocean. It is bounded north by Guinea-Bissau, Senegal, and Mali, east by Ivory Coast, and south by Liberia and Sierra Leone.

Most of Guinea's area of 96,865 square miles is devoted to agriculture and animal husbandry. Agricultural products include rice, cassava, bananas, palm nuts, coffee, pineapples, and oranges. Guinea has one of the world's richest deposits of bauxite, and this, together with alumina, iron ore, and aluminum are the leading exports.

Guinea was one of the few former French dependencies which elected to separate itself from the French Community, although French remains the official language and French technical assistance is provided under an agreement made in 1963. The capital is Conakry. Population, about 4,010,000.

Ivory Coast. A republic of western Africa with a southern coast line of 34 miles on the Gulf of Guinea. It is bounded west by Liberia and Guinea, north by Mali and Upper Volta, and east by Ghana. Its area is 127,520 square miles.

About 90 per cent of the population is engaged in agriculture, animal husbandry, fishing, and forestry. The leading products are yams, cassava, bananas, corn, and rice. Mahogany is obtained from the forests. Diamonds and manganese are exported. The population numbers about 4,100,000. The capital is Abidjan. The Ivory Coast is a member of the French Community.

Kenya. A constitutional democracy of East Africa with an eastern coast line on the Indian Ocean. It is bounded south by Tanzania, north by Sudan and Ethiopia, west by Uganda, and east by Somali Republic and the Indian Ocean. Its area is 224,960 square miles.

The northern three-fifths of the country is arid. Production comes chiefly from the south, which consists of a low coastal plain and a plateau varying from 3,000 to 10,000 feet in altitude. The forests of the uplands are preserved to conserve the water supply. Kenya is the largest source of tea in Africa. Other products are coffee, cereals, cotton, sisal, dairy products. Copper, gold, and salt are among the products of the mines.

The capital is Nairobi. Kenya is a member of the British Commonwealth of Nations. Population, 10,209,000.

Lesotho. An enclave within South Africa, known as Basutoland before emerging in 1966 from colonial status to Great Britain. Agriculture and stock raising are the chief occupations. Its area is 11,716 square miles and the capital is Maseru. Population, 1,081,000.

Liberia. A republic of western Africa with 350 miles of southern coast line on the Atlantic Ocean and stretching inland from 75 to 190 miles. It is bounded west by Sierra Leone, north by Guinea, and east by Ivory Coast. Its area is about 43,000 square miles.

Most of the country is covered with tropical forest. Rubber is the chief export, Liberia providing the United States with about one-tenth of its imports of natural rubber. Iron ore also is exported.

Liberia was founded by settlement of American slaves at the site of the present capital, Monrovia, by philanthropic societies, beginning in 1822. English is the official language, although the many indigenous tribes speak their own languages. Population estimated at 1,500,000.

Libya. A republic of north Africa on the Mediterranean Sea between Egypt and Algeria. Its southern, desert region borders Chad and Niger. The northern region is fertile and produces dates, olives, almonds, figs, and grapes. Petroleum is the most important mineral and accounts for nearly all of Libya's exports. Its area is 679,358 square miles; the population, 2,260,000. Tripoli is the largest city and shares with Benghazi the governmental administration.

Malagasy. An island republic in the Indian Ocean off southeast Africa, from which it is separated by the Mozambique channel, 240 miles wide at its narrowest point. The island, formerly known as Madagascar, is 980 miles long in a generally north-and-south direction with a maximum width of 360 miles and an area of 229,975 square miles. The interior is a plateau 3000 to 5000 feet in height, rising in the northwest to mountains with a maximum height of 9490 feet. Around the plateau are extensive plains, up to 50 miles wide on the eastern side and up to 100 miles on the western side.

Cattle breeding and agriculture are the chief occupations. The principal farm animal is the humped zebu. Agricultural products of the greatest importance are rice, cassava, sugar cane, coconuts, and bananas. Others include corn, vanilla, and potatoes. Among mineral products are graphite, mica, and phosphates. Cotton and silk weaving are carried on as well as food-processing industries.

The capital is Tananarive. The republic is a member of the French Community. Population, 7,185,000.

Malawi. A land-locked republic of southeastern Africa. It is bounded north by Tanzania, west by Zambia, and south by Mozambique. Its area is 46,686 square miles. Until 1964 it was the British dependency of Nyasaland. Principally an agricultural country, tea, tobacco, cotton, and peanuts are its leading products. Lilongwe is the capital. Population, 1975, 5,040,000.

Mali. A land-locked republic of western Africa, bounded north by Algeria, east by Niger, south by Upper Volta, Ivory Coast, and Guinea, and west by Senegal and Mauritania. Its area is about 450,000 square miles. It is traversed west to east by the upper reaches of the Niger River. On this river small steamboats connect Gao and Timbuktu with a railway leading through the capital Bamako and continuing in Senegal to Dakar, which port Mali has the right by treaty to use. Agriculture is being organized on collective principles. Cattle number about 4,000,000. The chief exports are groundnuts, gum, dried fish, and hides. Mali is a member of the French Community. Population, about 5,600,000.

Mauritania. An Islamic republic of west Africa with a western coast line on the Atlantic Ocean. It is bounded east by Mali and south by Mali and Senegal. The area is 418,810 square miles, much of which is desert. Agriculture and animal husbandry are the main occupations, products including millet, rice, and corn. There are about 700,000 camels. Iron and copper have been discovered. The capital is Nouakchott. Population, about 1,120,000.

Morocco. A constitutional monarchy on the northwest coast of Africa and separated from Spain by the Strait of Gibraltar. With a northwestern coast line on the Atlantic Ocean and a northern coast line on the Mediterranean Sea, it is bounded east and south by Algeria and south by Spanish Sahara. At the north facing Gibraltar are the Riff mountains and behind them run the Atlas mountains. The rest of the area consists of fertile alluvial plains and plateaus, but in the south and west the land is arid—the beginning of the Sahara desert. The area is estimated at 171,305 square miles.

Agriculture is the leading industry, supporting 70 per cent of the population, but phosphates make up the bulk of the exports. Farm products include wheat and barley, vegetables, canary seed, olives, almonds, and citrus fruits. Morocco is the world's leading producer of cork. Wine is produced in quantity, and sardines are exported. Mineral products, in addition to potash, include coal, iron, manganese, silver, and zinc. Islam is the established state religion. The capital is Rabat, and the largest city is Casablanca. Population, 16,309,000.

Mozambique. Formerly a Portuguese colony, Mozambique is bordered on the north by Tanzania, Zambia, and Malawi; on the west by Rhodesia and South Africa; and on the east by the Mozambique channel. The land area is 303,070 square miles. The eastern region is mostly coastal lowlands, while the interior is highland plains. Aluminum, asbestos, tin, tungsten, and coal are mined in the northwest, but the chief exports are cashew nuts, sugar, and cotton. Many Mozambicans travel to South Africa to work in the mines. The population is estimated at about 9,300,000; the capital city is Maputo.

Niger. A land-locked republic of north central Africa, bounded north by Algeria and Libya, east by Chad, south by Nigeria, and west by Benin, Upper Volta, and Mali. Its area of 490,000 square miles lacks water except in the west, which is watered by the Niger River and its tributaries, and in the south, where water is obtained from wells. The country is a plateau, and access is chiefly by air.

Agricultural products include peanuts, millet, cassava, cotton, and rice. The capital is Niamey. Niger is a member of the French Community. Population, about 4,239,000.

Nigeria. A republic of west central Africa with a southern coast line on the Gulf of Guinea, into which flows the country's principal river, the Niger. It is bounded west by Benin, north by Niger, east by Chad and Cameroon. Its area is 356,669 square miles. The coast is a belt of mangrove swamps, behind which is a belt of tropical forest 50 to 100 miles wide. Farther north the level rises, and open woodland and treed plains afford facilities for agriculture. The extreme north is desert.

Agriculture and stockraising are the principal industries, the northern regions producing groundnuts, cotton, and hides, while cocoa, timber, and rubber come from the south. Minerals produced include tin, gold, coal, and petroleum. Among leading manufactures are soap, cigarettes, beer, margarine, textiles, cement, and canned foods. Of the estimated 62,650,000 inhabitants, nearly 14 million are Moslems and about 7 million are Christians. Nigeria is a member of the British Commonwealth. The capital is Lagos.

Rhodesia. A land-locked, south-central African republic, Rhodesia covers 150,820 square miles. It is bounded on the north by Zambia, on the east by Mozambique, on the south by South Africa, and on the west by Botswana. Most of the country is a high, rolling plateau; the chief rivers are the Zambezi and Limpopo. The land abounds in minerals—asbestos, coal, chrome ore, copper, gold, iron, lithium, nickel, phosphate, and tin. The Wankie colliery is the largest coal mine in the world. Tobacco is the main export yield; corn is the staple food and most important crop. Major industries include textiles, chemicals, and metal products. The population is 6,100,000; of these, 512,940 live in Salisbury, the capital, largest city, and industrial center of Rhodesia.

Rwanda. A republic of east central Africa, 10,169 square miles in area, bounded north by Uganda, east by Tanzania, and south and west by Zaire. Its agricultural industry produces coffee and cotton. The capital is Kigali. Formerly a Belgian trusteeship, it asserted its independence in 1962. Population, about 5,500,000.

Senegal. A republic of west Africa, on the Atlantic Ocean. Its capital, Dakar, is the extreme western point of Africa. Senegal is bounded north by Mauritania, east by Mali, and south by Guinea and Guinea-Bissau. Its area is 76,000 square miles. The surface is mainly sandy and supports an agriculture of which peanuts are the leading product. Dakar is the country's port and has a considerable concentration of industry, including cement and titanium concentrates. Ground-nuts and phosphates are exported in quantity. Senegal is a member of the French Community. Population, about 4,100,000.

Sierra Leone. A republic of western Africa with a southwestern coast line 212 miles long on the Atlantic Ocean. Having an area of 27,925 square miles, it is bounded north and east by Guinea and southeast by Liberia. The principal occupation is agriculture. Exports include palm kernels, coffee, cocoa, iron ore, and diamonds. The capital, Freetown, is one of the finest ports in Africa. It was founded in 1787 by the British government as a home for destitute free slaves. Sierra Leone is a member of the British Commonwealth. Population, about 2,475,000.

Somali Republic. A republic of east central Africa with a northern coast line on the Gulf of Aden and a southeastern coast line on the Indian Ocean. Its eastern tip is the most easterly point of the continent. Having an area of 262,000 square miles, it is bounded west by Kenya and Ethiopia. About 80 per cent of the inhabitants depend on the livestock industry, most of the country being adapted to grazing rather than agriculture. Large uranium deposits were found in 1968. The capital is Mogadisho. It was previously an Italian colony. Population, about 2,745,000.

South Africa. A republic at the southern extremity of Africa, 472,494 square miles in area, with the Atlantic Ocean westward and Indian Ocean eastward meeting off its southern coast. South Africa is bounded north by its own dependency of Southwest Africa, Botswana, Rhodesia, and Mozambique. Lesotho and the former British dependency of Swaziland are enclaves within South Africa.

The surface is, for the most part, a high plateau, interrupted by isolated flat-topped hills called kopjes. The plateau slopes rapidly down near the coasts. A ridge, low in the west, passes around the southern and eastern parts of the plateau, reaching its highest point in the east central region of the country. This eastern ridge is the divide separating a large number of short rivers, draining toward the east and the south, from the Orange river, which flows westward across the country and empties into the Atlantic Ocean. Farther north, the Limpopo river rises on the interior plateau and makes its way north of the eastern ridge; then, turning southeast, it flows into the Indian Ocean.

The climate of South Africa is warm, and the soil is fertile. The precipitation varies greatly, being nearly 50 inches on the southeastern coast and falling to less than 3 inches farther north on the western coast. In the western part of the country, semiarid conditions prevail, and grazing rather than agriculture is the principal industry. Wool is one of the chief exports, and about half the world's supply of mohair comes from the Republic. Corn, wheat, oats, barley, and tobacco are also grown, and such products of subtropical agriculture as cotton, tea, and sugar cane are raised in the lower and moister coastal regions. The operation of ostrich farms constitutes a distinctive industry.

The exports of the greatest value are the products of the mining industry. South Africa is the world's chief source of diamonds and is by far the greatest gold producing region of the world. The output of gold is several times that of Canada, the country which ranks second to South Africa. Other minerals obtained in important quantities include coal, tin, and copper.

The white population in 1961 was 3,067,638, while the native population stood at 10,807,809. The 1968 estimate of the total population was 19,167,000. About one-half those of the white race are of Dutch descent. The religion is predominantly Protestant. There are 16 universities, 11 for whites, 5 for nonwhites. Most of the country's 13,284 miles of railway is owned by the government.

South Africa is divided into four provinces. Cape of Good Hope is in the extreme south, and Transvaal, on the eastern side of the country, lies farthest north. Between the two lie the inland province, called Orange Free State, and Natal, which borders on the Indian Ocean. In eastern Transvaal is the Kruger national park, a 5-million acre sanctuary for big game, which attracts thousands of visitors each year. The center of governmental administration is Pretoria, but the legislature sits at Cape Town, which is the terminus of the partially constructed "Cape to Cairo" railway. The largest city is Johannesburg, situated in the Witwatersrand, which is among the richest gold-mining districts of the world. Kimberley is the chief diamond-mining center.

Spanish Africa. The possessions of Spain in Africa were diminished when, in 1968, it granted independence to *Equatorial Guinea*, which includes Rio Muni, Marcias Nguema, and a number of small islands in the Gulf of Guinea. The capital of the new Republic of Equatorial Guinea is Malabo. Ifni, an enclave on the Atlantic coast of Morocco, was turned over to that country by Spain in 1969.

The following is the only remaining province in Africa belonging to Spain:

Canary Islands, 2807 square miles in area, in the Atlantic off the coast of Spanish Sahara, with an estimated population of 944,448.

Sudan. A republic of northeast Africa lying directly south of Egypt and with a northeastern coast line on the Red Sea. With an area of 967,000 square miles, it is the largest country in Africa. It is bounded east by Ethiopia, south by Uganda, Zaire, and the Central African Republic, and west by Chad and Libya.

Nearly half the country is desert or semidesert, and grazing of cattle, sheep, goats, and camels is a principal occupation. Cotton is by far the most important crop and provides most of the exports, although the Sudan is the world's chief source of gum arabic. The Nile River flows north through Sudan, and its waters are used for extensive irrigation works, an agreement having been made with Egypt for diversion of the available water.

About four-fifths of the 14,770,000 inhabitants are Moslem Arabs. The capital is Khartoum.

Tanzania (*Tăn-zȧ-nē'ȧ*). A united republic of eastern Africa, formed in 1964 of the former Tanganyika, fronting on the Indian Ocean and the large island of Zanzibar off its eastern coast. The new republic has a combined area of 362,820 square miles, and has a population of 12,590,000. The capital is Dar es Salaam.

The mainland is bounded by Kenya and Uganda on the north; Malawi, Mozambique, and Zambia on the south; Lake Tanganyika, Burundi, and Rwanda on the west. Its area is 361,800 square miles. The surface slopes upward from the coastal plain on the east to a high plateau and the western mountain slopes. The forests produce camphor and mahogany. About half the world's supply of sisal, Tanzania's chief agricultural product, is grown here. As Tanganyika, the country was colonized by Arabs as early as the 8th century A.D. and was a possession of Germany before World War I.

The island of Zanzibar lies about 22 miles off the coast east of the mainland. Politically it includes also the island of Pemba, 25 miles to its northeast. The total area of the two islands is 1020 square miles. Often referred to as the "Isle of Cloves," the islands supply about 80 per cent of the world's cloves. Coconuts are also produced in quantity. Chief port is the city of Zanzibar. Population about 354,360.

Togo. A western African republic fronting southward on the Gulf of Guinea and stretching northward to Upper Volta with Ghana on the west and Benin on the east. Its area is about 22,000 square miles. The surface is hilly, rising to a maximum altitude of 3600 feet. It is partly forested. The rest of the surface consists of plains, some dry and others cultivated. Coffee is the main export, but Togo produces also cocoa, copra, cotton, kapok, groundnuts, and cassava. The capital is Lome. It was a German colony before World War I and is now a member of the French Community. Population, about 2,197,000.

Tunisia. A republic of north Africa with the Mediterranean Sea on the north and east. It is bounded southeast by Libya and west by Algeria. Its area is 63,362 square miles. The principal occupation of its estimated 5,270,000 inhabitants is agriculture, with large estates predominating. Chief products of the soil are cereal grains, olives and olive oil, citrus fruits, dates, grapes, and wine. Phosphates, iron ore, and silver ore are mined. Local and cottage industries produce wool, textiles, carpets, leatherwork, pottery, and copper ware. The population is predominantly Arab and Berber, but there is a large French minority. The capital is Tunis.

Uganda. An inland republic of central east Africa with an area of 91,343 square miles. It is bounded north by Sudan, east by Kenya, south by Tanzania and Lake Victoria, the world's second largest fresh-water lake, and west by Zaire. Its territory is traversed by the Nile River. Uganda is the largest coffee producer in the British Commonwealth, of which it became a member in 1962. Other products are tea, cotton, peanuts, sisal, and sugar. Copper and tin are the leading mineral products. Fresh-water fish are caught in large quantities commercially. The capital is Kampala. Population, about 11,171,900.

Upper Volta. An inland republic of western Africa, about 500 miles north of the Gulf of Guinea. It is bounded north and west by Mali, east by Niger, and south by Benin, Togo, Ghana, and Ivory Coast. Its area is 105,900 square miles. The surface is mainly a plateau of 600 to 1000 feet in altitude, on which are raised cattle, cotton, rice, and peanuts. The capital is Ouagadougou. Upper Volta is a member of the French Community. Population, about 5,870,000.

Zaire. With 904,757 square miles, it is the second largest country in Africa. It is bounded north by Central African Republic and Sudan, east by Uganda, Rwanda, Burundi, and Tanzania, south by Zambia and Angola, and west by the Atlantic Ocean and Congo.

The country is one of the richest sources of copper in the world, and its mineral wealth places it at the forefront of the African countries. Besides copper, it exports gold, radium, uranium, diamonds, cobalt, tin, zinc, tungsten, manganese, and silver.

The Congo River flows through the country. It and its tributaries provide transportation and extensive hydroelectric power. Tropical forests cover a considerable part of the country, and from them are exported mahogany, ebony, teak, and other valuable woods. Wild life includes elephants, lions, leopards, chimpanzees, apes, gorillas, giraffes, rhinoceroses, hippopotami, buffalo, hyenas, crocodiles, pythons, cobras, parrots, flamingoes, heron, and vultures. Ivory is exported.

Animal husbandry and agriculture form the occupation of most of the approximately 21,638,000 inhabitants, the chief exportable products being animal and vegetable oils, cotton, coffee, rubber, bananas, and manioc.

Zambia. An inland republic of south central Africa bounded north by Zaire and Tanzania, east by Malawi and Mozambique, south by Rhodesia and South West Africa, and west by Angola. The area is 290,586 square miles. Part of the southern boundary is the Zambesi river, from which hydroelectric power is developed in large quantities, particularly near Victoria falls, the world's largest cataract. The area is mostly a plateau with an equitable climate. The leading agricultural products are corn and tobacco. The country is one of the largest copper producing regions of the world.

Zambia, formerly a British protectorate, became in 1964 an independent republic within the British Commonwealth. The capital is Lusaka. Population, 4,751,000.

CITIES AND OTHER POINTS OF TRAVEL INTEREST

The following section contains descriptions of the principal cities and of other places in the continent which merit especial attention.

Addis Ababa. The capital of Ethiopia, situated in the center of the country at an elevation of about 8000 feet. It is connected by a 486-mile railway with Djibouti on the Gulf of Aden. It has a vast central market place where native and imported goods are sold. Population is estimated at 560,000.

Alexandria. The chief seaport of Egypt situated at the west of the Nile delta. The city has an industrial district with asphalt works and oil, rice, and paper mills. The chief exports are cotton, grain, rice, and sugar.

Alexandria was founded in 332 B. C. by Alexander the Great and was, for several centuries, the chief commercial city of the world. In ancient times, its harbor was famous for the Pharos, or lighthouse, a huge structure completed in 282 B. C. and regarded as one of the seven wonders of the ancient world.

In the 7th century, Alexandria was captured and sacked by the Arabs. Its importance in modern times dates from the construction of the Suez canal. Population, 1,801,056.

Algiers. The capital and chief seaport of Algeria. It lies near the center of the country's Mediterranean coast. The lower part, built by the French, has modern hotels, spacious squares, and ornamented parks, which present a marked contrast to the narrow streets and characteristic mosques of the Moorish section.

Algiers is one of the most important coaling stations on the Mediterranean Sea. It has an important trade, mainly with France. The chief exports are wine, fruits, olive oil, and cork. Population, 943,142.

Aswan Dam. A dam on the Nile River in Egypt at Philae about 700 miles up-stream from its mouth in the Mediterranean Sea. A dam was first completed there in 1902 and was heightened several times before construction was begun in 1960 on the "high dam." The "high dam" which required 10½ years to build at a cost of more than a billion dollars, partly supplied by Russia, was designed to increase 25-fold the water impounded for irrigation, to raise the water level 600 feet above sea level, and to back up the Nile for 300 miles, including 100 miles in Sudan. Development of over 9 million KW of power was envisaged, and Egypt's arable land would be enlarged by 30 per cent. Since the flood waters were scheduled to cover some 58 historic monuments, archeologists and governments hastened to devise and execute plans for their preservation. With an American contribution of a third toward the $31-million project, work was begun in 1964 on the dismantling at Abu Simbel of a temple hewn in rock containing four 65-foot statues of Rameses II. This monument, dating from 1300 B. C., was reconstructed from its parts on the heights above. At Philae, dikes were built to preserve a temple of Isis about 2000 years old.

Cairo (*ki'ro*). The capital of Egypt, and the largest city of Africa, situated on the Nile River about 100 miles from its outlet in the Mediterranean Sea. The city is an important center of trade.

Chief of the numerous sacred edifices of Cairo is the Sultan Hassan Mosque, which is regarded as the finest example of the Byzantine-Arabian architecture in existence. The El Azhar university, situated in the city, holds the leading place among the world's institutions for Mohammedan education. Cairo's site covers the remains of many cities that had fallen into ruins before the founding of the present city in 968 A. D. Population, 4,219,853.

Cape Town. The legislative capital of South Africa, occupying a picturesque site on the southwestern coast of the Republic. It stands at the head of Table bay, an inlet of the Atlantic Ocean. The city and several beautiful suburbs extend along a narrow coastal strip between the water and a group of precipitous mountains.

Cape Town is the chief seaport of South Africa, the exports ranking highest in value being diamonds and bar gold. Among the notable features of the city are the Parliament buildings, the public library; a 14-acre botanical garden; the Cape observatory; and the Castle. The last-named edifice was built as a defensive work in 1666, 14 years after the founding of a Dutch colony on the present site of the city. Cape Town passed into the hands of the English in 1806. Population, 807,211.

Casablanca. The chief city and seaport in Morocco. It has a large airport as well as a fine harbor. Following its capture by American forces in 1942, Casablanca became headquarters for the movement of Allied troops on their way to North Africa and the Mediterranean region. Population, 1,120,000.

Dakar. The capital and chief port of Senegal. It is the westernmost point on the coast of Africa and terminus of transatlantic flights between Africa and South America. Prior to Senegal's independence, Dakar was the administrative center of French West Africa. It has numerous industrial establishments. Population, 374,700.

Dar es Salaam. The capital and chief port of Tanzania. It is carefully laid out with wide streets and substantial buildings—features which it owes to the Germans, who made it the administrative center of German East Africa. The British took it in 1916. Population, 250,000.

Giza (*gē'zĕ*). A village of Egypt about three miles from Cairo. It is notable for the pyramids which stand in the vicinity. The largest was erected by Cheops, an Egyptian king who lived about 3000 B. C. According to Herodotus, 100,000 men were employed for 20 years in building it, while 10 years were occupied in transporting the stones. It is about 480 feet in height with a base 764 feet square. The pyramid is believed to have been originally encased with marble. Since 1000 A. D., however, the exterior stones have been removed, leaving visible a structure of rough limestone blocks forming steps with a platform of considerable area at the top. This pyramid was one of the seven wonders of the ancient world and is the only one of the seven still in existence. Two other major pyramids and nearly 40 minor ones are included among the pyramids of Giza. They were intended to serve as tombs for their builders. The great sphinx is located in the approach to Giza, where it might serve to frighten evil spirits away from the pyramid tombs near by. The sphinx is an image of the head of the god Harmachis attached to the body of a lion. The whole figure is 66 feet high and about 172 feet long and is carved out of the solid rock.

Johannesburg (*yô-hän'ĕs-bûrg*). The largest city and commercial metropolis of South Africa, lying in the south central part of the Transvaal province. The city was founded in 1886 and owes its importance to its location on the Witwatersrand, in the midst of the richest gold field in the world. Johannesburg is regularly laid out and well built, presenting a more completely modern appearance than any other city on the continent of Africa. It contains the University of the Witwatersrand.

Johannesburg was the center of the agitation which resulted in the Boer war. The days of the Boer régime are recalled by a dismantled fortress overlooking the city and by a monument, which stands in a nearby field, commemorating the Boer declaration of independence in 1880. The city was occupied by the British in 1900. Population, 1,152,525.

Karnak, El (*kär'näk*). A village of Egypt on the right bank of the Nile River about 400 miles southeast of Cairo, famed for its ruins of ancient Egyptian temples. The chief one is the temple of the god Amen-Ra. It was erected about 4000 years ago and is the largest temple in the world. There is comfortable standing room for as many as 90 people on the top of many of the columns still erect.

Luxor. A village of Egypt near the Nile River a short distance southwest of El Karnak and about 400 miles above Cairo. Luxor is known for the numerous tombs nearby, which contain the mummies and treasures of ancient Egyptian monarchs. These treasures, which were intended to serve the spirits of their deceased owners, amount to millions of dollars in value. The tombs are hewn in the rock and usually have, on their walls, elaborate carvings, which have done much toward the unfolding of early Egyptian history. One of the more remarkable of such tombs was that of Tutankhamen, discovered by Lord Carnarvan in 1922.

In Luxor stand two colossal statues, one of which is said to represent the god Memnon. It is a Roman restoration of a former statue, which, before its destruction by an earthquake, is said to have given forth a sound each morning when struck by the rays of the rising sun.

Nairobi. The capital of Kenya, situated about 300 miles inland from Kenya's port Mombasa, with which it is connected by rail. Its altitude is 5000 feet, and its climate is favorable. Population 314,760.

Port Said (*pōrt sä-ēd'*). A seaport of Egypt at the Mediterranean end of the Suez canal. It has an export trade in cotton and is an important coaling station. Its features include a large lighthouse, whose light is visible 24 miles out at sea, and a colossal statue of De Lesseps, the French engineer under whose direction the Suez canal was constructed. Population, 282,977.

Pretoria. The administrative capital of the Republic of South Africa. It is an inland city, situated in the northeastern part of the Republic in the Transvaal province. Its streets are broad and regularly laid out. The outstanding architectural feature of the city is the large group of government offices. They are in the Renaissance style of architecture and have a central tower surmounted by a statue of Liberty. Pretoria is the seat of Transvaal University college. Population, 1960, 422,590.

Timbuktu. An inland city of Mali near the southern border of the Sahara desert and on the edge of the marshes of the Niger River. The city was formerly one of the chief centers of Mohammedan influence in Africa, the center of an immense caravan trade in gold, ivory, wax, salt, hardware, beads, and cloth. The principal buildings—a large Mohammedan library and several mosques of striking appearance—date back beyond the 18th century. Population, about 8735.

PRINCIPAL WORLD PORTS*

Port traffic statistics for ocean-borne cargoes are difficult to make comparable owing to the different methods used in measuring cargoes. The following table showing ship entrances with net registered tonnage gives a fair idea of the traffic and importance of the ports listed. Figures are from the Bureau of Foreign and Domestic Commerce.

Rank	Port and Country	Number of Vessels	Net Register Tons	Rank	Port and Country	Number of Vessels	Net Register Tons
9.	Antwerp, Belgium	11,125	18,730,000	15.	Marseille, France	9,135	16,612,000
6.	Baltimore, U.S.A.	56,067	21,008,000	38.	Melbourne, Australia	3,396	7,613,000
41.	Bombay, India	33,731	6,547,000	36.	Montevideo, Uruguay	1,631	8,087,000
17.	Boston, U.S.A.	7,340	14,978,000	33.	Montreal, Canada	5,725	8,516,000
20.	Buenos Aires, Argentina	14,826	13,435,000	29.	Naples, Italy	9,008	10,809,000
48.	Calcutta, India	1,296	4,059,000	32.	Newcastle, England	8,532	8,596,000
43.	Capetown, South Africa	1,629	5,454,000	21.	New Orleans, U.S.A.	16,287	13,319,000
50.	Charleston, S.C., U.S.A.	10,668	3,226,000	1.	New York, U.S.A.†	92,032	68,598,000
42.	Cherbourg, France	952	6,478,000	24.	Norfolk, U.S.A.	7,089	12,222,000
7.	Colombo, Ceylon	2,708	20,425,000	8.	Osaka, Japan	18,999	19,600,000
39.	Copenhagen, Denmark	25,432	7,452,000	11.	Philadelphia, U.S.A.‡	8,302	17,907,000
49.	Curacao, Dutch West Indies	5,047	3,700,000	37.	Piraeus, Greece	13,396	7,758,000
22.	Duluth, U.S.A.	2,807	12,882,000	40.	Portland, Oregon, U.S.A.	9,548	7,051,000
44.	Galveston, U.S.A.	1,762	5,383,000	27.	Rio de Janeiro, Brazil	3,924	11,226,000
28.	Genoa, Italy	5,421	10,860,000	5.	Rotterdam, Netherlands	110,406	22,415,000
10.	Hamburg, Germany	16,141	18,418,000	18.	San Francisco, U.S.A.	17,353	14,974,000
25.	Havre, France	9,018	11,572,000	47.	Savannah, U.S.A.	1,395	4,075,000
16.	Hong Kong, China§	5,947	15,340,000	35.	Seattle, U.S.A.	3,416	8,210,000
30.	Houston, U.S.A.	7,275	10,091,000	12.	Shanghai, China	8,488	17,418,000
46.	Jacksonville, U.S.A.	1,810	4,523,000	19.	Singapore, Straits Settlements	5,934	14,800,000
45.	Jakarta, Indonesia	2,183	5,338,000	23.	Southampton, England	15,628	12,509,000
3.	Kobe, Japan	26,776	28,334,000	31.	Sydney, Australia	6,855	10,057,000
14.	Liverpool, England	14,614	16,640,000	26.	Vancouver, Canada	16,970	11,488,000
2.	London, England	29,137	29,673,000	4.	Yokohama, Japan	5,757	26,785,000
13.	Los Angeles, U.S.A.	5,369	17,211,000				

*Statistics for United States ports include barges but exclude tugs and ferries. †Upper bay shipping only. ‡On Delaware River, Philadelphia to the sea. §Excluding 9,304 junks.

SCENES IN AFRICA

These four 65-foot statues are all of the Egyptian King Rameses II, who defeated the formidable Hittites about 3300 years ago. The Egyptians used repetition for emphasis—hence the four statues before a temple at Abu Simbel. They were threatened with flooding by the Nile backed up behind the Aswan dam in 1967. To save them, money poured in from all over the world, and work began on an unexampled engineering feat—to raise these statues intact to the top of the cliff above.

Parker Collection

The biggest man-made hole in the world. The old South African Kimberly diamond mine.

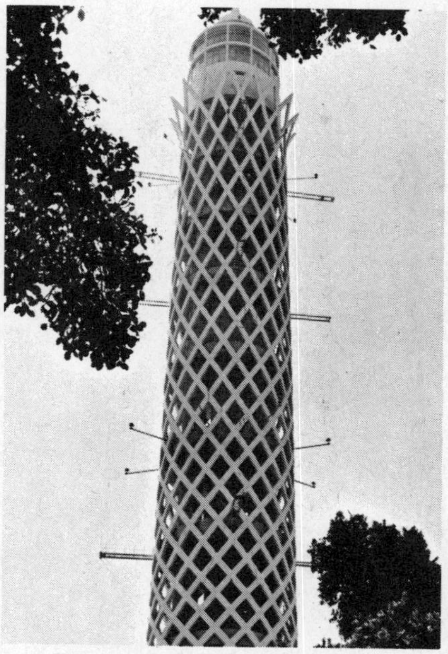

The Cairo Tower at Guezi Reh, Egypt, 618 feet tall, is the highest building in Africa and the Middle East. Built in the shape of a lotus flower, it has a revolving restaurant at the top which gives a panoramic view up to 30 miles.

UAR Tourist Office

The Voortrekker Monument at Pretoria honors the pioneers (Voortrekker) who settled the Union of South Africa.

SATOUR

New University building at Nsukka, Nigeria.

Wide World

VIEWS IN AUSTRALIA

Left Wheat field near Forbes, New South Wales. Wheat for grain is the main crop in Australia representing about half the total area cultivated. The leading Australian wheat states are New South Wales, Victoria, and Western Australia.

Right A view from Bald Hill, Stanwell Park on the south coast of New South Wales, about forty miles from Sydney, where the Pacific Ocean surf rolls against beach and cliff, overlooked by small towns and pleasant little farms.

Left Skiing is a popular sport in Australia during the months of June through August. The snow fields in the Snowy Mountains or Australian Alps, which rise to about 7300 feet, are lower than those in Europe and America, but are relatively safe because there are few ridges and rocks.

Right Blast furnaces at Newcastle, New South Wales. Newcastle, 100 miles north of Sydney, and Wollongong, 60 miles south of Sydney, are the manufacturing centers of Australia's iron and steel industry. Rayon is also made at Newcastle.

Left Temporary Parliament House in Canberra, the national capital city. Australia is an independent dominion within the Commonwealth of Nations. Its legislative bodies are the Senate and the House of Representatives.

Left Kangaroos and wallabies carrying their young in their pouches are a common sight on the plains and in the hill country of Australia. These animals are capable of speeds up to 40 m.p.h. and can jump up to 30 feet in a single leap.

Right Martin Place, Sydney, one of the principal business centers of the capital city of New South Wales. Sydney is the most important seaport in Australia and has a population of almost 2,000,000.

AUSTRALIA

An island continent lying southeast of Asia between the Indian and the Pacific Ocean. The western portion of Australia forms one of the oldest land surfaces of the globe. The continent is about one-fourth less in area than Europe, but is nearly as large as the continental United States and, with the exception of Antarctica, is the only continent lying wholly in the southern hemisphere. Australia is 1800 miles from Asia, 4500 miles from Africa, 6300 miles from South America, 6700 miles from the United States, and 11,000 miles from England. The island lies between 10° 39′ and 39° 11′ south latitude and between 113° 5′ and 153° 16′ east longitude, and from east to west is 2400 miles long and from north to south, 1971 miles. The total area is 2,971,081 square miles, of which 1,149,320 square miles, or about five-thirteenths, are within the Torrid Zone. The population is 12,099,100.

Surface. Strong contrast in elevation above sea level is strikingly absent in Australia. The highest point is Mount Kosciusko, which has an elevation of 7328 feet. The greater part of Western Australia consists of a low plateau averaging about 1000 feet in height. This plateau extends eastward into South Australia and Northern Territory. To the eastward of this plateau lie the lowlands of the Lake Eyre and Murray River basins. Along the eastern coast of the continent the land rises to an average elevation of from two to three thousand feet, forming the Great Dividing range. This range extends practically the full length of the eastern coast. At the southern end of the coast, the range turns westward and disappears in western Victoria. The most elevated area, the Australian Alps, is in the southeastern part of the continent, near the border of New South Wales and of Victoria. The low-lying coastal strip is very narrow along eastern Australia, but it widens about the Gulf of Carpentaria in the north and around Western Australia. The main watershed of the continent is formed by the Great Dividing range, from which practically all the rivers of importance rise. The country around Lake Eyre is a basin of internal drainage. The West Australian plateau is an arid region with only a few short streams flowing down the western scarp.

Climate. The climate of northern Australia is tropical, and the mean annual temperature rises in places to 85° F. The range of temperature in the interior is very great. In central Australia, heavy frosts occur at night during the winter, while in summer the temperature in the shade may rise above 130° F. The southern part of Australia lies within the South Temperate Zone and near the south coast the mean annual temperature is about 60° F. In summer, the southern coastal areas are tempered by sea breezes, but are subject to extremely sudden changes of temperature. Hot north winds from the interior may be replaced by cold south winds, the thermometer showing a fall of 20° or more in about 20 minutes. These southerly changes rarely occur in the inland districts, and within 100 miles of the coast the temperature at midday may rise to 100° F. or over for days or even for weeks.

Snow may lie for months on the higher portion of the Australian Alps, but over the greater part of the continent snow is rarely, if ever, seen.

Rainfall. A line running generally from Sharks' bay on the west coast to Sydney on the southeast coast divides the northern area of summer rains from the southern area of winter rains. In the winter months, June to September, areas of low pressure move northward from the antarctic region to a latitude sufficiently low to bring rain to Tasmania and the southern projections of the continent. In the summer, however, these areas do not move so far to the north. As a result, summer rains seldom occur, except on the west coast of Tasmania. In summer, the thermal equator is over northern Australia, and the northwest monsoons bring rain to the northern coast line, January and February being the wettest months. Monsoonal tongues sometimes extend southward as far as northern Victoria and produce extremely useful rains.

The rainfall in the remaining portion of Australia is governed mainly by the southeast trade winds. These winds bring summer and autumn rains to the eastern coast. The greater part of the moisture is deposited on the eastern highlands. The trade winds pass on as dry winds and, becoming heated, absorb moisture rapidly, thereby causing the aridity which characterizes large parts of central and western Australia. Cairns, on the northeast coast, receives over 100 inches per annum, while a large portion of the interior receives less than 10 inches. Wheat may be grown in some areas in the south, which have about 10 inches of rain, because the rain that does fall comes at the right time.

The rains of northern and of southern Australia are fairly reliable, but the central area shows great variation, and disastrous droughts sometimes occur over a large portion of the continent. During such drought periods, there is an immense loss of cattle and sheep, as it is impossible, under present conditions of transportation, to move the vast numbers of stock to the better-watered areas. Artesian wells have improved conditions somewhat by affording a supply of drinking water for the stock; but unfortunately the water is not suitable for irrigation.

Irrigation. Owing to the small rainfall over large portions of Australia, irrigation is impracticable except in limited areas, such as the Murray River basin. In recent years considerable areas in New South Wales and Victoria have been irrigated as a result of progress on the Snowy Mountains Project which diverts waters from the Australian Alps into the Murray-Murrumbidgee Irrigation Area. The Goulburn valley is served from the Waranga basin. Water for the Mildura and Red Cliff fruit growing settlements is pumped from the Murray River.

Rivers. The interior of the continent being dry, there are comparatively few rivers. Australia has only the one small snowfield, which feeds the Murray River. Of the streams flowing into the Pacific, the Burdekin and the Fitzroy, both in Queensland, are the largest. Each drains an area of about 55,000 square miles. The chief river of the north, the Roper, flowing into the Gulf of Carpentaria, is navigable for 75 miles from its mouth. The largest river system is the Murray with its tributaries—the Darling, the Murrumbidgee, and the Lachlan. These rivers drain south Queensland, western New South Wales, and northern Victoria. There are other streams, such as Cooper's Creek, which, in time of abnormal rains, carry enormous volumes of water inland to lakes which have no outlet, such as Lake Eyre, Lake Gairdner, and Lake Frome. Generally, however, these streams contain water in their upper courses only, because, by evaporation and soakage, the water is lost, and the remainder of their channels is marked by occasional water holes, which also dry up in time of drought.

On the east, north, and west coasts, short rivers flow from the mountain slopes to the sea. But there are no long navigable waterways penetrating far into the interior, like the Mississippi in North America and the Nile in Africa. Hence the development of the continent has been much retarded.

Minerals. Australia is fairly rich in mineral resources. Gold, discovered here in 1851, has yielded the most valuable returns. In the early days most of the gold was obtained from alluvial deposits or gold placers. Deep leads or deeply buried alluvial deposits also gave splendid returns. When the alluvial areas were worked out, the miners turned their attention to the quartz reefs from which the alluvial gold had been derived, and more costly methods of winning the gold were introduced. Copper, tin, lead, silver, zinc, manganese, antimony, wolfram, and bismuth have been mined, and important deposits of such minerals as gypsum and phosphates are being worked.

Precious stones, including diamond, sapphire, topaz, and opal, are found. Agates are fairly abundant.

Black coal occurs in large areas in eastern Australia and in Tasmania. Western Australia draws its supply largely from the Collie coal field, situated in the state. Thick seams of brown coal occur in southeastern Australia, especially near Morwell in Victoria. Building stones have been quarried in all the states.

Mineral Production of Australia, 1967

Item	Quantity	$A1,000*
Black coal	34,799,000 t.	160,099
Brown coal	23,386,000 t.	20,686
Copper	90,252 t.	72,515†
Gold	801,000 f.oz.	24,371†
Iron ore	18,536,000 t.	82,994
Lead	375,031 t.	73,654†
Silver	19,783,000 f.oz.	N.A.
Zinc	399,582 t.	29,354†
Value of all mining & quarrying 696,701		

* Value at mine; includes value of materials used in production process. † Value of all minerals containing the metal.

Vegetation. The continent has over 7000 species of plants found nowhere else in the world. Many of them have fossil representatives in America and in Europe. Characteristically Australian are the gum trees, or eucalyptus, and the acacias. Eucalypts number over 230 species and are found in all places capable of supporting vegetation. Some are only a few feet in height, as the mallee and snow gum; some rival California's giant sequoias. Oil is secreted in the leaves of numerous species, and a gumlike resin exudes from the trees when the bark is injured. Some of the most durable timber known is furnished by various eucalypts, as the jarrah, red gum, and ironbark.

Much sunshine and too little rain compel many Australian trees to hang their leaves vertically, only the edges being turned to the sun. By this means the amount of evaporation from the leaves is diminished. The eucalypts are evergreens, but in many cases they shed their bark. The acacias, or wattles, constitute another important group, the members of which vary, according to their environment, from small shrubs to trees 100 to 150 feet in height. The bark of some varieties is used for tanning. The golden wattle is regarded as Australia's national flower.

Other forms of natural vegetation include the grass tree, resembling a tall stump from which grass sprouts at the top; tree ferns as large as palm trees; the banksia or Australian honeysuckle; and the native cherry, noted for having the stone outside the fruit.

Fodder Plants. Many acacias provide fodder for sheep and cattle. Other shrublike fodder plants, growing in the dry interior, are saltbushes, cotton bushes, and bluebushes. Australia's saltbushes have proved so valuable as sheep foodplants that they have been introduced into the arid regions of the southwestern United States.

Timber. Forest areas occupy 24,500,000 acres, which is about one-twentieth of the surface of Australia. Of this total, 15,895,781 acres are held as timber reserves. Soft woods, such as kauri pine, red cedar, silky oak, and Queensland maple, are found in the tropical forests of Queensland. Murray pine and Huon pine, the latter growing in Tasmania, are other important soft woods. The hard woods include many species of eucalypts, such as ironbark, red gum, gray box, yellow box, blue gum, and stringybark. These grow mainly on the highlands of eastern and southeastern Australia. Jarrah and kauri flourish in southwestern Australia. Blackwood, a species of acacia, is used extensively for furniture.

Grassland. The eastern half of the interior is a vast sheep pasturing country, though the rainfall is light. The soil is rich alluvium, and in good seasons grass is abundant. In time of drought the grass dries and is scattered by the wind, leaving the land perfectly bare. When the drought breaks, the grass springs up and grows with great rapidity. European fodder grasses have been planted over considerable areas. Farther west, plants needing but little water, wattles and saltbushes, mallee and mulga scrub, and the wiry spinifex, or porcupine grass, cover a large part of Australia's semidesert.

Jungles. In the northern part of Australia, a region of tropical heat and of heavy rains, there are found, in all the lowland districts, dense forests containing eucalypts, bamboos, palm trees, beautiful orchids with singular flowers, and gigantic lilies six to eight feet high, bearing dark red blossoms. Such jungle growth is variously known as bush, brush, or scrub. The term "bush" is frequently applied to any area in which the natural trees have not been cleared off to any extent.

Fauna. The fauna of Australia is quite distinct from that of the northern hemisphere. It is most closely related to that of South America. The characteristic mammalian forms are the marsupials, which, with few exceptions, are found elsewhere only in the fossil state. The higher mammals are represented only by the dingo, or native dog, probably introduced by the aborigines, and by a few rodents. The marsupials, or pouched animals, include the kangaroo and the wallaby, which are typically Australian. Other forms are the wombats, bandicoots, opossums, or possums, and the native bear, or koala. The Tasmanian wolf and Tasmanian devil are marsupials now confined to Tasmania. Outside the Australian area the only living pouched animals are the Patagonian opossum-rat and the North American opossum. The Monotremes, which are the lowest order of the mammals, have no living representatives outside Australia. The Australian forms include the duck-billed platypus and the echidna, or anteater. Both are egg laying forms and constitute a link between the mammals of today and the great reptile family from which the birds and mammals have developed.

Among the more remarkable birds are the emu, cassowary, kookaburra (laughing jackass or giant kingfisher), native turkey, black swan, lyre bird, and bower bird. Brilliant plumaged parrots and the yellow-crested cockatoo are abundant.

Two species of crocodiles are found in north Queensland. The largest lizard is called the "iguana" or "goanna" and may reach a length of 5 feet. Snakes, both venomous and nonvenomous, are fairly abundant.

Fish. Excellent food fish of many kinds abound in Australian coastal waters and in most of the rivers. The remarkable ceratodus or lungfish occurs in the Burnett and the Mary River in Queensland. Several species of European fish have been acclimatized. Trout may now be caught in a number of the mountain streams.

Pearling. Pearl fishing is a lucrative occupation off the northern and northwestern coasts of the continent. Some of the nearer pearl-oyster banks, however, have been practically exhausted, owing to persistent gathering of the shellfish and failure to allow the beds time enough to restock.

Sheep Raising. Gold brought Australia into the circle of the nations, but her greatest source of wealth is her merino sheep. Sheep raising is the continent's main industry. Pasturage for sheep is less dependent on rainfall than is pasture for cattle; sheep thrive where cattle would starve. Australian wool is the thickest and finest in the world. Hence wool growing is a profitable industry in the east central part of Australia. Wire fencing is used to enclose the "stations" or "runs" on which sheep are grazed. Merino sheep, improved wonderfully from the old Spanish stock, form the largest flocks. The stations vary greatly in size and in the number of sheep carried. Many of the very large stations have been subdivided, but recently, in the Riverina, there was one station which carried 150,000 sheep. Australia has over 120,000,000 sheep and exceeds in number any other sheep raising area in the world.

Large cattle stations are situated in the northern parts of Australia, especially Queensland. Dairy farms are abundant in the well watered districts of eastern and southern Australia. Horses and pigs are also raised.

ANIMAL INDUSTRY OF AUSTRALIA

ITEM	Season 1967–68	Season 1960
Cattle, No.	19,218,000	16,503,000
Pigs, No.	2,056,000	1,424,000
Sheep, No.	166,912,000	155,171,000
Butter produced, lbs. .	432,284,000	436,633,000
Wool produced, lbs. . .	1,769,688,000	1,680,000,000

Agriculture. The area under cultivation in Australia is gradually extending. In the southern coastal regions the rainfall is generally good; and oats, barley, maize, and lucerne are the principal crops. Apples, pears, peaches, and other such fruits are largely grown. Inland, wheat is extensively cultivated, the area under cultivation increasing as means of communication are improved. Apples, oranges, lemons, peaches, apricots, grapes, and currants are readily grown in the irrigation areas. In the coast regions of Queensland, sugar cane, bananas, pineapples, and other tropical fruits are cultivated. Rice, cotton, and tobacco have been grown in various portions of the Commonwealth.

Manufacturing. Manufacturing is rapidly developing. Flour, woolen goods, leather, boots and shoes, furniture, iron and steel goods are among the products made for home consumption; and an export trade in manufactured articles is gradually developing.

VALUE OF CHIEF CLASSES OF PRODUCTS

ITEM	Value 1965–66 $A1,000	Value 1967–68 $A1,000
Agricultural	861,115	925,941
Pastoral	1,188,536	1,059,600
Dairying, Poultry and Bee-Farming . . .	416,003	453,381
Forests and Fisheries .	170,152	165,717
Mining	441,558	564,386
Manufacturing . . .	6,275,355	7,430,738
Total	9,354,369	10,599,763

Commerce. Imports are principally European manufactures. Most of the trade is with Great Britain. Australia exports more wool than any other country. Among the other exports are wheat, butter, hides, tallow, and dressed meats, comprising chiefly beef, mutton, and rabbit. Summer dairy products, shipped on fast steamers with cold-storage chambers, reach Great Britain in a few weeks when the cows in that country are housed for the winter.

Canada and New Zealand are linked by cable with Australia. Most of the foreign capital invested in Australia is British. The country has about 28,000 miles of railway, of mixed gauges. A railway gauge unification scheme is being considered. The state governments own the railways while the Federal government owns the telegraph and telephone services, an interstate and the overseas airline.

The Federal District. In 1911, the Commonwealth acquired from New South Wales an area of approximately 912 square miles to be used as a Federal district. An additional area of 28 square miles on Jervis bay was obtained in 1917 to be used as a naval station. This Federal district was named Canberra. Building operations began in 1923, and the Australian parliament convened there for the first time in May 1927.

Inhabitants. The population of Australia in 1968 was estimated at 12,099,100. Protestants constitute the larger proportion of the inhabitants, but there is an influential Catholic minority. The Federal constitution forbids the establishment of any state-supported religion. In all parts of the Commonwealth, education is free, secular, and obligatory. Illiteracy is virtually unknown. The population is almost entirely of British origin, less than 5 per cent being of any other extraction. These figures do not include about 50,000 aborigines.

Name. The continent was formerly called New Holland. *Australia*, from the Latin word for southern, was suggested by Captain Matthew Flinders (1774–1814), an English navigator, who had explored the southern part of the island. The name came into use in 1817.

STATES OF THE COMMONWEALTH

The Commonwealth of Australia, a self-governing British Commonwealth member, was formed Jan. 1, 1901. It consists of six states—New South Wales, Queensland, South Australia, Tasmania, Victoria, and Western Australia—the Northern Territory, and the Australian Capital Territory. The following section contains a brief description of the states and of the Northern Territory.

New South Wales, a state of southeastern Australia. The Great Dividing range extends along the east side at a distance of 20 to 100 miles inland. On the west is a magnificent pastoral country which gradually changes to arid plains farther inland. The pastoral area is the basis for Australia's great sheep industry. There are 48,000,000 sheep in this area alone. Also this state includes Australia's most important mining, farming, and industrial developments. Coal, gold, silver, lead, tin, antimony, manganese, bismuth, and copper are locally mined and iron ore is nearby and available. Farm crops are wheat, maize, barley, oats, potatoes, lucerne, tobacco, sugar cane, and grapes. Sydney, Newcastle, Broken Hill, Tamworth, Bathurst, Goulburn, Wagga Wagga, and Albury are important urban centers.

Forests cover the western slopes of the mountains and include such trees as the red cedar, eucalyptus, red gum, and murray pine. Acacias and mulga are shrubs of the arid regions. Unusual animal life is found, as kangaroos, platypuses, and echidnas. Rabbits introduced from Europe have multiplied and become a serious menace to sheep grazing since they also are herbivorous.

Queensland lies in the northeast part of the continent. The climate is subtropical to tropical. Along the coast and on the windward eastern side of the Great Dividing range the rainfall is heavy. Across the mountains and inland to the "Never, Never Country" the land is arid, again supporting immense herds of cattle and sheep. Tropical crops, as sugar cane, bananas, and rice, are grown along the coastal plains. Wheat is prominent about Brisbane. Natural forests still abound including such valuable trees as cedar, kauri, pine, silky oak, and maple. Leading cities are Brisbane, Rockhampton, Towns-ville, Maryborough, Gympie, Ipswich, Toowoomba, and Charters Towers.

South Australia lies in south central Australia. The Flinders range, Spencer's Gulf, and a series of shallow saline lakes divide it into eastern and western sections. The east is well watered and fertile; the west is desert. The Murray River flows through the southeastern corner. Temperatures are extremely high in desert sections in summer but frosts occur in the higher lands in winter. Ranching prevails, with sheep the most prominent. Adelaide is the state capital and most important city. Other cities are Whyalla, Port Pirie, Port Augusta, and Gawler.

Tasmania, originally called Van Diemen's Land, is an island state lying to the south of Victoria, from which it is separated by Bass strait. It consists of one large and numerous small islands. The climate is temperate and moist. Mines produce silver, lead, copper, gold, zinc, tin, and coal. Besides metals, Tasmania exports fruits dairy products, potatoes, wool, hides, and timber. Hobart is the capital and principal port.

Victoria is a comparatively small state on the southeast corner of Australia. The section of the Great Dividing range known as the Australian Alps is in the eastern part. The coastline is 680 miles long on the south and the Murray River forms the north boundary. As in Tasmania, just across the straits, the climate is temperate with moderate temperatures and sufficient rainfall for cropping except in the northwest. Grazing is important with sheep raising first. Farming and manufacturing are rapidly developing. Melbourne is the capital. Other important cities are Ballarat, Bendigo, and Geelong.

Western Australia comprises all of western Australia to the 129° Meridian east. It is a huge area with greatest dimensions being 1480 miles north-south and 1000 miles east-west. It is largely an arid tableland with a narrow strip of coastal lowland. The southwest corner of the state has moderate temperatures and sufficient rainfall, crops and livestock. The extreme north is tropical with abundant rainfall. Gold is the most valuable in mineral output. About Perth, the capital city, a wide variety of temperate and subtropical crops are grown, such as wheat, oranges, grapes, lemons, and olives. Other important cities are Fremantle, Midland, Albany, Coolgardie, Kalgoorlie, Geraldton, Northam, Collie, Bunbury, and the port of Broome.

Northern Territory is the northern central section of the continent and includes the Arnhem Land peninsula. Its dimensions are 900 miles north-south by 560 miles east-west. The coastline is 1040 miles in length. The area is largely tableland with a low narrow tropical coastal plain in the north. This state is not especially well developed because of heat and aridity. The northern part has tropical rainfall mainly in summer. Darwin is a port, has an important international airport and is the center of the Territory Administration. Alice Springs is the other important town in the Territory.

STATISTICS OF AUSTRALIA

States and Territories	Area in sq. mi.	Pop. 1968 est.	Capital
New South Wales	309,433	4,430,200	Sydney
Victoria	87,884	3,356,900	Melbourne
South Australia	380,070	1,136,400	Adelaide
Queensland	667,000	1,751,800	Brisbane
Tasmania	26,215	386,000	Hobart
Western Australia	975,920	930,800	Perth
Northern Territory	520,280	64,000	Darwin
Federal District (A.C.T.)	939	117,200	Canberra

PRINCIPAL CITIES

The following section contains a brief description of the chief cities of Australia, including each of the state or territorial capitals. The population of Australia shows a marked tendency to concentrate in the cities, the five largest of which contain almost 50 per cent of the country's inhabitants.

Adelaide. The capital of South Australia, situated in the southern part of the state on the Torrens River, about six miles from its mouth in the Gulf of St. Vincent. A dam here forms the river into a lake a mile and a quarter long. The city stands on a wide plain near the base of the Mt. Lofty range and is divided by the Torrens into South Adelaide and North Adelaide.

The manufactures comprise iron wares, leather, woolens, pottery, starch, soap, flour, and malt liquors. Adelaide is the trade emporium of South Australia and has a large commerce. Port Adelaide, the seaport of the city, is about 7 miles distant by rail. It is the seat of considerable manufacturing; is a port of call for vessels from Europe; and is connected by railway with the principal cities of the Commonwealth. Near by is the summer resort of Glenelg.

Adelaide was founded in 1836 and was named in honor of Queen Adelaide, consort of King William IV of England. Population, 794,300.

Ballarat. A prosperous inland city of Victoria, Australia, the center of a rich gold yielding district. It was the finding of gold nuggets near the present site of Ballarat in 1851 that started the rush of gold seekers into Australia. At Bakery Hill, there was found, in 1858, a nugget that was sold for about $50,000. Population, 41,037.

Brisbane. The capital of Queensland, Australia, situated in the southeastern part of the state on the Brisbane River, about 25 miles from Moreton bay. Brisbane is the center of commerce and of manufacturing for southern Queensland.

Steamers ascend the river and berth at the wharves. There is a regular steamer communication with other ports in Australia and with the chief ports of Europe, and of the United States. Among the manufacturing establishments are flour mills, tobacco factories, breweries, tanneries, and shoe factories. Coal is mined in the vicinity.

The climate is healthful though the mean yearly temperature is 68.9° F. in the shade. Higher education is afforded by a Teachers College, a Technical College, and the University of Queensland. Population, 813,300.

Canberra (*kăn'bĕr-ȧ*). The capital of Australia. It is a Federal territory, 912 square miles in area, situated about 150 miles southwest of Sydney and 60 miles inland from the east coast of Australia. The city is built on the Molonglo River and is picturesquely surrounded by mountains. It was laid out by W. Burley Griffin, of Chicago, whose plans were adjudged the best in a world-wide competition. These plans call for streets in concentric circles with radiating avenues. The National War Memorial Museum, Institute of Anatomy, overseas embassies, Australian National University (1949), National Observatory and Canberra University College (1932), and government buildings are tourist attractions. Population, 110,000.

Darwin. A port city, named after Charles Darwin, and the government seat of the Northern Territory, Australia. Almost 2000 miles from the nearest metropolis, Darwin is the terminus of the overland telegraph and of the cable to Java and Singapore. In 1974, a cyclone struck Darwin, leaving 50 dead and destroying 90 per cent of the city. Reconstruction started immediately and it was estimated that it would take 5 years to complete. Population, 45,000.

Hobart. The capital of the Australian island state of Tasmania. The city is situated on the Derwent estuary.

The manufactures include woolens, hats, flour, pottery, leather, and jam.

Most of the exports consist of fruits, hops, grain, wool, and timber. Many Australian visitors are attracted to Hobart by the cool and invigorating climate. The city is the seat of the University of Tasmania.

Hobart was founded in 1804 and was named Hobart Town in honor of Lord Hobart, then secretary of state for the colonies. In 1881 the name was changed to Hobart. Population (with suburbs), 144,000.

Melbourne. The capital of Victoria, on the Yarra River about two miles from its mouth in Hobsons bay, an arm of Port Phillip bay. The river is navigable by vessels drawing less than 22 feet of water, but large steamers usually anchor in the bay at Port Melbourne.

The University of Melbourne stands in the foremost rank of institutions of higher learning.

Melbourne has large docks. Served by regular steamer communication with ports in Asia, Europe, and America, the city is a great emporium of foreign commerce. Railroads connect it with all the chief cities in Australia.

From 1901 to 1927 it served as the temporary capital of the Commonwealth. Population, 2,319,700.

Perth. The capital of Western Australia, occupying a picturesque site in the southwestern part of the state on

Melville water, an expansion of the Swan river. The city is 12 miles by rail from its port, Fremantle, a town at the mouth of the river on the Indian Ocean.

The University of Perth was founded in 1912. Population, (with suburbs) 499,494.

Sydney. The largest and oldest city in Australia and the capital of New South Wales. Sydney is picturesquely situated on Port Jackson, a magnificent expanse of water, which forms a landlocked harbor extending 20 miles inland. The harbor is spanned by a steel arch bridge having a main span of 1650 feet, one of the longest in the world. The water in the harbor is deep enough to permit ocean-going ships to dock at the wharves and quays. Favored by this advantage, the city has become a naval station of the first rank.

Sydney has an enormous commerce. The harbor is crowded with shipping from foreign ports, and the staple Australian products are exported in immense quantities. Favored by the proximity of vast coal deposits, Sydney is also a manufacturing city. Cars, locomotives, hardware, foundry and machine shop products, clothing boots and shoes, textiles, machinery, and malt and distilled liquors are some of the manufactures. An annual sheep show is an event of great commercial importance.

Sydney has 647 acres of parks within the city boundary and 680,000 acres of reserves and commons in the metropolitan area.

Adjoining Victoria park stands the sumptuous main edifice of the University of Sydney with the Macleay museum of natural history.

The city's mean annual temperature is about 63.1° F., which is nearly the same as the average yearly temperature of Lisbon. Sydney was founded in 1788 by Captain Arthur Phillip, who had been sent by the British government to select a site for a colony. Population, 2,444,735.

NEW ZEALAND

A self-governing country consisting of two large islands to which are attached politically a number of small islands lying at some distance from the main group. New Zealand is situated in the south Pacific Ocean about 1200 miles east of Australia. It lies 7000 miles almost due south from Alaska and is 4000 miles west of the coast of Chile. It is 5400 miles by direct route from San Francisco. The two large islands are called North island and South island and are separated by Cook strait, which has a width varying from 16 to 90 miles. The two islands lie entirely in the South Temperate Zone and form a group stretching about 1000 miles in a general northeast and southwest direction and having a maximum width of 180 miles. The total area of New Zealand including Stewart Island and the Chatham Islands is 103,736 square miles.

North Island. The northern portion of New Zealand has an area of 44,281 square miles. It is 515 miles long, and its greatest breadth is 180 miles. The island may be likened to an inverted shoe the toe of which is a long irregular peninsula extending to the northwest. This peninsula is attached to the rest of the island by a narrow isthmus, consisting of a neck six miles in width separating Hauraki gulf on the east from Manukau harbor on the west. The arch of the shoe is represented by the Bay of Plenty in the north. The only remaining inlet of any considerable size is Hawke bay on the east. North island has the two best ports of New Zealand, Port Nicholson in the south and Waitemata at the isthmus in the northwest.

Most of the surface is gently undulating with low, heavily forested hills. A volcanic area, beginning in the south, passes through the center of the island as far as the Bay of Plenty. Much of this region will not support grasses, but trees cover parts of it. It occupies the southern extension of the island from coast to coast, but, where the width of the island increases, a fertile area spreads out on each side and runs along each coast in a belt averaging about 40 miles in width. These tracts are well adapted for grazing. The northwestern peninsula is in large part covered with a heavy clay, which yields returns only in response to intensive cultivation. The peninsula has areas of rich alluvium, however, in which the mangrove, the orange tree, various palms, and the giant kauri pine flourish. The partially fossilized resin of this pine is excavated and exported in quantity to be used in the manufacture of varnish and of linoleum.

The volcanic area of North Island contains many notable features. The highest volcano is Mount Ruapehu, which has an altitude of 9175 feet. It is situated in Tongariro national park, about 20 miles southwest of Lake Taupo, New Zealand's largest inland body of water. Stretching north from the mountain is a region of about 5000 square miles abounding in hot springs, geysers, pools of boiling mud, and colored lakelets. This region formerly contained a famous series of pink and white terraces of volcanic formation. In 1886, however, they were blown up in an eruption which tore a chasm in the earth nine miles in length. Farther south, on Cook strait, stands one of the most beautiful mountains of the island, Mount Egmont, an extinct volcano 8340 feet in height. No country has so large a proportion of its area incorporated in national parks as New Zealand. Covering over 2,500,000 acres, these reserves embrace a variety of scenery unmatched in any other park system of the world.

The rivers of the island are short. The longest is the Waikato River, which drains the waters of Lake Taupo northward to an outlet on the west coast. It is navigable for 70 miles of its course, but it shares with nearly all the other rivers of New Zealand the disadvantage of having at its mouth a bar which obstructs navigation.

South Island. The southern portion of New Zealand is slightly larger than the northern, having an area of 58,092 square miles. Off its southern coast, and separated by Foveaux strait, lies Stewart Island, which has an area of 670 square miles. About 350 miles to the east lie the Chatham Islands, 372 square miles in area. The length of South Island is 530 miles. It has a fairly uniform breadth of about 100 miles.

The outstanding feature of the surface is a mountain range called the Southern Alps, which runs from end to end near the western coast of the island. The mountains reach a maximum elevation at Mount Cook, which has an altitude of 12,349 feet. The scenic grandeur of the region is comparable to that of the European Alps. On the western slope, many glaciers flow down to the edge of the coniferous forests which cover a large part of the mountain sides. East of the divide are several long glacial lakes. The largest, Lake Wakatipu, has a depth of more than 1500 feet, and its wild, mountainous surroundings impart to it a beauty rivaling that of Lake Lucerne in Switzerland. The eastern slope descends to a plateau flanked on the east by a ridge of mountains passing through the center of the island. East of this ridge the land inclines toward the sea in grassy terraces, which provide the largest stretch of arable land in New Zealand.

Other Islands. New Zealand controls a number of islands in the south Pacific Ocean. They have a total area of about 500 square miles and a population of approximately 15,000. The more important of these islands are Cook Islands, about 1500 miles northeast of North Island, and Auckland Islands, uninhabited, 200 miles south of New Zealand. The Cook Islands support about 21,000 inhabitants, mainly of Polynesian race, who export tropical fruit and coffee. New Zealand formerly held a mandate over Western Samoa, which became independent in 1962. This group of fertile islands of 1130 square miles is about 1000 miles to the north and had an estimated population of 137,000 in 1968.

Climate. The prevailing winds of New Zealand blow from the west. They carry sufficient moisture to foster everywhere on the islands a vegetation of a uniform greenness that recalls the verdure of Ireland. In South island, where the mountains reach a greater height, much of the moisture is precipitated as rain on the plateau, and the warm, dry winds, descending from the elevated regions into the eastern plains, occasionally cause droughts of sufficient duration to injure the crops. Except in the mountains, New Zealand is free from severe frosts, while in North island, where two-thirds of the population is concentrated, the climate is subtropical. Tempering breezes, however, blow incessantly from the ocean; yellow fever is unknown, and there are few mosquitoes or other pests usually found in subtropical regions. As a result, the mortality rate of New Zealand is one of the lowest in the world.

Flora and Fauna. The most characteristic plant of New Zealand is the fern, which flourishes in great variety everywhere. The so-called tree fern often reaches a height of 40 feet. About two-thirds of the indigenous species of vegetation are found nowhere else, and most of the others resemble those of Australia. The eucalyptus and acacia, however, which predominate in Australia, are not found in New Zealand. The nikau palm occurs even on South island, which is the southern limit for true palms. The kauri pine, the beech, and many other hardwood trees formerly covered much of the region's surface. Phormium, or New Zealand flax, is the country's outstanding contribution to the economic plants of the world. The fiber is used for binder twine and ropes. The cultivation of phormium has been introduced into Ireland, America, and several other regions of the earth. A noticeable feature of New Zealand's flora is the comparative absence of brilliant flowers.

New Zealand has not a single indigenous mammal. The dog and the rat, however, were brought by Polynesian settlers, and wild pigs, rabbits, and many other forms of animal life have been introduced by Europeans. There are no snakes, but there are a few lizards peculiar to the country. The area is the sole habitat of many species of birds, including the kiwi, or apteryx, a wingless and tailless bird the size of a hen. The kiwi is related to the moa, a bird which was formerly very numerous in New Zealand but which has been exterminated within the past few centuries.

Stock Raising. The bulk of New Zealand's wealth is derived from sheep and cattle. The wool clip normally amounts to more than 200 million pounds, approximately 20 to 25 per cent of that of Australia. Sheep skins to the value of 10 to 15 million dollars are exported annually. Frozen meat exports are valued at more than 50 million dollars, and 60 to 80 million dollars worth of butter and cheese is shipped. The stock is carried and fattened mainly on cultivated grasses, although in North island most of the pasturage is unplowed.

Agriculture. The greater part of the land sown to field crops is in South island. The produce, absorbed almost entirely by the domestic market, consists principally of wheat, oats, barley, and potatoes. Grain growing is not a specialized occupation, but is carried on along with stock raising. About two-thirds of New Zealand's surface is said to be capable of successful cultivation.

Mining. The four minerals produced in quantity by New Zealand are coal, gold, kauri gum, and silver. Most of the coal is mined in South island, but very little is sent out of the country. Gold is found in both islands, and heads the list of mineral exports. Gold mining was an attraction which drew large numbers of settlers in the decade 1861-71.

Manufacturing and Trade. The chief manufactures of New Zealand are connected with stock raising and dairying. After meat packing and the making of dairy products, the most important industries are lumber mill operations, printing, and the manufacture of flour, textiles, leather, and metal products. Industrial disputes are settled by compulsory arbitration.

Most of the trade is with Great Britain. The United States, Canada, and Australia rank next in order. The exports normally amount to over 300 million dollars in value, most of which is represented by the products of New Zealand's characteristic industry, the raising of sheep and other livestock. The imports usually approximate the same value as the exports, the chief articles being iron and steel products, textiles, motor cars, oils, clothing, paper, and tobacco products.

Internal Communications. New Zealand has about 3450 miles of railroads, practically the entire mileage being owned and operated by the government. The greater part of the mileage is on South island. The telephone and the telegraph system are also under government ownership.

Inhabitants. The aborigines of New Zealand are called Maoris, a Polynesian people which is believed to have displaced an earlier race some six centuries ago. They were polygamous, and occasionally indulged in cannibal feasts. Among them, it was supposed that the seat of the soul was the left eye. In warlike arts, wood carving, dyeing, and tattooing, they had developed a considerable skill. After a desperate resistance to the British settlers, they accepted the religion and the manner of life of the newcomers. In 1968, the Maoris in New Zealand numbered 219,042.

The population of New Zealand, 1968 estimate, was 2,776,266, nearly all of whom were of British descent. A little less than two-thirds of the population resides in North Island, the rest living in South Island and the dependencies. The capital is Wellington and the largest city is Auckland, both of which are in North Island.

There is an excellent educational system, at the head of which stands the University of New Zealand with four affiliated colleges. The university is not a teaching body. It has the power of granting degrees and is charged with conducting the examination of students prepared by the colleges. Over one-third the population are members or adherents of the English Church. The Catholics number about 11 per cent of the total.

New Zealand is divided into nine provincial districts, of which four are in North island, five are entirely in South island, and one is partly in South island and partly in other islands. Those in North island are Auckland, Wellington, Hawke's Bay, and Taranaki. Within South island are the provincial districts of Canterbury, Nelson, Westland, Marlborough, and the greater part of Otago. Otago includes also Stewart and other outlying islands.

PRINCIPAL CITIES

Auckland. The largest city of New Zealand, beautifully situated on a cluster of extinct volcanoes at the neck of the northwestern peninsula of North Island. The isthmus is six miles in width, thus providing the city with two natural harbors, one on each side of the isthmus. The eastern harbor is protected by a volcanic cone rising to a height of 1000 feet. This harbor has been elaborately improved and is the point of export for kauri gum and a large part of the lumber shipped abroad. The chief industries include shipbuilding, sugar refining, and the manufacture of rope and of machine shop products.

Auckland is the seat of Auckland University College and has an art gallery, a library with a valuable collection of rare manuscripts, and a museum containing many Maori relics. The mountain sides in the vicinity are terraced by former Maori fortifications. The Domain, one of the four parks of the city, contains a fine botanical garden. Auckland was until 1865 the capital of New Zealand. Population, 548,293.

Christchurch. The capital of the provincial district of Canterbury and the second largest city of New Zealand, situated near the center of the eastern coast of South island on the Avon River seven miles from its mouth. The city lies on a fertile plain and is the center of the surrounding agricultural and grazing interests. Frozen meats, wool, and lumber are exported. The chief manufactures include agricultural machinery, leather goods, furniture, and clothing.

Christchurch was founded by the "Canterbury pilgrims," a group of churchmen who left England about 1849. Many of the streets are named after English dioceses. Canterbury college is the leading educational institution. The Anglican cathedral with its dominating spire is the finest piece of church architecture in New Zealand. A museum contains numerous remains of the moa, an extinct wingless bird which is peculiar to New Zealand. Population, est., 250,000.

Dunedin. The capital of the provincial district of Otago, situated on Otago harbor, an inlet on the southeastern coast of South Island. The chief exports are wool, frozen meat, and gold. Dunedin is the seat of Otago College, the largest institution for higher education in New Zealand.

Dunedin is connected by rail with Christchurch to the north and with Invercargill to the south. The population is about 80,000.

Invercargill (*ĭn'vẽr-kär'gĭl*). A port and city at the southern extremity of South Island. Invercargill is the regular starting point for journeys to Lake Wakatipu and other glacial lakes of the Southern Alps. It has several woolen and lumber mills. Population, 43,800.

Wanganui (*wŏ'ngä-nōō-ē*). The principal port on the west coast of North island, lying about 120 miles north of Wellington. It is regularly laid out at the foot of low hills, from the summit of which may be seen the snow-clad volcano of Mount Ruapehu. Wanganui is the export center for a pastoral and agricultural region. Population 36,000.

Wellington. The capital and third largest city of New Zealand, situated at the geographical center of the country, on a mountainous site at the southern end of North Island. It fronts on Lambton harbor, the most commodious in New Zealand. The port is equipped with modern facilities for handling the city's extensive commerce, which includes a large export trade in wool, meat, hides, skins, butter, cheese, and hemp. Wellington's manufactures embrace chiefly packed meats, woolen goods, soap, matches, rope, and brick. Printing and the assembling of motor vehicles are other important industries.

The government and principal office buildings are substantial, modern structures. The city has a university, two museums, an art gallery, and a modern research laboratory. Besides 1613 acres of parks and reserves in the city, Wellington owns a 970-acre belt of grazing land, accessible to the public, and Williams park, a seaside resort on Days bay. The 30-mile drive around the Wellington waterfront is one of the finest scenic routes in Oceania. Population, 167,859.

GREAT CITIES OF THE WORLD

City and Country	Population		City and Country	Population	
	City Proper	Urban Agglom.		City Proper	Urban Agglom.
Ahmedabad, India	1,585,544	1,950,000	Los Angeles, USA	2,750,000	8,960,000
Alexandria, Egypt	2,032,000	2,250,000	Madras, India	2,469,449	3,200,000
Algiers, Algeria	1,503,720	1,800,000	Madrid, Spain	3,247,108	3,785,000
Amsterdam, Netherlands	770,805	1,780,000	Manchester, England	516,100	2,865,000
Athens, Greece	867,023	2,540,541	Manila, Philippines	1,435,500	5,000,000
Bagdad, Iraq	1,300,000	2,183,800	Marseille, France	889,029	1,015,000
Baku, USSR	927,000	1,555,000	Melbourne, Australia	74,400	2,620,400
Baltimore, USA	847,000	1,920,000	Mexico City, Mexico	7,768,000	10,700,000
Bangkok, Thailand	1,867,297	3,125,000	Milan, Italy	1,743,427	3,725,000
Barcelona, Spain	1,800,274	3,365,000	Milwaukee, USA	685,000	1,388,000
Belgrade, Yugoslavia	770,140	1,150,000	Montevideo, Uruguay	1,202,757	1,300,000
Berlin (W.), Germany	2,047,948	3,860,000	Montreal, Canada	1,214,352	2,743,408
Beirut, Lebanon	470,870	1,010,000	Moscow, USSR	7,469,000	10,650,000
Birmingham, England	1,086,500	2,660,000	Munich, Germany	1,336,576	1,895,000
Bogota, Colombia	2,855,065	2,925,000	Nagoya, Japan	2,082,235	3,500,000
Bombay, India	5,970,575	6,750,000	Nanking, China	1,455,000	....
Boston, USA	601,000	3,855,000	Naples, Italy	1,221,859	1,975,000
Brussels, Belgium	153,405	2,020,000	New Orleans, USA	569,000	1,131,000
Bucharest, Rumania	1,528,562	1,642,651	New York, USA	7,605,000	17,150,000
Budapest, Hungary	2,049,100	2,475,000	Odessa, USSR	1,002,000	1,050,000
Buenos Aires, Argentina	2,972,453	8,625,000	Osaka, Japan	2,802,065	14,350,000
Cairo, Egypt	4,961,000	6,600,000	Paris, France	2,290,900	9,150,000
Calcutta, India	3,148,746	9,100,000	Peking, China	4,800,000	7,570,000
Canton, China	1,867,000	....	Philadelphia, USA	1,820,000	5,280,000
Caracas, Venezuela	1,658,500	2,475,000	Pittsburgh, USA	472,000	2,240,000
Casablanca, Morocco	1,506,373	1,575,000	Prague, Czechoslovakia	1,091,449	1,230,000
Chicago, USA	3,115,000	7,655,000	Pusan, Korea	1,880,710	....
Chungking, China	2,165,000		Rangoon, Burma	1,854,000	....
Cleveland, USA	750,903	2,361,100	Rio de Janeiro, Brazil	4,252,009	7,000,000
Cologne, Germany	832,396	1,700,000	Rome, Italy	2,833,103	3,075,000
Copenhagen, Denmark	562,405	1,515,000	Rotterdam, Netherlands	635,910	1,100,000
Dallas, USA	859,000	2,470,000	Saigon, Vietnam	1,804,880	2,750,000
Denver, USA	506,000	1,285,000	St. Louis, USA	538,000	2,270,000
Delhi, India	3,706,558	4,500,000	San Diego, USA	765,000	1,355,000
Detroit, USA	1,355,000	4,530,000	San Francisco, USA	675,000	4,450,000
Genoa, Italy	813,256	880,000	Santiago, Chile	517,473	2,925,000
Glasgow, Scotland	905,032	1,925,000	São Paulo, Brazil	5,921,796	8,050,000
Gorki, USSR	1,283,000	1,775,000	Seattle, USA	490,000	1,788,000
Guadalajara, Mexico	1,411,900	1,800,000	Seoul, Korea	5,536,377	5,900,000
Hamburg, Germany	1,751,621	2,300,000	Shanghai, China	7,900,000	10,820,000
Harbin, China	1,814,000	....	Shenyang, China	2,423,000	....
Havana, Cuba	1,755,400	1,800,000	Singapore, Singapore	2,074,507	2,225,000
Houston, USA	1,369,000	2,140,000	Sofia, Bulgaria	919,000	1,035,480
Hyderabad, India	1,607,396	2,000,000	Stockholm, Sweden	1,353,359	671,226
Istanbul, Turkey	2,376,300	3,250,000	Sydney, Australia	55,770	2,898,330
Jakarta, Indonesia	4,576,009	4,650,000	Taipei, Taiwan	2,003,604	3,050,000
Johannesburg, S. Africa	654,682	2,550,000	Tehran, Iran	3,858,000	4,400,000
Kanpur, India	1,154,388	1,320,000	Tel Aviv, Israel	367,600	1,215,000
Karachi, Pakistan	2,850,000	3,498,634	Tientsin, China	3,800,000	4,280,000
Kharkov, USSR	1,357,000	1,625,000	Tokyo, Japan	8,678,642	23,800,000
Kiev, USSR	1,947,000	2,140,000	Toronto, Canada	712,786	2,628,043
Kobe, Japan	1,351,651	....	Tsingtao, China	1,144,000	....
Kyoto, Japan	1,438,714	....	Turin, Italy	1,199,006	1,670,000
Lahore, Pakistan	2,050,000	2,200,000	Victoria, Hong Kong	521,612	3,575,000
Leningrad, USSR	3,850,000	5,000,000	Vienna, Austria	1,614,841	1,940,000
Lima, Peru	340,339	3,350,000	Warsaw, Poland	1,410,000	1,875,000
Lisbon, Portugal	774,500	1,800,000	Washington, D.C., USA	715,000	3,190,000
Liverpool, England	561,100	1,595,000	Wuhan, China	2,226,000	....
London, England	7,167,600	10,475,000	Yokohama, Japan	2,562,291	....

The source of the above data was the *Rand McNally Commercial Atlas & Marketing Guide*, 1976. The figures for the cities in the U.S. are 1975 Rand McNally estimates. The populations for the foreign cities were derived from censuses, official estimates and unofficial estimates.

ANTARCTICA

Isolated, inaccessible, and for a long time undiscovered, the continent of Antarctica received special attention from several nations during the International Geophysical Year of 1957–58. Improved equipment and techniques made possible the accumulation of much new data concerning the area, topography, sea bottom, weather, depth of ice, mineral resources, animal and vegetable life, fossils, and other aspects of the great Ice Age land mass which surrounds the South Pole.

To analyze and evaluate all the information thus obtained is a major undertaking which may require several years during which important additional findings are certain to be made in the continuation of some investigations beyond the time originally fixed for the IGY studies.

Conditions are such as to make international cooperation in Antarctic exploration cordial and promising. It is true that some overlapping territorial claims here have been made by different countries from time to time, dating back to Kerguelen's identification of "South France" at longitude 50 in 1771 and English explorer Cook's discovery of new land in 1773, when he made the first recorded crossing of the Antarctic Circle. As additional land masses were discovered, other claims were entered, particularly by Britain, Australia, and New Zealand and, by implication, the United States through the establishment of outposts in "Little America" by Admiral Richard Byrd. However, since the continent is not suitable for colonizing, and since the utilization of its mineral resources is not feasible at this time, there has been comparatively slight political rivalry between the nations that have sent exploring parties.

Because of Antarctica's remote location, immense area, and forbidding climate, its exploration is a major challenge to world scientists. Being an irregular land mass of 6,000,000 miles, extending roughly in a circle from the South Pole to meet the Atlantic, Pacific, and Indian oceans, it contrasts sharply with the Arctic region, whose center is an ice-covered sea and whose land boundaries within the Arctic Circle are marked by Canada, Alaska, and Siberia. People, timber, vegetation, and rich animal and mineral resources are found within the Arctic Circle, but not within the Antarctic, where winds reaching 100 miles an hour blow across snow-covered plateaus and temperatures of -80 are not uncommon. In earlier periods of exploration, sailing through "pack ice" or traversing frozen surfaces by dog sledges called for unexampled heroism and hardihood. More recently, the problem of transportation has been made easier by the use of airplanes and motor-driven vehicles such as the modern "snocats" and "weasels," but the storms and crevasses remain, and also the "white-out" peril to flyers.

For the United States, "Operation Deepfreeze," organized by the late Admiral Byrd and commanded by Admiral George Dufek brought to the task of IGY exploration the experience gained by Admiral Byrd's epoch-making 1928 expedition and such later ones as "Operation Highjump" of 1947 and its sequel "Operation Windmill." For the British, a Commonwealth Transantarctic expedition featured cooperation and friendly rivalry between Dr. Vivian Fuchs and Sir Edmund Hillary of New Zealand, best known as the conqueror of Mount Everest. In their race by separate overland routes to the South Pole, Hillary arrived first, on January 4, 1958, and Fuchs on January 19. Explorers had flown over the Pole not long before, but Hillary and Fuchs were the first in 46 years to reach it by the land route. In fact, there was a striking resemblance between this latest venture and the one that led to the reaching of the South Pole five weeks apart by Amundsen and Scott in the Antarctic "summer" of December-January, 1911–12. The tragic fate of Captain Scott soon after his triumph and his personal record of the last days have made his story one that is both inspiring and poignant.

To review the less dramatic and more prosaic aspects of the latest Antarctica explorations, we may note a few of the observations and estimates that have so far been reported. It is too soon to use the word "conclusions," for scientists are notably careful about expressing final judgments. However, some typical researches and their tentative results may be cited at this early stage of the investigation. For example, studies of the sea bottom were made to determine approximately when the Ice Age took over. It was believed that the seas were free of ice until about 3000 B. C. The Geomagnetic South Pole was relocated about 600 miles west of its earlier assumed location. Ore specimens of high-grade manganese silicate were found on Clark Peninsula. Seismic soundings proved some ice-covered land to be 7,000 feet above sea level. In addition to previously-known mountain peaks 15,000 feet high, new ones ranging up to 11,000 feet were sighted. Bedrock at the South Pole was estimated to be 903 feet above sea level but covered by 8,297 feet of snow and ice. Along a bank of the Upper Mawson Glacier, a New Zealand party found a coal field of six seams, each 6 to 12 feet thick. A Japanese party reported finding uranium. Valleys almost free of ice and snow were found extending north from the Hill Glacier in the Great Antarctic Horst Mountains. One party discovered a glacier-made gorge 9,000 feet deep and 30 miles long. When these countless other facts have been brought together and studied, the hitherto mysterious continent of Antarctica will be much better understood.

NOTED WATERFALLS

NAME	Location	Height (feet)
Angel	Venezuela	3,300
Bridal Veil	Yosemite, Cal.	620
Gastein	Austria	480
Gavarnie	Pyrenees	1,385
George VI	British Guiana	1,600
Grand Falls	Labrador	316
Great Falls	Montana	526
Great Falls	Potomac River	35
Great Umgeni	Natal	364
Harsprang	Sweden	110
Iguassu	Argentina	215
Illilouette	Yosemite, Cal.	370
Juanacatlan	Mexico	70
Kar Kloof	Natal	350
Krimmler	Austria	1,300
Kukenaam	Guiana	2,100
Minnehaha	Minnesota	60
Montmorency	Quebec	265
Multnomah	Oregon	607
Nevada Falls	California	594
Niagara Falls	New York	167
Portage Falls	Portageville, N. Y.	110
Rhine Falls	Schaffhausen	710
Ribbon Falls	Yosemite, Cal.	1,612
Roraima	Guiana	2,000
Ruikanfos	Norway	805
St. Anthony	Minnesota	50
Seculéjo	Pyrenees Mts.	820
Sellesche	Switzerland	128
Seneca Falls	New York	50
Shoshone	Idaho	210
Skykjefos	Norway	660
Snoqualmie	Washington	267
Staubbach	Switzerland	870
Sutherland	New Zealand	1,904
Takakkow	British Columbia	1,400
Taughannock	New York	215
Tequendama	Colombia, S. Am.	475
Terni	Italy	650
Trollhattan	Sweden	108
Twin Falls	British Columbia	400
Vernal Fall	California	320
Victoria	Africa	343
Voringsfos	Norway	520
Widow's Tears	Yosemite, Cal.	1,170
Yellowstone (2 falls)	Wyoming	420
Upper	Wyoming	110
Lower	Wyoming	310
Yosemite (3 falls)	California	2,370
Upper	California	1,430
Middle	California	620
Lower	California	320

NOTED WATERFALLS

At George VI Falls, in tropical Guyana, the Uitshi River drops 1600 feet.

The Great Falls of the Potomac River, in Maryland, is an interesting and picturesque example of the cascade type of waterfall.

Niagara Falls undoubtedly is the world's best known waterfall. This view shows the American side of the falls, which drops 167 feet.

Montmorency Falls, 265 feet, is one of Canada's most beautiful waterfalls. It is eight miles from Quebec.

Iguassu Falls is on the river which is the boundary between Argentina and Brazil. The water drops 215 feet.

Victoria Falls, on the Zambesi River in South Africa, is 343 feet high and is one of the world's most spectacular.

There are two great falls on the Yellowstone River in Wyoming. This is the Lower Falls. It is 310 feet high.

FAMOUS VOLCANOES

The beautifully shaped Mayon volcano rises 8000 feet on Luzon, P. I. It has a perfect cone and is the most active of the Philippine volcanoes. Mayon erupted 26 times during the 19th Century and in 1914 destroyed several villages and killed several persons. The volcanoes in this area are a part of the volcanic mountain chain known as the Circum-Pacific system, often called the "Circle of Fire."

Vesuvius is the world's best-known volcano. It is in Italy, southeast of Naples, and is the only active volcano on the mainland of Europe. Its earliest recorded eruption was in A.D. 79, when it buried Pompeii. Its latest eruption was in 1944.

Caroli is a beautiful but dangerous Aleutian volcano. A wisp of smoke at its top shows that it is active. The most recent Aleutian eruption was Shisaldin volcano, which burst into action in 1947.

On the Lipari Islands, north of Sicily, is Stromboli volcano. It is about 3000 feet high and is called the *Lighthouse of the Mediterranean* because of its activity. In ancient times, these islands were identified with Vulcan, fire god of Roman myths.

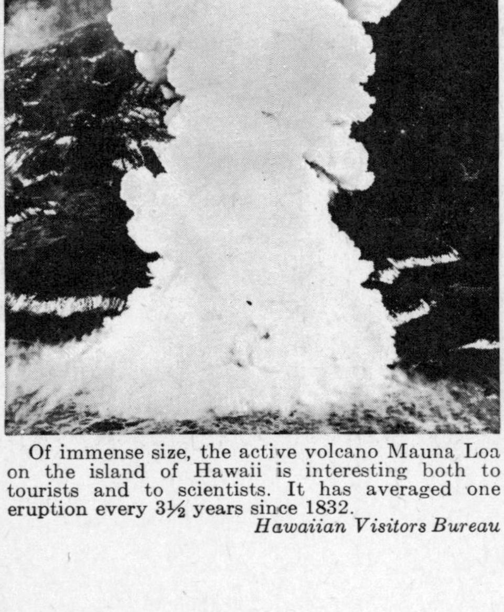

Of immense size, the active volcano Mauna Loa on the island of Hawaii is interesting both to tourists and to scientists. It has averaged one eruption every 3½ years since 1832.

Hawaiian Visitors Bureau

Beginning in 1943 with smoke, then lava, issuing from the surface of a cornfield near San Juan, Mexico, Paricutin rose within a year to a height of over 2000 feet.

NOTED MOUNTAINS AND VOLCANOES

The following list is a selection representative of important mountains. It contains one or more of the higher peaks in various regions of the world, includes some of the greatest volcanic mountains, and embraces also a number of the most active volcanoes. All volcanic mountains, including extinct, quiescent, and active volcanoes, are in italics; some of the more active volcanoes are indicated by an asterisk thus, *Stromboli**.

Name of Mountain or Peak	Location	Height Feet
Aconcagua	Chile-Argentina	22,835
Adams	Washington	12,307
Altar	Ecuador	17,300
Ancohuma	Bolivia	21,489
Antisana	Ecuador	18,714
Apo	Philippine Is.	9,690
Ararat	Turkey	16,945
Arequipa (Misti)	Peru	20,013
*Asama**	Japan	8,200
*Aso-San**	Japan	5,225
Baker	Washington	10,750
Baldy Peak	New Mexico	12,491
*Bandai-San**	Japan	5,968
Ben Nevis	Scotland	4,406
Blackburn	Alaska	16,140
Borah Peak	Idaho	12,655
Bruce	Australia	4,024
Cayambe	Ecuador	19,014
Cenis, Mt.	France	11,755
Chimborazo	Ecuador	20,577
Chinati Peak	Texas	7,730
Clingmans Dome	Tennessee	6,642
*Colima**	Mexico	14,240
Cook	New Zealand	12,349
Cosiguina	Nicaragua	2,776
*Cotopaxi**	Ecuador	19,344
Cradle	Australia	5,069
Crillon	Alaska	12,725
Demavend	Iran	18,600
Dhaulagiri	Nepal	26,810
Elbert	Colorado	14,431
Elbrus	Russia	18,481
Elgon	Uganda-Kenya	14,178
*Erebus**	Antarctica	13,202
*Etna**	Sicily	10,705
Everest	Nepal	29,002
Fairweather	British Columbia	15,300
*Fuego**	Guatemala	12,582
Fuji	Japan	12,388
Galdhoppigen	Norway	8,097
Gannett Peak	Wyoming	13,785
Godwin-Austen (K 2)	Kashmir	28,250
Haleakala	Hawaii	10,032
*Hekla**	Iceland	4,707
Hermon	Syria-Lebanon	9,232
Holy Cross	Colorado	13,986
Hood	Oregon	11,245
Huascaran	Peru	22,205
Humphreys Peak	Chile-Argentina	19,130
Illampu (Sorata)	Bolivia	21,275
Illimani	Bolivia	21,185
*Izalco**	El Salvador	6,184
Iztaccihuatl	Mexico	17,342
Jorullo	Mexico	4,330
Jungfrau	Switzerland	13,653
Kanchenjunga	India-Nepal	28,156
Katahdin	Maine	5,268
*Katmai**	Alaska	7,000
Kenya	Kenya	17,040
*Kilauea**	Hawaii	4,000
Kilimanjaro (Kibo Peak)	Tanzania	19,565
Kings Peak	Utah	13,498
Kosciusko	Australia	7,305
*Lassen**	California	10,453
Lebanon	Lebanon	10,131
Llullaillaco	Chile	22,015
Logan, Mt.	Yukon	19,850
Loma Tina	Dominican Rep.	9,239
Longs Peak	Colorado	14,255
McKinley	Alaska	20,270
Maipu	Chile-Argentina	17,355
Marcy	New York	5,344
Margherita	Uganda-Congo	16,795
Matterhorn	Switzerland	14,701
Mauna Kea	Hawaii	13,825
*Mauna Loa**	Hawaii	13,675
Mercedario	Argentina	21,885
Mitchell	North Carolina	6,684
Mont Blanc	France	15,781
Monte Rosa	Italy	15,203
Morrison	Formosa	14,000

NOTED MOUNTAINS AND VOLCANOES—Con.

Name of Mountain or Peak	Location	Height Feet
Mount of Olives	Jordan	2,680
Olympus	Greece	9,570
Orizaba	Mexico	18,700
Orohena	Tahiti	7,618
Parnassus	Greece	8,062
Peaks of Otter	Virginia	4,001
*Pelée**	Martinique, W.I.	4,429
Perdu, Mont	France	10,997
Perote, Cofre de	Mexico	14,048
Pico, Peak of	Azores	7,611
Pikes Peak	Colorado	14,110
Popocatepetl	Mexico	17,877
Rainier	Washington	14,408
Robson	British Columbia	12,972
Rogers	Virginia	5,720
Roraima	Venezuela	9,219
Ruapehu	New Zealand	9,175
Sajama	Bolivia	21,047
Saint Elias	Alaska	18,008
Saint Helens	Washington	9,671
San Francisco	Arizona	12,655
*San Miguel**	El Salvador	7,064
Shasta	California	14,162
Simplon	Switzerland	11,117
Sinai, Mt. (Jebal Musa)	Egypt	7,359
Sir Sanford	British Columbia	11,590
Snehaetta	Norway	7,550
Snowdon	Wales	3,560
*Soufrière, La**	St. Vincent, W.I.	4,048
Spruce Knob	West Virginia	4,860
*Stromboli**	Lipari Is., N. of Sicily	3,038
Teide	Canary Is.	12,000
Terror	Antarctica	10,750
Tolima	Colombia	18,438
Toluca	Mexico	15,020
Truchas	New Mexico	13,110
*Tungurahua**	Ecuador	16,512
Tupungato	Chile-Argentina	21,490
Vancouver	Alaska-Yukon	15,700
*Vesuvius**	Italy	3,891
Washington	New Hampshire	6,288
Wheeler Peak	Nevada	13,058
Whitney	California	14,495
Wrangell	Alaska	14,005

IMPORTANT MOUNTAIN PASSES

Pass	Location	Altitude (feet)
Athabaska	Alberta	5,736
Berthoud	Colorado	11,314
Bolan	Baluchistan	5,880
Brenner	Austrian Alps	4,495
Cajon	California	3,800
Chilkat	Yukon	4,950
Chilkoot	Alaska	3,500
Crownest	Alberta	4,450
Donner	California	7,135
Fremont	Colorado	11,318
Kearsarge	California	11,823
Khyber	Afghanistan	3,500
Kicking Horse	Alberta-Br.Col.	5,339
Kootenay (North)	Alberta	6,774
Kootenay (South)	Alberta	7,100
La Veta	Colorado	9,382
Logan	Montana	6,664
Loveland	Colorado	11,992
Mont Cenis	France	6,831
Rabbit Ears	Colorado	9,680
Raton	Colorado	7,834
Rogers	British Columbia	4,340
St. Bernard, Great	Swiss Alps	8,100
St. Gotthard	Swiss Alps	6,936
San Gorgonio	California	2,804
Shipka	Bulgaria	4,166
Simplon	Swiss Alps	6,589
Simpson	Alberta	6,650
Tehachapi	California	3,790
Tennessee	Colorado	10,424
Truckee	California	5,800
Uspallata (Cumbre)	Chile	12,650
Vermilion	Alberta	5,264
White Pass	Alaska-Br.Col.	2,888
Wolf Creek	Colorado	10,850
Yellowhead (Tete Jaune)	Alberta-Br.Col.	3,711

PRINCIPAL ISLANDS OF THE WORLD

Name	Location	Dependency, Territory, or part of	Discovery, Conquest, or Settlement: By Whom †	Date	Area Sq. Mi.	Population	Chief City or Town
Aleutian	Bering S.-Pac. O.	Alaska	Russians	1741	6,821	8,500	Unalaska
Azores	Atl. O. W. of Port.	Portugal	Cabral, *P.*	1432	893	603,000	Ponta Delgada
Baffin	Arctic O.	Canada	Baffin, *E.*	1616	183,870	2,052	Cape Dorset
Bahama	Atl. O. E. of Fla.	Bahama*	Columbus, *S.*	1492	5,353	168,812	Nassau
Balearic	Mediterranean S.	Spain	Romans	123‡	1,936	542,000	Palma
Barbados	West Indies	Barbados*	British	1625	166	254,000	Bridgetown
Bermuda	Atl. O. N. of W. Ind.	Great Britain	Bermudez, *S.*	1515	21	53,000	Hamilton
Borneo	East Indies	Indonesia, Malaysia	De Gomez, *P.*	1518	288,150	5,200,000	Banjermasin
Bornholms	Baltic Sea	Denmark	Norse	B.C.?	217	47,017	Rönne
Canary Is.	Atl. O. W. of Afr.	Spain	French	1334	2,807	1,160,000	Las Palmas
Cape Verde	Atl. O. W. of Afr.	Portugal	Cadamosta, *P.*	1456	1,557	272,071	São Vicente
Ceylon	Ind. O. S. of India	Sri Lanka*	Portuguese	1505	25,332	12,711,143	Colombo
Corsica	Mediterranean S.	France	Phocaeans	560‡	3,367	219,300	Bastia
Crete	Mediterranean S.	Greece	Prehistoric	3400‡	3,218	456,642	Heraklion
Cuba	West Indies	Cuba*	Columbus, *S.*	1492	44,206	9,170,000	Havana
Cyprus	Mediterranean S.	Cyprus*	Egyptians	1500‡	3,572	631,778	Nicosia
Elba	Mediterranean S.	Italy	Romans	B.C.	86	28,500	Portoferraio
Falkland Is.	Atlantic O.	Great Britain	Davis, *E.*	1592	4.700	1,759	Stanley
Faroe	N. Atlantic O.	Denmark	Norwegians	9th c.	540	40,441	Thorshavn
Fiji	S. Pacific Ocean	Fiji*	Tasman, *D.*	1643	7,055	535,357	Suva
Gotland	Baltic Sea	Sweden	Swedes	9th c.	1,225	54,174	Visby
Great Britain	Atl. O.-North Sea	Great Britain	Romans	55‡	88,752	53,978,538	London
Greenland	Arctic O.	Denmark	Norwegians	982	840,000	49,502	Julianehaab
Guadeloupe	West Indies	France	Columbus, *S.*	1493	657	334,000	Pointe-à-Pitre
Guam	East Indies	United States	Magellan, *P.*	1521	209	86,926	Agana
Hawaiian Is.**	Pacific Ocean	United States	Jas. Cook, *E.*	1778	6,425	769,913	Honolulu
Hispaniola	West Indies	Haiti Dom. Rep.*	Columbus, *S.*	1492	29,400	8,456,005	Port au Prince
Iceland	No. Atlantic O.	Iceland*	Norwegians	870	39,758	216,628	Reykjavik
Ireland	Irish S.-Atl. O.	British Isles	Ancient Celts	B.C.	32,598	4,514,313	Dublin
Isle of Man	Irish Sea	Great Britain	Ancient Celts	B.C.	211	56,289	Douglas
Isle of Wight	English Channel	Great Britain	Romans	43	147	109,284	Newport
Jamaica	West Indies	Jamaica*	Columbus, *S.*	1494	4,411	1,861,300	Kingston
Japan ††	S. of Japan-Pac. O.	Japan*	Portuguese	1542	142,726	108,430,000	Tokyo
Java	East Indies	Indonesia	Portuguese	1511	51,032	76,000,000	Jakarta
Long Island	Long Is. So.-Atl. O.	New York	Hudson, *E.*	1609	1,723	6,403,852	Brooklyn
Macias Nguema	G. of Guinea, Afr.	Equatorial Guinea	Portuguese	1486	782	62,612	Malabo
Madagascar (Malagasy)	Ind. O. E. of Afr.	Malagasy*	Portuguese	1506	229,233	7,185,000	Tananarive
Madeira	Atl. O. W. of Afr.	Portugal	Portuguese	1419	308	269,000	Funchal
Malta	Mediterranean S.	Malta*	Phœnicians	1000‡	122	317,980	Valletta
Manhattan	Hudson R.-East R.	United States	Verrazano, *I.*	1524	22	1,509,327	New York§
Marshall Is.	N. Pacific	U. S. Trustee	British	1788	160	25,044	Jabor
Martinique	West Indies	France	Spanish	1493	420	342,000	Fort de France
Mauritius	Ind. O. E. of Afr.	Mauritius*	Portuguese	1505	720	826,199	Port Louis
Nantucket	Atlantic O.	Massachusetts	Gosnold, *E.*	1602	57	3,824	Nantucket
New Caledonia	Oceania	France	Jas. Cook, *E.*	1774	7,374	131,665	Noumea
Newfoundland	Atlantic O.	Canada	Cabot, *E.*	1497	143,045	522,104	St. John's
New Guinea	East Indies	Australia	Portuguese	1526	316,615	2,489,935	Port Moresby
New Zealand‡‡	Tasman S.-S. Pac.O.	New Zealand*	Tasman, *D.*	1642	103,736	3,105,400	Auckland
Novaya Zemlya	Barents S.-Kava S.	Russia	English	1556	31,900	100	
Orkney	Atlantic Ocean	Scotland	Ancient Picts	B.C.?	376	17,462	Kirkwall
Philippines§§	East Indies	Philippines*	Magellan, *P.*	1521	115,830	42,517,330	Manila
Prince Edward	G. of St. Lawrence	Canada	Cabot, *E.*	1497	2,184	111,641	Charlottetown
Puerto Rico	West Indies	United States	Columbus, *S.*	1493	3,435	2,712,033	San Juan
Réunion	Ind. O. E. of Afr.	France	Portuguese	1513	969	476,700	St. Denis
Saint Helena	S. Atl. O. W. of Afr.	Great Britain	Portuguese	1502	47	4,952	Jamestown
Sakhalin	Okhotsk S.	Russia	Dutch	1650	24,560	631,000	Alexandrovsk
Samoa, Amer.	S. Pacific Ocean	United States	Roggoveen, *D.*	1722	76	27,159	Pago Pago
Santa Catalina	G. of St. Catalina	California	Cabrillo, *P.*	1542	85	1,457	Avalon
Sardinia	Mediterranean S.	Italy	Carthaginians	500‡	9,301	1,473,800	Cagliara
Shetland	Atl. O.-North Sea	Scotland	Ancient Picts	B.C.?	550	18,445	Lerwick
Sicily	Mediterranean S.	Italy	Phœnicians	1000‡	9,925	4,680,715	Palermo
Spitsbergen (Svalbard)	Arctic Ocean	Norway	Barents, *D.*	1596	24,294	3,472	Longyearbyen
Staten	New York Bay	United States	Verrazano, *I.*	1524	60	221,981	New York§
Sulawesi (Celebes)	East Indies	Indonesia	Portuguese	1512	72,986	8,500,000	Makassar
Sumatra	East Indies	Indonesia	Portuguese	1508	167,480	20,800,000	Medan
Tahiti	S. Pacific Ocean	France	Spain	1606	402	84,552	Papeete
Taiwan (Formosa)	China Sea	Nationalist China	Portuguese	1590	13,892	16,500,000	Taipei
Tasmania	Bass St.-Ant. O.	Australia	Tasman, *D.*	1642	26,215	400,431	Hobart
Tierra del Fuego	St. of Magellan-Antarctic O.	Chile-Argentina	Magellan, *P.*	1520	8,074	8,000	Ushuaia
Trinidad	West Indies	Trinidad and Tobago	Columbus, *S.*	1498	1,864	892,317	Port of Spain
Vancouver	St.of Georgia-Pac.O.	Brit. Columbia	Vancouver, *E.*	1792	12,408	333,950	Victoria
Victoria	Arctic O.	Canada			81,930	41,878	
Virgin Is.	West Indies	United States	Columbus, *S.*	1493	133	63,200	Charlotte Amalie
Zanzibar	Ind. O. E. of Afr.	Tanzania	Egyptians	B.C.	640	190,117	Zanzibar

* Independent state. † Capital letters in italics, following names, indicate nationality of the discovery, thus *D.* signifies Dutch; *E.*, English; *I.*, Italian; *P.*, Portuguese; *S.*, Spanish. ‡ Before Christ. § Island forms part of New York City. ** Seven inhabited is., largest being Hawaii (4,021 sq.m.), Maui (728 sq.m.), Oahu (589 sq.m.). †† Four main islands, largest being Honshu (88,925 sq.m.). ‡‡ Two largest islands in group: South I. (58,093 sq.m.) and North I. (44,281 sq.m.). §§ Two largest islands in group: Luzon (40,420 sq.m.) and Mindanao (36,537 sq.m.).

IMPORTANT RIVERS OF THE WORLD

Name	Location	Length Miles	Drainage Basin Sq. Miles	Outlet	Largest City or Town on Banks
Amazon	South America	3,400	2,500,000	Atlantic Ocean	Pará
Amur	Northeastern Asia	2,700	780,000	Sakhalin Gulf	Blagovieschtchensk
Arkansas	United States	2,000	189,000	Mississippi R.	Tulsa
Assiniboine	Manitoba-Saskatchewan	450	52,600	Red R. of North	Winnipeg
Athabasca	Alberta	765	58,910	Lake Athabasca	Athabaska
Brahmaputra	India-Pakistan	1,800	425,000	Bay of Bengal	Dibrughur
Clyde	Scotland	100	1,480	Irish Sea	Glasgow
Colorado	United States-Mexico	2,000	250,000	G. of Cal.	Yuma
Columbia	Canada-United States	1,400	298,000	Pacific Ocean	Vancouver, Wash.
Congo	W. Equat. Africa	3,000	1,500,000	Atlantic Ocean	Kinshasa
Connecticut	New England	350	11,000	Long Is. Sound	Hartford
Cumberland	S. E. United States	688	18,000	Ohio River	Nashville
Danube	Southeastern Europe	1,750	300,000	Black Sea	Vienna
Darling	Australia	1,160	200,000	Murray River	Bourke
Delaware	E. United States	360	12,012	Delaware Bay	Philadelphia
Dnieper	S. European Russia	1,400	202,000	Black Sea	Kiev
Don	S. E. European Russia	1,300	166,000	Sea of Azov	Rostov
Douro	Spain-Portugal	500	37,500	Atlantic Ocean	Porto
Dvina	Russia	1,000	140,000	White Sea	Archangel
Ebro	Spain	470	30,000	Mediterranean Sea	Saragossa
Elbe	Germany	700	55,000	North Sea	Hamburg
Euphrates	Syria, Iraq	1,700	260,000	Persian Gulf	Basra
Fraser	British Columbia	750	91,700	Strait of Georgia	New Westminster
Ganges	India	1,500	400,000	Bay of Bengal	Cawnpore
Hudson	New York	300	13,000	New York Bay	New York
Hwang	China	2,600	400,000	Gulf of Pechili	Lanchow
Indus	Pakistan	1,800	372,000	Arabian Sea	Hyderabad
Irrawaddy	Burma	1,250	158,000	Bay of Bengal	Mandalay
Jordan	Jordan	200	1,500	Dead Sea	
Kuskokwim	Alaska	700	50,000	Bering Sea	Bethel
Lena	Siberia	2,800	900,000	Arctic Ocean	Yakutsk
Loire	France	650	45,000	Bay of Biscay	Nantes
Mackenzie	N. W. Terr., Canada	2,525	680,000	Arctic Ocean	Ft. Providence
Marne	France	325	4,894	Seine	Chalôns-sur-Marne
Mekong	Indo-China	2,600	280,000	South China Sea	Phnom Penh
Meuse	Belgium-France	575	12,740	North Sea	Liège
Mississippi	United States	2,500	725,000	Gulf of Mexico	Saint Louis
Missouri	United States	3,000	525,000	Mississippi R.	Kansas City
Missouri-Mississippi*	United States-Canada	4,200	1,250,000	Gulf of Mexico	Saint Louis
Murray	Australia	1,450	270,000	Indian Ocean	Albury
Nelson*	Canada	1,660	370,000	Hudson Bay	Port Nelson
Niger	Western Africa	2,600	600,000	Gulf of Guinea	Bamako
Nile	Cent. and N. E. Africa	4,145	1,100,000	Mediterranean Sea	Cairo
Ob	N. W. Siberia	2,500	1,125,200	Gulf of Ob	Barnaul
Oder	Germany-Poland	560	43,000	Baltic Sea	Breslau
Ohio	Eastern United States	975	214,000	Mississippi R.	Pittsburgh
Orange	Southwestern Africa	1,300	400,000	Atlantic Ocean	Hopetown
Orinoco	South America	1,500	368,000	Atlantic Ocean	Ciudad Bolivar
Ottawa	Ontario-Quebec	685	86,000	St. Lawrence R	Ottawa
Peace	British Columbia-Alberta	1,065	117,000	Slave River	Peace River
Plata-Parana*	South America	2,500	1,200,000	Atlantic Ocean	Rosario
Po	Italy	420	27,000	Adriatic Sea	Turin
Potomac	Eastern United States	450	15,000	Chesapeake Bay	Washington
Red	Texas-Arkansas	1,200	90,000	Mississippi R.	Shreveport
Red River of the North	United States-Canada	545	63,400	Lake Winnipeg	Winnipeg
Rhine	N. W. Europe	800	75,000	North Sea	Cologne
Rhone	France	500	38,000	Mediterranean Sea	Lyon
Rio Grande	S. W. United States	2,000	240,000	Gulf of Mexico	El Paso
Sacramento	California	400	27,100	Suisun Bay	Sacramento
Saguenay	Quebec, Canada	405	35,900	St. Lawrence	Chicoutimi
St. Lawrence	United States-Canada	750	500,000	Gulf of St. Law.	Montreal
San Francisco	Eastern Brazil	1,800	200,000	Atlantic Ocean	Penedo
San Joaquin	California	350	30,000	Sacramento R.	Stockton
Seine	France	480	30,000	English Channel	Paris
Shannon	Ireland	250	4,500	Atlantic Ocean	Limerick
Susquehanna	N. E. United States	500	....	Chesapeake Bay	Harrisburg
Tagus	Portugal	565	31,850	Atlantic Ocean	Lisbon
Tennessee	S. E. United States	1,200	44,000	Ohio River	Knoxville
Thames	England	215	6,000	North Sea	London
Tiber	Italy	240	6,840	Mediterranean	Rome
Ural	Russia	1,400	85,000	Caspian Sea	Orenburg
Vistula	Poland-Danzig	650	76,000	Baltic Sea	Warsaw
Volga	Russia	2,300	563,300	Caspian Sea	Saratov
Weser	Germany	300	18,530	North Sea	Bremen
Yangtze	China	3,300	650,000	East China Sea	Nanking
Yenisei	Mongolia-Siberia	3,000	1,000,000	Arctic Ocean	Krasnoyarsk
Yukon	Alaska-Canada	2,300	330,000	Bering Sea	Dawson
Zambezi	South Africa	2,200	600,000	Indian Ocean	Livingstone

* River system.

Country	Area (sq. miles)	Population		Capital	Largest City	Form of Gov't[1]
		Thousands	No. Per Sq. Mile			
Afghanistan	252,000	18,796	74.6	Kabul	Kabul	P.D.
Albania	11,100	2,578	214.2	Tirana	Tirana	P.R.
Algeria	896,593	16,275	18.2	Algiers	Algiers	Isl. Rep.
Argentina	1,072,168	25,050	23.4	Buenos Aires	Buenos Aires	M.O.
Australia	2,967,900	13,339	4.5	Canberra	Sydney	P.D.
Austria	32,375	7,528	282.5	Vienna	Vienna	Rep.
Bahamas	5,382	197	36.6	Nassau	Nassau	B.C.R.
Bahrain	256	239	933.6	Manama	Manama	
Bangladesh	55,126	74,991	1,360.4	Dacca	Dacca	B.C.R.
Barbados	166	244	1,469.9	Bridgetown	Bridgetown	B.C.R.
Belgium	11,782	9,772	829.4	Brussels	Brussels	C.M.
Benin (Dahomey)	43,475	3,029	69.7	Porto-Novo	Cotonou	M.O.
Bhutan	18,000	1,146	63.7	Thimphu	Thimphu	A.M.
Bolivia	424,165	5,470	12.9	Sucre[2]	La Paz	Rep.*
Botswana	222,000	661	3.0	Gaberones	Kanye	B.C.R.
Brazil	3,286,488	104,243	31.7	Brasilia	Sao Paulo	M.O.
Bulgaria	42,823	8,706	202.7	Sofia	Sofia	P.R.
Burma	261,789	30,310	115.8	Rangoon	Rangoon	M.O.
Burundi	10,747	3,678	342.2	Bujumbura	Bujumbura	Rep.
Cambodia (Khmer Rep.)	69,898	7,888	112.9	Phnom Penh	Phnom Penh	Rep.
Cameroon	179,558	6,282	35.0	Yaounde	Douala	Rep.
Canada	3,851,809	22,479	5.8	Ottawa	Montreal	P.D.
Cape Verde Is.	1,557	291	186.9	Praia	Mindelo	Rep.
Central African Rep.	241,305	1,752	7.3	Bangui	Bangui	M.O.
Chad	495,750	3,949	8.0	Fort-Lamy	Fort-Lamy	Rep.
Chile	292,258	10,405	35.6	Santiago	Santiago	Rep.
China (Communist)	3,691,500	824,961	223.5	Peking	Shanghai	P.R.
China (Nationalist)	13,893	15,701	1,130.1	Taipei	Taipei	Rep.
Colombia	439,737	23,952	54.5	Bogota	Bogota	Rep.
Comoro Islands	863	298	345.3	Moroni	Moroni	Rep.
Congo (Brazzaville)	132,047	1,313	9.9	Brazzaville	Brazzaville	Rep.*
Costa Rica	19,652	1,921	97.7	San Jose	San Jose	Rep.
Cuba	42,827	9,090	212.2	Havana	Havana	Rep.*
Cyprus	3,572	641	179.5	Nicosia	Nicosia	B.C.R.
Czechoslovakia	49,374	14,686	297.4	Prague	Prague	S.R.
Democratic Yemen	61,890	1,590	25.7	Aden	Aden	Rep.
Denmark	16,630	5,045	303.4	Copenhagen	Copenhagen	C.M.
Dominican Republic	18,658	4,562	244.5	Santo Domingo	Santo Domingo	Rep.
Ecuador	109,484	6,552	59.8	Quito	Guayaquil	Rep.*
Egypt	386,900	36,417	94.1	Cairo	Cairo	Rep.
El Salvador	8,124	3,980	489.9	San Salvador	San Salvador	Rep.
Equatorial Guinea	10,830	303	28.0	Santa Isabel	Santa Isabel	Rep.
Ethiopia	471,800	27,239	57.7	Addis Ababa	Addis Ababa	C.M.
Fiji	7,055	560	79.4	Suva	Suva	B.C.R.
Finland	130,129	4,682	36.0	Helsinki	Helsinki	Rep.
France	210,039	52,507	250.0	Paris	Paris	Rep.
Gabon	103,347	1,106	10.7	Libreville	Libreville	Rep.
Gambia	4,467	510	114.2	Bathurst	Bathurst	B.C.R.
Germany, East	41,768	17,166	411.0	East Berlin	East Berlin	D.R.
Germany, West (F.R.)	95,985	62,041	646.4	Bonn	Hamburg	F.R.
West Berlin	186	2,173				
Ghana	92,100	9,607	104.3	Accra	Accra	Rep.
Greece	50,960	8,962	175.9	Athens	Athens	C.M.*
Grenada	133	107	804.5	St. George's	St. George's	B.C.R.
Guatemala	42,042	5,175	123.1	Guatemala City	Guatemala City	Rep.
Guinea	94,926	4,309	45.4	Conakry	Conakry	Rep.
Guinea-Bissau	13,948	517	37.1	Bissau	Bissau	Rep.
Guyana	83,000	774	9.3	Georgetown	Georgetown	B.C.R.
Haiti	10,714	4,514	421.3	Port-au-Prince	Port-au-Prince	Rep.*
Honduras	43,277	2,654	61.3	Tegucigalpa	Tegucigalpa	Rep.
Hungary	35,920	10,458	291.1	Budapest	Budapest	P.R.
Iceland	39,769	215	5.4	Reykjavik	Reykjavik	Rep.
India	1,266,602	586,266	462.9	New Delhi	Bombay	B.C.R.
Indonesia	782,663	127,586	163.0	Jakarta	Jakarta	Rep.
Iran	636,000	31,955	50.2	Teheran	Teheran	C.M.
Iraq	168,928	10,765	63.7	Baghdad	Baghdad	Rep.*
Ireland (Eire)	27,136	3,086	113.7	Dublin	Dublin	Rep.
Israel	7,992	3,299	412.8	Jerusalem	Tel Aviv-Jaffa	Rep.
Italy	116,313	55,361	476.0	Rome	Rome	Rep.
Ivory Coast	123,484	6,673	54.0	Abidjan	Abidjan	Rep.
Jamaica	4,244	1,998	470.8	Kingston	Kingston	P.D.
Japan	145,747	109,671	752.5	Tokyo	Tokyo	C.M.
Jordan	36,832	2,618	71.1	Amman	Amman	C.M.
Kenya	224,961	12,912	57.4	Nairobi	Nairobi	B.C.R.
Korea, North	46,800	15,439	329.9	Pyongyang	Pyongyang	P.R.
Korea, South	38,130	33,459	877.5	Seoul	Seoul	Rep.
Kuwait	6,880	929	135.0	Kuwait	Kuwait	R.M.
Laos	91,400	3,257	35.6	Vientiane	Vientiane	C.M.
Lebanon	3,950	2,782	704.3	Beirut	Beirut	Rep.
Lesotho	11,720	1,016	86.7	Maseru	Maseru	R.M.*

Note: For footnotes, see end of tabulation.

Country	Area (sq. miles)	Population		Capital	Largest City	Form of Gov't[1]
		Thousands	No. Per Sq. Mile			
Liberia	43,000	1,667	38.8	Monrovia	Monrovia	Rep.
Libya	675,000	2,352	3.5	Tripoli & Benghazi	Tripoli	M.O.
Luxembourg	999	342	342.3	Luxembourg	Luxembourg	C.M.
Malagasy, Rep. of	226,444	7,785	34.4	Tananarive	Tananarive	Rep.
Malawi	45,747	4,900	107.1	Zomba	Blantyre-Limbe	B.C.R.
Malaysia	127,316	11,700	91.9	Kuala Lumpur	Kuala Lumpur	C.M.
Maldive Islands	115	129	1,121.7	Male	Male	Rep.
Mali	478,822	5,557	11.6	Bamako	Bamako	Rep.*
Malta	122	298	2,442.6	Valletta	Valletta	B.C.R.
Mauritania	398,000	1,290	3.2	Nouakchott	Nouakchott	Isl. Rep.
Mauritius	787	872	1,108.0	Port-Louis	Port-Louis	B.C.R.
Mexico	761,604	58,118	76.3	Mexico City	Mexico City	Rep.
Mongolia	604,000	1,403	2.3	Ulan Bator	Ulan Bator	P.R.
Morocco	177,117	16,880	95.3	Rabat-Sale	Casablanca	C.M.
Mozambique	308,642	9,029	29.3	Maputo	Maputo	Rep.
Nepal	54,362	12,321	226.6	Katmandu	Katmandu	C.M.
Netherlands	15,892	13,541	852.1	Amsterdam[3]	Amsterdam	C.M.
New Zealand	103,736	3,027	29.2	Wellington	Christchurch	P.D.
Nicaragua	50,000	2,084	61.7	Managua	Managua	Rep.
Niger	489,000	4,476	9.2	Niamey	Niamey	Rep.
Nigeria	356,669	61,219	171.6	Lagos	Lagos	Rep.*
Norway	125,053	3,987	31.9	Oslo	Oslo	C.M.
Oman	82,000	743	9.1	Muscat	Salalah	Rep.
Pakistan	307,374	68,214	221.9	Islamabad	Karachi	Isl. Rep.
Panama	29,209	1,631	55.8	Panama City	Panama City	Rep.*
Papua New Guinea	178,260	2,652	14.9	Port Moresby	Port Moresby	B.C.R.
Paraguay	157,048	2,572	16.4	Asuncion	Asuncion	Rep.
Peru	496,224	14,531	29.3	Lima	Lima	M.O.
Philippines	115,800	41,457	358.0	Quezon City	Manila	Rep.
Poland	120,725	33,691	279.1	Warsaw	Warsaw	P.R.
Portugal	35,383	8,735	246.9	Lisbon	Lisbon	Rep.
Qatar	4,400	170	38.6	Doha	Doha	Rep.
Rhodesia	150,873	6,100	40.4	Salisbury	Bulawayo	B.C.R.
Rumania	91,700	21,029	229.3	Bucharest	Bucharest	S.R.
Rwanda	10,169	4,123	405.4	Kigali	Kigali	Rep.
Sao Tome & Principe	373	79	212.4	Sao Tome	Sao Tome	
Saudi Arabia	872,000	8,702	10.0	Riyadh	Riyadh	Mon.
Senegal	78,685	4,231	53.8	Dakar	Dakar	Rep.
Seychelles	107	58	542.1	Victoria	Victoria	B.C.R.
Sierra Leone	27,925	2,707	96.9	Freetown	Freetown	B.C.R.
Singapore	227	2,219	9,775.3	Singapore	Singapore	B.C.R.
Somalia	246,300	3,086	12.5	Mogadisho	Mogadisho	M.O.
South Africa	471,445	24,920	52.9	Pretoria[4]	Johannesburg	Rep.
Spain	194,885	35,225	180.7	Madrid	Madrid	C.S.
Sri Lanka (Ceylon)	25,332	13,679	540.0	Colombo	Colombo	B.C.R.
Sudan	967,500	17,324	17.9	Khartoum	Omdurman	M.O.
Surinam	70,060	385	5.5	Paramaribo	Paramaribo	Rep.
Swaziland	6,704	478	71.3	Mbabane	Mbabane	R.M.
Sweden	173,732	8,161	47.0	Stockholm	Stockholm	C.M.
Switzerland	15,943	6,481	406.5	Bern	Zurich	Rep.
Syria	71,772	6,303	99.6	Damascus	Damascus	Rep.*
Tanzania	364,943	14,763	40.5	Dar es Salaam	Dar es Salaam	B.C.R.
Thailand	198,250	39,950	206.7	Bangkok	Bangkok	C.M.
Togo	21,925	2,171	99.0	Lome	Lome	M.O.
Trinidad & Tobago	1,980	1,062	536.4	Port-of-Spain	Port-of-Spain	B.C.R.
Tunisia	63,379	5,641	89.0	Tunis	Tunis	Rep.
Turkey	300,948	38,270	127.2	Ankara	Istanbul	Rep.
Uganda	91,452	11,172	122.2	Kampala	Kampala	B.C.R.
U.S.S.R.	8,649,500	252,064	29.1	Moscow	Moscow	S.R.
United Arab Emirates	37,000	430	11.6	Abu Dhabi	Dubayy	Rep.
United Kingdom	94,217	56,056	595.0	London	London	C.M.
United States	3,615,122	211,909	58.6	Washington, D.C.	New York	Dem.
Upper Volta	105,869	5,895	55.7	Ouagadougou	Ouagadougou	Rep.
Uruguay	68,536	2,764	40.3	Montevideo	Montevideo	Rep.
Venezuela	352,144	11,557	32.8	Caracas	Caracas	Rep.
Vietnam	130,653	43,349	331.8	Hanoi	Hanoi	D.R.
Yemen Arab Rep.	77,200	5,238	67.8	Sana	Sana	Rep.
Yugoslavia	98,766	21,153	214.2	Belgrade	Belgrade	F.R.
Zaire	905,365	24,222	26.8	Kinshasa	Kinshasa	Rep.*
Zambia	290,586	4,751	16.3	Lusaka	Lusaka	B.C.R.

Present (1970) form of government, which may differ from the form that is supposed to exist. An asterisk (*) indicates that the basic form of government is being influenced by the military; the actual difference between Rep.* and M.O., thus, may be very little in many cases. Abbreviations used: B.C.R.—British Commonwealth member with republican government; C.M.—Constitutional Monarchy; C.S.—Corporate State; D.R.—Democratic Republic (Communist); F.R.—Federal Republic; I.P.—Indian Protectorate; Isl. Rep.—Islamic Republic; M.O.—Military Oligarchy; P.D.—Parliamentary Democracy; P.R.—People's Republic (Communist); Rep.—Republic; R.M.—Representative Monarchy; S.R.—Socialist Republic (Communist). [2] Actual seat of government is La Paz. [3] Actual seat of government is The Hague. [4] Administrative capital. Legislative capital is Capetown; judicial is Bloemfontein.

Source: 1969 population estimates by UN; local estimates used when no UN figures were available.

PRINCIPAL FRESH-WATER LAKES OF THE WORLD

Name	Location	Area Sq. Miles	Elevation Above Sea Level	Depth	Discovery or Early Exploration: By Whom	Date
			Feet	Feet		
Albert	Central Africa	1,800	2,100	20	Speke and Grant	1862
Athabasca	Alberta	2,762	697	Shallow	Hearne	1771
Baykal	Eastern Siberia, Asia	13,200	1,500	5,306		
Bangweulu	Central Africa	1,670	3,700	15	Livingstone	1868
Cayuga	New York	75	381	400		
Chad	French Sahara-Nigeria	10,000	850	20	Denham and Clapperton	1823
Champlain	New York	600	93	300	Champlain	1609
Chapala	Mexico	1,400	6,000			
Chautauqua	New York	35	1,300	....	La Salle	1669
Como	Italy	55½	650	1,365	Mentioned by Virgil	30 B. C.
Constance	Switz.-Ger.-Aust.	208	1,309	827	Lake Dwellers	Stone Age
Crater	Oregon	20	6,177	2,001	Hillman	1853
Edward	Central Africa	1,500	3,000	....	Stanley	1876
Erie	United States-Canada	9,968	573	210	Chaumont and Brebeuf	1640
Garda	Italy	189	216	1,916	Described by Virgil	35 B. C.
Gatun	Panama, Cent. Amer.	164	85			
Geneva	Switzerland-France	225	1,230	1,095	Lake Dwellers	Stone Age
George	New York	50	323	400	Friar Jogues	1642
Great Bear	N. W. Terr., Canada	12,200	450	270		
Great Slave	N. W. Terr., Canada	11,170	391	650	Hearne	1771
Huron	United States-Canada	22,978	581	750	Brulé and Le Caron	1615
Itasca	Minnesota	2	1,457	50	Schoolcraft	1832
Ladoga	European Russia	7,000	55	730		
Lake of the Woods	Ontario-Manitoba	1,485	1,058	....	De Noyon	1688
Lucerne	Switzerland	49	1,435	700	Scene of Tell legends	
Maggiore	Italy	82	636	1,220	*L. Verbanus* of Romans	B. C.
Managua	Nicaragua, Cent. Amer.	560	154	Unknown	Cordoba	1522
Michigan	United States	22,336	581	870	Nicolet	1634
Mweru	Congo (Kinshasa)-Zambia	1,700	3,189	....	Livingstone	1867
Neuchatel	Switzerland	90	1,420	472	Lake Dwellers	Stone Age
Nicaragua	Nicaragua, Cent. Amer.	3,000	106	260	Cordoba	1522
Nipigon	Ontario	1,590	850			
Nipissing	Ontario	330	640	....	Brulé and Le Caron	1615
Nyasa	Equatorial Africa	14,200	1,645	2,580	Livingstone	1859
Okeechobee	Florida	730	16	15	Spaniards—Fontaneda?	1552?
Onega	European Russia	3,764	125	400		
Ontario	United States-Canada	7,243	246	738	Champlain	1615
Rangeley	Maine	80	1,350			
Reindeer	Manitoba-Saskatchewan	1,765	1,150			
Rudolf	Equatorial Africa	3,500	1,250	....	Count Teleki	1888
Seneca	New York	75	445	630		
Simcoe	Ontario	271	130	....	Champlain	1615
Superior	United States-Canada	32,060	602	1,012	Brulé	1622
Tahoe	California	200	6,275	1,650	John C. Fremont	1844
Tanganyika	Equatorial Africa	12,700	2,600	2,000	Speke and Burton	1858
Tezcuco	Mexico	85	7,300	2	Cortes	1519
Titicaca	Bolivia-Peru	3,200	12,500	900	Ancient Incas	
Victoria	Equatorial Africa	27,000	3,775	270	Speke	1858
Winnepesaukee	New Hampshire	178	475	300	Johnson and Willard	1652
Winnipeg	Manitoba	9,398	710	70	Verendrye	1733
Winnipegosis	Manitoba	2,086	828	40	Verendrye	1736
Yellowstone	Wyoming	140	7,740	300	Colter	1807

PRINCIPAL SALT-WATER LAKES OF THE WORLD

Name	Area Square Miles	Location	Elevation Above Sea Level*	Depth
			Feet	Feet
Aral, Sea of	26,200	Kirghis-Khiva, W. Asiatic Russia	155	220
Balkash	8,600	Russian Central Asia	780	135
Caspian Sea	170,000	S. E. Europe-Western Asia	−86	3,000
Dead Sea	340	Palestine, S. W. Asia	−1,290	1,280
Eyre	3,600	South Australia	−35	Shallow
Great Salt Lake	1,750	Utah, W. United States	4,218	40
Issyk-Kul	2,230	Asiatic Russia	5,400	Unknown
Kuku-nor	2,300	Central China	10,000	Unknown
Maracaibo†	8,000	Venezuela, South America	Sea level	500
Salton Sea	266	S. E. California, North America	−280‡†	Shallow
Urumia	1,795	Azerbaijan, S. W. Asia	4,100	40
Van	1,400	Armenia, S. W. Asia	5,214	Unknown

* A minus sign indicates below sea level. † Partially fresh. ‡ Approximate level before the inflow from the Colorado river in 1905-06.

FAMOUS CATHEDRALS

Cologne Cathedral, with twin steeples 515 feet high, is Germany's finest example of decorated Gothic architecture. Begun about 1250, on the site of a 500-year-old church destroyed by fire, it was some 600 years in building. In World War II it escaped damage from bombs falling on the city, one having torn a hole in the earth only 50 yards away. The picture shows the cathedral with night-time illumination.
Lufthansa German Airlines

Saint Paul's Cathedral in London. Constructed during the years 1675–1710. Designed by Sir Christopher Wren, it is considered the finest example of Renaissance architecture in England.

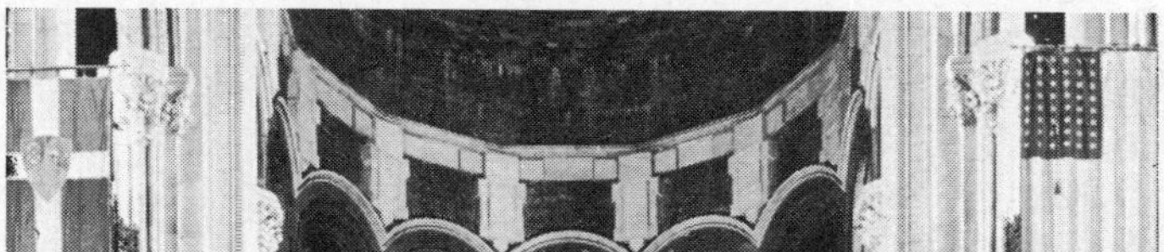

Cathedral of Saint John the Divine in New York City. Completed in 1911, the original style was Romanesque. In 1928, Cram and Ferguson, architects of Boston, undertook to remodel the nave along Gothic lines.

WORLD TRAVELS

An illuminated backdrop provides an appropriate setting for the Christmas toy market (*Christkindles-markt*) in Nurnberg, Bavaria.

Lufthansa

Entrance to the Tiger Balm Gardens at Singapore, built as a memorial to his family by a man whose wealth came from the sale of "Tiger Balm" ointment.

Keystone Press

A focus of interest for students of Egyptian archaeology and for tourists with cameras is the Sphinx beside the pyramids.

Lufthansa

Tolerated as a commercial bridge between Communist China and the outside world, the British crown colony of Hong Kong flourishes as a busy modern city.

Keystone Press

Built by the Turks, this medieval bridge spans the Naretva River near Mostvar, Yugoslavia.

European Travel Commission

Prominent among hostelries awaiting the world traveler is the luxurious Dan Carmel Hotel on top of Mt. Carmel, overlooking Haifa, Israel and its harbor.

Sadeh

The Komazawa Swimming Pool above was completed along with other modern structures for the 1964 Olympic Games at Tokyo, Japan.

Japan Nat'l Tourist Ass'n

MEANINGS OF PLACE NAMES

It is part of man's inquiring nature to be interested in the origin of things, but it was not until the 19th century that scholars began to investigate the origin of place-names by using scientific method. Before this, legend was usually employed to give meaning to a name whose origin was no longer self-evident. Historical documents are now carefully searched to find the earliest written form of a name and this is then interpreted by the language or dialect spoken in the area at that time. Even this is not valid if the meaning does not correspond with geographical or historical fact. Thus it is that many of the ancient names are still unintelligible.

This science of place-name study is called *toponymy* and it is a branch of *onomastics*, or the study of names in general. Apart from its intrinsic value in satisfying man's natural curiosity, toponymy also serves the student of language and history. Place-names often contain the only record of an extinct language and they can supply much valuable information on the origins and social customs of early peoples.

There are three main types of place-names and most names may be so classified, whether they originated in 10th century Asia, 15th century Europe, or 20th century America. *Habitation* names have evolved from the name of a tribe who once inhabited the area, or from the name of an individual who once owned the land. The countries of Iran, Bulgaria, Finland, France, and Belgium are but a few which have received their names from tribes who lived there. Nearly all the major tribes of the American Indians have left their trace on the map. Usually the names of individuals are commemorated in the names of villages or small towns.

Nature names describe the place itself, its surroundings, or its position relative to an outstanding landmark or other town. Often these names are composed of only one element, such as Bonn, Vigo, Chester, and Mons, which mean simply "the city," 'the village," "the castle," "the mountain." More often they have a qualifying element as is found in the names of Tallahassee, Casablanca, and Reykjavik, which mean "old town," "white house," and "smoky bay."

Commemorative or *historical* names form the final group. These may recall either an historical event, a famous person, or another place. Nice and Tirana, Washington and Constantinople, New York and New Orleans, are all names of this type.

The map of North America contains a rich variety of names because they have been contributed by men of many nationalities. The French in Quebec and Louisiana, the Spanish in California and the Southwest, the Dutch in New York, as well as the native Indians have all left their mark. In addition, the names of many towns were given by settlers to recall their homes in Europe.

Meanings of the names of American states will be found on page 36; those in the Canadian provinces, on page 108.

Acapulco (*ä'kä-pōōl'kō*). Mexican town. From the Aztec *acatl,pul,co,* "place covered with thick reeds."

Accra (*ăk'rȧ*). Capital of Ghana. The original tribe of fishermen who lived here were known to the natives of the interior as *Accras* derived from *nkran,* "ant."

Addis Ababa (*ăd'ĭs ăb'ȧ-bȧ*). Ethiopian city. Founded in 1887 as the new capital and named by the Empress Taitu. The name is Amharic for "new flower" and refers to its ideal situation.

Adirondacks. The Algonquin Indians who lived in these mountains were nicknamed *Ratirontakeke,* "they eat, i.e., live from, the forest." Adirondack is a Mohawk variation.

Alcantara (*ăl-kăn'tȧ-rȧ*). Town in Spain. Arabic *Al-Kantara,* "the bridge." The Romans built a famous bridge here which was constructed without the use of mortar.

Alcatraz. Island in San Francisco Bay. Site of former U.S. penitentiary. Spanish *Isla de Alcatraces,* "island of pelicans." The Spaniards found the place covered with these birds when they discovered it in 1769.

Al-Mausil. City in Iraq. Arabic for "place of connection." It is the meeting place of the ancient trade routes. The cloth called *muslin* was formerly made here.

Amalfi (*ä-mäl'fē*). Italian resort. Arabic *Al-Marfa,* "the port, landing-place."

Amarillo. Texas city. Suggested by the yellow banks of the nearby creek or the yellow flowers that cover the prairie in the spring. Buildings were painted bright yellow after the town was named. *Amarillo* is Spanish for "yellow."

Amritsar (*ŭm-rĭt'sẽr*). Sacred city of India. Built around a pool named "nectar of immortality." The name is Sanskrit.

Amsterdam. Dutch city. Low German name meaning "dam of the people living on the Amstel River." Amstel itself means "water-bank."

Anaconda. City in Montana. The mine here was named from a newspaper account during the Civil War when "Grant circled Lee like a giant anaconda."

Anacortes (*ăn'ȧ-kôr'tĕs*). City in Washington State. Originally named after the wife of the founder, Anna Curtis. Later altered to agree with the Spanish sound of other local names.

Anatolia. Ancient name of Asia Minor. From the Greek *anatole,* "rising of the sun."

Andes. South American mountain range. This Quichu Indian name means "metal" but refers especially to the copper which is mined here.

Androscoggin (*ăn'drŭs-kŏg'ĭn*). Maine river. Abnaki Indian for "place where fish are cured" by drying or smoking.

Angostura. Now Ciudad Bolivar, Venezuela. Located on the narrowest point on the Orinoco, it receives its name from the Spanish word for "narrow." Angostura bitters are from here.

Anticosti. Large island in the Gulf of St. Lawrence. Most authorities see in the name a transposition of the Montagnais Indian name *Natiscotec* which means "place where bears are hunted."

Antigua (*ăn-tē'gȧ*). West Indian island. Columbus named the island in honor of the church of Santa Maria la Antigua ("the old") in Seville.

Antofagasta. City in Chile. "Place where copper is hidden" in the Quechuan Indian language.

Antwerp. Belgian port. Old Low German *aend-werp,* "against the dike or dam" referring to the original site of the city.

Aorangi (*ä'ô-räng'ē*). Maori name for Mt. Cook, highest peak in New Zealand. Maori *ao,* "cloud" and *rangi,* "sky." The peak is often covered with clouds.

Aral Sea. U.S.S.R. Its many willow-covered islands give this large inland sea its name. From the Kirghiz *aral,* "willow-plot."

Arctic (*ärk'tĭk*). The northern constellation known as the Great Bear is seen in this region. From the Greek *arktos,* "bear."

Argentina. The poet Barco Centenera first used the word Argentina in his poem of the same name in 1602. He was referring to the country's situation on the banks of the Plata River. The name is Spanish for "silvery."

Aroostook. River in Maine. Micmac Indian for "shining river."

Ascot. Village in England, the home of the Royal Ascot races. "Eastern cottage or sheep shelter." From Old English *east-cot.*

Asuncion. Capital of Paraguay. Named in honor of Our Lady of the Assumption. The name is Spanish.

Atacama. Desert in Chile. The Spanish form of Quechua Indian *tacama,* a type of black duck. These birds inhabit the area near the coast.

Atchafalaya (*ȧ-chăf'ȧ-lī'ȧ*). River and bay in Louisiana. "Long river" in the Choctaw language.

Atlantic. The ocean is named after the mythical island of Atlantis which was supposed to lie in the waters west of Mt. Atlas from which the name originated.

Australia. As early as the 16th century, various terms derived from the Latin *australis,* "southern," were applied by mapmakers to lands south of Asia.

Austria. Latinized form of German *Oster-reich,* the "eastern kingdom" of the Franks.

Azores. Islands in the Atlantic. Portuguese *Ilhas do Acores,* "Islands of hawks."

Bahrein (*bȧ-rīn'*). Islands in the Persian Gulf. Arabic "two seas," applied to land having water on both sides.

Baikal (*bī-käl'*). The largest lake of Siberia. The lake has an abundance of fresh-water salmon. The term *bai-kol* is Turko-Tatar for "rich take."

Balkan. Mountain range and peninsula in southeastern Europe. This Turkish term meaning "mountain" was first used in 1808.

Ballarat. City of Australia. Officially *Ballaarat*, an aboriginal name meaning "camping-place." A swamp which was here was a favorite with the natives.

Baltimore. Maryland city. Cecil Calvert, Lord Baltimore, opened up the colony of Maryland. The barons of Baltimore came from *Bailena-tigh-mhor*, "town of the large house" in Ireland.

Bangkok. Capital of Thailand. In the Thai language this means "the place where the wild olives grow."

Basel (*bä'zĕl*). Swiss city. This name is derived from Celtic word which means "boar." The Gauls were devoted to a God in the form of a pig whose image has been found on many coins.

Beirut (*bā-rōōt'*). Capital of Lebanon. From the Phoenician *b'eroth*, "wells."

Belem. City in Brazil. Named in honor of Our Lady of Bethlehem, Portuguese *Belêm*. The mental hospital in London, England called St. Mary of Bethlehem is the origin of our word *bedlam*.

Belfast. City in Northern Ireland, hence the town in Maine. Gaelic *Beal-feirste*, "ford at the sandbar" was the place where the Lagan River was crossed.

Belgrade. Capital of Yugoslavia. Serbian *Beograd*, "White City." In olden times the city shone white in the sun.

Belleek. Town in Ireland famous for its pottery. Gaelic *Beal-leice*, "ford-mouth of the flagstones."

Berezina. Russian river. Scene of battle during Napoleon's retreat from Moscow. Old Slavic *beréza*, "birch tree." The river banks were formerly covered with birch.

Berlin. German city. A wooden scaffolding was formerly erected over the river and was used to collect floating timbers and for fishing. Old Slavic *bruleni*, "water-rake."

Bethlehem. A village in Palestine. The name is from the Syrian *beit el lehm*, "house of bread." The city in Pennsylvania was named while some German settlers were singing carols in a stable there on Christmas Eve in 1741.

Biarritz (*byä'rēts'*). French city. "Place of the twin oaks," from the basque *haritz*, "oak-tree."

Bihar (*bê-här'*). Town and state in India. The Sanskrit word *vihara* means "monastery." There was formerly a large Buddhist monastery here.

Bismarck. Capital of North Dakota. Originally Edwinton, but the name was changed by an overseas shipping agent in 1873 in honor of the German Chancellor. It was hoped that German settlers would thus be attracted.

Biwa. Largest lake in Japan. The lake is similar in shape to the Japanese *biwa*, a mandolin-type musical instrument.

Bizerte (*bē'zĕrt'*). Tunisian city. A gross Arabic corruption of *Hippo Diarrhytus*, a hybrid name from Phoenician *hippo*, "city" and a Greek term meaning "traversed by running waters."

Blarney. Castle in Ireland containing the Blarney stone Irish *Blárna*, diminutive of Middle Irish *blár*, "field."

Blenheim. German *Blindheim*. Village in Bavaria; site of famous battle in 1704. "Settlement in a blind valley."

Bombay. City in India. Portuguese corruption of the vernacular name *Mumbai*. There was a temple here dedicated to the goddess of the Koli fishermen, *Mumba*, or the "Great Mother."

Bonin Islands. South of Japan. Corrupted from Japanese *Munin*, "uninhabited." There were no natives on the islands when discovered by the Japanese about the year 1600.

Bonn. Capital of West Germany. Originally a Gaulish settlement whose name is simply a Celtic word for "city."

Bothnia. Gulf between Sweden and Finland. Lies on the eastern shores of *Botten*, a Swedish district. Old Norse *botn* means "valley bottom."

Bowery. Street in New York City. English spelling of Dutch *boererij*, "farm." Originally this was a lane which led to the farm of Peter Stuyvesant.

Brazos. River of Texas. Originally Spanish *Brazos de Dios*, "Arm of God." A mission on the river was destroyed by the Indians but the Spaniards believed it to be the work of God.

Bremen. German port. Middle High German *brĕme*, "bank, shore."

Britain. From the Old French Bretaigne. Great Britain refers to the British Isles as opposed to Little Britain or *Brittany* in France. Both names refer to the home of the *Britons*, who were a Celtic people. The name is related to the Welsh word *pryd*, "picture," and refers to the custom of the Britons of tattooing themselves.

Brooklyn. Named by Dutch settlers after the town of Breukelen in the Netherlands. This name, originally *Broklede*, means "water-course through a swamp."

Bruges (*brōōzh*). City in Belgium. Although this name is usually associated with Low German *brügge*, "bridge," it is actually the Old Norse *bryggja*, "quay or landing-place." Named by the Vikings.

Brussels. Capital of Belgium. Records of the year 1107 show *Brucsella*, "house in the swamp."

Bryn Mawr. Suburb of Philadelphia. The railway station here was named after a local country estate which was so called after an ancestral seat in Wales. It is Welsh for "great hill."

Buffalo. This city in New York State was built on Buffalo Creek. The creek name is probably derived from the name of a local Seneca chief rather than from the animal itself.

Bulawayo. City in Southern Rhodesia. Zulu for "place of killing." Rebellious members of the Indunas tribe were formerly executed here.

Bulgaria. "Country of the Bulgars." From the Old Turkish *bulgar*, "mongrol, cross-breed," alluding to the mixture of races in this people.

Cadiz. City in Spain. Arabic *Gades*, from a Phoenician word related to the Hebrew *gader*, "protecting wall."

Cairo. Capital of Egypt. A Venetian corruption of the Arabic *Qahir al-Falak*, "The Triumphant of Heaven." The planet Mars was in the ascendant when the city was laid out.

Calcutta. City in India. Sanskrit *Kali-ghat*, "ghat of the Goddess Kali." A ghat is a flight of stairs leading to a river for the convenience of ritual bathers.

Calicut. City in India. Officially *Kozhikode*, meaning "cockfort." On his retirement, the last king of Malabar gave the Zamorin of Calicut as much land as was within earshot of a cock's crow.

Callao. Peruvian seaport. A Spanish word meaning "gravel" referring to the stony nature of the beach.

Calumet. River in Illinois which has given its name to the industrial district at the southern end of Lake Michigan. The name is French for "reed." The reeds which grew along the banks of the river were made into "pipes," *calumets*, by the Indians.

Cambodia. Republic in southeast Asia. A European form of *Kambuja*. Kambu was the mythical founder of the Khmer race which settled here.

Cambridge. University town in England and city in Massachusetts. Old English *Grantebrycg*, "Bridge on the Granta River." *Granta*, which is from a Celtic root meaning "muddy," was altered to *Cam* through Norman French influence.

Cameroon. African republic. Named for the Cameroon River. Early navigators found many prawns here and called the river, *Rio dos Camaroes*, "River of shrimps, or prawns."

Canada. Apparently derived from the Huron-Iroquois *kanata*, "village, collection of tents." The name is first mentioned in Jacques Cartier's narrative of 1534 and referred to a village called Stadacona where Quebec City now stands. Gradually extended to southern Ontario and Quebec and thence to the whole dominion.

Cannes (*kăn*). Resort on the French Riviera. This was originally a Phoenician settlement and contains the same Semitic root found in the name of the Biblical town of Cana. The name means "place of reeds." The English word *cane* is related.

Canton. City in China. This is a variation of *Kwangtung*, the Chinese province of which Canton is the capital. The area in southern China formerly known as *Kwang* was divided into the two provinces of *Kwangtung*, "Eastern Kwang," and *Kwangsi*, "Western Kwang."

Canton. City in Ohio. Named in the mistaken belief that it was directly opposite the city of Canton in China.

Cardiff. Chief city of Wales. The Welsh name is *Caer ar Daf*, "Fort on the Taff River." A Roman station was established here during the conquest of Britain.

Carlow. County in Ireland. Irish *Cetherloch*, literally "Quadruple Lake." The Barrow River anciently formed four lakes here.

Carmel. Mountain in Israel and many places in America. In historical times Mount Carmel was famous for the luxurious growth of plants on its slopes. Hebrew for "garden, orchard."

Carnegie. Old Scottish barony which was the seat of the Carnegie family. Gaelic *Cathair-an-eige*, "Fort at the Gap." This would refer to a mountain pass.

Carrara (*kȧ-rär'ȧ*). Italian town famous for its marble. From the Ligurian *caris, cararis*, "rock, stone."

Cartagena. City in Spain whose name has been transferred to cities in South America. Named after the ancient city of Carthage in North Africa. Phoenician for "new city."

Castile. Medieval kingdom of Spain. Spanish *Castilla* means "place of many castles."

Catamarca. City and province in Argentina. From the Kechua Indian *q'atamarca*, "village of the mountain slope." This city lies at the foot of the Sierra de Ambato.

Catskill. Creek and mountains in New York. *Kill* is a Dutch word for "creek" and the name means "creek of the cats or panthers."

Caucasus. Mountain range in southeastern Europe. The modern name comes from the Greek *Kaukasia*. The basic Indo-European root is seen in the Lithuanian word *kaukas*, "hill," and the English word *high*.

Chattanooga. City in Tennessee. A simplification of the Cree Indian *Chat-to-to-noog-gee*, "rock rising to a point." This was the native name for Lookout Mountain.

Cheddar. Gorge in England famous for its cheese. Earlier recorded as *Ceodre*, from the Old English *ceod*, "pouch." This would refer to the shape of the gorge.

Chemnitz. City in East Germany. A Slavic name meaning "stony river."

Chesterfield. Town in England. Old English *Cestrefeld*, "field by the Roman fortification." The word *cestre* is derived from Latin *castrum*, "fort" which is the origin of the French *chateau* and place-names such as *Castile, Lancaster, Winchester*.

Cheyenne. Capital of Wyoming. Named after the Cheyenne Indians. This is a French version of the name given to them by the Dakota Indians meaning "the red-talkers," that is, "those who speak in a strange tongue."

Chicago. French rendition of a native name. It is Algonquin Indian for "wild-onion place." The wild-onion or garlic formerly covered the low, marshy plain.

Chimborazo. Volcano in Ecuador. From the Kechua Indian *cimpu*, "multi-colored woolen threads" and *rasu*, "snowy peak." The debris on the slopes resembles the woolen threads in the *llautu* or headband worn by the Incas.

China. Named after the Ts'in Dynasty which ruled in China in the Third Century B. C.

Cimarron. River in New Mexico. Originally the Spanish word *cimarron* meant "wooded; mountainous," but later it was applied to anything that was wild or unruly.

Cincinnati. This city in Ohio was named in honor of the Society of the Cincinnati. This society was formed in 1783 by a group of officers in the Continental Army before its disbanding and was named after the Roman hero Cincinnatus.

Clare. Town and county of Ireland. A board was once used to cross over the River Fergus at this point. *Clar* is the Irish word for "plank."

Clyde. Scottish river famous for its shipbuilding. From a Celtic root meaning the "cleanser." Possibly in honor of a river goddess.

Coburg. City in West Germany. Formerly *Choburg* from a Slavic *chov*, "shelter." It means "the fort of refuge."

Cochabamba. City and department in Bolivia. Literally, Kechua Indian for "lake-plain." The natives used the term *bamba* (from which the word *pampas* is derived) for any barren expanse,

Cochise. Town and county in Arizona. Named in honor of Chief Cochise, the leader of the Chiricahua Apaches.

Coeur D'Alene. City in Idaho. This is the French name of the Skitswash Indians and means "awl-heart." It is said to have been applied by an Indian chief to indicate the size of a trader's heart.

Coleraine. Town in Northern Ireland. Gaelic *Cuil Raithin*, "ferny nook or corner."

Cologne. West German city where *eau-de-cologne*, or "water of Cologne" was originally made. Established by the Emperor Augustus as *Colonia Agrippina*, "colony or settlement of Agrippina." It was the birthplace of Agrippina, the wife of Augustus.

Colon. City in the Canal Zone. This place-name, like Columbus, Colombia, British Columbia, etc., was named in honor of Christopher Columbus. It is the Spanish form of the name.

Concepcion. City in Chile. Like many places in South America, this name commemorates a Feast of the Blessed Virgin. Concepcion alludes to her Immaculate Conception.

Connemara. District in the west of Ireland. Gaelic *Conmacne-Mara*, "place by the sea where the descendants of Chief Conmac reside."

Constantinople. Old name of Istanbul, Turkey. A Greek name meaning "City of Constantine." The Emperor Constantine made the old city of Byzanz the capital of Eastern Roman Empire in the year 330. The Greek word *polis*, "city" enters into the names *Naples, Tripoli*, and others.

Copenhagen. Capital of Denmark. Old Danish *København*, "Port of merchants." Copenhagen was the center of commerce for the western Baltic.

Corcovado. Mountain at Rio de Janeiro whose summit supports a famous statue of Christ. Portuguese *corcovado*, "hunchbacked," describes the shape of the peak.

Cork. City and county of Ireland. Originally *Corcachmor* which is Gaelic for "great swamp." A district in the city is still known as "The Marsh."

Corregidor. Island at the entrance to Manila Bay, Philippines. Ships formerly stopped here to have their paper checked and corrected. Spanish *corregidor* means "corrector."

Correggio. Town in northern Italy; home of Correggio, the artist. In the dialect of northern Italy the word *coréza*, from which this place-name is derived, means "a strip of land in the middle of a marsh."

Corvallis. Town in Oregon. From the Latin words *cor*, "heart" and *vallis*, "of the valley." Corvallis lies in the middle of the Willamette Valley.

Cotopaxi. Volcano in Ecuador. Kechua Indian *q'utu p'asi*, "smoky mound."

Couchiching. Ontario lake. The lake discharges the waters of Lake Simcoe into the Severn River. From Algonquin *kotchichi*, "discharge, emptying."

Coventry. English cathedral city. Old English *Cofentreo*. The town grew up around a tree belonging to a man called Cofa.

Crimea. Russian peninsula in the Black Sea. At the time of the Bosphoran Empire a protective moat and embankment were built across the isthmus here. From the Turkish word for "trench," *kyrym*.

Croatia. Ancient kingdom, now a federated republic of Yugoslavia. "Land of the Croats." The Croats are a Slavic people whose name originally derives from Old Persian *haurvata*, "shepherd." The French form of the name, *Cravate*, is the origin of our word *cravat*. This was originally a neckpiece worn by Croatian soldiers.

Cuba. Arawak Indian for "land." The apparent reference is to the island as the Mainland as opposed to the Lesser Antilles.

Cumberland. County in England, thence Cumberland Gap in Tennessee and many American place-names. "Land of the Cumbrians." The Cumbrians were Britons who inhabited the ancient kingdom of Strathclyde, which embraced Cumberland. Their name derives from Welsh *Cymry*, "compatriots."

Curitiba (*kōō'rē-tē'vȧ*). City in Brazil. Guarani Indian *curi*, a type of pine tree, probably the Araucaria. Literally, a "place of pine trees."

Cusco. City in Peru; former capital of the Incas. From the Kechua Indian word *qusqu*, "navel." The city lies in the middle of a valley.

Dachau (*däĸ'ou*). City in West Germany. From Old High German *daha*, "clay," and *aue*, "watery place." The site of the original settlement was in a clay-rich swamp.

Dahomey. Republic of Africa. In the native language this is literally "the belly of Dan." In the 17th century a native king murdered a petty chief and built a house over his corpse. The chief's name was Dan, hence the original name, *Danhomé*.

Dalmatia. Coastal region of Yugoslavia. Home of the Illyrian tribe called *Delmatae* or "shepherds." Dalmatian dogs originated here.

Danube. European river. Its Celtic name was *Danuvius*, from an Indo-European root with the basic meaning of "that which flows or gushes."

Dar es Salaam. African seaport. Arabic *Bandar es Salaam,* "Harbor of Peace." So called by the Sultan of Zanzibar when he established a base here in the mid-19th century.

Darjeeling. Indian town in the Himalayas. From the Tibetan *Rdo-rje-gling,* "place of the dorje." A *dorje* is a mystical thunderbolt in Lamanist religion.

Darmstadt. City in West Germany. "Town on the Darm River." The Darm is named from Old High German *darm,* "intestine." There are many twists and turns in the river.

Denmark. Old Norse *Danmork,* "Country of the Danes." The Danes were originally a Germanic people who inhabited the marshy hollows of southern Jutland. Their name is related to the Old English word *dene,* "hollow, small valley."

Denver. English village. Ancestral home of the Denver family. From Old English *Dena faer,* "passage or road of the Danes." Denver, Colorado was named in honor of J. W. Denver, a Governor of Kansas Territory.

Derbent. City of the U.S.S.R. on the Caspian Sea. A defile here, called the Caspian Gates, locked the route through the Caucasus Mountains. From Persian *derbend,* "bolt, lock."

Derby. County town of Derbyshire, England. The 12th Earl of Derby established the Derby stakes at Epsom Downs; hence any similar annual race is called a *derby.* From Old Norse *djur-byr,* "homestead frequented by deer."

Detroit. City in Michigan. Founded in 1701 as Fort Pontchartrain du Detroit. The French word *detroit,* "straight, narrows," refers to the Detroit River.

Dnepr, Dnestr. Two great rivers of the U.S.S.R. Formerly *Danapris* and *Danastius,* which are Scythian names with the probable meaning of "nearer river" and "further river."

Dominica. Island in the West Indies. Spanish for "Sunday." It was discovered on a Sunday by Columbus.

Donegal. Irish county. English version of *Dun-na-nGall,* "fort of the foreigners." The "foreigners" were the Danes, who had an earthen fortification here before the 12th century.

Dordrecht. City in the Netherlands. Middle Dutch *Thur-drecht,* "through-channel." The city was built on a short stretch of water between the Dubbel and Mewerde Rivers.

Drammen. Norwegian river and city. Old Norse *Drofn,* related to the German word *trübe,* "gloomy." Indo-European rivers often have names signifying "dark, dismal, gloomy."

Dresden. City in East Germany. A Slavic name from Wendish *Drazhdzhanj,* "home of the forest-people."

Dublin. Capital of the Republic of Ireland. Irish *Dubhlinn,* "black pool." This was the name of that part of the Liffey River on which the city is built. Irish-speaking people refer to the city as *Baile-atha-cliath,* "town of the ford made of hurdles."

Dubuque. City in Iowa. Julien Dubuque, a French-Canadian trader settled here in 1788 in order to mine.

Dundee. Scottish city. Gaelic for "Fortress on the Dee River." The Dee, originally *Devona,* honors a river goddess.

Dunkirk. Town on the Belgian coast. Flemish *Dunkerque,* "church on the sand-dunes."

Durham. English city and county. Norman corruption of Old English *Dun-holm,* "hill-island." The city is built on a rocky hill nearly surrounded by the Wear River.

Durham. City in North Carolina. Originally Plattsburg, the name was changed in 1851 to honor Dr. Bartlett Durham whose forebears were from Durham, England.

Dusseldorf. City in West Germany. German *dorf* means "village." The name of the Dussel River derives from Old High German *doson,* "to rage, roar." Hence, "village on the banks of the roaring river."

Eboli. Town in Italy. Modern form of Celtic *Eburum,* "place of the yew tree."

Edmonton. Town in England and city in Alberta. Old English *Eadhelmstun,* "the homestead of Adhelm."

Egypt. Probably from an epithet of the city of Memphis, "Hi-ku-Ptah," which means "house of the spirit of Ptah." Ptah was one of the chief gods of ancient Egypt.

El Paso. City in Texas. In the year 1598, the Spaniards crossed the Rio Grande here and called the ford *El Paso del Norte,* "The Pass of the North."

El Salvador. Republic of Central America. So named in 1524 by Pedro de Alvarado in honor of Our Blessed Saviour (Span. *Salvador*).

Engadine. Swiss alpine valley. *En co de Ino* is the Raeto-Romansch form of Latin *in capite Eni,* land lying at "the head or source of the Inn River."

Erfurt. East German city. "Ford on the Erf River." *Erf* is a Germanic river-name meaning "brown-colored."

Erie. One of the Great Lakes and a city in Pennsylvania. Named after the Erie Indians. It is a French form of their original name of *Yenrish,* "Long-tailed." This tribe held the panther sacred.

Eritrea. Self-governing state in the Ethiopian federation. This territory lies on the shore of the Red Sea and its name is derived from the Greek *Ereuthre thalassa,* "Red Sea."

Essen. Industrial city in West Germany. In 898 written *Astnide* from Middle Low German *ast,* "forge." Therefore, "place of the forge."

Essex. County in England and many towns in North America. Old English *East Seaxe,* "East Saxons" as distinguished from the West and South Saxons.

Estonia. One of the Baltic states. "Land of the *Aestii.*" This was a Germanic tribe who once lived on the shores of the Gulf of Riga and whose name possibly derives from the Latin *aestuarium,* "tidal waters, estuary."

Ethiopia. Republic in northeast Africa. From the Greek *aithein,* "to burn," and *ops,* "sight, face." This is the land of the people who have dark skin, literally, "burnt faces."

Faroe. Danish islands in the North Atlantic. Old Norse *faer,* "sheep." The islands still support large herds of sheep.

Foggia. Italian city. This name is derived ultimately from the Latin word *fossa,* "ditch, trench." In the dialect of North Italy, however, it refers to a place for threshing grain.

Formosa. The name the Portuguese navigators gave to the island of Taiwan in 1590. It is Portuguese for "beautiful."

Forth, Firth of. The long estuary of the Firth River, Scotland. Gaelic *Foirthe* from a Celtic *Vo-ritia,* "running under," hence, "the river with strong undercurrents."

France. "The land of the Franks." The name of the Franks is probably derived from a Germanic word related to Old English *franca,* "spear, javelin."

Frankfurt. The name of two German cities. German for "Ford of the Franks." The *frankfurter* originated here.

Fresno. City and county in California. From Spanish *fresno,* "ash-tree."

Funchal. City in the Madeira Islands. "Place where fennel grew," from the Spanish word for fennel, *funcho.*

Fundy. Bay between New Brunswick and Nova Scotia. It is an Anglicized form of the name *Fond de la Baie,* "far end of the bay," which appeared on French maps.

Galapagos (*gȧ-lä'pȧ-gŭs*). Pacific islands belonging to Ecuador. This is the Spanish name for a species of turtles found here.

Galilee. Sea in Israel and district of Palestine in Biblical times. From the Aramaic *galil,* "ring or circle," with reference to the fact that it was surrounded by Gentiles or foreigners.

Galle. Seaport of Ceylon. The place is built on a rocky promontory and named Haycock Hill. In the Sinhalese language, *gala* means "rock, hill." The Portuguese confused this with the Latin word for "rooster," *gallus.*

Garda. Lake in northern Italy. Named after the Veronese castle which *guarded* the military road near here.

Gaspe (*găs'pā*). Peninsula in the province of Quebec. Micmac Indian for "end of the earth."

Gaza. Town and strip of land between Egypt and Israel. A stronghold of the Phoenicians in ancient times, the place derives its name from their word *'azzah,* "firmness, strength." Gauze is said to have been first made here.

Gdansk. Polish city on the Baltic Sea. Germanic *Gutiskandje* means "end or coast of the Goths." Danzig is the German name.

Gdynia. Polish city. German *Gdingen,* from *G(u)dingen,* "place of the Goths."

Geneva. Swiss city. Originally *Genava,* a Ligurian name which means "knee or bend." The city is situated in a deep corner at the east end of Lake Geneva.

Gethsemane. Garden outside Jerusalem. This is the Aramaic name for a vat in which oil was stored after being pressed from olives. There was probably such a vat here as it is close to the Mount of Olives.

Gibralter. Named after Tariq Ben Zaid, the Moorish conqueror of the Visigoths. Arabic *Gabal Tariq*, "Mount of Tariq."

Gilead. Mountainous region of Palestine. Aramaic for "rugged country" as opposed to the fertile plain of Bashan.

Ginza. Main street of Tokyo. Literally "silver place." It derives the name from the silver mint which was located here.

Gonzaga. Town in northern Italy; home of St. Aloysius Gonzaga. Originally *Verecundiaca* or "property of Verecundius." Verecundius is a Latin personal-name meaning "modesty."

Gouda. Dutch town famous for its cheese. The town lies near the Gouwe River which was called *Golda* in the 12th century. It is Low German for "gold river" and refers to the yellowish-colored, muddy water.

Gramercy Park. New York City. Known to the Dutch settlers as *Krum Marisje*, "crooked little swamp."

Greenland. An English literal translation of Old Norse name. It actually means "new land" and not "green-colored land."

Guiana. Region in northern South America shared by the English, French, and Dutch. English spelling of Spanish *Gauyana*. The parrot which is native to the area is called by the Carib Indians *wayana*, and this is the origin of the place-name.

Guinea. Republic in northwestern Africa. The name is a European form of a Berber phrase meaning "land of the black men."

Hague, The. Capital of the Netherlands. Officially *'s Gravenhage*, "The Count's Hedge." First mentioned in the year 1242 as the residence of Count William II of Holland, *Die Haghe.*

Hainan. Chinese island. From the Chinese *hai*, "sea," and *nan*, "south." It lies in the sea south of the southern mainland.

Hainault. Province of Belgium. "Meadow on the Hagna River." The name Hagna comes from a Low German word meaning "hedge."

Haiti. Republic in the West Indies. The Arawak natives called the country *Aiti*, which in their language meant "mountainous."

Halifax. Cities in England and Nova Scotia. In the 12th century, *Haliflax*, Old English for "sacred flax field."

Hamburg. City in West Germany. From Old Saxon *hamme*, "enclosed place." The fort built here in the 9th century was once surrounded by trees.

Hanover. Cities in Germany and the United States· The German spelling is *Hannover*. From the German phrase *zum hohen Ufer*, "at the high bank." The city is built on the bank of the Leine River.

Hardwar (*hŭr'dwär*). Sacred town in India. Sanskrit *Hari dwara*, "capital of Hara." Hara is a title of the Hindu god Siva.

Harlech, Welsh castle and town. The Romans built a castle on a rock here. Welsh *hardd*, "beautiful," and *llech*, "rock." The same Celtic root may be seen in the name *Belleek*.

Hartford. City in Connecticut. Founded by settlers from Massachusetts led by Samuel Stone who was born in Hertford (originally *Hartford*), England. It means "Ford of the stag."

Heidelberg. City in West Germany. "Mountain of the heathberry." This is the same as the English bilberry.

Hereford. Town and county in England; many American towns. Old English *here-ford*, "army ford." This would be where a marching column could cross the river in closed order.

Hialeah. Suburb of Miami with famous racetrack. Named by Willie Willie, an Indian chief, whose town occupied the site until the end of the 1920's. Seminole-Creek Indian *haiyakpo-hili*, "pretty prairie."

Himalayas. Asian mountain range. The peaks are perpetually covered with snow. The name is Sanskrit for "abode of the snows."

Hiroshima. Japanese city. In 1594 a feudal lord built his castle here and named it *Hiro-shima-jo*, "Castle of the Broad Island."

Hoboken. City in New Jersey. Dutch settlers named the place after the town of Hobuechen, Holland. It means "place of the tall beech tree."

Holland. Former name of the Netherlands and still the name of a region. Originally *Holtland*, "wood-land." This part of the country was densely wooded in ancient times.

Holstein (*hōl'stīn*). Former duchy of Denmark and now part of the province of Schleswig-Holstein, West Germany. The Old Low German name was *Holt-seten*, "home of the forest-dwellers."

Honduras. Republic in Central America. Spanish for "depths." It is not known if the reference is to the coastal waters or to the inland valleys.

Hong Kong. British colony off the Chinese coast. Chinese *H'eng K'eng*, "Water-channel or harbour of the fragrant flowers."

Honolulu. Capital of Hawaii. The first element *hono* is common to many Hawaiian place-names and means "bay, gulch, or valley." Honolulu is "the sheltered bay."

Honshu. Largest island of Japan. Japanese for "mainland."

Hunan. Chinese province. Region "south of the lakes."

Hungary. The area was settled by the Ten Tribes of Oguz, Turkish *on ogur*, whose name was Latinized to *Ungari*. The initial *H* is by attraction to the name of the Huns.

Innsbruck. City in Austria. German for "bridge on the Inn River." The river-name is Celtic but the meaning is doubtful.

Iran. Old Persian *Airyana*, "Land of the Aryans." The Aryans were an Indo-European people who occupied the major portion of the country in historical times.

Iraq. That part of the Tigris-Euphrates Valley known as Babylonia was once called *'Iraq*, which is Arabic for "cliff."

Irrawaddy. River of Burma. Sanskrit *Iravati*, "giver of refreshment."

Israel. The origin of the name given in Genesis 32:22 is merely folk-etymology. More probably from the Semitic root *ishr*, "reliable, happy," referring to an ancient Canaanite god of fertility.

Istanbul. Capital of Turkey. The Byzantines referred to Constantinople, which was the former name, simply as *The City*. Hence the Greek phrase, *eis ten polin*, "to or in the city," from which the modern name is derived.

Italy. "Land of the Itali." The tribal name is derived from the Oscan dialect *Viteliu*, "young cattle," honoring Mars who was the god of bulls.

Iwo Jima. Japanese island. Japanese *iwo-shima*, "sulphur island." At one time there were important sulphur mines here.

Jaffa. City in Israel. A city established by the Phoenicians and mentioned in the Bible as *Joppa*. The name is Semitic and means "beautiful place."

Jakarta. Capital of Indonesia. It was named *Jayakarta*, "prosperous on account of victory," in 1527 after a successful battle there.

Jamaica. The abundance of springs on this West Indian island prompted the Arawak Indians to call it *Jaymaca* or "Island of Springs."

Japan. This is a 15th century Dutch corruption of the Chinese name *Jih-pen*, "Place of the Sun's Origin."

Jena. City in East Germany. Middle High German *jan*, "row of mowed hay or compost."

Jerusalem. Shalem was the local god of pre-Israelite Jerusalem. The name may be interpreted as "the foundation or city of Shalem."

Jodhpur. City in India. It was established by Rao Jodha in the year 1459 and called "City of Jodha." Riding breeches known as *jodhpurs* originated here.

Jordan. River of the Bible; thence the country through which it now flows. The river drops 1300 feet in its course and was known to the Hebrews as "the descender."

Kalgoorlie. Town and famous gold field in Australia. A shrub known to the aborigines as *galgurli* was a prominent feature of the local landscape.

Kanchenjunga (*kŭn'chĕn-jŭng'gä*). Mountain in the Himalayas and the 3rd highest in the world. Its five peaks are perpetually covered with snow, hence the Tibetan name, "the five repositories of the great snow."

Kandahar. City in Afghanistan. Founded in 330 B. C. by Alexander the Great. The name is a corruption of the original *Alexandria Arachosiarum*, "Alexandria of the Arachosian people."

Kanpur. City in northern India known as Cawnpore during the British rule. Sanskrit for "City of Kahn." Kahn is one of the names of the Hindu god Krishna and means "husband."

Katmandu. Capital of Nepal. A wooden temple was built here in 1596 for religious mendicants. Sanskrit *kath*, "wood," and *mandu*, "palace, temple."

Kennebec. River in Maine. The Abnaki Indian name meaning "long water" originally referred to the stretch between Skowhegan and Merrymeeting Bay.

Kent. County in England, and the name of many American towns. Known to Julius Caesar as *Cantium*, the area's name probably derives from Celtic *canto-*, "rim, border" as applied to a coastal district.

Khartoum. Capital of the Sudan. The Arabic name is *Rasel-Khartum*, "Cape of the Elephant's Trunk." At high water on the Nile, a spit of land having the shape of an elephant's trunk appears near here.

Kiel. City and canal in Germany. From the Low German phrase *tom Kyle*, "on the creek or inlet," referring to its position on Kiel Bay. The same word is the second element of the *Catskills*.

Kilimanjaro. Mountain in Tanganyika; highest in Africa. A native name which may be roughly translated as "mountain of the cold devils."

Killarney. Town and lakes in Ireland. Irish *Cill-airne*, "church of the sloes or blackthorn bushes."

Kirghiz. Soviet Republic in Asia. Home of the Kirghiz people. Their name comes from Kirghiz *kyr*, "wilderness" and *gizmak*, "to wander." It refers to their nomadic life.

Klondike. River and gold field in the Yukon Territory. This is a mispronunciation of the Indian *Thron-diuk*, "hammer-water." The natives hammered stakes across the shallow mouth of the river on which they hung their nets.

Koevorden. Town in the Netherlands. From Dutch *koe-voord*, "ford of the cows or oxen." This is the ancestral home of Capt. George Vancouver whose family name was originally Van Koevorden.

Kostroma. River, city and oblast of the U.S.S.R. Russian *koster'* is a type of sturgeon which abounded in the river.

Kuala Lumpur. Capital of Malaysia. In the Malayan tongue, *kuala* refers to any place where a river empties. *Lumpur* means "muddy." The waters here were muddied by the work of Chinese miners.

Kuwait. A shiekdom on the Persian Gulf. The name, which is a diminutive of Arabic *kut*, and meaning "small fort," was given by early settlers to the stronghold built in the center of the original tented village.

Labrador. That part of the Province of Newfoundland which is on the Canadian mainland. First noted on a map of 1534 as "land of the Labrador." The pilot on the English ship which sighted land here was a labrador (Spanish for "laborer") from the Azores.

Ladoga. Large lake in northwestern U.S.S.R. From the Finnish *aaldokas*, "tossed, disturbed." The waters of this lake are extremely rough in bad weather.

Lagos. Capital of Nigeria. Named by Portuguese explorers for the many lagoons and coastal lakes in the neighborhood. Portuguese *lago* means "lake."

La Jolla. Suburb of San Diego, California. This is a variant spelling of Spanish *hoya*, "pit, cavity," hence the pronunciation. It was the name of a rancheria in a hollow.

Lancaster. County town of Lancashire, England and a city in Pennsylvania. Old English *Loncestre*, "Roman fort on the River Lune." Lune is a Celtic river-name meaning "health-giving."

La Paz. Capital of Bolivia. Originally, in Spanish, *Pueblo Nuevo de Nuestra Senora de la Paz*, "New Town of Our Lady of the Peace." The name commemorates the treaty signed between two rival groups of Spanish *conquistadores* in 1548.

Laredo. Village in Spain and city in Texas. Nuevo Laredo is a Mexican city across the Rio Grande from Laredo. The name is related to Spanish *gleria*, "gravel" and refers to the stony river banks.

Las Vegas. City in Nevada and town in New Mexico. The Spanish word *vega*, "open plain," aptly describes the surrounding desert.

Latakia (*lăt'ȧ-kē'ȧ*). City and territory of Syria, famous for its tobacco. The Greek name was *Laodicea*, given by Seleucus Nicator in honor of his mother Laodice.

Latvia. Former Baltic state now part of the U.S.S.R. The country is named for the Late River near the Lithuanian border. The river-name is Lettish for "marshy, swampy."

Lausanne. City in Switzerland. Like many names in this area, this one is Celtic and proves that the Celts were here in ancient times. It means "river of the flat stones."

Lebanon. A country in Western Asia on the Mediterranean. From a Semitic word meaning "the white." It probably refers to the snowy peaks of the Lebanon Mountains.

Leipzig. City in East Germany. This is the German form of Slavic *Lipsk*, from *lipa*, "linden tree."

Lepanto. Strait in Greece where a famous naval battle was fought between the European powers and Turkey in 1571. An Italian corruption of Modern Greek *Epaktos*, originally *Naupaktos*, "place where ships were built."

Levant. Name applied to the eastern regions of the Mediterranean. A French term from the Latin *levans*, "rising," referring to the rising of the sun.

Lhasa. Capital of Tibet. Long known as "The Forbidden City" because of its inaccessibility. Tibetan *lha-sa*, "land of God." It is a holy city and the residence of the Dalai Lama.

Liberia. Republic of western Africa. The American Colonization Society settled emancipated American slaves here in 1822. The Latin name, meaning "land of the free," commemorates their new-found freedom.

Lido. Island reef off Venice, Italy, famous as a resort. Latin *litus*, "beach."

Lille. French city where lisle fabric was first made. In the 11th century Flemish counts built a chateau here in the midst of a marsh. French *l'isle* is an old spelling for "island."

Lima. Capital of Peru. Spanish corruption of *Rimac*, the name of the river on which it lies. It is Kechua Indian *rimaq*, "talking," hence "noisy."

Limburg. Provinces of Belgium and the Netherlands famous for Limburger cheese. The castle of *Lintburch*, "fortress of the linden tree," gives the modern name.

Limehouse. District of London. There were many limekilns here from medieval times until quite recently. From Old English *lim-ast*, "lime oast or kiln."

Limerick. City and county of Ireland. Irish *Luimneach*, a diminutive form of *lomm*, and meaning "little bare spot of land."

Limoges. French city famous for its porcelain. In ancient Gaul this was the home of the tribe of *Lemovici*, or "warriors of Lemos." The modern name is derived from the tribal name.

Lincoln. Cities in England and Nebraska. The Latin name was *Lindon colonia*, "colony or settlement of Lindon." Lindon is a Celtic name meaning "lake" and refers to the widening of the Witham River here.

Lithuania. Former Baltic state now part of the U.S.S.R. This is a Latinization of Lithuania *Lietuva*, "coastland."

Liverpool. English seaport and towns in New York and Pennsylvania. The name refers to a pool of thick, clotted water.

Lorelei. Rock in the Rhine River on which a siren is supposed to have sat and lured sailors to their destruction. From Middle High German *lure-lei*, "ambush-rock."

Los Angeles. Originally *Reina de los Angeles*, "Queen of the Angels," a name given by the Spanish in honor of Our Lady of the Angels of Portiuncula. The stream on which the city was built was discovered on this feast-day.

Lourdes. French town and shrine. From the Basque *lorr-d-e*, "rocky height extending into space."

Loyola. Castle in Spain where St. Ignatius Loyola was born. From the Basque *lloi-ola*, "muddy place."

Luxembourg. Duchy in Europe and province of Belgium. Formerly *Lutzelburg*, from Old High German *luzzilburh*, "little fortress."

Madeira. Portuguese islands off the coast of Morocco. They are famous for their wines. Early navigators were impressed by the forests of large, unusual trees which they brought back to the King of Portugal. It is the Portuguese word *madeira*, "wood."

Madrid. Capital of Spain. First mentioned as *Magrit*, a name from a north African dialect meaning "aqueduct." There were many aqueducts built here by the Arabs to bring water from the mountains to the dry plains.

Majorca. The largest of the Balearic Islands in the Mediterranean. From the Latin *major*, "older, larger," as opposed to Minorca from the Latin *minor*, "younger, smaller."

Malaga. City in Spain. Founded as a commercial center by the Phoenicians and called by them *Malaka*, "workshop, factory."

Mali. Republic of northwest Africa. The Mandingo tribe called any capital city *Mali*, or "place where the king lives." The name was later extended to their entire empire.

Managua. Capital of Nicaragua. Named after the Barbados cherry tree which grew there. It is a name given by the Arawaks.

Mangalore. City in India. Sanskrit *Mangalapura,* "City of Good Fortune."

Manila. Former capital of the Philippines. Tagalog *ma-nilad,* "place of nilads." The nilad is the plant *Ixora Manila,* a white, blossoming shrub which once grew here in profusion.

Mauna Loa. Semi-active volcano of Hawaii. A native name which means "long mountain."

Mayo. Irish town and county. St. Colman established a monastery here in the 12th century which he called *Magh-eo,* "plain of the yew trees."

Mazatlan. City on the west coast of Mexico. "Place of deer," from the Aztec word *mazatl,* "deer."

Mecca. One of the capital cities of Saudi Arabia. Arabian *Makkah,* "Sanctuary." This holy city of the Moslems is surrounded by an inviolable territory.

Mecklenburg. Former German state and the name of two American counties. *Mikilinburg* was the chief fortress of the Obortites, a Slavonic tribe who succeeded the Teutons in the 6th century. Its name is Germanic, however, and means "large fortress."

Melanesia. One of the three great divisions of the Pacific islands. The name is a Greek formation and means "island of the blacks." The Papuans, who are the prevailing tribe, have very dark skin.

Memphis. Capital of ancient Egypt and largest city in Tennessee. The old name, *Menfi,* is from the Egyptian name of the pyramid of Pepi I, *Men-nefer.* It probably means "his goodness endures."

Menlo Park. Village in New Jersey where Thos. Edison lived, and city in California. From Menlo Castle, Ireland, whose Irish name is *Mion Loch,* "small lake" as contrasted with Lough Corrib.

Menominee. River in Wisconsin. From the name of an Indian tribe which means "wild rice men." They lived mainly on the wild rice found in the lakes and rivers of their country.

Merrimack. River in Massachusetts and New Hampshire. This is a Pennacook Indian name meaning "deep place." The river is navigable as far as Haverhill.

Mesopotamia. Historical region now occupied by modern Iraq. The area between the Tigris and the Euphrates, hence its Greek name meaning "in the middle of the rivers."

Miami. City in Florida. Fontanedo spelled the name *Mayaimi* in 1575 and stated that it meant "very large." It is probably a compound of Choctaw *maiha,* "wide," and *mih,* "it is very." The Laguna de Mayaimi, which gave its name to the city, is now Lake Okeechobee.

Milan. City in northern Italy. Those who imported silks and ribbons from Milan for making hats, etc., were called Milaners; hence our word *millinery.* The Gaulish name was *Mediolanum,* "cleared portion of a wood."

Milwaukee. A Wisconsin river and city at its mouth. From Algonquin Indian *milo-aki,* "good land," referring to the country through which the river flows.

Minneapolis. Largest city in Minnesota. A name formed by adding the Greek word *polis,* "city," to the root of *Minnehaha,* "curling water," the name of the falls which are in the city still.

Mobile. City in Alabama. Name of an Indian tribe. It is probably connected with the Choctaw word *moeli,* "to row, paddle;" hence "the rowers."

Mojave. River and desert in California. Named after the Mojave Indians who lived here. Their name *Hamakhava* referred to the center of tribal activities in the vicinity of the mountains known as the Needles and means "three mountains."

Moluccas. Indonesian islands. The Arabians gave them the name *Jazirat-al-Malik,* "Islands of the Kings." Each island used to have its own king.

Monaco (*mon'ȧ-kō*). Independent principality in southern France. Originally a Phoenician settlement dedicated to *Melkarth,* "The Solitary One," a god corresponding to the Greek god Herakles. The Greeks later translated this as *Monoikos,* hence the present name.

Mongolia. Region in central Asia. "Land of the Mongols." The name of these people is generally believed to come from the Tartar word *mong,* "brave." The word *mogul* derives from the Persian form of their name.

Monrovia. Capital of Liberia. Named in honor of President James Monroe "as an acknowledgment of important benefits conferred on the Settlement by the present illustrious chief magistrate of the United States," in the words of the founders.

Monterey. City and bay in California. **Monterrey.** City in Mexico. Both named after the Count of Monterrey who was Viceroy of Mexico 1595–1603.

Moose Jaw. City in Saskatchewan. The Moose Jaw River makes a 90-degree turn here resembling the outline of a moose's jawbone.

Mostar. City in Yugoslavia. Serbo-Croatian *most,* "bridge," and *stary,* "old." The Turks built a bridge over the Neretva here in 1556.

Mourne. Mountains in Northern Ireland. Irish *Mughdhorna,* the tribal name of the MacMahons who lived here. They are descendents of the Celtic *Mugdornai,* "wearers of ankle-bands."

Multnomah. County in Oregon. This is the former name of the Willamette River and referred to that part of the river below the falls. It is a corruption of the Chinook *nematlnomag,* "down-river."

Munich. City in West Germany. The German name, *München,* is from the phrase *bei den Mönchen,* "near the monks." The reference is to its proximity to a monastery on the Tegernsee.

Murmansk. Port in the northern U.S.S.R. The name is a Russian corruption of Old Norse *Northmadhr,* "Northmen." It is literally "place of the Northmen," referring to the foundations of the early Vikings.

Muskegon. River and city in Michigan. Chippewa Indian *muskig,* "grassy bog." The course of the river through swamp land. The same Indian word has given us the word *muskeg.*

Mysore. City and state in India. From *Mahisur,* "buffalo town."

Nagasaki. Japanese city. In the latter part of the 12th century the district was given as a fief to Nagasaki Kotaro by the founder of the Kamakura Shogunate Government.

Nanking. Chinese city. "Southern Capital." This was the capital of China from 1928–1949.

Naples. City in Italy. From the Greek *Neapolis,* "New City." This type of name was often given to a place in a new colony.

Natchez. City in Mississippi. This is the name of an extinct Indian tribe who lived in the area. From Caddo Indian *Na'htcha,* "forest, timber-land."

Netherlands. European kingdom. Often called Holland from the name of two of its provinces. The name means "low-lying lands" and much of the country is below sea-level. Belgium and the Netherlands were once called the Low Countries.

Nevis. River and mountain in Scotland and island in the West Indies. A Celtic name meaning "misty, watery river."

Newark. Towns in England and city in New Jersey. Old English *niwe,* "new" and *(ge)weorc,* "fortification."

New Guinea. Island in the southwest Pacific. Named by the Spaniard Ynigo Ortiz de Retes in 1545 because he thought the natives resembled the Negroes of Guinea in Africa. Also called **Papua.**

New Orleans. Originally named by its French founders *La Nouvelle Orleans* after a city in France. See *Orleans.*

New Zealand. English form of the Dutch *Nieuw Zeeland.* Tasman gave this name to the islands to commemorate the Dutch province of *Zeeland,* "land reclaimed from the sea."

Niagara. River and falls between Canada and the United States; also two cities named after the falls. From Iroquois *Ongniaahra,* "point of land cut in two." Once a place near Lake Ontario where the wide river cut through the land.

Nice (*nēs*). City on the French Riviera. Founded by the Greeks and called by them *Nikae,* "victory." They won a battle against the coast-dwellers here and erected a defensive bastion in 300 A. D.

Nimes (*nēm*). French city. Originally *Nemausus,* from a Celtic root meaning "holy place, sanctuary." The fabric *denim* was once called *serge de Nimes,* or "serge from Nimes."

Niobrara. River in Nebraska. Corruption of Omaha Indian *ni,* "water" and *bthatha,* "spreading."

Nome. Town in Alaska. When the chart of this area was being drafted, attention was drawn to the fact that the cape here had no name. The notation *? name* was made and this was misread as Nome.

Norway. Old Norse *Norvegr,* "the north-way." This refers to the coastal route used to travel to the northern regions.

Novgorod. City of the U.S.S.R. Russian for "New City."

Nubia. Former kingdom in northeastern Africa. From Egyptian *noub*, "gold." Gold was found here in historical times.

Nunassiaq. Territory of northern Canada. In 1963 the Northwest Territories Council named the eastern part of the Territories *Nunassiaq*, an Eskimo name for "beautiful land."

Nuremberg. The English spelling of Nurnberg, West Germany. From Middle High German *knur*, "rock, cliff or any barren spot of ground."

Nyasaland. Former British protectorate in Africa. Named after Lake Nyasa on which it borders. This is a corruption of the Bantu name Nyanza from the root word *anza*, "body of water."

Oahu. One of the Hawaiian Islands. From a Polynesian word *ahu*, "heap." In this case it refers to a storehouse or place where things gathered were kept in a heap.

Oaxaca. Mexican city and state. Spanish transcription of Nahuatl *Huaxinyacatl*, "place where the guaje trees start to grow."

Oberammergau. Town in Bavaria famous for its Passion Play. "Upper district of the Ammer River."

Odense. City in Denmark. Old Norse *Odin's ve*, "place sacred to the god Odin."

Odessa. City in the Ukrainian S.S.R. Founded as a Russian trading center in 1795 on the site of the Turkish fortress of Hadzhibej. Named in memory of the ancient city of Odessa which was near the present site of Varna, Bulgaria. This name was from the Thracian word *bedu*, "water."

Okefenokee. Swampy region in Georgia. From Hitchiti Indian *oki-finoki*, "shaking water."

Okhotsk. Sea east of Siberia, really an arm of the Pacific. The name of the sea derives from that of the Okhot River which empties into it. The Tungus word *okat* means simply "sea."

Okinawa. Island between Japan and Formosa. The literal meaning of this Japanese name is "rope offshore." It refers to the shape of the long, low island which suggests a knotted rope.

Omaha. City in Nebraska. Commemorates the Omaha Indians whose name is Siouxan for "those going against the current or wind." They once lived on the banks of the Ohio and Wabash rivers, but later migrated up the rivers to the west.

Orense (*ô-rān'sâ*). City of Spain. From the Latin name *Auriensis*, a derivative of *aurum*, "gold." Gold was formerly found there.

Orinoco. River of Venezuela. The Carib Indians made pottery along the banks. This would verify the meaning of "clay river."

Orkney. Islands north of Scotland. A translation of Old Irish *Insi Orc*, "islands of the Uirc tribe." The tribal name means "pigs" and has pagan connotations.

Orleans. City in France. *Aurelianum* was the name given to the ancient Gaulish city of Genabum in honor of Aurelianus, Emperor of Rome, 270–75 A. D.

Osaka. Japanese city. In 1583 the great Japanese warrior, Hideyoshi, built a magnificent castle on a hill here. He called it *O-saka* or "great hill." The name of the castle was later given to the entire city.

Ottawa. Capital of Canada situated on the Ottawa River. The river-name is Iroquois and means "boiling" with reference to its many rapids and falls.

Oxford. City and county in England and town in Mississippi. "Place where the oxen forded the river."

Ozarks. Range of mountains in the Southern States. The French had a custom of shortening long Indian names, thus Arkansas became Ark. The phrase "aux Arks," referred to the range of mountains which lay in the direction of the Arkansas River.

Pakistan. Moslem students in England during the 1930's took the first letters of Punjab, Afghania, Kashmir and Sind, which are all regions of Pakistan, and added the suffix *-stan*, "land."

Palestine. From the name of the Peleshtim or Philistines, one of the tribes of sea peoples who invaded the coastal plain in the 12th century B. C.

Palomar. California mountain which supports a famous observatory. A Spanish name meaning "place of doves."

Panama. Central American Indian word meaning "butterflies." During the migration of butterflies in the summer months the multitudes were so vast that the sky was darkened for days.

Papua. British territory on the island of New Guinea. Portuguese explorers named the aborigines *Papuas* from the Malayan word for "frizzled or curly hair." During World War II, the Australian soldiers in New Guinea called them "fuzzy-wuzzies."

Paris. Name of the French capital and of many American towns. Commemorates the Gaulish tribe of the *Parisii*, "the bold ones."

Passamaquoddy. Bay in Maine. Malecite Indian for "place where pollack abound." The pollack is a fish related to the cod.

Pawtucket. City in Rhode Island. Narragansett Indian for "at the falls on the tidal stream." The Pawtucket Falls on the Blackstone River are here.

Pecs. City in Hungary. Known in ancient times as *Quinque Ecclesiae*, "Five Churches." From Old Slavic *piec*, "five."

Peking. Capital of the People's Republic of China. "Northern Capital," as opposed to Nanking. From 1928 to 1949 the city was known as *Peiping* or "Northern Peace."

Pembroke. Welsh town and county and many towns in America. Old Welsh *pen-brog*, "head of land." It is at the western extremity of Wales.

Pensacola. City in Florida. It is the name of a Muskhogean Indian tribe, who were called by the Choctaws *panshi-okla*, "hair people." Both men and women of the tribe wore their hair long.

Pernambuco. Former name of Recife, city of Brazil. From the Guarani Indian *paranambuku*, "long river."

Persia. Historical name of Iran. Named for the Parsa, an Indo-European people who lived here. Their name probably derives from Sanskrit *parashu*, "battle-axe," and refers to their use of these weapons in battle.

Perth. City in Scotland, Australia, and America. From a Pictish word related to the Welsh word *perth*, "bush, hedge."

Peru. The Spanish heard of a place called Viru by which entrance to the Incan Empire was presumably gained. The name was ultimately given to the entire country in a corrupted form. It is from Kechua Indian *wiru*, a species of South American bamboo.

Phoenicia. Ancient kingdom in vicinity of modern Syria and Israel. Famous for its purple dye industry, the name is from the Greek *phoenix*, "purple."

Platte. River in Nebraska. This is a misspelling of the French word *plate*, "flat." The river is extremely shallow and wide.

Polynesia. Pacific islands. Greek for "many islands."

Pomerania. Former German province on the Baltic; home of the pomeranian dog. Old Slavic *po-morije*, "seacoast."

Pondicherry. City in India, formerly a French dependency. Earlier *Podutscheri*, from Dravidian *podu*, "new," and *tscheri*, "city."

Popocatepetl (*pō-pô-kăt'ĕ-pĕt'l*). Mexican volcano. An Aztec name meaning "smoky mountain," referring to its volcanic activity.

Portugal. From *Portucale*, the name given to the region behind the "port of Cale." The name Cale is Celtic and means "shelter."

Potomac. American river. Name of an Algonquin town erroneously applied to the river. It means "where things are brought," probably tributes to a neighboring tribe.

Prague. Capital of Czechoslovakia. An Old Slavic word meaning "clearing burnt by the sun."

Recife (*rĕ-sē'fĕ*). City in Brazil. An enormous reef (Portuguese *recife*) encloses the harbor.

Regina. Capital of Saskatchewan. Honors Queen Victoria, called Victoria Regina in Latin.

Reykjavik (*rā'kyä-vēk'*). Capital of Iceland. Old Norse *reykr-vik*, "smoky bay." The first settlers mistook the clouds of steam from local hotsprings for smoke.

Riga. Capital of Latvia. From Lithuanian *ringa*, "something crooked," with reference to the stream on which the city was built.

Rostock. City in East Germany. Old Slavic *rastok'*, "fork in a river."

Rotorua. Thermal spa in New Zealand. It was the second big lake discovered by the Maori explorer Ihenga, hence its Maori name, "Second Lake."

Rotterdam. City in the Netherlands. Low German for "dam on the Rotte River." Rotte is the river "of duckweed."

Ruhr. German river and valley. Old High German *ruora*, "following with a strong, swift course."

Russia. Swedish tribes living around Kiev were called *Rus*. The name was gradually extended to the whole country.

Santos. City in Brazil. From the Portuguese *Hospital dos Santos*, "Hospital of the Saints." This was a hospital for sailors built in the 16th century.

Saskatoon. City in Saskatchewan. A kind of Juneberry called by the Cree Indians *missaskatoomina* grew here in abundance.

Saxony. Former German kingdom. "Land of the Saxons." The tribal name derives from Old High German *sahso*, "one-edged sword." This was their battle-weapon.

Sedalia. City in Missouri. Named by George R. Smith after his daughter Sarah, whom he called "Sed."

Shanghai. Chinese for "upper sea." Two arms of the sea extended inland at one time and Shanghai was on the upper arm.

Shantung. Chinese province famous for its silk. Chinese *shan*, "mountains" and *tung*, "east." It is the province "east of the mountains" while Shansi is "west of the mountains."

Sheffield. City in England. "Field by the River Sheaf." The *Sheaf* is Old English for "boundary river" and it separates Derbyshire and Yorkshire.

Sorrento. City in Italy. Modern form of Latin *Surrentum* from Greek *Seiren*, "siren or sea-nymph." The city faced the Sea of the Sirens.

Staten Island. Between New Jersey and Long Island. Named *Staaten Eylandt* during the Dutch period in honor of the States (Staaten) General, the governing body of the Netherlands at that time.

Stockholm. Capital of Sweden. Old Norse *stokkr* is the first element of Stocksund, "Sound of stakes or stumps." Stockholm is the *holm*, or island, in Stocksund.

Strasbourg. French city. Formerly *Stratesburg*, "fortress on the Roman street or road."

Sudan. African republic. Arabic *Blad-es-Soudane*, "Country of the Blacks." Originally referred to people not of Semitic stock but later extended to the entire area.

Susquehanna. River in Pennsylvania. Delaware Indian *Assisku-hanne*, "muddy stream."

Sussex. County in England and counties in the U.S. Old English *Suth-Seaxa*, "South Saxons."

Syracuse. Cities in Sicily and New York State. From the Greek *Syrako*, the name of a swamp in Sicily where the Greeks established a colony. It means "sour or brackish water."

Tahoe. Lake between California and Nevada. Corrupted form of the Washoe Indian word for lake, *da'au*.

Tallahassee. City in Florida. Creek Indian *talwa-hasi*, 'old town."

Tasco. Mexican town and art colony. The name is related to the native word *tlachtli*, "ball." The place was once consecrated to the ritual games of the Aztecs.

Thames. River in England and rivers in North America. A British river-name, formerly *Tamesis*, "dark river."

Ticonderoga. Fort and town in New York State. Lake George empties into Lake Champlain here, hence the Mohawk name "where two currents join."

Timor. Indonesian island. Malayan word for "east." Timor is the most easterly of the Sunda Islands.

Tirana. Capital of Albania. Founded in the early 17th century by the Turks and named after Teheran, Persia, after a Turkish victory there.

Titicaca. Lake in Bolivia. Kechua Indian *titi*, "lead," and *gaga*, "rock." The name was originally applied to the rocks which surround the lake.

Tobruk. Town in Libya. Arabic pronunciation of the Greek *Antipyrgos*, "opposite the rock." A firm rock in the harbor protected ships from the east wind.

Tokyo. City in Japan. "New Capital." Kyoto was the the "Old Capital."

Toronto. City in Ontario. An Iroquois name meaning "tree or stump projecting out of the water."

Transvaal. Province of the Republic of South Africa. Named by the Boers when they settled "across the Vaal River." *Vaal* is Dutch for "yellow."

Tripoli. Capital of Libya. A union of three ancient cities called Oea, Leptis Magna, and Sabata. Greek for "three cities."

Tucson. City in Arizona. Derived from the Papago Indian name of *Tuqui-son*, "black-based." The base of the Sentinel Mountains here is darker in color than the summit.

Tunis. Capital of Tunisia, Africa. The Berber root *ENS*, "to sleep" suggests that this was once a place for passing the night; an encampment.

Turkey. "The country of the Turks." These people were originally inhabitants of Mongolia and received their name from living near a hill called *Turku*, "helmet." The hill was helmet-shaped.

Tuskegee. City in Alabama. From the name of a Muskhogean tribe. They were "warriors" and Creek Indian word for warriors, *taskialgi*, is related.

Ukraine. Part of the U.S.S.R. From the Slavic *ukrai*, "on the edge," hence "boundary." This territory separated the Poles from the Mongolian Tartars.

Vaduz. Capital of Liechenstein. Formerly *Valdulz*, from *Vallis Dulcis*, which is Latin for "Sweet Valley."

Valparaiso. Seaport in Chile. Spanish for "valley of paradise," referring to the beautiful situation and lush plant growth.

Vancouver. Cities in Washington State and British Columbia and island off British Columbia. Named after Capt. George Vancouver, an English navigator who explored this coast 1792–94.

Venezuela. South American republic. When Spanish explorers saw the native huts built on pilings off Maracaibo, they were reminded of the city of Venice, Italy, and gave the name *Venezuela*, which is Spanish for "Little Venice."

Waco. City in Texas. Named after the Waco Indians. Their name was originally *Wehiku*, a corruption of Mexico, and they were so-called because they were always fighting the Mexicans.

Waikiki. Beach at Honolulu. Hawaiian for "spouting water."

Wichita. City in Kansas. From an Indian tribe of that name which means simply "the men."

Winchester. City in England and many places in America. Earlier *Ventacestre*, Old English for "fort on the Venta River." *Venta* is a Celtic river-name meaning "smiling, pleasant."

Windsor. Town in England and city in Ontario. Old English *Windlesora*, "windlass-shore." This was a landing-place with a windlass for pulling the boats up the river-bank.

Winnebago. Wisconsin lake. The name signifies "dirty, stinking water," in the Fox and Sauk Indian languages. The English called the Winnebago Indians "The Stinkards.'

Winnipeg. Capital of Manitoba. The name is Cree Indian *win*, "dirty" and *nipi*, "water." The reference is to the waters of Lake Winnipeg which lies to the north.

Yemen. Independent kingdom in Arabia. From the Arabic *yaman*, "to the right-hand." Yemen is on the right side of the region of Hejaz, while Syria is on the left or north side.

Yokohama. City and seaport of Japan. Japanese for "sheltered beach."

York. City and county of England; hence New York. In the year 730 the name was *Eburacum* which is Celtic for "place of the yew tree." Later the Old English word *wic*, "village" was added and finally the Scandinavians contracted the name to its present form.

Yosemite. National park in California. This is a name which was given to a band of renegades from various tribes who once lived here. In the local Indian dialect it means "killers."

Yugoslavia. The name of this European republic is Serbo-Croatian for "South Slavs," as distinguished from East and West Slavs to the north.

Yuma. Town in Arizona. The Yuma tribe received their name from their habit of making huge fires to induce rain. It derives from the Spanish *umo*, "smoke."

Zaragoza. City in Spain; often spelled *Saragossa*. An Iberian city which received the name *Caesaraugusta* in 27 B. C. in honor of that emperor. Zaragoza is an Arabic corruption.

NATIONAL AND STATE EMBLEMS

The human sentiments of fealty to rulers and of tribal or national loyalty have been embodied in many different symbols. On the other hand, for rulers and reigning houses there have been evolved, through the science of heraldry, elaborate emblems and arms. Heraldry has devised an extensive and intricate system of patterns and colors by which to depict the relationships and the history of families.

In the Old World, national coats of arms have often combined the personal emblems of rulers with symbols of the composition and the authority of the state. Primitive tribes had their totems, or figures of animals or birds, which served as tribal symbols. These emblems carried more or less religious meaning. In the ancient Eastern nations, the emblem of the ruler was frequently some animal form which represented a deity.

For the Romans, the *fasces*, or rods, of the lictor became the symbol of civil authority, while the eagle was adopted as the sign of the conquering might of Roman legions. Both these symbols have persisted down to modern times. The official seal of France, for example, carries a seated female figure representing the republic, bearing the fasces.

The eagle and the lion have been the favorite animal emblems of European states. The Byzantine emperors adopted the double-headed eagle as representing their sovereignty over the East and the West.

American Eagle, The. The white-headed or bald eagle is the emblem on the coat of arms of the United States, and is also the adopted badge of the order of the Cincinnati. Owing to the alleged cowardice and predatory habits of the white-headed eagle, Benjamin Franklin is said to have expressed regret that it had been chosen as America's national emblem. Geographically, however, the choice of this bird is appropriate, since its habitat extends over the whole of North America.

Among European states, the lion as a heraldic device symbolizes power and has shared honors with the eagle. The arms of Great Britain, Belgium, Bulgaria, Holland, and Norway bear each a golden lion; those of Denmark carry blue lions; while those of Spain bear a red lion. Rumania and Sweden have in their arms both an eagle and a lion. On the arms of Czechoslovakia, two gold lions support a shield, in the quartering of which appear eagles.

Latin American states have generally avoided in their emblems all suggestions of Old World royalty. In their official arms, the liberty cap and flags frequently appear. For Bolivia, Colombia, and Ecuador, the condor, native to these countries, takes the place which the eagle holds in the heraldry of other nations.

Greece and Switzerland have a cross as the chief emblem in their arms, the former silver, the latter white. In Japan, the imperial emblem is the golden chrysanthemum.

Flowers or plants have frequently been chosen as national emblems. The following list gives those that by tradition have come to be regarded as emblems of various nations.

Australia	Golden Wattle
Canada	Maple Leaf
China	Narcissus
Egypt	Lotus
England	Rose
France	Fleur-de-lis
Germany	Cornflower
Greece	Violet
India	Lotus
Ireland	Shamrock
Italy	White Lily
Japan	Chrysanthemum
Mexico	Nopal Cactus, or Prickly Pear
Persia	Rose
Scotland	Thistle
Spain	Pomegranate
Switzerland	Edelweiss
United States	Goldenrod (by popular choice)

Practically all the American states have chosen official state flowers and state birds. These will be found in the table immediately following this section.

NATIONAL FLAGS

In ancient times, just as a motto was usually a slogan, or battle cry, an emblem or a banner was a symbol of religious or patriotic devotion that was calculated to rouse the fighting spirit of a group of warriors. Banners with tribal or national significance are mentioned in Biblical references, as in Psalm 20:5, 60:4, and Isaiah 13:2. There is abundant evidence that similar devices were used by Persian, Greek, and other national armies among the ancients. Sometimes an emblem was restricted to a particular group or leader, but with the merging of military units there was need for a symbol to stand for the army as a whole, and for the nation which it served. Thus the eagle became the official emblem for all the Roman legions and was recognized as the symbol of national authority throughout the Roman empire. In medieval times the standard often took the form of a banner borne upon a lance, or "flagstaff," and in appearance was comparable to a pennant flying from the mast of a ship.

Design of National Flags

Modern national flags are distinguished principally by the colors they display and the patterns in which they display them.

Here are briefly described the official flags of the countries of the world with the exception of the American flag. For an illustrated account of its evolution, see *Stars and Stripes*. In the descriptions below, the colors if vertical are given in the sequence of left (mast end) to right; if horizontal, they are given in the sequence of top to bottom.

Afghanistan. Three vertical bars—black, red, white. In the center is a white ensign.

Albania. Red, with black double-headed eagle and yellow-bordered red star above.

Algeria. Green and white vertical bars with a red crescent and a red star.

Argentina. Three horizontal bands—blue, white, blue, with gold sun in the white.

Australia. Blue field with union jack in upper left with large seven-pointed star below and southern-cross constellation of five stars on field.

Austria. Three horizontal stripes—red, white, red, with black double-headed eagle in the white.

Belgium. Three vertical bars—black, yellow, red.

Bolivia. Three horizontal stripes—red, yellow, green, with national arms in center of yellow.

Brazil. On a green field, a yellow lozenge containing a blue circle in which is represented a heavenly constellation. Across the blue circle runs a white band bearing the motto, *Ordem e progresso*, "Order and Progress."

Bulgaria. Three horizontal stripes—white, green, red, with coat of arms (gold-crowned lion) in upper left corner.

Burma. Red with dark blue upper left corner, in which is a large white five-pointed star surrounded by five smaller stars.

Cambodia. Three horizontal stripes—blue, red, blue, with a white emblem in the larger red stripe.

Canada. Red maple leaf with 11 points on white square flanked by vertical red bars one-half width of square.

Ceylon. Two vertical stripes of green and saffron at left of dark red field having yellow lion in center, the entire flag being bordered with yellow.

Chile. Two wide bands, white and red, with blue upper left section containing a five-pointed white star.

China, Nationalist. Red with blue upper left section, in which appears a white sun.

China, People's Republic of. Red, with white upper left section.

Colombia. Upper half is yellow band, below which are two horizontal bands of blue and red.

Congo (Brazzaville). Gold diagonal stripe from lower left to upper right divides green upper left triangle and red lower right triangle.

Congo (Kinshasa). Blue field with diagonal stripe from lower left to upper right corner, stripe being red with yellow border on each side. Gold five-pointed star is in blue upper left triangle.

Costa Rica. Five horizontal bands—blue, white, red (wide), white, blue, with emblem in red band.

Cuba. Five horizontal stripes—blue, white, blue, white, blue; red triangle at left containing large white star.

Cyprus. White field containing gold map of Cyprus above crossed olive branches.

Czechoslovakia. Two horizontal bands, white and red, with blue triangle at left, the base extending full width of flag.

Dahomey. One vertical green bar and two horizontal bands, yellow and red.

Denmark. A red field divided by a white cross, the vertical element being closer to the left. This is the oldest national flag design in the world, said to date from 1219.

Dominican Republic. A white cross divides the field into quarters—upper left, blue; lower left, red; upper right, red; lower right, blue. The national emblem is centered in the white cross.

Ecuador. Three horizontal bands—yellow, blue, red, the yellow being twice the width of each of the others. The arms of the state are superimposed.

Egypt. See *United Arab Republic.*

Eire. Three vertical bars—green, white, orange.

Ethiopia. Three horizontal bands—green, yellow, red, with a lion in the yellow band.

Finland. A blue cross in a white field, the vertical element being closer to the left.

France. Three vertical bars—blue, white, red.

Gabon. Three horizontal bands—green, gold, blue.

Germany, East. Three horizontal stripes—black, red, gold, with hammer and sickle superimposed.

Germany, West. Three horizontal stripes—black, red, gold.

Ghana. Three horizontal bands—red, gold, green, with a black star in the center.

Great Britain. Union jack, consisting of a blue field with three superimposed crosses—St. George's for England (red on white field), St. Andrew's for Scotland (white on blue field), and St. Patrick's for Ireland (red on white field). The first is horizontal and vertical, while the last two run diagonally. To preserve the identity of the white St. Andrew's cross, the white borders of the diagonal are unequal, the white on one side being twice the width of the white on the other.

Greece. Nine horizontal stripes of alternating blue and white, with a white cross on blue field in upper left section.

Guatemala. Three vertical bars—blue, white, blue, with the national arms in the white bar.

Guinea. Three vertical bars—red, yellow, green.

Haiti. Two vertical bands of black and red.

Honduras. Three horizontal bands—blue, white, blue, the central band containing five blue stars.

Hungary. Three horizontal bands—red, white, green.

Iceland. Blue, with a white-bordered red cross, the vertical element being closer to the left.

India. Three horizontal bands—saffron, white, and dark green, with 24-spoke wheel of Asoka in the center of the white band.

Indonesia. Black with two horizontal stripes of red and white.

Iran. Three horizontal bands—green, white, red, with golden lion and sun in white band.

Iraq. Three horizontal bands—red, white, black, with two green stars on the white band.

Israel. White with two horizontal blue stripes above and below blue star of David.

Italy. Three vertical bars—dark green, white, red.

Ivory Coast. Three vertical bars—orange, white, green.

Jamaica. Two horizontal bands, green and black with a diagonal gold cross.

Japan. White ground with red sun.

Jordan. Three horizontal bands—black, white, green. At left is red triangle containing seven-pointed white star.

Kenya. Three horizontal bars—black, red, green separated by white stripes with a shield and crossed spears in the center.

Korea (South). White with large circle in center, this being divided by a curved line into red above and blue below. Near each corner is a set of black bars, some long and some short, arranged in different combinations.

Kuwait. Three horizontal bands, with a black trapezoid superimposed on the left.

Laos. Red with white three-headed elephant supporting parasol.

Lebanon. Three horizontal bands—red, white, red. The white band is twice the width of each red band and has a green cedar tree in the center.

Liberia. Eleven horizontal stripes, red and white alternating. At upper left is a blue square with a white five-pointed star.

Libya. Three horizontal bands—red, black, green, with a white crescent and star in the center of the black, which is twice the width of each of the others.

Liechtenstein. Two horizontal bands, blue and red.

Luxembourg. Three horizontal bands—red, white, blue.

Malagasy. A white bar at left and two horizontal bands, red and green.

Malawi. Three horizontal bands—black, red, and green, with red rising sun in black band.

Malaysia. Fourteen red and white alternating horizontal stripes with a crescent and 14-pointed star in upper left corner.

Mali. Three vertical bars—green, yellow, red.

Malta. Two vertical bars, white and red, with red-edged cross in white bar.

Mauritania. Green with gold crescent and star.

Mexico. Three vertical bars—green, white, red, with eagle and cactus emblem on the white bar.

Monaco. Two horizontal bands, red and white.

Morocco. Red with green five-pointed star.

Netherlands. Three horizontal bands—red, white, blue.

New Zealand. Blue with union jack at upper left corner and four five-pointed red stars with white borders in the blue field.

Nicaragua. Three horizontal bands—blue, white, blue, with national ensign on the white band.

Nepal. Double-peaked red standard with sun and moon with blue borders.

Niger. Three horizontal bands—orange, white, and green, with orange sun in center of white band.

Nigeria. Three vertical bars—green, white, green.

Norway. Red with white-bordered blue cross superimposed, its vertical element being closer to left.

Pakistan. Dark green with white vertical bar at left and white heraldic five-pointed star in a white crescent in center of green bar.

Panama. Four quarters as follows: upper left, white with a blue star; upper right, red; lower left, blue; lower right, white with a red star.

Paraguay. Three horizontal bands—red, white, blue. White band has the national ensign on the obverse side and, on the reverse side, a lion with the inscription *Paz y Justicia* "Peace and Justice."

Peru. Three vertical bars—red, white, red, with the coat of arms on the white.

Philippines. Two horizontal bands, blue and red, with white triangle at left containing a gold sun and three gold stars.

Poland. Two horizontal bands, white and red.

Portugal. Two vertical bars, green and red with widths in proportion of 2 to 3. Superimposed on the dividing line is a blue-bordered white shield on a gold circle, the latter commemorating Prince Henry, the 15th century explorer.

Rumania. Three vertical bars—blue, yellow, red, with the national ensign in the center.

Russia. Red with five-pointed gold star in upper left corner, below which is a gold hammer and sickle.

Rwanda. Three vertical bars—red, yellow, green, with a black R in the yellow.

Salvador. Three horizontal bands—blue, white, blue, with coat of arms on the white.

San Marino. Two horizontal bands, blue and white.

Saudi Arabia. Green with a white sword below white Arabic characters.

Senegal. Three vertical bars—green, gold, red, with a green star in the center of the gold bar.

Sierra Leone. Three horizontal bands—green, white, blue.

Singapore. Two horizontal bands of red and white with a white crescent and five stars in the left half of the red.

Somali Republic. Light blue with large five-pointed white star in center.

South Africa. Three horizontal bands—orange, white, blue, the white having superimposed on it the flags of Great Britain, the South African Republic, and the Orange Free State.

Spain. Three horizontal bands—red, yellow, red, with the coat of arms in the yellow, which is twice the width of each of the other bands.

Sudan. Three horizontal bars—blue, yellow, green.

Sweden. Yellow cross on a medium blue field, the vertical element being closer to the left.

Switzerland. White cross on a yellow field.

Syria. Three horizontal bands—red, white, black, with three green stars in the white.

Tanzania. Green triangle upper left, blue triangle lower right, separated by a gold-bordered diagonal black stripe.

Thailand. Five horizontal stripes—red, white, blue, white, red, the blue being double the width of each of the others.

Togo. Five horizontal stripes—green, gold, green, gold, green with a red upper left section containing a white star.

Trinidad. Red with white-bordered black stripe running diagonally from upper left corner.

Tunisia. Red with a white circle enclosing a red crescent and star.

Turkey. Red with white crescent and five-pointed star. The star and crescent was the ensign of Byzantium (later Constantinople, now Istanboul) said to have been adopted after the city defeated an attack on a moonlight night by Philip of Macedon in 339 B.C.

Uganda. Six horizontal stripes—black, yellow, red, black, yellow, red, with white circle in center enclosing a crested crane.

United Arab Republic. Three horizontal bands—red, white, black, with two green stars in white.

United Nations. Light blue with white global map of the world in center supported by two olive branches.

Upper Volta. Three horizontal bands—black, white, red.

Uruguay. Nine alternating white stripes and blue stripes, with a rising sun on white in the upper left section.

Vatican City. Two equal horizontal bands, white and yellow, the white containing the papal insignia—a tiara above two crossed keys, one gold and one silver.

Venezuela. Three horizontal bands—yellow, blue, red, with an arc of seven white stars in the blue band.

Viet-Nam, North. A five-pointed yellow star in a field of red.

Viet-Nam, South. Yellow, with three thin horizontal red stripes near the center.

Yemen. Three horizontal bands—red, white, black, with a green star in the white.

Yugoslavia. Three horizontal bands—blue, white, red, with a five-pointed yellow-bordered red star in the white.

Zambia. Green with a block of vertical red, black, and orange bars in the lower right corner surmounted by an orange eagle.

STATE MOTTOES, NICKNAMES, BIRDS, AND FLOWERS

State	Motto, with Year of Adoption	Translation	Nickname of State	State Bird	State Flower
Alabama	Audemus Jura Nostra Defendere.	We Dare Defend our Rights, 1939	Cotton	Yellowhammer	Camellia
Alaska	None		"The Last Frontier"	Willow Ptarmigan	Forget-me-not
Arizona	Ditat Deus. 1863	God Enriches	Grand Canyon	Cactus Wren	Saguaro Cactus
Arkansas	Regnat Populus. 1864	The People Rule	Wonder	Mocking Bird	Apple Blossom
California	Eureka	I Have Found It	Golden	Valley Quail	Golden Poppy
Colorado	Nil sine Numine	Nothing without the Deity	Centennial	Lark Bunting	Rocky Mountain Columbine
Connecticut	Qui Transtulit Sustinet 1842	He Who Transplanted Continues to Sustain	Constitution (Nutmeg)	Robin	Mountain Laurel
Delaware	Liberty and Independence		Diamond (Blue Hen)	Blue Hen Chicken	Peach Blossom
Florida	In God We Trust. 1846		Peninsula	Mocking Bird	Orange Blossom
Georgia	Wisdom, Justice, Moderation		Cracker	Brown Thrasher	Cherokee Rose
Hawaii	Ua Mau Ke Ea O Ka Aina I Ka Pono	The life of the land is perpetuated in righteousness.	Aloha	Nene (Hawaiian goose)	Hibiscus
Idaho	Esto Perpetua. 1886	Mayest Thou Endure Forever!	Gem	Mountain Bluebird	Syringa

STATE MOTTOES, NICKNAMES, BIRDS, AND FLOWERS—Con.

STATE	Motto, with Year of Adoption	Translation	Nickname of State	State Bird	State Flower
Illinois	State Sovereignty, National Union. 1818	. . . .	Prairie (Sucker)	Cardinal	Native Violet
Indiana	The Crossroads of America	. . . .	Hoosier	Cardinal	Peony
Iowa	Our Liberties We Prize, and Our Rights We Will Maintain	. . . .	Hawkeye	Eastern Goldfinch	Wild Rose
Kansas	Ad Astra per Aspera. 1861	To the Stars through Difficulties	Sunflower (Jayhawker)	Western Meadow Lark	Native Sunflower
Kentucky	United We Stand, Divided We Fall. 1792	. . . .	Blue Grass (Corncracker)	Cardinal	Goldenrod
Louisiana	Union Justice, and Confidence	. . . .	Pelican (Creole)	Eastern Brown Pelican	Magnolia
Maine	Dirigo	I Guide	Pine-Tree	Chickadee	Pine Cone and Tassel
Maryland	Scuto Bonæ Voluntatis Tuæ Coronasti Nos	With the Shield of Thy Good-Will Thou Hast Covered Us	Old-Line	Baltimore Oriole	Black-eyed Susan
Massachusetts	Ense Petit Placidam sub Libertate Quietem. 1780	By the Sword We Seek Peace, but Peace only under Liberty	Bay (Old Colony)	Chickadee	Mayflower
Michigan	Si Quæris Peninsulam Amœnam Circumspice. 1835	If You Seek a Pleasant Peninsula, Look around You	Wolverine	Robin	Apple Blossom
Minnesota	L'étoile du Nord. 1858	The Star of the North	Gopher	American Goldfinch	Moccasin Flower
Mississippi	Virtute et Armis. 1894	By Valor and Arms	Bayou (Magnolia)	Mocking Bird	Magnolia
Missouri	Salus Populi Suprema Lex Esto. 1822	Let the Welfare of the People Be the Supreme Law	Show-Me	Bluebird	Hawthorn
Montana	Oro y Plata. 1864	Gold and Silver	Treasure	Meadow Lark	Bitterroot
Nebraska	Equality before the Law. 1867	. . . .	Corn Husker (Tree-Planter)	Western Meadow Lark	Goldenrod
Nevada	All for Our Country. 1866	. . . .	Sagebrush (Silver)	Mountain Bluebird	Sagebrush
New Hampshire	Live free or die	. . . .	Granite	Purple Finch	Purple Lilac
New Jersey	Liberty and Prosperity. 1776	. . . .	Garden	Eastern Goldfinch	Violet
New Mexico	Crescit Eundo. 1850	It grows as it goes	Sunshine	Road Runner	Yucca Flower
New York	Excelsior. 1809	Higher	Empire	Eastern Bluebird	Rose
North Carolina	Esse quam Videri. 1893	To Be rather than to Seem	Tar Heel (Turpentine)	Cardinal	Dogwood
North Dakota	Liberty and Union, Now and Forever, One and Inseparable	. . . .	Sioux (Flickertail)	Western Meadow Lark	Wild Prairie Rose
Ohio	With God, all things are possible. 1959	. . . .	Buckeye	Cardinal	Scarlet Carnation
Oklahoma	Labor Omnia Vincit	Labor Conquers All Things	Sooner	Scissortailed Flycatcher	Mistletoe
Oregon	The Union	. . . .	Beaver	Western Meadow Lark	Oregon Grape
Pennsylvania	Virtue, Liberty, and Independence. 1809	. . . .	Keystone*	Ruffed Grouse	Mountain Laurel
Rhode Island	Hope. 1864	. . . .	Little Rhody	Rhode Island Red	Violet
South Carolina	Animis Opibusque Parati.	Ready in Soul and Resource	Palmetto	Carolina Wren	Yellow Jessamine
South Dakota	Under God the People Rule	. . . .	Coyote	Ringnecked Pheasant	Pasque Flower
Tennessee	Agriculture and commerce. 1797	. . . .	Volunteer	Mocking Bird	Iris
Texas	Friendship. 1930.	. . . .	Lone-Star	Mocking Bird	Bluebonnet
Utah	Industry	. . . .	Beehive	Seagull	Sego Lily
Vermont	Freedom and Unity. 1866	. . . .	Green Mountain.	Hermit Thrush	Red Clover
Virginia	Sic Semper Tyrannis	Thus ever to Tyrants	Old Dominion	Cardinal	Dogwood
Washington	Alki	By and By	Evergreen	Willow Goldfinch	Western Rhododendron
West Virginia	Montani Semper Liberi. 1863	Mountaineers Are Always Free Men	Panhandle	Cardinal	Big Rhododendron
Wisconsin	Forward	. . . .	Badger	Robin	Violet
Wyoming	Cedant Arma Togæ. 1868	Let Arms Yield to the Gown	Equality	Meadow Lark	Indian Paintbrush

*Reference is to situation at apex of arch formed by states from North Carolina to New England.

HOLIDAYS IN THE UNITED STATES

Although the term "national holiday" is popularly applied to the Fourth of July and other generally observed holidays, the term is really a misnomer. Congress can point the way by legislating holidays for the District of Columbia and the territories under Federal control, but legal holidays are established by statute in the various states, as shown in the following list. Unless otherwise stated, Labor Day is the first Monday in September.

HOLIDAYS IN THE VARIOUS STATES

Alabama.—Jan. 1; Jan. 19 (Lee's birthday); Feb. 22 (Washington's birthday); Mardi Gras; Apr. 13 (Jefferson's birthday); Apr. 26 (Confederate Memorial day); June 3 (Jeff. Davis's birthday); July 4; Labor day; General Election day; Nov. 11; Thanksgiving day; Dec. 25; Arbor day.

Alaska.—Jan. 1; Feb. 12 (Lincoln's birthday); Feb. 22; Mar. 30 (Seward day); May 30; July 4; Oct. 18 (Alaska day); Thanksgiving day; Dec. 25.

Arizona.—Jan. 1; Feb. 14 (Admission day); Feb. 22; May 30; July 4; Labor day; Oct. 12 (Columbus day); General Election day; Nov. 11; Thanksgiving; Dec. 25; Arbor day.

Arkansas.—Jan 1; Jan. 19; Feb. 22; June 3; July 4; Oct. 12; Labor day; General Election day; Nov. 11; Thanksgiving day; Dec. 25, Arbor day.

California.—Jan. 1; Feb. 12; Feb. 22; May 30; July 4; Sept. 9 (Admission day); Labor day; Oct. 12; General Election day; Nov. 11; Thanksgiving day; Dec. 25; Arbor day.

Colorado.—Jan. 1; Feb. 12; Feb. 22; May 30; July 4; Aug. 1 (Colorado day); Labor day; Oct. 12; General Election day; Nov. 11; Thanksgiving day; Dec. 25; Arbor day.

Connecticut.—Jan. 1; Feb. 12; Feb. 22; Good Friday; May 30; July 4; Labor day; Oct. 12; General Election day; Thanksgiving day; Dec. 25; Arbor day.

Delaware.—Jan. 1; Feb. 12; Feb. 22; Good Friday; May 30; July 4; Labor day; Oct. 12; General Election day; Thanksgiving day; Dec. 7 (Delaware day); Dec. 25; Arbor day.

District of Columbia.—Jan. 1; Jan. 20 (Inauguration day); Feb. 22; May 30; July 4; Labor day; Nov. 11; Thanksgiving day; Dec. 25; Arbor day.

Florida.—Jan. 1; Jan. 19 (Lee's birthday); Feb. 22; Mardi Gras; Good Friday; April 26 (Confederate Memorial day); June 3 (Jeff. Davis's birthday); July 4; Labor day; Oct. 12; General Election day; Nov. 11; Thanksgiving day; Dec. 25; Arbor day.

Georgia.—Jan. 1; Jan. 19 (Lee's birthday); Feb. 12 (Georgia day); Feb. 22; Apr. 26 (Confederate Memorial day); June 3; July 4; Labor day; General Election day; Thanksgiving day; Dec. 25; Arbor day.

Hawaii.—Jan. 1; May 30; June 11; July 4; Labor day; Thanksgiving day; Dec. 25.

Idaho.—Jan. 1; Feb. 22; May 30; June 15 (Pioneer day); July 4; Labor day; General Election day; Thanksgiving day; Dec. 25; Arbor day.

Illinois.—Jan. 1; Feb. 12; Feb. 22; May 30; July 4; Labor day; Oct. 12; General Election day; Nov. 11; Thanksgiving day; Dec. 25; Arbor day.

Indiana.—Jan. 1; Feb. 12; Feb. 22; May 30; July 4; Labor day; Oct. 12; General Election day; Thanksgiving day; Dec. 25; Arbor day.

Iowa.—Jan. 1; Feb. 12; Feb. 22; May 30; July 4; Labor day; General Election day; Nov. 11; Thanksgiving day; Dec. 25; Arbor day.

Kansas.—Jan. 1; Feb. 12; Feb. 22; May 30; July 4; Labor day; Oct. 12; General Election day; Thanksgiving day; Dec. 25; Arbor day.

Kentucky.—Jan. 1; Feb. 12; Feb. 22; May 30; July 4; Labor day; Oct. 12; General Election day; Thanksgiving day; Dec. 25; Arbor day.

Louisiana.—Jan. 1; Jan. 8 (anniversary of the battle of New Orleans); Feb. 22; Mardi Gras; Good Friday; June 3 (Jeff Davis's birthday); July 4; Labor day; Oct. 12; Nov. 1 (All Saints' day); General Election day; Nov. 11; Thanksgiving day; Dec. 25; Arbor day.

Maine.—Jan. 1; Feb. 22; Apr. 19 (Patriots' day); May 30; July 4; Labor day; General Election day 'Courts only'; Thanksgiving day; Dec. 25; Arbor day.

Maryland.—Jan. 1; Feb. 22; Mar. 25 (Maryland day); Good Friday; May 30; July 4; Labor day; Sept. 12 (Defenders' day); Oct. 12; General Election day; Thanksgiving day; Dec. 25; Arbor day.

Massachusetts.—Jan. 1; Feb. 12; Feb. 22; Apr. 19 (Patriots' day); May 30; July 4; Labor day; Oct. 12; Thanksgiving day; Dec. 25; Arbor day.

Michigan.—Jan. 1; Feb. 12; Feb. 22; May 30; July 4; Labor day; General Election day; Thanksgiving day; Dec. 25; Arbor day.

Minnesota.—Jan. 1; Feb. 12; Feb. 22; Good Friday; May 30; July 4; Labor day; General Election day; Nov. 11; Thanksgiving day; Dec. 25; Arbor day.

Mississippi.—Jan. 1; Jan. 19; Feb. 22; Apr. 26 (Confederate Memorial day); June 3; July 4; Labor day; Thanksgiving day; Dec. 25; Arbor day.

Missouri.—Jan. 1; Feb. 12; Feb. 22; May 30; July 4; Labor day; Oct. 1 (Missouri day); Oct. 12; General Election day, Nov. 11; Thanksgiving day; Dec. 25; Arbor day.

Montana.—Jan. 1; Feb. 12; Feb. 22; May 30; July 4; Labor day; Oct. 12; General Election day; Nov. 11; Thanksgiving day; Dec. 25; Arbor day.

Nebraska.—Jan. 1; Feb. 12; Feb. 22; May 30; July 4; Labor day; Oct. 12; General Election day; Nov. 11; Thanksgiving day; Dec. 25; Arbor day.

Nevada.—Jan. 1; Feb. 12; Feb. 22; May 30; July 4; Labor day; Oct. 31 (Admission day); General Election day; Thanksgiving day; Dec. 25; Arbor day.

New Hampshire.—Jan. 1; Feb. 22; fast day appointed by the governor; May 30; July 4; Labor day; Oct. 12; General Election day; Thanksgiving day; Dec. 25; Arbor day.

New Jersey.—Jan. 1; Feb. 12; Feb. 22; Good Friday; May 30; July 4; Labor day; Oct. 12; General Election day; Nov. 11; Thanksgiving day; Dec. 25, Arbor day.

New Mexico.—Jan. 1; Feb. 12; Feb. 22; May 30; July 4; Labor day; General Election day; Thanksgiving day; Dec. 25; Arbor day.

New York.—Jan. 1; Feb. 12; Feb. 22; May 30; July 4; Labor day; Oct. 12; General Election day; Thanksgiving day; Dec. 25; Arbor day.

North Carolina.—Jan. 1; Jan. 19; Feb. 22; Apr. 12; May 10 (Confederate Memorial day); May 20 (anniversary of the signing of the Mecklenburg declaration of independence); July 4; Labor day; General Election day; Nov. 11; Thanksgiving day; Dec. 25; Arbor day.

North Dakota.—Jan. 1; Feb. 12; Feb. 22; May 30; July 4; Labor day; Oct. 12; General Election day; Nov. 11; Thanksgiving day; Dec. 25; Arbor day.

Ohio.—Jan. 1; Feb. 12; Feb. 22; May 30; July 4; Labor day; Oct. 12; General Election day; Thanksgiving day; Dec. 25; Arbor day.

Oklahoma.—Jan. 1; Feb. 22; May 30; July 4; Labor day; General Election day; Thanksgiving day; Dec. 25; Arbor day.

Oregon.—Jan. 1; Feb. 12; Feb. 22; May 30; July 4; Labor day; General Election day; Thanksgiving day; Dec. 25; Arbor day.

Pennsylvania.—Jan. 1; Feb. 12; Feb. 22; Mar. 4 (Pennsylvania day); Good Friday; May 30; July 4; Labor day; Oct. 12; General Election day; Nov. 11; Thanksgiving day; Dec. 25; Arbor day.

Puerto Rico.—Jan 1; Feb. 22; Mar. 22 (Emancipation day); Good Friday; May 30; July 4; July 25 (Occupation day); Labor day; Oct. 12; General Election day; Thanksgiving day; Dec. 25; Arbor day.

Rhode Island.—Jan. 1; Feb. 22; May 30; July 4; Labor day; Oct. 12; General Election day; Nov. 11; Thanksgiving day; Dec. 25; Arbor day.

South Carolina.—Jan. 1; Jan. 19 (Lee's birthday); Feb. 22; May 10 (Confederate Memorial day); June 3 (Jeff. Davis's birthday); July 4; Labor day; General Election day; Thanksgiving day; Dec. 25; Dec. 28 (Woodrow Wilson's birthday); Arbor day.

South Dakota.—Same as in North Dakota, excepting Oct. 12.

Tennessee.—Jan. 1; Jan. 19; Feb. 12; Feb. 22; Good Friday; May 30; June 3; July 4; July 13 (Glen Bedford Forrest's birthday); Labor day; General Election day; Nov. 11; Thanksgiving day; Dec. 25; Arbor day.

Texas.—Jan. 1; Feb. 22; March 2 (anniversary of Texas independence); Apr. 21 (anniversary of battle of San Jacinto); June 3 (Jeff. Davis's birthday); July 4; Labor day; Oct. 12; General Election day; Nov. 11; Thanksgiving day; Dec. 25; Arbor day.

Utah.—Jan. 1; Feb. 12; Feb. 22; May 30; July 4; July 24 (Pioneer day); Labor day; Oct. 12; General Election day; Thanksgiving day; Dec. 25; Arbor day.

Vermont.—Jan. 1; Feb. 22; May 30; July 4; Aug. 16 (Bennington Battle day); Labor day; Oct. 12; Nov. 11; Thanksgiving day; Dec. 25; Arbor day.

Virginia.—Jan. 1; Jan. 19; Feb. 22; May 30; June 3; July 4; Labor day; General Election day; Nov. 11; Thanksgiving day; Dec. 25; Arbor day.

Washington.—Jan. 1; Feb. 12; Feb. 22; May 30; July 4; Labor day; Oct. 12; General Election day; Thanksgiving day; Dec. 25; Arbor day.

West Virginia.—Jan. 1; Feb. 12; Feb. 22; May 30; June 20 (West Virginia day); July 4; Labor day; Oct. 12; General Election day; Thanksgiving day; Dec. 25; Arbor day.

Wisconsin.—Jan. 1; Feb. 22; May 30; July 4; Labor day; General Election day; Thanksgiving day; Dec. 25; Arbor day.

Wyoming.—Jan. 1; Feb. 12; Feb. 22; May 30; July 4; Labor day; General Election day; Thanksgiving day; Dec. 25; Arbor day.

NATIONAL HYMNS AND ANTHEMS

Argentine Republic. *Oíd, mortales, el grito sagrado* (Hear, O Mortals, the Sacred Call). Music by D. V. Lopez.

Australia. "Advance, Australia Fair." Words and music by Peter D. McCormick.

Austria. (*Oesterreichische Bundeshymne* (Austrian Federal Hymn). Words by Viktor Keldorfer; music by W. A. Mozart.

Belgium. *La Brabançonne.* Words by Jenneval; music by F. van Campenhout.

Brazil. *Hymno da Proclamacão da Republica* (Hymn of the Proclamation of the Republic). Words by Medeiros e Albuquerque; music by Leopoldo Miguez.

Canada. "God Save the King." Also "O Canada," composed in French by A. B. Routhier and translated into English by R. S. Weir; music by C. Lavallée.

Chile. *Dulce Patria;* national air, by Carnicer.

Costa Rica. *De la Patria.* Words by J. M. Zeledón; music by M. M. Gutierrez.

Czechoslovakia. *Kde Domor Muj* (Where is My Homeland?) Words by J. R. Tyl; music by F. Skroup.

Denmark. *King Kristian stod ved höien Mast* (King Christian Stood beside the Mast). Words by Ewald; music by Hartmann.

Ecuador. *Salve. O Patria.* Words by J. L. Mera.

Eire. *Amhrán na bfFiann* (The Soldier's Song). Words by Paeder Kearney; music by Patrick Heaney.

Finland. *Vårt Land* (Our Land). Words by J. L. Runeberg; music by F. Pacius.

France. *La Marseillaise.* Words and music by Rouget de Lisle.

Germany. *Deutschland-Lied* (Germany Song). Words by Heinrich H. von Fallersleben; music by Josef Haydn.

Great Britain. "God Save the King." Composed by Henry Carey. The words were in part adapted from verses written by others; the air was adapted from the French.

Greece. "Sons of Greece, Come, Arise." Words by Dionysus Solomos; music by N. Mantzaros.

Hungary. *Isten áld meg a Magyart* (Lord Bless the Hungarian). Music by F. Erkel.

India. *Jană Gană Mană.* Words and melody by Rabindranath Tagore.

Israel. *Hatikvah* (The Hope). Words by Naftali Herz Imber; traditional melody.

Italy. *Fratelli d'Italia* (Brothers of Italy). Words by Goffredo Mameli; music by Michele Novoro.

Japan. *Kimi Ga Yo Wa.* Composer, Hayhasi Hironokami.

Mexico. *Mexicanos, al grito de guerra* (Mexicans, at the Cry of War). Words by F. G. Bocanegra; music by James Nunó.

Netherlands, The. *Wilhelmus van Nassouwe* (William of Nassau) and *Wein Neerlandsch Bloed* (Old Dutch Blood), the latter by H. C. Tollens.

Nicaragua. National air, by Blas Villatas.

Norway. *Sang for Norge* (Song for Norway). Words by Björnstjerne Björnson.

Peru. *Somos libres, seámoslo siempre* (We Are Free, Let Us Be So Ever).

Poland. *Jeszcze Polska Nie Zginela* (Poland's Not Yet Dead). Words and music by General Josef Wybicki.

Russia. "Sing to our Motherland." Words by S. Mikhalkov and El-Registan; music by A. V. Alexandrov.

Salvador. *Saludemos la Patria* (Let Us Hail Our Country). Words by J. J. Canas; music by J. Aberle.

Sweden. *Ur Svenska Hjertans djup* (From the Depths of Swedish Hearts). Words by Strandberg; music by Lindblad.

Switzerland. *Dem Vaterland* (To the Fatherland). Words by J. R. Wyss. The music is that of "America."

United Arab Republic. Music from Verdi. No words.

United States, The. "Star-Spangled Banner," officially adopted in 1931. Words by Francis Scott Key. Music adapted from an old drinking song, "To Anacreon in Heaven."

"America." Words by Samuel F. Smith; music that of "God Save the King."

Uruguay. *Orientales, la patria ó la tumba* (Uruguayans, fatherland or death). Words by Juan Coppetti.

Venezuela. *Gloria al bravo pueblo* (Honor to a Brave Nation). Words by V. Salvias; music by J. Landaeta.

Yugoslavia. *Hej Slaven* (Fellow Slavs). Words anonymous; music traditional.

RELIGIOUS BODIES—FACTS AND PHILOSOPHIES

For understandable reasons, statistics concerning church organizations are subject to frequent revision. Variations from year to year are explained partly by the growth of population, by increased or decreased activity of church bodies, and sometimes, particularly in the United States, by the merging of related sects. Owing to changes in classification, a detailed comparison of statistical tables by decades is not practical. However, a summation of totals reported by the various groups gives a fairly accurate picture of church membership as of a particular date.

The assembling of information concerning 259 religious organizations in the United States is a continuing process which depends upon voluntary reporting of statistics by the various groups. At present the compiling is done by the Bureau of Research and Survey of the National Council of the Churches of Christ in the U.S.A. The membership data thus collected, along with many additional facts, can be found in the *Yearbook of American Churches*. In this volume, and in *Statistical Abstract of the United States*, which summarizes information from it, a breakdown of membership figures is given, both for groups numbering 50,000 or more and for branches and smaller organizations.

CHURCHES IN THE UNITED STATES
(A partial list of larger groups)

Name	Members	
	1960	1968
Adventists	354,184	396,000
Assemblies of God, General Council	508,602	627,000
Baptist Bodies, Grand Total	21,374,126	25,143,000
Brethren (German Baptists, Dunkers)	248,249	188,000
Church of Christ, Scientist	*	*
Churches of God	392,635	465,000
Church of the Nazarene	307,629	365,000
Congregational Christian Churches	6,957,000†	†
Eastern Orthodox (Eight groups)	2,718,110	3,526,068
Evangelical and Reformed	809,000	†
Evangelical United Brethren	751,763	‡
Friends	126,233	69,000
Jewish Congregations	5,500,000	5,780,000
Latter Day Saints	1,647,524	2,180,000
Lutheran (All branches)	8,101,306	8,996,000
Mennonite (Combined totals)	158,998	122,000
Methodist (All branches)	12,585,394	13,558,000
Presbyterian (All branches)	4,277,947	4,274,000
Protestant Episcopal	3,444,265	3,374,000
Reformed Bodies	485,025	665,000
Roman Catholic	42,104,899	47,873,000
Salvation Army	273,319	330,000
Unitarian	151,557	282,000§
United Church of Christ		2,033,000†

*** Membership figures not available.** † Represents merger of Congregational Christian Churches and the Evangelical and Reformed Church. ‡ Merged with Methodist Church to form United Methodist Church (10,790,000 members). § Now Unitarian Universalist Association as a result of a 1961 merger with the Universalist Church.

Some groups not represented in the foregoing table are given below, with their latest available totals:

African Orthodox, 6,000; Buddhist Churches of America, 100,000; Christian Union, 5,821; Churches of God in Christ, 581,005; International Church of Four Square Gospel, 98,893; Jehovah's Witnesses, 359,146; Moravian Bodies, 66,040; New Apostolic Church of North America, 20,923; Pentecostal Assemblies, 449,394; Polish National Catholic Church, 282,411; Reformed Episcopal, 7,061; United Brethren, 24,661; Volunteers of America, 31,780.

BIBLIOGRAPHY ON WORLD RELIGIONS

Since the formation of the United Nations organization, comprising member countries with widely divergent religious backgrounds, new impetus has been given to the study of world religions, their traditions and philosophies. For the guidance of persons seeking information concerning this field of knowledge, a "Committee on College Reading" has recently compiled a carefully selected group of references dealing with various aspects of the subject.* By permission, the following titles, with the Committee's descriptive notes, are given here.

Apocrypha (tr. by Goodspeed) *Univ. Chicago Press*
Religious writings similar to the books of the Old and New Testament, but not universally accepted.

Ballou, Robert (Ed.)—World Bible . . . *Viking*
Comprehensive selections from basic texts of Hinduism, Buddhism, Confucianism, Taoism, Zoroastrianism, Judaism, Christianity, and Mohammedanism.

Bates, E. S. (Ed.)—The Bible Designed to be Read as Living Literature . . *Simon and Schuster*
Largely the King James version, but modernized and arranged chronologically by subject matter.

Browne, Lewis—This Believing World. *Macmillan*
An objective summary and analysis of the chief religions of the world.

The New Catholic Encyclopedia . . *McGraw-Hill*

Burrows, Miller—The Dead Sea Scrolls.

Fosdick, Harry E.—A Guide to Understanding the Bible . . . . *Harper*
Traces the development of concepts of God, man, right and wrong, suffering, fellowship with God, and immortality.

Goodspeed, E. J.—The Story of the Bible. *Univ. of Chicago Press*
An account of the manuscripts that form the Bible.

James, William—Varieties of Religious Experience. *Modern Library*

Jurgi, E. J. (Ed.)—The Great Religions of the Modern World . . . . . *Princeton Univ. Press*
Ten essays, each by an authority, on the ten great living religions.

Roth, Cecil—The Jewish Contribution to Civilization . . . . *Harper*
An authoritative account of the part that the Jewish people have played in western civilization.

Sheen, Fulton J.—Preface to Religion . *Kenedy*
A presentation of the Catholic philosophy in answer to the quest for happiness and peace.

Williams, Michael—Christian Classics . *Liveright*
An anthology of religious autobiography, of spiritual counsel, of English mysticism and of religious poetry.

*Published by Hendricks House, Farrar Straus, N. Y. (library edition). New American Library, N. Y. pocket book)

RELIGIONS OF THE WORLD (1969 est.)

Name	North America[1]	South America	Europe	Asia	Africa	Oceania[2]	Total
Total Christian	214,258,000	150,426,000	442,006,000	61,473,000	42,056,000	14,055,000	924,274,000
Roman Catholic	126,468,000	147,219,000	226,303,000	47,622,000	28,751,000	4,107,000	580,470,000
Eastern Orthodox	3,675,000	47,000	114,103,000	2,819,000	4,956,000	84,000	125,684,000
Protestant	84,115,000	3,160,000	101,600,000	11,032,000	8,349,000	9,864,000	218,120,000
Jewish[3]	6,035,000	705,000	4,025,000	2,460,000	238,000	74,000	13,537,000
Moslem	166,000	416,000	13,848,000	374,167,000	104,297,000	118,000	493,012,000
Hindu	55,000	660,000	160,000	434,447,000	1,205,000	218,000	436,745,000
Buddhist	187,000	157,000	8,000	176,568,000	......	......	176,920,000
Confucian & Taoist	112,000	128,000	67,000	425,538,000	9,000	57,000	425,911,000
Miscellaneous[4]	83,626,000	21,754,000	190,865,000	434,028,000	180,329,000	3,605,000	899,221,000
Total	304,439,000	174,246,000	636,993,000	1,907,481,000	328,134,000	18,127,000	3,369,420,000

[1] Includes Central America and West Indies. [2] Includes Australia and New Zealand. [3] Includes total Jewish population, whether or not related to the synagogue. [4] Including primitive or none (atheist).

POPULAR NAMES OF CITIES

Aberdeen, Scotland. Granite City, from its many granite buildings.

Amsterdam, The Netherlands. Venice of the Netherlands, from its many canals.

Athens, Greece. City of the Violet Crown, in reference to beautiful effects of sunset light on the Acropolis.

Baghdad, Iraq. City of Peace, a name acquired during the reign of the Abbassides.

Baltimore, Md. Monumental City, from the fact that it was the first to erect a monument to the memory of George Washington.

Birmingham, Eng. The Midland Capital, from its central geographical position.

Boston, Mass. Athens of America; City of Notions, from the amount of "Yankee notions," so called, manufactured there; Hub of the Universe, so called by Dr. Oliver Wendell Holmes; Tri-Mountain City, from the three hills on which it was originally built.

Brighton, Eng. Queen of Watering Places, from its popularity as a seaside resort.

Brooklyn, N. Y. City of Churches, from the number of churches it contains.

Buffalo, N. Y. Queen City of the Lakes, from its importance as a lake port.

Chicago, Ill. Garden City, from the number and beauty of its private gardens; Windy City, from the prevalence of strong winds.

Cincinnati, Ohio. Queen City, so called when it was the commercial metropolis of the Middle West.

Cleveland, Ohio. Forest City, from the number of trees on its streets.

Columbus, Ohio, Rose capital of the world.

Constantinople (Istanbul), Turkey. City of the Golden Horn, from the name of its harbor.

Damascus, Syria. Pearl of the Desert, from the beauty of its situation.

Detroit, Mich. City of the Straits, from its location on the strait connecting Lake Saint Clair and Lake Erie; also Automobile City, from its primacy in the motor industry.

Duluth, Minn. Zenith City of the Unsalted Seas, from its position at the head of the Great Lakes.

Edinburgh, Scotland. Modern Athens, from its fame as a center of learning.

Foochow, China. Happy City, from meaning of name.

Halifax, N. S. Warden of the North, from its importance as a British fortified post and naval base.

Hannibal, Mo. Bluff City, from its location on the bluffs of the Mississippi river.

Hartford, Conn. Charter Oak City, in reference to the oak tree in which the charter of the colony of Connecticut is said at one time to have been concealed.

Indianapolis, Ind. Railroad City, from its prominence as a railroad center.

Jerusalem, Palestine. Holy City; City of David; City of Peace.

Keokuk, Iowa. Gate City, from its situation at the foot of the Mississippi rapids.

Lhasa, Tibet. Forbidden City, from the former rigid exclusion of foreigners.

Little Rock, Ark. City of roses.

Liverpool, Eng. The Modern Tyre, from its importance as a seaport.

Louisville, Ky. Falls City, from the falls of the Ohio River.

Lowell, Mass. Spindle City, from its large textile mills.

Manchester, Eng. Cottonopolis, because of its great cotton mills.

Milwaukee, Wis. Cream City, from cream-colored brick manufactured there.

Minneapolis, Minn. Flour City, from its great mills.

Montpelier, Vt. Green Mountain City.

Nashville, Tenn. City of Rocks, from its natural surroundings.

New Haven, Conn. Elm City, from the number of its elms.

New Orleans, La. Crescent City, from its position on a curve of the Mississippi.

New York, N. Y. Empire City, from its being the chief city of the United States; also Gotham, applied by Washington Irving in his *Salmagundi.*

Niagara Falls, N. Y. Power City, from immense amount of electric power generated there.

Paris, France. City of the Lily; City of Louis.

Philadelphia, Pa. City of Brotherly Love, from the meaning of the name; also Quaker City.

Pittsburgh, Pa. Iron City, from the extent of its iron manufactures.

Portland, Me. Forest City, from the number of its trees.

Portland, Oreg. Rose City, from its prolific rose gardens.

Quebec, Que. Gibraltar of America, from the almost impregnable heights upon which the city stands.

Rochester, N. Y. Flower City, from the profusion of flowers and extensive nurseries there; also Kodak City, from its extensive manufacture of photographic cameras.

Rome, Italy. City of the Seven Hills, from the seven eminences over which the city extends. Eternal City.

Saint Louis, Mo. Mound City, from the many ancient mounds found in the vicinity.

San Francisco, Cal. City of the Golden Gate, from its location at the entrance to San Francisco bay.

Savannah, Ga. Garden City, from its parks and gardens.

Springfield, Mass. City of Homes, from the many people of the city who own their homes.

Springfield, Ohio. Flower City, from the beauty of its surroundings.

Stockholm, Sweden. Venice of the North, from its many islands and waterways.

Venice, Italy. City of Saint Mark; City of the Seventy Isles; Queen of the Adriatic.

Washington, D. C. City of Magnificent Distances, from its being laid out on a large and regular scale; also Federal City.

Worcester, Mass. The Faithful City, so called from its motto: *Floreat Semper Civitas Fidelis.*

BIBLIOGRAPHY

The following titles of books have been selected chiefly from lists of standard works recommended by librarians for the guidance of general readers.

GENERAL GEOGRAPHY

Chase, Ilka—Second Spring and Two Potatoes. *Doubleday '65* (around the world)
Davies, Clarice S.—Exploring the World : *Roy '66*
Hall, Ernie—Flotsam, Jetsam, and Lagan from the Seven Seas, the Five Great Lakes, and Our Inland Rivers . . . . *Cornell Maritime '65*
James, Preston E.—A Geography of Man. 2nd ed. *Blaisdell '66*
Jones, Emrys—Human Geography; an Introduction to Man and His World . . . . . . *Praeger '66*
Perpillou, Aime V.—Human Geography . *Wiley '66*
Rand McNally New Cosmopolitan World Atlas. *Rand McNally '65*
Scott, Jack D.—Passport to Adventure *Random '66*

REGIONAL GEOGRAPHY AND TRAVEL

United States
Brooks, Maurice G.—The Appalachians. *Houghton '65*
Carpenter, John A.—Alaska, From Its Glorious Past to the Present . . . Chicago, *Children's Pr. '65*
Davenport, William W.—Hawaii, 1966 *McKay '66*
Ford, Norman D.—What to See in All America. *Crown '64*
Hollon, William E.—The Great American Desert, Then and Now. . . . . *Oxford '66*
Mandell, Muriel—The 51 Capitals of the U.S.A. (grades 5–8) . . . . *Sterling '65*
Paterson, John H.—North America, 3rd ed. *Oxford '66*
Perry, George S.—Cities of America . . *McGraw*
Platt, Rutherford Hayes—The Great American Forest . . . . *Prentice '65*
Road Atlas and Travel Guide . *Rand McNally '66*
Steinbeck, John—Travels with Charley; in Search of America . . . . . . *Viking '62; Banton '63*

Canada
Canadian Almanac and Directory for 1966 (119th yr.). . . . . *Pittman '66*
McDougall, Robert L., ed.—Canada's Past and Present . . . . *U. of Toronto Pr. '65*
Myers, B. R.—North of the Border . *Vantage '64*
Nicholson, N. L.—Canada in the American Community . . . . *Van Nostrand '63*
Scarfe, N. V. & others—A New Geography of Canada . . . . *Gage '63*
Wilson, George W.—Canada; an Appraisal of Its Needs and Resources . . . *Twentieth Century '65*

Mexico, Central America, West Indies
Fodor's Guide to the Caribbean, Bahamas, and Bermuda, 1966. . . . . *McKay '65*
MacPherson, John—Caribbean Lands; a Geography of the West Indies . . . . *Longmans '65*
Nicholson, Irene—The X in Mexico; Growth Within Tradition . . . . *Doubleday '66*
Rodman, Seldon—The Road to Panama. *Hawthorne '66*
Woodman, Jim—Discovering Yucatan. *Doubleday '66*
The World and Its Peoples: the Caribbean Region and Central America . . . . *Greystone '65*

South America
Clark, Sydney A.—All the Best in South America, East Coast . . . . *Dodd '66*
Clark, Sydney A.—All the Best in South America, West Coast . . . . *Dodd '66*
Clissold, Stephen—Latin America; a Cultural Outline . . . . *Harper '66*
Fodor's Guide to South America, 1966. *McKay '66*
Johnson, William W.—The Andean Republics: Bolivia, Chile, Ecuador, Peru . . . *Time, Inc. '65*
MacEoin, Gary—Colombia and Venezuela and the Guianas . . . . *Time, Inc. '65*
Schneider, Ronald M.—An Atlas of Latin American Affairs . . . . *Praeger '65*

Europe
Clark, Sydney A.—All the Best in France. *Dodd '66*
Fielding's Travel Guide to Europe, 1966. *Morrow '66*
Fodor, Eugene, ed.—Britain and Ireland. *McKay '66*
Fodor's Guide to Europe, 1966; a Comprehensive Handbook of 34 countries . . . . . *McKay '66*
Houston, James M.—A Social Geography of Europe. Rev. . . . . *Hillary House '66*
Latham, Peter—The German Federal Republic. *Blackie '65*
Latham, Peter—Italy . . . . *Blackie '65*
Salisbury, Harrison E.—Russia . . *Macmillan '65*
Shakleton, Margaret Reid—Europe; a Regional Geography. 7th ed . . . . *Praeger '65*
Waldo, Myra—Travel Guide to Europe, '66–'67. *Macmillan '66*
The World and Its Peoples: Austria, Hungary, Czechoslovakia, Poland . . . . *Hawthorne '65*

Asia
Gary, Dorothy H.—Splendors of Asia. . *Viking '65*
Gellhorn, Eleanor C.—McKay's Guide to the Far East and Hawaii . . . . *McKay '65*
Gellhorn, Eleanor C.—McKay's Guide to the Middle East . . . . *McKay '65*
Hammer, Ellen Joy—Vietnam, Yesterday and Today. . . . . *Holt '66*
Lamb, Beatrice (Pitney)—India; a World in Transition. Rev. ed. . . . . *Praeger '65*
Langer, Paul F.— Japan, Yesterday and Today. *Holt '66*
Lindqvist, Sven—China in Crisis . . *Crowell '65*
McCune, Shannon B.—Korea, Land of Broken Calm . . . . *Van Nostrand '66*
Tayyeb, Ali—Pakistan; a Political Geography. *Oxford '66*
Tregear, Thomas R.—A Geography of China. *Aldine '66*
Walz, Jay—The Middle East . . . *Atheneum '65*

Africa
Ady, Peter H.—Africa . . . . *Clarendon Pr. '65*
Nelson, Nina—Your Guide to Egypt. *Intl. Pubns. Serv. '66*
Sillery, Anthony—Africa; a Social Geography. *Humanities '65*
Steffen, Don Carl—The Splendor of Africa. *Walker '65*
Wattenberg, Ben and Smith, Ralph—The New Nations of Africa . . . . *Hart '63*

The Pacific
Berney, Maurice, ed.—Australia. *Rand McNally '65*
Briggs, Donald S.—Orient-Hawaii Guide; Introducing Hawaii, Japan, Hong Kong, and the Philippines . . . . *Crown '62*
Corpuz, Onofre D.—The Philippines. *Prentice '66*
Horne, Donald—The Lucky Country: Australia in the Sixties. 2nd ed. London, *Angus & Robertson '66*
Waldo, Myra—Travel Guide to the Orient and the Pacific . . . . *Macmillan '65*

Polar Regions
Debenham, Frank—In the Antarctic; Stories of Scott's Last Expedition . . . . . . *Verry '65*
Dukert, Joseph M.—This is Antarctica. *Coward '65*
Eklund, Carl R. and Beckman, Joan—Antarctica. *Holt '63*
Silverberg, Robert, ed.—Antarctic Conquest; the Great Explorers in Their Own Words . *Bobbs '65*
Simmons, George—Target: Arctic; Men in the Skies at the Top of the World . . . *Chilton '65*

Space Exploration
Alexander, Thomas W.—Project Apollo: Man to the Moon . . . . *Harper '64*
Emme, Eugene M.—A History of Space Flight. *Holt '66*
Faget, Maxime A.—Manned Space Flight. *Holt '65*
Hilton, William F.—Manned Satellites, Their Achievements and Potentialities . . *Harper '66*

ATLAS of the WORLD

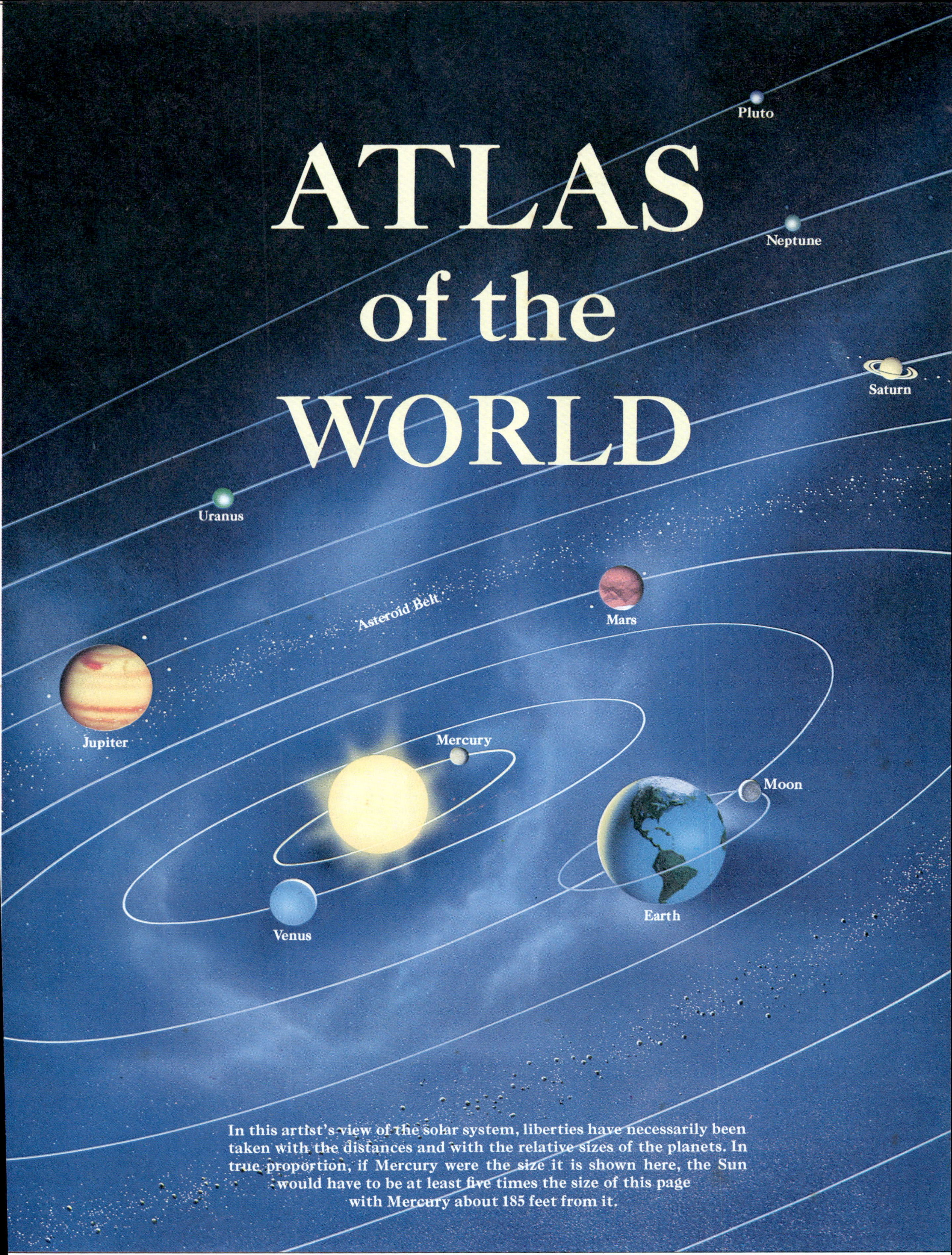

In this artist's view of the solar system, liberties have necessarily been taken with the distances and with the relative sizes of the planets. In true proportion, if Mercury were the size it is shown here, the Sun would have to be at least five times the size of this page with Mercury about 185 feet from it.

THE MOON

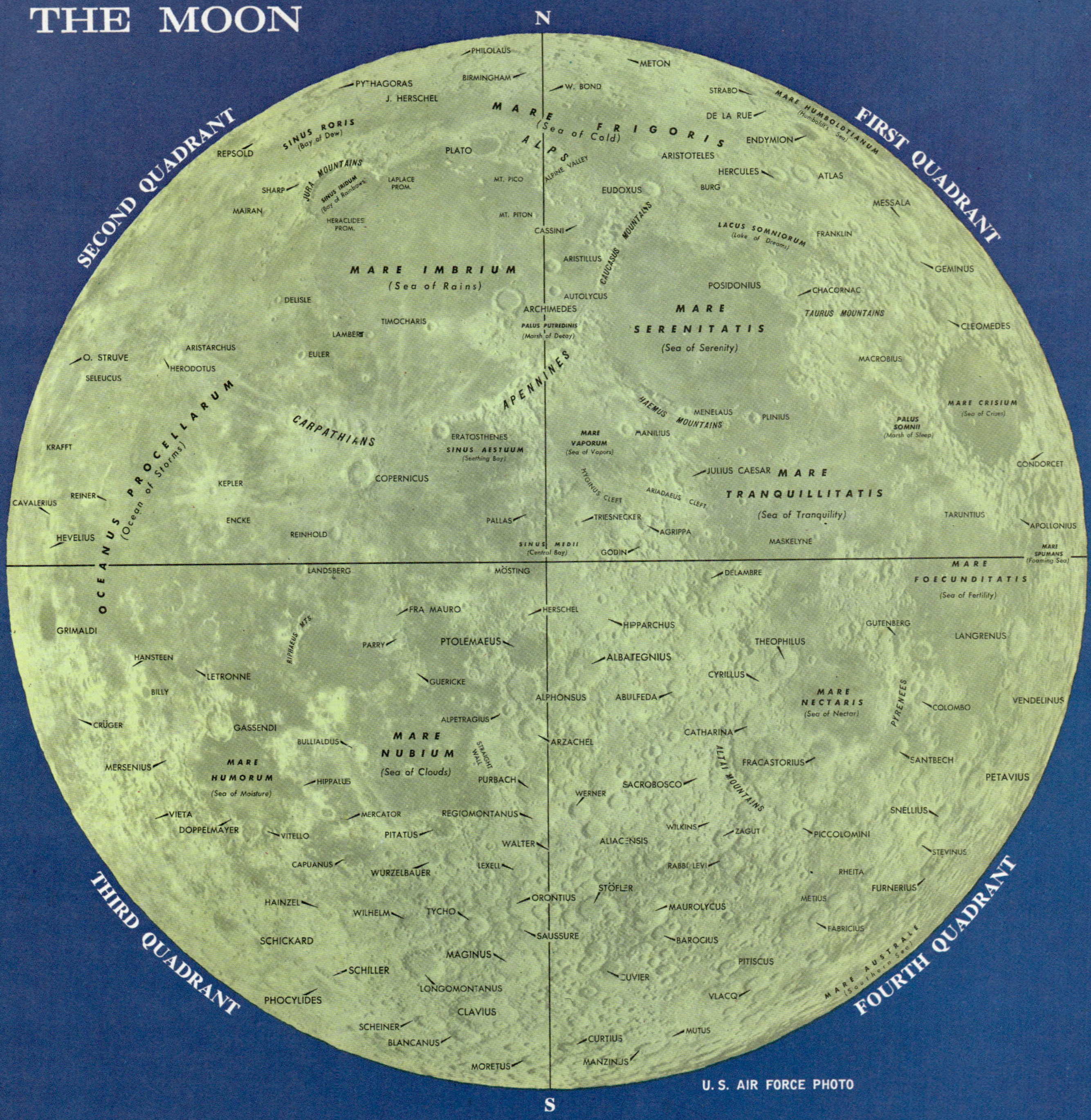

U. S. AIR FORCE PHOTO

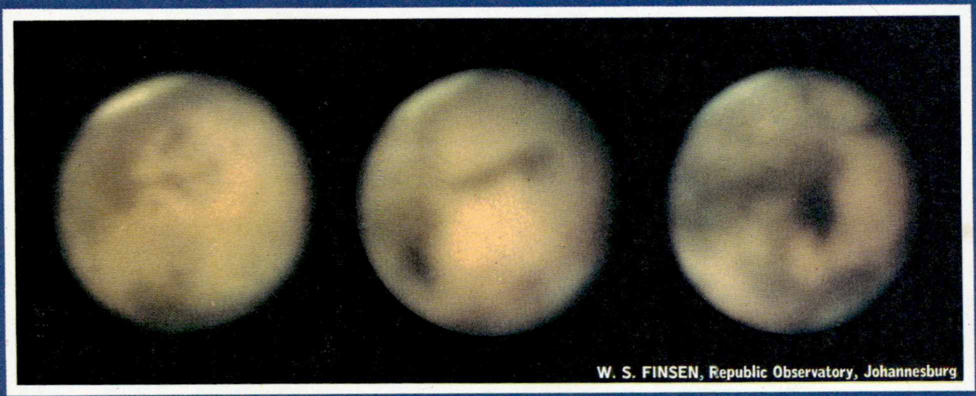

W. S. FINSEN, Republic Observatory, Johannesburg

THREE VIEWS OF THE PLANET MARS

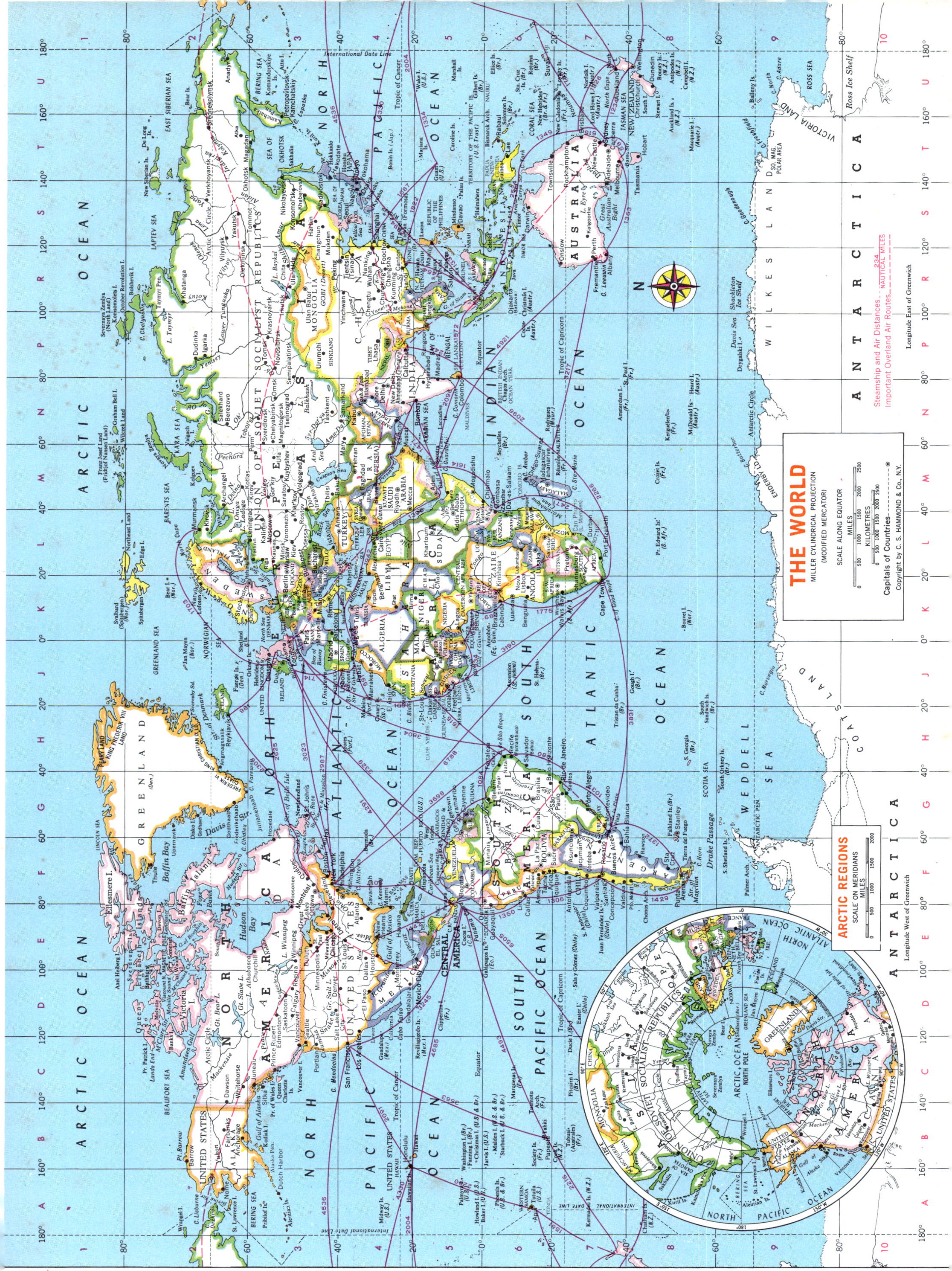
THE WORLD
MILLER CYLINDRICAL PROJECTION
(MODIFIED MERCATOR)
SCALE ALONG EQUATOR
MILES
KILOMETRES
Capitals of Countries
Copyright by C. S. HAMMOND & Co., N.Y.
Steamship and Air Distances... 234 NAUTICAL MILES
Important Overland Air Routes
Longitude East of Greenwich
ARCTIC REGIONS
SCALE ON MERIDIANS
MILES
Longitude West of Greenwich
ARCTIC OCEAN
NORTH PACIFIC OCEAN
SOUTH PACIFIC OCEAN
NORTH ATLANTIC OCEAN
SOUTH ATLANTIC OCEAN
INDIAN OCEAN
ANTARCTICA
NORTH AMERICA
SOUTH AMERICA
EUROPE
ASIA
AFRICA
AUSTRALIA

THE OCEANS

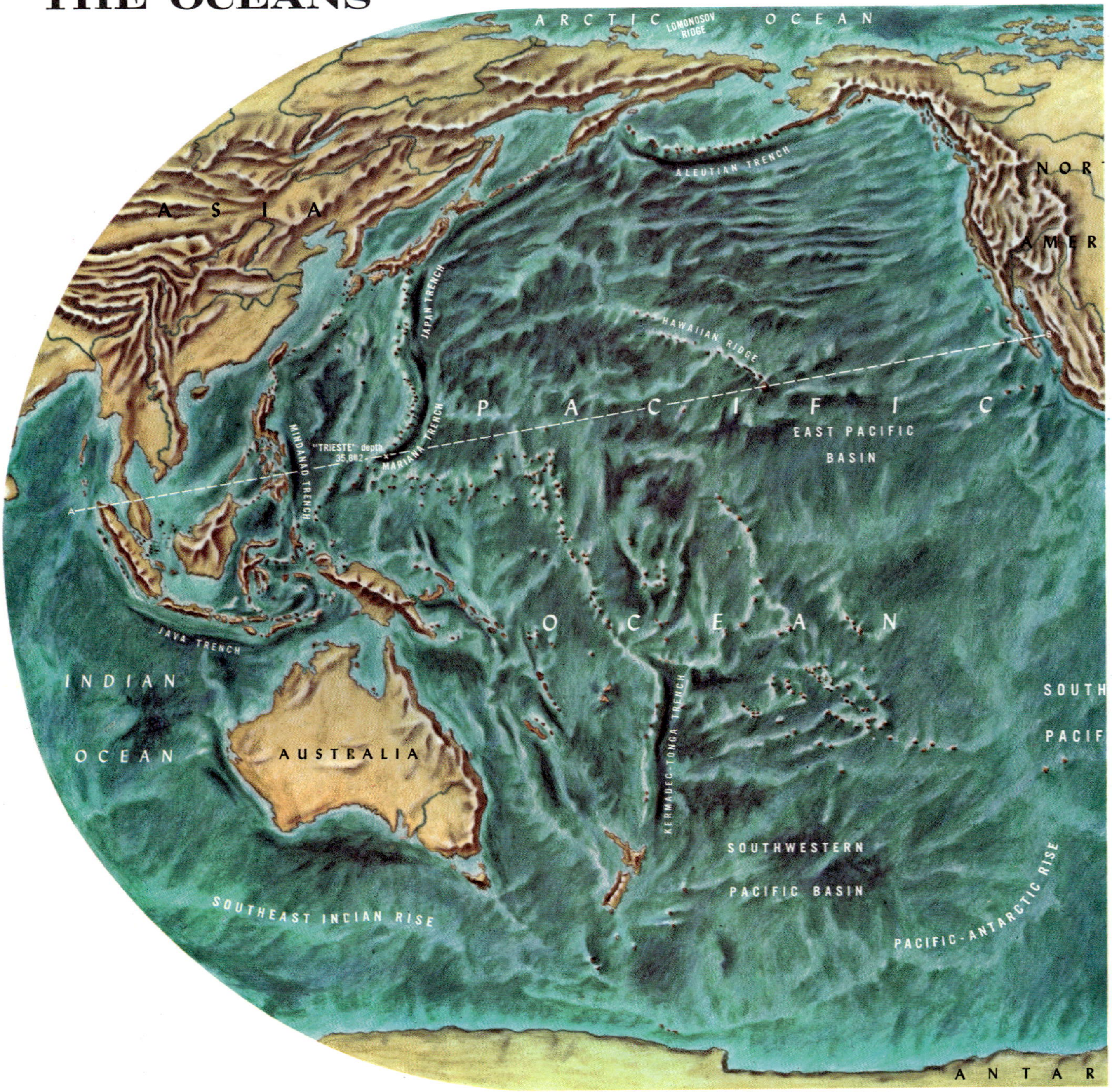

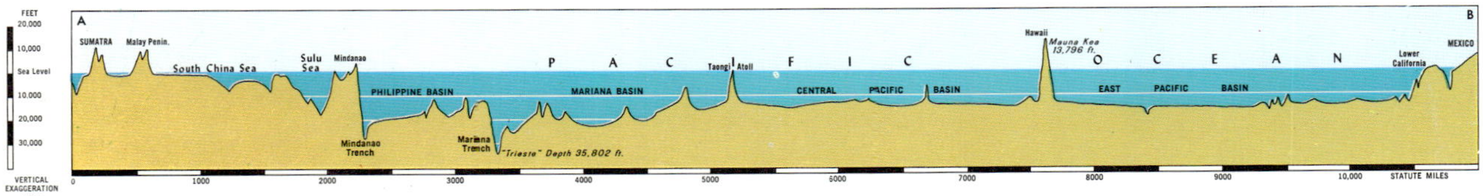

PROFILE OF THE PACIFIC OCEAN

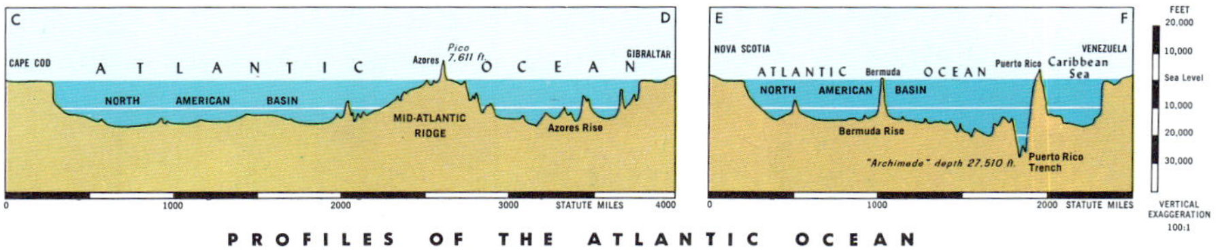

PROFILES OF THE ATLANTIC OCEAN

ARCTIC OCEAN
GREENLAND
ICELAND
EUROPE
ASIA
U.S.S.R.
ALASKA
UNITED STATES
YUKON TERR.
NORTHWEST TERRITORIES
DISTRICT OF MACKENZIE
DISTRICT OF KEEWATIN
DISTRICT OF FRANKLIN
BRITISH COLUMBIA
ALBERTA
SASKATCHEWAN
MANITOBA
ONTARIO
QUEBEC
LABRADOR
NEWFOUNDLAND
HUDSON BAY
BAFFIN BAY
Davis Strait
Denmark Strait
LABRADOR SEA
GREENLAND SEA
NORWEGIAN SEA
NORTH SEA
BARENTS SEA
KARA SEA
LAPTEV SEA
EAST SIBERIAN SEA
CHUKCHI SEA
BEAUFORT SEA
BERING SEA
GULF OF ALASKA
QUEEN ELIZABETH ISLANDS
North Pole
Arctic Circle

NORTH AMERICA
LAMBERT AZIMUTHAL EQUAL-AREA PROJECTION
SCALE OF MILES
0 100 200 300 400 500 600 700
SCALE OF KILOMETRES
0 100 200 300 400 500 600 700
National Capitals
State, Provincial & Territorial Capitals
International Boundaries
State & Provincial Boundaries
Copyright by C. S. HAMMOND & CO., N.Y.
PACIFIC OCEAN
UNITED STATES
MEXICO
GULF OF MEXICO
CARIBBEAN SEA
GREATER ANTILLES
LESSER ANTILLES
SOUTH AMERICA
BAHAMAS
Tropic of Cancer
Equator
Gulf of California
Sierra Madre Occidental
Bay of Campeche
Yucatán Peninsula
Yucatán Channel
GALÁPAGOS ISLANDS (Ecuador)
Clipperton Island (Fr.)
REVILLAGIGEDO IS. (Mex.)
VENEZUELA
COLOMBIA
ECUADOR
PERU
BRAZIL
Longitude West of Greenwich

WESTERN CANADA
SCALE OF MILES
0 50 100 200
SCALE OF KILOMETRES
0 50 100 200
Provincial and Territorial Capitals
International Boundaries
Boundaries of Provinces
Copyright by C. S. HAMMOND & Co., N. Y.

EASTERN CANADA
CONIC PROJECTION
SCALE OF MILES
0 50 100 200 300
SCALE OF KILOMETRES
0 50 100 200 300
Capital of Canada
Capitals of Provinces
International Boundaries
Boundaries of Provinces
Canals
ARCTIC CANADA
HUDSON BAY
Hudson Strait
Ungava Bay
James Bay
NEWFOUNDLAND
QUEBEC
ONTARIO
MANITOBA
NEW BRUNSWICK
NOVA SCOTIA
PRINCE EDWARD I.
Gulf of St. Lawrence
Cape Breton I.
UNITED STATES
Lake Superior
Lake Huron
Lake Michigan
Lake Erie
MONTREAL
TORONTO
Ottawa
Québec
Copyright by C.S. HAMMOND & Co., N.Y.

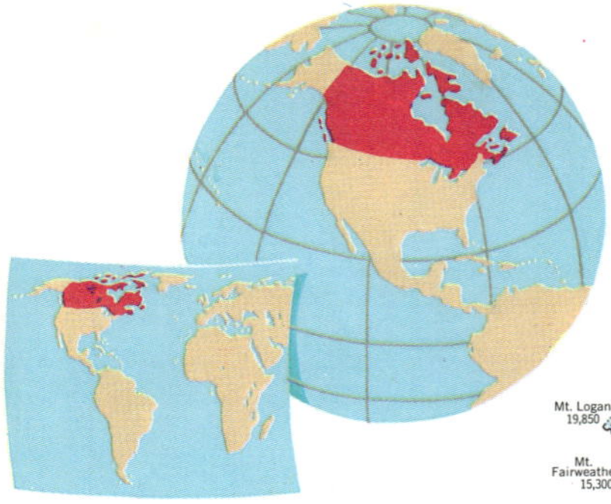

CANADA

CAPITAL	Ottawa
HIGHEST POINT	Mt. Logan
MONETARY UNIT	Canadian dollar
MAJOR LANGUAGES	English, French
MAJOR RELIGIONS	Protestant, Roman Catholic

TOPOGRAPHY

AGRICULTURE, INDUSTRY and RESOURCES

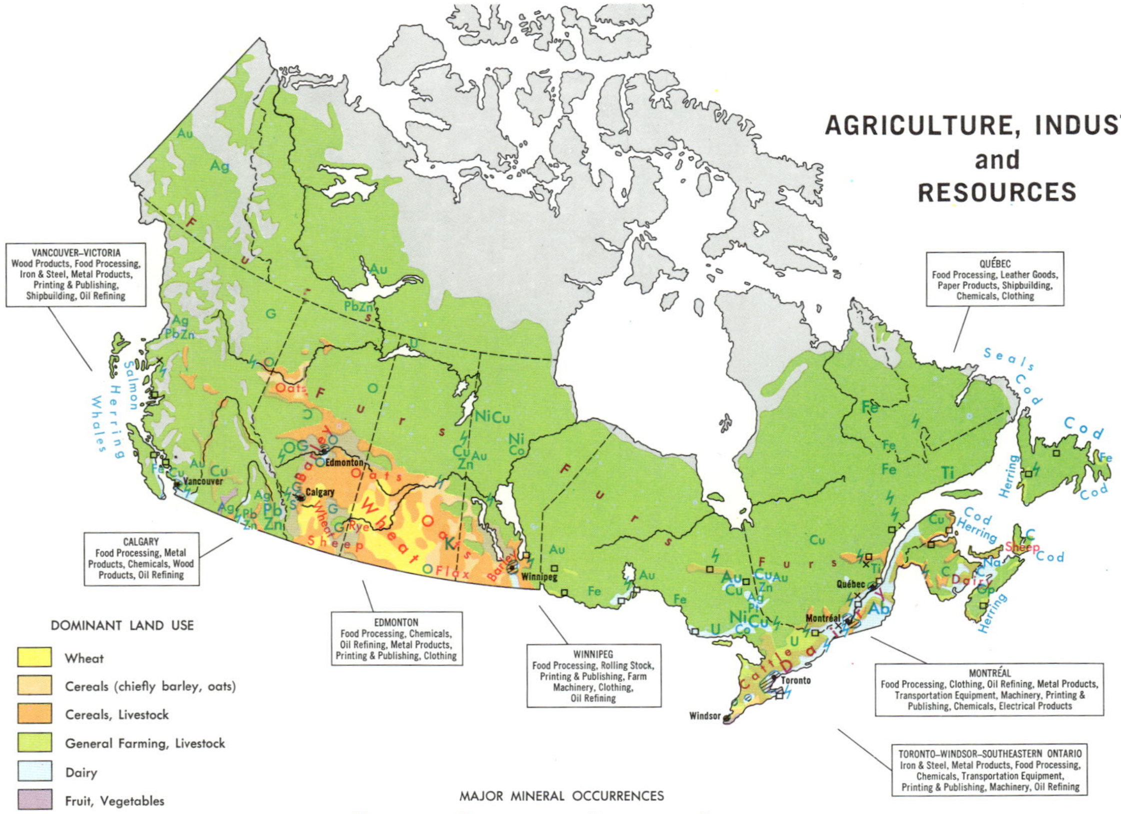

DOMINANT LAND USE

- Wheat
- Cereals (chiefly barley, oats)
- Cereals, Livestock
- General Farming, Livestock
- Dairy
- Fruit, Vegetables
- Pasture Livestock
- Range Livestock
- Forests
- Nonagricultural Land

MAJOR MINERAL OCCURRENCES

Ab Asbestos	Cu Copper	Na Salt	S Sulfur
Ag Silver	Fe Iron Ore	Ni Nickel	Ti Titanium
Au Gold	G Natural Gas	O Petroleum	U Uranium
C Coal	Gp Gypsum	Pb Lead	Zn Zinc
Co Cobalt	K Potash	Pt Platinum	

- Water Power
- Major Industrial Areas
- Major Pulp & Paper Mills
- Aluminum Smelters

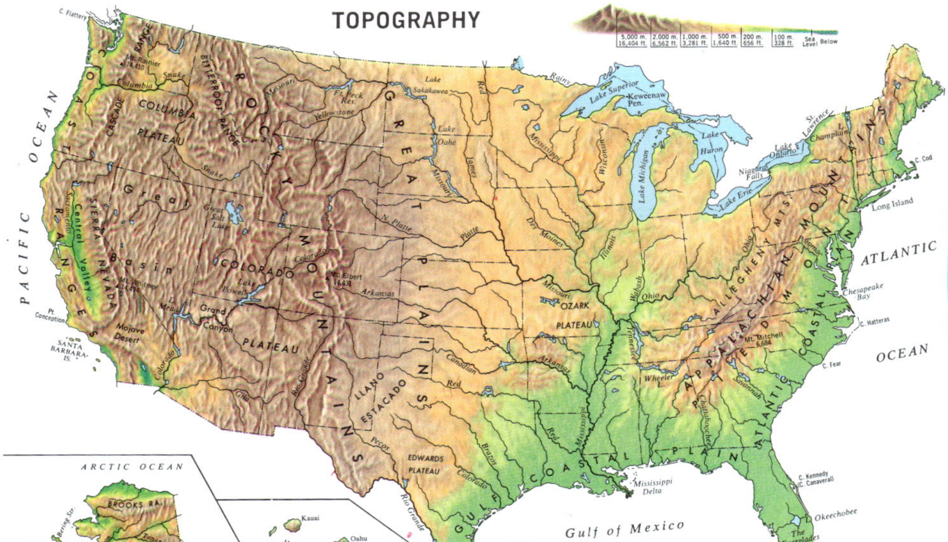

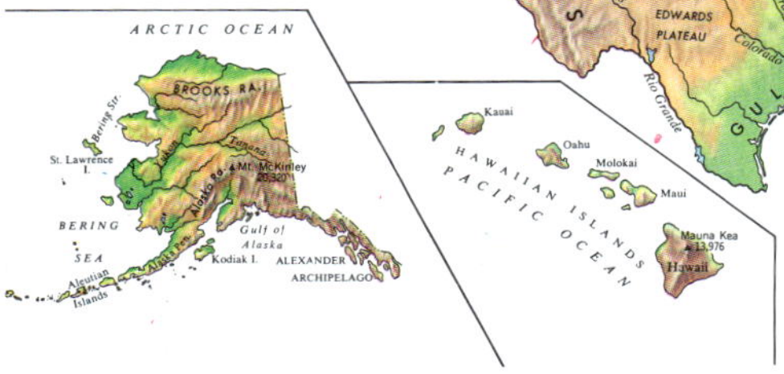

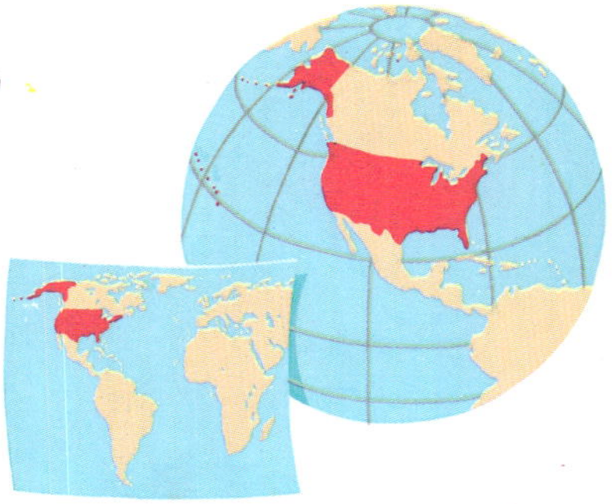

UNITED STATES

CAPITAL	Washington
HIGHEST POINT	Mt. McKinley
MONETARY UNIT	dollar
MAJOR LANGUAGE	English
MAJOR RELIGIONS	Protestant, Roman Catholic

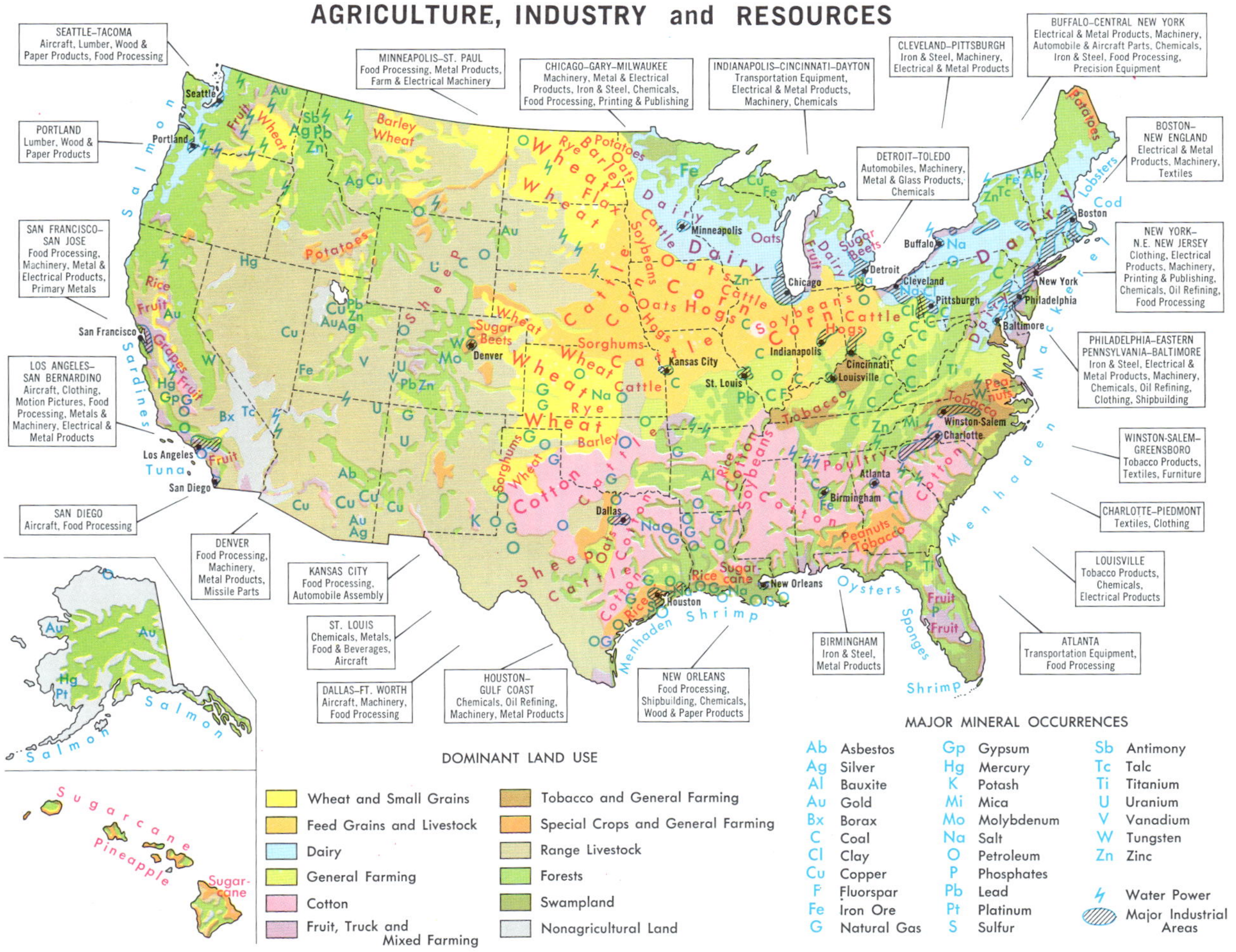

BRITISH COLUMBIA
ALBERTA
SASKATCHEWAN
MANITOBA
CANADA
PACIFIC OCEAN
WASHINGTON
OREGON
CALIFORNIA
NEVADA
IDAHO
MONTANA
WYOMING
UTAH
COLORADO
ARIZONA
NEW MEXICO
NORTH DAKOTA
SOUTH DAKOTA
NEBRASKA
KANSAS
OKLAHOMA
TEXAS
MEXICO
BAJA CALIFORNIA
GULF OF CALIFORNIA
CHIHUAHUA
COAHUILA
NUEVO LEON
TAMAULIPAS
Seattle
Spokane
Portland
San Francisco
Sacramento
Los Angeles
San Diego
Salt Lake City
Denver
Phoenix
Tucson
Albuquerque
Santa Fe
El Paso
Boise
Helena
Cheyenne
Bismarck
Pierre
Lincoln
Omaha
Wichita
Oklahoma City
Dallas
Fort Worth
Austin
San Antonio
Calgary
Edmonton
Regina
Vancouver
Victoria
Alaska
Anchorage
Fairbanks
Nome
Juneau
YUKON TERRITORY
BERING SEA
Gulf of Alaska
U.S.S.R.
Aleutian Is.
Hawaii
Honolulu
Oahu
Kauai
Molokai
Maui
Lanai
Tropic of Cancer
MISSOURI
ILLINOIS
St. Louis
OHIO
KY.
IND.
Cincinnati
Dayton
Newport
Covington
Berkeley
Oakland
San Jose
LOS ANGELES
Long Beach
Santa Monica
Pasadena
Longitude West of Greenwich

UNITED STATES
POLYCONIC PROJECTION
SCALE OF MILES
0 50 100 200 300
SCALE OF KILOMETRES
0 50 100 200 300
Capitals of Countries
State and Provincial Capitals
International Boundaries
State and Provincial Boundaries
Copyright by C. S. HAMMOND & CO., N. Y.
GULF OF MEXICO
ATLANTIC OCEAN
LAKE SUPERIOR
LAKE HURON
LAKE ONTARIO
LAKE ERIE
GULF OF ST. LAWRENCE
CHICAGO
DETROIT
NEW YORK
PHILADELPHIA
Longitude West of Greenwich

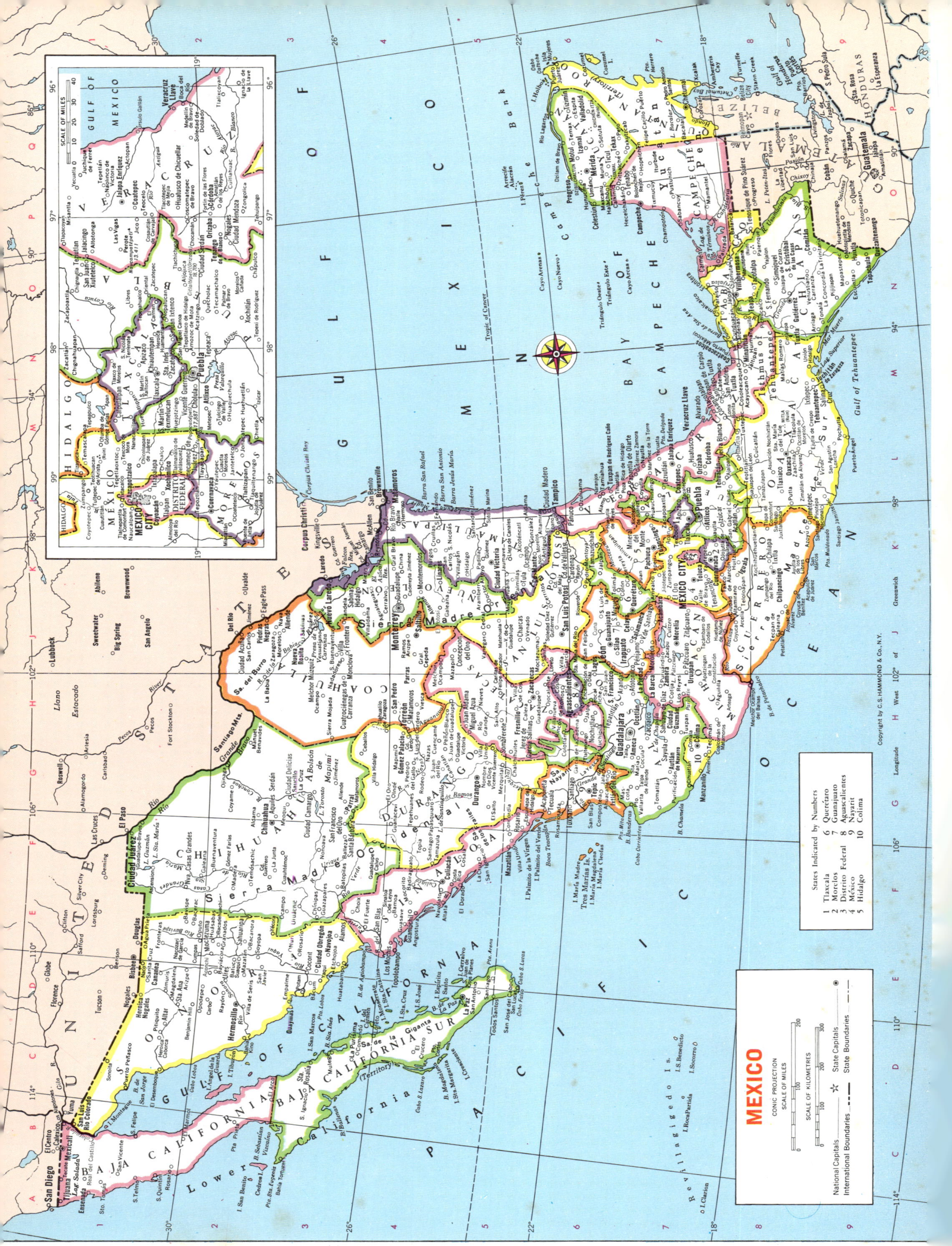
MEXICO
CONIC PROJECTION
SCALE OF MILES
SCALE OF KILOMETRES
National Capitals
State Capitals
International Boundaries
State Boundaries
States Indicated by Numbers
1 Tlaxcala
2 Morelos
3 Distrito Federal
4 México
5 Hidalgo
6 Querétaro
7 Guanajuato
8 Aguascalientes
9 Nayarit
10 Colima
Copyright by C.S. HAMMOND & Co., N.Y.

MEXICO

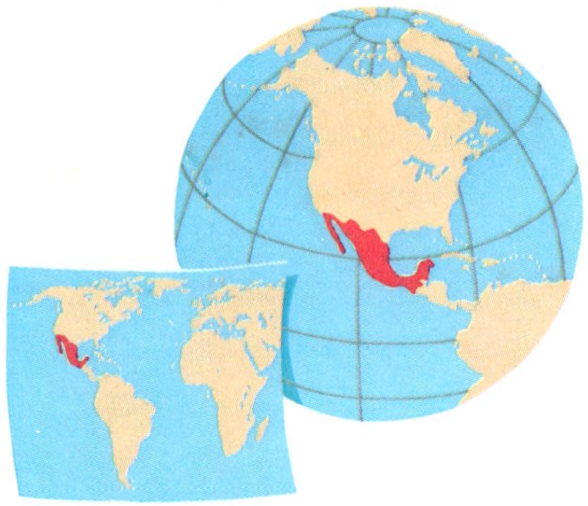

CAPITAL	Mexico City
HIGHEST POINT	Citlaltépetl
MONETARY UNIT	Mexican peso
MAJOR LANGUAGE	Spanish
MAJOR RELIGION	Roman Catholic

TOPOGRAPHY

AGRICULTURE, INDUSTRY and RESOURCES

DOMINANT LAND USE

- Wheat, Livestock
- Cereals (chiefly corn), Livestock
- Diversified Tropical Cash Crops
- Cotton, Mixed Cereals
- Livestock, Limited Agriculture
- Range Livestock
- Forests
- Nonagricultural Land

- Water Power
- Major Industrial Areas

MAJOR MINERAL OCCURRENCES

Ag	Silver	G	Natural Gas	O	Petroleum
Au	Gold	Gr	Graphite	Pb	Lead
C	Coal	Hg	Mercury	S	Sulfur
Cu	Copper	Mn	Manganese	Sb	Antimony
F	Fluorspar	Mo	Molybdenum	Sn	Tin
Fe	Iron Ore	Na	Salt	W	Tungsten
				Zn	Zinc

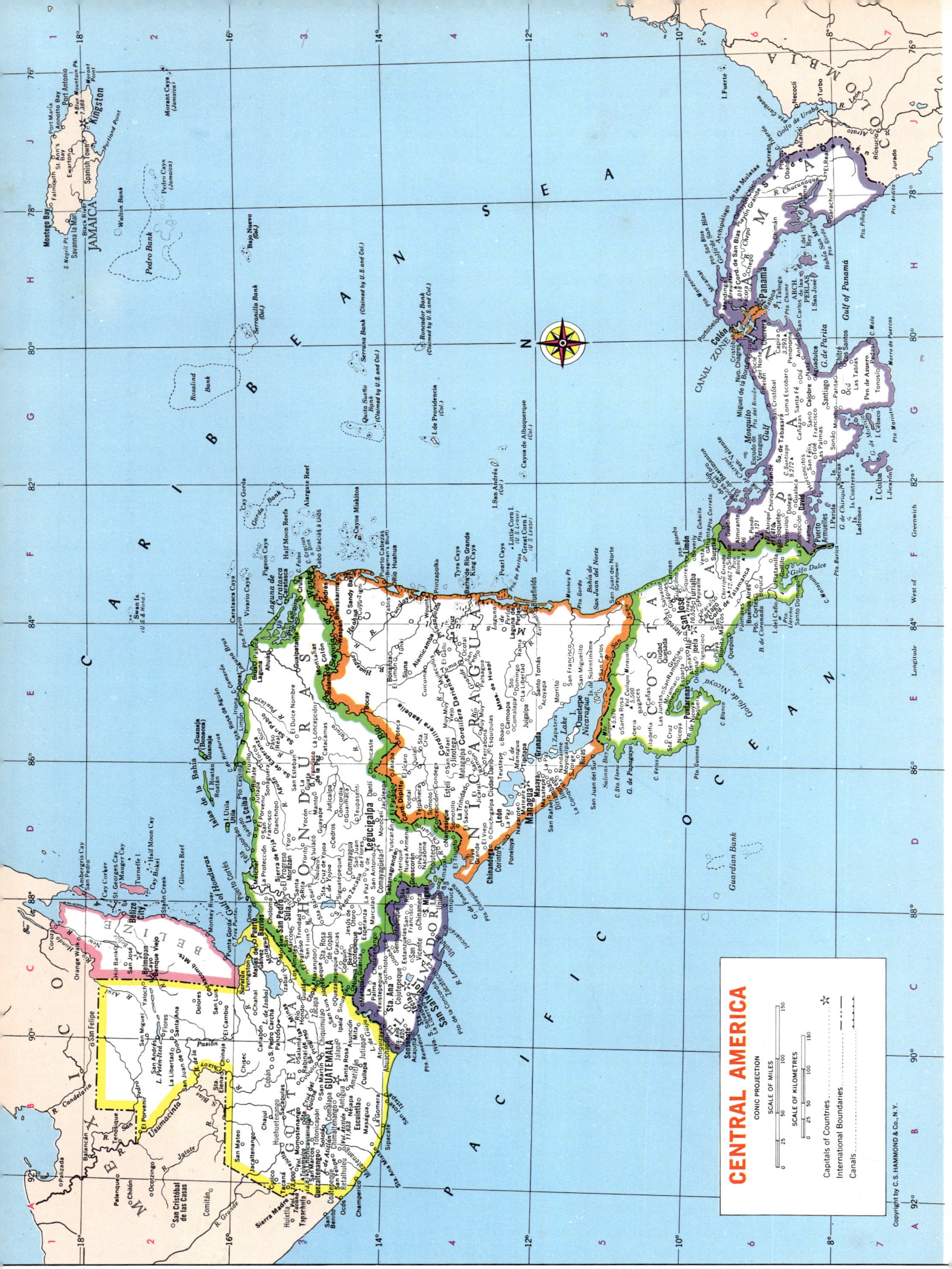
CENTRAL AMERICA
CONIC PROJECTION
SCALE OF MILES
SCALE OF KILOMETRES
Capitals of Countries
International Boundaries
Canals
Copyright by C. S. HAMMOND & Co., N. Y.
CARIBBEAN SEA
PACIFIC OCEAN
MEXICO
BELIZE
GUATEMALA
HONDURAS
EL SALVADOR
NICARAGUA
COSTA RICA
PANAMA
COLOMBIA
JAMAICA
CANAL ZONE
Gulf of Honduras
Gulf of Panamá
Gulf of Fonseca
G. de Papagayo
Golfo de Nicoya
Mosquito Gulf
Golfo de Urabá
Kingston
Belize City
Guatemala
San Salvador
Tegucigalpa
Managua
San José
Panamá
Colón
Longitude West of Greenwich

CENTRAL AMERICA

	GUATEMALA	HONDURAS	EL SALVADOR	BELIZE	NICARAGUA	COSTA RICA	PANAMA
CAPITAL	Guatemala	Tegucigalpa	San Salvador	Belmopan	Managua	San José	Panamá
HIGHEST POINT	Tajumulco	Las Minas	Santa Ana	Victoria Peak	Cerro Mocotón	Chirripó Grande	Vol. Chiriquí
MONETARY UNIT	quetzal	lempira	colón	Belize dollar	córdoba	colón	balboa
MAJOR LANGUAGE	Spanish	Spanish	Spanish	English, Spanish, Mayan, Creole	Spanish	Spanish	Spanish
MAJOR RELIGION	Roman Catholic	Roman Catholic	Roman Catholic	Roman Catholic, Protestant	Roman Catholic	Roman Catholic	Roman Catholic

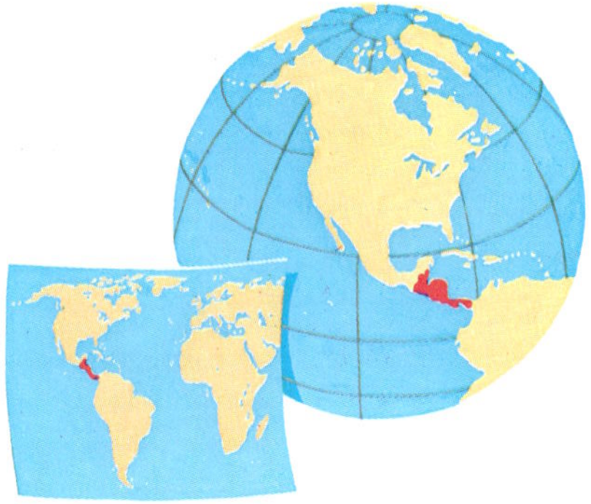

TOPOGRAPHY

AGRICULTURE, INDUSTRY and RESOURCES

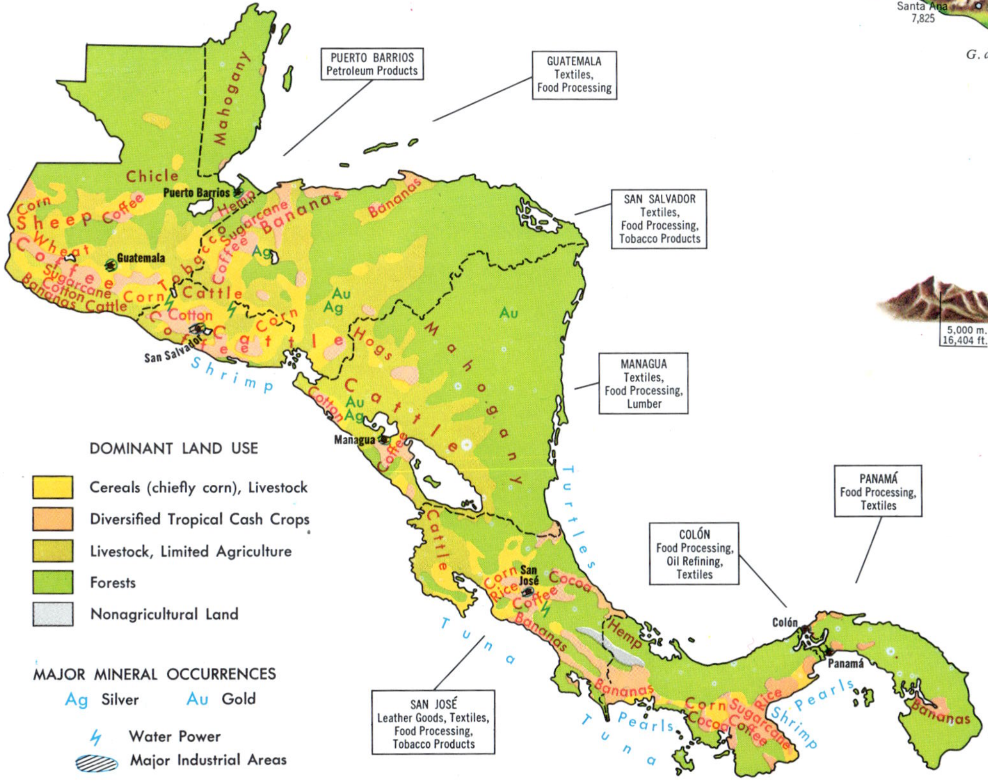

DOMINANT LAND USE

- Cereals (chiefly corn), Livestock
- Diversified Tropical Cash Crops
- Livestock, Limited Agriculture
- Forests
- Nonagricultural Land

MAJOR MINERAL OCCURRENCES

- Ag Silver
- Au Gold
- Water Power
- Major Industrial Areas

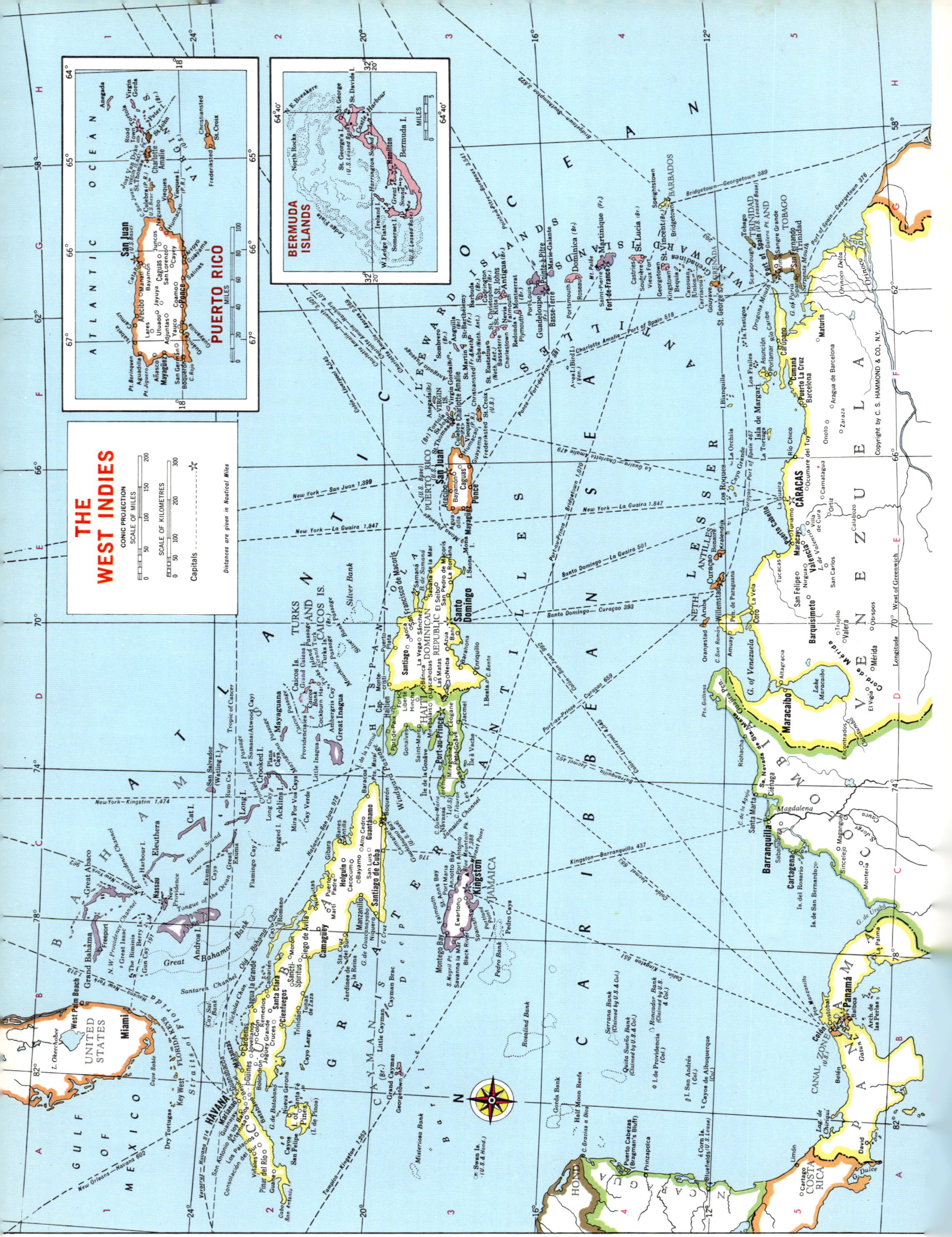
THE WEST INDIES
CONIC PROJECTION
SCALE OF MILES
0 50 100 150 200
SCALE OF KILOMETRES
0 50 100 200 300
Capitals
Distances are given in Nautical Miles
PUERTO RICO
BERMUDA ISLANDS
ATLANTIC OCEAN
CARIBBEAN SEA
GULF OF MEXICO
GREATER ANTILLES
LESSER ANTILLES
LEEWARD ISLANDS
WINDWARD ISLANDS
BAHAMA IS.
TURKS AND CAICOS IS.
HISPANIOLA
PUERTO RICO
JAMAICA
VENEZUELA
COLOMBIA
PANAMA
UNITED STATES
Copyright by C. S. HAMMOND & CO., N.Y.

THE WEST INDIES

CUBA

CAPITAL	Havana
HIGHEST POINT	Pico Turquino
MONETARY UNIT	Cuban peso
MAJOR LANGUAGE	Spanish
MAJOR RELIGIONS	Roman Catholic

JAMAICA

Kingston
Blue Mountain Peak
Jamaican pound
English
Protestant, Roman Catholic

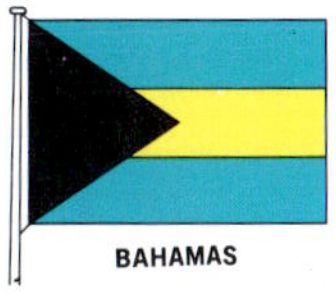

BAHAMAS

Nassau
Mt. Alvernia
Bahamian dollar
English
Protestant,
Roman Catholic

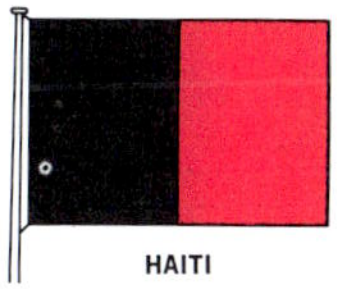

HAITI

CAPITAL	Port-au-Prince
HIGHEST POINT	Pic La Selle
MONETARY UNIT	gourde
MAJOR LANGUAGES	Creole, French
MAJOR RELIGIONS	Roman Catholic

DOMINICAN REPUBLIC

Santo Domingo
Pico Duarte
Dominican peso
Spanish
Roman Catholic

TOPOGRAPHY

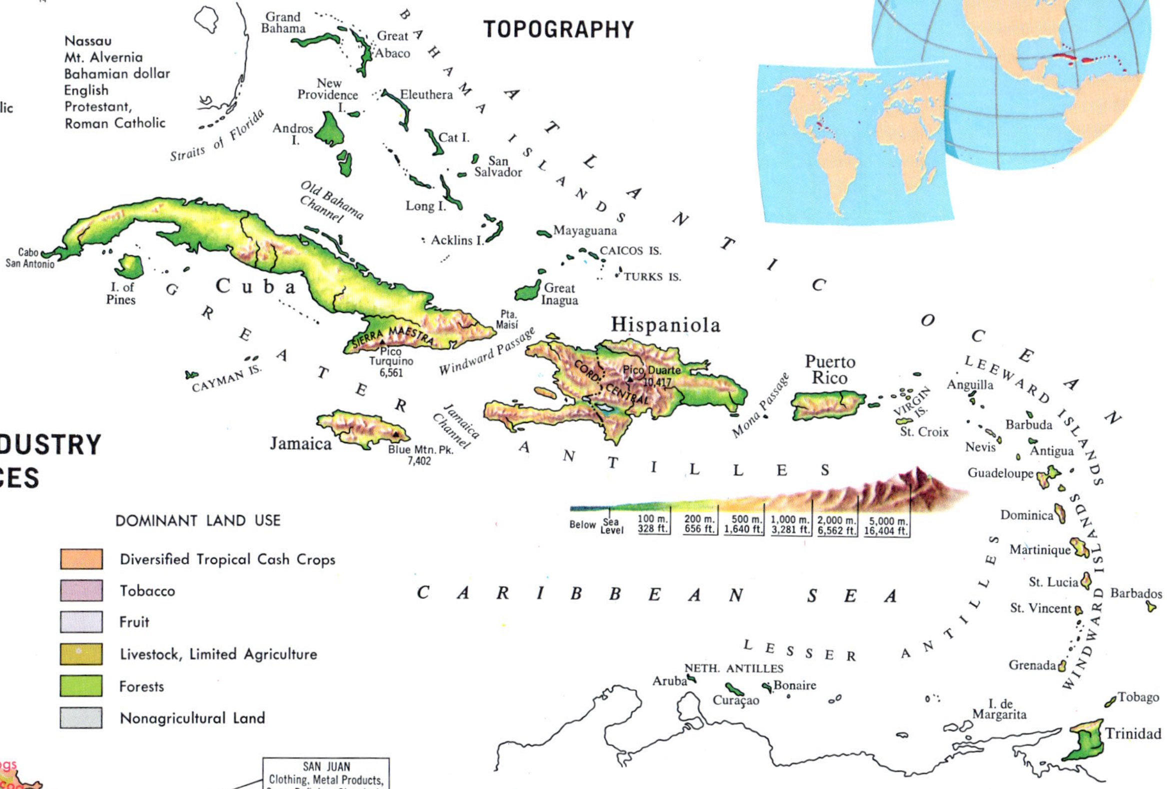

AGRICULTURE, INDUSTRY and RESOURCES

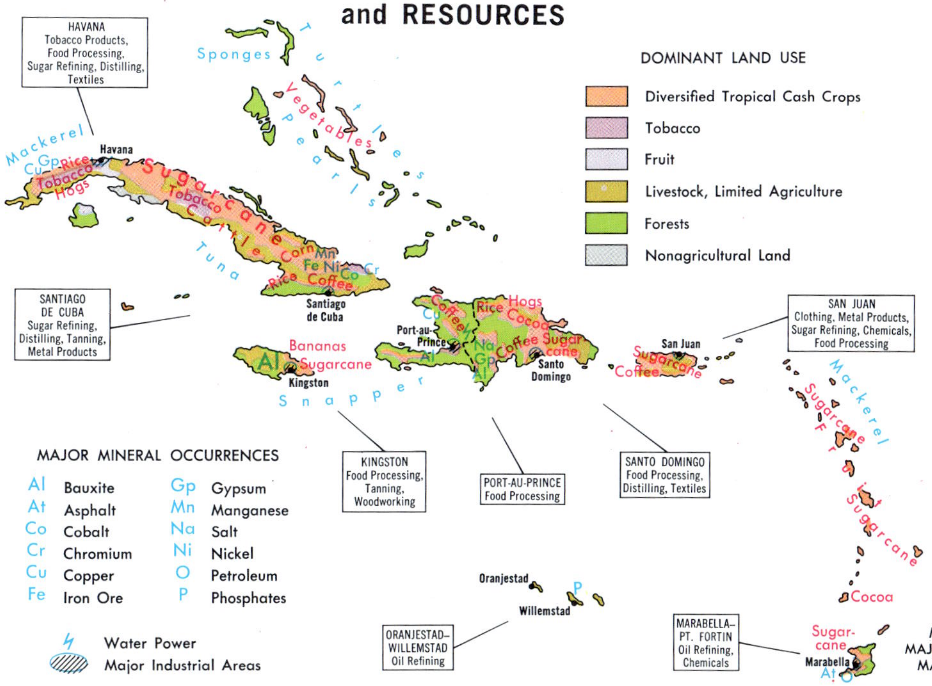

DOMINANT LAND USE

- Diversified Tropical Cash Crops
- Tobacco
- Fruit
- Livestock, Limited Agriculture
- Forests
- Nonagricultural Land

MAJOR MINERAL OCCURRENCES

Al	Bauxite	Gp	Gypsum
At	Asphalt	Mn	Manganese
Co	Cobalt	Na	Salt
Cr	Chromium	Ni	Nickel
Cu	Copper	O	Petroleum
Fe	Iron Ore	P	Phosphates

Water Power
Major Industrial Areas

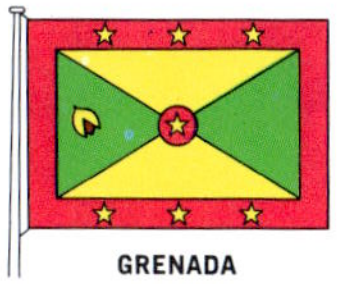

GRENADA

CAPITAL	St. George's
HIGHEST POINT	Mt. St. Catherine
MONETARY UNIT	East Caribbean dollar
MAJOR LANGUAGES	English, French patois
MAJOR RELIGIONS	Roman Catholic, Protestant

BARBADOS

Bridgetown
Mt. Hillaby
British West Indian dollar
English
Protestant, Roman Catholic

TRINIDAD & TOBAGO

Port of Spain
Mt. Aripo
British West Indian dollar
English
Roman Catholic, Protestant, Hindu

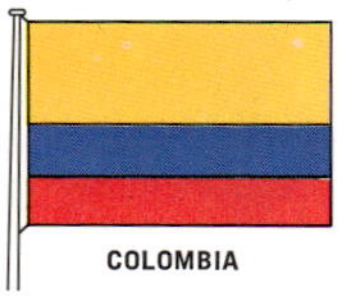

COLOMBIA

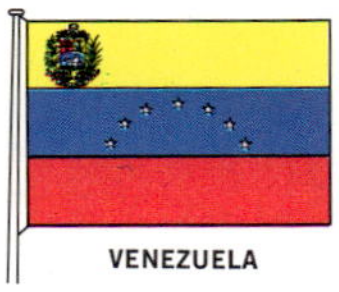

VENEZUELA

ECUADOR

PERU

BRAZIL

	COLOMBIA	VENEZUELA	ECUADOR	PERU	BRAZIL
CAPITAL	Bogotá	Caracas	Quito	Lima	Brasília
HIGHEST POINT	Pico Cristóbal Colón	Pico Bolívar	Chimborazo	Huascarán	Pico da Banderia
MONETARY UNIT	Colombian peso	bolívar	sucre	sol	cruzeiro
MAJOR LANGUAGES	Spanish	Spanish	Spanish, Indian	Spanish, Indian	Portuguese
MAJOR RELIGIONS	Roman Catholic	Roman Catholic	Roman Catholic	Roman Catholic	Roman Catholic

BOLIVIA

PARAGUAY

	BOLIVIA	PARAGUAY
CAPITAL	La Paz, Sucre	Asunción
HIGHEST POINT	Nevada Ancohuma	Amambay Range
MONETARY UNIT	Bolivian peso	guaraní
MAJOR LANGUAGES	Spanish, Indian	Spanish, Indian
MAJOR RELIGION	Roman Catholic	Roman Catholic

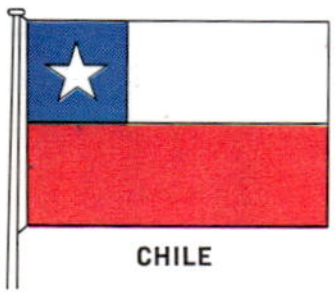

CHILE

	CHILE
CAPITAL	Santiago
HIGHEST POINT	Ojos del Salado
MONETARY UNIT	Chilean escudo
MAJOR LANGUAGE	Spanish
MAJOR RELIGION	Roman Catholic

ARGENTINA

URUGUAY

	ARGENTINA	URUGUAY
CAPITAL	Buenos Aires	Montevideo
HIGHEST POINT	Cerro Aconcagua	Mirador Nacional
MONETARY UNIT	Argentine peso	Uruguayan peso
MAJOR LANGUAGE	Spanish	Spanish
MAJOR RELIGION	Roman Catholic	Roman Catholic

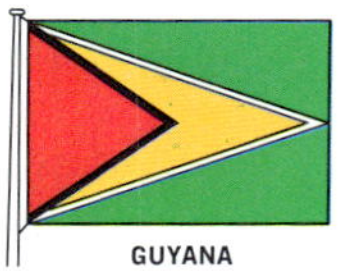

GUYANA

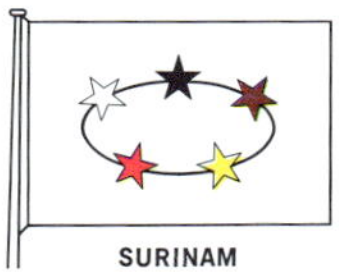

SURINAM

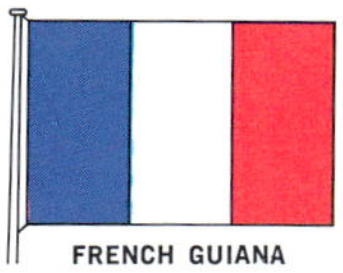

FRENCH GUIANA

GUYANA	SURINAM	FRENCH GUIANA
Georgetown	Paramaribo	Cayenne
Mt. Roraima	Wilhelmina Mts.	Chaîne de Milthaide
Guyana dollar	Surinam guilder	French franc
English, East Indian	Dutch	French
Christian, Hindu, Mohammedan	Christian, Mohammedan, Hindu	Roman Catholic, Protestant

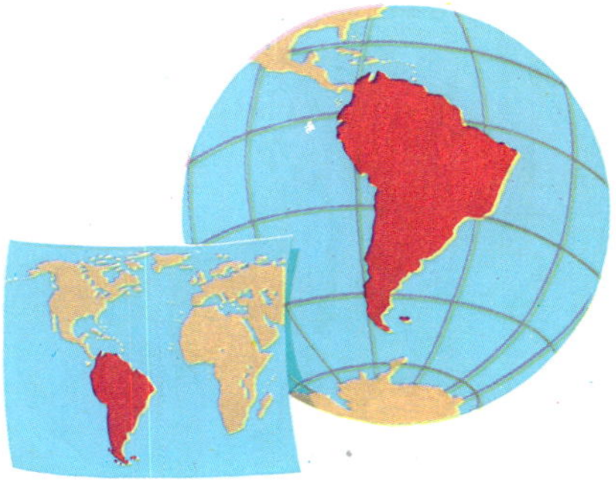

SOUTH AMERICA

AGRICULTURE, INDUSTRY and RESOURCES

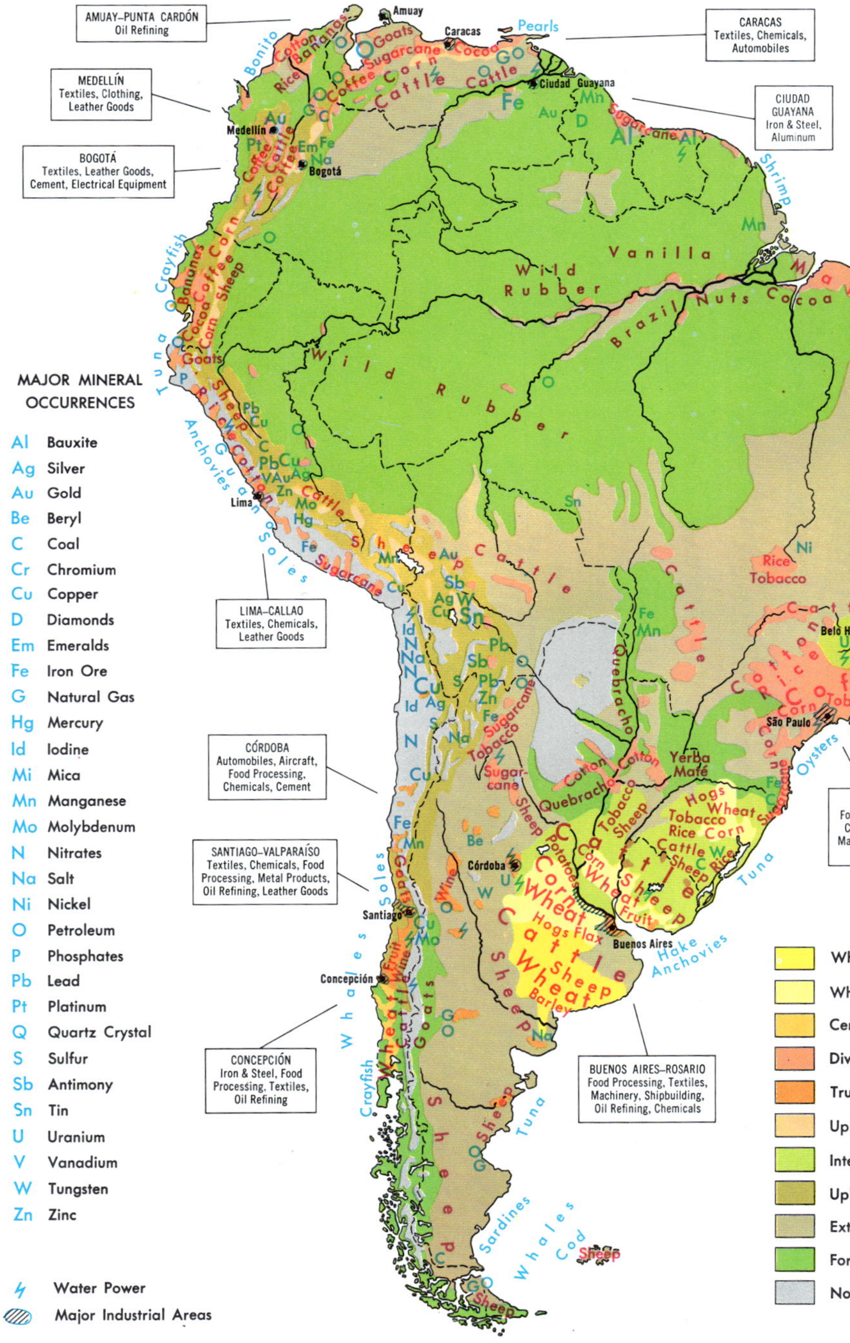

DOMINANT LAND USE

- Wheat, Livestock
- Wheat, Corn, Livestock
- Cereals, Livestock
- Diversified Tropical Crops (chiefly plantation agriculture)
- Truck Farming, Horticulture, Special Crops
- Upland Cultivated Areas
- Intensive Livestock Ranching
- Upland Livestock Grazing, Limited Agriculture
- Extensive Livestock Ranching
- Forests
- Nonagricultural Land

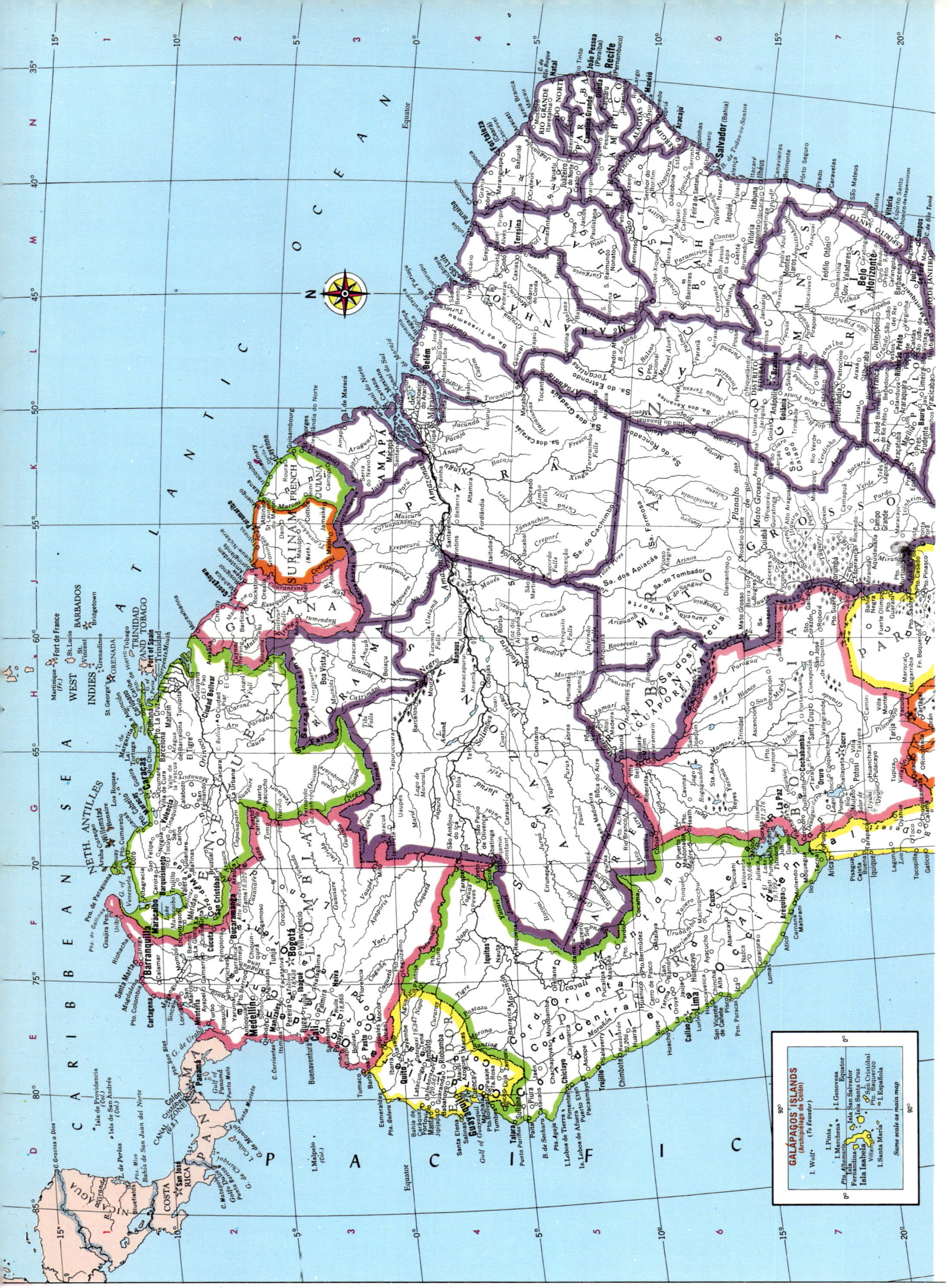
CARIBBEAN SEA
ATLANTIC OCEAN
PACIFIC
WEST INDIES
NETH. ANTILLES
BARBADOS
TRINIDAD AND TOBAGO
VENEZUELA
COLOMBIA
GUYANA
SURINAM
FRENCH GUIANA
ECUADOR
PERU
BOLIVIA
PARAGUAY
PANAMA
COSTA RICA
NICARAGUA
GALÁPAGOS ISLANDS
(Archipiélago de Colón)
(To Ecuador)
Same scale as main map
Equator

SOUTH AMERICA
LAMBERT AZIMUTHAL EQUAL-AREA PROJECTION
SCALE OF MILES
0 100 200 300 400 500
SCALE OF KILOMETRES
0 100 200 300 400 500
Capitals of Countries
Other Capitals
International Boundaries
Other Boundaries
Copyright by C.S. HAMMOND & Co., N.Y.
PACIFIC OCEAN
ATLANTIC OCEAN
DRAKE PASSAGE
FALKLAND ISLANDS (Br.)
SOUTH SHETLAND IS.
SOUTH ORKNEY IS.
JUAN FERNÁNDEZ IS. (Chile)
Tropic of Capricorn
BUENOS AIRES
Montevideo
Santiago
Asunción
RIO DE JANEIRO
SÃO PAULO
URUGUAY
ARGENTINA

WESTERN and CENTRAL EUROPE
CONIC PROJECTION
SCALE OF MILES
SCALE OF KILOMETRES
National Capitals
Administrative Centers
International Boundaries
Internal Boundaries
Canals
The government of the United States has not recognized the incorporation of Estonia, Latvia and Lithuania into the Soviet Union, nor does it recognize as final the de facto western limit of Polish administration in Germany (the Oder-Neisse line).
Arctic Circle
NORWEGIAN SEA
NORTH SEA
ATLANTIC OCEAN
Bay of Biscay
MEDITERRANEAN SEA
TYRRHENIAN SEA
IONIAN SEA
LIGURIAN SEA
Gulf of Bothnia
Gulf of Finland
Gulf of Riga
BALTIC SEA
GREAT BRITAIN
UNITED KINGDOM
IRELAND
NETHERLANDS
BELGIUM
FRANCE
SPAIN
PORTUGAL
SWITZERLAND
WEST GERMANY
EAST GERMANY
POLAND
CZECHOSLOVAKIA
AUSTRIA
HUNGARY
ITALY
NORWAY
SWEDEN
FINLAND
DENMARK
ESTONIAN S.S.R.
LATVIAN S.S.R.
LITHUANIAN S.S.R.
ALGERIA
TUNISIA
MOROCCO
FAERØE IS. (Den.)
SHETLAND ISLANDS
ORKNEY IS.
HEBRIDES
CHANNEL IS. (Br.)
BALEARIC IS.
Corsica
Sardinia (Sardegna)
Sicily (Sicilia)
LIPARI ISLANDS
EGADI IS.
GIBRALTAR (Br.)
ANDORRA
MONACO
SAN MARINO
VATICAN CITY
MALTA
LONDON
PARIS
BERLIN
Copenhagen
Stockholm
Helsinki
Oslo
Brussels
Amsterdam
Bonn
Vienna
Prague
Budapest
Warsaw
Madrid
Lisbon
ROME
Dublin
Bern
Luxembourg
Copyright by C. S. HAMMOND & Co., N.Y.
Longitude West of Greenwich
Longitude East of Greenwich

TOPOGRAPHY

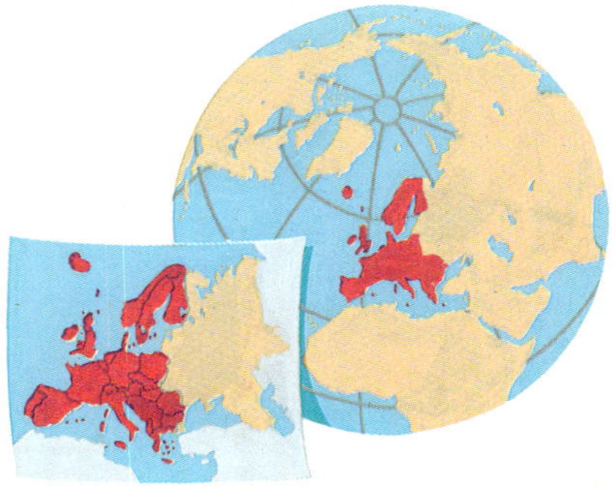

WESTERN and CENTRAL EUROPE

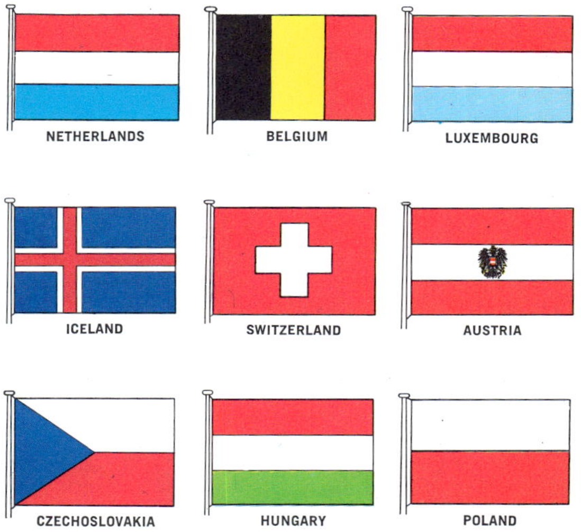

AGRICULTURE, INDUSTRY and RESOURCES

DOMINANT LAND USE

- Cereals
- Fruit, Horticulture
- Special Crops, Truck Farming
- Dairy, Livestock
- Mixed Farming
- Pasture Livestock
- Forests
- Nonagricultural Land

MAJOR MINERAL OCCURRENCES

Ag	Silver	K	Potash		
Al	Bauxite	Lg	Lignite		
C	Coal	Mg	Magnesium		
Cr	Chromium	Mo	Molybdenum		
Cu	Copper	Na	Salt		
Fe	Iron Ore	O	Petroleum	Ti	Titanium
G	Natural Gas	Pb	Lead	U	Uranium
Gr	Graphite	S	Sulfur	W	Tungsten
Hg	Mercury	Sb	Antimony	Zn	Zinc

Water Power — Major Industrial Areas

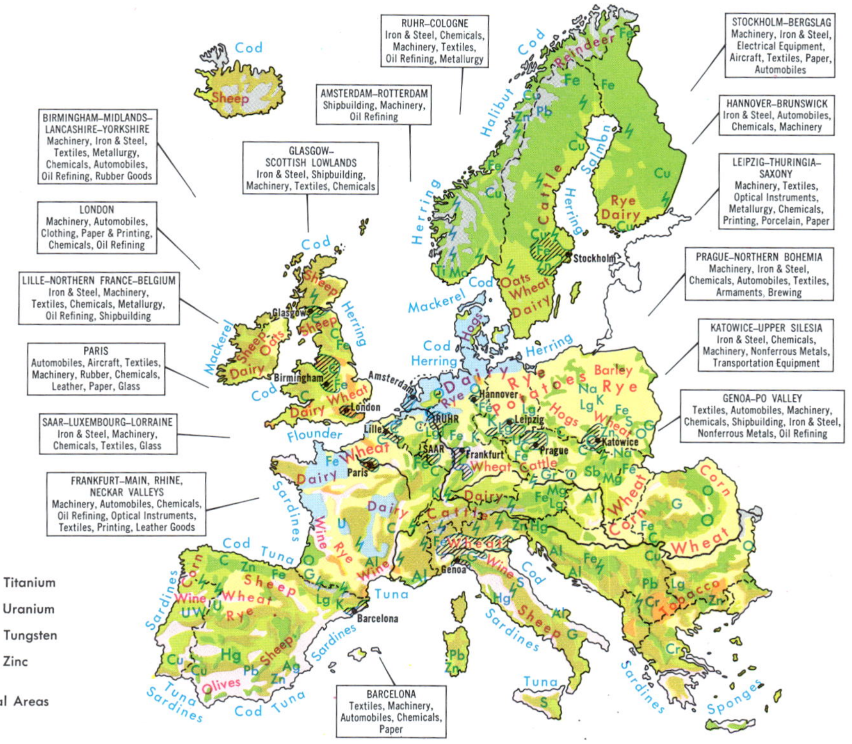

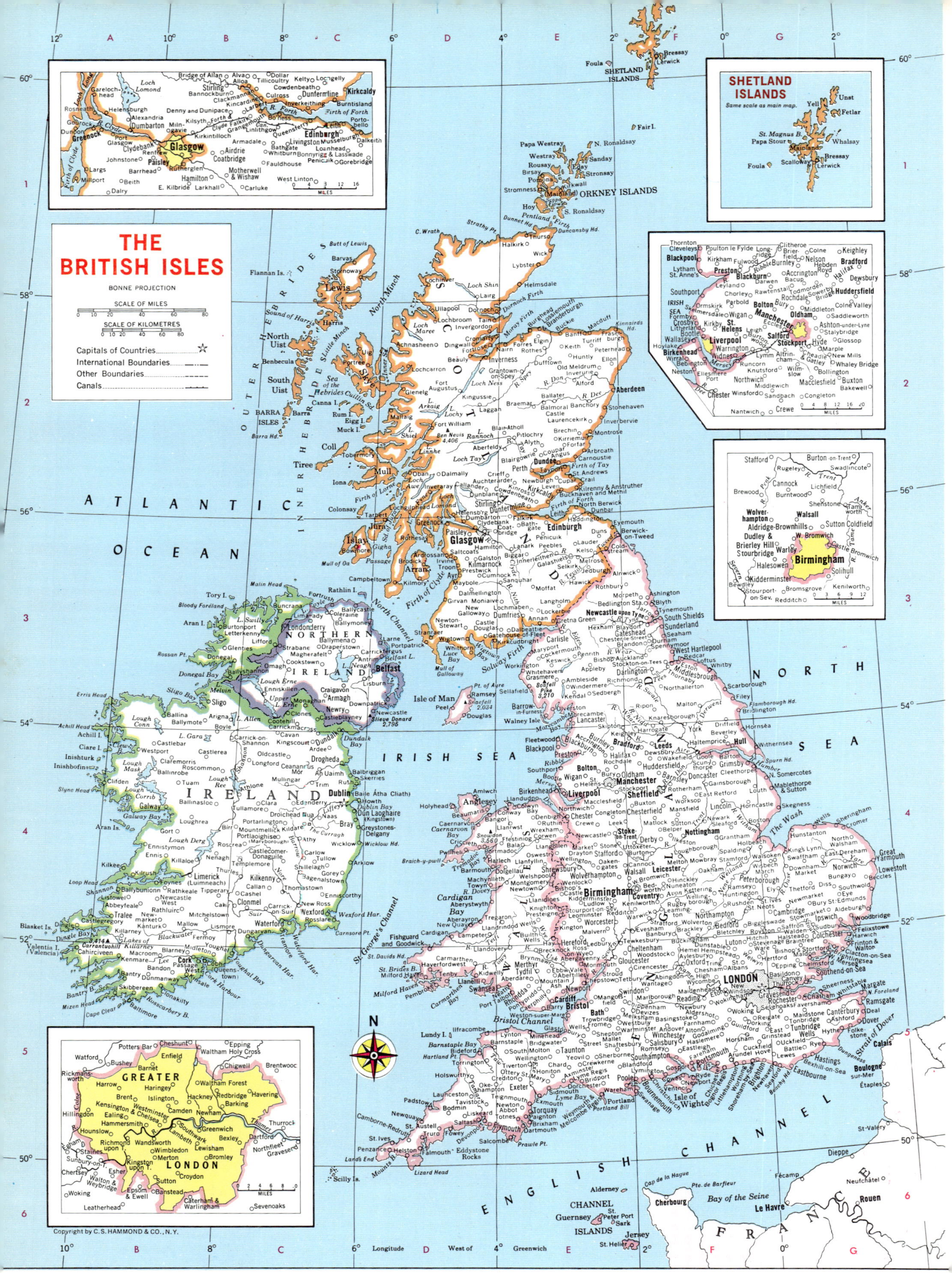
THE BRITISH ISLES
BONNE PROJECTION
SCALE OF MILES
SCALE OF KILOMETRES
Capitals of Countries
International Boundaries
Other Boundaries
Canals
SHETLAND ISLANDS
Same scale as main map.
ORKNEY ISLANDS
SCOTLAND
NORTHERN IRELAND
IRELAND
ENGLAND
WALES
ATLANTIC OCEAN
NORTH SEA
IRISH SEA
ENGLISH CHANNEL
CHANNEL ISLANDS
FRANCE
GREATER LONDON
LONDON
Edinburgh
Glasgow
Belfast
Dublin
Birmingham
Manchester
Liverpool
Cardiff
Longitude West of Greenwich
Copyright by C. S. HAMMOND & CO., N.Y.

THE BRITISH ISLES

TOPOGRAPHY

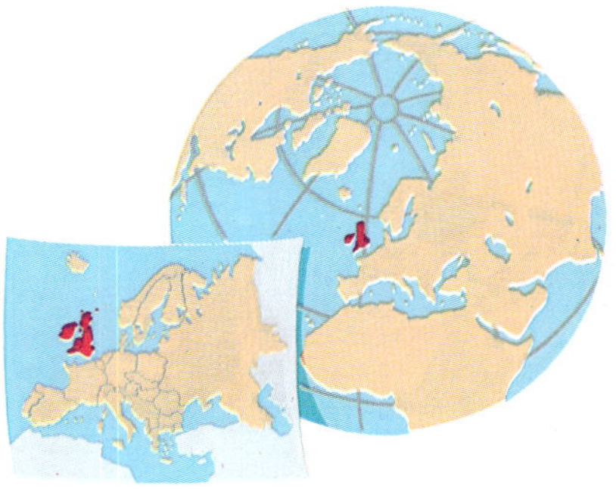

UNITED KINGDOM

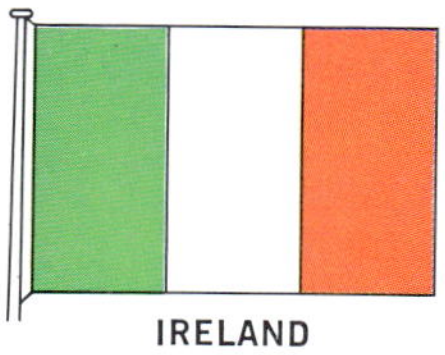

IRELAND

	UNITED KINGDOM	IRELAND
CAPITAL	London	Dublin
HIGHEST POINT	Ben Nevis	Carrantuohill
MONETARY UNIT	pound sterling	Irish pound
MAJOR LANGUAGES	English, Gaelic, Welsh	English, Gaelic
MAJOR RELIGIONS	Protestant, Roman Catholic	Roman Catholic

AGRICULTURE, INDUSTRY and RESOURCES

DOMINANT LAND USE

- Cereals (chiefly oats, barley)
- Truck Farming, Horticulture
- Dairy, Mixed Farming
- Livestock, Mixed Farming
- Pasture Livestock

MAJOR MINERAL OCCURRENCES

- C Coal
- Fe Iron Ore
- Ka Kaolin (china clay)
- Na Salt
- Sn Tin

- Water Power
- Major Industrial Areas

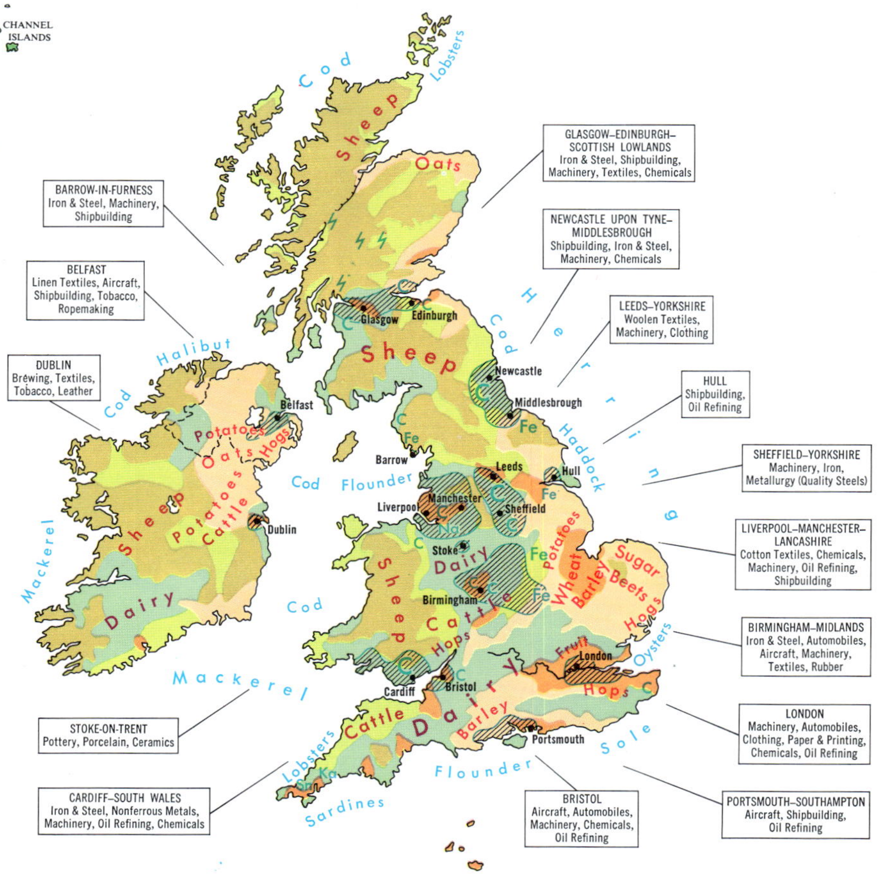

FRANCE
CONIC PROJECTION
SCALE OF MILES
SCALE OF KILOMETRES
Capitals of Countries
Capitals of Departments
International Boundaries
Department Boundaries
Canals
© C.S. HAMMOND & Co., N.Y.
PARIS AND ENVIRONS
CORSICA
Same Scale as Main Map
UNITED KINGDOM
ENGLAND
BELGIUM
NETHERLANDS
GERMANY
LUXEMBOURG
SWITZERLAND
ITALY
SPAIN
ANDORRA
ENGLISH CHANNEL (La Manche)
BAY OF BISCAY
MEDITERRANEAN SEA
NORTH SEA
Gulf of Lions
PARIS
LONDON
Longitude West of Greenwich
Longitude East of Greenwich

TOPOGRAPHY

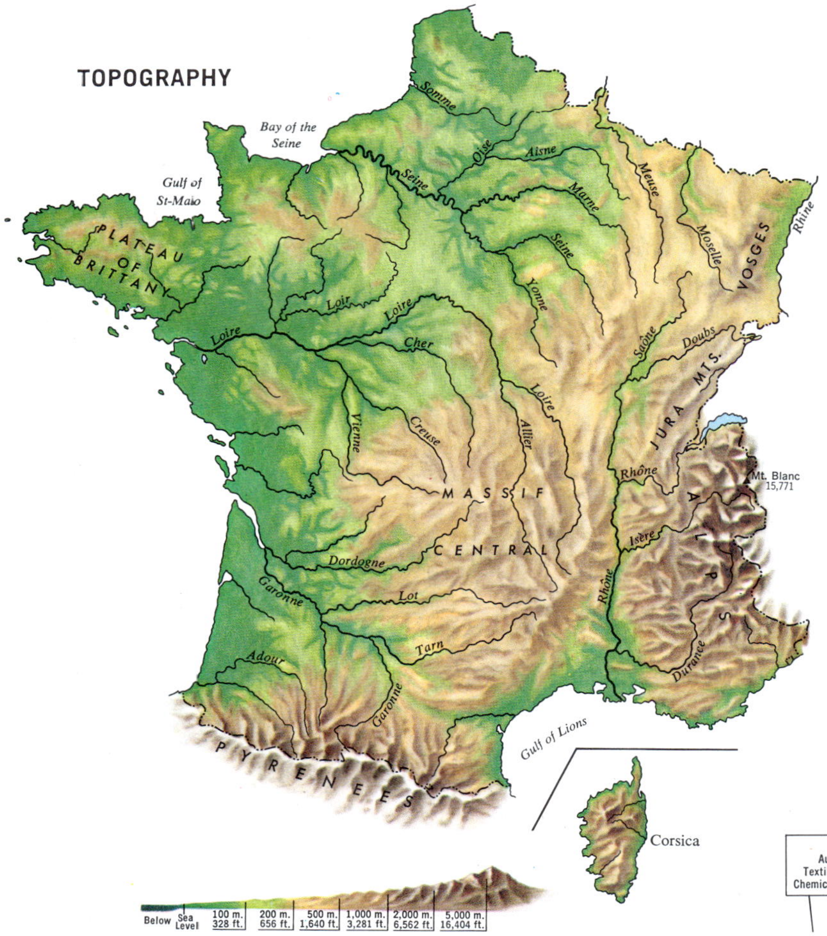

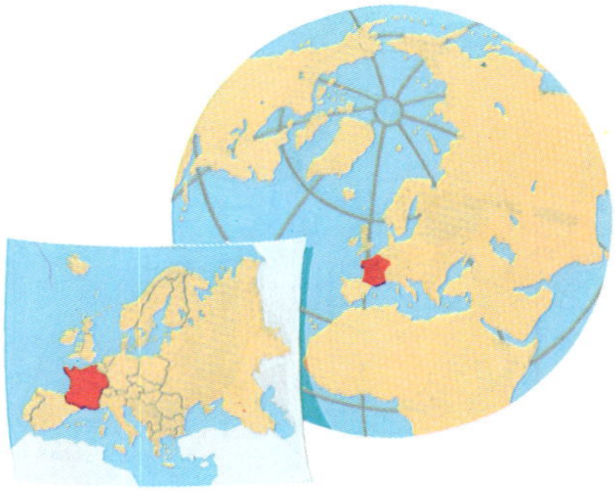

FRANCE

CAPITAL	Paris
HIGHEST POINT	Mont Blanc
MONETARY UNIT	franc
MAJOR LANGUAGE	French
MAJOR RELIGION	Roman Catholic

AGRICULTURE, INDUSTRY and RESOURCES

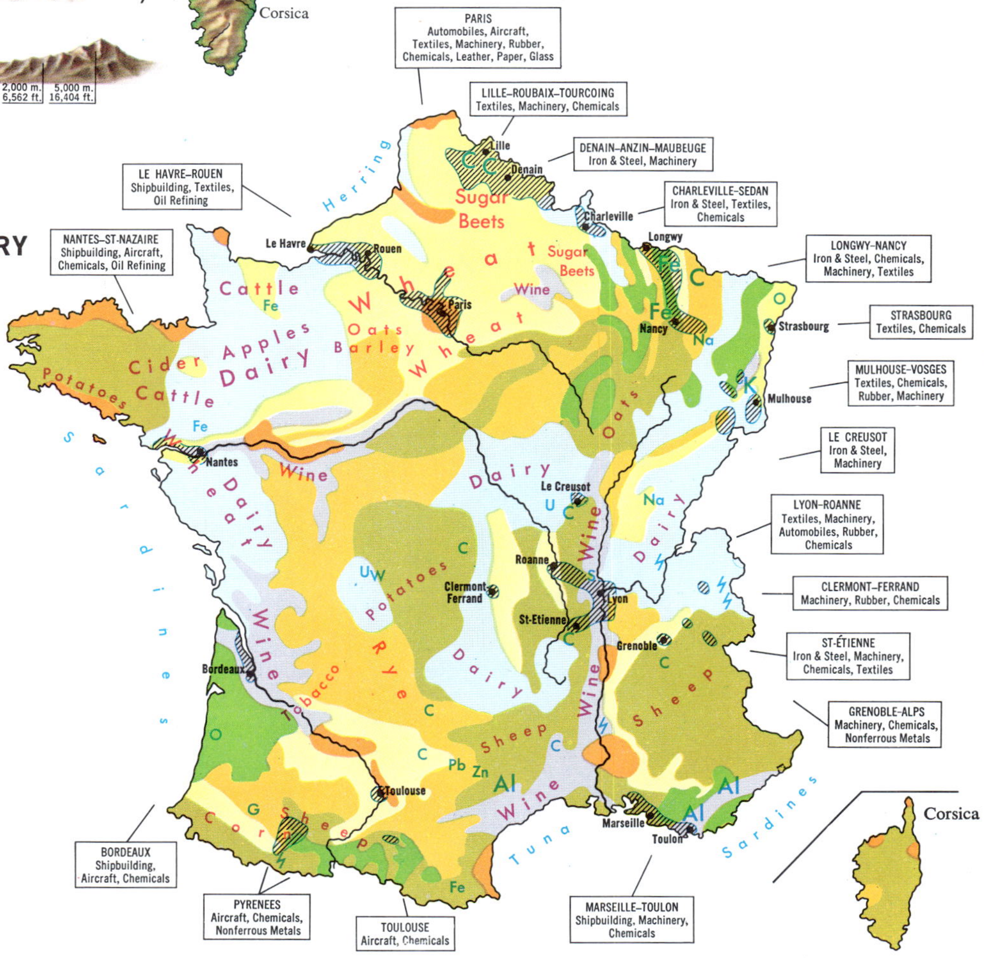

DOMINANT LAND USE

- Cereals (chiefly wheat)
- Cereals (chiefly rye, oats, barley)
- Dairy
- Pasture Livestock
- Truck Farming, Horticulture
- Grapes, Wine
- Forests

MAJOR MINERAL OCCURRENCES

Al	Bauxite		Petroleum
C	Coal	Pb	Lead
Fe	Iron Ore	S	Sulfur, Pyrites
G	Natural Gas	U	Uranium
K	Potash	W	Tungsten
Na	Salt	Zn	Zinc

Water Power
Major Industrial Areas

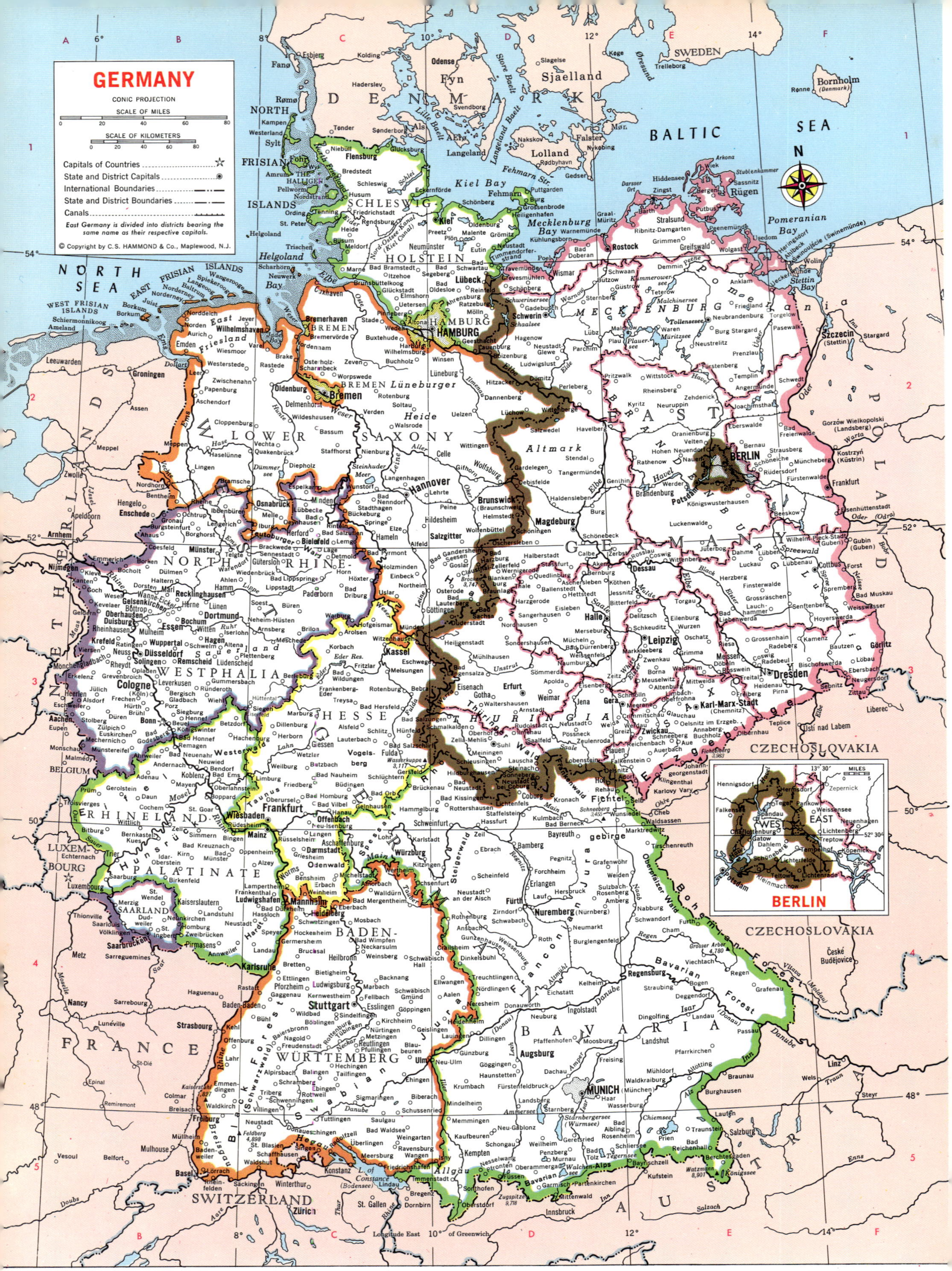

GERMANY
CONIC PROJECTION
SCALE OF MILES
0 20 40 60 80
SCALE OF KILOMETERS
0 20 40 60 80
Capitals of Countries
State and District Capitals
International Boundaries
State and District Boundaries
Canals
East Germany is divided into districts bearing the same name as their respective capitals.
© Copyright by C.S. HAMMOND & Co., Maplewood, N.J.
NORTH SEA
BALTIC SEA
DENMARK
SWEDEN
NETHERLANDS
BELGIUM
LUXEMBOURG
FRANCE
SWITZERLAND
AUSTRIA
CZECHOSLOVAKIA
POLAND
SCHLESWIG-HOLSTEIN
LOWER SAXONY
NORTH RHINE-WESTPHALIA
HESSE
RHINELAND-PALATINATE
SAARLAND
BADEN-WÜRTTEMBERG
BAVARIA
EAST GERMANY
MECKLENBURG
BRANDENBURG
SAXONY
THURINGIA
BERLIN
WEST
EAST
Longitude East 10° of Greenwich

TOPOGRAPHY

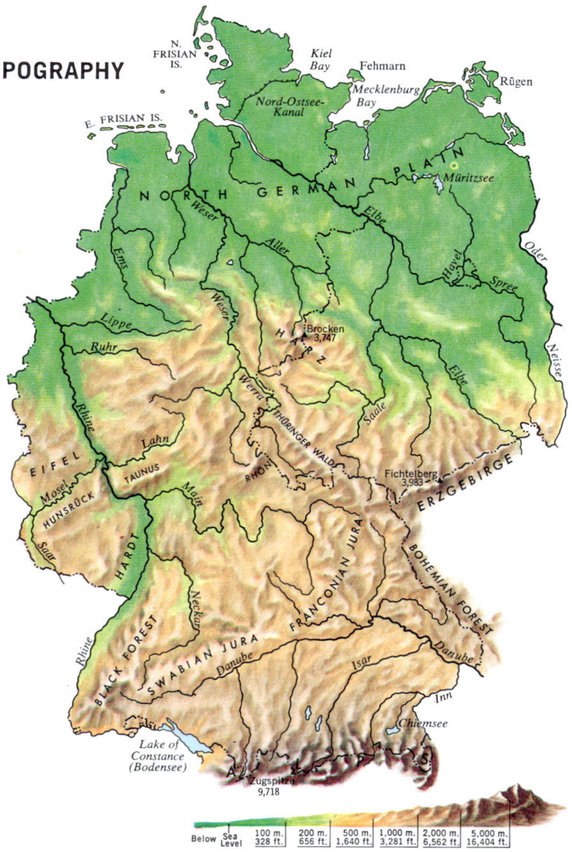

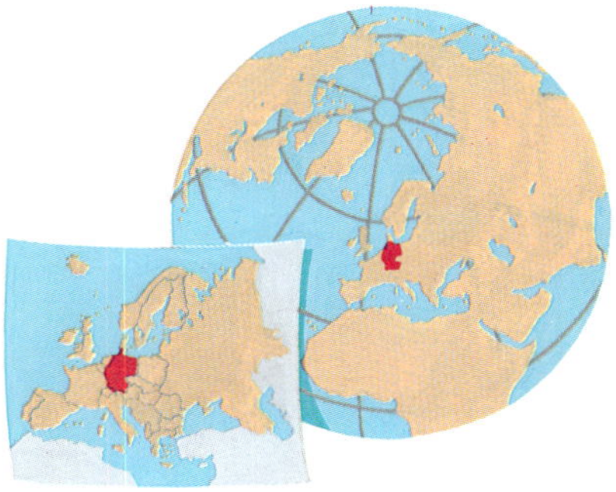

GERMANY

WEST GERMANY

EAST GERMANY

	WEST GERMANY	EAST GERMANY
CAPITAL	Bonn	Berlin (East)
HIGHEST POINT	Zugspitze	Fichtelberg
MONETARY UNIT	West German Deutsche mark	East German Deutsche mark
MAJOR LANGUAGE	German	German
MAJOR RELIGIONS	Protestant, Roman Catholic	Protestant, Roman Catholic

AGRICULTURE, INDUSTRY and RESOURCES

DOMINANT LAND USE

- Wheat, Sugar Beets
- Cereals (chiefly rye, oats, barley)
- Potatoes, Rye
- Dairy, Livestock
- Mixed Cereals, Dairy
- Truck Farming
- Grapes, Fruit
- Forests

MAJOR MINERAL OCCURRENCES

- Ag Silver
- C Coal
- Cu Copper
- Fe Iron Ore
- G Natural Gas
- Gr Graphite
- K Potash
- Lg Lignite
- Mg Magnesium
- O Petroleum
- Pb Lead
- U Uranium
- Zn Zinc

- Water Power
- Major Industrial Areas

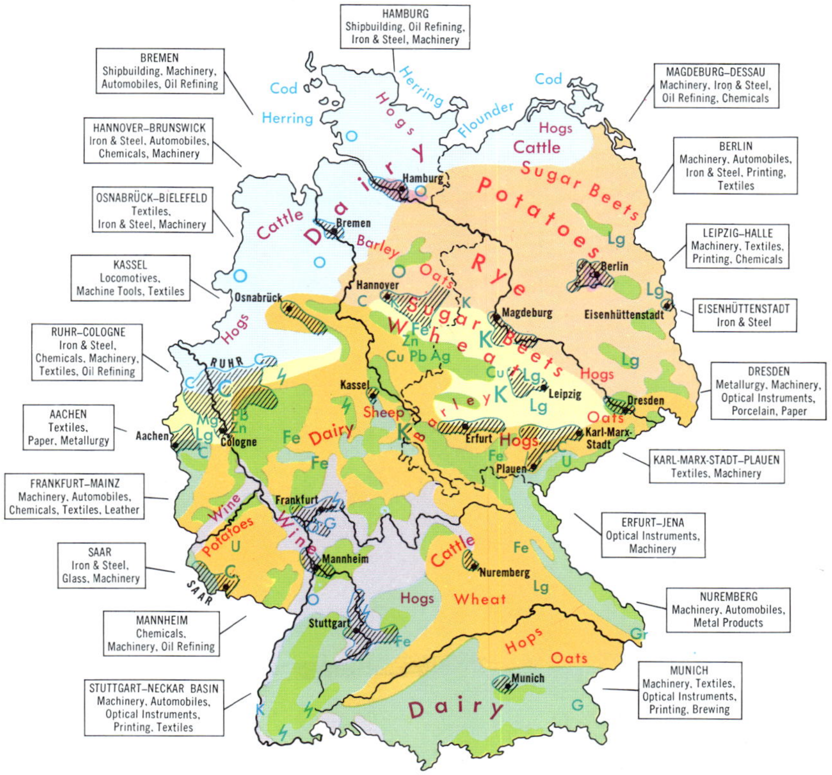

SCANDINAVIA and FINLAND
CONIC PROJECTION
SCALE OF MILES
0 50 100 150
SCALE OF KILOMETRES
0 50 100 150 200
Capitals of Countries
Administrative Centers
International Boundaries
Internal Boundaries
Canals
SUBDIVISIONS Indicated by Numbers
Fylker in NORWAY
1 Akershus G6
2 Vestfold G7
3 Østfold G7
4 Oslo G7
5 Bergen D6
Oslo is the administrative center for Akershus and Oslo Fylker; Bergen for Hordaland and Bergen Fylker
Lan in SWEDEN
6 Göteborg och Bohus G7
7 Västmanland K7
8 Södermanland K7
9 Östergötland J7
10 Malmöhus H9
11 Kristianstad J8
Copyright by C. S. HAMMOND & CO., N. Y.
SVALBARD
NORWEGIAN SEA
Nordaustlandet
Spitsbergen
Edgeøya
Bjørnøya
STOCKHOLM
Oslo
ARCTIC OCEAN
BARENTS SEA
NORWEGIAN SEA
ATLANTIC OCEAN
NORTH SEA
SKAGERRAK
KATTEGAT
GULF OF BOTHNIA
BALTIC SEA
Gulf of Finland
Gulf of Riga
Lake Ladoga
Lake Imandra
DENMARK
COPENHAGEN
Göteborg
Helsinki
LENINGRAD
Tallinn
Riga
Bergen
Trondheim
Stavanger
Malmö
GOTLAND
Öland
Bornholm
AHVENANMAA (ÅLAND)
NORRBOTTEN
LAPPI
OULU
VAASA
U. S. S. R.
EAST GERMANY
WEST GERMANY
HAMBURG
BERLIN
POLAND
WARSAW
Gdańsk (Danzig)
Szczecin (Stettin)
Kaunas
Murmansk

TOPOGRAPHY

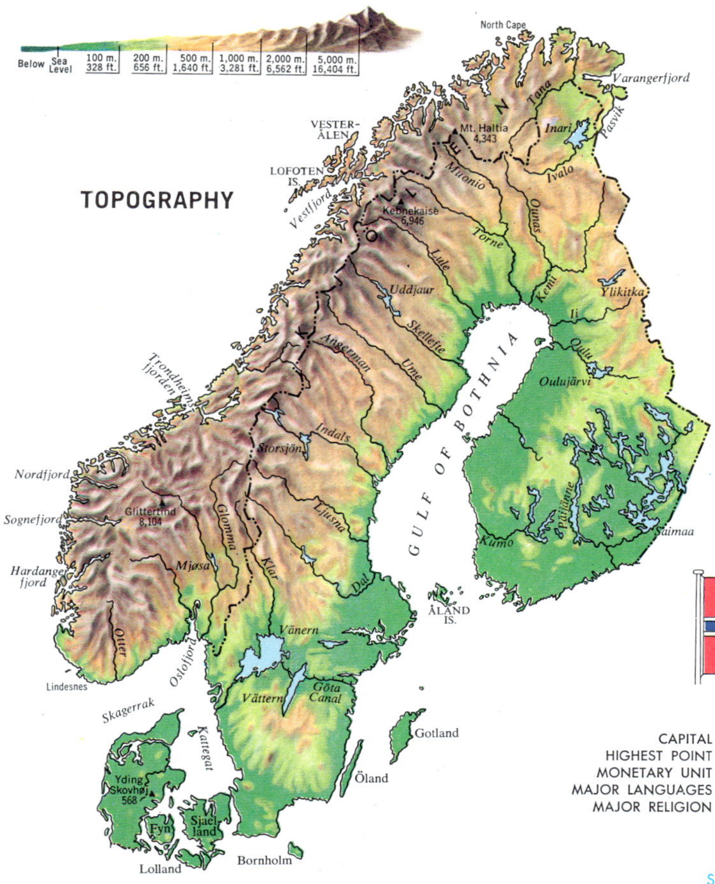

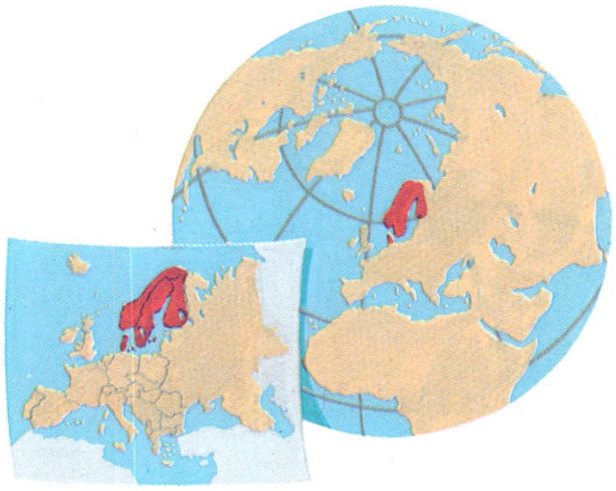

SCANDINAVIA and FINLAND

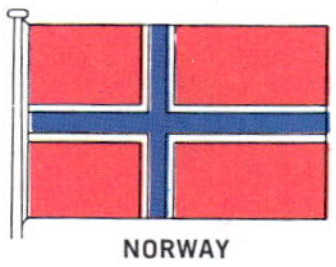

NORWAY

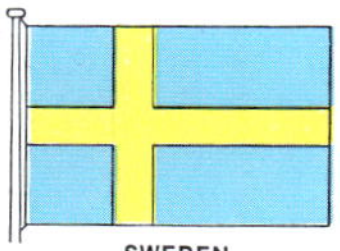

SWEDEN

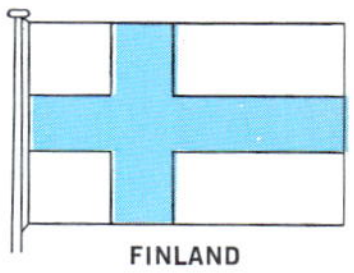

FINLAND

	NORWAY	SWEDEN	FINLAND
CAPITAL	Oslo	Stockholm	Helsinki
HIGHEST POINT	Glittertind	Kebnekaise	Mt. Haltia
MONETARY UNIT	krone (crown)	krona (crown)	markka (mark)
MAJOR LANGUAGES	Norwegian	Swedish	Finnish, Swedish
MAJOR RELIGION	Protestant	Protestant	Protestant

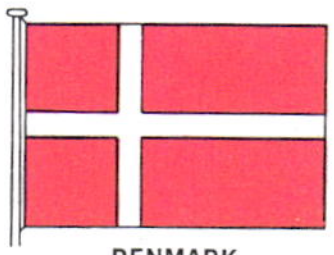

DENMARK

CAPITAL	Copenhagen
HIGHEST POINT	Yding Skovhøj
MONETARY UNIT	krone (crown)
MAJOR LANGUAGE	Danish
MAJOR RELIGION	Protestant

AGRICULTURE, INDUSTRY and RESOURCES

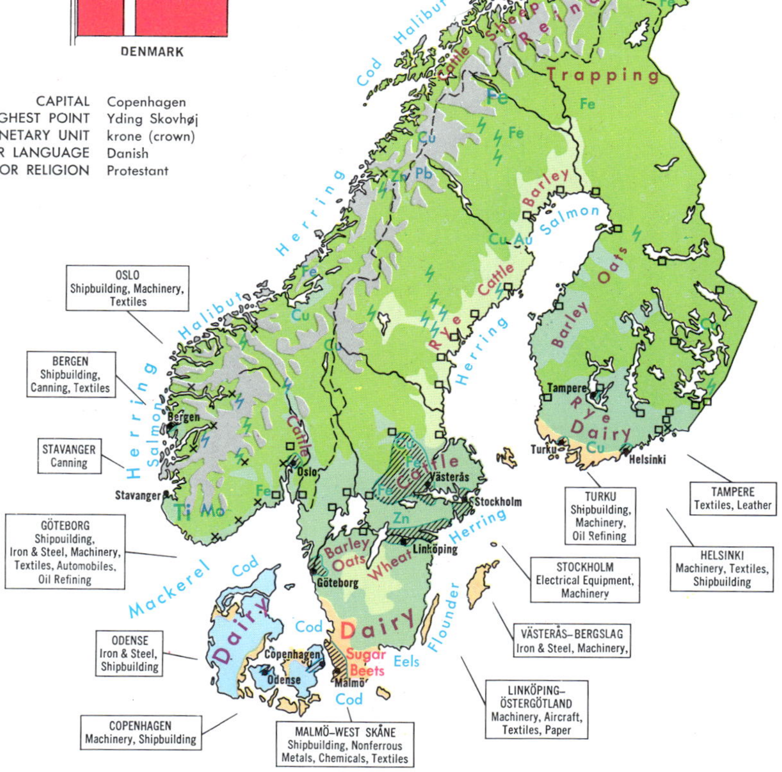

DOMINANT LAND USE

- Cash Cereals, Dairy
- Dairy, Cattle, Hogs
- Dairy, General Farming
- General Farming (chiefly cereals)
- Nomadic Sheep Herding
- Forests, Limited Mixed Farming
- Nonagricultural Land

MAJOR MINERAL OCCURRENCES

- Au Gold
- Cu Copper
- Fe Iron Ore
- Mo Molybdenum
- Pb Lead
- Ti Titanium
- Zn Zinc

- Water Power
- Major Industrial Areas
- × Electrochemical & Electrometallurgical Centers
- □ Paper, Pulp & Sawmilling Centers

THE MEDITERRANEAN
SCALE OF MILES
0 50 100 200 300 400
SCALE OF KILOMETRES
0 50 100 200 300 400
Capitals of Countries
Canals
Copyright by C. S. HAMMOND & Co., N.Y.
Longitude West of Greenwich 0° Longitude East of Greenwich
ATLANTIC OCEAN
Bay of Biscay
MEDITERRANEAN
TYRRHENIAN SEA
IONIAN SEA
ADRIATIC SEA
Ligurian Sea
Gulf of Lions
Gulf of Sidra
Strait of Gibraltar
FRANCE
SPAIN
PORTUGAL
WEST GERMANY
CZECHOSLOVAKIA
POLAND
AUSTRIA
SWITZERLAND
HUNGARY
RUMANIA
YUGOSLAVIA
BULGARIA
ALBANIA
GREECE
ITALY
MOROCCO
ALGERIA
TUNISIA
LIBYA
PARIS
MADRID
ROME
Vienna
Budapest
Belgrade
Bucharest
Sofia
Athens
Tunis
Algiers
Tripoli
Lisbon
Barcelona
Marseille
Naples
Palermo
Sicily
Sardinia
Corsica
Crete
Malta
BALEARIC ISLANDS
Majorca (Mallorca)
CYCLADES
DODECANESE IS.
Istanbul
Casablanca
Rabat
Benghazi

Bay of Biscay
Iberian Peninsula
CANTABRIAN MTS.
PYRENEES
SIERRA MORENA
SIERRA NEVADA
Mulhacén 11,411
Str. of Gibraltar
MASSIF CENTRAL
THE ALPS
Mt. Blanc 15,771
JURA
CARPATHIANS
TRANSYLVANIAN ALPS
DINARIC ALPS
APENNINES
BALKAN MTS.
RHODOPE
Balkan Pen.
Mt. Olympus 9,570
Vesuvius 4,190
Mt. Etna 11,053
MEDITERRANEAN SEA
TYRRHENIAN SEA
IONIAN SEA
ADRIATIC SEA
LIGURIAN SEA
SEA OF CRETE
BLACK SEA
Sea of Azov
Sea of Marmara
CAUCASUS
El'brus 18,481
PLATEAU OF ANATOLIA
TAURUS MTS.
LEBANON MTS.
ATLAS MOUNTAINS
ER RIF
Great Western Erg
Great Eastern Erg
Qattara Depression
Nile Delta
Suez Canal
Sinai Pen.
RED SEA
Dead Sea
Crimea
Corsica
Sardinia
Sicily
Malta
Crete
Rhodes
Cyprus
© C. S. HAMMOND & Co.

THE MEDITERRANEAN

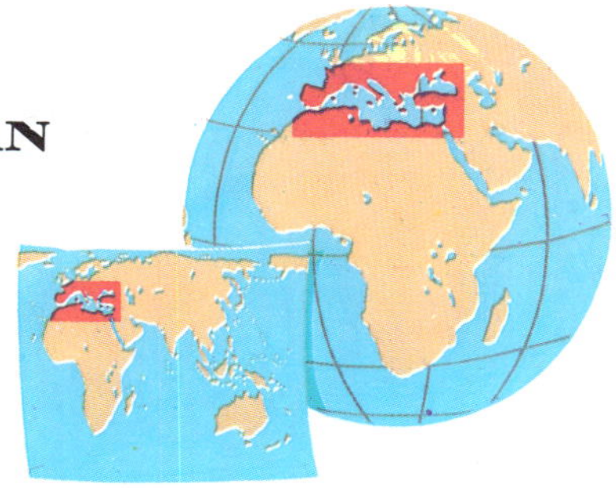

DISTANCES BETWEEN MAJOR PORTS

Distances in Statute Miles	Alexandria	Algiers	Barcelona	Genoa	Gibraltar	İstanbul	Marseille	Piraiévs	Port Said	Tunis
Alexandria	•	1602	1704	1513	2076	853	1618	592	189	1209
Algiers	1602	•	324	611	483	1602	472	1241	1741	451
Barcelona	1704	324	•	509	593	1709	217	1433	1840	566
Genoa	1513	611	509	•	978	1485	235	1125	1640	543
Gibraltar	2076	483	593	978	•	2075	797	1714	2214	923
İstanbul	853	1602	1709	1485	2075	•	1590	419	925	1208
Marseille	1618	472	217	235	797	1590	•	1229	1745	547
Piraiévs	592	1241	1433	1125	1714	419	1229	•	689	848
Port Said	189	1741	1840	1640	2214	925	1745	689	•	1348
Tunis	1209	451	566	543	923	1208	547	848	1348	•

THE ROMAN EMPIRE AT ITS GREATEST EXTENT ABOUT 117 A. D.

ITALY
CONIC PROJECTION
SCALE OF MILES
0 20 40 60 80 100
SCALE OF KILOMETERS
0 20 40 60 80 100
Capitals of Countries
Regional Capitals
Provincial Capitals
International Boundaries
Regional Boundaries
ITALY is divided for administrative purposes into 20 regions, shown on the map in separate colors. The regions of Friuli-Venezia Giulia, Sardinia, Sicily, Trentino-Alto Adige and Valle d'Aosta enjoy special autonomy.
The regions are subdivided into provinces bearing the same names as their respective capitals, except:
PROVINCE
CAPITAL
MASSA-CARRARA
Massa
PESARO-URBINO
Pesaro
SWITZERLAND
AUSTRIA
YUGOSLAVIA
FRANCE
LIECHTENSTEIN
MONACO
SAN MARINO
CORSICA
SARDINIA
SICILY
TUNISIA
MALTA
LIGURIAN SEA
TYRRHENIAN SEA
ADRIATIC SEA
IONIAN SEA
MEDITERRANEAN SEA
Gulf of Venice
Gulf of Genoa
Gulf of Gaeta
Gulf of Salerno
Gulf of Taranto
Gulf of Squillace
Gulf of Sant'Eufemia
Gulf of Tunis
Gulf of Hammamet
Strait of Sicily
Strait of Messina
Strait of Bonifacio
Strait of Otranto
Malta Channel
TUSCAN ARCH.
LIPARI ISLANDS
EGADI ISLANDS
PONTINE ISLANDS
PELAGIE ISLANDS
ROME
MILAN
NAPLES
Turin
Genoa
Venice
Florence
Bologna
Trieste
Palermo
Bari
Cagliari
Catania
Messina
Taranto
VATICAN CITY
ROME and ENVIRONS
Copyright by C.S. HAMMOND & Co., N.Y.
Longitude East of Greenwich

TOPOGRAPHY

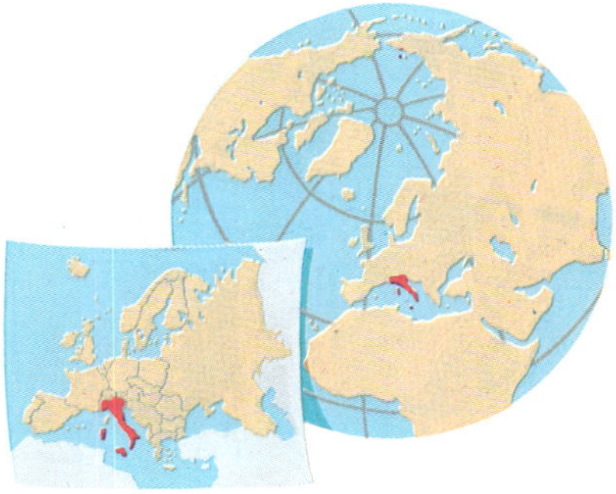

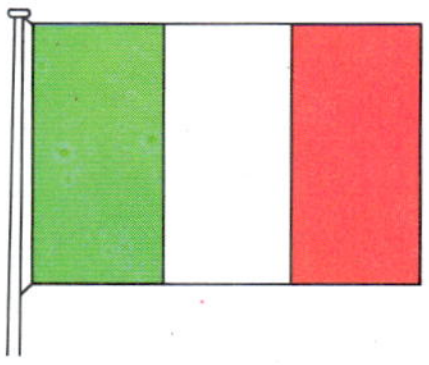

ITALY

CAPITAL Rome
HIGHEST POINT Dufourspitze (Mte. Rosa)
MONETARY UNIT lira
MAJOR LANGUAGE Italian
MAJOR RELIGION Roman Catholic

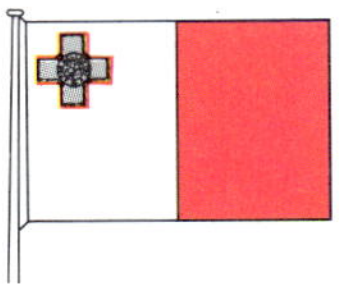

MALTA

AGRICULTURE, INDUSTRY and RESOURCES

DOMINANT LAND USE

- Wheat, Rice, Dairy
- Pasture Livestock
- Cereals, Livestock
- Fruit, Truck and Mixed Farming
- Grapes, Wine
- Forests
- Nonagricultural Land

MAJOR MINERAL OCCURRENCES

Al	Bauxite	Hg	Mercury	O	Petroleum
C	Coal	Lg	Lignite	Pb	Lead
Fe	Iron Ore	Mr	Marble	S	Sulfur, Pyrites
G	Natural Gas	Na	Salt	Zn	Zinc

Water Power
Major Industrial Areas

SPAIN and PORTUGAL
CONIC PROJECTION
SCALE OF MILES
0 20 40 60 80 100
SCALE OF KILOMETRES
0 20 40 60 80 100
Capitals of Countries
Provincial Capitals
International Boundaries
Provincial Boundaries
© Copyright by C.S. HAMMOND & Co., Maplewood, N.J.
BAY OF BISCAY
ATLANTIC OCEAN
MEDITERRANEAN
BALEARIC ISLANDS (BALEARES)
Gulf of Lions
Gulf of Valencia
FRANCE
ANDORRA
MOROCCO
MADRID
LISBON (Lisboa)
CANARY ISLANDS (Spain)
MADEIRA (Portugal)

SPAIN and PORTUGAL

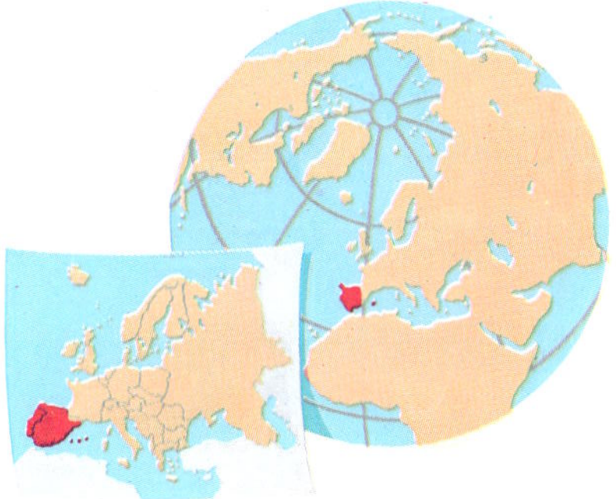

TOPOGRAPHY

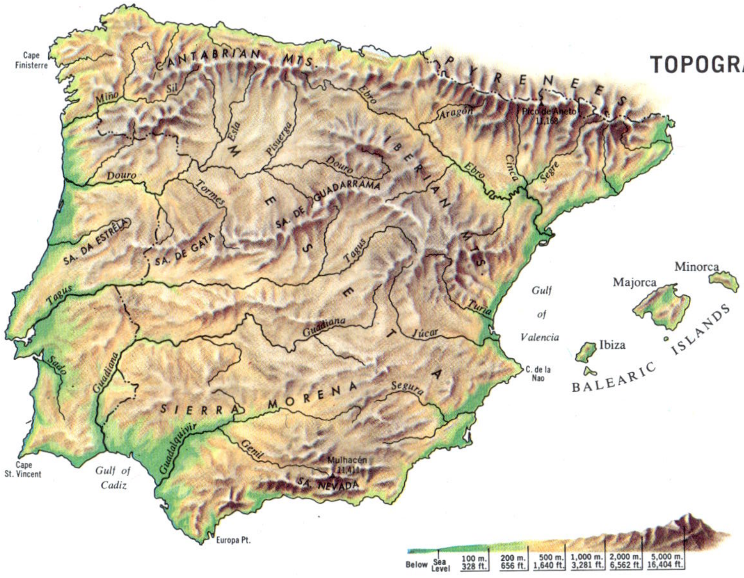

SPAIN

CAPITAL	Madrid
HIGHEST POINT	Pico de Teide (Canary Is.)
MONETARY UNIT	peseta
MAJOR LANGUAGES	Spanish, Catalan
MAJOR RELIGION	Roman Catholic

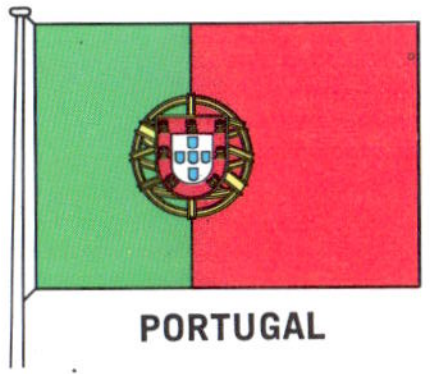

PORTUGAL

CAPITAL	Lisbon
HIGHEST POINT	Malhão da Estrêla
MONETARY UNIT	escudo
MAJOR LANGUAGE	Portuguese
MAJOR RELIGION	Roman Catholic

AGRICULTURE, INDUSTRY and RESOURCES

DOMINANT LAND USE

- Cereals (chiefly wheat)
- Livestock (chiefly sheep, goats)
- Mixed Cereals, Livestock
- Olives, Fruit
- Grapes, Fruit, Nuts, Mixed Cereals
- Forests
- Nonagricultural Land

MAJOR MINERAL OCCURRENCES

Ag	Silver	Na	Salt
C	Coal	Pb	Lead
Cu	Copper	S	Sulfur, Pyrites
Fe	Iron Ore	Sn	Tin
Hg	Mercury	U	Uranium
K	Potash	W	Tungsten
Lg	Lignite	Zn	Zinc

Water Power

Major Industrial Areas

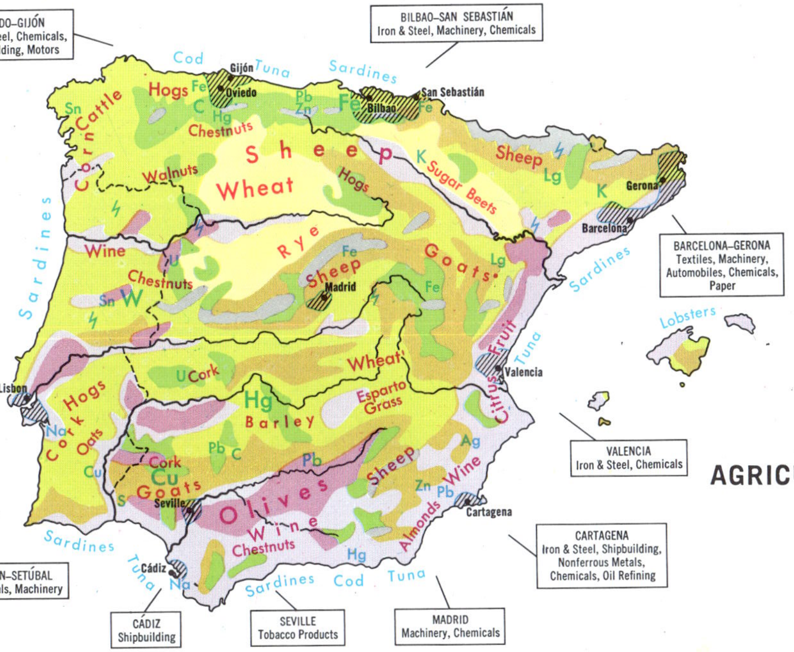

THE BALKAN STATES
CONIC PROJECTION
SCALE OF MILES
0 25 50 75 100 125 150 175
SCALE OF KILOMETRES
0 25 50 75 100 125 150 175
Capitals of Countries
Administrative Centers
International Boundaries
Major Internal Boundaries
Minor Internal Boundaries
Canals
BULGARIA and GREECE are divided into counties and departments, respectively. Because of the scale no attempt has been made to delimit and name these subdivisions; their administrative centers have, however, been designated.
The larger divisions named in Greece are well-known geographical regions, without administrative function.
RUMANIA consists of thirty-nine counties and three cities of regional status, Bucharest, Constanţa and Petroşeni. Scale does not permit delimiting these counties.
ALBANIA is divided into twenty-seven districts. Scale does not permit the delimitation of these divisions.
YUGOSLAVIA is a federation of six republics. The Serbian republic includes an autonomous province (Voyvodina), and an autonomous region (Kosovo-Mitohiyan).
POLAND
CZECHOSLOVAKIA
U. S. S. R.
GERMANY
AUSTRIA
HUNGARY
RUMANIA
YUGOSLAVIA
BULGARIA
ALBANIA
GREECE
TURKEY
ITALY
VIENNA
BUDAPEST
Belgrade
BUCHAREST
Sofia
Tiranë
Athens
İSTANBUL
ADRIATIC SEA
BLACK SEA
AEGEAN SEA
IONIAN SEA
TYRRHENIAN SEA
MEDITERRANEAN SEA
SEA OF CRETE
SEA OF MARMARA
Crete
CYCLADES ISLANDS
DODECANESE IS.
Longitude East of Greenwich
Copyright by C.S. HAMMOND & Co., N.Y.

THE BALKAN STATES

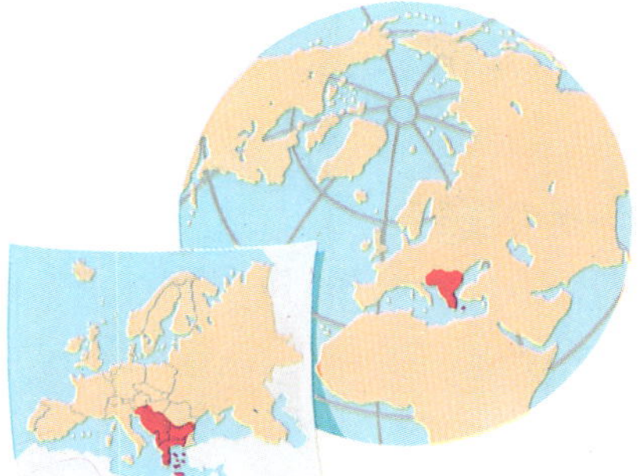

TOPOGRAPHY

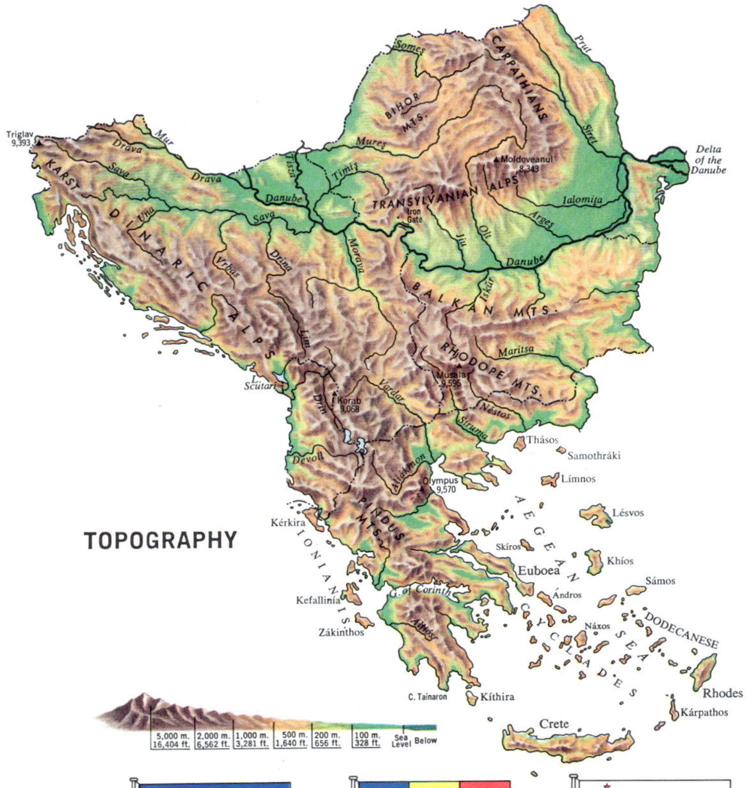

ALBANIA

GREECE

	ALBANIA	GREECE
CAPITAL	Tiranë	Athens
HIGHEST POINT	Korab	Olympus
MONETARY UNIT	lek	drachma
MAJOR LANGUAGE	Albanian	Greek
MAJOR RELIGIONS	Mohammedan, Eastern Orthodox, Roman Catholic	Greek Orthodox

YUGOSLAVIA

RUMANIA

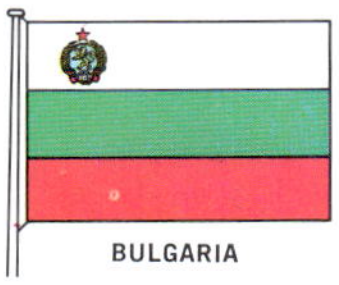

BULGARIA

	YUGOSLAVIA	RUMANIA	BULGARIA
CAPITAL	Belgrade	Bucharest	Sofia
HIGHEST POINT	Triglav	Moldoveanul	Musala
MONETARY UNIT	Yugoslav dinar	leu	lev
MAJOR LANGUAGES	Serbian-Croatian, Slovenian, Macedonian	Rumanian	Bulgarian
MAJOR RELIGIONS	Eastern Orthodox, Roman Catholic	Rumanian Orthodox	Eastern Orthodox

AGRICULTURE, INDUSTRY and RESOURCES

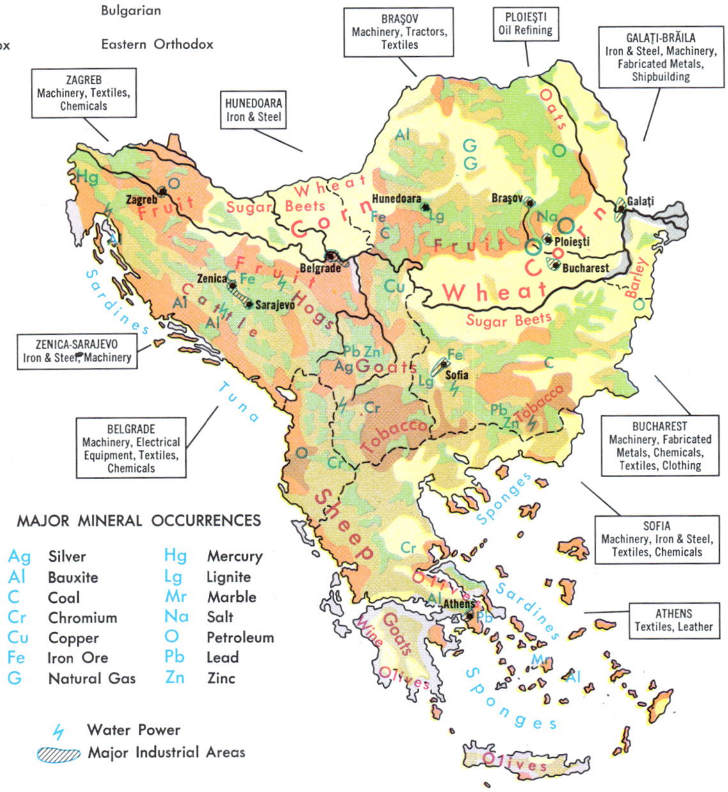

DOMINANT LAND USE

- Cereals (chiefly wheat, corn)
- Mixed Farming, Horticulture
- Pasture Livestock
- Tobacco, Cotton
- Grapes, Wine
- Forests
- Nonagricultural Land

MAJOR MINERAL OCCURRENCES

Ag	Silver	Hg	Mercury
Al	Bauxite	Lg	Lignite
C	Coal	Mr	Marble
Cr	Chromium	Na	Salt
Cu	Copper	O	Petroleum
Fe	Iron Ore	Pb	Lead
G	Natural Gas	Zn	Zinc

Water Power

Major Industrial Areas

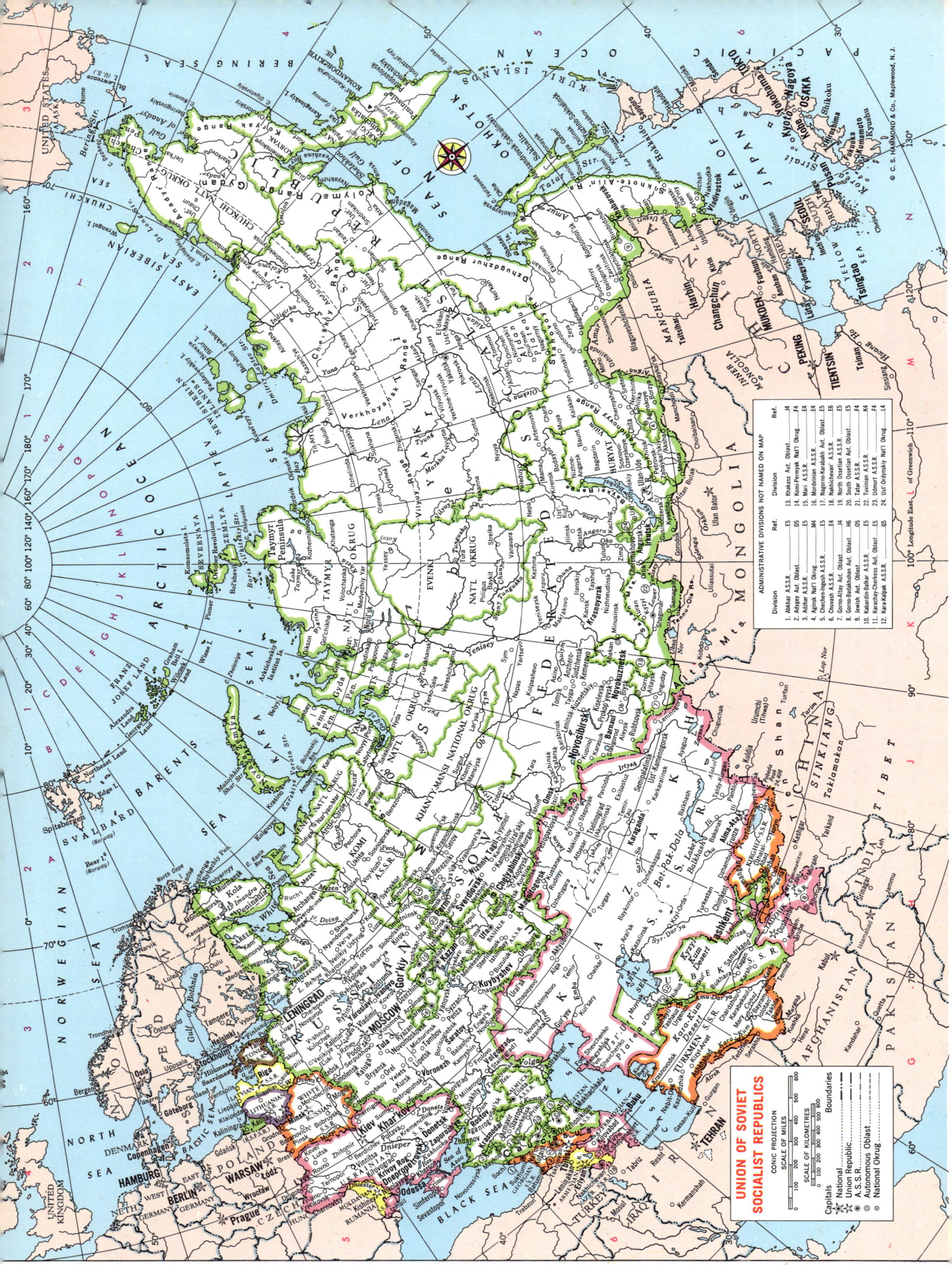
UNION OF SOVIET SOCIALIST REPUBLICS
CONIC PROJECTION
SCALE OF MILES
0 100 200 300 400 500 600
SCALE OF KILOMETRES
0 100 200 300 400 500 600
Capitals
National
Union Republic
A.S.S.R.
Autonomous Oblast
National Okrug
Boundaries
ADMINISTRATIVE DIVISIONS NOT NAMED ON MAP
Division Ref. Division Ref.
1. Abkhaz A.S.S.R. E5 13. Khakass Aut. Oblast J4
2. Adygey Aut. Oblast D5 14. Komi-Permyak Nat'l Okrug F4
3. Adzhar A.S.S.R. E5 15. Mari A.S.S.R. E4
4. Aginsk Nat'l Okrug M4 16. Mordvinian A.S.S.R. E4
5. Chechen-Ingush A.S.S.R. E5 17. Nagorno-Karabakh Aut. Oblast E5
6. Chuvash A.S.S.R. E4 18. Nakhichevan' A.S.S.R. E6
7. Gorno-Altay Aut. Oblast J4 19. North Ossetian A.S.S.R. E5
8. Gorno-Badakhshan Aut. Oblast H6 20. South Ossetian Aut. Oblast E5
9. Jewish Aut. Oblast O5 21. Tatar A.S.S.R. F4
10. Kabardin-Balkar A.S.S.R. E5 22. Tuvinian A.S.S.R. K4
11. Karachay-Cherkess Aut. Oblast E5 23. Udmurt A.S.S.R. F4
12. Kara-Kalpak A.S.S.R. G5 24. Ust'-Ordynskiy Nat'l Okrug L4
100° Longitude East of Greenwich 110°
© C. S. HAMMOND & Co., Maplewood, N. J.

TOPOGRAPHY

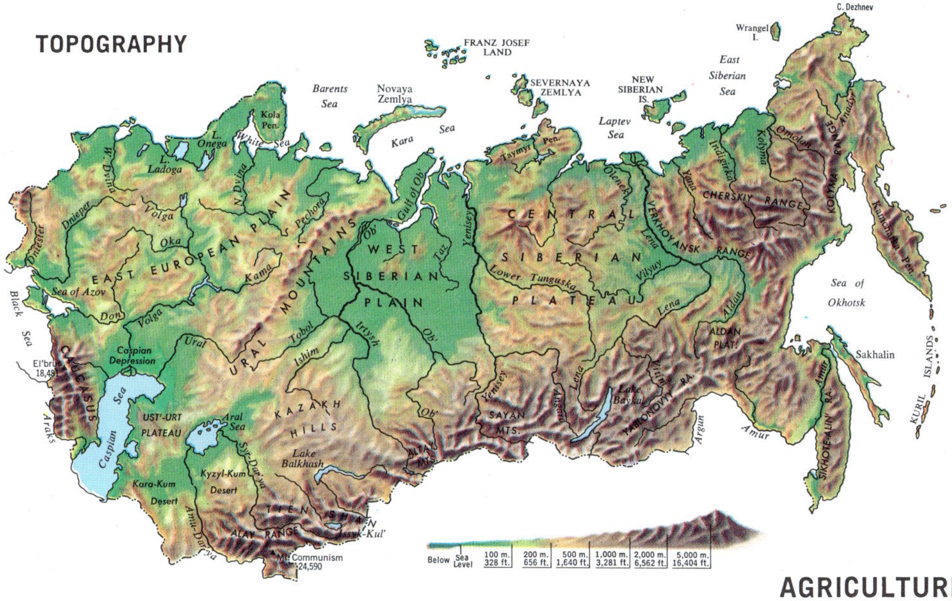

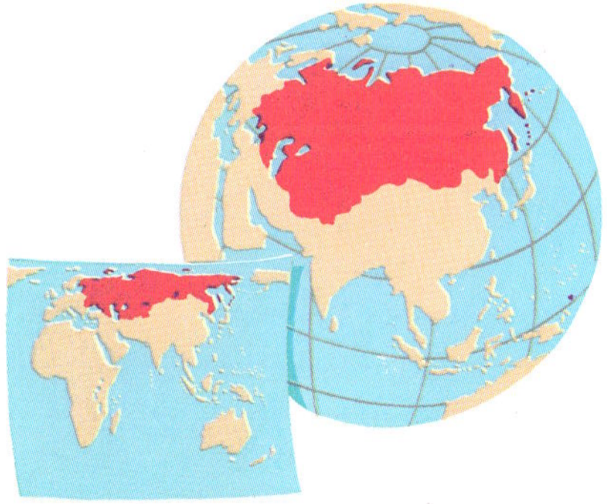

UNION OF SOVIET SOCIALIST REPUBLICS

CAPITAL	Moscow
HIGHEST POINT	Mt. Communism
MONETARY UNIT	ruble
MAJOR LANGUAGES	Russian, Ukrainian, White Russian, Uzbek, Azerbaidzhani, Tatar, Georgian, Lithuanian, Armenian, Yiddish, Latvian, Mordvinian, Kirghiz, Tadzhik, Estonian, Kazakh, etc.
MAJOR RELIGIONS	Russian Orthodox, Moslem, Tribal religions

AGRICULTURE, INDUSTRY and RESOURCES

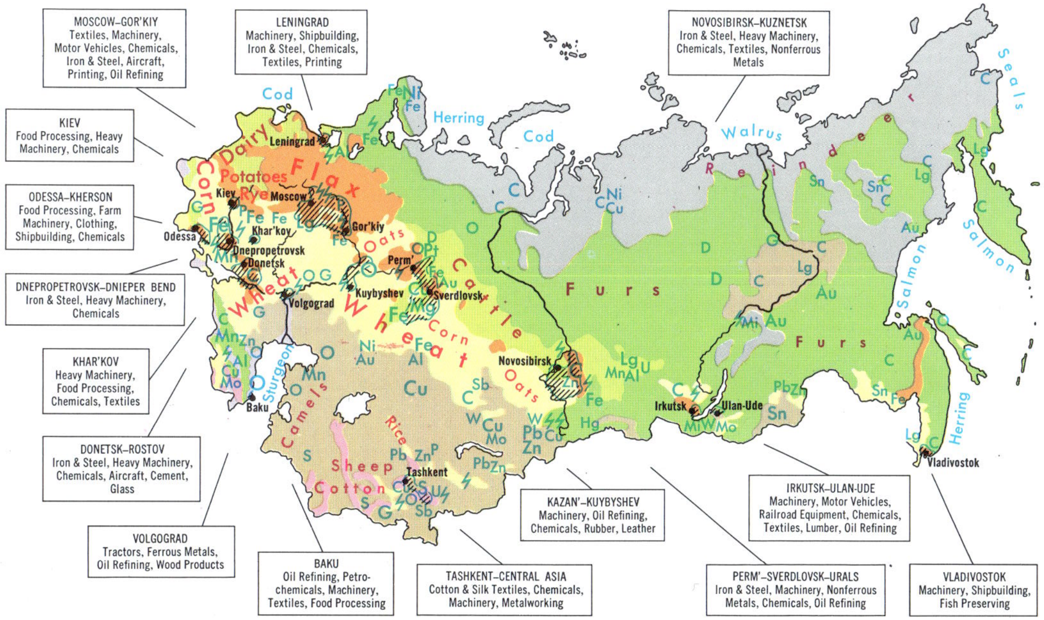

DOMINANT LAND USE

- Cereals
- Dairy, Livestock, Hogs
- Truck Farming, Potatoes, Dairy, Flax
- Sheep Herding, Limited Agriculture
- Cotton
- Vineyards, Horticulture
- Forests
- Nonagricultural Land

MAJOR MINERAL OCCURRENCES

Al	Bauxite	Lg	Lignite	Pb	Lead
Au	Gold	Mg	Magnesium	Pt	Platinum
C	Coal	Mi	Mica	S	Sulfur, Pyrites
Cu	Copper	Mn	Manganese	Sb	Antimony
D	Diamonds	Mo	Molybdenum	Sn	Tin
Fe	Iron Ore	Ni	Nickel	U	Uranium
G	Natural Gas	O	Petroleum	W	Tungsten
Hg	Mercury	P	Phosphates	Zn	Zinc

- Water Power
- Major Industrial Areas

Administrative Divisions bear same names as their respective Capitals or Centers, except:

Abkhaz A.S.S.R.	Sukhumi	F6
Adygey Aut. Oblast	Maykop	F6
Adzhar A.S.S.R.	Batumi	F6
Bashkir A.S.S.R.	Ufa	J4
Chechen-Ingush A.S.S.R.	Groznyy	G6
Chuvash A.S.S.R.	Cheboksary	G3
Crimean Oblast	Simferopol'	D6
Dagestan A.S.S.R.	Makhachkala	G6
Kabardin-Balkar A.S.S.R.	Nal'chik	F6
Kalmuck A.S.S.R.	Elista	F5
Karachay-Cherkess Aut. Obl.	Cherkessk	F6
Karelian A.S.S.R.	Petrozavodsk	D2
Komi A.S.S.R.	Syktyvkar	H2
Komi-Permyak Nat'l Okrug	Kudymkar	H3
Mari A.S.S.R.	Yoshkar-Ola	G3
Mordvinian A.S.S.R.	Saransk	G4
Nagorno-Karabakh Aut. Obl.	Stepanakert	G7
Nenets Nat'l Okrug	Nar'yan-Mar	H1
North Ossetian A.S.S.R.	Ordzhonikidze	F6
South Ossetian Aut. Obl.	Tskhinvali	F6
Tatar A.S.S.R.	Kazan'	G3
Trans-Carpathian Oblast	Uzhgorod	B5
Udmurt A.S.S.R.	Izhevsk	H3
Volyn Oblast	Lutsk	C4

ASIA
LAMBERT AZIMUTHAL EQUAL-AREA PROJECTION
SCALE OF MILES
0 150 300 600 900 1200
SCALE OF KILOMETRES
0 300 600 900 1200
Capitals of Countries
Canals
International Boundaries
Elevations in Feet
Copyright by C. S. HAMMOND & CO., N.Y.
ATLANTIC OCEAN
ARCTIC OCEAN
North Pole
GREENLAND
Iceland
BARENTS SEA
KARA SEA
LAPTEV SEA
BERING SEA
SEA OF OKHOTSK
PACIFIC OCEAN
SEA OF JAPAN
SOUTH CHINA SEA
BAY OF BENGAL
ARABIAN SEA
INDIAN OCEAN
UNION OF SOVIET SOCIALIST REPUBLICS
SIBERIA
MONGOLIA
CHINA
MANCHURIA
JAPAN
INDIA
PAKISTAN
AFGHANISTAN
IRAN (PERSIA)
IRAQ
TURKEY
SAUDI ARABIA
BURMA
THAILAND (SIAM)
MALAYSIA
INDONESIA
REPUBLIC OF THE PHILIPPINES
SRI LANKA (CEYLON)
AUSTRALIA
AFRICA
Madagascar
MOSCOW
PEKING
TOKYO
Equator
Tropic of Cancer
Tropic of Capricorn
Longitude East of Greenwich

SOUTHWEST ASIA
CONIC PROJECTION
SCALE OF MILES
SCALE OF KILOMETRES
Capitals of Countries
Other Capitals
International Boundaries
Copyright by C. S. HAMMOND & CO., N. Y.

SOUTHWEST ASIA

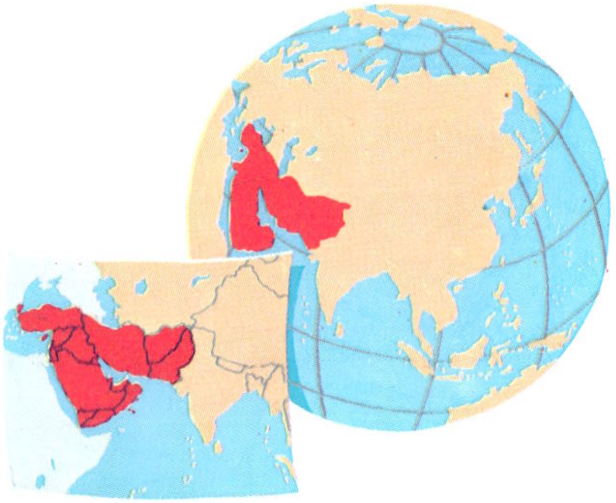

TOPOGRAPHY

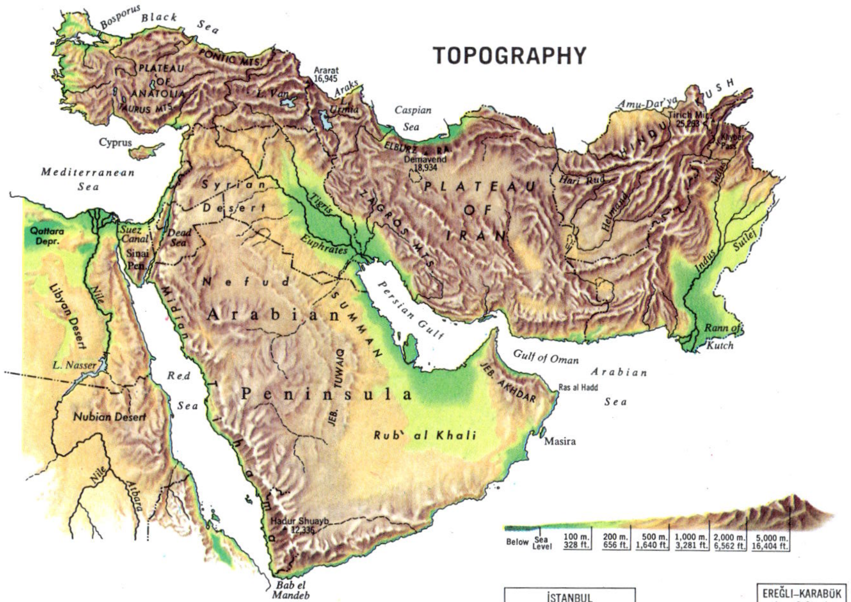

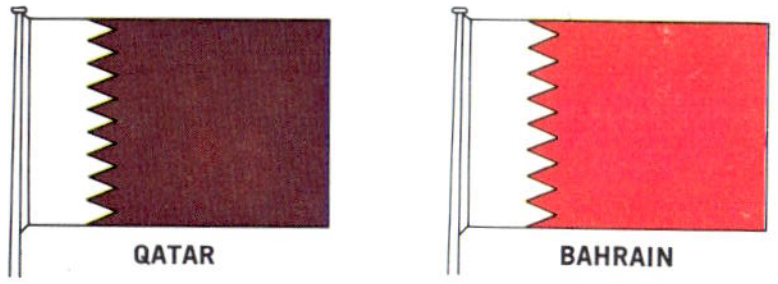

AGRICULTURE, INDUSTRY and RESOURCES

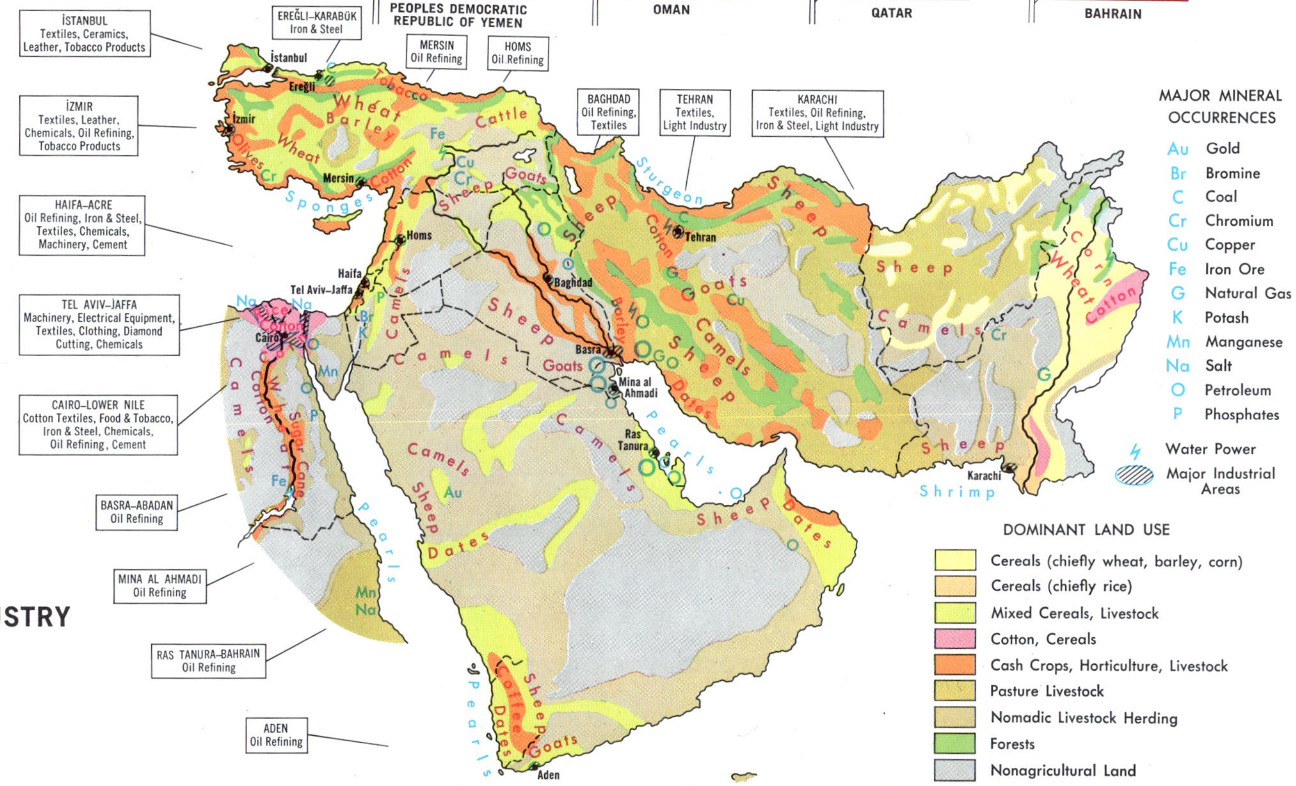

SOUTHERN ASIA
CONIC PROJECTION
SCALE OF MILES
SCALE OF KILOMETRES
Capitals of Countries
Provincial and State Capitals
International Boundaries
Provincial and State Boundaries
Canals
ARABIAN SEA
BAY OF BENGAL
INDIAN OCEAN
ANDAMAN SEA
CALCUTTA
BOMBAY
Copyright by C. S. HAMMOND & Co., N.Y.

SOUTHERN ASIA

TOPOGRAPHY

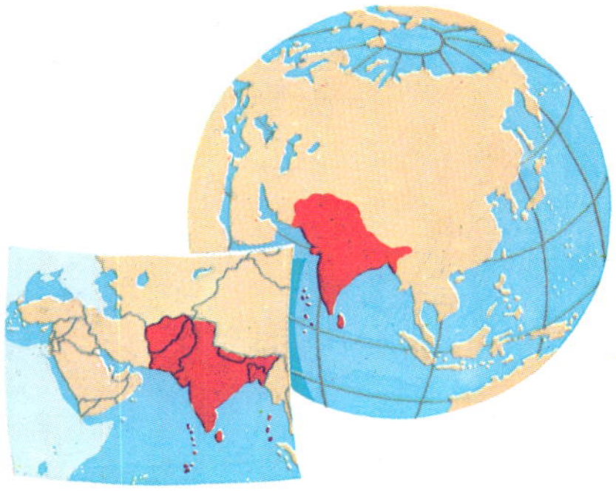

AFGHANISTAN

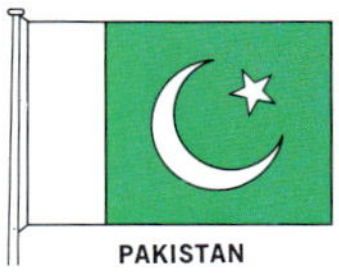
PAKISTAN

INDIA

NEPAL

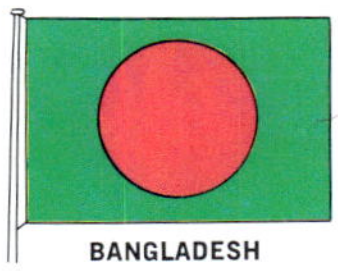
BANGLADESH

BHUTAN

AGRICULTURE, INDUSTRY and RESOURCES

DOMINANT LAND USE

- Cereals (chiefly wheat, barley, corn)
- Cereals (chiefly millet, sorghum)
- Cereals (chiefly rice)
- Cotton, Cereals
- Pasture Livestock
- Nomadic Livestock Herding
- Forests
- Nonagricultural Land

MAJOR MINERAL OCCURRENCES

Ab	Asbestos	Gr	Graphite
Al	Bauxite	Lg	Lignite
Au	Gold	Mg	Magnesium
C	Coal	Mi	Mica
Cr	Chromium	Mn	Manganese
Cu	Copper	Na	Salt
Fe	Iron Ore	O	Petroleum
G	Natural Gas	Ti	Titanium
U	Uranium		

- Water Power
- Major Industrial Areas

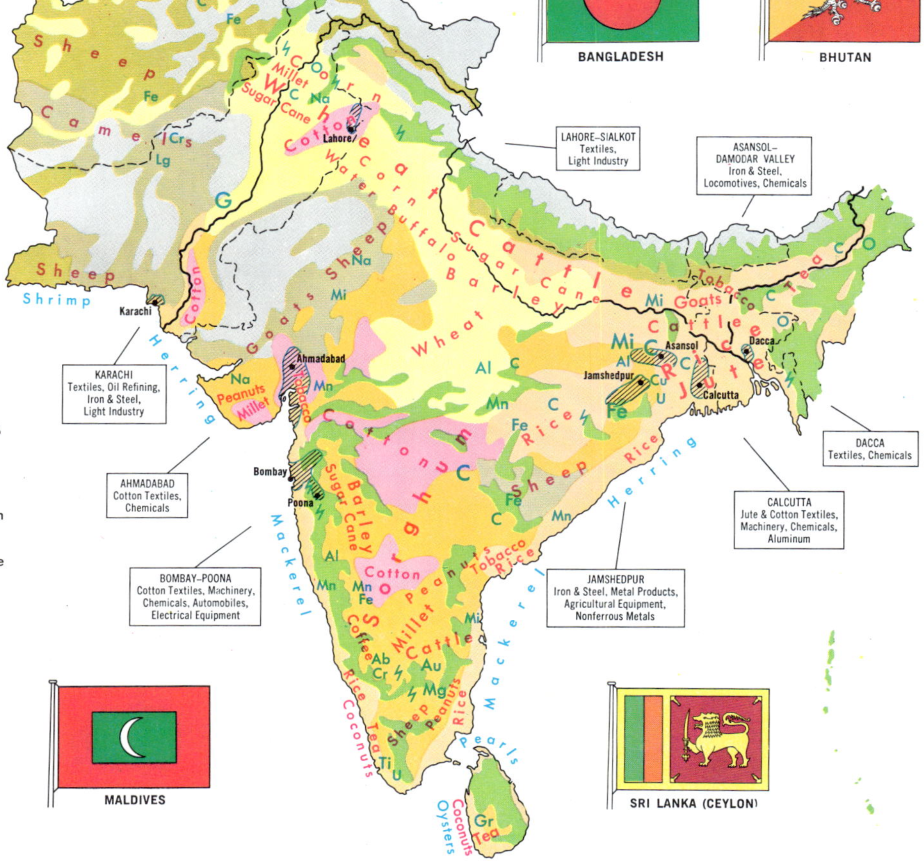

MALDIVES

SRI LANKA (CEYLON)

EAST ASIA
CONIC PROJECTION
SCALE OF MILES
SCALE OF KILOMETRES
Capitals of Countries
International Boundaries
Provincial Capitals
Provincial Boundaries
Canals
Walls
© Copyright by C.S. HAMMOND & CO., N.Y.
*Wuhan municipality consists of Hankow, Hanyang and Wuchang
†Lüta municipality includes Port Arthur and Dairen

EAST ASIA

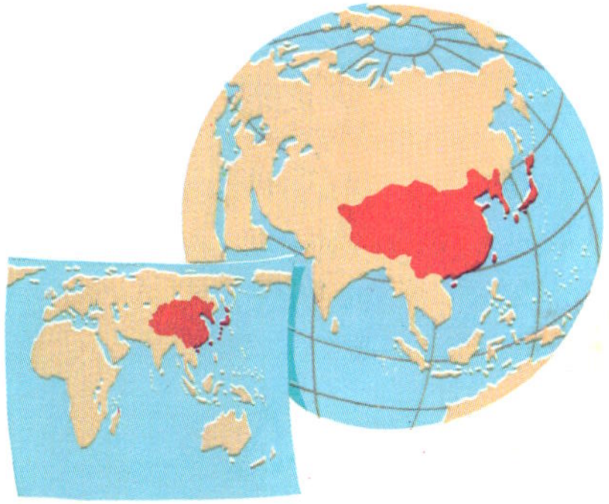

TOPOGRAPHY

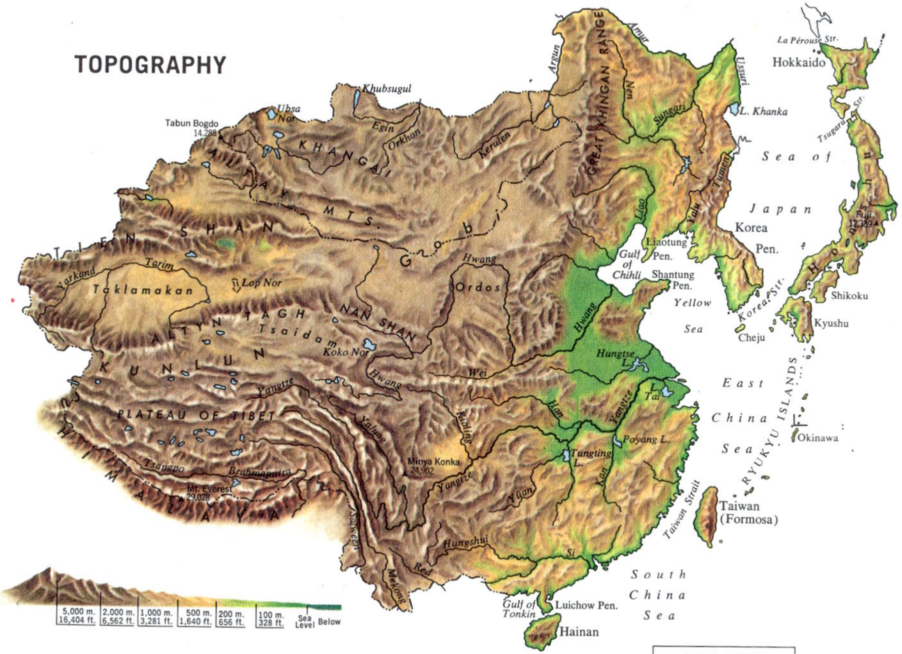

JAPAN

NORTH KOREA

SOUTH KOREA

CHINA (MAINLAND)

CHINA (FORMOSA)

MONGOLIA

AGRICULTURE, INDUSTRY and RESOURCES

DOMINANT LAND USE

- Cereals, Rice, Cash Crops
- Livestock Herding, Limited Agriculture
- Forests, Scrub
- Nonagricultural Land

MAJOR MINERAL OCCURRENCES

Ag	Silver	Mn	Manganese
Al	Bauxite	Mo	Molybdenum
Au	Gold	Na	Salt
C	Coal	O	Petroleum
Cu	Copper	Pb	Lead
Fe	Iron Ore	S	Pyrites
G	Natural Gas	Sb	Antimony
Gr	Graphite	Sn	Tin
Hg	Mercury	U	Uranium
J	Jade	W	Tungsten
Mg	Magnesium	Zn	Zinc

Water Power

Major Industrial Areas

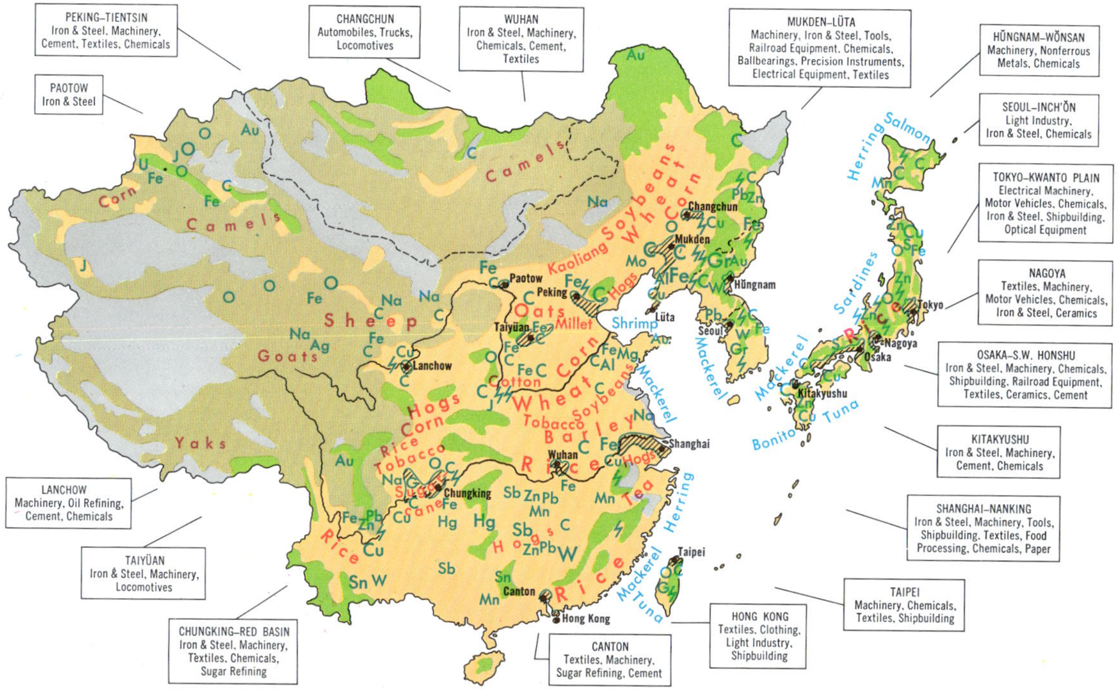

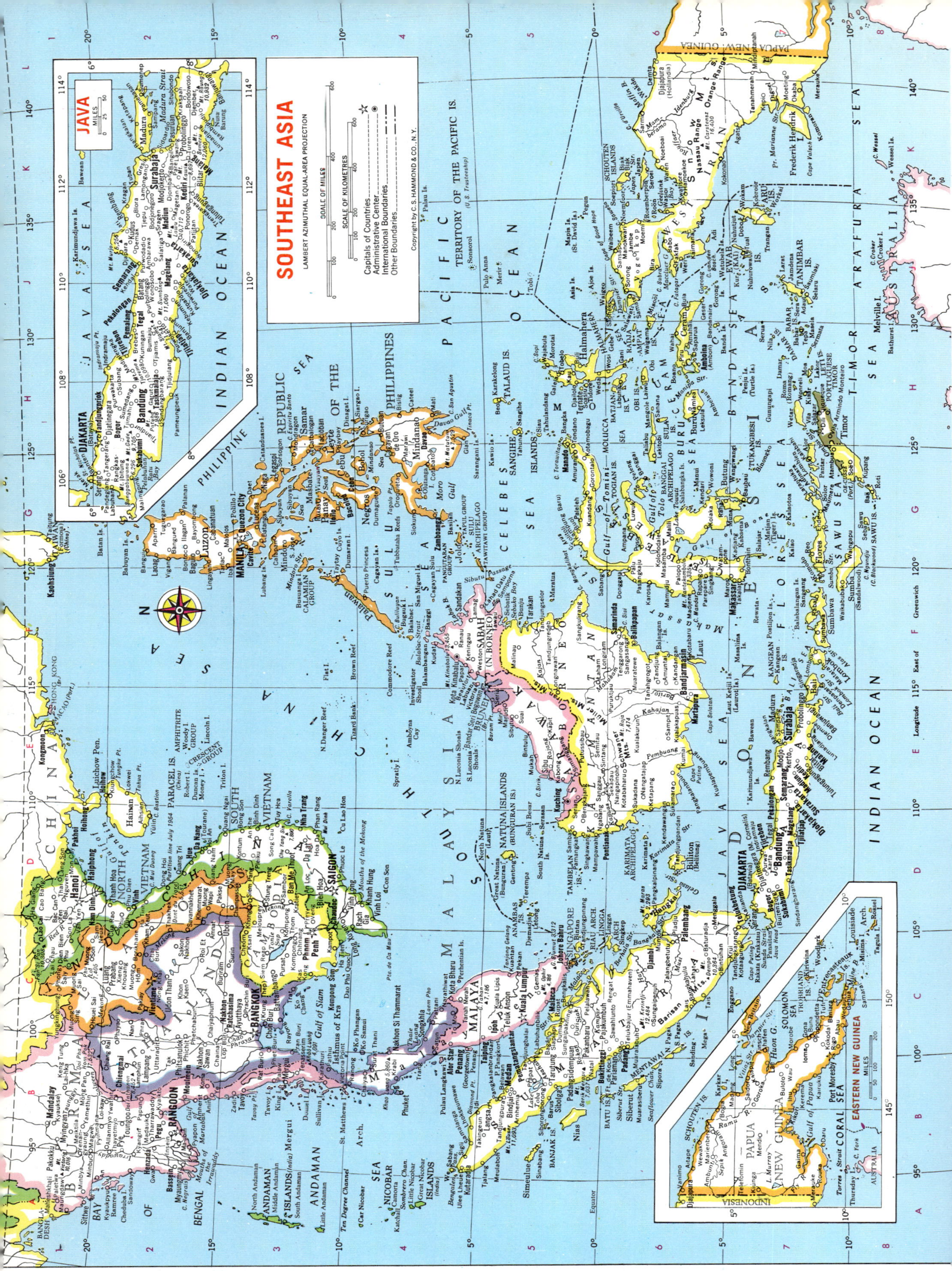

SOUTHEAST ASIA
LAMBERT AZIMUTHAL EQUAL-AREA PROJECTION
SCALE OF MILES
SCALE OF KILOMETRES
Capitals of Countries
Administrative Center
International Boundaries
Other Boundaries
Copyright by C. S. HAMMOND & CO., N.Y.
JAVA
EASTERN NEW GUINEA
SOUTH CHINA SEA
INDIAN OCEAN
PACIFIC OCEAN
CELEBES SEA
JAVA SEA
BANDA SEA
ARAFURA SEA

SOUTHEAST ASIA

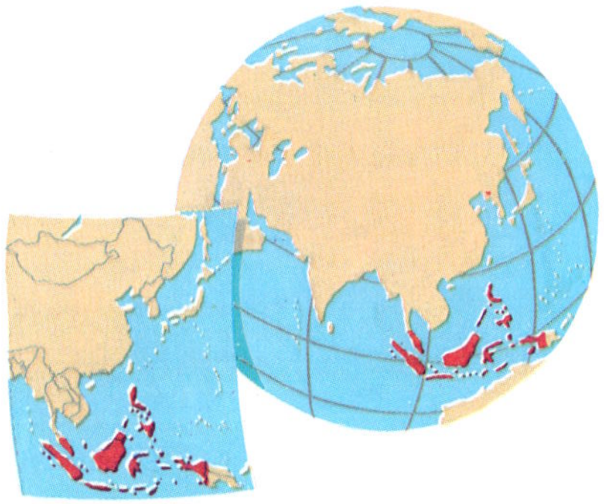

TOPOGRAPHY

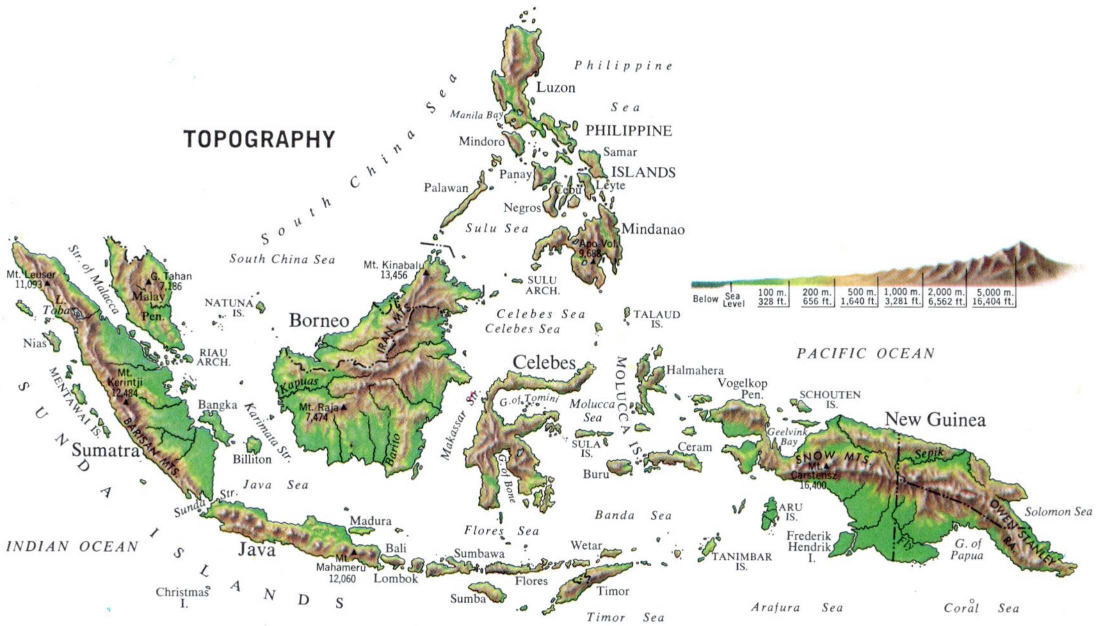

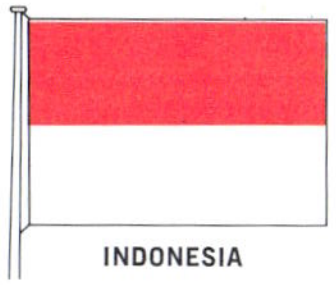

INDONESIA

CAPITAL	Djakarta
HIGHEST POINT	Mt. Kerintji
MONETARY UNIT	rupiah
MAJOR LANGUAGES	Indonesian (Malay, Javanese, etc.)
MAJOR RELIGIONS	Mohammedan, Tribal religions, Christian, Hindu

PHILIPPINES

CAPITAL	Quezon City
HIGHEST POINT	Apo
MONETARY UNIT	Philippine peso
MAJOR LANGUAGES	Malayan languages (Tagalog, etc.), English, Spanish,
MAJOR RELIGIONS	Roman Catholic, Mohammedan, Tribal religions

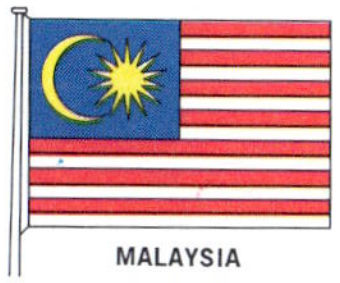

MALAYSIA

CAPITAL	Kuala Lumpur
HIGHEST POINT	Mt. Kinabalu
MONETARY UNIT	Malayan dollar
MAJOR LANGUAGES	Malay, Chinese, English, Indonesian, Hindu
MAJOR RELIGIONS	Mohammedan, Confucianist, Buddhist, Tribal religions, Hindu, Taoist

AGRICULTURE, INDUSTRY and RESOURCES

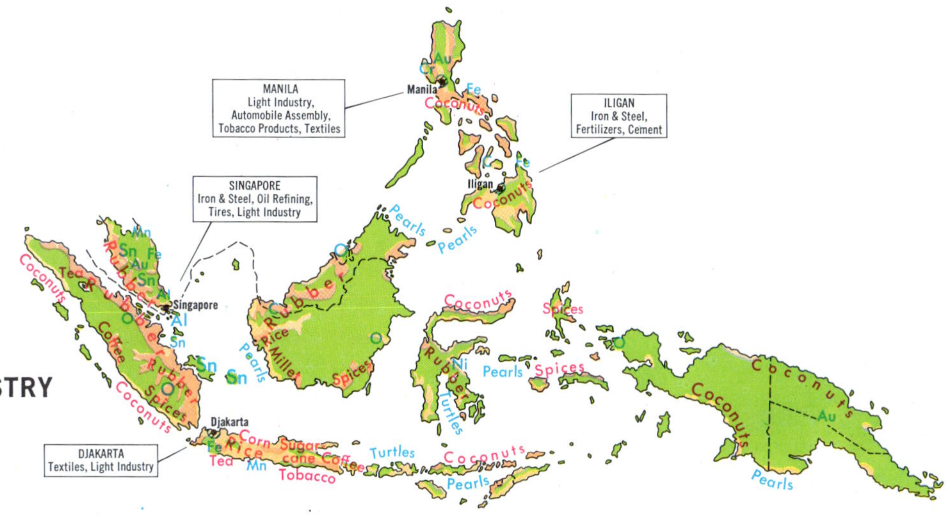

DOMINANT LAND USE

- Cereals (chiefly rice, corn)
- Diversified Tropical Crops
- Forests

MAJOR MINERAL OCCURRENCES

Al Bauxite	C Coal	Mn Manganese	O Petroleum
Au Gold	Fe Iron Ore	Ni Nickel	Sn Tin

Major Industrial Areas

INDOCHINESE
and
MALAY PENINSULAS
CONIC PROJECTION
SCALE OF MILES
SCALE OF KILOMETRES
International Boundaries
Provincial and State Boundaries
Capitals of Countries
Provincial and State Capitals
Copyright by C. S. HAMMOND & Co., N. Y.
Longitude East 96° of Greenwich
BHUTAN
INDIA
BANGLADESH
CHINA
KACHIN STATE
SHAN STATE
SAGAING
BURMA
KAYAH STATE
MANDALAY
RANGOON
BAY OF BENGAL
ANDAMAN SEA
ANDAMAN IS. (India)
NICOBAR IS. (India)
THAILAND (SIAM)
BANGKOK
GULF OF SIAM
LAOS
Vientiane
CAMBODIA
Phnom Penh
NORTH VIETNAM
Hanoi
SOUTH VIETNAM
SAIGON
GULF OF TONKIN
HAINAN
SOUTH CHINA SEA
Paracel Is.
MALAYA
MALAYSIA
Kuala Lumpur
Strait of Malacca
SUMATRA
INDONESIA
SINGAPORE
JOHORE
Kunming
Isthmus of Kra
Partition line July 1954 (Demilitarized Zone)

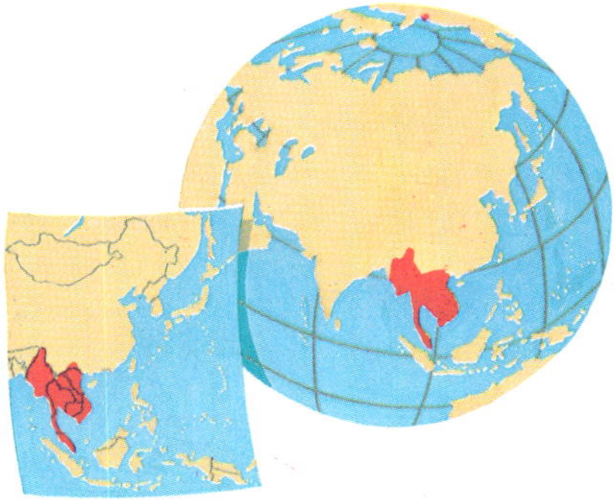

INDOCHINESE and MALAY PENINSULAS

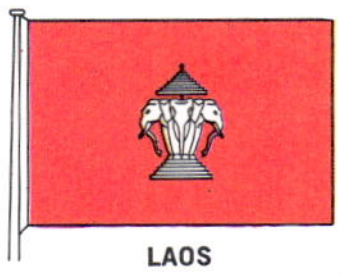
LAOS

NORTH VIETNAM

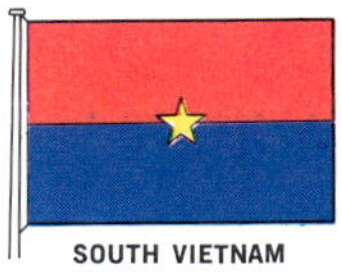
SOUTH VIETNAM

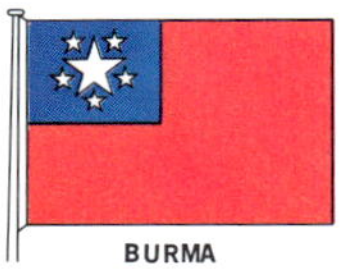
BURMA

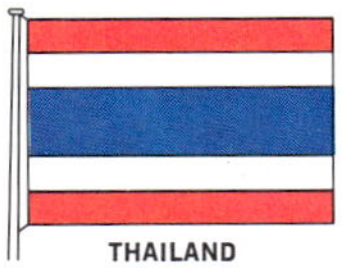
THAILAND

CAMBODIA

SINGAPORE

AGRICULTURE, INDUSTRY and RESOURCES

DOMINANT LAND USE

- Rice
- Diversified Tropical Crops
- Livestock Grazing, Limited Agriculture
- Tropical Forests

MAJOR MINERAL OCCURRENCES

Ag	Silver	Cr	Chromium	O	Petroleum	Sn	Tin
Al	Bauxite	Cu	Copper	P	Phosphates	Ti	Titanium
Au	Gold	Fe	Iron Ore	Pb	Lead	W	Tungsten
C	Coal	Mn	Manganese	Sb	Antimony	Zn	Zinc

Water Power
Major Industrial Areas

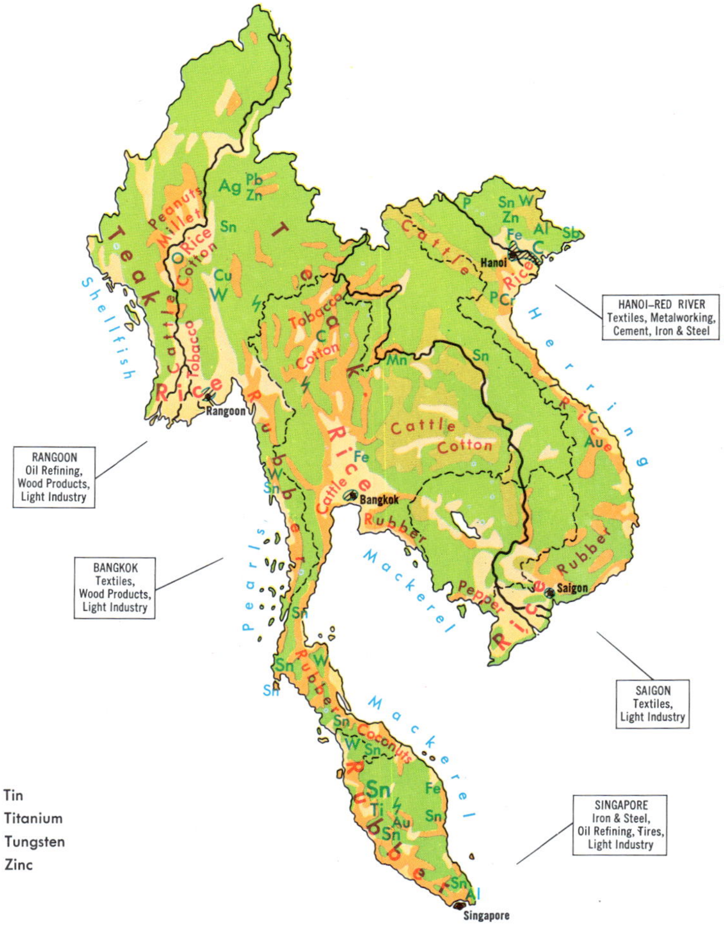

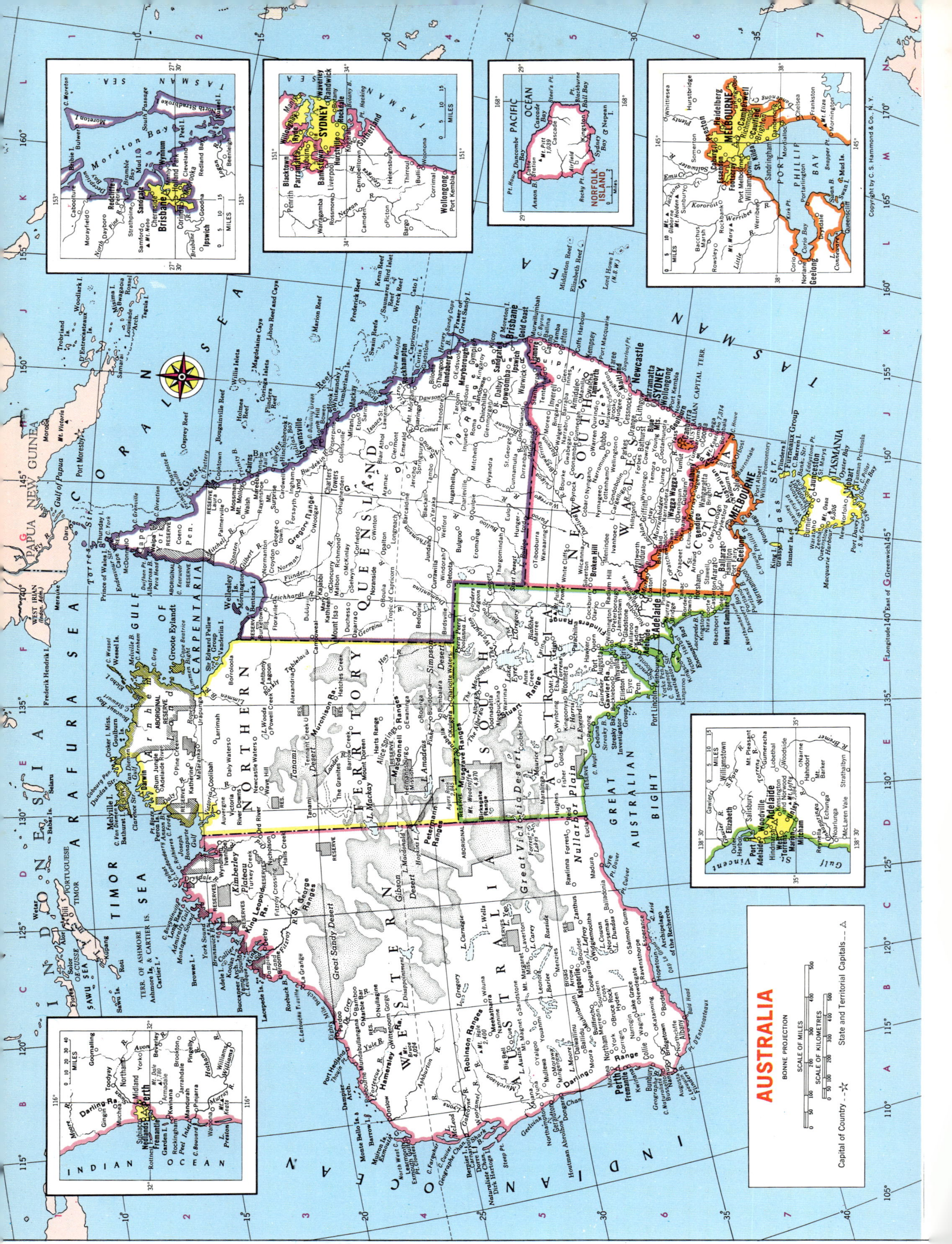
AUSTRALIA
BONNE PROJECTION
SCALE OF MILES
SCALE OF KILOMETRES
Capital of Country
State and Territorial Capitals
Copyright by C. S. Hammond & Co., N. Y.
WESTERN AUSTRALIA
NORTHERN TERRITORY
SOUTH AUSTRALIA
QUEENSLAND
NEW SOUTH WALES
VICTORIA
TASMANIA
PAPUA NEW GUINEA
INDONESIA
ARAFURA SEA
TIMOR SEA
CORAL SEA
TASMAN SEA
INDIAN OCEAN
GREAT AUSTRALIAN BIGHT
GULF OF CARPENTARIA
BASS STR.
NORFOLK ISLAND
PACIFIC OCEAN
Perth
Adelaide
Melbourne
Sydney
Brisbane
Hobart
Darwin
Canberra

AUSTRALIA

TOPOGRAPHY

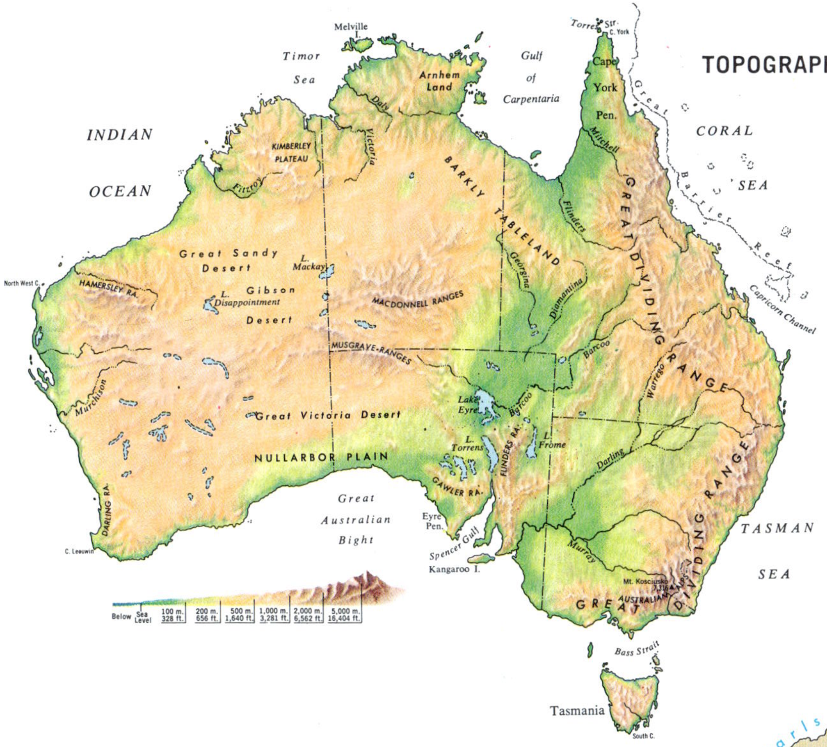

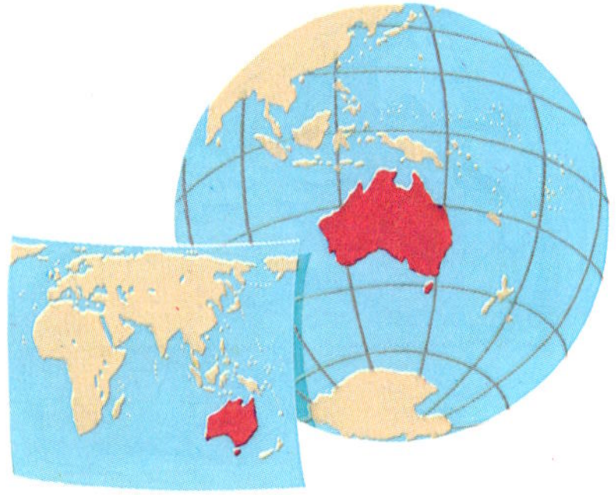

CAPITAL	Canberra
HIGHEST POINT	Mt. Kosciusko
MONETARY UNIT	Australian dollar
MAJOR LANGUAGE	English
MAJOR RELIGIONS	Protestant, Roman Catholic

AGRICULTURE, INDUSTRY and RESOURCES

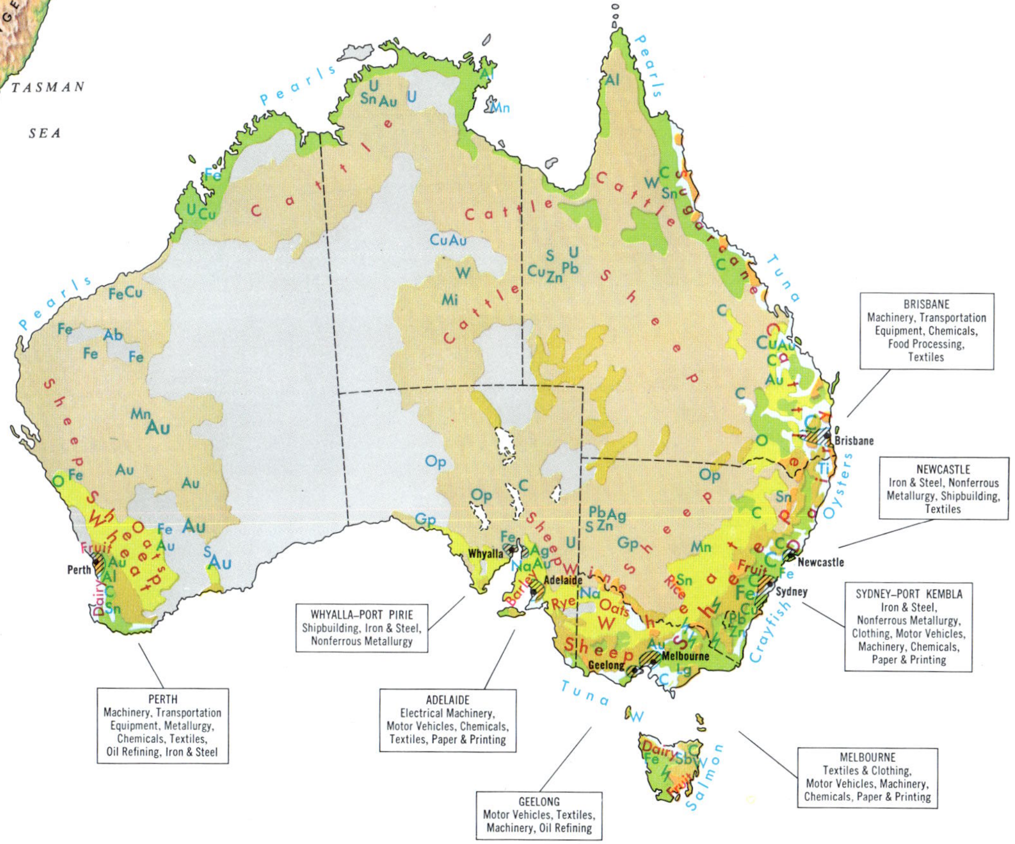

DOMINANT LAND USE

- Cereals (chiefly wheat), Livestock
- Dairy, Truck Farming
- Cash Crops, Horticulture, Fruit
- Pasture Livestock
- Range Livestock
- Forests
- Nonagricultural Land

MAJOR MINERAL OCCURRENCES

Ab	Asbestos	Na	Salt
Ag	Silver	O	Petroleum
Al	Bauxite	Op	Opals
Au	Gold	Pb	Lead
C	Coal	S	Sulfur, Pyrites
Cu	Copper	Sb	Antimony
Fe	Iron Ore	Sn	Tin
Gp	Gypsum	Ti	Titanium
Lg	Lignite	U	Uranium
Mi	Mica	W	Tungsten
Mn	Manganese	Zn	Zinc

Water Power
Major Industrial Areas

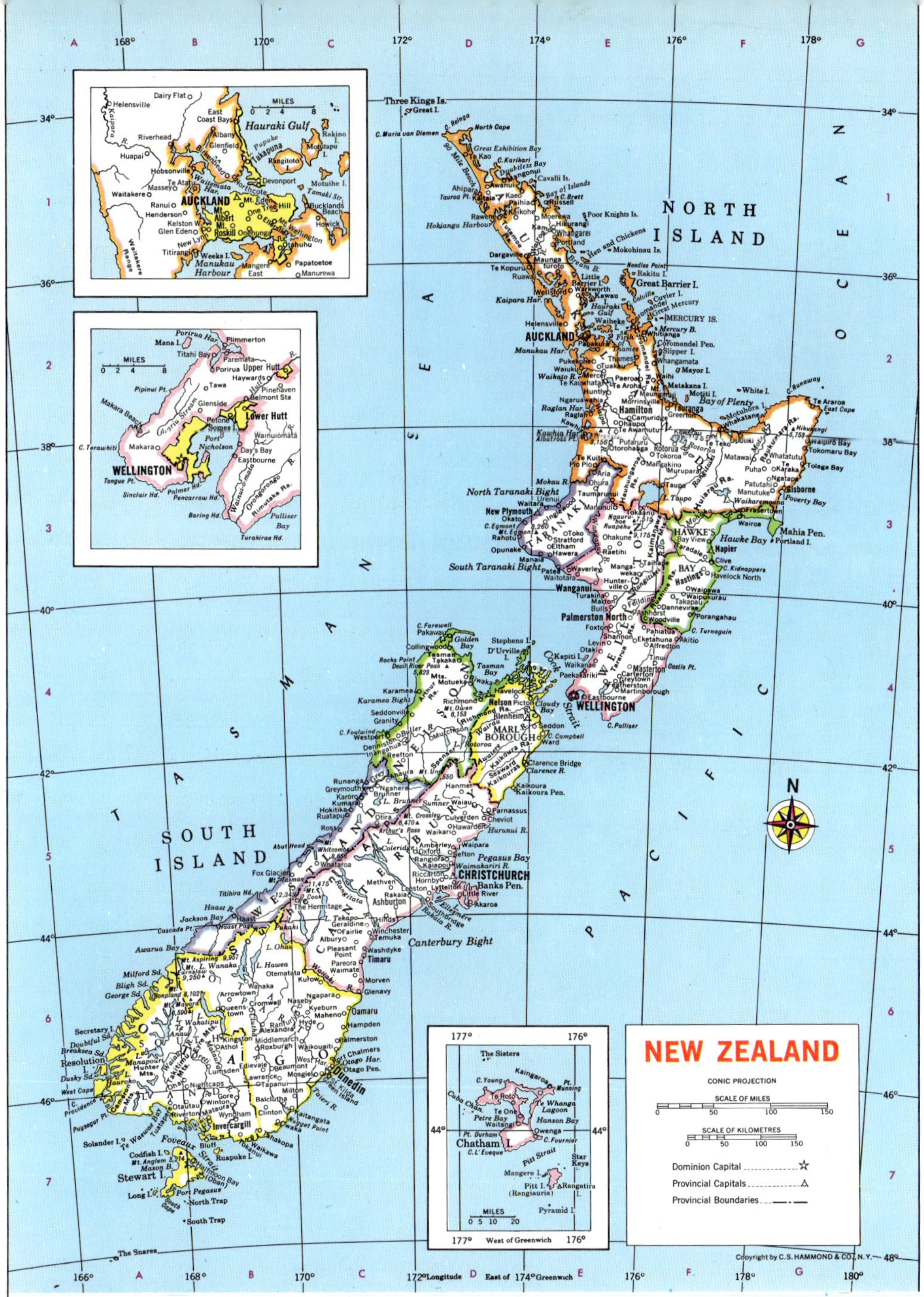

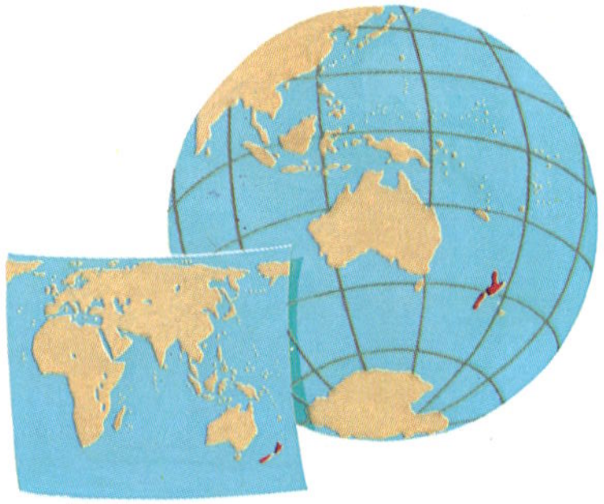

NEW ZEALAND

CAPITAL	Wellington
HIGHEST POINT	Mt. Cook
MONETARY UNIT	New Zealand dollar
MAJOR LANGUAGES	English, Maori
MAJOR RELIGION	Protestant

TOPOGRAPHY

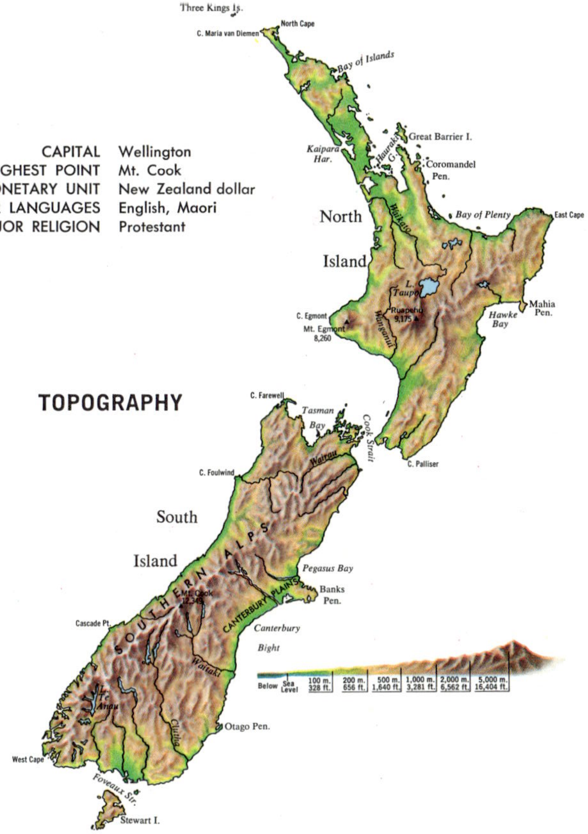

AGRICULTURE, INDUSTRY and RESOURCES

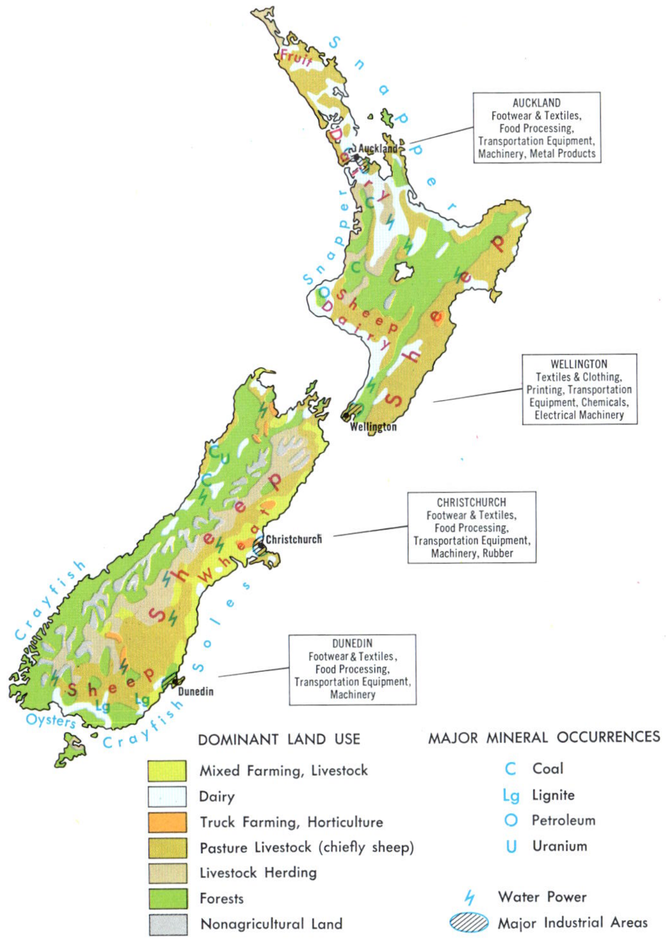

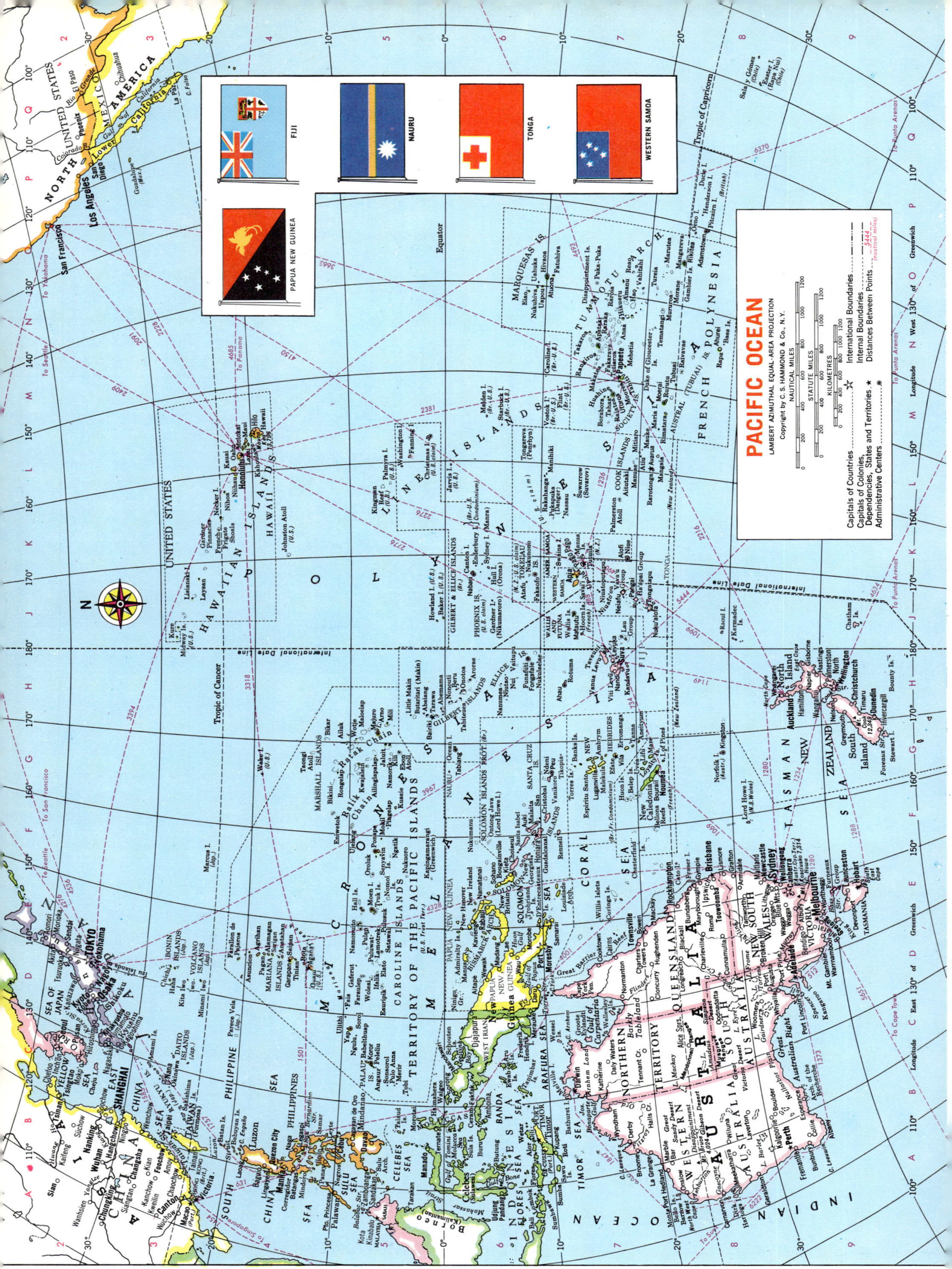
PACIFIC OCEAN
LAMBERT AZIMUTHAL EQUAL-AREA PROJECTION
Copyright by C. S. HAMMOND & Co., N.Y.
NAUTICAL MILES
STATUTE MILES
KILOMETRES
Capitals of Countries
Capitals of Colonies, Dependencies, States and Territories
Administrative Centers
International Boundaries
Internal Boundaries
Distances Between Points
FIJI
NAURU
TONGA
WESTERN SAMOA
PAPUA NEW GUINEA
Equator
Tropic of Cancer
Tropic of Capricorn
International Date Line
POLYNESIA
MICRONESIA
MELANESIA
AUSTRALIA
NEW ZEALAND
TASMAN SEA
CORAL SEA
PHILIPPINE SEA
SOUTH CHINA SEA
INDIAN OCEAN
HAWAIIAN ISLANDS
MARSHALL ISLANDS
TERRITORY OF THE PACIFIC ISLANDS
SOLOMON ISLANDS
NEW HEBRIDES
NEW CALEDONIA
FRENCH POLYNESIA

AFRICA

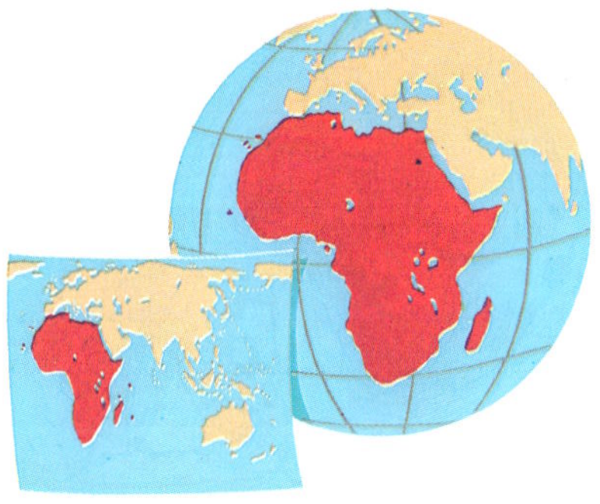

TOPOGRAPHY

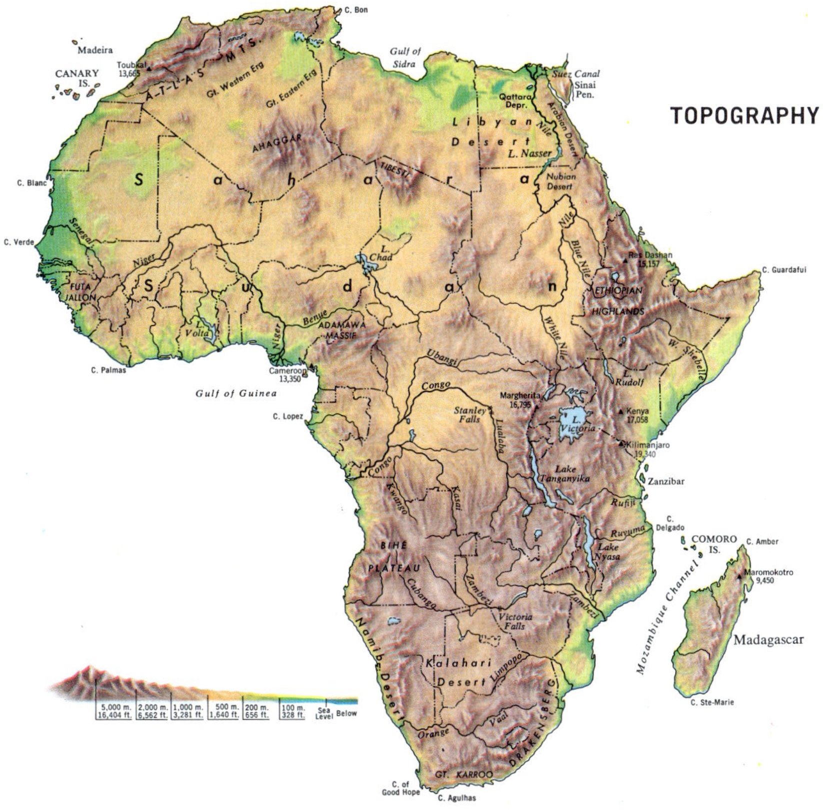

AGRICULTURE, INDUSTRY and RESOURCES

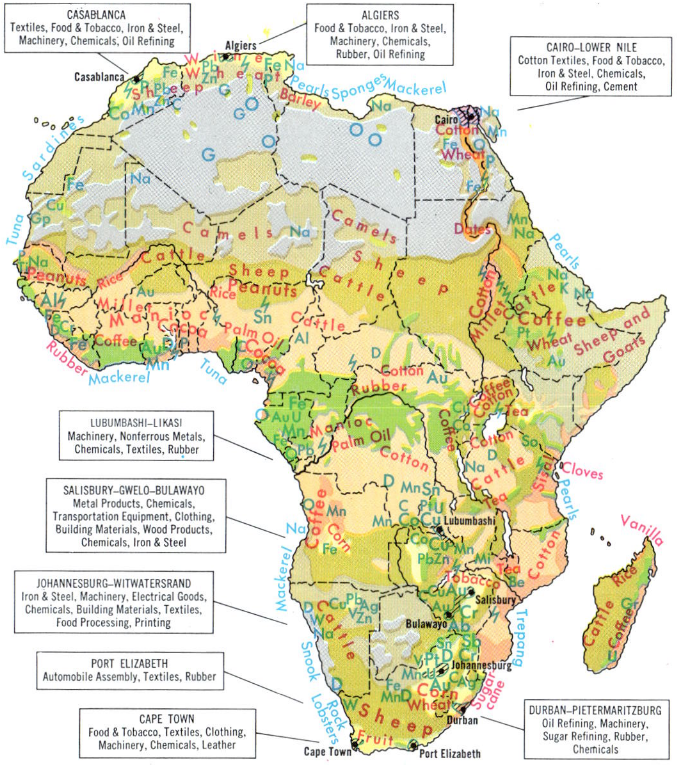

DOMINANT LAND USE

- Cereals, Horticulture, Livestock
- Cash Crops, Mixed Cereals
- Cotton, Cereals
- Diversified Tropical Crops
- Plantation Agriculture
- Oases
- Pasture Livestock
- Nomadic Livestock Herding
- Forests
- Nonagricultural Land

MAJOR MINERAL OCCURRENCES

Ab	Asbestos	G	Natural Gas	Sb	Antimony
Ag	Silver	Gp	Gypsum	Sn	Tin
Al	Bauxite	Gr	Graphite	So	Soda Ash
Au	Gold	K	Potash	Ti	Titanium
Be	Beryl	Mi	Mica	U	Uranium
C	Coal	Mn	Manganese	V	Vanadium
Co	Cobalt	Na	Salt	W	Tungsten
Cr	Chromium	O	Petroleum	Zn	Zinc
Cu	Copper	P	Phosphates		
D	Diamonds	Pb	Lead		Water Power
Fe	Iron Ore	Pt	Platinum		Major Industrial Areas

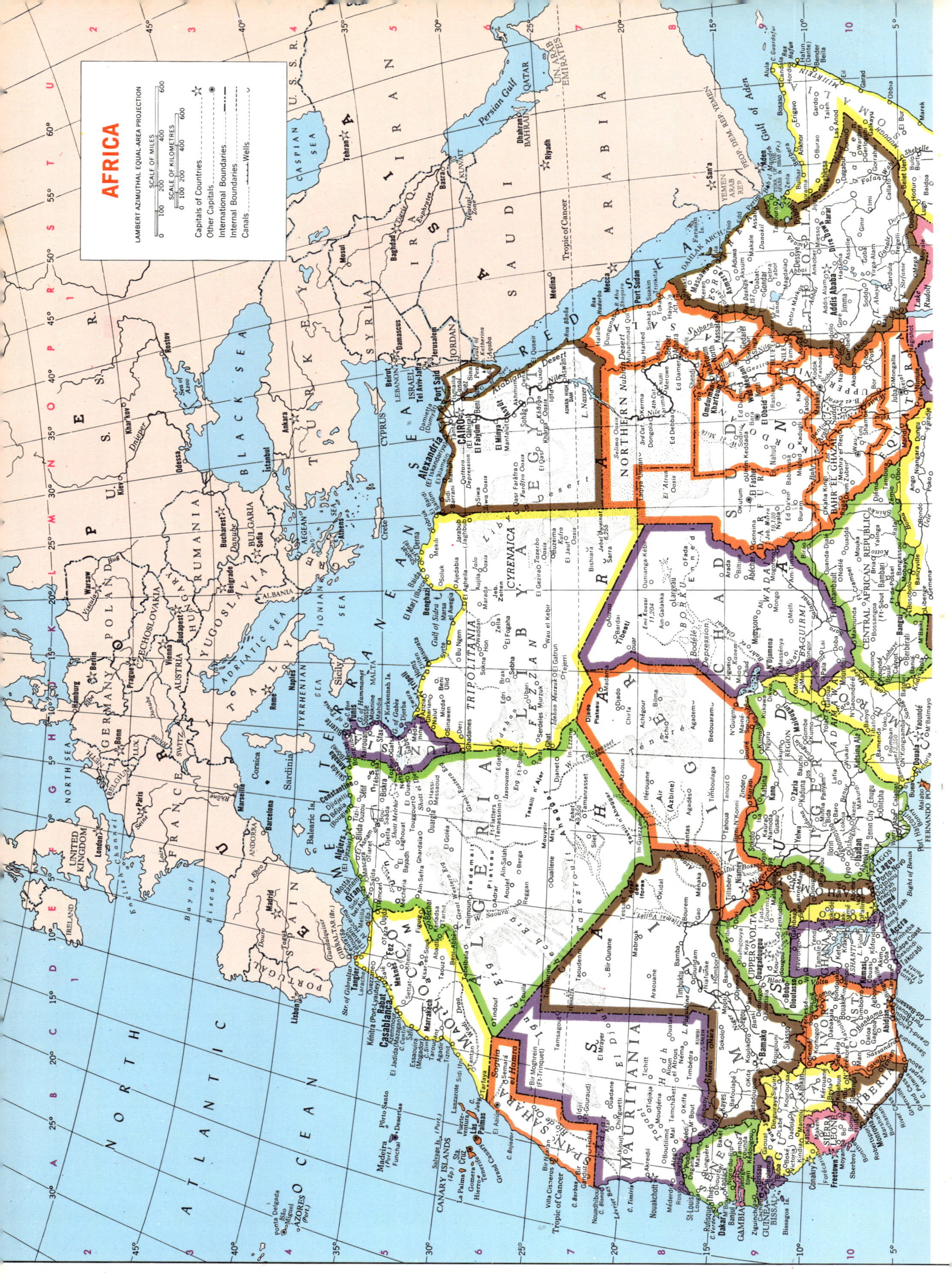
AFRICA
LAMBERT AZIMUTHAL EQUAL-AREA PROJECTION
SCALE OF MILES
SCALE OF KILOMETRES
Capitals of Countries
Other Capitals
International Boundaries
Internal Boundaries
Canals
Wells

GULF OF GUINEA
SOUTH ATLANTIC OCEAN
INDIAN OCEAN
Equator
Tropic of Capricorn
KENYA
TANZANIA
ANGOLA
ZAMBIA
RHODESIA
BOTSWANA
SOUTH-WEST AFRICA
MADAGASCAR
MALAGASY REPUBLIC
CAPE OF GOOD HOPE
MAURITIUS
RÉUNION
Longitude West of Greenwich
Longitude East of Greenwich
Copyright by C.S. HAMMOND & CO., N.Y.

FLAGS OF AFRICA

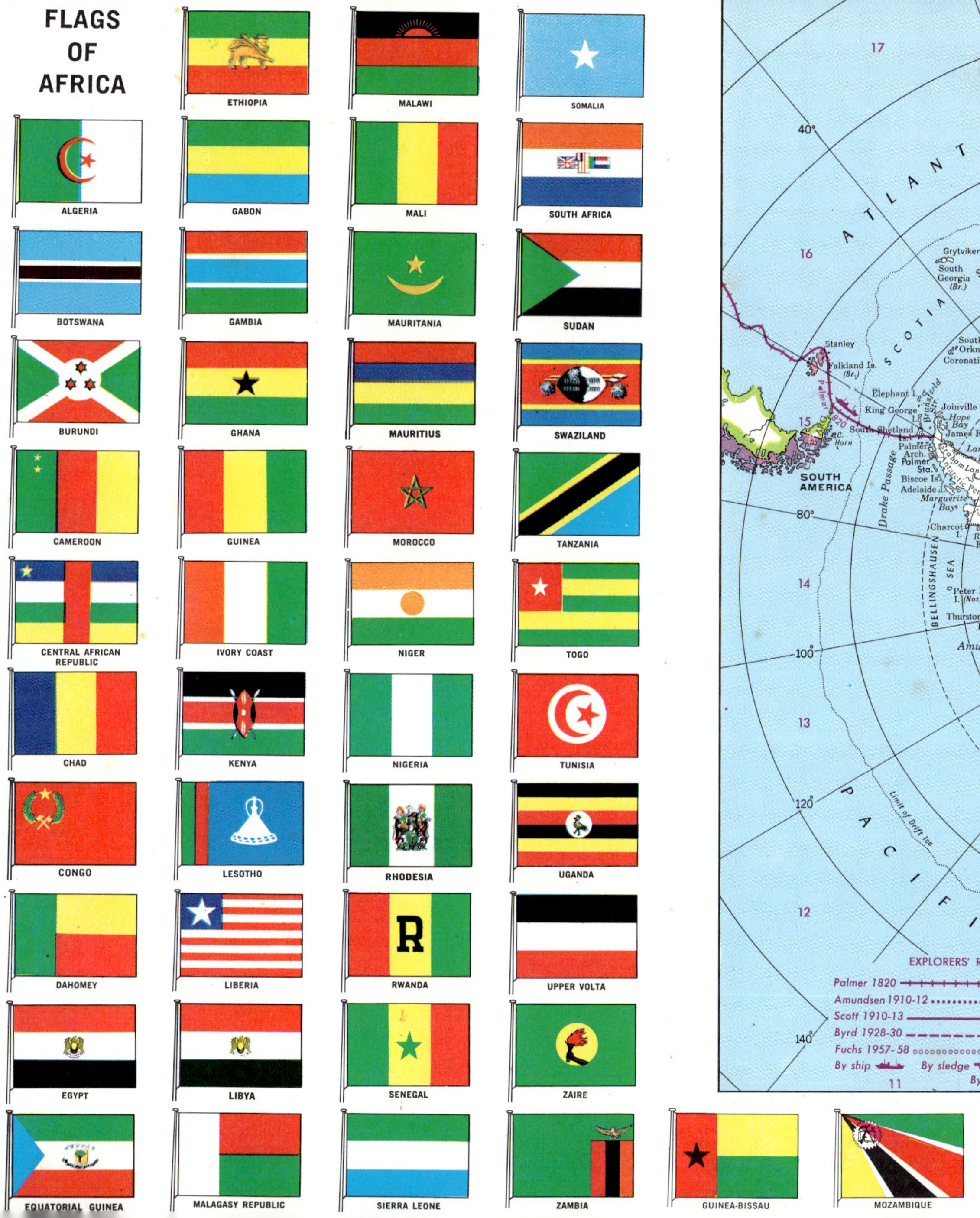

Economics and Useful Arts

SUBJECT GUIDE

Machines in the Field. Top: **Tractor-Pulled Harrow**—Used to break up clods of earth and destroy weeds in preparing land for seeding. Lower left: **Cultivator**—In operation to loosen and aerate the earth during the early stage of growth of field crops. Lower right: **Field Baler**—The sweep moving through the fields of cut straw feeds the crop into a pressure chamber to make firm, square bales for easy handling and storage. (*Courtesy Sperry Rand and Caterpillar Tractor Company*)

Modern Farm Machinery. Top. **Combine:** A self-propelling machine for harvesting that cuts, threshes, and cleans the grain while moving through the fields. Bottom. **Automatic Baler:** Pickup balers such as this lift the hay to a conveyor that carries it to a baling chamber, where it is compressed into bales weighing as much as 125 pounds and automatically bound with heavy twine or wire. Balers handle such crops as alfalfa, maize straw, or prairie hay. *(Sperry Rand/New Holland)*

1. SNOW AND ICE: Polar and mountainous regions of perpetual ice and snow cover one-tenth of the earth's land areas. Windswept, always below freezing, it can support life only peripherally, if at all.

As much as the character of the Eskimo seal hunter differs from that of the Bantu tribesman, so does the character of vegetation differ according to the land and climate which support it.

In its various forms, vegetation is nature's wild harvest . . . a gift to man. From the forests of the world, the tropical rain forests of the equator, the broadleaf forests of the middle latitudes and the coniferous forests of pine and evergreen found nearly as far north as the Arctic Circle, comes the wood he has used in a hundred thousand ways through every civilization.

His herds and flocks have grazed upon the tropical savannas where the grass grows luxuriously to heights of eight to fifteen feet, and on the prairies and the steppes of the temperate regions.

From nature's harvest has come much of his food . . . coconuts, coffee, bananas, oranges, olives, nuts, peaches, pears, lemons and dates. She has given man rubber, cork, hemp, resin and many of his medicines.

A number of these and other wild crops he has "domesticated" and improved through cultivation, fertilization and crossbreeding. They have been his for so long that man scarcely thinks of wheat, rice, corn and cotton as anything but his own, or remembers that all of them once grew wild.

His domestication of flora does not end here. With an increased awareness that no natural abundance is unending, today man "farms" the forests, replacing the trees that he cuts down and replenishing the woodlands which he has decimated throughout his history.

Nature's gifts to man have been many but none is richer than the bounty of the earth.

2. TUNDRA: The tundra of the far north is a place of mosses, lichens and stunted flowering plants and trees. About 6% of all land area is tundra, some rocky and barren and the rest covered with seasonally boggy earth over perpetually frozen subsoil, an area so marginal that only specially adapted life forms, such as reindeer, can live here.

VEGETATION

3. CONIFEROUS FOREST: The coniferous forests of Europe, Asia and North America cover about 9% of the earth's land. The soil is poor for farming and the people live primarily on forestry, mining and the manufacture of wood products.

4. TEMPERATE FOREST: Over half of the world's population lives and works in the regions of temperate broadleaf forests which comprise only 7% of the world's land, including parts of the United States, Europe, China and Japan. The climate here is invigorating, characterized by changeable weather, warm summers and frosty winters.

5. PRAIRIE AND STEPPE: On th[e] grassy prairies and steppes are foun[d] many of the sheep and cattle ranches o[f] the earth, and where the land has bee[n] successfully cultivated, the great grai[n] fields.

The Holstein-Friesian breed originated in the province of Friesland in northern Germany. The first importations of Holsteins into the United States were made in 1795. The Holsteins are the largest of the dairy breeds. The color is black and white, with the colors sharply defined rather than blended. Cattle qualify for registration that are nearly all white or black, but no solid-color animal can be registered. A Holstein herd test of upwards of 100,000 cows shows an average annual production of 11,208 lbs. of milk with a fat test of 3.44% and a total average production of 385 lbs. of butterfat. Official records show that scores of Holstein cows have produced in excess of 30,000 lbs. of milk in a year.

The Guernsey breed originated in the Channel Islands, near the north coast of France. The first cattle brought to the United States were called Alderneys. Gradually the cattle on the islands of Alderney, Sark, and Guernsey became known as the Guernsey breed. The color of the Guernseys is fawn and white, with fawn predominating. A light cherry red with white is not unusual. The horns are of moderate size and amber in color. The skin is yellow. In a recent American Guernsey Cattle Club herd improvement registry covering several thousand cows on annual test the average production was 8688.5 pounds of milk and 425 pounds of butterfat.

The Jersey breed originated on the island of Jersey, one of the Channel Islands. In 1789 a law was passed prohibiting the importation of cattle into Jersey Island except for immediate slaughter. The first importation of Jerseys into the United States was made in 1850. Jerseys are more evenly distributed in the United States than any other breed. The color is usually some shade of fawn or cream, though different shades of mouse color, gray and brown are common. Some individuals are almost black. They may be a solid color of any of these shades, or spotted with white. The muzzles and tongues are usually black or lead colored, and around the muzzle is a white or mealy ring. Jerseys surpass all other breeds in the production of butterfat. Several cows have produced in excess of 1000 lbs. of butterfat in a year.

The Brown Swiss breed is one of the oldest in existence and was developed in Switzerland over a period of many centuries. The first importation of Brown Swiss into the United States was made by Henry M. Clark of Belmont, Massachusetts. It included 1 bull and 8 heifers. The bull, named William Tell, became number one in the herdbook of the Brown Swiss Cattle Breeders' Association. The color varies from dark to light brown. There is usually a light stripe of gray along the back. The nose, switch, tongue, and horn tips are always black, and there is usually a light or mealy ring around the muzzle. The cows have made good at the milk bucket. Well-culled, well-fed farmer herds average 10,000 pounds of 4% milk year after year.

The Ayrshire breed originated in southwestern Scotland, in the county of Ayr. The first importations into the United States occurred in 1822. The color varies from almost pure white to nearly all cherry red or brown, with any combination of these colors. The horns turn gracefully, giving a distinctive appearance to the head. Ayrshire cows have more of the beef type conformation than most other dairy breeds. They produce milk that tests around 4% butterfat. In order for a bull to meet Approved Sire Plan adopted by the Ayrshire Breeders' Association, 70% of all tested daughters must each produce 8,500 pounds of milk or 340 pounds of fat in a 305-day lactation period.

AMERICAN DAIRY CATTLE

Engineering in Modern Construction. The new Denver Convention Hall above encloses 100,000 square feet of column-free area beneath a 46-foot-high steel roof. The construction (shown in skeletal form in the bottom picture) is based on a 10-by-10-foot module. It was one of the primary features that brought an outstanding engineering award. At top, the hall is shown with the outer façade in place, while the essential construction module system of the roof is exposed as an architectural feature. Opened in 1969, the center contains a floor area 680 feet long and 240 feet wide, having a seating capacity of 14,000. The space-frame roof of webbed steel is painted white and is completely exposed to view on the interior. The façade of the building is rust-brown, with tall, narrow windows extending to the full height of the structure. Designed by the architectural firm of Muchow, Ream & Larson, the center was completed at a cost of $14 million. (American Iron and Steel Institute)

CALCULATOR PLOTTER

Modern Mechanical Research. This prototype of a 4-legged quadruped machine was developed by General Electric engineers. It was designed to spur development of equipment to improve the mobility and materials-handling capabilities of workers under the most severe conditions. By an advanced control system, the machine mimics and amplifies the linear movements of the operator. The front legs of the unit are controlled by the operator's arms and the rear legs by his legs. The research prototype—11 feet high and 3000 pounds in weight—was built by GE under a joint U.S. government agency contract.

Economics and Useful Arts

INTRODUCTION

Economics is the study of the means by which people obtain their livelihood and satisfy their wants. Many thinkers maintain that the economic system under which a people lives largely determines the form of all its institutions, including its morality, family life, religion, and art. Whether or not this view is entirely correct, there can be no doubt that, along with political government, economic conditions constitute a factor of supreme importance in the life of man.

The economic system touches the life of every man, woman, and child, primarily through their jobs or other sources of income or support and through the prices which must be paid in securing what they want. When jobs fail or prices fluctuate unduly, the average person senses that something is wrong. On giving it proper attention, he begins to perceive that he is part of a vast system of world-wide sweep. If he is to be an intelligent citizen and understand the forces which have such a large part in determining his well-being, it is essential that he study the economic system under which he lives.

The Economic System. In the normal course of events, every one of us, unless he is altogether dependent on others, contributes something to the common store of goods and services. In return, he receives, through the agency of money, the right to a certain share of that common store.

The present economic system of production, distribution, and consumption has been built and rebuilt by many generations, the results differing according to each generation's degree of intelligence, skill, and invention, its command over nature, and its social relationships. The system rests on such institutions as property and contract, the division of labor, competition, and combination. Behind all the factors of an economic system are the laws of human nature. These laws, working through the instincts to acquire, to possess, and to provide for family and dependents, operate to convert the vast resources and powers of the earth into human service.

Under the impact of two world wars, the economic system has been subjected to tremendous strains and shocks of abnormal periods. We have seen inflation and deflation at their greatest extremes, high prices, scarcity of raw materials, rationing and governmental price fixing, excess profits tax, and other programs and policies necessitated by world conflict. The divergent interests of workers and employers, labor and capital, have frequently set class against class, while the intensive research in products and methods has given us great improvements in machines and time-saving devices, all of which have displaced great numbers of workers from one form of employment into other forms, causing a change in the personal life of the individual affecting his housing, type of employment, wage, and social position.

The economic system of a democratic country must assume that the right of private property is an inalienable right. With this right of ownership and possession for use, man becomes a dignified human being and possesses initiative and an incentive to achieve a better education, and a better position so that he may provide more adequately for himself and his family

Today, millions of people live under one or the other of two world economic systems designated as Capitalism and Communism. In the "free world," where people are self-governed, Capitalism prevails. The economic life of the country is carried on by private enterprise instead of government directives. The individual citizen can choose his own occupation, invest his savings as he wishes, and otherwise manage his personal and business affairs. Competition is essentially free, and the hope of profit provides an incentive for industry and thrift. In Russia, which operates under a system of modified Marxist Communism, production has been placed on a basis of use rather than profit, and the strong central government allocates production, regulates prices, and assigns positions. Under this "controlled economy" the individual surrenders his independence and initiative and has his entire future education, work, and leisure time planned for him. While Russia has recently made some concessions to the individual citizen by increasing the supply and availability of consumer goods, an extreme form of Communism exists in mainland China.

In the United States of America, which has the world's highest standard of living, it is recognized that the government, as a servant of all the people, must provide for laws and regulations so that all persons, regardless of race, creed, or color, may have the opportunity of training and work so that they in return may provide for themselves and their families. The purpose of a government in our economic system is simply to outline the rights and responsibilities of each group, so that no one transgresses upon the rights of others.

The Division of Labor. This is the key to the understanding of the whole economic order. If every man or every family produced only for himself or itself, there would be no exchange, no markets, no money, no means of transportation; in fact, no economic system. Some such situation actually existed in the more primitive ages of the world where each household was almost self-sufficient. With the advance of civilization, however, came the division of labor. Men have discovered that it is far more profitable to co-operate with one another, each finding and keeping to his own special task.

Ours is an age of specialization. To provide the breakfast of even the humblest family in a modern country, all parts of the earth are drawn upon. To serve our needs we have thus built up the vast network of modern trade and commerce.

Linking the World. The greatest benefits of the division of labor are reaped when cities and districts and countries exchange with one another those products which they can produce most advantageously. Such advantages in the production of certain commodities may arise in a particular place by reason of its climate, soil, natural resources, and the capacities of its inhabitants. The United States, with its wide range of soil and climate, is more self-sufficient than most countries. But it needs the rubber and tin of the East Indies, the silk of Japan, the nickel of Canada, and a thousand other products which commerce brings to our shores.

In a similar way, different parts of the same country specialize and create domestic trade. Indiana specializes in corn; South Dakota, in wheat; California, in oranges. Each produces the crops which it can raise to the greater advantage. Likewise, the city depends on the country, but so also does the country depend on the city.

By aid of the means of communication, we have today markets that are nation-wide and even world-wide for the main articles of commerce—wheat, cotton, wool, rubber, and so forth. By aid of the system of transportation, the resources of the world are exploited and brought wherever there is a demand for them. Nowhere have these agencies been more highly developed than in the United States, and nowhere have they been such important factors in the building up of a national life.

Capital and Labor. We often speak of capital as a form of wealth. It also has another aspect, which appears when we contrast capital with labor. The relationships among these two contributors to economic production constitute one of the most interesting and dynamic aspects of society. Before the Industrial Revolution, workers generally owned the tools of their craft. The mechanization of industry, however, separated workers from the tools of production, which became too costly and impersonal to be owned by each man. Ownership passed to the company or corporation employing the workers. Consequently, interest in the products of the economic unit became divided, with portions going to both owners and workers. During the 20th century, ownership claims became further separated from management, as a third specialized contributor to economic activity. The expectations of all three have now to be balanced and reconciled.

The diverse interests of all contributors and claimants against the economic product or output are in conflict among themselves, but coordination of them is essential in the harmonious functioning of the economic system. They *must* work together. The dominance of any one of the interests shifts the balance of power. Owners originally held dominion —with the rise of labor unions, however, control over economic processes passed more to workers collectively. More recently, managers have enjoyed a type of supremacy. Inability to resolve conflicts among these parties has led to the government's increasingly mediating and regulating their respective activities. These issues are treated in the *Labor Relations* section.

From Producer to Consumer. When production takes place on a large scale, the consumer is no longer in direct and personal relation to the producer. Hence arises the need for agencies to bring the two together. Modern business makes necessary a system of commission houses, jobbers, wholesalers, and retailers. They all have their parts to perform in the division of labor, and, as such, they serve useful economic functions. The practical aspect of this subject is taken up in the discussion of *Marketing*, and *Selling and Advertising*.

Money as the Medium of Exchange. All this interchange requires a scale of value and an exchange system. This is achieved through the modern use of money. Direct barter, various commodities, and silver and gold have served as means of exchange, but today money serves this function and, depending upon a convention or custom, it includes anything *generally* acceptable as a means of making payments. Thus, in the U.S. today, money includes coins, paper bills, and demand (or checking) accounts.

For the creation and control of money, a vast system of institutions has arisen, consisting in the U.S. of individual banks and other financial institutions, as well as the Federal Reserve System—and, on the international level, there are such institutions (with the U.S. and other nations as members) as the International Monetary Fund and the International Bank for Reconstruction and Development, generally known as the World Bank.

Pervading the monetary system is the very important element of credit. In effect, credit is a special form of money which expands and contracts as loans are made and then repaid. It permits purchase in advance of immediate ability to pay, thereby generating a chain of economic activity from borrower, to retailer, to manufacturer or builder, and thence to employees and purchasers.

The control of credit is the key to the expansion of the means of production, the level of employment, and the scale of living. Governments ultimately hold this key. In the modern world they recognize this responsibility and devote much of their attention to it in order to keep as even a keel as possible between inflation with rising prices and deflation with attendant unemployment and loss of purchasing power. These subjects are treated under *Insurance*, *Investments*, *Money and Banking*.

The Stages of Production. In a study of Useful Arts, we begin with the land, for on it or out of it (including, as economists do, the oceans and inland waters as part of the "land") are produced all the raw materials which the labor and organization of men turn into the means of satisfying their numerous wants. Thus we have first in order the extractive industries, which are described under the titles *Agriculture*, *Animal Industry*, *Fisheries*, and *Mining and Mineral Production*.

Most raw materials—wheat, cotton, wool, silk, iron, copper, lumber, and a host of others—go through many and elaborate processes before they are ready for their final use. They must be conveyed by land and water, they must pass through many hands, they must be treated by complicated machinery. Production calls for the work of the inventor and of the engineer no less than that of the farmer and of the miner. Hence the division on *Inventions* and on *Engineering and Building*.

Then comes the last stage, that of manufacturing. In the plant of the manufacturer, the work of the farmer, the miner, the inventor, and the engineer is brought together. Out of the factory the results of their labor pass at last as finished goods, and the whole roundabout process of production is complete. The more important aspects of this last step are treated under *Manufacturing*.

The Age of Industry. One man today can do the work which hundreds or even thousands were needed to perform in the pre-industrial age. Power has been harnessed and applied in countless ways. Steam and electricity and oil and gasoline serve the desires of man. The blast furnace, the power loom, the self-binding reaper, the linotype machine—to mention at random a few of our innumerable inventions—make possible an efficiency of production which surpasses the wildest dreams of the past. The standard of living of ever-greater populations has risen vastly. The ordinary man has at his command commodities that in earlier times were the rare luxuries of kings. Thus has industry, aided by invention, revolutionized the world. The Industrial Revolution is well named because, of all the great changes society has known, none has been at once so rapid and so extensive as this development. A period of much less than a hundred years saw the transformation of the everyday life of our Western civilization, saw a remarkable change in the habits and thoughts and modes of work of many millions, saw a new power over nature created, and saw the very face of the country completely altered.

To understand these things is to understand our own age and civilization. Through a study of economics and the arts of production, we may attain this understanding and learn in a new way the meaning of the world and the society in which we live.

Mass Production. A logical modern extension of the Industrial Revolution has been the introduction of large-scale manufacturing operations. These cut unit costs, thus permitting lower prices, wider markets, and greater profits. The next step is investment of part of the profits and new money in developing new products through research and utilization of the advances of science.

As a final stage comes the application of the computer for making automatic numerous steps in manufacture, control of operations, and even many decisions of management.

COMMERCE

COMMERCE consists of all those processes of trade involved in the general distribution of commodities from the producer to the consumer. However, the term generally implies an exchange of large volumes of merchandise between different places or communities rather than the trade carried on between individuals. Traffic passing from one nation to another is *foreign*, or *international*, commerce; that moving between localities included within national boundaries is *internal*, or *domestic*, commerce. In the United States, commercial shipments of merchandise from one state to another are said to enter into *interstate* commerce.

Origins. The desire of man to satisfy his wants as easily as possible supplies the primary reason for commercial transactions. However, there can be comparatively little exchange between countries or districts inhabited by people who produce the same type of commodities; for then, neither locality has anything required by the other. Commerce, therefore, depends upon existing differences in temperature and climate, in natural resources, in industrial development, or in racial and cultural characteristics.

Transportation and Commerce. Wherever such differences exist, the inhabitants of one district will generally have a surplus of certain commodities which they are anxious to exchange for the surplus from other places. But, before the exchange can be accomplished, the goods must be transported to the locality where they are needed. For this reason commerce and transportation are mutually dependent to such an extent that the condition of one is almost invariably indicated by a corresponding degree of development in the other.

Because of this intimate relationship, the history of commerce may be divided into three fairly distinct periods: First, that in which transportation was accomplished by man or by beasts of burden on land, and by coasting vessels on the water. Second, that in which mariners, by the aid of the compass, were able to guide their sailing vessels upon the open seas. Third, that in which transportation depended chiefly on the power of steam, internal combustion, and other forms of engines. The first period, of possibly 5000 years' duration, extended from the beginning of commerce well into the 15th century, in spite of the fact that the compass was known in parts of Europe as early as 1200; the second period, of about 400 years' duration, may be said to have terminated in 1838, when the first line of commercial steamships began. The third period is that of the past century.

ANCIENT COMMERCE

Early exchange centered on Mesopotamia, the "Great Road" between Central Asia, the Mediterranean Sea, and Egypt. Commerce was related to geographic location and raw material shortages. Metals, semiprecious stones, building stone, timber, and aromatic woods and spices were important commodities. Manufacturing of woolen cloth and bronze work occurred. Until 3000 B.C., trade was by barter and controlled by the temple. Early legal codes, and even the beginning of civil law, evolved from the commercial experience and early guilds were formed. In this period, Damascus in Syria emerged as a major trade center for the caravan routes crossing the region from the Mediterranean and Red Seas to the interior.

The Phœnicians. The first people devoted chiefly to commerce were the Phœnicians, who inhabited a strip of land about 100 miles long and 10 miles wide on the eastern coast of the Mediterranean. Forced upon the sea as fishermen, these people gradually developed commercial fleets which in time extended their voyages to the Strait of Gibraltar and even north to England. The ships brought back ivory, tin, copper, and precious metals, while caravans sent inland brought spices and frankincense from India. Manufacturing produced glassware, linen and woolen cloth, and metal work. Profits from commerce and manufacturing supported the merchant and leisure class. Great cities such as Sidon and Tyre emerged and extensive colonization, such as the founding of the great city of Carthage, took place on Mediterranean shores and parts of the Atlantic coast. For perhaps 1000 years, the Phoenicians dominated commerce and served not only to exchange commodities but ideas and cultures, as well.

The Greeks. Eventually, the commercial supremacy of the Phœnicians passed to the Greeks, who excelled both as sailors and as business men. Their homeland, which in area was smaller than the state of Maine, nevertheless offered great incentives to commerce. It was sufficiently fertile to afford a surplus of some products, such as wine, figs, and olive oil, but it did not produce enough grain to feed the population. Mountains on the north protected it fairly well from attack by land; it was centrally located in relation to other countries of the Mediterranean; and its extensive coast line afforded many good harbors.

The conditions of living in a small, well populated country having an insufficient supply of grain were conducive to emigration; ships furnished an easy means of travel. Consequently, for a period of about 500 years, the Greeks followed a consistent policy of founding and of developing settlements in fertile sections of foreign lands, notably on the Black Sea, in Asia Minor, and in southern Italy and Sicily. Malaga, in Spain, and what is now Marseille, in France, were sites of thriving Greek colonies. From these colonies, grain and raw materials were supplied to the mother country, which developed many manufacturing industries, especially the production of bronze, clay, marble, and woolen products.

The Greeks were quick to adopt new devices for facilitating commerce. From contact with the Phœnician traders, they acquired an alphabet, which they greatly improved. From the Lydians of Asia Minor, they learned to mark pieces of silver with an official seal and to use these coins as money.

In spite of the success of the Persians, who broke the Greek power in the East, the Western colonies developed more rapidly than before, while Greece itself, under the leadership of Athens, reached the pinnacle of its power.

Empire of Alexander. The enormous eastern empire held by the Macedonian, Alexander the Great, took away from Athens the control of commerce and led to the development of great commercial cities farther east. Of these, the largest was Alexandria, located near the western corner of the Nile delta. As the greatest of Hellenistic cities, it surpassed all previous commercial centers in volume of trade and was a cosmopolitan economic and intellectual center. The Pharos, the 370-foot-high harbor lighthouse, was considered one of the seven wonders of the ancient world.

The Romans. The expansion of Roman power outside of Italy is said to have begun in 241 B. C., when Sicily was taken from the Carthaginians. Ninety-five years later, the great commercial cities of Carthage and Corinth were destroyed by Roman soldiers, and Greece and Macedonia were reduced to the position of Roman provinces.

Although Rome ruled the Western world, she never became a commercial city. Captives of war were extensively sold as slaves, and great quantities of foodstuffs, manufactured products, and luxuries were sent to the capital by sea, and over the fine roads that were constructed by Roman engineers, even in the farthest provinces. These products, however, to a large extent, did not represent commercial transactions but were the tributes and taxes imposed upon conquered peoples. What Rome gave in return was almost five centuries of comparative peace and security, during which time commerce developed wherever conditions permitted.

MEDIEVAL COMMERCE

During the "dark ages" that followed the fall of Rome, commerce was almost entirely in the hands of the Mohammedans, with centers at Baghdad, Damascus, Cairo, Alexandria, and the Moorish cities in Spain.

Western and northern Europe became divided under the feudal system into thousands of tiny units, each attempting to be complete within itself, and entirely independent of all external sources of supply. Roads were totally neglected; strangers were regarded with suspicion; robbery was a common practice; and commerce, under such conditions, was quite naturally almost nonexistent.

Growth of Towns. Soon after 1000 A. D. the need for places where an interchange of commodities might be carried on was filled by the widespread development of towns. In these growing communities, manufacturing and trading not only became possible, but were necessary in order to provide something to exchange for the food and raw materials brought in at first from the surrounding country, and, later, from other parts of the world.

Under these conditions some men were enabled to devote all of their time to trading and dealing in commodities. The fear of the townspeople that these traders would take undue advantage of their opportunities, coupled with the prevalent suspicions of all strangers, next led to the establishment of *public markets*, where commercial transactions might be carried on under official supervision. As the markets increased in size and prosperity, traders customarily united for mutual benefit, forming *merchants' guilds*. Somewhat later, the craftsmen also combined, according to their special trades, to form *craftsmen's guilds*. The guilds provided the merchants and artisans with a position in the social order, a monopoly of the town's trade, and considerable power in local government.

Fairs. European trade expanded in the 11th century to meet the demand for goods from beyond local regions. This led to the establishment of fairs, usually held annually and under the protection of powerful lords. Participants were guaranteed protection and safe conduct, and efforts were made to ensure honest dealings. The fairs of Champagne, in northern France—in a fertile region crossed by major trade routes—were the most famous. Each country and region, however, had its own fair. As the most important form of commercial activity in their time, medieval fairs had a profound influence: they served to promote Western civilization by destroying the provincialism and bigotry of the "Dark Ages," and by establishing the basis for expanded trade, monetary economies, and commercial law.

Risks of Medieval Commerce. The extensive commerce of the latter part of the medieval period was carried on at very great risk, because of constant rivalry and open warfare between great commercial cities. There was no central government sufficiently powerful to enforce its laws and to guarantee security. Shipments on land and by inland waterways were subject both to innumerable and excessive tolls and to constant danger from highway robbers. Similarly, coasting vessels always had to be ready for battle with pirates or with ships from rival cities.

Venice and the Hanse. In the north of Europe, during the 13th and the 14th century, the great commercial cities of Lubeck, Hamburg, Cologne, Danzig, and many others united, for mutual protection, into an organization known as the Hanse, or Hanseatic league. This league became extremely powerful and had complete control of commerce with the countries on the Baltic and, to a large extent, with those on the North Sea.

On the Mediterranean the struggle for supremacy was largely between Venice and her chief rivals, Genoa and Pisa. Leadership was secured to Venice by the crafty manner in which the doge, Enrico Dondolo, directed the energies of the Fourth Crusade, first to the capture of Zara, a rival Christian city, and next, in 1203, to the subjugation of Constantinople. Venice then completely dominated the trade with the East, and developed commerce to a degree never before attained. Venetian methods of banking and bookkeeping represented standards that were copied throughout the commercial world.

Between Venice and northern Europe, commerce was carried on in two ways: Traders from central and southern Germany were permitted to bring their metals, furs, coarse textiles, twine, and leather over the Alps by way of the Brenner or the Saint Gotthard pass, to Venice. By sea, the Venetian galleys, with their precious cargoes of spices, dyes, alum, fine textiles, weapons, and paper, traveled to Flanders. Bruges, which was succeeded in the 15th century by Antwerp, was the common center at which the wares of Venice were traded for the fish, furs, coarse textiles, wax, grain, and salt meat brought by the ships of the Hanseatic league, and for the wool, tallow, leather, tin, and lead of England. English exports at this time were almost entirely under the control of the "Merchants of the Staple," a society composed chiefly of foreigners.

MODERN COMMERCE

During the 14th and the 15th century, England, France, and Spain were becoming nations in which many loosely connected feudal divisions were gradually merged under comparatively strong central governments. Then, for the first time, the individual cities of Italy and the weak organization of the Hanse came into conflict with commercial rivals who had less experience but were more powerful and determined than themselves.

Portugal, under the direction of wise rulers, had already attained the leadership in navigation; not because the Portuguese were better sailors than the Venetians, the Genoese, or the mariners of the Hanseatic league, but because they received encouragement and assistance from their government.

New Trade Routes. In the East, the ancient land routes by which the commerce of India and of China had reached Venice were gradually cut off by the spread of Turkish power. As a result, each of the important European nations was actively searching for the "Eastern passage" by which their ships could reach the fabulously rich countries of the Orient.

In 1492, Columbus, a Genoese in command of Spanish vessels, sailed west until he reached the New World, which blocked the direct route to Asia. Cabot, an Italian master of an English ship, reached North America in 1497. Finally, by sailing around Africa, Vasco da Gama, a Portuguese, established trade by sea with India in 1498, and returned home the next year with goods that sold for sixty times the cost of the voyage. In 1522 the expedition which had set out from Spain three years before under command of Magellan completed the first voyage around the world.

The Portuguese obtained the rewards due the winner of the race to the East, for to them Pope Alexander VI assigned all of Africa and of Asia, with the exception of the Philippines. The Americas, except Brazil, were allotted to Spain.

The Struggle for Supremacy. The open seas now became the highway on which the ships of Portugal, Spain, France, and England speeded in order to obtain as much as possible from the newly found sources of wealth. Portuguese ships brought back great quantities of Eastern products which, because of the increased supply, eventually sold at prices low enough to change such important commodities as tea, coffee, and sugar from luxuries to necessities. Lisbon for a time succeeded Antwerp as the most important city of commerce.

Spain. During the century which followed the discovery of America, Spain became the richest and most important country on the earth. From her colonies she received enormous quantities of gold

WORLD'S PROGRESS IN COMMERCE AND PRODUCTION

Year	Population	Total Commerce $	Commerce per Capita $	Ships, Sail Tons	Ships, Steam Tons	Railways Miles
1850	1,075,000,000	4,049,000,000	3.76	11,470,000	864,000	24,000
1860	1,205,000,000	7,246,000,000	6.01	14,890,000	1,710,000	67,400
1870	1,310,000,000	10,663,000,000	8.14	12,900,000	3,040,000	139,900
1880	1,439,000,000	14,761,000,000	10.26	14,400,000	5,880,000	224,900
1890	1,488,000,000	17,519,000,000	11.80	9,166,000	8,295,000	390,000
1900	1,543,000,000	20,105,000,000	13.02	6,674,000	13,857,000	500,000
1910	1,616,000,000	33,634,000,000	20.81	4,624,000	22,046,000	637,000
1920	1,730,000,000	61,277,000,000	35.42	4,066,000	32,092,000[3]	710,600
1930	2,000,000,000	69,526,000,000[1]	34.28[1]		69,734,310[4]	706,090
1940	2,170,000,000	27,706,000,000[2]	12.92[2]	....	69,439,659[5]	756,781[6]
1950	2,400,000,000	58,400,000,000	24.31	....	75,718,000	783,679
1960	3,005,000,000	264,000,000,000[10]	113.80	61,655,000[11]	74,261,000	N.A.
1968	3,483,000,000	491,000,000,000[10]	141.00	119,889,000[12]	74,263,000	N.A.
1974	3,890,000,000	1,584,500,000,000[13]	407.32	215,979,000[12]	126,184,000	N.A.

Year	Telegraphs Miles	Cables[8] Miles	Cotton Pounds	Coal Short tons	Pig Iron Long tons	Gold Production $
1850	5,000	25	1,435,000,000	81,400,000	4,700,000	363,900,000
1860	100,000	1,500	2,551,000,000	142,300,000	7,200,000	1,334,000,000
1870	281,000	15,000	2,775,000,000	213,400,000	11,900,000	1,263,000,000
1880	440,000	49,000	3,601,000,000	340,000,000	18,000,000	1,150,800,000
1890	768,000	132,000	5,600,000,000	466,000,000	27,200,000	1,060,100,000
1900	1,180,000	200,000	6,247,000,000	800,000,000	40,400,000	2,100,000,000
1910	1,307,000	291,000	9,013,000,000	1,141,600,000	65,800,000	3,780,700,000
1920	1,592,000	....	9,405,000,000	1,305,000,000	68,300,000	4,253,800,000
1930	7,119,665	360,613	12,900,000,000	1,196,003,000	80,289,000	3,846,848,000
1940	6,730,500[7]	344,079[2]	14,770,820,000	1,615,972,000[2]	104,000,000	8,562,100,000
1950	5,089,000	344,079[2]	13,750,000,000	1,441,257,000	112,800,000	8,610,000,000
1960	N.A.	N.A.	22,000,000,000	2,170,000,000	286,000,000	1,175,000,000
1968	N.A.	N.A.	25,000,000,000	2,217,000,000	425,000,000	1,420,000,000
1974	N.A.	N.A.	27,000,000,000	1,870,000,000	485,000,000[13]	1,371,000,000

[1] 1929. [2] 1938. [3] Includes motor ships. [4] Gross Tons, includes motor and sail ships. [5] Includes barges, motor and sail ships, 1939. [6] 1937. [7] 1939. [8] Nautical miles. [9] For decade ending year named. [10] Imports and exports. [11] Motor, 1961. [12] Motor. [13] 1975.

and silver, and also many valuable cargoes of hides, drugs, dyes, cocoa, vanilla, and sugar. Manufacturing industries at home were developed on a large scale for the production of silk and woolen textiles, wines, soap, salt, and many other commodities. In addition to manufactured articles, Spain exported figs, raisins, olives, olive oil, iron ore, and large amounts of mercury for use in obtaining gold and silver at the mines of Mexico and Peru.

All of these great advantages were nullified and finally destroyed by a prolonged period of bad government, marked especially by exorbitant taxes of every kind, and by a policy of exploitation rather than assistance in connection with the colonies. So serious were the results that the population declined rapidly, and some great commercial cities retained only one-fourth of their former inhabitants.

Portugal. The commercial greatness of Portugal was open to attack by her rivals, because it lacked the firm foundation of domestic production. The Portuguese were excellent traders, but their country was small and was not developed industrially. Manufactured articles for export were not made at home but had to be purchased from other European countries. Consequently, England and the Netherlands were eventually able to cut off Portugal's supply of export goods, and to fill the Eastern demand themselves. In addition to this fundamental lack of commercial stability, Portugal fell under the harmful rule of Spain during the 60 years between 1581 and 1640. By the time the Spanish yoke was cast off, England had broken Portuguese control in India, and the Netherlands had taken the islands of Ceylon, Sumatra, Java, and the valuable Moluccas, or Spice islands.

The Netherlands. Dutch traders were quick to take advantage of the opportunities offered by the decline of Spain and Portugal. Their ships traveled to India and to the Eastern islands, and were equally active in European trade. Most of the wool exported by Spain was carried to northern countries by Dutch vessels, which also entered the Baltic and returned with cargoes from Russia.

At home, large business companies grew up, the manufacture of silk and of leather was developed, the fishing industry increased until more than 2000 fishing boats were regularly employed, and business of all forms was greatly stimulated. The Netherlands became the financial center, and Amsterdam the most important commercial city, of Europe.

Unfortunately for the country, a strong central government was lacking, corruption became common among high officials, and taxes were greatly increased. The volume of commerce ceased to grow after 1730. In 1798 the Dutch East India Company, which had ruled all of the Eastern possessions and for 180 years had paid average annual dividends of over 18 per cent, came to an end. Its debts of more than 50 million dollars were assumed by the government.

France. Among the five European nations that achieved commercial power during the modern period of 1500 to 1800, France was one of the two which a historian in the 16th century would probably have selected as most likely to reach and to keep first place. Portugal and the Netherlands were obviously handicapped by their lack of area and domestic resources. But France and Spain were the largest and richest countries of western Europe, and both had extensive coast lines. In exploration, France surpassed both the English and the Dutch, while in area of foreign colonies, she was second only to Spain.

France did develop a prosperous trade with the Levant and with Italy and Spain, but this could not become of first importance because faulty political organization raised almost insuperable obstacles to the free flow of commerce.

The greatest checks to commerce within the country were due to the existence of feudal divisions which prevented national unity, to the continuance of the guilds long after these organizations had been displaced in more progressive nations, and to the establishment of an absolute monarchy wherein the correction of existing evils was impossible unless the ruler was unusually strong and wise. High customs duties were collected whenever goods entered the country and also when they crossed from one internal division to another. The quarrels and the strict regulations of the numerous guilds

CANADIAN SHIPPING, 1972

Cargo Loaded and Unloaded, 15 Major Ports
(in 1,000-ton units)

Ports	International		Coastwise		Total
	Loaded	Unloaded	Loaded	Unloaded	
Vancouver, B.C.	24,358	2,918	3,546	4,074	34,987
Sept.-Iles, Que.	17,779	391	3,418	734	22,324
Montreal, Que.	4,738	5,779	5,171	10,024	25,513
Port Arthur, Ont.	4,533	148	17,599	812	23,094
Hamilton, Ont.	350	7,619	219	4,991	12,680
Port Cartier, Que.	11,594	650	38	2,804	15,088
Halifax, N.S.	3,685	5,434	1,885	710	11,715
Quebec, Que.	4,323	5,772	1,512	3,226	14,385
Toronto, Ont.	267	2,298	122	1,579	4,267
St. John, N.B.	2,346	6,019	1,818	133	10,317
New Westminster, B C.	728	352	994	946	3,020
Sault Ste. Marie, Ont.	212	2,755	185	1,764	4,917
Baie Comeau, Que.	3,768	1,240	181	2,724	7,826
Port Alfred, Que.	445	3,589	4.4	472	4,512
Sorel, Que.	2,624	4,607	2,531	604	8,085

Source: *Canada Year Book, 1974.*

largely prevented any improvements in methods of manufacture, and, finally, selfish monarchs entered upon a series of wars which gained nothing at home and lost most of the colonies abroad.

England. In spite of serious wars and intense commercial competition with larger countries, England, by 1750, had become the dominating factor in world commerce. Of the various reasons for her success, two may be considered as fundamental: First, she was a part of Europe and yet was separated from the continent by a wide channel which effectively prevented invasion by land; this condition made the possession of a powerful navy a primary necessity for national safety. Second, England acquired a coherent central government much sooner than did her rivals, and this government was far more flexible and democratic than theirs.

As a basis for exchange with other countries, England had from very early times the products of her sheep industry and of her mines. Manufacturing industries were gradually developed, which changed these raw materials into cloth and metal products. Ships were required to carry the excess production to other countries, and ships were needed also for protection and to supply trained sailors to the navy in time of war. The government, therefore, adopted the policy of encouraging shipping and commerce. Whenever possible, special privileges were secured by the state for English merchants, and success in battle usually meant the addition of foreign colonies in which an extension of trade could be expected.

English Trading Companies. During the 17th century, English commerce was to a large extent controlled by trading companies such as the East India Company, the Guinea Company, the Virginia Company, and the Hudson's Bay Company. A trader who was not a member of one of the companies could deal only with France, Spain, or Portugal. The strict control and regulations of the companies provoked so much antagonism that they finally lost their power and disbanded. The Hudson's Bay Company, however, still exists as an ordinary business corporation.

Having extensive colonies which supplied raw materials and required manufactured articles in return, together with a powerful merchant marine for the distribution of her products, England experienced at home a high degree of industrial development. Textiles and products of iron and steel were the chief commodities manufactured and exported. Homeward bound ships brought wool, cotton, naval stores, grain, sugar, tea, coffee, spices, tobacco, and rum; also silk, linen, and other foreign

CANADIAN COMMERCE

Imports and Exports to Selected Countries, 1930–1973
(add 000's)

Year	Imports (in dollars)					Exports (in dollars)				
	From U. K.	From Common-wealth	From U. S.	From Others	Total	To U. K.	To Common-wealth	To U. S.	To Others	Total
1930	227,816	*	653,676	126,987	1,008,479	316,342	*	373,424	173,917	863,683
1935	173,889	*	312,417	64,009	550,315	377,644	*	261,685	85,648	724,977
1940	267,383	*	744,231	70,336	1,081,950	655,957	*	442,984	80,013	1,178,954
1945	271,668	*	1,202,418	111,689	1,585,775	1,486,848	*	1,196,977	534,506	3,218,331
1950	400,811	240,988	2,089,531	393,901	3,125,231	467,896	184,362	2,020,703	431,055	3,104,016
1951	415,194	305,522	2,752,087	532,136	4,004,939	630,124	239,982	2,296,235	730,741	3,897,082
1952	351,541	183,911	2,887,628	493,338	3,916,418	744,461	260,788	2,302,673	974,339	4,282,261
1953	445,441	169,666	3,115,301	517,400	4,247,808	663,785	231,412	2,413,318	788,596	4,097,111
1954	382,229	180,759	2,871,279	533,134	3,967,401	651,033	193,768	2,308,670	706,746	3,860,217
1955	393,117	208,940	3,331,143	634,554	4,567,754	767,642	235,867	2,547,636	707,183	4,258,328
1956	476,371	220,437	4,031,394	818,749	5,546,951	811,113	242,011	2,803,085	904,233	4,760,442
1957	507,319	237,937	3,887,391	840,704	5,473,351	720,898	231,637	2,846,646	989,699	4,788,880
1958	518,505	208,702	3,460,147	863,138	5,050,492	771,576	281,435	2,808,067	930,358	4,791,436
1959	588,573	239,240	3,709,065	972,043	5,508,921	785,802	273,305	3,083,151	879,414	5,021,672
1960	588,930	279,069	3,693,189	931,160	5,492,348	915,290	326,958	2,932,171	1,089,633	5,264,052
1967	673,050	435,291†	8,016,341	1,950,517	11,075,199	1,169,053	638,201†	7,079,396	2,224,930	11,111,580
1973	1,005,397	1,991,296†	16,483,587	3,822,294	23,302,574	1,581,845	2,477,608†	16,611,868	4,629,694	25,301,005

† Commonwealth and preferential countries. Source: *Canada Year Book, 1974.*

textiles. It must not be thought that all of this commerce depended on the colonies, for, at the end of the 18th century, more than half of England's trade was carried on with Europe. The trade with America ranked second in value. That with Africa was very much smaller, but was considered important because it furnished a supply of slaves for sale in America and the West Indies.

Canadian Commerce. The early commerce of Canada was controlled largely by monopolistic companies chartered by France. After the English conquest, control passed to British traders who confined their commerce almost entirely to the homeland. Early trade with the United States was by smuggling until Great Britain removed restrictions on normal traffic.

In 1975, Canada's foreign trade amounted to over $66 billion, with about two-thirds of its exports going to the United States, compared to about 6% to Great Britain. The United States supplies Canada with about 60% of its imports, while Great Britain supplies about 4½%. Major exports to Great Britain include foodstuffs and tobacco (about 20% of the total in value), aluminum, copper, nickel, newsprint, and lumber. Exports to the United States include raw materials, petroleum, lumber, and wood pulp. Canadian imports are largely manufactured goods, such as auto parts, machinery, and vehicles. The accompanying tables indicate the character of Canadian trade.

In 1975, Canada ranked 11th in world trade. It has enjoyed the trade advantages associated with membership in the British Commonwealth. In 1974 Canada entered into a comprehensive trade agreement with the European Common Market. This was an attempt to reduce its commercial dependence on the United States.

Class of Merchandise	Imports of Canada, 1973 (Thousand dollars)			Exports of Canada, 1973 (Thousand dollars)		
	From United Kingdom	From United States	From All Countries	To United Kingdom	To United States	To All Countries
Live Animals	1,527	131,007	137,105	1,433	117,821	144,688
Food, Feed, Beverages and Tobacco	68,164	861,073	1,844,380	332,575	861,562	3,007,857
Crude Materials, Inedible	33,115	780,215	2,016,253	311,685	2,733,613	5,019,059
Fabricated Materials, Inedible	252,470	2,823,959	4,281,513	774,718	5,697,755	8,194,083
End Products, Inedible	638,765	11,695,214	14,776,578	160,591	7,161,256	8,308,116
Special Transactions—Trade	11,356	192,119	246,747	843	39,855	45,355
Total	1,005,397	16,483,587	23,302,576	1,581,845	16,611,869	24,719,157

Source: *Canada Year Book, 1974.*

UNITED STATES

The preceding sections relate the story of commercial progress on the earth, from the days of ancient Babylon to the beginning of the 19th century. At the conclusion of this 4800-year period of development, world commerce had reached a yearly value of about one and one-half billion dollars. Of the total, the United States of America was credited with about one-tenth.

World commerce, due to advanced methods of transportation and communication, increased tremendously from 1800 to the present time, while from 1800 to the beginning of World War I the rise of American foreign commerce was almost proportional to that of the rest of the world. Assembly line methods in production of ships and planes enabled America to lead the world in World War II in its merchant marine tonnage, rail transportation, and air transport.

In the following paragraphs, the development of foreign commerce in the United States is given especial attention. The corresponding growth in other nations is indicated by the commercial relations of these countries with America, and by the comparative importance of each in world trade.

The commerce of the English colonies in North America was such as would be expected between fertile, newly discovered lands, and the older, more advanced countries. Food and raw materials, consisting chiefly of flour, grain, tobacco, lumber, fish, potash, and indigo, were exported in exchange for textiles and other manufactured articles, and for colonial products such as sugar, molasses, coffee, and tea.

It is surprising to note that after the Revolution the United States continued to trade chiefly with England, although that country closed the ports of the West Indies to American ships. The European wars between England on one side, and France, Spain, and the Netherlands on the other, afforded the new nation its first great commercial opportunity. Having ships and sailors equal to any in the world, the American merchant marine developed rapidly, and carried a large share of the world's commerce while Europe was busily engaged in warfare.

This commercial growth received serious checks when France and England both placed arbitrary restrictions on neutral shipping. A general embargo, ordered by the American government in 1807 as a means of retaliation, proved even more disastrous. Commerce declined until the conclusion of the War of 1812, and then, after a few years of sharp fluctuations, experienced a long period of slow growth.

Expansion and Development. This period was, for the United States, one of active territorial expansion and economic development. The West grew rapidly, and in various parts of the country improved highways, new canals, or steamboats on the large rivers supplied better means of transportation. At the same time, more and better manufactured commodities were produced by industries which had originated or developed during the seven years between the passing of the Embargo act and the end of the War of 1812. Domestic manufacturers fought hard to retain the home market which had been created by the temporary shortage of foreign goods. They succeeded to a notable extent because their increased *production* was accompanied by an even greater increase in *demand*, together with great improvements in the natural means of *distribution*. Although the *per capita* consumption of foreign goods decreased, the total amount of foreign trade continued to increase, and was carried chiefly by American ships. During this period the American merchant marine approached very closely in size that of Great Britain, and was second to none in skill and efficiency.

The change in the economic condition of the country is well shown by the changes in the list of exports. In 1800, grain amounted to one-third, and cotton to less than one-fourteenth, of all exported merchandise; in 1860, cotton accounted for four-sevenths of the total, and grain for only one-thirteenth. Manufactured goods, which stood low on the earlier list, were second only to cotton in 1860.

Triangular Exchange. The South gave all of its energies to the production of cotton. The North developed extensive manufacturing industries, but it also produced sufficient grain and meat to supply the entire nation and still had a surplus for export. From New Orleans, enormous quantities of cotton were shipped to Europe. Europe returned to New York textiles, articles manufactured from iron and steel, and luxuries. Finally, the cycle was completed and the South received compensation for its cotton in the form of food and manufactured products sent from the North.

Effects of Civil War. Intersectional warfare checked for a time the development of American commerce. With the war's end, slavery had been abolished and the nation was again a political unit. The war also had the effect of influencing the economic futures of the two opposing sections. The world demand for cotton, and the consequent high prices paid for this staple, forced the South to resume the production of white fiber as rapidly as possible. In the North, a shortage of labor accentuated the advantages that were to be obtained by the extensive use of machinery in the factories and on the farms.

1850 to 1900. During the second quarter of the 19th century the annual production of coal increased from one-half million to six million tons, and the economic value of railroads was clearly demonstrated. Between 1850 and 1860, thousands of miles of track were laid, especially in the Middle West. Our domestic exports, which amounted to 316 million dollars in 1860, averaged less than 225 million dollars a year until 1870; but by 1880 they became 824 million, and in 1892 they exceeded one billion dollars tor the first time.

The last half of the 19th century was marked throughout the civilized world by the expansion of industrial and commercial activities. That the United States was able to hold a position of decided commercial importance is shown by the tables, *A Century of Growth of the United States* and *World's Progress in Commerce and Production.*

Merchant Marine. This position was retained in spite of a great decline in American shipping. Many conditions contributed to this marked decrease in tonnage. The country was expanding and developing so rapidly that there were unusual opportunities for profits in domestic rather than in foreign trade. Higher tariff rates gave protection to home industries but did not help the merchant marine. Lower priced, foreign-built ships were not purchased because, according to the law, they could not obtain American registry. And, finally, we were not prepared to build iron ships at a cost that could compete with those built in England.

In 1860, 70 per cent of our exports and 63 per cent of the imports were carried by American vessels. These ratios fell to about 10 per cent in 1910 but rose to more than 35.8 per cent by 1935. The foreign commerce of the United States amounted to $21.26 *per capita* in 1860. Fifty years later, although population was three times as great, the figures had increased to $34.78. In 1920, following World War I, the amount became $120.81, but fell to $77.59 by 1929. It was $48.92 in 1940; $137.63 in 1964.

U.S. Exports and Imports. Historically, U.S. exports were characterized by large quantities of relatively few products, largely agricultural in nature. In 1860, 80% of the exports were in this category, reflecting the impact of colonialism upon the country. In 1975 exports from the U.S. amounted to over $106 billion, consisting largely of manufactured products. Principal exports included various machinery (almost one-third of the total), grain, industrial chemicals, iron and steel mill products, automobiles and aircraft.

While major imports emphasize raw materials and food requirements, the U.S. also purchases manufactured goods abroad. While manufactured items accounted for more than half the imports in 1860, by 1975 they accounted for only slightly more than one-third. Major imports include machinery and vehicles, petroleum, electrical apparatus, iron and steel products, wood pulp and paper products, metals, chemicals, sugar and coffee. Many of these items come from the uuderdeveloped countries of the world.

UNITED STATES EXPORTS AND IMPORTS, 1974 (Million Dollars)

Exports		Imports	
Rank	$ Value	Rank	$ Value
1. Total Machinery	38,189	1. Petroleum & products	24,210
2. Grains and preparations*	11,898	2. Total machinery	11,862
3. Chemicals	8,822	3. Automobiles (and parts)	10,640
4. Automobiles (and parts)	7,878	4. Iron & steel mill products	5,013
5. Aircraft (and parts)	5,766	5. Chemicals	3,991
6. Iron & steel mill products	2,500	6. Nonferrous base metals	3,925
7. Coal	2,487	7. Pulp, paper, and products	2,572
8. Textiles and apparel	2,196	8. Sugar	2,256
9. Cotton	1,335	9. Metal manufactures	2,053
10. Nonferrous base metals and alloys	1,300	10. Coffee	1,504
Total	82,371	Total	68,026

* Including soybeans.

U. S. Foreign Trade. The foreign trade of the United States amounted to $4.2 billion in 1913. Principal participants included Great Britain, an 18% share, Canada 13%, Germany 12.5%, France 7%, and several other nations significant largely in terms of a single commodity—Cuba and sugar, Brazil and coffee.

By 1975, not only had total U.S. foreign trade increased to nearly $200 billion, but the importance of the various countries had changed. Canada continues to develop as a major source of trade, with more than 20% of the total. Other large participants include Japan, with about 10%; West Germany, about 6%; the United Kingdom, about 5%; and Mexico, about 4%.

Internal Commerce of the U. S. Although the United States ranks high in world commerce, the internal or domestic trade is of far greater importance. Within American boundaries, sections of widely diversified economic and geographical character specialize in the production of commodities to which the locality is best adapted. Excess production may be transported to any part of the country, or may be shipped out without any hindrance of toll or tariff except the cost of transportation. The great size of this free market has been a vital factor in American economic development.

Europe's Common Market. The existence of this huge free market in the United States provided the basic argument for the economists and statesmen who created the European Common Market. Western Europe possessed a pool of skilled labor, capital, and population greater than that of the United States, but their potential was not realized because of trade and political barriers. The Treaty of Rome in 1957 provided for gradual reduction of tariffs and aimed at unified labor and social-welfare conditions and freedom to travel, trade, employ, and invest without border hindrances. Political integration was set as the ultimate goal.

Governments as Traders. Meanwhile world commerce contended with a refractory element—the Communist regimes which barred private trading and channeled all exchange of goods through their governments. The element of political policy was thus injected into the global market place. Lacking also was the element of stability since the Communist market might disappear overnight. Commerce between the free world and the Communist powers tended to be dictated by the needs of the latter and by their ability to pay in gold, since the goods they had available for export were severely restricted.

To a limited extent, the proliferation of new and underdeveloped nations had a like effect, since many of them had no individuals or business organizations capable of foreign trade. The rulers perforce set limits on what could or could not be bought or sold.

This situation forced on governments of the United States and other freely trading nations the task of handling a considerable part of the distribution of goods where such nations were involved.

FOREIGN TRADE (COMMERCE) OF LEADING COUNTRIES, 1975

Showing their trade with the United States

Country	Exports		Exports to U.S.		Imports		Imports from U.S.	
	Total ($000,000)	Per Cap. ($)	($000,000)	%	Total ($000,000)	Per Cap. ($)	($000,000)	%
Algeria	4,377	254.50	1,359	29.5	4,035	234.60	632	15.6
Argentina	3,191	131.60	215	6.3	3,656	141.90	628	17.1
Australia	11,575	857.40	1,147	9.9	9,811	726.25	1,816	18.5
Austria	7,518	1002.40	238	3.1	9,319	1252.10	181	1.9
Belgium/Luxembourg	28,807	2880.45	1,190	4.1	30,691	3069.10	2,247	7.3
Bolivia*	548	96.10	89	16.2	196	34.35	138	70.4
Brazil	8,656	82.45	1,464	16.9	13,558	129.10	3,056	22.5
Canada	31,881	1518.10	21,747	67.7	34,306	1559.40	21,756	61.7
Chile	2,408	204.80	138	5.7	1,911	191.10	533	27.8
China (Taiwan)	5,232	337.50	1,938	37.0	6,906	445.50	1,660	24.0
Colombia	1,358	56.55	590	43.4	1,558	64.90	643	41.2
Costa Rico	454	227.05	195	42.9	637	318.50	212	33.2
Czechoslovakia	8,358	597.00	NA	NA	9,081	648.60	NA	NA
Denmark	8,716	1743.25	461	4.5	10,366	2073.20	445	3.8
Ecuador	844	125.95	461	54.6	943	140.70	414	43.9
Egypt	1,402	36.80	28	1.9	3,951	103.95	683	13.0
El Salvador	463	115.80	180	38.8	562	140.50	194	34.5
Finland	5,487	1192.80	148	2.6	7,602	1652.65	261	3.4
France	52,214	1004.10	2,137	4.0	54,247	1043.20	3,031	5.5
Germany, West	91,620	1527.00	5,382	5.7	64,925	1082.00	5,194	8.0
Germany, East	10,088	600.50	NA	NA	11,290	672.00	NA	NA
Ghana	720	72.05	150	20.8	805	80.55	100	12.5
Greece	2,288	254.20	111	4.8	5,457	606.30	450	8.2
Guatemala*	586	97.60	173	29.5	700	116.60	255	36.4
Honduras	283	94.30	145	57.2	400	133.30	151	37.7
Hungary	6,091	609.10	NA	NA	7,176	717.65	NA	NA
India	4,365	7.30	548	12.5	6,094	10.10	1,290	21.1
Indonesia	7,103	54.60	2,221	30.9	4,708	36.20	810	17.2
Iran	20,249	613.60	1,400	14.4	10,343	313.40	3,242	31.0
Iraq	8,756	796.00	19	0.02	2,365	215.00	310	13.1
Ireland	3,177	1024.80	176	5.5	3,768	1215.45	190	5.0
Israel	1,835	539.70	313	17.0	4,140	940.90	1,551	37.4
Italy	34,821	633.15	2,397	6.6	38,366	697.60	2,867	8.0
Japan	48,452	440.40	11,260	23.0	47,825	434.70	9,565	20.0
Korea, Rep. of	4,948	145.50	1,416	28.5	7,275	213.90	1,761	23.6
Libya	6,454	2581.60	1,046	15.6	2,762	1104.80	232	8.3
Mexico	5,821	92.30	3,059	53.0	6,331	105.30	5,144	77.0
Morocco	1,542	88.10	10	0.06	2,560	146.30	200	7.8
Netherlands	35,075	2598.15	1,083	2.8	34,573	2560.00	4,183	11.8
New Zealand	2,152	694.20	246	11.4	3,152	1016.80	414	13.1
Nicaragua	376	167.10	131	34.8	517	229.80	156	30.1
Nigeria	8,078	126.20	3,282	40.6	6,103	98.45	536	8.7
Norway	7,207	1801.75	403	5.5	9,718	2429.50	510	5.2
Pakistan	1,005	13.95	49	4.8	2,125	29.50	372	17.5
Peru	1,514	94.60	NA	NA	1,531	95.70	904	59.0
Philippines	2,241	52.10	754	33.6	3,375	78.50	832	24.6
Poland	10,283	302.45	NA	NA	12,536	380.70	NA	NA
Portugal	1,939	228.10	194	10.0	3,840	451.75	349	9.0
Rumania*	4,874	232.10	NA	NA	5,144	244.95	NA	NA
Singapore	5,376	2443.60	532	9.9	8,133	3696.80	994	12.1
South Africa, Rep. of	12,026	462.50	841	7.0	8,137	312.95	1,302	16.0
Spain	7,691	219.75	831	10.8	16,097	459.90	2,161	13.4
Sweden	17,439	2179.90	877	5.0	17,874	2234.25	925	5.1
Switzerland	3,317	518.30	867	26.1	13,305	2078.90	1,153	8.6
Thailand	2,485	60.60	217	8.7	3,143	76.65	357	11.3
Turkey	1,401	35.00	145	10.3	4,640	116.00	608	13.1
United Kingdom	43,760	781.40	3,784	8.6	53,232	951.10	4,525	8.4
Uruguay*	382	127.30	24	6.2	487	162.30	51	10.4
U.S.S.R.	33,310	130.10	NA	NA	53,262	951.10	NA	NA
Venezuela	10,214	851.15	3,624	35.4	5,359	446.60	2,243	41.8
Yugoslavia	4,061	193.40	260	6.4	7,697	366.50	328	4.2

* 1974

Sources: Data for calculating information from Department of Commerce, Domestic and International Business Administration, and from *Statistical Yearbook* (*UN*), *1976*.

Hence the rise of so-called foreign aid, under which credit or outright grants of money were extended to foreign governments to purchase goods. An example is the sale of American agricultural surpluses to India. Since such countries lacked exportable goods with which to make payment, the United States accepted payment in local currency and left it there on deposit.

Balance of International Payments. This term refers to the net result of a nation's transactions with the outside world in a given period. It is derived from statistics showing to what extent domestically produced goods and services have been exchanged with foreign countries, and how the differences in credits have been financed. The chief factors producing the balance are 1) exchanges of merchandise, services, and income on investments, 2) unilateral transactions like individual gifts and government grants, 3) transfers of long-term capital, and 4) movements of gold and short-term capital.

ECONOMIC DEPENDENCE OF THE UNITED STATES

The United States is more favorably situated in regard to raw materials than any other country. Nevertheless, her high scale of living and enormous consuming power create many needs that cannot be satisfied by materials obtainable within her own territories. The following table presents some of the commodities for which she is dependent chiefly on foreign sources of supply. Those in *italics* are of especial importance for national defense in the event of war. An asterisk (*) appears after those of which there is practically no supply native to the United States.

Material	Chief Uses	Quantity Imported 000 omitted	Chief Sources
Abaca	paper products	36 tons	Philippines
Aluminum	construction of airplanes, automobiles	457 tons	Japan, Canada
*Antimony**	printing glass	2,174 tons	Mexico, Bolivia
Arsenic	pesticides, medicines	13 tons	France, Sweden
Barley	food, livestock feed	2,000 bushels	Canada
Bismuth	glass, clothing, paint, medicines	1,331 lbs.	Japan, Peru, Bolivia
Black Pepper	food seasoning	51,049 lbs.	Indonesia, India, Malaysia
Cadmium	plating for mechanical equipment	5,928 lbs.	Canada, Australia
Chinawood Oil (Tung)	paints, varnishes, insulation	21,000 lbs.	Paraguay, Argentina
Chromite	hard steel, paint	1,350 tons	USSR, S. Africa, Philippines
*Cobalt**	steel alloys, colored enamels	5,200 tons	Belgium, Zaire
Cocoa	candy, beverages	233 tons	Ghana, Brazil
Coconut Oil	food, cooking materials	890 lbs.	Philippines
Coffee*	beverage	2,683 lbs.	Colombia, Brazil, Portugal
Hides and skins	shoes, leather, travel goods	69,000 lbs.	Canada, Brazil, India, New Zealand
Jute	twine, burlap, linoleum, carpet bags	250,000 lbs.	Pakistan, Thailand, India
Kapok	lifeboats, buoys, mattresses	9.8 tons	Thailand, Philippines
Lumber	construction	6,114,000 bd. ft.	Canada
Manganese	structural steel	766 tons	Brazil, West Germany, France, S. Africa
Mercury	electrical apparatus, medicinal agent	3,380 lbs.	Canada, Spain
*Nickel**	steel, electroplating	162,000 tons	Canada, Norway
Nutgalls*	dyeing, inks, color printing	N.A.	China
Nux Vomica*	medicinal agent	N.A.	Korea, Cambodia, India, Laos
Palm Oil	soap, tin plate	900,000 lbs.	Singapore
Petroleum, (crude)	fuel oils, gasoline, lubricants	1,498,181 bar.	Saudi Arabia, Nigeria, Canada
Petroleum, (refined)	gasoline, fuel oils, lubricants	666,858 bar.	Saudi Arabia, Iran, Canada
Platinum	electrical equipment, jewelry, chemical industries	1,900 oz.	Canada, United Kingdom
Rattan*	furniture	N.A.	Indonesia, Philippines, China, Malaysia
Rubber (crude)	footwear tires, electrical equipment	657 tons	Thailand, Ceylon, Indonesia, Liberia, Malaysia
Sisal Hemp	binder twine	N.A.	Mexico, Brazil, Haiti
Tea*	beverage	159,467 lbs.	India, Ceylon, China, Japan
Tin	canning, dyeing, textile manufacturing, solder	43,663 tons	Malaysia, Thailand
Wool (carpet)	rugs	119,600 lbs.[1]	Argentina, Pakistan, India, New Zealand, Australia, Syria, Lebanon, Iraq
Wool (unmanufactured)	clothing	33,600 lbs.	Argentina, Uruguay, Brazil, New Zealand, Australia

Data concerning imports are mostly 1975 figures taken from *Commodity Year Book, 1976*, or 1974 figures taken from *Statistical Abstracts, 1975.* [1] 1968.

COMMERCIAL RAW MATERIALS

By far the most important commercial raw materials are those commodities which are utilized for food, for clothing, for the production of machinery and of power, and for structural purposes. These are obtained from all parts of the earth as contributions from the three kingdoms of nature—the vegetable, the animal, and the mineral.

The following classification is based primarily on this natural division, and secondarily on the purpose for which each commodity is generally employed. In the various groupings are included the most important commercial raw materials, together with representative examples of a vast number which are of minor importance.

VEGETABLE PRODUCTS

Cereals: Wheat—including emmer and spelt—rice, corn, oats, rye, barley, the sorghums, millet, and buckwheat (not a true cereal but used as such).

Other Starchy Foods: Potatoes, yams, sweet potatoes, arrowroot, cassava (tapioca). See *Starch.*

Pulses: Peas, beans, lentils, soy beans.

Sugars: Cane sugar, beet sugar, maple sugar, palm sugar (jaggery), and glucose.

Vegetables: Artichoke, asparagus, beans (string), beet, cabbage, carrot, cauliflower, celery, cucumber, eggplant, endive, garlic, kohl-rabi, leek, lettuce, mushrooms, okra, onion, parsnip, peas (green), pumpkin, radish, rhubarb, spinach, rutabaga, squash, tomato, turnip, and various others.

Fruits: Orchard fruits—apple, apricot, cherry, peach, pear, plum, prune, and quince; various grapes—table, raisin, wine, and currant; berry fruits—blackberry, blueberry, cranberry, currant, gooseberry, huckleberry, loganberry, mulberry, raspberry, and strawberry; melon fruits—cassaba melon, muskmelon, watermelon; citrus fruits—citron, grapefruit, kumquat, lemon, lime, and orange; subtropical fruits—carob (Saint-John's-bread), date, fig, olive, persimmon, and pomegranate; tropical fruits—avocado, banana, guava, mango, papaw, soursop, and prickly pear.

Nuts: Almond (sweet and bitter)—Jordan almonds are a choice hard-shelled variety of sweet almond from Malaga, Spain; chestnut, native to the eastern United States, also imported from southern Europe; cashew nut, from India and Brazil—poisonous until roasted; coconut, commonly grown in tropical countries; filbert, grown in southern Europe; hickory nut, native to the eastern United States; litchi nut, a dried fruit from China; peanut, not a true nut but the fruit of a legume; pecan, both wild and cultivated in the southern United States; pine nuts, oily seeds of pines native to southern Europe and southwestern Asia; pinons, nuts from pines native to the southwestern United States and Mexico; pistachio, grown in Mediterranean countries; and the English walnut, extensively cultivated.

Beverages. The plant materials chiefly used for making beverages are coffee, the cleaned seeds of the coffee tree; cocoa, prepared from the seeds of cacao; maté, the dried leaves of a South American holly; and tea, the variously cured leaves of the Asiatic tea shrub. With these are sometimes grouped fermented beverages, such as beer, wine, sake (Japan), and pulque (Mexico), and also distilled liquors, such as whisky, brandy, rum, gin, mescaline (Mexico), arrack (Orient), and vodka (Russia), which, strictly speaking, are manufactured products.

Timber. Of imported woods, the most valuable include mahogany, teak, lignum-vitæ, Spanish cedar, Circassian walnut, rosewood, or Jacaranda (from Brazil), satinwood (from the East Indies and West Indies), ebony, greenhart (from South America), lancewood (from Jamaica), and rule boxwood (from West Indies and South America).

Fibers. Textile and cordage fibers include cotton, flax, hemp, jute, ramie, manila hemp, sisal hemp, bowstring hemp, sunn hemp, coir, pineapple fiber, and raffia. Among brush fibers are broom corn, piassaba (from the West Indies and from Brazil), saw palmetto (from Florida), and palmyra (from Ceylon). Other fibers or fiber-like products are kapok, or silk cotton; luffa, a vegetable sponge; Spanish moss, from the southern United States, used for upholstery; rattan, from the East Indies, used in making furniture, baskets, and whips. Fibers used for paper making are exceedingly numerous (See *Paper.*). Panama hat straw, or toquilla, is prepared from the young leaves of a South American screw pine.

Alkaloidal Stimulants and Narcotics. These include tobacco, the most extensively used narcotic, cola leaves, chewed by the Indians of South America; pituri leaves, used by the natives of Australia; the kola nut, containing caffeine, chewed by the natives of Africa; betel leaf and betel nut, widely used by Malayan peoples; hashish, from Indian hemp, used by the peoples of southern Asia; and opium, the dried juice of the poppy, used widely in the Orient.

Medicinal Plants. Many plants contain medicinal principles which experience has proved to be of such value that they are employed more or less widely by all civilized nations. Among plants used for their leaves are belladonna, one source of atropin; coca, the source of cocaine; digitalis, or purple foxglove, grown in Europe and in America; and senna, from Egypt and India. Some of the best-known medicinal roots are aconite, hydrastis (golden seal), gentian, ginseng, licorice, may apple, rhubarb, and sarsaparilla.

Among the most highly prized medicinal barks are cascara sagrada, native to California and Oregon, and cinchona, or Peruvian bark, the source of quinine, now obtained chiefly from cultivated trees in Java. Nux vomica (the source of strychnine), chaulmoogra, and the castor oil plant are valued for the medicinal properties of their seeds. Plants yielding medicinal juices include aloes and also the poppy, the source of opium. Among medicinal resins are asafetida, balsam of Peru, and guaiac.

Gums and Resins: Rubber, gutta-percha, balata, chicle, gum arabic, gum Senegal, gum tragacanth, turpentine, rosin, and copal.

Tanning Materials. These include various barks, woods, roots, fruits, and nuts which contain tannin. Among these are oak bark, hemlock bark, chestnut bark and wood, sumac leaves, canaigre root, myrobalans (unripe fruit), divi-divi (seed pods), quebracho wood, gambier (twigs and leaves), mangrove bark, and oak galls.

Dyestuffs: Logwood, fustic, Brazilwood, Lima wood, Osage orange, indigo, archil, and cudbear.

Vegetable Oils. *Drying oils,* used extensively in paints and varnish, include linseed oil, perilla oil, Chinese wood oil (tung oil), candlenut oil, hempseed oil, walnut oil, soy bean oil, poppy-seed oil, and sunflower oil. *Semidrying oils,* used for various purposes, include corn oil, cottonseed oil, sesame oil (benne oil), rape oil (colza oil), olive oil, apricot kernel oil, peach kernel oil, almond oil, castor oil, and peanut oil.

Vegetable Fats. These substances, which are solid at ordinary temperatures, include cocoa butter (See *Chocolate.*), coconut oil, palm oil, palm kernel oil, and Japan wax.

Essential Oils. Many of these form the basis of natural perfumes; as, for example, attar of roses, geranium oil, lemon-grass oil, lavender oil, neroli, ylang-ylang oil, and patchouli oil. Peppermint oil and spearmint oil are widely used for many purposes.

Spices and Condiments: Allspice (or pimento), cinnamon, cloves, mace, mustard, pepper, tonka bean, and vanilla.

ANIMAL PRODUCTS

Food. Beef, pork, mutton, poultry, and game form the chief items in the meat supply of most civilized countries. In some parts of the world, meat from the whale, horse, camel, and reindeer is also used. Eggs, almost universally an important article of food, are a commercial source of albumin and are used also in tanning. Milk is the source of butter, cheese, casein, milk sugar, and various fermented beverages, such as koumiss and leben. Butter, cheese, condensed milk, preserved meats, canned meats, and meat extracts, though often classified as manufactured products, may also be listed here.

Fish, oysters, clams, lobsters, crabs, and shrimps, marketed fresh, dried, canned, or otherwise preserved, are used in great quantities for food. See *Fisheries*.

Animal Oils. Oils used for food include butter, lard, tallow, and oleo oil (See *Oleomargarine.*). Medicinal cod-liver oil is expressed from the livers of freshly caught cod. Large amounts of other fish oils are obtained, especially menhaden oil. (See *Fisheries.*) Sperm oil, valued as a lubricant, is obtained from the sperm whale. Wool wax, widely used in making salves and ointments, is the natural grease from sheep's wool.

Animal Fibers. Wool, produced chiefly by the sheep, is obtained also from the alpaca in Peru and from the Kashmir goat of central Asia. Silk, produced by the silkworm, ranks next in value to wool among animal fibers. Long hair from the tails of cows and from the manes and tails of horses is used in making bows for musical instruments, for weaving into haircloth, and for stuffing mattresses. Short hair from various animals is used as stuffing material and in making plaster. Swine bristles from Russia and China are largely used in making brushes. The hair of the Australian rabbit is one of the most important materials entering into the manufacture of felt hats.

Hides and Skins. See *Leather*.

Furs. The most expensive furs are probably those of the sea otter, the Russian sable, and the silver fox. Among other valuable furs are those of the seal, ermine, marten, weasel, mink, skunk, mole, chinchilla, beaver, muskrat, karakul sheep (yielding the Persian lambskin), various species of fox, wolf, and bear, and the larger cats, such as the lion, the tiger, and the leopard.

Horns, Hoofs, Bones, and Tusks. Ivory is obtained chiefly from the tusks of the elephant but also from the tusks of the hippopotamus, the horn of the narwhal, the tusks of the walrus, and the tusks of the extinct mammoth whose remains are still found in Siberia. Horns and hoofs are utilized for the production of buttons, combs, ornaments, and of cyanide compounds. Bones are used for making buttons and ornaments, for the production of fertilizer, and for the preparation of bone black and bone charcoal.

Bird Products. Besides eggs, the most important bird products include feathers, plumes, edible birds' nests, eider down, and guano (See *Fertilizer.*).

Insect Products. In addition to silk, the most valuable of all, insect products include honey, beeswax, lac, and cochineal.

MINERAL PRODUCTS

The immense number of commercial products obtained from the mineral kingdom may be classified as (1) ores, met ls, and other minerals; (2) fuels; (3) building materials; and (4) gems and precious stones.

COMMUNICATION

By communication is meant the transference of thoughts and of information from person to person. Underlying, as it does, all human cooperation, it has an importance which can scarcely be exaggerated. The initial step, and unquestionably the most important in making possible an unimpeded exchange of ideas, was the invention of spoken and, later, of written language.

A great length of time elapsed during which communication between distant points could be effected only by means of messages, oral or written, which were carried by messengers. The great development of electrical signaling devices and the vast improvements which have taken place during the past century in the means of transportation have reduced to comparative insignificance the time element in communication. With the help of the printing press, radio, and television, they bring to the population of all civilized nations a knowledge of the events of importance in the whole world within a few hours of the time of their occurrence.

Early Postal Systems. The complicated postal organization of today had its origin in the system of private messengers employed by ancient rulers. Each messenger was given a fixed station where he should always hold himself in readiness to receive a message and to carry it to the next post. The emperor Diocletian was apparently the first to establish such a post open to the use of private persons. In the 12th century a commercial post was organized by the Hanse Towns of northern Germany, and in the 13th century a postal system was developed by the University of Paris for the benefit of its students. The national postal system in France was established by Louis XI in 1464.

Postal System in England. In England, private postal systems were used in the 14th century, but it was not until 1533 that Sir Brian Tuke was appointed the first "Master of the Post" by Henry VIII. Improvements in the service were gradually made, but, in 1812, the cost of sending a single sheet varied from 8 cents to 35 cents according to the distance. A money order system was begun in 1792 for the convenience of soldiers and sailors.

Due to reforms initiated by Sir Rowland Hill, a rate of one penny was established throughout the United Kingdom in 1840. The first adhesive postage stamp was issued in May of that year. This one-penny stamp was black and carried the profile of Queen Victoria. It had to be cut from the printed sheet. Perforated stamps were not officially issued until 1854. If the postage was not prepaid by means of a stamp, a double rate was charged upon delivery of the letter. The use of postage stamps made possible the mail box, which was first introduced in 1855.

Universal Postal Union. In 1874 an International Postal Union was organized at Berne, Switzerland. This was followed in 1878 by a larger organization known as the Universal Postal Union, which includes practically all nations on the globe. All these countries are declared to be "a single postal territory for the reciprocal exchange of correspondence." Postal accounts between countries are adjusted every three years by checking the amount of correspondence for a month. In all countries the one-cent stamp, or its equivalent, is green, the two-cent stamp, pink, and the five-cent stamp, blue.

Postal System in America. The general court of Massachusetts in 1639 ordered that the house of Richard Fairbank was to be the official distributing point for overseas mail. In 1691, Thomas Neale was by royal patent granted authority for the establishment and control of an American post, and, in 1693, Andrew Hamilton was appointed the first colonial postmaster-general. In 1707, control of the post was purchased from Neale by the English government, which held it until the Revolution.

Under the new order, Benjamin Franklin was appointed the first postmaster by the Continental Congress in 1775. The first Federal postage stamps were issued in 1847, although in 1845 the postmasters of various large cities were permitted to issue five- and ten-cent stamps at their own expense. Stamped envelopes were first used in 1853.

It was not, however, until 1856 that prepayment was required and stamps came into general use. In 1851 the rate was reduced to three cents up to a distance of 3000 miles, and in 1863 under Lincoln, this rate was established for all distances and free delivery was begun in some of the larger cities. A money order system was established in 1864; postal cards came into use in 1873; a two-cent rate went into effect for the first time in October 1883; a special delivery service, for which an extra charge was made, began in October 1885; and rural free delivery was inaugurated in 1896. In 1971 the Post Office Department was replaced by an independent U.S. Postal Service in the executive branch.

Parcel Post. By the provisions of the general parcel post act which took effect January 1, 1913, and by its subsequent revision, the transportation of parcels within certain limits of size and weighing up to 70 pounds is undertaken by the post office department. By facilitating the cheap transit of merchandise, this service has opened up throughout the entire country a market for goods sent by mail. For rate making purposes, the United States and certain other territories are divided into units of area which are the basis of eight postal zones. The zones represent an area having a mean radial distance of 50, 150, 300, 600, 1000, 1400, 1800, all beyond 1800, miles from the center of any given unit of area which is the mailing point.

The value of the parcel post service is enhanced by the privilege of insuring the contents of the parcel against loss by the payment of a small additional fee. Parcels may also be sent C. O. D., special delivery, or as first class mail.

Air Mail Service. In 1918 the regular use of airplanes was initiated by the United States government for the carrying of air mail. By 1969, each of the 50 states had air mail service and many foreign countries were included in regular air mail service with the United States.

Since the first air mail service, accomplished by the U.S. Army for the government in 1918 with one round trip a day between Washington, D.C. and New York, delivery and receipt of mail by air has grown immensely. From time to time, Congress has authorized increased air mail rates to help the Post Office department reduce operating losses. In 1977 the air mail rate for a letter was 13¢ an ounce and for an air postal or post card, 9¢ each, when mailed from any point in the U.S. to any other point in the U. S. or its possessions. The same air rates apply also to 1) first class letters and cards addressed in care of an APO and/or a Fleet Post Office for delivery outside the U.S., and 2) Canada and Mexico. The air mail rate to all countries besides Canada and Mexico is 31¢ for each half ounce. Aerogrammes may be sent by air to all countries and purchased at the post office for 22¢ each.

Dead Letter Office. Every year about 23,000,000 pieces of mail matter are received by the Post Office so carelessly or incorrectly addressed that they cannot be delivered. These are sent to the Dead Letter Office at Washington, D. C. where, by means of maps and directories, skilled clerks are able to guess correctly the destinations of about one-half the items. The others are opened and those with addresses inside are returned to the sender.

Currency, checks, and money orders amounting to more than $1 million are received annually. Merchandise which cannot be delivered or returned to the sender is sold at auction, letters are burned. and thousands of magazines, picture cards, and holiday cards are sent to hospitals. Insured parcels are held for six months; ordinary parcels for 60 days. Parcel sales are held periodically at each Dead Letter branch post office from two to six times a year. The fees from return postage from unclaimed packages along with the money which was inclosed in some of the letters amounts to about $250,000, which is only $20,000 less than the entire operating expense. The Dead Letter office originated in 1825.

Postal Service in Canada. The postal system of Canada is similar to that of the United States in its main features, and includes the services comprised under the headings of registration, insurance, money orders, postal savings, parcel post, and C. O. D. delivery systems. Rural free delivery was inaugurated in 1908, and an air mail service in 1927. The latter is of especial value in Canada in establishing communication between isolated settlements and the more populous portions of the country. Thus in 1929 an air mail route was established southward from Aklavik, which lies 300 miles within the Arctic Circle.

Telegraphic Communication. Postal communication depends for its speed on the available means of transportation. Although modern air mail service has effected great improvements in speed, it was preceded by Morse's telegraph, which began commercial operations in 1844.

The advantages of a land telegraph system quickly became apparent and in 1861 the first transcontinental system opened between San Francisco and New York. Telegraphic communication between water-separated places was first attempted in 1842 in New York harbor; by 1851, a line crossed the English Channel. After unsuccessful efforts, the first transatlantic cable was completed in 1866. Since then, 21 cables (about 1½" thick) have been laid in the North Atlantic. A lesser number cross parts of the Pacific Ocean.

Telephony. Vocal communication over long distances became possible when Bell invented the telephone in 1876. Improvements on the original device were made by many of the greatest inventors of the world. The advantages of the telephone have been so obvious that in the United States there is an average of one telephone for every 1.5 persons. Sweden has one telephone for every 1.6 persons. In the per capita use of telephones the following nations rank in order after the United States and Sweden: Switzerland, Canada, New Zealand, Denmark, United Kingdom, Finland, Norway, Australia, the Netherlands, and Japan.

COMMUNICATIONS OF PRINCIPAL COUNTRIES
(add 000's)

Country	Telephones*	Radio Sets*	Television†
United States	143,972	368,000	121,100
Japan	39,405	70,794	25,500
United Kingdom	20,536	39,000	17,725
Germany, Fed. Rep.	18,767	20,586	17,600
U.S.S.R.	15,782	110,300	50,000
Canada	12,454	19,133	9,800
France	12,405	17,034	13,712
Italy	13,695	12,448	12,805
Sweden	5,178	262	4,115
Spain	7,043	8,000	6,125
Australia	5,000	2,815	4,250
Netherlands	4,679	3,811	3,545
Switzerland	3,790	2,003	1,800

* For 1974. Source: *Statistical Yearbook, 1975* (*UN*).
† For 1975. Source: *Encyclopedia Year Book, 1976*.

Teletypewriter. A service was inaugurated in 1931 by which two-way communication by typewriter became possible over telephone or telegraph wires. By this system, two people, equipped with teletypewriters, on being connected through a central exchange, can converse in type, the words of both parties being recorded for future reference. This instrument, operating at about 60 words per

GROWTH OF UNITED STATES POSTAL SERVICE, 1900-1975

Item	1900	1920	1940	1960	1975
Post offices, no.	76,688	52,638	44,095	35,238	30,754
City carriers, no.	15,322	36,142	58,551	109,749	166,946
Money orders	$255,670,027	$1,365,659,884	$2,094,543,479	$5,030,614,549	$5,194,000,000
Gross revenue	$102,354,579	$437,150,212	$766,948,627	$3,276,818,000	$11,585,400,000
Gross expenditures	$107,740,267	$454,322,609	$807,629,180	$3,873,953,000	$12,574,205,000
Total Number Pieces of Mail Handled	7,129,990,000	....	27,749,467,000	63,674,609,000	89,270,000,000

Source: *Annual Report of the Postmaster General.*

minute, is employed extensively also for one-way communication, where it is desirable to send the same message to numerous places throughout the country. Market quotations, financial news, and weather reports for airports are broadcast by wire in this manner.

Radio Communication. With the beginning of the 20th century, radiotelegraphy became a practical means of transmitting messages, so that ships at sea were enabled to keep in continuous communication with each other and with many stations ashore. Navigation became at once more safe and more accurate, because a captain could obtain the exact time and, during a fog, could usually obtain his bearings from a land station equipped with direction-finding apparatus known as the radio compass. All seagoing passenger ships must now be equipped with radio apparatus.

Long distance conversation by means of the radiotelephone became possible in 1915. Owing to developments made in the research laboratory of the American Telephone and Telegraph Company, the wire systems may be used in connection with the radiotelephone. By this method it is now possible to establish communication with a properly equipped ocean liner at sea from any commercial telephone in North America. On January 7, 1927, a regular transatlantic radiotelephone service was inaugurated between New York and London. This was followed by extensions which made possible direct vocal communication between any telephone in North America with any telephone in Europe. See *Cable, Submarine; Radio; Telegraph; Telephone; Phototelegraphy.*

Newspapers. The preceding articles have outlined the development of two-way communication. But of no less significance for the world's history is the growth of one-way communication from its primitive forms to the high-speed printing presses and radio broadcasts of the present day.

The prototype of the modern newspaper is to be seen in the *Acta Diurna* ("Daily Events") issued during the Roman Empire and posted in a public place. Copies were made by hand and dispatched to subscribers at a distance.

The invention of printing made possible the first genuine newspaper to be regularly published. It was the *Avisa Relation oder Zeitung*, printed first in 1609 in Germany. In 1622 appeared the first newspaper in England, *The Weekly Newes from Italy, Germany, etc.*, published in London. The earliest news sheet to appear in the Western Hemisphere was the *Relación*, issued in 1594 at Lima, Peru, but it was not until 1620 that a regular newspaper was published there. The first regular newspaper in British America was *The Boston News-Letter*, begun in 1704.

Before the days of the telegraph, enterprising newsmen employed carrier pigeons, fast ships, pony expresses, and even semaphore signaling systems for gathering news. With the rise of telegraph and telephone systems, this task was greatly simplified and was put on an organized basis. See *Newspaper Press Associations.* With the development of phototelegraphy, it has become possible to transmit news in picture form with practically the same speed as verbal messages. Improvements in printing presses make it possible now to issue editions containing latest news within a few minutes.

Broadcasting. Within the decade 1920–30, a second means of rapid dissemination of information grew into effective rivalry with newspapers. This was the system of radio broadcasting.

Experimental dissemination of speech and music from a central sending station to owners of receiving sets began some years prior to 1920. Lee De Forest was one of the leaders in this development. Station KDKA, operated by the Westinghouse Electric and Manufacturing Company at East Pittsburgh, Pa., broadcast the presidential election returns in 1920. The popularity of this broadcast led the way for a phenomenal increase in the number of receiving sets owned and for a corresponding increase in broadcasting stations. By 1940, there was an average of one radio receiving set for each 2.4 persons in the United States, and programs for every taste and purpose had become routine.

By utilizing telephone wires, chains of stations may be connected so as to send out identical programs. In this manner, nation-wide and world-wide "hook-ups" afford opportunities for statesmen, entertainers, or advertisers to reach the ears of millions of listeners. By 1940, there were 675 broadcasting stations in the United States. Canada and Russia ranked next in number, the total for the world being a little fewer than 2000.

Radio broadcasting has remained an important means of communication even with the introduction of television in 1939, when the first station (WRGB) began operating in Schenectady, New York. By 1976 there were 7,307 radio stations operating in the United States, a 110% increase since 1960. Television stations increased from 50 in 1950 to 961 in 1975. Nearly every city in the U.S. is served by one of the three major networks: the American Broadcasting Company, the Columbia Broadcasting System and the National Broadcasting Company. In addition, there were 152 non-commercial stations in operation at the end of 1975. By 1973, more than 368 million radios and 120 million televisions were in use in the U.S.

Communication Satellites. These are satellites of the earth which (1) have an approximately circular orbit and travel at such a speed that they remain a constant distance above a given point on the earth's surface and (2) are able to receive, amplify, and reflect electrical impulses produced on the earth by radio and television transmitters. By means of a number of such satellites properly spaced, impulses may be transmitted from any point on earth and reflected to any point without having to contend with difficulties created by the curvature of the earth's surface. The first such satellite designed as a part of this system was Early Bird, launched April 6, 1965. Since that time the growth of the communications satellite system has been spectacular. In 1975, 15 satellites were launched by governments, private industries and international organizations.

TRANSPORTATION

Transportation is conducted chiefly by the use of vehicles operated upon the water, upon the land, and, more recently, through the air. Water transportation was early conducted by means of sailing vessels. Land transportation, except upon pack animals, required the construction of roads and railways, as well as the invention and improvement of appropriate vehicles.

Sailing Vessels. Long before the Christian era, the Egyptians, the Phœnicians, and the Greeks made use of sails to propel the small vessels of their time. To a large extent the Greeks, and especially the Romans, propelled by oars the ocean craft with which they navigated the Mediterranean. In the larger boats, called galleys, the oars were arranged in two or three rows or banks. The largest type of vessel widely used in ancient times for commercial or war purposes was the trireme, equipped with three banks of oars. The life of the oarsmen in these galleys was a hard one, and slaves were commonly employed. This practice gave rise to the term "galley slave."

The sailing vessels employed by the Venetians, Italians, Spanish, Portuguese, Danes, Norsemen, and the early English navigators were small craft, which seldom ventured far from sight of land. But beginning with the 14th century, the increasing use of the mariner's compass made it possible for sailing vessels to make voyages of great length.

According to present standards, the ships then employed seem small. Few people now living would willingly undertake a transatlantic voyage in a ship of the size of the *Mayflower*, in which the Pilgrims, early in the 17th century, came to their new home in America. But, in small sailing vessels of these or similar types, men in those days were making voyages halfway round the world, and, in a few instances, daring sailors circumnavigated the globe.

Steamships. The great revolution in transportation came when mechanical power was substituted for wind power on the ocean and for muscle power on the land. In performing the service of transportation, mechanical power was first applied to vessels. As early as 1787, John Fitch, a Pennsylvania farmer, propelled a boat on the Delaware by steam power. The *Charlotte Daudas* in 1802 towed two vessels of 140 tons 3½ miles an hour against a strong wind in the Forth and Clyde canal. Robert Fulton five years later ran the *Clermont* from New York to Albany by steam power and demonstrated the practical success of steam navigation.

A few years more were to pass before a vessel crossed the ocean entirely by steam power. The first transatlantic voyage of a steamer was the one made by the *Royal William*, which sailed from Quebec to the Isle of Wight in 1833. This was a wooden vessel, but in 1845 an iron steamer, the *Great Britain*, built by I. K. Brunel, a celebrated British engineer, was put in operation upon the transatlantic service.

The latter vessel is notable also because it was the first large merchant ship driven with a screw propeller. While its basic principle had long been known, the modern practical screw propeller was invented almost simultaneously in 1836 by Francis B. Smith, an English farmer, and by John Ericsson, a Swedish engineer.

Highways. The extensive use of vehicles upon the land could not precede the building of roads. The earliest road building on a large scale was carried on by the Romans. By maintaining order and by building permanent highways in the lands about the Mediterranean and in far-away Britain, the Romans made possible the development of Western civilization.

The first of the modern nations to undertake road building on an extensive scale was France. Beginning in 1597 under Sully, this progressive country proceeded to construct 15,000 miles of surfaced road. Colbert, who became prime minister in 1661, introduced the corvée system of forced labor upon the roads. The method was bad, but it gave France good roads in advance of other nations.

Two Scottish engineers, Thomas Telford and John L. McAdam, who did their work between 1800 and 1830, have fixed their names permanently to types of roads now largely built. Both men emphasized the necessity of providing adequate drainage for roads. Telford roads have a foundation of large broken stones surfaced by more finely broken or crushed rock; macadam roads are built without the foundation of larger stones. Hard surfaced roads are now constructed of the following materials: Sand clay, gravel, water bound macadam, surface treated macadam, bituminous macadam, cement concrete, brick and other block paving materials. The development of the motor car has given great impetus to road construction.

Canals. Canals are nearly as old as human history. The Assyrians built them. The Egyptians connected the Nile with the Red Sea by a canal. The Chinese are said to have constructed canals more than 2000 years ago. They built their Grand Canal, a system about 1000 miles long, in the 13th century. In the 15th century the famous artist, Leonardo da Vinci, invented the canal lock which was introduced into the canals of Milan. France began her existing system of canals early in the 17th century. England built her canals in the 18th century. In the first half of the 19th century numerous canals were built in North America.

Along with the construction of canals went the canalization of rivers until various countries, such as France and England, were equipped with a coordinated system of canalized rivers connected by canals. During the early development of the United States and Canada, however, it was impossible, because of physical obstacles, to create a fully co-ordinated system of inland waterways.

Railways, Steam and Electric. Before the system of inland navigation was completely worked out in the United States and Canada, the superiority of the railroad had been demonstrated. In 1829, the steam locomotive was perfected by the English engineer, George Stephenson, whose famous "Rocket" was successfully developed. By 1830, the Baltimore and Ohio, the Mohawk and Hudson, predecessor of the present New York Central, and a few other railroad systems began to operate in a small way. The completion of the Union Pacific in 1869 opened the first transcontinental span of railroad in America.

By 1890 the electric railway became commercially important for its passenger travel and cargo transport. Today, because of its cleanliness in operation and speed, it is utilized in mountainous areas throughout the world where hydroelectric power is available and on such heavily travelled passenger lines as in Washington and New York.

OCEAN TRANSPORTATION

Ocean Vessels in Colonial Times. The *Mayflower*, in which the Pilgrims came to America, was a typical sailing vessel of its time. It was a three-masted, square-rigged ship, only 100 feet long, and between 20 and 25 feet wide. It was registered as of 180 tons burden or, as it would be measured today, of about 160 tons gross register. Aboard this ship were 102 Pilgrims and the crew. The *Speedwell*, which started across the ocean with the *Mayflower* but which had to turn back, was only one-third the capacity of the *Mayflower*.

At the beginning of the 19th century, many ships were owned and operated by the merchant princes of America; as, for example, Elias Haskett Derby of Salem, Mass., and Stephen Girard of Philadelphia. The ships were square-rigged sailing vessels—ships and barks with three masts and brigs with two masts—of 100 or 200 tons register, a few being as large as 300 tons. The American merchants, lumbermen, planters, and fishermen of that period usually operated their own vessels instead of employing the services of common carriers. Derby, with his fleet of small sailing vessels, built up an extensive trade with the East Indies. Stephen Girard used forty sailing ships to carry on his trade with the West Indies and other parts of the world. The small vessels which these men used were well adapted to the service requirements of their time and brought fame and wealth to their owners.

Common Carriers on the Ocean. In American commerce, the common carrier on the ocean dates from 1816, when the Black-Ball Line was established from New York to England. Even in Great Britain the common carrier was hardly known until the beginning of the 19th century. For hundreds of years men had owned ships for hire or for charter to those who desired to use them, but transportation services on the ocean were not organized and conducted by common carriers until the early 1800s. The early common-carrier lines employed sailing vessels, but, from about 1840 in England and from about 1870 in America, steamship lines began to replace sailing vessels.

American Clipper Ships. In the 1840's the Cunard and other British companies began to use steamships and iron vessels. Thereupon the shipbuilders and seamen of America sought to increase the size and speed of the wooden sailing vessel so as to enable it to compete successfully with its new rival. Out of this competition grew the famous American clipper ships of the late 1840's and early 1850's. These were square-rigged sailing vessels, some of them between 2000 and 3000 tons gross register—fifteen times the size of the *Mayflower*. They derived their name from their long, overhanging prow and their sharp lines forward.

For a time the swift-sailing clippers held their own in competition with the steamship. But, as the marine engine became more efficient and iron and steel vessels of increasing dimensions were constructed, sailing tonnage rapidly declined. The last serious effort to enable the sailing vessel to maintain its place on the high seas was made at the close of the 19th century. About that time huge six- and seven-masted, steel-hulled sailing vessels of over 5000 tons register were built. Some of these vessels could carry 7000 tons of cargo.

Ocean Steamships. The steamship has had an interesting history. The marine engine, first successfully employed in the 1830's to propel vessels entirely across the Atlantic, was installed in wooden vessels with paddle wheels. English builders began to use the screw propeller for transoceanic service in the 1840's. It was more than a decade later before American builders substituted the screw for the less efficient paddle wheels. Indeed, even some of the British lines, such as the Cunard, kept to the use of paddle wheels until after 1860. The celebrated *Great Eastern*, completed in 1859, was equipped both with screw and with paddle wheels. This ship marked the transition from the older to the newer type of steam vessel. The *Great Eastern* was too large to be successfully driven by the engines of its day.

The Marine Engine. Most steamships are equipped with the inverted direct-acting marine engine. This type was used first in 1854, and most of the early engines were single expansion, although from the beginning some double expansion engines

FOREIGN COMMERCE AT SELECTED U.S. PORTS: 1974

(Figures in thousands of short tons of cargo)

PORT	IMPORTS	EXPORTS
Baltimore Harb. & Channels, Md.	25,231	12,876
Baton Rouge, La.	12,427	7,660
Beaumont, Tex.	6,205	4,232
Charleston Harbor, S.C.	3,113	1,302
Coos Bay, Oreg.	1	5,467
Corpus Christi, Tex.	11,143	4,598
Galveston, Tex.	1,093	4,110
Houston, Tex.	18,763	15,908
Jacksonville Harbor, Fla.	5,329	1,707
Long Beach Harbor, Calif.	11,943	6,125
Los Angeles Harbor, Calif.	10,463	3,348
Marcus Hook & vicinity, Pa.	9,515	146
Mobile Harbor, Ala.	9,416	3,963
New Castle & vicinity, Del.	4,652	—
New Orleans, La.	13,537	37,188
Norfolk Harbor, Va.	8,913	33,345
Paulsboro & vicinity, N.J.	13,191	63
Philadelphia Harbor, Pa.	33,112	6,025
Port Arthur, Tex.	7,789	3,021
Port Everglades Harbor, Fla.	3,778	319
Portland Harbor, Maine	22,791	17
Port of Boston, Mass.	8,397	881
Port of Longview, Wash.	331	3,986
Port of Newport News, Va.	1,063	10,482
Port of New York, N.Y. & N.J.	58,666	7,862
Port of Portland, Oreg.	2,245	6,821
Richmond Harbor, Calif.	3,432	634
San Juan Harbor, P.R.	4,208	451
Savannah Harbor, Ga.	4,252	1,981
Seattle Harbor, Wash.	3,670	2,020
Tacoma Harbor, Wash.	2,178	3,169
Tampa Harbor, Fla.	5,803	12,883

Source: U.S. Corps of Engineers.

were constructed. The triple expansion marine engine made its appearance in 1881. However, it was not until 1894, when the *St. Louis* and the *St. Paul* of the American Line were built by the Cramps of Philadelphia, that the quadruple expansion marine engine was constructed.

During this same year, 1894, an entirely new type of engine, the turbine, was also applied to the propulsion of vessels. The first large ocean vessel to be equipped with turbines was the *Carmania* of the Cunard Line, built in 1905.

The Diesel Engine. Earlier types of marine engines are, however, being displaced by an entirely different kind of engine, which is far more efficient and requires much less fuel. This is the internal combustion engine, named after its inventor, Rudolf Diesel. This engine has no boilers or furnaces but burns oil as fuel in the cylinders. The principal limitation upon the immediate use of the Diesel engine is its relatively large cost, but, in 1927, the tonnage of new ships being equipped with this type of engine exceeded for the first time that of steamship construction. See *Internal Combustion Engine*.

The Diesel driven engines were extensively constructed and used in World War II and proved so efficient that in 1948 practically every major railroad line in America had Diesel engines on order.

Ocean Leviathans. The large vessels of today have little resemblance to the ocean vessels of a century ago. The remarkable increase in the size of vessels is indicated by the developments of the first thirty years of the 20th century. The *Mauretania* (I), which began operation in 1908, was considered a marvel because she registered nearly 30,700 tons gross. She held the transatlantic speed record until 1929. In 1910 the *Olympic* was launched. This ship's length was slightly over 850 feet; its gross registered tonnage was 46,439.

Then, in 1912 and shortly thereafter, came the *Imperator* (renamed the *Berengaria*), the *Vaterland* (renamed the *Leviathan*), and the *Bismarck* (renamed the *Majestic*), all approximately 900 feet long.

The *Bremen* (1st), also about 900 feet long, was launched in 1929. It crossed the Atlantic in nearly 9 hours less time than the *Mauretania*. The first liner to exceed this length substantially was the *Normandie*, (renamed *Lafayette*), which was launched in 1932, and later burned in New York harbor. The greatest speed attained by any Atlantic (screw) steamship was 35.59 knots per hour in 1952 by the American-built liner *United States* on her passage from New York to Bishop's Rock in 3 days, 10 hours, and 40 minutes, a total of 3144 sea miles.

Oil Tankers. An outstanding development of marine traffic is the oil tanker. The evolution of super-tankers reflects increased world demand for petroleum products and a drastic reduction in transport costs. When the 38,000-ton *W. Alton Jones* joined the Cities Service fleet in June 1954, it was the largest tanker afloat. By 1960, the *Universe Apollo*, a 106,416-ton super-tanker built in Japanese shipyards by a U.S. company, exceeded in tonnage any other vessel. The largest super-tankers are now 1135 feet long, with a tonnage of 327,000 deadweight tons. Tankers of nearly a million tons are now on order. The world's tanker fleet has grown to more than 3,825 vessels and total capacity has risen to about 150 million tons. The super-tanker has been developed to transport more economically the oil products of the Middle East to the industrial powers. Japan is the world leader in construction of the tankers.

The majority of the world's tanker fleets are controlled by individuals such as the Onassis family and Stavros Niarchos, the Greek shipowners, and Daniel Ludwig, owner of National Bulk Carriers, Inc., an American firm. Major oil companies operate about 30 per cent of the fleet and national governments 10 per cent.

Although some countries may appear to have large merchant fleets most of the ships using their flags are owned by foreigners. The Liberian government, for example, requires only a small registration fee and an almost nominal annual charge. They maintain no control over the operation of ships flying the Liberian flag. Ships registered in Panama have the advantages of low fees and lenient labor laws.

The American Marine. The British colonists in America were a maritime people. They had to build ships in order to market their products in the West Indies and in Europe. With low-priced material for shipbuilding from the abundant forests, American shipping prospered until the Civil War.

During the Civil War there was a shrinkage of nearly a million tons in American shipping on the high seas. Four-fifths of this shrinkage was due to war losses and to the transfer of American vessels to foreign flags to escape the hazards of war. Moreover, this blow to the American marine came at the time when the steamship was taking the place of the sailing vessel, and when iron was supplanting wood in the shipyards of the world.

The American merchant marine of 1860 was composed largely of wooden sailing vessels; by 1870, the marine engine provided the steamship with a basis for superiority over the sailing vessel. The American marine began a decline that was to continue to the present due to the relatively high cost of shipbuilding and operation in the U.S. Generally, this reflects high labor costs and expensive material costs. Federal subsidization of construction and operating expenses amounting to 40 to 50 per cent of the total cost is required.

In 1975, the U.S. operated 3.9% of the world's 22,600 merchant vessels. In 1968, the U.S. operated 21.5% of the combination passenger-cargo vessels, 14% of the freighters, 8.7% of the tankers, and 2.8% of the bulk carriers. Of the 622,900,000 tons of cargo shipped and received by the U.S. in 1973, only 6.4% was carried on U.S. vessels. In 1950, U.S. vessels carried 39.3% of the much smaller total tonnage.

WORLD'S MERCHANT MARINE

Flag	Merchant Fleet as of June 30, 1975 (In 1000 tons)		
	Number	Gross Tons	Dwt. Tons
United States	891	12,359	17,608
Albania	10	50	68
Algeria	27	212	288
Argentina	158	1,310	1,805
Australia	88	1,032	1,492
Austria	19	77	115
Bangladesh	15	82	119
Belgium	76	1,265	2,000
Brazil	256	2,583	4,098
Bulgaria	114	851	1,230
Burma	10	58	73
Canada	69	365	503
Chile	44	390	588
China (Rep.)	370	2,763	3,994
China (Nat'l)	153	1,382	2,117
Colombia	38	212	281
Costa Rica	1*	5*	8*
Cuba	61	404	544
Cyprus	575	3,302	4,839
Czechoslovakia	12	123	180
Denmark	314	4,179	6,997
Ecuador	16	122	170
Egypt	57	287	402
Ethiopia	5†	35†	52†
Finland	186	1,740	2,740
France	436	10,382	17,740
Germany (West)	620	8,110	12,948
Germany (East)	147	1,180	1,706
Ghana	19	127	166
Greece	1,802	22,118	36,563
Honduras	11	52	53
Hungary	14	46	64
Iceland	26	50	73
India	301	4,065	6,39[illegible]
Indonesia	164	595	750
Iran	39	458	696
Iraq	17	278	455
Ireland	17	164	247
Israel	49	453	587
Italy	630	9,772	15,427
Ivory Coast	17	124	170
Japan	2,033	36,090	60,720
Korea (South)	154	1,294	2,154
Kuwait	39	936	1,617
Lebanon	46	139	194
Liberia	2,491	66,709	125,308
Malaysia	24	322	459
Mexico	49	465	689
Monaco	4†	35†	51†
Morocco	19	62	93
Netherlands	442	5,107	7,793
New Zealand	35	121	160
Nicaragua	5†	14†	21†
Nigeria	18	118	170
Norway	985	26,054	45,180
Pakistan	55	479	633
Panama	1,499	12,972	20,809
Peru	41	358	536
Philippines	153	781	1,123
Poland	285	2,542	3,726
Portugal	106	1,090	1,625
Rumania	92	747	1,118
Saudi Arabia	20	66	85
Singapore	376	3,926	6,295
Somalia	243	1,810	2,625
South Africa	56	451	579
Spain	437	4,599	7,642
Sweden	325	7,125	11,968
Switzerland	26	233	342
Thailand	28	149	244
Tunisia	12	37	52
Turkey	106	847	1,229
United Kingdom	1,592	32,240	53,121
Uruguay	17	155	240
U.S.S.R.	2,375	13,920	17,758
Venezuela	42	417	597
Yugoslavia	218	1,784	2,586
Zaire	10	96	137
Total	22,591	320,275	530,669

* 1968 † 1969

Source: Maritime Administration, U.S. Dept. of Commerce.

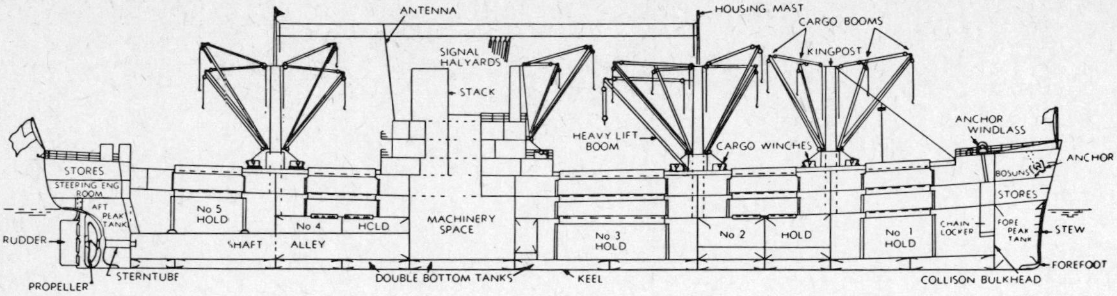

TYPICAL CARGO VESSEL, UNITED STATES MERCHANT MARINE

During the year 1935 the water-borne foreign commerce of the United States was valued at $3,786,000,000, of which 35.8 per cent was carried in American vessels and 64.2 per cent in foreign. If the commerce is measured by tonnage, however, the proportion of the total commerce carried in ships of American registry rises to approximately 40 per cent, indicating that a larger amount of goods bulky in relation to their value, such as grain and petroleum, are carried in American ships. These figures show clearly that, in the overseas commerce of the United States, American vessels in 1935 were playing a minor rôle. This rôle, which had diminished steadily since 1830, expanded remarkably during and immediately after World War I, then fell, but climbed precipitately during World War II.

TRANSPORTATION ON LAKES, RIVERS, AND CANALS

River Navigation. Long before men had the capital or the knowledge required for the construction of highways, and centuries before railroads were thought of, rivers and lakes were used wherever possible for inland transportation. Not only in ancient Egypt, Babylonia, and China, but in modern European countries, such as Austria, Germany, France, Holland, England, and others having navigable streams, the rivers were the only avenues over which traffic could move from interior points to seaboard markets.

For a long time rivers were used without improvement. Later their channels were improved by the removal of obstacles and, to some extent, by the construction of dams, locks, and canals past the rapids in the streams. The importance of rivers as avenues of inland transportation in Europe during the middle ages is indicated by the practices established by the feudal barons. These medieval rulers often maintained their power by constructing castles and barriers along the rivers. Possessing these strategic strongholds, they secured their revenues by exacting tolls from all those who used the streams for commercial purposes.

Canal History. As a result of improving their rivers and of constructing canals during the 17th and the 18th century, Holland, France, and England in turn acquired the economic leadership of other European countries. By building canals to connect their natural waterways, each of these countries was able to develop industrially, to accumulate capital, and successively to play an important rôle in international affairs.

Canal construction in the Netherlands required no special engineering skill, and it was to be expected that the people of that country would extend their numerous natural waterways by artificial channels. In countries like France and England, however, superior engineering skill was required. To France first credit must be given, for in that country as early as 1605, during the reign of Henry IV, construction was begun on the Briare canal to connect the Seine and the Loire rivers. It took until 1642 to finish the work. In 1675 the Orleans canal connected the same rivers by another route, and in 1681 the celebrated Languedoc canal was completed, connecting the Bay of Biscay with the Mediterranean. The summit level of this canal was 600 feet above the sea.

The greatest names in English canal history are Francis, duke of Bridgewater, and his engineer, James Brindley. The Bridgewater canal, connecting Manchester and Liverpool, was begun in 1759. During the succeeding 75 years one inland canal after another was constructed in England and Scotland until the principal streams of the island were connected by a network of waterways. Until after the middle of the 19th century, the waterways of Great Britain, France, and of several other European countries were far more important as freight carriers than were the railways.

Canals in the United States. River and canal transportation in the United States dates from colonial days. The first great leader in the development of inland waterways was George Washington. Washington was a surveyor, and the knowledge he gained in the French and Indian war, which took him as far west as the Ohio river, gave him a lifelong interest in waterways. In 1774, before the Revolution, he brought about the establishment of a company, chartered by Virginia and Maryland, for the improvement of the Potomac river. The ultimate purpose of this company was to connect the Chesapeake bay and the Ohio river by a canal, if possible, or at least by a portage road westward from Cumberland on the Potomac river.

The Revolutionary War interrupted the plans of the colonies for joining the Potomac and Ohio. However, upon the termination of the Revolution, Washington again returned to the prosecution of the project, only to be interrupted once more by being called to the presidency of the new republic. Much later, and in a different manner than Washington had planned, the Chesapeake bay and the Ohio river were connected by the construction of the Baltimore and Ohio railroad which reached Wheeling on the Ohio river in 1851. Forty years earlier, a highway, called the National Pike, had joined the two waterways.

The first man to plan a comprehensive system of inland navigation and of inland waterways and highways in the United States was Albert Gallatin, who for twelve years served as secretary of the treasury under Jefferson and Madison. In the year 1808 Gallatin made a report to Congress outlining

SOME IMPORTANT CANALS

Name	Location	Length (miles)	Width (feet)*	Minimum Depth (feet)†	Number of Locks	Opened	Approximate Cost
Albert	Antwerp-Liège, Belgium	76	52.5	11.5	6	1939	$ 80,000,000
Amsterdam Ship	Ijsselmeer—North Sea, Netherlands	16.7	164	32.1	5	1876	12,700,000
Cape Cod	Buzzards Bay—Barnstable Bay	7.68	250	27	none	1914	13,500,000
Chesapeake-Delaware	Delaware and Maryland	13.63	24	19	none	1829	‡9,000,000
Chicago Drainage and Ship	Chicago—Lockport, Ill.	38.6	174	22	1	1900	55,250,000
Corinth	Gulf of Corinth—Ægina Gulf	4	69	26	none	1893	13,750,000
Cronstadt	Leningrad—Bay of Cronstadt	18.75	275	22	none	1884	10,000,000
Hohenzollern	Berlin—Stettin, Germany	136	32	9.8	19	1914	12,500,000
Houston Ship	Galveston Bay—Houston, Texas	50	150	30	none	1925	20,000,000
Kaiser Wilhelm (Kiel)	Baltic—North Sea, Germany	61	147.6	36	2	1895	95,000,000
Lake Washington	Seattle—Puget Sound	8	80	34	1	1916	3,500,000
Languedoc	Garonne R.—Mediterranean, France	148	19.7	6.5	119	1681	3,500,000
Manchester	Manchester—Mersey River, England	35.5	80	28	4	1894	90,000,000
Moscow-Volga	U.S.S.R. Moscow to Volga River	80	279	18	11	1937	
New Orleans	Mississippi River—Lake Pontchartrain	5.5	300	30	1	1923	20,000,000
New York Barge	Lake Erie—Hudson River	540.8	44.44	12	57	1918	168,000,000
Panama	Through Isthmus of Panama	50.5	110**	41	6	1914	400,000,000
Port Arthur	Taylor's Bayou—Sabine Pass, Texas	7	150	26	none	1899	1,500,000
Sabine Neches	Sabine River—Port Arthur Canal	23	150	30	1	1926	18,100,000
Sault Ste. Marie, U. S.	Lake Superior—Lake Huron	1.6	100	25	1	1896	17,500,000
Sault Ste. Marie, Can.	Lake Superior—Lake Huron	1.41	60	19.5	1	1895	5,000,000
Suez	Mediterranean to Red Sea	104.5	196	46	none	1869	136,000,000
Great Lakes Canals, including St. Lawrence Seaway							
Lachine	Lachine—Montreal, St. Lawrence R.	8.7	45	14	5	1826	14,043,000
Soulanges	St. Lawrence River	14.6	45	15	5	1899	7,897,000
South Cornwall	St. Lawrence River at Cornwall Is.	2	500	29.5	none	1958	17,000,000
Trent	Georgian Bay—Lake Ontario	275.4	33	6	42	1826	19,951,000
Welland Ship	Lake Ontario—Lake Erie	27.6	80	30	8	1930	131,860,000
Wiley-Dondero	St. Lawrence R., south of Long Sault Island	9	442	27.5	2	1958	11,000,000
Williamsburg	St. Lawrence River	12.5	45	14	6	1847	13,550,000

*Width of locks or bottom of channel. †A depth greater than 20 feet indicates a ship canal. ‡Converted, 1926, from lock to sea-level canal. **300 feet minimum through the Divide.

in detail a plan for a system of inland waterways and of highways extending throughout the then settled portion of the United States. But again an armed conflict, the War of 1812, interrupted transportation development.

History of "Internal Improvements." During the War of 1812–15 the United States had great difficulties in conducting land campaigns. The practical failures of most of the land campaigns of that war made it clear to everyone that both military and economic considerations demanded the development of transportation facilities. The railroad had not been invented, and the public naturally turned to improving the rivers, constructing canals, and building highways. The movement for "internal improvements" was led by the ardent young statesman Henry Clay, and was supported by John Quincy Adams. For a time, leaders of the South, such as John C. Calhoun, advocated Federal support for canals and roads.

But, from 1820 on, the conflict over slavery and state rights caused the leaders of the South to oppose internal improvements by direct action of the Federal government. During the administration of John Quincy Adams, 1825–29, the Federal government gave active support to canal and road building. But after Andrew Jackson became president he supported the strict constructionists, and took the position that the Federal government could not constitutionally carry on works of internal improvement within the states. His popularity and powerful personality put an end to the policy of Federal aid for canals and roads.

During the year that Andrew Jackson was inaugurated president, the construction of railroads was begun in the United States. Within a decade it became evident that the railroads were to be efficient carriers of freight as well as of passengers, and that the inland waterways must at least share their traffic with the railroads. Indeed, as time went on, the waterways lost most of this traffic to the rival railroads. Nevertheless, the states which had begun works of internal improvements during the two decades following the War of 1812 continued to carry on such works until the Civil War and in some cases beyond that period. See table *Some Important Canals*.

River and Harbor Works. The Civil War settled the controversy as to the power of the Federal government. After 1865 no question was raised as to the power of the United States to expend funds upon the improvement of harbors, upon the channels of the Hudson, the Mississippi, the Ohio, and other rivers, and upon the connecting channels and the ports of the Great Lakes. From 1870 on, the Federal government regularly appropriated funds for rivers and harbors.

River Traffic. Railroads are now so generally used for freight traffic and passenger travel that it is hard to realize the great role played by the Mississippi, Missouri, Ohio, Kentucky, Tennessee, and other rivers, in the development of the country from 1840 to 1870. The steamboat, which began to run on the Hudson in 1807, made its appearance on the Ohio in 1811, and its use increased with the settlement of the Mississippi Valley states. St. Louis, on the Mississippi, near the mouth of the Missouri, became the principal trading city of the Mississippi valley, and New Orleans became the chief export city of the United States. The traffic of the great Middle West and of much of the South moved with the river currents to the Gulf, borne by the busy steamboats.

The Erie Canal. The canal which most influenced economic development in the United States was DeWitt Clinton's "Big Ditch"—the Erie

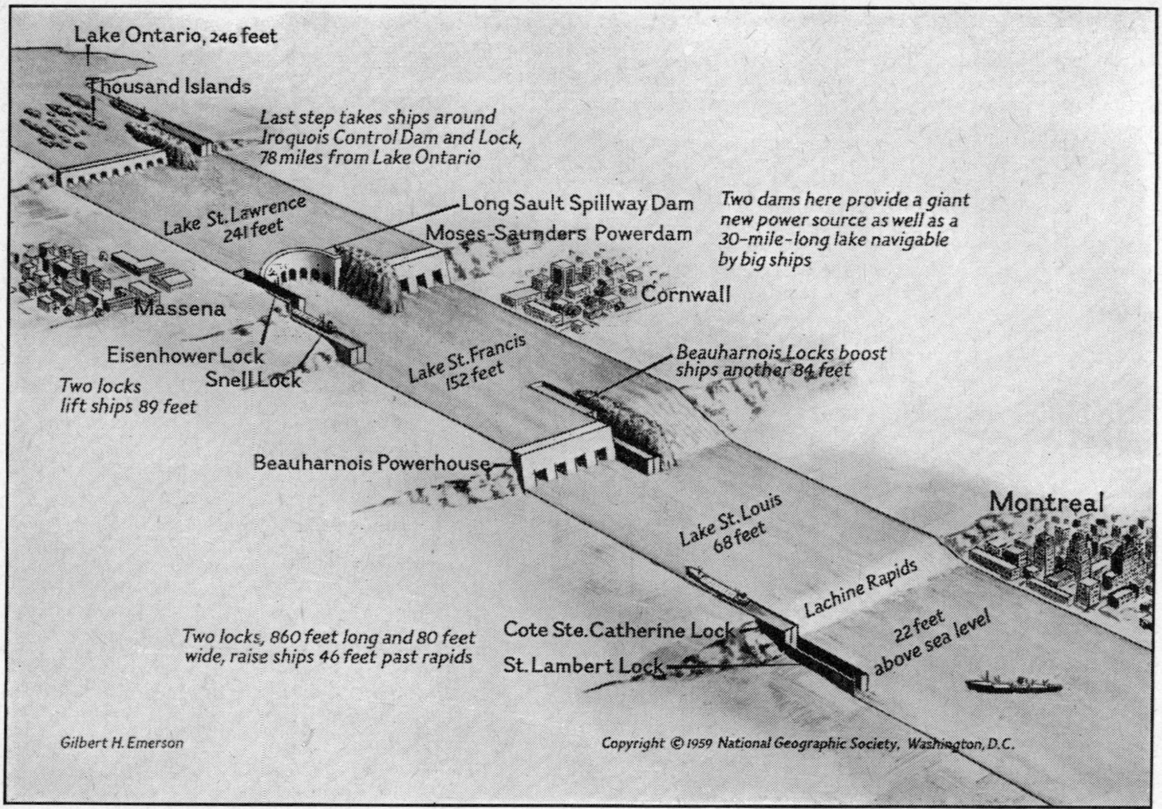

"Drawn by Gilbert H. Emerson. Reprinted by special permission from the March, 1959, National Geographic Magazine."

DIAGRAMMED STEP-DOWN OF SEAWAY IN ST. LAWRENCE RIVER

Canal—constructed by the State of New York from 1817 to 1825. By connecting the Hudson River and New York City with the Great Lakes via the Mohawk Corridor, it permitted the expansion of trade between the mid-west and eastern coast. New York City emerged as the great metropolis of the nation and its leading port. In the Midwest, the success of the Erie Canal stimulated the construction of numerous canals, notably in Ohio and Indiana. By the 1870's, competition from the railroads and rate wars caused canal traffic to decline.

New York State Barge Canal System. Presently, the Erie Canal is part of this System. The entire System, including the Champlain, Oswego, and Cayuga-Seneca canals in addition to the Erie, extends over 801.3 miles. The canals are at least 12 feet deep with a minimum bottom width of 75 feet when dredged through earth and of 94 feet where cut through rock. The 56 concrete locks built by the state are 300 feet long and 45 feet wide. The Federal lock at Troy is 44.4 feet wide. The largest barge that can be accommodated would be 300 feet long and 43 feet wide with a 4000-ton capacity.

The lock at Little Falls has a 40½-foot lift, one of the highest in the world. The five locks at Waterford raise a vessel 169 feet, twice as great as that to the summit of the Panama Canal.

Canals in Canada. Canada had an exceptional opportunity for the development of river and lake transportation by canalizing the St. Lawrence River and by connecting Lake Erie with Lake Ontario. The possibility of connecting Georgian Bay with the Ottawa River, and thus with the St. Lawrence River at Montreal, was also early apparent.

The St. Lawrence River has four rapids, which render upstream navigation impossible except by the construction of canals and locks along the river past the rapids. The Lachine Rapids are just above Montreal, and a canal past those rapids was begun in 1824. At later dates, canals past the other rapids of the river were constructed. These were equipped with locks 270 feet by 45 feet, and 14 feet deep.

The first Welland Canal, enabling boats to pass from Lake Erie to Lake Ontario, was opened in 1829. This waterway has been enlarged from time to time, and work completed in 1930 gave the waterway the dimensions of an ocean ship canal. In addition to one guard lock, there are seven lift locks, each of which is 800 feet in length by 80 feet in width, with a depth of 30 feet of water above the sills, each lock having a lift of 46½ feet. The canal connects Port Colborne, on Lake Erie, with Port Weller, on Lake Ontario. The total cost exceeded $122 million.

The St. Lawrence Seaway. The feasibility of a Seaway was studied in 1895 but not until May 13, 1954 was legislation signed authorizing the U.S. to join Canada in its construction. Congress acted after Canada announced plans to construct the Seaway within its boundaries. Passage of the bill was urged for reasons of national security.

The dredging of the St. Lawrence River and construction of locks and canals permits 27-foot draft ocean-going vessels (80 per cent of the world's shipping) to proceed beyond Montreal to Detroit and on to Duluth, Minnesota.

In 182 miles from Lake Ontario to Montreal, the river drops 224 feet. Canada undertook construction of facilities in the 68-mile section from Montreal to the International Rapids. The U.S. built the Wiley-Dondero Canal and three locks in the 46-mile International Rapids section between Cornwall, Ontario, and Ogdensburg, New York.

Another project, the joint development between

New York and Ontario in the International Rapids section of hydro-power facilities capable of producing 13 billion k.w.h. annually, began operations on July 1, 1958. The cost of the power project exceeded $600 million.

Chesapeake and Delaware Canal. In 1824, the Chesapeake and Delaware Canal Company constructed a canal connecting the Chesapeake and Delaware bays. This canal was acquired by the United States government in 1919. The Engineer Corps of the Army took in hand the work of improving the canal by the elimination of curves and the removal of locks, converting it into a sea-level canal. These improvements, completed in 1926, were calculated to reduce a ship's transit time from ten hours to four hours or less.

The Panama Canal. Encouraged by their success at Suez, the French sought to build a canal across the Isthmus of Panama. Under a concession from the Colombian government, work was begun in 1881. Unexpected physical obstacles and the prevalence of malaria and yellow fever caused the enterprise to be abandoned in the late 1880's. About this time an American company was considering the construction of a canal across Nicaragua, but this project, too, was abandoned and it became evident that if a canal was to be built it would have to be done by the United States government. As between the two locations, the United States in 1902 decided in favor of the Panama route after the French agreed to sell their interest for $10 million. In this same year Congress authorized the President to negotiate with the Colombian government for a concession to build the Canal. However, the two governments were far apart in their valuations of this permission. Colombia wanted $50 million and the United States considered the concession to be worth $10 million.

During the delay thus caused, the Republic of Panama declared its independence from Colombia. The United States promptly recognized the new government and made a treaty with it whereby permission was granted for building the Canal and for permanent occupancy of a strip ten miles wide along the canal route. The U.S. Secretary of War, assisted by a commission, began the construction in 1904.

This time, under the leadership of Col. Wm. C. Gorgas, measures were taken to prevent the diseases that had plagued workers on the French project. Sanitary precautions that eliminated disease-carrying mosquitoes made the Canal Zone completely safe from a health standpoint. U.S. Army engineer Col. George W. Goethals was equally successful in overcoming the many physical obstacles that had baffled the French. Both men were raised to the rank of Major General in recognition of their services.

The length of the Panama Canal is about 44 nautical miles or 50 statute miles. The minimum depth is 41 feet, and the minimum bottom width through the Divide is 300 feet. Navigation for most of the distance is in lake channels. A vessel passing from the Caribbean Sea to the Bay of Panama proceeds through a sea-level channel across the swamp district to Gatun, where by means of three locks the vessel rises to the level of the lake. Thence, the channel is through the lake to the Continental Divide, where, through a cut nine miles in length, the vessel passes to within a few miles of the ocean. At Pedro Miguel the vessel is lowered 30 feet to Miraflores Lake. Two locks at Miraflores lower the vessel to mean sea level.

Transit from sea to sea occupies 7 to 8 hours, with passage through the locks 3 to 3½ hours. In 1974 there were 15,269 transits carrying a record of 147,907,000 tons of cargo. Tolls on commercial ships totaled $119,419,878. The canal is operated and regulated financially by the Panama Canal Company, a governmental agency.

The total cost of the Panama Canal has been over $400 million. Under a new treaty signed with Panama in 1955, the United States raised the annuity paid Panama for the use of the Canal Zone from $430,000 to $1,930,000 annually and, among other concessions, agreed to return land no longer needed for canal operation. In 1974, a U.S.-Panamanian agreement set guidelines for the negotiation of a new treaty under which the Canal Zone would eventually revert to Panama.

The Suez Canal. The Suez Canal, connecting the Mediterranean with the Red Sea, was the first inter-ocean canal constructed. Begun in 1859 and opened in 1869, it was constructed by the Suez Canal Company under the leadership of Ferdinand de Lesseps.

This sea-level canal, 105 miles in length, is the world's busiest international waterway. Originally 26 feet in depth and with a bottom width of 72 feet, successive enlargements have given it a depth of 46 feet (capable of handling 35-foot draft vessels) with a minimum bottom width of 196 feet. The original cost was $80 million; total capital investment, approximately $136 million.

Canal use developed slowly since sailing vessels, the only ones employed in the Europe and Orient traffic in the mid-1800's, could not use the route. Traffic increased considerably with the introduction of steam vessels and stockholders realized dividends of 25 to 30 per cent. Approximately 176,000 shares of Canal stock, including that held by Egypt, were purchased by Disraeli for the British government in November 1875. The British government became the largest stockholder, although never controlling the majority of the 400,000-share stock.

Tonnage on the Canal increased from 20 million tons annually prior to World War I, to over 270 million tons in 1966. Nearly three-fourths of the northbound traffic is pêtroleum. The distance from the Persian Gulf to London via the Canal is 7000 miles; via South Africa, 12,900 miles. A 30,000-ton tanker saves over $100,000 by using the Canal.

The Canal company's 99-year concession was to revert to Egypt in 1968, but in July 1956 the Egyptian government seized and nationalized the Canal. Warfare followed in which Egypt was attacked by Israel, Britain, and France. From October 1956 until mid-April 1957, the Canal was closed while war-damage was being repaired. Since then Egypt has operated the Canal. From 1967 to 1975 the canal was closed due to the Arab-Israeli wars.

RAILROAD TRANSPORTATION

When in 1829 Stephenson succeeded in running "The Rocket" at the rate of 44 miles an hour in the contest at Rain Hill near Liverpool, England, he inaugurated a new epoch in the world's history. The effect of Stephenson's achievement was greater even than that of Watt, for the influence of the locomotive upon the industrial and social life of the world has been more fundamental than that of the stationary engine. The locomotive has made possible the rapid settlement and development of the continents of North and South America and of Australia, and is rapidly opening up Africa.

History of American Railroads. The railroad has had its most rapid and its largest development in the United States. The chartering of railroad companies in the United States began in 1826, and construction, on a small scale at first, soon followed.

The first locomotives were run in 1830. Several roads, the antecedents of the present Baltimore and Ohio, New York Central, and Pennsylvania systems, started at about the same time. The Baltimore and Ohio was chartered in 1827, and the first rail of this historic road was laid July 4, 1828, by Charles Carroll who was then the only surviving signer of the Declaration of Independence.

The Mohawk and Hudson, from which the great New York Central system has developed, was chartered in 1826. Construction was begun in 1830, and the first 17 miles of the line were opened in 1831. These early roads developed slowly, but Buffalo was reached in 1842. The Baltimore and Ohio reached Wheeling in 1851. The most active center of railroad construction in the 1830's was Philadelphia, which was connected with the Susquehanna River by rail in 1834 and thus with Pittsburgh by rail and canal lines. The Camden and Amboy connected the Delaware River with New York bay in 1837, and Baltimore was reached by rail in the same year.

Between 1830 and 1835 three lines were built out from Boston, one north to Lowell, one south to Providence, and the other west to Worcester. By 1841 this third line had been extended to Albany, and before the close of the following year one could travel from Boston to Buffalo by an all-rail route.

Periods of Railroad Construction. The historic growth of American railroads and the decline in mileage since World War I may be observed in the table *Railroad Mileage in the United States, 1845–1974*. Slow initial growth was followed by a 240 per cent increase in mileage in the decade 1850–1860. In no subsequent period did the railroads experience such a rapid rate of increase. In this decade prior to the Civil War, growth occurred principally in two regions, the South and the trans-Appalachian west. Vigorous railroad construction by the southern states provided them with the economic strength to wage four years of Civil War. The extension of northern railroads west beyond the Appalachian Mountains to the Mississippi River and to some extent beyond enabled the North to defeat the South.

From the close of the Civil War to 1880, rapid construction of railroads and the westward extension of the lines were plagued by intermittent panics. The severe panic of 1873, whose effects lasted for five years, resulted in large measure from the over-extension of railroads into the west in advance of traffic requirements. This distinctive railroad panic and its effects were ended by 1880.

From 1880 to 1890, more than 70,000 miles were added to the railroad network of the United States, the largest total in any 10-year period. Expansion occurred in all parts of the country but notably in the new states of the central west.

RAILROAD MILEAGE OF THE UNITED STATES BY STATES

State	Miles of Line 1940	Miles of Line 1960	Miles of Line 1974
Alabama	4,996	4,647	4,541
Alaska	536	572	538
Arizona	2,228	2,166	2,034
Arkansas	4,482	3,950	3,559
California	7,947	7,758	7,335
Colorado	4,552	3,786	3,499
Connecticut	887	825	656
Delaware	295	293	291
District of Columbia	35	30	....
Florida	5,218	4,670	4,143
Georgia	6,334	5,864	5,414
Hawaii*	192	25	....
Idaho	2,746	2,685	2,659
Illinois	11,949	11,211	10,607
Indiana	6,889	6,601	6,419
Iowa	8,950	8,569	7,644
Kansas	8,564	8,239	7,621
Kentucky	3,691	3,543	3,518
Louisiana	4,357	3,938	3,752
Maine	1,882	1,786	1,667
Maryland	1,367	1,146	1,099
Massachusetts	1,793	1,654	1,405
Michigan	7,303	6,665	6,032
Minnesota	8,421	8,205	7,382
Mississippi	3,919	3,659	3,645
Missouri	7,042	6,595	6,082
Montana	5,149	4,969	4,900
Nebraska	6,044	5,721	5,334
Nevada	1,941	1,647	1,573
New Hampshire	1,002	869	751
New Jersey	2,108	1,915	1,708
New Mexico	2,812	2,473	2,087
New York	7,739	6,541	5,325
North Carolina	4,668	4,310	4,115
North Dakota	5,266	5,255	5,079
Ohio	8,501	8,334	7,746
Oklahoma	6,302	5,802	4,946
Oregon	3,385	3,149	3,041
Pennsylvania	10,328	9,126	8,064
Rhode Island	194	184	139
South Carolina	3,466	3,282	3,016
South Dakota	4,006	3,920	3,363
Tennessee	3,573	3,402	3,207
Texas	16,356	14,769	13,320
Utah	2,082	1,734	1,734
Vermont	919	811	765
Virginia	4,261	4,133	3,873
Washington	5,243	4,979	4,807
West Virginia	3,831	3,680	3,508
Wisconsin	6,639	6,191	5,832
Wyoming	2,008	1,881	1,780

Source: Interstate Commerce Commission; annual reports, *Statistics of Railways in the U.S.*, and *Transport Statistics in the U.S.*

* Figures do not include approximately 670 miles of plantation railway lines.

By 1890, the principal railway systems required to meet the commercial needs of the nation had

RAILROAD MILEAGE IN THE UNITED STATES, 1845-1974

Year	Miles of Line in Operation	Change in Mileage	Year	Miles of Line in Operation	Change in Mileage	Year	Miles of Line in Operation	Change in Mileage
1845	4,633	......	1890	163,597	35,277	1935	241,822	−7,230
1850	9,021	4,388	1895	180,657	17,060	1940	233,670	−8,152
1855	18,374	9,353	1900	193,346	12,689	1945	226,696	−6,974
1860	30,626	12,252	1905	218,101	24,755	1950	223,779	−2,917
1865	35,085	4,459	1910	240,293	22,192	1955	220,670	−3,109
1870	52,922	17,837	1915	253,789	13,496	1960	217,100	−3,570
1875	74,096	21,174	1920	252,845	− 944	1965	211,384	—4,284
1880	93,262	19,166	1925	249,398	−3,477	1970	205,782	−5,602
1885	128,320	35,058	1930	249,052	− 346	1974	201,555	−4,227

Statistical Abstract of the United States, 1975.

PASSENGER TRAFFIC, 1930–1974
Millions of Passenger Miles and Percentage of Total*

Year	Rail-roads	%	Busses	%	Air Carriers	%
1930	26,876	68.5	7,100	18.1	73	0.2
1940	23,816	64.5	9,800	26.5	1,052	2.8
1950	31,790	45.3	26,436	37.7	10,072	14.3
1960	21,284	27.2	19,896	25.5	33,958	43.5
1961	20,308	26.3	19,703	25.6	34,642	44.9
1963	18,600	21.6	21,700	25.3	42,900	49.9
1968	13,265	9.4	26,211	18.6	101,189	72.0
1974	10,500	5.9	26,700	15.1	135,474	76.7

* Excludes miles traveled in private automobiles. Sources: *Railroad Information Yearbook* and *Statistical Abstracts*.

been built. From that time on, most additions were built to supplement or extend existing systems. Peak mileage was reached in 1916 when the net extended to 254,037 miles. Since then, nearly 53,000 miles of line have been abandoned, primarily because of the growth of other forms of transportation. The change also reflects the decline in passenger traffic and efforts to economize by reducing redundant services.

Distribution of Railroad Mileage. Approximately 29 per cent of the railroad mileage of the world is in the United States. The combined countries of Europe have approximately 30 per cent and the remainder of the world 40 per cent of the total.

The mileage by state is given in an accompanying table. Texas, with 13,951 miles of railway, surpasses the mileage of France or Germany. New Jersey ranks first among the states in the number of miles of railroad per hundred square miles of area whereas Nevada has the lowest ratio.

Standard Gauge. The standard gauge of railroads is 56.5 inches from the inside of one rail to the inside of the opposite rail, measurement being made about ⅝ of an inch from the top of the rail head.

History of Canadian Railroads. In many respects the development of Canadian railways corresponds with that of the United States. As was the case in the States, the Canadian colonies devoted their attention first to canal building and the establishment of inland waterways. During the first half of the 19th century, these were the chief improvements made in transportation.

The first railway in Canada was placed in operation in 1836. This was a line 16 miles in length, connecting Montreal and St. John's on the Champlain route to New York. Up to 1850 only 50 additional miles of railway had been constructed. But the great activity in American railroad building during the 1840's convinced the Canadians that they too must have railroads to supplement their canals.

In 1849 the Canadian government adopted a vigorous policy regarding railway construction by undertaking to guarantee 6 per cent interest on a sum not to exceed one-half the cost of railways 70 miles in length or longer. As a result, the St. Lawrence and Atlantic railway, connecting Montreal and Portland, Maine, was completed in 1853, and, during the same year, the Northern railway from Toronto to Collingwood was placed in operation. In 1854 the Great Western railway, connecting Niagara and Detroit, was opened. The Grand Trunk railroad, chartered in 1852, operated the St. Lawrence and Atlantic under a lease, and, in 1856, completed the main line from Toronto to Montreal, thereby connecting the chief commercial districts of Canada with the Atlantic seaboard.

By 1860 more than 2000 miles of Canadian railways were in operation. These were constructed largely by heavy outlays of British capital. But the financial crisis of 1857, together with the pecuniary embarrassments of most of the lines, prevented extensive railway construction for the ensuing 10 years. Except for the completion of local lines, there was but little additional railway building until after the confederation of the various provinces of the Dominion was effected in 1867.

Fulfilling a condition of Confederation in the East, the Dominion government undertook the completion of the Intercolonial railway between the province of Quebec and the ice-free Atlantic ports of Nova Scotia and New Brunswick. In 1876, at a cost exceeding $20,000,000, this line was completed. A corresponding condition of western federation, demanded by British Columbia, was fulfilled by the construction of the Canadian Pacific railway. At a cost to the country of $62,000,000 in cash and 25,000,000 acres of land, this notable enterprise in railway transportation was begun in 1881 and completed in 1885. It is worthy of note that in the United States at this time only three transcontinental railway connections with the Pacific coast had been established. These were the Central Pacific, from Ogden to San Francisco, finished in 1869; the Southern Pacific, from the Texas seaboard to San Francisco, completed in 1877, and the Atchison, Topeka, and Santa Fé, from the Missouri river to Los Angeles, opened in 1885.

The railways of Canada have been built largely under various forms of government aid, consisting of land grants, cash subsidies, loans, and guarantee of bonds or interest. The total so granted, up to 1940, exceeded 47,000,000 acres.

Government Railways in Canada. A feature wherein railway development in Canada sharply differs from that in the United States is found in the large mileage owned or controlled by the national government. The Prince Edward Island railway, completed in 1875, and the Intercolonial railway, completed in 1876, were the earliest government owned lines. In 1903 the national government began the construction of the eastern division of the National Continental railway from Moncton, N. B., to Winnipeg. This line was to be leased to the Grand Trunk railway. Upon the failure of the latter to operate the new road after it had been completed at a cost of $165,000,000 up to 1919, the national government undertook its operation.

At the beginning of 1918 the Canadian government railways had a total mileage of 5150, comprising the Intercolonial, 2305 miles; St. John and Quebec railway, 128 miles; Prince Edward Island railway, 314 miles, and National Continental railway, 2403 miles. During 1918 branch lines in New Brunswick aggregating 143 miles were taken over for operation. In the same year the national government acquired the capital stock and control of the Canadian Northern Railway Company. The Canadian Northern system at this time had a total mileage of 9566 miles. With the later acquisition of various subsidiaries, including the Hudson Bay railway, the Canadian Northern system, as controlled by the government, comprised fully 10,000 miles of line. In 1920, the Grand Trunk Pacific railway, having a mileage of about 2700 miles, was taken over and operated by the government. The Grand Trunk railway, also, with about 3600 miles, was placed under government management in 1921.

In this manner the government acquired about 21,500 miles of railway; the total was increased to over 24,000 in 1935. This is over one-half the total mileage in Canada, which in 1973 amounted to 44,230, of which 90% is controlled by the government-owned Canadian National and the privately owned Canadian Pacific.

Technical Triumphs of American Railroads. The triumph of American railroads has been as significant in the development of equipment as in track construction. The success of U.S. railroading depended upon the ability to move heavy loads over long distances and over such grades as were required to surmount the Appalachian and Rocky mountains.

In a country of three million square miles, resources are scattered and occasionally remote. The great distances and the diversity of economies and resources suggest the complex nature of the transport problem which the railroads solved. With major markets in the northeastern quarter of the country and on the west coast fringe, extensive transportation systems became a necessity. The wheat and corn of the mid-west and Great Plains must travel 1000 to 1500 miles to the markets and ports of the east. Vast quantities of coal move from the Appalachian fields by rail to the industrial centers of the interior; non-ferrous metals cross the nation from the mines of the west to eastern markets; and the forests of the west, south, and north-central states transport their products by rail to the rest of the nation.

Steam Locomotives. To provide transportation for the products of forests, mines, and fields, the steam locomotive was enormously increased in size and tractive power. From the tiny locomotives of the 1830's and 1840's, weighing from 5 to 20 tons, was developed the huge triplex articulated locomotive of recent years, which had 24 driving wheels and a total weight of 853,000 pounds. This extraordinarily large locomotive was intended for work on heavy mountain grades. But the standard freight locomotives, with eight driving wheels, had a total weight of about 500,000 pounds. The average tractive power of locomotives in the United States more than doubled in the first 40 years of the 20th century, being over 50,000 pounds in 1940. The number in use was 44,333. The maximum of 65,358 was attained in 1924.

Since World War II, however, there has been a sudden and dramatic change from steam locomotives to Diesel engines. By 1957 the railroads owned only 2,404 steam locomotives as against 27,211 Diesel units. Diesels now perform almost all freight, passenger, and switching service. The average traction power of over-the-road locomotives increased from 45,225 pounds in 1930 to 60,311 pounds in 1964.

The Car. Such heavy trainloads would not be possible except for the size and the strength of the freight cars now in use. At the close of the Civil War, the standard freight car had a capacity of about 20 tons. By the end of the 19th century the standard had been raised to 40 tons. The average capacity climbed from 42.5 in 1921 to 58.2 tons in 1964. The only limit to the size of the car is the strength of the tracks and bridges.

The Electric Locomotive. The earliest electric locomotive was used to haul cars in mines in 1882, but the most important early use of this form of traction was in subways and tunnels, where it has obvious advantages in the fact that electric locomotives do not emit smoke and noxious gases. The first tunnel in which electric locomotives were used was that of the City and South London Railway under the Thames River, opened for traffic in 1890.

Other situations in which electric locomotives have proved of value sufficient to justify the high initial cost are: in terminals and suburban divisions; on steep mountain grades; and on routes carrying heavy traffic and requiring fast service.

Diesel-Electric Locomotive. Although electrically driven, this type of locomotive does not require that tracks be electrified so as to transmit current from a central station. On the contrary, it generates its own current by means of a dynamo driven by a Diesel engine. The current drives motors geared to the wheels. The Diesel uses much less fuel than the steam locomotive. It also requires less maintenance and inflicts less wear and tear on tracks. It allows easier starting for heavy loads, and can maintain higher speeds for longer periods. The first Diesel-Electric locomotive for commercial use was built in 1925, the Jersey Central Railroad's No. 1000.

Streamlined Passenger Trains. The streamlining of passenger trains has the primary purpose of economy through reduction of air resistance at high speeds. A second advantage of molding the outline of locomotive and cars is to increase the beauty of the train as an attraction to customers. The first completely streamlined train in America was the "Zephyr," put into service by the Chicago, Burlington & Quincy Railroad on November 11, 1934, to run between Lincoln, Nebraska, and Kansas City, Missouri. Lightweight low-slung coaches able to take curves faster and cars with observation domes and with rubber used to make a smoother ride were other improvements designed to offset the attraction of transport by air, bus, and private automobile. In the years of explosive growth in travel, the number of passengers carried by railroads declined between 1950 and 1975 from 488 million to 269 million.

Competition with Trucks. In the years after World War II, the tonnage of goods hauled by trucks gained rapidly on the static or declining volume of goods hauled by railroads. The answer of the railroads was directed toward the twofold goal of cutting expenses and making its service more efficient and attractive. These developments included (1) discontinuance of uneconomic runs, with government consent, (2) conversion to Diesel locomotives, and (3) construction of larger and more specialized freight cars. These latter included cars adapted for transporting automobiles and particularly those which could carry truck trailers deliv-

INTERCITY FREIGHT TRAFFIC, 1930–1974*
(Millions of Freight in Ton-Miles)

Year	Railroads	%	Motor Vehicles	%	Inland Waterways**	%	Oil Pipeline	%
1930	389,648	74.3	20,345	3.9	86,453	16.5	27,900	5.3
1940	379,201	61.3	62,043	10.0	118,057	19.1	59,277	9.6
1950	596,940	56.2	172,860	16.3	163,344	15.4	129,175	12.1
1955	631,385	49.4	222,254	17.5	116,508	17.0	203,244	15.9
1960	579,130	43.7	297,662	22.4	220,253	16.6	228,626	17.2
1961	569,997	42.9	313,141	23.6	209,706	15.8	233,172	17.6
1962	599,977	43.1	331,319	23.8	223,089	16.0	237,723	17.0
1963	629,457	43.1	347,865	23.8	240,000	16.4	243,286	16.6
1964	666,207	43.5	347,470	22.7	250,165	16.3	265,826	17.4
1965	721,055	43.67	359,218	21.76	262,421	15.89	306,393	18.56
1966	761,044	43.71	380,917	21.85	265,000	15.20	332,916	19.10
1968	768,538	41.63	396,300	21.46	287,000	15.55	391,300	21.20
1974	855,700	38.6	495,000	22.3	354,882	16.1	506,000	22.8

* Airlines percentage of total was less than 1/10 of 1% before 1964; slightly above thereafter.
** Inland waterways consist of Great Lakes and Rivers & Canals. In the 35-year period, the share of traffic carried on the Great Lakes dropped from 14.8% to 6.7% whereas the share of traffic carried by Rivers & Canals increased from 1.7% to 9.3%.
Source: *Statistical Abstract.*

ered to the railroad by trucks and delivered again to trucks to take them to their ultimate destination. This was known as "piggy-back" service; it represented a measure of co-operation instead of competition. Similar in effect was the increasing use of standardized freight containers that could be reloaded directly for truck, ship, or air transportation.

Other improvements by the railroads were (1) the use of machines in laying rails, which could be fused into lengths of 2000 feet or more, and (2) the use of computers to make up freight trains in switchyards and to keep hour-by-hour record of where each shipment was.

TRANSPORTATION UPON ELECTRIC RAILWAYS

Tramways. The first electric railways were built to take the place of horse-car lines or tramways in the cities. The tramways had been preceded by bus lines, which began to run in New York City in 1830 and in Philadelphia the following year. It was not until 1832 that the first horse car was built in the United States. The first street railway in Boston dates from 1853, and, in Philadelphia, from 1858. Chicago's first line was started in 1859. These horse-car lines provided a service of four or five miles an hour, and were fairly adequate for the transportation needs of the times.

Cable and Elevated Roads. By 1870, more rapid transit than could be provided by horse-car lines had become necessary, and in one important city, San Francisco, steep hills made horse cars impracticable. The cable lines were the first to provide rapid transit. San Francisco opened a cable line in 1873, Chicago in 1878, Philadelphia in 1884.

In New York City, rapid transit was provided by the construction of elevated railways. The franchise for the first of these elevated railways was granted in 1867. Construction followed in due course, and by 1879 New York City had a fairly complete system of elevated roads. It was intended at first to use cable traction upon these elevated lines, but, before operation began, it was decided to use dummy locomotives. Twenty-five years later these steam locomotives were displaced by electric locomotives. Chicago began the construction of elevated roads in 1888; Boston, in 1903; and Philadelphia, in 1907.

Subways. The earliest underground railway for passengers was opened in London in 1863. It was operated with steam locomotives at first, but electric traction began to be used in 1890. The term "tube" is ordinarily applied in England to these railways. Budapest and Glasgow followed with the inauguration of electric train subways in 1896. A subway was opened in Boston in 1898. A subway service in Paris was initiated in 1900. The first line of the New York subway system was opened in 1904. Construction in this city presented peculiar difficulties. The subways had usually to be blasted through rock and, in certain sections, buildings of enormous weight had to be safeguarded while tunnels were driven beneath them. In later years, Philadelphia, Rochester, Toronto, Berlin, Tokyo, Moscow, Stockholm, and Montreal constructed transit facilities of this type. Chicago has a freight subway with a network of tunnels beneath the street level.

Technical Development. The electric railway was made possible by the dynamo, which was developed for practical use shortly after the middle of the nineteenth century. However, it was not until 1888 that an electric trolley line was actually demonstrated to be commercially practicable. After its introduction during that year, the electric railway made rapid progress in all cities. By the end of the century it had almost completely displaced horse-car lines.

Early in the 20th century, long-distance electric railway and electric interurban traffic developed rapidly and served as a decentralizing force. The increasing use of the automobile and motor bus, and the economic impact of the depression of the 1930's upon the over-extended lines resulted in their decline.

Transportation in Cities. The popularity of the private automobile caused a rapid and long decline in rapid-transit systems using electric power to carry people from one part of a metropolitan area to another. Transit companies in practically all cities converted to the use of buses, although electrically driven trains continued to operate in subways.

But the rapid growth of cities and the increase in car ownership produced transit difficulties of crisis proportions. Streets were widened; elevated roads were constructed; beltways were built around

RURAL ROADS IN THE UNITED STATES—1973

State	State Control	Local Control	Federal Control	Total Mileage
Alabama	19,831	47,741	275	67,847
Alaska	4,351	1,559	1,701	7,611
Arizona	5,590	21,156	18,100	44,846
Arkansas	13,779	52,758	1,802	68,339
California	14,263	71,477	37,137	122,877
Colorado	8,493	67,119	95	75,707
Connecticut	1,518	3,908	......	5,426
Delaware	4,348	......	......	4,348
Florida	13,349	57,035	1,390	71,774
Georgia	15,857	68,356	1,003	85,216
Hawaii	895	1,680	77	2,652
Idaho	4,741	25,462	22,504	52,707
Illinois	13,389	88,856	242	102,487
Indiana	10,224	65,078	56	75,358
Iowa	9,089	89,922	69	99,080
Kansas	10,081	113,098	94	123,273
Kentucky	23,846	39,314	609	63,769
Louisiana	14,231	28,160	323	42,714
Maine	10,960	7,841	162	18,963
Maryland	4,964	17,541	144	22,649
Massachusetts	1,193	4,908	49	6,150
Michigan	8,014	88,035	2,660	98,709
Minnesota	11,107	98,054	1,539	110,700
Mississippi	9,742	49,863	239	59,844
Missouri	29,908	68,451	740	99,099
Montana	12,158	53,823	9,471	75,452
Nebraska	9,793	80,719	563	91,075
Nevada	6,161	41,577	......	47,738
New Hampshire	3,056	7,006	111	10,173
New Jersey	1,579	12,005	13	13,597
New Mexico	11,666	46,575	6,819	65,060
New York	12,518	44,130	35	56,683
North Carolina	71,537	......	1,829	73,366
North Dakota	6,692	95,035	1,298	103,025
Ohio	17,036	68,971	29	86,036
Oklahoma	11,513	81,948	34	93,495
Oregon	9,279	35,213	50,179	94,671
Pennsylvania	42,491	46,784	858	90,133
Rhode Island	500	519	......	1,019
South Carolina	32,123	20,637	490	53,250
South Dakota	8,823	69,260	1,623	79,706
Tennessee	8,162	59,202	1,211	68,575
Texas	61,578	136,172	1,021	198,771
Utah	4,826	22,151	16,110	43,087
Vermont	2,593	10,129	185	12,907
Virginia	49,687	870	2,337	52,894
Washington	14,335	39,598	17,177	71,110
West Virginia	31,902	......	776	32,678
Wisconsin	10,772	78,871	68	89,711
Wyoming	5,918	20,879	12,500	39,297
Total	710,461	2,249,446	215,747	3,175,654

Source: Dept. of Transportation, Federal Highway Adm., *Highway Statistics, 1973.*

many cities; even hours of work were staggered in some places to avoid traffic tie-ups at the rush hours. Space had to be found for parking the automobiles. One result was a trend for businesses to move into the suburbs.

The problem was attacked in some cases by a revival of public mass transportation systems. San Francisco began construction of a suburban electric rail system with maximum train speed of 80 miles an hour, the tracks going overhead in some places and underground in others. Montreal and Stockholm constructed subways. Los Angeles also began work on a rapid transit system. Many other cities proceeded to enlarge their existing surface systems or subways, including Chicago, Cleveland, Boston, Detroit, and Toronto. Tokyo put up a monorail system as a partial answer, and Seattle continued to operate the monorail trains used for its world's fair.

TRANSPORTATION ON THE PUBLIC ROADS

Highway History. In colonial days and until within a few decades, road building in the United States was carried on mainly by local governments. The work of construction was done by townships and towns in the middle and eastern states, and by counties and subdivisions of counties in the southern states. These local highways were mostly dirt roads and were not suitable for the handling of freight and passenger traffic between distant points. The first long distance or through-transportation highways were the turnpike roads, built by corporations chartered by the several states. The first important turnpike was the one from Philadelphia to Lancaster, Pa., begun in 1792 and completed two years later. Early in the 19th century, turnpike roads in large numbers were built in Pennsylvania, New York, and other states.

For a time the government of the United States gave aid to highway construction. Works of internal improvement then included highways as well as canals. But the policy of national aid to public highways came to an end in the 1830's, when it was held that Federal works of internal improvement were unconstitutional. By 1850 most of the states had come upon financial difficulties in attempting to build or aid canals, railroads, and highways.

Good Roads Movement. About 1890 a "good roads" movement started in Massachusetts, New Jersey, New York, and other states. Following 1910, this movement was powerfully re-enforced through the need for roads more suitable for motor vehicles, which by that time were coming into general use. The way had been prepared abroad, where the first asphalt highway was constructed in Paris in 1870 and the first cement highway was built in Grenoble in 1876.

Motor Trucks and Buses. The decade of 1920-30 saw public conveyances on the highways developed to the point of near approximation with the railroads in the transportation picture. This was due to improvements both in trucks and buses and in the highways on which they traveled. The highways were, of course, built at public expense. The federal government alone was soon spending a billion dollars a year to construct a system of national (United States) highways and assisting states and municipalities to improve their roads. Truck and bus lines were made subject to regulation by the Interstate Commerce Commission in 1935.

In 1940, the first motor toll road was opened, the Pennsylvania Turnpike, a divided highway with restricted entry and no traffic lights. It was followed by many others, constructed by state governments which expected to liquidate the cost by toll revenues. The private automobile was the beneficiary even more than the public conveyance.

The Motor Age. Before the mid-20th century, the private automobile had become a necessity rather than a luxury. Its appeal was irresistible, giving its occupants a sense of being at home wherever the car traveled. The result was more and more intolerable traffic congestion. Again the federal government stepped in.

In 1956, Congress passed the Federal Aid Highway Act authorizing expenditure of $33 billion over 13 years, primarily for a 41,000-mile system of *interstate* highways, multi-lane divided roads with limited access and engineered for maximum speed and safety. Ninety per cent of the cost was borne by the federal government, as was the case also for improvement of 190,000 miles of state roads and 510,000 miles of secondary roads. Gasoline and other taxes were imposed to produce the needed revenue. Traffic on the interstate system was enabled to pass between, into, and around the larger cities; railroad and highway crossings were eliminated by overpasses. The original cost authorizations were later substantially increased. Apart from the direct transportation benefits of lower operating cost of vehicles, increased safety, and saving of time for travelers and shippers, the system had an important impact on the pattern of economic life. The new highways attracted industrial, commercial, and residential development with consequent enlargement of economic opportunities.

MOTOR VEHICLE REGISTRATION IN UNITED STATES
Privately Owned Vehicles*

Year	Passenger Cars	Trucks		Buses	Total
		Number	% of total		
1900	8,000	......	...	......	8,000
1910	458,377	10,123	2.2	......	468,500
1915	2,332,426	158,506	6.4	......	2,490,932
1920	8,131,522	1,107,639	12.0	......	9,239,161
1925	17,439,701	2,483,215	12.5	17,808	19,930,724
1930	22,972,745	3,518,747	13.3	40,507	26,531,999
1935	22,494,884	3,675,865	14.0	58,994	26,229,743
1940	27,372,397	4,590,386	14.3	72,641	32,035,424
1945	25,691,434	4,834,742	15.8	112,253	30,638,429
1950	40,333,591	8,604,448	17.5	223,652	49,161,691
1955	52,135,583	10,302,987	16.4	255,249	62,693,819
1960†	61,558,847	11,937,589	16.2	272,129	73,768,565
1961	63,260,416	12,286,430	16.4	279,668	75,826,514
1962	65,928,547	12,809,150	16.2	285,219	79,022,916
1963	69,026,690	13,423,327	16.2	297,864	82,747,881
1964	71,984,540	14,019,143	16.2	305,415	86,309,098
1966	78,331,488	15,522,114	16.4	323,197	94,176,799
1969	86,710,000	17,155,000	16.3	‡	105,404,000
1974	104,898,256	24,598,284	18.0	446,547	134,904,676

* Figures from 1950 through 1974 are for privately and publicly owned vehicles, excluding military vehicles. † Increase over 1955 due in part to addition of Alaska and Hawaii. ‡ Buses included with figure for trucks.
Source: Dept. of Transportation, Federal Highway Adm.; annual reports, *Highway Statistics*, *Drivers Licenses*, and unpublished data.

TRANSPORTATION BY AIR

Early History of Aircraft. The earliest *attempts* at flight were made with craft heavier than air. This fact was probably due to the every-day example of the flight of birds.

The Greek inventor Archytas is said to have constructed, about 400 B. C., a wooden pigeon which maintained itself for a short time in the air. About 1500 A. D., Leonardo da Vinci constructed models of helicopters, with propellers rotating in a horizontal plane, which hovered in the air. He is, therefore, properly credited with the invention of the helicopter and also of the propeller with rotating blades. He first conceived also of the parachute and he drew plans for ornithopters, that is, for aircraft to be propelled by flapping wings. These were to be operated by the arms and legs of the aeronaut. Many later inventors continued to experiment on these lines despite the fact that Giovanni Borelli (1606-79) pointed out that man's pectoral muscles have less than one-tenth the power possessed by the wing-operating muscles of birds when the weight of the body is taken into consideration.

Attempts at gliding are said to have been made in Rome in the time of Nero. About 1660, a French acrobat named Allard undertook a gliding flight in Paris before Louis XIV. These and many subsequent attempts ended in injury or death to the would-be aeronauts.

Aeronautics. Mechanical flight is pre-eminently a development of the 20th century. Its success demanded the improved gasoline engine, a light, strong metal, such as duralumin, and a knowledge of air dynamics. These discoveries led to the evolution of the airship from the balloon and to the building of successful heavier-than-air machines, or airplanes. See *Airplane* and *Airship*.

The flight of an airplane is analogous to that of a kite. The string by which the kite is drawn forward corresponds to the forward drive of the propeller, and the upward pressure of the air on the kite corresponds to the lift exerted on the wings of the airplane. This lift is due partly to the pressure exerted on the under side of the wings, and partly to the suction caused by a partial vacuum on the upper side of the wings. Neither surface of the wing is flat. The cross section of the wing follows certain streamline designs which are a balance between three requirements—maximum lifting power, strength, and minimum resistance in passing through the air. The last mentioned requirement demands also that the body of the airplane should conform to streamline design.

To exert effective lifting power the wings must be driven forward at a certain minimum speed and must be inclined upward at an angle of from 2° to 20°. Below this limit, or above it, the air resistance, or "drag," causes the plane to "stall;" that is, to fall below the minimum speed necessary for horizontal flight or control. The minimum speed required to keep the average plane in the air is about 35 miles an hour. Airplanes driven by piston engines travel from 200 to 350 miles per hour at top speed. But those propelled by jet, which were introduced into commercial flying in the 1960's, attain speeds of from 500 to 600 miles per hour. This velocity approaches the speed of sound, which is approximately 770 miles per hour. Plans soon were laid for introducing supersonic turbojet planes which would operate at nearly 2000 miles an hour.

The jet planes are pushed forward, not by revolving propellors pressing against air, similar in principle to the screw of a ship, but by thrusting backwards an explosive mixture of compressed air and fuel. Their propulsion is independent of air. Hence at high altitudes, up to 42,000 feet, where air is rarified and presents much less resistance to the plane's forward movement, far greater speeds can be obtained with the same expenditure of fuel. This is the chief factor in making their flight more economical.

The mechanisms for stabilizing the airplane's course include a vertical tail fin and a horizontal tail plane. Control of its course is effected through an "elevator," jointed to the tail plane, a rudder, jointed to the fin, and ailerons, or adjustable wing flaps. Landing on rough ground is facilitated by the use of pneumatic tired wheels on axles fitted and designed for maximum shock absorbing capacity.

While the control of an automobile involves only two main factors—speed and steering in a horizontal plane—the control of an airplane involves at least two additional factors. One is steering in a vertical plane; that is, going upward, downward, or on the level. The other is maintaining an even keel; that is, avoiding undue tipping, or "banking." Most planes have a so-called stick control. Moving the "stick" forward or backward causes a fall or rise in height; moving it sideways causes tipping to the right or left. Steering right or left is accomplished by a foot bar.

Important Dates in Aircraft History.

Aug. 27,1783—Hydrogen first used in a balloon by Prof. J. A. C. Charles, of Paris.

Jan. 7, 1785—The first crossing of the English channel in a balloon, by J. J. Blanchard, a Frenchman.

Jan. 9, 1793—The first ascent of a balloon in America, at Philadelphia, by J. J. Blanchard, in the presence of George Washington.

1848—The first power-driven airplane which actually flew, a 9-pound model, steam-driven, constructed by John Stringfellow, an Englishman. It flew 120 feet.

Dec. 17, 1903—First successful piloted flight in a power-driven airplane, at Kitty Hawk, N.C., by Wilbur Wright, 120 feet in 12 seconds. Nine days previously Samuel P. Langley's 'aerodrome" had crashed in a take-off, but was later proved capable of flight by Glenn Curtiss and flown successfully at Hammondsport, N.Y. Sept. 17, 1914.

1904—The first airship built in the United States, the *California Arrow*, by Captain T. S. Baldwin.

Aug. 22, 1906—First successful flight in Europe and first in the world without launching aids, by Alberto Santos-Dumont at Bagatelle, France.

July 25, 1909—First airplane flight across the English Channel, by Louis Bleriot, 20 miles in 37 minutes.

June 22, 1910—The first flight of an airship on a regularly operated transportation service, by Count Zeppelin at Friedrichshaven, Germany.

May 15, 1918—First regular air mail route in America inaugurated, between New York and Washington.

June 14, 1919—First non-stop transatlantic airplane flight, by Alcock and Brown, Newfoundland to Ireland, 1936 miles in 15 hours, 57 minutes.

1924—First aerial circumnavigation of the globe, by United States Army planes in 175 days.

1930—Development of "blind flying."

1931—Aerial circumnavigation of the earth in 8 days, 15 hours, 51 minutes, by Post and Gatty, as compared with the first circumnavigation in 1519 by Magellan, which required 37 months.

1934—First west to east crossing of the Pacific, by Sir Charles Kingsford-Smith and Capt. P. G. Taylor, 7365 miles in 51 hours flying time.

Nov. 1935—First transpacific air mail service—San Francisco to Manila.

June 17, 1939—Transatlantic passenger service inaugurated between U.S. and Europe.

1940–45—World War II mass production of aircraft; emergence of the helicopter as a useful craft; development of jet aircraft and V-2 rockets by German scientists.

1950–53—Korean War saw the military use of advanced jet aircraft.

1953–57—Development of turbo-prop, turbo-jet, and pure-jet commercial aircraft; experimental VTOL (vertical take-off and landing craft) introduced; advanced development of military rockets and missiles.
1958—First U.S. commercial jet aircraft capable of speeds up to 615 m.p.h. and reducing flying times by nearly one half.
1965–67—Pilot studies by the United States and jointly by France and Britain for development of commercial supersonic planes.

Air Travel. Air transportation is mainly passenger transportation, although carrying of mail has played a large role in development of the line. Volume of air freight is insignificant in comparison with passenger traffic.

The development of air travel was slow at first since it represented such a sharp break with past habits. Fear had to be overcome by confidence based on proven safety. European air lines, with government subsidies, progressed rapidly in the 1920's. In 1930, Congress authorized air mail subsidies, and the routes selected by the postmaster general helped develop the pattern of routes which formed the basis for today's system. The government established beacons and radio stations for the guidance of fliers. Terminals were constructed by municipalities, usually with government assistance.

Established in 1938, the Civil Aeronautics Board was given broad powers to regulate non-military flying and to lend assistance to commercial air lines. This law and the sale of surplus military aircraft after World War II provided the impetus for a crescendo in air travel which, by the 1960's, placed it at the head of all forms of travel except the private automobile. Transoceanic air passengers far exceeded in number those using ships. The use of private planes also grew apace. Traffic congestion at the larger airports became a serious problem.

Airplane safety depends on numerous sophisticated instruments. The pilot uses a radio range instrument to keep to a course marked by a radio beam, any deviation from which is registered on the panel instruments. An "omnibearing instrument" gives him his exact location. When he is near an airport landing, his instrument landing system enables him to follow a radio beam sent from his landing point. At the airport, a control officer, by means of radar, is made aware of every aircraft within range and issues instructions for orderly landing.

Planes that fly above 10,000 feet are equipped with pressurized cabins. Those going more than 25,000 feet are equipped with separate facilities to distribute oxygen to all occupants should the pressure system fail.

Commercial Air Transportation. At the end of the second decade of commercial air transport in the U.S. in 1940, there were 2331 airports in operation and 16,903 aircraft which carried 3,185,278 passengers and over 14 million pounds of freight and express traffic. By 1968, there were 10,470 airports in the United States. The number of aircraft on regularly scheduled flights was 2583. In addition, many others operated on unscheduled flights, with a total of 116,794 classed as eligible to operate. Domestic flights carried 145,774 passengers and about 1.6 billion ton-miles of freight.

One of the drawbacks of air transport is the fact that airports must be so far from cities which they serve that a disproportionate amount of time is spent traveling between home and airport. This gap can seldom be filled by private automobile. Limousines, buses, or taxicabs are the usual means of connection, with helicopters in some instances. There were 21 helicopters so operating in 1965.

Federal Control. Federal promotion and regulation of civil aviation are carried out by two bodies—the Civil Aeronautics Board and the Civil Aeronautics Administration. The Civil Aeronautics Board is an independent agency concerned primarily with the issuance of certificates of public necessity, economic regulation, the formulation of safety regulations, and the investigation of accidents in civil aircraft. The Civil Aeronautics Administration is an operating agency of the Department of Commerce. Its principal activities are the building and operation of air navigation aids, the enforcement of safety regulations, and the promotion of a national airport system.

TRANSPORTATION VISTAS

The demand for fast transportation in a world rapidly filling with people pointed by the middle of the 20th century to intolerable traffic congestion on highways and in the air. Radical new methods came under study and testing. Some of these are described below.

Air Cushion Vehicles. These operate on the principle of the jet. Air is forced downward so as to exert a lift on the car or boat sufficient to free it of contact with the surface of the ground or water. Propulsion also is by jet action.

This type of craft was invented by the British engineer Christopher S. Cockerell. His air-cushion boat, the hovercraft, was demonstrated successfully with the financial aid of the National Research Development Corporation of Great Britain. A land vehicle was developed also to follow a rail in the form of a V.

In France, a so-called aero train was built which uses a rail embedded in the center of a smooth reinforced concrete roadway. This rail also fits into a deep groove in the car but, when the car attains operating speed, does not touch the surfaces of the groove. Jets of air prevent the contact. Thus there is no friction either with the roadbed or the rail. Speeds of 175 miles per hour are envisaged.

In the United States a similar vehicle known as the levacar was constructed by the Ford Motor Company in 1961. It, however, utilizes two rails instead of one but is raised so as to have no direct contact with them, as in the aerotrain. A possible speed of 500 miles an hour was claimed for it.

Train in a Tube. A more radical device worked out by the Lockheed Corporation replaces the roadbed and guide rails with a giant tube within which the vehicle is propelled. The car would be fitted with precision to the walls of the tube. No attention is paid to getting rid of friction since at high speeds this would be at a minimum. The work of the engine is to take the air ahead and force it at great pressure to the rear. This jet effect would propel the car at a speed which theoretically could be supersonic. In some respects, the train would operate like a piston or like a mail carrier in a pneumatic tube.

Another device, using both a tube and air cushion, is one developed by the Rensselaer Polytechnic Institute. The air cushion centers the car in the tube so as to avoid contact with the walls of the tube, and the car is propelled by sucking in the air ahead and ejecting it in the rear.

The RRollway. This word is formed from "railroad" and "tollway." It is applied to a proposed electric train of cars about 24 feet wide operated on four tracks. Its purpose is to provide a rapid mode of transporting passengers and also, if they wish, their automobiles, which can be driven in and parked transversally across the car. The width of the track assures stability. Speeds up to 300 miles an hour are envisaged. Operation would be automatic by computer so that a service as frequent as one each 90 seconds could be maintained. According to the developer, General American Transportation Corporation, the terminals would be outside cities in view of the wide tracks required and the requisite large areas of the terminals.

LABOR RELATIONS

SINCE the days of feudalism, much of the world's work has been done under what is known as the system of free contract which means that the employee delivers his work to his employer for a stipulated price. Forced labor, as under slavery, and labor exacted as a duty because of social status, which prevailed under feudalism, theoretically at least have no part in labor relations today among democratic nations.

Before the rise of large-scale industry, as on many farms today, the relation between employer and employee was close and personal. But as the small property owner yielded to the large corporation as the typical employer, the relation of employee to employer became rather that of production worker to manager with personal acquaintance replaced by rules and policies. In a corporation, the management itself consists of employees of the corporation. Its interests, however, lie chiefly with the owners of the corporation rather than with the production workers. This fact provides the setting for the problems of labor relations in industry.

Management and Workers. The interests of management and workers conflict in so far as each group seeks to obtain a larger share of the revenue of the enterprise. Their interests overlap, however, in that neither could operate the enterprise without the aid of the other and both stand to prosper by enlarged revenue. Under normal conditions, ownership and management have the initial advantage in that they do not need workers as much as the workers need them. That is to say, the workers are usually much more dependent upon the weekly or monthly pay check than the owners of capital are upon profit or dividends from business. The owners are likewise able, as a group, to employ their superior money resources as a purveyor of power through political activity, use of the courts, and publicity. To offset this advantage, workers eventually built up strong organizations—labor unions—to mobilize countervailing economic and political power.

Role of the Government. For these reasons the labor problem in an industrialized nation enters vitally into government itself. Two groups, one wealthier and the other more numerous, compete for control. But the government, which represents all other interests as well as these, has a primary concern in seeing that industrial peace is preserved, that production and distribution of goods and services are promoted and that causes of strife are kept to a minimum. The government also has an interest in seeing that the health and the physical and mental well-being of its citizens are not impaired by substandard conditions of work, prolonged unemployment, and discriminatory employment practices.

INDUSTRIAL CONFLICT

In the early 19th century, the legal relation of employer and employee was still that of master and servant, a relic of the feudal system. Concerted action by employees to obtain better wages or working conditions was punishable by the courts as conspiracy, for which prison sentences might be imposed. In 1842, however, the Supreme Judicial Court of Massachusetts, then perhaps the most influential court in the country, ruled that employees might lawfully organize for mutual aid.

This right was slow in obtaining recognition. Its practical exercise, however, and the use of it to better the conditions of labor provide the key to most of the economic conflict between capital and labor both before and since.

The ultimate weapons of industrial conflict are the strike on the part of employees and the lockout on the part of employers. These simple forms of economic pressure, however, are usually supplemented by other actions intended to break the resistance of the opposing parties. Strikes, cessation of work by a group of employees until certain issues are settled, are usually accompanied by picketing and may be supplemented by boycotts. In the past, especially in the late 1930's, the stay-in or sit-down strike technique was used. Lockouts are much rarer than strikes. Most employer action in industrial disputes, therefore, takes the form of combating strikes.

Early History of Unions. The first recorded strike in America took place in the colonial period, when in 1741 New York bakers quit work as a protest against a municipal ordinance regulating the price of bread. The earliest known strike for higher wages took place in 1786, when the Philadelphia printers ceased work as a means of enforcing their demand for a minimum weekly wage of six dollars. A sympathetic strike took place in 1799, when the shoemakers, belonging to the organization known as the Federal Society of Journeymen Cordwainers, were compelled to lay down their tools in order to aid the bootmakers, who were seeking an increase in wages. This action may be regarded also as the first *organized* strike in America. Sympathetic strikes, however, did not play an important part in industrial disputes until the last two decades of the 19th century.

A successful attempt to establish a 10-hour working day was made by the unions of Philadelphia in 1835. Fifty-one years later, in 1886, occurred the first nation-wide strike for an eight-hour day.

Many trade unions were formed in the period between 1792 and 1810, especially in the cities of New York, Baltimore, Philadelphia, and Pittsburgh. The first central organization of trades in one city was formed at Philadelphia in 1827. It was called the Mechanics Union of Trade Associations.

In 1833, there were 29 organized trades in New York City. Many of these affiliated to form the New York Trades Union. Similar organizations followed quickly in other cities, so that when a convention was called in New York in August 1834, delegates were present representing the trades unions of Boston, Brooklyn, Philadelphia, Poughkeepsie, New York, and Newark. At this convention was inaugurated the National Trades Union. A trades union, comprising as members *unions* in various trades, must be distinguished from a trade union, which comprises as members *individual workers* in *one* trade only.

The printers were apparently the first craft to unite their local units into a national association, so that the Typographical Union, organized in 1850, is the oldest *national* trade union in America. The Stonecutters effected a national organization in 1853; the Hat Finishers, in 1854; the Molders, and the Machinists and Blacksmiths, in 1857.

In addition to unions of the workers in a particular trade, two organizations on a national scale arose prior to 1870, each of which admitted workers of any trade. The first was known as the National Labor Union, founded in 1866. The second, established in 1869, was called the Noble Order of the Knights of Labor. It began as a secret society, but the policy of secrecy was abandoned in 1878. Dissensions within these organizations led, in 1881, to the formation at Pittsburgh of the Federation of Organized Trades and Labor Unions of the United States and Canada. This federation merged with a separate trade union conference on December 8, 1886, forming the present American Federation of Labor. In 1889, the new federation recognized the continuity of its existence by dating its records from 1881.

Strikes. A strike is a concerted cessation of work on the part of the employees to compel an employer to meet their wishes as to wages or other conditions. It is a two-edged weapon, however; sometimes it cuts three ways. While its purpose is to cause loss to the employer, it also cuts off earnings of employees and may entail serious consequences for the public.

To enable employees to stand the loss of wages, labor organizations usually accumulate strike funds from which payments may be made to needy strikers in the form of strike benefits.

When the effect of strikes on the public goes beyond mere inconvenience and threatens disorganization of customary ways of living, as when electric power is cut off, the government is likely to intervene. Some states make strikes against public utility companies unlawful. The Federal government has the power by law to delay strikes which the president finds to imperil the public health or safety.

Sit-down Strike. This is a term applied when strikers, instead of leaving their jobs, remain at their places and refuse to work. Such action amounts practically to taking over the shop. When first used, in 1937, the sit-down strike brought workers some conspicuous successes, but in 1938 it was held by the U.S. Supreme Court to be illegal, and participants were deprived of the protection of Federal labor laws which they would otherwise have enjoyed.

Sympathetic Strike. This is a strike called by a union against an employer with whom the union has no quarrel, the purpose being to aid a sister union involved in a dispute with another employer.

Picketing. The picket line is the commonest means of adding to the effectiveness of a strike. It usually takes the form of a file of strikers carrying signs near a plant entrance, the signs conveying in simplified form the strikers' version of the dispute. The signs, for example, may read, "Unfair to organized labor." Sometimes sound trucks are pressed into service to give the public a more detailed account of the strikers' case.

The effectiveness of a picket line may be much greater than the number involved would lead one to expect. This is because crossing a picket line is regarded by large numbers of people as a species of treason to the employee class or the labor movement. The picket line helps to make a strike complete.

When feelings run high, picketing may become much more than an advertisement of the strikers' case. The pickets may attempt forcibly to prevent nonstrikers or customers from entering the employer's premises. This is sometimes known as obstructive or violent picketing as opposed to peaceful picketing.

Peaceful picketing has been declared by the United States supreme court to be a right protected by the Constitution as a form of free speech. On the other hand, courts ordinarily take the view that violent picketing is unlawful and may be forbidden by injunction. Even peaceful picketing when engaged in for unlawful purposes falls under the ban of many laws which define such purposes.

Boycotts. In addition to picketing, unions frequently seek to exert pressure on employers with whom they are in controversy through destroying their markets by means of boycotts. That is to say, members and others are asked not to patronize the employer concerned.

Secondary Boycott. A boycott is secondary when it is aimed only indirectly at the employer with whom the union has a quarrel. It seeks to reach him by forcing his customers, suppliers, or employees to cease doing business with him until he consents to what the union wants. An example would be picketing a radio store to prevent it from handling radios made by a company against which the union was striking. Such tactics are forbidden by Federal law and by some state laws.

Union Label. The use of a special label for goods made in factories where labor is unionized is another form of aiding a consumer's boycott. In another sense it is a form of advertising so as to permit preferential buying, comparable to the injunction to "buy home goods."

Strikebreaking. The usual strategy of the employer in combating a strike, the picket line, and boycott is to attempt to operate his business with nonstrikers or new employees and weaken the morale of the strikers. Injunctions against picketing and boycotts may be sought.

If the strike is "economic," that is, not motivated by the employer's unfair labor practices, the employer may lawfully replace the strikers by permanent employees. Otherwise, the strikers are entitled to their jobs back with regular pay for the time they were on strike. For this reason, employers have largely abandoned the cruder forms of strikebreaking formerly used. In most large strikes, there is no attempt to operate until the dispute is settled. But sometimes picketing continues even years after the business has been operating normally.

LABOR INJUNCTIONS

It is impossible to understand industrial conflict without appreciating that, while the objective of employees is better pay and working conditions, these can be achieved as a rule only when the employees are able to act together effectively. Only by organizations can strikes, picketing, or boycotts be made into effective instruments.

For this reason, in the earlier stages of the industrial age, employers' efforts to combat employee demands were aimed at preventing employees from organizing. One method used was to insist that new employees sign what came to be called "yellow-dog contracts." These were undertakings not to join a labor organization on pain of discharge. Even without such contracts, many employers considered membership in such organizations ground for discharge.

When conflicts came into the open through strikes and picketing, the weapon of court injunctions was relied on. An injunction is a court order usually issued to prevent the violation of someone's right. If it is disobeyed, the violators may be punished at the court's discretion through fines or imprisonment.

The first labor injunction by a Federal court was issued in 1885 (*U. S. v. Kane*) to prevent an act threatening a bankrupt property which was directly under the guardianship of the court. This precedent was extended to protect private property rights in the case of Casey v. Cincinnati Typographical Union, decided in 1891. Thereafter injunctions were used freely to prevent picketing and other strike action, frequently without the union being notified or given a chance to reply.

Antitrust Laws. In 1890 Congress passed the Sherman Antitrust act designed to break up combinations of capital. Combinations in restraint of interstate commerce were made subject to injunctions and to suit for triple damages by persons injured by the combinations. This law was utilized to prevent picketing and boycotts where interstate commerce was affected.

The supreme court of the United States, in 1906 and 1908 respectively, decided that a boycott conducted by a labor union against goods of a manufacturer with which the union has a dispute and a boycott against retailers buying from such a manufacturer fall under the prohibitions contained in the Sherman act. (See *Buck Stove and Range Case* and *Danbury Hatters' Case.*) The Clayton act, amending the Sherman act in 1913, provided that the antitrust laws should not apply to labor unions acting lawfully in pursuit of their legitimate purposes. The courts held, however, that action which interfered with interstate commerce was not part of the legitimate activity of unions, thus leaving the earlier decisions of the supreme court in effect.

Norris-LaGuardia Anti-Injunction Act. This act, passed in 1932, attempted, among other things, to do what the Clayton act failed to do. It forbids Federal courts to issue injunctions in labor disputes except under narrowly defined circumstances. The result was that labor organizations were pretty largely freed of injunctions issued by Federal courts. A seeming exception was the 1947 injunction to prevent a coal strike, but this applied to a government-operated industry.

Injunctions Under Taft-Hartley Act. The Labor-Management Relations act, 1947, popularly known as the Taft-Hartley act, punched at least two holes in the Norris-LaGuardia act. First, it allows injunctions in labor disputes at the instance of the national labor relations board, an agency established for regulating labor relations. This agency is *required* to seek orders to stop secondary boycotts and certain other kinds of "unlawful" acts by unions. It is *permitted* to seek such orders to stop "unfair labor practices." (See *Taft-Hartley Act* below.)

The other major modification in the Anti-Injunction act is a provision of the Taft-Hartley act under which the attorney general of the United States may obtain injunctions to delay up to 80 days any strikes found by the president to affect the public health or safety.

RIGHT TO ORGANIZE

As stated above, a key objective of employees in industrial conflict is the right to organize for mutual aid and protection. The chief obstacles to the exercise of this right have been these: (1) the discharge of employees known to be members of unions or active in forming unions; (2) refusal by employers to recognize and deal with unions organized by employees to act as their agents; and (3) undermining the unions of employees by organizing so-called company unions which the employer could control.

After decades of costly controversies in which these tactics were combated by unions through the use of their economic weapons of strikes, picketing, and boycotts, Congress adopted legislation to curb those employer practices which undercut the right of employees to organize. The six principal steps in this legislation are as follows:

In 1926, the Railway Labor act asserted the duty of railroads to deal with freely chosen representatives of their employees for the establishment of wages, hours, and other conditions of employment. In 1929, the United States supreme court held that employers violate this law by forming company unions and dealing with them as though they were the freely chosen representatives of employees (*Railway Clerks v. Texas & New Orleans Ry.*).

In 1932, the Norris-LaGuardia act, already referred to, forbade "yellow-dog contracts." It thereby put an end to the practice of requiring employees to consent in advance to their discharge if they joined a union.

In 1933, the National Industrial Recovery act authorized industry codes in which it was obligatory to incorporate terms which (1) prohibited employers from discriminating against employees for union activity and (2) required employers to recognize as bargaining agent of employees any union selected by the majority of the employees. The act was declared unconstitutional in 1935.

In 1934, the Railway Labor act was amended to provide for designation of employees' bargaining agents by a government agency, the national mediation board. That representative—union or person—must be designated for which the majority of the employees in any craft or class have voted to represent them in dealing with the railroad employing them.

Wagner Act. In 1935, Congress adopted the National Labor Relations act, popularly known as the Wagner act. This law served as a basic guarantee of the right to organize and bargain collectively. There were two principal reasons for its effectiveness.

First, it brought under Federal regulation nearly all forms of business except small local enterprises.

Second, the act provided an enforcing agency, the national labor relations board, which prosecuted violations at government expense and without cost to the complainant.

In 1947, this basic labor law was made still more sweeping by a new act. At the same time its emphasis was changed. While the purpose of the Wagner act was to remove certain causes of labor strife by restraining conduct of employers, the Labor Management Relations act, 1947, was designed to guard rights of the public, of employers, and of individual employees. In doing so, it abridges in some respects the collective rights of employees which had been guaranteed by the Wagner act.

TAFT-HARTLEY ACT

The Taft-Hartley act, officially known as the Labor Management Relations act, 1947, contains as Title I the National Labor Relations act (the Wagner act of 1935) as amended in 1947. The other titles, or divisions, of the act relate to restrictions on payment of benefits to employees or unions, outlawry of certain kinds of union conduct, suability in the Federal courts for breach of agreements, and handling of disputes imperiling the national health or safety. The act also establishes the United States mediation and conciliation service and defines its rôle in the settlement of labor disputes.

The most publicized part of the law is Title I. This is the part which forbids as "unfair labor practices" certain types of conduct on the part of employers and of unions. It describes the methods by which the conduct may be stopped through action by the national labor relations board and the courts. It also prescribes means by which the union chosen by the majority of employees may be given official status through "certification." Finally, it imposes certain conditions with which unions must comply before they are permitted to use the services of the board.

Unfair Labor Practices. This is the term with which Title I of the act brands forbidden conduct. There are five principal unfair labor practices of employers and six unfair labor practices of unions or their agents. Those of employers were forbidden by the Wagner act of 1935 and are carried forward with a few changes into the later law. Those of unions were added by the Taft-Hartley act in 1947.

Practices Forbidden Employers. Employers are forbidden to engage in the following practices:

(a) *Discrimination for Union Activity.*—This prohibition acts as a limitation on the right of employers to hire and fire at will. It means in practice that employers may not discharge or otherwise discriminate against workers for the reason that they are or are not union members or that they have engaged in concerted activity (or refused to do so) to advance their interests.

(b) *Domination of a Labor Organization.*—This means organizing, or encouraging employees to organize, an inside labor union or it may mean merely giving financial or other support to a union which the employees have organized on their own initiative. The reason which frequently actuates employers in supporting inside unions is the desire to forestall organizers from outside. When organized from outside, employees typically affiliate their local organization with a national union and draw strength and support from it in dealing with their employer. An inside group dominated by the employer is frequently referred to as a "company union."

(c) *Refusal to Bargain.*—This is an unfair labor practice which has an exact counterpart among those forbidden to unions. The meaning of it will be described below.

(d) *Interference with Employee Rights.*—This also has its counterpart among unfair practices of unions. The rights with which interference is forbidden are the rights to join, and refrain from joining, unions formed for the purpose of dealing with employers. As applied to employers, the term has a very broad meaning. It may include the conduct described in (a), (b), and (c) above and many other acts. Some acts which have been forbidden under this head include: Insisting on employees' signing of individual contracts in place of bargaining collectively through a union; espionage and questioning employees about their union membership; and maneuvers to weaken unions, such as transferring production from a plant where the union is strong to a plant where it has not obtained a foothold.

Discrimination for Giving Testimony.—The employer may not discriminate against an employee for filing charges or giving testimony under the Act.

Practices Forbidden Unions.—Unions and their representatives are forbidden to engage in these unfair labor practices:

(a) Coercion of employees in their right to join or refrain from joining labor organizations formed for the purpose of collective bargaining or coercion of employers in the selection of their agents in dealing with employees either when bargaining or handling grievances.

(b) Causing or attempting to cause an employer to discriminate against a worker who has been denied membership in a union for reasons other than certain ones specified in the Act.

(c) Refusal to bargain with employers, provided the union represents the majority of employees.

(d) Participation in secondary boycotts or striking and picketing for three other specified improper purposes. The purposes which are declared improper or unlawful are: (1) Organization from the top down through picketing, as when a union, without any members among employees, goes to their employer and compels him, by picketing, to give it a contract covering his employees; (2) supplanting an officially certified bargaining agent by compelling the employer to recognize the picketing union instead; and (3) forcing the solution of a dispute over work jurisdiction, as when a carpenters' union pickets an employer to compel him to let its members do work which he is having members of a machinists' union do.

(e) Charging excessive or discriminatory fees to members where the employee is permitted to hold his job only if he joins the union. There are special rules under the law which govern such compulsory membership. They are explained below.

(f) Compelling an employer to pay money, in the nature of an exaction, for work which is not intended to be performed.

Some of these unfair labor practices—those of employers—have been defined more concretely by judicial interpretation over a period of years. The one known as refusal to bargain, which is forbidden both to employers and unions, is defined at some length in the law itself. Important points in the elaboration of "discrimination," "domination," and "refusal to bargain" follow.

Discrimination Interpreted. In determining whether the discharge of an employee was for union activity or for some reason not forbidden by the law, such considerations as the following are taken into account.

1. Did the employer know of the employee's union membership? If he did not, the discharge could not have been for this reason.

2. If the alleged ground of discharge is inefficiency, were non-union employees of less efficiency for the same kind of job retained? If so, the employer's defense is weak.

3. If the discharge is said to be because the employee broke a rule against engaging in union activity on company time, are other rules against outside activity similarly enforced? If not, there is a presumption that the discharge is unlawful.

When persons unlawfully discharged are ordered reinstated, persons hired to replace them must be dismissed by the employer if necessary to make room for them. The same applies when employees are ordered reinstated after participating in a strike caused by an employer's unfair labor practice. If the strike, however, is economic, that is, for the purpose of obtaining better wages or working conditions, the strikers are entitled to their jobs back only if the jobs are still available.

Strikers or unlawfully discharged employees are not entitled to reinstatement if they have been guilty of crimes in connection with the labor dispute, have participated in sit-down strikes, or have, through their union, breached a contract with an employer.

Unlawful Aid to Unions. Support or aid which the law forbids employers to give to organizations of employees has been held to include the following procedures:

1. Suggesting the formation of a union, either personally or through supervisors, or facilitating its formation by advice or by provision of space or supplies free of charge.

2. Pressure placed on employees to join, particularly if the pressure includes threats of reprisals or promises of benefits.

3. Paying officers of the organization for time spent on the activities connected with it.

4. Eagerness in recognizing and executing a contract with the organization or giving it credit for wage increases granted, particularly if an outside union claims at the same time to represent a majority of the employees.

Duty to Bargain. The courts have held that, by making unlawful a refusal to bargain, Congress has created a positive duty to bargain in good faith. The Taft-Hartley act imposes this duty on both employers and unions, whereas the Wagner act imposed it on employers only.

The Taft-Hartley act defines the duty to bargain to include meeting at reasonable times, conferring in good faith on conditions of employment, negotiating an agreement or a dispute arising out of an agreement, and executing a written contract on request embodying the points agreed upon. The law, however, does not compel either party to agree to a particular proposal or to make a concession.

Freedom of Speech. The unfair labor practice of interference with employees' organizational rights was interpreted in the early years of the Wagner act to prevent employers or supervisors from expressing their views to employees about unions. The courts held that the words of employers were "loaded" in view of the employers' economic power over their employees. The Taft-Hartley act, however, provides that an employer may lawfully express his opposition to unionism in general, provided that he does not promise special benefits or suggest that employees will be penalized for failing to adopt his views.

Union Security. This term is applied to agreements between employers and unions under which employees must belong to the union if they are to continue in their jobs. It has a very special relation to the unfair labor practice of discrimination.

It should be explained first that carrying out such an agreement by discharging an employee who is not a union member amounts on its face to discrimination in respect of union membership. The Taft-Hartley act, however, permits this exception to its ban on discrimination but hedges it about with a number of conditions.

In the first place, the law forbids the closed shop. The *closed shop* is an arrangement under which the employer is restricted to hiring persons who are members of the union.

The law does permit the union shop or a membership-maintenance agreement—but with some "ifs."

The *union shop* is an arrangement whereby employers may hire regardless of union membership, but employees, to keep their jobs, must join the union within a stated period (30 days under the Taft-Hartley act) and must thereafter remain members in good standing. Otherwise, the employer is required to discharge them.

Membership maintenance is an arrangement whereby those employees who are members of the union on a given date or who later become members must remain members if they are to keep their jobs. An "escape period" of limited time is usually provided to allow members to renounce membership. Hence, all employees need not be members of the union.

Preferential hiring requires the employer to hire union members to the extent that the contracting union is able to supply a sufficient number of qualified employees. This provision is lawful today, under certain conditions.

The agency shop does not require union membership, but does require as a condition of employment the payment of the same lawful union dues required of members.

While the Taft-Hartley act allows the negotiation of the union shop, the agency shop, and membership-maintenance provisions, it permits individual states to outlaw such clauses.

This recognition of states rights is a one-way affair. A state may not enact a law that allows greater union security, say a closed shop, and have this law take precedence over the Taft-Hartley prohibition of such clauses. The federal law specifies that it is to be superseded by state law only if the state law is more restrictive of union security than the federal enactment. In 1970 nineteen states had enacted so-called "right-to-work" laws which outlawed any kind of union security clause.

Under the Taft-Hartley law, failure of the employees to continue their membership for any reason other than nonpayment of dues will not justify discharge. For example, if a member is expelled from the union for violating its rules of conduct but offers to pay his dues, he may not be discharged from his job by the employer.

If these conditions are ignored, it becomes an unfair labor practice for the employer to discharge the employee for nonmembership in a union and it becomes an unfair labor practice for the union to try to force the employer to make the discharge. Either the employer or the union or both may be required to make good the wages lost by an employee discharged under these circumstances.

Bargaining Agents. It is a basic principle of labor law that, if a majority of the employees concerned select a union to represent them in bargaining, the employer has the duty of dealing with that union. But the determination of whether a particular union is the majority's choice is beset with difficulties.

The first problem is, who are the "employees concerned"? Are they the employees in one department, in the entire plant, or in some other grouping? To solve this problem, the national labor relations board is given the duty of deciding which employees are in a bargaining unit.

The second problem is, do the employees really wish the union to represent them? The difficulty is solved by having a secret election conducted by the national labor relations board to determine the free choice of the employees.

Unit for Bargaining. Establishing the unit appropriate for collective bargaining corresponds, in its field, to determining in political life what classes of persons are eligible to vote in an election. The process, however, is frequently much more complicated. Bargaining units fall principally into one of the following types:

1. *Craft unit*, which consists of those employees of a firm who follow one craft or occupation, such as carpenters, molders, or machinists.
2. *Plant unit*, which consists of all employees working in one plant. Supervisory personnel are excluded by law, while guards or watchmen and professional employees have separate provisions.
3. *Employer unit*, which consists usually of all those working for one employer, who has a number of plants. The term is sometimes extended to include all persons working for members of an association of employers, which is authorized by its members to bargain for them.

The term *industrial unit* is sometimes applied to cover plant and employer units. It is used to point a contrast with craft unit, since the industrial unit takes in all workers without distinction of special skills.

Craft unions ordinarily seek to have craft units established, while industrial unions prefer plant or employer units. In practice, however, a number of craft unions may act together through a joint council in a form very similar to an industrial union. Industrial unions, on the other hand, may make special contracts for special classifications of their members, with a result similar to that secured by cooperating craft unions.

Determination of Units. In establishing units for bargaining, the National Labor Relations Board first excludes all persons whose interests are held to lie with the employer rather than with the other employees. These ordinarily include executives, supervisors, secretaries, and personnel directors. The rule is that those who have power to hire and fire or whose recommendations on employment are given weight are considered to be on the side of management. Supervisory employees are excluded from bargaining units because the law excludes them from the definition of "employee."

The law also provides that plant guards may not be in the same unit with other employees, nor may they be represented by a union which is affiliated in any way with a union representing the other employees in the plant. Professional employees and office workers must be given the option of inclusion with other employees or constituting a unit of their own. Craft employees also are usually given a choice of bargaining in a separate unit.

Within these limits, the labor board usually decides the question of unit by the test of effectiveness in bargaining. This test has been interpreted to mean:

1. Where bargaining has been effectively carried on in the past, the unit used should not be disturbed. This is sometimes known as the history-of-bargaining rule.
2. When a union and an employer differ as to the proper unit, the union's preference is usually given the greater weight, provided it does not do violence to the way the employer's business is organized.

Employee Elections. An election to choose a bargaining agent will usually be held if a union can show that it has a following of 30 per cent of the employees concerned. An employer may ask for an election if one or more unions claim to represent the majority of employees. Individual employees also, with support of 30 per cent of their unit, may secure elections. If there is no legal obstacle, the NLRB sets up a polling booth and the election is on.

Where only one *bona fide* union is seeking to be certified as agent for employees, the ballots present a choice for the union or against it. If two or more unions compete, the employee is permitted to vote for either or for no union. If no one choice receives more than 50 per cent of the votes, the choice obtaining the lowest number is eliminated and a run-off election is held.

If a union wins an election which the board directs, it is "certified" as bargaining agent. If no union is selected, collective bargaining need not take place.

A union once certified remains the bargaining agent until displaced by another in a subsequent election or until it is "decertified." Decertification by the board takes place only after a decertification election, which may be asked for by 30 per cent of the employees or by another union. If the challenge fails, the union is recertified.

NLRB. This federal agency, the National Labor Relations Board, is responsible for the application of the Taft-Hartley act and related labor legislation. Its main responsibilities are: (1) the determination of employee representation (described earlier), and

(2) handling unfair labor practice charges—which may be initiated by an employee, a union, or an employer. The board is composed of 5 members appointed by the President of the U.S., with Senate approval, for 5-year terms.

The regional directors of the NLRB investigate charges brought for unfair labor practices. If the charges appear valid, the directors seek informal settlement or issue a "complaint" and hearing notice. Trial attorneys of the NLRB's general council prosecute the charge before a trial examiner appointed by the board. Following such a hearing, the trial examiner prepares an "intermediate report," with a recommended order, which normally becomes final after 20 days, unless appealed to the board within that time. If the order is contested, the NLRB itself reviews the charge and issues a "Decision and Order." Compliance with the order may be voluntary or it may be forced by a circuit court of appeals or a district court. The court's decree is final, subject to petition to the U.S. supreme court.

Injunctions to Stop Unfair Labor Practices. As stated above, the labor board gets its orders enforced by securing a decree from a United States circuit court of appeals. Disobedience to such orders may be penalized by fine or imprisonment. But the board has recourse also to United States district courts to secure speedier action.

The general counsel of board is authorized to seek injunctions to stop any unfair labor practice after he has issued a "complaint," that is, after he has begun formal action in prosecuting a violation.

In respect of one group of unfair practices, however, the board is directed to seek an injunction as soon as it is determined that a complaint should be issued. This group comprises the practices listed under **Practices Forbidden Unions,** paragraph (d). They may be roughly identified as secondary boycotts, organizational picketing, striking to displace a lawful bargaining agent, and striking over a work-jurisdiction dispute.

National-Emergency Disputes. The Taft-Hartley act lays down special procedures for postponing or halting national-emergency strikes, that is, strikes affecting all or a large part of an industry and imperiling the national health or safety. If the president so identifies a dispute, he may appoint a board of inquiry to report on the issues. The government may then go into court for an injunction to stop or postpone the strike until these three steps are taken: (1) The parties negotiate with governmental assistance through mediation; (2) if no agreement is reached in 60 days, the board of inquiry reports the position of the parties, which is made public by the president; and (3) the national labor relations board in the next 15 days polls employees on acceptance of the employer's last offer. If the offer is rejected, the injunction is dissolved, and the parties are left to the arbitrament of economic weapons, unless Congress intervenes. Settlement of the dispute, of course, at any time in this period would also lead to dissolution of the injunction.

LABOR-MANAGEMENT REPORTING AND DISCLOSURE ACT OF 1959

Presumably this law, popularly referred to as the Landrum-Griffin act, was to correct abuses in union and management behavior publicized by the McClellan Committee hearings. However, it went further than simply correcting abuses—it made a number of changes in prior labor legislation and significantly modified Federal labor policy.

The Act sought to protect the rights of union members and insure democratic union administration. Local unions must elect officers at least every three years, and nationals at least every five, by secret ballot. Locals may not raise dues without majority approval by secret ballot and certain restrictions are put on dues increases by organizations other than locals. Members are insured freedom of speech in union meetings, the right to nominate candidates, to vote in union elections, and to examine union books records, and accounts.

Unions must adopt constitutions and by-laws and file with the Secretary of Labor copies of these and a variety of reports on finances and administrative practices. Union officers are required to file reports which would show financial connections that could influence their dealings with management; employers must make reports showing dealings with union officials. Labor relations consultants must also report compensation, disbursements, and the nature of their activities.

Some modifications in the Taft-Hartley law are technical. Employment, by unions, of Communists is prohibited for five years after membership. Revisions insure that, if the National Labor Relations Board does not take jurisdiction in an issue, a State agency may do so, thus eliminating a "No Man's Land" that evolved under Taft-Hartley. Secondary boycotts, attempts by a union to persuade persons not involved directly not to patronize the boycotted concern, were restricted further, but in construction and garment manufacture the provisions were softened. The act declared "hot cargo agreements" between employers and unions an unfair labor practice. In such agreements, the employer agrees not to handle, use, sell, transport, or otherwise deal in any of the products of another employer.

In general, violations of the Act are punishable by fines and imprisonment. Administration of the Act throws a major responsibility on the Secretary of Labor. The Secretary is empowered to conduct investigations when it is believed that violations (other than those arising from the "Bill of Rights of Members") have occurred or are threatened. The numerous reports and other data required under the Act go to the office of the Secretary; he must supervise the internal affairs of unions much more closely than ever before. The results of the law depend primarily on the actions of the staff of the Secretary.

PUBLIC EMPLOYEE UNIONISM

The Lloyd-LaFollette act, of 1912, allowed postal employees to join unions. In 1962, Executive Order 10988 specifically recognized the right of employees in the administrative branch to organize and to present their views on employment terms to agency management.

Organizational rights and certain bargaining privileges were further spelled out in Executive Order 11491, in 1969. A Federal Labor Relations Council and a Federal Service Impasse Panel were established to implement the labor-management program.

The various states have also adopted legislation regulating unionism within such public agencies and institutions as elementary and secondary schools, hospitals, correctional institutions, police and fire departments, mental institutions, public health services, and others. In general, the laws are aimed at controlling strikes that would hamper the effective provisions of such institutions and services.

COLLECTIVE BARGAINING CONTRACTS

The purpose of collective bargaining is to arrive at a contract between employer and union which will govern relations between the parties for a definite period of time—usually a year. Among the subjects which collective bargaining contracts typically cover are these:

1. Union recognition, with a description of the unit of employees represented by the union.
2. Wage rates, possibly with provision for renegotiation after a certain time.
3. Hours of work, with provision for premium rates of pay for hours in excess of the standard day or week.
4. Holidays, with the rate of pay when work is performed on holidays.
5. Vacations, showing eligibility and length, with the amount of vacation pay to be given.

6. Seniority and other ground for promotions and for the selection of those to be laid off and rehired in business fluctuations.

7. Employee benefits, such as sick leave or pension plans.

8. Guarantees of various kinds, such as (1) an employer's undertaking not to discriminate among employees on specified grounds or (2) a union's promise not to strike.

9. Grievances, with procedures for settlement. The procedures usually culminate in arbitration of unsettled grievances arising out of disputed points in the contract or even of all disputes.

10. Union security, which might include the union shop or checkoff.

11. Management prerogatives, outlining management's authority relative to such functions as plant layout and location, product design, production processes, work scheduling, new product development, pricing policies, and other areas of decision.

12. Termination, often with a provision for automatic renewal if neither party gives notice before a certain date that it desires a change in terms.

Limitations on Contracts. The Taft-Hartley act, as noted above, forbids closed-shop clauses. Other contract terms limited by the law are those providing for the checkoff and employee welfare funds.

Checkoff.—This is an arrangement whereby the employer holds back from the employees' pay envelopes the amount of union dues and pays the proceeds over to the union's treasurer. The law permits the checkoff only if the employee authorizes the employer in writing to make such deductions from his pay. The authorization may not be made irrevocable for longer than one year.

Welfare Funds.—The law permits the setting up of trust funds under contracts, but, if the employer contributes to such a fund, the money must be used only for genuine welfare purposes of employees and their families. Management must be given an equal voice in control of the fund, disputes to be resolved by having a third, neutral member on the governing committee.

AVOIDANCE OF DISPUTES

In advance of the acceptance of collective bargaining, a large number of employers put into practice arrangements designed to give employees a sense of unity with the enterprise, thus mitigating or obscuring any division of interest which might lead to disputes. Under collective bargaining, the approach toward elimination of controversy takes typically the form of methods for disposing of grievances. In some instances, a more positive step has been taken through mutual arrangements to increase efficiency or expand markets on the understanding that wages are to be increased, or not decreased, if the efforts are successful.

Methods adopted on employer initiative are usually considered as part of personnel management. Undertaken as a long-range means of increasing efficiency, this form of management aims to keep employees satisfied, loyal to the company, and disposed to give their best services. Methods include wage incentive systems, and granting of special benefits, such as insurance and profit sharing. Labor leaders frequently oppose their use on the ground that they detract from loyalty to the labor movement on which employees in general, it is stated, must depend for safeguarding of their interests.

Settlement of Grievances. Nearly all collective bargaining contracts prescribe steps to be taken for settlement of disputes arising under their terms and provide that no strike or lockout is to take place during the life of the contract when such steps are available. Some contracts go still further and prohibit all work stoppages. Under most contracts the final step in settlement of disputes is arbitration, both sides binding themselves in the contract to abide by whatever award is made.

The following generalized description illustrates the manner in which a dispute arising under a contract may be settled.

Workman Smith complains that, having been told to report for work, he did so, found no work available, and yet was not paid for four hours as required under terms of the contract applying to this situation. The foreman giving no satisfaction, Smith carries the complaint to the shop steward. The shop steward is a union member elected by the "local" for the purpose of taking up grievances of employees with supervisors. The status of shop steward is recognized by the company under the contract.

The steward is told by the foreman that he had not notified Smith to report. The dispute thus hinges on a question of fact, which must be decided on the basis of evidence, if any.

At the next meeting of the union's grievance committee, the status of which also is recognized under the contract, the steward reports the complaint, the statements of Smith and the foreman, and the evidence which each is able to adduce. If the committee, possibly after discussion with both parties, thinks Smith was mistaken, the complaint is dismissed. If it disbelieves the foreman, the chairman of the grievance committee takes up the matter with the supervisor or other superior official. Failing settlement here, an officer of the national union may be called in to speak with the highest executive officer of the company. This completes the grievance procedure where there is no absolute prohibition of strikes or arbitration clause.

Arbitration. This term applies to the settlement of a dispute by the decision of an umpire or impartial committee, both sides agreeing in advance, or being required by law, to accept the award. If acceptance is required by law, the arbitration is said to be compulsory; if by agreement, the arbitration is called voluntary.

There are two different kinds of situations to which arbitration of labor disputes is applied. One is a dispute over rights arising under a contract, such as the dispute outlined above. Arbitration in such a situation is sometimes known as arbitration of rights. This is the most usual type of arbitration.

The other type of dispute—interest—arises during the negotiation of contract terms. Here the services of the Federal Mediation and Conciliation Service may be utilized in the search for a compromise solution.

Railway Labor Disputes. The Railway Labor act of 1926 set up a special procedure for avoiding strikes which was the precedent for the Taft-Hartley act's provision respecting national-emergency disputes described above. If a strike is threatened, the president may appoint an "emergency board" to investigate the dispute and make recommendations within 30 days. For that period and an additional 30 days the parties are forbidden to make any change in conditions, but no penalties are prescribed for violating the prohibition.

LABOR UNIONS—A SUMMARY

As indicated in the foregoing account, labor unions have evolved into major types through a long period of strife, adjustment, and progress. As their membership has increased in numbers and in variety of occupation, the interests which they represent have ceased to be limited to labor and management and have involved a third party, the general public, whose disapproval or sense of unfairness could place either of the bargaining groups at a serious disadvantage. Although in most cases the leaders have been responsive to the challenge and have moved to correct injustices by or within their own organizations, there have been instances in which pressure from the public has been exerted to insure reasonableness and equity in the conduct of one group or the other. Practices on either side that the public considered arbitrary, monopolistic, or unduly selfish have sometimes led to stringent regulation by Federal authorities or to proposals for local remedies such as the "right to work" laws that have recently been enacted in several states. Both the efforts of unions to achieve economic betterment and those of management to obtain productivity with economy have become increasingly subject to public scrutiny.

Types of Unions. Organizationally, unions may be divided into craft unions and industrial unions.

A *craft union* embraces workers in a single craft, irrespective of industry, plant, or employer. Thus all carpenters are eligible in one union whether hired by a building firm, a mining company, or a ship builder. Craft unions frequently provide insurance and unemployment benefits for members.

An *industrial union* embraces workers in a single plant or industry regardless of the type of work done by members. In mass-production industries, this type of union has advantages over craft unions, since modern factory production breaks down the older classifications of skill and craft and opens the way for enrollment of all workers.

The existence of these two types of labor organization has given rise to numerous disputes since a given craft employee may be claimed by both types.

Jurisdictional Disputes. These are controversies between two unions as to which one is entitled to enroll a certain type of worker. The term is sometimes applied to conflicts between craft and industrial unions, but it more typically describes a conflict between craft unions. Some long-standing jurisdictional disputes include one over drivers of beer trucks as to whether they belong to the brewery workers (industrial union) or to the truck drivers (craft or class union). Another involves two crafts—carpenters and machinists—and concerns work on a considerable number of jobs which had not been envisioned when the unions were chartered, such as installation of metal-frame windows.

Strikes over work-jurisdiction disputes are forbidden as unfair practices by the Taft-Hartley act, which authorizes the National Labor Relations Board to settle the question at issue unless the parties work out some other acceptable method of settlement.

National Labor Unions. The earlier unions in the United States adopted the craft form of organization. The Knights of Labor championed the industrial type, but the ascendency of the American Federation of Labor, representing the craft type predominantly, gave this type the advantage until the formation of a rival group in 1935, which later became the Congress of Industrial Organization. The latter body and the Federation embrace the great majority of organized workers.

The American Federation of Labor (A. F. of L.). This organization was an association of trade unions in the United States and its dependencies. Some unions, however. known as international unions, had local units in Canada also.

The basic unit in the Federation was the local union. Most local unions belonged to national or international unions, which were associated in the A. F. of L. as more or less autonomous bodies. They were chartered by the A. F. of L., and the charters could be revoked for non-payment of dues or assessments.

Other local unions were directly affiliated with the A. F. of L. and were known as federal unions. They belonged to crafts or industries for which no national union had been chartered.

Congress of Industrial Organizations (C.I.O.). Formally organized on November 16, 1938, this rival labor group stems from the Committee for Industrial Organization, a committee of the A. F. of L. formed for the purpose of promoting the industrial type of union. Its members were A. F. of L. unions of the industrial type. In 1936, these unions were suspended and later expelled. Meanwhile, many new unions were chartered by the C. I. O. before it had adopted a constitution.

The formation of the C. I. O. was in protest against the failure of the A. F. of L to organize mass production industries, this failure being attributed to a desire to protect the jurisdictions of craft unions over skilled workers within these industries. The first fruits of the C. I. O.'s efforts were the organization of most of the steel and automobile industries.

In many other industries the C. I. O. and A. F. of L. directly competed for members, the A. F. of L. frequently opening membership to all employees irrespective of craft and thus competing on an industrial union basis.

AFL—CIO Merger. On December 5, 1955, these two great unions were merged in a single federation, The American Federation of Labor and Congress of Industrial Organizations.

Following the merger at the national level, began the slow process of merging state federations of labor (of the former A. F. of L.) and state industrial union councils (of the former CIO) and city organizations of like nature. Most, but not all, local unions are affiliated with the appropriate state and city "central labor body." The mergers of state and city bodies progressed slowly.

There remained also the problem of many international unions affiliated with the AFL-CIO with seriously overlapping jurisdiction. For example both AFL and CIO had affiliates that assumed jurisdiction over workers in aircraft manufacturing. The same situation prevailed in many other industries. Also certain craft unions of the old AFL felt they should have jurisdiction over some workers organized by industrial unions of the former CIO. Thus jurisdictional problems abound within the merged labor body.

Railway Brotherhoods. Traditionally workers on the railways were in unions unaffiliated with either the AFL or CIO. The major unions of this group are the Brotherhood of Locomotive Engineers, Brotherhood of Locomotive Firemen and Enginemen, Brotherhood of Railroad Trainmen, Order of Railway Conductors and Brakemen, and the Yardmasters of North America. The Switchmen's Union of North America is affiliated with the A. F. of L.

These are sometimes referred to as operating brotherhoods to distinguish them from unions of other railroad employees who do not actually operate trains. After the merger of AFL and CIO the Brotherhood of Locomotive Firemen and Enginemen and the Brotherhood of Railroad Trainmen affiliated with the merged federation. In addition, most of the unions of non-operating railroad employees are affiliated with the A. F. of L. Nevertheless for purposes of negotiations these unions and the operating brotherhoods frequently act through a joint body known as the Railway Labor Executives' Association.

In addition to the above there are a number of independent unions, most of them being plant or local organizations. A considerable proportion of them are successors of company-supported unions, reorganized after withdrawal of employer support.

In addition some major unions of national importance are non-affiliates of AFL-CIO. These include the United Mine Workers and the Teamsters (Chauffeurs) Union, the latter expelled from the AFL-CIO in 1957 because of its failure to remove corrupt officials from positions in the union. In 1968, the powerful United Automobile workers (UAW) joined the ranks of the non-affiliates by splitting away from the AFL-CIO.

EMPLOYER ASSOCIATIONS

When unions become strong, employers frequently form their own organizations to bargain on behalf of their members with the unions and to take concerted action if necessary in resisting union demands or pressing their own. Such associations may be formed on an industry basis, as among coal mine owners, or on a regional basis, taking in employers in a given area, as is done in San Francisco.

When collective bargaining has reached this stage, individual employers no longer negotiate with unions but accept the terms reached in conversations between the association and the union. Disputes become fewer. The magnitude of a possible strike or lockout tends to impress a sense of caution on both sides. Well defined procedures are usually established for handling disagreements under the contracts negotiated. Not infrequently a permanent arbitrator is appointed whose duty is to settle such disagreements, building up a body of precedents into an accepted code of labor practices. Unions and associations in some instances work out programs of joint action to aid the industry.

WAGE AND HOUR REGULATION

While, in general, employment conditions are a matter of free arrangement between employers and employees, there are several segments of economic life in the United States in which such freedom of contract is rigidly limited by law.

Industrial employment of children is limited by all states and is prohibited for interstate enterprises by the Federal government.

Hours which women may be permitted to work are restricted in a majority of the states.

A lower limit is placed on the wages for which women may be permitted to sell their labor in approximately half the states.

Both hours and wages of industrial workers in interstate commerce, men and women, are regulated by the Federal government under the Fair Labor Standards Act of 1938.

Child Labor. The first child labor law in the United States was adopted by Massachusetts in 1836. It required that children under 15 years of age employed in manufacturing establishments should be required to attend school at least three months in the year.

In 1842, the hours of children under 12 were limited to ten a day in Massachusetts; in Connecticut this provision was applied to children under 14. Rhode Island in 1853 restricted hours of labor for children under 12 to eleven a day.

In the decade of 1850-60, a number of states prohibited altogether the employment of children under certain ages in manufacturing industries. Other states limited their employment with varying requirements as to age and hours.

In 1907 the Federal government took cognizance of the problem in a comprehensive investigation into the condition of women and child wage earners. The findings of this report, added to years of effort to secure a Federal child-labor law, culminated in the passage of the Keating-Owen bill by Congress in September 1916. This act was declared unconstitutional in a 5-to-4 decision by the supreme court on June 3, 1918 (247 U. S. 251). An attempt was next made to achieve the same purpose by levying a tax of 10 per cent on the annual net profits of any establishment employing child labor in violation of the standards it set. But on May 15, 1922, this act was declared unconstitutional by an 8-to-1 decision of the supreme court (259 U. S. 20).

In 1924, Congress approved a resolution for submitting to the states a proposed amendment to the Federal constitution giving Congress the power to "limit, regulate, and prohibit the labor of persons under 18 years of age." By 1938, only 28 out of the requisite 36 states had ratified the proposed amendment. In that year the United States supreme court upheld a wage regulation law of the State of Washington in terms which led to the belief that the earlier child labor decisions would be reversed. The same year Congress passed the Fair Labor Standards act, which forbids interstate shipment of goods made at a plant where, within the previous 60 days, minors below 16 years of age (18 in hazardous occupations) were employed.

Regulation of Hours by States. The earliest law in America regulating hours of work for women was passed by New Hampshire in 1847. This measure became a dead letter through the practice of employers in requiring employees to contract away their rights under the act as a condition of employment. The next such law was passed by Massachusetts in 1874. It limited hours worked by women in manufacturing to 10 daily and 60 weekly.

All such state laws until recent years applied to women and children only. Then men in certain occupational groups began to be given similar protection. Pennsylvania in 1937 passed a law applying to both men and women in all occupations. It was declared unconstitutional on technical grounds.

Regulation of Wages by States. The pioneer in legislation setting minimum wages was Massachusetts, which passed the first law of this type in 1912. It covered only women and children with provision for gradual application from industry to industry. The first such law to be applied also to men was passed by Oklahoma in 1938. It was held unconstitutional on technical grounds but upheld in other respects. Connecticut in 1939 became the first state to extend the coverage of its minimum-wage law to men. As of 1968, 39 states, Puerto Rico, and the District of Columbia had enacted minimum wage laws, almost all of which covered both men and women.

The prevailing pattern of state wage laws of general application calls for appointment of committees to study the need for wage minima in different occupations. The recommendations of such committees, if accepted by a designated administrative agency, become effective as wage orders. In some cases the wage order is "directory" for a period, during which violation incurs the penalty of publicity only. It later became "mandatory," and violations then are punishable by criminal penalties.

Fair Labor Standards Act. Effective October 24, 1938, this law established in general a 44-hour week, hours worked in excess of the standard calling for pay at the rate of time and one-half. After one year, the standard week was reduced to 42 hours and a year later reached the permanent form of 40 hours. A 1965 amendment also required the time-and-one-half rate for hours over 8 a day, a practice that was already almost universal in most industries.

A "floor" was placed beneath wages, it being unlawful to pay an employee engaged on work for interstate commerce a wage less than 25 cents an hour. This figure was raised to 30 cents after the first year and to 40 cents by the end of the seventh year. Provision was made for increasing the minimum wage in individual industries to the 40-cent level in less than the seven years.

The federal minimum wage rate was raised to the hourly rate of 75 cents in 1949, $1.00 in 1956, $1.25 in 1961, $1.40 in 1967, and $1.60 in 1968.

In 1974 legislation was passed covering new minimum wage rates for nonfarm workers, farm workers, federal, state, and local government workers, domestic service, and retail and service employees of chain-store operations. The minimum wage is to be increased in stages until 1978, when all are to receive $2.30.

Enforcement. For violation of the law, fines may be levied and second offenders may be imprisoned. Injunctions also may be issued against such practices in violation of the law as failure to pay the minimum wages or pay for overtime work, failure to keep records or falsification of records, employment of minors without permits, and shipment in interstate commerce of goods produced in violation of the law. Also, employees who believe they have been underpaid on the basis of the law may sue to recover wages allegedly due. If successful, they are entitled to collect double the amount due as wages and reasonable legal expenses in addition.

Public Contracts. Another way in which the government influences wages and hours is through the power of its purse. By requiring that all enterprises doing business with it should stipulate that, in carrying out the contract, they will observe specified standards, the government is able to extend these standards at least as widely as work done under such contracts. In practice, the influence extends much further, since a firm filling contracts both for the government and other customers frequently finds it impossible to separate the work and maintain one standard for government work and a lower standard for other work.

This form of leverage is applied by the Davis-Bacon act, of 1931. It requires contractors in construction work valued at $2000 or more, and paid for by federal funds, to pay at least the prevailing minimum wage to all construction employees. This type of regulation was extended in 1965, by the O'Hara-McNamara Services act, to government contract on-site services other than construction.

Portal-to-Portal Act. This act, amending the Fair Labor Standards act and Public Contracts act, was passed in 1947 to limit liability of employers for wages of employees. Primarily it was to mitigate the effect of a decision by the United States supreme court in *Anderson v. Mt. Clemens Pottery Co.* The court held that time spent by employees in subsidiary activities outside their principal jobs, such as traveling from entrance to job and back, must be paid for as time worked. The law forbids courts to treat such time as working time unless it has been so treated by contract, custom, or practice.

Wage Stabilization. During World War II, a somewhat flexible ceiling was placed over wages as a means of controlling inflation. Employers were forbidden by the Economic Stabilization Act of 1942 to increase or decrease compensation except by permission of designated government agencies, especially the National War Labor Board. While wage rates were stabilized, employees increased their earnings by overtime, promotion increases, shift differentials, and other benefits, such as paid holidays and health and welfare plans. During the Korean conflict, wages and prices were temporarily frozen in 1951, and a Wage Stabilization Board promulgated regulations outlining conditions under which such increases as those based on merit, seniority, promotion, inequity, and other factors could be granted.

UNEMPLOYMENT

Defenses against Unemployment. In seasonal employments. the laborer has tried to prolong his job by curtailing daily production until the piece-work system has been substituted for the day wage. Similarly, low employment periods have been met by union men through restriction of days of work so as to make available work go around among the existing number of trained workers in the craft. Monopoly of labor supply through restricted apprenticeship and membership is another means used to prevent unemployment.

Labor-saving Machinery. There is an increasing realization among labor leaders that machinery, by increasing possible production per hour, increases possible earnings per hour. On the other hand, not only may the impact of rapid mechanization on a society geared to private profit be disastrous to those whose skill is rendered useless, but it is believed by many to be a cause in recurrent depressions.

Technological Unemployment. This is a term used to describe unemployment which results from the introduction of labor-saving machinery. In some favorably situated industries, those displaced through machinery may be equalled in number by those absorbed again into employment by the industries as mechanization brings enlarged demand.

Featherbedding. This term is used to mean employment and payment of a worker, pursuant to a union contract, for work not intended to be performed. Typically, it means payment of a worker whose task has disappeared because of technological changes, such as firemen no longer needed when Diesel locomotives replaced steam locomotives. It is an extreme form of union efforts to limit output of work so as to limit unemployment.

Seasonal Unemployment. To a certain extent, unemployment of this type is inevitable, as for instance in farming, where the chief demand for labor is at seeding or harvest time. In other cases, buying habits of the public are responsible.

Cyclical Unemployment. The use of this term is based on the expression "business cycle," referring to the cycle, or recurrent sequence, of booms and depressions. Loss of work opportunities is the most serious feature of depressions. Not only does it fall with cruel force on those who are denied the opportunity of earning a living, but, by drastically cutting the productivity of all industry, it decreases the wealth available for distribution.

Measurement of Unemployment. The United States Labor Department publishes monthly figures on the percentage of the labor force actively seeking jobs. It is based on the survey of a sample of about 35,000 households. It is possible, however, that total personal income may rise even when reported unemployment is increasing. Reasons include the facts that unemployment compensation is paid and that the figures take no account of many persons having second or part-time jobs.

Employment Act of 1946. Consideration of the losses occasioned by cyclical unemployment was behind the declaration of congressional policy contained in the Employment act of 1946. The declaration states that it is the responsibility of the Federal government to use all practicable means, consistent with other aspects of national policy, to coordinate its efforts with those of industry, agriculture. labor, and state governments to promote maximum employment, production, and purchasing power.

In the early 1960's, Congress passed a sequence of acts—the Area Redevelopment act in 1961, the Manpower Development and Training act in 1962, and the Economic Opportunity act in 1964—aimed at the expansion of employment opportunities, providing for the training of workers and attacking the roots of poverty. In 1968, the "Job Opportunities in the Business Sector" (JOBS) program was launched in a widespread attempt to combat hard-core unemployment.

The first national fair employment or equal employment opportunity legislation was incorporated as Title VII of the 1964 Civil Rights act. In general, Title VII makes it unlawful for an employer to refuse to hire or to discharge or otherwise to discriminate against an individual on the basis of race, color, religion, sex, or national origin.

Unemployment Compensation. The most common measure designed to aid in meeting the problem of involuntary idleness is unemployment compensation. Each state, prompted by the offset provision of the Social Security act of 1935, has enacted unemployment compensation legislation. Extensive variation exists among these laws with respect to their coverage, eligibility requirements, and benefit amounts. Generally, these laws exempt farm workers, casual workers, and frequently workers in very small establishments. Benefit funds are raised by employers' payment of taxes on wages earned during periods of employment. Benefits allowed tend to be roughly half of lost wages, and generally may not be paid for more than 26 weeks in a year, but some states responded to encouragement by the federal government to extend the benefits to 39 weeks.

In response to severe recessions and resultant lengthy periods of unemployment, Congress in 1958 and again in 1961 enacted temporary legislation urging states to lengthen the duration of benefit payments. The first such legislation provided federal loan assistance, while benefits provided by the second legislation were financed by a temporary increase in payroll taxes.

Some of the more powerful industrial unions, notably those in automobile, rubber, and steel manufacturing, have negotiated agreements with employers to pay supplemental unemployment benefits in addition to the unemployment compensation payment. These supplemental benefits are financed by the employer based on employee hours worked. The benefits are retained in a trust fund, added to state benefits to constitute from about 80% to 95% of take-home pay, and are usually payable up to 52 weeks.

MARKETING

Marketing is a specialized type of economic activity that has been developed during the 20th century, largely in the United States. The broad activity of which "marketing" is the specialized name, however, is common to all people and all times. This basic activity of distributing products that people consume arises from the separation of producing and consuming as specialized economic activities.

Thus, the term "marketing" has several meanings: it covers a highly specialized consumer-related service, a type of business undertaking, a far-reaching economic process, or a form of social activity.

A Social Institution. When a pattern of activity and personal relationships spreads throughout and characterizes a society, it is regarded as an institution. As marketing forms a meaningful element in present-day society, it may be said to be institutionalized. However, while marketing has been an important influence on society, it is society which has created and approved the manner in which distribution is performed. Marketing is an expression of society's values and goals, as well as forming the best judgment of how to attain those goals and to relate the activity with other social patterns. Every society has its own structure, relationships, goals, values, and resources, and marketing is the product of all of them. Therefore, the distributive processes and systems of one society may not be appropriate for another. Nevertheless, every society will work out some form of distribution, and one of the more highly specialized and technical forms of distribution is termed "marketing."

Viewed in this sense, marketing is not merely the means by which *businessmen* meet the needs of society for consumer goods and services, it is also a means by which *society*, acting as a whole, meets its own needs.

An Economic Process. As an economic process, marketing is the manner in which economic resources are organized by society for reaching its consumption goals. Marketing is the manner in which factors of economic production—land, labor, capital, and management skill—are combined in the processes of distribution. Marketing is the process of creating additional values in products by making them available to the market at the time, in the place, and in the manner desired. Marketing is the carrying into effect by suppliers of the conception, creation, and communication of a standard of living for society. It is the means by which a uniform pattern of consumption is provided through mass distribution to a large community. It is the process of effecting through the market mechanism the assignment and use of scarce resources.

Viewed thus, marketing is concerned mainly with economic factors such as values, prices, costs, utility, scarcity, economies, profits, production, and efficiency. It is not thereby concerned with some of the broader social implications.

A Business Undertaking. Business is a managed aspect of the market economy, and marketing is a phase of business management: that which relates to the analysis of markets, the conception of marketable products, their physical distribution, and transfer of title.

As a business undertaking, marketing is a broad technical activity; the general function of assembling, sorting, and dispersing goods; the control of the flow of values through successive stages of ownership; the utilization of the mechanism of the market for private and public economic and social ends. Marketing is typically a seller-initiated management process.

From the conception of "marketing" early in the 20th century, it has always been a *compound* activity and not merely the *single* process of selling, distributing, etc.

A Consumer-Oriented Service. Finally, marketing is management of business enterprise based upon primary motivation to render a customer service. Marketing is characteristically a matter of viewpoint, and nothing less than consumer orientation is marketing in the highest sense.

Adoption of this viewpoint in marketing management is a contemporary development. It has long been held that business is primarily for producing profit, that it performs best when "let alone" (*laissez faire*), and that buyers should look after their own defense (*caveat emptor*). Marketing practice in the United States has shown the fallacy of this philosophy and the profitability of conforming business undertakings to the needs and wishes of the market. This viewpoint has evolved with development of scientific marketing practice.

Thus marketing is the conduct of the distributive function in business, approached from the interest of the market served. This concept of marketing is consistent with the idea of marketing as a social institution, for society approves only institutions which meet its needs. The marketing mechanism which is consumer-oriented fulfils both a business and a social purpose.

HOW SOCIETIES SUPPLY THEIR NEEDS

The role which marketing plays in modern society is outlined more boldly by contrasting the marketing process with its counterparts in other societies. In ancient societies, as in some underdeveloped ones even today, needs were met through exchange carried on *without markets* and *without marketing.* The market economy has evolved only during the past 400 years, since the Industrial Revolution. The practice of modern marketing began about 1900.

In general, older societies have accomplished the distribution of products by three principles of human behavior which are not primarily economic in nature: reciprocity, redistribution, and householding. A fourth principle, which is primarily economic, is that of the market organization; marketing relates only to this.

Reciprocity is that conduct of society whereby one gives from the harvests of his production, not for immediate material benefit in exchange, but for the approbation which society places on good husbandry and fine citizenship. Credit due to good behavior and civic virtue is the well-spring of motivation in such dissemination of one's goods. The recipients, according to the society and the scale of the operation, may be one's sister and her family, or a paired counterpart in another tribe or village. Supply for one's own needs is assured in the measure that he has earned social esteem through his own generosity. Social values are paramount; the economic effect is secondary. This system has been effective where society is organized on a family or kinship basis.

Redistribution is the principle employed in societies of a territorial character, under a common chief, whereby a substantial part of production is delivered to village headmen who keep it in storage. Redistribution of the provision is made according to a plan of differentiated rations to both producing and non-producing parts of the population and to members of other distant communities on ceremonial and festival occasions. Redistribution was practiced in the kingdom of Hammurabi in Babylonia and in the New Kingdom of Egypt as well as in medieval feudal systems, which were also based on this principle.

Householding is that principle of economic organization whereby production is carried on by a closed group, such as a family, a village settlement, or a political unit, for supplying the needs of the group. *Personal* self-sufficiency has never existed, and such *group* self-sufficiency is achieved only in a fairly advanced stage of agriculture; it is not more primitive than systems of reciprocity and redistribution. Production in a householding economy is for use, not for exchange; storage may or may not be performed. In certain circumstances, surpluses may be sold, but inasmuch as gain through sale is not the motive for producing, the essential character of the economy is not disturbed thereby.

In these three forms of the economy, there is no instance of trade or markets, where equivalencies are determined and expressed as a price. Where there is no market, there obviously is no marketing.

However, before markets developed, trade existed and was widely carried on. The development of markets antedated the rise of the market economy. And the existence of the market economy was prerequisite to the modern conception of marketing.

Trade developed in three distinct and separate realms: foreign trade, local trade, and national trade. Foreign or long-distance trade arose originally out of exploration, adventure, hunting, piracy, and war. Later, it was characterized by barter, and ultimately markets for trade developed at seaports, fords, riverheads, caravan junctures, and sites of fairs. Such trade was external to the economy of a society. Its transactions were consummated by rulers and headmen; its functionaries were not middlemen, but hired servants; and its markets were segregated from local distribution by regulations prohibiting retail sale of goods by long-distance traders.

Local markets were within the towns and did not extend into the countryside. In them were dispersed products which could not stand long travel and which supplied the common needs of the community. While foreign trade was conducted *outside* the economy, local trade was made to conform to the prevailing principles of economic and social behavior. Trade was restricted in the community to prevent its encroaching upon the prevailing economic organization of society. The values of society superseded those of the local market place.

National or interior markets were not the outgrowth of either local or long-distance trade. Regulations specifically prevented such spread of trade. Rising territorial states, however, adopting a policy of mercantilism, removed barriers to trade and opened the countryside and provinces to the competitive commerce. The impetus to this move was political, for the national state was forced to draw its resources from a wider territory and to foster more extensive interchange among its regions. Freeing trade from restrictions which confined it to the town or to long-distance dealing, however, did not remove all restrictions from it. On the contrary, the national market was still kept subordinate to social objectives; practices in the new market did not interfere with the prevailing manorial economy.

Between the development of national markets and the later rise of the market economy, prevailing concepts of the relationship between the economy and society were changed. Production was carried on primarily for sale on the market; incomes were derived from sales on the market; personal gain became the principal motivation of exchange; and social values became subordinated to economic value. Such was the conceptual transition from the non-market to the market economy accompanying the Industrial Revolut on.

In their early stages, the market economy and market society were fraught with commercial tyranny and social depredations. Such was the character of trade in the United States, even until the late 19th century. Then social resistance to predatory business practices began to express itself in legislation and in other ways intended to improve trade and market practices. At the same time, scientific methods were introduced into business management. These several circumstances led to the development of the body of thought and practice known as Marketing.

SOCIAL ORIENTATION OF MARKETING IN THE UNITED STATES

The nature of marketing in any country is determined largely by two factors: 1) the character of society which determines the behavior of people in the market as consumers and as businessmen, and 2) the types and quantities of products which must be distributed.

Marketing in the United States is affected by certain basic facts, one of which is that ours is a theistic society, predicated upon the principle of man's divine rights. Precocious and preoccupied with success, however, it presents paradoxes as a market economy. Ours is a new culture. It has not been weighted with historical precedents that have hampered many countries of Western Civilization and the Oriental societies. Not only have we been receptive to new ideas, we have been quick to translate ideas into institutions, products, and practices. Willingness to experiment and to find better ways of doing things has characterized our life. This attitude has accustomed us to continual change, to anticipation that, although present achievements are good, better ones are on the threshold. While this youthful attitude has encouraged progress, it has left some traditional values undeveloped. Short-lived values have been preferred to more permanent ones; appearance has been more important than quality; and mere change has been accepted in place of improvement.

Notwithstanding the youthful character of our society, many of our attitudes are deeply rooted in ancient Judeo-Christian concepts, one of which relates to the importance and the dignity of individual man. From this stems our ideal of equality—that all men are created equal and that men should enjoy equal opportunity. This concept relates to the absence of formal class or caste structure in our society, to the provision of education for the masses, to freedom of initiative in business undertakings, to equality of the sexes, to uniformity of living level among different groups. It is interpreted in our concept of the "average man," in glorification of the "middle income" group, in protection of the "little" fellow.

Our society emphasizes also the importance of mental enlightenment. Respect for the ability to think things through has produced theories of rationalism and pragmatism and placed great hope upon science for meeting human needs. It is related to the fact that in the United States more than 38 million pupils are enrolled in elementary and secondary public and private schools, and more than 3 million in institutions of higher education. It is related also to the vast and numerous programs of adult education and executive development. Logic and reason are replacing ignorance, mysticism, and emotionalism. It has been assumed, therefore, that individuals are rational in the market place as well as in their other behavior. Standards of fairness, justice, and ethics also stem from rationality.

In an environment offering opportunity and equipped with rationalism, man in our society is under social pressure to produce—to achieve, to get ahead. Fortunately, we have been exceedingly inventive in our scientific pursuits, and rich rewards have befallen individuals. Rewards, however, rather than contributions have become the social criterion for bestowing homage and respect. Ability to show affluence and material possessions has become an important end and motivation; when satiety with things is reached the quest for power and prestige continues. The urgency to evidence success has encouraged aggression and risk taking, countenanced brashness and egoism, and deplored weakness and failure.

Toward the end of achieving its objectives, our society has widely adopted the concept of specialization. We are a society of interrelated parts and individuals, but specialization rather than integration is stressed. Occupations in both the professions and trades have taken on assembly-line characteristics. Even education has become compartmented and not dedicated to development of the whole man. Society exploits specialized talents and personal idiosyncracies. The effect has been an increased dependence of the individual upon the whole, loss of pride in craftsmanship, and resort to hobbies, adult education, and vicarious enjoyment as compensation for the imbalances of over-specialization.

As the basic needs of our people have become satisfied, we have indulged in leisure, diversion, mobility, and pleasure. Approximately 20 per cent of the American families change their dwelling place every year. We travel widely. We seek comfort, ease, and entertainment, on the assumption that *now* is the time for *enjoyment*. Abstinence, sacrifice, and self-discipline are unpopular. Pleasure is pursued vigorously, usually with gadgets and extra equipment. While there has been an increase in reading and educational undertakings, we often reach for fragments of knowledge which are not integrated. Personal interests have often precluded interest in broader social issues, and satisfaction with our own institutions has prevented us from becoming sufficiently informed about those of other people.

The family, long a significant social unit, has some unique characteristics in our society. It is typically a small group expressing considerable independence, both economically and socially. It consists typically of parents and their unmarried children, although the latter often establish independent households. Since 1900, private households have increased 205 per cent, while population has increased 120 per cent. Although about one-third of our families have liquid savings and no debt, personal debt in general is commonplace. Consequently, training in personal finance and encouragement in economic independence is begun early in one's life. The family is often a unit of decision, action, and consumption.

THE AMERICAN MARKET

In this social setting lies the American market, which is the object of the marketing task. It consists of approximately 213,000,000 individuals, about two-thirds of whom reside in urban areas. In 1975, the per-capita income was $5,834. The per-capita personal income in 1975 was as follows:

Alabama	$4,557	Montana	$5,434
Alaska	8,815	Nebraska	6,175
Arizona	5,329	Nevada	6,524
Arkansas	4,383	New Hampshire	5,210
California	6,555	New Jersey	6,629
Colorado	5,839	New Mexico	4,482
Connecticut	6,854	New York	6,603
Delaware	6,800	North Carolina	4,801
Dist. of Columbia	7,750	North Dakota	5,855
Florida	5,517	Ohio	5,883
Georgia	4,969	Oklahoma	4,996
Hawaii	6,426	Oregon	5,611
Idaho	4,980	Pennsylvania	5,874
Illinois	6,750	Rhode Island	5,917
Indiana	5,587	South Carolina	4,521
Iowa	5,899	South Dakota	4,980
Kansas	5,968	Tennessee	4,766
Kentucky	4,668	Texas	5,387
Louisiana	4,729	Utah	4,819
Maine	4,785	Vermont	4,926
Maryland	6,437	Virginia	5,671
Massachusetts	6,159	Washington	6,226
Michigan	6,240	West Virginia	4,815
Minnesota	5,754	Wisconsin	5,627
Mississippi	4,041	Wyoming	5,941
Missouri	5,387		

Source: Bureau of Economic Analysis, 1976.

Although personal consumption is regarded as household consumption, not all of it occurs in the home. In addition, people consume in restaurants, hotels, private clubs, schools, trains and airplanes, churches, student organizations, boarding houses, and in welfare, charity, and emergency institutions. The durable and nondurable goods and services consumed through *personal* expenditures are about 62 per cent of the Gross National Product.

Business institutions constitute another large market, buying products which they either convert into other products or which they consume in their business activities. Such industrial consumers are the market for 45 per cent of all manufactured goods, 80 per cent of all farm products, about 50 per cent of all imports, the bulk of products mined and quarried, and practically all products of wells, fisheries, and hunting and forest industries.

Personal and business domestic investment accounts for another 15 per cent of the Gross National Product. This includes new construction—residential, non-farm, and other; producers' durable equipment; and changes in business inventories.

Governmental agencies—federal, state, and local—are the market for about 19 per cent of the Gross National Product. They consume vast quantities of commodities in performance of administrative work, in military activity, in carrying out public projects, in fulfilling price support programs, and in granting foreign aid assistance.

Finally, the market for some 4.5 per cent of the Gross National Product is abroad, where American products are marketed to personal consumers, business establishments, and government organizations.

PRODUCTS TO BE MARKETED

Another factor affecting the marketing task in the United States is the variety and quantity of products which are produced. In 1975, the Gross National Product amounted to approximately $1,500 billions. The magnitude of the marketing task, however, is a multiple of the value either of goods produced or consumed, for in the channels of distribution one product may be resold several times. For example, agricultural products may be sold at the farm, through a broker, to wholesalers, then to jobbers, then to retailers, and ultimately to consumers.

THE MARKETING TASK

Whatever the form of society and the nature of its products and disposition of its consumers, the responsibility for distributing its products constitutes a collective undertaking. In our society, this responsibility for effecting distribution and exchange is known as *the marketing task*. When transaction occurs and goods are acquired, the marketing task is fulfilled.

The performance of the marketing task in our society is a vast and complex undertaking. It employs uncounted millions of people in the marketing activity of manufacturers and other producers, in advertising agencies, research organizations, credit information bureaus, market news agencies, and transportation companies, as well as in almost 2,100,000 marketing establishments. The number employed in retail and wholesale establishments alone comprise more than 20 per cent of our gainfully employed citizens.

The task to which these people are dedicated is the creation of those services required to make desired products available to consumers at the place, at the time, and in the manner preferred. The task of marketing is twofold: first, to distribute physical products; second, to provide with those products such service or services as the market may wish. Such services may include personal salesmanship, credit, delivery, adjustments, guarantees, assortment, continuous availability, convenience, pleasant surroundings, and the like. The *primary* task of marketing is the distribution of *commodities*. The performance of related services is secondary and incidental but in our society highly important.

THE MARKETING FUNCTIONS

Circumstances of the market define the need for marketing, and this need prescribes the types of marketing service supplied. Thus because they are *functions* or variants of the marketing task to be performed, these services or processes are known as "marketing functions." The following functions are implicit in a concept of marketing:

Market Research
Conception and Identification of Products
Selling
Buying
Transporting
Storing
Market and Marketing Finance
Merchandising
Market Risk Bearing

Not all of these functions must be performed in every instance of marketing. In the simplest market situations, a minimum of marketing activity occurs. It must be remembered that, insofar as the marketing of products is concerned, it is the *product* that is wanted. The services which constitute marketing are desired and bought only in order that the *product* may be obtained at the time, in the place, and in the manner desired. The *transaction* conveying the product is the object of primary interest. Marketing services are performed only in order that the transaction may occur. Marketing, therefore, is the means by which a transaction is brought about; it is not primarily the transaction itself.

Market Conditions. A market may be defined as demand and supply existing in a relationship which results in transaction and in transfer of goods. Markets, however, have a variety of demand-supply relationships, and the state of the market determines the functions to be performed. When buyers and sellers have mutual knowledge of each other's need, transaction or fulfillment of the market may depend upon only negotiation and establishment of a price. It is impossible that such markets exist to any large extent in a vast economy, for several reasons. First, mutuality of knowledge does not exist; consequently, both buyers and sellers are obliged to share an information function. Sellers seek to know what needs exist, what capacities are unsatisfied, where markets are located. Buyers at the same time study their needs and the offerings of which they know, and they seek additional information about the market. Sellers interpret their market information into products, whose qualities they make known through means of identification and communication.

When knowledge of the market is shared by traders, transaction may still not occur because of other maladjustments of demand and supply. Space and time factors may prevent the fulfillment of a transaction, until additional services have been performed. When buyers and sellers are separated by space, transaction is dependent upon transportation. When time interferes, transaction depends upon products being stored if supply antecedes demand, or upon the transaction being financed if demand antecedes effectual demand. Acts counteracting time and space facilitate transaction and bring markets to fulfillment.

In addition to the relationship existing be ween any pair of demanders and suppliers who may make an individual transaction, there are other significant factors affecting the need for marketing in the *aggregate market*. A single transaction occurs at but one place and at a particular time. Satisfaction of the demand which constitutes the aggregate market requires making products available *within the bounds of the market* in the assortment, at the place, and at the time preferred by a *variety* of buyers. Transaction thus depends upon merchandising, or the providing of products for the *collective* market. To the physical product is thus added *availability*.

The service of availability is provided by the function of merchandising and also by the bearing of market risk. Unless market risks are borne, the responsibility for making goods available to the market is not undertaken.

Utility Created. In the mass market economy, marketing in some form or combination of functions is practically indispensable, for there is almost always need for one or more of the functions of transportation, storage, finance, or availability. Because value is placed upon these services, marketing, through the functions which produce these services, creates five types of economic utilities:

Information Utility, by market research, product identification, selling, and buying
Place Utility, by transporting
Time Utility, by storing
Possession Utility, by market and marketing finance
Availability Utility, by merchandising and bearing of market risk

Creation of form utility is the province of production, in contrast to marketing. The greater the demand for marketing service, the greater is the justification for incurrence of functional costs, and the greater the value which is added to products through the performance of marketing functions.

The nature of the marketing functions needs to be understood in detail, for upon them depends the system of marketing institutions and policies governing the practice of marketing.

Market Research. Research in connection with marketing includes both market research or investigation of characteristics of the market, and marketing research or inquiry into the means and practices of marketing. Both represent the quest for information to guide the economic processes of production and distribution to maximum satisfaction of society's wants and needs.

The nature of research has varied throughout the years, depending largely upon the nature of marketing problems and the prevailing concept of marketing. Its fields of study include the consumer, internal functions of business management, economics of the market, marketing channels, and trade practices. It employs both quantitative and qualitative data drawn from private and public, internal and external sources. Its methods are those of scientific inquiry developed in the physical and social sciences, including survey, observation, and experimentation. Techniques are borrowed from fields of statistics, accounting, engineering, mathematics, economics, psychology, and sociology. Among the methods of analysis employed are questionnaire survey, ratio analysis, depth interviewing, simulation, business games, correlation analysis, cost and budget analysis, copy testing, opinion research, and others.

Conception and Identification of Products. Information gathered through research is a guide to the invention and production of products for which there is a market. Products produced, however, must be recognizable as possessing qualities desired by buyers. For some products this assurance can be gained only by first-hand inspection. For others with less perceptible qualities, assurance depends upon adequate identification of the products. This is achieved through establishment of standard grades for products, through informative labeling and sales promotion, and through branding.

Standards developed in the interest of the public pertain to various aspects of identification and are usually the product of the collective efforts of agencies and businessmen. Standards convey information concerning size, quality, number of units, composition, strength, purity, etc. Among the agencies co-operating in the development of standards are the Agricultural Marketing Service of the U.S. Department of Agriculture, the Commodity Standards Division of the U.S. Department of Commerce, the Food and Drug Administration, the Federal Trade Commission, and the American Standards Association.

The identity of products is also established by the use of brand labeling. Using private marks of identification, producers distinguish their products both through word descriptions and through association and imagery. Symbols as well as words convey to buyers information which sellers wish them to have about their products.

Selling. Selling is the communication to a prospective buyer of information intended to show the likelihood of a product's meeting a buyer's need. It ranges in type from the mere listing of sales facts to aggressive presentation of sales claims or to efforts designed to create wants rather than merely to satisfy known needs. It includes personal selling, advertising, and other forms of sales promotion such as contests, displays, premiums, sale events, sampling, dealer aids, demonstrations, trading stamp plans, and the like.

The need for selling arises from 1) the separation of buyers and sellers, 2) buyers' unfamiliarity with new products, 3) sellers' opportunities for lowering costs through increased scale of operation, and 4) the stimulus given improvement of products and services through open announcement of offerings.

Although vast sums of money and effort are expended in selling—more for personal selling than for advertising—the beneficial contributions of this function are greater in value than the cost of performing it. Advertising expenditures are estimated to amount to between 3 and 4 per cent of personal consumption expenditures; the advertising expenses of most retail stores amount to between 1 and 2 per cent of their sales.

Buying. Buying is, in part, performance of the information function on the part of the buyer and, in part, the buyer's effort to consummate a transaction. It is a function known as procurement, purchasing, shopping, or simply "buying." It may be carried on for purposes of one's own use or as an intermediary activity on behalf of another.

Personal buying stems from the level of living which one maintains or from that to which he aspires. It is likely to conform to the pattern of consumption of the economic or social level with which one associates himself. The order in which one buys various products is determined by the priority of his need, by the channels in which his living flows, and by the appearance of especially favorable buying opportunities. Buying usually requires, first, choice between two or more potentially satisfying prospects. This may be followed by selection of a particular brand or style of produce, and by selection of the vendor from whom the purchase is to be made. Rational and emotional motivations enter into the buying calculation.

Business buying is somewhat predetermined for a distributor by what he can sell, and for an institutional consumer by the operation he conducts. The rate and timing of purchases is affected by the necessity of maintaining an inventory of supply or stock, by seasonal factors, by costs of acquisition, special buying opportunities, discounts, condition of one's liquid working capital, and the like.

Transporting. Movement of products from one place to another is feasible simply because 1) a market for them exists at a distance, in addition to or in place of a market for them at their origin, and 2) the value of the product in the distant market is sufficiently higher than in the other to warrant the incurrence of the necessary transportation costs. Such markets in different positions may be called "space markets." They are linked by transportation, the performance of which in accommodating distant markets creates place utility.

The extent to which transportation is performed in marketing depends upon several factors. If production costs are identical in different markets, products will tend to be produced in each market and not to move between them. If there is a differential in production costs, producers in the two markets compete in the intervening space to the extent that production costs plus transportation costs become equal. The differential may be so great as to permit one producer to compete even in the local market of the other. The sum of production plus transportation costs, however, may not exceed any fixed sense of value in a distant market, else it may be found that for products delivered at prices above that value no market exists. Value in the buyers' minds justifies incurrence of costs; transportation may create place utility, but it cannot create a market for that utility.

Market patterns change with changes in the variables of which transportation is a function. Thus changes in production costs, in freight rates, in methods of shipment, in insurance rates, etc. affect the markets for products and for transportation service.

Storing. The need for storage arises from the separation of markets by time. Producers frequently have a choice in disposing of their goods in the present local market, in the present distant market, or in a future market, be it local or elsewhere. Value of the product at a future time, however, must exceed present value by at least the cost of storage. Through storage, therefore, is created time utility or the service which is warranted by anticipated values in a future market.

The performance of the storage function is affected by the cost of storing, by production cost differentials at different times, and by the relative competition between time and space markets.

An important factor in storing is the financing of the investment in products during the storage period. The development of means in recent years whereby this is facilitated has made storing more feasible and has thus prolonged markets. These facilities have included bonding of public warehousemen, field warehousing, and the rise of companies financing particularly goods in storage.

Financing. Many transactions would never materialize if immediate payment of cash were always necessary. The ability to obtain goods before paying for them is often important to both businessmen and consumers. Only by so obtaining goods may businessmen have them to sell or fabricate, and so conduct their business. Likewise is this the means by which consumers may have enjoyment of products sooner than they would if cash were required. Possession, therefore, has a value to both business and household buyers, and the financing of possession creates possession utility.

Financing the market involves assuming three responsibilities: 1) providing capital for receivables, 2) assuming credit risk, and 3) performing investigation, authorization, collecting, etc. inherent in the operation. Thus is produced credit service, a utility for which there is a wide market, a variety of prices, and definite production costs. Both vendors, in connection with sale of goods, and lenders, in connection with loans, provide such credit service. All or part of these responsibilities may be shifted from vendors and lenders to an array of credit specialists which have arisen in the banking and commercial fields.

The basis of a system providing credit service is confidence in the promise to pay extended by the one who offers his credit. One's credit is good in proportion to his ability to redeem his credit through ultimate payment. Thus it is directly related to potential income, although moral considerations and other resources are also important.

Merchandising. Merchandising is that service provided in distribution which makes products available in the market at the time, at the place, and in the manner desired. In contrast to transporting and storing, which carry products into *other markets*, merchandising provides for the availablity of goods with a *given market*. It is a function which is performed in storekeeping, stock keeping, etc. It caters to the desire of consumers that goods be available when they are in the market for them.

Aggregate markets, unlike single transactions, embrace a period of time and a span of space, in which all buyers desiring to make a transaction may do so. For example, the "Christmas market" covers a period of two or three months, during which some people prefer to buy early, others late. Markets for automobiles, clothing, and garden equipment are also periodic; those for grocery staples, birthday cards, and gasoline are continuous. Providing availability satisfies a value and creates a utility in addition to the mere value of the product itself. This is the contribution of the merchandising function. Merchandising differs from mere storing for value increases with storage time, whereas no such increase occurs during the time goods are in inventory for availability. To the contrary, if value does not remain constant, it may even decline toward the end of a market period.

Similarly, markets have spatial dimensions embracing a city, a metropolitan area, or a neighborhood, in which products are transported for the simple reason of making them available *in the market* rather than moving them to *other markets* where they have greater value.

Merchandising provides products not only at the time and place, but also in the manner desired. By this function are assembled goods in assortment making choice possible, goods so related as to make shopping convenient, and goods surrounded with an environment pleasant and appropriate for buying. All of these functions of merchandising provide in some way the service of availability.

Market Risk Bearing. In a broad sense, products are brought to the market only because someone assumes entrepreneurial responsibilities, including the risks which are inherent in the market situation. In a market economy, it is normal and to be expected that transactions will be consummated. It is normal also, however, that failure in the fulfillment of other marketing functions sometimes prevents the occurrence of transactions. Lack of information, faulty communication, improper estimation of the market, failure to provide goods at the place and time and in the manner desired—these occasion risk which must be borne in an economy such as we have. The dynamic nature of the market imposes also risks which result from price changes.

Marketing Processes: Wholesaling and Retailing. Although the concept of marketing may be refracted into the spectrum of marketing functions, the distributive operation itself occurs neither as a composite activity of marketing nor as the separate activities of the marketing functions. It consists rather of the complementary processes of retailing and wholesaling, retailing being selling to ultimate, household, or personal users, and wholesaling being selling to all others—to distributors and to business and institutional buyers. All of the marketing functions are performed on both levels of distribution, but the two levels represent the performance of dissimilar processes.

The wholesaling process, in general, is one of assembling products, of moving them toward their markets in bulk, to points where bulk is broken by making them available in smaller quantities to industrial buyers or to subsequent distributors. It is that stage of distribution wherein time utility is generally created and wherein major responsibility for financing distribution *within the channels* is assumed. It is the stage wherein purchases are large, consisting of great quantities of given products, but sales are large consisting of a great number of smaller quantities of a variety of products. The assembly process of wholesaling may also combine small quantities at the point of origin, as in distribution of agricultural products, before moving them on in bulk.

The retailing process, on the other hand, is essentially one of dispersion. It is a further step in the breaking down of homogeneous or heterogeneous bulk which has moved through wholesaling processes. It provides for satisfaction of the individual want or need at the termination of mass production and mass distribution. It offers availability, both through variety and assortment of products and through presentation in keeping with the time and space dimensions of the market. It furnishes information not only as to what supplies are available, but also as to where they may be obtained. It provides for, although it does not generally assume, responsibility for financing the consumer market.

MARKETING FUNCTIONARIES—THE MARKETING SYSTEM

When functions must be performed, there emerge individuals and institutions to perform them. Marketing functions are performed by a variety of functionaries. While the needs for functionaries differ with the combinations of functions inherent in different market situations, needs differ also depending upon the manner in which the functions are performed in any given situation. A range of choices lies between extremely specialized functionaries, on the one hand, and highly integrated functionaries, on the other.

One classification of functionaries is made on the basis of the extent to which they combine or segregate production and marketing. Some producers perform no marketing functions, even in connection with their own products; they are obviously specialists solely in production. Other producers undertake a full range of functions in connection with their products, some marketing them to the first specialist in the channel of distribution, others marketing them to their final market destination; thus they combine production and marketing. Still others market not only their own products, but also some purchased for resale. If their sales of purchased goods exceed the sales of goods produced, they cease to be classifiable as a producer and are in fact distributors, or specialized marketing functionaries.

Apart from producers (manufacturers, farmers, extractive industries, and others) who perform some marketing functions, the bulk of the marketing work is done by functional specialists. Some perform single marketing functions, such as transportation by carriers, storage by warehouses, financial assistance by banks, sales information by advertising agencies. Others perform not only such functions, but also through selling contribute directly to the transfer of title of goods. Those are known as *marketing establishments*.

Marketing establishments are of two types: middlemen and others. Middlemen are independent, autonomous organizations—*merchant middlemen*, who take title to the goods they handle, and *functional middlemen*, who do not take title to goods in whose distribution they assist. Other than the middlemen, there are marketing establishments which are not independent entrepreneurs, inasmuch as they are owned by producers (manufacturers' branches), by consumers (consumer co-operatives), by independent distributors (chain store warehouses), or by governmental agencies (military post exchanges). To be classifiable as marketing establishments, even those owned by producers must be physically separate from the parent producers, a separate place of business specializing in marketing.

Marketing establishments are also distinguished as *retailing establishments* and *wholesaling establishments*. Retailing establishments are those the bulk of whose sales are made to ultimate consumers. Wholesaling establishments are those whose business is primarily with industrial buyers and distributors.

Determination of the type and identity of marketing functionaries is of practical significance. Whether one is engaged in retailing or wholesaling determines prices at which he buys and sells, wages which he is required by law to pay, taxes levied upon him, the market which he can reach, and the nature of his business operation. Whether he is independently or producer-owned determines the character of his competition, whether he must earn a full measure of operating profit on his distributive activity, the risks he bears, or the price at which he obtains his merchandise.

A Marketing Establishment. Collectively, the various types of marketing establishments comprise what is known as the marketing structure or marketing system. An understanding of their varying roles, their differences, and their competitive advantages requires understanding of the essential character of a marketing establishment.

Basically, it is an entrepreneurial business venture. In the process of meeting a market need, it represents an effort to maximize profit through the utilization of invested and borrowed funds in the usual fixed assets (building and equipment) and current assets (inventory, accounts receivable, and cash). Gross profits tend to be maximized by increasing the volume of sales of the enterprise. Maximization of net profit depends upon the most favorable relation between sales volume and operating costs. It may be achieved by increasing sales without a proportionate increase in costs, or by a decrease in sales with a greater than proportionate decrease in operating costs.

This expansion and contraction of income and costs results from the efforts of management to manipulate several of the fundamental characteristics of the business: the variety and assortment of items handled, the number of store units operated, the number and types of services provided, the types of clientele or markets served, the radius of the market, and the types and intensity of promotional effort employed. An infinite number of combinations of these factors is possible, but certain combinations of them have become common, and enterprises so characterized are familiar to us as our well-known types of retail and wholesale establishments: department stores, chain stores, single-line stores, merchant and functional wholesalers, manufacturers' sales branches, etc.

THE RETAILING STRUCTURE

While there is no such thing as a standard variety or assortment of goods offered in a given establishment, a large part of our marketing effort and structure has been based upon the concept of a "line" of goods. This signifies a group of products which are related through common physical properties, in use, in purchase, or in origin. The traditional "lines" have been the grocery, drug, hardware, and dry goods line. During the 19th century, those products were the principal ones marketed, and they were typically segregated in distribution and made available through what have been called "single-line stores": grocery, drug, hardware, and dry goods stores.

Multiple-Line Stores. The efforts of management to increase volume through expansion and combination of lines, thus providing a broader base for the allocation of overhead, has resulted in the fusions represented by the general store, the department store, the modern drug store, mail order house, and others, wherein products of different lines are combined, as in supermarkets, automotive supply stores, and variety stores. There has been a strong tendency in recent years for many retail stores to offer items from different lines in the name of providing shopping convenience known as "one-stop shopping."

Simultaneously, there has been a contrary trend toward line specialization through reduction of items handled. Thus have arisen such specialized retailing establishments as those handling only neckties, paint, millinery of a particular price, dietetic foods, toys, and the like. Through such restriction of the line, it is expected either that costs will be disproportionately cut or that volume will be increased through more effective promotional emphasis.

Multiple-Unit Stores. Historically, retail establishments have been operated as single units, even though several may have fallen under common ownership. Contemporary marketing, however, exploits the merchandising potentialities of multi-unit establishments linked in horizontal integration. Chain organizations and branch establishments are typical. Not only is increased volume made possible by the addition of outlets, but multiple-unit operations also provide for economies through large-scale buying, apportionment of overhead, experimentation, research, and risk. Thus have developed on the basis of multiplicity of horizontally integrated units four types of retail enterprises: 1) the corporate chain store organization, which is typically found among single line and specialty stores, although also among the smaller department stores; 2) voluntary chain organizations representing independent ownership but integrated merchandising; 3) ownership groups, as among large department stores, representing centralized ownership but decentralized merchandising; 4) branches, also typical of department stores, representing the integration not of comparable and equal units, but of dominant and subordinate ones, with centralization of both ownership and merchandising.

In addition to their horizontal linkage, retail stores have also been affiliated in vertical channels by several means: in corporate systems initiated by producers, wholesalers, and retailers alike; in contractual systems, such as wholesale-sponsored voluntary chains, retailer-cooperative organizations, and franchising organizations; and in administered systems wherein vendor-developed comprehensive programs for distribution integrate the entire channel.

Multiple-Service Stores. Throughout a century, the principal service provided by retail establishments has been that of availability. Additions and subtractions of other services have from time to time been made to accommodate the market and to maximize profit. Chain stores originally represented not only a multiplicity of units, but also a reduction of the services of credit and delivery which were customarily provided by retail groceries. The department store, on the other hand, epitomizes the combination of a full range of services with merchandise: credit, delivery, returns, adjustments, guarantees, nursery facilities, club rooms, restrooms, shopper service, etc. Discount houses are typically a withdrawal of services customary in connection with durable goods, including personal salesmanship and even convenient availability, insofar as the discount house is located more or less remotely. Mail order establishments, by the very nature of their operation, curtail the service of availability, while attempting to compensate for non-store inconvenience by substitution of the service of catalogue selling, telephone ordering, and liberal adjustments.

Multiple Customers. Markets are stratified on several bases, and the effort to serve either more or fewer market classifications is a management decision which also has helped to form the retailing structure. Some establishments sell at both wholesale and retail. Some cater to high, medium, and low income classes. Some solicit the patronage of minors as well as adults. Some make direct solicitation of the consumer while concurrently selling also to other distributors. Conversely, managements contrariwise minded follow the opposite policy of serving selective types of customers in their effort to achieve their operating objectives.

Multiple Territories. As with customer types, merchants differ with respect to the distance they will go in seeking customers. Some operate wholly on a local basis, customarily providing over-the-counter sales service. Supermarkets have greatly extended the circumference of the market formerly served by the neighborhood grocer. Department stores draw patronage from large metropolitan markets and, even more extensively, through the use of mail order selling. Some enjoy even a national patronage as a result of advertising placed in such media as the *New York Times* Sunday edition.

Thus it is apparent that, while physically retail establishments may be characterized by size, location, and commodities handled, conceptually from the management standpoint they represent so many integrations and specializations of line, unit, service, market, and territory. The manner of merchandising which these combinations provide determines the market appeal of the establishments and their competitive stature among the trade.

Environmental Influences. The managerial concept of the best way in which to perform the necessary marketing functions is not the sole determinant of the nature of the establishments which are created. Environmental influences also determine the manner in which the various factors may profitably be combined as a market offering. This is the influence which social change holds over the entire marketing process.

One need go back no more than one hundred years to observe some of the principal environmental influences which have helped to shape the retailing establishments of our marketing system.

1. Department Stores. Following the Civil War, four circumstances contributed to the growth of department stores: a) the increase of urban population, b) increased manufacture of textiles, c) increasing disposition of consumers to buy ready-made clothing, and d) a growing higher income class which constituted a market for the more luxurious commodities and services which department stores were offering.

Late 19th century improvements in urban transportation augmented department store growth by making downtown shopping areas more readily accessible to people in all sections of the widening metropolitan areas. These factors continued almost uninterrupted until the 1930's with post-war migration from rural to urban areas and with growing markets for department store type merchandise. However, growth of large metropolitan family-owned department stores was paralleled by growth of chains of smaller department stores locating particularly in the rising number of small towns. At the same time, the financial merger movement of the 1920's stimulated integration of large department stores in ownership groups for both financial and merchandising advantages. Enlargement of cities gave rise in the 1930's to department store branches in secondary shopping areas, and in the 1950's to branches in shopping centers. Complex downtown traffic problems have posed a counteracting influence upon central department store popularity and accessibility, but this has been compensated somewhat by the department store's development of parking facilities.

2. Chain Stores. The growth of retail chains, particularly in groceries, was the result of population growth prior to 1920, and of widening realization of advantages to be gained through horizontal and vertical integration and through elimination of some services. During the early 19th century, the number of chain organizations increased rapidly. They too were influenced by the mergers of the 1920's with resulting reduction in the number of chains but increase in the number of stores comprising chains. Depression conditions of the 1930's, coupled with punitive graduated license taxes imposed upon chains and the rising competition of supermarkets in the grocery field, wrought enlargement of the chain stores and reduction of their number. Later, chain groceries adapted themselves to expanding use of the supermarket techniques.

3. Mail Order Establishments. The custom of American farmers to live on their farms, in contrast to the European practice of settling in villages adjacent to agricultural areas, contributed to the crossroads location of numerous general stores combining the lines of consumer goods common in the 19th century. Their unwillingness or inability to handle the increasing number of products, or to satisfy farmers' desire for urban contacts which would break their isolation, prepared the way for the catalogue-promoted mail order selling. Such business was made feasible by improvements in rail transportation, by provision of rural free delivery and parcel post service, and by achievement of a high rate of literacy through general educational programs. The popularity of mail selling, however, met head-on the counteracting influence of automobiles and improved rural highways in the 1920's, which shifted much buying from home ordering to small town shopping. The adaptive response of mail order establishments to that development was their opening in towns of catalogue order offices, display rooms, and ultimately retail stores, which are in fact chain department stores.

4. Consumer Co-operatives. Co-operative establishments differ from those privately owned mainly in ownership and not in merchandising conception. In a given field, both have responded to the same external influences. However, co-operatives have felt the added stimulus of depression-born emphasis upon low price and savings and of socialistic philosophies antagonistic to capitalistic enterprise. Consequently, those influences, particularly during the 1930's, stimulated growth of co-operatives, but their competitive status and service to consumers are to be judged primarily from a managerial rather than from a legal standpoint.

THE WHOLESALING STRUCTURE

Social circumstances affect first that level of marketing practice which directly serves society, namely, retailing. Changes in retailing and in the retailing system in turn affect wholesaling practice and wholesaling establishments.

Whereas in retailing the character of marketing establishments is determined almost wholly by decisions made locally within those establishments, in wholesaling their character is the effect of the joint and/or separate decisions of producers and wholesale middlemen. Between them occurs such a play of integration and specialization of activities, whereby the functions inherent in a given market situation are divided, that a producer's assumption of wholesaling functions is usually attended by a corresponding reduction in wholesaling functions performed by independent wholesale middlemen. This process whereby functions of wholesaling sometimes performed by wholesale middlemen are shifted backwards or forwards in the distributive channel is termed *circumvention*, indicating a tendency to "go around" but signifying management decisions making a new allocation of the functions involved.

The performance of wholesaling occurs in three stages representing degrees of specialization and integration: 1), producers performing the entire function of wholesaling involved in the distribution of their goods; 2), producer-owned marketing establishments physically separate from the production facilities; 3), independent wholesale undertakings representing complete separation of production and marketing functions.

Channels. In a market as large and diversified as that of the United States, competitive initiative has produced a variety of combinations of marketing establishments involved in the performance of the functions. These combinations are called "channels" for the flows of various elements. Some handle the flow of products, others the flows of title, information, payments, service, and the like.

The circumstances of the market—of the buyer, of the seller, and of the product—prescribe the functions which must be performed. Differences in market situations result in a variety of channels functioning side by side, even in the same line or trade. Dissimilar channels are also found serving in *identical* market situations, as a result of differences in competitive strategy and efficiency.

Wholesaling components of vertical channels include both *wholesale middlemen* and *other wholesale establishments*. They range from those establishments performing a minimum of functions (such as brokers and drop shippers) through those middlemen performing a wide range of functions (such as the selling agent and the regular wholesaler) to producers' own distributive outlets, with or without stocks.

The regular wholesaler represents a full combination of marketing functions; other establishments represent a lesser combination, and therefore a relegation of residual functions to other buyers and sellers in the channel.

In the channels for manufactured products, the following are the principal establishments and their functions:

I. Limited Function Middlemen
a) Not taking title.

1) *Brokers*. One of the most highly specialized independent middlemen is the broker, whose almost sole function is representation of buyers and sellers in negotiations. He does not take title, handle goods, render financial assistance, or determine the sale price. He is engaged either by buyers or sellers on a temporary basis and is paid a commission for his service. He is most useful in the sale of highly standardized goods, particularly of a seasonal nature, and in negotiating between widely scattered buyers and sellers.

2) *Commission Merchants*. Commission merchants also do not take title, but, in addition to the negotiatory functions of the broker, they may handle, or temporarily store commodities, and on occasion render financial assistance to buyers. They serve mainly in distribution of grocery specialities, and in the wholesale marketing of dry goods.

b) Taking title.

1) *Drop Shippers*. Buying, selling, and financing of marketing are the principal functions of drop shippers, who do not handle physically the commodities they sell. They deal primarily in the distribution of bulky products bought in large quantities.

2) *Cash and Carry Wholesalers*. Buying, selling, and storing are the main functions of cash and carry wholesalers, who omit delivery and marketing financing.

3) *Wagon Distributors*. Simultaneous sale and delivery are the chief functions of the wagon distributor, who omits storage and financing in the limited line of specialty items which he carries.

II. Full Function Establishments
a) Not taking title.

1) *Manufacturers' Representatives*. Manufacturers' representatives are, with selling agents, one of the two types of functional middlemen who maintain continuous contractual relations with producers whom they represent. They sell, handle products, and provide market information, but they do not buy, render financial assistance, select the market in which they sell, or determine the selling price. They serve the principal in the manner and place of his determination. This middleman is employed by producers needing economical sales assistance in selling a narrow line of products in sparce, scattered, distant, or new markets.

2) *Selling Agents*. Selling agents are independent, multiple-line establishments substituting for a manufacturer's own sales organization. They may perform all functions except buying. Handling the producer's entire output, they sell, store, finance, gather market information, determine price and territory. Combining the product with non-competing lines of other producers, particularly in the field of textiles but also in other lines, they serve manufacturers who are least able or willing to perform any of the marketing functions themselves.

b) Taking title.

1) *Regular Wholesalers*. Independent merchant wholesalers perform in some channels the dual processes of assembly and disposition. They are most useful in distributing products which, for efficiency and economy, must be gathered from many sources and distributed to many outlets and buyers. They take title, buy, sell, store, break bulk, deliver, and both gather and disseminate market information. When handling manufactured goods intended for the household consumer market, this middleman is called a wholesaler; when handling products for the industrial or institutional market, he is known as an industrial distributor. Regular wholesalers provide economical distribution for a great number of related products.

Producer-Owned Establishments. Producers desiring to perform and control their own marketing activity find certain circumstances favoring the establishment of a distributive branch, in contrast to direct distribution from the place of production. Such branches may be either with stocks or without stocks, being in the latter case sales offices. When branch distribution is undertaken, existing circumstances must warrant it. Branches without stocks are made feasible by the production of a diversified line of products, by concentrated markets, and by technical products requiring expert salesmanship. Branches with stocks are inspired by the market's need for accessible inventories for repair and replacement, for installation and repair service, and for small-scale delivery of products moved major distances in bulk for reasons of economy.

Distribution of Agricultural Products. The markets, horizontal outlets, and vertical channels for agricultural products differ from those of manufactured goods. Markets for agricultural products impose a marketing task in some respects unique. Primary production, in contrast to manufacturing, is generally on small scale, requiring assembly of products into marketable quantities before they can be economically moved long distances to urban markets where they are disseminated in vertical channels to retail outlets. On the other hand, many industrial users of agricultural raw materials, such as canners, meat packers, tanners, cotton mills, etc., are located in the vicinity of farms and purchase directly from the producers of those materials.

For agricultural commodities which must be assembled in the local areas, the establishments which have arisen there to perform this function include independent cash buyers, traveling buyers, cooperative assemblers, representatives of distant merchants and industrial consumers. Depending upon the product, these local agencies in the channel may buy, sell, store, transport, grade, finance, bear market risk, and provide market information. In the central market, where the process of dispersion begins, an important role is played by functional middlemen: brokers, commission merchants, and auction houses. Negotiating and dealing in large quantities, they facilitate the distribution of farm products to wholesalers, jobbers, and large retail chain organizations.

MARKETING MANAGEMENT

While marketing is a social phenomenon and its institutional structure is an example of economic specialization, the management of marketing is a role in business which has become highly professionalized. Within a business organization, the function of marketing is an area of decision making, corresponding in importance to production, finance, and personnel, with which it must be integrated for effective and profitable operation. Responsibility for the marketing function, itself a complex and coordinated activity, is being placed in modern organizational structures with a position known as "Vice President in Charge of Marketing," "Director of Marketing," or "Marketing Manager." In top management deliberations, the marketing manager has a leading responsibility, inasmuch as the total undertaking of the individual firm must begin with the market—with understanding of its needs and wants, its character, size, location, etc. Marketing management is responsible for preserving this viewpoint in the various undertakings of the firm.

The Marketing Mix. Within the scope of its own technical responsibility, marketing management is charged with planning, organizing, and controlling a variety of activities which, combined in different proportions, constitute the "marketing mix." It is the administration of the means of accomplishing the marketing objective. Those means include personal selling, advertising, credit selling, product styling, packaging, branding, choice of both horizontal and vertical channels, price structure, guarantees, service policies, etc. Specialization in the performance of marketing gives rise to subordinate organizational specialization in the positions of sales manager and salesmen, director of marketing research, advertising manager, merchandising manager, manager of credit sales, service manager, adjustments manager, etc. It is the duty of the co-ordinative manager of marketing to proportion and combine these various activities of the "mix" in the manner most appropriate to the prevailing circumstances.

The actual management of marketing is regarded as a process of decision making, primarily in determination of policies and secondarily in the application of them. Decisions must be based upon a knowledge of theory and facts. Theory, embracing concepts and principles, is drawn from economic theory, sociology, psychology, law, accounting, finance, management, statistics, and mathematics, not to speak of marketing theory. The facts upon which marketing decisions are based are ascertained both within and without the business organization.

The actual processes of marketing decision making are too complex for a brief treatment of them; however, the following are some of the areas of decision and a few of the factors which management takes into consideration.

1) MARKET AND PRODUCT DECISIONS. Every marketing venture begins with an assumption that a market exists. The entrepreneur must determine, however, whether it is a household or industrial market, whether demand is elastic or inelastic, whether it is an effectual or potential market, whether its wants have been articulated or must be cultivated with information, whether it is of such dimensions that it can be reached economically. It must be considered whether a product of desired character can be made to sell at an acceptable price, whether a single item or a line of products should be made, whether they should be of staple or changing characteristics, sold in bulk, packaged, or branded.

2) CHANNEL DECISIONS. As the necessary channel is a function of the market, the producer, and the product, marketing management must ascertain the functions required for the distribution of a product, the costs involved, and the likelihood of selling at a price which justifies the costs. If multiple channels are required, the manufacturer's price structure must provide for both the functions performed and the functionaries that are essential in different channels.

3) PRICE DECISIONS. Price is a focal point of a variety of administrative decisions. It is in one sense an expression of the vendor's concept of his costs; it is also an indication of the buyers' valuation of the goods. Administratively, price determination is not a simple task. It is the effect of policies embodied in accounting practices, implicit in the marketing structure of the firm, or expressed in its promotional strategy. Price may be stated simply and directly as a net amount, or as a gross sum subject to trade, functional, quantity, cash, and other discounts. It may be a mill-based or a delivered price. In many other ways, price decisions are a means of management for achieving its marketing objectives.

MARKETING LEGISLATION

While sanctioning the general institution of marketing in our market economy, society has not completely surrendered control over it to the competitive business mechanism. Evidence to the contrary implied by attitudes of *laissez faire* and *caveat emptor* in trade during recent centuries, is refuted by reconstruction of social sanctions through legislation in the United States beginning about 1890. At that time, in the name of the Sherman Antitrust Act, appeared the beginnings of social policy which have since then been amplified and clarified by legislative, judicial, administrative, and "semi-judicial-administrative" agencies, in both federal and state governments. While aimed at "business," the regulation has pertained specifically to marketing—both wholesaling and retailing.

Underlying the philosophy of marketing regulation are the principles of the superiority of the interests of consumers over those of business, of the freedom to undertake and carry out business enterprise, and of conformity to fair play, insofar as that can be defined in business practice. Several lines of social policy are apparent in marketing legislation:

First, a concept of fairness in competitive price determination underlies portions of the following related statutes: The Sherman Antitrust Act (1890), the Clayton Act (1914), the Robinson-Patman Act (1936). They deal in part with the question of trade-restraining price discrimination, sanctioning price differences based upon, and to the extent of, differential distribution costs incurred in selling different quantities or under different conditions. Restraint is exercised over competition-impeding dealership contracts of vendors and horizontal agreements among competitors relating to price and trade practices.

Second, vertical agreements relating to price maintenance have been sanctioned, with exceptions in some states, by the Miller-Tydings Act (1937) and the McGuire Act (1952), as well as by similar state legislation. Such laws undertake to prevent socially undesirable predatory price-cutting practices through the interest which sellers claim to have in protection of their brand name and distributive organizations.

Third, protection of the public against false, deceptive, and misleading statements in advertising is provided in the Federal Trade Commission Act (1914) and the Wheeler-Lea Act (1938) whereby jurisdiction over this area of business practice is established with the Commission. Similar guard over statements made in product labels is effected through the Pure Food and Drug Act (1906) and the Food, Drug and Cosmetic Act (1938).

Fourth, encouragement as well as discouragement of certain marketing practices is given in the Webb-Pomerene Act (1918) and the Capper-Volstead Act (1922), which sanction agreements among competitors otherwise prohibited by the Sherman Act, in certain matters relating to export trade practice and the establishment of agricultural marketing cooperatives, respectively.

Fifth, a variety of regulation is provided in a number of lesser acts such as the Wool Products Labeling Act (1939), the Fur Products Labeling Act (1951), the Lanham Trademark Act (1946), unfair trade practice acts, municipal vending ordinances, and the like.

MARKETING IN DIFFERENT COUNTRIES

The concept of marketing was originated and developed in the United States, but every country has its own practices and system for the distribution of its products. There are notable differences between markets and marketing in different countries; yet there are similarities which cannot be overlooked. The differences stem from the fact that different societies provide for meeting their material needs in different ways. Thus, the socially sanctioned systems reflect the productivity, the aspiration, the ideals, the needs and wants of the respective peoples. On the other hand, common to world-wide market economies is specialization giving rise to a marketing structure. Examples drawn from a few selected countries will serve to illustrate.

Mexico. Mexico typifies a developing agricultural nation in the process of industrializing. Its people comprise a small, literate, cultured minority and a large, illiterate, uncultured, poor majority. Trade, barter, and public market distribution have characterized rural agriculture. The poorer population presents a market for only simple necessities, whose distribution is along primitive lines. To the affluent urban dwellers a whole range of the conveniences and luxuries of American and European markets is provided.

Channels are short, in consideration of the small assembly and dispersion function yet required by the markets. Emphasis is placed upon maximizing profit in the individual transaction, and business is generally conducted without a sense of social responsibility, which is essential to the modern concept of marketing.

Credit is little used. Prepackaging and branding are increasing. Selling occurs in both personal salesmanship and advertising. Principal modernization of marketing establishments appears to be occurring on the retail level, where private supermarkets and improved farmers' markets are found in food distribution and where in the department store field Sears, Roebuck de Mexico is doing an outstanding job of industrial and merchandising development.

Switzerland. Switzerland is a highly developed small country lacking productive land and raw materials and having high density and wide dispersion of its population. With incomes yielding savings, the Swiss have a standard of living which is one of the highest in Europe and in the world. Producers of quality products, they value quality and service in what they buy.

Convenience is often desired, but it appears to be of less value than in the United States. Because no advertising appears on television or radio, a large part of the selling function is performed by sales personnel, who complete a three-year apprenticeship in certain branches of the market and who, having an excellent knowledge of the products they sell, can assist the customer intelligently. There is little tendency of customers to bargain for prices, for a one-price policy is widely adopted.

Consumers have undertaken to provide commodities for themselves at minimum prices through consumer co-operatives, such as the Migros Cooperative chain developed by Gottlieb Duttweiler, which has more than 500,000 members. It is active in the distribution of goods, insurance, and gasoline products. Research of the market is widely conducted in Switzerland; one of the principal centers for this activity is the School of Economics at St. Gall. Brand names are widely used in Switzerland, as is prepackaging.

Retail stores, on the whole, are smaller than those in the United States, although in recent years department stores and supermarkets have gained in importance. The single-line independent store is still the principal type. In wholesaling, farmers' cooperatives have assumed most of the assembly function. Manufacturers have few distributive branches.

The Soviet Union. Although the Union of Soviet Socialist Republics is based upon a political philosophy completely in contrast to that of the United States, Russia nevertheless has a marketing task of meeting the needs of its citizens. In general, both the means of production and distribution are publicly owned, and their operation is subject to governmental planning. Consumption conforms to what is made available.

In its early years, the Soviet government mistakenly attempted to eliminate marketing functionaries without providing for performance of the necessary functions, with the result that chaos was introduced into wholesale distribution. Today more attention is given to scientific marketing, although prevailing practices are still outmoded. Little use is made of brands, because almost all products are state produced. Advertising also is sparingly used. Installment credit has only recently been introduced to facilitate purchase of more expensive goods; credit payments are deducted directly from payments due the wage earner. Such conveniences as delivery, servicing, adjustments, and returns are rarely found in the Soviet trading mechanism.

Since the outlawing and elimination of private merchants in the early 1930's, the Soviet distribution system has been composed of three sectors: the state trading network, the co-operative trading network, and the free farm markets. The *Torg* is the main retail sales unit of the Ministry of Trade. It usually has subordinate to it a chain of stores in a particular city or locality selling a specified group of products. It is managed by a government-appointed official. The stores within the *Torg* system supply the main bulk of necessities to most urban customers, but there are other stores that cater to demands of the higher income groups for better quality and more diversified merchandise.

On the wholesale level, the most important state organization is the Ministry of Requisitions, which procures agricultural products delivered to the state by the collective farms in fulfillment of their compulsory obligations and in payment for the use of the tractor and machine station services. Actual wholesale distribution of industrial goods is organized around the *Prombazy*, which is a large system of warehouses receiving goods from factories and delivering to retail outlets of both state and cooperative organizations. There is also a cooperative wholesaling system.

Japan. Japan presents a market of great density with high urban concentration and low per capita purchasing power. Like its production and foreign trade, its distribution has been dominated by influential wealthy families and powerful financial institutions. Retail business is handled mainly by small shops which specialize in one or several related items. There are also numerous large and modern department stores in the large cities.

Wholesalers dominate distribution and influence heavily the practices of both retailers and manufacturers. They control distribution financing, inasmuch as banks are reluctant to make loans to retailers and producers but will discount wholesaler-endorsed drafts given by both. Wholesalers control even small details like design and style of goods; they determine the prices at which manufacturers sell, thus leaving producers to be little more than contract manufacturers. Carrying these responsibilities, however, wholesalers do not engage extensively in market research, and many of their decisions are made without much understanding of the ultimate market.

In addition to financing, wholesalers are important in the functions of assembly and distribution and in the storage of commodities. While small producers and small retailers engage somewhat in storage, wholesalers perform almost all of the storage function for large producers and for department stores, neither of whom maintains any significant inventories.

SELLING AND ADVERTISING

Among the marketing functions, two are of special importance in business practice and social influence: selling and advertising. Business efficiency as well as business morality are often judged in terms of their performance of these functions.

Selling and advertising are activities which are usually associated with business, but they are not peculiar to business. The techniques which they employ are used by government, religious, social, and other organizations as well as by business enterprises. In all instances, selling and advertising are communications functions. Selling is a personal form of communication; advertising is an impersonal form. The current significance of these functions may be considered from several standpoints: historical development, economic service, psychological implications, management role, and social impact.

Historical Development. Historically, advertising and selling have a long heritage. Personal selling characterized earliest trade transactions. It was employed by importers who, by caravans and merchant ships, brought treasures of the East to Mediterranean shores. It was also used by vendors who, in stalls at local markets and fairs, supplied the daily needs of common people in ancient times; by medieval guildsmen and itinerant merchants; by American Colonial traders, village hucksters, and metropolitan wholesalers and retailers. Advertising, too, appeared early, as wall signs in the period of the Roman empire, as shop identifications and handbills during the handicraft era, as classified and display advertisements, and as radio, television, and outdoor ads of the 19th and 20th centuries. Selling and advertising have been employed in some form in all ages; their specific expressions, however, have changed with social and technological evolution.

Economic Service. As used in business, selling and advertising render an important economic service. They influence the demand of persons who are in the market. It has long been understood in economic theory that in a purely competitive market no selling effort is exerted. Demand and supply are assumed to be known to each other, and because products are, moreover, assumed to be uniform, no amount of cost or effort expended upon promotion of sales would be economical or profitable. The presumed conditions of such a market, however, do not exist in reality. On the contrary, separated from sellers by physical distances, by levels of middlemen, and by different states of knowledge, buyers are in need of information as to what is available, where it is, and at what price. Similarly, sellers, instead of offering homogeneous, uniform products, present to the market items differentiated as a result of production policy or in consideration of market desires. Consequently, an important function of selling and advertising lies in their furnishing the market with information in order to facilitate transactions.

They are also important for the "creation" of demand. In a dynamic economy, where many people have discretionary purchasing power (more than is necessary for meeting bare essentials of living), formation of demand is susceptible to sales influences which encourage spending at the expense of saving, which reveal new combinations of pleasures in consumption, or which switch preferences from one product to another. Imaginative and aggressive selling is the means by which innovators in a free competitive market vie with one another in making a superior offering. Advertising and selling, in other words, are normal, essential, and effectual means of achieving some of the objectives of our competitive market economy.

Psychological Implications. Selling and advertising have also long been a subject of interest to psychologists, who have brought to the study of them several interpretations of human behavior. According to one theory, these functions furnish the stimuli for evoking conditioned responses on the part of consumers. Another theory holds that selling effort initiates a series of steps by which the consumer mentality is transported from interest, through desire and conviction, to action in accord with the proposition made by the seller. Still another theory holds that men are motivated not only by rationality but also by irrationality. Thus selling and advertising employ techniques for prevailing upon both the logical and the emotional faculties of people.

Management Role. However selling and advertising are conceived as psychological stimuli or as economic functions, in practice they remain activities to be administered by business management. Enterprises today are guided increasingly by objectives, in terms of which selected means are chosen. Selling and advertising are two of the means by which managers seek to achieve the maximization of sales and profits, the introduction of new products, the capturing of a share of the market, or some other objective. They are two means for achieving the marketing or sales objective designated "the marketing mix," as previously described.

Personal selling and advertising are themselves alternatives to each other, and although one may be used to supplement the other, there are bases upon which a choice between them may be made: the type of information to be conveyed, the number of people to be contacted, the budget available for promotional activities, or the facilities at the seller's disposal. In general, personal selling is employed when products are complex or technical and require detailed, interpreted sales presentations, when the number of prospective customers is relatively small, or when a service is needed in connection with the transaction. By contrast, the impersonal medium of advertising is often preferable when the obverse conditions prevail: a simple message needs to be communicated to many prospects; a step in the sales process other than the transaction needs to be accomplished; or when the timing of the sales presentation is achieved other than by a personal visit.

Social Impact. The forms of selling, while gaining business acceptance, have evoked also social appraisal, for the character of advertising and personal selling has an impact upon social conditions. Needing market information, the public is dependent upon various forms of selling. This dependence, in turn, gives the public an expectation of reliability in the information—an expectation that sellers will give an honest and fair representation of their products and services. It is recognized that in the competitive system claims and counterclaims are to be expected, and courts have sanctioned trade puffery while denying deceptive selling.

Several types of social control over selling and advertising practices have been developed: Better Business Bureaus, organizations sponsored mainly by retail businesses to police selling practices; fair trade commissions, whose responsibility is to administer laws of the state relating to unfair selling; and finally, the Federal Trade Commission. Created in 1914 with powers mainly to act upon the initiative of businessmen injured by the selling practices of others, the Commission, in 1938 through the Wheeler-Lea Act, was empowered to take, upon its own initiative, preventive measures to protect the public from misleading or deceptive advertising. Such guides to selling action have tended to aid sellers in establishing policies by which social responsibility is fulfilled.

In summary, selling and advertising are communications functions employed by business for the achievement of selected management objectives. Because they have such broad economic and social effects, they are subject to social review as well as to business appraisal.

POWER

THE satisfaction of human needs rests fundamentally on labor. Consequently, the more labor procurable at the least cost in human energy, the greater is the human energy set free for other purposes—for the enjoyment of leisure, for progress, for civilization. Past civilizations were built up and supported largely on the labor of slaves maintained at a subsistence level. Modern civilization rests on the utilization of mechanical power, which, in an ever increasing degree, is made to do work formerly done by human beings. Revolutionary changes in the development and use of power have done more than any other factor to raise the standard of well-being in the 20th century.

The application of mechanical power to human productivity multiplies the amount and the value of goods which each individual worker can produce. The following table, showing the estimated daily output of various kinds of workmen in the year 1800 and in 1925, brings home vividly the advantages created largely by the use of power-driven appliances.

ESTIMATED DAILY PRODUCTIVITY PER WORKMAN IN 1800 AND 1925

PRODUCT	1800	1925
Iron	500 lbs.	5000 lbs.
Lumber	100 bd. ft.	750 bd. ft.
Nails	5 lbs.	500 lbs.
Shoes	1/4 prs.	10 prs.
Coal	1/2 ton	10 tons
Paper	20 sq. ft.	200 sq. ft.
Bricks laid	500	3600*

*By electric brick layer.

No degree of finality is to be expected of such figures as the above. They depend first on the degree to which various labor saving devices, available to an industry, are actually adopted by the industry. They depend also on the continued discovery of still newer devices, a process which, while going on constantly, is nevertheless very unequal and largely unpredictable. An example is the mechanical blowing of glass bottles, which almost overnight multiplied many-fold the output per man. The flour milling and automobile industries represent continuous and progressive advances over decades. The figures given are regarded as conservative. Their value is chiefly in illustrating the most fundamental fact in the evolution of our economic system—the multiplication of productive capacity by the development of mechanical power.

Early Sources of Power. The adoption of draft animals as a substitute for human labor was an extraordinary advance in the economy of primitive man. This change dates from prehistoric times. Draft animals performed heavy work on the farms, as well as providing power for transportation throughout the world during the entire period of recorded history. They were also employed by the Romans and later peoples in turning mills for grinding grain. Comparatively little additional progress in the utilization of non-human power was made until the invention of steam-driven appliances for pumping water in the late 17th century. The Romans, however, are credited with the first use of the water wheel to turn grinding mills. The wheel was connected with the mill stone by a horizontal spindle through the intervention of bevel gearing.

The water wheel of the Romans was introduced into various parts of Europe and into Britain. At the time of the Norman Conquest of England, 1066 A. D., two counties alone, Norfolk and Suffolk, had 500 mills driven by water power. Windmills were introduced from the East by the Crusaders.

Steam Engines and the Industrial Revolution. The 18th century is notable for the invention of the steam engine and for the beginnings of its application to industries, notably mining, textile and steel manufacture, and flour milling. This development occurred first in England, where, in the 19th century, an industrial society first began to take shape. Urban population increased rapidly. Despite recurrent crises of overproduction, unemployment, booms, and panics, British wealth grew rapidly, due to the fact that machines driven by steam multiplied the productive power of each laborer. Steam power at the same time was vastly increasing the facilities for transportation on land and sea. By the close of the century, Germany and Belgium had been largely industrialized, but the most striking transformation of all was under way in the United States.

The Early Twentieth Century. In 1900, the United States contained two-fifths of the steam railway mileage of the world—about 198,000 miles of track. The country's installed power, not used for transportation, was about 15,278,000 horse power, of which nearly two-thirds was used for manufacturing, the balance being divided almost equally between public utility plants and mineral production. For about 88 per cent of the power the prime mover was steam, that for the balance being practically all water power.

The beginning of the 20th century was notable for two developments in the utilization of power which were of fundamental importance.

The first was the adaptation to wide practical use of the internal combustion engine. The world is most largely indebted for this device to Nicholas Otto, who in 1877 developed the first successful engine of this type, and to Gottlieb Daimler, who in 1884 adapted this engine for use in road vehicles. In 1900, Rudolf Diesel exhibited at Paris the Diesel engine, a much more economical type, particularly for heavy uses. In the following quarter-century the internal combustion engine made possible the universal employment of the automobile for transportation and travel; it also led to the solution of the problem of air travel. In marine transportation, the Diesel engine made rapid inroads on the use of steam. By 1927, the tonnage of ships constructed with oil-burning motors exceeded the year's construction of ships equipped for steam propulsion. Petroleum, the chief source of the motive power for these engines, took its place with coal as one of the most indispensable of raw materials.

The second epochal development of the 20th century in the use of power was the wide utilization of electricity as a means of distributing energy and of making it flexible in application.

Dynamos and electric motors respectively are the instruments by which power is made to take the form of electricity and by which electricity is reconverted to mechanical energy. The principle governing these machines was discovered by Michael Faraday in 1831. Important improvements were made by Werner Siemens in 1854 and by H. Wilde in 1863. In the period from 1880 to 1900, electric railways were constructed in most of the principal cities. It was not until the 20th century, however, that the importance of electricity as a form of power was adequately realized.

Technical improvements in the steam engine, the internal combustion engine, and electrical machinery were largely responsible for the phenomenal growth of power used in the 20th century. The total installed horsepower in the U.S. increased rapidly after 1900, but changes since World War II have been even more phenomenal. The total horsepower of all prime movers was 2.8 billion in 1940, with just over 90% produced by automotive engines. The total increased by more than 500% by 1968 to 17.9 billion; more than 94% was produced by automotive engines. All other sources of horsepower production, including factories, power plants, railroads and other forms, contribute only about 6% of the total horsepower, an indication of the tremendous importance of the automotive engine to society.

PRODUCTION OF ELECTRIC ENERGY IN THE U. S., 1930–1970

Source: *The Federal Power Commission.*

Year	Electric Energy Produced				Fuel Consumed in the Year		
	Total	Hydro	Steam	Internal Comb't'n	Coal	Oil	Gas
	1,000 Kw. hrs.	1,000 Kw. hrs.	1,000 Kw. hrs.	1,000 Kw. hrs.	Short tons	42 Gal. Barrels	1,000 Cu.ft.
1930	91,111,548	31,189,554	59,293,363	628,631	40,277,989	8,804,530	119,552,711
1935	95,287,390	38,372,154	56,144,412	770,824	32,714,761	11,256,565	124,117,769
1940	141,837,010	47,321,278	93,001,735	1,531,997	51,473,881	16,325,122	180,096,185
1945	222,486,283	79,970,312	140,435,268	2,080,703	74,724,956	20,228,215	326,211,969
1950	329,141,343	95,938,317	229,543,366	3,659,660	91,870,770	75,420,490	628,918,834
1951	370,672,814	99,750,579	267,251,680	3,670,555	105,768,006	63,944,724	763,898,241
1952	399,223,620	105,102,458	290,384,847	3,736,315	107,071,241	67,218,426	910,116,741
1953	442,664,515	105,233,348	333,541,535	3,889,632	115,897,204	82,237,712	1,034,272,333
1954	471,686,354	107,068,508	360,834,386	3,783,460	118,384,671	66,744,754	1,165,498,360
1955	547,037,985	112,975,069	430,119,086	3,943,830	143,759,195	75,273,862	1,153,279,586
1956	600,667,750	122,028,608	474,552,045	4,087,097	158,278,996	72,710,841	1,239,310,686
1957	631,507,224	130,232,457	497,212,384	4,082,383	160,769,232	79,692,910	1,336,140,626
1958	645,098,000	140,262,000	500,764,000	4,072,000	155,724,000	77,668,000	1,372,853,000
1959	710,006,000	137,782,000	567,839,000	4,385,000	164,431,000	88,263,000	1,628,509,000
1960	753,350,000	145,516,000	603,342,000	4,492,000	176,634,000	85,340,000	1,724,762,000
1966	1,144,350,138	194,755,781	944,430,145	5,164,212	266,476,823	140,948,854	2,609,948,660
1967	1,211,749,276	220,043,018	986,782,770	4,923,488	273,972,576	161,274,680	2,743,251,360
1970	1,529,581,307	247,327,890	1,260,580,532	6,038,373	322,357,138	332,104,404	3,894,017,643

Electrification. Electricity is not a primary source of power, like steam, waterfalls, and gas engines. It is a means of making prime movers more useful. Through the generation of electricity by prime movers and the subsequent reconversion of this electricity into power through electric motors, primary energy can be used with greater flexibility in time and space. Power through electricity can be used *when* and *where* it is wanted far more readily than power delivered directly from steam engine or water wheel.

Not only may factories using electricity for power be located at points more advantageous for utilizing raw materials, markets, and labor, but electricity enables power to be used in private homes and on farms. This results in two chief developments of great social significance. First, labor in homes and on farms for the first time in the world's history may be largely freed from drudgery, thereby releasing an incalculable amount of human time and energy for other purposes. Secondly, factories need no longer be located in centers of congested population. New centers of industry may be semi-rural in character, with marked improvement in living conditions. Individual factories need not, as a rule, have their own power plants. Expensive and dangerous beltings and shaftings may be dispensed with. The control of machine processes is more exact and is effected with less labor.

Electricity has the further merit of being instrumental in turning power into other useful forms of service. The most obvious of these is light. The first electric lighting plant was established by Thomas Edison in Brooklyn, beginning operation on September 4, 1882. By November 1883, only 508 premises were wired for 12,732 lamps, none being in private homes. By 1937, about 21,500,000 homes in the United States were served with electricity, in addition to more than 4,000,000 commercial or industrial establishments. Since then, of course, millions of other homes and business establishments have been provided with electrical energy. Lighting now takes a variety of forms developed from the incandescent carbon lamp and the tungsten. Fluorescent lighting and neon lights have become quite common, the latter used especially for advertising purposes.

In addition to light, electric power is essential for the operation of telephones, telegraphs, and radio, where it results in the production of sound. As heat, it performs essential work in electric ranges, furnaces, irons, toasters, grills, and numerous other devices. As an agent of chemical change through electrolysis, it plays a necessary part in the chemical industry. Another important use is for the precipitation of dust from the air in factories. It is essential to the production of talking motion pictures. By facilitating automatic control of numerous processes, it releases an enormous amount

DIVISIONS OF INDUSTRY

Industry	April 1970			Total 1965
	Male	Female	Total	
Employed Persons	48,686,000	29,722,000	78,408,000	72,179,000
Professional and technical workers	6,890,000	4,431,000	11,322,000	8,883,000
Managers, officials, and proprietors	6,896,000	1,301,000	8,198,000	7,340,000
Clerical workers	3,497,000	10,337,000	13,834,000	11,166,000
Sales workers	2,724,000	1,990,000	4,714,000	4,715,000
Craftsmen, and foremen	9,737,000	290,000	10,027,000	9,221,000
Operatives	9,539,000	4,272,000	13,811,000	13,390,000
Private household workers	26,000	1,559,000	1,585,000	2,251,000
Other service workers	3,185,000	4,954,000	8,139,000	7,091,000
Farmworkers	2,692,000	472,000	3,164,000	4,265,000

Source: *Statistical Abstract of the U.S., 1970.*

of human labor. A remarkable instance of such control is found in three water reservoirs at Washington, D. C. These were equipped in 1928 with automata which would report by telephone the depth of the water on receipt of a telephone inquiry from the War Department. Finally, electricity has given the world automatic refrigeration and the control of atmospheric humidity through air conditioning.

Growth of Electric Power in American Industry. The first quarter of the 20th century witnessed the electrification of over three-fourths of American industry. The following summary presents the factual basis for this statement:

In 1899, the total horse power in electric motors was 492,936 out of a total of 10,097,893 primary horse power—4 per cent of the total.

In 1927, the total horse power in electric motors was 30,361,106 out of a total of 39,040,563 of primary horse power—78 per cent of the total.

In other words, electrification in American industry rose from 4 per cent in 1899 to 78 per cent in 1927.

In the same period the amount of power developed in factories and used directly without being transformed into electricity showed only a moderate increase, reaching a high point in 1909 (13,734,597) and steadily declining thereafter. On the other hand, electricity developed in individual factories increased from 310,374 horse power in 1899 to 11,216,111 in 1927—36-fold. Electricity used in the factory but developed in central stations increased from 182,562 horse power in 1899 to 19,144,995 in 1927—105-fold.

Electric Power in Other Countries. The output of light and power in the United States is more than half that of all the rest of the world combined. Norway rates first in per capita output of electric power, followed by Canada, Switzerland, and Sweden.

Chief Sources of Electricity. In presenting the available information on this subject, it must be remembered that for a substantial part of the electricity generated there are no authentic records. Every gasoline automobile, for instance, generates electricity for setting off the cylinder explosions and for other purposes. Motor ships generate electricity which in turn drives the propelling machinery.

Most electricity, however, is generated in central plants or by individual industrial concerns which report their production. Data for 1965 disclosed that electricity in the United States is generated to the extent of 55% from coal, 21% from natural gas, 6% from oil, and 18% from water-power sources. Currently, 60% of the coal produced is used by electric utilities in generating power, as is 16% of the natural gas, 3% of the petroleum, and virtually all the water power. In Canada most of the electric energy is produced by water power.

Conservation of fuel is a long-range motive for preferring water power to coal or oil as a source of electricity, yet immediate economic factors are necessarily the ones which determine the development of the electric industry. Chief among these factors are the location of mineral fuels and of water-power sites in relation to the centers of population. The cost of transmission of current rises rapidly with increase of distance, not only on account of the cost of transmission lines but through losses of energy in transmission.

More than 75% of the undeveloped water power and 65% of the developed power of the United States is found west of the Mississippi; the greatest demand for power is in the East. On the other hand, coal is plentiful in the Eastern States. This situation, together with the plentiful supply of oil, is largely responsible for the greater use of fuel for developing electric power in the United States. In Canada, however, fuel is relatively expensive, and water power is available nearer the centers of population. Consequently, electric power in Canada is almost synonymous with hydroelectric power.

Electricity Generated by Fuel. Electric generating plants operated by steam are normally located in or near industrial centers, in order to be close to their customers and in order to have available a water supply for use in condensing steam as required by the turbine type of steam engine.

Unlike hydroelectric power, the output of steam-driven generators can be counted on at all times irrespective of season. Installations may be added, unit by unit, as the market requirements demand. While operating costs were traditionally higher than those for hydro plants because of labor and fuel costs, improved technology and efficiency in operation have made many steam plants highly competitive. For example, the amount of coal required to produce one kilowatt-hour of electricity was reduced by more than one-third between 1940 and 1968. In some regions, fuel oil and natural gas may be more economical fuels.

Atomic Power. In 1954, the Atomic Energy Commission launched an experimental program to test different types of reactors to produce electric power. Although strongly criticized, five plants, to cost about $120 million, were developed. Results proved the technical feasibility of atomic power if not its economic feasibility in the U.S. where alternative low-cost fuels are available. The first nuclear power reactor was started up at Shippingport, Pennsylvania, in 1957. By 1970, 27 reactors were scheduled to be in operation.

An atomic-powered submarine, the USS *Nautilus* was launched early in 1955; during 1961, the 22nd nuclear-powered submarine was commissioned. The nuclear-powered merchant vessel *Savannah*, a 22,000-horse power ship whose keel was laid on May 22, 1958, was completed in 1961. The world's largest nuclear-powered vessel, the USS *Enterprise*, an 86,000-ton and 1101-foot aircraft carrier, put to sea on October 29, 1961, from Newport News, Va.

Hydroelectric Power. By this term is meant electricity developed by water power, usually through the medium of water turbine generators.

The first hydroelectric plant began operation at Appleton, Wisconsin, in 1882, a few weeks after the opening of Edison's electric lighting plant in Brooklyn. The Appleton plant had a capacity of 250 sixteen-candlepower lights. The largest hydro plant in the world, Grand Coulee, in Washington, is to have an ultimate capacity of 9.8 million kilowatts. Other large units in the United States include John Day Dam, 2.7 million kilowatts, and Chief Joseph Dam, 2 million kilowatts, both in the Pacific Northwest, and the Robert Moses plant, at Niagara, New York, with a capacity of 2 million kilowatts.

The economic advantages of hydroelectric power include the low cost of operation, since no fuel is required and very few men are needed to operate the plant. On the other hand, hydroelectric plants require a large initial investment, since complete installation for all requirements must be made at the outset, even though much of it may be usable only for a brief flood season or may not be required for years. It is often necessary also to construct dams and artificial water channels, and the power houses themselves must be more substantially built in order to withstand the surge of the water.

Tennessee Valley Authority. A new emphasis was placed on these and subsequent developments by the Tennessee Valley Authority act, approved May 18, 1933. Under this act, a government corporation, the Tennessee Valley Authority, was created not only for the purpose of improving navigation and controlling floods, but to generate and sell power with a view to determining the relative cost of public and private power operations. For this reason, the corporation (TVA) was designated by President Roosevelt as a "yardstick of power costs." The private utility industry bitterly contested the validity of the "yardstick," maintaining that the two costs were not on a comparable basis.

Another part of the TVA's purpose was declared to be the maximum utilization of electricity within its territory, this to be brought about partly by low promotional rates and partly by education of residents in the advantages of greater use.

The TVA operates in 40,600 square miles of territory drained by the Tennessee River. It comprises parts of seven states—Alabama, Georgia, Kentucky, Mississippi, Tennessee, and the Carolinas—embracing an area inhabited by two million people, with four million more in territory within transmission range of its electric power. TVA took over Wilson Dam and proceeded to build more than 20 major dams providing, in part, a 750-mile waterway, nine feet deep, between Knoxville, Tennessee, and Paducah, Kentucky, where the Tennessee River joins the Ohio.

Electrical energy is produced by water power and by steam, with coal-generated steam plants producing nearly three-fourths of the energy today. About 60 per cent of the energy goes to the Atomic Energy Commission but 148 municipal and rural co-operatives are served, distributing billions of k.w.h. to businesses, industries, and farms.

The TVA has provided cheap electric power, flood control, improved river navigation, and extensive recreational facilities. In fiscal 1954, the TVA's power revenues were $133,948,000.

Municipal Power Systems. Prior to 1933, about 1750 municipalities operated their own electric systems as compared with 13,665 communities which were served by privately operated systems. Most of these municipal plants were small, however, and they generated little more than 4.5 per cent of total power produced. The largest included those in Los Angeles, Seattle, Cleveland, and Springfield, Ill.

With the establishment of the TVA and the building of large governmental dams in the Columbia basin and elsewhere, a powerful impulse was given to municipal power distribution. Numerous Federal loans and grants were made to local bodies for building or buying the necessary facilities, this being a means of finding a market for power developed at the dams.

The production of electric energy amounted to 795,251 million kilowatt-hours in 1959 of which nearly three-fourths was produced by private utilities. Of the electric power produced by publicly-owned utilities, 65 per cent comes from Federally-owned facilities, 20 per cent from municipal power plants, and 15 per cent from co-operatives. According to the Municipal Year Book, of the 131 cities with a population of more than 100,000 in 1961, 105 operated water supply and distribution systems, 17 electric generating and distributing systems, 14 transit systems, and 7 gas manufacturing and distributing systems.

Transmission of Electricity. One of the chief advantages of electricity as a form of power is its ability to be transmitted long distances. In 1889, seven years after the construction of the first electric plant, it was a notable achievement to transmit electricity 13 miles at a pressure of 4000 volts. Today currents of 220,000 volts are frequently sent upwards of 250 miles by straightaway transmission.

High voltage transmission systems usually employ overhead conductors. These ordinarily consist of twisted strands of copper or of aluminum wire with steel cores, supported either by poles or steel towers with arms, to which the wires are attached through the medium of insulating porcelain plates.

High voltages used for long distance transmission are transformed to lower voltages at distributing stations and substations until the current is of the proper character for the ultimate user.

Interconnection of Electric Systems. This is frequently referred to as superpower, which may be defined as a system of hydroelectric and steam generating plants within a given territory interconnected into a power pool, which draws on the various generating stations according to their capacities, subject to the dictates of economy, and dispenses electricity to various communities according to their needs. The policy of interconnecting power systems took shape in the period 1917-1919.

The advantages of such interconnection may be seen from the fact that water power is subject to wide fluctuations. During the late spring and early summer, when the rivers are full, the requirements for power are reduced by the contributing factors of daylight, temperature, and the tendency of industry to relax. During the early fall, when these requirements are at their height, the rivers are at their lowest. To cut down on requirements for reserve equipment and to provide greater security against interruptions in service, many power companies provide supplementary steam plants, which need operate only when water power is deficient.

The Electrical Power Industry. By 1937, the electrical power industry in the United States represented a capital investment of about 12 billion dollars. Annual revenue exceeded 2600 million dollars. Municipalities also had invested more than 700 million dollars in electrical properties.

Operating companies in the United States which produce electric power are required by law to be local monopolies under the control of a state regulating commission. The standard method is to place each local monopoly under the regulation of a state commission charged with the duty of seeing that the service is adequate and that the prices are just and reasonable.

In the 1930's, the Federal government became a factor in the production and distribution of electric power. Although faced with opposition from private power groups contending that they could not compete with the non-profit operations and low-interest financing of the government, public power has expanded. Major developments include the Tennessee Valley Authority and various Columbia River projects. Recently, feelings were aroused over the Dixon-Yates contract for private power expansion in the Tennessee Valley and the Hell's Canyon project in Idaho. In both cases, public versus private power has been the issue.

Electric Industry in Canada. The potential hydroelectric power in Canada is estimated at 33,617,200 horse power at ordinary six-month flow or 20,347,400 horse power at the minimum flow. Installations totaled in 1942 approximately 8,845,000 horse power. Capital invested in the industry represented about 1,564 million dollars, the annual gross revenue being approximately 152 million dollars. Over 70 per cent of all industrial and domestic power used is in the form of electricity.

The electrical industry of Canada presents two noteworthy features. One is its close association with the pulp and paper industry. Many pulp companies, having developed electricity in excess of their own requirements, found the sale of surplus current an increasingly important part of their business. The other noteworthy feature is the large part played by municipal and governmental bodies in the generation of electricity. More than one-third the electric power in Canada is generated by governmental units.

Power on Farms. The power available on farms in the United States is approximately equal to that available in the combined factories, public utility plants, and mines of the country—upwards of 60 million horse power. The horse power per capita at the service of those engaged in agriculture has exceeded that at the service of each wage earner in industry since 1870, with the exception of the period 1904-1914, when agriculture lagged behind industry in the adoption of mechanical aids to production.

In 1870 practically the entire non-human power on farms was in the form of farm animals. Even in 1900, they represented about 80 per cent of the available power, the remainder being steam engines, gas engines, and windmills. By 1923, however, according to estimates by the United States Department of Agriculture, mechanical power exceeded animal power.

INSURANCE

THE gigantic nature of the private insurance business in the U.S., in the early 1970's, is summarized in the following figures: about 5,000 insurance companies had more than $250 billion in assets, received $70 billion a year in premium volume (sales), and employed 1,400,000 persons.

In addition, various forms of social (government) insurance required the expenditure, largely in taxes paid by employers and employees, of more than $40 billion a year. About three-fourths of social insurance costs were accounted for by the federal Old Age, Survivors', Disability and Health Insurance (OASDHI) program, which provides basic retirement, death, and disability protection for hospital and medical costs of the elderly, was also a rapidly expanding part of OASDHI. Other important social insurance programs were administered through the states: unemployment compensation, workmen's compensation (for work injuries and diseases), and temporary nonoccupational disability income insurance.

A more detailed review of the private sector of the field is best approached by a division into (1) *life* insurance, (2) *health* insurance, and (3) *property-liability* insurance. The basic purpose of all these types is the reduction of risk or uncertainty in regard to economic losses. The principle of loss sharing among large groups of exposures is used to apportion equitably the dollar value of losses for such events as death, disability, medical treatment, automobile collision, fire, windstorm, theft, riot, and a variety of other causes of loss. Many of these occasions (difficult to predict for individuals or businesses) become reasonably predictable through the institution of insurance.

LIFE INSURANCE

Life insurance has for its basis the *potential income-earning* ability of an individual. This is one of the greatest assets that individuals and families have. Few other assets begin to compare with the importance of this "human life value." Life insurance protects the insured, his family, creditors, and others against the financial loss occasioned by death. Almost $1.5 trillion dollars of life insurance in force—with more than 1800 companies holding $200 billion of assets to guarantee future payment to 130 million individual policyholders—is clear evidence of the popularity and significance of the field of life insurance.

Purpose and Extent. In the vast majority of instances, life insurance is taken to protect the family against the loss of the earning capacity of the breadwinner through untimely death. But, in recent years, business uses of life insurance have also shown marvelous growth. Life insurance can help offset financial loss when a key man in the firm dies. Partners can insure each other so that funds will be available to buy out the interest of the one dying first. Stockholders in closely held corporations often hold life insurance to provide funds for the firm's purchase of the shares of a deceased shareholder.

Increasingly, also, businesses are using group forms of life insurance, whereby large groups of employees are protected under a single policy for a stated amount for each employee, usually the equivalent of one or two years' wages. The "Life Insurance in the U.S." table will make clear the extent of this extraordinary growth. Annual income of U.S. life insurance companies grew nearly eightfold between 1940 and 1970, doubling during the last decade. Benefits increased from $2.7 billion in 1940 to $15.5 billion in 1970. Assets grew from $30 billion to $200 billion, while total life insurance in force rose from $.1 billion to $1.4 billion during the same period.

Group life insurance accounted for almost 40% of the total insurance in force in 1970 with legal reserve life insurance companies. From 23,000 policies involving 8.8 million certificates and $15 billion of life insurance in 1940, the field expanded to include 289,000 policies involving 75 million certificates and $483 billion of life insurance at the beginning of the 1970's. Group life insurance has been among the fastest-growing types of insurance. More than $500 billion of such insurance is in force, providing at least some basic protection for many families. The principle of group insurance is also used in the sizable Servicemen's Group Life Insurance and Federal Employees Group Life programs. Another type with rapid growth from 1950 to 1970 is group credit life insurance, used to repay a loan when an individual borrower dies.

In Canada, life insurance ownership equals 197% of national income, the highest such ratio for any country. The total life insurance in force as of 1970 was $110 million, of which 54% was individual life insurance and 46% was group life insurance. Eleven million Canadians owned life insurance in 1970, with some 70% held in Canadian companies. Benefits paid during the year totaled $1.3 billion; death payments were $425 million, while "living benefits," such as annuities, surrender values, dividends, and matured endowments made up the remainder.

Additional forms of life insurance in the U.S. at the end of 1969 included veterans life insurance, with $38 billion in force; fraternal life insurance, with $23 billion (including Canada); and savings bank life insurance, with $3.6 billion in force.

Basic Principles. Life insurance differs from other forms of insurance in one vital respect. In other forms, the contingency insured against may never happen, and, as regards the great majority of policies written, does not happen. Life insurance, however, protects against the event of death, which, under a whole-life policy, is a "hazard converging into certainty." It is, therefore, necessary to provide not only against the risk of death each year, but also "to accumulate a fund sufficient not only to meet a claim whenever occurring, but also to provide at the ultimate limit of human life an absolutely certain claim.

To accomplish this, it is necessary to have life insurance companies base their premium charges upon a mortality table, which includes the death rate per 1000 persons and the expectation of life for each age. The U.S. death rate as a whole has remained approximately the same from 1955 to 1970. However, considerable improvement in the rate came early in the century with advances in medicine. Life expectancy at birth is now close to 70 years.

MORTALITY TABLE

Age	Number Living at Beginning of Designated Year	Number Dying During Designated Year	Deaths per 1,000	Expectancy Years	Per Cent Living to 65
0	1,000,000	7,080	7.08	68.30	68.01
1	992,920	1,747	1.76	67.78	68.49
2	991,173	1,507	1.52	66.90	68.61
3	989,666	1,445	1.46	66.00	68.72
4	988,221	1,384	1.40	65.10	68.82
5	986,837	1,332	1.35	64.19	68.91
6	985,505	1,281	1.30	63.27	69.01
7	984,224	1,240	1.26	62.35	69.10
8	982,984	1,209	1.23	61.43	69.18
9	981,775	1,188	1.21	60.51	69.27
10	980,587	1,186	1.21	59.58	69.35
11	979,401	1,205	1.23	58.65	69.44
12	978,196	1,233	1.26	57.72	69.52
13	976,963	1,289	1.32	56.80	69.61
14	975,674	1,356	1.39	55.87	69.70
15	974,318	1,423	1.46	54.95	69.80
16	972,895	1,498	1.54	54.03	69.90
17	971,397	1,574	1.62	53.11	70.01
18	969,823	1,639	1.69	52.19	70.12
19	968,184	1,685	1.74	51.28	70.24
20	966,499	1,730	1.79	50.37	70.36

MORTALITY TABLE—Con.

Age	Number Living at Beginning of Designated Year	Number Dying During Designated Year	Deaths per 1,000	Expectancy Years	Per Cent Living to 65
21	964,769	1,765	1.83	49.46	70.49
22	963,004	1,791	1.86	48.55	70.62
23	961,213	1,817	1.89	47.64	70.75
24	959,396	1,832	1.91	46.73	70.88
25	957,564	1,848	1.93	45.82	71.02
26	955,716	1,874	1.96	44.90	71.16
27	953,842	1,898	1.99	43.99	71.30
28	951,944	1,932	2.03	43.08	71.44
29	950,012	1,976	2.08	42.16	71.58
30	948,036	2,019	2.13	41.25	71.73
31	946,017	2,072	2.19	40.34	71.89
32	943,945	2,124	2.25	39.43	72.04
33	941,821	2,185	2.32	38.51	72.21
34	939,636	2,255	2.40	37.60	72.37
35	937,381	2,353	2.51	36.69	72.55
36	935,028	2,469	2.64	35.78	72.73
37	932,559	2,611	2.80	34.88	72.92
38	929,948	2,799	3.01	33.97	73.13
39	927,149	3,013	3.25	33.07	73.35
40	924,136	3,262	3.53	32.18	73.59
41	920,874	3,536	3.84	31.29	73.85
42	917,338	3,826	4.17	30.41	74.13
43	913,512	4,138	4.53	29.54	74.44
44	909,374	4,474	4.92	28.67	74.78
45	904,900	4,841	5.35	27.81	75.15
46	900,059	5,248	5.83	26.95	75.56
47	894,811	5,691	6.36	26.11	76.00
48	889,120	6,179	6.95	25.27	76.49
49	882,941	6,710	7.60	24.45	77.02
50	876,231	7,291	8.32	23.63	77.61
51	868,940	7,916	9.11	22.82	78.26
52	861,024	8,576	9.96	22.03	78.98
53	852,448	9,283	10.89	21.25	79.78
54	843,165	10,033	11.90	20.47	80.65
55	833,132	10,831	13.00	19.71	81.63
56	822,301	11,685	14.21	18.97	82.70
57	810,616	12,597	15,54	18.23	83.89
58	798,019	13,566	17.00	17.51	85.22
59	784,453	14,583	18.59	16.81	86.69
60	769,870	15,659	20.34	16.12	88.33
61	754,211	16,774	22.24	15.44	90.17
62	737,437	17,927	24.31	14.78	92.22
63	719,510	19,117	26.57	14.14	94.52
64	700,393	20,340	29.04	13.51	97.10
65	680,053	21,592	31.75	12.90	100.00
66	658,461	22,874	34.74	12.31	
67	635,587	24,178	38.04	11.73	
68	611,409	25,484	41.68	11.17	
69	585,925	26,724	45.61	10.64	
70	559,201	27,842	49.79	10.12	
71	531,359	28,773	54.15	9.63	
72	502,586	29,477	58.65	9.15	
73	473,109	29,929	63.26	8.69	
74	443,180	30,189	68.12	8.24	
75	412,991	30,301	73.37	7.81	
76	382,690	30,302	79.18	7.39	
77	352,388	30,200	85.70	6.98	
78	322,188	29,983	93.06	6.59	
79	292,205	29,568	101.19	6.21	
80	262,637	28,885	109.98	5.85	
81	233,752	27,898	119.35	5.51	
82	205,854	26,590	129.17	5.19	
83	179,264	24,986	139.38	4.89	
84	154,278	23,143	150.01	4.60	
85	131,135	21,131	161.14	4.32	
86	110,004	19,011	172.82	4.06	
87	90,993	16,846	185.13	3.80	
88	74,147	14,700	198.25	3.55	
89	59,447	12,630	212.46	3.31	
90	46,817	10,681	228.14	3.06	
91	36,136	8,881	245.77	2.82	
92	27,255	7,248	265.93	2.58	
93	20,007	5,788	289.30	2.33	
94	14,219	4,502	316.66	2.07	
95	9,717	3,413	351.24	1.80	
96	6,304	2,525	400.56	1.51	
97	3,779	1,846	488.42	1.18	
98	1,933	1,291	668.15	.83	
99	642	642	1,000.00	.50	

The assumption is that the death rate of the future will be approximately that demonstrated by the past. Given the age of the insured, the kind and amount of the policy desired, and the maximum rate of interest which the company will guarantee on its funds, it is possible to compute a premium based on the particular mortality table in use. That premium is known as the "net premium," and is intended to cover only the actual mortality cost of the company. To this "net premium" the company must add a percentage to cover expenses of operation and contingencies, thus giving the so-called "gross premium," actually charged the policyholder.

Should the premium be found to be too large, owing to a more favorable death rate than was indicated by the mortality table, or because expenses are smaller and interest earnings larger than anticipated, the company may have agreed to return to the policyholder all or a portion of such gains in the form of a "dividend." When this is done, the insurance is known as "participating." When the insurance is "nonparticipating," the premium charged the policyholder is usually considerably smaller. This is due to the fact that the company, as distinguished from the policyholder, remains entitled to all the gains which may accrue.

While the premium may be increased from year to year as the age of the insured increases, this is seldom done. Experience has shown that life insurance, in order to be practicable, must be based on a uniform annual premium during the premium-paying period. Such a plan requires the company, during the early years of the policy, to charge a premium more than sufficient to pay the current cost of insurance. The excess portions of the annual premiums are thus accumulated in a fund, known as the "reserve." This will be drawn upon in later years when, owing to the increasing hazard connected with increasing age, the uniform annual premium becomes insufficient to meet the current cost.

When a large number of policies are considered, the reserve (the overcharge or unearned premium) may be defined as representing that "sum which, together with future premiums paid by policyholders, will just enable the company to meet its claims according to the mortality table in use." Accumulation of such a reserve fund is fundamental to any sound plan of life insurance. Its absence in the past has been the cause of failure of many insurance institutions. Even today, it is the one great distinguishing feature between the sound and the unsound. It is for this reason that all regular life insurance companies are required by law to operate on the so-called "legal reserve basis."

Who Can Be Insured. Unlike the various kinds of property insurance, life insurance has not been construed by the courts as furnishing contracts of indemnity for loss suffered. It is well settled in the law that an individual possesses an insurable interest in his own life to an unlimited extent. Likewise, the insured may make his life insurance payable to his own estate, or to any beneficiary he may choose.

In view of the above ruling, it is necessary for insurance companies to protect themselves against the acceptance of risks which are either substandard in quality or which involve amounts of insurance greatly out of line with the earning capacity of the applicants. The protection needed is secured in several ways. A medical examination of the prospect is often required in the case of individual applicants. This precaution may be dispensed with in the case of policies of limited size or for group insurance. The prospect is required also to give true answers to numerous questions, relating to his health, family history, habits, and other points, contained in the application for his insurance. Where the insurance applied for is apparently too large, inquiry will also be made into the financial status of the applicant.

The problem of providing insurance for substandard applicants is receiving careful study in insurance circles. It is recognized that applicants for insurance are by no means equal in the quality of the risk involved. Numerous features, involving occupation, state of health, nationality, stature, weight, family history, and various other points, need to be considered if due allowance is to be made for the actual merits of the case. It is now felt that substandard lives should be given the benefits of life insurance, although at premiums sufficiently increased to meet the additional hazard associated with the substandard character of the applicant.

Almost all applicants for life insurance today are able to obtain policies. About 97% of applications for individual contracts are accepted. Only 3% are rejected because of serious health impairments or extremely hazardous occupations. Only 5% of policyholders pay higher than standard rates for "extra risks," such as heart disease, weight problems, or work hazards.

Who May Be a Beneficiary. As already noted the insured has an insurable interest in his own life to any extent. Further, in the absence of policy conditions to the contrary, he may name his own estate, or any individual he chooses, as beneficiary. But what is the situation when the insurance is taken out by a person other than the one insured?

Here we unfortunately meet with a great variety of judicial decisions. With respect to ties of affection, blood, or marriage, the courts have generally held that certain of such ties create an insurable interest even though the element of financial dependence is not present. The weight of authority holds that a parent has an insurable interest in the life of a child. Husband and wife are conclusively presumed to have an insurable interest in each other's life.

As regards all other relations, however, the courts have generally taken the position that the interest of the beneficiary, when taking out the insurance, must be based upon a reasonable expectation of deriving pecuniary benefit from the continuance of the insured's life. The weight of legal opinion is to the effect that the insurable interest of a beneficiary taking out insurance "must exist at the time the contract is made and that a policy valid at its inception will not, therefore, be voided if it should happen that the interest ceases before the maturity of the contract, unless the provisions of the policy are such as to bring about that result."

A creditor has an insurable interest in the life of a debtor. This interest has been held even to survive a discharge of a debtor in bankruptcy. The only question about which there is variance relates to the amount of insurance that the creditor may obtain on the life of the debtor. Usually, the creditor may only take out insurance up to the amount of the debt. Some states allow an additional amount to repay the creditor for the insurance premiums and/or the loss of interest.

What Type of Policy to Select. When considering the fundamental whole type of policies—term, life, and endowment—the average applicant unfortunately gives too little thought to the importance of making the proper selection. No one type of contract serves all persons equally well. In every case the applicant's special circumstances should be considered by the salesman, and the insurance recommended should be such as will meet the needs of the prospect.

The size of the premium varies greatly with the kind of policy, depending mainly on the extent to which a savings fund is provided for in addition to the current cost of protection. When a term policy grants protection only, and contains no savings fund accumulation, the premium outlay is small. The company's promise is limited to $1000 in the event of death during the term, nothing being paid in case of survival. The whole life policy, on the contrary, promises, not only $1000 upon death at any time, but also the same amount upon survival at age 100. As compared with short term policies, it represents a gradually increasing savings fund, thus requiring a higher premium to be paid throughout life.

The whole life policy offers permanent rather than temporary protection. There are two basic types: the "ordinary" (or "straight") life insurance contract, and the "limited-payment" contract. The ordinary life contract is based on the assumption that premium payments will be continued as long as the insured is living.

The limited-payment whole life policy resembles the ordinary whole-life contract in every respect, except that premium payments are limited to a term of years, like 20 years, instead of being continued throughout life. Since the liability is the same under the two contracts, the insurance company must collect the same amount, considering an assumed rate of interest. If all payments are, therefore, completed within 20 years, as under a 20-payment life policy, the premium rate must necessarily be higher than when the payments continue indefinitely for life. As distinguished from the above, endowment insurance—using a 20-year endowment for illustrative purposes—promises $1000 upon death during the 20-year term as well as an equal amount upon survival at the end of the term. Since this policy involves, in addition to the term insurance, a rapidly increasing savings fund (amounting to $1000 in 20 years), the premium must be correspondingly large. The difference in cost between the aforementioned types of policies may be illustrated at age 25 with the following rates charged by a certain company per $1000 of insurance: 10-year level term (renewable to age 70), $6.20; ordinary life, $15.20; 20-payment life, $25.20; and 20-year endowment, $45.50.

Owing to the low premium, term insurance gives the largest protection for the smallest possible outlay. It, therefore, meets the insurance needs of the young man with a small income and with a family on his hands. Here no surplus earnings exist to pay for the accumulating savings fund under other types of policies. Even where there is some small surplus, it may probably be used to better advantage in the profession or business, which are in the formative stage. Moreover, in the average man's family there is a peculiarly hazardous period, the child-raising period, when the death of the income producer proves a calamity. Accordingly, many who carry a substantial line of higher premium insurance supplement the same with additional 10- or 20-year term insurance to cover the period mentioned. The total insurance is thus substantially increased without undue strain.

The essential purpose of term insurance is to protect a *known temporary hazard*, under conditions when no other form of policy can be purchased in adequate amount. Its great disadvantage lies in the

LIFE INSURANCE IN CANADA

(Millions of Canadian Dollars)

	1960	1974	1975
Insurance in Force:			
Ordinary	$31,016	$ 37,673	$ 98,478
Group	14,739	100,998	121,865
Industrial	1,112	...	...
Total	$46,867	$188,671	$220,343
Benefit Payments:			
Death Benefits	$ 197	$ 614	$ 700
Matured Endowments	46	80	82
Disability Payments	6	23	26
Annuity Payments	71	393	486
Surrender Values	128	269	271
Policy Dividends	113	303	336
Total	$ 561	$ 1,760	$ 1,984
Income:			
Premium Income	$ 953	$ 3,099	$ 3,549

Source: *1976 Life Insurance Fact Book* (New York: Institute of Life Insurance).

LIFE INSURANCE IN THE UNITED STATES

INCOME, PAYMENTS, ASSETS AND RESERVES OF LIFE INSURANCE COMPANIES 1900–1975 (000,000 Omitted)

Date	Premium Income	Investment Income	Total Income	Benefit Payments	Assets	Reserves
1900	N.A.	N.A.	$ 401	$ 169	$ 1,742	$ 1,443
1910	N.A.	N.A.	781	387	3,876	3,226
1920	$ 1,381	$ 383	1,764	745	7,320	6,338
1930	3,517	1,077	4,594	2,247	18,880	16,231
1935	3,673	1,399	5,072	2,535	23,216	20,404
1940	3,887	1,771	5,658	2,664	30,802	27,238
1945	5,159	2,515	7,674	2,667	44,797	38,667
1950	8,189	2,075	11,337	3,730	64,020	54,946
1951	9,040	1,948	12,012	3,984	68,278	58,547
1952	9,883	2,160	13,076	4,146	73,375	62,579
1954	11,563	2,590	15,280	4,947	84,486	70,903
1955	12,546	2,801	16,544	5,382	90,432	75,359
1956	13,584	3,063	17,865	5,878	96,011	79,738
1960	17,365	4,304	23,007	8,119	119,576	98,473
1961	18,258	4,668	24,397	8,811	126,816	103,285
1967	28,277	7,917	38,248	13,300	177,361	142,217
1969	33,996	9,354	45,628	15,525	197,208	158,550
1975	58,575	16,488	78,022	22,536	289,304	235,057

Before 1947 the business of accident and health department of life companies was not included. N.A.—Not available.
Source: *1976 Life Insurance Fact Book.*

fact that the temporary nature of the hazard may be misjudged. At the expiration of the term policy, insurance protection may still be needed, and yet be unobtainable because of inability to meet the medical standard. For this reason term policies usually contain a renewable provision allowing extensions of the original term period. Term policies may also be convertible, which means they may be exchanged for higher premium form by paying the extra cost. Both of these provisions are recommended if the insured's needs so dictate.

The shortcomings just noted with respect to term insurance are obviated by the ordinary policy. This represents *permanent* protection at a very moderate cost. It also combines protection with reasonable saving. Whenever possible, this type of insurance should be preferred to the term plan. Many who take term insurance could, through a little additional effort, pay the extra premium on an equal amount of ordinary insurance. Many argue that they prefer to place the difference in premium in bonds, stocks, real estate, or some other investment. Yet this seems inadvisable, even assuming the resolution is carried out, owing to the absolute security of the life insurance investment and the approximate return of 4–5½%. Careful evaluation of the net effects (after taxes) over a long period of investment, such as 20–40 years, is necessary to justify a decision to purchase term insurance only. The normal family situation suggests a combination of both term and whole-life protection for the husband.

A substantial variety of special forms have become important in life insurance. The so-called "preferred risk" or "special" policies are sold at a reduced rate per $1,000 of insurance because the insured agrees to buy a certain minimum amount, such as $5,000, $10,000, or $25,000. The reduced rate represents a discount for a quantity purchase and recognition of the more careful selection process followed in reviewing applications for insurance. These contracts contain essentially the same provisions as ordinary life forms.

Another development which has appealed to many buyers of life insurance is the "family plan" under which standard packages of coverage apply to all members of the family. The insurance is generally an amount of ordinary life, such as $5,000, on the father, with perhaps $1,000 of term on the life of the wife and each child (to age 18). The premium remains constant even if the wife dies or additional children are born.

Methods of Paying the Proceeds at Maturity of the Policy. The proceeds of life policies may be paid either in a lump sum or in installments. In the latter case, commonly known as the annuity option, monthly installments are usually paid for ten or twenty years, irrespective of the life of the beneficiary and, therefore, as much longer as the beneficiary may survive the 10- or 20-year period.

The lump sum payment plan has little to commend it where the purpose of the insurance is to give an income to dependents. The fairness of giving 20 or 50 thousand dollars in one lump sum to a widow may well be questioned. The underlying purpose of life insurance is to *assure an income* to dependents *as long as needed.* This the lump sum payment method does not guarantee. The life annuity plan, on the contrary, "insures the insurance," and is just as necessary a form of protection to the beneficiary as the original insurance itself.

Under the life annuity plan the policy proceeds constitute an "insurance estate" administered by the insurance company. It relieves the beneficiary of all expenses of reinvestment, and of all exercise of judgment in the placing of investments and of their supervision thereafter. Administration of the insurance estate by the insurance company also compares very favorably with the administration of an estate through other channels. There are no legal contests between heirs, no legal expenses of administration, no income taxation, and no fluctuation in either the value of or the income obtained from the estate. Moreover, there is no danger of loss of the principal. The only significant danger is that the value of the proceeds will diminish due to inflation. The dollars paid the beneficiary continue at a constant amount while the purchasing power of these dollars diminishes. Thus, in many situations it may be advisable to use a portion of the total estate values for other investments—such as stocks, bonds, or mutual funds—to hedge against the inflationary trend of the economy.

Disposal of Policy before Maturity. In many instances, however, life insurance policies terminate

INSURANCE IN FORCE, 1900–1969 (000,000 Omitted)

Year	Ordinary	Group	Industrial	Credit	Total
1900	$ 6,124	. .	$ 1,449	. .	$ 7,573
1910	11,783	. .	3,125	. .	14,908
1920	32,018	$ 1,570	6,948	$ 4	40,540
1930	78,576	9,801	17,963	73	106,413
1935	70,684	10,208	17,471	101	98,464
1940	79,346	14,938	20,866	380	115,530
1945	101,550	22,172	27,675	365	151,762
1950	149,071	47,793	33,415	3,889	234,168
1951	159,054	54,398	34,870	4,818	253,140
1952	170,795	62,913	36,448	6,435	276,591
1954	198,419	86,395	38,664	10,241	333,719
1955	216,600	101,300	39,682	14,750	372,332
1960	340,268	175,434	39,563	31,183	586,448
1961	364,347	192,202	39,451	33,493	629,493
1966	538,992	343,362	39,663	62,672	984,689
1969	678,887	483,240	38,614	83,788	1,284,529
1975	1,083,421	904,695	39,423	112,032	2,139,571

Source: *1976 Life Insurance Fact Book.*

by lapse or surrender instead of by death. Various circumstances may be responsible for this, such as inability to pay premiums, death of the named beneficiary without leaving other dependents to be protected, or impairment of the insured's health to such an extent as to make further payments of premiums inadvisable in view of the "extended insurance option" granted by the policy.

Cash or Loan Value.—When a policy terminates by surrender, the insured has the option of selecting any one of a number of "guaranteed values," set forth in the contract. One of these values is called the "cash" or "loan value." This value represents the amount of the reserve value of the policy which may be borrowed, if it is intended to keep the policy alive, or which may be taken in cash, if the policy is to be terminated. Usually, such a value is granted after the second annual premium has been paid. Competition is now leading many companies to offer cash values after the first year of the policy. The amount, however, will not represent the full reserve value, in most cases, until a considerable number of years have elapsed. Usually, the full reserve value is given or loaned after the payment of ten annual premiums. With the rise of interest rates after 1969, the policy loan feature of permanent contracts became more valuable to policyowners. A loan rate of 5% is guaranteed in most such contracts, while alternative sources of credit may cost much more.

Paid-up and Extended Insurance.—Instead of the cash value of the policy, the insured may, upon terminating his policy, take either "paid-up insurance" or "extended insurance." The "paid-up insurance" represents that amount of insurance which may be purchased with a net single premium equal to the amount of the cash value of the policy. "Extended insurance," on the contrary, means insurance of the same kind on a term basis and for the original amount for as long a period as may be purchased with a net single premium equal to the cash value at the attained age.

In a typical case, the cash value of a $10,000 20-payment life policy at age 35 amounts to $682 at the end of the third year. Instead of taking the $682 in cash, the policyholder may obtain $1540 of paid-up whole-life insurance, or $10,000 of extended term insurance for a period of 7 years and 334 days. In other words, all three of these options are mathematically equivalent, assuming a given mortality table and a stipulated interest rate. Aside from these options, many companies give the insured, upon termination of his policy, the privilege of utilizing the cash value to purchase an annuity, or some other type of life insurance contract.

Industrial Insurance. As its name implies, industrial insurance is a form of life insurance especially adapted for wage-earners. Its purpose is to enable the large industrial portion of our population to have the funds necessary to meet the expenses connected with medical attendance during their last illness and to assure a decent burial. But, while these are its special purposes, industrial insurance has proved a great educator to the masses in that it has conveyed a proper appreciation of the value of ordinary life insurance.

Although originally sold on the basis of units of premiums of 5 cents a week or multiples thereof, with collection by the agent each week, improved machine accounting techniques and rising income levels for policyholders have resulted in policies being stated in terms of their face amount (usually $250–$1,000) and in monthly premium collections. Such insurance is more expensive than ordinary life, but it has served a real need in the insurance market. The average size policy in the U.S. in 1969 was just under $500. Although this type of life insurance decreased during 1950–70 from 15% of all life insurance in force to less than 3%, 79 million persons held such contracts for a total of $39 billion in protection by 1970.

Industrial life insurance contracts contain a few provisions that differ from other individual policies, but they are based on the same general principles that serve as the foundation for ordinary life insurance. The legal reserve basis is used and the contracts contain practically all of the leading provisions found in regular policies. Premiums are calculated upon an actuarial basis, although a different mortality table is necessary to indicate the higher death rate that prevails among this type of policyholders.

Group Insurance. This form of insurance was introduced in 1911. It is designed to enable an employer to insure employees under one policy. The employer holds a master policy, which covers the employees insured, and each of the employees so insured holds an individual policy. The premium may be paid entirely by the employer or its cost may be shared between employer and employee. At least 10 to 25 employees (depends on state law) must be covered, although so-called wholesale policies are written covering from 5 to 9 employees. Most group insurance policies are for term insurance. No medical examination is necessary. Consequently this is the only form of insurance which some people can obtain. For employees advanced in years, the cost is much less than for equivalent insurance in any other form. In case of the termination of employment, the holder of an individual policy ordinarily has the privilege of converting his insurance into some other type, on which, of course, he pays the premiums.

The employer ordinarily receives whatever dividends are paid on group policies. These may in some cases equal the amount the employer has contributed toward meeting the premium. If the dividends are less than the amount paid by the employer, the difference may be regarded as an increased wage payment or an investment in employee good will.

An important recent development is group creditor insurance under which a lending institution purchases a group contract on all borrowers to cover the loan in the event of the borrower's death. The average credit life insurance policy is written for about $1000, compared with the average contract for other group life insurance, which is $6500.

Fraternal Insurance. Fraternal societies usually observe some ritual, and their government is purely democratic. With respect to insurance, their chief purpose has been to enable the members to secure protection at the smallest possible cost.

Owing to this desire, many of the societies ignored the "reserve basis" of life insurance and charged premiums wholly inadequate to prevent numerous failures. This situation led to the adoption in many states of laws making it compulsory, for the orders to employ the legal reserve basis. In 1970 fraternal insurance in force in the U.S. and Canada was only about $23 billion, and assets of these companies were $4.7 billion.

Whereas an ordinary life policy is a definite promise to pay a stated sum in return for a fixed annual premium, the benefit certificate of a fraternal society has, in the past, merely recognized the holder's rights as a member in the society to share in its benefits if the same can be paid out of the assessments levied on the membership. With the adoption of actuarial methods, however, a fraternal benefit certificate can be made as definite a promise as an ordinary life policy.

Usually, the holder of a certificate can name as beneficiary only some member of his family, or other dependent recognized by the society, and for an amount not to exceed a limited sum, such as two or three thousand dollars. Many societies also extend to their members sickness and accident benefits.

HEALTH INSURANCE

Just as life insurance serves to protect dependents against financial need through the death of the insured, so health and accident insurance are intended to protect dependents against a similar need arising out of the incapacitation of the insured through sickness or accident. For the average family this form of protection is indispensable. Industrial accidents are covered today in most states by workmen's compensation insurance. But the largest number of accidents do not occur in industry and must be covered by private insurance. Moreover, loss due to sickness is equal to many times the loss resulting from accidents. It is estimated that about 250,000,000 working days are lost annually in the United States through sickness.

Various methods of granting protection against sickness and accident have been adopted by private insurance companies. Most life insurance companies grant protection, in the form of a monthly income for life, in the event of the total and permanent disability of the insured. But fully 97 per cent of all sickness and accident claims are for temporary disability. Many accident and health companies also issue "limited policies" at comparatively small premiums since the coverage is confined to a limited number of diseases or accidents and the compensation to a comparatively short period.

Much more adequate are the health and accident policies which are "general" in their coverage. These cover against disability from every variety of sickness or accident. They may be issued either separately or in combination, that is, as either health or accident policies or both.

Under accident policies a certain principal sum, such as $5,000, is paid in the event of death, the loss of sight, both hands, both feet, or one hand and one foot. Smaller sums are paid for the loss of one eye, or one hand, or one foot. Weekly or monthly compensation is also provided either for a definite period or for life, in the event of permanent disability, and a smaller compensation when the disability is only partial. Almost invariably indemnities are doubled if the accident occurs on a public conveyance.

In health insurance no principal sum is paid in case of death, and the payments are limited to a weekly compensation for a stipulated period. Often, both health and accident policies provide for extra payments covering hospital and surgical expenses. Until recently all health and accident policies were subject to cancellation by the company. But recently various companies have undertaken to issue so-called "non-cancellable policies," which may be renewed from year to year at the option of the insured until a stipulated age is reached.

More than 85% of all Americans have one or more forms of private health insurance. By 1969 the coverage was: hospital expense, 170 million; surgical expense, 156 million; regular medical expense, 129 million; major medical expense, 67 million; disability income loss, 63 million. One of the fastest-growing was major medical insurance, offering maximum benefits of $5000 to $20,000 or more. In 1955 fewer than 5 million persons had this coverage—by 1969 the number had grown by more than 13 times.

For those 65 and over, federal Medicare, since 1966, has provided considerable protection against rising costs. Compulsory coverage of most hospital expenses is provided by employer and employee taxes. A second part of the program (physician's expenses and other medical costs) is financed by the government and by voluntary contributions by participants (95% of all eligible have chosen this coverage). More than 20 million persons are covered by Medicare, in which selected companies and Blue Cross-Blue Shield organizations participate as intermediaries to pay benefits of more than $5 billion a year.

PROPERTY-LIABILITY INSURANCE

Property-liability insurance in the U.S. includes more than 2500 companies. Some firms write many or all kinds of "multiple-line" insurance; others cover only a few specialized lines (or types) of insurance, such as automobile or fire insurance. Most of the $29 billion of annual premiums in this sector are written by approximately 1000 companies, operating in all or many states.

Automobile Insurance. The "automobile economy" of today is reflected in the more than $12 billion a year of the direct insurance cost of the mobile society of the U.S. Nearly 60,000 automobile accident deaths and 5 million annual injuries emphasize the need for improved motor vehicle safety as one of the most vital current issues.

Numerous industry proposals and government regulations are aiming at solutions to the "automobile problem," which is really a complex of related problems of increasing costs, difficult apportionment of individual and societal responsibility, dissatisfaction with present conditions, and evolving changes in the legal and economic systems. Some current criticism is directed at auto manufacturers, while other comment takes to task the liability system on which auto insurance is based, the rating structure used by insurers, enforcement of traffic safety by government, and the irresponsibility of some drivers.

Kinds of Automobile Insurance. Under this area of coverage there are six headings:

Bodily injury liability insurance protects against legal claims arising from personal injuries or death caused by the use of a motor vehicle. The policy covers the person or corporation responsible for the operation of the car. It usually also covers any licensed driver the policyholder or adult members of his family permit to drive the car. Usual protection covers defense of all claims and suits for injury and payment of any costs assessed against the insured, up to the policy limit, which may range from $5000 for one person and $10,000 for all claims from one accident to as much as $300,000 and $1 million limits, respectively.

Property damage liability insurance protects against losses incurred through damage done in use of the car to the property of other people. In case the damaged property cannot be used and its withdrawal from use imposes additional losses to its owner, these losses, assessed against the insured, are also covered by the policy. But the policy does not cover damage done to the car of the policyholder.

Collision insurance covers damage to the policyholder's car caused by collision with any other object, moving or stationary. If the driver strikes a tree, the policy protects him no less than if he collides with another car. The amount he can collect, however, is limited to the actual cost of repairs or the actual value of the car at the time of the accident. Moreover, the accident must have taken place within certain geographical areas. Under many policies, no idemnity can be collected unless the damages are over a certain minimum amount, such as $50 or $100, called the deductible.

Comprehensive insurance pays for all physical damage to the vehicle, with certain exceptions specified in the contract. Such losses to the insured car as fire, hail damage, lightning, theft, riot damage, or glass breakage are covered to the extent of the actual cash value of the item damaged.

Medical payments coverage provides for reimbursement to the insured for any medical expenses incurred by him or by persons in the car, to the limits stated. Some automobile policies also include a lump sum payment for death and a weekly benefit for total disability.

Uninsured motorists' coverage is a recent and important part of most present contracts. On either a mandatory or optional basis, the insured is protected against bodily injury losses (medical expenses, loss of income) caused by negligent but uninsured motorists. The coverage applies to "hit-and-run" and stolen-car accidents, including protection up to specified limits for the insured, his family, and other riders in the car of the insured.

Workmen's Compensation Insurance. Accidents and diseases affect thousands of employees each year. Without insurance, many would suffer severely as a result of medical expenses and income loss.

Workmen's compensation insurance provides benefits through a combination of social and private insurance. State laws require most employers to purchase workmen's insurance. Some states provide funds for writing this protection, but in 44 states most of the policies are written by private insurers.

Standard contracts include: (1) a promise by the insurer to pay the employees those benefits provided in the law, and (2) employers' liability coverage for basic limits of about $25,000. Most benefits are paid under the workmen's compensation portion of the contract—in which the employer pays the employee regardless of fault, or of who is to blame for the loss. The concept of employer liability, based on negligence and proven fault by the employer, is important in understanding the derivation of the present workmen's compensation system.

Laws Formerly Adverse to Employees. Employers' liability insurance indemnifies "against loss from liability imposed by law upon the insured." Thus, it is important to note the nature of the law of the particular jurisdiction under consideration as it governs the liability of employers.

In the 1800's, a mass of special law between employer and employee—so-called judge-made law—developed both in England and in America.

The adverse character of this law from the employee's standpoint is indicated by the following doctrines or practices: (1) the *contributory negligence doctrine*, which held that an employee must show his freedom from negligence, and cannot collect if he has failed to use reasonable care and if that neglect contributed to his injury; (2) the *fellow-servant rule*, which provided that an injured employee could not recover from the employer if the injury was caused by the negligence of a fellow servant; and (3) the *assumption of risk rule*, which was to the effect that "an employee entering employment is held to assume and consent to the ordinary and obvious risks incident to the employment."

With the increasingly harsh application of these rules, various statutes were enacted with a view to increasing the employee's protection. But this tendency was soon counteracted by the development of the "*contracting-out privilege*," according to which the employer could request his employees to contract away their rights under the law, thus relieving the employer of all liability in case of injury.

Under such a system of law it naturally followed that little financial redress was obtainable for injured employees. Criticism of the system was well merited, but should have been directed against the law itself, and not against the form of insurance which merely sought to protect against the law as it existed. The fault was with the system of law. This forced upon the employee the burden of proof and yielded substantial compensation to only a small proportion of injured employees. This system led also to excessive delay owing to the slow operation of court trials.

Workmen's Compensation Laws. In view of such shortcomings it was only natural that the public should demand a more definite and rational system of law with respect to employers' liability for industrial accidents. This was accomplished through the passage of so-called workmen's compensation laws. Within the decade 1910–20 practically every state enacted such legislation.

While lacking uniformity in details, the various laws have a common purpose. All of the objectionable doctrines mentioned in the preceding paragraphs are abrogated. Employers who refuse to come under the act are compelled to take their chances in a court of law without the support of any of the aforementioned legal rules.

At first, only hazardous occupations were covered by workmen's compensation laws, but gradually coverage has been extended to more than two-thirds of all U.S. workers. Some smaller employers and agricultural, domestic, and casual help are usually excluded. Basic benefits are for medical expenses, loss of income due to death or disability, and rehabilitation expenses resulting from all work accidents and from many diseases caused by work conditions. Although medical expenses are usually paid without limit, income payments normally aim at replacing about two-thirds of income within a stated maximum duration.

All features of administration are clearly defined and are designed to overcome the delay occasioned under the previous system. Specific payments are provided for each of the following: death, total disability, partial disability, or specific injuries. The compensation is based upon the wage of the injured person; and, in addition, in the event of death, upon the number and the degree of consanguinity of the dependents.

All employers, if choosing to come under the act, are compelled to protect their legal obligation under the law through insurance. In most states, the insurance may be taken either with a state fund or with an insurance company. In most instances self-insurance is permitted only when authorized by the administrative authorities, and may subsequently be revoked at any time. A few states make it compulsory to take the insurance in the state fund. Whatever insurance institution is selected, the policy must be based on the compensation law under consideration, and any provisions to the contrary are declared null and void.

FIRE AND MULTIPLE-PERIL INSURANCE

Fire insurance is an important form of indemnity in the field of property insurance. This line of insurance also embraces such perils as windstorm, riot, explosion, water overflow, vandalism, and collapse. Also, contracts protecting the insured against consequences of such perils which cause his business or residence to be closed are part of the fire insurance field.

A significant development since the early 1950's has been the expansion of many contracts to include multiple-peril insurance of fire, theft, and liability perils. Package policies insuring these basic perils have become popular, and the average home now has the broad protection of a homeowner's policy. A variety of commercial multiple-peril policies are also available to most firms and institutions, in which broad coverage, convenience, and lower cost are obtained in a single contract.

Purpose of Fire Insurance. Like other forms of insurance, fire insurance has for its fundamental purpose the "substitution of certain for uncertain loss." As regards a great and everpresent hazard, it serves to stabilize business, to reduce all costs to consumers, and to enhance production by eliminating fear of loss and by increasing initiative.

Fire insurance also serves as the support of commerce and of industry, in so far as it and its companion, marine insurance, are the basis of our whole credit system. The significance of this function becomes apparent when we reflect that fully 90 per cent of the world's business is conducted on credit, and that nearly all transactions involving goods, buildings, and ships, are confronted with the danger of ruinous loss through fire or marine disaster.

As has been elsewhere stated: "It can be shown in a hundred ways that fire and marine insurance have become absolute necessities of trade, without the assuring protection of which the large undertakings of today would be a gigantic gamble and would never be attempted if liable to miscarry through a single fire or marine disaster. As it is, enormous sums are borrowed on stocks and bonds and warehouse receipts; merchants sell their wares on credit; investors furnish millions for the upbuilding of vast industries supporting whole towns;

capitalists make loans on buildings worth many times the value of the ground upon which they are built—all being willing to do this because they know that the insurance policy stands between them and loss."

Personal Character of the Contract. Fire insurance policies are personal contracts, that is, strictly speaking, they do not insure the property but the persons who own the same or have an interest therein. Two buildings may be just alike in all respects, except that one is owned by an honest person whereas, with respect to the other, the owner may be grossly careless or even inclined to profit from a dishonest fire. The importance of this factor cannot be overemphasized. Probably no other type of contract places one party (the insurer) so much at the mercy of the other (the insured). With reference to over-insurance, therefore, as well as the determination of rates, it is highly important that the insurance company know the character of the property-owner.

Nature of the Indemnity. The fire insurance contract is also one of indemnity for actual loss. Irrespective of any value stated in the policy, insurance companies are not liable for more than the "actual value of the property at the time of the fire." Any other rule might work the greatest injustice to companies, and might even result in fraud, owing to the constant and frequently great fluctuations in values as regards both buildings and goods. Should companies be obliged to pay the full face of the policy in the event of total loss, irrespective of an actually lower value, the policyholder would be enabled to profit from a fire. Such a result is contrary to the very idea of "indemnity," which "implies that the insured should be compensated for loss actually incurred, but should never find the insurance contract a source of profit."

Two other concepts, relating to the nature of the indemnity, should be mentioned. Only the loss of material values is indemnified, i. e., the fair cash market value of the property at the time of the fire. Sentimental values, such as those associated with gifts, documents, and objects of art, are not covered unless there is an express agreement to the contrary. In case of inability to reach a fair settlement with the insured as to the fair value of the property damaged or destroyed, the insurer is given the option, under the terms of the policy, of replacing or reconditioning the property. Moreover, in the event of agreement as to the value of all the property, damaged and undamaged, the insurer is given the option of settling at that figure and taking title to the undamaged portion.

Restriction of Liability. The company's liability is also limited to "loss or damage directly traceable to fire." Small fires, working through a chain of circumstances, such as charged wires and explosives, may result in enormous loss for which the insurer becomes liable. In all such cases the question is: "Is fire the real cause, and if so, is the sequence of events between the origin of the fire and the destruction of the property an unbroken one or has some outside force, such as an act of God, intervened to bring about or increase the loss?"

Who May Insure. Since fire insurance policies are contracts for indemnity and not for profit, it follows that only those who have a pecuniary interest—an insurable interest—in the property under consideration have a right to insure. Insurable interest, however, has been given a very broad meaning by our courts. Eliott defines it as "every interest in property or in relation thereto, or liability in respect thereof, of such a nature that a contemplated peril may directly damnify the insured."

Such an interest does not necessarily imply ownership or even possession of the property. Thus insurable interest has been held to extend to the following: (1) custodians of property intrusted to their care, to the extent of their interest or liability, such as administrators of estates, agents in property held for the principal, assignees in insolvency, trustees, common-carriers, warehouse men, and commission merchants; (2) creditors or debtors, such as mortgagees, debtors with respect to property seized for debt, pledgees to the value of the property pledged, and those who have by agreement expended money on the property of others; and (3) those possessing contract rights depending upon the preservation of the property, such as consignees and consignors, contractors whose payment is deferred until completion of the contract, patentees possessing a right to royalties, and even insurers in the property they have insured.

The last illustration serves as the basis for the important practice of reinsurance, whereby an insurance company may reduce its risk by reinsuring all or a part with other insurers.

Use of a Standard Policy. In probably no form of insurance is it so essential to have a uniform or standard policy as in fire insurance. Prior to 1870 there was an utter lack of uniformity. The first state to attempt a remedy was Massachusetts, which adopted a standard form in 1873. New York followed in 1887, and the so-called New York Standard Fire Policy, although improved from time to time, has been adopted as the standard in all but a few states on a mandatory basis. Even where not enacted into law, this policy is generally used by all the companies.

Standard policies are necessarily drawn to meet a general situation, and cannot be designed to cover the numerous special needs surrounding the many different types of property or the various insurable interests therein. All such exceptional circumstances must be arranged for through so-called "endorsements" attached to the policy.

Coinsurance. With comparatively few exceptions, fire insurance on commercial and industrial properties is written subject to coinsurance. This means that the insured will have any claim paid in the proportion that the insurance taken bears to the insurance required. The advantage offered the insured for accepting a coinsurance clause is a reduced rate per $100 of insurance.

For example, with a building valued at $10,000, let us assume that the insurance required is $8000 (80 per cent), that only $4000 of insurance was taken, and that a loss of $2000 occurred. Under the circumstances the $2000 loss is paid only in the proportion that $4000 (the insurance taken) bears to $8000 (the insurance required), or to the extent of only one-half, or $1000.

Usually the amount of insurance required is 80% of the value, representing the proportion of the property value subject to destruction by fire. Where, however, the property is subject to total destruction, a 100% coinsurance clause may be used. In other cases much lower percentages, as, for instance, 70 or even 50% are applied.

Where property appreciates materially during the term of the policy, it is highly important that the owner should correspondingly increase his insurance in order to comply with the coinsurance requirement. The purpose of coinsurance is to secure justice between property owners and to enable the companies to derive an adequate premium income. The overwhelming majority of fires result merely in partial losses.

Without a coinsurance requirement, many of those insured would be encouraged to purchase only small amounts of insurance in relation to their exposed property values. With coinsurance, all of the insured are encouraged to purchase amounts that will provide protection against serious losses. Equity among policyholders is achieved in applying the fire insurance rate, as if the rate were proportionally decreased when larger amounts were purchased.

TRANSPORTATION INSURANCE

Often referred to as "marine" insurance, transportation insurance has two basic divisions: (1) ocean marine insurance, and (2) inland marine insurance. The first primarily covers sea perils of ships and cargoes; the second generally covers a wide variety of movable property in transit, as well as fixed property used in connection with transportation, such as bridges, docks, and tunnels. Ocean marine insurance is used here to illustrate the unusual aspects of transportation insurance.

Ocean marine insurance has for its purpose the indemnification of interested parties "against loss, damage, or expense, occasioned accidentally in connection with vessels, cargoes, and freight charges, through any of the numerous perils incident to transportation by water." In fact, the so-called "warehouse-to-warehouse clause," used in insuring cargo, covers goods from the time they leave the shipper's warehouse in the interior—through all the various stages of the journey, rail, truck, dock, ship, and port of destination—until they reach the warehouse of the consignee in the foreign country.

Types of Losses Covered. Policies of marine insurance may vary according to the type of losses they cover. Marine losses are either "total" or "partial." Total losses, in turn, may be either "actual" or "constructive," the latter comprising those cases where the property has not actually been destroyed but where the cost of repairing or reconditioning is so great, as compared with the restored value, as to make the attempt financially inadvisable.

Partial losses may be classified as "general average," "particular average," and "salvage." General average has been defined as comprising "losses and expenditures which result from the sacrifice of any interest voluntarily made by the master of the vessel, in time of real distress, for the common safety of vessel, cargo, and freight, and which must be repaid proportionately by all the parties benefited." Any partial loss which does not meet this definition is regarded as a "particular average loss." "Salvage" represents the remuneration recoverable under maritime law by a salvor for saving property at sea.

SURETY, FIDELITY, TITLE AND CREDIT INSURANCE

In the field of property insurance, there should be mention of surety and fidelity bonds, and title insurance, and credit insurance. A surety bond is a guarantee, and has been defined as a "written obligation to pay a sum of money under one or more expressed conditions, among which may be found negligence, breach of trust, disobedience of a law, failure to pay a judgment, failure to pay a debt voluntarily assumed, and other conditions under which losses may be sustained by personal acts." Hundreds of kinds of policies are issued to meet every possible variety of obligation. Some bonds are much like insurance, protecting against crime perils such as fidelity losses due to employee dishonesty. Broadly speaking, bonds may be classified as falling under fidelity, judicial (court bonds), license and permit, contract, and depository bonds.

Title insurance, as defined elsewhere, "promises to protect the owner of real estate, or the lender of money thereon, against loss or damage, not exceeding the amount stated in the policy, sustained by reason of any defect of title assumed under the policy, or because of the unmarketability of the title or by reason of unknown liens or encumbrances against the property at the time the policy is issued."

Credit insurance has for its purpose "the indemnification of losses, coming within the coverage of the policy and exceeding the normal loss of the business under consideration, suffered by manufacturers and jobbers through the insolvency of their customers."

BUSINESS CYCLES

It is a matter of historical observation that aggregate business activity pursues a distinct course of expansion and contraction, prosperity and depression. This more or less rhythmic succession of business conditions is known as the *business cycle*. The layman refers to its alternative phases as good times and bad times.

Prosperity is characterized by full employment. Consumers and businesses spend freely, frequently with borrowed money, and prices are firm or rising. Profit margins are generally favorable. New enterprises are undertaken and old businesses expand. The total output of the economy increases and a spirit of optimism prevails. Depression is associated with opposite conditions. There is widespread unemployment and jobs are scarce. There is a reluctance to spend, accompanied by a contraction of credit. Prices usually decline and profit margins narrow or disappear. Business firms contract, some failing altogether. Total output of goods and services declines and optimism gives way to fear and pessimism.

Business Crises. The change in business from prosperity to depression used to be abrupt and decisive. Now, with government assistance in moderating crises, it is usually more gradual.

Frequently in the 18th and 19th centuries, the prosperity phase of business cycles was associated with the doubtful and unscrupulous promotion of some particular enterprise accompanied by excessive and unsound credit expansion. Normal business was displaced by frenzied speculation. Ultimately, some prominent firm or individual became overextended in the speculation and was forced to liquidate its holdings. Thus, the speculative mania was broken.

The abrupt reversal of outlook resulted in the calling of loans, a desperate scramble for money, frantic sale of securities, and sharp declines in prices. Instead of the pessimism of a normal business crisis, the community was gripped by overpowering fright. When crises became thus violent, they were called panics. There have been 11 such panics in the U.S., the last one in 1929.

Since then, instead of panics, there are periods of reduced activity such as in 1957–58, 1960–61, and 1969–70, when stock markets decline, unemployment increases, and business activity in general slows down. These are called recessions.

True, the business cycle has become milder as a result of a favorable conjuncture of structural changes and because of better and wider understanding of the requirements of business cycle policy. However, the forces that tend to generate cyclical movements have not vanished.

Causes. The annals of business record crises from the beginnings of commercial capitalism. There is little doubt that crises are as old as trade itself. However, up to the Napoleonic era of the early 19th century, and to a limited extent thereafter, each crisis had a special cause usually of a non-business nature. The business reversals were attributable to what we would now call random events such as a bad harvest, riots, wars, or acts of God. The periods of depression were viewed as abnormal deviations from the normal course of prosperous economic growth.

As capitalism matured and modern industrial economies developed, crises became more regular in occurrence and more similar in nature, especially in their financial aspects. Instead of being viewed as random abnormal events, they became recognized as a recurrent and inherent feature of a business economy. Statisticians detected a rhythm and regularity which seemed periodic and the concept of a business cycle evolved. Although modern data do not support the thesis of periodic recurrence, the name "business cycle" has remained, and more or less regular fluctuations are considered a normal attribute of modern business societies.

A problem of such long standing and such social

importance has attracted many great minds to its study. Consequently there are many theories or explanations of business cycles.

Since many of the theories differ more in their emphases than in fundamentals, most of them may be classified under one of three headings: business economy theories, monetary theories, and savings and investment theories.

Business Theories. These explanations rest on the general hypothesis that prosperity, through its effects on business expectations, breeds maladjustments which ultimately undermine prosperity. They run somewhat as follows. Business is speculative by nature and therefore prosperity breeds overoptimism and overexpansion. Productive capacity and goods are created in anticipation of future markets and inventories are accumulated. This process strains the capacity of the whole economy. Labor efficiency declines as marginal workers are employed, wage rates rise, raw materials rise in price, credit becomes scarce, and interest rates rise. Eventually costs rise faster than selling prices, profits are reduced, and some of the weaker businesses fail. These conditions convert overoptimism into overpessimism and contraction begins. Inventories are reduced, loans cancelled or paid off, and prices decline. These developments set the stage for recovery, optimism returns, and the process is repeated. These theories are realistic and conform with observed behavior, but they are somewhat superficial. They are more descriptive than explanatory.

Monetary Theories. These explanations emphasize the key role of the money supply and bank policies. They may be summarized in the following manner. Economic activity expands and contracts with changes in total spending, and this spending is done with money. Spending is influenced largely by changes in the supply of money. In a modern credit economy, bank deposits constitute the main form of money. Consequently the behavior of banks in expanding and contracting the money supply is responsible for business fluctuations.

In the early phases of prosperity, banks extend credit at low interest rates. This leads to business expansion, inventory accumulation, and the spread of optimism. This process gains momentum until the banks are unable or unwilling to continue the credit expansion and interest rates rise. Businesses are forced to curtail activities and reduce inventories. The decline begins. When contraction has gone far enough, bank reserves are adequate for a new round of expansion. Theories of this type make the monetary system and its interest-rate movements the sole originating force in cycle turns. However, once the turn has been taken and a new direction of movement charted, the economic system will respond with a complex interplay of other forces which further influence interest rates and are influenced by them in a cumulating movement away from equilibrium.

Savings and Investment Theories. These theories are more general and analytical than the others. They do, however, usually incorporate elements of the other two in them. Most currently accepted explanations are of this type. A general outline of such theories is as follows.

In a modern business economy, any given level of production generates a flow of money income equal to it. That is, the total market value of the goods produced is distributed among the populace in the various forms of income payments such as wages, rents, profits, etc. If the total of income payments is spent, the spending will exactly absorb the output, and that level of production will be perpetuated. This exact balancing of the flow of production and the flow of spending would constitute an equilibrium from which the economy would not fluctuate. The existence of business cycles stems from imbalances between these two flows. The imbalances occur through the savings and investment processes.

Since, historically, business cycles have not been government caused but are distinctly an attribute of a private enterprise economy, we may, for purposes of analysis, assume government to be non-existent. Or, more realistically, we may assume government to be neutral in its effects on business fluctuations, which it would tend to be, if its budget were in balance.

Total spending in the private sector of the economy is the sum of consumer spending plus business investment spending. Total private spending must equal private incomes after taxes, if the economy is to remain in equilibrium. Income receivers as a group typically save part of their incomes; thus consumer spending is less than total income and production. This leaves some income, the savings, available for investment spending. If businesses decide to invest an amount exactly equal to these savings, the total flow of consumer and business spending will equal the flow of incomes. The economy would not fluctuate under such conditions.

Saving out of income is carried on by the populace at large, including business firms, for various reasons, many of them habitual in nature. The decisions to save are changeable and largely independent of business investment plans. Investment is carried on by business firms mainly to exploit the profit opportunities of new resource discoveries, new technology, new products, and population growth. These decisions are largely independent of the savings plans of the public.

Thus savings decisions and investment decisions are carried out by different groups with different motivations and independent of each other. Furthermore, the nature of each is such that both are quite variable. There is no assurance that plans to save will match plans to invest. For this reason the flow of total spending can have a tendency to either exceed or fall short of the total income flow. Since equilibrium requires a balance of the two flows, this imbalance leads to fluctuations.

If technological developments, discoveries, population growth and related stimuli are such as to cause investment plans to exceed planned savings, banks can create money through credit expansion—thus lending non-saved money. This permits the total spending flow to exceed the income flow. Equilibrium is destroyed and the economy expands until the flow of production and income rises to a level equal to the new spending level. At first such expansion is usually real in that physical output expands along with the monetary expansion. Once all labor and other resources are employed, any further expansion must be strictly monetary, and inflation sets in. Whether the expansion is real, monetary, or both, it continues until the income and spending flows are again in balance. At this point, savings out of the enlarged income flow would equal the investment spending and equilibrium would be reestablished. The expansion or the new equilibrium may continue for an indefinite period of time—business cycles vary in duration.

If for some reason investment plans should become less than planned savings, due either to an increase in savings or to a decline in investment, savings will begin to pile up in banks and other financial institutions. The spending flow becomes less than the income flow. Inventories accumulate and production is reduced. The income flow declines until it is in balance with the spending flow. At this lower level of income, savings would be reduced to equal investment and the contraction would cease. Equilibrium would exist at this depressed level until either savings or investment decisions changed so as to set off a new expansion.

This analysis stresses the divergence between the plans to save and the plans to invest. Actually it is possible that savings and investment may be planned equal, and still turn out unequal, causing fluctuations in the economy. In some instances new products and new technology may stimulate investment plans which equal savings. But the actual investment may require such radical shifts in the structure of output that it is impossible to move the men and resources quickly enough. In such instances actual investment would be forced to fall short of plans and thus be less than savings.

Possibility of Control. In view of past experience and the nature of business activity, it is not considered possible entirely to eliminate business cycles while still maintaining a private enterprise economy. However, some control is possible and fluctuations may be modified.

To the extent that cycles are accentuated by overoptimism and speculation during prosperity, government, through the control of banking, can curtail credit whenever signs point to excessive borrowing. In this way purely monetary and inflationary expansion can be curbed. This should make less severe the declines following an expansion. Likewise, centrally-controlled banks can be liberal in their credit policies during a decline, thereby relieving some of the stress on business and reducing the number of failures. It was to facilitate such policies that the Federal Reserve system was revamped in 1935. See *Federal Reserve System.*

A balanced budget means that taxes are equal to government spending, which means that the government extracts from the income flow by taxation an amount equal to what it extracts from the production flow by its spending. Under such conditions any imbalance between total spending (including government spending) and total income (including taxes) would stem from the private sector.

Economic contraction and expansion are situations of imbalance between income and spending. If the economy is declining, income is greater than spending because savings are greater than investment. The government can counteract the decline by unbalancing its budget so as to spend more than it taxes, financing the difference by borrowing. In this manner government increases public spending more than it reduces private spending, thereby causing total spending to rise. This brings spending and income into equality, halting the decline.

If the economy is in an expansion running into inflation, spending is greater than income because savings are less than investment. The government can curb the inflationary expansion by unbalancing its budget so as to tax more than it spends. The excess revenue can be used to pay off past borrowing or to add to the government's cash balance. This action would decrease private spending more than it increased public spending, causing total spending to decline. Income and spending are made equal and the expansion ceases.

Since periods of depression and prosperity are approximately balanced in duration, the government could alternately increase and reduce its debt, thus acting as a stabilizer without going progressively farther into debt. The policy then becomes essentially one of timing public expenditures. However, for this policy to control the business cycle completely, the government would need the ability to forecast business conditions perfectly and the administrative and political flexibility constantly to adjust its taxing and spending activities.

Built in "Stabilizers." There are, however, certain means of control that act more or less automatically. When times are good, progressive income taxes, both personal and corporate, and taxes for unemployment compensation usually take more from spendable income than is paid out in benefits and subsidies, thus acting as a brake. When times are bad, less is collected from both personal and corporate income taxes and more is paid out in unemployment insurance and other forms of social security. The result increases purchasing power, thus stimulating demand and employment.

Explanatory Table. In the examination of the table which follows, the above discussion should be borne in mind. Under the heading "Special Causes," attention is drawn only to particular events which precipitated the crisis, it being unnecessary to mention in each case the general causes of overspeculation and its concomitants. Similarly, in the column headed "Special Consequences," no mention is made of the normal features accompanying and succeeding the crisis—the fall in prices, slack trade, unemployment, and so forth—unless these features showed some special character.

IMPORTANT BUSINESS CRISES

Date	Countries Chiefly Affected	Special Causes	Special Consequences	Period of Depression
1809	England, United States	Speculation connected with Napoleonic war which led to credit and note inflation.	Bullion committee's recommendation for resumption of cash payments not accepted; depreciation of notes continued.	2 years
1815	England . .	Close of Napoleonic wars; vast production of English manufactured goods which European countries were too much impoverished to buy.	Much unemployment, machine-breaking, fall of prices.	About 2 years
1836–1839	England, U. S. A., France, Belgium . .	Railway speculation in England and U. S. A. Land speculation and paper money inflation in U. S. A. Collapse occurred simultaneously in England, Ireland, and U. S. A., in 1836. Bad harvest of 1838 caused another crisis in which Bank of England was threatened with ruin.	Failure of many banks and speculators; much unemployment. Drain of bullion from England was finally checked by raising discount rate and by aid of Bank of France. Bank Act of 1844.	7 years
1857	United States, nearly all other countries . . .	American crisis due to great discoveries of gold, railroad extension, development of banking and speculation.	Suspension of Bank Act in England. Very great unemployment in all countries.	3 years
1866	England . .	Wild speculation in limited liability companies, excessive borrowings by means of "finance bills," unsound banking practices.	Universal distrust of English investments. The failure of the weaker banks left the well-established banks stronger.	About 1 year
1869	United States	Operations of Jay Gould, made possible by unsound paper money system.	Many failures. (Black Friday, Sept. 24, 1869).	
1873	Nearly all countries .	Payment of French indemnity to Germany loosed a speculative mania in Germany and Austria; railway boom in U. S. A.; excessive construction of permanent works and "overproduction" at high prices.	Failures of banks and commercial houses; unemployment (3,000,000 "tramps" in U. S. A. during winters of 1873 and 1874). Shrinkage of prices, stagnation, glut.	6 years

IMPORTANT BUSINESS CRISES—Con.

Date	Countries Chiefly Affected	Special Causes	Special Consequences	Period of Depression
1882	France, England . . .	Wild speculation inspired by Union Generale, a company promoted among French and Austrian Catholics to destroy financial supremacy of Jews.	Collapse of this company and of the boom in general. Long period of depression.	5 years
1884	United States	Railroad speculation; large foreign wheat crops caused low prices for US grain and lessened US railroad earnings.	Very low prices.	2 years
1890–1894	England, Germany, France	Speculation in South America. Revolution in Argentina.	Support of Bank of England, aided by Bank of France, averted panic.	4 years
1893	United States	Good harvest of 1891 stimulated business; smaller harvest of 1892, low agricultural prices, heavy gold exports, fear that gold standard might be abandoned, and doubtful bank loans occasioned crisis.	Widespread failures, unemployment, and industrial unrest; march of Coxey's Army. Political and tariff uncertainties prevented thorough recovery until latter part of 1897.	4 years
1900	England, Germany, France	Great prosperity in England in 1898; business further stimulated by war in 1899 till it reached highest point in 1900 and then receded; high taxation and dear coal (both due to South African war) held responsible.	In England, unemployment but no spectacular failures. In Germany alarming failures occurred.	4 years
1903–4	United States	Decline of security prices after speculation of 1900 and 1901, precipitated by withdrawal of European funds—("Rich man's panic").	A few corporations failed, idle money accumulated in banks, but abundant harvests of 1904 hastened recovery.	About 1 year
1907	United States, Europe . .	Failure of Knickerbocker Trust Co. inaugurated panic in New York which spread over the whole country. American panic caused rise of bank rates in London, Paris, Berlin, and intensified depression there.	Failures, but not extensive scale. US government aided banks; Clearing House certificates issued; gold shipped to US from Europe. This crisis strengthened movement to Federal Reserve System.	1½ years
1914	United States, Europe . .	Crisis due to overspeculation transformed into special financial crisis by outbreak of World War I.	Many normal features of depression disappeared in the increased business activity due to the war.	About 2 years
1920–1922	United States, England, Europe . .	Increase of productive capacity in victorious countries accompanied with loss of purchasing power in defeated countries partly due to collapse of national currencies.	Widespread unemployment and business losses; famines and pestilence in some countries.	Less than 2 years in the US. Continued depression in Europe
1929–1933	World wide except in Russia . . .	Cumulative result of over expansion in agricultural and industrial productiveness. Reparations and war debt payments combined with trade restrictions.	Unprecedented unemployment. Practically all countries off gold standard. Banking crisis in United States. Free play of economic forces curbed by governments.	About 8 years
1937–1938	United States	Sharp change of federal fiscal policies from deficit to balanced budget. Excessive credit restraint by Federal Reserve Banks.	Renewed large government deficits	About 1 year
1945	United States	Reconversion from a war to a peacetime economy. Sharp reduction in defense spending.	None. Surprisingly rapid recovery.	Less than 1 year
1948–1949	United States	Rapid inflation following end of wartime price controls.		About 1 year
1953–1954	United States	Close of Korean War and sharp reduction of military spending.	Exceedingly liberal credit policies.	1 year
1957–1958	United States	Excess industrial capacity developed in preceding boom. Cutbacks in defense spending.	Large Federal deficit.	About 1 year
1960–1961	United States	Unemployment caused by restrictive monetary policy, automation, and monopoly in the bear markets.	Chronic unemployment.	About 1 year
1970	United States	Efforts to counteract inflation characterized by restrictive monetary policy.	Very high interest rates.	
1971		Vietnam war limitations reduced military spending. Aerospace cut also brought lower federal outlays.	The US balance-of-trade deficit was triple that of 1970. Import taxes rose, and wage-price freezes were imposed. The US Gross National Product continued upward, despite inflation. World inflation continued.	
1972		The US move toward a peacetime economy spurred growth. Wage-price controls were continued.	US inflation increased 3.5%; consumer prices rose, and employment increased. Interest rates rose and the foreign-trade deficit moved higher. The Gross National Product again moved upward.	
1973–1976	United States	Arab oil embargoes and shortage of domestic fuel caused "energy crisis" and programs for development of other sources of energy. The change from war to peacetime economy slowed. Urban centers faced financial difficulties.	Inflationary trends continued and unemployment rose to highest rates since the great depression of the 1930s. The housing industry suffered as homeowners faced increasing mortgage rates. The federal government was forced to aid urban areas. Despite the struggling economy, the Gross National Product continued upward.	

INVESTMENTS

INVESTMENT has been defined as the exchange of money for property rights from which a gain is expected. This definition must be qualified somewhat for the purpose of the present discussion. All such exchanges are not investments in the true sense of the word. The true investor receives his gain in the form of an annual income upon his commitment rather than from an appreciation in the value of his investment. One who buys American Telephone and Telegraph Company stock to procure an annual income of five per cent is an investor; another who buys the same security in anticipation of a rise in price is a speculator. A true investment, therefore, is a commitment of capital (1) for use in production; (2) entrusted to the management of another; and (3) for which the primary purpose of the investor is to receive income by reason of the use in production.

In making any investment, the individual investor should be primarily concerned with the safety of the principal amount invested and with the certainty and regularity of income. In addition, the investor will be interested in marketability and yield. An absolutely safe investment does not exist. Since safety is a relative term, all securities have a certain element of risk. The yield which the safest security offers may be considered as the true rate of investment income. The higher yield obtainable from all other securities may be considered as a premium received for the additional risk assumed in the purchase of securities less desirable than the best. The yield on long-term United States government bonds may be accepted as the "true" rate at any given time.

Since no security other than those issued by the United States government is completely safe, a basic principle of investment is "diversification." Diversification involves selecting investments in several different securities or areas so that gain in one may be used to offset losses in another. Diversification is obtained by investing in different types of securities (bonds, stocks, etc.), securities in different industries (railroads, utilities, steel, etc.), securities with different maturity dates (short-term, long-term, no maturity, etc.), or securities in companies operating in different geographic areas.

Determination of Yield. The annual return or yield of an investment is the percentage relationship between the amount of the annual income obtained therefrom and the amount invested. In the case of stocks, the method of determining current yield is fairly simple. The rule is to divide the number of dollars received in annual dividends per share by the number of dollars paid as the original cost per share. To illustrate: a certain stock pays dividends at the rate of $9 per share and is quoted at $180; 9 divided by 180 gives 5 per cent, which is the current yield.

The determination of bond yields is somewhat more involved as the good bond will be paid at par at maturity date regardless of the purchase price. If the bond is purchased below par, it is assumed that the holder will receive, in addition to the annual interest, an increase in the value of the bond as the bond approaches the due date. Conversely, if the bond is purchased above par, the holder is obliged to charge against his current income a certain amount to cover the decrease in the value of the bond as it nears maturity.

To illustrate: a 6 per cent bond due in ten years is quoted at 105; from the annual income of $60 on a thousand dollar bond, a deduction of $5 must be made for premium write-off, leaving $55 net return. This is divided by the average investment of $1025 (average of $1050 cost price at time of purchase and $1000 maturity value) for a yield of 5.37 per cent net to maturity. The amount of the premium write-off was determined by dividing the number of dollars paid as premium ($50) by the number of years (10) in the period during which the bond will run.

Classes of Securities. Investment securities may be divided into two classes, owner obligations (preferred and common stocks) and creditor obligations (bonds, notes, debentures, etc.). A fundamental difference exists between owners and creditors. The owners (stockholders in a corporation) are a part proprietor in the enterprise and must be prepared to share both in profits and in losses according as the business prospers. The stockholder in a corporation is normally limited in loss absorption to the amount of his investment in the corporation. The creditor (bondholder, etc.) has legally loaned money or capital to the business and, therefore, expects the payment of interest regularly and of principal at maturity, regardless of the incidental prosperity of the company. If the company cannot pay the creditor his interest when due or his principal at maturity, the creditor has the right to sue and demand foreclosure on the assets of the business.

The income of a bondholder is said to be fixed, regular, and certain within limits. This is because the bond bears a fixed rate of interest, such as 5 per cent; because the interest must be paid regularly irrespective of earnings; and because default in payment to the bondholder usually brings foreclosure upon the corporate property or a reorganization of the enterprise.

The income of the stockholder is not so satisfactorily assured. The amount will depend upon the prosperity of the company and the discretion of the directors of the corporation. During poor years, his income may cease entirely. His right to receive income is subordinate to that of all others who have a claim against the corporation.

Preferred stockholders are owners who normally have a preference to earnings over other stockholders (common stockholders). Preferred holders will receive their stated dividend before common stockholders receive anything. However, their dividend income is normally limited to a stated maximum amount, while common stockholders have no limit on the amount they may receive. While preferred stockholders have a right to receive their dividend before common stockholders, they do not have the right of foreclosure on property for nonpayment as creditors do. If the company pays no dividends to its common stockholders, it is under no obligation to pay anything to preferred stockholders. Preferred stockholders normally have a preference over common stockholders as to assets in the event of dissolution. However, in dissolution, creditors would have to be paid in full before preferred stockholders could receive anything.

Creditors are divided into two major classes: secured and unsecured. Secured bondholders are protected by a mortgage or certain corporate property in addition to the legal promise to pay. Holders of unsecured bonds (debentures) do not have a lien on specific property but do have all the rights of general creditors including the right of suit and foreclosure.

Tests of Investments. What comprises a good investment? Of many attributes, the most important are: (1) safety of the principal; (2) satisfactory income; (3) marketability; (4) a favorable tax position; (5) a satisfactory denomination and maturity date; and (6) a good collateral value.

Safety of principal depends chiefly upon the true value of the assets of the company which is, in turn, dependent upon the earning power of those assets. Satisfactory income comprehends both stability and amount of income. This depends upon the nature of the business and the efficiency of the management. The amount of income received on any investment should be adequate to compensate the investor for the risk he undertakes. Marketability of a security means that it can be disposed of at a fair price in a reasonable time. Marketability depends in part upon the volume of the security outstanding in the hands of the public, but much more largely upon the reputation of the company. These are the three major tests, and unless the prospective security meets each of these satisfactorily, the other tests may be eliminated.

Public Bonds. Public bonds may be divided into two classes: federal and municipal. Federal bonds are the bonds of the United States government. They are regarded as the premier investment security of the country because they are secured by the credit of the United States. Bonds guaranteed as to principal and interest by the United States government are in the same class. No question exists as to the ability of the government to arrange payment at maturity. The market price of the bonds will change from month to month with changes in the market rate of interest, but this is in no way attributable to apprehension over their repayment.

Municipal bonds comprise state, county, city, and all local government obligations. These bonds are often desirable investment securities. They are secured by the taxing power of the communities. While it is true that the respective states are sovereign powers and, as such, cannot be sued in the event of default of payment of their bonds, it is also true that constitutional restrictions upon the creation of debt have kept the bond issues within conservative limits. There has been no default in the payment of state bonds since the early 1890's. The value of a state bond depends upon (1) the good faith of the people, (2) the financial standing of the state, and (3) the constitutional restrictions on the amount and purpose of issue.

County and city bonds are also highly regarded as investment securities. Unlike a state, a municipality may be sued. The first test, therefore, is ability to pay. Experience has shown that a net debt of ten per cent of the value of the taxable property marks the ordinary limit of safety in municipal borrowing. For small communities, seven per cent is a safer limit. The second test is validity of issue. Unless the bonds have been issued in accordance with existing laws, there is constant danger that the issue may be declared invalid. The average investor is not in a position to pass upon questions of validity. His chief protection is to buy municipal bonds only through reliable bond houses which have had the advice of counsel in this respect. The third test is the good faith of the citizens of the municipality with regard to the payment of their debts. State, county, city, and local government bonds are regarded as tax-exempt securities, as the income received is exempt from Federal income taxes.

Corporate Securities in General. Corporate securities include the stocks and bonds of all privately-owned profit corporations. They are generally divided into railroads, public utilities, financial, and industrial. From the standpoint of investment desirability, corporate securities range from very good to very bad. In general, the nature of the business has material effect upon the prosperity of the companies. The income of public utility companies has a greater inherent stability than that of industrial companies. Consequently, the utilities are more highly regarded in the investment field.

The stability of income depends upon the product the corporation makes or the service it sells and upon the character of the management. The bonds of Pacific Gas and Electric Company are better than those of Bethlehem Steel Company because there is a more constant demand for electricity than for steel products. Also, the bonds of a company which is efficiently managed by men of great ability are better than those of another company which is less fortunate in this respect.

The strength of a corporate security may best be judged from the financial statements of the company and from past payment records. The balance sheet shows the assets and liabilities; the income statement shows the income and expense items and the profit or loss for the period covered. Past payment records give an indication of future payments and trends. From the balance sheet may be determined the valuation of assets which represent the capital behind the stocks and bonds. From the income statement may be judged the earning power of the company. Of the two, the earning power is by far the more significant.

Before purchasing any security an individual investor should make a careful study of all available information pertaining to the particular industry, company, and security. In the case of many large companies, there is a considerable volume of material available through banks, brokerage houses, and libraries. Certain financial services are available through the above sources which summarize information on securities and/or corporations of interest to the general public. These services offer up-to-date data through daily, weekly, or monthly supplements to annual publications. The leading services are Fitch Investors Service, Moody's Investors Service, and Standard & Poor's Corporation. A considerable amount of investment information can also be obtained from current business magazines and newspapers.

Railroad Securities. From the time railroads were first constructed in this country until the time of World War I, railroad stocks and bonds enjoyed a high rating in investment circles. With the introduction of other forms of motive transportation (especially automobile, truck, and plane) railroad earnings have trended downward. The tremendous increase in traffic during World War II greatly improved the position of railroads and enabled many of them to pay off millions of dollars of indebtedness. This improvement in financial position carried into the early postwar period, but competition from other forms of transportation continued to increase and the railroads again experienced a long-run downward trend.

The roads sought to combat this trend by such moves as abandoning unprofitable passenger runs, use of specialized types of cars for freight, and application of computers to speed freight shipments. In the 1960's, a number of railways worked out mergers into fewer but larger systems to reduce overlapping services and strengthen the financial position of the corporations. Such moves were subject to approval of the Interstate Commerce Commission, which has the duty of regulating rates and services from the public's point of view. This includes consideration of the interests of displaced employees.

Railroad companies issue more different classes of securities than any other enterprise. The senior bonds are those which are protected by a first lien or mortgage on the property. Junior bonds follow senior issues in their claim and are given names such as consolidated, general, refunding, and debenture. The rolling stock is usually bought on the installment plan and is financed through the sale of equipment trust certificates which are generally very safe investments. Most railroads issue both preferred and common stock.

Public Utility Securities. Public utility securities comprise those issued by electric light and power companies, by natural and artificial gas companies, by water companies, by electric railways, and by telephone and telegraph companies. The types of securities issued are much simpler than in the case of the railroads. They comprise mortgage bonds, collateral trust notes, debenture bonds, preferred stocks, and common stocks.

The utility companies (particularly the electric and gas companies) enjoy many advantages over other corporations. They operate under public service commissions in the different states which set rates sufficiently high to insure a fair return. They have a virtual monopoly in supplying their product under the franchises granted by the communities in which they operate. The demand for their products is growing steadily. Rate increases seem to have little effect on demand for their products. High grade public utility bonds have taken the place formerly held by railroad bonds as the safest corporate bonds.

Prior to World War II, the best-known public utility securities were those issued by the large holding companies in the field. These holding companies do not conduct any direct operations but simply buy and hold the securities of operating companies, frequently managing them and financing them through other subsidiaries. Since the gradual enforcement of the Public Utility Holding Company Act of 1935, holding companies have become much less important in the field and the leading companies today are primarily operating companies or holding companies with only one layer of operating companies beneath them.

The chief tests of public utility securities are the earnings records and the rate of return. Operating companies should have earned the total interest charges an average of four times per year during the preceding seven years. The rate of return tends to be lower than for comparable railroad and industrial securities due to the reduced risk of public utility investment. A third test of importance is the location of the communities served. In this connection, the effect of competition with publicly-owned utilities along with the rate of growth of the community should be considered.

Industrial Securities. Industrial securities comprise the stocks and bonds issued by all privately-owned corporations outside the railroad, public utility, and finance fields. Industrials include agriculture, manufacturing, wholesaling, retailing, service, mining and petroleum industries. Thus, it is difficult to generalize about the field as a whole due to its diverse nature. Generally, industrial corporations issue primarily common stock. Only a small percentage of the companies have preferred stock or bonds outstanding. When bonds are outstanding, they are generally less important percentage-wise to the company than they are for utilities and railroads.

The profits of industrial companies vary to a marked degree with changing business conditions. When business is booming, most industrial companies realize large profits; when business is dull, many suffer losses or barely avoid them. Retailing, service, food processing, and tobacco companies tend to fluctuate less with business conditions than do other types of industrials.

Industrial securities, notably the common stocks of companies which are leaders in essential and growing industries, have gained greatly in public esteem in recent years. Common stocks of these companies are particularly popular as a hedge against inflation as it is anticipated that their earnings and market price will increase as prices of goods and commodities increase. Considerable caution is necessary in choosing good industrial securities.

In testing industrial securities, consideration should be given to the nature of the industry and the type of product or service handled. The growth rate of the industry as well as of the specific company should be considered along with past dividend record. Stability and trend of earnings becomes particularly important in choosing a good industrial investment.

Investment Companies. Investment companies or trusts are financial organizations which make a business of investing the funds supplied by their shareholders in selected stocks and bonds, the investors sharing in the income and profits from the securities held by their company, according to the number of shares they own. These companies have proved attractive to small investors, with perhaps little knowledge of financial markets, because the companies are managed by specialists in the investment field, and because the "mutual fund" permits the buying of a diversity of investments, thus minimizing the risk of loss.

There are two main types of investment companies, the "closed-end" company which has a set capitalization, and the "open-end" company which keeps offering new shares for sale. The companies are regulated by the Federal Investment Company act of 1940, and have, since 1950, been obliged to conform to the rulings of the Securities and Exchange Commission in their dealings with the public and with their stockholders. They are also subject to state regulation.

Real Estate Mortgages. Real estate mortgages have long been one of the most popular forms of investment in this country. The chief concern of the investor should be to secure ample margin of safety. In no case should the mortgage exceed two-thirds of the conservative value of the property pledged. The average investor should avoid all but first mortgages and then only on property which is more likely to appreciate in value than to decline. Moreover, he should invest with particular care during times when rents are abnormally high as this condition makes for inflated real estate values. The mortgage should contain a condition that the entire principal becomes immediately due and payable in the event of default. The average investor in mortgages should confine his holdings to residential property. "Special utilizations," such as office buildings, hotels, and stores, are likely to have wide fluctuations in value. Mortgages on vacant land are likewise inadvisable.

Foreign Securities. Two primary reasons exist for foreign investing: At times, the income return in the domestic market declines to such an extent that investors are compelled to invest abroad to get a satisfactory yield, even at the increased risk of loss. The second reason is the desire to facilitate the financing of foreign trade. Long-term credits make a strong appeal in international trade and are made possible through the willingness of the nationals of the exporting countries to advance the necessary funds by purchasing foreign securities offered directly or indirectly in payment.

Foreign investment (other than in Canadian securities) is not recommended for the average investor due to the high degree of risk involved and the possible problems of fluctuating exchange rates.

Effect of Taxation. Present tax laws materially affect investment income. The Federal normal and surtax applies on all bond interest with the exception of municipal and certain government bonds. In addition to the Federal taxes, many of the states impose additional taxes upon income.

Current income taxes are established on a graduated scale under which those having the largest income are required to pay the highest rate of tax. The maximum is over 75 per cent for the Federal tax. This means that more than three-fourths of the taxable income is taken from the wealthy investor by the government. As a result, rich investors have been driven to purchase tax-exempt securities. Consequently, tax-exempt securities are selling at too high a price (conversely, too low a yield) to make them attractive to the average investor in the lower tax brackets.

The fact that capital gains are taxed at a maximum of twenty-five per cent has made them more desirable to wealthy investors than dividend or interest income. Thus, certain investors will give up stability of income for gains made through buying and selling securities.

Economic Conditions. Business conditions are constantly changing. Periods of prosperity and depression have followed alternately during the entire commercial experience of this country. Interest rates are high when business is active, and low when business is dull. Stock prices are high when business is booming, and low when business is poor. Bond prices, peculiarly, are low during periods of activity and high during periods of inactivity. See *Business Cycles*.

The most favorable time to buy stocks is when prospective earning power is good but has not yet been reflected in the market, and the most favorable time to sell is when the price already discounts a long period of increasing profits. Generally, the most advantageous time to buy bonds is when market interest rates are high, and the best time to sell bonds is when interest rates are low.

Needless to say, there is no unfailing method of telling when the conditions are ripe for buying and selling, since only later events can provide the answer to the question of whether given conditions are the end of a "movement" or midway within it.

Security Regulation. The Federal securities acts consist of a series of measures passed in the period 1933–40 inclusive with amendments since that time. These statutes are all concerned with the subject of investment and are designed to protect the investor against dishonest and misleading practices as well as against irrational actions on his own part. The first of these measures is the Securities Act of 1933 which calls for registration of most large new issues of securities. The Act does not attempt to control the quality of the issues, but rather it is an attempt to give the investor complete and accurate information regarding possible investments. The Securities Exchange Act of 1934 was designed to control certain types of manipulations on security exchanges and to make information available on issues traded on organized exchanges. Other Acts in this group deal with public utility holding companies, over-the-counter securities, corporate reorganizations, bond indentures, investment companies, and investment advisers.

The administration of these Acts is in the hands of the Securities and Exchange Commission. This is a Commission of five members appointed by the President with the consent of the Senate. The SEC accepts all registrations of new issues and polices the organized security exchanges and security dealers. The basic philosophy of the commission and the legislation which it has fostered is to place the potential security purchaser on a more equal plane with the seller so that the purchaser may make rational and intelligent investment decisions.

Security Middlemen. Corporate securities are purchased generally through investment bankers, security dealers, and brokerage houses. Publicly-traded securities are normally not purchased direct from the issuing company. Investment bankers act as dealers rather than brokers and normally handle new issues of securities or very large offerings in the secondary market. Brokerage houses act as agents for buyers and sellers and accept a commission for their services. They deal primarily in the secondary markets. Secondary markets are those in which securities are bought and sold after the original sale by the issuing corporations. Organized security exchanges (such as the New York Stock Exchange) are the major secondary markets. However, large numbers of securities are bought and sold in the secondary market outside the organized exchanges by brokers and security dealers. This is called the over-the-counter market.

UNITED STATES SAVINGS BONDS

The tremendous amount of governmental borrowing in World War II and since has been met to some extent by United States Savings Bonds. As a medium of investment for people of moderate means, these securities have proved highly popular.

Among the reasons for their attractiveness to the mass of the people are:

1. They are made available in small denominations.

2. They can be liquidated without loss at any time after a minimum period.

3. Their purchase is supported by patriotic motives.

4 During most periods of time, they have offered the best return available for minimum risk fixed-value investment.

Purpose of Savings Bonds. Savings bonds grew out of the old postal savings system bonds. Before 1935, persons with postal savings accounts could exchange their savings for postal savings bonds. When issuance of postal savings bonds was discontinued in 1935, the government brought out savings bonds to take their place. Series E savings bonds were first issued in 1941. The guaranteed redemption value forestalled losses to the investor while the graduation of yield, rising in later years, discouraged liquidation before maturity.

An additional merit in this type of financing for government is that, unlike borrowing through the banking system, it does not create inflationary tendencies. Savings bonds may not be purchased by commercial banks and, therefore, cannot be used as a base for further credit expansion.

During World War II, the savings bond, renamed defense savings bond and later war savings bond, assumed an additional function of great importance. The war economy brought a huge increase in purchasing power accompanied by a diminution of goods and services available for purchase. To avoid the bidding up of prices, a draining off of purchasing power became essential. The leading instrument available for this purpose was the war savings bond.

Following World War II, the bonds were renamed savings bonds and have continued to be important in government finance although the total amount outstanding has not risen to any great extent in recent years.

Features of Savings Bonds. There are two major series of savings bonds of interest to the average investor. These are Series E and Series H bonds.

Series E bonds are discount bonds. They are sold at 75 per cent of their face value. Interest is not paid semi-annually as in the case of most bonds; instead, bonds are redeemed at face value at maturity with the gain on cost representing the interest on the bonds. Since the introduction of E bonds, Congress has several times shortened their maturity to increase the yield and make it competitive with that available to investors on other types of fixed-income securities. Series E bonds purchased on or after December 1, 1973, return 6 per cent interest, compounded semiannually, when held to maturity of 5 years. Outstanding E bonds that as of December 1, 1973 had not reached their first maturity receive a ½-percent increase in yield for semiannual interest periods beginning on or after December 1, 1973, payable as a bonus at maturity. Series E bonds may be redeemed at any time after 2 months after purchase and be purchased in amounts up to $5,000 per investor per year. They are non-negotiable, but a fixed market for them is maintained at all times since they are redeemable at set prices.

Series H bonds are current income bonds. They are issued in larger amounts (the smallest is $500) and mature in 10 years. The interest checks vary in amount from small to large as the period of time the bond is held increases. Series H bonds purchased on or after December 1, 1973, yield 6 per cent from date of issue to date of maturity.

All existing Series E and H savings bonds have provision for extension beyond the stated maturity if the investor so desires. They may be held for additional periods with the same yield to maturity. A substantial number of matured bonds have been held by investors for continued investment.

MONEY AND BANKING

Money plays a substantial and significant role in the determination not only of the welfare of individuals, but also of the growth and stability of the entire economy. Available and quite reliable statistics for the last century indicate that major economic fluctuations in the United States have been characterized by significant monetary and banking disorders.

Without an understanding of the monetary powers and operations of the Federal Reserve system and certain government departments, particularly the Treasury, it is impossible to comprehend the nature of domestic monetary policy problems and their international ramifications, as well as the underlying theories of the ways in which money affects the economy. While monetary policy actions are directed primarily at commercial banks, they also have an impact in varying degrees on other financial institutions.

The world is becoming increasingly characterized as one global market in which multinational industrial corporations and banks participate. The types of monetary and fiscal policies pursued by the various countries are associated with and largely determine flows of funds in financial markets within and among nations, the relative amounts of individual commodities and services produced and marketed, the total volume of employment and output, and the distribution of income and wealth. In the international realm, also, the policies and operations of two institutions with common membership, the International Monetary Fund and the International Bank for Reconstruction and Development, popularly known as the World Bank, have an important bearing upon the world economy.

What Is Money? Because of the difficulties of direct barter of goods for other goods or services and the obvious advantages of the division of labor and specialization, even primitive societies developed money relatively early in their existence. In bygone days commodities such as wheat, tobacco, or salt have served as media of exchange. The American Indians used wampum, or shells, for money. Gourds were formerly used as money in Haiti, and the monetary unit of Haiti still carries that name. The Latin word for money, *pecunia*, is derived from *pecus*, "cattle," and survives in the English word pecuniary, thus reflecting an early use of cattle as money. For thousands of years silver was a rival of gold in the coinage systems of most advanced countries of the world and was not decisively replaced by gold until the 19th century.

Gold was first coined by Croesus, King of Lydia in the 5th century B. C., and was long the most popular form of actual money. It had many attributes that made it especially valuable, both as money and as a monetary standard. These included beauty, indestructibility, high value in small bulk, homogeneity, malleability, and scarcity. The annual production, even under the most favorable conditions, never exceeded five per cent of the existing stocks. This tended to give to gold a stability in value greater than that of any other commodity. Other commodities had certain of these attributes of gold, but in the case of no other metal did the combination exist so favorably.

Today, money is no longer defined in terms of its physical substance. Instead, economists favor a broad, functional definition. Within a single society, money may take more than one form at any one time; within the same society at some other time, money may take other forms. Thus, in a given society at a given time, what is money depends upon a convention or custom and includes anything *generally* acceptable as a means of making payments. Following this definition, in the United States today, the Federal Reserve and most economists define money to include coins, paper bills, and demand (or checking) deposits. The last form is the most popular form of money, mainly because of its convenience. Some economists would even broaden the definition of money to include, for example, savings accounts and time deposits, which usually have been classified as "near monies" because they are not immediately spendable in their present form, but may ordinarily be converted to money in a short time and at little or no financial loss.

Functions of Money. Money serves several important functions quite well. It is used as a medium of exchange, as a standard of value, as a store of value, and as a standard of deferred payment. While money does not perform these functions perfectly and, indeed, at times may not perform some of them as well as something else might, the important thing to note is that money has performed this combination of functions better than any substitute.

Money is most popularly known as a medium of exchange. Without money, men with commodities and services to dispose of would be compelled to exchange them directly for other commodities or for other services. The farmer who produces wheat and desires shoes would be obliged to find someone who had shoes to exchange and who wanted wheat. Under a monetary system, producers simply exchange their production for money, and exchange the money for the commodities and services desired. The barter system of exchange is both slow and inconvenient; the money system has made possible a method of exchange infinitely more efficient.

Complementary with its use as a medium of exchange, money serves as a standard of value. Value is expressed in terms of price. Other things being equal, when the quantity of money is increased, the general price level tends to rise, and when the quantity of money is decreased, the general price level tends to fall. The general price level may change, since the values of all of its components are expressed in terms of money, whose quantity varies in accordance with central banking policy. The function of money in acting as a common denominator of values for individual commodities is decidedly useful also in enabling one to remain acquainted with the relative values of different goods without necessarily desiring immediately either to buy or to sell.

Money also serves as a store of value. People often have goods or services to dispose of without a concurrent desire for other commodities or services. By exchanging the goods immediately for money, one may hold the money indefinitely, awaiting the desired time for exchanging it. In the meantime, the money represents so much stored value. The modern form of hoarding money consists of more than holding of coins and paper notes and includes the holding of idle demand (checking) deposits.

Finally, money serves as a standard of deferred payment. All credit transactions represent the postponed payment of money. If the transaction is not immediately completed, there must be some agreement between the buyer and the seller, or between the borrower and the lender, as to the method of settlement at the due date. The purchasing power of the money may substantially change in the meantime: nevertheless, the number of dollars agreed upon remains the basis of the settlement.

The Purchasing Power of Money. The purchasing power of money is its worth in exchange for goods and services. It is highly desirable that this power be stable, but experience has shown that such is far from the case. When prices advance, the purchasing power of money falls; when prices decline, the purchasing power rises. For example, prices were much lower in 1958 than in 1970. It required $1.36 in 1970 to buy what $1 bought in 1958.

Changes in price levels represent concurrent changes in the value of money. It is important to appreciate the large influence these changes exert on business conditions. They profoundly affect credit transactions because they create risk for all parties.

They affect production, as changes in the value of materials during processing interfere with expected profits. Since interest on debt and some other charges are fixed, the effect on profits is much greater proportionately than the alterations in price level would suggest.

But most important is the fact that prices do not change uniformly. There is a wide variance, both in degree and in time. The position of the farmer in 1932, for example, was especially unfavorable because the prices of farm products had fallen much lower than other prices. This uneven variance is the main reason that many people favor a program for price stability.

CONSUMER PRICE INDEX—SELECTED ITEMS

All index figures are based on an arbitrary figure of 100 for 1967.

Item	1960	1965	1970	1975 May
Food	88.0	94.4	114.9	171.8
Meats	87.2	93.9	117.6	167.9
Dairy Products	88.4	90.0	111.8	153.6
Housing	90.2	94.9	118.9	165.3
Gas & Electricity	98.6	99.4	107.3	167.3
Health & Recreation	85.1	93.4	116.2	152.3
Medical Care	79.1	89.5	120.6	166.8
Movie Admissions	65.0	86.5	130.0	170.0
Transportation	89.6	95.9	112.7	147.4
Cars, new	104.5	100.9	107.6	126.8
Bus Fares	NA	93.7	118.4	175.5
All Items	88.7	94.5	116.3	159.3

Source: *Statistical Abstracts 1975.*

The Measurement of Prices. The general level of prices is measured through the use of index numbers. Current prices on a great many commodities are taken and a general average is secured after giving weight in accordance with the importance of each commodity. This permits one to judge the general trend of prices, not only from week to week, but also over a period of years. The Bureau of Labor Statistics issues monthly indices of wholesale prices for some commodities, consumer prices for some commodities and services, and a weekly index for a few commodities. The wholesale price index, begun in 1890, is the oldest continuous statistical series issued by the government. Since January 1971, it has been relative to the arbitrary figure of 100 for the average price of commodities in 1967. Whenever possible, the prices used are collected directly from sellers and apply to the first large-volume commercial sale of each item. The consumer index is also relative to 100 for 1967 and the prices used are for the weights of commodities that the average consumer might buy. It is with this index that the variation in the cost of living is calculated.

What Establishes the Value of Money? Money's value is determined by the relationship between demand and supply. The demand for money constantly varies. Of course, in the popular sense, there is no limit to the demand for money. The ordinary person really does not demand money, but rather the goods or the services which money commands. The demand for money depends upon the volume of transactions, upon the population, and upon the extent of the use of credit. In the period before World War II the famous British economist J. M. Keynes developed an analysis of the motives for holding money. The transactions demand for money depends largely upon the quantities of goods and services produced in the community, and thus upon the level of national income. Also, there is a precautionary motive for holding money. It arises from the desire to be able to meet possible emergencies. While the size of one's precautionary balance is related to income, it is also related to the level of interest rates, that is, to the income that would be forgone if money were held idle. Lastly, there is a demand for money for speculative purposes. This will be small when interest rates are already high. When rises in interest rates are expected, there is a preference for holding cash in order to speculate, in effect, on bond prices.

In the post World War II period, building upon the Keynesian analysis, economists have viewed money as an asset. In this light, they regard monetary demand as the choice of money from among other assets by those holding wealth in various forms. Thus, one's demand for money is related to his total wealth and to the rate of return he expects on money in comparison with other kinds of assets. Therefore, monetary theory is part of the theory of wealth.

For the most part, the supply of money is determined by the Federal Reserve through its control over the monetary base, especially the reserve component of this base.

Formulations of the Quantity Theory of Money. The quantity theory in its various versions is perhaps the oldest of monetary theories. Dating from before the Middle Ages, it survives today and has recently had an upsurge in popularity.

Earlier forms of the theory were directed toward explaining movements of the price level by relating them to changes in the quantity of money. Modern quantity theorists are less interested in price levels and more interested in the relation between fluctuations in monetary growth and changes in the volume of economic activity and, thus, income. These, of course, have a bearing on price levels.

In their statements of causation, quantity theorists make use of the equation of exchange, an identity or truism, expressed in algebraic terms. This equation, though not a theory itself, sets forth the factors involved in the traditional theory. The equation is the most convenient approach to the study of the interdependent and interacting forces that effect changes in the level of prices in general. The most familiar form of the equation of exchange, expressed in algebraic terms, is that developed by Irving Fisher as follows: $MV + M'V' = PT$. In this equation, M equals the average quantity of money, including metallic and paper money, in circulation during a year's period, V represents the velocity or speed of circulation of money, which means the number of times the total supply of money turns over during the course of a year in facilitating trade. If the velocity of circulation of money happens to be twenty-five, only one twenty-fifth as much money is required as if its velocity were one.

The rapid turnover of money increases the efficiency of its use. M′ stands for demand deposits. Actually, the "dollar on deposit" as represented by M′, directly facilitates much more trade than the dollar represented by M. V′ represents the velocity of circulation of bank deposits, the number of times on the average that the "dollar on deposit" does duty in an exchange transaction annually. P represents the average price paid for all units of goods acquired in an exchange transaction, and T represents the total number of units so exchanged, or the volume of trade.

If the algebraic symbols are translated into their meanings, the equation of exchange may be expressed as follows: the average quantity of money in circulation, multiplied by its velocity of circulation, plus the average quantity of bank deposits for checking, multiplied by their rate of turnover, equal the average price per unit paid for goods multiplied by the volume of trade. The total of money payments must equal the total value of all the goods acquired in exchange. Quantity theorists, by transposition, often wrote the equation: $P = \frac{MV+M'V'}{T}$. This equation indicates that prices vary directly with the quantity of money and of substitutes for money, together with their velocities of circulation, and inversely with the volume of trade. In general, it was then concluded, after examining the factors in the equation, that M + M were the causal factors, and the ultimate effect of changes in the quantity of money was to change the price level in the same direction and even, according to the earliest theorists, in the exact proportion.

In this transactions form, the quantity theory proved relatively useless to policy makers because they had incomplete data to analyze T, P, and V. Also, many transactions involved merely a transfer of existing goods.

Since modern quantity theorists are vitally interested in the rate of economic growth, which is measured by changes in GNP (gross national product), for which the government has reliable data reflecting the output of currently produced goods and services, it became customary to use an income version of the quantity theory. Thus, more recently, the equation of exchange has been condensed and refined. Usually it is now written as either $MVy = PyTy$ or $Vy = \frac{GNP}{M}$. M is the money supply as defined today; PyTy or GNP represents currently produced output (or income); and Vy refers to the income velocity of money, the number of times on the average and for the period (usually one year) that a dollar is spent for final goods or services produced during this period. In recent years, Vy has been quite constant and has averaged about 3, as calculated by dividing GNP by the money supply. In other words, on the average, $1 has accounted for $3 of income for the annual period. Because of the relative constancy of V, the modern quantity theorist argues that changes in M are the usual factor in the determination of the level of GNP.

Two leading present-day quantity theorists, Milton Friedman and Anna Schwartz, have analyzed a century of statistics comparing fluctuations in business activity with the rate of growth of the money stock and have found close correspondence between the two, as evidenced by variable lags in which monetary changes consistently have led changes in economic activity by periods of at least months and sometimes a year or more.

The Use of Credit. The extent of the use of credit has been given as one of the factors affecting the demand for money. Credit is also an economic contrivance enabling society to allocate resources. It is a device that not only makes it possible for individuals to spread their consumption over time, but also provides business with large-scale capital formation, and the economy with technological progress and economic growth.

It is important to note that credit and debt are two aspects of the same thing. For every creditor (lender) there is a debtor (borrower). A potential debtor's ability to obtain credit is based upon his present and expected future income, the amount and nature of his assets and collateral, and, of course, upon his character, particularly his willingness to meet obligations promptly.

Credit or debt is usually evidenced by either open-book accounts or by written instruments such as promissory notes, drafts, acceptances, or bonds. Oral agreements are much less satisfactory, partly because there is difficulty in proving their existence. Bank loans, as well as loans extended by other financial institutions, are, of course, examples of credit transactions.

PUBLIC DEBT OF THE UNITED STATES
Source: *U.S. Treasury Department*

June 30	Amount in Millions of Dollars	Per Capita Dollars
1800	83	15.87
1900	1,263	16.56
1920	24,299	228.33
1930	16,185	131.49
1940	40,440	308.29
1950	257,357	1,696.11
1955	274,374	1,660.56
1956	272,825	1,621.82
1959	284,706	1,607.57
1960	286,331	1,586.07
1961	288,971	1,574.80
1962	298,201	1,600.53
1963	305,860	1,619.32
1964	312,526	*1,627.00
1965	317,864	*1,634.00
1967	326,221	*1,637.00
1969	353,720	*1,741.00
1970	382,603	*1,875.00
1975	544,131	*2,542.00

*Based upon Bureau of Census est. of pop.

The Gold Coin Standard and the Limited Gold Bullion Standards. In 1900 the United States legally established the gold coin standard and remained on it until 1933. Many other countries also have made use of this standard. Each nation had its own distinctive unit of account. In order that commerce could be carried on readily among nations, it was essential that there be some common standard for determining the relative values of these national currencies. That standard was provided by gold. Nations defined their units of account as a definite weight of pure gold. Thus, par value could be expressed for the various currencies by comparing their gold equivalents.

The gold content of the dollar was originally 24.75 grains, being so defined in 1792. In 1834, it was altered to 23.22 grains.

The gold dollar retained its 1834 value for a century. In 1933 Congress voted to end the gold coin standard and authorized the president to reduce the dollar's gold equivalent by as much as 50%. On January 31, 1934, President Franklin D. Roosevelt established a $35 price per ounce (480 grains) of gold and defined the American dollar, therefore, as equivalent to 13.71 grains of gold. At this time, the country changed to the limited gold bullion standard, under which gold coins and gold certificates were exchanged for other money, and gold was henceforth kept in bar form in several depositories, of which Fort Knox, Kentucky, is the best known. Gold certificates became the legal reserves of the twelve Federal Reserve banks.

Modifications of a Full Gold Standard. A nation may be legally on a gold standard, and yet the circulation of gold may be modified in various degrees. The chief restrictions include:

1. Circulation of coinage is forbidden, but paper money is convertible into gold bars or bullion. Countries having this system are said to be on the *gold bullion standard.* The purpose is to discourage the circulation of gold, which can be used more economically as a basis for credit money.
2. All domestic circulation of gold is forbidden, both that of coin and of bullion.
3. Export of gold is forbidden except under governmental license.

Devaluation. When the United States suspended the operation of the gold coin standard in 1933, restrictions numbered 2 and 3 were used. At the same time all gold was nationalized. By this move the Federal government obtained all "profit" from the procedure by which the same amount of gold was made to represent 69 per cent more dollars.

Of this profit, amounting to about 2,800 million dollars, approximately two billion dollars was used as a *stabilization fund,* the purpose of which was to keep on an even keel the foreign exchange rate between the dollar and other currencies.

Other things being equal, devaluation of the currency has a tendency to raise domestic prices. It acts most quickly on those of goods which are bought abroad, the effect then spreading slowly to other prices. Until this process is completed, there is a stimulus to export trade.

Stabilization of Currencies. The chief purpose of a freely operating gold standard was to make possible the conversion of one national currency into others at an approximately constant level. Foreign currencies or short-term credit instruments payable in them are known as pieces of foreign exchange when held by residents of other countries.

In practice, conversion was a market transaction, the price of each currency being determined by supply and demand. Price changes in foreign exchange, however, usually received an automatic check when they rose above, or fell below, a certain point. When gold flowed freely, this point was known as the *gold export point*. Under managed currencies, it is known as the point of support or the *stabilization point*.

The gold export point under a full gold standard may be defined as the point of price increase in a foreign currency at which it becomes more profitable to ship gold instead of buying the foreign currency.

In theory, inequalities in the distribution of gold among nations should be self-correcting. When one country receives an unduly large supply, prices would normally rise. This rise would make it easier for foreign countries to sell in that market and harder for producers there to sell abroad. Hence the imports would tend to be larger than the exports, and would have to be paid for by the export of gold. This in turn would tend to lower domestic prices and encourage export trade.

Difficulties in Maintaining a Full Gold Standard. Many obstacles to this self-corrective process arose. In the first place, the increase of gold may or may not be followed by a proportional increase of currency and credit, which are actual determinants of price level. Central bank policies and national habits may prevent such increases in money and credit. The normal effect of the gold influx is thereby "sterilized." This result occurred in France and, to a certain extent, in the United States in the years 1928-30, when these two countries together acquired about two-thirds of the world's monetary gold.

Even though the price level does rise, tariff barriers and other restrictions may be imposed to prevent the inflow of goods. Other countries, therefore, have no opportunity to acquire claims to the excessive gold so as to bring about its redistribution.

Balance of Payments. The United States "balance of payments" is an expression used to designate an estimated (by the Commerce Department) and itemized account of all the transactions that lead to flows of funds between U.S. residents and those of other countries.

Balance of payments accountants use a double-entry format showing the goods, services, and securities that are exported or imported, as well as how these transactions are financed. Since the means of finance is not always known for particular transactions, some estimates are incomplete. Others are inconsistent because they are based upon a number of statistical sources. For these reasons an errors-and-omissions entry is used to make the balance of payments actually balance.

Even though receipts and expenditures relative to other countries are equal, the balance of payments may be said to be in disequilibrium if the U.S. either loses or gains monetary reserves, or if its short-term monetary liabilities to foreigners are increased or decreased. The prevalence of these situations means that payments and receipts are equal only because of "induced" or "accommodating" capital flows in the form of movements of official reserves, that is, gold and convertible currencies. Autonomous outflows do not equal autonomous inflows when induced capital flows are necessary. The country is said to be in a state of surplus when it acquires monetary reserves, and in deficit when it loses monetary reserves.

Managed Currencies. The great depression beginning in 1929 led to partial or complete suspension of full gold standards by every nation in the world. Stability of exchange rates was made to depend on action by governments or central banks. Such action is known as currency management, and nations were said to be on managed, inconvertible paper standards domestically, whereas gold was used chiefly as an international monetary reserve.

The plan adopted by the United States, as by Great Britain and France, was the use of a stabilization fund. Thus when the dollar price of the pound or franc deviated by a certain amount from a point chosen as normal, the Treasury of the U.S. would buy or sell pounds or francs until the normal price was restored. This action was called "pegging" or "supporting" the foreign exchange rate.

Many other countries met the situation by limiting transactions in foreign currencies so as to make purchases balance sales. German nationals, for instance, could not obtain dollars until Americans had purchased an equivalent value of marks.

International transactions after 1950 multiplied many times in volume while gold stocks increased very moderately. A world-wide credit shortage developed into crisis proportions in 1966. Remedies proposed included devaluation of gold in terms of the leading currencies to creation of an international medium of exchange. Ultimately, through the auspices of the International Monetary Fund, the SDR (special drawing rights) plan was adopted, under which bookkeeping entries known as SDR's were created for use by governments and central banks to serve as an addition to the existing pool of international reserves.

The Rate of Interest. Interest is the cost of borrowing money. The rate changes with conditions of business, and is determined by the demand for and the supply of loanable funds. The businessman seldom withdraws actual money at his bank when arranging a loan. He secures a credit to his deposit account which he draws against in payment of his obligations.

The average business man is a constant borrower at his bank. He needs additional capital for the operation and expansion of his business, and secures it through his banks and other institutional lenders or through the selling of negotiable short-term, intermediate, or long-term credit instruments in the open market. The extent to which he borrows depends upon the relationship between the cost of borrowing—the rate of interest—and the return he can obtain in his business from the added investment. There must be or appear to be a profit margin, or he will not borrow. Low rates of interest therefore tend to encourage borrowing by businessmen and make

MONEY IN CIRCULATION, BY DENOMINATION: 1960 TO 1974
(In millions of dollars. As of December 31.)

Denomination	1960	1965	1970	1972	1974
Total*	32,869	42,056	57,093	66,516	79,743
Coin and small denomination currency	23,521	29,842	39,639	45,105	51,606
Coin†	2,427	4,027	6,281	7,287	8,332
$1	1,533	1,908	2,310	2,523	2,720
$2	88	127	136	135	135
$5	2,246	2,618	3,161	3,449	3,718
$10	6,691	7,794	9,170	9,827	10,503
$20	10,536	13,369	18,581	21,883	26,197
Large denomination currency	9,348	12,214	17,454	21,411	28,137
$50	2,815	3,540	4,896	5,868	7,444
$100	5,954	8,135	12,084	15,118	20,298
$500	249	245	215	193	179
$1,000	316	288	252	225	209
$5,000	3	3	3	2	4
$10,000	10	4	4	4	4

* Outside Treasury and Federal Reserve Banks. † Paper currency only; $1 silver coins reported under coin.
Source: *Statistical Abstracts, 1975.*

for increased business activity. High rates of interest may, depending upon profit prospects, discourage borrowing and make for decreased business activity.

Money in the United States. The present monetary standard of the United States may be described from the domestic standpoint as an inconvertible managed paper standard, and from the international standpoint as a restricted or limited gold bullion standard.

Credit Money in the United States. Credit money is also called representative money. All money which circulates freely in the United States is credit money. This applies to metallic coins as well as to paper money.

By far the greatest part of representative money in the United States consists of Federal Reserve notes, described below. These and subsidiary coins are the backbone of the money system, although there are a number of other types, most of which are gradually being withdrawn from circulation.

National bank notes in the later 19th century constituted a principal form of currency, supplemented by gold certificates and silver certificates. Gold certificates were withdrawn from circulation in 1934, when the dollar was devalued in terms of gold. Silver certificates, however, in that year were given a larger role in credit money. The treasury was directed by the Silver Purchase Act to buy silver and add it to the total money stock until its value, computed at $1.29 an ounce, was equal to one-fourth of the money stock or until its market price reached $1.29 an ounce.

In 1963, however, when the market price did reach about $1.29 an ounce, the act was repealed, and the treasury was directed to gradually withdraw silver certificates from circulation and replace them by Federal Reserve notes. Other metals were substituted also for silver in subsidiary coins to prevent them from being melted down for the silver in them. Redemption of silver certificates ended on June 30, 1968.

Advantages of Credit Money. The wide use of credit money as a substitute for standard money is due to two important advantages:

It is more economical. The use of credit money, which is easily and quite inexpensively manufactured, relieves the demand for gold, which is much more difficult and costly to produce.

It makes possible an elastic currency supply. In view of the fact that the demand for money is constantly changing, it is highly desirable that the supply be regulated accordingly; otherwise, price levels will constantly fluctuate. Elasticity of currency means the power to expand and to contract according to the needs of business. The supply of gold currency in circulation may be increased or decreased only with extreme difficulty; the supply of paper currency and other credit money may be easily regulated, as in the case of Federal Reserve notes. Yet paper currency has value because its supply is controlled.

Federal Reserve Notes. The most important currency used in the United States today is the Federal Reserve note. These are issued by the Federal Reserve banks and are essentially promissory notes of these banks. For each of these notes outstanding the Federal Reserve Bank must maintain certain assets. The reserve for these notes is no longer partly gold certificates as in the past.

An example of a traditional rediscount (or discount, the term preferred by the Federal Reserve) follows. This particular example results in the creation of Federal Reserve notes. Jones, a rancher in Montana, borrows $500 from the National Bank of Butte for sixty days to enable him to market his wool crop. The banks may rediscount the promissory note given by Jones with the Federal Reserve Bank of Minneapolis, receiving Federal Reserve notes. When Jones repays his loan, the rediscount can be paid off, and the Federal Reserve notes retired.

DEPOSITS IN U.S. COMMERCIAL BANKS

December 31, 1974
(In millions of dollars)

State	Total	Demand	Time
Alabama	8,367	3,669	4,698
Alaska	1,004	494	510
Arizona	5,710	2,147	3,563
Arkansas	5,428	2,477	2,951
California	79,184	27,916	51,268
Colorado	6,989	3,360	3,629
Connecticut	6,983	3,584	3,399
Delaware	1,840	816	1,024
Dist. of Columbia	3,586	2,069	1,517
Florida	24,094	10,694	13,400
Georgia	12,157	5,905	6,252
Hawaii	2,444	964	1,480
Idaho	2,433	999	1,434
Illinois	58,610	21,729	36,881
Indiana	16,513	6,271	10,242
Iowa	10,589	4,127	6,462
Kansas	7,964	3,662	4,302
Kentucky	9,090	4,412	4,678
Louisiana	11,017	4,897	6,120
Maine	1,825	730	1,095
Maryland	8,012	3,557	4,455
Massachusetts	14,788	7,407	7,381
Michigan	28,101	9,263	18,838
Minnesota	13,887	5,263	8,624
Mississippi	5,144	2,335	2,809
Missouri	16,159	7,781	8,378
Montana	2,617	977	1,640
Nebraska	5,767	2,681	3,086
Nevada	1,752	710	1,042
New Hampshire	1,485	546	939
New Jersey	20,882	8,215	12,631
New Mexico	2,651	1,115	1,536
New York	132,712	65,943	66,769
North Carolina	11,895	5,177	6,718
North Dakota	2,235	907	1,328
Ohio	29,636	11,194	18,442
Oklahoma	9,210	4,111	5,099
Oregon	5,577	2,281	3,296
Pennsylvania	42,661	15,480	27,181
Rhode Island	3,099	905	2,194
South Carolina	3,867	2,193	1,674
South Dakota	2,614	911	1,703
Tennessee	12,287	4,849	7,438
Texas	42,516	20,692	21,824
Utah	2,959	1,269	1,690
Vermont	1,237	349	888
Virginia	13,084	4,914	8,170
Washington	8,699	3,549	5,150
West Virginia	4,980	1,855	3,125
Wisconsin	13,951	4,899	9,052
Wyoming	1,422	572	850
United States	741,713	312,858	428,855

Source: *Statistical Abstract of the United States, 1975.*

Thus the commercial bank rediscounted its customers' promissory notes with the Federal Reserve Bank. The provision of this facility was one of the most important innovations of the Federal Reserve Act. However, today banks do not have to rediscount their customers' promissory notes in order to obtain funds from the Federal Reserve Banks. They can obtain advances secured by government securities. Under the Banking Act of 1935 the Federal Reserve Banks can also make longer-term advances secured by any assets which the Federal Reserve banks approve.

Rediscounts and advances normally do not result in the creation of Federal Reserve notes. The funds may merely be added to the reserve balances, which the member banks are required to hold with the Federal Reserve banks. (Part of a member bank's deposit balance constitutes required legal reserve. The rest is called an excess legal reserve. The sum of the two constitutes the bank's total portion of legal reserve on deposit. The remainder of its legal reserve consists of vault cash.) Similar results can be obtained through purchases of government bonds by the Federal Reserve system. See *Open Market Operations*. Today most money is created by the latter method.

Legal Tender. Any form of currency which the law states must be accepted in payment of obligations is known as legal tender. Since 1933 all forms of United States currency have been fully legal tender. Before that date, a large proportion of it was not, notably Federal Reserve notes and silver certificates. Some of the coins had only limited legal tender qualities. But since all forms of currency bore the promise of the government to redeem in lawful money on demand, the distinction between what was and what was not legal tender was of little practical importance.

Money and the Banks. In the popular sense, banks are institutions where money is stored for safe-keeping. This is far from being the case, however. A bank may be holding many thousands of dollars on deposit for its patrons. But, under ordinary circumstances, only a very small fraction of this amount is carried as money in the vaults of the bank. One may wonder why banks are willing to safeguard the funds of their depositors without making a charge for the service. The answer is that the bank lends money to depositors and others and receives interest payments upon the loans. In some cases, the bank shares this revenue with its patrons by paying interest on the deposits. American banks are forbidden to pay interest on demand deposits.

Kinds of Banks. Just as there are different kinds of stores at which we may purchase various kinds of commodities, so there are various kinds of banks with which to do business. The percentage of the country's banking strength represented in the Federal Reserve system is evidenced by the following statistics:

NUMBER OF COMMERCIAL BANKS IN U.S.

June 30, 1975

Member banks		5,794
National banks	4,730	
State banks	1,064	
Non-member banks		8,779
Insured	8,526	
Non-insured	253	
Total number of banks		14,573

Numerically, over one-third of the banks of the country are members of the Federal Reserve system, but these banks hold approximately 80% of all commercial assets.

Commercial Banks. Commercial banks are unique in that their demand or checking deposits circulate as money and are the largest component of our money supply. The name "commercial" was first widely applied to these banks over a century ago when the view was held in both England and the United States that institutions accepting and creating demand deposits should restrict their lending for the most part to short-term, self-liquidating business loans extended for working capital purposes such as meeting the payroll or acquiring raw materials. However, these banks today are allowed to lend for a wide variety of purposes and to extend loans in all maturity ranges.

Since depositors may at any time without notice draw against their demand deposits by writing checks, the banks must exercise extreme caution in lending because they often cannot tell in advance just when the depositor is going to withdraw or transfer his funds. Banks know from experience, however, that it is extremely unlikely that all the depositors will ask repayment on the same day. They know also that the new deposits each day tend to equal the amount of the withdrawals. Consequently they feel safe in lending an amount equal to the larger share of their deposits.

Sometimes a rumor of unsatisfactory conditions at a bank will cause depositors to become apprehensive of the safety of their deposits and will result in large withdrawals in short intervals. This is known as a "run" on the bank. Unless the bank can meet the sudden demand, it will be obliged to suspend operations. The Federal Reserve banks enable a solvent but hard-pressed bank to turn some of its loans and other assets into cash to pay insistent depositors. Also, existence of the Federal Deposit Insurance Corporation makes runs less likely.

This machinery, particularly as recently liberalized to permit rediscounting of "approved" assets instead of "commercial paper" only, is designed to make longer-term loans no less safe for commercial banks than the 60- and 90-day loans to which they largely confined themselves in the past.

Bank Deposits. Banks accept funds on deposit from their patrons and make a corresponding credit in the deposit book of the patron and on their own books of account. It should be appreciated that the funds deposited immediately become the property of the bank and that the depositor becomes a creditor of the bank to that amount. Items which are payable at other banks are credited conditionally, subject to collection. If payment is refused at the other bank, the credit at the first bank is canceled.

Deposits are of two kinds, demand and time or savings. A demand deposit is subject to withdrawal at any time at the option of the depositor. A time deposit may not be withdrawn before the expiration of the definite period for which the deposit was made. Time deposits are more satisfactory to the bank, because the institution knows in advance when withdrawal may be expected. Savings accounts may be withdrawn after advance notice is given unless this requirement is waived by the bank.

Deposit Insurance. Through an agency known as the Federal Deposit Insurance Corporation, the United States government insures all deposit accounts in all member banks of the Federal Reserve system and in other banks which are willing and able to pay for the service. On the failure of one of these banks, depositors are paid up to the amount insured.

Each deposit is insured up to $20,000. Cost of the insurance is defrayed by assessing a modest premium, usually 1/12 of 1% of total deposits. All national banks having deposits insured are required to join the Federal Reserve system, but state banks may insure without joining.

Bank Checks. A check is an order drawn upon a bank by one who has funds in that bank to pay a certain sum to another party upon demand. The party to whom the check is payable may possibly present the check to that bank and secure cash from the bank. More probably, he will deposit the check in his own bank for credit to his account. Each day the banks exchange these checks, usually through a clearing house. In this way, the payee receives his funds without being obliged personally to present the check for payment, and the banks are relieved of the obligation of carrying large cash reserves to meet checks presented by individuals for payment. The depositors in a certain bank may during one day draw checks aggregating $10,000; yet that same day the bank may receive in deposits $15,000 in checks on other banks. The net result is an increase of $5000 in the funds of the bank, despite the fact that checks for $10,000 were drawn against it.

Payment by check is the most popular method in this country. At least three-quarters of the daily business transactions are settled on this basis.

Bank Loans. From the banker's viewpoint, he is in business to make loans and investments. Deposits and withdrawals are simply a service which he offers as an inducement for customers, but which, of themselves, bring no profit to the bank unless service charges are set high enough to do so. The bank profits, as has been stated before, from the interest it receives upon its loans and securities.

Loans differ in thousands of ways. One man desires to borrow $1000 for ten days to meet his payroll at a time when his cash balance is low; a second man desires to borrow $10,000 to finance the purchase of one hundred shares of United States Steel Common Stock as a speculation for an indefinite period; a third man wishes to borrow $5000 for five years to buy a home; and so on.

Commercial loans should never exceed one year initially, but they may be renewed. A depositor is usually permitted to borrow in proportion to his bank balance. If he is well and favorably known, he will secure the credit upon his simple promissory note; otherwise, he may be obliged to pledge collateral as security. The more marketable the collateral, the more satisfactory it is to the banker. The interest charge is often collected in advance when the loan is made. The bank is usually less interested in what the borrower is going to do with the funds than it is in the chance for repayment; yet the two are closely interrelated. Often the depositor is expected to allow a part of his loan—about one-fifth—to remain on deposit. This portion is called a compensating balance. For the ordinary bank, the loans average about three-quarters of the deposits in prosperous periods.

The total loans outstanding in the commercial banks of the United States run into enormous figures. At the present time, the total is over $750,000,000,000.

Rediscounting Loans. Banks which are members of the Federal Reserve system are permitted to rediscount customers' promissory notes. All loans are not eligible for this purpose, especially those which are made for stock speculation. The Cleveland Trust Company may lend $5000 to a manufacturer in Cleveland, and then have the Federal Reserve bank of Cleveland rediscount it, in the same manner as was previously mentioned in connection with the Montana bank. The rediscount privilege greatly increases the lending power of the member banks. But, more important, it allows the bank quickly to convert loans into cash in times of emergency. This rediscount privilege used to be much more important than it is today. The Federal Reserve now has more effective ways to increase the lending power of banks.

Other Forms of Loans. Other forms of loans handled by commercial banks include drafts and acceptances. Brown in Albany buys merchandise from White in Buffalo on terms of thirty days. White may immediately draw an order upon Brown, payable in thirty days, and have this order, or draft as it is called, discounted at his Buffalo bank in the same manner in which he would discount his personal promissory note. An acceptance is a draft which bears the written acceptance of the party upon whom it is drawn that payment will be made when due. Many firms now have their customers sign acceptances upon receipt of goods. In this manner the firm is able to receive immediate payment through discounting the acceptance at its local bank. Otherwise the firm would have to wait until the invoice was due before receiving the money.

Types of Commercial Banks. Commercial banks are divided into two classes, depending upon the method of incorporation. National banks receive a Federal charter. State banks receive charters from the states in which they are located.

National banks are required to operate under the provisions of the National Banking Act, as amended. Minimum capital requirements are established for country and city banks. With certain exceptions, loans cannot be made to any individual in an amount in excess of 10% of the capital of the bank. In addition, there are other loan limitation provisions. These banks were formerly permitted to issue circulation notes backed by government bonds, but this privilege was discontinued on August 1, 1935.

National banks are permitted to have branches under the same terms as state banks within states which grant this privilege to state banks. National banks must be members of the Federal Reserve system and of the Federal Deposit Insurance Corporation.

State banks operate under the banking laws of the respective states. These laws vary widely but, in the main, follow closely the Federal law. State banks are permitted, though not required, to join the Federal Reserve system if they can qualify.

ASSETS, LIABILITIES AND CAPITAL ACCOUNTS OF ALL COMMERCIAL BANKS

(Money in $ Billions, at Year-End)

Item	1950	1974
Number of Banks	14,164	14,448
Assets	170.5	927.5
Loans & Securities	128.0	750.3
Cash, balances with banks, etc.	40.4	128.8
Liabilities & Capital Accounts	170.5	927.5
Deposits	156.1	753.6
Demand	118.8	317.5
Time	37.3	436.1
Business & Personal	129.4	608.9
Government	12.6	74.6
Capital Accounts	11.7	64.0
Capital Notes and Debentures	0.0	4.4
Equity Capital	11.6	59.6
Stock	3.6	15.0
Surplus	5.3	25.3
Undivided profits & reserves	2.7	19.1

Source: *Federal Reserve Bulletin.*

Federal Reserve System. The Federal Reserve system is the machinery by which a central control may be exercised over the expansion and contraction of the money supply and credit. The Reserve system may be said to be the most potent instrument for good or ill in American economic life.

Before this machinery for credit control is described, it should be noted that it cannot actually produce credit if there is no demand for credit, that is, if people do not wish to borrow. What it can do is to make credit easier or more difficult to obtain.

The Reserve system comprises 12 Federal Reserve banks and about 6400 member banks. The Federal Reserve banks are located in the following cities: Boston, New York, Philadelphia, Cleveland, Richmond, Atlanta, Chicago, Saint Louis, Minneapolis, Kansas City, Dallas, and San Francisco. Each Reserve bank may have branches under certain conditions.

The Federal Reserve banks are bankers' banks. Except under emergency conditions, they deal only with banks and governments. Their capital is subscribed to by the member banks to an amount equal to 6 per cent of the capital and surplus of each subscribing bank. Each Reserve bank is permitted to pay to stockholders from its earnings a cumulative dividend of 6 per cent of its paid up capital. The balance is transferred to reserve.

Purposes of the System. The two most important dates in the history of the Federal Reserve system are 1914 and 1936.

On the first of these dates, the system was established and most of the control mechanisms were established.

On the second date, 1936, additional controls were provided, and all of them were placed in the guiding hands of one authoritative commission, known as the Board of Governors of the Federal Reserve System. The enabling law was passed in 1935. Since that time there have been many more amendments to the Act.

The Reserve banks were created in the first place to prevent recurrence of the "money squeeze" known as the currency panic of 1907. They provided elasticity or flexibility of the currency supply.

The system was strengthened in 1936 to avoid, as far as possible, a recurrence of an unstable boom, such as that which preceded 1929, and the collapse of credit which followed.

The following paragraphs outline the chief features of the system. Under the headings *Legal Reserves*, *Rediscount Rate* and *Open Market Operations* are described the credit control methods originally provided. The additional controls established in 1936 are explained under the heading *Margin Requirements*, while, under *Board of Governors*, is described the way in which central control may be excercised.

Legal Reserves. Each member bank is required to keep on deposit with the Federal Reserve Bank of its district a sum which, in addition to its vault cash, constitutes the member bank's legal reserve. This reserve must be maintained at a certain minimum percentage of deposit liabilities, the percentage depending on the type of deposit and the location of the bank, and being subject to change by the Board of Governors of the Federal Reserve System. See *Raising of Reserves*.

Lower reserves are required against time deposits than against deposits payable on demand. The pooling of a part of reserves in central institutions has one distinct advantage. It reduces to a minimum the transfer of actual cash from one part of the country to another. When a check on a member bank in Bangor, Maine, is paid by a member bank in Fresno, California, money is not sent from Bangor to Fresno in settlement, but the transfer is effected by a debit and credit entry in the Federal Reserve books. This entry signifies the transfer of a definite amount of ownership in the so-called gold settlement fund, which is held in Washington. It is due to this procedure that there is usually no collection charge for checks drawn on member banks. All member banks have been classified according to their location as either Reserve City or Country banks.

FEDERAL RESERVE SYSTEM

ASSETS AND LIABILITIES OF ALL MEMBER BANKS

(All money in $ millions)	1947	1960	1970	1974
Loans	$32,628	$99,933	$253,936	$429,537
U.S. Treasury Securities	57,914	49,106	45,399	38,921
Other Security Investments	7,304	16,579	66,604	100,073
Total Deposits	122,528	193,029	384,596	575,563
Cash Assets	32,845	45,756	81,500	106,995
Borrowings	54	130	18,578	52,850
Capital Accounts	8,464	17,398	34,100	48,240
Number of Banks	6,923	6,174	5,767	5,780

Source: *Federal Reserve Board.*

Rediscount Rate. The Federal Reserve banks may exert a considerable effect on the expansion or contraction of business by two devices intended as general or quantitative controls. One is raising or lowering of the rediscount rate. The other is known as open-market operations.

A member bank may command the liquid resources of its reserve bank by rediscounting "eligible paper" that it holds. Or it may borrow on its own promissory note secured by eligible paper or United States government obligations, such as bonds and Treasury certificates.

By raising the rate of interest charged member banks when they wish to borrow on eligible paper, a reserve bank tries to discourage borrowing and serves notice to the business community that it regards current expansion as excessive. On the other hand, by lowering the rediscount rate, it tries to encourage borrowing and the consequent expansion of credit.

Open-Market Operations. By this term is meant the purchase or sale of government securities, bankers' acceptances, foreign exchange, and a few other things by the Federal Reserve banks. These operations automatically expand or contract the nation's monetary base and money supply. When Jones sells a $1000 bond to Smith, there is merely a transfer of funds or credit from one individual to another. But when a Federal Reserve bank buys a $1000 bond, it issues new funds in payment. When it sells a bond, it withdraws the funds it receives. Since the funds so created or destroyed may be the basis of many times their face value in bank credit, one can see how large an influence the reserve banks can exert on economic activity.

Variation of Reserve Requirements. All member banks have been classified as either reserve city or country banks. Congress has fixed a range of from 10 to 22% for reserve requirements against net demand deposits (gross demand deposits less balances due from other domestic banks and cash items in process of collection) for reserve city member banks and 7 to 14% for country member banks. For all member banks, Congress has set a range of 3 to 10% against time and savings deposits. The Board of Governors of the Federal Reserve System may vary reserve requirements within these limits to offset or to prevent undesirable changes in the money supply. If it wishes, the Board may apply differential reserve requirements; that is, it may break each type of deposit into two or more brackets and apply a lower percentage to, for example, the first $5 million of deposits than to amounts above that. Reserves are now computed on a weekly basis. Weekly average required reserves are not based on average net customers' deposits and average vault cash held two weeks earlier but on the bank's own average deposits at the Federal Reserve as of the current week. There is a 2% carry-over of excesses or deficiencies.

While originally reserve requirements were meant to compel banks to maintain adequate liquidity, today they are used for purposes of control. In general, this tool is used relatively infrequently because of its uneven impact on banks and the serious side effects associated with it.

Margin Requirements. To check speculation on the stock exchanges, the Board of Governors of the Federal Reserve is empowered to set rules to govern the amount of money which may be lent to finance the purchase of a given value of securities. This applies both to member banks and to brokers doing business on stock exchanges. See *Margin*.

Board of Governors. The most important change in the banking system effected in 1936 was to place more authority in the hands of the reserve board. The old board had the right to recommend use of controls and to see that policies pursued by the twelve Reserve banks were within the law. Actually, control over each of the twelve banks was exercised by officers of those banks, who were private bankers and not public officials. Concerted action by the entire system was difficult if not impossible to effect.

The new board, consisting of seven members appointed for 14-year staggered terms by the president, with the advice and consent of the Senate, is armed with actual control. Its decisions are mandatory in setting the rediscount rate, reserve requirements, and margins for security speculators. Policies for open-market operations are set by a committee consisting of these seven board members and five senior officers of the reserve banks, chosen regionally on an alternating basis.

Furthermore, the presidents of the twelve Reserve banks must be acceptable to the board of governors. Additional assurances that the system shall be operated in the public interest rather than for the profit of bankers include a provision that members of the board of governors may not return to the private banking business for two years after the expiration of their terms of office.

The policy of the board is insulated from influence of the executive branch of the government through a requirement that the terms of members expire in rotation at two-year intervals. It would take six to eight years for a president to have his appointees form a majority of the board.

The reason for this precaution is to prevent the government from using the banking system as a source of indefinitely large Federal loans if the Federal Reserve board does not agree with government policy. It should be noted that, while the Federal Reserve banks are privately owned, the central banks of other major nations are owned by their governments. The Federal Reserve system is legally and structurally independent of the national government, yet it was created by Congress and can be abolished by Congress.

Government as Banker. The Federal government began providing credit for its citizens with the establishing of the Farm Loan Banks in 1916. See *Farm Loan Banks*. These banks were provided for farmers who demanded mortgage money for farm property at rates comparable to those prevailing in cities.

World War I, the Depression of the Thirties, and World War II brought a vast expansion in government lending. Through the War Finance Corporation, Federal funds were advanced to private corporations for the purpose of enabling them to forestall serious failures in financial institutions during the deflation period of the early 1930's. Banks, insurance companies, and later, railroads, states, school districts, and even private individuals were beneficiaries. The Federal Deposit Insurance Corporation was created by the Act of 1933 and made permanent in the Banking Act of 1935. Through this act the insurance of deposits was made mandatory for members of the Federal Reserve system and optional for sound non-member banks. Deposits in insured banks are fully protected up to $20,000 for each depositor. This provides 100 per cent insurance coverage to the vast majority of all the depositors in the insured banks of the country.

Two forms of credit constitute the credit structure of American business, namely: investment credit and commercial credit. The Federal government adopted the National Banking Act of 1863, by which it chartered national banks; about 5000 such banks were in existence at the beginning of 1951. Twelve Federal Reserve banks were chartered by the U. S. Government in 1914 and since then have established 24 branches. In 1916, the Federal Farm Loan act authorized the creation of special types of mortgage banks, designed to help finance agriculture. In 1932 a system of Federal Home Loan banks was established to provide a nationwide credit facility to mortgage lending institutions to help meet extraordinary needs of savers and borrowers. In the same year the Reconstruction Finance Corporation was created by Congress to help meet an emergency situation. With a capital of 500 million dollars, the RFC loaned to banks themselves funds to liquidate frozen credits and to strengthen their capital structures. The Home Owners Loan Corporation provided capital for individual home purchasers and, in the financial operations of World War II, the Reconstruction Finance Corporation, through such affiliates as the Defense Plant Corporation and the Defense Supplies Corporation, provided investment of billions of dollars.

In 1933 there were organized the Federal Farm Mortgage corporation, to refinance farm mortgages in distress, and the Home Owners Loan Corporation, to provide emergency relief to home owners under threat of foreclosure of their homes, and to refinance their homes on easier terms that they might retain ownership. During their statutory lending period, 1,017,821 loans were made in the aggregate amount of $3,093,451,321. Financial institutions and individual lenders received $2,750,000,000 from the HOLC for frozen mortgages and paid $490 million to local cities and towns for delinquent taxes of its borrowers, and taxes on its own acquired properties. 800,000 homeowners were saved from loss of their property through foreclosure. Liquidation of the Corporation was completed in October 1950, and in the following year $14,023,649.82 was paid to the Treasury of the United States.

Additional banking aid for farmers includes: 12 intermediate credit banks, which discount agricultural paper as the Federal Reserve banks do commercial paper; 12 production credit corporations, which lend money for general farm transactions much as the Federal Land banks do for purchase of farms; and one central bank and 12 regional banks for financing farm co-operatives. In all these agencies, the government owns the stock but most of the capital comes from private investors.

Thousands of co-operative savings and loan associations have been organized pursuant to the Federal Credit Union act of 1934 and subsequent amendments, and pursuant to similar legislation enacted in all but a few of the 50 states.

Truth-in-Lending. A bill passed by Congress in 1968 requires lenders to list credit costs of all transactions in terms of approximate "effective annual" rates. Credit information must be complete, true, and comparable—that is, calculated at annual rates under the same specifications by all lenders. "Extortionate extension of credit" was barred by the bill and made punishable by imprisonment and fine. A significant provision also required disclosure of "true" annual interest rates on first mortgages on housing.

Credit Cards. These cards permit holders to obtain goods or services without immediate payment. Of plastic or cardboard, the cards are numbered and often carry photographs for identification. In the 1960's millions used them for travel, telephone calls, and to buy all types of goods. Cards are issued to those with good credit, and businessmen are heavy users since the cards provide full expense records. Bank, hotel, restaurant, auto rental, airline, and oil company cards are among the most common. Charges are usually billed for the preceding month and prompt payment is normally expected.

Savings Banks. As the name indicates, savings banks aim to provide a place to safeguard the savings of the people. The funds are invested in securities of the highest class, and the income is distributed to the depositors in the form of interest. In New York State, all savings banks are mutual, which means they are owned by and operated for the depositors. The entire investment income becomes the property of the depositors after the payment of expenses. The entire amount is seldom distributed, however, as a certain part is placed in a surplus account for the protection of the accounts. It is the custom to limit the maximum balance to a few thousand dollars.

Savings and Loan Associations. This type of financial institution is chartered by both state and Federal governments. All federally chartered associations use "Federal" as a part of their corporate name. In certain areas state-chartered associations use building and loan association, building association, homestead association, and co-operative bank, as a part of their corporate name. The major function of savings and loan associations is to accept savings from the public in large and small amounts, regularly or irregularly, at the convenience of the savings customers. Investments are generally limited by Federal or State law to loans for building or buying homes, and U. S. Government obligations. To a limited degree funds can be invested in loans on other types of real estate. As a result of specialization in home financing, savings and loan associations provide more home loans than any other type of financial institution.

The channeling of these funds into home financing not only encourages and makes home ownership possible, but performs a basic economic function by providing jobs for construction workers, income for suppliers of materials and orders to factories.

All Federally chartered associations are required by law to be members of the F.S.L.I.C. State-chartered associations are insured upon application and meeting the F.S.L.I.C. requirements. Of the 6300 associations in existence, 4500 are members of the F.S.L.I.C. The Federal Home Loan Bank System (see below), of which all insured associations are members, makes available credit to meet unusual demands and for seasonal mortgage lending.

Federal Savings and Loan Insurance Corporation. This Corporation was created in 1934 by an Act of Congress to insure savings accounts in savings and loan associations, up to the legal authorization of $20,000. The original capital of $100 million was provided by the Federal government. This has been retired in full by the Corporation. The premium for insurance protection is paid by the insured associations at a rate fixed by law, currently $1/12$ of 1% of aggregate liabilities.

In the event of default by an insured institution, the Corporation, as soon as possible, pays the saver up to 100% of insurable limit in cash or makes available an insured account in another insured association. In order to prevent default, the Corporation is authorized to take steps to restore an insured association to normal operating conditions.

Federal Home Loan Bank System. Federal Home Loan Banks were established in 1932 by an Act of Congress to provide a system of reserve credit banks for thrift institutions of the savings and loan type engaged in long-term home mortgage financing. Eleven regional Federal Home Loan Banks, and the districts they serve, are designated by the Federal Home Loan Bank Board. Membership in a Federal Home Loan Bank is by approval by the Federal Home Loan Bank Board, upon meeting eligibility requirements.

Principal functions of these banks are to provide additional liquidity for members by making advances when needed to meet unusual or heavy withdrawal demands and to meet seasonal mortgage lending demands. The Federal government supplied the initial capital of $125 million; this has been fully retired. Each member association is required to hold stock equal to 1 per cent of its total mortgage loans and is entitled to obtain advances on an unsecured basis for a term up to one year or on a ten-year term basis where the loans are secured by mortgage loans. The system raises its funds through consolidated obligations of the eleven banks in the system. Members of the bank system may deposit funds with the Bank of which it is a member.

Federal Housing Administration. This corporation was established in 1934 to insure mortgage loans made to finance the construction, improvement or purchase of all types of residential property. Loans made on the FHA plan are originated by any type of financial institution that is making mortgage loans. The loans to be insured are submitted to the FHA and upon acceptance a premium of ½ of 1 per cent per annum is paid by the borrower. The protection of insurance is given to the lender in return for his willingness to make high-percentage, long-term loans tailored according to standards set by the Federal Housing Administration. Whereas most lending institutions are confined, on their loans on residential property, to 60 to 80 per cent of value, FHA loans can be made for as high as 95 per cent.

The Veterans Loan Guarantee. As a part of the Veterans Rehabilitation Act of 1945, provision was made for loans to be made by private lending institutions to honorably discharged veterans for as much as 100 per cent of the purchase price or the construction cost of homes for terms up to 25 years at a rate of 4 per cent. Also, certain business and farm loans to honorably discharged veterans could be insured. The lenders making these loans were originally protected with a guaranty up to $2000 or 50 per cent of the loan. These guaranties were increased in 1950. In the first five years of the operation of this program, 2½ million veterans acquired homes on this plan.

TOTAL RESERVE ASSETS: 1970 TO 1974

Figures are in millions of U.S. dollars. Assets include gold stock, holdings of convertible foreign currencies, special drawing rights and reserve position in International Monetary Fund.

Country	1970	1972	1974
All countries[1]	92,449	158,067	217,912
United States	14,487	13,150	16,058
Algeria	339	493	1,689
Argentina	673	465	1,315
Australia	1,693	6,141	4,269
Austria	1,751	2,719	3,430
Belgium	2,847	3,870	5,345
Brazil	1,187	4,183	5,252
Canada	4,679	6,050	5,825
Central Africa	102	84	(NA)
China (Taiwan)	480	1,039	1,191
Colombia	206	325	449
Cyprus	209	320	269
Denmark	484	855	935
Ecuador	83	143	350
Egypt	167	149	104
Finland	480	758	708
France	4,960	10,015	8,851
Germany, F. R. of	13,610	23,785	32,399
Ghana	58	107	94
Greece	310	1,032	936
India	1,006	1,180	1,325
Indonesia	160	574	1,492
Iran	208	960	8,383
Iraq	462	782	3,273
Ireland	697	1,126	1,266
Israel	449	1,222	1,202
Italy	5,352	6,079	6,941
Japan	4,840	18,365	13,519
Jordan	256	270	350
Korea, Rep. of	610	740	1,056
Kuwait	203	363	1,397
Lebanon	386	675	1,674
Libyan Arab Rep.	1,590	2,925	3,616
Malaysia	664	981	1,618
Malta	158	275	402
Mexico	744	1,164	1,395
Morocco	140	237	417
Netherlands	3,241	4,785	6,958
New Zealand	258	833	566
Nigeria	224	385	5,629
Norway	813	1,325	1,929
Oman	129	164	225
Pakistan	190	281	460
Panama	17	44	(NA)
Peru	329	460	(NA)
Philippines	251	551	1,504
Portugal	1,504	2,312	2,354
Saudi Arabia	662	2,500	14,285
Singapore	294	873	(NA)
South Africa	1,012	1,290	1,159
Spain	1,817	5,014	6,485
Sweden	761	1,575	1,735
Switzerland	5,132	7,488	9,011
Syria	55	135	835
Thailand	906	1,052	1,855
Tunisia	60	223	418
Turkey	431	1,401	1,861
United Kingdom	2,827	5,647	6,939
Uruguay	175	198	217
Venezuela	1,021	1,732	6,529
West Africa	259	323	338
Yugoslavia	140	733	1,139
Zaire	186	178	140
Zambia	514	165	172

NA—Not available. [1] Includes countries not shown separately.
Source: *Statistical Abstracts 1975.*

BUSINESS, BANKING, AND LEGAL TERMS

The everyday life of the average man or woman brings frequent occasions which demand the ability to understand and use many terms peculiar to business, banking, or the law. To know the nature and the meaning of commercial forms and legal instruments is to be acquainted with the necessary working tools of the business world. Every person needs to know what these tools are and how they are used.

The treatment of the topics in the following dictionary of business, banking, and legal terms is adapted to meet such everyday needs. This alphabetic list will supply definite information upon specific subjects, and it will supplement with greater detail the chapters that precede it in the department of Economics.

Acceptance. A term designating any bill of exchange which has been accepted by the drawee—the party upon whom it is drawn.

The term is used with reference to the act of the drawee in accepting the bill of exchange, by writing upon the face of the bill the word "accepted" and signing his name as acceptor. The date of acceptance and the place of payment are generally added. These, however, are not essential to the validity of the acceptance. After the bill has been accepted, it becomes the direct obligation of the acceptor, and the drawer of the bill then becomes liable to pay the amount of the bill only in the event that the acceptor does not pay it.

A bank or banker's acceptance is a bill of exchange of which the acceptor is a bank or trust company or some other financial person, firm, or corporation which makes a business of lending its credit by accepting bills of exchange.

A trade acceptance is a bill of exchange drawn by a seller upon a purchaser to cover a current sale of goods. Ordinarily, the trade acceptance is drawn by the seller payable to himself, and the acceptance of the bill by the purchaser converts the bill into what is substantially the same as a promissory note. The trade acceptance, however, bears upon its face the statement: "The obligation of the acceptor hereof arises out of the purchase of goods from the drawer"; and it is made a crime under the Federal laws to use a trade acceptance in interstate commerce for any other purpose than in payment for an original purchase of goods. See *Bill of Exchange*, *Payee*.

Acceptor. One upon whom a draft or bill of exchange is drawn, and who, by writing his acceptance upon the face of the bill, has undertaken to pay the amount of the bill.

Acceptor for Honor. One who accepts a bill drawn upon another, in order to prevent the bill from being protested for nonacceptance or nonpayment. Thus the acceptance is deemed to be for the "honor" of the person upon whom the bill is drawn.

Accommodation Paper. An instrument by which one person lends his credit to another. Usually, but not necessarily, the transaction involves no financial profit to the person lending his credit. The accommodation may take the form of signing a note as maker or endorser, or of drawing, accepting, or endorsing a draft or bill of exchange, or otherwise affixing one's name to a commercial instrument in such manner as to become liable in the event that the instrument is not paid when due by the person receiving the accommodation.

Accounts Payable. Sums owed by a person, partnership, or corporation to others upon open account, the obligations not being represented by notes, bills, or other instruments of indebtedness. See *Bills Payable*.

Accounts Receivable. Sums due to a person, partnership, or corporation from others upon open book account, the obligations not being represented by notes, bills, or other instruments of indebtedness. See *Bills Receivable*.

Accrued Dividends. A term improperly applied to dividends which have not been paid or declared, but which are loosely regarded as having "accrued" because the stock upon which the dividends are payable entitles the holder to cumulative dividends at a specified rate. In fact, a stockholder can have no right to dividends until they have been declared by the board of directors of the company. See *Preferred Stock*.

Accrued Interest. While interest upon an obligation usually becomes due and payable at the termination of some definite period or periods of time, the interest upon the obligation, in fact, accrues from day to day. In the purchase and sale of securities between interest payment dates, the amount of interest accrued must be added to the face value of the obligation in order to determine the actual present value. Similarly, an exact statement of the financial condition of a business at any particular moment must include among the liabilities of the company the item of accrued interest upon interest-bearing obligations of the company held by others. A similar item will also be included among its assets, representing interest accrued upon interest-bearing obligations of others held by the company. Interest already due and unpaid is not properly included in the item of accrued interest.

Active Stocks. Stocks that are frequently bought and sold in considerable quantities upon the general market.

Actuary. One whose business is the calculation of insurance risks and premiums.

Ad Valorem Duties. Tariffs imposed upon articles according to their value.

Affidavit. A written statement sworn to or affirmed before some person who has authority by law to administer an oath. Affidavits are prescribed by law for proper execution of many documents. They are frequently used in place of oral evidence at court trials. Their proper substance is confined to statements of fact regarding which the witness has certain knowledge. Making a false statement in an affidavit is the crime of perjury.

Agent. One hired to carry on certain activities for an employer. The person employing the agent is known as the principal, and is bound by any acts performed by the agent within the scope of the agent's employment. The principal is liable also for any damages sustained by third persons from wrongful acts committed by the agent in the course of his employment.

Frequently it is difficult to distinguish an agent from an independent contractor. Under a mere agency, the employer may direct and supervise the work of his agent, both in large matters and in details. In the case of the independent contractor, this power of supervision does not exist.

Amortization. The periodic setting aside of revenue or earnings in a definite proportion to the initial cost of machinery, plant, or other capital investment, for the purpose of providing a fund with which to replace the machinery or equipment when it has become worn out.

The term is applied also to the building up of a fund for the retirement of a loan when it becomes due.

Ancillary Receiver. A receiver appointed in a state or a district other than the one in which the principal or original proceedings have been begun. The duties of an ancillary receiver are to gather in and administer property in the state or the district of his appointment. See *Receiver*.

Annuity. An annuity has been defined as a series of equal payments made or due at equal intervals of time. Although the term is most commonly associated with payments made at stated intervals to insurance policy holders or beneficiaries, it applies also to bond coupons, preferred stock dividends, and other periodic payments.

Arbitrage. The almost simultaneous purchase and sale of foreign exchange, securities, or commodities in two or more different markets with the motive of making a profit.

Assessed Valuation. The value placed upon property by government officials as a basis for the imposition of taxes. Frequently the assessed valuation of property is considerably below its real or market value.

Assessment. (1) A charge imposed upon properties to defray a part of the cost of a local improvement by which most, if not all, of the properties are directly benefited. Assessments for paving and cleaning streets, for installing sewers, and for widening streets are of this character.

(2) A levy made by a company upon its shareholders for the purpose of securing additional capital. The stock of most business corporations is today nonassessable if the par value of the stock has once been fully paid in cash or its equivalent.

Assets. Anything of value belonging to a person, firm, or corporation. The term includes, not merely real property and tangible personal property, but also good will, copyrights, patent rights, and all other rights, privileges, franchises, and property interests having value.

Assignee. One to whom any contract, right, security or interest has been assigned.

Assignment. The transfer to another of one's interest in a contract, security, or any other thing of value. Except in the case of negotiable instruments, an assignee receives no better title to the thing assigned than his assignor had.

A "general assignment for the benefit of creditors" is sometimes made by a debtor who is insolvent or financially embarrassed. The assignment takes the form of a transfer, by the debtor, of all his assets to a trustee. The purpose of such an assignment is to show the good faith of the debtor and his willingness to distribute his assets among his creditors. If satisfied that the debtor has not withheld assets from the trustee, the creditors will join in a composition agreement whereby each creditor agrees to accept, in satisfaction of the debt, a certain percentage of the amount due him. If all the creditors join in the composition agreement, the property of the debtor can be equitably distributed among the creditors, without the stigma and the wastage of assets which bankruptcy proceedings would entail. Any group of creditors, however—sometimes one creditor is sufficient—may refuse to enter into this plan for an informal distribution of the debtor's assets, and may insist upon formal bankruptcy proceedings; and the general assignment is itself a sufficient ground for the institution of bankruptcy proceedings against the debtor.

Assumed Bonds. Bonds issued by one corporation and assumed by another, as a result of a merger or consolidation of the two companies, or as a result of the acquisition of the control of the former company by the latter. The bonds so assumed become the liabilities of the second corporation as though originally issued by it.

Attachment. A writ issued by a court of competent jurisdiction, authorizing the seizure of a person or of designated property.

Audit. An official examination of the accounts and records of a person, firm, or corporation, to determine whether there are any arithmetical errors or fraudulent entries in the accounts, or whether any improper methods of accounting have been employed.

Available Assets. Unencumbered real or personal property that can be sold, pledged, or mortgaged as security for a proposed indebtedness.

Balance of Trade. A part of the balance of payments, the relation between the merchandise exports and imports of a country. When the exports exceed the imports during any period, the balance of trade is said to be "favorable." When imports exceed exports, the balance of trade is "unfavorable." It is so regarded largely because an excess of exports is likely to be accompanied by an influx of gold or other international reserves in payment of the excess of products sent abroad. And, vice versa, an excess of imports may result in an outward flow of international reserves.

In actuality, however, an excess of imports frequently indicates merely that the citizens of a country have lent or invested heavily abroad and are receiving the income upon their investments, or repayment of the principal, in merchandise. When this is the case, there can be no harm in an "unfavorable" balance of trade.

Balance Sheet. A statement of the assets, liabilities, and net worth of an individual, firm, or corporation as of a certain date.

Bank Acceptance. See *Acceptance.*

Bank Balance. The amount credited to a customer by a bank at any particular time. This sum does not represent actual currency in the custody of the bank to the amount of the balance; rather, it represents the amount of an obligation due from the bank to the customer. In the ordinary deposit in a commercial bank, the amount of this balance is subject to withdrawals upon written orders called checks, drawn by the depositor upon the bank.

Bank Discount. Simple interest deducted in advance from the face value of a loan, the principal of which is payable at a definite future date. By thus taking the interest before it is earned, a slightly higher rate of interest than the rate nominally charged is actually received by the bank, since the full amount of the principal is never turned over to the borrower, who does repay the full amount.

Bank Draft. An order in writing, drawn by one bank upon another, directing the latter to pay a designated sum of money to a third person. The draft may be payable at sight, that is, on demand, or at a definite or determinable future time.

Banker's Acceptance. See *Acceptance.*

Bank Examiner. Both state and national banks, as depositories of the funds of the general public, are subjected to stringent control and supervision by state and/or federal authorities. This control is exercised by examinations of the banks, made periodically by bank examiners acting under the authority of the Comptroller of the Currency, the Federal Reserve, the Federal Deposit Insurance Corporation, or the banking department of a state. Such examinations supplement and check the statements which banks are required to furnish, setting forth in detail their financial condition. Any fraudulent or false entries or unsafe practices discovered by the bank examiners are reported to the proper officials, and the bank guilty of the improper practice or false entry is promptly required to rectify the situation or sometimes to drop its membership in the FDIC, Federal Reserve System, or both. In extreme cases banks may be placed in receivership or reorganized.

Bank Holding Company. Any company which holds a controlling interest in one or more banks and often provides certain services for the members of the group. This type of organization is also referred to as group banking.

Bankruptcy. Proceedings under which the property of an insolvent debtor may be distributed ratably among his creditors under the supervision of a court, and the bankrupt be thereupon discharged of his debts. Bankruptcy proceedings thus serve two purposes: (1) the equitable distribution of the property of the debtor among his creditors; (2) the release of the debtor from his obligations, giving him a fresh start in the business world.

Bankruptcy proceedings in the United States are governed by the Federal Bankruptcy act of 1898 and the amendments thereto. Under this act, proceedings may be either "voluntary" or "involuntary." In the former, the debtor himself institutes the proceedings by filing a voluntary petition showing that he owes debts to the amount of at least $1000, which he is unable to pay. In involuntary proceedings the creditors file the petition. Three or more creditors with unsecured claims amounting to at least $500, or, if there are fewer than twelve creditors, one creditor with a claim amounting to $500 may institute the proceedings.

A debtor may be adjudicated an involuntary bankrupt only if, within four months prior to the filing of the petition, he has done one or more of the following acts: (1) concealed, removed, or otherwise fraudulently disposed of property with intent to hinder, delay, or defraud his creditors; (2) transferred property, while insolvent, to any creditor, with intent to prefer that creditor over others; (3) permitted a creditor to obtain a preference by legal proceedings, as by attachment or levy upon goods of the debtor, and failed to vacate the preference at least five days before a sale under the levy or attachment; (4) made a general assignment for the benefit of creditors; (5) being insolvent, applied for a receiver, or if a receiver has been appointed at the request of creditors.

Bank Statement. A statement issued by a bank or trust company, setting forth in detail its assets and liabilities, together with its capital accounts.

Basing-Point Price. This term means primarily the price for a commodity plus transportation charges. Thus more distant customers pay more than nearer ones. However, a company with widely separated plants may average total shipping charges and, by adding this average to the factory price, sell at a uniform price everywhere. The Supreme Court has held that this practice may violate the antitrust laws.

Bear. A stock or commodity speculator who gambles on the prospect of prices going down. The "bear" sells, for future delivery, stock or wheat which he does not then have, expecting to cover, that is, buy in, at a lower price than that for which he has agreed to sell, at some time before delivery must be made.

Bear Market. A condition of declining prices in securities or commodities, generally accompanied by little activity in the market and by a general depression in trading.

Bear Panic. When those who have sold "short" in any security or commodity find that the market is rising, they attempt to cover in order to keep their losses as low as possible. When the rise in prices is very sudden or very pronounced, the haste of the "bears," to cover their sales by buying in on the market, reaches the point of a veritable panic. See *Cover, Selling Short.*

Bear Raid. A concerted movement by those traders who make a business of selling "short" on stock or commodity exchanges, the purpose of which is to cause the market price of a certain stock or commodity to fall. This result is effected by sales of the stock, against which the raid is directed, at prices below the true market value of the stock. In the case of a successful "bear raid," these sales, which usually provide for delivery at some future time, result in a very pronounced temporary fall in the price of the stock, the public being afraid to hold a stock, the price of which is apparently on the down grade. When the market price has thus been hammered down to an artificially low price, the bears "buy in" and so cover at a profit their earlier sales for future delivery.

Bids and Offers. The rules of the New York stock exchange provide definite terms upon which bids and offers must be made and construed in dealings upon the exchange. These are: "cash," that is, for delivery upon the day of contract; "regular way,"—for delivery upon the business day following the contract; "at three days,"—for delivery upon the third day following the contract; "buyers' or sellers' options,"—for not less than four days nor more than sixty days. Unless otherwise specified, bids and offers are deemed to be "regular way."

Bill of Exchange. An unconditional order in writing, addressed by one person (called the drawer) to another (called the drawee), ordering the person to whom it is addressed to pay on demand, or at a fixed or determinable future time, a definite sum of money to the bearer or to the order of a third party (called the payee). Often the term "draft" is used in the United States particularly with respect to domestic bills of exchange.

A check is in effect a bill of exchange drawn upon a bank, payable upon presentation or at sight. See *Acceptance, Check, Draft.*

Bill of Lading. A receipt and contract and, in some forms, a document of title given by a railroad or other carrier, stating that the goods described have been received by the carrier for transportation to a designated point, and setting forth the terms of the contract between the carrier and the shipper under which the goods are transported. There are two kinds of bills of lading in use in the United States. One is the so-called "order (or negotiable) bill of lading," and the other the so-called "straight (or non-negotiable) bill of lading."

In the "order bill of lading," the carrier undertakes to deliver to the *order of* a designated person, and only upon the surrender of the document. In the "straight bill of lading," the carrier merely undertakes to transport and to deliver to the person named as consignee in the bill of lading; the surrender of the bill of lading is not made a condition precedent to the surrender of the goods by the carrier.

The distinction between the order bill and the straight bill has become very important by reason of the effect which the law has given to order bills of lading. Since the order bill may be negotiated from one holder to another by mere endorsement and delivery, and since the carrier undertakes to deliver the goods represented by it only upon a surrender of the document, the order bill has come to be dealt with commercially as the symbol of the goods. Thus loans are frequently made upon the security of properly endorsed bills of lading, the lender being protected by the assurance that the carrier will not deliver the goods represented by the bill of lading except upon the surrender of that instrument properly endorsed.

In order to further the use of the order bill of lading as an instrument in commerce and as the basis for the advance of credit to owners of goods in transit, all states have passed the Uniform Bill of Lading act, which makes the order bill of lading in effect a negotiable instrument and protects from loss all bona fide purchasers of such bills, as well as persons who lend upon the instruments, even though the bill of lading itself may have been lost by, or even stolen from, the true owner. The Uniform Bill of Lading act also forbids any attachment of, or interference with, goods in transit represented by an order bill of lading, unless the negotiation of the bill has first been enjoined and thus its transfer to a bona fide purchaser or lender has been rendered impossible. The Uniform Bill of Lading act has been passed by Congress, and has thus been made applicable to all shipments in interstate and foreign commerce.

The straight bill of lading possesses none of these peculiar attributes that the law has given to the order bill. The straight bill of lading, therefore, does not in any sense represent the property in the possession of the carrier, and cannot form the basis for a loan upon the goods. The duty of the carrier, where a straight bill of lading has been issued, is merely to deliver to the person named as consignee, and this duty remains unchanged and unaffected by any attempted dealing with the bill of lading.

Bill of Sale. A written instrument transferring or assigning, from one person to another, personal property or an interest therein.

Bills Payable. Obligations owing to others, represented by bonds, notes, or other instruments of indebtedness.

Bills Receivable. Obligations due from others, represented by notes, bills, or other instruments of indebtedness.

Bimetallism. A monetary standard in which the monetary unit is defined in terms of two metals. All provisions with regard to such metals—coinage, redeemability, legal tender characteristics, etc.—apply equally to both metals.

Black Friday. September 24, 1869. A day when the "bears" of the New York stock exchange were practically ruined by a "bull" movement engineered by Jay Gould and Jim Fisk, which caused an unprecedented rise in the prices of speculative stocks upon the exchange. The movement was precipitated by the redemption by the United States of $4,000,000 of its bonds in gold.

Blanket Mortgage. A mortgage which covers several different properties, or one mortgage which is issued in place of several existing mortgages. Such a mortgage is not necessarily a first mortgage.

Block of Stock. A number of shares of stock held by an individual or by a group in a particular corporation.

Bond. A long term instrument by which a person, corporation, or government agrees to pay a certain sum of money on a determinable date. Bonds are usually given under seal and, in many states, are enforceable for a period of twenty years after their maturity; while the ordinary promissory note, or contractual obligation, is not enforceable after the lapse of six years from the date when the obligation matured.

Bonded Debt. The amount of the indebtedness of a government, a corporation, or an individual, represented by bonds issued and outstanding. The bonded debt is taken to represent the fixed or permanent indebtedness, as opposed to current or short time indebtedness, which must be paid or renewed currently.

Books Closed. The books of a corporation are usually closed as of a certain date, for the purpose of determining what persons are entitled as stockholders to share in a dividend to be declared, or in other distributions to be made by the company, or to determine who are entitled to vote as stockholders in any stockholders' meeting of the company. During the period when the books are closed, no transfers of stock are made on the books of the company. For all corporate purposes, the holders of record, as of the date upon which the books are closed, are deemed the stockholders of the company until the books are again opened to transfers of stock.

The term "books closed" is sometimes used also with reference to subscriptions to a new issue of securities, when the issue has been fully subscribed. In the event of oversubscription, the issue is frequently prorated among all who have sent in subscriptions. But, unless the right to prorate the issue among the subscribers has been specifically reserved in the offer of sale of the securities to the public, a subscriber is not obligated to accept less than the full amount called for by his subscription.

Book Value. The value of the assets of a company as set forth upon the books of the company.

The book value of a share of stock issued by a company, as distinguished both from its par value and from its market value, or selling price on the market, may be obtained by dividing the net assets of the company by the number of outstanding shares. If the books of the company are accurately kept, the book value of any share of stock is thus a closer approximation to the amount of capital investment represented by each share than either the par or the market value of the stock.

Boom. Unusual activity and enthusiasm in any line of business, or prosperity in business generally, resulting in a marked rise in prices, employment, output, and profit.

Bottomry. Lending money upon the security of vessels or their cargo.

Bourse. The stock exchange of Paris; by extension, any exchange in continental Europe.

Break-even Point. Point in a firm's operations where revenue from sales just equals overhead and current costs, thus showing neither profit nor loss. It is usually expressed as a percentage of maximum productive capacity.

Break in the Market. A sharp and rapid decline in the prices of stocks or bonds, generally coming at the end of a period of violent speculation and rising prices.

Broker. One who, for a commission or other fee, buys or sells personal or real property for others.

Brokerage. Fee charged by a broker for his services.

Bull. A speculator in the stock market who gambles upon the expectation of a rise in prices; one who manipulates the market in such a manner as to bring about a rise in prices.

Bullion. Uncoined gold or silver, generally in the form of bars or ingots, ready to be turned into coins. Bullion is frequently used in payment of obligations due from persons of one country to those in another. See *Dollar Exchange.*

Bull Market. A bull market is one of activity and rising prices. The term is particularly applied to such a condition in the stock market.

Buyer's Option. A special term applied to a contract permitted by the rules of the New York stock exchange, whereby the buyer of stock is not compelled to accept and pay for the securities purchased until the expiration of a specified time. The buyer has the privilege, however, of demanding delivery of the stock upon one day's notice. The rules of the New York stock exchange provide that such a contract must be for a term of not less than four days and not more than sixty days. A buyer's option, the term of which is four days, is called "buyer's four"; if the term is ten days, it is called "buyer's ten"; and so forth.

Buying Outright. A purchase of stock or other security by a payment of the full purchase price at once or within a definite period after the purchase. This is distinguished from buying "on margin," where only a portion or percentage of the purchase price is paid by the purchaser, the remainder of the price being loaned to the purchaser by the broker. See *Margin*.

Callable Bonds. Bonds issued with a right reserved by the issuing corporation to redeem or "call" the issue, in whole or in part, after a specified date, at a designated price. The "call" price is generally five to ten points above par. A redemption provision is now commonly inserted also in issues of preferred stock.

Call Loan. The lending of money repayable on demand. Loans of this character used to be very common in New York City, where brokers and speculators upon the various exchanges borrowed large sums of money from the banks upon securities as collateral. In this type of loan, both the borrower and the lender have the right to terminate the loan at any time. The advantage to the bank of such a loan is that it enables the bank to make some profitable use of its available funds during any period of temporary abundance; while leaving the bank free to terminate the loan at any time, should any extraordinary demand for cash arise. Its advantage to the borrower is that, as soon as the temporary need of cash or credit has passed, the loan may be repaid and the incurring of interest may at once be terminated.

Calls. Transactions upon stock and commodity exchanges in which one person is given an option to require another to deliver a specified amount of stock or of a commodity at a particular price at any time within a specified period. A "call" is frequently referred to as a "buyer's option."

The term "call" is used also with reference to a notice issued to stockholders or subscribers to the stock of a corporation, requiring payment to the corporation of sums upon stock purchased or held by them. In this sense a "call" may be issued either before or after the stock has been paid in full. If issued prior to full payment, it is nothing more than a notice that an installment is due upon the purchase price of the stock. Where a call is issued after the stock has once been fully paid for, it amounts to an assessment of stockholders to enable the corporation to carry on its business. Most stock is now issued as nonassessable after it has once been paid for in full. In that event, a "call" of the latter character cannot be made.

Capitalism. The economic system of private enterprise in industry and trade in which capital and capitalists play the chief rôle, subject to regulation by the state. Capitalism emphasizes freedom of individual initiative in business. Its greatest development has been since the Industrial Revolution in the 19th century, but it has been known to most civilizations.

Carrier. Any person or company that purports to engage in the business of transporting passengers or freight for hire. The more appropriate term is "common carrier," the term "carrier" being used as a colloquial abbreviation of the longer term. Included within the general class of common carriers are railroads, steamships, ferries, street railways, airplanes, trucks, and other vehicles which make a business of carrying persons or property from one place to another. An elevator has been held not to be a common carrier.

From the early days of feudal England down to the present time, common carriers have been subjected to special rules of law, at least with respect to the transportation of property.

From early times, too, the law limited the charge which a common carrier may make, for transporting persons or property, to such sum as was deemed a reasonable compensation for the service rendered. In modern times, common carriers have come to be strictly regulated by statutes administered by governmental commissions; and the more important carriers, such as the huge railroad systems and steamship lines, as well as street railway systems, are looked upon as quasi public corporations. The Interstate Commerce act, originally enacted by Congress in 1887, and amended from time to time since then, created a commission with power to regulate the service rendered and the rates charged by any carrier engaged in interstate traffic. The commission may also prescribe rules to insure safety of operation. In most states, there are similar regulatory statutes.

Carrying Charges. Interest on moneys advanced by banks or brokers, insurance, storage charges, and similar costs incurred by one who has purchased goods or securities on credit or on margin.

The term is sometimes used also as the equivalent of "fixed charges," that is, costs incurred regardless of the volume of operations or the amount of business done.

Cartel. This is a formal or informal agreement between rival firms controlling production and distribution of certain products to divide the market regionally so as to maintain prices. This is a form of monopoly barred by antitrust laws in the United States, but it is not uncommon in Europe. Its economic effect is to retard consumption and to place little premium on efficiency of operations.

Cashier's Check. A check, sometimes called an officer's check, issued by a bank, usually signed by the cashier (whence the name is derived), and drawn against the bank itself or against a metropolitan bank with which the drawing bank keeps an account. New York funds are generally provided in the form of cashier's checks. The cashier's check differs radically from an uncertified check drawn by a depositor of the bank. The cashier's check gives the holder an obligation against the bank itself, while the ordinary check gives the holder no claim against the bank, but only a claim against the depositor in the event that the check is not honored.

Center Spread. A preferred position for advertisements, since the two facing pages offer a continuous surface and the double-page text and illustrations can be printed on a large sheet with no interference from center margins or "gutters."

Certificate of Deposit. A certificate or receipt, in which a commercial bank or savings and loan association acknowledges that it has received a certain sum of money from the person to whom the certificate is issued, and agrees to pay the sum to the person named in the certificate, or to his endorsee, upon demand or at a definite future date. Such a certificate bears interest and is often negotiable, and the amount represented by a certificate of deposit is generally not subject to withdrawal by check. In the case of a negotiable time certificate of deposit, that is, one payable at a definite future date, the holder of the certificate may not be a depositor of the bank, but may have purchased his instrument through the open market.

Certified Check. A check having the word "certified" stamped or written upon it, and bearing the signature of an official of the bank upon which the check is drawn. The effect of the certification is merely to furnish a guarantee from the bank that the amount to the credit of the drawer of the check is adequate to meet the check, and that the amount of the check will be set aside for the purpose of paying the check when presented for payment. It is not true, as is sometimes thought, that a certified check constitutes a direct obligation of the bank to pay the amount of the check. Thus, if the check is a forgery, the bank may subsequently refuse to pay the check, even though it be certified, without liability to any holder or endorsee. Or, if the amount of the check has been fraudulently raised before certification, a subsequent holder of the check can recover only the amount for which the check was originally drawn.

Chain Banking. The control of two or more banks by an unincorporated individual or group of individuals through stock ownership in the various banks and/or interlocking directorates.

Chattel Mortgage. A lien given upon personal property, generally as security for a loan or other obligation. Nominally, a chattel mortgage takes the form of a transfer of title of the personal property to the person to whom the mortgage is given (called the mortgagee). In almost all states, however, a chattel mortgage is now regarded, not as a transfer of the title to the property, but as merely giving a lien upon the property.

Generally, a chattel mortgage, to be valid against creditors of the mortgagor or against subsequent transferees of the property, must be recorded in the city or town where the mortgagor resides. Chattel mortgages usually provide for a sale of the property in the event of nonpayment of the debts they are given to secure. The method of sale, however, is usually expressly prescribed by statute.

Check. A check is a written order directed to a bank, ordering the bank to pay a specified sum of money to the order of the person named in the check or to the bearer of the check.

A check payable to "cash" is equivalent to a check payable to bearer, and may be negotiated from one person to another without endorsement. It is the practice of banks, however, to require one who presents a check payable to bearer or payable to cash to endorse the check. Such an endorsement, however, merely operates as a receipt to the bank.

Checks should be presented promptly for collection or payment. Where a check is not presented promptly for payment and the bank upon which it is drawn becomes insolvent during the interval, the holder may in some cases be compelled to shoulder the loss. Moreover, death or bankruptcy of the drawer of the check renders the instrument void, and relegates the holder to the status of a mere general claimant against the drawer's estate.

C. I. F. An expression used in quoting prices, particularly in the export trade, to indicate that the price includes the cost of the goods plus insurance and freight.

Clearing House. The place at which the banks of a particular city or region customarily present checks drawn upon each other. A definite debit or credit balance against or in favor of each of the member banks is made on the basis of these balances.

The method by which the local clearing house operates is as follows: Each bank sends a messenger to the clearing house with the checks which it has received that are drawn against the other members of the clearing house. Each bank assorts the checks it receives, placing all of the checks drawn against one bank in an individual folder, to which is attached an itemized statement of all of the checks contained and their total amount. Each bank has a designated desk as the clearing house, and, at an appointed time the messenger of each bank distributes to the desks of the other banks the checks drawn upon the latter, retaining a duplicate memorandum of each amount. When the distribution is complete, each bank is in possession of all the checks which have been drawn upon it and deposited in other banks. The amount of such checks is then totaled,and, in the event that this total exceeds the amount of the checks presented by it against the other banks, a debit balance is entered against the bank. In the event that the amount of checks presented by any bank against the other banks exceeds the amount of checks presented by the other banks against it, a credit balance is entered for the particular bank.

If there is a debit balance, the amount thereof is paid by the particular bank to the clearing house; if there is a credit balance, the amount of the credit is received by the bank having the credit balance from the clearing house. Under the Federal Reserve system, member banks may use the reserve banks as clearing houses. Under special arrangements non-member banks also may clear checks through the regional reserve banks.

In the larger cities, clearing house organizations have functions wider than those of the ordinary clearing house.

Clearing House Balance. Applied both to an amount due from a clearing house to a creditor bank and to an amount due from a debtor bank to the clearing house. In the former case the balance is called a favorable balance, and in the latter it is called an adverse balance, at the clearing house.

Co-insurance Clauses. Under a co-insurance clause, the insured party agrees to maintain other insurance in an amount equal to a specified percentage of the property's total value. If the insured should carry less than this designated percentage, the payment for any loss he incurs would be reduced in proportion to the percentage by which he has fallen below the co-insurance requirement stipulated by the insuring company.

Collateral Loan. A loan secured by a pledge of securities or other personal property.

Collateral Note. A form of note commonly used by banks and other financial institutions making secured loans. This type of note not merely recites the promise of the borrower to pay but also sets forth the terms upon which the security is deposited with the lender. The terms of the collateral note are designed to relieve the bank or other lender from the obligations imposed by law upon pledgees who undertake to sell the pledged property.

Collision Deductible Insurance. If an insuring company should assume entire coverage for loss resulting from automobile collisions, the premium it would have to charge would be very high, and to many owners would seem almost prohibitive. However, if the insured agrees to assume liability for a certain amount of the damage, for example, the first $100, the premium can be greatly reduced. In that case, a great many small claims would not need to be brought to the attention of the insuring company. Its only liability would be for damage in excess of the deductible amount.

Commercial Agencies. Organizations which make a business of compiling and furnishing to their subscribers information with respect to the assets and liabilities, promptness of payment of obligations, and general solvency and credit of individuals, firms, and corporations engaged in business. This information is given out in the form of general ratings, furnished to all subscribers, and in special reports with respect to any particular concern, furnished upon the special request of a subscriber.

Dun and Bradstreet, Inc. is the leading commercial agency in the United States. The credit ratings and reports given by this agency constitute an important basis for extending or withholding of credit to prospective borrowers or to purchasers on credit.

Commercial Paper. Short-term notes of business concerns and sales finance companies of national reputation, which either may be purchased by dealers and then distributed by them among various banks and other investors throughout the country, or may be placed directly with interested buyers, usually by telephone. Dealers usually make a profit or commission of one-quarter of one per cent upon the principal of these notes. By using this type of commercial paper, these large borrowers may supplement their bank loans and at times borrow at a lower rate than they would be compelled to pay for current loans obtained from local banks.

This type of security, by reason of its general marketability, has come to be highly regarded throughout the banking community as an excellent mode of investment for secondary reserve purposes. The notes, commonly in amounts of $2500 and $5000, run for periods varying from one month to one and one-half years, and can be made to bear such a maturity as will fit in with the needs of the banks purchasing the securities. While these notes are not guaranteed by the houses which buy and sell them, the larger note brokerage houses have made a practice of virtually protecting their purchasers against loss, both by thorough examination of the businesses of those whose notes are purchased and by taking control of such businesses, if necessary, in order to save purchasers from loss.

Commission House. A firm which buys and sells commodities or securities, as a broker or agent for others, receiving a commission on the purchases or sales, or upon both, in compensation for the service rendered.

Common Stock. That class of stock which is entitled to receive dividends or otherwise share in the earnings of a company only after all preferential rights to payments out of the earnings of the company have been satisfied. The term common stock is also used with reference to all of the stock issued by a corporation where only one class of stock has been created. Usually the control of the company is vested in the holders of the common stock. This, however, is not necessarily so, and sometimes the holders of preferred stock are given an equal or greater share in the control of the corporate affairs.

While the common stock usually receives no dividends until the preferential dividends to which any class or classes of preferred stock may be entitled have been paid, the common stock is normally entitled to receive all of the surplus after the preferential payments to the preferred stockholders have been made. The relative rights of holders of any particular issue of preferred or common stock depend, however, upon the special provisions of the certificate of incorporation of the company which issues the stock, and, to determine what these rights are, resort must always be had to the certificate.

Usually, the holder of preferred stock is assured the more continuous and steady return upon his investment. On the other hand, the common stock carries with it the possibility of great profits, in the event that the enterprise proves especially profitable. See *Preferred Stock.*

Congeneric. In the banking field, the term is applied to only bank holding companies whose non-bank subsidiaries engage in financial activities other than commercial banking.

Conglomerate. A merging of a company in one industry with one or more companies in other unrelated industries. In the field of banking, a one-bank holding company having subsidiaries which engage in business activities unrelated to the financial field. It is now illegal for holding companies controlling two or more banks to have affiliates in either nonfinancial fields or even in most financial fields, though in the latter case there are certain exceptions.

Consignee. A person named in a bill of lading as the one to whom goods are to be delivered by a railway or other carrier.

Consignment. Goods are said to be shipped upon "consignment" when they are forwarded by a seller, called the principal in the transaction, to a broker or sales representative, pursuant to an arrangement whereby the broker is to sell the goods and remit to his principal the proceeds less his commission, the broker undertaking no responsibility for the purchase price of the goods until they are actually sold. However, when a sale has in fact been made, if the goods were shipped upon consignment, the broker becomes personally responsible for the sale price, less the commission to which he is entitled. In this respect, such a broker is similar to a "*del credere factor*" who insures the financial responsibility of his purchasers.

Consignor. One who delivers goods to a railway or other carrier for transportation to a designated point.

Consols. The name applied to the 3 per cent "consolidated annuities," sometimes referred to as "consolidated threes," issued by the government of Great Britain, entitling the holder to a certain sum from the government annually. These annuities are obligations of the British government, but differ from other bonds in that they have no definite date of maturity. The government, however, reserves the right to pay the principal represented by the securities at any time. They are, therefore, callable. See *Callable Bonds*.

The full name, "3 per cent consolidated annuities," had its origin in the fact that this form of obligation was issued to replace the entire or consolidated debt of Great Britain, and a purchaser received 3 per cent annually upon the amount paid to the government for the consol.

Controlling Interest. A phrase used to indicate a person, or a body of persons united in mutual interest, who have secured the right, by purchase or by proxy, to vote a majority of the shares of capital stock in a corporation at any stockholders' meeting.

Convertible Bonds. Bonds which are issued subject to a provision for their surrender and cancellation at some future time and the issuance of stock in their place. The provision for conversion may make the conversion optional in the bondholder or in the company, or may be made absolute upon the fulfillment of some condition, depending in each case upon the particular provision contained in the bond.

Corner. The acquisition by an individual, or by a group of speculators, of the larger part or of all of the available supply of a particular stock, or of a commodity such as cotton, wheat, copper, or sugar. When a corner has been successfully effected, one who has sold the stock or commodity short, or who must have the commodity to carry on his business, is compelled to pay any price demanded.

The most notable corners in American financial history were the successful corner of Harlem Railroad stock by Commodore Vanderbilt in 1863 and the attempted corner of gold by Jay Gould in 1869.

Corporation. A corporation is a legal creation whose rights and liabilities as a single person are stated in its charter. The most common form is the joint stock corporation, which is organized for the profit of its members, known as stockholders. Stockholders are not liable for the corporation's debts. Consequently, capital may be invested in a corporation without jeopardizing the estate of the investor. Stockholders have no claim on the corporation's assets. Hence the corporation may carry on indefinitely, irrespective of the death or withdrawal of any of the investors. Through these two advantages, the corporate form of organization has made possible the concentrations of capital on which modern industrial society rests.

A corporation is formed by applying to the state or Federal government for a certificate of incorporation. When granted, this document entitles the corporation to carry on the type of business described therein. The business is managed by officers chosen by a board of directors, who have previously been elected by the stockholders. A typical set-up would be a board of directors consisting of three or more people and executive officers known as president, vice president, secretary, and treasurer.

The owners of a corporation are the stockholders. Their degree of ownership depends on the number of shares of stock they hold and on the special rights which these shares may confer. Profits are distributed to the shareholders at the discretion of the directors. See. *Common Stock, Preferred Stock.*

Cost, Insurance, Freight. See *C. I. F.*

Country Banks. A term used to designate Federal Reserve member banks in small communities. They are required to hold lower legal reserves than are city member banks.

Coupon. A certificate attached to a bond, representing the interest for a given period, to be detached and forwarded to the corporation or government which has issued the bond when such interest becomes due. The coupon generally bears the name of the debtor or obligor upon the bond, the number of the bond, the rate of interest, and the amount due or payable upon the coupon.

Coupon Bonds. Bonds issued with coupons attached, representing the interest falling due from time to time. The interest upon coupon bonds is obtained by detaching or clipping the coupons as they fall due and forwarding them to the debtor corporation for payment.

Cover. Where a person has sold for future delivery stocks or commodities which he does not actually own at the time he makes the sale, he is said to "cover" when he buys in such stocks or commodities.

Curb. The name given originally to the group of brokers who formerly made a practice of meeting daily in Broad street, New York, one block from the New York stock exchange. There they bought and sold securities of both the better and the cheaper grades. This practice of congregating at a point near the financial center of New York City, for the purpose of engaging in stock transactions, began as early as 1869, and continued until 1920, when an ordinance was passed by the city of New York prohibiting the carrying on of brokerage transactions upon the public streets. As a result of the enforcement of this ordinance, the so-called curb brokers organized and erected their own exchange, which is called the American Stock Exchange. Here is now carried on the business which formerly was transacted upon the street and sidewalks of Broad Street.

Currency Denominations. Identification of denominations of U.S. currency is made in terms of the portraits they carry as well as the amount printed on their face. Historical celebrities associated with the different denominations are as follows: \$1, Washington; \$2, Jefferson; \$5, Lincoln; \$10, Hamilton; \$20, Jackson; \$50, Grant; \$100, Franklin; \$500, McKinley; \$1,000, Cleveland; \$5,000, Madison; \$10,000, Chase; \$100,000, Wilson. There are now plans to drop the large denominations.

Current Assets. Assets which are readily convertible into cash and which change in amount from day to day. Cash on hand, bank deposits, merchandise, and accounts and bills receivable are all regarded as current assets.

Current Liabilities. Obligations which fall due from day to day or which will mature in the near future. Included within this designation are accounts payable, notes payable, wages unpaid, interest due or accrued, and similar obligations which are immediately payable or of short term duration.

Dating. An agreement between a buyer and a seller of goods, providing that the date of purchase shall be deemed to be of a later date than the actual date of purchase. The purpose of "dating" is to extend the period or term of credit beyond that normally allowed.

Debenture Bonds. In the United States, an evidence of indebtedness issued by a corporation and not secured by a mortgage or other lien upon property of the corporation. Such a bond is similar to an ordinary promissory note, except that it normally runs for a longer period.

Deed. An instrument signed and sealed, purporting to convey an interest in real property from one person to another.

A *quitclaim deed* is one in which the grantor purports merely to convey such right, title, or interest as he may have in the property described in the deed. Such a conveyance does not carry with it any representation of ownership vested in the grantor, and, in the event that it is later discovered that the title to the property is encumbered or was vested in some other person than the grantor, no recourse can be had against the grantor.

A *warranty deed* is one in which the grantor covenants that he is the owner of the property and that there are no encumbrances upon the property (except such as are expressly excluded from the covenants), and that the grantee will enjoy quiet and peaceful possession of the property. A grantor who executes a warranty deed may be called upon to defend the title to the property, should the grantee's title or possession be attacked. He may also be compelled to respond in damages, should the title prove to be defective.

Deferred Dividend. When dividends are not regularly paid upon preferred stock, carrying cumulative dividends, such unpaid dividends are regarded as "deferred," and ordinarily must be paid before any dividends can be paid upon the common stock.

Demurrage. A charge imposed upon a shipper for detaining a railroad car, or other vehicle of transportation, for a longer time than that allowed by the agreement with the carrier for loading or unloading the cargo.

Deposit. Funds deposited with a bank, entailing an obligation upon the bank to repay an amount equal to the sum deposited. The ordinary deposit with a commercial bank involves an undertaking by the bank to honor withdrawals, in the form of checks drawn upon the account, until the amount of the deposit is exhausted. A deposit of this character is a "demand deposit," being payable at any time upon presentation of a check drawn upon the bank. Interest is not paid on demand deposits; a service charge may be imposed if the balance is too small in relation to the checks drawn. Time deposits, on which interest is paid, are those which must be left with the bank for a definite period.

Depreciation. Diminution in the value of any property, real or personal, whether due to ordinary wear and tear or to any other cause resulting in the lessened value of the property, during any period of time

Diminishing Returns. The law of diminishing returns was formulated by Malthus (1766–1834). Land, he said, becomes more productive with the application of more fertilizers and more labor but only up to a point. Beyond this point their application is not justified by the increase in production. The law has been generalized and applied to production generally.

Direct Mail Selling. This term usually applies to letters, booklets, brochures, or a combination thereof, addressed to individual prospects and designed to secure an order without the necessity of visits by a salesman. Successful selling by direct mail depends upon several factors, including an article, product or service that is not too expensive, yet costing enough to absorb its share of the selling campaign; a list of prospects carefully selected and with verified up-to-date mailing addresses; and a sales presentation that is interesting in content and attractive in form, besides being complete enough to answer a prospect's questions. The usual sequence of 1) getting attention, 2) arousing interest, and 3) creating desire is essentially the same in direct mail campaigns as in personal selling.

Discount. This term has several meanings. It is applied to a loan made by a bank to a customer upon his note, where the interest which is to accrue upon the loan during the term of the note is deducted in advance. Thus, if a customer wishes to borrow $1000 for six months at 6 per cent, the bank "discounts" his note and credits him with the sum of $970. The $30, which is deducted from the principal of the loan, is termed discount or unearned interest, and the entire transaction is called a "discount."

The term discount is applied also to the purchase by a bank, from the payee or holder, of a note having a definite maturity. In such a purchase, as in a direct loan upon the paper of the borrower himself, the interest to become due upon the note during the term it has to run is deducted in advance, and the net proceeds only are credited to the seller of the note.

Another use of the term discount is with reference to the amount or percentage by which the market price of a particular kind of domestic or foreign currency, or of a bond or other obligation, falls below its nominal or par value. Thus, when bonds of the United States government, having a face value of $100, sell for $98, they are said to sell at a discount of $2 or of 2 per cent.

Dishonor. The refusal of one upon whom a draft or bill of exchange is drawn to pay or to accept the bill in accordance with the terms of the instrument.

Disintermediation. Direct investment by individuals in assets, such as Treasury bills, other government securities, acceptances, and commercial paper, as opposed to indirect investment through deposits in banks and other savings institutions. In the last decade, interest rate ceilings on the savings deposits of commercial banks have been set by the Board of Governors of the Federal Reserve system under its Regulation Q. At times when interest yields on open market instruments have risen above these ceilings, disintermediation has occurred. Savings and loan associations faced a similar problem during much of this period because, for one thing, the depressed state of the construction industry made them unable to compete with either commercial banks or open market instruments.

Disposable Income. This refers to income after taxes, which is available for purchase of goods or services and for savings. It is not necessarily the same as "take-home pay," since this may be smaller by reason of "check-off" items that are part of voluntary expenses or savings. Disposable income on a national scale is a key factor in planning for stabilization of prices. An increase of taxes will curtail disposable income and therefore reduce private demand; and this in turn will tend to lower certain prices. Lowering taxes operates in the opposite direction.

Dividend. A proportionate distribution of past and/or present earnings by a corporation among its stockholders. Where the stock of the company has a nominal or par value, the dividend will be payable in terms of a certain per cent of this nominal or par value. Where, however, the stock has no nominal or par value, the dividend merely represents a distribution of cash among the stockholders, out of the earnings or surplus profits of the company, in proportion to their respective holdings in the company. The laws of practically all the states prohibit the payment of dividends to stockholders except out of earnings or surplus profits, in order that the capital of the corporation may be kept intact for the benefit of creditors. Any violation of this prohibition usually renders the directors participating in the declaration or payment of the dividend guilty of a crime.

A stock dividend is entirely different from a cash dividend, and represents merely a distribution of additional evidences of ownership in the corporation, no property of the company being turned over to the stockholders.

Dollar Exchange. Bills of exchange, drawn in foreign countries upon banks or business concerns of the United States, and payable in United States money.

Domestic Exchange. Drafts or bills of exchange, drawn upon banks or commercial houses located in New York or other important commercial centers, used in making remittances from one part of the country to another. Bank drafts upon New York City formerly constituted the greater part of domestic exchange. In recent years, however, bank drafts upon Federal Reserve banks have in large measure replaced drafts upon New York.

Double Taxation. Frequently the same person or the same property is taxed by more than one governmental authority. The most common instance of double taxation of this sort is taxation by both the Federal and the state government. But sometimes the same person or interest in property may also be taxed by more than one state. Thus, where a person residing in the state of New York owns property which is physically present in the state of Ohio, a tax may be imposed by both states, one by reason of jurisdiction over the person owning the property, and the other by reason of jurisdiction over the property or "*res*" itself.

Likewise, where two different states or countries impose income taxes, a tax may be imposed by one state or country, by reason of the income being derived within the limits of its territorial sovereignty; and an income tax may be imposed upon the same income by another state or country, by reason of its jurisdiction over the person earning the income. Frequently, too, succession or inheritance taxes seem to operate to impose double or multiple taxation, where the decedent was a resident of one state and had property subject to the jurisdiction of other states. Double or multiple taxation of this sort may sometimes appear to operate unjustly, but the courts have uniformly held that such taxation is entirely lawful and constitutional.

Draft. A written order drawn by one party (drawer) directing a second party (drawee) to pay a definite sum of money to a third party (payee). The drawer and the payee may be the same person. Also, the drawee and the payee may be the same person. Thus three parties, but not necessarily three persons, are involved. A draft may be drawn payable at sight or on demand, that is, upon presentation; or it may direct payment at a definite or determinable future time. A draft is a bill of exchange. In the United States, however, the term draft has come to be applied to ordinary domestic bills of exchange, as distinguished from bills of exchange used in foreign commerce.

Duebill. A written nonnegotiable acknowledgment of a credit to the account of the person to whom the bill is addressed. This type of instrument is usually given by merchants to persons who have purchased goods and have subsequently returned them.

E. & O. E. Abbreviation for "errors and omissions excepted." This term appearing upon any financial statement negates any representation of the one furnishing the statement that it is absolutely accurate. Its use absolves the one furnishing the account from personal liability for errors in the statement, other than those due to fraud or willful misrepresentation.

Employee Benefit Plans. In the policy and practice of an increasingly large number of companies, there is a tendency to supplement the direct payment of wages or salaries to employees by "fringe benefits" of various kinds. Examples are group insurance, pension plans, and profit-sharing, either current or deferred. Such items are incorporated in "package agreements" between the firm and its employees.

Endorse. To write one's name upon the back of a note, check, or other instrument, for the purpose of transferring the instrument to another, or for the purpose of lending one's credit as a guarantor of the payment of the obligation. An endorsement by one whose name already appears upon the instrument as a payee or endorsee should be made without variation from the form in which it first appears upon the instrument. An endorsement, however, is legally sufficient if, in fact, the person who endorses the instrument is the same person as the one to whom the instrument was payable as payee or endorsee.

Endorsee. One to whom a note or other negotiable instrument has been transferred by endorsement by the holder of the instrument.

Endorsement, Anomalous. Where one who is not a party upon the face of a note or other instrument writes his name upon the back of the instrument, as a guarantor of its payment at maturity, such endorsement is termed anomalous.

Endorsement, Restrictive. An endorsement which indicates that the holder or endorsee of the instrument is not the owner of the instrument, but has merely been intrusted with it for certain definite purposes specified in the restrictive endorsement. Thus, a note or check may be restrictively endorsed, "Pay to the First National Bank for collection only," or "Pay to John Jones as agent," signed by the holder of the instrument.

Endorsement, Special. Where a payee or endorsee of a note or other instrument, upon transferring it, designates upon the back of the instrument the particular person to whom or to whose order the instrument shall be paid, such endorsement is termed a special endorsement. When an instrument has been thus endorsed, it may be further negotiated or transferred only by an endorsement of the person named in the special endorsement.

Endorser. One who has signed his name upon the back of a note, check, or other commercial instrument, to lend his credit to the maker or to the holder of the instrument, in which case he may be an anomalous endorser; or one who, being the holder of the instrument, endorses the instrument in order to negotiate it or sell it to another. Unless an endorser has signed his name "without recourse," he may be held liable for the payment of the instrument, in the event that the maker fails to pay it at maturity. The endorser may, however, be released from liability if the instrument is not duly presented to the maker and protested, and notice of the protest given to the endorser within 24 hours.

Engel's Law. This is a rule formulated by the German statistician Ernst Engel (1821–96) to the effect that, as a family's income increases, the proportion of it spent for food decreases, the proportion spent for advancement (education, luxuries, and savings) increases, and the other items remain about the same.

Escrow. An instrument deposited with a third party, to be delivered to the grantee named in the instrument upon the performance of some condition or upon the happening of a certain event.

Eurodollars. Bank demand and/or time deposits denominated in United States dollars and located in banks outside the United States (but not necessarily in Europe).

Excess Profits Tax. A federal levy imposed several times throughout the twentieth century during war periods. The tax base is that portion of profit that is above normal for the industry, each firm being given a choice of alternative methods of defining abnormal profit.

Exchange. Claims upon foreign merchants or banking institutions, usually in the form of bills of exchange or drafts accepted or drawn upon them, arising out of the export of goods to foreign countries or out of other international transactions. These instruments are bought by persons who are obliged to make remittances to such countries. The result of this buying and selling of "exchange" is that claims by individuals in one country against individuals or banks in another country are offset by claims which individuals in the latter country have against individuals and banks in the former country.

Excise. Any tax imposed by a government upon commodities manufactured, sold, or used, or upon activities carried on, within its territorial jurisdiction. The tax upon cigars and cigarettes, and the tax upon liquors, formerly constituted the most important excise taxes in the United States. In recent years the scope of excise taxes in the United States has been very much widened.

Ex Dividend. Literally, without dividend. When stock is sold during a period when the stock books of the particular company are closed in anticipation of the payment of a dividend, no transfers of ownership being recorded by the company during this period, the stock is said to sell on the market "ex dividend." This is because the purchaser of the stock during such a period will not be entitled to receive the dividend about to be paid by the company.

External Loan. A loan which a country obtains by selling its bonds or other obligations to investors in other countries; it is to be distinguished from an internal loan, which is obtained by the sale of securities to the country's own citizens. Frequently, in the case of an external loan, securities are made payable in the currency of the country in which they are intended to be sold.

Face Value. The value noted upon the face of a check, note, bond, certificate of stock, bank note, or unit of currency. The term "face value" is used in contradistinction to the actual value of the instrument, which may be either greater or less than its face value. See *Par*.

Factor. One who sells goods for another upon commission. See *Agent, Consignment*.

Fair Trade Laws. These are laws designed to limit price cutting. The Robinson-Patman Act bars discrimination between purchasers unless based on specified economic reasons. The Miller-Tydings Act permits states to enact laws for maintenance of resale prices by manufacturers. Courts decisions have severely curtailed the scope of such laws.

Farm Loan Bank. Banks organized pursuant to the Federal Farm Loan act of July 17, 1916. This act provided for the creation of a Federal land bank in each of eleven designated farm loan districts. Most of the original capital was provided by the Federal government, but now all the capital of the banks is owned by national farm loan associations. The act provides for the lending of funds to farmers, but only upon the security of first mortgages on farm land; and the loans are to be made, not directly to the farmer, but through advances to local farm loan associations. In order to obtain a loan under the provisions of this act, an intended borrower has to become a member of one of these associations and subscribe to stock in the association to an amount equal to at least 5 per cent of the amount to be borrowed.

F. A. S. Free alongside ship. This term is used to indicate the extent of the obligation of the seller with respect to delivery of goods sold. Where the goods are sold "F. A. S.," the seller's obligation is fulfilled when the goods are delivered to a wharf from which the goods can be loaded into a vessel for transportation to the port of destination. Where it is necessary to carry the goods from the wharf to the vessel by means of small tugs or lighters, the seller would be obligated to bear the expense of this part of the transportation in addition to carrying the goods to the wharf.

Federal Funds. Funds on deposit and immediately available at the twelve Federal Reserve banks. These are largely the excess reserves of member banks. Federal funds are the customary means of settling certain transactions in the short-term money market. Important among these is the demand for Federal funds by certain commercial banks, which pay interest to borrow the funds, and then make use of them to avoid deficiencies in legally required reserves.

Federal Reserve Bank Notes. Currency formerly issued by Federal Reserve banks in denominations of one, two, five, and ten dollars, secured by deposit, with the Secretary of the Treasury, of certain issues of United States bonds to an amount equal to the bank notes issued. In 1945 the Federal Reserve banks lost the right to issue these notes.

Federal Reserve Notes. Currency issued by Federal Reserve banks, for which these banks pledge collateral consisting of certain assets. The Federal Reserve note has introduced an elastic element into the currency of the

United States. Its volume can be increased or decreased in accordance with seasonal and extraordinary demands. At present these notes account for 90 per cent of the total amount of currency in circulation.

Fee Simple. The absolute, unconditional ownership of real property. The fee simple is the highest estate known to the law. The ownership of the fee simple in any particular parcel of property is not inconsistent with the existence of restrictions or encumbrances upon the property.

Fiduciary. One who occupies a position of trust, or who receives and dispenses funds for another. Executors, administrators, trustees under wills and deeds of trust, directors of corporations, agents, committees of the estates of lunatics, and guardians of infants are all within the general class designated as fiduciaries.

First Mortgage Bond. A bond secured by a first or prior lien upon a part or all of the assets of the company issuing the bond. The extent of this lien depends upon the particular terms of the mortgage in each case. Some so-called "first mortgage bonds" cover only a very limited part of the tangible assets of the issuing company. Others purport to cover not merely specific physical property described in the mortgage, but also property both tangible and intangible which may subsequently be acquired. In the event of a default in the payment of interest or principal upon first mortgage bonds, a foreclosure of the mortgage securing the bonds would bar all secondary or subsequent liens or mortgages upon the property.

Fiscal Year. Any twelve consecutive months used as a period of financial accounting by an individual or a corporation. The fiscal year of any business concern may or may not coincide with the calendar year.

Fixed Charges. The fixed expenses of a business, which can be determined in advance, and which do not vary in proportion to the amount of business carried on. Fixed charges include interest upon bonds or other fixed or long-time indebtedness, taxes upon property, rent, insurance, and depreciation.

F. O. B. Free on board. This term is used in price quotations to indicate the extent of the undertaking of the seller with respect to defraying the cost of transportation, at the price quoted. Thus, if flour is quoted at ten dollars a barrel, f. o. b. cars Buffalo, the seller undertakes merely to deliver the flour to the railroad company at Buffalo, and the cost of transportation from that point on must be borne by the purchaser.

Foreclosure. A remedy provided by the law for realizing upon the security given for a loan or other obligation, in the event of a failure of the obligor or debtor to comply with the terms of his agreement. The usual mortgage upon real property, for example, provides that in the event of a failure to pay any installment of principal when due, or to make any payment of interest within thirty days after the payment is due, the mortgagee may sell the property at a foreclosure sale and receive payment out of the proceeds of the sale. If, upon a mortgage foreclosure, the amount received from a purchaser is more than sufficient to satisfy the claim of the mortgagee and the expenses of sale, the surplus is turned over to subsequent lienors or, if there are none, to the mortgagor.

The term foreclosure applies, not merely to the sale of real property to realize upon sums advanced upon real property as security, but also to sales of personal property under like circumstances. A foreclosure sale may take place also to satisfy a judgment obtained against the owner of the property or to obtain payment of taxes which have been imposed upon the property.

Fractional Currency. Coins of less than one dollar.

Fully Paid. Stock is "full paid" or "fully paid" when it has been completely paid for by the stockholder and no further payment or assessment can legally be demanded from or imposed upon the stockholder by reason of his ownership of the stock. In order that stock be fully paid, it must have been issued in exchange for cash, property, or services having some reasonable relation in value to the par value or amount of the stock issued.

The practice of issuing so-called fully paid stock, bearing a par value of a particular amount, for worthless patents, fictitious good will, and highly overvalued services of promoters, together with the associated practice of issuing shares of stock as bonuses to subscribers or purchasers of stock, has rendered this term in practice almost meaningless. The misleading character of issues of this sort has led to the introduction of non-par-value stock. This becomes fully paid when any sum, however small, is paid to the corporation for the stock, if the agreement between the stockholder and the corporation does not require any further or other payment.

Funding. The floating of a new issue of securities to pay off obligations which have matured or are about to mature. The term is used also with reference to the replacing of a number of outstanding issues of securities by a single new issue, generally for a longer term than the outstanding issues. Such a funding plan frequently provides economies in administration, in addition to extending the period during which the obligations will remain outstanding.

Futures. Contracts for the delivery of stocks or commodities at a future date. Dealing in futures is a very legitimate and even a necessary element in the conduct of some businesses. Thus, a flour manufacturer, in order to make his plans of production for the ensuing quarter or half year, must make his purchases in advance of his actual needs. Only by so doing can he, with any safety, make quotations to his customers for future delivery to them. But speculators upon the commodity and stock exchanges deal in futures in a manner which amounts to plain gambling. These speculators, however, by selling for delivery in the future, relieve the business man of the risks incident to possible fluctuations in prices, and enable him to do business upon a safe, carefully calculated basis.

Garnishee Proceedings. Legal proceedings by which a creditor reaches an obligation owed to his debtor by a third person. Thus, if A owes B $50 and C owes A $50, B may garnishee the sum which C owes to A and thus obtain payment of B's claim against A. In these proceedings, C, the debtor's debtor, is known as the garnishee

Gold Bond. Long-term debt instruments payable in gold coin and issued by governmental units and by private corporations in the days of the gold coin standard. The term "gold" in this connection was intended to promote the sale of such bonds by promising their redemption in the legal tender of that day. After the gold coin standard was abandoned and the dollar was devalued (1934), the Supreme Court refused to enforce payment of the bonds in an amount of dollars having the same total gold equivalent as the dollars originally lent. The Court held that the value of the dollar is determined by its purchasing power rather than its gold equivalent.

Gold Certificates. Paper money issued by the Treasury and which was formerly circulated as legal tender and later, under the limited gold bullion standard, served as legal reserves of the Federal Reserve banks. Recently this requirement has been removed so that the gold certificate is merely a warehouse receipt for gold owned by the Treasury, most of which is part of our international monetary reserve.

Gold Reserve. The term applied to the stocks of gold in the various government depositories, the largest being Fort Knox in Kentucky.

Good Will. Reputation enjoyed by a company or its product, which gives to the product a ready and wide marketability and attracts repeat customers. Frequently, good will constitutes the most valuable single asset a business possesses. Where the good will has been acquired through the expenditure of large sums in advertising, it is deemed proper accounting to set forth as an asset the good will achieved by the advertising at a valuation approximately equal to the sum spent in advertising.

Greenbacks. See *United States Notes.*

Gresham's Law. The principle that, if there is money of different kinds in a country, the better appearing money, or that which intrinsically is more valuable, will either go out of circulation into hoarding or into industry or will be exported, and that that kind of money which is less attractive or of less intrinsic value will tend to become the sole currency of the country.

Gross National Product. This is the market value of all goods and services produced by a nation in a given year. It is the obverse of gross national income, which is the total money value received by the nation for the gross product. The two are equal. The gross national income is measured by (a) compensation to employees, (b) income of proprietors, (c) rental income, (d) corporate profit, including adjustment of inventory values, and (e) net interest received. Gross national product consists of (a) personal consumption expenditures, (b) gross private domestic investment, (c) net export of goods and services, and (d) government purchases of goods and services. In order to show year-to-year trends, the total values are adjusted by price indexes so as to be expressed in dollars of constant value. The totals, as computed by the Commerce Department, have excluded all goods and services that do not enter the market, such as do-it-yourself projects and unpaid housework.

Guarantee. The undertaking by one who is not a direct party to a transaction to perform the promise or obligation made or assumed by another, in the event that the latter does not himself perform the promise or obligation. Bonds of subsidiary corporations are frequently guaranteed by the principal or holding corporation. It is not legally possible, however, for a company to guarantee the payment of the principal or interest upon its own bonds or the payment of dividends upon its own stock. For, in order to have a true guaranty, there must be three parties in the transaction,—the creditor, the debtor, and the guarantor.

Hedging. Either buying or selling in such a manner as to curtail threatened losses through speculative sales or purchases in stocks or commodities. Thus, for example, a speculator agrees to deliver a certain number of units of stock or of a commodity at a certain price at a future time. He intends to cover the sale by purchasing at some time before delivery is due, at a price lower than that named in his contract of sale. Prices then begin to advance in such a manner as to indicate that there probably will be a continuous advance rather than any decline in prices. The speculator will then at once "cover" by buying in the amount of stock or commodity that he has sold, and thus limit his loss to the difference between the price at which he has sold and the price at which he has covered.

Holder in Due Course. One who has acquired a promissory note or other negotiable instrument for value, without notice of any defect in the instrument or in the title of the transferor. A holder in due course may ordinarily recover upon the instrument, regardless of defenses claimed by the maker or by other parties to the instrument. The defense of forgery, however, is available even against a holder in due course.

Holding Company. A corporation whose chief function is the holding of stock in other corporations, the latter being sometimes referred to as its "subsidiaries."

Hypothecation. Depositing stocks or bonds with a creditor as security for the payment of a debt.

Income. Gains received in any form capable of valuation, including compensation for services rendered, interest, dividends, gains from sales and exchanges of personal or real property, profits derived from the conduct of a business, and any other thing of value received during any period.

Income Tax. Federal, state, or city levies imposed upon a person and measured by the income he receives. A state may impose an income tax by reason of the fact that gain has been derived from sources within that state's jurisdiction, even though the person upon whom the tax is imposed has never been, by citizenship or residence, or otherwise, personally subject to the jurisdiction of the state imposing the tax. Income taxes are direct and usually are characterized by progressive rates.

A second type of income tax is one imposed on corporations. As levied in the United States, it presents two differences from the income tax on individuals.

First, the rate is not increased to so high a figure for large incomes. Prior to 1934, a flat rate on earnings was applied irrespective of the amount of earnings. In that year for the first time a slightly higher rate was imposed on larger profits. The change was designed to encourage small enterprises.

Second, higher rates have at times been imposed on companies which retain larger proportions of their earnings to add to surplus. First used under the Revenue act of 1936, this principle is for the purpose of encouraging larger distributions in dividends during the depression period. The money thus distributed is taxable under the individual income tax schedules.

Indenture. An agreement or deed under seal, executed by two or more persons. The origin of the term was in the practice, now obsolete, of executing an agreement in duplicate, or in as many counterparts as there were parties, the copies being separated unevenly in such manner as to create indentures, those in one copy fitting into those in another.

Inheritance and Estate Taxes. Federal and state levies upon the succession to property of a deceased person. Thus, the term "transfer" tax or "succession" tax is sometimes applied to this tax.

Usually, an estate tax is imposed upon the entire estate of the decedent by the state in which he resided at the time of his death, regardless of the situs or physical location of the property left by him. Most states, however, also impose a so-called inheritance tax upon the transfer of property from a deceased person to his heirs at law, or other beneficiaries, if any of the property of the deceased lies within the territorial limits of those states. A so-called inheritance tax is sometimes imposed upon a beneficiary also, by reason of his succession to property, whether under a will or by operation of law, even though the property had no situs or physical presence within the taxing state and the decedent had no residence or domicile there.

Insolvent. Formerly one was deemed insolvent if he was unable to meet his obligations as they matured. The repeated failure of anyone engaged in business to pay definitely maturing obligations upon their due dates was regarded as conclusive evidence of his insolvency.

The term has acquired a new meaning. This meaning has been legislated into legal and commercial usage by the Federal Bankruptcy act of 1898. This act defines an insolvent as one whose liabilities exceed his assets at a fair market valuation. Obviously, under this latter definition, one who fails to meet his obligations as they mature may nevertheless be solvent.

Interest. A periodical return paid for the use of money or other capital. Fundamentally, interest is regarded as a compensation paid to those who deprive themselves of the present use of their funds or capital, in order that these funds may be put to productive and profitable employment. The average rate of interest has been viewed by economists to be determined by two factors—the amount necessary to induce individuals to sacrifice the present for the future, and the amount of additional value that can be created by using the capital thus set aside in producing goods to be consumed in the future. With reference to business loans made by banks, the most important variable in determining the rate is probably the size of the loan, interest rates being scaled upward from the prime rate, that rate which is extended to the top business firms.

Interim Certificates. Frequently, in the reorganization of corporations, considerable time is consumed in carrying into effect the plans of reorganization. It is then customary for stockholders who join in the plan of reorganization to deposit their certificates of stock with designated trustees or with a stockholders' committee, who act for the participating stockholders. These trustees—commonly a single trust company is designated to perform this function—issue to the stockholders interim certificates in exchange for the stock certificates deposited with the trustees. The interim certificate is issued only as a temporary evidence of the interest of the holder.

Interlocking Directorate. The holding by the same persons, of directorships in two or more corporations. When the corporations have dealings with each other, the results may be prejudicial to the interests of one corporation or the other, or outsiders. This circumstance has given rise to criticism of the practice and to restriction of it by Federal law in several fields.

International Bank for Reconstruction and Development (World Bank). A sister institution to the International Monetary Fund (see below), with which it has common membership. This bank makes long-term productive loans to member countries, chiefly for developmental purposes; however, it supplements rather than replaces private investment.

International Monetary Fund. An international financial institution created near the end of World War II and now having 116 members. This bank has the resources to substantially aid members facing temporary balance of payments problems, with the result that these countries have less need to resort to any of the various forms of foreign exchange controls that distort international trade and investment. The Fund extends short and intermediate term loans to members who meet the qualifications.

Internal Loan. A government loan, the securities for which are intended by the government for flotation and sale primarily among its own citizens; as distinguished from an external loan, which is intended primarily for foreign investors. See *External Loan.*

Inventory. An itemized statement or schedule of the assets of an individual, a firm, or a corporation, usually accompanied by a statement of the value of each of the separate items set forth in the schedule.

Investment Banker. One who buys securities wholesale and sells them retail. It is the practice of the well established investment bankers to underwrite or purchase blocks of new securities of corporations and then to market them to their customers. The investment banker is thus the connecting link between persons who have funds in large amounts to invest and persons actively engaged in existing industries or in the promotion of new enterprises.

Invoice. Statement furnished by a seller to a buyer, setting forth in detail the character, quantity, and price of goods sold, and any other terms of the sale.

Jetsam. Goods thrown overboard to lighten a vessel in distress; also called jettison.

Judgment. A determination of a judicial tribunal, reached at the conclusion of legal proceedings. The judgment may impose upon the defendant an obligation to pay a certain sum of money; it may order him to do or to refrain from doing certain acts; or it may merely state a conclusion of law as to what are the rights of the parties.

Judgment Debtor. A debtor against whom a creditor has obtained from a court a judgment which has been placed on record.

Judgment Note. A promissory note containing a power of attorney, authorizing the holder of the note to confess judgment on behalf of the maker or obligor in the event the note is not paid at maturity. The purpose of such a provision is to avoid the necessity of bringing formal legal action against the maker for the recovery of the amount due upon the note. In many states such a power of attorney, if incorporated in the note itself, is given no legal effect.

Killing. The making of exceptionally large profits in a speculative transaction. The word "coup" is sometimes used in a similar sense.

Kiting. A method of obtaining from banks the use of funds for a short period, without paying interest therefor, by the exchange of checks between two or more individuals having accounts in different banks. Thus, if A desires the use of $1000 and is unable or unwilling to borrow the sum from a bank, he may, by prearrangement with a friend, B, who has an account in another bank, request the friend to forward to A a check for $1000. A deposits B's check in the bank with which A keeps his account, and receives credit therefor immediately. A then draws upon the amount thus placed to his credit in his bank, either by obtaining cash from the bank or by issuing checks, to pay his current obligations.

Before B's check reaches the bank with which B keeps his account—and several days may elapse between the deposit of the check in A's bank and its presentation to B's bank—A forwards to B a check drawn upon A's bank for a similar sum, and B deposits the check of A in B's bank, thus obtaining a credit upon the books of the bank sufficient to meet the check drawn by B in A's favor. B then draws a second check in favor of A in the sum of $1000, or in some other sum, which A again deposits in the bank with which A deals. Again A forwards a check to B in a similar amount, which B deposits in time to meet the second check drawn by B in favor of A. By continuing this exchange of checks, it is possible for A to carry indefinitely a fictitious credit in his favor, upon which he can draw in the form of cash or otherwise, depending upon the practice and rules of the particular bank.

Kiting is, therefore, merely a method of taking advantage of the delay incident to the collection of checks. Ordinarily, depositors are not expected to draw checks unless they have on deposit, at the time the check is drawn, sufficient funds to meet the checks. Improved check clearance methods make this practice less prevalent, as will the checkless society of the future. It is now predicted that by about 1980 the transfer of funds may be entirely automated at reasonable cost to the public. One making a payment will merely dial his bank's computer.

Lamb. An amateur speculator upon the stock market who is shorn of his money as the lamb is shorn of its fleece. Thus, buyers of worthless securities, or others deprived of their savings in near-fraudulent transactions, are said to have been "fleeced."

Latin Union. Agreement in 1865 of France, Belgium, Italy, Greece, and Switzerland to adopt a common gold monetary unit as the basis of their systems of currency. In Italy this monetary unit was called the lira; in Greece, the drachma; and in France, Belgium, and Switzerland, the franc. The unit was equivalent to 19.3 cents in United States currency. World War I disrupted the agreement.

Lawful Money. A term covering broadly any form of currency in common use and accepted by government for payment of taxes and fees, whether or not it be legal tender in a technical sense. Prior to 1933, Federal Reserve notes, silver certificates, and national bank notes were lawful money but were not legal tender. In that year the distinction was wiped out as affecting currency in the United States. See *Legal Tender*.

Legal Investment. By law, savings banks, commercial banks, and insurance companies are required to invest their funds in limited classes of high grade securities. These securities consist of Federal, state, county, and municipal bonds; first mortgages on real estate in an amount not exceeding, under the laws of most states, 60 per cent of the value of the real property; and bonds of certain designated companies. A further limitation with respect to investment in railroad and municipal bonds is frequently imposed, to the effect that the bond of a particular municipality or of a particular railroad may not be the subject of investment if there has been, at any time during the preceding five years, or sometimes a longer period, a failure to pay interest upon its bonds; and, in the case of some railroad bonds, if there has been, for a certain period preceding the investment, a failure to pay dividends.

Either by statute or by repeated rulings of the courts, fiduciaries (in which class are included trustees under wills and under deeds of trust, executors and administrators, and guardians of the estates of minors and incompetents) are required to invest the funds of the trust estate in securities which are legal investments for savings banks. This rule, where not prescribed by statute, is not an absolutely hard and fast limitation upon the investments of fiduciaries. But, if investments are made in any other securities or property than the so-called "legal investments," the fiduciary runs a very serious risk of being held liable personally for any diminution or depreciation in the value of the principal of the estate.

Legal Rate of Interest. The maximum rate of interest fixed by the laws of a state or country as a lawful charge for the use of money. Each state in the Union may fix its own lawful rate of interest. Where individuals of different states, having different legal rates of interest, are involved in a transaction, that rate governs, which is fixed by the laws of the state in which the transaction takes place, or in which it is to be performed.

Where interest in excess of the rate allowed by law is charged, the rate is usurious, and the lender is guilty of usury. Under the laws of most states, if the facts are proved, the lender can then recover neither the interest nor the principal. In some states usury is also made a misdemeanor, punishable under the penal law.

Legal Tender. Currency which a creditor is compelled to accept in payment of a debt, in the absence of an express agreement prescribing the specific kind of money to be paid by the debtor, or no further interest on the debt may be collected.

Before 1933, when all lawful money in the United States was made fully legal tender, gold certificates, gold coin, United States notes, originally issued during the Civil War and known as greenbacks or legal tenders, United States treasury notes of 1890, and silver dollars were full legal tender in unlimited amounts. Silver coins of less than one dollar had limited legal tender qualities.

Letter of Advice. A formal notification sent by the drawer of a bill of exchange to the one upon whom the bill is drawn, generally a banking house with which the drawer has made arrangements for the acceptance of bills drawn by him, advising the latter of the drawing of the bill and of the amount and terms of the instrument.

Letter of Credit. A formal letter, issued by a bank or banking firm on behalf of a customer, requesting correspondents of the bank to honor drafts drawn by the person named in the letter of credit, and to charge the amounts thereof to the issuing bank.

Letters of credit are of two general classes—travelers' letters of credit and commercial letters of credit. The traveler's letter of credit is merely a letter addressed generally to the correspondents of the issuing bank, introducing the person for whose benefit the letter has been issued, and requesting that his drafts be honored up to a named amount by any correspondent bank. The signature of the one in whose favor the letter is issued is written at the bottom of the letter at the time it is issued. With this letter in his possession, a traveler may, at the office of any correspondent bank, obtain currency in any sum up to the amount named in the letter of credit, by writing a draft for the amount desired. The signature upon the draft is compared with the signature upon the letter of credit, and, if it appears to be in proper form, the desired funds will be paid to the holder of the letter of credit in any form of currency he may desire. Whenever any payment is made pursuant to the letter of credit, an entry is made on the reverse side of the letter, showing the date of payment, the bank making the payment, and the amount paid.

Commercial letters of credit are drawn by a bank at the request of a customer, usually in order to facilitate purchases abroad. Thus, if an importer desires to purchase goods in a foreign country on credit, he obtains a letter of credit from his bank or from another bank with which his bank has made arrangements for the issuance of letters of credit. This document may be addressed to a foreign correspondent of the issuing bank, or it may be addressed by the issuing bank directly to the foreign exporter.

The letter in effect is an undertaking or a guaranty that the issuing bank will accept and/or pay all drafts drawn in accordance with the terms specified in the letter of credit. Where the letter specifies that drafts will be honored only when accompanied by negotiable bills of lading, consular invoices, and, sometimes, also by policies of insurance, the instrument is called a "documentary" letter of credit. Where there is no requirement that drafts shall be accompanied by bills of lading or other instruments of title, the letter is called a "clean" letter of credit.

The letter may be a "revocable" letter of credit or an "irrevocable" letter, depending upon the particular terms of the instrument. In the former, the bank reserves the privilege of withdrawing the credit at any time before drafts have been drawn against it. Where the letter is "irrevocable," it remains in effect until it is exhausted or expires by its terms.

Where the letter of credit is forwarded first to a correspondent of the issuing bank, and the correspondent notifies the exporter and undertakes on behalf of the issuing bank to accept drafts drawn by the exporter, pursuant to the letter of credit, the letter is said to be "confirmed." Where, however, the correspondent or notifying bank merely advises the exporter of the receipt of the letter of credit, without itself undertaking to accept or guarantee drafts drawn against it, the letter is "unconfirmed."

Lien (*lē'ĕn*; *lēn*). A legal right of a person to detain or control property belonging to another until certain charges upon it have been paid, or until some pecuniary claim against the owner has been satisfied.

Lighterage. Transferring goods from a dock or wharf to a lighter or barge, and then from the lighter or barge to a ship, or vice versa. The term is applied also to the expense involved in thus loading or unloading a vessel, This expense will be incurred whenever the shallowness of the water or the lack of proper dock facilities makes it impossible to load or unload directly from wharf to ship.

Limited. See *Ltd.*

Limited Partnership. A partnership in which the liability of one or more of the members is limited to the amount invested in the business. Such a partner, in the event of the insolvency of the partnership, cannot be held liable for any of its obligations beyond the amount which, under the partnership agreement, he has undertaken to place at the disposal of the business.

Usually, limited partnerships are strictly regulated by statute, the purpose of such regulation being to provide adequate notice to the public of the limited liability of one or more of the partners. These laws generally provide that the active management of the partnership shall be vested solely in the general partners—those members of the firm who are liable, without limitation, for any and all debts contracted by the partnership.

Liquidation. The conversion of the assets of a corporation, firm, or partnership into cash, and the distribution of its assets among the creditors and stockholders or other persons having an interest in the company or business.

A liquidation is known as a "voluntary" liquidation where it results from the mere desire of the owners of the business, or the stockholders of a corporation, to terminate the business and distribute its assets. The liquidation is a "forced" liquidation where the pressure of creditors has thrown the business, or has threatened to throw it, into receivership, and liquidation is the only method by which creditors can receive payment of the sums due them.

Listed. Before a stock or bond may be bought and sold on any of the larger stock exchanges, the security must be submitted to the governors of the exchange or to a special committee appointed to pass upon the character of the security and the qualifications of the corporation issuing the stock or bond. Certain definite requirements usually must be met to qualify the security for listing. When the stock or bond has been approved as fulfilling these requirements, it becomes "listed" on the particular exchange.

Sometimes the term listed is used with reference solely to listing on the New York stock exchange.

Lombard Street. The name applied to the financial section of London, of which Lombard street forms a part. The use of this term corresponds to the use of the term "Wall Street" in this country, as expressive of the entire metropolitan financial district.

Ltd. Abbreviation for the word limited, required to be included in the names of companies organized under limited liability statutes in Louisiana, Great Britain, Canada, and in some other countries. The term "Ltd." is used with the same purpose and effect as the abbreviation "Inc."—which is more commonly used in the United States—to indicate that the company is one in which the liability of the stockholders is limited to the amount invested in the corporation.

Manifest. A complete list of the passengers or freight carried upon each voyage made by a vessel. This list must be signed by the captain or other person in charge of the ship. If a passenger ship, it must contain, in addition to the name of every passenger, a complete record of the voyage, including particularly the name of the port of embarkation and that of the port of landing. Where the manifest covers a shipment of freight, it must contain the name of each shipper or consignor, the character of the freight, the number of packages, and the ports of loading and destination.

Margin. A sum deposited with a broker for the purchase of stocks or commodities on speculation. The "margin" so deposited constitutes a protection against loss to the broker, in the event of a fall in the value of the securities purchased. The amount of the margin required by the broker varies with the speculative quality of the security or commodity to be purchased for the customer. In the case of stocks traded on national exchanges and certain other securities, margin rules are set by the Federal Reserve Board of Governors.

Whenever the price or quotation of a security purchased for a customer on margin falls to such a point that the margin is reduced below the stipulated percentage, the broker calls upon the customer for additional margin. If this is not forthcoming, the broker "sells out" the customer before the fall in price has completely wiped out the margin deposited.

Matched Order. An order to buy, given simultaneously with an order to sell a similar number of shares of the same stock or an equal quantity of a commodity. Such an order really amounts to a fictitious sale and gives an appearance of activity in the particular stock or commodity which has no basis in actual demand. The purpose of "matched orders" is usually to cause an artificial or temporary rise in prices. Penalties are prescribed against traders on national exchanges who use this device. Detection is a duty of the Securities and Exchange Commission.

Mechanic's Lien. Under the laws of many states, one who performs labor or provides materials used in the construction of a building may obtain a lien upon the building for the value of the labor or materials rendered, by filing a notice in the office of the county clerk or registrar of deeds. Such a lien is called a mechanic's lien. The purpose of these statutes is to provide security and some assurance of ultimate payment to those who render services or provide materials by which the owner of the building benefits.

In order to obtain a mechanic's lien, it is not necessary that the work or materials be rendered directly to the owner at his request. A notice of lien may be filed by one who performs work for a contractor or subcontractor. But, in that event, under the laws of most states, the lien is valid only to the extent to which money is or may become due from the owner to the contractor or subcontractor, by reason of work performed upon the structure. The filing of a notice of a mechanic's lien, therefore, operates as a notice to the owner that, if any sums are or may become due to his contractor, he must set aside out of these sums, an amount sufficient to pay the mechanic's lien asserted against the building. To avoid double payment, it is customary for the owner to require a contractor to file a bond, protecting the owner against the possibility of having his property subjected to liens of persons hired by the contractor to perform services upon the building.

Middleman. One who stands between the producer or manufacturer and the consumer. Distributors of all kinds, such as jobbers, wholesalers, retailers, brokers, factors, and commission merchants, are included within this class.

Money. Any generally recognized medium of exchange. In a more limited sense, and as the term money is now commonly used, it applies to the currency or coin either issued or recognized by governmental authority, whether or not it is legal tender, and to demand deposits. See *Legal Tender*.

Money Order. An order payable at sight to a person designated in the instrument, the amount to be charged to the account of the drawer. Money orders are issued by express companies and by the post-office department of the United States government, and, more recently, also by bankers' associations. They are quite similar to cashiers' checks in their essential character and in the purpose which they serve. By reason of their almost universal acceptability and further by reason of the fact that they are made payable to a designated party—so that one not entitled to the money order cannot avail himself of it—they provide a safe and convenient means for transmission of payment through the mails.

Moratorium. An act of the government providing that, during a certain period, creditors shall have no right to bring proceedings against debtors for the collection of debts.

Mortgage. Technically, a transfer of title to real or personal property as security for a loan or other obligation.

Formerly a mortgage was deemed to convey to the mortgagee the ownership in the property subject to defeasance; that is, subject to termination upon payment of the debt for which the mortgage was given as security. Today, however, mortgages, upon either real or personal property, are commonly regarded as giving to the mortgagee merely a lien upon the property mortgaged, and not as conveying any actual rights of ownership.

In most states, statutes provide specifically how mortgages may be foreclosed in the event of nonpayment of the debt for which the mortgage was given, the purpose of these statutes being to protect the mortgagor—the one who gives the mortgage—from a forfeiture of his interest in the property.

In order that the mortgagee shall have a valid lien upon the property mortgaged, as against a person to whom the property may be sold by the mortgagor, or, in most states, even as against judgment creditors of the mortgagor, the mortgage must be recorded. If the mortgage is upon real property, it will be recorded in the office of the clerk or the registrar of deeds of the county where the property is located. Chattel mortgages must generally be recorded in the office of the clerk of the town or municipality in which the mortgagor resides.

Mortgage, Insured. Congress set up in 1934 a Federal Housing Administration, one of whose functions is to insure approved mortgages on homes. The mortgage is insured in favor of the lender of the money, and the insurance is paid for by the borrower. If the borrower defaults, the housing administration makes good the loan. One purpose of the law is to create a class of negotiable mortgages. Insurance eligibility requirements vary from time to time, depending upon economic conditions.

Mortgage Bond. A bond secured by a mortgage upon real or personal property.

Municipal Bonds. Obligations of a city, school district, incorporated village, or other municipality, issued to provide funds for municipal purposes. The term is often used more broadly to include the obligations of the state as well.

National Bank. A bank organized under the National Banking Act of the United States, and subject to regulation by the Comptroller of the Currency and Administration of National Banks, United States Treasury Department. The present national banks have been organized pursuant to acts passed on February 25, 1863 and June 3, 1864, as a part of the general financing plan of the Northern states during the Civil War. These banks were specifically given the power to issue bank notes upon depositing with the Treasury certain types of bonds of the United States. When the eligible types of bonds were called for redemption in 1935, the note-issuing privilege of the national banks lapsed. All national banks are required to be members of the Federal Reserve system and of the Federal Deposit Insurance Corporation.

National Income. See *Gross National Product.*

Negotiable Paper. A check, draft, bill of exchange, or other commercial instrument payable to bearer or to order, the title to which may be transferred by delivery or by endorsement. An instrument is not negotiable unless it is payable to "bearer" (or a recognized equivalent of the term bearer, such as "cash") or to "the order of" a designated person. In order to be negotiable, the instrument must have also a definite or ascertainable date of maturity, and must contain an unconditional obligation to pay a definite sum of money. One who acquires a negotiable instrument for value, prior to maturity and without notice of any defect in the title of previous holders of the instrument, usually may recover against those who appear to be liable upon the instrument, irrespective of any defenses which they may claim against previous holders of the instrument.

Negotiable Securities. Bonds payable to bearer and therefore transferable by delivery, as distinguished from registered bonds, which can be effectively transferred only by changing the registration of the bond at the office of the issuing corporation.

Net. A term applied to a price or to an amount after all discounts and other deductions have been made.

The net weight of a commodity sold in a container is the weight of the contents alone, free from the container.

No Account. When a check, drawn upon a bank in which the drawer is not a depositor, is presented at that bank, it is stamped with the words "no account."

Nonassessable. A term applied to stock in a "limited liability" corporation, which has been paid for in full, and the owner of which, under the terms of the issuance of the stock, cannot be required to make further contributions to the capital or business of the corporation. When such stock has once been fully paid for, the ownership of it entails no further liability on the part of the owner, either to the corporation or to its creditors.

No Protest. An instrument that is not subject to protest is marked with these words. See *Protest.*

Note. An unconditional written promise to pay a specific sum of money at a definite or determinable future date, signed by the person making the promise.

Oath. In law, an oath is a solemn affirmation, usually accompanied by a set formula, such as the words "I do hereby solemnly swear that", etc. One who swears falsely is liable to criminal penalties in nearly all jurisdictions.

Option. A right or privilege to buy (or sometimes to sell) property upon designated terms. An option differs from a contract in that the person to whom the option is given is under no obligation to buy or to sell, whichever the case may be. He may or may not exercise his privilege, as he chooses. In order that an option may be valid and binding, usually something of value must be given to the person granting the option. Otherwise, it is a mere offer, which may be withdrawn at any time.

Outlawed. A colloquial term applied to the barring of rights by the failure to enforce them within a certain period.

The practical administration of justice requires that a definite limitation be placed upon the time within which those who claim rights against others shall enforce these rights in courts of justice. The principle upon which statutes of limitation rest is that the facts about a matter are likely to be obscured by the lapse of time, and also that it is socially desirable that a long existing situation should not be disturbed by reason of long past events.

The period within which an action must be commenced upon a note or other contractual obligation is, under the laws of most states, six years. An instrument under seal, however, does not become outlawed in some states until twenty years have elapsed from the date when the obligation matured. Tort actions—actions for injuries to person or property—are usually "outlawed" in two, three, or four years, the term varying in different states.

Overdrawn. When a depositor draws checks to an amount in excess of the credit to his account, his account is said to be overdrawn. Where such an overdraft is permitted by a bank, it constitutes, in effect, a loan by the bank to the depositor. Such a loan, however, often is not represented by any written instrument from the depositor to the bank.

Paper Money. Any paper currency, whether or not it is legal tender.

Par. The face value of a note, security, or other instrument. A stock or bond is said to sell at par, above par, or below par, accordingly as its sale price is equal to, greater than, or less than, the nominal value stated upon the instrument itself.

Parity Price. This term, used in connection with American farm legislation, means the price of a farm commodity which has the same purchasing power as the price which that commodity had, as an average, in a selected base period. Thus, if a bushel of wheat sold at $1.00 in the base period and the consumer price index later doubled, the parity price would be $2.00 a bushel.

Pass Book. A term sometimes applied to a bank book. See *Bank Book.*

Payable to Bearer. An instrument payable to "bearer" is payable to the holder of the instrument, and may be transferred from one holder to another by mere delivery, without endorsement. Where an instrument is made payable to "cash," it is regarded as payable to bearer.

Payee. The one to whom a note, draft, or other instrument is made payable.

Payor (Payer). The maker or drawer of a promissory note, or of a similar instrument.

Personal Property. Any property, whether tangible or intangible, that is not affixed to land. Stocks, bonds, jewelry, furniture, live stock, automobiles, trade-marks, good will, patents, and leases for definite periods of years are all included within the general class of personal property.

Pit. The trading room of the Chicago board of trade, in which grain, rye, oats, barley, and other commodities are bought and sold.

Point. The unit used in designating the extent of a rise or fall in the market price of a security or a commodity. A point may indicate different amounts for different securities or commodities. Thus, a rise or fall of a point in the quotation of a stock ordinarily indicates a rise or fall of one dollar. In quotations of cotton, a point is $1/100$ of a cent, and a rise of 25 points in the price of cotton would indicate merely an increase of one-quarter of a cent per pound.

Pool. A combination of individuals or interests for the purpose of creating an artificial rise or fall in the price of securities or commodities dealt in upon the stock or commodity markets. The members of the pool combine their resources and, under the management of a designated individual or group of men, buy and sell in a particular stock or commodity with the purpose, either of hammering down the price of the stock or commodity, or of artificially raising the price to a point that will enable them to unload the security or commodity upon the public at a profit.

Operations of these types on national security exchanges were forbidden by law in 1933; those on the commodity exchanges, in 1936. Security traders are now required to obtain licenses from the Securities and Exchange Commission; commodity traders from the Commodities Exchange Commission. The penalty for engaging in pool operations may be revocation of the trader's license.

Postdated Check. A check bearing a later date than the date upon which it was actually drawn. A postdated check will not be honored by a bank until the date indicated upon the check arrives.

Power of Attorney. A writing or instrument signed by one person and giving to another person authority to perform certain acts on behalf of the signer of the instrument. A power of attorney, in most states, must either be witnessed, or be acknowledged before a notary public or other official authorized to take acknowledgments. The power of attorney may be very general in its scope, or it may be limited to a single specific act.

A power of attorney may be terminated at any time by the grantor of the power, unless the holder of the power of attorney has some pecuniary interest of his own which would be violated or infringed by the termination.

For some purposes, a power of attorney may be conferred by one person upon another by mere oral or parol authorization, without any instrument in writing. An authority conferred in this manner is more properly termed a mere agency rather than a power of attorney.

Preferred Creditor. A creditor entitled to payment of his claims before the claims of mere general creditors are paid. Whether a creditor has a preferred claim becomes important where a debtor has become insolvent or has been adjudicated a bankrupt. Claims arising out of personal services rendered within two years of the filing of a petition in bankruptcy are entitled to a preference, and such claims must be paid in full before other debts may be paid.

Preferred Stock. Stock in a corporation, which confers upon the holder a prior right to dividends or to payment out of the assets of the corporation, in the event that the corporation is dissolved.

The usual preference given to holders of preferred stock is one entitling the holders to dividends of a certain per cent upon the par value of their stock in each year, before any dividends shall be paid to holders of the common stock. This preference as to dividends may be either cumulative or noncumulative. If the dividend preference is cumulative, then, if no dividends, or dividends less than the amount of the dividend preference, are paid in any year upon the preferred stock, the amount unpaid must be paid to the holders of the preferred stock before any dividends can be paid upon the common stock in any subsequent year. If the preference as to dividends is noncumulative, then, if no dividends are paid upon the preferred stock in any year, such omission of dividends does not affect the relative rights of the holders of preferred and common stock in any subsequent year, the prior omission of payment of dividends to the preferred stockholders being disregarded.

Generally, the dividends which holders of preferred stock may receive from the corporation are limited to a definite rate or amount. Thus, if the preferred stock entitles the holder to dividends of 7 per cent upon the par value of the stock, all of the profit in any year, in excess of the dividends to which the preferred stock is entitled, goes to the holders of the common stock. This, however, is not necessarily the case. For, in the absence of a provision limiting the holders of preferred stock to dividends of a certain per cent, preferred stockholders are entitled to share equally with the common stockholders in any excess profits distributed by the corporation, after the common stockholders have received dividends at a rate equal to that paid to the holders of the preferred stock. See *Common Stock.*

Premium. When any security having a par value sells at a price above par, it is said to be quoted at a premium.

The term is used also in transactions in international or foreign exchange, with reference to the amount above the normal exchange rate at which any particular currency is quoted.

Price Index. This term applies to a measure of prices. To prices in a base period is assigned the number 100 on the scale, and a change of one point represents a change of one per cent of the prices in the base period.

The prices are weighted by the amount of each commodity or service usually purchased. From time to time the items priced are reviewed and altered or changed in weight to reflect current spending habits.

Both consumer and wholesale price indices are calculated and used by the federal government to compute the present purchasing power of the dollar as compared with its purchasing power in other years.

Principal. The capital sum due upon a bond or other obligation as distinguished from the interest which accrues or becomes due upon the principal from time to time.

Profit. This is the excess of a firm's revenue in a given period over all operating and overhead costs, including depreciation and pro-rated cost of capital invested. If revenue is insufficient to cover the costs, there is a loss.

It is from profits that dividends normally are paid. On the average, about two-thirds of profits are paid in dividends and one-third is retained for reinvestment in the business. This fact helps account for the long-term upward bias in stock prices, since capital is continually accumulated in this way for further earnings.

Corporations are taxed by the federal government on the basis of their profits. Profits after taxes form the chief determinant of the market value of the firm's stock. Since rising stock values facilitate the raising of new capital, as well as benefiting the stockholders, management has a strong incentive to increase profits by improving and diversifying the products offered for sale and by reducing the costs of doing business. It is this characteristic of the profit system that is responsible for the dynamic nature of capatilistic economies in comparison with communistic regimes, in which the profit motive is discouraged.

Profiteering. Selling goods or services at a price yielding an unusually large profit. In 1918, Congress passed a law designed to prevent and punish profiteering in certain businesses. This law, however, was held unconstitutional.

Promissory Note. An instrument containing an unconditional promise to pay a definite sum of money to a particular person or to his order, or to bearer, either on demand or at a definite future time. A promissory note may be either negotiable or nonnegotiable. It is nonnegotiable when it is payable to a definite person only, and not to his order or to bearer, or when it does not meet any of the other requirements of the negotiable instruments law.

Promoter. One who makes a business of floating or financing new enterprises or of obtaining additional capital for already existing enterprises.

Pro Rata. In proportion to their respective rights or liabilities. Thus, it is the policy of the law that creditors of an insolvent debtor shall share pro rata in his assets; that is, in proportion to their respective claims. Conversely, where several persons are engaged in a joint enterprise, it is the policy of the law that they shall, as among themselves, be liable pro rata for any obligations incurred; that is, they share the burden in proportion to their interests in, or contributions to, the entreprise.

Protest. The formal step necessary to fix the liability of the endorsers of a check, note, or other instrument which has been presented to the maker or acceptor for payment and has been refused. In the case of a note or of a draft or bill of exchange payable at a definite future date, the instrument must be presented formally to the maker or acceptor during business hours upon the date of maturity. If the instrument is not paid before the close of business on that day, the notary who made the formal presentation of the instrument for payment certifies over his seal and signature that the instrument was presented and payment was refused. This certification is the "protest" of the instrument.

It is usually not necessary, particularly in domestic, as opposed to foreign, business, that the note or draft be presented and protested for nonpayment in order that the maker shall remain liable upon the instrument.

Proxy. An authorization from one person to another to act in his place and on his behalf. It is customary for stockholders of a corporation to vote their stock by proxy; that is, by executing a written authority authorizing another to act on their behalf at a meeting of the stockholders.

Put. An agreement to accept and pay for a certain amount of a stock, or of a commodity, at a fixed price at any time before the expiration of a designated period.

Pyramiding. Buying additional blocks of a particular stock or commodity upon margin, with the book profits yielded by a rise in prices. Thus, a customer requests a broker to buy 100 shares of a particular stock at 25 dollars a share, on a five-point margin, that is, a margin of 20 per cent, and gives directions to the broker to buy additional stock upon the same margin upon each advance in the market price of the stock. If the stock advances five points, the broker, under his instructions, will buy another hundred shares upon a similar margin upon the basis of the five-point paper profits yielded by the first purchase. As the stock continues to rise in price, the paper profits furnish additional margin for further purchases, until a large quantity of the stock has been purchased; and, if the stock so purchased is unloaded before a fall in the price of the stock, a very handsome profit upon the original investment will result.

Quotation. A price bid or asked for a stock, bond, or commodity. Sometimes a quotation may represent an actual market price based upon actual sales.

Rate of Exchange. The actual price at which a unit of currency of one country exchanges for a unit of currency of another country. Under normal conditions, the monetary unit of one country has a definite par in terms of the currency of any other country, generally based upon the amount of pure gold represented by the respective monetary units. When exchange is at par—one of the possible rates—, then the currency of one country has a value, in transactions with persons of the other country, equal to the relative amount of gold represented by the monetary units when operating under gold standard conditions.

Where paper currency which is not redeemable in gold, circulates within a country, a new element is introduced. The currency of such a country will be exchangeable for the currency of other countries at a rate established by other factors. Under "managed currencies," such as Great Britain's became in 1931 and that of the United States became in 1933, the par may be set by tacit agreement and with an eye to its effect on internal prices. Sometimes each government, in such cases, uses a large "stabilization fund" to support at a definite level the value of its own currency through buying or selling those of other countries. In other cases an international financial institution may carry on these support or pegging operations.

Rating. The credit worth of an individual, firm, or company, as estimated by Dun and Bradstreet, Inc., or any other recognized mercantile agency.

Real Property. Land and all things permanently attached to the land. Thus, real property includes structures erected upon the land and intended to remain affixed for an indefinite time, minerals, water flowing through the land, trees and other issues of the soil (excepting crops which are planted and reaped yearly or more frequently), rights of way and other easements, and rights of every nature in land and in waters, not including, however, leases for years or mere licenses.

Rebate. A return of part of a sum received for goods, for services rendered, or for taxes overpaid. Some uses of the rebate device are now illegal. For example, at one time it was customary for railroads to make rebates to large or favored shippers. The result of this practice was that certain large corporations were able to save sufficiently upon their transportation costs to undersell their smaller or less favored competitors. The result of this was to crush the smaller concerns out of existence. The Interstate Commerce Act of 1887 and the amendments which have since been made to that act have had, as one of their chief objects, the prevention of this practice. Under this act, the giving of a rebate by any railroad or other common carrier in interstate commerce was made a crime.

Receiver. Person appointed by a court to manage the property of a person or a company, pending the termination of legal proceedings affecting the property or its owner. Thus, a receiver may be appointed to receive the rents and profits of a property with respect to which mortgage foreclosure proceedings have been instituted. Similarly, a receiver may be appointed to receive the rents and profits of property the ownership of which is disputed.

The type of receiver that is most common, however, is the receiver who is appointed ostensibly to take over the assets and continue the business of a corporation, pending its dissolution. Frequently this means of preserving the property of a corporation until its affairs can be liquidated is abused by those in charge of the affairs of the corporation. Thus, the receiver may be appointed at the behest of friendly creditors, with the sole purpose of preventing unfriendly creditors from pressing their claims and levying execution upon the property of the company. No bona fide purpose to dissolve the corporation or to liquidate its affairs then exists; but the protection which receivership proceedings provide against the collection of claims by creditors is obtained. In these cases, therefore, a receivership merely grants the corporation a moratorium —a suspension of payment of its debts—and serves no other purpose than to carry the corporation through temporary financial straits.

Refunding. Floating a new issue of securities to replace outstanding issues which are about to mature.

Registered Bonds. Bonds payable to a definite person designated in the face of the bond, and transferable only by endorsement properly witnessed and by an entry of the transfer upon the books of the issuing corporation. Where the bond is registered not merely as to principal but also as to interest, the interest is paid by check to the record holder of the bond, without the necessity of the transmission of any coupons to the corporation. When the bond is registered as to principal only, and not as to interest, it usually bears coupons representing the interest due or to accrue upon the bond, the coupons being payable to bearer and cashed upon presentation as they mature.

Registrar. One who records original issues and transfers of stock or bonds of a corporation. The functions of the registrar generally include the duty of safeguarding against a fraudulent or erroneous overissue of stock or bonds by the officers of the corporation. The registrar must then make certain that no certificates of stock or bonds are issued unless they are part of a duly authorized original issue or are issued in place of surrendered and canceled certificates of like amount.

Reserve. Funds set aside to meet a contingent or definite future expenditure.

Most corporations have a reserve for obsolescence and depreciation, the purpose of which is to provide a fund with which to replace capital assets when they have become worn out or useless. Where a company carries its own insurance—that is, does not take out insurance with regular insurance companies, but carries its own risks as to fire loss or other damage—a reserve will be accumulated from year to year so that, in the event of a loss by fire or otherwise, there will be sufficient funds set aside to cover the loss. It is also customary for companies that have issued bonds or other long-term notes to set aside annually a certain amount as a so-called reserve, with which to fund or pay the bonds or notes when they become due. Banks are required by law to maintain a reserve consisting of cash or its equivalent, amounting to a certain proportion or percentage of their deposits. See *Bank Reserves.*

Rights. The term applied to the privilege given to existing stockholders of a corporation to purchase a proportionate number of shares of any new issue of the company's stock.

Under the law which has grown up with respect to the rights of stockholders in corporations, a stockholder is entitled to subscribe to any new issue of stock that the corporation may make, in proportion to his holdings in the corporation, before the stock may be offered to the general public. Where the outstanding stock of the corporation has a market value higher than par, this privilege of purchasing stock of the new issue, at par or at any price lower than the market quotation for the outstanding stock, is a valuable one. Thus, assuming that there are 10,000 shares of the stock of a corporation outstanding, the shares having a par value of $100, but selling on the market at $150, if a new issue of 5000 shares is to be offered at $100 per share, each stockholder would be entitled to purchase one share of the new issue for each two shares which he already owns in the corporation. The holder of 100 shares would then be the owner of 50 so-called "rights," a right being the privilege of purchasing one share of stock of the new issue. If the new stock is issued at $100 and the stock outstanding is quoted at $150, then the value of a right would be something less than $50. These rights may be bought and sold and, in the case of stocks having a wide market, are sometimes the subject of considerable speculation.

Savings Banks. Banks organized for the purpose of receiving deposits from small savers, and utilizing these savings in the form of investments in high-grade bonds and in loans upon real estate. Savings banks are very strictly regulated by statute in nearly all states, with the purpose of insuring the utmost safety to depositors. Thus, savings banks are generally prohibited by law from investing their funds in other than Federal, state, or municipal bonds and bonds of certain designated railroads, and in loans secured by first mortgages upon real estate, where the loan is not in excess of 60 per cent of the value of the property. Generally, deposits in savings banks are not subject to check or to withdrawal upon demand, although banks frequently waive the requirement that they receive a certain period of notice of an intended withdrawal.

Scrip. A form of promissory note or certificate of indebtedness, issued by a corporation to its stockholders in lieu of cash dividend payments. A corporation will resort to the use of scrip dividends when, although the profits of the company are such as to warrant some return being made to the stockholders upon their holdings in the company, the amount of actual cash on hand is not enough to permit immediate payment of cash to the stockholders.

Second Mortgage. A mortgage upon property which is already subject to a prior or first mortgage. Mortgages are called first, second, third, or fourth mortgages, according to the order in which they have been placed upon the property, and they are entitled to payment out of the property in order of their priority. Thus, if a second mortgage is foreclosed on default in the payment of interest or principal, the property can be sold only subject to the first mortgage. In other words, only the equity of the owner above the first mortgage can be relied upon to pay the amount of the second mortgage. In the event that the interest or principal due upon the first mortgage is not paid when due, the first mortgage may be foreclosed, and, in that event, the amount of the first mortgage must be paid out of the proceeds before any sum will be paid to the holders of the second or subsequent mortgages. If, after payment of the amount of the first mortgage and the expenses of the foreclosure sale, there is any residue, this will be paid to the second and subsequent mortgagees or lienors, in order of their priority.

Secured Creditor. A creditor who has security or collateral, in the form of personal or real property, for a sum due him from a debtor.

Securities. Stocks, bonds, and other evidences of long-term indebtedness or of ownership in a corporation.

Seigniorage. A profit-yielding charge made by a government for coining bullion into money.

Sellers' Option. A contract entered into in a stock or commodity exchange, whereby the seller is given the option of delivering at any time during a specified period upon one day's notice to the buyer. Under New York Stock Exchange rules, the period of a sellers' option cannot be less than four days nor longer than sixty days. "Sellers' option four" or "sellers' option ten" designates the period during which delivery may be made. See *Bids and Offers*, *Buyer's Option*.

Selling Short. Selling for "future delivery." One who sells short makes an agreement whereby he agrees to deliver at a future time, a stock or commodity which he does not possess at the time he enters into the contract to deliver, with the expectation that he will be able to purchase the stock or commodity, before delivery is due, at a lower price than he sold for. One who habitually sells short is called a "bear." See *Bear*.

Sight Draft. An order due and payable upon presentation to the person upon whom it is drawn. The ordinary bank check is, in effect, a sight draft. See *Draft*.

Silent Partner. One who has money invested in the business of a partnership and shares in its profits and losses, but whose interest in the business is not known to the general public. A silent partner is usually liable without limit for all of the debts of the partnership but only for those incurred while he maintained his interest in the business. He may, however, retire from the partnership at any time without giving notice to the public. See *Limited Partnership*.

Silver Certificate. Prior to the summer of 1968, this was paper currency issued by the government of the United States as a substitute for, and representative of, silver dollars deposited with the United States treasury.

Simple Interest. Interest computed on the principal only. Simple interest is to be distinguished from compound interest. In the latter, at regular intervals, interest due or accrued is added to the principal, and interest is computed thereafter upon the principal plus the interest so credited.

Single Standard. A phrase used to describe a monometallic monetary system in which one metal is used as the sole standard of value. Formerly, nearly all countries had a bimetallic system, or double standard, in which both silver and gold were freely coined at a certain ratio. Values were then determined in terms of either silver or gold. England was the first country formally to adopt the single gold standard, the act accomplishing this reform having been passed in 1816. The single gold standard was formally adopted by the United States in 1900.

Sinking Fund. A fund created by setting aside periodically, out of earnings or revenue, sums with which to pay bonds or other long-term obligations when they mature. A sinking fund may be created also for the purpose of replacing worn-out machinery or other capital assets. See *Amortization*.

SDR (Special Drawing Rights). Reserve assets created in the form of book entries by the International Monetary Fund and divided among member countries in proportion to their present IMF quotas. Within limits, each member country is required to accept SDR balances in exchange for convertible currency, from other countries offering them in the settlement of balance of payments obligations. In general, the SDR's may be used by national governments in the same ways as gold and other international reserve items are used.

Specie. Coined money.

Spot. A term used in quotations on commodity exchanges to indicate that the price is for immediate delivery and cash payment.

Standard Weight and Fineness. A phrase referring to the weight and purity of the metal in a monetary unit established by law. Thus, the gold dollar, existing since 1934 only in the form of bullion, has a standard weight of $15^5/_7$ grains, $^9/_{10}$ fine, that is, $^9/_{10}$ pure gold and $^1/_{10}$ copper alloy, or $13^5/_7$ grains of pure gold.

State Banks. Banks organized under the laws of a particular state and subject to state regulation.

Sterling. Abbreviation for the pound sterling, the unit of account of the English monetary system. For nearly a century the pound sterling at par was equivalent to $4.86. Its par is now $2.40.

Sterling Exchange. British money or bills of exchange payable in British money.

Stock. The capital stock of a corporation represents the amount invested by stockholders in the business of a corporation. From the point of view of the law, the capital so invested represents a fund to which creditors may look for payment of debts incurred by the corporation.

The capital stock of a corporation is usually divided into a number of shares which are held by the various stockholders of the company. These shares, evidenced by certificates of stock, represent the proportionate interest which each stockholder has in the corporation.

Stock Certificate. A printed or engraved certificate issued as an evidence of ownership of stock in a corporation. This certificate must be signed by authorized officials of the company; sometimes also by a "registrar of transfers."

Stock certificates may be transferred by endorsement upon the reverse side of the certificate, or by a separate instrument of transfer. The transfer, however, vests no rights in the one to whom the transfer is made, as against the corporation, until a record of the transfer has been made on the books of the corporation.

Under these statutes, if a certificate is endorsed in blank by the holder of record, it becomes similar to a negotiable instrument, the ownership of which can be transferred by mere delivery from one person to another. Under the Uniform Stock Transfer act, which has been adopted in a majority of states, one who, in good faith, purchases a certificate which bears a valid endorsement may obtain a good title even though the certificates have been stolen from, or lost by, the true owner.

Stock Dividend. Nominally, a distribution of surplus or earnings to stockholders, in the form of additional stock, rather than in the form of cash. The use of the term distribution, in connection with stock dividends, is, however, misleading. For, in a stock dividend no property is turned over by the corporation to its stockholders. The stockholders merely receive additional evidences of their ownership or interest in the company. Thus, if a stock dividend of 100 per cent has been declared and made by a corporation, each stockholder merely holds two shares of stock where he formerly held one. The net assets of the company remain unchanged, and the proportionate interest of each stockholder in the net assets of the company remains the same. His interest in the company, however, is evidenced by a greater number of shares of stock.

Where the stock has a par value, a stock dividend operates to convert surplus on the books of the company into capital stock.

Stop-loss Order. An order left by a customer with his broker directing the broker to sell stock owned by the customer in the event of a fall in the price of the stock below a certain point. The object of such an order is to check further loss where there appears a definite tendency to a decline in the price of the stock.

Where a stock or commodity has been sold short by the customer, an order would be placed with the broker to buy as soon as the price had risen to a definite point, in order to avoid greater losses, which would be incurred if the customer were compelled to cover at a still higher price.

Stop Payment. An order by a customer to a bank, directing it to refuse payment of a check or other instrument drawn by the customer upon the bank, or made payable at the bank.

A bank owes no obligation to the holder of a check drawn upon the bank by a customer, in the absence of a certification of the check by the bank. The bank may, therefore, with entire impunity, refuse payment of a check upon which the drawer has stopped payment. If the check, however, has been transferred by the payee or any other holder to a bona fide purchaser, either by endorsement or, if payable to bearer, by delivery, then the drawer of the check may be held liable to such a transferee for the amount of the check. No claim, however, can be made against the bank by any holder or transferee of the instrument.

Subpœna. A writ issued by a court of law commanding a person to appear on a certain day and at a place designated under a penalty for nonappearance or default.

Subpœna Duces Tecum (*sŭb-pē'nȧ dū'sēz tē'kŭm*). A court order in an action, directing a witness to bring with him any books, documents, or other papers in his possession or control which may or can be used as evidence. Such an order must describe with reasonable clearness what is wanted.

Supplementary Proceedings. A statutory remedy brought against a judgment debtor in aid of execution, for the purpose of locating and setting apart property of his to be applied in satisfaction of the judgment.

Surplus. The net worth of a firm or corporation, above its capital or capital stock. The term nominally includes both earnings from business operations and increases in the value of capital assets.

Tare. The difference between the gross and the net weight of an article in a container or vehicle. The gross weight of a barrel of flour is the total weight, including the container. The net weight is the weight of the flour itself. The difference between the gross and the net weight is the "tare."

Teller. A paying teller is an officer of a bank who pays out cash over the counter upon checks and other instruments made payable at the bank.

A receiving teller is a bank officer who receives and counts sums deposited with the bank, giving receipts for the funds deposited.

Ticker. An instrument, operated by telegraph, which automatically types messages transmitted from a central station. The instrument is used in brokers' offices, primarily for receiving prompt information with regard to stock transactions.

Time Deposit. A deposit of funds with a bank, under an agreement that the bank shall be entitled to the use of the funds for a definite period, or until a certain number of days have elapsed after notice has been given of an intention to withdraw the deposit.

Trade Acceptance. See *Acceptance*.

Trade Discount. A deduction, usually on a percentage basis, from the retail or "list" price of goods, allowed to a merchant by the manufacturer or jobber.

Trade-Mark. A special mark or symbol used for the purpose of identifying a certain product, or the products of a certain merchant or manufacturer. A trade-mark is protected under the law against use or appropriation by others than the one first to use the particular mark. The purpose of this protection given by the law is chiefly to prevent fraud upon the public.

Trade-marks may be registered at the United States patent office. Such registration does not add to the rights already possessed, without registry, by the owner of a trade-mark. Registration, however, provides conclusive evidence of a time since which the trade-mark has been used, and may prove of considerable value in the event of any litigation respecting the particular trade-mark.

Transfer Agent. Custodian of the stock book of a corporation, whose duty is to record transfers of stock and to issue new stock certificates in place of the surrendered certificates.

Transfer in Blank. Normally, stock is transferred by delivery, accompanied by an endorsement upon the reverse side of the stock certificate, made by the one in whose name the certificate has been issued. Where the name of the person to whom the stock is transferred is left blank, the stock certificate is said to be endorsed "in blank," and may then be transferred from one person to another by mere delivery, without further endorsement.

The stock is not effectually transferred, as against the corporation, however, until an entry of the change of ownership has been made upon the books of the corporation. And all rights of participation in benefits accruing to stockholders, including the right to dividends and the right to vote at stockholders' meetings, are determined by the record of stock ownership kept by the corporation.

Treasury Certificates. Short-term obligations bearing interest, issued by the United States government.

Treasury Notes. Certain paper currency issued by the United States government at intervals beginning in 1862 and now mostly retired. Today the term is used mainly to denote an intermediate credit instrument issued and sold by the United States Treasury.

Trust Companies. Corporations organized under state and federal laws, usually with powers to carry on a general commercial banking business and to act in various fiduciary capacities. These fiduciary capacities include acting as an executor under a will; administrator of the estate of a deceased person; trustee under a will, a deed of trust, or a mortgage indenture; guardian of the estate of an infant; committee of the estate of an incompetent; registrar and transfer agent of a corporation; and fiscal agent for a person, a corporation, or a municipality.

Trustee. One to whom property or rights are transferred, to be administered for the benefit of a certain person or group of persons known as the beneficiaries of the trust, or the *cestuis que trustent.*

A trustee under a will or a deed of trust is usually given the custody of property or securities, for the purpose of collecting and distributing the income for a designated period—during the minority of an infant or during the life of the beneficiary—the principal to be preserved intact by the trustee and distributed to certain persons at the termination of the trust.

A trustee under a corporate mortgage is appointed to safeguard the interests of numerous bondholders scattered throughout the country. It is the duty of such a trustee to see that the corporation which has given the mortgage does nothing to lessen the value of the property which forms the security for the bonds issued.

Underwriting. An agreement to share in the risk of a proposed venture or undertaking. Before the rise of the large insurance corporation, it was customary for a group of capitalists to underwrite a policy of fire, marine, or other insurance, each underwriter, or person who subscribed his name to the agreement, undertaking to pay a definite proportion of the loss.

The term is now frequently applied to an agreement by private banking houses, or by other dealers in securities, to provide a market for a proposed issue of bonds or other securities. Such an underwriting agreement normally contains a promise by the underwriters that they will dispose of a certain proportion of the securities to the general public on or before a certain date, and, if all of the securities are not taken up by the general public, that the underwriter will himself purchase the remainder. Where the proposed issue is large, a number of private banking houses form a "syndicate" and together underwrite the issue. They then proceed to use their joint efforts to dispose of the stock to the public. A generous commission is usually paid to the underwriters for the service rendered.

Unearned Increment. The increase in the value of land, resulting from an increase in population or from any other cause not traceable to the expenditures or efforts of the individual owner.

United States Notes. Paper money of the United States, originally issued under the act of February 25, 1862. This currency was merely a promise by the government to pay the bearer, on demand, the face amount of the note in gold. In fact, however, the notes were not redeemable until 1879, when specie payments were resumed by the government. These notes, when issued, were expressly made legal tender for all debts, and were received in payment for all public dues except customs and excise taxes. By reason of their legal-tender quality, they were popularly called "legal tenders." They were also called "greenbacks," from the color of the reverse side of the notes. Some of these notes still circulate, having been replaced when worn out as required by special and long-standing legislation.

Unlisted Securities. Stocks and bonds not listed upon the recognized stock exchanges. Frequently the term is applied to any security not listed upon the New York stock exchange. See *Listed.*

Upset Price. The price below which a security or a commodity will not be offered: as, for example, by an auctioneer at a public sale.

Voucher. A receipt, evidencing a payment of money, together with a statement of the items for which the payment was made.

Wall Street. Name popularly given to the financial district of New York City, of which Wall street itself forms the center.

Warehouse Receipt. A receipt issued by a warehouseman, evidencing a deposit of certain goods with him. The warehouse receipt may be negotiable; that is, it may run to the bearer or to the order of the depositor of the goods, in which case it may be transferred by delivery or by endorsement from one holder to another. When a negotiable receipt has been issued, the goods will be surrendered by the warehouseman only upon a surrender of the receipt. For many purposes, such a receipt may then be dealt with in commerce as though it were the goods themselves, since the possession of the receipt gives control over the goods. Thus, banks frequently make loans upon these negotiable receipts as collateral, and the goods themselves are bought and sold in the market by mere negotiation or delivery of the receipt.

The Uniform Warehouse Receipt act, which has been passed in most states, is designed to further the commercial dealing in negotiable warehouse receipts as the representatives of the goods. This act, however, differs from that governing negotiation of "order bills of lading," in that a pledgee or purchaser of a warehouse receipt from or through a thief or a finder gets no title to the receipt or to the goods represented by it.

Warrant. In law, a warrant is a precept, or writ, issued by a court, authorizing a public official to do some special act; as, for example, to make an arrest. In business, a warrant is a written authorization proceeding from a competent source to a proper individual, conveying power to receive either money, its equivalent, or other personal property, or to pay money to one who is entitled to receive it. In England, the term is in general use to designate a receipt for goods which have been deposited in a warehouse, showing the date of entry, the person or persons to whom the goods are deliverable, the date upon which rent commences, and all other details necessary to identify the particular parcels for which the warrant is issued. The warrant is transferable by endorsement.

Warrant, Bench. A warrant issued by a court "in bench," authorizing an officer to arrest and bring before the court persons who are in contempt, or who have disobeyed a court order, or who have been indicted. The name distinguishes this writ from warrants issued by inferior judicial officials.

Warrant, Search. A written authority of state, issued by a court, directing some judicial officer to examine a named place for articles alleged to be unlawfully concealed there. The articles most commonly searched for are stolen and embezzled goods, counterfeit money, gambling implements, and other unlawful possessions.

Wash Sales. Fictitious sales made for the purpose of creating an artificial market price for a stock or commodity. Wash sales on national exchanges are now forbidden under penalty of law. See *Pool, Bear.*

Watered Stock. Where stock has been issued, having a total nominal or par value in excess of the capital actually invested in a corporation, the stock is said to be "water." And the amount of stock issued in excess of the actual assets held by the corporation is called "water." The result of watering stock is to mislead creditors of the corporation and the general public who form a market for the sale of the stock of the corporation.

When, As, and If Issued. Frequently, when a corporation plans to issue stock or bonds to the public, a campaign for the sale of the securities will be undertaken before the necessary legal steps involved in creating the new issue of securities have been completed. The corporation, or the banking house through which it has arranged to dispose of the securities, in order to safeguard itself against the possibility of some legal obstacle preventing the proposed issue, will then offer the securities to the public "when, as, and if issued." In the event that, for any reason, the securities are not issued, the corporation or the banking house through which it operates will then not be liable to those who have given orders for the proposed stock or bonds.

Will. A formal, written instrument executed pursuant to provisions prescribed by law, providing for the distribution of the property of the testator—the person making the will—at his death. Normally, a will may be revoked or amended by the testator at any time before his death.

Under the laws of most states, a will is invalid unless it is subscribed by the testator and declared by him to be his last will and testament, in the presence of two witnesses who, at his request, also subscribe their names to the will in the presence of the testator and in the presence of each other. In some states, three witnesses are necessary. Under exceptional circumstances, as in the case of a soldier dying on the field of battle, the ordinary formalities necessary to render a will valid may be omitted.

Without Recourse. One who endorses a note, check, or other commercial instrument is usually liable to subsequent holders of the instrument, in the event of the nonpayment of the instrument at maturity, if proper presentation and protest of the instrument is made. If one desires to relieve himself from this liability, he must prefix or append to his endorsement the words "without recourse." His endorsement then merely operates to transfer such title as he has to the instrument, and carries with it no implied promise to pay the instrument in the event that the maker does not pay it at maturity.

AGRICULTURE

The story of modern agriculture is one of man's inventive mind, his observation, experimentation, innovation, and adaptation. The annual abundance created by modern agriculture is often taken for granted in Western society. It should not be, as it is a triumph only recently achieved by man in managing nature's elements. Furthermore, world population pressures are constantly challenging man's ingenuity in the food production-consumption cycle.

Today the skilled commercial farm operator in the United States has the resources and ability to produce enough food for himself and at least 50 others. Only five percent of the nation's people live on farms and ranches, yet they produce ample food and fiber for themselves and the other 95 per cent of the population. In addition, there is enough left to export to other areas of the world. American consumers are the primary beneficiaries of this agricultural production-marketing miracle, since they need spend only about 17 per cent of their disposable income for food, the lowest in man's experience.

The background of modern agriculture, like that of the human race itself, begins in prehistoric times. Nevertheless, to a certain limited extent, it can be told. Through the discovery of various tools used by the ancient races, scientists have been able to trace the development of man, from the stone ages, through the periods when bronze implements were substituted for stone and when iron displaced bronze. By a somewhat similar method, the story of prehistoric agriculture has been pieced together.

Emerson has written that "the first farmer was the first man," but, according to archeological records, the earlier man knew nothing of agriculture. He was a hunter who was probably forced by hunger to eat wild fruits, grasses, and roots, when he could capture no game. Such was the condition of the men of the Paleolithic or Old Stone Age. They were hunters and fishers who had fire and probably the bow and arrow, but no domestic animals, with the possible exception of the dog.

Prehistoric Agriculture. Sometime during the Paleolithic period, possibly some 25,000 to 50,000 years ago, man acquired his first ideas of planting the edible seeds from wild plants, thus producing crops of grain. The men of the next period, the Neolithic or New Stone age, not only polished their stone tools and kept dogs, sheep, goats, and oxen, but also learned to raise wheat, barley, and millet. Where wheat was first found is an unsolved question that has provoked much discussion. Many scientists now believe that it originated as a wild grass, somewhere in the region of the eastern Mediterranean. The grain was gradually improved and ultimately carried to all parts of the earth. It did not reach the American continent until after Columbus' voyage, nor was it known in Australia until 1788.

Although Neolithic man had learned some of the benefits of keeping domestic animals and of planting grain, he nevertheless depended on hunting and fishing for a large part of his food and clothing. But the hunters slowly changed their modes of living to those of shepherds or farmers. Some tribes increased their herds of cattle and sheep, and adopted the nomadic life necessary to guarding their animals and leading them to new pastures. Others found that in certain rich valleys food was most easily obtained by erecting permanent dwellings and devoting their energies to tilling the soil. From farming settlements of this kind, made in Mesopotamia and Egypt, came the first civilized communities of which any record can be found.

Ancient Agriculture. Five thousand years before Christ, both in the valley of the Nile and in the rich country between the Tigris and Euphrates rivers, crops of bearded wheat, six-rowed barley, millet, flax, and durra, which is a variety of sorghum, were raised by tillage and irrigation. The earliest Egyptians seem to have known onions, garlic, radishes, beans, chick-peas, lentils, and the castor bean. Cattle grazed on the grass-covered range; poultry and swine were well known; sheep were raised for their wool, goats for their milk, and camels and donkeys for burden-bearers. Horses were not introduced until 1900 B. C., when the nomadic shepherd kings from Asia conquered the country. For fruit the Egyptians had watermelons, grapes, olives, figs, pomegranates, and dates.

On coming further down the scale of time, we find that the Greeks raised wheat and barley as their chief cereals, and that they had hemp as well as flax. They had mules and commonly kept swarms of bees. To the vegetables known to the Egyptians, the Greeks added beets, cabbage, lettuce, turnips, kidney beans, and garden peas. Naturally they did not have the date palm, but they had the almond tree, and also apples, quinces, cherries, pears, and plums. The Greeks are said to have been the first to apply manure to the fields, and to plow under a growth of green lupine in order to enrich the land.

The Romans gave much attention to agriculture, and fortunately left many accurate records telling of their crops and the methods used to produce them. They carefully plowed and harrowed their fields and were acquainted with methods of drainage. Oxen were used as work animals on the Roman farms, and mules as beasts of burden. Much attention was given to breeding fine horses, sheep, swine, cattle, many kinds of poultry, and even hares, fish, snails, and dormice. Oats and rye, celery, peaches, apricots, and melons were added to the list of products known to the older nations, and alfalfa was raised for fodder. Milk was obtained chiefly from sheep and goats, and was made into cheese by curdling with lamb's or kid's rennet. As the Romans came into possession of great tracts of land taken from vanquished nations, they developed an extensive system of working large foreign estates by means of slaves. The popular demand for the division among the common people of these great holdings of state-owned land was resisted by the aristocratic possessors, and this dispute led to one of the greatest internal struggles in the history of Rome.

Medieval Period. During the dark ages that followed the conquest of Rome, agriculture made very little progress, for the conquerors were a war-like people who had reached a stage of development not far above the pastoral. There were, however, two agencies that carried on agricultural work with great activity. In Spain, the Moors, or Arabs, who were also great engineers, brought in rice, cotton, and sugar, and when necessary used irrigation to bring the land to a high degree of cultivation. At the same time, in western Europe, the members of many religious brotherhoods studied the manuscripts left by the Romans, and worked with great energy to improve on the crops and the methods of producing them. Much later, toward the end of the Middle Ages, the people of the Low Countries—the Netherlands and Belgium—gained a great reputation as farmers and dairymen, and northern Italy was so intensively cultivated during the 13th and 14th centuries that it not only supported a large population, but it also exported much grain.

Contemporary with the development in Europe, the Chinese, and the Incas of Peru had reached a very high state of agricultural production. Both nations understood the use of fertilizers and of methods of irrigation. The important crops of the Chinese have for centuries been wheat, rice, tea, cotton, and silk for which large amounts of mulberry leaves are required. The ancient Peruvians terraced the hillsides in order to make use of all available ground. Their principal crops were corn, potatoes, and cotton; much coca also was grown for the alkaloid contained in its leaves. The chief beast of burden was the llama, and the alpaca was raised for its hair. Neither of these nations has made any permanent impression on modern methods of agriculture. The civilization of the Incas is extinct, and the typical Chinese farmer of today still prefers the methods of cultivation used by his ancestors of one or two thousand years ago.

Modern Improvements. The two greatest innovations in modern agriculture may be said to be the proper rotation of crops and a chemical knowledge of fertilizers. The value of the first was demonstrated when Lord Townsend established in England the Norfolk system, consisting of the annual rotation of wheat, turnips, barley, and clover. This permitted half of the land to be used for grain, while the other half produced fodder with which to fatten cattle. Under this system, the land was neither exhausted by the continuous growth of one crop nor unproductive from lying fallow, cattle-raising was promoted, and much of the product of the land was returned to it as manure.

A knowledge of the chemical composition of plants and of soils came at first from the work of Liebig in the beginning of the 19th century. This led to the scientific use of artificial fertilizers containing potash, phosphorus, and nitrogen. Breeding experiments have led to better types of all farm animals, and, by means of modern methods of transportation, the most satisfactory breeds of plants or animals can be quickly sent to any part of the world.

Investigations in agricultural science are promoted by the governments of practically every civilized nation, with the result that modern agricultural practice is based on knowledge rather than on the Chinese system of adherence to the ways of their ancestors.

AGRICULTURE IN THE UNITED STATES

The first farmers of North America were the Indians, who, long before the coming of the white race, were accustomed to raising beans, pumpkins, squashes, peppers, onions, sunflowers, tobacco, and, most important of all, maize or Indian corn. This was most fortunate for those pioneers who arrived in 1607 and 1620, for, without the corn which they obtained from the Indians, the settlers both of Jamestown and of Plymouth would have starved during their first winters in America.

First Experiments. The early history of agriculture after the arrival of the settlers is one of adaptation and adjustment. The summers at Jamestown were so warm that it seemed that semitropical vegetation should be successful. Consequently, pineapples, French grapes, olives, figs, ginger, and sugar cane were planted, and attempts were made to raise silkworms. Naturally these undertakings, begun in ignorance of the colder winters, were failures. Furthermore, because of the high summer temperature and very rich earth, the wheat plant grew luxuriantly but failed to produce much grain. Tobacco was an early success and proved so profitable that all other crops were neglected until laws were made requiring each planter to raise a certain amount of corn and other food products.

In New England, a friendly Indian named Squanto taught the newcomers to plant corn. The earth was exposed to the sun by girdling the trees and burning the branches and underbrush. Four grains of corn and two beans were then dropped at four-foot intervals into openings made with an ax or hoe. If possible, a fish was placed in each hill for fertilizer. Later, when the plants were high enough, the ground was piled up around the base of the stalks. White potatoes, which are native to South America, were brought from England by the settlers and were not previously cultivated by the Indians, although the natives in the South were well acquainted with the sweet potato. Cattle and hogs, both in the North and in the South, were allowed to run wild in the woods, where they developed rapidly and often formed large herds.

Experiments gradually taught what crops were most satisfactory and profitable in each section. Buckwheat was introduced into New York by the Dutch in 1625. Apples were planted on Governors Island in Boston Harbor, and the first fruit was picked October 10, 1639. Cherries were brought first to Virginia, in 1641. Rice, which in 1647 had been a failure in Virginia, was tried at Charleston in 1693, and, together with indigo, soon became the principal crop of South Carolina and Georgia. Long fiber or sea-island cotton was introduced into these states in 1786, and, by this time, the best crops were so well established that, except for sorghum and alfalfa, nothing new was introduced during the next century.

Regional Differences. Agriculture as practiced in the southern colonies soon became differentiated from that in the North.

In New England the growing season was shorter. Land was harder to prepare for use because of its stony character and the extensive forests. Help was hard to obtain and the climate did not lend itself to any one highly profitable crop. Consequently each family raised most of the products necessary for its subsistence—grain, vegetables, fruit, cattle, swine, and other farm animals. Lumbering, fishing, and shipbuilding sometimes provided auxiliary sources of income.

In the South, however, the land was richer and the growing season was long and warm. Rice, indigo, sugar cane, and cotton proved highly profitable, especially when cultivated on a large scale with the help of cheap labor. This was supplied by indentured servants, convicts, and, later, by Negro slaves. The typical farm, or plantation, was about 5000 acres, about 50 times the size of the Northern farm. It was operated as a source of profit for the owner rather than as a means of family subsistence.

Cotton. The use of the newly invented spinning jenny and power loom between 1767 and 1790 produced a large demand in England for American cotton. In 1793 the difficult problem of separating the cotton fiber from the seeds was solved by Eli Whitney's invention of the cotton gin. The result was a vast increase in cotton production, exports rising 200-fold between 1791 and 1803. Its cultivation, formerly confined to Georgia and North Carolina, had, by 1815, spread north to Virginia and west and south to Alabama and Mississippi. As the soil became exhausted under this one-crop agriculture, new land was brought under cultivation in Louisiana, Texas, and Oklahoma. The United States instantly assumed and maintained a position of dominance in the world's cotton production. The cotton crop was admirably adapted to Negro labor, a fact which made Negro slavery the outstanding feature of Southern economic life until the Civil War.

Wheat and Corn. While the South was devoting all its energies to the production of cotton, settlers were moving west across the northern and central states. By its policy in granting small homesteads, the government encouraged family-sized holdings. Labor was difficult to obtain, since few men cared to work for others when they could take up new government land at a very small cost and work for themselves. The farmers produced principally corn, wheat, and other grains, besides potatoes, fruit, and live stock. Much of the grain was fed to live stock, which commanded a ready and profitable market. Excess production was sold in the South.

In the meantime the cultivation of corn in the region lying roughly between the winter wheat area and the spring wheat area increased rapidly. This region became known as the corn belt. It included chiefly western Ohio, Indiana, Illinois, Iowa, Missouri, eastern Nebraska, and southeastern South Dakota. Some corn was exported, but principally it was used to fatten hogs. The United States thus became the largest producer of corn and of hogs.

Farm Animals. Cattle and hogs were first brought to Florida from the West Indies in 1638; to Newfoundland by the Portuguese in 1553; and to Canada and Virginia in 1608. Although horses were taken to Florida in 1527, all of these were killed, and it was not until much later that others were imported. In the early days the sheep were small, with a light coat of coarse wool, the hogs were long-legged and thin, the cattle were light and wiry, and the cows produced only enough milk for their calves. Gradually, however, fine animals were imported from Europe, and, from these, careful breeding produced the splendid present-day herds of dairy and beef cattle, the large meat-type hogs, sheep that yield from 15 to 30 pounds of wool at a clip, and flocks of hens that average approximately 240 eggs per year instead of one or two dozen.

In the second half of the 19th century the western plains supported huge herds of cattle on unfenced ranges. As the area of cultivation was extended, the ranges were fenced off, but the amount and the quality of beef production increased as a result of better breeding. The fattening of cattle for market, like the raising of hogs, became especially important in the corn-growing regions because, by feeding the grain to animals, a higher-priced product was obtained. For the same reason the combination of grain raising and milk production was profitable near the large cities.

Farm Machinery. In the first half of the 19th century, farming was carried on almost entirely by hand labor with the help of a few simple tools, much as it had been since the dawn of history. From 1830 to 1860, horse-drawn implements were made available in considerable variety, but only after the Civil War was there a sweeping adoption of them. Seeders and cultivators replaced the hoe; mowing machines, the scythe; reapers, the cradle; threshing machines, the flail. Among scores of other important farm machines are cream separators and milkers, corn cutters, hay loaders, and manure spreaders. Illustrative of the economic and human value of such devices is a statement issued by the United States Department of Agriculture, that the human labor required to produce a bushel of grain had decreased on the average from 3 hours and 30 minutes in 1830 to 10 minutes in 1896, the cost of this labor declining from 17¾ cents to 3⅓ cents. By the 1960's the application of new technology to mechanization had reduced the average time to produce a bushel of corn to 4.8 minutes and wheat to 6.6 minutes.

Power Farming. In 1870, practically the entire non-human power on farms was in the form of farm animals. Even in 1900 they represented about 80 per cent of the available power, the remainder being steam engines, gas engines, and windmills. By 1919, however, the number of horses and mules on farms reached its maximum, 26,436,000, and thereafter declined with increasing rapidity. By 1923, mechanical power exceeded animal power, the principal forms being stationary gas engines, gasoline tractors and trucks, steam engines, electricity, and windmills. In the years from 1920 to 1940, the number of tractors on farms increased over 14-fold, and had increased to 4,263,000 by 1975. The total power available on the farm is approximately equal to that at the service of the combined factories, public utility plants, and mines of the country—over 60 million horse power.

The use of the tractor has made it possible for individuals to work much larger areas than formerly. Plowing and cultivating can be done much more quickly and at the most suitable time. Harvesting grain with the combine, which cuts and threshes or husks in a single operation, greatly reduces the cost of this process when a sufficiently large area of suitable land is worked. There were approximately 678,000 such combines on United States farms in 1975. Even in the raising of cotton, mechanical methods have made rapid headway, particularly in western Texas and Oklahoma. The tractor-drawn plow, the "sled", which strips the cotton bolls, opened and unopened, at a single operation, and the cotton cleaner, used in connection with the gin, radically reduce the unit cost of production.

Automobiles and trucks effect great saving of time in marketing and in moving about the farm, making possible the cultivation of more land at a greater distance from shipping points. Electricity has been made increasingly available to farms, so that many minor operations can be performed through electric motors, particularly dairying and household operations, by which much of the former domestic drudgery is eliminated.

Economic Change. The pressure of demand, the scarcity of labor, and the attractive prices for farm products occasioned by World Wars I and II hastened the adoption of labor-saving devices and the use of power machinery on the farm. The result after World War I was a world-wide surplus, despite Russia's withdrawal from the export market, and prices fell rapidly. War-impoverished importing nations lacked purchasing power and the increasing replacement of the horse by the automobile cut down the market for hay and oats. The productive capacity of Canada, Argentina, Australia, and certain other countries had increased at even faster rate than that of the United States. The result was a market in which only the most efficient producers could make a profit. Road and other improvements increased taxes while farm income decreased. Small-scale farmers were forced, in large numbers, to abandon their farms. The earlier scale of land values was completely upset, with the resulting failure of many banks.

Between 1920 and 1930 there was a net decrease of farm population in the United States of about 3 millions, which was only slightly increased later. Cultivated land also decreased by more than 13,000,000 acres. Yet, in the same period the total crop production increased about 20 per cent and the productivity of each worker increased by about 30 per cent. This situation indicated, after World War I, heightened efficiency of agriculture, but the distress caused by the process made the relief of agriculture a political question of importance.

Today American farms are outstanding in producing food to feed, not only Americans, but people more or less dependent upon the United States for subsistence since World War II.

International Trade. The typical farm in the U.S. has increased average production rapidly in the past several decades, and has an absolute production advantage in total resources used. Specialization and trade, in the absence of political or other barriers, are based on the principle of comparative advantage. That is, each nation produces those products for which it has the greatest comparative advantage, and trades its surplus to other nations that can only produce at a comparative disadvantage.

Thus, the U.S. was a net exporter of agricultural products in 1975, exporting some $21.6 billion worth, while importing $9.6 billion. The primary U.S. agricultural exports are oilseeds and products, wheat and flour, feed grains, animal and animal products, and tobacco, in that order. Principal imports are coffee, meats and poultry, sugar, rubber, and vegetables. Major receivers of American agricultural products in 1975 were Japan, Canada, the Netherlands, and West Germany. The principal sources of American agricultural imports in that year were Brazil, Mexico, Australia, and the Philippines.

An estimated 17 per cent of all U.S. farm products are sold to other countries. For some commodities, such as wheat and soybeans, the percentage may be as high as 50 or 60 per cent. International trade in agricultural commodities produced in the U.S. is important to the American economy and to world consumers.

POPULATION: TOTAL AND FARM, UNITED STATES, 1917-1975

Year	Total Population 000 omitted	Farm Population: Number 000 omitted	Farm Population: % of total	Year	Total Population 000 omitted	Farm Population: Number 000 omitted	Farm Population: % of Total
1917	103,052	32,326	31.4	1940	131,820	29,047	22.0
1918	104,266	31,741	30.4	1941	133,076	28,786	21.6
1919	104,935	30,886	29.4	1942	134,483	27,895	20.7
1920	106,089	31,556	29.7	1943	136,278	25,757	18.9
1921	108,023	31,638	29.3	1944	138,016	24,647	17.9
1922	109,676	31,558	28.8	1945	139,584	24,342	17.4
1923	111,476	30,873	27.7	1946	141,032	25,543	18.1
1924	113,573	30,493	26.8	1947	143,478	26,147	18.2
1925	115,402	30,440	26.4	1948	146,044	25,093	17.2
1926	117,007	30,162	25.8	1949	148,562	25,134	16.9
1927	118,628	29,647	25.0	1950	151,132	24,335	16.1
1928	120,135	29,599	24.6	1951	153,699	23,276	15.1
1929	121,453	29,564	24.3	1952	155,761	24,283	15.6
1930	122,775	29,447	24.0	1953	158,313	22,679	14.3
1931	123,841	29,723	24.0	1954	161,191	21,890	13.5
1932	124,658	30,229	24.2	1955	164,303	22,158	13.4
1933	125,401	31,198	24.9	1956	167,261	22,257	13.3
1934	126,192	31,071	24.6	1957	170,293	20,396	11.9
1935	127,057	30,887	24.3	1958	173,260	20,827	12.0
1936	127,886	30,420	23.8	1959	177,131	21,172	12.0
1937	128,649	29,903	23.2	1960	179,323	13,475	11.4
1938	129,589	29,573	22.8	1969	201,921	10,307	5.1
1939	130,642	29,388	22.5	1974	211,523	9,264	4.4
				1975	213,135	8,864	4.2

RURAL POPULATION BY STATES, 1970*

State	Population	State	Population	State	Population
Alabama	1,432,224	Louisiana	1,235,156	Ohio	2,626,320
Alaska	154,870	Maine	487,891	Oklahoma	819,092
Arizona	362,036	Maryland	917,436	Oregon	688,681
Arkansas	962,430	Massachusetts	922,477	Pennsylvania	3,363,499
California	1,817,089	Michigan	2,321,310	Rhode Island	122,422
Colorado	473,948	Minnesota	1,277,663	South Carolina	1,366,018
Connecticut	686,657	Mississippi	1,230,270	South Dakota	368,879
Delaware	152,535	Missouri	1,398,818	Tennessee	1,618,380
Florida	1,321,306	Montana	323,733	Texas	2,275,784
Georgia	1,821,501	Nebraska	570,733	Utah	207,801
Hawaii	129,878	Nevada	93,402	Vermont	301,441
Idaho	327,133	New Hampshire	321,641	Virginia	1,713,653
Illinois	1,884,155	New Jersey	794,759	Washington	932,701
Indiana	1,821,609	New Mexico	315,420	West Virginia	1,064,746
Iowa	1,207,971	New York	2,633,254	Wisconsin	1,506,854
Kansas	779,625	North Carolina	2,796,891	Wyoming	131,305
Kentucky	1,534,653	North Dakota	344,319	Total	53,884,804

* Figures include persons living on farms or in places of less than 2500 population.
Source: Bureau of the Census

NUMBER, ACREAGE, AND VALUE OF FARMS BY STATES

State	Number of Farms (1,000)		All Land in Farms (thousands of acres)		Average Acreage per farm		Average Value per farm ($1000)	
	1959	1969	1959	1969	1959	1969	1959	1969
Alabama	116	72	16,543	13,654	143	188	13	38
Alaska	*	*	888	1,604	2,421	4,832	48	62
Arizona	7	6	40,203	38,203	5,558	6,486	270	452
Arkansas	95	60	16,459	15,695	173	260	19	68
California	99	78	36,888	35,722	372	459	131	218
Colorado	33	28	38,787	36,697	1,162	1,313	61	124
Connecticut	8	4	884	541	107	121	47	111
Delaware	5	4	763	674	146	182	35	91
Florida	45	36	15,237	14,032	338	394	74	140
Georgia	106	67	19,658	15,806	185	234	18	55
Hawaii	6	4	2,461	2,058	394	528	*	157
Idaho	34	25	15,232	14,417	452	566	51	100
Illinois	155	124	30,327	29,913	196	242	62	119
Indiana	128	101	18,613	17,573	145	173	38	70
Iowa	175	140	33,831	33,570	194	239	49	94
Kansas	104	86	50,153	49,390	481	574	48	91
Kentucky	151	125	17,031	15,968	113	128	15	32
Louisiana	74	42	10,347	9,789	139	232	24	74
Maine	17	8	3,082	1,760	178	221	25	63
Maryland	25	17	3,457	2,803	138	163	39	104
Massachusetts	11	6	1,142	701	102	123	32	69
Michigan	112	78	14,783	11,901	132	153	26	50
Minnesota	146	111	30,796	28,845	211	260	33	59
Mississippi	138	73	18,630	16,040	135	221	14	52
Missouri	169	137	33,155	32,420	197	237	22	53
Montana	29	25	64,081	62,918	2,213	2,522	77	150
Nebraska	90	72	47,756	45,834	528	634	47	98
Nevada	2	2	10,943	10,708	4,649	5,070	142	271
New Hampshire	7	3	1,124	613	172	211	18	50
New Jersey	15	8	1,379	1,036	89	122	46	133
New Mexico	16	12	46,293	46,792	2,908	4,020	68	168
New York	82	52	13,490	10,148	164	196	24	53
North Carolina	191	119	15,888	12,734	83	107	15	36
North Dakota	55	46	41,466	43,118	755	930	39	87
Ohio	140	111	18,507	17,111	132	154	33	61
Oklahoma	95	83	35,801	36,008	378	434	32	75
Oregon	43	29	21,236	18,018	499	620	44	93
Pennsylvania	100	63	11,862	8,901	119	142	22	53
Rhode Island	1	1	138	69	99	98	38	72
South Carolina	78	40	9,149	6,992	117	177	16	46
South Dakota	55	46	44,851	45,584	805	997	41	83
Tennessee	158	121	16,081	15,057	102	124	13	33
Texas	227	214	143,218	142,567	631	668	52	99
Utah	18	13	12,689	11,313	712	867	42	80
Vermont	12	7	2,945	1,916	243	279	20	62
Virginia	98	65	13,126	10,650	135	165	19	47
Washington	52	34	18,717	17,559	363	516	48	115
West Virginia	44	23	6,063	4,341	138	188	10	25
Wisconsin	131	99	21,156	18,109	161	183	21	42
Wyoming	10	9	36,200	35,476	3,715	4,014	79	164
Total	3,711	2,730	1,123,508	1,063,347	303	390	35	76

* Statistics not available.
Source: *Department of Commerce, Bureau of the Census*

LEADING U.S. AGRICULTURAL IMPORTS BY COMMODITY 1972 AND 1974

Commodity	1972 Million $	1974 Million $
Coffee	1,169.1	1,803.6
Meats and Poultry	1,096.2	1,794.0
Sugar	839.9	1,220.9
Rubber	202.5	483.4
Vegetables and Preparations	329.1	401.1
Oils and Fats	166.8	342.2
Cocoa Beans	169.9	288.8
Fruits and Preparations	168.0	228.8
Bananas	177.9	197.5
Tobacco	159.2	189.6

These commodities account for about 73 per cent of total agricultural imports.

Total Agricultural imports, 1974 (preliminary data), 9,551,930,000.

Total Imports—all commodities, 1974 (preliminary data), 82,494,219,000.

Source: *Agricultural Statistics 1975*, ERS, U.S. Department of Agriculture.

LEADING COUNTRIES BY VALUE OF AGRICULTURAL IMPORTS ENTERING THE U.S. IN 1972 AND 1974

Country	1972 Million $	1974 Million $
Brazil	617.3	820.4
Mexico	536.2	728.5
Australia	408.9	709.2
Philippines	376.1	573.3
Canada	321.6	544.0
New Zealand	222.3	396.0
Colombia	160.9	330.0
Dominican Rep.	195.6	380.7
Indonesia	122.0	316.8
Denmark	165.8	266.2

Source: *U.S. Foreign Agricultural Trade by Countries*, ERS, USDA, 1975.

U.S. AGRICULTURAL EXPORTS: MAJOR COUNTRIES OF DESTINATION

Country	Value of Total Exports (Million $)	Principal Product Exported
Japan	3,355.8	Feed grains
West Germany	1,540.7	Feed grains
Netherlands	1,473.2	Feed grains
Canada	1,194.8	Fruits and preparations
China, People's Rep. of	851.5	Wheat and flour
Italy	757.9	Wheat and flour
United Kingdom	683.6	Tobacco
Rep. of Korea	659.8	Feed grains
Spain	643.7	Feed grains
Mexico	610.3	Feed grains
Total	11,771.3	

Source: *U.S. Foreign Agricultural Trade by Countries, Fiscal Year ending June 30, 1974*, ERS, USDA.

U.S. AGRICULTURAL EXPORTS: VALUE UNDER SPECIFIED GOVERNMENT PROGRAMS AND COMMERCIAL SALES BY COMMODITY GROUPS[1]

Commodity	Under Government Programs[2] (Million $)	Commercial (Dollar) Sales[3] (Million $)	Total Exports (Million $)
Wheat	180.2	4,376.2	4,556.4
Corn	35.4	3,693.7	3,729.1
Rice, milled	323.4	428.9	752.3
Wheat flour	69.9	69.1	139.0
Tobacco, unmanufactured	30.0	783.6	813.6
Grain sorghum	67.2	565.3	632.5
Cotton	34.3	1,259.7	1,294.0
Hides and Skins	.2	460.3	460.5
Soybean oil	72.2	222.4	294.6
Soybeans	...	3,272.8	3,272.8
Others	126.3	5,251.4	5,377.7
Total	939.1	20,383.4	21,322.5

Source: *Agricultural Statistics 1975*, ERS, U.S. Department of Agriculture.

[1] Data for year ending June 30, 1974.

[2] Public Laws 83-480 (Agricultural Trade Development and Assistance Act) and 87-195 (Act for International Development).

[3] Includes commodities bought with Export-Import Bank loans and guarantees and credits extended by CCC; exports assisted by payments in cash or by sales from CCC stocks below domestic market price; and exports under barter contract for overseas procurement for U.S. agencies, which benefit the balance of payments and rely primarily on authority other than P.L. 480.

FARM TENANCY

Source: U. S. Bureau of the Census

Year	Farms Operated by Tenants	Total Farms	Tenancy as of % of total
1900	1,295,000	4,565,000	28.4
1910	2,355,000	6,362,000	37.
1920	2,455,000	6,448,000	38.1
1930	2,664,000	6,289,000	42.4
1940	2,361,000	6,097,000	38.7
1950	1,444,000	5,382,000	26.8
1964	539,921	3,157,867	17.1
1969	353,000	2,730,250	12.9

RETAIL FOOD PRICE SPREADS

Source: U. S. Department of Agriculture

Year	Retail Cost[1] ($)	Farm Value[2] ($)	Farmer's Share (%)
Average:			
1913–19	484	224	46
1925–29	588	241	41
1933	371	119	32
1937	486	199	41
1939	426	161	38
1945	615	324	53
1950	870	409	47
1953	949	421	44
1957	953	380	40
1960	991	383	39
1965	1,038	408	39
1967	1,080	414	38
1968	1,118	435	39
1969	1,173	477	41
1970	1,228	478	39
1971	1,250	480	38
1972	1,311	524	40
1973	1,537	701	46
1974	1,750	746	43

[1] Retail cost of average quantities purchased annually per household in 1960-61 by urban wage-earner and clerical-worker families and single workers. [2] Farm value of equivalent quantities sold by producers adjusted for value of by-products.

CIVILIAN CONSUMPTION OF PRINCIPAL FOODS
(in pounds per capita)
Source: *Agricultural Statistics 1975*, ERS, USDA

Foods	1959	1966	1974 (prel.)
Meat	146.6	151.4	165.0
Poultry	35.6	44.3	50.7
Fish	13.7	13.9	15.0
Eggs	44.7	39.7	36.4
Dairy Products including butter	393.0	371.0	343.0
Fats and oils excluding butter	41.7	47.2	51.3
Fruits, fresh	92.1	79.6	78.1
Fruits, processed	48.4	41.4	54.4
Vegetables, fresh	146.7	138.4	142.6
Vegetables, processed	50.4	56.1	64.3
Flour and other cereal products	148.0	143.0	138.0
Sugars and other sweeteners	107.7	113.0	121.5
Coffee, tea, cocoa	15.2	15.1	13.2
All foods, total	1,450.0	1,427.0	1,428.0

Agricultural Adjustment. The first governmental attack on the problem was an attempt to support prices of farm products. Tried out in 1929-33, it failed because of uncontrolled production.

The second attack was through the Agricultural Adjustment act of 1933. This law empowered the secretary of agriculture to pay producers for withholding a proportion of their normal acreage from production of certain basic crops. The law was declared unconstitutional by the Supreme Court in January 1936. This act was supplemented by the Agricultural Adjustment Act of 1938, which had the following principal features designed to provide an "ever normal granary":

Acreage allotments are made annually for growing these major crops—corn, wheat, cotton, rice, and tobacco. Farmers who consent to abide by the allotments and who observe specified soil-conserving practices obtain benefit payments based on various factors and preference in access to federal crop loan facilities. If any major crop is estimated to be above normal by a certain amount, marketing quotas are set which, if made effective, may not be exceeded by farmers without payment of a fine. Such quotas become effective only if approved in a referendum by at least two-thirds of the farmers affected. Wheat crops may be insured with the Federal Crop Insurance Corporation on payment of a premium either in cash or wheat. The secretary of agriculture is authorized to make so-called parity payments to producers of the major crops if funds are appropriated for the purpose.

Parity payments are payments designed to raise farm per capita income to the point at which it bears the same relation to non-farm per capita income as farm income bore to non-farm income in the period from August 1909 to July 1914.

The Agricultural Act of 1948 introduced the concept of a "flexible price support" feature in farm legislation. This allowed the price of peanuts, corn, wheat, cotton, rice, and tobacco to vary, depending on the amount of the commodity that was produced. The range of flexibility was set at 60 to 90 per cent. If the supply of the crop were 70 per cent (or below normal), the support level would be the maximum 90 per cent of parity. The 1948 act also introduced the new parity formula, designed to eliminate distortions due to changes in the cost of production.

Legislation in the 1960's was by no means limited to the basic commodities. Efforts were begun early in 1961 to expand the existing program authorizing food distribution to needy persons. A pilot food stamp program was begun. Expansion of the School Lunch and Special Milk programs was undertaken. The Feed Grain Act (March 22, 1969) and the Agricultural Act of 1961 (August 8, 1961) provided the basic framework for legislation in the next decade. Also undertaken were specific programs for wheat and feed grains, with provisions for crop acreage diversion to soil-conserving crops and methods (practiced extensively in the Soil Bank Program of the late 1950's), authorization of marketing orders for specific crops, and extensions of the National Wool Act of 1954 and Public Law 480 to help supply needy nations with surplus American food stocks.

The Food and Agriculture Act of 1965 broke the tradition of annual Congressional battles and outlined legislation covering a four-year period. Essentially, the 1965 Act carried forward many of the provisions of previous legislation.

Co-operatives. The procedure of pooling farm produce in America for the purpose of selling it to better advantage is carried on voluntarily by farmers through associations known as Co-operatives.

The Capper-Volstead act of 1922 protected these associations at first, when properly conducted, from

CHIEF CROPS FOR UNITED STATES 1930-1974
Source: *Economic Research Service; Dept. of Agriculture*

Year	All Corn	Oats	Barley	Sorghums for grain	Wheat	Rye	Buckwheat	Rice
	1,000 bushels	1,000 bushels	1,000 bushels	1,000 bushels	1,000 bushels	1,000 bushels	1,000 bushels	1,000 bags
1930	2,080,130	1,274,592	301,619	37,561	886,522	45,383	6,967	20,218
1935	2,299,363	1,210,229	288,667	57,610	628,227	56,938	8,488	17,753
1940	2,457,146	1,246,450	311,278	85,824	814,646	39,725	6,476	24,495
1944	3,087,982	1,149,240	276,275	184,978	1,060,111	22,525	8,956	30,974
1945	2,868,795	1,523,851	266,994	96,063	1,107,623	23,708	6,467	30,668
1946	3,217,076	1,477,573	265,059	106,025	1,152,118	18,487	6,812	32,497
1947	2,354,739	1,176,142	281,868	93,217	1,358,911	25,497	7,177	35,217
1948	3,605,078	1,450,186	315,537	131,384	1,294,911	25,886	6,085	38,275
1949	3,238,618	1,254,855	237,071	148,299	1,098,415	18,102	4,956	40,737
1950	3,057,803	1,410,464	303,533	233,278	1,019,389	21,257	4,439	38,689
1951	2,941,423	1,316,396	254,668	159,265	987,474	21,410	3,340	43,805
1952	3,279,403	1,260,127	226,014	83,024	1,298,957	16,046	3,205	48,107
1953	3,192,491	1,209,458	242,544	109,353	1,169,484	18,163	3,193	52,607
1954	2,964,639	1,499,579	370,126	204,087	969,781	23,688	2,719	58,853
1955	3,229,743	1,503,074	401,225	242,526	934,731	29,055	1,934	55,902
1956	3,455,283	1,163,160	376,873	206,205	1,004,272	21,155	2,032	49,459
1957	3,422,231	1,300,954	437,170	564,324	950,662	27,243	1,871	42,935
1958	3,799,844	1,422,164	470,449	614,845	1,462,218	32,485	1,783	47,015
1960	3,908,070	1,555,312	431,309	619,867	1,357,272	33,052	810	54,591
1961	3,625,530	1,011,398	395,669	479,751	1,234,743	27,476	864	54,198
1969	4,578,000*	950,000	417,000	743,000	1,458,900	31,000	N. A.	91,300
1974†	4,651,167*	620,539	308,077	628,081	1,793,322	19,293	N. A.	114,096

* Corn raised for grain. † Preliminary data.

Chief Crops for United States 1930-1975—Cont.

Year	Flaxseed	Cotton		Tobacco	Hay	Sorghums for forage	Sorghums for silage	Beans dry edible
		Lint	Seed					
	1,000 bushels	1,000 bales	1,000 tons	1,000 pounds	1,000 tons	1,000 tons	1,000 tons	1,000 bags
1930	21,673	13,932	6,028	1,648,037	74,527	6,326	572	14,341
1935	14,914	10,638	4,634	1,302,041	90,364	12,052	3,133	14,335
1940	30,924	12,566	5,286	1,460,441	96,050	16,110	6,217	16,945
1944	21,665	12,230	4,902	1,950,940	102,889	11,552	5,644	16,147
1945	34,557	9,015	3,664	1,991,108	107,438	9,543	3,570	13,091
1946	22,588	8,640	3,513	2,314,807	99,518	8,181	3,587	15,840
1947	40,618	11,857	4,681	2,107,160	100,576	5,666	3,338	17,268
1948	54,803	14,877	5,945	1,979,581	96,172	3,633	4,318	20,816
1949	42,976	16,128	6,559	1,969,100	95,055	5,729	3,626	21,379
1950	40,236	10,012	4,105	2,030,645	102,340	6,592	4,926	16,886
1951	33,802	15,290	6,186	2,282,386	108,351	6,410	5,622	17,446
1952	30,174	15,139	6,109	2,254,271	104,345	4,358	3,821	16,235
1954	41,534	13,569	5,568	2,200,134	104,380	6,431	6,890	18,899
1955	41,243	14,721	6,043	2,192,852	112,736	6,877	9,402	16,649
1956	48,009	13,310	5,407	2,175,556	108,680	4,613	8,843	17,218
1957	25,919	10,964	4,609	1,667,544	120,977	7,508	15,157	15,626
1958	39,543	11,512	4,798	1,736,204	121,924	4,936	12,268	18,981
1960	30,402	14,272	5,886	1,944,175	118,236	3,859	12,547	17,917
1961	22,178	14,318	5,978	2,061,392	116,819	3,413	12,996	20,287
1969	27,264	10,015	4,186	1,807,000	127,000	9,567†	10,948†	19,000
1975	14,557	8,326	3,030	2,184,237	132,917	. . .	7,259	17,196

Year	Peas dry field	Peanuts picked and threshed	Soybeans	Potatoes	Sugar cane		Sugar beets	Oranges and Tangerines
					Sugar and seed	Sirup		
	1,000 bags	1,000 pounds	1,000 bushels	1,000 bushels	1,000 tons	1,000 gallons	1,000 tons	1,000 boxes
1930	2,114	697,350	13,929	343 817	3,153	16,602	9,199	55,060
1935	3,385	1,152,795	48,901	378,895	4,954	24,509	7,908	52,073
1940	2,192	1,766,590	78,045	376,920	4,218	13,360	12,194	85,510
1944	8,894	2,080,825	192,121	383,926	6,144	19,897	6,718	113,210
1945	5,915	2,042,235	193,167	419,399	6,707	28,251	8,616	104,350
1946	6,679	2,038,005	203,395	487,315	5,962	23,335	10,560	118,540
1947	6,322	2,181,695	186,451	388,985	5,289	18,545	12,503	114,510
1948	3,640	2,335,840	227,217	449,895	6,768	11,245	9,424	104,120
1949	3,212	1,864,780	234,194	402,353	6,541	9,745	10,196	108,465
1950	3,206	2,021,730	299,279	429,896	6,944	9,230	13,535	121,610
1951	3,763	1,595,025	280,512	325,708	5,601	5,140	10,584	122,900
1952	2,610	1,366,225	298,052	349,098	7,605	6,005	10,169	125,080
1954	3,484	1,043,560	342,795	355,099	6,940	4,795	14,027	141,475
1955	2,525	1,548,010	373,522	227,046	7,248	4,910	12,228	137,015
1956	4,639	1,607,810	449,446	243,716	6,483	3,895	12,993	136,705
1957	3,326	1,435,945	483,715	239,539	6,750	3,225	15,530	111,155
1958	2,475	1,864,725	574,413	265,729	6,681	3,770	15,183	130,620
1960	3,241	1,786,266	555,307[a]	257,435	16,456	3,558	16,421	121,535
1961	3,543	1,742,960	679,566	293,594	19,737	3,425	17,704	138,095
1969	3,738†	2,553,000	1,117,000	511,666	22,615	2,482†	28,518	188,090
1975	2,731	3,857,122	1,521,370	315,647	28,499	. . .	29,270	237,910

Year	Grapefruit	Lemons	Apples	Peaches	Pears	Grapes	Cranberries	Strawberries
	1,000 boxes	1,000 boxes	1,000 bushels	1,000 bushels	1,000 bushels	1,000 tons	1,000 barrels	1,000 crates
1930	18,690	7,950	. . . . . .	56,392	27,167	2,458	584	9,143
1935	18,347	7,787	140,398	55,440	25,943	2,477	516	10,811
1940	42,883	17,236	111,436	57,832	29,590	2,466	570	12,319
1944	52,180	12,550	121,266	78,191	31,337	2,712	376	4,366
1945	63,450	14,450	66,796	81,548	33,042	2,781	656	5,201
1946	59,520	13,800	119,410	86,643	34,447	3,160	856	7,004
1947	61,630	12,870	113,041	82,270	35,312	3,036	790	8,895
1948	45,530	10,010	88,407	65,352	26,334	3,078	968	10,224
1949	36,500	11,360	133,742	74,818	36,404	2,650	840	8,795
1950	46,580	13,400	123,126	53,485	31,140	2,707	984	11,295
1951	40,400	12,900	112,935	70,265	32,687	3,281	932	11,846
1952	38,360	12,590	92,489	62,560	30,947	3,164	804	11,794
1954	46,120	14,600	103,773	60,794	30,077	2,607	1,012	11,874
1955	45,380	13,250	107,157	51,852	29,622	3,241	1,026	223*
1956	44,790	16,200	100,852	70,079	32,322	2,912	970	275*
1957	39,780	16,900	118,548	61,518	31,676	2,599	1,050	277*
1958	43,500	17,000	126,610	71,069	28,890	3,026	1,166	267*
1960	43,300	14,340	108,515	74,315	25,621	2,997	1,341	233*
1961	42,910	16,740	126,565	77,895	27,080	3,092	1,236	255*
1969	54,170	15,810	140,873	77,000	29,625	3,874	1,468†	243*
1975	61,370	29,400	7,087,100[a]	2,818,000[a]	739*	4,300	2,075	5,420[b]

* Thousand tons. † 1968 preliminary. [a] lbs. [b] cwt.

FARM INCOME AND GOVERNMENT PAYMENT BY STATES—1974

Source: *Economic Research Service; Department of Agriculture*

State	Cash Receipts from farming (000 omitted)				Farm Income (000,000 omitted)		
	Livestock and Products	Crops	Government Payments	Total	Gross Income	Expenses	Total Income *
Alabama	$679,000	$511,000	$9,220	$1,199,220	$1,352.5	$1,165.7	$264.4
Alaska	4,000	2,000	59	6,059	7.3	6.6	0.6
Arizona	583,000	613,000	5,252	1,201,252	1,255.5	903.2	337.8
Arkansas	827,000	1,260,000	7,417	2,094,417	2,240.5	1,741.9	650.4
California	2,788,000	5,863,000	18,285	8,669,285	8,963.0	6,399.4	2,733.0
Colorado	1,409,000	744,000	12,533	2,165,533	2,264.7	1,705.9	494.3
Connecticut	125,000	88,000	505	213,505	234.1	195.3	52.9
Delaware	164,000	108,000	254	272,254	282.8	199.1	83.5
Florida	549,000	1,695,000	12,548	2,256,548	2,362.2	1,604.5	858.5
Georgia	1,027,000	1,072,000	10,364	2,109,364	2,280.8	1,767.9	598.3
Hawaii	58,000	579,000	8,310	645,310	661.9	245.1	419.1
Idaho	411,000	1,043,000	11,151	1,465,151	1,556.5	1,008.9	604.4
Illinois	1,789,000	3,937,000	9,755	5,735,755	6,173.6	4,489.8	1,250.2
Indiana	1,162,000	1,888,000	6,591	3,056,591	3,395.7	2,494.8	547.1
Iowa	3,786,000	3,495,000	16,596	7,297,596	7,658.0	5,650.4	1,204.4
Kansas	1,835,000	2,140,000	22,457	3,997,457	4,186.0	2,973.1	944.6
Kentucky	585,000	903,000	5,813	1,493,813	1,729.5	1,249.3	639.0
Louisiana	335,000	1,046,000	13,591	1,394,594	1,478.0	957.5	567.1
Maine	226,000	213,000	1,656	440,656	473.3	316.4	212.6
Maryland	369,000	253,000	1,023	623,023	693.1	549.0	136.1
Massachusetts	105,000	96,000	487	201,487	223.8	185.1	45.7
Michigan	707,000	1,050,000	10,438	1,767,438	1,952.2	1,352.0	656.0
Minnesota	1,950,000	2,591,000	18,420	4,559,420	4,849.6	2,851.5	1,752.4
Mississippi	602,000	873,000	7,944	1,482,944	1,630.9	1,284.7	385.0
Missouri	1,441,000	1,289,000	22,549	2,752,549	3,024.7	2,407.4	513.5
Montana	430,000	760,000	14,998	1,204,998	1,294.1	872.2	694.2
Nebraska	2,265,000	1,964,000	20,970	4,249,970	4,396.2	3,188.1	681.1
Nevada	101,000	35,000	305	136,305	151.1	118.8	30.1
New Hampshire	51,000	20,000	654	71,654	82.6	65.9	17.6
New Jersey	114,000	236,000	660	350,660	393.2	299.3	98.6
New Mexico	410,000	156,000	13,341	579,341	627.7	552.1	93.8
New York	1,026,000	506,000	6,003	1,538,003	1,737.0	1,458.7	367.6
North Carolina	920,000	1,712,000	8,125	2,640,125	2,925.9	1,858.5	1,087.8
North Dakota	490,000	2,080,000	30,968	2,600,968	2,706.8	1,314.6	1,126.0
Ohio	998,000	1,508,000	7,419	2,513,419	2,833.3	2,242.4	646.3
Oklahoma	1,117,000	830,000	14,355	1,961,355	2,124.4	1,835.1	397.8
Oregon	328,000	775,000	4,137	1,107,137	1,212.9	815.1	408.0
Pennsylvania	1,097,000	504,000	4,916	1,605,916	1,801.5	1,469.6	407.1
Rhode Island	12,000	14,000	63	26,063	28.4	22.0	6.6
South Carolina	255,000	572,000	5,591	832,591	924.6	685.5	243.0
South Dakota	1,279,000	816,000	33,443	2,128,443	2,218.3	1,403.6	572.3
Tennessee	459,000	546,000	8,979	1,013,979	1,213.0	1,091.3	234.5
Texas	2,972,000	2,848,000	80,552	5,900,552	6,335.8	5,275.4	813.4
Utah	220,000	101,000	2,946	323,946	351.9	286.2	82.8
Vermont	197,000	17,000	1,573	215,573	240.7	198.7	42.6
Virginia	453,000	519,000	7,825	979,825	1,157.3	869.3	316.1
Washington	458,000	1,525,000	9,829	1,992,829	2,108.4	1,236.4	908.8
West Virginia	100,000	43,000	1,496	144,496	191.5	174.7	27.2
Wisconsin	1,919,000	526,000	13,298	2,458,298	2,718.0	2,007.7	750.3
Wyoming	237,000	132,000	4,784	373,784	410.2	359.9	67.6
Total	$41,424,000	$52,097,000	$530,448	$94,051,448	$101,112.0	$73,405.0	$26,072.0

* Of farm operators (net income).

prosecution under the antitrust laws. They are fostered by the Farmer Co-operative Service of the U.S. Department of Agriculture which disseminates information concerning supply, demand, prices, and those practices found advantageous by co-operative organizations.

Another form of co-operative enterprise which, in America, has developed chiefly in farm communities is the so-called "consumer" co-operative. Its aim is to secure for members the price benefits of large-scale buying. In many cases, these associations own their own stores, warehouses, and factories. Business done through them by farmers reached a pre-war high of $250,000,000 in 1938. They have been chiefly active in the purchase of gasoline, seed, and fertilizer and in the building and operation of rural electric distribution systems under the encouragement of the rural electrification administration.

The increase in business done by farmers' marketing and purchasing co-operatives since 1915 is shown by the following table:

AGRICULTURAL CO-OPERATIVES

Source: *Farmer Cooperative Service*

Marketing Season*	Number	Estimated Membership (thousands)	Estimated Business (Millions of $)
1915	5,424	651	636
1925	10,803	2700	2400
1930	11,950	3000	2400
1935	10,500	3660	1840
1940	10,600	3400	2280
1941	10,550	3600	2840
1942	10,450	3850	3780
1943	10,300	4390	5160
1944	10,150	4505	5645
1945	10,150	5010	6070
1946	10,125	5436	7116
1949	10,035	6584	8,726
1954	9,903	7604	9,642
1959	9,345	7273	12,036
1964	8,583	7082	14,742
1967	7,940	6445	17,034
1970	7,790	6355	19,080

*Ends June 30 of the following year.

OPERATIONS OF COOPERATIVES, 1972-73

Leading States	Associations Number	Membership Number	Business ($1000)
California . .	308	91,850	2,655,901
Iowa	499	373,385	1,827,430
Minnesota . .	1,117	591,990	1,766,161
Wisconsin . .	538	422,040	1,763,497
Illinois . . .	329	318,285	1,427,847
New York . .	296	135,900	1,238,710
Texas	484	142,630	964,329
Kansas . . .	288	202,980	959,004
Ohio	218	217,630	929,699
Nebraska . .	374	263,870	841,790
All others . .	3,403	3,366,190	12,123,374
Total . . .	7,854	6,126,750	26,497,742

Source: *Agricultural Statistics 1976*.

HORTICULTURE

Originally the term horticulture meant the cultivation of a garden. It now includes the art and science of vegetable growing or *olericulture*, fruit growing or *pomology*, flower growing or *floriculture*, and landscape gardening. Horticulture, therefore, might justly be called applied botany, and it bears much the same relationship to botany as do any of the branches of engineering to mathematics and physics.

In a new and undeveloped country, horticulture, as a branch of agriculture, usually receives comparatively little attention. But it increases rapidly in importance as the primary problems of producing a sufficient supply of grain, potatoes, and live stock are gradually solved. The phenomenal development of horticulture in America is shown by the great and increasing number of horticultural publications, by the extent to which the subject is taught in the schools, by the obvious importance of the canning and preserving industries, greenhouses, nurseries, and seed raising, and by the accompanying tables. Factories devoted to the manufacture of boxes, baskets, barrels, glass jars, and tin cans depend for their existence largely on the success of horticultural enterprises.

Robert Squibb's *Garden Kalendar*, published at Charleston, South Carolina in 1787, was probably the first separate book on horticulture printed in America. Since that time, more than 10,000 books have been published (a conservative estimate), in addition to numerous journals, many of which are still in circulation. There are also a number of national or regional horticultural societies and many local organizations.

Elementary instruction in horticulture is often given in both primary and secondary schools of cities, as well as in rural districts. This training is given not only to teach horticulture, but also to help develop growing minds. Advanced courses in horticulture are given by some 70 colleges and universities located in every state and territory of the United States.

Vegetables. The chief sources of fresh vegetables are large commercial farms, often distant from market areas, and greenhouses, usually located near large cities. With intense cultivation, $1,500 to $2,500 worth of crops for fresh market may be taken from a single acre. Other farms are devoted to raising vegetables for commercial processing. Numerous families have home gardens.

Modern transportation facilities and refrigeration have made possible large-scale truck farming at a distance from cities. For some time the South and West have specialized in supplying the North with out-of-season vegetables. A great deal of the marketing is done co-operatively, shipments in carload lots being made up with the produce of a number of growers, who might separately have difficulties in filling a freight car as their crops are harvested.

Fruits and Nuts. The orange is the most important fruit produced in the United States, both in quantity and in value. Apples rank second in value, while grapes are second in quantity produced. Citrus production has become the most highly organized of the fruit industries. Much of the fruit produced in the U.S. is processed, as consumers use more fruit canned, frozen, dried, and in juice form, than in the fresh form. Nut production has declined in recent years. English walnuts, pecans, and almonds are the most important ones, in that order.

Flowers. In the commercial production of flowers, the chrysanthemum is the most valuable crop, followed by the carnation, and then the rose. An important branch of this industry is the forcing of bulbs and plants in order to produce potted flowers for sale, not only for holidays, but during the entire year. Although it has been demonstrated that bulbs can be produced in America, they are nearly all imported from Holland.

Landscape gardening consists in the arrangement of growing trees, shrubs, and other ornamental plants in connection with walks, drives, and other features of the landscape, so that together they form an artistic and pleasing view.

COMMERCIAL TRUCK CROPS

Crop	Acreage (1,000)		Production (tons)		Value ($1,000)	
	1974*	States Leading	1974*	States Leading	1973	1974*
Artichokes	10.8	Calif.	35.1	Calif.	8,699	12,152
Asparagus	112.5	Calif., Wash.	130.2	Calif., Wash.	66,411	74,277
Beans, lima	72.2	Calif., Del.	86.0	Calif., Del.	20,714	26,786
Beans, snap	372.1	Wisc., N.Y.	887.4	Oreg., N.Y.	130,430	167,765
Beets	18.5	Wisc., N.Y.	240.7	N.Y., Wisc.	5,520	9,636
Broccoli	48.7	Calif., Oreg.	188.2	Calif., Oreg.	42,476	52,859
Brussels sprouts	6.3	Calif.	33.1	Calif.	8,894	11,524
Cabbage	106.2	Tex., Fla.	953.4	Tex., Fla.	121,416	92,519
Cantaloupes	69.9	Calif., Tex.	473.0	Calif., Ariz.	91,322	94,686
Carrots	79.0	Calif., Tex.	1,154.3	Calif., Tex.	105,450	124,017
Cauliflower	34.6	Calif., N.Y.	147.6	Calif., N.Y.	33,902	38,771
Celery	32.4	Calif., Fla.	805.6	Calif., Fla.	101,352	91,806
Corn, sweet	628.1	Wisc., Minn.	2,705.4	Minn., Wisc.	157,334	211,748
Cucumbers	177.3	N.C., Mich.	820.9	Mich., Calif.	98,879	124,626
Eggplant	3.3	Fla., N.J.	30.0	Fla., N.J.	5,164	6,969
Escarole	8.3	Fla., N.J.	55.7	Fla., N.J.	13,943	12,191
Garlic	9.0	Calif.	58.5	Calif.	10,522	14,284
Honeydew melons	11.4	Calif., Tex.	91.5	Calif., Tex.	18,324	15,610
Lettuce	226.2	Calif., Ariz.	2,486.1	Calif., Ariz.	374,923	352,731
Mint for oil	87.1	Oreg., Wash.	2.4	Oreg., Wash.	36,112	61,274
Onions	109.9	Calif., Tex.	1,670.8	Calif., Tex.	207,046	158,494
Peas, green	425.6	Wisc., Wash.	572.7	Wisc., Wash.	59,694	112,071
Peppers, green	47.8	Fla., Calif.,	238.3	Calif., Fla.	65,739	70,110
Spinach	34.5	Calif., Tex.	204.5	Calif., Tex.	17,579	19,108
Strawberries	39.6	Calif., Oreg.	266.6	Calif., Oreg.	131,592	152,759
Tomatoes	464.5	Calif., Fla.	8,013.8	Calif., Fla.	561,233	797,625
Watermelons	215.2	Tex., Fla.	1,159.8	Fla., Tex.	77,465	88,468

* Preliminary. Source: *Statistical Abstract of the U.S. 1975.*

PRINCIPAL CANADIAN AGRICULTURAL CROPS

Crop	Area in Acres		Yield per Acre (Bushels)		Total Production (Bushels)	
	1974	1975	1974	1975	1974	1975
Winter wheat	420,000	455,000	45.4	50.0	19,070,000	22,750,000
Spring wheat	18,807,300	19,337,800	21.9	25.5	412,043,000	492,450,000
Durum wheat	2,850,000	3,650,000	20.1	25.1	57,400,000	91,500,000
All wheat	22,077,300	23,442,800	22.1	25.9	488,513,000	606,700,000
Oats for grain	6,106,000	6,058,000	41.7	47.5	254,745,000	287,898,000
Barley for grain	11,799,500	10,991,200	34.3	38.6	404,286,000	423,797,000
Fall rye	801,000	746,000	22.7	26.4	18,164,000	19,698,000
Spring rye	42,000	42,000	17.9	20.6	750,000	865,000
All rye	843,000	788,000	22.4	26.1	18,914,000	20,563,000
Mixed grains	1,810,900	1,835,400	44.6	48.5	80,754,000	88,991,000
Flaxseed	1,450,000	1,400,000	9.5	12.2	13,800,000	17,100,000
Rapeseed	3,160,000	4,020,000	16.2	17.8	51,300,000	71,600,000
Corn for grain	1,460,000	1,539,000	69.8	83.6	101,910,000	128,624,000
Buckwheat	63,600	47,200	19.1	20.3	1,216,000	959,000
Peas, dry	78,500	74,500	21.4	24.6	1,680,000	1,834,000
Beans, dry	171,500	147,000	20.7	18.3	3,548,000	2,695,000
Soybeans	445,000	390,000	24.8	31.0	11,040,000	12,090,000
Potatoes*	282,600	257,300	193.9	169.0	54,783,000	43,482,000
Tame hay†	13,033,000	13,014,000	1.95	1.95	25,402,000	25,342,000
Fodder corn†	1,048,000	1,021,000	10.56	12.35	11,070,000	12,606,000

Source: Statistics Canada. * In cwt. † In tons.

LEADING AGRICULTURAL PRODUCTS OF CANADA, 1974*

By Provinces on Basis of Bushels Produced
(000 omitted)

Province	Wheat	Oats	Barley	Grain Corn	Tame Hay	Potatoes	Fodder Corn	Mixed Grain
Alberta	110,000	80,000	188,000	....	6,700	4,000	....	14,600
British Columbia	1,900	3,500	6,400	....	1,600	3,200	330	300
Manitoba	63,000	43,000	53,000	190	2,400	4,900	210	6,000
New Brunswick	144	2,295	447	....	277	13,398	....	252
Nova Scotia	120	920	271	....	317	638	....	369
Ontario	19,370	23,415	15,470	90,200	6,320	8,120	8,485	43,800
Prince Edward Island	444	2,805	1,048	....	225	10,304	....	4,358
Quebec	1,535	23,810	1,650	11,250	4,980	8,425	2,045	4,675
Saskatchewan	326,000	75,000	128,000	....	3,200	378	....	6,400
Canada	522,513	254,745	394,286	101,910	26,019	53,363	11,070	80,754

* Estimated.

DRAINAGE AND RECLAMATION

In agricultural practice the term drainage generally refers to the removal of excess water from the soil by means of open ditches, or to drainage below the surface using drain tile or tubing (plastic is sometimes used for this purpose today) in which the water collects and is carried away under the force of gravity. Where the ground is so low that the water collected by the system must be removed with pumps, the process is termed pump drainage.

Drainage was used to a certain extent by the Romans, and during the 17th century attention was occasionally called to its advantages; but the methods practiced by James Smith, of Perthshire, England, about 1823, are generally considered to have introduced the modern systems of farm drainage. In America, John Johnson imported tiles from Scotland in 1835 and placed them in the wet ground of his farm near Geneva, New York. The improvement in his crops was so noticeable that the advantages of draining were quickly appreciated.

The simplest way of draining wet soil is to dig ditches from 3 to 5 feet deep and connect these with a main ditch that is somewhat deeper. Because this method cuts up the ground, tubing or 4- to 7-inch tiles are generally placed at the bottom of the ditches, which are then refilled. The ground water filters through openings into the tile or tubing, then flows through drains of larger diameter, and thence to the outlet.

Among the more important advantages of drainage are:

1. Excess water is removed from the ground, providing aeration of the root zone.
2. Nutrients are made more readily available to plants.
3. Farmers are enabled to prepare soil for planting earlier in the spring and to perform field operations at the appropriate time.
4. Better environment is provided for plants, resulting in higher yields of better-quality crops.
5. Drained regions provide a more healthful environment.
6. Excess soluble salts are more efficiently removed from alkaline land.

Drainage in the United States. In the United States about 9 percent (nearly 100 million acres) of all farmland had drainage in 1960. The number of drained acres in cropland amounted to around one-fourth of the total cropland in the country. However, since a large part of the drainage in the country operates in land not now used as farms for the raising of crops, the above figures give a very inadequate picture of drainage enterprises.

In order to drain a farm, an entire district often must be embraced in a drainage operation, known officially as an enterprise. Such enterprises are organized under state laws and may be undertaken by state governments, counties, or townships. If supported and operated by organizations having their own executive officers, enterprises are known as drainage districts. There were 8,461 drainage enterprises in the United States in 1960. Other enterprises are individually owned, being constructed for various uses by the land owner.

Nearly two-thirds of the lands in drainage enterprises are located north of the Ohio and Missouri rivers. These are usually small enterprises and, with the exception of those draining swampy areas in Wisconsin and northern Michigan, they were undertaken to improve farm land already under cultivation.

The enterprises along the lower Mississippi and in the plains along the southern Atlantic and Gulf of Mexico coast lines are, in the main, large scale undertakings. They have been instrumental in draining huge swamps and making them fit for cultivation.

Drainage enterprises in the arid southwestern states are practically all located on irrigated land. Their purpose is to prevent damage from seepage of water and to carry off excess salts from the soil. Frequently, the water drained off is collected in drainage wells and is pumped from them to be used again for irrigation.

Old World Projects. The Fens on the east coast of England, the valley of the Po, in Italy, the south of France, and Egypt have all benefited from extensive reclamation projects. These are not as famous as those in the Netherlands, where, by an elaborate system of dikes and canals, many marshes have been changed to fertile regions known as "polders." In the Haarlem Meer, 44,724 acres which had been covered with 13 feet of water were surrounded by a dike, and, after 39 months of pumping, the water was removed. Even this project is dwarfed by the reclamation of the Zuider Zee, a branch of the North Sea which was formed in 1170 when a terrific storm broke down the sand dunes on the coast. An 18-mile dike was completed in 1932, which cut off the inland water. The pumping out of this water provides 523,000 acres of reclaimed land, leaving a lake named Ijsselmeer.

DRAINAGE OF FARMS IN THE UNITED STATES*

State	Area Drained and Used for Agriculture (acres)	Cost of Draining: Works and Services incl. maintenance, repairs & administration, 1950–59 (dollars)
Alabama	65,901	31,061
Arkansas	4,680,966	20,488,266
California	1,911,251	29,065,257
Colorado	55,496	178,196
Delaware	340,922	476,944
Florida	4,855,327	91,627,636
Georgia	93,228	118,012
Idaho	110,982	2,011,573
Illinois	5,563,426	28,691,965
Indiana	11,053,446	13,598,832
Iowa	6,871,339	21,032,299
Kansas	373,110	1,665,416
Kentucky	888,799	897,753
Louisiana	7,110,624	45,796,344
Maryland	350,447	409,398
Michigan	9,877,049	37,186,074
Minnesota	10,560,808	41,809,993
Mississippi	3,040,607	9,557,061
Missouri	3,097,316	12,138,381
Montana	60,112	721,491
Nebraska	739,220	1,388,581
Nevada	41,521	219,902
New Jersey	10,956	40,617
New Mexico	31,593	127,433
New York	49,616	202,013
North Carolina	1,320,503	2,959,290
North Dakota	1,641,183	1,672,790
Ohio	8,809,415	8,268,377
Oklahoma	133,796	249,053
Oregon	270,454	5,002,268
South Carolina	338,066	824,238
South Dakota	658,580	298,591
Tennessee	590,879	2,136,236
Texas	5,691,130	28,895,392
Utah	66,910	558,392
Virginia	92,778	401,765
Washington	241,182	4,404,324
Wisconsin	584,093	1,579,398
Wyoming	23,833	145,293
United States	92,296,864	416,875,865

* Last reported in the *1959 Census of Agriculture*, Vol. III.

IRRIGATION

The practice of supplying water to the fields by artificial means has been known for thousands of years. The ancient Egyptians, the Babylonians, the Chinese, and the natives of India—all made use of irrigation. In the western hemisphere, the Incas of Peru, the Aztecs of Mexico, and the Pueblo Indians of New Mexico employed artificial methods of watering very similar to those of the Old World.

In many parts of the earth, the soil is extremely fertile, but vegetation is scanty because the annual rainfall either is less than 20 inches or is concentrated in a relatively short season and followed by a long period of drought. In such regions, the ability to obtain water and distribute it to the fields when needed means the difference between a comparative desert and a rich region capable of supporting a large population.

Water is usually obtained from a river having its source in a more humid region. Lakes, wells, and springs also serve as sources of water. During the rainy season in India, many small reservoirs, called tanks, become filled by the floods.

Irrigation is practiced more extensively in India than in any other country. However, in the Middle East, United States, and other countries with large areas having arid and semi-arid climates, irrigation systems are being expanded with governmental assistance.

Methods of Irrigation. A large proportion of all irrigated lands receive water from rivers and streams. During the season of flood, these streams usually carry far more water than can be used, while later in the year their volume is much less than is needed by the surrounding country. By means of a dam equipped with control gates, a reservoir can be created which may be filled when the river is high and gradually emptied when the river would otherwise be too low.

Most of the great dams of the world, that at Aswan, Egypt, being a notable example, have been constructed as the most important feature of some irrigation project. The force of falling water is frequently sufficient to generate electric power, which is especially valuable in irrigated regions where fuel is generally scarce. The water is usually distributed from the river by main canals, with ditches branching from it to carry the water to the fields. Irrigation is accomplished by running the water in shallow channels until it is absorbed by the earth, or by flooding the entire field. Another method of irrigation is effected with sprinklers. Water is lifted from its source—well, stream, or reservoir—and pumped through pipes to sprinklers.

Irrigation in America. In the United States, irrigation was at first carried on by private enterprise, but the capital required was so great and the payments were necessarily spread over such a long period that the work on many projects was finally undertaken by the government. By the terms of the National Reclamation act, which was passed in 1902, a large part of the money received from the sale of public lands in sixteen Western states was to be used for the construction of reclamation projects under the direction of the department of the interior. But, when the equipment has been paid for, the control passes to the owners of the irrigated land.

More irrigated acres are devoted to raising alfalfa than to any other crop. Much of the irrigated land, however, is concentrated in specific areas: in the cotton-, fruit-, and vegetable-producing areas of California; in the high plains and the lower Rio Grande valley of Texas; in southern Idaho; in a few valleys in Oregon, Washington, and Colorado; and on livestock ranches scattered throughout the West, where irrigated land produces hay for use between grazing seasons. More than half of the 11.2 million-acre increase in irrigated land from 1950 to 1964 occurred in the Great Plains states. As a result, cereals account for about one-third of the total crops irrigated.

The Arrowrock dam on the Boise project, built in Idaho in 1915, was long the highest in the world (350 feet), but the Hoover (Boulder) dam, finished in 1936, is more than twice as high (726), and a dozen or more other dams also outrank Arrowrock. Many of these, in addition to irrigation, are used for flood control, power production, and river regulation. The total area of irrigated land in the United States approaches 35 million acres. Nearly 10 per cent of all U.S. farms have some irrigation. For details, see tables on *United States Government Irrigated Land Enterprises*. Large-scale irrigation projects are also being carried out in western Canadian provinces.

Old World Irrigation. As already stated, India is the most extensively irrigated country in the world, with a total area of projects in excess of 80 million acres, or more than 20 per cent of the total area occupied. The Sukkur barrage in the Sind province is designed to irrigate 5,500,000 acres. It is part of a larger plan for impounding the waters of the Indus river by works estimated to cost 250 million dollars. The annual value of crops on irrigated land in India approximates an average of 1½ times the total cost of the works.

Virtually 100 per cent of the cultivated land in Egypt is irrigated because of the arid climatic conditions. In 1955 this amounted to more than 7 million acres, with another 2 million acres in the planning stages for irrigation. The Aswan Dam, constructed in 1902 and more than doubled in storing capacity in 1912, is credited with having saved Egypt from famine and economic disaster in the low-flood year of 1913. Russia and Japan rank ahead of Egypt, however, in the total area of their irrigated soil. France, Italy, and Spain follow in the order named. China has a large area of irrigated land, but no authentic statistics are available by which its extent may be determined.

FORESTRY

Forestry is the art and the science of the economical management of existing communities of trees, and the development of new forests upon land unsuited to agriculture.

Value of Forests. Forests supply fuel and timber; they break the force of strong winds; they are warmer in winter and cooler in summer than open country; they afford parks for amusement; and they protect game for the hunter. Finally, forests exert a very noticeable influence upon the flow and character of neighboring streams. This effect has three principal causes: First, the trees break the direct force of the rainfall so that the earth on wooded hillsides is not cut up and washed into the valley. Second, water accumulates in the porous bed of a forest, and escapes to the stream gradually, thus tending to produce a continuous flow rather than a series of sudden, disastrous floods. Third, trees draw from swampy ground a large amount of water, which is evaporated through their leaves, thereby substantially decreasing the volume to be drained off by streams.

The purpose of forestry is to secure the greatest possible utilization of forests and forest products for the present, and, at the same time, to provide new growth for the future. To attain these results, existing forests must be protected from their chief enemies, fire and insects; lumbering operations must be performed with a minimum of waste; and cut-over areas must be replanted. Replanting may be done by allowing seed trees to remain standing, by artificial distribution of seed, or by setting out young trees which have been raised in nurseries.

Forestry has been practiced in Europe for several centuries, especially by the Germans and the French. England depended largely upon her commercial organizations to provide a supply of timber from foreign lands, but for a time during the World War she could obtain only that wood which France was able to spare. Because of this experience, England, shortly after the war, planned

UNITED STATES GOVERNMENT IRRIGATED LAND ENTERPRISES*

State	Area Irrigated (in acres) 1949	1959	1964	Percent Increase 1959–64	Capital Invested 1959 ($1,000)
Alaska	N.A.	N.A.	158	...	N.A.
Arizona	979,014	1,152,450	1,125,376	−2.3	168,000
Arkansas	418,644	974,297	711,812	36.9	N.A.
California	6,618,595	7,395,570	7,598,698	2.7	898,000
Colorado	2,940,502	2,684,757	2,690,018	0.2	204,000
Florida	362,909	413,526	1,217,192	194.3	N.A.
Hawaii	...	141,179	143,940	2.0	N.A.
Idaho	2,168,323	2,576,580	2,801,500	8.7	148,000
Kansas	140,992	762,101	1,004,210	31.8	43,000
Louisiana	598,056	484,850	580,687	19.8	11,000
Mississippi	...	99,686	123,398	23.8	N.A.
Montana	1,809,908	1,874,520	1,893,360	1.0	96,000
Nebraska	887,505	2,077,926	2,169,317	4.4	56,000
Nevada	722,896	542,976	824,511	51.9	17,000
New Mexico	691,429	731,835	812,723	11.1	59,000
North Dakota	35,759	40,000	...	...	N.A.
Oklahoma	44,189	197,632	302,081	52.9	N.A.
Oregon	1,338,226	1,384,284	1,607,659	16.1	71,000
South Dakota	84,356	115,629	130,050	12.5	10,000
Texas	3,148,115	5,655,638	6,384,963	12.9	88,000
Utah	1,166,659	1,061,683	1,092,270	2.9	92,000
Washington	617,362	1,006,969	1,149,842	14.2	369,000
Wyoming	1,475,069	1,469,911	1,571,192	6.9	79,000
All Others	...	2,217,800	1,121,126	...	...
Total	26,248,508	33,021,799	37,056,083	12.2	2,411,000

* Statistics from Census Bureau, 1950, and *U.S. Census of Agriculture, 1964.*

	Diversion Dams number	Reser-voirs number	Reservoirs with capacity reported: Reservoirs number	Total Capacity acre-feet	Canals miles	Pipe Lines miles	Wells number: Flow-ing	Pumped
Arizona	562	269	237	3,625,629	4,898	316	245	4,361
Arkansas	108	86	74	40,431	684	19	27	3,662
California	4,706	1,687	1,507	8,711,658	20,188	10,091	572	72,163
Colorado	7,713	1,182	1,105	2,021,343	18,833	251	1,451	4,988
Florida	355	180	168	3,343	692	485	4,181	3,381
Idaho	5,108	366	313	5,124,969	15,321	437	490	887
Kansas	127	52	42	25,505	546	14	12	1,340
Louisiana	319	61	56	31,249	3,675	61	844	7,590
Montana	8,134	629	577	1,598,898	15,498	109	100	142
Nebraska	488	117	96	133,934	4,628	90	100	7,176
Nevada	4,046	202	176	687,179	3,390	124	293	254
New Mexico	1,286	476	448	3,186,401	5,769	167	106	3,832
North Dakota	15	11	6	1,101	92	7	—	4
Oklahoma	20	29	27	148,945	355	20	—	160
Oregon	6,218	528	470	2,369,138	8,395	573	148	2,770
South Dakota	281	100	94	204,693	968	7	14	27
Texas	439	570	508	1,402,689	9,892	758	163	15,065
Utah	3,080	511	474	2,424,093	9,622	299	1,920	565
Washington	1,859	224	205	6,436,541	3,977	1,515	87	2,098
Wyoming	5,237	458	415	4,370,844	9,724	59	225	248
Total	50,101	7,738	6,998	45,548,583	137,147	15,402	10,978	130,713

to plant one million acres of forest within forty years, and appropriated 17 million dollars to be used for this purpose within a period of ten years.

Forestry in the United States. During the early days of American history, the entire country, with the exception of the treeless plains of the mid-continent, was heavily wooded. Forestry, therefore, received little attention. In 1962 there were approximately 508 million acres of commercial forest land in the United States. Of this, 72 per cent was owned privately and 28 per cent by local, state, and federal governments.

In recognition of the pressing need for conservation of a dwindling national asset, Congress, in 1891, empowered the president to create forest reserves. Yellowstone Park Timberland reserve, the first to be established under the new law, was created by President Harrison. There are now national forests in 44 states and Puerto Rico, with a total area of approximately 226.5 million acres. These are under the control of the forest service of the Department of Agriculture and are chiefly located in the Western states.

Within the national forests, cutting of mature trees and replanting of new crops is continually going on. Fuel and fencing may be obtained free by local settlers, but most of the timber is sold. Grazing of live stock within the areas of the national forests is a practice of great importance. About 5 per cent of the cattle and 17 per cent of the sheep and lambs slaughtered annually are fed on national land during some part of the year.

Possibly the most important function of the national forests is to safeguard the streams which supply water for the famous Western irrigation projects. Without water there can be no irrigation, and without the forests the supply of water would be irregular and uncertain.

TOTAL AREA OF NATIONAL FORESTS EXTENDING INTO TWO OR MORE STATES

Forest	States	Net Area Acres
Apache	Arizona and New Mexico	1,569,090
Ashley	Utah and Wyoming	1,076,367
Bitterroot	Idaho and Montana	1,900,814
Black Hills	South Dakota and Wyoming	660,085
Cache	Idaho and Utah	712,890
Caribou	Idaho and Wyoming	845,497
Cherokee	North Carolina and Tennessee	547,489
Coronado	Arizona and New Mexico	1,442,277
Custer	Montana and South Dakota	1,201,317
Eldorado	California and Nevada	600,526
George Washington	Virginia and West Virginia	920,647
Harney	South Dakota and Wyoming	539,147
Inyo	California and Nevada	1,582,046
Kaniksu	Idaho, Montana, and Washington	1,487,698
Klamath	California and Oregon	1,511,832
Kootenai	Idaho and Montana	1,800,782
La Sal	Colorado and Utah	534,299
Lolo	Idaho and Montana	1,692,392
Minidoka	Idaho and Utah	592,968
Mono	California and Nevada	1,262,773
Ouachita	Arkansas and Oklahoma	1,491,818
Rogue River	California and Oregon	906,195
Siskiyou	California and Oregon	1,379,479
Tahoe	California and Nevada	606,154
Targhee	Idaho and Wyoming	1,365,574
Umatilla	Oregon and Washington	1,303,208
Wasatch	Utah and Wyoming	845,296
White Mountain	Maine and New Hampshire	704,196

In addition to national forests, there are forested tracts totaling about 8 million acres which have been created as reserves by a number of the states. New York State leads with forest reserves in excess of 2 million acres, chiefly in the Adirondack and Catskill parks. Pennsylvania and Washington have about 1.3 million acres of state forest land each. Other states with forest reserves over 500,000 acres are Montana and Michigan.

According to estimates made by the U. S. Department of Agriculture, about one-third of the total land area of the U.S. is forested, or 758 million acres out of 2.2 billion acres in the 50 states. Of this total, 508.8 million acres are classified as commercial forest land, either incapable of producing in excess of 25 cords of timber growth per acre per year, or protected by statute from commercial use. Of the 508.8 million commercial acres, 151 million acres are on farms, 216 million are owned by forest industry firms, and the balance are owned by state, local, and federal governments.

Progress of Forestry. By the enactment, in 1924, of the Clarke-McNary forestry law, the United States government became committed to a definite national forestry policy, embracing alike the publicly and the privately owned forest lands of the nation. The provisions of this act insure increased protection to immature forests and a larger measure of Federal assistance in fire prevention. Provision is made for the systematic study of the problems of forest taxation with the specific purpose of developing equable laws to encourage timber growing. Appropriations also are authorized for supplying nursery stocks of young forest trees to the farmer and for aiding him in caring for his tree plantations, the latter work to be carried out in co-operation with the agricultural extension service and forestry department of his own state.

The aim of forestry is to make the forest lands a perpetual source of needed supplies of wood. This will be accomplished when the annual growth equals or exceeds the amount of timber cut, and lost through fire, insects, and disease.

Civilian Conservation Corps. A major step in forestry conservation was taken in 1933, when provision was made for a "forest army," or Civilian Conservation Corps (CCC), employed by the Federal government to plant trees, combat fire and tree diseases, and otherwise to add to the value of the forest domain. A project was begun in 1935 for planting a tree shelter belt 100 miles wide from the Texas Panhandle to Canada to check erosion by the wind, the trees being designed to retard the evaporation of moisture from the soil. Trees are planted in strips 70 feet wide, spaced at one-mile intervals. The CCC was disbanded during World War II.

Forestry in Canada. Approximately 94.4 per cent of Canada's forested land is publicly owned. The Canadian government administers about 12,000 square miles of forest within national parks. Apart from these areas, there are no national forests in Canada. The other publicly owned forests belong to the provinces, whose governments administer a total of 97,600 square miles of provincial forest reserves and, in addition, about 13,000 square miles of forested lands within the provincial parks.

Forest reserves are intended to supply timber for local use and to protect the watersheds. The export of unmanufactured timber or pulpwood cut from public lands is prohibited in every province except Nova Scotia.

All the provinces provide means of protection against forest fires, including the patrolling of the forest areas, building of roads and telephone lines, and the maintenance of airplane and motor service for reporting or combating fires. Many millions of trees are distributed annually free of charge from governmental nurseries.

PREVENTION OF SOIL EROSION

Agricultural scientists estimate that 64 per cent of the cropland in the United States is in need of better conservation practices. Approximately 16 million acres need to be converted from cropland to permanent cover of trees or grass.

Removal of forest and grass cover to permit intensive cropping of the land has had a triple effect. First, a large proportion of the rain, instead of being held back and absorbed to form a sub-surface reservoir, runs off, forming gullies and carrying

UNITED STATES NATIONAL FORESTS

State or Dependency and Forest	Net Area Acres**
Alabama:	
Wm. B. Bankhead	178,736
Conecuh	83,790
Talladega	357,726
Tuskegee	10,777
Total for State	631,317†
Alaska:	
Chugach	4,726,082
Tongass	16,015,912
Total for State	20,734,673†
Arizona:	
Apache*	1,190,068
Coconino	1,800,786
Coronado*	1,724,147
Kaibab	1,718,043
Prescott	1,247,622
Sitgreaves	768,994
Tonto	2,894,314
Total for State	11,429,833†
Arkansas:	
Ouachita*	1,321,689
Ozark	1,046,649
St. Francis	20,611
Total for State	2,442,924†
California:	
Angeles	648,739
Cleveland	391,312
Eldorado*	640,872
Inyo*	1,774,236
Klamath*	1,667,669
Lassen	1,667,669
Los Padres	1,749,082
Mendocino	867,433
Modoc	1,688,789
Northern Redwoods (Purchase Unit)	14,491
Plumas	1,147,415
Rogue River*	49,261
San Bernardino	613,886
Shasta	986,585
Sequoia	1,118,508
Sierra	1,295,745
Siskiyou*	31,740
Six Rivers	935,266
Stanislaus	895,820
Tahoe*	694,123
Toiyabe	629,745
Trinity	1,051,173
Total for State	19,994,773†
Colorado:	
Arapaho	984,489
Grand Mesa	360,963
Gunnison	1,660,147
Manti-La Sal*	26,631
Pike	1,084,873
Rio Grande	1,800,322
Roosevelt	776,882
Routt	1,144,792
San Isabel	1,103,859
San Juan	1,849,635
Uncompahgre	957,004
White River	1,960,714
Total for State	14,319,757†
Florida:	
Apalachicola	556,496
Ocala	361,243
Osceola	157,233
Total for State	1,075,712†
Georgia:	
Chattahoochee	679,660
Oconee	96,056
Total for State	806,063†
Idaho:	
Bitterroot*	460,812
Boise	2,633,534
Cache*	262,897
Caribou*	963,939
Challis	2,447,363
Clearwater	1,250,772
Coeur d'Alene	723,408
Kaniksu*	891,348
Kootenai*	48,851
Lolo*	426,062
Nezperce	2,196,029
Payette	2,307,328
St. Joe	868,650
Salmon	1,768,728
Sawtooth	1,731,563
Targhee*	1,319,293
Total for State	20,347,244†
Illinois:	
Shawnee	210,953
Total for State	229,248†
Indiana:	
Hoosier	125,000
Total for State	146,169†
Kentucky:	
Cumberland	459,661
Total for State	538,893†
Louisiana:	
Kisatchie	591,566
Total for State	593,416†
Maine:	
White Mountain	41,004
Total for State	50,016†
Michigan:	
Hiawatha	476,653
Huron	414,918
Manistee	446,403
Marquette	354,270
Ottawa	861,459
Total for State	2,633,127†
Minnesota:	
Chippewa	594,292
Superior	1,929,533
Total for State	2,784,143†
Mississippi:	
Bienville	175,657
Delta	58,956
De Soto	500,405
Holly Springs	145,432
Homochitto	189,070
Tombigbee	65,232
Total for State	1,134,495†
Missouri:	
Clark	824,118
Mark Twain	391,702
Total for State	1,400,811†
Montana:	
Beaverhead	2,130,936
Bitterroot*	1,113,814
Custer*	1,097,784
Deerlodge	1,134,572
Flathead	2,336,388
Gallatin	1,700,139
Helena	966,613
Kaniksu*	447,142
Kootenai*	1,769,404
Lewis and Clark	1,862,018
Lolo*	2,076,641
Total for State	16,699,099†
Nebraska:	
Toadstool Park (National Grassland)	100
Nebraska	339,716
Total for State	349,543†
Nevada:	
Eldorado*	400
Humboldt	2,507,870
Inyo*	60,576
Toiyabe	2,489,181
Total for State	5,073,657†
New Hampshire:	
White Mountain	677,660
Total for State	678,807†
New Mexico:	
Apache*	542,443
Carson	1,225,408
Cibola	1,690,738
Coronado*	69,567
Gila	2,715,706
Lincoln	1,087,909
Santa Fe	1,233,419
Total for State	9,153,364†
North Carolina:	
Croatan	152,351
Nantahala	448,334
Pisgah	479,722
Uwharrie	43,391
Total for State	1,127,418†
North Dakota:	
Total for State	1,104,958†
Ohio:	
Wayne	113,000
Total for State	127,381†
Oklahoma:	
Ouachita	180,977
Total for State	287,119†
Oregon:	
Deschutes	1,659,380
Fremont	1,254,608
Klamath*	29,795
Malheur	1,204,834
Mount Hood	1,115,327
Ochoco	845,880
Rogue River*	837,235
Siskiyou*	1,047,101
Siuslaw	622,180
Umatilla*	1,075,959
Umpqua	983,982
Wallowa	979,279
Whitman	1,511,613
Willamette	1,665,835
Winema	908,963
Total for State	15,471,213†
Pennsylvania:	
Allegheny	471,077
Total for State	479,762†
Puerto Rico:	
Caribbean	21,499
Total for Territory	27,916†
South Carolina:	
Francis Marion	245,650
Sumter	341,610
Total for State	588,928†
South Dakota:	
Black Hills	1,047,106
Custer	73,707
(Norbeck Wildlife Preserve)	(46,000)
Total for State	1,982,433†
Tennessee:	
Cherokee	594,770
Total for State	603,601†
Texas:	
Angelina	154,392
Davy Crockett	161,563
Sabine	183,844
Sam Houston	158,205
Total for State	775,375†
Utah:	
Ashley*	1,282,829
Cache*	391,720
Dixie	1,851,341
Fishlake	1,415,665
Manti-La Sal*	1,237,128
Sawtooth*	71,117
Uinta	774,901
Wasatch*	822,197
Total for State	8,000,169†
Vermont:	
Green Mountain	231,825
Total for State	235,558†
Virginia:	
George Washington*	903,748
Jefferson	543,501
Total for State	1,495,080†
Washington:	
Colville	928,312
Gifford Pinchot	1,263,300
Kaniksu*	287,684
Mount Baker	1,818,294
Okanogan	2,042,213
Olympic	621,756
Snoqualmie	1,207,815
Umatilla*	313,780
Wenatchee	1,205,437
Total for State	9,710,815†
West Virginia:	
George Washington	98,259
Monongahela	805,721
Total for State	920,212†
Wisconsin:	
Chequamegon	827,067
Nicolet	640,448
Total for State	1,478,984†
Wyoming:	
Big Horn	1,113,768
Black Hills*	199,466
Bridger	1,699,878
Caribou*	7,829
Medicine Bow	1,069,283
Shoshone	2,430,028
Targhee*	344,573
Teton	1,700,766
Wasatch	36,880
Total for State	9,165,186
Aggregate for the National Forests	186,921,196

* Forest extending into more than one state.

** Acreage includes land area and water.

† Totals include National Grasslands land utilization projects and other special areas administered by the Forest Service.

top soil into streams and rivers. Secondly, the soil, containing a smaller amount of permanent moisture, is more susceptible to drought. Thirdly, during dry spells, high winds strip off enormous amounts of top soil, carrying it away as dust.

As compared with plowed land, it is estimated that grass-covered soil retains two to three times as much water from a given rainfall and that forests in turn retain twice as much as do pastures.

Prescriptions to retard damage include:

1. Contour farming across the slopes, rather than up and down the slopes.
2. Building brush and log dams across gullies and small streams.
3. Retention and/or development of woodlots on farms and planting of trees to serve as windbreaks to prevent wind erosion.
4. Rotation of crops, including in the cycle the raising of grasses and soil-enriching plants, such as clover and other legumes.

Partly to encourage this form of conservation, Congress passed a Soil Conservation Act in 1936. The Soil Conservation Service was established as a result of this act, making technical service available to farmers for the development of soil and water conservation practices. In addition to this technical assistance from the U.S. Soil Conservation Service and local Soil and Water Conservation Districts, farmers also receive payments from the Federal government to help share the cost of establishing soil and water conservation practices.

ANIMAL INDUSTRY

During the early period of man's development, wild animals were a valuable source of food and of clothing. Later, certain of the larger animals were tamed and used as beasts of burden. Fine furs are still taken chiefly from wild animals; but, as the population of the earth increased in numbers and advanced in the arts of civilization, man learned that better meat, more comfortable clothing, and superior types of motive power could be obtained from domestic animals. By careful selection and breeding, he gradually developed these animals to suit his needs.

Nevertheless, the number of species used by man is very small. Swine, cattle, sheep and goats, horses, mules, and asses comprise more than 99 per cent of all live stock exclusive of poultry. These animals are extensively distributed throughout the temperate zones, the type or species most suitable to any locality depending almost entirely on the climate and on the condition of the soil.

Swine. The total number of swine in the U.S. in 1969 was 57 million. This was more than double the number of sheep and lambs, estimated at 21 million, but only about one-half of the 110 million cattle and calves on farms that year. Nevertheless, because of its rapid growth and great rate of reproduction, the hog is the chief meat-producing animal of the world. Hogs cannot live upon grass, but require a more concentrated food. They are found, therefore, wherever grain is raised, because the feeding of grain to hogs usually results in a more valuable food product. A large part of the American corn crop goes to market as pork. In fact, the corn belt is the center of the hog-raising industry.

Modern breeds of swine are meat-type hogs. The Hampshire, Duroc, Yorkshire, Chester White, and Poland China breeds are popular domestic types and produce excellent hams, bacon, and other cuts. Breeding stock, such as the Landrace breed, developed in Denmark, have also been introduced into the U.S. from Europe since World War II as the newer meat-type animals have gained in popularity over older lard-type strains. In number of swine produced, China, Brazil, the United States, and Russia are the four leading countries.

Sheep. Just as pork is the principal meat of grain-producing countries, so mutton and wool are the chief animal products of all dry, rough, and thinly settled, grass-growing regions. Tunis, Algeria, and Morocco are known as the "sheep countries," and for centuries the shepherd has been representative of one of the most important industries of Syria, Palestine, and the great dry steppes of southern Russia and the Crimea. The semiarid regions of western United States and the high plateaus of Mexico are largely devoted to sheep raising. Australia leads all countries in number of sheep, Russia is second, United States third, and Argentina fourth. The number of sheep in the United States reached its maximum in 1903.

Draft Animals. The horse is the most important and the most valuable of all draft animals; nevertheless, for this purpose, it is exceeded in numbers, even at the present time, by the ox. In the production of horses, Russia is first, followed by the United States, Argentina, Brazil, China, Germany, and Canada. In Canada, horse raising is of unusual importance. The number of horses sometimes exceeds that of sheep and is almost equal to that of swine.

The United States produces more than half of the world's supply of mules. The greatest horse and mule market in the world is at East Saint Louis, Illinois.

The Percheron, which is considered by many to be the finest type of draft horse, was developed by French breeders in the south of Normandy. The English Shires are the largest of all horses. The breeding of thoroughbreds is most extensive in Great Britain.

As a beast of burden, the camel is especially well adapted to traveling in the desert, the reindeer to the plains of the arctic regions, and the yak to cold places of high altitude, such as Tibet. The llama performs in the Andes the same services as does the yak in the Himalayas. The elephant is extensively used in India as a draft animal, and his great power is utilized by almost every traveling circus. The dog is very useful for drawing sleds in the snow regions of North America, and is commonly used for hauling wagons in the densely populated sections of northwestern Europe.

Cattle. India, the United States, Russia, Argentina, Brazil, Germany, and China are the chief cattle producing countries of the world; but the chief beef exporting nations are Argentina and Australia. The cattle of India consist largely of the humped Brahman variety, and of the water buffalo. They are not used to any great extent for food. Cattle raising is quite generally divided into the production of beef cattle of the Hereford, Angus, Shorthorn, and newer cross-breed types such as the Santa Gertrudis, and of milk-producing breeds, such as the Holstein, Guernsey, and Jersey. In a new, level, thinly settled country, well covered with rich grass, beef cattle are raised on a large scale for the export of meat, hides, and tallow. Fresh beef can be shipped to any part of the world because of modern methods of artificial refrigeration. But, as the population increases, cattle ranges give place to farms, and the type of cattle gradually changes from beef producers to dairy animals. In order to produce more beef from fewer animals, the tendency of modern breeding is towards early maturing cattle. In Europe, where extensive pastures are no longer available, practically all cattle are stall-fed.

Poultry. Poultry raising is the most universal form of animal industry. All countries raise poultry, chiefly chickens. China leads in the production of eggs, with Russia second. The average commercial egg farm in the U.S. has 10,000 hens in its flock; some have as many as 2 million hens under single management with automated facilities. The U.S. produces in excess of 69 billion eggs per year. The U.S. is also a world leader in the production of turkeys, some 106 million in 1969, valued at nearly $415 million. Today in the United States, egg-producing hens, called layers, are either hybrids or

Leghorns. Meat-type birds come from highly specialized breeders; some breed only for the male line and others for only the female line.

Silk Culture. Annual production of silk amounts to about 75 million pounds, of which Japan produces more than half. Other important silk-producing countries include China, Russia, India, and Korea. The silk industry has become relatively less important as synthetic fibers have been developed and accepted. Annual importation of silk into the United States exceeds $300 million in value.

Bees. The production of honey is an industry that depends upon the food-storing instinct of the honeybee, and upon a supply of growing flowers to provide the nectar. Total production of honey in the U.S. is over 200 million pounds annually. This amount has declined steadily in recent years. Of even greater value is the service performed by bees in pollinating flowers of fruit trees and other useful plants.

Farm Animals in U. S. In 1940, each of the 6.1 million farms of the United States had on the average seven swine, ten cattle, seven sheep, two horses or mules, and 55 chickens, valued in all at $740.49. These animals produced, besides what was consumed on the farms, 399 dozen eggs, 49 pounds of wool, and 1916 gallons of milk, including that sold for making butter and cheese. The farm value of these products amounted to an average of $275.77 for each farm. The inhabitants of the Oceanic countries are the greatest meat-eaters in the world, with an average annual consumption exceeding 200 pounds per person. Per-capita consumption of meat in the United States in 1969 was 182 pounds. Beef consumption, in particular, has increased in recent years in the U.S.—from 82.1 pounds in 1957–59 to 110.5 pounds per person in 1969.

The most important breeding grounds of beef cattle in the United States are the western portion of the Corn Belt, the Great Plains, the valleys and high plateaus of the Far West, and the Gulf coast from Georgia to Texas.

Milk. The insuring of an adequate daily supply of fresh milk of standard quality in the large centers of population necessitates elaborate organization, specialized transportation, and rigid inspection. Most milk offered for sale is pasteurized, that is, heated to 161 degrees Fahrenheit for 15 seconds, or to as high as 190 degrees for one-half second in the flash pasteurization process, to kill all pathogenic bacteria. Many municipalities have insisted on a unified system of grading milk as A, B, and C. Grade A, either raw or pasteurized, must have not more than 10,000 bacteria per cubic centimeter; grades B and C, not more than 50,000. Grade B must be pasteurized under official supervision; grade C is pasteurized, but not under official supervision. By the Babcock test, devised in 1890 by S. M. Babcock, the proportion of fat in milk is readily determined. This normally varies from 3 to 6%. Large amounts of milk are concentrated and shipped in air-tight tins for use in the home or food factories. Wisconsin and New York are the leading states in milk production.

Serums and Vaccines. Employment of animals for the preparation of serums and of vaccine used in the treatment and prevention of diseases is a small but exceedingly important branch of animal industry. For example, diphtheria antitoxic serum is developed within the blood of healthy horses, while the vaccine used for preventing smallpox is generally obtained from calves.

There is a marked difference between antitoxin and vaccine. Diphtheria antitoxin, as its name implies, contains substances which, when injected into the blood of a person suffering from diphtheria, neutralize the poisons already produced in the blood by the active germs of that disease. A vaccine is the exact opposite of an antitoxin. Smallpox vaccine, for example, contains, in a greatly diluted or weakened form, the virus which tends to produce smallpox, or, rather, cowpox. When, by the process of vaccination, a minute quantity of vaccine is allowed to enter the system, the blood soon proceeds to develop within itself quantities of antitoxin which neutralize the virus.

In the preparation of diphtheria antitoxin, a very small amount of the poison produced by growing diphtheria germs is injected into a healthy horse. The horse develops a very mild fever, which soon disappears. Successively larger doses are administered at intervals until the horse receives without injury an amount of the toxin many hundreds of times that which would kill an ordinary animal.

Smallpox vaccine is obtained by vaccinating healthy young calves with smallpox or cowpox virus. The virus is applied in long narrow scratches, which, in about a week, develop the characteristic swelling that contains vaccine lymph. The virus produced in these lesions is collected, purified, diluted with glycerin, and quickly distributed.

Insulin. This extract, secured chiefly from the pancreas of cattle and hogs, is used extensively in the treatment of diabetic patients. It occurs in certain interior portions of the pancreas, known as the "islands of Langerhans." Diabetes is caused by a failure of the liver to act normally in transforming sugar into glycogen, and as a result the blood becomes surcharged with unassimilated sugar. Insulin, when injected into the blood, temporarily enables the liver to take this sugar from the blood.

DAIRYING

This term embraces the production of milk and the manufacture of milk products. While goats, sheep, camels, reindeer, mares, and the Asiatic buffalo are sometimes used as a source of milk, the cow alone is bred for the purpose and supports a huge dairy industry. The dairy industry was revolutionized in the late 19th century by the introduction of the centrifugal cream separator and of the Babcock test for determining the fat content of milk. The latter, invented in 1890, made possible the purchase of milk, for manufacture and distribution, on the basis of quality and greatly stimulated the improvement of herds.

The same period saw the rise of education in dairy management. A school of agriculture was opened in 1873 at Copenhagen, Denmark, which country has shown the most marked improvement in the quality of its milch cows. In 1890, at Madison, Wis., the first American school for dairying was opened, under the direction of W. A. Henry. Since that time numerous schools for dairying, experimental stations, and co-operative cow-testing associations have come into existence in the United States, Canada, and other countries. Australia, New Zealand, Argentina, Russia, and Switzerland are also large producers of milk and milk products.

Dairying in North America. In 1969 there were about 13 million dairy cows on U.S. farms, and the average milk produced per cow was 9,000 pounds. A United States gallon of milk weighs about 8.6 pounds; the Canadian gallon, about 10.3 pounds. Each person in the United States annually consumes about 5.4 pounds of butter, 10.8 pounds of margarine, 10.9 pounds of cheese, and 18.1 pounds of ice cream, in addition to 271 pounds, or about 31.5 gallons, of fluid milk and cream.

The chief dairying states are Wisconsin, New York, Iowa, Minnesota, California, and Pennsylvania. Wisconsin produces the greatest amount of butter, cheese, and condensed milk; New York, the most milk for market. The dairy production of the United States is valued at about $6.2 billion, or $31 per capita. Among the Canadian provinces, Ontario leads in the production of cheese and butter; Quebec ranks second.

Cheese and Other Milk Products. Cheese was a common article of diet at least as early as 1400 B. C. It is made from milk by separating the curd, or casein, portions of the fat, and other constituents from the whey, shaping the mass into different forms, and usually curing it. The separation is ordinarily effected by rennet, prepared from the stomachs of young calves or pigs. Upward of 150 kinds of cheese are made in Europe and America, the differences being dependent on the kind and condition of milk used, the manufacture, the seasoning, and especially the curing.

Milk is preserved either in the form of powder; as a sweet, slow-flowing liquid; or as an unsweetened, creamlike liquid. In these forms, which were first made about 1855, milk is now susceptible of much wider use than was formerly the case. It has become an important article of international commerce, and its use by bakers has resulted in a marked improvement in the quality of factory-made bread.

When used for ice cream, milk is generally *homogenized*, the fat globules being thereby rendered so small that they do not rise in the form of cream.

Casein obtained from milk is used in the manufacture of glue and also, in a plastic form, as a strong, elastic, noninflammable product resembling celluloid. Its uses include electric insulation and ornamental objects.

FISHERIES

The three greatest commercial fishing grounds of the world are located near the coasts of northwestern Europe, northeastern North America, and northeastern Asia. In these places, where the ocean is comparatively shallow, enormous "schools" of valuable food fishes congregate in order to obtain the food that they find near the bottom. A second important type of fisheries takes advantage of the spawning habits of certain fish, which, at the spawning season, travel up rivers or to the shores, where they are easily caught. The cod and haddock are chief examples of bottom feeders, while salmon and shad are the most valuable of the second group.

The rank of various nations in order of the size of their fish catch is approximately: Peru, Japan, Russia, Norway, United States, India, Spain, Canada, Denmark, and South Africa. In terms of value of catch, Japan ranks first, followed by the United States, the Philippines, Spain, and France. Data regarding value of the catch in mainland China and Russia are not available. Although the United States is among the top-ranked nations, the fishing industry is of less relative importance than in many other countries. The total catch of fish in the United States in 1974 was 4.9 billion pounds, valued at $898 million. In addition, 2.2 billion pounds of fish were imported from other countries, at a value of nearly $1.5 billion.

The development of the freezing process has increased the consumption of fish to an annual total of 15.01 pounds per person in the United States.

Fisheries in the U.S. Because of its great extent, the United States affords almost all kinds of fishing, from seal-fishing in Alaska to sponge-gathering in Florida. Shrimp are the most valuable product of the country's fisheries, with salmon second, tuna third, crabs fourth, and oysters fifth. The menhaden, though inedible, is important for its use in manufacturing fertilizer and for the industrial use of its oil.

Canadian Fisheries. Salmon caught in the Pacific regions of Canada are the most valuable product of the country's fisheries. Lobster and cod are second and third in value, with flounder and haddock together in fourth place. The total Canadian catch amounts to some 2.3 million tons annually, valued at nearly $545 million.

Secondary Products. In addition to food, there are many other uses for fishery products. From the whale are obtained the ordinary whale oil and whalebone, and also sperm oil, spermaceti wax, and ambergris, which is highly valued for use in fine perfumes. True caviar is prepared from the roe of the sturgeon, and the swimming bladder of the same fish is the source of the finest isinglass. Liquid glue is prepared from fishskins and offal, while crushed oyster, clam, and other shells are used for poultry grit, for surfacing roads, and for making lime. Sealskin, pearls, and corals are among the luxury products of the fisheries. Fish scales enter into *essence d'orient*, used in making artificial pearls.

ANIMAL INDUSTRY IN CANADA, 1974

PROVINCE	Milk Cows	Other Cattle	Sheep and lambs	Swine	Poultry
Alberta	190,000	3,920,000	181,000	1,195,000	3,132,000
British Columbia	109,000	490,000	34,000	56,000	4,215,000
Manitoba	118,000	1,076,000	21,000	635,000	3,735,000
New Brunswick	39,000	65,000	8,000	45,000	715,000
Nova Scotia	50,000	82,000	19,000	72,000	1,330,000
Ontario	847,000	2,464,000	138,000	1,900,000	13,375,000
PEI	28,000	73,000	5,000	87,000	159,000
Quebec	1,125,000	687,000	42,000	1,215,000	5,295,000
Saskatchewan	93,000	2,562,000	91,000	660,000	1,530,000
Canada	2,080,000	12,898,000	784,000	6,564,000	34,996,000

LEADING UNITED STATES CATTLE STATES, 1975

Rank	State	Number	Rank	State	Number	Rank	State	Number
1	Texas	15,600,000	6	Oklahoma	6,400,000	11	Kentucky	3,450,000
2	Iowa	7,500,000	7	California	5,000,000	12	Illinois	3,400,000
3	Missouri	6,600,000	8	Wisconsin	4,550,000	13	Colorado	3,250,000
4	Nebraska	6,550,000	9	South Dakota	4,500,000	14	Montana	3,150,000
5	Kansas	6,450,000	10	Minnesota	4,430,000	15	Tennessee	3,100,000

Source: U.S. Department of Agriculture.

POULTRY AND EGG PRODUCTION IN THE UNITED STATES, 1975

Source: Department of Agriculture, Statistical Reporting Service; annual report, *Agricultural Statistics.*

State	Eggs Produced on Farms (millions)	Chickens Raised on Farms (1,000)	Commercial Broilers Produced (1,000)	Turkeys Raised (1,000)	Chicks Hatched by Commercial Hatcheries (1,000)
Alabama	2,951	14,330	398,303	17	432,399
Alaska	5	36	.....	.....	.....
Arizona	159	518	.....	.....	.....
Arkansas	3,594	20,092	482,399	7,100	561,820
California	8,467	22,122	90,377	15,771	148,157
Colorado	473	2,188	.....	3,620	.....
Connecticut	798	3,100	1,836	36	4,733
Delaware	115	650	146,945	.....	145,462
Florida	2,779	11,300	59,727	.....	116,557
Georgia	5,284	20,800	426,857	1,216	487,191
Hawaii	209	565	1,900	.....	.....
Idaho	184	760	.....	.....	.....
Illinois	1,483	5,500	.....	445	10,750
Indiana	2,609	12,500	11,679	5,135	51,087
Iowa	2,006	10,600	3,615	6,260	20,645
Kansas	599	2,900	780	154	5,830
Kentucky	518	3,000	6,885	.....	.....
Louisiana	658	3,100	54,443	2	.....
Maine	1,650	8,300	77,426	6	98,510
Maryland	331	1,500	189,709	39	210,603
Massachusetts	541	1,800	.....	125	.....
Michigan	1,303	6,000	577	700	10,675
Minnesota	2,209	9,572	10,815	22,752	34,095
Mississippi	1,707	10,300	227,220	.....	248,419
Missouri	1,241	7,078	19,796	8,125	17,683
Montana	197	1,050	.....	.....	.....
Nebraska	782	2,400	2,312	487	4,173
Nevada	4.3	17	.....	.....	.....
New Hampshire	283	1,300	.....	21	.....
New Jersey	620	2,200	.....	74	.....
New Mexico	234	1,300	.....	.....	.....
New York	1,984	8,500	1,580	145	9,560
North Carolina	2,802	14,000	286,558	14,400	316,756
North Dakota	132	800	.....	911	.....
Ohio	1,999	8,900	11,900	2,835	.....
Oklahoma	430	2,100	29,560	1,370	1,698
Oregon	519	1,640	14,253	1,025	28,522
Pennsylvania	3,299	12,440	63,649	2,838	107,227
Rhode Island	69.5	220	.....	9	.....
South Carolina	1,385	6,180	31,552	2,585	32,645
South Dakota	702	3,550	.....	860	.....
Tennessee	949	2,300	42,586	4	.....
Texas	2,360	11,000	173,588	8,845	201,949
Utah	321	922	.....	3,446	883
Vermont	105	350	.....	7	.....
Virginia	765	4,400	77,220	5,972	95,921
Washington	1,068	4,460	16,730	225	18,825
West Virginia	256	1,050	18,293	1,530	.....
Wisconsin	1,194	4,300	11,274	4,894	.....
Wyoming	29.7	95	.....	.....	.....
Total	64,362	274,085	2,992,344	124,255	3,622,875

PRODUCTION OF FARM CROPS AND MEAT OF LEADING COUNTRIES, 1968

Source: *Statistical Abstract of the United States, 1970.*

In Thousands of Short Tons

Country	Wheat	Rice	Cotton	Corn	Potatoes	Sugar	Meat
Argentina	6,327	312	79	7,231	2,168	1,028	3,248
Australia	16,189	244	21‡	222	737	3,086	1,932
Austria	1,152	—	—	440	3,828	330	511
Belgium	942	—	—	3	1,726	634	668
Brazil	944	7,332	657	14,125	1,770	4,824	2,446
Canada	19,495	—	6	2,261	2,655	130	1,615
Chile	1,345	103	—	354	799	187	280
China (mainland)	28,329*	101,412†	1,602	N.A.	N.A.	2,756	N.A.
Colombia	143	860	132	970	937	731	530
Cuba	—	210	—	132†	116†	5,859	270
Denmark	511	—	—	—	955	376	1,020
Ecuador	84	—	—	220	389	—	—
Egypt (UAR) . .	1,652	2,851	482	2,532	520	456	482
Finland	569	—	—	—	1,001	54	193
France	16,144	91	—	5,897	11,016	2,536	3,289
Germany, Fed. Rep.	6,832	—	—	316	21,154	2,176	3,677
Greece	1,670	119	82	413	714	132	226
Hungary	3,704	45	82	4,204	1,799	465	517
India	18,232	65,743	1,195	6,284	4,665	2,618	642
Indonesia	—	17,093	—	3,368	46‡	661	227
Iran	5,486	1,055	176	......	......	......	......
Iraq	1,500	384	......	......	......	......	......
Ireland	448	—	—	—	1,791	168	430
Italy	10,571	704	2	4,396	4,365	1,422	1,372
Japan	1,116	20,685	—	56	4,471	669	847
Korea, Rep. of . .	94‡	2,756‡	4	69	680	—	108
Mexico	2,088	502	592	10,318	441	2,575	653
Netherlands . . .	748	—	—	1†	5,561	787	1,006
New Zealand . .	487	—	—	227	331	—	1,048
Norway	......	......	—	—	1,005	—	146
Pakistan	7,341	22,118	585	693	993	473	408
Paraguay	......	......	11	198	11	41	159
Peru	165	441	111	650	1,874	829	163
Philippines . . .	—	5,326	—	1,603	13†	1,819	358
Poland	5,148	—	—	14	56,016	2,041	2,008
Portugal	879	169	—	583	1,147	15	192
Rumania	5,344	66	—	7,832	4,085	457	449
South Africa . . .	1,350	2†	17	5,700	548†	1,895	685
Spain	6,041	399	78	1,624	4,118	789	902
Sweden	1,167	—	—	—	1,570	326	438
Switzerland . . .	411	—	—	—	1,210	75	353
Syria	661	9	......	......	......	......	......
Turkey	10,584	226	480	1,102	1,990	772	205
U.S.S.R.	102,947	1,172	2,255	9,731	112,637	10,784	11,739
United Kingdom .	3,824	—	—	—	7,546	1,033	2,230
United States . .	47,289	5,265	2,737	122,493	14,700	5,626	17,618
Uruguay	534	115	—	76	103†	77	459
Venezuela	—	299	14	661	175	373	250
Yugoslavia . . .	4,809	20	3	7,507	3,186	477	713
World Total . .	366,100	314,300	12,500	275,800	346,500	73,700	85,600

* 1966. † 1967. † 1965. — None or negligible.

DOMESTIC ANIMALS ON FARMS

	Horses and Mules	All Cattle		Milk Cows		Sheep and Lambs	Hogs and Pigs
	1959	1964	1975	1964	1974	1975	1975
Alabama	93,000	1,848,000	2,700,000	160,800	95,000	4,400	820,000
Alaska	N.A.	8,000	9,300	2,000	1,700	12,400	700
Arizona	51,000	1,104,000	1,170,000	46,000	62,000	510,000	97,000
Arkansas	77,000	1,574,000	2,680,000	132,000	92,000	5,500	302,000
California	77,000	4,303,000	5,200,000	732,000	797,000	1,100,000	138,000
Colorado	65,000	2,499,000	3,375,000	93,000	76,000	990,000	290,000
Connecticut	4,000	123,000	110,000	72,000	55,000	5,500	6,800
Delaware	3,000	37,000	33,000	18,000	12,200	1,900	55,000
Florida	27,000	1,822,000	2,950,000	176,000	201,000	4,200	240,000
Georgia	71,000	1,747,000	2,420,000	153,000	130,000	3,500	1,300,000
Hawaii	7,000	218,000	250,000	14,000	12,800	....	58,000
Idaho	50,000	1,603,000	2,150,000	165,000	149,000	595,000	90,000
Illinois	74,000	3,751,000	3,200,000	422,000	262,000	229,000	5,600,000
Indiana	53,000	2,053,000	2,125,000	328,000	220,000	196,000	3,900,000
Iowa	81,000	7,285,000	7,350,000	736,000	407,000	460,000	12,600,000
Kansas	68,000	5,150,000	6,400,000	241,000	147,000	200,000	1,650,000
Kentucky	145,000	2,341,000	3,750,000	407,000	297,000	40,000	1,000,000
Louisiana	87,000	1,867,000	1,832,000	187,000	137,000	15,000	170,000
Maine	8,000	158,000	138,000	76,000	60,000	13,000	7,300
Maryland	15,000	415,000	444,000	175,000	136,000	17,000	235,000
Massachusetts	5,000	127,000	107,000	79,000	54,000	7,900	55,000
Michigan	36,000	1,725,000	1,640,000	574,000	420,000	167,000	700,000
Minnesota	58,000	4,281,000	4,430,000	1,237,000	890,000	390,000	3,000,000
Mississippi	141,000	2,351,000	3,000,000	248,000	129,000	7,000	351,000
Missouri	102,000	4,522,000	6,800,000	461,000	314,000	194,000	3,200,000
Montana	86,000	2,873,000	3,340,000	55,000	28,000	710,000	145,000
Nebraska	68,000	5,987,000	6,900,000	250,000	158,000	280,000	2,700,000
Nevada	19,000	609,000	657,000	13,000	14,000	151,000	9,000
New Hampshire	4,000	82,000	71,000	44,000	32,000	5,600	8,700
New Jersey	7,000	153,000	117,000	97,000	50,000	10,100	98,000
New Mexico	43,000	1,203,000	1,720,000	35,000	31,000	578,000	53,000
New York	47,000	1,959,000	1,875,000	1,134,000	905,000	79,000	90,000
North Carolina	145,000	906,000	1,120,000	198,000	152,000	11,000	1,900,000
North Dakota	57,000	2,465,000	2,635,000	229,000	125,000	315,000	350,000
Ohio	74,000	2,164,000	2,350,000	544,000	407,000	517,000	1,675,000
Oklahoma	90,000	4,200,000	6,500,000	168,000	124,000	89,000	300,000
Oregon	44,000	1,620,000	1,470,000	126,000	91,000	415,000	90,000
Pennsylvania	58,000	1,789,000	1,960,000	791,000	687,000	125,000	660,000
Rhode Island	1,000	16,000	12,000	10,000	5,900	2,500	9,000
South Carolina	68,000	555,000	710,000	77,000	57,000	1,400	540,000
South Dakota	61,000	4,144,000	4,950,000	223,000	164,000	792,000	1,400,000
Tennessee	139,000	2,136,000	3,300,000	370,000	218,000	19,000	920,000
Texas	237,000	9,766,000	16,600,000	392,000	349,000	2,688,000	780,000
Utah	30,000	748,000	900,000	75,000	78,000	697,000	43,000
Vermont	9,000	368,000	336,000	230,000	193,000	6,300	4,500
Virginia	84,000	1,312,000	1,750,000	246,000	159,000	177,000	660,000
Washington	38,000	1,376,000	1,420,000	192,000	181,000	93,000	71,000
West Virginia	38,000	482,000	540,000	84,000	42,000	128,000	50,000
Wisconsin	59,000	4,384,000	4,640,000	2,083,000	1,801,000	105,000	1,150,000
Wyoming	49,000	1,348,000	1,690,000	23,000	13,200	1,350,000	30,000
Total	2,953,000	105,558,000	131,826,000	14,623,000	11,219,000	14,512,000	49,602,000

Source: *1959 data, 1959 Census of Agriculture; 1964 data, Dept. of Agriculture, Statistical Reporting Service; 1975 data, Agricultural Statistics, 1976.*

PUREBRED BEEF AND DUAL-PURPOSE CATTLE

Source: *Breeder's Gazette, March 1964*

Number of new registrations each year, as reported by breed associations, United States

Year	Aberdeen Angus	Devon	Hereford	Polled Hereford	Red Poll	Shorthorn	Brahman
1936	15,023	208	124,278	8,000	1,382	36,521	....
1937	17,278	236	134,679	6,732	1,418	34,424	....
1938	19,248	214	135,454	7,946	1,624	33,575	....
1939	25,308	259	159,408	8,717	2,350	41,025	....
1940	40,778	285	191,405	10,848	2,876	41,431	4,409
1941	38,737	336	207,517	15,244	2,724	50,120	4,132
1942	46,820	338	250,527	17,372	2,522	54,471	[1]
1943	52,432	398	288,675	17,034	3,155	52,845	8,536
1944	57,717	443	298,421	18,881	4,267	60,504	7,054
1945	66,020	401	316,081	31,863	3,958	63,988	10,954
1946	71,968	397	336,193	24,200	4,088	69,418	10,623
1947	81,992	403	356,530	33,000	4,366	80,853	14,928
1948	84,548	365	352,888	37,121	4,296	58,538	15,145
1949	87,722	...	370,015	37,179	4,689	73,986	17,220
1950	110,442	601	426,971	44,263	4,782	76,965	19,177
1951	138,896	511	506,061	61,513	5,093	108,565	20,610
1952	164,329	500	548,418	71,580	5,011	47,938	24,013
1953	160,754	710	560,794	78,152	4,225	47,674	17,873
1954	213,410	534	552,554	80,020	3,834	48,487	17,010
1955	186,316	560	522,639	101,084	3,443	48,963	16,564
1963	345,576	5,308	513,076	174,575	2,135	38,294	13,791

[1]No report of registration received.

PUREBRED DAIRY CATTLE

Number of new registrations, by breeds, United States

Breed	1948	1949	1950	1951	1952	1953	1954	1955	1963
Ayrshire:									
Bulls	4,175	3,904	3,412	3,458	2,604	2,357	2,178	2,018	*
Cows	21,938	22,413	20,824	22,005	20,604	22,013	20,815	21,017	*
Total	26,113	26,317	24,236	25,463	23,208	24,370	22,993	23,035	14,605
Brown Swiss:									
Bulls	6,295	5,637	5,759	5,827	*				
Cows	16,330	15,678	16,962	19,936	*				
Total	22,625	21,315	22,721	25,763	23,385	21,854	22,854	21,667	16,854
Guernsey:									
Bulls	18,939	17,227	16,013	14,181	13,669	9,622	7,882	7,589	*
Cows	77,956	72,679	78,888	79,448	100,240	79,986	73,663	73,977	*
Total	96,895	89,906	94,901	93,629	113,909	89,608	81,545	81,566	55,670
Holstein-Friesian:									
Bulls	35,576	36,329	36,662	36,629	32,424	25,752	23,539	23,469	*
Cows	132,762	141,596	147,584	155,009	157,266	163,810	172,424	174,139	*
Total	168,338	177,925	184,246	191,638	189,690	189,572	195,963	197,608	258,568
Jersey:									
Bulls	12,152	11,273	10,654	9,145	7,934	7,841	6,041	5,777	*
Cows	56,974	54,701	58,325	59,506	62,924	79,741	54,555	54,483	*
Total	69,126	65,974	68,979	68,651	70,858	87,582	60,596	60,260	43,363

*Individual figures not available.

AGRICULTURAL INDUSTRY IN

State	Electricity*	Electric water pump*	Telephones*	Distance to trading Center most frequently used		
				1 to 4 miles	5 to 9 miles	10 miles and over
Alabama	144,589	31,857	17,442	80,801	56,360	50,501
Arizona	8,062	4,630	4,408	3,421	2,308	3,176
Arkansas	121,916	30,808	19,201	77,044	50,517	34,350
California	124,613	85,194	78,720	64,636	32,625	20,450
Colorado	36,541	18,623	27,048	13,828	11,349	16,298
Connecticut	14,425	11,175	13,081	6,940	4,795	1,835
Delaware	6,112	4,665	4,990	3,263	2,662	491
Florida	40,535	24,235	10,253	19,220	16,776	13,711
Georgia	149,271	52,916	18,624	73,390	66,754	40,656
Idaho	37,232	25,874	22,264	14,457	12,433	9,832
Illinois	169,645	105,237	127,618	81,116	65,093	31,351
Indiana	152,864	99,299	102,904	68,422	57,180	26,767
Iowa	184,787	116,983	166,380	78,935	73,690	32,858
Kansas	97,668	41,245	89,760	41,610	44,185	32,347
Kentucky	145,246	28,940	45,808	90,410	52,607	41,129
Louisiana	83,191	30,485	14,364	53,779	29,948	20,187
Maine	26,200	14,798	19,467	12,821	8,568	5,370
Maryland	30,302	20,765	19,457	15,749	10,121	6,348
Massachusetts	20,365	10,294	17,319	10,930	5,526	2,306
Michigan	146,902	114,255	83,136	66,687	55,320	22,426
Minnesota	150,755	101,391	107,359	65,896	69,101	33,833
Mississippi	140,695	36,188	16,425	97,035	75,862	55,320
Missouri	159,165	53,461	106,673	91,862	72,121	41,903
Montana	26,335	15,134	9,995	7,353	7,956	17,636
Nebraska	83,309	38,115	69,541	34,285	38,741	24,949
Nevada	2,184	1,457	1,550	949	700	1,056
New Hampshire	12,696	7,904	10,055	5,690	4,150	2,118
New Jersey	23,281	19,427	17,829	10,922	7,567	3,113
New Mexico	14,037	5,595	3,500	6,381	4,500	9,657
New York	117,262	79,735	87,767	55,746	38,471	16,417
North Carolina	219,417	71,021	23,347	111,337	85,498	62,154
North Dakota	44,200	19,812	27,214	15,894	22,791	22,711
Ohio	185,681	118,286	119,721	85,869	65,452	31,115
Oklahoma	93,315	30,512	47,161	45,054	47,291	38,594
Oregon	56,618	37,762	30,104	22,740	16,072	14,970
Pennsylvania	133,919	85,391	77,211	58,291	46,106	28,561
Rhode Island	2,411	1,862	1,998	1,011	746	489
South Carolina	95,025	32,961	11,901	51,902	47,985	29,191
South Dakota	45,898	16,631	37,221	16,690	22,242	23,650
Tennessee	165,541	41,694	43,541	94,713	57,025	45,843
Texas	260,373	89,647	79,080	106,288	100,888	93,197
Utah	21,602	5,448	12,515	8,397	4,574	4,460
Vermont	17,533	7,595	13,267	8,899	5,133	2,591
Virginia	114,273	40,701	35,853	56,202	37,830	38,524
Washington	64,599	42,293	40,166	29,037	19,397	14,287
West Virginia	59,141	13,915	21,724	32,736	19,683	19,003
Wisconsin	156,382	121,229	99,821	71,273	61,036	24,004
Wyoming	9,432	4,716	4,735	2,958	2,284	6,428
Total	4,213,563	2,011,162	2,059,625	2,072.940	1,640,239	1.117.473

* Latest available statistics. Based on reports for sample of farms.

THE UNITED STATES **

Motor Trucks*		Tractors*		Automobiles*		Farms Operated by Full Owners	State
Farms Reporting	Number	Farms Reporting	Number	Farms Reporting	Number		
56,000	70,000	53,000	79,000	64,000	82,000	92,530	Alabama
5,000	17,000	4,000	14,000	5,000	11,000	6,477	Arizona
60,000	81,000	54,000	105,000	53,000	65,000	79,898	Arkansas
64,000	126,000	62,000	158,000	36,000	49,000	80,852	California
27,000	56,000	26,000	68,000	27,000	39,000	29,798	Colorado
5,000	10,000	5,000	13,000	6,000	9,000	6,068	Connecticut
3,000	5,000	4,000	10,000	4,000	6,000	4,401	Delaware
24,000	41,000	24,000	46,000	31,000	43,000	40,542	Florida
57,000	77,000	59,000	97,000	67,000	90,000	83,366	Georgia
26,000	48,000	27,000	66,000	27,000	37,000	29,661	Idaho
99,000	121,000	125,000	335,000	125,000	166,000	132,822	Illinois
78,000	99,000	98,000	231,000	99,000	137,000	108,082	Indiana
97,000	107,000	144,000	352,000	149,000	201,000	154,162	Iowa
80,000	134,000	85,000	194,000	86,000	115,000	92,440	Kansas
74,000	90,000	88,000	144,000	102,000	131,000	133,038	Kentucky
40,000	51,000	36,000	65,000	46,000	56,000	62,466	Louisiana
9,000	15,000	10,000	20,000	11,000	15,000	12,875	Maine
14,000	21,000	18,000	45,000	18,000	28,000	20,760	Maryland
6,000	11,000	6,000	14,000	7,000	10,000	8,019	Massachusetts
63,000	80,000	88,000	204,000	88,000	122,000	93,504	Michigan
91,000	113,000	125,000	308,000	126,000	175,000	131,163	Minnesota
61,000	75,000	53,000	95,000	71,000	88,000	109,141	Mississippi
100,000	123,000	126,000	256,000	124,000	150,000	141,315	Missouri
25,000	58,000	25,000	69,000	25,000	35,000	27,020	Montana
64,000	93,000	75,000	190,000	77,000	106,000	80,163	Nebraska
2,000	4,000	2,000	6,000	2,000	3,000	2,156	Nevada
3,000	6,000	4,000	8,000	4,000	6,000	4,648	New Hampshire
9,000	17,000	9,000	26,000	10,000	15,000	10,641	New Jersey
12,000	23,000	9,000	19,000	11,000	15,000	14,206	New Mexico
43,000	63,000	62,000	157,000	61,000	84,000	66,510	New York
84,000	101,000	102,000	164,000	116,000	151,000	148,202	North Carolina
45,000	82,000	47,000	130,000	46,000	65,000	48,836	North Dakota
74,000	91,000	109,000	249,000	111,000	160,000	120,381	Ohio
73,000	105,000	66,000	116,000	71,000	87,000	88,726	Oklahoma
32,000	54,000	34,000	76,000	36,000	49,000	39,757	Oregon
54,000	70,000	75,000	173,000	75,000	110,000	83,086	Pennsylvania
1,000	2,000	1,000	2,000	1,000	2,000	1,100	Rhode Island
30,000	39,000	33,000	54,000	44,000	58,000	56,248	South Carolina
39,000	57,000	47,000	125,000	47,000	66,000	49,703	South Dakota
74,000	86,000	86,000	138,000	97,000	122,000	133,446	Tennessee
152,000	211,000	152,000	285,000	163,000	205,000	205,110	Texas
13,000	20,000	13,000	25,000	14,000	19,000	15,759	Utah
6,000	8,000	8,000	19,000	8,000	12,000	9,247	Vermont
46,000	59,000	56,000	103,000	59,000	78,000	80,354	Virginia
36,000	64,000	39,000	83,000	42,000	60,000	45,574	Washington
20,000	24,000	23,000	39,000	24,000	29,000	34,504	West Virginia
82,000	97,000	113,000	285,000	113,000	154,000	116,816	Wisconsin
8,000	18,000	8,000	23,000	8,000	11,000	9,038	Wyoming
2,167,000	3,030,000	2,520,000	5,486,000	2,675,000	3,593,000	3,157,857	Total

* Based on reports for sample of farms. ** Source: U.S. Census of Agriculture 1964 Vol. II.

MINING AND MINERALS

Mining includes all methods and processes involved in obtaining valuable mineral materials—organic and inorganic—from the earth's crust. Technically defined, minerals are earth substances with definite chemical compositions; however, in common usage the term mineral includes all elements and compounds occurring naturally. Consequently, coal and petroleum, which do not have definite chemical compositions, are classified as minerals. Most minerals must be treated, refined, or purified before they can be used. The processing of mined products is included in the science of metallurgy.

Mining is purely an extractive process. For this reason it is the most destructive of the primary industries by which man satisfies his wants. A ruined forest may be replaced, if necessary, within a few generations; even the number of fish in the sea may be greatly increased by artificial propagation. But, when a ton of coal or of iron ore has once been mined, the store available to future generations has been decreased by just so much. There can be no replacement. Mineral reserves may, however, be enlarged by new discoveries, mining improvements, and new economic developments.

The distinctive character of modern commerce, industry, and civilization is due largely to the extensive employment of mined products. In addition to the important role mineral resources have in establishing living standards, they also have been and continue to be an extremely important element of international politics.

Historical. In human development, the acquirement of a knowledge of mining and metallurgy marks the change from savagery to barbarism. This change has not been made by all peoples at the same time. Copper was obtained from the mines of Sinai by the Egyptians 5000 or more years ago, while this stage was not reached in Europe until about 2000 B.C. Gold and meteoric iron, which are found as free metals, were used even earlier. Similarly, the natives of North America employed copper which they found near Lake Superior.

Copper was the first metal to be reduced from its ore. The Phoenicians, about 1000 B.C., obtained copper from Cyprus and Spain. They also got silver from Spain, and, for the tin needed to alloy with copper in making bronze, they sailed to the British Isles. The Romans mined iron on the island of Elba. In the 16th century the search for gold drew the Spanish to South America. There they found gold in vast quantities, although the Aztecs still used weapons and tools of bronze.

Mining Products. These important substances may be classified as metals or nonmetals. The first group supplies the materials from which tools and machines are constructed. Examples of metals are: iron ore, manganese ore, copper, aluminum, gold, and uranium.

Nonmetals are divided into mineral fuels and other nonmetallic minerals. The mineral fuels include liquid (petroleum), gaseous (natural gas), and solid (hard and soft coal) minerals. The nonmetallic minerals include building, chemical, fertilizer, ceramic, and insulating materials; refractory (or heat-resistant) materials used in making asbestos fabrics, insulation, and furnace linings; abrasives; pigments and fillers; and precious and semiprecious stones.

Types of Mines. Heavy minerals, of which gold is the most important, are frequently found disseminated throughout an alluvial or a glacial deposit. A mineral-bearing bed of this type is known as a placer, from the Spanish word *placel*, meaning sand bank. The simplest form of placer mining consists in shaking the gold-bearing earth in a pan of water with such a motion that the heavier particles sink to the bottom while much of the lighter material can be thrown over the side.

In *sluicing*, an operation which depends on the same principle, a stream of water flows through a wooden trough or other form of channel provided with corrugations, or riffles, on the bottom. Mercury is placed in the riffles. When placer dirt is shoveled into the sluice, the current carries away the lighter substance while the gold settles into the riffles, where it amalgamates with the mercury and is retained. The amalgam is collected and heated in a retort, from which the mercury distills, leaving the gold.

Hydraulicking is placer mining on a large scale. In this process the gravel bank is washed down into sluices by means of a stream of water under a pressure of 250 to 400 pounds per square inch. Huge dredges are also used on placer deposits, the buckets dropping the sand on screens, from which the fine particles pass to sluices, where the gold is recovered.

Where bodies of ore are to be found comparatively near the surface, *open-pit* mining is frequently most satisfactory. By this process the overburden of useless earth is removed so that the ore may be taken up by steam shovels and dropped directly into railroad cars. *Quarrying* is removing nonmetallic rock from shallow open-pit mines.

Drilled wells are used chiefly to obtain petroleum, natural gas, salt, and sulphur.

Underground mines are reached by tunnels entering the side of a hill or mountain, by shafts sloping gradually, or by vertical shafts. When the veins of mineral are reached, various systems of cutting away the ore are used so as to obtain as much of the valuable material as possible, consistent with economy, safety, and ease of working. Some of these methods are known as *stoping*, *room-and-pillar* mining, the *longwall* method, *milling*, and *caving*. Removal of the coal or ore may be accomplished by pick-and-shovel methods or by machines.

Development. The search for valuable bodies of minerals in the earth is known as prospecting. An oily spot on the surface of the ground an outcropping vein, rusty places, or a strip of unusually rich or poor vegetation may call attention to a useful deposit. Modern methods of prospecting are generally carried out by large companies in the light of geological knowledge supplied by scientific experts. Any region that gives indication of mineral wealth may be tested by means of core drills which bring up a section of the material through which they pass. Careful geological and chemical examination of the core forms a basis for a fairly accurate estimate of the amount and the quality of ore that may be expected.

Having established a promising location, shafts must be sunk, the ore blocked out by further drilling, and provision made for drainage and ventilation of the tunnels. If early indications are confirmed, machinery is installed, a mill or a cleaning house is constructed, and the mine is placed in operation.

Technical Processes. Magnetic ores are frequently separated from nonmagnetic substances by passing the powdered material through a magnetic field. A similar separation of conducting and nonconducting minerals may be produced by means of an electrostatic field. Gold-bearing ore taken from the lodes of underground mines usually consists chiefly of quartz. This hard material is reduced to powder by stamp mills or by other types of machinery and is then passed over copper plates coated with mercury. Much of the gold is retained by these plates. The remainder of the metal may be obtained by treating the powder with chlorine gas.

Production in the U.S. Although the U.S. has never been self-sufficient in minerals its total mineral production, since at least 1900, has been greater than total mineral imports. The Depression of the 1930s drastically slowed mineral production but before that, from 1900 to 1929, the U.S.

produced 89 per cent of all the minerals it consumed. After 1939 U.S. mineral production began to increase and has continued to increase; however, production has not increased at the same high rate as consumption.

In 1971 the U.S. was self-sufficient in molybdenum, phosphate, diatomite, talc, vermiculite, magnesium, bromine, clay, feldspar, boron minerals, coal, lime, and cement. Metal production is low in the U.S.; in 1972, the U.S. was self-sufficient in only two metals, molybdenum and magnesium.

For some time the U.S. was the world's principal market for raw minerals; but, since 1945 world mineral production has increased more rapidly than U.S. production. In the early 1970s the value of U.S. mineral imports was more than three times the value of U.S. mineral exports. The U.S. is still an important supplier of coal, molybdenum, phosphate, boron minerals, and sodium minerals. Of 35 major mineral commodities, the U.S. ranked first in production of 12, including natural gas, in 1974; the U.S. ranked second in production of 4, including coal and crude petroleum, in 1974.

In the early 1970s the U.S. consumed about one-quarter of the world's annual mineral production. Every year the U.S. is demanding more raw mineral materials than it can produce.

Bureau of Mines. This branch of the Department of the Interior was established by an act of Congress that became effective July 1, 1910.

It is the duty of the bureau to conduct scientific investigations with the objectives of improving technical processes and conditions of labor involved in the production and use of mineral wealth, and assisting industries in the reduction of pollution due to the mining and processing of minerals. As a result of the bureau's efforts, legislation has been passed to improve safety conditions and reduce pollution.

Economic Significance. Among the scores of minerals which the world produces, certain ones stand out as pre-eminently important by reason of their utility in our civilization. Among them are coal, gas, petroleum, iron, and gold.

Coal, gas, and petroleum are the basic fuels for the production of power, on which industrial civilization rests. Coal and gas are of primary importance for industrial power, and petroleum for motive power in transportation by sea, highway, and air.

Iron is by far the most essential metal in the machine age. When iron deposits are found close to coal deposits, the material elements are present for building up an economic empire. These conditions account to a large extent for the industrial growth of the U.S., Britain, Western Europe, and Russia.

Gold is placed among the premier minerals because of its unique value as a promoter of trade and commerce.

World Energy Crisis. By 1973 a grave and persisting crisis in energy faced the Western world. The problem was rooted in widespread wastage of power and was marked by factors of limited choice. The U.S., representing 6 per cent of the world's population, was consuming 30 per cent of the available world energy supplies. At the same time, three-quarters of current U.S. energy needs were met by gas and oil. American production of both of these sources of energy was declining, and only sharply limited resources remained for future production. Other sources of energy for the U.S. were more abundant in the form of adequate coal deposits, oil-rich rock shale, and the virtually unlimited resources of nuclear and solar energy. Yet the inherent restrictions in the complex of use, demand, price, choice, and availability of energy resources—and the long-standing reliance on imported sources of energy—endangered the economic security, as well as the foreign and domestic policy independence of the U.S., Japan, and other nations of the Americas, Europe, and Africa.

The situation worsened in 1973. That year war broke out once more between Egypt and Syria and Israel. Arab countries had been taking over more and more control of their own oil production and had formed the Organization of Petroleum Exporting Countries to control the price and distribution of oil. In the years that followed, world oil prices were quadrupled and embargoes were established against Western nations in an attempt to force Israel to withdraw from Arab lands. The rise in oil prices and the cutback in production increased world inflation, and intensified the already existent crises in energy and food supplies.

At the peak of the crisis the need was clear for a shift to new and primary forms of energy production. Such major changes had occurred twice before—from the use of wood as fuel in the mid-1800's to coal in the early 1900's, and a later shift from coal to oil and gas fuels. The two changeovers had each required some 60 years to accomplish. But in the troubled world of the mid-1970's it was clear that the West could not afford any such span of time to complete the needed shift in fuel use and sources.

Another factor emerged in the harsh winter of 1976-77. When record-breaking sub-zero weather hit the Eastern part of the country, natural gas companies found they did not have adequate supplies to meet the heavy demand. Some factories and schools had to close so that private homes could remain heated. Although many were surprised by these drastic measures, others had been predicting a crisis in natural gas. In preceding years, industry had begun to rely heavily on gas for their energy needs. In 1962, 45% of all energy consumed by manufacturers was natural gas; in 1974, the amount had risen to 54%. During the same period, the use of coal resources dropped from 24% to 10%. Natural gas use increased not only because it is efficient and non-polluting, but also because the price of gas passing through interstate pipelines was regulated by the federal government and did not increase at the same rate as other energy resources, such as coal. Under controlled prices, gas suppliers claimed they lacked "incentive" to develop more of the known reserves. From 1969 to 1976, total production remained about the same while demand greatly increased. The shortages of supplies became apparent to the public in late 1976. A short-term answer proposed was the deregulation of gas prices. Others thought the crisis had been artificially created to achieve a price increase. But almost everyone agreed that the country could no longer count on abundant supplies of natural gas.

Faced with these problems, three sets of priorities emerged. For the present near-term (until 1985) and beyond, the priorities were: (1) To preserve and expand major existing energy systems—coal, nuclear reactors (industrial furnaces for converting energy in atomic nuclei into heat energy), and gas and oil from new sources, together with improved methods of recovery. (2) To increase conservation and to improve the efficiency of energy use in all sectors of national economies.

For the mid-term (1985 to 2000) and beyond, the priorities were: (1) To accelerate the development of new processes to produce synthetic fuels from coal, to extract oil from rock shale, and to find alternate sources, such as the production of fuel alcohols from plant life. (2) To increase the use of underdeveloped energy forms such as natural springs of hot water and steam from underground, to make solar-energy devices available, and to extract more usable energy from waste heat.

For the far-term (past the year 2000), the following priorities appeared: (1) To pursue vigorously other possible technologies that would make available the unlimited resources of nuclear power reactors. (2) The fuller exploitation of solar energy through collection and transmission by space satellites. (3) The development of major devices to use wind power. (4) The perfection of other devices to harness the energy potentials of ocean forces.

CRUDE PETROLEUM PRODUCTION

(Crude oil and natural gas liquids; in 1,000 metric tons)

	1950	1960	1970	1975*
NORTH AMERICA				
Canada†	3,800	27,480	69,954	80,000
U.S.A.†	285,200	384,080	533,677	485,500
Mexico	10,296	14,125	21,877	37,500
CARIBBEAN				
Trinidad	2,980	6,075	7,225	10,000
Colombia	4,850	8,100	11,071	8,000
Venezuela ‡	78,140	148,690	193,209	124,000
SOUTH AMERICA				
Brazil	40	4,050	8,009	8,400
Ecuador ‡	360	390	191	8,050
Peru	2,050	2,680	3,450	3,500
Bolivia	80	450	1,128	2,000
Chile	80	990	1,620	1,200
Argentina	3,460	9,160	19,969	19,550
MIDDLE EAST				
Turkey	30	350	3,461	3,150
Iraq ‡	6,650	47,480	76,600	111,300
Iran ‡	32,260	52,065	191,663	268,200
Saudi Arabia ‡	26,620	61,090	176,851	337,300
Kuwait ‡	17,290	81,860	137,397	93,300
Kuwait neutral zone ‡	—	7,270	26,724	25,400
Bahrain	1,560	2,250	3,834	3,100
Qatar ‡	1,640	8,210	17,257	20,000
Abu Dhabi ‡	—	—	33,288	64,600
Dubai ‡	—	—	4,306	12,600
Oman	—	—	17,169	16,500
Syria	—	—	4,350	9,000
Egypt§	2,370	3,600	16,404	15,750
Sharjah	—	—	—	2,000
FAR EAST				
India	315	440	6,809	8,300
Pakistan	250	360	486	400
Burma	125	530	750	900
Indonesia ‡	6,450	20,560	42,102	63,000
Brunei	4,340	4,690	6,916	9,550
Japan	350	510	750	600

	1950	1960	1970	1975*
EUROPE				
Austria	1,600	2,440	2,798	2,000
Germany (West)	1,120	5,560	7,536	5,750
Netherlands	700	1,920	1,919	1,400
U.K.	40	90	84	1,130
France	120	2,260	2,308	1,050
Italy	8	1,990	1,408	1,030
Spain	—	—	156	1,888
Norway	—	—	—	9,350
Denmark	—	—	—	160
AFRICA (EXCLUDING EGYPT)				
Algeria ‡	80	8,630	47,253	42,600
Tunisia	—	—	4,151	4,500
Libya ‡	—	—	159,201	71,000
Gabon ‡ and Congo	—	850	5,460	13,800
Angola	—	70	5,066	7,000
Nigeria ‡	—	880	53,420	87,800
OCEANIA				
Australia	—	—	8,292	19,250
COMMUNIST COUNTRIES				
U.S.S.R.	37,500	148,000	352,667	490,000
Rumania	4,100	11,500	13,377	14,600
Yugoslavia	110	1,040	2,854	3,700
Hungary	500	1,215	1,937	2,000
Poland	175	195	424	550
Albania	395	600	1,199	2,300
Bulgaria	—	200	334	120
Czechoslovakia	50	140	203	150
Germany (East)	—	—	60	200
China‖	—	5,000	20,000	78,000
ESTIMATED TOTAL WORLD PRODUCTION#	538,470	1,090,680	2,336,153	2,702,140

* Provisional estimates. † 1970–1975 figures refer to all hydrocarbon liquids; 1950–1960 figures refer only to crude oil proper. ‡ OPEC member. § Including the Sinai fields. ‖ From 1963 the figures include shale and coal-based oil. # Estimates differ widely because of conversion difficulties of barrels to metric tons.

U.S. PETROLEUM IMPORTS: 1974–1976

(Quantity in barrels; value in dollars)*

	GENERAL IMPORTS†					
	December 1974		December 1975		March 1976	
COUNTRY OF ORIGIN	NET QUANTITY	VALUE	NET QUANTITY	VALUE	NET QUANTITY	VALUE
Canada	26,969,377	$326,091,774	22,721,799	$279,553,321	13,132,845	$164,411,764
Mexico	377,899	3,764,951	3,156,195	38,168,038	3,210,824	38,907,792
Trinidad	3,282,182	41,341,215	3,670,862	48,061,359	4,810,299	64,046,723
Venezuela	15,616,059	169,825,698	13,639,749	156,345,865	8,310,679	93,830,057
Ecuador	940,139	10,211,009	2,793,733	31,184,728	895,590	10,361,323
Iran	13,415,077	146,539,707	10,454,630	125,840,817	9,335,058	112,796,424
Kuwait	—	—	1,743,276	18,866,564	—	—
Saudi Arabia	22,462,804	242,298,573	30,528,842	351,257,167	35,046,306	411,718,075
Qatar	864,238	10,114,219	—	—	668,383	8,062,856
Arab Emirates	2,709,830	30,792,378	4,744,160	54,422,302	6,270,627	74,853,370
Indonesia	10,802,857	137,479,884	11,201,073	142,445,953	17,070,905	218,116,923
Algeria	8,309,887	103,486,750	6,162,862	78,325,606	12,390,951	159,719,111
Tunisia	49,119	610,057	443,458	5,654,089	414,282	5,364,952
Libya	—	—	10,616,623	131,485,522	11,649,986	143,854,909
Nigeria	24,685,879	294,709,315	24,469,311	309,065,517	28,312,098	363,826,669
Angola	295,278	3,428,178	1,587,453	18,557,326	41,734	521,675
Norway	—	—	839,397	9,713,148	624,474	7,930,819
Oman	443,181	4,879,425	491,367	5,827,613	51,668	617,949
Egypt	153,733	1,583,307	686,886	6,900,294	1,148,527	13,017,306
Gabon	702,419	7,716,930	968,631	11,206,006	1,081,177	12,508,990
Bolivia	—	—	273,031	3,677,728	—	—
Malaysia	—	—	220,620	2,786,431	225,994	2,854,304
TOTAL	132,079,958	$1,534,873,370	151,413,958	$1,829,345,394	154,692,407	$1,907,316,991

Source: Social and Economic Statistics Administration, U.S. Dept. of Commerce. * Data for U.S. Trade Statistics commodity numbers 475.0510 and 475.1010 combined. † General imports are a combination of entries for immediate consumption and entries into bonded warehouses. Imports for consumption are a combination of entries for immediate consumption and withdrawals from warehouses for consumption.

INVENTIONS

Primitive man became safely established in his supremacy over the lower animals when he invented the bow and arrow. Since that prehistoric time, millions of inventions have been made, each adding a part to the total sum of knowledge by which mankind is gradually achieving mastery of space and control of the forces of nature. Some inventions are of trifling importance; others are so fundamental that their development affects the lives of all civilized people. The history of human progress has been marked by a series of epoch-making inventions.

At Ghent, in Flanders, on December 14, 1814, a treaty was signed which formally declared at an end the War of 1812 between England and the United States. Nevertheless, fighting was still going on in Louisiana 59 *days* later, because news of the treaty had not yet arrived. Few examples could more strikingly illustrate the progress of invention during the last century. Today, an event of similar importance could be known throughout the country in less than 59 *minutes*.

An invention is considered to be any new and useful machine, art, manufacture, or composition of matter, or any new and useful improvement thereon. All civilized nations recognize the right of an inventor to his product, and, when all requirements have been fulfilled, will issue a written contract or *patent*, guaranteeing to him the exclusive right to the use of his invention for a definite period of time. The life of a United States patent is 17 years. Approximately 3.5 million patents have been issued by the United States patent office. Comparatively few have shown themselves to be valuable.

SOME NOTED INVENTIONS OF MODERN TIMES

Certain inventions have proved to be of special importance because of their marked influence upon the welfare and the progress of mankind. Talking machines, telephones, and motion pictures, for example, are so much a part of our daily life that the wonderful principles governing their operation usually receive but little attention. Some of the more noteworthy of these inventions are given special treatment in the articles that follow.

Air Brake. A device, invented by George Westinghouse, Jr. in 1869, for applying the brakes to the cars of a railroad train by means of compressed air. Although the original system has been greatly improved in many ways by Westinghouse and others, the following description applies to the mechanism common both to passenger and to freight trains.

Each car is equipped with a *brake cylinder*, in which there is a piston connected to the brake shoes by a rod; an *auxiliary reservoir* to hold compressed air; a *triple valve*; and a train pipe with flexible couplings at each end. On the locomotive, in addition to its own brakes, are a steam driven *air compressor* which supplies air to the whole system, a *main air reservoir*, and the *control valve* operated by the engineer.

Under normal conditions, equal pressures of about 70 pounds are maintained in the train pipe and in the auxiliary reservoirs, and this condition of equal pressure holds the triple valve in a position closing the brake cylinder. To *set* the brakes, the engineer allows air to *escape* from the train pipe, thus reducing the pressure below that of the auxiliary reservoir. The triple valve then changes so that air enters the brake cylinder and forces the brake shoes against the wheels.

To *release* the brakes, the engineer allows air from the main reservoir, which has about 110 pounds pressure, to enter the train pipe until it again has a pressure equal to that in the auxiliary reservoir. The triple valve then resumes its normal position and the pressure is removed from the brakes. It is obvious that, if the coupling of a car becomes detached or broken, the train pipe pressure is lowered and the brakes are immediately applied.

This system has been of great importance in the development of the railroads because it allows the engineer to have complete control of his train, and permits of quick stops at high speed, either in an emergency or under ordinary running conditions.

Airplane, or **Aeroplane.** A heavier-than-air flying machine that flies because of the lifting effect of *moving* air upon a surface inclined to the wind at a small angle. The necessary movement of the air is relative to that of the airplane. For example; a speed of about 35 miles per hour *with respect to the air* is generally required before a flying machine can leave the ground. If the air is still, the machine will have to travel along the ground at 35 miles per hour, but, if a 20-mile wind is blowing, the machine can rise when moving into the wind at only 15 miles per hour.

Airplanes are usually classified, according to the number of their supporting surfaces, as *monoplanes* or *biplanes;* the latter type is becoming less common. The planes are not flat, but are curved upward, with the greatest curve near the front edge. A two or three bladed propeller at the front is driven by a gasoline motor. The larger military and cargo planes have two or four engines.

Among notable attempts to solve the problem of artificial flight was the work of Lilienthal and Chanute, with gliders; and of Ader, Maxim, and Langley, who, with the aid of their respective governments, built power driven machines which were usually destroyed by accidents at the first trial.

Orville and Wilbur Wright, bicycle manufacturers of Dayton, Ohio, were interested in aviation, and they found after many tests that the current theories were partly correct and partly guesswork. The Wrights devoted their attention chiefly toward a means of securing stability of a machine when in the air. They succeeded in developing a system of maintaining balance and control by bending or warping the ends of the planes, and using an elevating rudder in front. On December 17, 1903, they achieved flights of from 12 to 59 seconds, Wilbur being the first to fly successfully in a heavier-than-air machine. Reports of this work traveled to Europe and encouraged the French school of enthusiasts to continue their efforts. Alberto Santos-Dumont was the first of these to succeed, when in 1906 he made flights of several hundred feet. The French airplanes differed from the Wright type in having a tail, which was not adopted by the Wrights until about seven years later. Glenn H. Curtiss, in America, developed a type of biplane, and in 1911 and 1912 he developed the hydro-airplane and flying boat, capable of rising from and landing on the water.

From 1908 the development of the airplane was very rapid, especially in France and Germany. Improved engines also supplied greater power although they weighed much less. Of these, the rotary engines are most peculiar because the cylinders are placed like the spokes of a wheel, and revolve around a fixed crank shaft. The motors commonly used average two pounds in weight per horse power; some racing motors are as light as .8 pounds per horse power.

In World War I airplanes carried machine guns and even small cannon. These guns were often geared to fire between the revolving blades of the propeller. In World War II the armament was greatly increased. Bombing planes can carry bombs weighing up to 4000 pounds. Photographic equipment is used for reconnaissance and for checking the damage done by bombing. Radio keeps the aviator in communication with other planes. By the use of gliders, engineless planes towed by another plane, an entire army may be transported by air and set down behind the enemy's lines. Since World War II the development of jet-propelled planes, particularly the propellerless jet and the turbo-propeller jet, has given military planes supersonic speed. In September 1948 the U. S. Air Force F-86 made 670 m.p.h., and the F-110 is capable of going 1500 m.p.h. Experimental craft have gone 4100 m.p.h.

Noteworthy aerial achievements include the first non-stop flight across the Atlantic Ocean, 1930 miles from Newfoundland to Ireland, in 16 hours, 12 minutes, made in 1919 by English aviators, Alcock and Brown; a discontinuous flight of 26,103 miles around the world in 365 hours, 11 minutes, of flying time, made in 1924 by U. S. Army Air Service planes; and an altitude record of 310,000 feet by Major Robert M. White, an American, in 1962. The first American passenger air line service was begun on November 1, 1920, between Key West and Havana.

Various types of airplanes have been built for vertical ascent. The most successful is the autogiro, invented in 1923 by De la Cierva, a Spaniard. It differs from all other heavier-than-air craft in the source of its lifting power. This lift is given, not by wings, but by four rotating blades hinged to a nearly vertical spindle and moving in a horizontal plane. They rotate by wind pressure, and are not driven by the engine, the sole function of which is to propel the machine. The autogiro can climb steeply and descend almost vertically at a speed less than a man with a parachute, thereby eliminating the hazards of landing which attend the usual type of airplane. Moreover, it is proof against falling into a spin, and can maintain itself in the air at a forward speed as slow as 25 miles an hour. See *Aeronautics, Transportation by Air.*

Airship. A dirigible balloon as distinguished from an airplane. Ordinary balloons were invented by the Montgolfier brothers in 1783, and in the same year Pilâtre de Rozier made the first ascension. Attempts were made, almost from the beginning, to control the direction of flight. However, the first successful dirigible was not built until 1852 when Henri Giffard propelled a balloon at six miles per hour by means of a three horse power steam engine. Alberto Santos-Dumont constructed 14 dirigibles. As all of the earlier airships were handicapped by lack of light, powerful motors, it remained for the Lebaudy brothers, Major Parseval, and Count Ferdinand von Zeppelin to develop dirigibles capable of fulfilling the requirements for military use.

Dirigible balloons may be classified as rigid, semirigid, and nonrigid. The rigid type has a strong skeleton or framework inside the envelope; the semirigid is held by a network of wires and rods; the nonrigid is merely a large bag of gas. Successful development of the rigid type is due largely to Zeppelin, whose airships were all rigid.

The zeppelin was developed commercially for mail and passengers before World War I and in that war was used for bombing expeditions. The United States tried dirigibles, but gave them less attention after several accidents. They proved of great value, however, in World War II in combating submarines. Captive balloons were used for observation during World War I, and, in World War II, to support cables and nets for air raid protection. Blimps are non-rigid airships. A U. S. Navy blimp set a world record in 1954 by staying aloft more than 8 days.

The lifting power of airships has customarily been provided by the use of hydrogen, although in recent years helium has been increasingly employed. The buoyancy of helium is somewhat less and the cost is higher, but it has the merit of not being inflammable. This advantage of helium received a tragic confirmation in 1937, when the German zeppelin *Hindenburg* was destroyed by flames, with most of its passengers, its hydrogen having ignited from an unknown cause as the craft was mooring at Lakehurst, N. J.

Amplifier. This is a general term applied to devices for magnifying variations in electric currents. The commonest form is the three-electrode vacuum tube. It has made possible such recent achievements as transatlantic radiotelephony, phototelegraphy, television, speaking motion pictures, a radically improved type of phonograph, and the "loud speaker."

The idea is already familiar that the sound variations constituting speech or music can be rendered as equivalent grooves on the record of a phonograph and then reconverted into sound. It is equally true that a modulated electric current can be produced which will represent such sound variations. The current may also represent light variations, through the agency of the photoelectric cell, the action of which is explained under *Phototelegraphy*. The amplifier is used to magnify the modulated electrical current to such a degree that, when this is converted to equivalent sound or light variations, the results will be easily heard or seen.

In speaking motion pictures, sound is converted to an equivalent band of light and shade, which is placed so accurately beside the pictures on the film that, on reconversion to sound, it produces an effect remarkably close to real life. The amplifier is essential to the process. Phonographs also owe much to the amplifier, both in improving the quality, and in enlarging the volume, of the sound reproduced.

Automobile. A self-propelled, four-wheeled vehicle designed to travel on highways. As steam and electric automobiles comprise less than 2 per cent of the total number, the term refers, when used without qualification, to a motor vehicle propelled by a gasoline engine. In Great Britain, gasoline is commonly called *petrol*; in Germany, *benzin*; and, in France, *essence de pétrole*, or simply *essence*.

Most standard automobiles of today consist essentially of a steel frame, attached through springs and axles to four pneumatic tired wheels. A four-cycle gasoline engine is mounted at the front, just behind a radiator through which water for cooling the engine is pumped. By means of a *clutch* operated by a left-foot pedal, the flywheel may be connected with the *transmission gears* which transmit the power through a driving shaft to bevel and differential gears attached to the middle of the rear axle.

Speed of the car is varied by shifting from one to another of the transmission gears, and by changing the amount of fuel supplied to the engine. The *differential gear* permits the rear wheels to revolve at different rates when the car rounds a curve and the outside wheel must move faster than that on the inside. The engine is started by means of an electric motor which receives power from a storage battery and is geared to the flywheel. When the engine is running, the battery is charged by a generator driven by the fan belt.

The front axle does not turn, but the wheels are attached to it by movable joints which are connected by a bar called a tie rod. The bottom of the post on which the steering wheel is mounted is fitted with a screw thread which causes a vertical *steering arm* to move forward or backward. This movement is transmitted to the *steering knuckle* by a rod.

The engine usually has from 4 to 12 cylinders, runs at from 800 to 4000 revolutions per minute, and weighs from 5 to 15 pounds per horse power. Some of the speed records which have been made are: 1 mile in 17.7 sec.; 10 miles in 4 min. 9.31 sec.; 50 miles in 26 min. 23.4 sec.; 100 miles in 54 min. 17.8 sec.; and 500 miles in 5 hr. 7 min. 26 sec.

It is probable that Siegfried Markus, a German, should be called the inventor of the gasoline automobile, for in 1875 he built a crude machine which carried him about the streets. Gottlieb Daimler is often called the "father of the automobile" because of the great improvement which he made in the gasoline engine, about 1884. In 1885 both Daimler and Karl Benz used gasoline engines to propel bicycles and tricycles. The first commercially manufactured car, made by Panhard and Levassor in 1891, used the Daimler engine. But the first automobile imported into the United States was a Benz, taken to the Chicago World's Fair in 1893.

The first successful American automobile was built by Charles E. and J. Frank Duryea in 1892. Henry Ford built a car in 1893, and Elwood Haynes in 1894. In 1896 these three cars and the imported Benz were the only ones in the United States; in 1948 there were 33¼ million passenger cars alone. The first public auto race was run in 1894 from Paris to Rouen; the first in the United States took place in 1895 from Chicago to Waukegan. The commercial history of gasoline automobiles in the United States may be said to date from 1898, when a Winton was the first car sold. The first commercially successful Ford was sold in 1903.

In 1879, George B. Selden, of Rochester, N. Y., applied for a fundamental patent on a road vehicle driven by a gasoline motor. The application was kept active, by perfectly legitimate methods, for 16 years, when a patent was taken out in 1895. Because of this patent, many of the leading manufacturers were forced to pay royalties of from .8 to 1.25 per cent of the retail price. Others refused to pay and, led by Henry Ford, carried the question to the United States circuit court of appeals which in 1911 decided in their favor and freed the industry of this burden. See *Internal Combustion Engine*.

Colorscope. This is an electrical device for matching colors. Each of two colors to be matched is placed before a photoelectric cell, which generates an electric current proportional in intensity to the light waves received by the cell. When the colors are exactly matched, the two currents are equal and register zero on a galvanometer. The instrument was invented by Dr. H. H. Sheldon and exhibited first in 1930.

Compass. A device designed to hold a certain definite direction, from which a ship or airplane may establish and maintain a true course. Prior to the 20th century, the only compass known was the magnetic, or *mariner's*, compass. This acted imperfectly in the presence of magnetized iron on ships, and the gyrocompass was devised to overcome this difficulty. The development of aeronautics demanded a different type. Several have been invented, of which the earth inductor compass is best known.

Magnetic Compass.—The action of this kind of compass depends on the magnetic force of the earth. The earth is a huge magnet, one pole being approximately at 70° N. lat. and 97° W. long. and the other at 72° S. lat. and 153° E. long.

One or more magnets, or needles, are mounted to move in a horizontal plane within a circular framework, the flat upper side of which is called the compass card. The magnet sets itself in line with the earth's "lines of force," thereby pointing in the general direction of the earth's magnetic poles. In order that motion may be as free as possible, the needle with its framework may be floated on a nonfreezing liquid within the compass bowl. This is the so-called liquid compass. In the dry compass, the entire weight of the needle and framework rests on a pivot within the bowl.

Since the compass needle points to the magnetic poles of the earth, not the geographic poles, it shows, for most places, a variation, or declination, from the true north and south. This angle of variation is known as the compass error. To enable navigators to make necessary corrections for declination, magnetic charts are prepared. They are revised periodically, since the location of the magnetic poles varies slightly from time to time.

Gyrocompass.—In the construction of this nonmagnetic compass, use is made of the fact that the axis of a freely suspended gyroscope wheel will tend to turn parallel to the earth's axis of rotation.

The most successful type of gyrocompass is that known as the *Sperry compass*, perfected about 1910 by Elmer A. Sperry.

The instrument consists essentially of a gyro wheel mounted so as to be free to spin, free to tilt about a horizontal axis, and free to turn about a vertical axis. The gyro wheel is about 9 inches in diameter and weighs 50 pounds. It revolves in a vacuum inside a metallic casing at a speed of about 8500 revolutions per minute.

Upon starting the gyro wheel in motion, it gradually assumes a position parallel to the earth's axis. In the course of a few hours it establishes a north and south direction, which is maintained with marked accuracy so long as the wheel is kept rotating at the right speed. As usually mounted, the instrument carries a compass card similar to that of the magnetic compass. See *Gyroscope*.

Earth Inductor Compass.—This instrument was invented by scientists in the United States bureau of standards. It consists of a generator, a direction controller, and a steering indicator. The generator is pivoted on a vertical axis. It contains two pairs of brushes, which are revolved in the magnetic field of the earth at the rate of 1400 revolutions per minute. Each pair of brushes collects a direct current.

When the generator is oriented properly, the currents are equal and register zero on a galvanometer, known as the steering indicator. If the generator is oriented at an angle to this position, one current is stronger than the other and deflects the steering indicator to the right or left. The direction controller is a crank for orienting the generator by reference to a compass card.

If the aviator wishes to change his direction, he moves the direction controller to the compass point indicating the desired direction. This changes the current strengths and deflects the steering indicator to the left or right until the plane is headed in the direction for which the control crank is set. To continue in this direction the aviator must steer so that the steering indicator remains at zero.

Boxing the Compass.—Around the outer edge of the circular compass card the degrees are marked from 0 to 360, beginning at north and numbering in the same direction as the hands of a clock move. Besides being marked in degrees, the compass card is marked also in points (11¼°), half points, and quarter points. The four primary directions—north, south, east, and west—are called the *cardinal* points. The points intermediate between these—northeast, southeast, southwest, and northwest—are called *intercardinal*. The point halfway between north and northeast is north-northeast, that between northeast and east is east-northeast, and so on for like subdivisions. Other points are named north by east, northeast by north, and similarly, according to the following table.

COMPASS CARD

N.	E.	S.	W.
N. by E.	E. by S.	S. by W.	W. by N.
N. N. E.	E. S. E.	S. S. W.	W. N. W.
N. E. by N.	S. E. by E.	S. W. by S.	N. W. by W.
N. E.	S. E.	S. W.	N. W.
N. E. by E.	S. E. by S.	S. W. by W.	N. W. by N.
E. N. E.	S. S. E.	W. S. W.	N. N. W.
E. by N.	S. by E.	W. by S.	N. by W.

Composing Machine. A machine which sets either type or type molds and arranges them in lines of the proper order and length for printing. The true typesetting machine has been almost entirely supplanted by those which set type molds from which castings are automatically produced. Of this second class, the linotype and monotype are best known, and, because of their extensive use in printing, are of greatest economic importance.

The linotype was invented in 1885 by Ottmar Mergenthaler, a German living in Baltimore. It is operated similarly to a typewriter, from a keyboard having 90 or more keys. When a key is pressed, the corresponding brass matrix is released from its compartment in a magazine and falls on a moving belt which carries it to a collector. At the end of each word a wedge-shaped spacer is inserted. When the molds for one line of type are assembled they are carried to a casting wheel and placed in front of a slot.

At this time the wedge-shaped spacers are pushed up between the matrices so that the words are spread until they exactly fill one line. A pump then forces molten type metal into the slot and against the matrices. The metal cools rapidly, so that the molds may be almost instantly removed and redistributed into the proper section of the magazine. The slug of metal is trimmed to exact size between knives and placed with others to form a column of type. Should any error be discovered, a whole line must be reset. Linotype machines may be operated electrically by the so-called teletypesetter, first used in 1928. This device makes use of ticker tape perforations transmitted by telegraph. These, corresponding to words, are fed into the teletypesetter, which depresses the proper keys of the linotype keyboard so as to reproduce the words of the message.

The monotype, as indicated by its name, casts each letter separately. It also differs from the linotype in that the composing and the type casting are done on different machines. The composing mechanism has a keyboard of 225 keys which cause holes corresponding to the proper letter to be punched in a moving strip of paper. When words have been set almost to fill a line, an automatic indicator shows the operator what size space is required to *justify*, or exactly fill the line. When this ribbon is passed through the casting machine, each type is cast separately and delivered in proper order of lines.

Photocomposition utilizes a filmsetting machine. A tape controls the movements of a matrix case through which a beam of light photographs each required letter. When the line is completed, the strip of film advances on a revolving drum. See *Books*.

Dynamo and Electric Motor. The dynamo, sometimes called a generator, is a machine for producing electric current. It is driven by mechanical power, usually steam or water power. The same machine, when reversed in action, is an electric motor. Driven by an electric current, it is capable of performing work, such as driving machinery or providing traction for cars. The dynamo and motor are sometimes referred to under the single term dynamo-electric machine.

Michael Faraday in England discovered, in 1831, the principle on which the dynamo is based, namely, that, if the lines of force between the poles of a magnet are cut by an electric conductor moving across them, an electric current is induced in the conductor. The dynamo consists essentially of one or more coils of insulated copper wire about a ring of soft iron, which revolves rapidly on its diameter between the poles of a magnet. The revolving part is called the *armature*. The ends of the wire lead to metal *collecting rings*, from which two metal brushes, connected through an external circuit, pick up the current. In this simple form, at each complete revolution of the armature, the current flows first in one direction and then in the opposite direction. The change from one point of maximum intensity in one direction to the next in the same direction is called a cycle. By adding two or more rings to the armature, a so-called two or many-phase current is produced, in which, for every revolution of the armature, there are two or more points of maximum current intensity in each direction.

If the collecting rings are replaced by a *commutator*, that is, by insulated ring segments placed opposite each other, a one-direction, or direct, current may be produced. It will fall to zero once during each revolution of the armature, but this pulsation may be virtually eliminated by increasing the number of armature rings and coils.

The magnets used for the early dynamos were permanent magnets, but later the electromagnet was substituted. For alternating currents, this is actuated by a separate circuit, but, with direct current machines, the current produced by the dynamo may be used in whole or part to actuate, and regulate the strength of, the magnet.

Designs of modern dynamos differ widely. One or many magnets may be used and either the magnets or the armature may revolve, the other remaining stationary. Motors have been adapted to innumerable uses, including electric railways, elevators, machine shops, and household appliances.

For long distance transmission, the alternating current is almost exclusively used in America, since this current may be readily transformed to a high potential and so transmitted over a much smaller copper or aluminum conductor than would otherwise be necessary. At the point of use, the current is "stepped down" by transformers and distributed to the users. It is common to transmit in this way currents of 220,000 volts over hundreds of miles.

When the peak requirements for electricity at different using centers occur at different times, economies can be effected by connecting many generating stations and consuming centers, thereby making available the surplus from any station for the center needing it.

Electric power is generated most economically where coal, natural gas, oil, or water power are readily available. The chief generating centers or regions in the United States include Niagara Falls; New York City; Chicago; Los Angeles; San Francisco; Pittsburgh; Muscle Shoals, Ala.; Butte, Mont.; and the North Pacific states. The electric power produced in the United States was over 1500 billion kilowatt hours in 1970, and the number of residential customers exceeded 63 million.

Electron Tube. A vacuum tube very similar in appearance to an incandescent electric lamp, but generally containing, in addition to the filament, a flat metallic plate and an irregularly shaped grid. When the filament is heated to glowing by means of an electric current, it emits *electrons* or negative charges of electricity, which ordinarily would return to the wire. If, however, a battery is connected to the filament and to the plate so that the plate is *positively* charged, the electrons will be attracted to the plate and a current of electricity will flow through the vacuum and around the circuit. If the plate is negatively charged, no current will flow; consequently, when connected with an alternating current, the tube acts as a valve which allows the electricity to pass through in one direction only, thus producing a direct current.

The grid is placed between the filament and the plate, so that, if a charge of varying strength is applied to the grid, corresponding changes will also be imposed on the current flowing through the tube. A weak current is thus enabled to control one that is much stronger. Because of these properties, electron tubes are used as relays, which make long-distance telephony possible; as converters, by which direct current may be obtained from an alternating source; as detectors, which amplify weak radio telegraph or telephone signals and make them audible; and as transmitters, which can be used to send out a continuous train of ether waves of almost any desired frequency.

Fathometer. An instrument for measuring the depth of water in the process of echo sounding. An electric oscillator on a ship makes a characteristic sound which is transmitted to the water. The instrument clocks the time of its production and the time when the echo, reflected from the floor of the ocean, returns to the instrument. Since sound travels about 4700 feet a second in water, the depth is calculated from the lapse of time, an indicator showing the result. By thus making possible the almost instantaneous recording of the contour of the sea floor, the instrument multiplies the speed and the economy with which the ocean bed can be mapped

Gyroscope. A mechanical device invented early in the 19th century, and at first used chiefly to illustrate certain laws of rotating bodies. It consists essentially of a wheel with a heavy rim, mounted on an axis which is pivoted at both ends within a light circular framework. Instruments of this type are frequently sold as toys under the name *gyro-top*. The more scientific form of gyroscope is so mounted that it is free to revolve about three mutually perpendicular axes, whose common center is the center of gravity of the spinning wheel.

When the wheel of a gyro-top is made to rotate rapidly,—usually by pulling away a string coiled about the axis,—two characteristics are noticeable. First, any attempt to change the direction of the axis meets with a surprising amount of resistance. Second, this resistance is so great that, if the gyroscope is turned on its side and supported at only one end, it will not fall, but will move in a horizontal circle about its point of support, apparently in contradiction of the laws of gravity. This circling movement, known as *precession*, takes place in the direction opposite to that in which the wheel is rotating.

A gyroscope resists any force which tends to change the direction of its axis for the same reason that the passengers on a moving train are jerked forward when the brakes are suddenly applied; that is, because of inertia The amount of inertia depends upon the speed of the wheel, its mass, and the average distance of the mass from the axis.

The act of precession is explained by the fact that a body moving under the influence of two forces must respond to both. The wheel which is rotating on one axis is also pulled downward because of gravitational attraction. The gyroscope then tends to place its axis parallel to a third, intermediate axis, and, as a result, moves backward. As the third axis also changes its position at the same time, precession continues as long as the inertia of the wheel is sufficient to prevent falling.

The earth acts as a huge gyroscope, spinning on an axis which points toward the polestar, and also rotating around the sun. As these two axes of rotation do not coincide, the earth, like the top, is forced to precess, thus causing the pole to move west in a small circle which is completed once in 25,900 years. For this reason, the star which indicated true north when the Egyptians built the pyramids is not the polestar of today.

The tendency of a gyroscope to rotate in one plane has been utilized for many purposes. By means of a gyroscope, Léon Foucault, about 1852, was able to demonstrate the rotation of the earth.

Gyroscopes are no longer scientific toys. The *Brennan monorail car* is capable of retaining perfect equilibrium upon a single rail, because of two heavy, motor-driven gyroscopes, which spin in opposite directions. Somewhat similar devices are used upon ships to prevent rolling, while, for ice-breaking vessels, the gyroscope is fastened so as to cause the vessel to roll. Torpedoes are held to their course by means of a controlling gyroscope which begins to spin when the torpedo is released. Gyroscopic apparatus for stabilizing airplanes is also in use. This stabilizing influence becomes more comprehensible in the light of Newton's third law of motion—to every action there is an equal and opposite reaction. Probably the most important application of the gyroscope is the gyrocompass which indicates true north regardless of any change in the magnetic field. See *Gyrocompass*.

Internal Combustion Engine. A heat engine which performs work because of the expansive energy of hot gases formed within a closed chamber. The fuel used may be a natural or an artificial gas, a volatile liquid such as gasoline or alcohol, a poorly volatile liquid such as kerosene, or heavy oils and tars. An engine is usually named for the fuel to which it is best adapted.

In order that such engines may operate continuously it is necessary that the fuel, together with the proper amount of air, be placed in the cylinder, compressed, burned, and allowed to expand, after which the spent gases must be removed and the series of operations repeated. When these processes are performed during four strokes of the piston the machine is called a *four-cycle* engine.

The action of a four-cycle gas or gasoline engine is as follows: At the first, or *intake stroke*, with the exhaust valve closed and the intake valve open, the piston moves away from the closed end of the cylinder, and fuel is sucked into the chamber. With both valves closed, the piston then returns on the *compression stroke* which forces the confined gas into a small space. The compressed gas is then ignited by means of an electric spark, and the chemical action of burning raises the temperature so that the gases expand and force the piston outward. After this *power stroke*, the exhaust valve opens and the piston returns on the *exhaust stroke*, forcing out the burned gas.

In a *four-cycle* engine there is one power stroke during two revolutions of the flywheel. In a *two-cycle* engine the same operations are performed during two strokes of the piston, so that there is an explosion at each revolution of the crank shaft. This is usually effected by making the crank case gas-tight and filling this space with the proper mixture of gas and air. At the end of the power stroke, two valves or ports are uncovered. One opens to the exhaust and the other to the crank case, which is under slight pressure, so that the burned gas flows out and fresh fuel is forced into the cylinder. As the piston returns, it covers the valve openings and compresses the gas, which is then ignited and the series repeated.

It is obvious that power thus imparted by a blow on the piston at every second or fourth stroke will be jerky. In order to prevent excessive vibrations a single-cylinder engine usually has a heavy flywheel, while larger engines have several cylinder, connected to one crank shaft and firing in rotation so that the pressure is more continuous. For automobile and aircraft engines, four and six vertical cylinders in a straight line, or eight and twelve cylinders in two equal rows inclined so as to form a V, have been most generally satisfactory. In some aircraft engines vibration is almost eliminated by having the cylinders rotate like a flywheel about a fixed crank shaft.

In gas engines the proper amounts of gas and air are easily adjusted in a mixing chamber; in the gasoline engine a jet of the volatile liquid is sprayed into a current of air as it is drawn through a *carburetor* into the cylinder. With kerosene or other less volatile fuels, a hot bulb or other form of heating device is often necessary. Ignition is almost universally caused by means of an electric spark produced by an induction coil or a high tension magneto.

The *Diesel* type of engine, which operates with heavy hydrocarbons such as tar oil, usually requires no ignition system when once in operation. Instead, air is drawn into the cylinder and highly compressed. The great pressure raises the temperature of the air to such a degree that, when the fuel is forced into the cylinder by means of a pump, spontaneous combustion occurs. The great advantage of the Diesel engine due to the low cost of fuel is partly offset by the heavier construction necessary to provide for the great pressure.

A theoretical plan for the four-cycle engine was originated by Beau de Rochas in 1862. The same plan was independently invented by Nicholas A. Otto, of Cologne, and was developed into a practical machine in 1877.

The power which a four-cycle engine will deliver is generally calculated by means of the formula,

$$\mathrm{DHP} = \frac{\mathrm{D}^2 \times \mathrm{S} \times \mathrm{RPM}}{18{,}000}$$

For example: the *delivered horse power* (DHP) of an engine having a 3-inch bore (D), a 4-inch stroke (S), and running at 1000 *revolutions per minute* (RPM) equals $3 \times 3 \times 4 \times 1000 = 36{,}000 \div 18{,}000$ or 2 horse power. The power of a two-cycle engine is obtained by dividing by 13,500 instead of 18,000.

For multicylinder engines the result is multiplied by the number of cylinders.

Microscope. An optical instrument consisting of a lens or combination of lenses, used to obtain a magnified image of minute objects. A *simple microscope* consists of a single convex lens composed of one or more parts, and is often called a magnifying glass. Instruments of this class have been known and used for centuries.

A *compound microscope* is composed of two lenses,—the objective and the eyepiece, or ocular,—mounted in opposite ends of a metal tube. The objective, being of short focus, is placed close to the object, of which it produces a magnified image within the tube. The eyepiece, which is generally of low power, magnifies this image a second time.

The first instrument of this type seems to have been made, about 1590, by Zacharias Janssen, a native of Holland. The magnifying power of a compound microscope depends on the power of the objective, the power of the eyepiece, and the distance between the two. It would thus seem possible to produce images of any magnification, but greatly enlarged images lack detail and sharpness, so that a power of 2000 diameters is seldom exceeded for visual work. It should be remembered that, as area increases with the square of the diameter, 2000 diameters means 4,000,000 times the area of the object.

The usual form of compound microscope consists of the lenses in an adjustable tube fastened above a platform having an opening in the center, across which the object is to be placed. Beneath the platform is a mirror which reflects rays of light from some source of illumination upward through a condenser. This, as its name indicates, concentrates the light from the mirror into a small bundle of rays which pass up through the stage, object, and lenses. For opaque objects the lighting must be from above.

Eyepieces which magnify from 4 to 20 diameters are generally used with objectives having a focal length of ⅔, ⅙, or 1/12 inch and a corresponding power of about 10, 44, and 90 diameters. A 1/12 inch objective with a 10-power ocular would therefore produce a magnification of 900 diameters. To prevent loss of light when using objectives of very short focus, a drop of cedar oil or similar fluid is placed so that it touches both the object and the lens. Objectives constructed to operate under such conditions are called *oil-immersion* lenses.

No microscope can show directly the true form of any object smaller than one-half the wave length of light by which it is seen. Much smaller objects, however, may be observed indirectly by means of two devices—the *ultramicroscope* and the *electron microscope*.

The ultramicroscope consists of an arrangement by which minute objects may be made visible as spots of light against a dark field. Light is sent across the field instead of up through it, so that any ultramicroscopic particles reflect light and are seen like dust in the air of a dark room through which a ray of sunshine is passing. In this way particles about six-millionths of an inch have been detected.

The electron microscope, invented in 1938, is a revolutionary contribution to microscopy. It employs the principle that electrons are, like light, reflected from what they strike. The electrons are focused, by a magnetic field within a cylindrical coil of electric wires, upon a glass plate treated chemically so as to become fluorescent where the electrons converge. The fluorescence reproduces the pattern of the minute object scanned.

The instrument is steel, about five feet high, with glass windows. Its interior is a vacuum. Within the vacuum a cathode-ray tube sends out a stream of electrons which strike the object to be scanned. Those reflected by the object are picked up by the magnetic field created by the coil of electric wire and are converged upon the chemically treated glass. The image may be projected in enlarged form on a phosphorescent screen.

Motion Pictures. A series of separate pictures projected upon a screen, and changed so rapidly that the eye receives the effect of continuous motion. This effect is due to a physiological property of the eye called *persistence of vision*, which causes an image to remain apparent for about 1/5 second after it has really disappeared. Standard pictures are projected at the rate of 16 per second. Each picture is shown perfectly still for 5/96 second, and the screen is dark for 1/96 second three times in the period during which one picture passes before the source of illumination.

After the invention and the development of photography, many investigators worked over the problem of picturing motion. Edward Muybridge, using methods devised by John D. Isaacs about 1872-73, studied the movements of a trotting horse by means of a row of 24 cameras, exposed in order as the horse passed before them. The photographs were projected in such a way as to simulate movement, but his apparatus was necessarily clumsy as he had only glass plates. A light, flexible, continuous film was needed as a substitute for the glass, and this was invented by Goodwin and produced by Eastman.

In 1894, Edison placed on the market his kinetoscope, which successfully depicts motion by means of photographs printed on an endless strip of celluloid film. But the pictures in this machine can be viewed by only one person at a time. In 1895, Thomas Armat of Washington was the first to produce motion pictures by modern methods. The essential point in the improvement made by Armat, with whom C. F. Jenkins was for a while associated as experimenter, was a device by which the film moved intermittently, having periods of rest and illumination largely in excess of the period of movement from image to image. Other projectors were made and exhibited in 1896. From 1897 to 1907 a violent war of litigation over patents disturbed the industry.

Motion picture film is so standardized that pictures made by one company may be exhibited on any machine in the world. It is usually prepared in strips 200 feet long by 1⅜ inches wide. On each side there is a margin of 3/16 inch in which perforations are cut. There are 16 photographs and 64 perforations to the foot. Each picture is thus 1 x ¾ inches. One thousand feet is the standard length to fill one reel.

The motion picture camera is equipped with a very fast, high grade lens of 2 to 3 inch focus. The shutter is a revolving, perforated disk driven by a crank which the operator usually turns at the rate of two revolutions per second. Eight exposures are made at each turn of the handle. Within the box the film passes from the original coil over several rolls. It is carried behind the lens, over other rolls which preserve an even tension and prevent tearing, and finally is rewound on a second reel. A delicate mechanism, catching in the perforated edges, holds the film firmly while the shutter is open and jerks it forward just ¾ inch when the shutter closes.

The exposed film is wound spirally on racks and is developed in huge tanks in a dark room. From the negative, any number of positives may be printed at the rate of from 5 to 8 pictures per second. These are made on similar strips of film coated with an emulsion which is not so sensitive but which gives greater contrast.

In the projecting machine, an electric arc is the usual source of illumination. The light passes first through heat filters and condensing lenses, and then through the film and the projecting lenses to the screen, where the picture is enlarged about 10,000 times. Most films are made of celluloid and are consequently highly inflammable. Non-inflammable films may be produced from cellulose acetate, but even these are melted by the heat from the arc if they are held too long between the lenses. The used and the unused reels of film are therefore held in asbestos lined boxes, and a safety shutter is provided, which automatically protects the picture from the light if the machine accidentally stops. The mechanism for moving the film is similar to that used in the camera, but the shutter disk which revolves once for each picture has two large openings instead of a single small one.

Animated cartoons are made by photographing a great number of single drawings each showing a different stage of the action. Colored "movies" are made by exposing through a series of color screens and projecting through similar screens in reverse order—the technicolor process. These pictures must usually be shown at about twice the normal speed. "Talking movies" depend for their success on the exact timing of picture and voice. This problem was solved by the use of the photoelectric cell and the amplifier. See *Amplifier*, *Photoelectric Cell*.

The motion picture industry as organized today has three principal divisions: production, distribution, and exhibition. Forty-five years after its birth, in about 1895, the industry in the United States had grown to such proportions that it employed nearly 300,000 people. Nearly one-fifth of the total of the world's motion picture theaters, approximating 100,000, are in the United States. Russia is credited with the largest number, about 30,000. It is estimated that one-eighth of the world's population attend motion picture theaters each week.

The first studio for making motion pictures was a little, black, paper covered shanty built by Edison near his factory in New Jersey. Today a whole community in California is given over to the staging and filming of picture stories. This community, Hollywood, in Los Angeles, produces over two-thirds of the world's output.

Phonograph. An instrument which records and reproduces sound by means of a moving diaphragm that is caused to vibrate by sound waves in the air. A stylus or chisel-like needle connected with the diaphragm is allowed to trace or engrave a spiral line upon a revolving cylinder or disk. The slightest movement of the diaphragm is thus recorded on the path of the needle. To reproduce the sound, the record is again revolved at the same speed and a smooth needle attached to a second diaphragm is allowed to travel over the engraved line. The irregular motion of the needle then forces the diaphragm to vibrate and produce sound waves similar to those first recorded.

The first phonograph, or "talking machine," was invented by Thomas A. Edison in 1877. It consisted of a cylinder having a spiral groove cut on its surface, and mounted on a screw passing through its center. A smooth layer of tin foil was placed on the cylinder, which was then revolved so that the groove was always under the point attached to the diaphragm. The movements of the diaphragm thus produced irregular indentations in the tin foil, which would impart similar vibrations when the stylus was again allowed to travel over the cylinder.

The *graphophone*, invented in 1885 by Chichester Bell and Charles Tainter, improved on the phonograph by substituting a wax tube for the tin foil. The *gramophone*, invented by Emile Berliner in 1887, differed fundamentally from the first two, in producing a tracing of the sound waves as a zigzag line of even depth, rather than an up-and-down engraving. This system was found more satisfactory on disks than on cylinders. Modern practice tends toward the use of wax cylinders for temporary records, such as those used for commercial dictation, and of hard disks for all permanent records. Some machines employ reproducing needles which are used but once, while others have a permanent diamond or sapphire point.

In preparing commercial records the original is recorded directly upon a wax tablet. This is carefully covered with graphite in order that it may conduct electricity, and is then electroplated with copper. The copper shell is stripped from the wax and then nickel-plated in order to harden it. From this *master record*, a second, mother record is prepared in the same way, and from the mother record several matrices are made which are used for molding the familiar commercial disks. These are generally composed of shellac, together with charcoal, barium sulphate, and other substances.

In the *auxetophone*, an ordinary record is used to control the action of a delicate valve which impresses the proper vibrations on a stream of air generated by an air compressor. The recorded sound is thus *reproduced* without the aid of a vibrating diaphragm.

Great progress has been made within the past few years in the recording and transmission of sound. A new accuracy and realism has been achieved by the introduction of high-fidelity (hi-fi) equipment, which reproduces sound with an amazing degree of faithfulness to the original. This has been accomplished largely by eliminating sound distortion caused by electronic deficiencies in the making of a record and in the transmitting equipment. Its popularity, especially among lovers of music, has proved a stimulus to the industry.

Photoelectric Cell. This device, often called the electric eye, is used for translating variations in the intensity of light into variations in intensity of an electric current. Since the electric current, properly amplified by electron tubes, can be made to perform innumerable operations, the photoelectric cell makes it possible to produce these results by changes in the light which falls on the cell. Possible applications are almost innumerable.

The effect of light on an electric current was first noted by Heinrich Hertz in 1887. Julius Elster and Hans Geitel constructed in 1890 the first photoelectric cell. In modern practice, this cell consists essentially of a glass bulb or tube, either evacuated of air or filled with an inert gas, such as argon or neon, having an anode of platinum or some other suitable metal. The cathode is usually a very thin coating of an alkali metal, such as potassium or cæsium, which has been found to emit particles of negative electricity, or electrons, when exposed to light. When an electric current is passed from the anode to the cathode, this current is decreased by the action of light on the cathode. This effect varies with the amount and the wave length (color) of the light, which is admitted through a small window. The current used is necessarily of extremely low voltage and must be magnified enormously by an amplifier before being put to effective use in the production of sound or the operation of mechanical devices. Another type of cell utilizes a property of selenium, which is a very poor conductor of electricity when in the dark but, when exposed to light, conducts an electric current much more readily.

Photoelectric cells differ in their sensitivity to light of different colors or wave lengths. Some are adapted to respond to infra-red light rays, which are invisible to the human eye. Such cells can "see" in the dark, and the resulting current fluctuations can be made to produce visible photographs of invisible objects.

The first important application of the photoelectric cell was in the production of audible motion pictures. It is the basic element in phototelegraphy and television. It may be used also for mechanically counting objects passing before its "eye," for sorting objects by their color, for analyzing and matching colors, for measuring illumination and ultra-violet radiation, for transforming the printed page into intelligible sound, and for picking up obscure or invisible light signals and performing operations in accordance with the signals. All these operations it can perform better than the human eye. With the development of television, it promises to enable man to see in the dark or through fogs.

Photography. The process of forming and fixing images of objects upon a sensitized surface by means of the physical and chemical properties of light. The question "Who invented photography?" is often asked, but cannot be definitely answered because modern photographic methods have been developed by contributions from many.

J. H. Schultz, in 1727, made the first photographic copy of writing. In 1802, Thomas Wedgwood copied pictures by the action of light. Joseph Nicéphore Niepce produced the first permanent pictures in 1814. Louis Jacques Daguerre, in 1839, made public the details of his *daguerreotype* process of sensitizing a silver plate with iodine, and developing, with vapors of mercury, the image produced on exposure. The next year Professor John W. Draper of New York university made by this method the first photograph of a human face. William H. F. Talbot, in 1841, presented his calotype process, which permitted many copies to be made from one paper negative.

In 1851, Scott Archer introduced the process in which sensitive silver salts are produced in a film of *collodion* supported on a glass plate. The American photographer Mathew Brady began using the new wet-plate process, called *ambrotypes*, in his New York studio around 1853. Later utilizing that method and a variant called *tintypes*, Brady documented the Civil War in over 7000 pictures. Because exposures required several seconds, he was unable to take action photography, but his portraits captured the destruction and desolation of the war.

The gelatin-silver bromide emulsion, the basis of modern dry plates, was discovered in 1871 by Dr. R. L. Maddox. In 1884, George Eastman patented a successful roll film of paper, and, in 1887, Rev. Hannibal Goodwin applied for a patent on a transparent, sensitive, celluloid-like pellicle which was the basis of the modern roll and cut film. Both films and glass plates are coated with gelatin containing bromide and iodide of silver.

Modern photographic apparatus usually consists of a light-tight box or camera, equipped with a lens which focuses an image upon the sensitive surface of a plate or film when the shutter is opened. No change can be seen on the exposed plate until it is *developed* by immersion in an alkaline, oxygen-absorbing solution of pyrogallol, metol, or similar reducing agent. In this solution the plate gradually darkens and the image appears. But, as the parts of any object which reflect the most light cause the greatest change in the silver salts, a reversed image, called a *negative*, is produced, in which the high lights of the object appear dark, and the shadows, light. Developing is done in the dark or in a red light, which does not affect ordinary plates. The negative is next *fixed* with a solution of sodium thiosulphate, commonly called *hypo*, which dissolves all *unchanged* silver salts. After further washing in fresh water, the negative is dried. Satisfactory negatives are produced almost mechanically by the system of *tank development*, in which the exposed plates are treated with a developer of known strength, for a definite time at a fixed temperature.

The final step consists in making a positive *print* by placing sensitized paper behind the negative and exposing these to the light. The dark parts of the negative hold back more light than the lighter shadows, so that the resulting image has the same light values as the original object. The principal kinds of photographic paper are: those which are printed by artificial light, developed, and fixed in the same way as the negative; and ordinary *printing out paper*, which is exposed to the sun until the image appears, and is then fixed, washed, and often given further treatment to improve the color.

Photographs in natural colors are generally produced by means of screens or filters which separate light into its red, green, and violet components. The finished photograph must usually be viewed through similar screens. The processes of Ives, Joly, Wood, and the Lumière brothers are best known. On the Lumière autochrome plate a permanent screen is formed by a layer of starch particles colored red, green, and violet.

By use of highly sensitized film, photography will produce results which far outdistance the capacity of the human eye. Rays, for instance, invisible to the eye may nevertheless produce pictures from objects which appear to be completely in the dark. In astronomical work, by long exposure, stars are photographed which are completely invisible to the human eye. In warfare, photographs made from airplanes will reveal changes in enemy forces which camouflage conceals from the eye. X-ray photography is one of the most valuable aids to surgery. Another important use is the photographing of documents or pages of books. The pictures are produced on a very small scale in a non-inflammable film, from which they may be projected by a lantern on a screen. The so-called candid camera depends on the use of very sensitive films and high speed exposure.

In 1947, American Edwin H. Land invented the Polaroid Land camera. This camera develops and prints the picture within seconds after it was taken.

Phototelegraphy. A process for sending photographs by telegraph or telephone, perfected in the Bell Telephone laboratories, New York City, about 1925. The apparatus consists of a transmitter and a receiver, which may be used at the ends of any telephone line. A positive film of the photograph to be transmitted is rolled into cylindrical form and inserted in the transmitter. This film is revolved, at the same time moving forward very gradually with a screwlike motion. A small intense ray of light is focused on the film and shines through it with intensities varying according to the lightness or shade of the portion traversed. The varying currents thus set up control a similar cell and a beam of light directed upon an unexposed photographic film at the receiving end which is geared to rotate synchronously with the film at the transmitting end.

Radar. This term means "radio direction and ranging," operating on the principle of high tension radio impulses sent out in a straight line and reflected directly back to the sending instrument. The time of travel gives the distance. A joint Army-Navy release proclaimed the existence of Radar April 25, 1943. The system operates with ultra-high-frequency radio waves and was discovered in September, 1922, by Dr. A. H. Taylor and Leo C. Young of the U. S. Naval Aircraft Radio laboratory. The battleship *New York*, in 1938, was the first ship to be equipped for its use.

Radio. This term is used to describe the transmission and reception of signals by means of radiated electromagnetic rays (radio waves).

The utilization of radio waves for sending messages by code is known as radiotelegraphy or wireless telegraphy. It may be accomplished by a series of interrupted waves to indicate dots and dashes, as in wire telegraphy. To transmit the tones of the voice or music, a continuous wave is required. To produce such radiations, an alternating current of very high frequency is necessary. This is supplied by electron tubes or transistors. Communication of this type is known as radiotelephony, or simply as radio.

The basis of modern systems of wireless or radiotelegraphy was laid down in 1864 when Clerk-Maxwell, by mathematical reasoning, predicted the existence of electromagnetic waves in the ether. In 1887 Professor H. Hertz proved by experiments that such waves existed, and later Edouard Branly and Sir Oliver Lodge each developed an instrument called a coherer, by which these waves could be detected. Hertz found that they could be produced in the ether by the discharge of an electric spark. The shortest of these waves is many times longer than the longest light wave, but they travel at the same speed, 186,284 miles per second.

Guglielmo Marconi, in 1895, was the first to combine the discoveries of earlier scientists into a practical method of signaling. In 1901 he signalled the letter S across the Atlantic. This achievement was surprising, since it meant that the waves must have changed their direction with the curvature of the earth. Professor Kennelly in the United States and Dr. Heaviside in England later proved that the Hertzian waves were reflected by a layer of ionized atoms produced about 50 to 100 miles above the earth's surface by ultra-violet rays from the sun. The existence of this celestial mirror, the so-called ionosphere, makes possible long distance communication by radio.

Marconi produced his signals by means of sparks formed by an induction coil and condenser. One side of the electric discharge was connected with the earth; the other, with a series of aerial wires or antennæ supported from tall poles. The current producing the spark was controlled by a telegraph key, so that long and short trains of waves, corresponding to the dashes and dots of the telegraph code, were radiated from the antennæ. At the receiving station, similar aerial wires conducted the incoming waves to a coherer which under their influence operated a local telegraphic circuit.

The coherer was soon replaced by electrolytic detectors and by crystals of carborundum, silicon, galena, and other minerals which, when used with telephone receivers, were much more sensitive. These in turn have been largely superseded by electron tubes and transistors which are used both for receiving and for transmitting.

A message sent out is radiated in every direction. To insure that the receiving station obtain only that message intended for it, the so-called wave antenna is employed, having a length approximately that of the wave used and pointed in the direction of expected messages. The antenna is not sensitive to waves coming crosswise. The large transatlantic stations are able to transmit two and receive six messages simultaneously. This result is possible partly through the use of different wave lengths and partly through the so-called barrage receiver, by which interfering waves from near-by stations are neutralized and the desired waves are amplified. In the short-wave "beam" system, reflectors are used at the sending and receiving ends, thereby greatly increasing the energy of the waves received.

The development of wireless telegraphy has been rapid. Three large systems are those of the Marconi and Telefunken companies, and of the Radio Corporation of America. In 1902 the first transatlantic message was sent, and later the value of the wireless telegraph on shipboard was proved by incidents such as the rescue of the survivors of the *Titanic* in 1912. Commercial service is regularly carried on throughout all parts of the world. All ships except the smallest are required to carry the necessary sending and receiving equipment.

Radio Broadcasting. Although all transmission by radio is broadcast in all directions, as distinguished from wire telegraphy and telephony, the term radio broadcasting is not applied to radiotelegraphy but only to wireless transmission by high frequency electromagnetic waves, or radiotelephony. These waves with their modulations corresponding to different sounds are produced through the medium of electron tubes or transistors in the sending instruments. Receiving instruments, also by means of electron tubes or transistors reconvert the modulations into air vibrations recognized by the ear as sounds.

The waves used in transmission differ in length according to the instruments producing them. If messages are sent out over waves having the same or not greatly different lengths the messages will "interfere." Consequently, to avoid "interference" no two or more stations within range of each other may be allowed to transmit over approximately the same length at the same time. For this reason, sending stations are licensed to broadcast with waves of a definite length and to broadcast at certain hours. Licensing is done by governments according to rules agreed on at international conventions. A high-power receiving station near Grand Island, Nebr., checks on American broadcasting stations to see that they observe the terms of their license.

Ordinary radio waves have lengths varying from 30,000 to 10 meters. "Short" radio waves have lengths from 10 meters down to lengths of microscopic proportions. The term *frequency*, measured in *kilocycles*, as applied to radio waves is the inverse of wave length. If a wave length is doubled, the frequency is halved.

Short-wave broadcasts have the advantage of being more readily reflected along the ionosphere. A system known as the national "hook up" is accomplished by the transmission of programs by wire to distant points where they are broadcast on long waves. Static refers to static electricity causing imperfect reception.

On September 29, 1915, the same year in which the first transcontinental telephone line was completed, a conversation over the wireless telephone occurred between New York and San Francisco and was heard in Panama and Honolulu. A regular transatlantic radiotelephone service was inaugurated in 1927. See *Electron Tube, Radio.*

Frequency Modulation. (F.M.) A circuit designed by Major E. H. Armstrong. The practical effect is to do away with static and man-made noises and interferences, also to permit a large number of stations to use a wave length.

Television. The method of broadcasting both sound and pictorial effects simultaneously. Transmission by wire or wireless of scenes or moving pictures by conversion of light rays to electrical waves, which are reconverted to reproduce the original image.

Refrigeration. While ice has been used at least as early as the Christian era to chill foods, and the addition of salt has been known for centuries to add to its effectiveness, the invention of a device to lower temperatures by mechanical means opened an entirely new chapter in refrigeration.

The first patent for a refrigerating machine was granted to Dr. John Gorie, Apalachicola, Fla., in 1851, and the first refrigeration plant to be operated commercially was opened in New Orleans in 1866.

Refrigerating machines are based on the principles (1) that a liquid absorbs heat ("produces cold") when it turns into a gas and (2) that a gas tends to turn into a liquid when the pressure upon it is increased and to return to a gaseous state when the pressure is lowered. These principles are applied as follows:

A gas is chosen as a "refrigerant" which will liquefy at a pressure not far above that of the atmosphere. Pressure is increased upon the gas, thus liquefying it. The liquid is led into pipes not subject to the higher pressure. The liquid becomes a gas, absorbing heat from the walls of the pipes and their surroundings, thereby cooling the surroundings. The gas is returned to the compression chamber, where it is again liquefied and the cycle repeats itself.

Gases commonly used as refrigerants include sulphur dioxide, ammonia, and carbon dioxide. They are usually compressed by a pump driven by an electric motor, although an alternative method is to heat a solution of ammonia gas in a closed boiler, the gas driven off increasing the pressure. Refrigerating machines are ordinarily automatic. This requirement involves (1) use of a thermostat to start the application of power when the temperature of the commodities to be chilled rises above a certain point and to stop the power when the temperature falls below another point and (2) valves which permit the flow of the refrigerant from the compression chamber to the cooling tubes and on to the compression chamber again when certain temperature conditions prevail.

Refrigeration machinery was first used in breweries and later was applied to the manufacture of ice. Its employment for the direct cooling of food storage chambers has had an influence on the diet of the world's population which is difficult to exaggerate. It has made possible, for instance, the storage and long-distance shipping of meat, fruits, and vegetables. The process of very rapid freezing of fresh fruits and fish has been found to preserve the original flavor without change.

One of the most important applications of refrigeration is so-called air conditioning, which usually involves the cooling of air and regulation of its humidity. The process involves sending air through a water spray chamber, the water ordinarily being cooled by refrigeration equipment.

For certain purposes, refrigeration is applied through the medium of solidified carbon dioxide, or "dry ice." The dry ice is produced under high pressure by refrigeration machinery, its temperature being about 110° F. below zero. In view of its low temperature, a much smaller bulk is required for a given amount of cooling than would be required if ordinary ice were used. As heat is absorbed, the dry ice turns into gas, leaving no liquid residue. The resulting carbon dioxide gas, being heavier than air, forms a protecting blanket around the solid, thus decreasing loss of heat to the surrounding air.

Sewing Machines. Modern sewing machines may be divided into two classes, chain stitch and lock stitch. The great majority of domestic machines make the lock stitch because the chain stitch is liable to ravel. Both types use a needle having the eye near the point, and usually a groove along the side so that the thread will not bind.

In making the chain stitch the needle plunges through the cloth and returns to its first position, leaving a loop of thread on the underside of the cloth. The material is advanced automatically, and the needle descends through the first loop, which is tightened while another loop is left. Through this the needle passes on the next stitch. The upper side of chain stitching appears as a straight line; the lower side forms a series of chainlike links. A second type of chain stitch machine employs a rotating hook to make a twisted loop.

Two threads are necessary to form the lock stitch. One passes from the spool, over various guides, and through the eye of the needle. The other is wound upon a bobbin that is attached beneath the sewing table to a vibrating shuttle or at the center of a rotating hook. When the needle descends, it throws out a loop, through which the shuttle or the hook passes with the second thread, thus locking the stitch. With a properly adjusted tension on the thread, the end of the loop is drawn to the middle of the cloth, so that both sides of the stitching present the same appearance.

An important device used on all domestic machines is the four-motion feed plate which lies under the material and moves it forward between stitches. The surface of this plate is covered with forward-pointing teeth which engage the cloth and with the first motion pull it toward the needle. The plate next drops down from the cloth, moves backward, then upward, and again travels forward for the length of the stitch.

Several hundred different types of sewing machines are used for commercial purposes. There are machines which sew on buttons, others which make the buttonholes, and delicate machines, having from four to a dozen needles, for sewing gloves. Carpet-sewing machines travel along the seam, because the material is too large and heavy to be moved to the needle. Sewing machines have had a predominating influence upon the garment making industry. The McKay stitching machine, invented by Lyman Blake, and the Goodyear welt-sewing machine have revolutionized shoemaking. By the Goodyear method, the insole of a shoe is fastened to the upper, and a narrow strip, called the welt, is sewed around the edge of the insole. The sole is then sewed to the welt.

The first sewing machine was invented in 1790 by Thomas Saint, an Englishman. Saint probably never built a machine, but a model constructed from his plans has been shown to be entirely practicable. In 1830, Barthelemy Thimonnier, a French tailor, produced a machine which was used for sewing uniforms for the French army. It was Thimonnier's factory that was destroyed by a mob. Later improvements of the sewing machine were made almost entirely by Americans.

About 1832–34, Walter Hunt, a machinist, first combined an eye-pointed needle with a lock stitch machine. He sold his interest in his invention to a blacksmith, who refused to apply for a patent. In 1853, Hunt himself applied, but the courts held that in waiting so long he had abandoned his rights to protection.

Elias Howe, in September 1846, received a patent for a sewing machine on which he had been working for three years. Howe's machines were the first to become a real competitor of hand labor. As the courts sustained the fundamental principles of Howe's patent, he is generally considered to be the inventor of the modern sewing machine. Howe was also the first to patent a lock stitch machine. He used in it an eye-pointed, grooved needle that moved horizontally.

In 1849, John Bachelder produced the first machine having a horizontal sewing table and a continuous feed. This feed consisted of an endless leather belt studded with pins.

Isaac Merritt Singer, in 1851, received patents for the first machine with a rigid, overhanging arm and a vertical needle. His machine made the lock stitch and was operated by a foot treadle.

The four-motion feed was invented in 1850 by Allen B. Wilson, a cabinetmaker. In 1857, A. E. Gibbs, a Virginia farmer, invented a rotary hook for making a chain stitch. As the fundamental patents have gradually expired, the most satisfactory features of the older machines have been adopted by all modern sewing machine manufacturers.

Steam Engine. A machine by which the expansive power of steam is transferred into mechanical energy and useful work.

The use of steam as a driving force is not new, for, in the first century A. D., Hero of Alexandria described a toy which revolved because of escaping steam. During the 17th century, steam appliances were used for pumping water, and, in 1705, Newcomen built for the same purpose the first practicable engine in which pressure was applied to a piston. In 1765, James Watt invented the separate condenser, and later made many other improvements of the greatest importance.

Modern steam engines may be divided into two types: the *reciprocating engine* and the *steam turbine*. In the first and more common type, steam acts alternately on either side of a *piston* which is forced back and forth within a hollow cylinder.

The piston is attached by a *piston rod* to a *crosshead*, which is in turn connected with the *flywheel* by a *connecting rod*. Through the action of valves, the steam is admitted behind the piston, while that part of the cylinder in front is connected with the exhaust. The piston moves toward the opposite end, and at the proper moment the steam is cut off, the piston finishes its stroke, and the valves automatically change so that the action is reversed. In a noncondensing engine the exhaust steam is forced out into the air against the atmospheric pressure of 14.7 pounds per square inch. In a *condensing engine* the exhaust steam is drawn off into a vacuum and condensed. By thus avoiding back pressure, more power is developed. In *expansion* engines the exhaust steam is forced into a second, larger cylinder, where it expands further and does more work. Marine engines are frequently of the *triple expansion* and even *quadruple expansion* type in which the steam, before it is exhausted, is allowed to expand into a third and a fourth cylinder, each larger than that preceding.

In spite of the great commercial importance of the reciprocating engine, it is very far from being efficient. In the best engines only about 12½% of the energy in the fuel is delivered as mechanical energy. The largest single units of this type are of about 10,000 horse power.

In the steam turbine, steam flows from an opening against vanes attached to a *rotor*, which revolves under the pressure of the moving steam. As the steam leaves the moving vanes, it strikes stationary blades, which again deflect it against another row of the vanes. The turbine is the most nearly perfect of all steam engines. It operates at very high speed and is especially effective in driving dynamos and in propelling ships. Turbine generators may attain a capacity of 160,000 kilowatts, or 251,000 horse power. The first vessel driven by turbines developed a speed of 34 ½ knots, so that large vessels were soon equipped with the new engines which give greater power and require much less space.

A further development in ship propulsion which provided greatly increased power with much greater economy in space was the introduction of atomic reactors, as in the pioneer U.S. ship *Nautilus* (See *Submarine Warfare*). The record of this vessel for long cruises submerged was enhanced when she made history, in 1958, by passing the North Pole under Arctic ice. Power plants similar to the one successfully demonstrated by the *Nautilus* are now standard for the U.S. submarine fleet.

The steam necessary for turbines is produced by heating water in a boiler. *Saturated steam* is in such a condition that any lowering of its temperature or increase of pressure will cause part of it to condense to water. One pound of such steam normally occupies 26.36 cubic feet. Saturated steam holding in suspension less than 3 per cent of water is called *dry steam*. Steam at a temperature higher than its normal condensing point is known as *superheated steam*. By its use and through improvements in design and fueling, boilers have been constructed to operate at a pressure of 3375 pounds to the square inch. Variant types of boilers include those which employ electricity for heating or which use mercury vapor instead of steam.

Telegraph. In its simplest form the telegraph is composed of a *line* of wire, usually galvanized iron; a key for sending; a sounder to make the signals audible; and some source of current such as a battery or dynamo. All are connected so that the current must pass through each one. Only one wire is generally used because the earth serves as a return wire to complete the circuit.

The *key* is merely a lever held in place by a spring. It has an insulated knob on one end, and carries a contact point underneath. The *sounder* consists of two electromagnets with a piece of iron mounted close to their ends. The iron armature is attached to a pivoted arm which strikes a brass anvil when it moves either up or down. When the key is *open*, no current can flow, but, when the knob is depressed, a contact is made which closes the circuit. The current then flows through the magnets, which pull the iron toward them, causing a click when the arm strikes the anvil. When the key is raised, the arm springs away from the magnets with another click.

The signals depend upon the time between the sounds of an up and a down click. A short period corresponds to a dot, a longer period to a dash, with a definite arrangement of dots and dashes for each letter. The Morse code, which is used in the United States and Canada, also makes use of a space in order to simplify the combinations. To avoid errors, the Continental Morse code using only dots and dashes is generally employed in Europe, and also in radiotelegraphy.

A commercial Morse telegraph key is equipped with a switch which is closed when the instrument is not in use. A current thus flows continually through all the instruments on a line until some operator wishes to send a message. He then opens his switch and sends the signals which are repeated in every office connected with the line. As the current flowing over a long line is usually too weak to operate a sounder, the main line is connected with a *relay*, which operates in the same way but is much more sensitive. The moving arm of the relay acts as a key to close a local circuit and operate a sounder. Very long lines, such as those from New York to Chicago, are generally divided into sections by *repeaters* which act as a reversible relay to repeat the signals with a stronger current.

By using currents differing in strength or direction, or both, it is possible by the *duplex* system to send a message in both directions at the same time. In 1873, Edison invented the *quadruplex* system whereby two messages may be sent in both directions at the same time. The *synchronous multiplex* system permits six operators to send over the same wire. Machines, such as the Wheatstone automatic telegraph, which use a perforated tape, are capable of transmitting 300 to 400 words per minute as compared with 25 to 40 by a good operator. With the multiplex *printing telegraph* system, messages are sent by pressing keys on a machine resembling a typewriter, and are automatically printed on telegraph blanks at the receiving end. Most telegrams are now sent in this way. Facsimile telegrams may be sent by phototelegraphic instruments. (See *Phototelegraphy*.)

The supreme court of the United States has decided that Samuel F. B. Morse was the inventor of the electromagnetic telegraph. Other famous scientists who worked on the same problem were the Englishmen, Wheatstone and Cook, whose five-wire system was the first to be tried commercially, and Professor Joseph Henry, an American, who in 1831 operated the first sounding electric telegraph. Steinheil of Munich also developed a similar system about 1837. Morse began his work in 1832. His first commercial line was constructed with government aid. It extended between Washington and Baltimore and was opened to the public April 1, 1844.

Morse Code. A•— B—••• C•• • D—•• E• F•—• G——• H•••• I•• J—•—• K—•— L— M—— N—• O• • P••••• Q••—• R• •• S••• T— U••— V•••— W•—— X•—•• Y•• •• Z••• •

Continental Code. A•— B—••• C—•—• D—•• E• F••—• G——• H•••• I•• J•——— K—•— L•—•• M—— N—• O——— P•——• Q——•— R•—• S••• T— U••— V•••— W•—— X—••— Y—•—— Z——••

Telephone. An instrument used for the purpose indicated by its name, which means a "voice from afar." Many inventors worked on the problem of an electric telephone. On February 14, 1876, Alexander Graham Bell applied for a patent, granted on the following March 7, which is fundamental for this method of transmitting speech by means of electricity.

Although it follows the basic principles of Bell's telephone, today's set possesses far better sending and receiving qualities. The telephone consists of two basic parts: 1) the handset which contains a receiver and transmitter, and 2) the base housing a ringer, an electrical network, a switch, and often a dial.

When the handset is lifted off the base, an electrical circuit is established through the telephone instrument. In the transmitter, this circuit passes through carbon granules in a chamber located immediately behind the diaphragm. Sound waves cause the diaphragm to vibrate, which in turn exerts pressure upon the granules, compressing them in varying densities. The varying resistance of the granules regulates the current flow. An electrical pattern of the voice is sent through a switching center to the other telephone.

In the receiver of the other telephone, a permanent magnet, surrounded by an electromagnet, exerts force on an iron-rimmed fabric diaphragm. As current passes through the electromagnet (coil), the magnet's attraction on the iron rim and attached diaphragm varies and the diaphragm moves accordingly. The surges of current dispatched from the transmitter set the pattern of vibration. This vibration sets sound waves in motion which the listener hears.

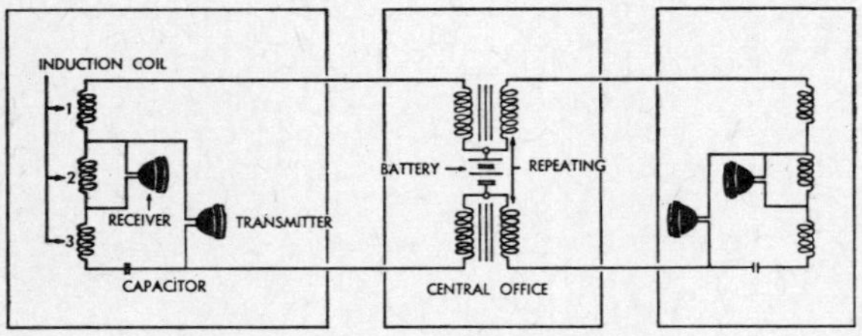

Diagram of a Telephone Circuit

One telephone is connected to another automatically (dial) or by hand in the switching center, called a central office. Today almost 90 per cent of all Bell telephones are dial operated. Three main types of dial apparatus are in use. Step-by-step, a switching system which connects a call in stages as each figure is dialed, is used mostly in smaller communities. In larger cities, or where switching requirements are complicated, "panel" and "crossbar" systems are most often found. Panel equipment has largely been replaced by "crossbar" for new installations. Unlike step equipment, crossbar switching of a call does not begin until the number is completely dialed. Then the entire operation is completed almost instantaneously. In conjunction with automatic accounting equipment, crossbar systems have opened the way for such modern, time-saving arrangements as operator long distance dialing and customer dialing to distant points. In 144 cities, in mid-1956, approximately 1,500,000 customers could dial long distance calls on a nationwide basis. Telephone connections now span the Atlantic and Pacific oceans.

Telephone conversations are carried over various types of voice highways. *Wire* transmission, the best known, basically depends on a pair of wires, providing metallic circuit. Two pairs form a quad and, when suitably arranged, can carry three conversations simultaneously. Telephone cables are made up of quads and pairs of various sizes. "*Carrier*" systems are today the principal method of long distance transmission. "Carrier" is the term given to a method by which a pair of wires, or other transmission medium, can be adapted to carry many simultaneous conversations. Conversations are put on different frequency bands. Filters at the receiving end sort out and "demodulate" (restore) the frequencies to those of the original voice band

"Coaxial" cable is one of the transmission media used for long distance carrier systems. Such cables usually have eight tubes. Tubes and a copper wire within have a common axis, or are coaxial. Voice signals are sent through the tubes on different frequency bands at speeds approaching light. With today's equipment, 1860 separate conversations or 660 conversations plus TV signals in each direction can be carried on a pair of tubes. Since two tubes are kept for emergencies, a coaxial cable thus can carry a maximum of 5580 separate simultaneous conversations. *Radio Relay*, a narrow beam radio system of super high frequencies (microwave), is another carrier communications system. The principal Bell Company radio relay systems can handle as many as six broad band communications paths in each direction. Two such highways in opposite directions can carry up to 600 conversations or two television programs. *V.H.F.(Very High Frequency) Radio* is used for communicating to and from moving vehicles, while *high frequency radio* is used for many overseas calls. In 1956, the first two major transoceanic telephone cable systems were laid—one between North America and Great Britain and the other between Alaska and the United States. The Trans-Pacific cable between U.S. and Japan was completed in 1964.

Television. This term is applied to the reproduction, transmission, and reception, through the medium of electromagnetic rays, of a series of rapidly succeeding photographic pictures which give the impression of a scene from life. The word means "seeing from a distance."

The central element in the process is a specialized form of electron tube known in different forms as an iconoscope or an image dissector. It contains a screen consisting of numerous minute light-sensitive cells. A photographic image is focused on the light-sensitive cells. The screen is scanned by an electronic beam, which has the effect of setting up in the cells currents proportional to the amount of light received. The currents on transmission to a receiving instrument are used to reconstruct the light pattern in the original image. A standard picture calls for the electronic beam passing across the image 440 times and making 30 complete pictures in a second.

Transmission requires the simultaneous use of numerous telephonic channels, a requirement which is met by the coaxial cable for wire transmission and short wave bands for wireless transmission.

Color television cameras contain three orthicon (image-dissecting) tubes. A system of mirrors and color filters enables the first tube to form a red image; the second, a green image; and the third, a blue image. Through use of an electronic transmission system, the three primary color signals are fed to three color picture tubes where they are simultaneously converted back into color images. A system of mirrors superimposes the three pictures so that the viewer sees one color-blended picture.

Thermostat. An instrument for automatically regulating the temperature produced by heating apparatus. When the temperature to be regulated rises to a certain point it causes an element of the thermostat, either a fluid or a metal bar, to expand and touch off a control which closes a draft or the fuel feed supplying the heat. Then when the temperature falls to a certain point, the sensitive element of the thermostat contracts and the control is actuated in such a way as to cause more heat to be supplied.

Thermostats in household use are ordinarily placed in a living room. The control actuated by the expanding or contracting element is connected electrically with a device for regulating the furnace. In a hot air furnace, if coal is burned, the device closes or opens the drafts; if oil or gas is used, the device partially cuts off the feed. In hot water furnaces, the action of the thermostat is to cut off or turn on an electric current operating a pump which, when in action, causes the hot water to circulate. A second thermostat regulates the temperature of the water.

Typewriter. An instrument for writing in characters similar to those used for printing. Christopher Latham Sholes is generally considered to be the inventor of the modern typewriter. On his first machine, completed in September 1867, many letters were written and sent to friends. One of these letters induced James Densmore, of Meadville, Pa., to take a large financial interest in the new invention, which was patented in 1868.

A famous firm of gunmakers, E. Remington and Sons, was then persuaded to manufacture the machine, which, in 1874, appeared on the market as the Remington typewriter.

Most of the standard modern typewriters are operated by 42 keys arranged in what has been found to be the most convenient order. This arrangement is known as the *universal keyboard*. Scores of other arrangements are used for writing in foreign languages, or for the use of special characters. Each key controls a steel type bar which carries two characters near the free end.

Selection of the desired character is obtained by means of a shift key.

The type bars are hinged in a basket-like group, so that each one may strike on a common center when the proper key is depressed. The paper is placed upon a rubber cylinder, which is mounted on a carriage moving from right to left. Under the control of a pawl and ratchet, the carriage moves one space to the left after each letter is printed or when the space bar is used. At the end of a line the carriage is pushed to the right by the operator. This pressure also serves to advance the paper for a new line.

Just before the type bar reaches the cylinder, an inked ribbon is raised into place so that the key strikes the ribbon and leaves a sharp impression upon the paper. Key and ribbon then drop back so that the writing is always visible. The ribbon, which is usually about 25 feet long, is stretched between two spools and moves at the same speed as the carriage. When most of the ribbon has been wound upon one spool, the direction of winding is automatically reversed.

The average operator writes about sixty words per minute, which is about three times as fast as the ordinary penman. Special typewriters are in use for bookkeeping and similar operations.

Outstanding among typewriter improvements was the early introduction of the warning bell which tells the typist the end of the line is approaching, the coming of the noiseless machine in 1909, and the advent of the electric typewriter about 1935.

The teletype or teletypewriter records messages by electrical transmission, as does also the machine known as the stock market ticker.

MODERN INVENTIONS

Invention, Inventor, and Country	Date
Adding machine; Blaise Pascal; France	1642
Recording; Burroughs; United States	1888
Air brake; George Westinghouse, Jr.; United States	1869
Airplane; Orville and Wilbur Wright; United States	1903
Airplane compass; Mendenhall and Williamson; United States	1917
Air pump; Otto von Guericke; Germany	1654
Airship; Henri Giffard; France	1852
Aluminum, Hall process of making; Charles M. Hall; United States	1886
Aniline dyes; W. H. Perkin; England	1856
Autogiro; J. de la Cierva	1920
Automobile, gas engine; Siegfried Markus; Germany	1875
First commercial; Levassor; France	1891
Babbitt metal; Isaac Babbitt; United States	1839
Bakelite; L. H. Baekeland; Belgium-United States	1907
Balloon; J. E. and J. M. Montgolfier; France	1783
Barbed wire machine; Glidden and Vaughan; United States	1874
Barometer; Torricelli; Italy	1643
Bicycle; Macmillan; Scotland	1840
Modern type; James Starley; England	1884
Bifocal lens; Benjamin Franklin; United States	1780
Calcium carbide, commercial production of; Thomas L. Willson; United States	1892
Carborundum; E. G. Acheson; United States	1891
Car coupler, automatic; E. H. Janney; United States	1873
Carding machine; Whittemore; United States	1797
Cartridge, metallic; Houiller; France	1847
Cash register; J. Ritty; United States	1879
Caterpillar tractor; Benjamin Holt; United States	1900
Caustic soda, Castner process; Hamilton Y. Castner; United States	1890
Cellophane; J. E. Brandenberger; France	1912
Celluloid; J. W. and Isaac Hyatt; United States	1869
Chrome tanning; Schultz; United States	1884
Clock, pendulum; Huygens; Netherlands	1657
Coach, steam; Richard Trevithick; England	1801
Coal, liquefaction of, for producing gasoline; Friedrich Bergius; Germany	1914
Coherer, for detecting "wireless" waves; E. Branly; France	1892
Color photography; F. E. Ives; United States	1892
Ruled screen process; John Joly; Ireland	1894
Autochrome process; A. and L. Lumière; France	1906
Cotton gin; Eli Whitney; United States	1793
Cream separator, centrifugal; De Laval; Sweden	1880
Cultivator, rotary disc; Mallon; United States	1878
Cyanide process for gold and silver ore; Forrest and MacArthur; Scotland	1890
Dental plate, rubber; Charles Goodyear, Jr.; United States	1855
Depth bomb; Unge; Sweden	1903
Improved; Godfrey Tait; United States	1916
Diesel engine; Rudolf Diesel; Germany	1893
Dynamite; A. Nobel; Sweden	1866
Dynamo-electric machine, first; Michael Faraday; England	1831
Drum wound armature; Werner Siemens; Germany	1854
Separately excited field; H. Wilde; England	1863
Electric arc lighting, practicable system; C. F. Brush; United States	1878
Electric battery, primary; Alessandro Volta; Italy	1799
Electric battery, storage; Gaston Plante; France	1859
Nickel-iron type; Thomas A. Edison; United States	1903
Electric furnace, arc type; Pichou and Johnson; France and England	1853
Resistance type; W. Borchers; Germany	1880
Electric lamp, carbon filament; Joseph W. Swan; England	1860
Improved carbon filament; Thomas A. Edison; United States	1879
Ductile tungsten filament; W. D. Coolidge; United States	1910
Electric motor, split phase; Tesla; United States	1887
Alternate current; Tesla; United States	1892
Electric welding, resistance process; Elihu Thompson; United States	1886
Electrocast blocks; G. S. Fulcher; United States	1927
Electromagnet; Wm. Sturgeon; England	1824
Electron tube, practical; J. A. Fleming; England	1904
Three-electrode; Lee De Forest; United States	1906
Electroplating; Luigi Brugnatelli; Italy	1805
Electrotyping; Moritz H. von Jacobi (Germany) and Thomas Spencer (England)	1838
Elevator, power; Elisha G. Otis; United States	1852
Flotation process, ore refining; Elmore; United States	1899
Food preservation, canning process; Appert; France	1810
Fourdrinier paper-making machine; Louis Robert; France	1798
Galvanometer; Sweigger; Germany	1820
Gas engine, electric ignition; Barsonti and Matteucci; Italy	1857
Four-cycle; Nicholas August Otto; Germany	1877
Successful; Gottlieb Daimler; Germany	1884
Gaslighting system; Wm. Murdock; England	1792
Gas mantle, incandescent; von Welsbach; Austria	1885
Gas meter, wet; S. Clegg; England	1815
Dry, modern; Wm. Richards; United States	1843
Gatling gun; R. J. Gatling; United States	1861
Gauge, steam pressure; Bourdon; France	1849
Gramophone; Emile Berliner; United States	1887
Graphophone; Bell and Tainter; United States	1885
Guncotton; Schönbein; Germany	1846
Gyrocompass; H. Anschutz-Kampfe; Germany	1906
Improved; Elmer A. Sperry; United States	1910
Gyroscope; Foucants; France	1852
Harvester and thresher, combined; S. C. Matteson; United States	1888
Holography; Dennis Gabor; England	1947
Hydraulic press; Joseph Bramah; England	1795
Hydrogenation, catalytic; Sabatier and Senderens; France	1902
Hydroplane; Glenn H. Curtiss; United States	1911
Ice machine, compressor system; Jacob Perkins; United States	1834
Absorption system; F. P. E. Carré; France	1860
Induction coil, modern; Ruhmkorff; Germany	1851
Injector, steam, for boilers; Henri Giffard; France	1858
Iron, galvanizing process; Henry Craufurd; England	1837
Knitting machine; William Lee; England	1589
Circular; M. I. Brunel; England	1816
Latch needle; Townsend and Moulding; England	1858
Kodak, roll-film hand camera; Eastman and Walker; United States	1888
Lacquer, synthetic—nitrocellulose; W. P. Field; United States	1890
Cellulose acetate; C. F. Cross, E. J. Bevan; England	1892
Laser; Charles Townes, Arthur Schawlos; U. S.	1958
Lathe, turret; Stephen Fitch; United States	1845
Lawn mower; A. M. Hills; United States	1868
Lewis gun; I. N. Lewis; United States	1912
Leyden jar, modern; John Bevis; England	1746
Lightning conductor; Benjamin Franklin; United States	1752
Linotype; Ottmar Mergenthaler; United States	1885
Lithography; Alois Senefelder; Bohemia	1798

MODERN INVENTIONS—Con.

Invention, Inventor, and Country	Date
Locomotive, steam, on rails; Richard Trevithick; England	1804
First successful; George Stephenson; England	1829
Loom, pattern; M. J. Jacquard; France	1801
Power; Edmund Cartwright; England	1785
Locomotive, electric; Vail; United States	1851
Machine rifle; John M. Browning; United States	1916
Maser, Charles Townes; United States	1954
Matches, friction; John Walker; England	1827
Safety; Lundstrom; Sweden	1855
Mercerized cotton; John Mercer; England	1844
Mercury vapor lamp; Peter Cooper Hewitt; U. S.	1900
Microphone; Emile Berliner; United States	1877
Microscope, compound; Zacharias Janssen; Netherlands	1590
Electron; E. Ruska, B. von Boris; Germany	1938
Monotype; Talbert Lanston; United States	1887
Motion picture machine; Thomas Armat; United States	1895
Mowing machine; Manning; United States	1831
With differential gear; Eickemeyer; United States	1876
Multiplying machine; G. W. Leibnitz; Germany	1671
Nails, machine cut; Ezekiel Reed; United States	1786
Naval telescope gun sight; Bradley A. Fiske; United States	1891
Nernst lamp; Walter Nernst; Germany	1897
Nitrogen fixation electric arc; C. Birkeland; Norway	1903
Catalytic process; Haber and Bosch; Germany	1911
Cyanamid process; Caro and Franke; Germany	1908
Nylon; E. I. du Pont de Nemours & Co., U. S.	1937
Oleomargarine; H. Mege-Mouries; France	1869
Opthalmoscope; Helmholtz; Germany	1851
Optophone, by which blind can read type; E. E. Fournier d'Albe; England	1914
Pen, steel; Samuel Harrison; England	1780
First successful fountain; L. E. Waterman; U. S.	1884
Percussion cap; Shaw; United States	1816
Phonograph; Thomas A. Edison; United States	1877
Photoelectric cell; J. Elster and H. Geitel; Germany	1895
Photography, daguerreotype process; L. Daguerre; France	1839
Bichromate process; Mungo Ponton; Scotland	1839
Use of hypo; John Herschel; England	1839
Collodion process; Scott Archer; England	1851
Gelatin-silver bromide emulsion; R. L. Maddox; England	1871
Roll-film, modern; Hannibal Goodwin; United States	1887
Phototelegraphy; Bell Telephone Laboratories; United States	1925
Piano; Bartollomeo Cristofori; Italy	1709
Piano player, first pneumatic; M. Fourneaux; France	1863
Pin-making machine; L. W. Wright; United States	1824
Plow, cast-iron, modern shape; Jethro Wood; United States	1819
Disk; Hardy; United States	1896
Pneumatic tire; R. W. Thompson; England	1845
Independently by John B. Dunlop, Ireland	1888
Pneumatic tool; George Law; England	1865
Portland cement; Joseph Aspdin; England	1824
Printing from movable type; J. Gutenberg; Germany	1450
Printing press, cylinder; F. Konig; Germany	1811
Double cylinder; R. Hoe & Co., United States	1845
Rotary; Thomas Nelson; England	1850
Gordon; George P. Gordon; United States	1850
Pulmotor; Alexander B. Dräger; Germany	1911
Radar; Dr. A. Hoyt Taylor and Leo C. Young of the Naval Aircraft Radio laboratory; United States	1922
Radiotelegraph; G. Marconi; Italy	1895
Radiotelephone; Lee DeForest; United States	1906
Long-distance; American Tel. & Tel. Co.; United States	1915
Rail, flanged; T. R. L. Stevens; United States	1831
Rayon; H. de Chardonnet; France	1889
Reaper, McCormick; Cyrus H. McCormick; United States	1831
Refrigerating machine; John Gorie; United States	1851
Revolver; Samuel Colt; United States	1835
Rifle, spiral grooves; Koster; England	1620
Breech-loading, successful; John M. Hall; United States	1810
Bolt action, military; Dreyse; Germany	1839
Repeating; Henry; United States	1860
Rock drill, percussion; J. J. Couch; United States	1849
Diamond bit; Herman; United States	1854
Safety lamp, miner's; Sir Humphry Davy; England	1815
Saw, band, wood; William Newbery; England	1808
Circular, wood; Samuel Miller; England	1777
Screw propeller, successful application; John Ericsson; Sweden	1841
Self-binding reaper, twine; J. F. Appleby; United States	1875
Sewing machine; Elias Howe; United States	1846
Four-motion feed; Allen B. Wilson; United States	1854
Shoe-sewing machine, McKay; Lyman Blake; United States	1858
Welt-sewing; Charles Goodyear, Jr.; United States	1871
Shotgun, practical breech-loading; Casimir Lefaucheux; France	1836
Hammerless, ejecting; J. Needham; England	1874
Silencer for firearms; Hiram P. Maxim; United States	1909
Smokeless powder; J. F. E. Schultze; Germany	1867
Spectroscope; Kirchhoff and Bunsen; Germany	1859
Spinning machine, jenny; James Hargreaves; England	1767
Roll-drawing; Richard Arkwright; England	1769
Mule-jenny; Samuel Crompton; England	1779
Ring spinner; John Thorp; United States	1828
Stainless steel; Brearley; England	1914
Steamboat, successful; Robert Fulton; United States	1807
Steam engine, atmospheric; Thomas Newcomen; England	1705
With separate condenser; James Watt; Scotland	1765
Double action, use of expanding steam; James Watt; Scotland	1782
Compound; Jonathan C. Hornblower; England	1781
High-pressure; Oliver Evans; United States	1799
Steam hammer; James Nasmyth; Scotland	1839
Steam turbine; Charles A. Parsons; England	1884
Steel, Bessemer process; William Kelly; United States	1847
Independently by Henry Bessemer; England	1855
Crucible process; Robert Huntsman; England	1740
Open-hearth process; Siemens and Martin; England	1866
High speed; F. W. Taylor and M. White; United States	1900
Manganese; Hadfield; England	1884
Stereoscope, lenticular; Sir David Brewster; England	1849
Stereotyping; William Ged; Scotland	1725
Stethoscope; Laënnec; France	1819
Submarine boat, first successful; John P. Holland; United States	1900
Submarine detector; Max Mason; United States	1917
Tack machine; Blanchard; United States	1806
Tank, military; Gen. E. D. Swinton; England	1914
Telegraph; S. F. B. Morse; United States	1837
Duplex system; J. B. Stearns; United States	1872
Quadruplex system; Thomas A. Edison; United States	1873
Submarine, siphon recorder; Wm. Thompson; England	1874
Telephone; A. G. Bell; United States	1876
Automatic; A. B. Strowger; United States	1889
Long-distance, by loading coils; Michael I. Pupin; United States	1900
Telephone transmitter, microphone; Emile Berliner and Thomas A. Edison, United States	1877
Telescope; Jan Lippershey; Netherlands	1608
Teletypesetter; Morkrum-Kleinschmidt Corporation; United States	1928
Television; J. L. Baird; England	1925
Independently by C. F. Jenkins; United States	1925
Thermit mixtures; H. Goldschmidt; Germany	1897
Thermometer; Galileo; Italy	1593
Threshing machine; Andrew Meikle; Scotland	1786
Torpedo, self-propelled; Whitehead; England	1868
Radio controlled; Bradley A. Fiske; United States	1897
Transistor; John Bardeen, Wm. B. Shockley, Walter H. Brattain, United States	1948
Trolley car, practical system; F. J. Sprague; U.S.	1888
Tunnel shield; M. I. Brunel; England	1818
Turbine, hydraulic; J. B. Francis; United States	1849
Turret, revolving, for floating battery; Theodore Timby; United States	1862
Typewriter, first practicable; C. L. Sholes; U.S.	1868
Vacuum bottle; James Dewar; England	1892
Valve gear, Stephenson link; William Howe; England	1843
Walshaert gear; Egide Walshaert; Sweden	1844
Vulcanized rubber; Charles Goodyear; United States	1844
Watches, machine-made; Dennison and Howard; United States	1850
Water gas, modern process; T. S. C. Lowe; United States	1873
Wood pulp, for paper, mechanical process; Keller and Voelter; Germany	1844
Sulphite process; B. C. Tilghmann; United States	1867
Sulphate process; Dahl; Sweden	1883

ENGINEERING AND BUILDING

An engineer directs the natural forces of nature to the uses of mankind. He must therefore be a scientist; for mathematics, physics, and chemistry are the foundation of most engineering training. Nevertheless, the pioneer of science who devotes his energies to solving the problems of physics or chemistry is not an engineer. To qualify as such, he must apply the knowledge obtained by research and testing, to the design, construction, and operation of works, machines, or processes.

The mathematician studies the mutual relations between the sides and the angles of a triangle; the engineer uses the knowledge thus obtained to measure the distance across a river or to the top of a distant peak. The physicist studies the laws of centrifugal force; the engineer applies these laws when he raises the outer rail at a curve, to prevent a train from leaving the track. The chemist discovers that starch can easily be changed into glucose; the engineer then designs and operates a factory where table sirups are made from corn or potatoes. Because of this practical side of his work, an engineer has been described as one who can accomplish with one dollar what an untrained worker can do, indifferently, with two.

The practice of engineering is not new, for the pyramids of Egypt with their perfectly placed masses of stone compare well with the greatest of modern structures; and some of the bridges and aqueducts constructed by the Romans are still in use. The earliest engineers were chiefly surveyors. Later, engineering became largely a military profession, because the chief demand of the time was for men who could plan strong fortifications and construct tunnels and the engines of war necessary to reduce opposing forts.

With the advance of civilization and the development of commerce, engineering projects, such as bridges and harbors, dams, roads, and canals, were required even more for civil than for military purposes. As a result, men capable of filling this need gradually developed the profession of *civil engineering*, which is now generally recognized as the first and largest division of engineering practice. Next, the rapid increase in the application of power to mechanical operations caused men to specialize in the design and the use of machines. Thus developed the second great branch of the engineering field—that of *mechanical engineering*.

Branches of Engineering. Civil and mechanical engineering represent the fundamental divisions of engineering practice. Mining, electrical, chemical, and sanitary engineering are specialized branches, each applying general engineering principles in connection with a particular division of science. The electrical engineer is probably the most highly specialized, but that each branch is closely related to every other is shown by the training given to students of engineering in the great technical schools. For the first two or three years of their work, students of electrical, mechanical, or chemical engineering study almost the same subjects; later they are permitted to specialize.

More than a hundred well recognized subdivisions might also be named, such as heat, hydraulic or water power, railway, locomotive, automotive, ventilation, highway, telephone, and aeronautical engineering.

Civil Engineering. The civil engineer may be compared to a general at war with the elements, for he strives to bring the land and the sea under his control. He is a builder, in order that commerce and industry may be more easily carried on. He designs, locates, and builds highways and railroads, and, if these are interrupted by a deep gorge or by wide rivers, bridges and tunnels are constructed under his direction. He deepens harbors, protects them from the open waters by means of breakwaters, places lighthouses to guide ships to safety, and builds docks at which cargoes can easily be handled.

Construction of canals and the development of inland waterways, the building of dams for purposes of irrigation and water power, the erection of a single skyscraper or the building of an entire city and of aqueducts to supply the city with water—all come directly within the province of the civil engineer.

Mechanical Engineering. The division of engineering which is concerned with the design, construction, and operation of machines. A civil engineer may plan and lay out a railroad, and a naval architect may design a fast and beautiful steamship, but it is the mechanical engineer who designs the locomotive that hauls the trains and the boilers and engines that drive the vessel. While an architect designs, and a civil engineer constructs, a mighty office building, the mechanical engineer provides for a suitable power plant, pumps, elevators, hot water, ventilation, heat, and often a system of refrigeration. A steel mill, with its enormous power plant and giant engines for handling and shaping iron and steel products, is one of the most impressive examples of mechanical engineering.

When a new type of machine is required for some special purpose, it must be designed by a mechanical engineer. However, standardized machines for many purposes are already on the market, so that in factory operation the mechanical engineer must frequently select and arrange the proper machines to produce a certain result in the most economical manner. The design and the improvement of automobiles have become so important that specialists in this branch of mechanical work are called *automotive engineers*.

Another important duty of the mechanical engineer is the testing of structural materials. The builder of a bridge knows that it will carry its load because a mechanical engineer has designed machines capable of testing steel beams by the application of enormous forces. In this age of machinery, no engineering problem of any considerable importance can be carried through without the aid of the mechanical expert.

Mining Engineering. A branch of engineering devoted to the surveying, testing, and evaluation of mineral deposits, and the planning and execution of the methods by which the mineral is obtained and treated. The mining engineer must decide on the methods to be used in removing the ore, in strengthening tunnel walls to prevent accidents, in providing drainage and ventilation for the mine, and in quickly and efficiently hoisting the mineral to the surface. He must, therefore, be especially trained in civil and mechanical engineering, and in chemistry, geology, and mineralogy.

Electrical Engineering. Engineering principles applied to the designing, building, and operating of dynamos and batteries, electric light and power systems, electric railways, motors, heating apparatus varying in type from a toaster to a giant furnace, telegraph and telephone systems including radio transmission, and various other types of electrical apparatus.

In co-operation with the mechanical engineer, the electrical engineer has done important work in providing mechanical equipment with electrical control. And, in co-operation with the chemical engineer, he has developed the important division of *electrochemical* engineering, which deals with the use of electricity in chemical processes. The products of the electrochemical industries include some of the most indispensable materials employed in manufacture, such as ferro-alloys, aluminum, electrolytic copper, caustic soda, chlorine, hydrogen, oxygen, carborundum, cyanamid, and calcium carbide.

SOME NOTED BRIDGES AND VIADUCTS OF THE WORLD*

Kind and Name	Location	Completed	Length Feet	Main Span Feet	Height Feet	Approximate Cost
Bascule [(1) one leaf; (2) two leaf]:						
Canadian Pacific Ry. (2)	Sault Ste. Marie canal (U. S.)	1914	426	336		$ 250,000
Michigan Ave. (2)	Chicago R., Chicago, Ill.	1920	300	256	16.5	
Wells S . (1)	Chicago R., Chicago, Ill.	1921		268		
Outer-Drive (2)	Chicago R., Chicago, Ill.	1937		264	24	1,800,000
St. Charles Air Lane (1)	Chicago R., Chicago, Ill.	1931	277	219.3	20	705,000
Arlington Memorial (2)	Potomac R., Washington, D. C.	1932	2,163	216	35	7,360,000
Tower (2)	Thames R., London, Eng.	1894	2,980	200	30	5,000,000
Cantilever:						
Quebec	St. Lawrence R., Quebec	1917	3,240	1,800	150	9,000,000
Forth	Firth of Forth, Scotland	1890	8,095	1,700	150	16,000,000
Rip Van Winkle	Hudson R., Catskill, N. Y.	1935	5,040	1,600	142	2,165,000
Victoria	St. Lawrence R., Montreal	1898	8,440	1,250	150	6,000,000
Longview	Columbia R., Wash.	1930	3,740	1,200	196	5,800,000
Queensboro	East R , New York City	1909	7,449	1,182	135	13,000,000
Carquinez	Carquinez Str., Cal.	1927	4,482	1,100	158	7,800,000
South Shore	St. Lawrence R., Montreal	1929	9,137	1,097	162	18,639,000
Cooper River	Charleston, S. C.	1929	14,313	1,050	160	6,000,000
Bluewater	St. Clair R., Port Huron	1938	6,539	871	210	3,250,000
Concrete Arch:						
Plougastel-Brest	Elorn R., France	1930	2,625	612	118	440,000
Westinghouse Memorial	Turtle Creek Valley, East Pittsburgh	1931	1,560	460	200	1,480,000
Pont de la Caille	Cruseilles, France			458.5		
Cappelen Memorial	Mississippi R., Minneapolis	1923	1,032	435	88	900,000
Pierre du Vauvray	Seine R., Ande, France	1924		432		
Royal Tweed	Tweed R., Edinburgh, Scot.	1928	1,400	361.5	45	800,000
Resorgimento	Tiber R., Rome, Italy	1911	492	328	47	238,000
Masonry Arch:						
Plauen	White Elster R., Germany	1903	492	295.2	58	125,000
Sidi Rached	Constantine, Algeria	1915	1,468	227	300	366,000
Cabin John	Cabin John Creek, Washington, D. C.	1864	420	220	101	237,000
London	Thames R., England	1831	928	152	56	7,241,500
Steel Arch:						
Kill van Kull	Staten Is.—Bayonne, N. J.	1931	5,780	1,652	150	18,000,000
Sydney Harbor	Sydney, Australia	1932	3,770	1,650	170	35,000,000
Birchenough	Sabi R., Southern Rhodesia	1935	1,080	1,080		500,000
Glen Canyon	No. Central Arizona	1964	1,271	1,028	700	
Hell Gate	East R., New York City	1917	17,868	977.5	135	15,000,000
Rainbow	Niagara R., Niagara Falls	1941	1,240	950	189	3,760,000
Henry Hudson	Harlem R., New York City	1936	2,000	800	142.5	1,137,876
McKees Rocks	Ohio R., near Pittsburgh	1930	3,600	750	100	6,000,000
West End	Ohio R., Pittsburgh	1931	1,889	780	73	
Suspension:						
Verrazano-Narrows	Brooklyn-Staten Island	1965	13,700	4,260	228	125,000,000
Golden Gate	San Francisco Bay, Cal.	1937	8,500	4,200	220	32,815,000
Mackinac	Straits of Mackinac, Michigan	1957	26,444	3,800	148	96,400,000
Washington Memorial	Hudson R., New York City	1931	8,243	3,500	213	60,000,000
Tagus River	Lisbon Harbor, Portugal	1966	3,323		230	75,000,000
Firth of Forth	Edinburgh, Scotland	1966	3,300			30,350,000
Severn River	Aust, England	1966	3,240		120	22,400,000
Bolivar	Orinoco R., Venezuela	1965	2,336		177	18,500,000
Transbay	San Francisco Bay, Cal.	1936	22,720	2,310†	200	77,600,000
Delaware Memorial	Delaware R. near Wilmington	1951	10,750	2,150	442	44,000,000
Ambassador	Detroit R., Detroit, Mich.	1929	8,000	1,850	152	22,500,000
Delaware River	Camden-Philadelphia	1926	9,570	1,750	135	24,600,000
Bear Mountain	Hudson R.	1924	2,257	1,632	155	5,000,000
Williamsburg	East R., New York City	1903	7,308	1,600	135	15,000,000
Brooklyn	East R., New York City	1883	7,580	1,595.5	135	18,000,000
Lions Gate	Vancouver Harbor, Vancouver, B. C.	1938	5,820	1,550	200	6,000,000
Mid-Hudson	Hudson R., Poughkeepsie, N. Y.	1930	4,200	1,500	135	5,622,700
Manhattan	East R., New York City	1909	6,855	1,470	135	17,000,000
Triborough‡	East and Harlem Rs., N.Y.C.	1936	4,318	1,380	135	42,000,000
Truss [(s) simple; (c) continuous]:						
Metropolis (s)	Ohio R., Ill.	1917	5,700	720	53	3,000,000
Paducah (s)	Ohio R., Ohio	1929	9,000	716	100	
St. Louis (c)	Mississippi R., Mo.	1930	5,350	700	55	
Tanana River (s)	Alaska	1923	700	700		1,370,000
Cincinnati (c)	Ohio R., Ohio	1929	1,575	675	104	1,750,000
Cape Girardeau (c)	Mississippi R., Mo.	1930	2,339	671	99	
Vertical Lift:						
Buzzards Bay	Cape Cod Canal, Mass.	1936	806	544	139	2,000,000
Marine Park	Jamaica Bay Channel, N. Y.	1937	4,802	540	55	3,800,000
Burlington-Bristol	Delaware R., N. J.—Pa.	1931	3,027	534	61	1,300,000
Kansas City	Missouri R., Kans.—Mo.	1912	5,340	428	65	2,200,000
Boonville, Mo., M.K.T.R.R	Missouri R.	1932	1,638	408	27	1,000,000
Hackensack River	P.R.R. near Jersey City	1930	2,950	331.5	40	
Suisun Bay	California	1930	5,603.5	328	70	12,000,000

*The bridges in this table are divided according to the type of their main span. In each division, the bridges are arranged in the order of the length of the main span.

†Two joined spans of 2310 feet each; also a main cantilever span of 1400 feet.

‡Suspension span over East River; vertical lift span, 310 feet long, over Harlem River.

Many bridges which are not remarkable for their main spans are nevertheless noteworthy on account of their lengths or their heights. Among the longest bridges in the world are the following:

Chesapeake Bay Bridge-Tunnel, length 17.6 miles, from Cape Charles to Chesapeake Beach, Va.

Transbay, 8 miles long.

Great Salt Lake cutoff, a railroad trestle 20 miles long.

San Mateo bridge across San Francisco bay, 7.1 miles.

Lake Pontchartrain railroad bridge, Louisiana, 7 miles.

James River Highway bridge, near Newport News, Va., with approaches, 6 miles; without approaches, 4½ miles.

Lake Pontchartrain highway bridge, Louisiana, 5 miles.

Huey Long cantilever bridge over Mississippi at New Orleans, completed 1935, totaling 4½ miles.

Rainbow Bridge, Niagara River, is the longest hingeless arch span in the world.

Among the highest bridges are the following:

Royal Gorge, a suspension bridge over the Arkansas River at Canon City, Colo., 1050 feet high; steel arch bridge over the Colorado River at Glen Canyon Dam, Arizona, 700 feet high; Snake River cantilever bridge near Twin Falls, Idaho, 502 feet high; Marble Canyon, a steel arch bridge over the Colorado River at Lee's Ferry, Arizona, 467 feet high.

Chemical Engineering. A chemical engineer designs and operates the process and special equipment necessary for commercial preparation of chemical substances. His field includes the production of acids and alkalies, dyes, fertilizers, gases, explosives, synthetic drugs and perfumes, and also of many products, such as leather, paper, soap, starch, glucose, and sugar, which frequently do not suggest the chemical methods by which they are prepared.

Sanitary Engineering. A branch of civil engineering which deals with problems such as providing a community with pure water, and disposing of sewage, garbage, and other refuse, in such a manner as to avoid danger to the public health. In addition to the fundamental civil engineering, a sanitary engineer must, therefore, have special training in biology, bacteriology, and chemistry.

Military Engineering. This consists in the application of engineering principles to military problems. The military engineer is essentially a civil engineer who has specialized in the design and construction of permanent forts, military bridges, roads, railroads, barracks, and camps. The plans for dugouts, trenches, tunnels, barbed wire entanglements, and the placing of mines and big guns are all under the direction of the military branch called, in the United States army, the Corps of Engineers. On graduation at West Point, the cadets ranking at the head of their class are usually assigned to this corps, which, in addition to purely military duties, has charge of navigable rivers and harbors, and also of the bridges and roads in Crater Lake and Yellowstone national parks.

The mechanical engineering involved in the production of guns and ammunition for the United States army is done under the direction of the department of ordnance. The magnitude of the work may be best appreciated after considering the size of one of the 16-inch guns guarding the Panama canal. It weighs 130 tons and is 49¼ feet long, tapering from a diameter of 28 inches at the muzzle to 5 feet at the breech. The projectile weighs 2400 pounds, and, when driven by a full charge of 667 pounds of powder, leaves the bore at the rate of about half a mile per second. When the gun is fired, the gas pressure on the base of the shell equals 19 tons to the square inch, or about 180 times the pressure on the foundations of a great skyscraper. If the tallest known building were placed on top of the earth's highest mountain, ten miles away from this gun, the engineers in charge could fire a shell over the obstacle with a fair chance of striking a target 21 miles distant.

Graduates of the United States Naval Academy are all trained as mechanical engineers. Those wishing to specialize in the designing of warships are given advanced courses in *naval architecture*; those who are to have control of a ship's engines, are given special courses in *naval engineering.* It is these specialists who decide upon the number and size of the guns, the type and size of the power plant, and the thickness of armor plate on a battleship; the size and equipment of submarines; the design of torpedoes, mines, depth bombs; and similar engineering problems relating to the navy.

Aqueduct (Latin, *aqua*, "water"; *ducere*, "to lead"). An artificial channel or system of conduits through which a large volume of water may flow for a long distance under the action of gravity. Aqueducts are generally used when a city is unable to obtain a near-by supply of water. And, because water is absolutely necessary, aqueducts were used by some of the most ancient cities of which there is any record.

The earliest aqueducts were tunnels, but the Romans developed the use of masonry conduits carried across the country on tall, arched piers. It is this type of structure which is generally associated with the name aqueduct. Modern engineers are returning more and more to the use of tunnels, preferring siphons—which are U-shaped tunnels—instead of bridges, for carrying the water across a river or a low level.

Rome was supplied with water by eleven aqueducts, constructed between 312 B. C. and 226 A. D. The longest of these, the *Anio Novus*, had a length of 62 miles. The *Aqua Virgo*, or *Aqua Vergine* as it is called in the modern Italian language, was restored by the popes Nicholas V and Pius IV and now supplies water for several fountains in Rome. Among the many aqueducts built throughout the Roman Empire, that at Segovia, Spain, and the Pont du Gard at Nimes, France, are probably most famous.

There are many modern aqueducts of great length. In England, Liverpool has a 68-mile aqueduct and Manchester one of 96 miles. Vienna, Austria, obtains water through a conduit 114 miles in length. Longest of all is the Pugliese aqueduct, which supplies 536 Italian towns with water, and has a total length of 1175 miles. The city of Winnipeg, Canada, has a 100-mile aqueduct, and Denver, Colorado, brings a part of its water a distance of 20 miles through large wooden pipes.

The Catskill aqueduct, built to supply New York City with an additional 600 million gallons of water per day, was completed in 1917 at a total cost of 177 million dollars. The water, obtained from the Esopus and Schoharie watersheds, is first stored in the Ashokan reservoir, which has sufficient capacity to cover all of Manhattan island to a depth of 30 feet. The aqueduct proper, 92 miles long, is composed of 55 miles of cut-and-cover conduit, 31 miles of tunnel, and 6 miles of steel pressure tubing. The cut-and-cover sections are made by excavating a channel, in which a 17-foot concrete conduit is built and then covered with earth. The water is carried under the Hudson river at Storm King, about 4 miles above West Point, by means of a siphon consisting of a tunnel 3022 feet long, bored through solid rock at a depth of 1100 feet below sea level. The aqueduct ends at Hill View reservoir, and the water is distributed to the city from a pressure tunnel 18 miles long, which passes the length of Manhattan island and into Brooklyn at a depth of 200 to 700 feet below the streets.

The Los Angeles aqueduct, built between 1908 and 1913, begins at the Owens river, which, with about 35 contributing streams, drains an area of 2800 square miles in the Sierra Nevada. The total length of the aqueduct is about 233 miles. For 60 miles the water is carried in open canal to the Haiwee reservoir. From the end of the reservoir, which is 3760 feet above sea level, the water flows to its destination through 98 miles of covered conduit, 43 miles of tunnel, and 12 miles of steel siphon. As Los Angeles has an elevation of only 275 feet, the water, in coming from the reservoir, has a total drop of almost 3500 feet and thus serves as a source of electrical energy capable of producing 120,000 horse power. The aqueduct is designed to carry 260 million gallons of water per day, and, as there is not yet need for so great an amount, the excess is used for irrigation purposes. The total cost of the aqueduct was about 24 million dollars.

The great Hetch Hetchy project for supplying water for the city of San Francisco involves the construction of an aqueduct 170 miles long.

Bridge. The first artificial bridges were probably tree trunks or strong vines used by primitive man to cross some narrow gorge or stream. Simple bridges, consisting of logs of wood or slabs of stone supported at each end, were used by the earliest known groups of mankind.

The arch bridge was probably first used by the Chinese. Simple brick arches have been discovered among Egyptian ruins, but whether or not the Egyptians used arch bridges is unknown. Bridges are not mentioned in the Bible, but according to other records a brick arch was erected across the Euphrates river within the city of Babylon. *Pontoon* bridges, which are carried on boats or other floating supports, were used for military purposes by Cyrus and other Persian kings as early as the 6th century B. C.

The stone arch was developed by the Romans, who used it especially for strong monumental bridges, some of which are still standing. Smaller Roman bridges usually consisted of wooden beams resting either on stone or on timber foundations. In the 16th century Leonardo da Vinci and Palladio invented the wooden truss and used it in constructing bridges. The first metal arch bridge was made of cast iron and erected at Coalbrookdale, over the Severn river, in 1776. Cast iron was displaced by wrought iron after the investigation carried out for Robert Stevenson when planning the famous tubular bridge across Menai Strait. Later, steel displaced wrought iron, and now ordinary steel is gradually giving way to special alloy steels. At the present time the principal structural materials for bridges are steel, concrete, and masonry.

Bridges may be classified, according to the methods used for supporting the weight, as girder or truss. suspension, arch, and cantilever.

A modern *girder bridge* rests upon strong beams or girders of steel or re-enforced concrete, supported by firm foundations at either end. The girders may be single steel I-beams for small crossings, or *plate girders* built up from steel plates carefully riveted together. Plate girder bridges are the standard type for distances of 20 to 100 feet. The longest plate girder is 130½ feet; another, of 122½ feet, is heavier, weighing 170 tons.

A *truss bridge* may be considered as one composed of enormous girders from which all excess material has been cut away, leaving only a network of braces and connecting members. The ribs of a truss are always arranged to form triangles, because triangular bracing gives the most rigid structure obtainable. Simple truss bridges have been built with spans up to 720 feet in length.

A *suspension bridge* is carried by ropes, chains, or cables, fastened at both ends. This type of bridge has frequently been used by primitive people; it is occasionally used for military purposes; and it has been employed for some of the most famous bridges in the world, notably those of New York City, San Francisco, Philadelphia, and Detroit. Of these, the Oakland Bay bridge at San Francisco, completed in 1936, has the longest span. 4620 feet. The weight of the cables supporting the Delaware River bridge connecting Philadelphia and Camden is 7000 tons. They contain a total of 25,100 miles of wire, a length exceeding the circumference of the earth. The oldest suspension bridge in the United States is the 1057 foot suspension bridge connecting Cincinnati, Ohio, with Covington, Kentucky, completed in 1867.

Arch bridges are so constructed that the load imparts an outward thrust which must be carried at each end by heavy structures, called abutments. In building a bridge of this type, false work or centering of some sort is necessary to carry the load until the arch is completed. It is interesting to note that the first masonry arch across the river Tiber—the Pons Æmilius—was begun about 179 B. C., and in 1911 the longest re-enforced concrete arch then built—the Risorgimento arch, with a span of 328 feet, 1 inch—was completed over the same river. One of the largest arch bridges in America is that over Hell Gate, New York City. It is made of steel, with a hinge at each end to relieve excessive strains. When the foundations for one of the abutments were being sunk, it was discovered that there was a wide crack in the rock, which had been thought to be solid. In order to prevent any settling, a concrete arch was built across the gap, so that the Hell Gate bridge is partially supported by another bridge that is buried 90 feet underground. The Kill van Kull bridge, New York, has the longest steel arch in the world, 1652 feet.

Cantilever bridges consist of trusses arranged like a bracket on a wall, that is, they are supported at one end, while the free arm reaches out over the space to be bridged. In practice, the heavy columns which are to carry the weight are usually erected on strong foundations, with an arm extending in opposite directions so as to give a balanced structure. The shore arm is then fastened to heavy anchor foundations. By placing a cantilever on opposite sides of a river, panel after panel can be added to the free arms until they meet at the center. The greatest bridge in the world of this type crosses the St. Lawrence river at Quebec, with a distance of more than one-third of a mile between the central piers. Construction was begun in 1903. In 1907, when the south cantilever was almost finished, one of the main supporting members gave way and the structure fell into the river. In the new bridge, begun in 1911, an opening of 640 feet was left between the arms. The truss to fill this span was constructed on the shore, floated out under the bridge, and lifted by means of hydraulic jacks. When about 15 feet above the water, the connections at one corner slipped, and the truss, weighing 5000 tons, collapsed and fell into the water. The following year, a second span was successfully raised into place. Seventy-four men were killed at the first accident, and eleven at the second.

The ordinary *bascule* or *jackknife bridge* is a girder or truss, hinged at one end and counterbalanced by weights so that it may be swung up like the blade of a pocketknife.

A *rolling lift bridge* is a bascule which turns up on the rounded ends of its own base instead of on a hinge.

A *vertical lift bridge* usually consists of a truss placed between two towers. Cables or levers connect the truss to counterbalancing weights, so that the power of a comparatively small motor is sufficient to raise the bridge straight up.

A *swing bridge*, erected on a turntable at its center, is sometimes preferred because it gives two channels, one on either side of the open bridge. When closed, a swing bridge is usually a simple truss, but the open bridge is a cantilever.

Viaducts, in the ordinary use of the term, are bridges carried across a valley or other low level, on towers. The towers may be high or low, and the spans are usually comparatively short.

A girder or truss bridge pushes down on its foundation piers, a suspension bridge pulls inward, and an arch pushes outward. A cantilever pushes down on its main pier, but may pull up on the anchorage. In addition to the *dead load* or weight of the bridge itself, the engineer must include in his calculations the *live load* which it is to carry, together with the added strain due to starting and stopping of trains, and a possible wind pressure of 30 or more pounds on each square foot of surface.

Canal Locks. Among the most important structures connected with a canal are the locks. These act as a step or as an elevator to raise or to lower a vessel from one water level to another. They are used where there is a change in the elevation of a canal.

An ordinary lock consists of a rectangular basin provided with heavy, water-tight gates at both ends. The sides of the lock and the top of the gates extend above the highest part of the canal. When the gates at one end are open, those at the other end must be closed in order to hold back the water.

When a vessel, traveling upstream, enters a lock, the gates are tightly closed behind it. Water is then admitted to the lock chamber, and the boat gradually rises until it reaches the upper level of the canal. The gates in front are then swung open, and the way is clear. To lower a vessel, the process is reversed, and the water flows from the lock until the lower level is reached.

Locks are occasionally constructed so that the entire chamber is raised or lowered. Sometimes two such chambers are connected and balanced so that one is raised when the other is lowered. In such cases only sufficient water is transferred to make the upper chamber slightly heavier than the other, so that the change in position is caused by gravity.

Dam. Any barrier used to stop the flow of a liquid is called a dam. In engineering, however, the term refers to a structure built across a watercourse, and provided with a spillway over which the water confined behind the wall can flow when it rises to the proper level.

By means of a dam, the depth of a shallow stream may be increased until it is sufficient for the passage of boats and barges; water can be stored for the use of municipalities, for manufacturing, or for irrigation; and power can be generated.

The design and construction of large dams requires a high degree of engineering skill because of the enormous pressure exerted by the water. This pressure depends not on the volume, but on the height, of the water held behind the dam. Each vertical foot of water imparts a pressure of .433 pounds on every square inch of surface, so that at the bottom of a dam where the water is 100 feet deep there is a pressure of 3.1 tons per square foot.

Few dams are more famous than that across the Nile river at Aswan. Since the dawn of civilization, the years of rich harvests and the periods of famine in the Nile valley have depended on the height to which the river would rise during the annual flood. The average rise has been about 25 feet; 30 feet meant destruction and ruin, while 18 feet meant poor crops and starvation. But now the reservoir behind the dam not only affords control of the river's flow, but supplies enough water to irrigate 6 million acres that formerly were desert.

Dams are built of timber, earth, concrete, masonry, and occasionally of steel. Earth dams frequently have a thin core of concrete, which prevents the water from trickling through the earth and ruining the dam. The center of the Gatun dam was pumped into place by hydraulic dredges which took up the mud from the river bottom and deposited it between walls of stone. The water drained away, leaving a very firm structure.

Automatic dams are frequently used on canals where it is desired to keep the water level as high as possible. Movable dams of the "bear-trap" type

SOME IMPORTANT DAMS OF THE WORLD

Name	Location	Completed	Type	Height Feet	Length on Top Feet	Width in Feet	
						Top	Base
Arrowhead	California	1909	Earth *	222	850	20	950
Arrowrock	Boise R., Idaho	1916	Concrete ([a])	349	1,100	15½	238
Ashti	Ashti R., India	1878	Earth	58	12,709	6	182
Aswan	Nile R., Egypt	1934	Masonry	174	6,970	36	92
Barossa	South Australia	1903	Concrete ([a])	112	472	4½	42
Bartlett	Verde R., Ariz.	1939	Multiple arch	287	750	20	1,700
Belle Fourche	South Dakota	1909	Earth	122	6,493	19	650
Bonneville	Columbia R., Wash., Ore.	1937	Concrete	170	1,282	40	180
Camarasa	Spanish Pyrenees	1920	Concrete	333	460	21	250
Cataract	Sydney N. S. W.	1908	Concrete ([a])	192	811	16½	158
Cheoah	Little Tennessee R.	1918	Concrete	225	725	12	175
Cobble Mountain	Little R.,Springfield, Mass.	1930	Earth	245	700	50	1,505
Columbia	Susquehanna R., Pa.	1875	Timber	11	6,847	16	30
Conowingo	Susquehanna R.	1928	Concrete	105	4,700	22	105
Coolidge	Gila R., Arizona	1928	Multiple dome	251	550	4	20
Dalles, The	Columbia R., Oreg.-Wash.	1961	Concrete-Earth	260	8,875	..	...
Daniel-Johnson	Canada	1970	Multi-arch	703	4000	..	...
Diablo	Skagit R., Rockport, Wash.	1930	Concrete arch	446	1,180	16	140
Dix River	Kentucky	1925	Rock-fill	278	1,020	20	650
Dnieprostroy‡	Dnieper R., Ukraine, Russia	1932	Arch gravity	200	5,000	73	140
Don Pedro	Tuolumne R., Cal.	1923	Concrete	280	1,040	16	177
El Azucar	San Juan R., Mexico	1945	Earth	138	19,360	26	1,661
Elephant Butte	Rio Grande R., New Mex.	1916	Concrete ([a])	305	1,310	18	215
Fort Peck	Missouri R., Mont.	1939	Earth *	242	20,000	13	2,875
Gatun	Panama	1913	Earth	105	7,800	400	2,600
Gilboa	Schoharie Creek, N. Y.	1926	Concrete, earth	160	2,300	15	158
Glen Canyon	Colorado R., Ariz.	1964	Concrete	710	1,550	25	340
Grand Coulee	Columbia R., Wash.	1942	Concrete	553	4,200	30	490
Grimsel	Central Switzerland	1930	Concrete gravity	373	656	15	224
Hetch Hetchy	Tuolumne R., Cal.	1922	Concrete	427	600	15	298
Hoover	Colorado R., Ariz. Nev.	1935	Concrete gravity	727	1,244	45	660
Kensico	White Plains, N. Y.	1917	Masonry	307	1,843	28	235
Keokuk	Miss. R., Keokuk, Ia.	1913	Concrete	53	4,649	29	42
Lake Cheesman	S. Platte R., Colo.	1904	Masonry	236	700	18	176
Morena	San Diego, Cal.	1909	Rock-fill	278	520	16	357
Norris	Clinch R., Tenn.	1936	Concrete	265	1,872	30	405
Necaxa No. 2	Necaxa R., Mex.	1911	Earth	190	1,220	54	975
New Croton	Croton R., N. Y.	1906	Masonry	297	1,168	18	206
Oahe	South Dakota	1958	Earth	242	9,360	..	...
Olive Bridge(Ashokan)	Esopus Creek, N. Y.	1913	Masonry	252	1,000	26	200
Owyhee	Owyhee R., Oregon	1932	Concrete	417	1,010	30	265
Pacoima	San Fernando, Cal.	1928	Concrete	372	640	10.4	100
Pardee	Mokelumne R., Cal.	1929	Concrete arch	358	1,337	..	241
Poona	India	1872	Masonry	108	5,136	14	61
Roosevelt	Salt R., Ariz.	1911	Masonry	280	1,125	16	158
Salt Spring	Mokelumne R.,Cal.	1932	Rock-fill	332	1,300	15	900
Saluda R.	S. Carolina	1930	Earth	208	7,838	25	1,150
Sautet	France	1934	Concrete arch	414	263	..	...
Seminoe	North Platte R.,Wyo.	1939	Concrete arch	261	560	15	85
Sennar	Nile R., Upper Egypt	1926	Masonry	130	9,915	15	50
Shasta	Sacramento R., Cal.	1945	Concrete gravity	602	3,500	..	...
Shoshone	Shoshone R., Wyo.	1910	Masonry	328	200	10	108
Sukkur	Indus R., India	1932	Masonry	185	4,725	..	...
Tansa	India	1891	Masonry	118	8,800	12	100
Tieton	Yakima project, Wash.	1925	Earth *	232	900	25	1,200
Wachusett	Nashua R., Mass.	1906	Masonry	228	1,476	25	187
Wilson Dam	Muscle Shoals, Ala.	1925	Concrete	137	4,860	..	105
Yellowtail	Big Horn River, Mont.	1965	Concrete	525	1,450	..	...

*With concrete core. ‡Destroyed by Russian army in 1941 to prevent use by invading Germans and later rebuilt.
([a]) Called also cyclopean masonry, because, where possible, enormous boulders are set in the concrete.

are equipped at the top with hinged, floating leaves, which rise and fall with the water level so that the depth of flow over the dam is always about the same. On small structures the water usually flows directly over the top, but, in large dams, the excess water passes through control gates and over a spillway. The highest dam in the world is the Hoover dam at Black canyon in the Colorado river, which rises 727 feet above the river bed.

The multiple arch, hollow, concrete dam is a form of structure which is coming into extensive use. The ability of this type to withstand great water pressure depends on the strength of comparatively thin, concrete arches, rather than on the weight of massive walls. The same principle is involved in the multiple dome dam, consisting of concrete forms facing upstream, each one shaped like one quarter of an egg shell cut axially.

Cofferdams are water-tight enclosures open at the top and used where it is necessary to work in places that would ordinarily be covered with water. In order to examine the sunken battleship *Maine*, which lay in Habana harbor at a depth of about 37 feet, an oval cofferdam was built around the vessel so that the water could be pumped away.

Embankments placed parallel to the course of a stream so as to prevent the flooding of the surrounding country are known as *levees*.

The term *dike* originally referred to an artificial ditch or canal. Later, it was also applied to the mound of earth thrown up beside the excavation, and eventually to any embankment or wall, especially one used to prevent floods.

Jetties are dikes built, usually at the mouth of a river or harbor, to direct the flow of the tide or the river current in such a way as to scour out a deeper channel. One of the most important uses of jetties has been to make navigable the mouth of the Mississippi river. The longest jetty in the world, 42¾ miles in length, was built to preserve a channel at the mouth of the Columbia river.

Locomotive. The first locomotive used commercially in the United States was called the *Stourbridge Lion*. It was built in England and was put into service in 1829. The first to be built in America for commercial purposes was the *Best Friend*, which was manufactured for the Baltimore and Ohio railroad in 1830. It was destroyed by an explosion after about seven months of service. In 1831, the *De Witt Clinton* was put into operation. On its first run from Albany to Schenectady, a stretch of 17 miles, it covered the distance in 1 hour and 45 minutes, but the return trip was accomplished in 38 minutes. Its weight was 12,098 pounds, or less than that of a single pair of driving wheels on a standard Pacific type engine of today.

The chief improvements in the locomotive have been devices to secure greater pulling power and more efficiency. These purposes have been effected partly by the use of stronger boilers and *greater steam pressure*. Some locomotives now operate at a boiler pressure of 250 pounds per square inch. Certain ones in Germany have been constructed to use a pressure of 750 pounds. A second improvement has resulted from *superheating the steam*. Superheated steam acts as a gas under pressure and can do a certain amount of work without condensing. A third improvement has been the introduction of *compound cylinders*, by which the engine is changed from the simple to the expansion type. See *Steam Engine*.

Among the largest and most powerful steam locomotives in the world is one built for the Northern Pacific railroad in 1928. It is 175 feet long, weighs 500 tons, generates 6000 horse power and is capable of hauling on the level a train over two miles long. It is driven by two pairs of cylinders, each connected with eight drive wheels. Electric locomotives weighing 600 tons and having a length of 150 feet are not unusual. The greatest speed attained by a locomotive, is 112 miles per hour, which was made in 1893 by the New York Central engine number 999 while hauling the Empire State Express.

In 1937, there were about 47,000 locomotives operating in the United States. This represents a decrease from the maximum of 65,358 in 1924 and indicates a trend toward fewer and more powerful locomotives, but since 1944 there has been a great upsurge in the use of Diesel-electric motive power. In 1952 it handled 65.5 per cent of freight traffic, compared with 32.6 per cent for steam locomotives and 1.9 per cent for other locomotives. The same advance has been made in passenger traffic, with Diesels hauling 71.5 per cent of the traffic in 1952.

In recent years, there has been a conspicuous trend toward the electrification of railroads. In a test made at Erie, Pa., an electric locomotive was pitted against two large steam locomotives of the New York Central railway in a pushing contest. It was found that the electric locomotive was able, not only to stop the two steam locomotives, which had been allowed first to develop a high speed, but forced them backward against the full force of their driving power.

The ordinary electric locomotive takes its power from an electrified line. Some locomotives, however, develop their own electric power either from Diesel engines or from a steam turbine engine.

Locomotives designed for high speed are usually streamlined to reduce air resistance. The necessity of providing for locomotives and cars a level track over or through natural obstacles has set for civil engineers many of the most difficult problems they have had to solve. Most of the great bridges and tunnels of the world have been built for railways and have been among the greatest triumphs of civil engineering.

The following table shows the standard types of American steam locomotives:

SYMBOL*	Type	Special Use
0–6–0	6-wheel switcher	Switching
2–8–0	Consolidated . .	General freight
2–8–2	Mikado	General freight—sharp curves
2–10–0	Decapod	Heavy freight
2–10–2	Santa Fe	Heavy freight—sharp curves
2–10–10–2	Mallet articulated†	Heavy freight
2–8–8–8–2	Mallet articulated triplex†	Heavy freight
4–4–0	American . . .	Passenger and freight
4–6–0	Ten-wheeler . .	Passenger, fast freight
2–6–2	Prairie	Heavy passenger, fast freight
4–4–2	Atlantic	High speed passenger
4–6–2	Pacific	Fast heavy passenger, fast freight
4–8–2	Mountain . . .	Heavy passenger

* The first figure in each entry indicates the number of smaller wheels under the front; the last figure denotes the number of trailing wheels under the rear; the intermediate figures indicate the number and the grouping of the driving wheels.

† In this type, the frame is jointed, or articulated, to facilitate the passing of curves.

Skyscraper. The first requirement of a modern skyscraper, and one of the most important, is a firm foundation. If possible, the foundation should rest on bed rock, but, where a heavy structure must be located over sand, soft clay, or peat, the difficulties of obtaining a solid foundation are often very great.

One of the most satisfactory methods is to drive piles through the soft earth until they reach solid rock. Or, if the ground is comparatively firm, a great number of piles may be driven until the total resistance of the earth to further settling of the piles is sufficient to carry the weight of the building. The Illinois Central Railway passenger station in Chicago is thus supported on about 1700 wooden piles, driven to a depth of from 40 to 60 feet by means of one-ton to two-ton drop hammers. In 1920, when an American firm received a contract to build modern steel office buildings in Japan, 13,000 piles of Oregon pine were shipped across the Pacific to form foundations in the city of Tokyo.

HIGHEST BUILDINGS AND TOWERS

Name and Location	Height in feet
Canadian National Tower, Toronto	1,815
Sears Tower, Chicago	1,454
World Trade Center, New York City	1,353
Empire State Building, New York City	1,250
Television Center, Moscow	1,179
Standard Oil Co. of Indiana Bldg., Chicago	1,136
John Hancock Center, Chicago	1,107
Chrysler Building, New York City	1,046
Eiffel Tower, Paris	984
60 Wall Tower, New York City	950
First Canadian Place, Toronto	935
40 Wall Tower, New York City	927
Bank of Manhattan, New York City	900
United California Bank, Los Angeles	858
Transamerica Pyramid, San Francisco	853
RCA Building, New York City	850
Water Tower Plaza, Chicago	850
U.S. Steel Building, Pittsburgh	841
One Chase Manhattan Plaza, New York City	813
John Hancock, Boston	812
Pan Am Building, New York City	808
First National Bank, Chicago	800
Woolworth Building, New York City	792
Gaspar Libero, São Paulo, Brazil	787
M. V. Lomonosov State University, Moscow	787
MLC Building, Sydney, Aus.	786
Commerce Court, Toronto	784
Bank of America, San Francisco	778
Canadian Imperial Bank of Toronto, Toronto	766
IDS Center, Minneapolis	752
Prudential Tower, Boston	750
Detroit Plaza Hotel, Detroit	748
U.S. Steel, New York City	743
City Bank Farmers Trust, New York City	741
Palace of Culture and Science, Warsaw	741
Toronto Dominion Bank, Toronto	740
Security Pacific, Los Angeles	738
Marine Midland Building, New York City	724
Peachtree Center Plaza Hotel, Atlanta	723
Exxon Building, New York City	720
First International, Dallas	710
Terminal Tower, Cleveland	708
Union Carbide Building, New York City	707
General Motors Building, New York City	705
One Penn Plaza, New York City	700
Metropolitan Life Building, New York City	700
One Shell Plaza, Houston	700
American Tobacco Building, New York City	700
500 Fifth Avenue, New York City	697
One Shell Square, New Orleans	697
IBM Building, Chicago	695
9 W. 57th Street, New York City	688
Chemical Bank New York Trust, New York City	687
McGraw-Hill Building, New York City	685
Chanin Building, New York City	680
Gulf and Western Building, New York City	679
55 Water Street, New York City	678
Lincoln Building, New York City	673
1633 Broadway, New York City	670
Atlantic Richfield Plaza (twin bldgs.), Los Angeles	667
National Bank of Tulsa, Tulsa	667
Civic Center (City Hall), Chicago	662
National Cathedral Tower, Washington, D.C.	660
Irving Trust Building, New York City	654
1100 Milam Building, Houston	651
One Astor Plaza, New York City	651
Ukraine Hotel (including tower), Moscow	650
American Brands, New York City	648
Lake Point Towers, Chicago	645
Burlington House, New York City	645
345 Park Avenue, New York City	634
Gateway Arch, St. Louis	630
1114 Avenue of the Americas, New York City	630
Home Insurance, New York City	630
Monsanto, New York City	630
One New York Plaza, New York City	630

Piles may be of wood, concrete, or steel. One of the most effective types consists of a hollow steel tube, driven with a pile driver. Earth and stones are blown out of the cylinder by compressed air, and the interior is filled with concrete.

When the piles are all in place, the tops are cut off at exactly the same height, and care must be taken that wooden piles are entirely below water level, because, when covered with water, wood is preserved almost indefinitely. The platform type of foundation usually consists of steel beams piled in layers to form a pyramid. Each layer is placed at right angles to that below, and all are covered with concrete.

To support the enormous weight of the skyscrapers of New York City, the foundations are sunk to bed rock by means of open cofferdams or closed pneumatic caissons. The caisson may be a huge timber box or steel cylinder, open at the bottom, but closed at a height of 8 or 10 feet so as to form a working chamber. Above the working chamber the caisson is filled with concrete, which is pierced by vertical shafts for the passage of men and materials. The top of each shaft is closed by an air lock, for, as the earth is removed at the bottom and the structure gradually sinks, the pressure of the air must be ra sed to prevent the surrounding water from flowing into the working chamber. When the edges of the caisson reach rock, the working chamber and shafts are filled with concrete, thus forming a solid pillar.

After the foundations have been completed, the steel skeleton is rapidly placed in position. First the massive columns are erected and bolted temporarily to the crossbeams that form the floor. At each floor the girders extend beyond the wall columns in order to form a short shelf, on which the wall for that floor is carried. Because of this arrangement, each floor supports its own wall. Floors are formed by brick or hollow tile arches, or by concrete slabs, placed between or over the beams.

Tunnel. The term tunnel, as generally used, refers to an artificial passageway, horizontal or nearly so, open at both ends, and constructed without removing the surface soil. Tunnels cut through solid rock with simple hand tools were built by many ancient nations, including the Egyptians, Assyrians, Greeks, Aztecs, Peruvians, and the natives of India. The oldest known tunnels were used as the entrance to a royal tomb or for religious purposes, but by 500 B. C. the Greeks were using tunnels for mining.

The Romans, who surpassed all previous nations as engineers, built tunnels for use as roads, aqueducts, sewers, and mine galleries, not only at Rome, but in what is now France, Switzerland, Spain, Portugal, Algeria, and Turkey. In order to drain Lake Fucinus, the emperor Claudius, about 52 A.D., completed a three-mile tunnel, 9 feet wide and 19 feet high. The Romans understood *fire setting*, which consists in first heating a rock surface by means of fires and then cooling it suddenly with water in order to produce cracks.

In the construction of large rock tunnels, small sections are first drilled and blasted out. These openings are then gradually enlarged to full diameter. In building the Connaught tunnel, a small pioneer tunnel, parallel to the main boring, was constructed first, so that, by cutting cross passages, work could be carried on in several sections at the same time. Of an entirely different type was the railroad tunnel under the river between Detroit, Michigan, and Windsor, Ontario. This tunnel was built on land in twenty sections having the form of enormous, hollow, steel cylinders. Each section was closed at both ends, floated into position, and then sunk to foundations which had been dredged on the river bed. The sections were joined, covered with concrete, and also given a concrete lining.

The first of the great transalpine tunnels, the Mont Cenis, was driven from both ends. The work was so accurate that, when the borings met after 13 years of labor, there was a difference in alignment of only one inch. During the construction of the St. Gotthard tunnel, conditions were so severe that 800 of the workers died. The Simplon tunnel, which now consists of two parallel tunnels 16½ feet in diameter, was most difficult of all. This tunnel passes through the mountains at a depth of 5000 to 7000 feet below the peaks. The pressure was so great that in places great steel beams were necessary to hold the rock walls in place. Cold springs at times poured as much as 17,000 gallons of water a minute into the first tunnel, and, near the center, hot springs were encountered which raised the temperature of the air to such a degree that it was necessary to spray the walls with cold water. The second tube was completed in 1921.

The many miles of tunnel under New York City represent one of the greatest achievements of engineering skill. The New York City extension of the Pennsylvania railroad, which crosses from New Jersey, under the Hudson river to the Pennsylvania terminal, and then under East river to Long Island, has a total length of only 13.68 miles. Yet the average cost of this short extension was almost 6 million dollars a mile. One of the chief engineering problems in the construction of the Holland vehicular tunnel was to provide proper ventilation. Powerful fans change the air completely 42 times each hour.

Construction of tunnels, such as the Pennsylvania and the Hudson and Manhattan tubes, through clay and silt, under a river bed, is much more difficult and dangerous than blasting through solid rock. The use of compressed air is often necessary in the head of the tunnel to balance the pressure of the surrounding water.

One of the greatest aids in soft ground tunneling is the *shield*, which is a short, hollow cylinder slightly larger in diameter than the tunnel. The forward end is closed and is provided with several strong doors through which the workman may pass to excavate, if the nature of the ground permits. The shield is pushed forward by hydraulic rams, and the cast-iron or concrete lining of the tunnel which is thus formed is constructed under the protection of the rear walls of the cylinder. Various unusual expedients are sometimes necessary. In tunneling through soft clay, huge torches have been used to bake the ground hard. In order to drive an opening through wet quicksand, the earth has been frozen by artificial refrigeration.

The largest tunnel in the world is the Rove, which forms a part of the canal between the Rhone river and Marseille, France. It is 4½ miles long and, with a height of 40 feet and a width of 72 feet, it is almost six times as large in cross section as an ordinary railroad tunnel.

The first transportation tunnel in the United States was a part of the Schuylkill Navigation canal, opened in 1821. The first railway tunnel in the United States was 901 feet long. It was constructed in Pennsylvania, between 1831 and 1833, for the Allegheny Portage railroad. Neither tunnel is now in existence.

SOME IMPORTANT TUNNELS OF THE WORLD

Name	Location and Use	Length Miles	Years in Construction	Approximate Cost
Appenine	Italy; Florence Bologna R. R.	11.5	1923–1928	$24,735,000
Arlberg	Austrian Alps; R. R.	6.23	1880–1884	7,500,000
Arthur's Pass	South Island, N. Z.; R. R.	5.38	1908–1912	3,000,000
Brooklyn-Battery	Brooklyn-Manhattan; under East R.; vehicular	1.72	1940–1950	80,000,000
Caldera	Peru, S. A.; R. R.	1.75	–1893	
Cascade	Cascade Mts., Wash.; Gt. N. R. R.	2.6	1897–1900	1,250,000
Cascade, New	Berne-Scenic, Wash.; R. R.	7.78	1925–1928	10,000,000
Choacella	Part of 240-mile Colorado River—Los Angeles aqueduct, costing $230,000,000	18.3	1933–1936	
City No. 1	New York City; Aqueduct	18.11	1911–1914	26,400,000
City No. 2	New York City; Aqueduct	20.0	1928–1932	42,700,000
Connaught	Selkirk Mts., B. C.; Can. Pac. R. R.	5.0	1913–1916	6,500,000
Detroit River	Detroit, Mich.—Windsor, Ont.; R. R.	1.6	1906–1910	10,000,000
Detroit International	Detroit, Mich.—Windsor, Ont.; vehicular	.95	1928–1930	10,000,000
Elizabeth Lake	Los Angeles Aqueduct, Cal.	5.1	1907–1911	1,088,000
Florence Lake	Southern Cal.; Aqueduct	12.8	1920–1925	17,000,000
Gravehals	Oslo—Bergen, Norw.; R. R.	3.3	1904–1909	
Great St. Bernard	Italy-Switzerland	3.6	–1964	35,000,000
Grenchenberg	Jura Mts., Switz.; R. R.	5.3	1912–1915	3,500,000
Gunnison	Montrose, Colo.; Aqueduct	5.8	1905–1909	2,170,000
Hetch Hetchy	San Francisco Aqueduct, Calif.	18.0	1920–1923	
Holland	New York—New Jersey; under Hudson R.; vehicular	1.75	1920–1927	48,400,000
Hoosac	Hoosac Mts., Mass.; R. R.	4.31	1856–1873	11,000,000
Hudson & Manhattan	New York City—New Jersey	8.50	1875–1911	75,000,000
Jungfrau	Swiss Alps; R. R.	4.47	1897–1912	1,375,000
Khojak Pass	Quetta-Chaman, India; R. R.	2.44	1889–1891	
Loetschberg	Bern-Brig, Swiss Alps; R. R.	9.05	1906–1913	10,000,000
Mersey	Liverpool-Birkenhead; vehicular	2.16	1925–1934	40,000,000
Moffat	James Peak., near Denver, Colo.; R.R.; water system	6.1	1922–1927	14,500,000
Mont Blanc	France-Italy	7.25	1959–1965	
Mont Cenis	France—Italy; R. R.	7.97	1857–1872	15,000,000
Mont d' Or	Jura Mts., France—Switz.; R. R	3.8	1910–1915	4,060,000
Mt. Royal	Montreal, Can.; Can. North. R. R.	3.22	1910–1916	
Newhouse	Idaho Springs, Colo.; drainage and transportation	4.17	1893–1910	
N. Y. City Extension	New Jersey—Long Island; Penn. R. R.	11.7	1905–1910	100,000,000
Pirahy River	Rio de Janeiro, Brazil; Aqueduct	5.25	1911–1913	
Posey (Oakland-Alameda)	San Francisco bay; vehicular, trolley	.67	1926–1928	4,500,000
Ricken	Swiss Alps	5.35	1904–1910	2,500,000
Rothschönberg	Freiberg, Sax.; mine drainage	18.0	1844–1887	
Rove	On Rhone canal, France	4.5	1901–1927	27,000,000
Saint Gotthard	Switzerland—Italy; R. R.	9.33	1872–1882	11,500,000
Severn	England—Wales	4.36	1873–1886	
Shandaken	Gilboa—Allaben, N. Y.; Aqueduct	18.0	1919–1923	12,138,000
Simplon	Switzerland—Italy (Second tunnel built 1912–1921)	12.45	1898–1906	21,000,000
Sutro	Virginia City, Nev.; drain mines	3.79	1869–1878	
Tanna	Japan; under mountains for Tokkaido R. R.	4.85	1918–1932	
Tauern	Austrian Alps; R. R.	5.31	1901–1909	6,062,500
Tequixquiac	Drains City of Mexico	6.25	1880–1898	6,760,000
Transandine	Chile—Argentina	5.0	–1911	

MANUFACTURING

The word manufacture is derived from the Latin *manus*, "hand," and *facere*, "to make." Literally, it means "made by hand." However, in modern usage, the term no longer imparts its intrinsic meaning, but almost invariably refers to the making of articles by power driven machinery rather than by hand-operated tools. This change in language is representative of far greater and more important changes in social and economic conditions, which were consequent to the Industrial Revolution that originated in England during the latter part of the 18th century.

For proper appreciation of the extraordinary effects of the Industrial Revolution, it is first necessary to consider the systems of manufacturing and the social conditions which this revolution displaced.

The Domestic System. Primitive manufacturing consists of the elemental processes involved in the preparation, for individual or family use, of food, shelter, clothing, ornaments, weapons, and tools. Manufacturing in the home, of products intended solely for domestic consumption, was customary in the earliest times of which there is any record. It was equally characteristic of the pioneers who settled the American West, and is always to be found where individual families must depend upon their own resources. The first advance in manufacturing practice came when some member of a household was able to produce a surplus of meal, cloth, leather, or other commodity, which could be sold outside of the home.

Origin of Handicrafts. Later, with the rise and development of large communities, specialization became possible. Men who were unusually skillful in building, weaving, metal working, or other handicraft were enabled to devote all their energies to their chosen occupations. Thus originated the numerous trades, such as those of carpenter, wheelwright, coppersmith, weaver, fuller, tanner, butcher, and baker. Eventually, the expert workers learned to combine for mutual benefit according to their distinctive handicrafts. Such combinations, which in Europe were known as craft guilds, gradually became very powerful and were able to exercise strict control over the individual members and their products.

As a rule, a master craftsman labored at home or in a shop connected with his dwelling place, carrying on his trade with the aid of apprentices and the help of journeymen who formed the intermediate grade of workers. His products were made to suit the demands of his customers, or were offered for sale to the public under regulations prescribed by the guild to which he belonged. The master generally owned his shop and tools, purchased his raw materials, changed them into the finished product, and disposed of the goods himself.

The Outwork System. The next step in the organization of manufacturing came with the growth of the outwork system. By this arrangement, raw materials owned by a merchant were distributed or "put out" among home workers, who made and returned the finished product and received payment for their labor. Under these conditions, the buying of raw materials and the selling of completed goods were controlled by the merchant. The workman, however, owned the tools required for production and was, to a certain extent, master of his time. He usually owned his home and a piece of ground, so that a shortage of work at his craft allowed him to give more time to his farm.

Hand Power and Machines. All of the foregoing systems of domestic production are still in existence. Bread is baked and clothing is made in many homes. And, frequently, a woman who has acquired unusual skill as a cook or as a seamstress devotes her spare time to preparing food or clothes for her neighbors. In almost every town, carpenters, cabinetmakers, tinsmiths, blacksmiths, tailors, and many other skilled craftsmen are to be found working with their own tools and in their own workshops in order to fill custom orders. Panama hats, Turkish rugs, Navajo blankets, and the fine laces of Switzerland, Italy, and Ireland are still prepared by the painstaking action of skilled fingers. Nor has the outwork system been entirely discarded. In a modified form it is still the basis of modern, successful, merchandising concerns which sell knitting machines and yarn to home workers, and buy, for resale, all of the hosiery which they are able to produce. Nevertheless, all of the foregoing examples are exceptions to the general rule that, today, manufacturing is done in factories equipped with complicated, power driven machinery. This change from handwork to the factory system of production was the outstanding feature of the Industrial Revolution.

Manufacturing before 1780. In the chapter on the history of commerce, it has been shown that manufacturing, transportation, and commerce are interdependent and have developed together from the earliest historical times. When, by 1750, England had become the chief commercial nation of the world, the most important products of her industries were woolen textiles, fabricated to a large extent from the fleece of domestic sheep.

Cloth making was a domestic industry in which the wool was washed, carded, and spun into yarn by women. The processes in use differed from those employed in the days of ancient Greece only because the spinning wheel had been substituted for the distaff and spindle sometime during the 15th century. Almost every cottage contained a loom, on which the yarn was woven into cloth by the master of the house. The methods of weaving, like those of spinning, had changed very little for centuries, although in 1733 John Kay invented the "fly shuttle," which made the process much more easy and rapid.

As several spinners were required to keep a weaver supplied with yarn, the weavers were usually glad to make cloth from yarn "put out" by a merchant. In this way the workers were able to keep continuously occupied, while the merchant insured a steady supply of cloth with which to meet the increasing demands of commerce. Fulling and finishing of woolen fabrics were generally done in a fulling mill located on the banks of a stream.

Practically all other operations were performed in the homes, although occasionally a merchant would erect and equip a weaving shed wherein a considerable number of hired weavers could work together under his supervision. Production of cotton cloth was small, the finest cotton goods being imported from India.

In the iron industry, charcoal furnaces were still extensively used, although the practice of smelting with coke, as introduced by Abraham Darby about 1735, was gradually spreading. This new demand for coke stimulated production of coal. In operating the coal mines, Newcomen's engine was found to be valuable for pumping out water which accumulated in the tunnels and galleries. Power for the operation of slitting mills and for producing the air blast for furnaces was obtained by water wheels. For this reason, ironworks were usually located beside streams.

Economic Conditions. A review of the general economic conditions existing in England about 1763 shows that commerce was actively increasing, transportation was being facilitated by the construction of turnpikes and canals, capital was accumulating, and industrial production, while very important in the aggregate, represented the contributions from farm homes and from many small shops or works, quite widely dispersed throughout the land. The country as a whole was fundamentally agricultural.

Living conditions were comparatively stable, because, if unable to obtain employment at his trade, a skilled worker could generally depend upon his small farm for the necessities of life.

At home, England possessed what seemed to be an adequate supply of coal, iron ore, and wool; her colonies were capable of producing large quantities of cotton, sugar, and natural dyes. All of these raw materials are adapted to large scale operations, and, as the demands for commercial products continued to increase, the need for machinery and improved methods of production was commonly recognized.

Epoch-making Inventions. In 1767, James Hargreaves invented his spinning jenny, capable of spinning eight threads of cotton instead of one. Arkwright, a barber by trade, followed, in 1769, with the roll-drawing spinner, which operated by water power, and therefore became known as the water frame. This machine produced thread strong enough to be used for the warp of cotton cloth, but insufficiently fine for the higher grades of muslin.

Ten years later, Samuel Crompton combined the best features of the jenny and the roll-spinner in a new power machine which, because of its hybrid origin, he called a "mule." The mule established the muslin industry in England. It also made it possible to spin cotton thread faster than the weavers could change it into cloth on the hand looms.

Improvements in the speed of weaving began in 1785 when Edmund Cartwright, a clergyman, obtained a patent for a power loom. This machine at first was far from successful; in fact, a practicable power loom did not come into use until about 1803. The great demand for cotton, caused by the application of the power loom, could not have been supplied at a reasonable cost had not Eli Whitney, in 1793, invented his cotton gin, whereby cotton fiber could be quickly separated from the seeds. It is interesting to note that these great inventions were all concerned with the manufacture of cotton, rather than of woolen fabrics. The use of power for spinning and weaving wool did not become general for several years after the beginning of the 19th century.

Water Power and Steam. In order to use the new textile machinery, many cotton mills were erected in the northern parts of England, where water power was most available. But the necessity of locating beside a waterfall was removed by Watt's condensing engine, invented in 1765 and greatly improved in succeeding years. Steam boilers heated by coal fires became a source of unlimited power. As the cost of transporting coal was greater than that of moving textiles or other finished commodities, the coal fields gradually became the center of manufacturing industries.

The iron trade also was greatly stimulated by the use of coal and of steam power. For example, the annual production of iron was doubled within eight years after the substitution of the steam engine for water power as a source of the air blast required in smelting. In 1783, Henry Cort invented the grooved rolling mill, and, in the following year, introduced the puddling process for making wrought iron from pig iron.

Thus, in response to the demands of commerce for large quantities of cheap textiles, we find that, in the last half of the 18th century, machines were invented which permitted of an increased volume of production. Steam engines were developed to drive the machinery. Cort's inventions made possible a more extensive application of iron, and from the improved iron many new types of machines and more efficient engines were constructed.

Effects of the New Inventions. Manufacturing by machinery, in buildings especially designed for that purpose, required a far greater outlay of capital than was necessary to provide the simple tools used by manual laborers. Nevertheless, costs of production were so greatly reduced by this method that a development of the factory system was inevitable. The widespread domestic system practically disappeared, because necessity forced the workers to leave their rural homes and to concentrate near the factories. The laboring population was gradually transplanted from the land to the cities. Master craftsmen, skilled in all branches of their trade, were no longer needed. For the factory system of production depends upon the use of labor-saving machinery wherever possible, and upon a systematic division of any complete manufacturing process into the proper number of parts. Each succeeding step is then performed by a worker who is able to acquire a high degree of skill in the accomplishment of a single operation. Under this system, production increased enormously, old industries expanded, and new ones came into existence.

Automation. Industrial development since World War II has been marked by the rapid progress made by automation, a new word meaning the use of machinery or mechanical devices instead of men in a production system. By the use of electronic equipment, the flow and quality of production can be regulated and co-ordinated. Production principles found effective in speeding the output of war materials are now used in civilian industries. Machines can operate continuously at higher speeds and more efficiently than men, and they do not tire as men do.

New models of specialized automatic labor-saving machines are constantly being introduced into industrial plants engaged in the mass production of standardized products. Development of mechanical ways of moving and handling materials has likewise contributed to the reduction of labor engaged in these operations. By the wider use of automatic controls, or the control of machines by other machines, many industries are becoming self-regulated. Not only does automation save labor, but it makes possible a better quality product. High-speed electronic computers and data-processing machines have helped to cut down the large clerical forces formerly required for the important work of handling information.

Whether automation presents an opportunity for labor or is a threat to it remains to be seen. If our economy continues to expand, the new machines may, through increased production, create more jobs than they eliminate. It seems inevitable that some readjustments will be necessary, but, as Norbert Wiener remarked, automation wisely applied holds promise of "more human use of human beings."

Industrial Advantages. Europe became the workshop of the world, and, until 1894, England surpassed all other nations in manufacturing. The advantages which caused her superiority are worthy of note because they are those which, today, will insure the success of any properly directed manufacturing concern. England controlled a plentiful supply of cheap *raw materials*. Her *workers* were skillful and adaptable. Her methods of *production*, because of the many great inventions and the early adoption of the factory system, were the most efficient known. She had, in her colonies and also in continental Europe, a ready *market* for her finished goods. And, as a means of *distribution*, her highly skilled commercial organization was second to none.

British Industrial Centers. Textiles are, as they always have been, the chief product of British manufacture. Before the advent of machinery, wool was the principal fiber used, but, early in the 19th century, cotton took the lead. Cotton was first imported into England in 1298 for use in making candlewicks. By 1801, England produced more cotton goods than did all of continental Europe. Manchester became the cotton manufacturing center of the world. Leeds is now the center of the

British woolen industry, of the manufacture of ready-made clothing, and of leather. Leicester is renowned for the production of woolen hosiery, as Nottingham is for cotton hosiery and for machine-made net. Silk weaving and dyeing is located chiefly in Derbyshire.

The iron and steel industry in England is second in importance only to that of textiles. Blast furnaces and rolling mills are concentrated at Middlesbrough, Newport, and Barrow, while Birmingham and Sheffield have become world famous for their manufactures of fine steel and of steel products. An example of extreme specialization is Redditch, whence a large part of the world is supplied with needles and fishhooks. The greatest shipbuilding district in the world is located along the banks of the Clyde river. The heart of the British ceramic industry is at Burslem in north Staffordshire.

INDUSTRIAL GERMANY

Germany's industrial revolution did not begin until the formation of the empire in 1871. But, when once begun, the transformation from an agricultural to an industrial basis was the most rapid and complete ever known. In 1845 Germany mined less coal than either France or Belgium. In 1880, Spain had more steam tonnage than Germany. Even as late as 1882, more than one-fourth of the German textile workers operated under the domestic system. But, by 1895, over 90 per cent were employed in factories. In 1871, about 64 per cent of the population of Germany was rural, while 36 per cent lived in cities. During the succeeding 40 years the intensive development of manufacturing caused towns to grow rapidly while the rural population remained stationary. In 1910, 60 per cent of the people lived in cities.

Fuel and Iron. Germany possessed or controlled abundant supplies of iron and coal. Nevertheless, her iron ore, derived chiefly from Lorraine and Luxemburg, contained a high proportion of phosphorus and was thereby rendered unsuitable for the production of Bessemer steel. This difficulty was removed in 1878 when Thomas and Gilchrist invented their basic method of making steel, by which phosphorus is removed from the molten metal and retained in the slag. When finely ground, "Thomas slag" becomes valuable as a fertilizer, so that the invention stimulated both manufacturing and agriculture, and was of fundamental importance to Germany.

Chemical and Other Industries. The German dye and fine-chemical industry, although depending primarily on the by-products from the coke ovens, is quite widely distributed, with the chief factories located on waterways at Ludwigshafen, Leverkusen (near Cologne), Frankfort, Hochst, and Berlin. The heavy-chemical industry is centered about the potash beds of Stassfurt. The largest salt works in the country is at Schonebeck.

Most of Germany's electrical machinery is made at Berlin and Nuremberg. Porcelain is produced chiefly at Meissen, Zwickau, and Berlin. Crefeld rivals Lyon as a center of the silk industry. Shipbuilding is important at Stettin, Hamburg, Kiel, and Lubeck. Textile factories tend to concentrate near the coal fields, but the industry as a whole is scattered over the entire country. Chemnitz is called the Saxon Manchester. As a nation devoted to manufacturing, Germany's policy has been to produce highly finished goods in which the greatest proportion of the cost is due to the application of skilled labor.

OTHER EUROPEAN NATIONS

France. In France the innovations which had so quickly transformed industrial conditions in England were adopted with much less haste. In 1848, factory methods of production were not yet customary, and typical French manufacturing was done in private workshops or in small establishments. One of the chief reasons why steam power was not more quickly applied in France was an insufficient supply of coal.

The famous French steelworks at Le Creusot were founded by royal charter in 1782, but this enterprise was not financially successful until the management was taken over by the Schneider family in 1836.

Production of textiles and of clothing is the most important branch of French manufacturing. Roubaix, Tourcoing, Fourmies, Reims, and Amiens are the chief centers of the wool industry. Mulhausen, in Alsace, and Rouen lead in the production of cotton fabrics. Paris has become the center of the production of jewelry, perfumes, gloves, shoes, and porcelain. Lyon is at the heart of the great French silk trade. Saint Etienne is known for the production of silk ribbons; Troyes, for hosiery; and Grenoble, for kid gloves. Lille is the largest manufacturing city of the North.

Switzerland. Switzerland, with very little coal or iron, is distinctly a manufacturing country which is forced, by a shortage of raw materials, to produce highly finished articles, such as silks, fine shoes, watches, and intricate machinery. The famous Geneva watches are so named because Geneva is the commercial center of the watch trade. They are made chiefly in the towns of Le Locle, La Chaux de Fonds, Bienne, Saint Imier, and Porrentruy. A shoe factory at Schonenwerd, near Olten, is said to be the largest in Europe. Saint Gallen is noted for the production of embroidered linen. Zurich and Basel are centers of the silk industry. Electricity generated by water power is extensively employed, notably in the production of aluminum at Rheinfelden.

Belgium. This country, where both coal and iron are available, was the only section of Europe which was able to follow the industrial pace set by England during the first half of the 19th century. Liege is one of the most successful metallurgical and manufacturing cities in Europe. It is famous for the production of all types of steel products, especially firearms. The production of textiles is even more important than that of steel and machinery. Cotton manufacturing is centered at Ghent, the making of linen at Ghent and Tournay, and the spinning and weaving of wool at Verviers.

Scandinavia. Sweden and Norway are noted for the production of wood pulp, matches, and paper, and for their electrochemical industries. In Norway electricity is used to manufacture large amounts of nitrogenous fertilizer at Odde, Notodden, and Sarpsborg. Stockholm, Goteborg, and Norrkoping are the chief industrial towns of Sweden. Perhaps the most famous manufactured product is the pure Swedish iron, reduced from domestic ore with charcoal from the extensive forests.

Czechoslovakia. This nation possesses a better supply of coal than of iron. Bohemia, however, is noted for its iron industry and especially for the manufacture of fine glassware, of which Eger is the center of production. Small articles of glass, such as buttons, beads, and imitation jewels are produced in enormous quantities at Gablonz.

Western Europe was the most important manufacturing district in the world. In 1880 the United Kingdom led all the other nations in this branch of industry, but by 1894 the United States assumed first place.

The highly developed production in Czechoslovakia far exceeds its domestic needs, and agricultural products, led by sugar, provide raw materials of great importance to its industry. The beer industry is world famous as are the spirits, malt and foodstuff industries. Metallurgical industry thrives here because of the abundant supply of iron ore and coal. Output of steel in 1970 was approximately 11 million metric tons (1 metric ton = 1.02 short tons). The Skoda steel works at Pilsen are among the largest in Europe. Other industries are glass, porcelain, pottery making, timber, paper and cellulose industries.

MANUFACTURING STATISTICS BY STATES, 1972

States	All employees		Production workers			Value added by manufacture million dollars
	Number (average for the year) 000 omitted	Salaries and wages, total million dollars	Number 000 omitted	Man-hours, total millions	Wages total million dollars	
Alabama	323	2,397	262	519	1,731	5,065
Alaska	8	75	6	12	57	170
Arizona	94	855	62	121	482	1,880
Arkansas	181	1,152	150	298	853	2,800
California	1,546	15,483	1,020	1,975	8,430	31,195
Colorado	133	1,298	89	177	770	2,504
Connecticut	399	3,860	258	521	2,069	6,828
Delaware	69	755	38	74	304	1,292
Dist. of Columbia	19	215	9	16	92	376
Florida	343	2,750	242	482	1,581	5,787
Georgia	468	3,336	369	738	2,243	7,386
Hawaii	25*	191	18	33	114	410
Idaho	43	340	34	66	245	821
Illinois	1,306	12,801	901	1,780	7,675	25,849
Indiana	704	6,882	526	1,042	4,641	14,112
Iowa	216	2,039	157	311	1,355	4,758
Kansas	137	1,181	101	203	783	2,915
Kentucky	259	2,160	200	393	1,480	5,682
Louisiana	179	1,601	134	275	1,072	4,273
Maine	100	699	83	162	513	1,383
Maryland	256	2,386	176	346	1,428	4,707
Massachusetts	619	5,486	416	812	3,027	10,678
Michigan	1,076	12,745	768	1,583	8,095	23,376
Minnesota	302	2,889	196	383	1,555	5,524
Mississippi	200	1,302	167	332	959	2,825
Missouri	434	3,897	300	584	2,305	8,169
Montana	21	185	17	34	138	463
Nebraska	85	704	63	128	469	1,733
Nevada	10	92	7	14	57	208
New Hampshire	90	663	68	131	414	1,279
New Jersey	836	8,107	547	1,071	4,354	16,409
New Mexico	24	157	17	33	96	358
New York	1,679	16,222	1,076	2,068	8,174	30,404
North Carolina	744	4,929	604	1,211	3,427	11,015
North Dakota	10	79	7	14	48	201
Ohio	1,346	13,810	940	1,888	8,717	27,171
Oklahoma	143	1,188	96	186	659	2,270
Oregon	179	1,627	142	271	1,170	3,490
Pennsylvania	1,418	12,794	1,015	1,954	7,886	23,519
Rhode Island	118	888	91	174	566	1,764
South Carolina	345	2,345	283	582	1,679	4,966
South Dakota	17	135	13	25	89	285
Tennessee	467	3,352	367	725	2,295	7,662
Texas	736	6,345	517	1,031	3,763	15,259
Utah	57	486	39	74	287	1,069
Vermont	37	311	26	52	176	576
Virginia	375	2,826	293	583	1,902	6,178
Washington	226	2,308	160	303	1,411	4,721
West Virginia	121	1,098	93	182	765	2,647
Wisconsin	501	4,722	361	721	3,063	9,443
Wyoming	7	57	5	10	39	144
Total	19,029	174,206	13,528	26,699	105,502	353,994

Source: *Statistical Abstract of the United States, 1975.*

SUMMARY OF MANUFACTURES FOR MAJOR INDUSTRY GROUPS, 1974

Industry	All Employees		Production Workers		Value added by manufacture (millions)
	Number (000 omitted)	Payroll (millions)	Number (000 omitted)	Wages (millions)	
Food and kindred products	1,553	$14,788	1,075	$9,196	$44,948
Tobacco manufactures	67	604	58	477	3,179
Textile mill products	933	6,684	813	5,195	13,199
Apparel and related products	1,317	7,642	1,147	5,793	14,926
Lumber & products, exc. furniture	675	5,490	583	4,294	11,561
Furniture and fixtures	459	3,570	381	2,577	6,983
Paper and allied products	646	6,995	507	4,995	18,957
Printing and publishing	1,076	11,139	639	6,131	23,610
Chemical and allied products	866	10,547	542	5,697	44,488
Petroleum and coal products	146	1,920	101	1,241	9,951
Rubber products	661	6,203	523	4,303	14,826
Leather and leather products	256	1,604	223	1,229	3,120
Stone, clay and glass products	637	6,414	508	4,720	14,566
Primary metal industries	1,248	15,900	1,001	12,102	37,297
Fabricated metal products	1,575	16,570	1,208	11,469	35,221
Machinery, except electrical	2,126	24,713	1,497	15,431	52,495
Electrical machinery	1,776	18,093	1,242	10,509	36,902
Transportation equipment	1,738	22,609	1,250	14,554	44,973
Instruments and related products	524	5,560	338	2,851	13,627
Miscellaneous manufactures	435	3,477	337	2,254	7,667
All industries, total	19,844	$208,312	13,927	$124,977	$452,497

Source: Bureau of the Census, *Annual Survey of Manufactures, 1974*, "General Statistics for Industry Groups and Industries."

MANUFACTURING CORPORATIONS—RELATION OF PROFITS TO SALES: 1960—74

(Averages of quarterly figures at annual rates, after taxes.)

Industry Group	Profits per dollar of sales (in U.S. cents)			
	1960	1965	1970	1974
Total	**4.4**	**5.6**	**4.0**	**5.5**
Durable goods[1]	**4.0**	**5.7**	**3.5**	**4.7**
Motor vehicles and equipment	5.9	7.2	2.6	2.6
Aircraft and parts	1.4	3.3	2.0	3.0
Electrical machinery, equip., & supplies	3.5	4.8	3.3	3.9
Machinery, except electrical	3.9	6.2	4.6	6.0
Fabricated metal products	2.4	4.5	3.0	4.6
Primary iron and steel	5.1	5.7	2.5	6.3
Primary nonferrous metal	5.4	7.3	6.2	7.0
Stone, clay, and glass products	6.6	5.9	3.6	4.4
Furniture and fixtures	2.1	3.7	2.5	(NA)
Other lumber and wood products	1.7	4.0	2.5	(NA)
Instruments and related products	5.9	8.6	7.3	9.2
Misc. manufacturing, inc. ordnance	3.5	3.8	3.4	(NA)
Nondurable goods[1]	**4.8**	**5.5**	**4.5**	**6.4**
Food and kindred products	2.3	2.7	2.5	2.8
Tobacco manufactures	5.5	5.9	5.8	9.1
Textile mill products	2.5	3.8	1.9	2.5
Apparel and related products	1.4	2.3	1.9	(NA)
Paper and allied products	5.0	4.9	3.4	7.1
Printing and publishing	3.6	4.8	4.2	4.7
Chemicals and allied products	7.5	7.9	5.9	8.4
Petroleum refining	9.9	11.1	9.3	12.6
Rubber and misc. plastic products	3.6	4.3	2.7	5.0
Leather and leather products	1.6	2.8	2.5	(NA)

NA—Not available. [1] Includes industries not shown separately. Source: *Statistical Abstracts 1975.*

MANUFACTURING IN THE UNITED STATES

The development of successful manufacturing requires, among other things, an adequate supply of capital and of labor, a steady market for the finished products, and regular means of transportation. None of these was available in the American colonies during the early period of their existence. Furthermore, almost all of the colonies were founded as commercial enterprises which were expected to serve their promoters and the homeland by becoming a source of raw materials and a market for manufactured goods.

First Colonial Manufactures. In the early colonial days of America, each home was of necessity self-sufficient. Grain was ground, wool was spun and woven, and hides were tanned only in order to supply the needs of the family. However, as the population increased and towns developed, these industries were divided among the members of each community. Each settlement was soon furnished with mills for grinding grain, for sawing lumber, and for the fulling and finishing of woolen cloth. Tanneries, also, were erected in many communities. The first sawmill was built at Dorchester (Mass.) in 1628. The first New England tannery was located at Lynn in 1629, and the manufacture of shoes was begun there in 1635.

Expansion of New England Industry. The American colonies as a group were essentially agricultural. But, in New England, where the land was not well adapted to farming, a large proportion of the settlers were forced to gain a livelihood by other means. Fishing, which, from the first, was an industry of primary importance, gave rise to a demand for ships. The finest materials with which to construct ships were available in the forests, and shipbuilding soon became one of the chief industries.

From fishing and shipbuilding, the New Englanders quite naturally advanced to maritime trade, which was carried on at first chiefly with the West Indies. These islands were glad to exchange their surplus sugar and molasses for salt fish and lumber. Thus, in addition to purely local manufacturing industries which sprang up in all of the settlements, New England developed others which were based on the necessity of equipping the ships, supplying food for the sailors, providing cargoes for export, and utilizing the commodities that were imported.

A ropewalk to supply vessels with cordage was erected in Boston in 1641, and, at many places along the coast, salt for the preservation of meat and fish was prepared by evaporating sea water over wood fires. Bakers found employment in shops devoted to the production of sea biscuit, or hard-tack. Rum was so extensively used on shipboard that the expense for liquor issued regularly to sailors was generally as great as the cost of their bread, and the production of rum by fermenting and distilling the West Indian molasses became a thriving New England industry. Since practically all commercial commodities, whether liquid or solid, were packed and shipped in barrels, the manufacture of barrels and barrel staves, buckets, and similar forms of cooperage from the white oak of New England became exceedingly profitable.

Ironworks. Iron was sorely needed in the colonies, not only to provide ships with anchors, bells, cannon, and shot, but also to supply the population with nails, hardware, cooking utensils, iron barrel hoops, and similar products. The earliest successful attempt to meet the demand was made at Lynn, Massachusetts, where a company organized by the son of Governor Winthrop erected a blast furnace in 1644. The first product from the furnace was a cast-iron kettle of about one quart capacity, made in 1645. In 1648 a refining forge was added to the equipment, so that refined iron products then became available. The making of nails, hammered from rods of iron obtained from slitting mills, was a domestic industry almost as widespread as the production of textiles

Growth of Manufacturing. The colonial population, which in 1640 numbered 25,000, increased to one million during the succeeding century, and amounted to 2¼ million in 1775. Manufacturing developed at a corresponding rate. Iron furnaces and refining forges became almost as common as sawmills, gristmills, and fulling mills. The abiilty of the colonial foundrymen is shown by the fact that in 1753 they melted and recast the bell for the Pennsylvania statehouse, which afterward became famous as the Liberty Bell. Four of the signers of the Declaration of Independence were financially interested in the iron industry. The Washington family owned a one-twelfth interest in the Principio ironworks of Maryland.

England encouraged the manufacture of pig iron, but passed laws against the production of steel and steel products, as well as that of other articles which competed with British industry. Although these prohibitory laws checked the growth of manufacturing industries, enforcement of them was found to be almost impossible except in the vicinity of the larger cities where the crown officers were stationed.

The Revolutionary War greatly stimulated American manufacturing, because raw materials accumulated and the supply of English products, on which the country had largely depended, was cut off. Necessity caused the growth of various industries. But, when peace was concluded, English manufacurers flooded the country with their products at prices so low that many American concerns were ruined.

Textiles. Competition of American made cloth with that of British manufacture was especially difficult, because the colonies were at first unable to utilize the newly invented textile machinery. England not only prohibited the exportation of designs or models of the machines, but even endeavored to prevent the emigration of mechanics skilled in the industry. However, in 1789, Samuel Slater, who had been employed in Arkwright's factory, came to America. He went first to Philadelphia, where a comparatively large amount of cotton spinning was carried on. Failing to interest the manufacturers in that city, he went to New York and then to Rhode Island, where, in 1790, on the falls of the Pawtucket river, he built for Moses Brown the first power driven cotton spinning mill in the United States. Andrew Jackson called Slater the "father of American manufacturers."

In 1805, there were only four cotton mills in America. But the passing of the Embargo act of 1807, followed by the Nonintercourse act and the War of 1812, prevented foreign commerce and again stimulated manufacturing. Twelve new spinning mills were opened in 1808; in 1811, spindles to the number of 80,000 were in use, and 10,000 bales of cotton were spun; in 1815, the spindles numbered 500,000. In 1814, Francis Cabot Lowell devised a power loom similar to those which he had seen while visiting England, and erected at Waltham, Massachusetts, the first complete cotton factory in the world. Practically all power mills were located on waterfalls, although steam engines came into use as a source of power after 1810. Most of the early mills obtained their cotton from the West Indies, because the Southern states marketed their product in Liverpool.

Tariffs and Railroads. At the close of the War of 1812, British manufactures were for a second time thrown on the American market at prices which brought disaster to many growing industries. After 1816, these industries received protection through a series of tariff acts, and manufacturing again expanded.

Even more important than the tariff, however, in its influence upon manufactures, was the development of railroads. The iron industry was directly affected, because the railroads proved to be the greatest consumers of iron products. Iron T rails were first rolled in 1844, in Maryland. Bessemer steel was first made on a commercial scale in 1864; in the following year, the Chicago Rolling Mills produced the first American Bessemer steel rails. Besides thus stimulating iron and steel manufactures, through enlarging the market for their products, the railroads promoted many types of industry by furnishing the necessary means for the interchange of goods between manufacturing centers and distant agricultural regions. The cotton growing South and the rapidly expanding agricultural regions of the West afforded rich markets where the demand for manufactured products seemed unlimited. By 1860 the annual production of agricultural implements alone amounted to $17.8 million.

Inventions and Industrial Progress. While the development of such agricultural machinery as the McCormick reaper added greatly to the farmers' ability to raise grain on a large scale, many other great inventions opened the way for new forms of manufacturing. (See table of *Modern Inventions.*) To choose a single example, the invention of the sewing machine laid the foundation for the great modern clothes making industries, and, when the machine was developed, it revolutionized the process of making shoes.

Manufacturing after the Civil War. During the Civil War, the lack of the customary supply of raw material from the Southern states checked the production of cotton goods, although other branches of manufacturing were unusually active. The coming of peace introduced an era of industrial progress in which large scale production was developed to a degree never before attained, and the United States advanced steadily to first rank among manufacturing nations. In 1820, America produced only 2 per cent of the world's pig iron; a century later the proportion had increased to 54 per cent.

GREAT MANUFACTURING INDUSTRIES

Group and Important Divisions	Value Added[1]
Machinery (except electrical)	$52,494,900,000
Construction, Related Machinery	8,886,900,000
Metalworking Machinery	7,395,900,000
General Industrial Machinery	7,147,100,000
Office and Computing Machines	7,141,100,000
Special Industry Machinery	5,071,600,000
Refrigeration and Service Machinery	4,715,300,000
Farm and Garden Machinery	4,214,000,000
Transportation Equipment	44,973,300,000
Motor Vehicles and Equipment	22,300,700,000
Aircraft and Parts	12,459,900,000
Guided Missles, Space Vehicles[2]	4,314,600,000
Ship, Boat Building and Repairing	3,061,300,000
Food and Kindred Products	44,947,500,000
Beverages	7,583,600,000
Meat Products	5,986,900,000
Preserved Fruits and Vegetables	5,416,700,000
Bakery Products	5,385,500,000
Grain Mill Products	4,942,400,000
Dairy Products	4,823,600,000
Chemicals, Allied Products	44,488,100,000
Industrial Organic Chemicals	9,384,200,000
Drugs	7,269,100,000
Plastic Materials, Synthetics	7,086,400,000
Soaps, Cleaners, Toilet Goods	7,072,700,000
Primary Metal Industries	37,297,300,000
Blast Furnace, Basic Steel Products	20,060,800,000
Nonferrous Rolling and Drawing	6,291,500,000
Iron and Steel Foundries	4,724,200,000
Electric, Electronic Equipment	36,901,500,000
Communication Equipment	9,978,900,000
Electronic Components, Access	6,963,000,000
Electrical Industrial Apparatus	4,532,400,000
Electric Lighting, Wiring Equipment	3,946,600,000
Fabricated Metal Products	35,221,000,000
Fabricated Structural Metal Products	9,153,300,000
Metal Forgings and Stampings	6,356,400,000
Misc. Metal Products	6,006,300,000
Cutlery, Handtools and Hardware	3,616,600,000
Metal Cans, Shipping Containers	2,986,000,000
Printing and Publishing	23,610,300,000
Newspapers	7,044,900,000
Commercial Printing	6,627,600,000
Books	3,009,400,000
Periodicals	2,435,800,000
Paper and Allied Products	18,957,200,000
Misc. Converted Paper Products	5,781,200,000
Paperboard Containers & Boxes	4,800,200,000
Apparel, Other Textile Products	14,925,800,000
Women's Outerwear	4,700,000,000
Men's Furnishings	3,703,300,000
Rubber, Misc. Plastics Products	14,826,200,000
Misc. Plastics Products	8,106,600,000
Tires and Inner Tubes	3,065,000,000
Stone, Clay, Glass Products	14,566,000,000
Concrete, Gypsum, Plaster Products	4,353,300,000
Misc. Nonmetal Mineral Products	3,065,000,000
Instruments, Related Products	13,627,400,000
Photographic Equipment, Supplies	5,075,000,000
Measuring, Controlling Devices	3,656,200,000
Textile Mill Products	13,199,000,000
Knitting Mills	3,268,900,000
Weaving Mills, Handmade Fiber	2,192,300,000
Lumber and Wood Products	11,561,200,000
Sawmills and Planing Mills	3,736,600,000
Millwork, Plywood, Struc. Mills	2,764,000,000
Petroleum and Coal Products	9,951,100,000
Petroleum Refining	8,363,500,000
Misc. Manufacturing Industries	7,666,500,000
Toys and Sporting Goods	2,285,900,000
Furniture and Fixtures	6,983,400,000
Household Furniture	4,249,000,000
Tobacco Products	3,179,100,000
Cigarettes	2,689,100,000
Leather, Leather Products	3,120,200,000
Footwear	1,859,600,000

[1] 1974 figures. [2] Not including government owned.
Source: *Annual Survey of Manufactures 1974.*

Distribution of Manufacturing. As the preceding table shows what manufactures in the United States have the greatest annual value, the next point of interest is, "Where are these industries chiefly located?" Inspection of the table, *Manufacturing Statistics by States*, shows that 40 states each had in 1972 an annual production exceeding $1 billion in value. To these states is to be credited over 95 per cent of all national manufactures.

According to the Bureau of the Census, the first census of manufactures covered the year 1809, and was then taken at ten-year intervals up to 1899. From 1904 to 1919 it was taken every five years, and from 1921 to 1939 every other year. The 1947 census of manufactures was the first since 1939. Present legislation provides for a complete census covering 1953 and every fifth year thereafter. An annual survey is part of this program.

Localization of Manufacturing. Economic factors such as raw materials, supply of power and labor, markets, and distribution facilities usually determine the location of manufacturing industries. Cotton and woolen mills require a moist atmosphere, while other industries depend on skilled labor or raw material supply. Water power and access to cheap coal were formerly major factors in attracting industry. Due to electric power today and its easy transmission, power requirements no longer force industries into certain areas. The West Coast today, with only 4 per cent of American industry, promises a future because of climate, availability of hydroelectric power, and future market demands.

Westward Movement of Industry. As the center of American population has moved westward, it has been followed, although with less speed, by the center of manufacturing. The early settler in the "West" obtained his ax, spade, and kettles from New England. Today the Western farmer obtains his plow or thresher from Illinois. The center of production of flour and gristmill products has moved from New York to Minnesota. Here the mills are close to the great wheat producing areas, power is available, and markets are easily accessible. Slaughtering and meat packing, which, as a separate industry, originated in Cincinnati about 1818, is now centered in Chicago. Kansas City, Kansas, ranks second in this industry, with Omaha, Nebraska, third. In these locations, the industry is close to the Western cattle raising area, its source of raw material.

Manufacturing in the South. One of the most notable developments connected with American manufacturing progress has been that of the production of cotton goods in the Southern states. North Carolina and South Carolina both rank in value of cotton manufactures above Massachusetts, which in 1920 was easily the leader. In 1880, North Carolina, South Carolina, and Georgia, together produced only 6.2 per cent of American cotton products. In 1910, their combined output equaled 29.7 per cent, and, in 1939, 58.8 per cent, of the total. In the production of iron and steel also the South is advancing steadily. A process by which paper may be made from slash pine grown in the South is the basis of an expanding industry. Large increases in chemical and other industries requiring cheap power took place as the result of the development of the Tennessee Valley, begun in 1933 under government initiative.

Easy access to raw materials and the shortage of energy supplies have been leading causes of the migration of certain industries to the South. The hope of obtaining labor at low wages was an important motive until government studies revealed that wage differences between the North and South had leveled out.

GROWTH AND SPECIALIZATION OF INDUSTRY

The 20th century witnessed a remarkable increase in specialization and an extraordinary rise in industrial efficiency. These were largely the result of the application of inventive genius and scientific research to the problems of production. Of chief importance was the exploitation of the possibilities in electricity as a means of transmitting power.

The Electrical Age. Power in the form of electricity can be used *when* and *where* it is wanted far more readily than power delivered directly from steam engine or water wheel. It facilitates the ready and precise control of machine processes, thereby making possible an increasing use of automatic machinery. In the first quarter of the 20th century electrification in American industry rose from 4 per cent to 70 per cent. It later became almost universal. Electricity used in factories but developed in central stations increased from 182,562 horse power in 1899 to 15,868,828 horse power in 1925—87 fold. The result has been a pronounced growth in production accomplished by a decreasing number of workmen. Wages have risen, yet many manufactured articles have become cheaper. At the same time, by making power available at long distances from its generating source, electricity has obviated the need for locating industries in centers of congested population. New industrial communities may be semi-rural in character, with marked improvement in living conditions.

The marked advance in the field of electric energy production in the United States is shown by the fact that the total production in 1950 was 389 billion kilowatt hours, while in 1970 it had risen to 1,640 billion. Production by the type of prime mover used in 1970 was hydro 247 billion KWh, steam 1,262 KWh, gas turbine 16 billion KWh, and internal combustion 6 billion KWh. Fuel consumed in the production was coal 321 million tons, oil 336 million barrels, and gas 3,932 billion cubic feet. By far the greater proportion of this energy was supplied by privately owned public utilities. The total number of power-generating plants in 1970 was 3,519, of which 1,183 were hydro, 1,009 were steam, 321 were gas, and 1,006 were internal combustion.

Specialization and Mass Production. The automobile industry and possibly the assembly line methods of shipbuilding and plane construction in World War II are the best examples of specialization and mass production. Operations are analyzed into their simplest constituent parts and each of these is performed by a worker, with or without a special machine. His work is confined, mechanical, and highly specialized.

MANUFACTURING, EMPLOYMENT AND VALUE ADDED—PER CENT DISTRIBUTION, BY GEOGRAPHIC DIVISIONS: 1947 TO 1972

Item	1947	1950	1954	1958	1963	1967	1970	1972
Employment								
New England	10.3	9.8	9.0	8.7	8.4	8.1	7.6	7.2
Middle Atlantic	27.7	26.9	26.6	25.7	24.0	22.6	21.8	20.7
East North Central . . .	30.2	30.0	28.6	26.6	26.4	26.7	26.0	25.9
West North Central . . .	5.5	5.6	6.0	6.0	6.0	6.2	6.2	6.3
South Atlantic	10.7	11.1	11.0	11.8	12.5	12.9	13.6	14.4
East South Central . . .	4.4	4.4	4.5	4.9	5.2	5.7	6.1	6.6
West South Central . . .	3.9	4.0	4.5	5.0	5.1	5.6	6.1	6.5
Mountain	1.0	1.1	1.1	1.4	1.7	1.6	1.8	2.0
Pacific	6.4	7.0	8.8	10.0	10.6	10.6	10.3	10.4
Value Added								
New England	9.2	8.3	7.8	7.4	7.1	7.2	6.8	6.4
Middle Atlantic	28.0	26.2	26.0	24.6	22.6	21.9	21.4	19.9
East North Central . . .	31.6	33.2	31.2	28.9	29.3	28.6	27.5	28.2
West North Central . . .	5.5	5.7	6.1	6.3	6.1	6.4	6.9	6.7
South Atlantic	9.3	9.4	9.1	10.1	11.0	11.2	11.8	12.5
East South Central . . .	3.9	3.8	4.0	4.5	4.8	5.2	5.7	6.0
West South Central . . .	4.1	4.3	4.9	5.5	5.7	6.3	6.7	7.0
Mountain	1.1	1.2	1.2	1.6	1.8	1.7	1.9	2.1
Pacific	7.5	7.9	9.7	11.1	11.5	11.3	11.1	11.3

Source: *Statistical Abstracts 1975.*

New Industries and Research. Through the expenditure of many millions of dollars on organized scientific research, industrial firms have evolved or perfected many important new materials and new products which have become the basis of new industries. Examples are the camera, synthetic lacquer, the radio, and a cheap method of producing aluminum. The electrical, rubber, and automobile industries have risen in the 20th century from very small beginnings to gigantic proportions, automobiles reaching the first place among American industries in 1925. Synthetic nitrates, rayon, and airplanes have likewise forged ahead under the powerful stimulus of well-directed research.

Manufacturing and Agriculture. In 1899, one out of every 16 persons in the United States, or 6.2 per cent of the population, was employed in manufacturing. The proportion increased moderately thereafter whereas the proportion of persons engaged in agriculture steadily declined. Not only, therefore, is manufacturing becoming more important because of the largely enhanced value of its product, but it produces a growing proportion of the total output of the country's industries, and it employs an increasing percentage of the working population. This condition became almost inevitable when the last of the rich American agricultural lands were settled. Fear is frequently expressed that manufacturing is making progress at the expense of agriculture. For any given locality this may at times be true, but, considered more broadly, manufacturing and agriculture must develop together. The great industrial cities could not exist for more than a day, or at most a week, if their incoming supply of food should be cut off, while the agriculturist, who finds his chief market in the industrial centers, would be unable to produce and distribute his crops if he did not have the advantages afforded by countless factory products.

The situation has been further affected by the recent enormous increase in the population of the United States, which between the 1950 and 1960 censuses increased nearly 28 millions, the greatest rise in the nation's history.

MANUFACTURES—STATISTICS FOR STANDARD METROPOLITAN AREAS WITH 40,000 OR MORE MANUFACTURING EMPLOYEES, 1973

Source: *Bureau of Census; 1973 Census of Manufactures*

STANDARD METROPOLITAN STATISTICAL AREA*	Rank	Establishments[4]	All employees[1]		Value added by Manufacture[2] $million	Capital Expenditure new[3] $million
			Number	Payroll $million		
Akron, Ohio	54	991	96,200	1,094.4	1,926.9	148.7
Albany-Schenectady-Troy, N.Y.	43	732	68,000	713.6	1,459.0	73.7
Allentown-Bethlehem-Easton, Pa.-N.J.	59	1,118	113,500	1,083.5	2,185.3	176.1
Anaheim-Santa Ana-Garden Grove, Calif.	19	2,820	144,300	1,536.9	3,085.7	149.6
Atlanta, Ga.	18	2,259	134,700	1,257.1	2,906.0	144.4
Baltimore, Md.	14	2,026	184,900	1,907.9	3,873.9	233.1
Binghamton, N.Y.-Pa.	112	361	42,200	463.9	617.5	56.7
Birmingham, Ala.	44	947	69,600	651.1	1,341.2	84.8
Boston, Mass.	8	5,229	280,800	2,917.6	5,283.2	284.7
Bridgeport, Conn.	86	926	63,800	643.4	1,286.0	45.2
Buffalo, N.Y.	26	1,632	160,300	1,838.6	3,720.4	242.9
Canton, Ohio	84	580	62,800	681.0	1,390.9	146.5
Charlotte-Gastonia, N.C.	62	1,197	91,100	679.3	1,331.8	104.3
Chattanooga, Tenn.-Ga.	90	635	57,300	481.4	989.2	69.7
Chicago, Ill.	2	14,004	953,100	10,119.7	19,938.8	1,015.6
Cincinnati, Ohio-Ky.-Ind.	23	2,046	164,600	1,805.6	3,960.1	198.0
Cleveland, Ohio	16	4,359	284,100	3,213.9	5,937.2	326.8
Columbus, Ohio	35	1,199	104,500	1,063.7	2,226.3	155.4
Dallas-Ft. Worth, Tex.	10	4,234	250,000	2,307.9	4,569.6	261.7
Davenport-Rock Island-Moline, Iowa-Ill.	96	417	46,000	549.0	980.4	51.9
Dayton, Ohio	42	1,149	118,100	1,382.5	2,427.9	184.2
Denver-Boulder, Colo.	24	1,808	95,700	1,001.5	1,967.9	178.3
Detroit, Mich.	5	7,510	589,500	8,234.8	13,563.7	872.1
Erie, Pa.	126	480	45,500	462.9	857.7	52.6
Gary-Hammond-E. Chicago, Ind.	57	456	106,500	1,311.8	2,792.7	276.4
Grand Rapids, Mich.	66	1,212	80,600	829.2	1,759.3	104.1
Greensboro-Winston-Salem-High Point, N.C.	46	1,559	144,000	1,129.3	2,847.5	165.2
Greenville-Spartanburg, S.C.	72	837	105,100	767.8	1,792.7	145.1
Hartford, Conn.	51	1,192	89,100	1,015.7	1,774.6	58.9
Houston, Tex.	13	3,169	170,600	1,834.9	4,797.2	530.3
Indianapolis, Ind.	31	1,506	129,500	1,487.3	2,830.7	179.0

For footnotes, see following page.

MANUFACTURES—STATISTICS FOR STANDARD METROPOLITAN AREAS WITH 40,000 OR MORE MANUFACTURING EMPLOYEES, 1973—Con.

Source: *Bureau of Census; 1973 Census of Manufactures*

STANDARD METROPOLITAN STATISTICAL AREA*	Rank	Establishments[4]	All employees[1]		Value added by Manufacture[2] $million	Capital Expenditure new[3] $million
			Number	Payroll $million		
Jersey City, N.J.	60	1,909	91,500	858.8	1,885.7	88.5
Kansas City, Mo.-Kans.	27	1,883	125,000	1,260.9	3,223.1	158.8
Lancaster, Pa.	107	719	56,100	513.3	1,084.7	73.5
Los Angeles-Long Beach, Calif.	3	18,025	816,700	8,376.5	18,136.0	750.0
Louisville, Ky.-Ind.	39	1,005	117,800	1,222.0	3,273.2	175.4
Memphis, Tenn.-Ark.	41	1,046	68,200	587.3	1,548.1	119.8
Miami, Fla.	25	2,890	89,100	661.7	1,286.8	86.8
Milwaukee, Wis.	21	2,623	211,600	2,324.2	4,186.6	296.8
Minneapolis-St. Paul, Minn.	17	3,217	215,400	2,283.3	4,530.3	179.6
Nashville, Tenn.	52	1,124	77,400	618.4	1,295.8	105.3
Nassau-Suffolk, N.Y.	9	4,193	157,000	1,590.9	2,936.2	102.7
New Haven, Conn.	82	818	47,600	444.7	933.3	44.5
New Orleans, La.	33	934	53,600	498.1	1,083.9	63.1
New York, N.Y.	1	28,419	938,700	9,146.0	15,666.2	524.5
Newark, N.J.	15	4,600	276,700	3,001.9	6,086.3	282.5
Oklahoma City, Okla.	49	856	42,300	377.5	813.0	54.6
Paterson-Clifton-Passaic, N.J.	74	1,591	77,600	697.4	1,304.9	55.9
Peoria, Ill.	98	364	48,300	634.1	1,336.9	136.8
Philadelphia, Pa.-N.J.	4	7,890	503,500	5,112.9	10,055.7	620.1
Phoenix, Ariz.	32	1,367	80,700	794.6	1,757.1	100.2
Pittsburgh, Pa.	12	2,531	269,900	3,171.4	5,070.9	246.3
Portland, Oreg.-Wash.	34	2,006	94,900	957.7	1,862.5	95.8
Providence-Pawtucket-Warwick, R.I.-Mass.	38	2,991	138,200	1,097.1	2,204.6	98.9
Reading, Pa.	111	631	53,300	471.6	978.1	52.5
Richmond, Va.	65	684	52,100	489.2	1,229.0	175.9
Rochester, N.Y.	36	1,292	151,300	1,836.4	5,196.8	282.8
St. Louis, Mo.-Ill.	11	3,215	264,100	2,870.4	5,644.2	262.4
San Bernardino-Riverside-Ontario, Calif.	29	1,311	62,100	581.9	1,190.1	63.1
San Diego, Calif.	20	1,400	70,000	737.7	1,332.1	83.5
San Francisco-Oakland, Calif.	6	4,933	188,900	2,109.2	4,429.5	308.1
San Jose, Calif.	30	1,743	145,400	1,804.2	3,317.3	236.6
Seattle-Everett, Wash.	22	2,159	121,400	1,390.3	2,729.5	127.8
Springfield-Chicopee-Holyoke, Mass.-Conn.	68	1,002	63,200	571.7	1,248.5	68.8
Syracuse, N.Y.	56	732	63,300	666.2	1,361.3	98.7
Tampa-St. Petersburg, Fla.	28	1,455	65,800	539.4	1,150.9	91.9
Toledo, Ohio-Mich.	45	1,197	95,600	1,113.3	2,156.2	129.8
Tulsa, Okla.	64	957	52,300	508.7	842.7	107.4
Washington, D.C.-Md.-Va.	7	1,727	58,900	668.8	1,107.2	79.9
Wichita, Kans.	94	564	45,900	435.1	982.0	54.5
Wilmington, Del.-N.J.-Md.	71	492	66,600	844.6	1,271.9	119.1
Worcester, Mass.	91	817	47,400	447.1	865.0	38.5
York, Pa.	104	699	58,800	510.0	1,062.4	53.2
Youngstown-Warren, Ohio	69	603	92,300	1,112.3	2,146.2	86.7

* A standard metropolitan statistical area is a county or group of counties (except in New England) which contains at least one city of 40,000 inhabitants or more, or "twin cities" with a combined population of at least 40,000. In New England, towns and cities are the units used in defining standard metropolitan statistical areas.

[1] Includes central administrative offices or units which serve the manufacturing establishments of a company.

[2] Value of shipments less cost of materials, supplies, fuel, electricity, and contract work.

[3] Includes expenditures for plants in operation and plants under construction.

[4] Figures for 1972.

LUMBERING

The lumber industry of the United States began in pioneering days in Maine, which held the lead for more than 200 years. With the increase in population and the westward trend of the people, the industry grew rapidly and the center of production shifted, first to New York about 1850, and then to Pennsylvania in 1860. From there it moved to Michigan, Minnesota, and Wisconsin, which from 1870 to 1895 were the principal lumber-producing states. Then the South sprang into the lead, notably Mississippi and Louisiana, but it was overtaken in 1920 by the West, particularly Oregon and Washington, an area which still dominates the industry. Oregon has been the leading lumber state since 1938.

The production of lumber is divided between the coniferous, or softwood, trees and the broadleaf, or hardwood, trees. In a general way, softwoods may be considered as the structural material used by carpenters, while hardwoods are more extensively utilized by cabinetmakers. The distinction, however, is not sharp, because some of the so-called "hardwoods" are, in fact, softer than certain of the so-called "softwoods."

Total lumber production in 1973 was 38,595,000,000 feet board measure, of which 31,586,000,000 feet was softwood and 7,009,000,000 was hardwood.

Industries depending on forest products are widely distributed throughout the United States. California manufacturing plants use the largest amount, followed by New York, Washington, Illinois, and Michigan.

On the basis of the quantity cut, yellow pine has been for many years the most important timber, although the amount of Douglas fir standing in forests in the United States is greater than that of any other single kind of wood. For the first time, in 1949, more Douglas fir was cut than yellow pine.

In recent years, the lumber industry has come to realize that trees are a crop and it engages in extensive tree planting, even maintaining nurseries to supply the seedlings.

LUMBER PRODUCTION AND CONSUMPTION

(In millions of board feet, except per capita.)

Item	1965	1973[1]
Total Production	36,762	38,595
Softwoods:		
Production[2]	29,295	31,586
Cedar	633	785
Douglas fir	8,783	8,686
Hemlock	2,576	2,494
Ponderosa pine	3,776	4,030
Redwood	1,087	1,227
Southern yellow pine	6,628	7,895
White fir	2,422	2,438
White pine	693	1,069
Hardwoods:		
Production[2]	7,467	7,009
Ash	141	140
Beech	182	176
Cottonwood	198	326
Elm	206	145
Maple	786	623
Oak	3,356	3,227
Sweet gum	387	342
Tupelo and black gum	385	309
Yellow poplar	681	701
Domestic consumption	40,782	45,919
Softwoods	32,701	38,452
Per capita (bd. ft.)	172	183
Mill stocks, yearend	4,539	3,998
Exports	777	1,773
Imports	4,895	9,002
Hardwoods	8,081	7,467
Per capita (bd. ft.)	39	35
Mill stocks, yearend	1,066	460
Exports	145	222
Imports	338	558

[1] Preliminary data.
[2] Includes kinds of wood not shown separately.
Source: *Statistical Abstracts 1975.*

SELECTED TIMBER PRODUCTS—WHOLESALE PRICE INDEXES: 1950–1974

(Based on an arbitrary designation of 100 for 1967. Prior to 1965, production in Alaska and Hawaii is not included.)

Product	1950	1955	1960	1965	1970	1974
All Lumber	**87**	**95**	**92**	**94**	**114**	**207**
Softwood lumber	88	98	93	93	113	211
Douglas fir	88	98	89	92	109	214
Southern pine	88	94	94	91	115	185
Ponderosa pine, #3 boards	100	110	104	94	116	246
Hardwood lumber	82	86	91	97	115	190
Oak, red, flooring, select	93	100	99	108	113	203
Gum #1, common	74	62	68	82	93	159
Poplar #1, common	77	83	80	86	105	173
Birch #1, common	71	80	89	96	91	140
Plywood	122	120	110	104	108	161
Softwood	148	143	113	106	114	187
Hardwood	99	100	105	101	103	130
Insulation board	83	101	114	98	111	134
Woodpulp	81	96	102	100	110	218
Paper	68	83	93	95	111	149
Paperboard	81	98	105	102	101	152

Source: *Statistical Abstracts 1975.*

BIBLIOGRAPHY

The literature covering the general field of economics and its many special divisions is very large and is constantly growing. Because of the current study and interest in the subject, new publications and revisions of texts are constantly in demand, particularly in the field of world economics, international trade, and labor relations. A carefully selected list of books both of popular and of scientific interest is here presented.

GENERAL WORKS

Behr, Michael R., and Nelson, Dennis L.—Economics: A Personal Consumer Approach *Reston '75*

Edel, Matthew—Economics and the Environment *Prentice-Hall '73*

Eells, Richard, and Walton, Clarence—Conceptual Foundations of Business, 3d ed. . . . *Irwin '74*

Fabrycky, W. J., and Thuesen, G. J.—Economic Decision Analysis . . . . . *Prentice-Hall '74*

Friedmann, John—Urbanization, Planning, and National Development . . . . *Sage '73*

Galbraith, John Kenneth—The New Industrial State . . . . *Houghton-Mifflin '71*

Ghelardi, Robert—Economics, Society, and Culture: God, Money, and the New Capitalism *Delacorte '76*

Harte, N. B.—The Study of Economic History *Frank Cass '71*

Loebl, Eugene—Humanomics . *Random House '76*

McNee, Robert B.—A Primer on Economic Geography . . . . *Random House '71*

Samuelson, Paul—Economics, 10th ed. *McGraw-Hill '76*

Schlossberg, S., and Sherman, F.—Organizing and the Law . . . . *Bureau of National Affairs '71*

Schneider, Harold K.—Economic Man; The Anthropology of Economics . . . . *Free Press '74*

Spencer, Milton H.—Contemporary Economics *Worth '71*

Turkel, Louis (Studs)—Working . . *Pantheon '74*

Weisskopf, Walter A.—Alienation and Economics *Dutton '71*

COMMERCE AND TRANSPORTATION

Ellsworth, P. T., and Leith, J. Clark—The International Economy, 5th ed. . . *Macmillan '75*

Farris, Martin T., and McElhiney, Paul T., eds.—Modern Transportation; Selected Readings, 2d ed. . . . . *Houghton-Mifflin '73*

Gunston, Bill—Transportation: Problems and Prospects . . . . *Dutton '72*

Pegrum, Dudley Frank—Transportation: Economics and Public Policy, 3d ed. . . . *Irwin '73*

Pisar, Samuel—Coexistence and Commerce; Guidelines for Transactions between East and West *McGraw-Hill '70*

Quandt, Richard E., ed.—The Demand for Travel: Theory and Measurement . . . . . *Heath '70*

William, E. W., Jr.—The Future of American Transportation . . . . . . *Prentice-Hall '71*

MARKETING

Boone, Louis E., and Johnson, James C.—Marketing Channels . . . . *General Living Corp. '73*

Corey, E. Raymond—Industrial Marketing: Cases and Concepts . . . . . . *Prentice-Hall '76*

Cundiff, Edward W.; Still, Richard R.; and Govoni, Norman A. P.—Fundamentals of Modern Marketing . . . . *Prentice-Hall '76*

Enis, Ben M.—Marketing Principles: The Management Process . . . . *Goodyear '74*

Enis, Ben M., and Cox, Keith K.—Marketing Classics . . . . *Allyn and Bacon '69*

Fisher, Lawrence—Industrial Marketing: An Analytical Approach to Planning and Execution *Brandon/Systems '70*

Gist, Ronald R.—Marketing and Society *Holt, Rinehart, and Winston '71*

Heskett, James L.—Marketing . . *Macmillan '76*

Rothberg, Robert R.—Corporate Strategy and Product Innovation . . . . *Free Press '76*

West, Christopher—Marketing on a Small Budget *Wiley '75*

INSURANCE, INVESTMENTS, MONEY, AND BANKING

Bracker, Lewis A., and Wagner, Walter—The Trouble with Wall Street . . *Prentice-Hall '72*

Goldsmith, Raymond William—Financial Structures and Development *Yale University Press '69*

Hallman, Victor, and Rosenbloom, Jerry S.—Personal Financial Planning . . *McGraw-Hill '75*

Hendrickson, Robert A.—The Future of Money *Prentice-Hall '70*

Jones, J. P.—The Money Story . . . *Drake '73*

Mehr, Robert I., and Neumann, Seev—Inflation, Technology, and Growth; Possible Long-Range Implications for Insurance . . *Indiana Univ. '72*

Mowbray, Albert H.; Blanchard, Ralph H.; and Williams, C. Arthur, Jr.—Insurance; Its Theory and Practice in the United States, 6th ed. *McGraw-Hill '69*

Pfeffer, Irving, and Klock, David R.—Perspectives on Insurance . . . . *Prentice-Hall '74*

Renwick, Fred B.—Introduction to Investments and Finance . . . . *Macmillan '71*

Riegel, Robert; Miller, Jerome S.; and Williams, C. Arthur, Jr.—Insurance Principles and Practices: Property and Liability, 6th ed. *Prentice-Hall '76*

Ritter, Laurence, and Silber, William—Principles of Money, Banking, and Financial Markets *Basic Books '74*

AGRICULTURE, FISHERIES, AND MINING

Cameron, Eugene N., ed.—The Mineral Position of the United States, 1975–2000 *Univ. of Wisconsin '73*

Hallett, Graham—The Economics of Agricultural Policy . . . . *Augustus M. Kelley '68*

Hickling, C. F.—The Farming of Fish *Pergamon '68*

McDivitt, James Frederick, and Manners, Gerald—Minerals and Men . . . . . *Johns Hopkins '74*

Mellor, John Williams—The Economics of Agricultural Development . . . . . . *Cornell '69*

Royce, William F.—An Introduction to the Fishery Sciences . . . . *Academic Press '72*

Temple, John—Mining; An International History *Praeger '73*

Wilcox, Walter; Cochrane, W. W.; and Herdt, R. W.—Economics of American Agriculture *Prentice-Hall '74*

INVENTIONS AND ENGINEERING

Abernathy, David, and Knipe, Wayne—Ideas, Inventions, and Patents; An Introduction to Patent Information . . . . *Pioneer Press '73*

Beakley, George C., and Chilton, Ernest G.—Design; Serving the Needs of Man *Macmillan '74*

Beakley, George C., and Leach, H. W.—Engineering: An Introduction to a Creative Profession, 2d ed. . . . . *Macmillan '72*

Bowker, Albert H., and Lieberman, Gerald J.—Engineering Statistics, 2d ed. . *Prentice-Hall '72*

Clarke, Arthur Charles—Profiles of the Future; An Inquiry into the Limits of the Possible, rev. ed. . . . . *Harper & Row '73*

Graham, A. Richard—An Introduction to Engineering Measurements . . . . . *Prentice-Hall '75*

Sociology and Civilization

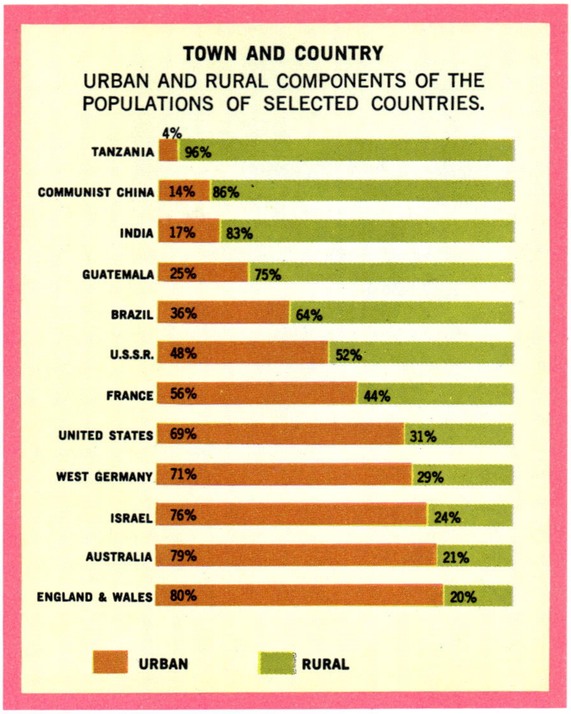

SUBJECT GUIDE

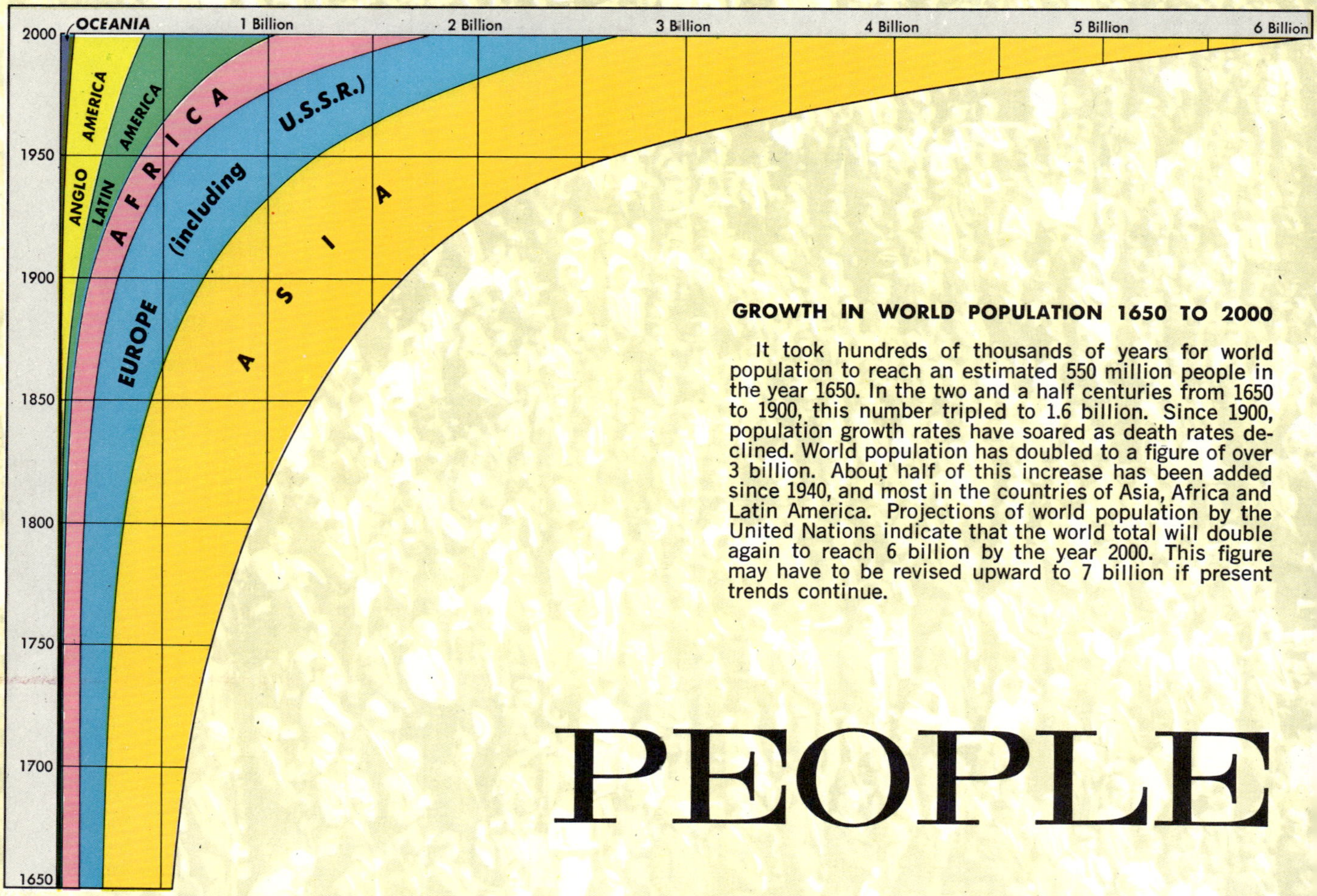

GROWTH IN WORLD POPULATION 1650 TO 2000

It took hundreds of thousands of years for world population to reach an estimated 550 million people in the year 1650. In the two and a half centuries from 1650 to 1900, this number tripled to 1.6 billion. Since 1900, population growth rates have soared as death rates declined. World population has doubled to a figure of over 3 billion. About half of this increase has been added since 1940, and most in the countries of Asia, Africa and Latin America. Projections of world population by the United Nations indicate that the world total will double again to reach 6 billion by the year 2000. This figure may have to be revised upward to 7 billion if present trends continue.

PEOPLE

Nearly three out of every hundred people born since the human race began are alive today. There are some three billion of us and at our present rate of growth, the population of the earth will double in another fifty years. Of this "population explosion" it has been said that modern man is less in danger of blowing himself out of existence with nuclear bombs than he is of squeezing himself to death. Although two-thirds of all the people of the earth now live on less than eight percent of its land surface, many of them already crowded in cities, within the foreseeable future, if the trend is maintained, there will be less than one square foot for every person on earth.

Why an exploding population? The age-old balance of life and death has been upset. The high death rate that offset a high birth rate and kept the population relatively static for thousands of years has been greatly reduced. Modern technology has provided more people with food to stay alive. Modern medicine has lowered infant mortality and, by conquering or controlling many of man's principal diseases, has given him the gift of many more years of life than had his forebears. Among the more backward areas of the world, medical science has virtually worked wonders. In Ceylon, the use of antibiotics, and DDT to wipe out the malarial mosquito cut the death rate in half in less than ten years.

And so there are more of us than ever before . . . nearly a hundred more each minute . . . who will require more food, homes, farms, schools, and jobs than can be provided to meet our growing needs. By solving a number of human problems, we now face a problem of human numbers.

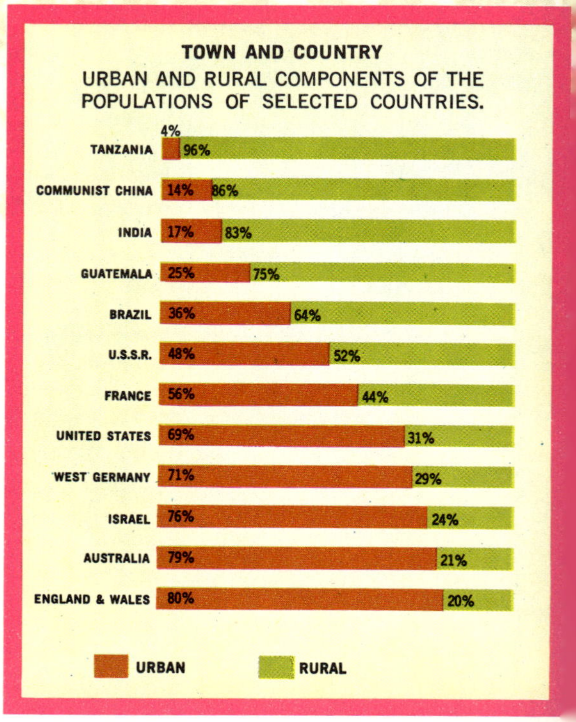

THE GREAT LANGUAGES: NUMBER OF SPEAKERS

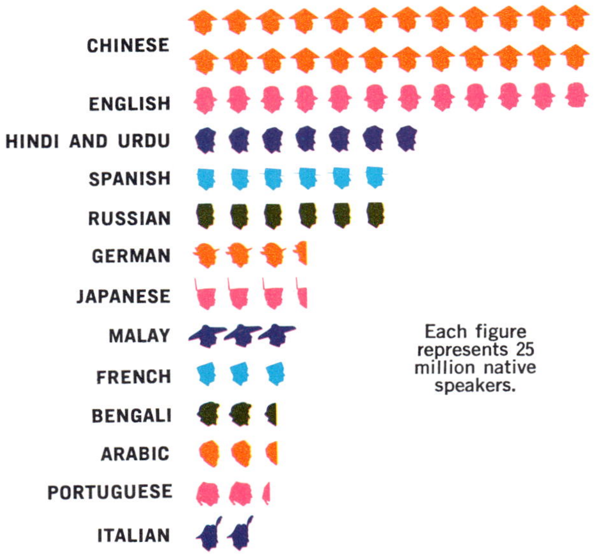

THE ENGLISH LANGUAGE TIME-RIVER

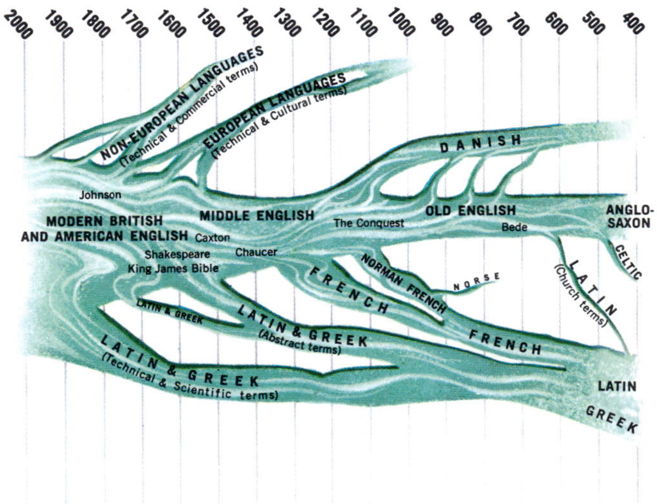

Mankind Divided

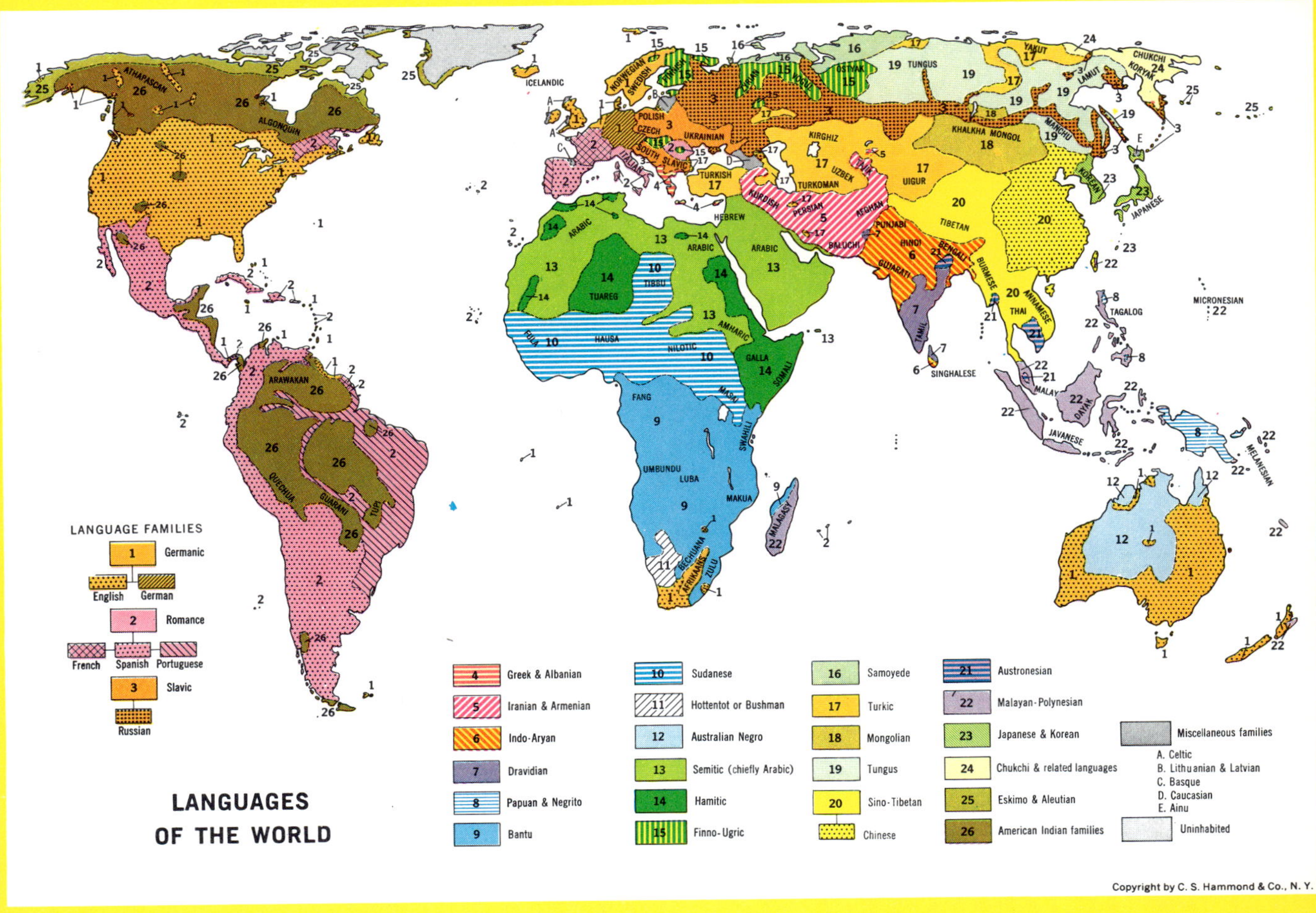

Therefore is the name of it called Babel; because the Lord did there confound the language of all the earth: and from thence did the Lord scatter them abroad upon the face of all the earth.

— GENESIS 11.9

The story of the Tower of Babel has not yet ended, for throughout the world men still speak a babble of over two thousand seven hundred various tongues and dialects that are a barrier between them.

It is difficult for men to "speak the same language" unless they all share the same language. The parochial prejudices and antipathies which have stood between them through the ages, have been caused, in part, by their fear, contempt or aversion of others who communicate among themselves in unintelligible sounds.

LANGUAGES

Under the demands of the modern world, speech barriers are breaking down to some extent. Many know or are learning one or more of our major languages and people of different lands have begun to converse more freely. But the concepts and nuances of one language . . . the essences . . . cannot always be translated literally into another, if at all.

Even within the confines of a single language, words sometimes fail us. As tools of communication, a number of them become dulled by overuse while others are burdened with a variety of meanings. The word "run," for example, has been defined in thirty-nine different ways as a verb, eighteen as a noun and four as an adjective. Of the more than one million words in the English vocabulary, whole segments comprise languages within the language . . . medical, technical, scientific and trade terminologies and jargons which, rather than informing the average person, often serve to exclude him.

While language is our most important means of communicating with one another, the number of languages, their elasticity and complexity, have served to divide us as well.

THE INDO-EUROPEAN LANGUAGE TREE

Dead branches denote dead languages.

Sociology and Civilization

SOCIOLOGY

INTRODUCTION

Development of Sociology. The beginnings of sociology as we know it today are found in the work of early reformers, ministers, and missionaries. Those early social thinkers were keen observers, noting differences in societies and levels of societies throughout the world. Their theories, based on critical observations, led ultimately to the scientific stature that this area of knowledge has attained.

As long as man has existed, he has thought about the realities of his life. Primitive tools and cave drawings indicate such thinking about the observed facts of prehistoric man's experiences. Cave drawings suggest that preoccupation with survival was not all that concerned those early men. Life meant more than food and shelter. The sociologist would call this area of interest "recreation." Burials may have meant that early man thought also about the hereafter; the sociologist calls this area of interest "religion." Man has continued to think about reality, and his speculations evolved until more systematic and reflective thinking emerged about the fourth century B.C., when Plato and Aristotle discussed social transition, change, and the problems and politics of their day.

Many thoughtful persons throughout time have attempted to explain and make clear the situations that have confronted them. These attempts gradually became increasingly exact and scientific. The Middle Ages did not present much of what can be called a social science, perhaps because during that period there was too little change to stimulate man's speculation about events. Not until 1842, when Auguste Comte published in France his *Positive Philosophy*, did sociology come into existence. Comte asserted that the tradition, speculation, and authority of past observations should now be developed into systematic observation and that a science of sociology could emerge as a distinct study. Comte is recognized as the father of sociology, and his writings stimulated others who were on the brink of this new approach to social reality, such as Herbert Spencer in England and Lester F. Ward in America. These early writers in sociology, the founders of this new study in the social sciences, were social philosophers. A quarter of a century later research studies began to replace the reform studies of the early sociologists. Theoretical formulations and practical studies proceeded from Charles H. Cooley, Robert E. Park, Ernest W. Burgess, W. I. Thomas, Max Weber, Emile Durkheim, and others, all important as the forerunners of the time when sociology would become a science.

Man has long sought for truth, as is evident even from the early interests in recreation and religion. The later and most exacting method of seeking truth is science, which differs from other methods that are concerned with final meanings and values. Sociology has attained scientific status, having emerged from the ideas of the early social reformers and philosophers. Contemporary social reformers and social idealists may be in a better position to help improve society, for the very reason that the study of sociology, which presents knowledge about society, is now more exact, more systematic.

Sociology is the scientific study of man's social relationships. These relationships are many and complex, consisting of various forms of group life, institutions, and social interaction, including problem behavior. Although man has long speculated about such concerns, his earliest ideas were very little like contemporary sociology.

The methods of sociology are neutral. To the sociologist himself is left the application of his findings about behavior.

Sociology and Other Studies. Thinking about the realities of experience may be traced to the beginnings of human knowledge. Over the centuries, these understandings have become more clearly defined until, during the ancient Greek era, ideas emerged from the writings of Plato, Aristotle, the early historians Herodotus and Thucydides, the Roman jurists, and the early Judaic and Christian writers. The ideas eventually took shape in the social sciences—during the middle of the 18th century in political science and economics, and during the middle of the 19th century in sociology.

It must be recognized, however, that any division of human knowledge into such specific areas as the natural sciences, social sciences, biological sciences, the various areas of business, and the humanities is merely determined on the part of man to enable him to get a mental grasp on human experience. In ordinary behavior, man simply behaves. However, he continually seeks answers to the why, how, when, and where of his experiences. His theories and ideas have developed into studies, some of which are highly exacting in their methods. Sociology is one such study.

Consider how many kinds of knowledge are involved in space exploration, for example. The natural sciences, physics, chemistry, geology, and geography are all involved in the complex problems of getting man to the moon and returning him safely to the earth, as well as in discoveries on the moon itself. The social sciences are involved as well. Economics, as indicated in budgeting; political science, as in international relations and the international concerns over the "space race"; and sociology in its studies of small group relationships involved in the confinement of persons in small areas for extended periods of time. All these things are involved in the same goal, getting man on the moon. Moreover, it is highly probable that all of man's accumulated knowledge has been involved in this single experience.

Man learns and transmits his learning through his group relationships. This vast body of knowledge is the human social heritage, which permits man to influence his environment as no other living species does.

Man in society, in social groups, is the observable fact for all of the social sciences. If a man were to stand in an ancient tower and look out through a niche, he would see only a small segment of the universe. For a complete picture of what surrounds his tower, he would have to view the universe through all the available niches, some of which would overlap the view from the previous niche. Thus it is with the social sciences. All are concerned with man in society, and each has a special point of view, parts of which clearly overlap with the points of view of some of the other social sciences. Each, therefore, helps to complete the total picture of "the universe out there"—man in society. What are these separate points of view of the various social sciences?

Some historians classify their study as social science, while others classify it as a humanity. Perhaps it is the approach involved that makes for this distinction. History is interested in reconstructing the past, the chronology of events. Its historical documentations is valuable to the sociologist, and sociological analyses are of value to the historian.

Political science is mainly concerned with the study of government in all its legal, administrative, and power functions. To the extent that the social organization, the culture of groups, and other aspects of political decisions in group life are involved, sociology and political science make valuable contributions to each other.

Economics deals with supply and demand, with all the facts of production, consumption, making a living, and distribution. To the extent that man's social goals, family life, migration, and public opinion become involved in the concerns of economics, sociology helps to explore these areas. In turn, the economic factors of social group life are of vital importance to the sociologist in his study of control, of change, and of industrial stability.

Anthropology in its study of man includes information on man's physical attributes as well as his social nature. Physical anthropology deals especially with contemporary primitive peoples. Anthropology, as all the other social sciences, has expanded its interests. It deals now with complex societies, and as such is called social anthropology, studying family arrangements, religion, and governments in their variations and similarities. The closeness to sociology is at once clear. Perhaps the line of differentiation between the two social sciences is mainly in methods of research.

All of the social sciences are expanding their interests and their research techniques. This leads to much overlapping with other disciplines, so that areas of behavior become the concern of two or more sciences. Psychology and sociology, for example, are both deeply involved in an area of behavior most frequently called social psychology—the effect of group experiences on the individual. Political science, psychology, and sociology are concerned with public opinion and communication. The specific techniques of inquiry and the philosophy of the sciences, as well as the reaults of their investigations, make for distinctions between them.

THE FIELD AND METHODS OF SOCIOLOGY

Modern Sociology, the Field and Perspective. Common-sense notions have developed about man's behavior, customs, institutions, forms of group life, and values. Sociology goes beyond such notions (sometimes termed myth, folklore, or old wives' tales) in seeking truth. It brings scientific methods to the study of these areas and the areas of interest and knowledge have become specialized fields.

With billions of people in the world, and more than 200 million of them in the United States, the possibilities for complex interpersonal relationships are astronomical. When two persons are in a room, there are two possible patterns of interrelationships. With three persons in a room, the patterns increase to at least six and possibly seven, if the total threesome become involved as one. Complexities in relationships are a fact, therefore. Yet there are dozens of other facts of relationships that are simple, perhaps slight at first glance, but that are equally meaningful as areas of inquiry to the sociologist. Such behavior patterns as tipping, coffee breaks, and a man's holding a door open for a woman are taken-for-granted instances of behavior which, under the inquiring techniques of the sociologist, may have special meaning and even surprising significance. The sociologist attempts to throw light on daily life and to increase knowledge of human relations.

Scientific Research. As there is a clear-cut distinction between common knowledge and the scientific knowledge stemming from the research of sociology, it is necessary to describe both science and scientific research in sociology. Science is an organized body of knowledge, which would include hypotheses, theories, laws, speculations, and facts, and as such might on occasion not be precise. Nevertheless, it does distinguish certain areas of knowledge from philosophical and humanistic areas. Most persons thinking about science are really thinking about methods of science, laboratories, test tubes, and experimentation. Human beings, of course, cannot be subjected to test-tube experimentation, but other devices and techniques have been developed in sociological investigation. In experimental research, sampling, collecting data, and the formulation of testable theories are essential to scientific inquiry. If one were asked whether the soup were good or not, he would not have to eat the whole kettle to answer. A spoonful or a dish of the soup would be enough for an opinion about the total. A scientifically selected sample, then, is important as a first step, followed by various means of collecting information about the sample. Participant observation, systematic observation, and observation of the situation are devices for obtaining data, depending on whether the observer is a member of the group, or a selector of only a portion of the total activities on which to comment, or the creator of an artificial situation in order to observe the behavior of the participants.

As an observer, the investigator has already determined what to observe. He has established in his thinking certain ideas he wishes to test. He has, thereby, limited the entire field of inquiry to observe items relevant to his thinking. By simple or complex statistical devices, he is then able to confirm his ideas or discover their falsity. The test of the accuracy of his findings could well be the duplication of his conclusions by the scientific inquiry of another investigator.

As a scientist, the sociologist has no particular axe to grind. He is interested in truth and presents findings derived from scientific inquiry. The sociologist is similar to other scientists in describing, interpreting, and predicting data relevant to his field. In the area of sociology, the scientist seeks to describe, interpret, and predict patterns of human interaction and behavior.

GROUP STRUCTURE OF SOCIETY

Primary Focus of Sociology. Man everywhere lives in groups. Isolated from group associations, man either willingly or unwillingly, begins to decline. Nourishment which comes from group interaction contributes to what is often called human nature, to the personality of man, to the fact that he is able to leave a cultural heritage to his descendants, and to man's socialization, distinguishing him from the occasionally found "wolf child" or savage man. The "group" is not simply a concept dreamed up by sociologists. It is a vital social fact, a social reality. One can test this for himself. Is he exactly the same person in every group to which he belongs? The chances are that he is not, and it would be unusual if he were. When having a good time with friends after a football game, why does he behave differently from the way he behaves in school?

Nevertheless, there is definitely a strain of consistency in all of a person's behavior. This is sometimes referred to as *character*, and character thus embodies a core of values and standards basic to a person.

The sociologist is interested in all groups that exist and in the patterns of interaction in all social situations. He is interested in group loyalties, in the effects of various group relationships on individuals, and in why the behavior of some persons differs from the social norms of the group.

Cultural Transmission. *Culture* is the man-made part of man's environment. Culture includes behavior norms of all kinds. Living in a particular culture, man tends to follow its norms. Consider; for example, that your wishes, dreams, goals, motives, hopes, achievements, even your rebellious notions are all the product of the values and standards of your culture. What becomes of the significant value of the individual under such conditions? Even highly personal values, embodied in such familiar statements as "think for yourself," and "make up your own mind" are part of Western culture. They are not universal. Assume for example that in a communist country a substantial grant for higher education in America were offered to an extremely bright young man employed by the government of his country. The Western system would allow such an individual to accept such a grant, based on his own individual merits. The political system in the communist country would not permit such a personal approach. Instead, the grant would have to be made to the government, which in turn would explore all professional areas of need and select someone to be nominated for the grant, who, in turn, might get the higher education in the field selected by the government. The individual is subject to the state. In Western countries the individual is the important value, and he contributes to the well-being of his country because of his own individual achievements. Both systems of values concerning the "individual" are reflections of the cultures of the respective countries.

Culture is an organized system of behavior; it serves many functions. It defines situations (eating with implements or with one's right hand); defines attitudes, values, and goals (what is beautiful, what one wants to become—both representing the related concepts of attitudes, values, and goals); gratifies human needs in prescribed behavior patterns (what and when and how to eat, how to find a mate); tends toward the unity of the group by the promotion of the loyalty and morale of the group; and acts as a preserving element in social change.

Individuals can and do make new contributions in culture, but for the overwhelming majority, the culture exists before the living individual. This means that man is born into the ready-made set of ways of behaving and thinking. The culture is transmitted to him, and it is the product of generations of his ancestors, who have developed ways of easing man's becoming a man.

Personality and Socialization. It is generally agreed that at birth the human infant does not possess personality. From that time on, there are experiences that are common to all infants, and those that differ with each individual person. The social and cultural experiences of the child make for uniformity within the group, and the differences in those same experiences make for individualism. Each child learns quickly to bring his own thinking to a situation. He learns that a prick from his diaper pin causes pain, and a cry is the result. This brings mother. Another kind of cry brings food, and still another produces love and a caress from mother. Original nature appears to be the biological inheritance of the child, which would make him differ from the young of another species. Human nature is original nature plus experience. One definition of *personality*, presented by the sociologist Milton Yinger, is that it is the totality of behavior of an individual whose "given tendency system" is said to be "interacting with a sequence of situations." If you examine the groups to which you belong, you will see certain consistent patterns in your behavior in each of the groups. This is the "given tendency system." And yet as you deal with your best friend, your parents, your teacher, your employer, your behavior is somewhat different (interacting with a sequence of situations). Your personality is the sum total of all of the roles you play in the varying situations you meet each day. You have learned to behave the way you do in all these roles from the social conditioning to which you have been exposed from birth. This is socialization, the process of fitting the individual into the organized and expected behavior of the group. This is a vast topic; it suggests the need for learning about the groups to which the individual belongs, the complex patterns of social interaction (including those termed deviant, or differing) and the institutions that establish the expected roles of the individual.

SOCIAL INTERACTION

Social Processes. In countless ways, an individual is continuously dealing with others. He is in communication with other people at practically every point of his daily life. This process of interstimulation and response is called *social interaction*.

Social interaction is the process of acting in awareness of others, molding our responses as we think others expect us to act. A student sits in the classroom where he is expected to sit; he does not go to the front of the room, where the teacher would normally be. His position as a student is his status, and where he sits in the classroom as a student is part of his role. *Status* is position in a group, and *role* is the behavior aspect of the status.

One can look at social behavior from these two views—status and role. In the social interaction of an individual in his daily experiences, one is playing many roles according to the statuses he may have. He is a child in the family, a student at school, a sacker in the grocery store. In the course of the individual's social interaction for a week, he may play many roles, corresponding to the various statuses involved. The concept of "social role" is a device that helps us to understand portions of social interaction.

Another concept, that of *social process*, gives us knowledge of other portions of social interaction. The occurrence of patterns of social interaction, with considerable repetition and regularity, is referred to as a social process. Social processes are the typical ways in which groups of people influence each other. Social processes include cooperation, competition, conflict, accommodation, and assimilation. An individual may not be particularly aware of these special forms of social interaction, but as a member of various groups, he may observe these processes in operation. It is important to realize that these processes exist in all societies, although there is great variety in the expression of them.

A *primary group* is the group to which "we" belong. There are strong feelings of loyalty, and *cooperation* is most frequently typical of the behavior of the group members in attaining the commonly desired goal. Groups also cooperate with each other, probably for the same ends—those of achieving commonly desired goals.

If the objects of the goal are scarce or are considered scarce, then competition is the process of distributing the scarce item among the competitors. In the primary group relations of a football team, each player cooperates with the other. Team activity cannot exist without the cooperation of its members. Only one team can win the football game, however, so the rival teams are engaged in competition to achieve the desired goal.

War is perhaps the most dramatic form of conflict. The process of attempting to destroy or eliminate the enemy is conflict. It develops when a contest itself is no longer important, but eliminating the contestants becomes most important. Despite the fact that social conflict is disruptive, it may serve several functions—such as defining issues, establishing a balance among contenders, or forming alliances with other groups.

There never has been an everlasting conflict. Every conflict eventually ends. Conflicts, however, may end with aggression directed toward a new enemy, or conflicts may end in some form of accommodation. *Accommodation* may settle issues temporarily or for long periods of time. Often, however, basic issues may still smolder. Some forms of accommodation are planned and formally negotiated, while others may arise in an unplanned way as the result of group interaction. Expected roles are accepted and adhered to if the two sides in the conflict want the conflict ended. Compromise involves conciliation, mediation, and arbitration, and a third party may be used to reach a settlement between the two sides.

Assimilation, or merging, is another social process in which two groups come to share a common culture and common goals. When this process is completely achieved, the two groups normally disappear as separate groups. Their separate identities become fused into one. This process is going on in the United States as certain racial and ethnic groups become fused into the dominant group. Complete assimilation of all differing groups may never occur; it seems to be blocked by such factors as prejudice, racial pride, and lack of opportunities.

Race and Minority Relations. Man has always lived in groups, and because of this, there has always been social interaction, and when groups interact with one another, the social processes mentioned earlier take place. In competing for position, one group almost invariably attempts to achieve a superior-inferior relationship with the other group, and various devices arise to accomplish this end. One such device is that of race. There is no general agreement as to why certain groups of people look different from other groups of people, but there is general agreement that physical differences exist. No definition of race is universally acceptable, but one which includes both physical meanings and cultural meanings is useful. A *race* is a group of people with a number of distinctive inherited characteristics, which become involved in behavior because of social definitions. If race were not involved in behavior, there might be no need for a definition of race, for persons would not see differences. When attitudes and behavior become involved in a biological occurrence, it becomes a matter of concern for the sociologist. Classifying peoples according to physical qualities is almost impossible, because of many overlapping areas, but in general most scientists agree on three basic races—white, black, and yellow—and many subdivisions.

In the processes involved in social interaction, race becomes a convenient label for assigning groups in patterns of social levels, such as the superior-inferior relationship. One race then becomes a minority group, which is a group having a low power position, a low prestige position, and most often a low economic position.

The difficulty of making race classification, however, is illustrated by what is termed the Jewish race. There are Negro Jews, Chinese Jews, and white Jews. Judaism is a religion, and technically speaking, there is no such thing as a Jewish race. In the social interaction of centuries in certain parts of the world, the sifting process into superior-inferior groups has used the device called race as a means of accomplishing that end. Thus, Jews in parts of the world have occupied inferior positions, not because they were an inferior race, for there is no such thing, but because people use the device of race to place one group, a religious group, in a lower position. It then becomes a minority group. If people think a thing is true, then it is true for them, and they act in terms of their beliefs, not in terms of the facts. Some persons therefore accept the mistaken idea that Jews are a race, and this false notion settles for them which group is superior and which group is inferior. The belief in a "super race" among Nazi Germans had in it the mistaken non-fact that Jews were a race and inferior; hence they were marked for extinction.

Under the enormous impact of beliefs, extraordinary things occur. People see what they believe, as truly as they believe what they see. Both majority and minority groups come to behave in their patterns of social interaction in ways conditioned by their respective beliefs. In the United States, the slogan "black is beautiful" is an understandable reaction on the part of the "black minority group" (using the phrase "minority group" as described above) to patterns of discrimination on the part of the white majority group, based on the same presumed racial quality of the color black.

Race, as a device of discrimination, exists in every society. It results in patterns of discrinination in many different forms, such as in occupation and employment, housing, education, and social life. The consequences of discrimination in minority relations are specific and measureable: poverty, high sickness and death rates, and family instability, to name a few. Anthropology and sociology have made great contributions to the study of race relations, particularly in the United States. If all the insights into the biological-social situation called race were accepted, racial problems would ultimately become non-existent. But this is hardly likely to occur as long as people everywhere find the device of race useful in dividing society into superior-inferior groups.

Collective Behavior. No topic in sociology is more fascinating than the study of collective behavior, and probably no topic is more difficult to study. The heightened emotions seen in crowds, mobs, panics, crazes, and mass hysteria contribute both to the fascination of collective behavior and to the difficulties involved in trying to study it. How is it possible to question the participants in a lynching? But studies do emerge and considerable insight is being achieved regarding such behavior.

In one sense all social interaction is collective behavior, but in order to make the term meaningful it is necessary to limit it to that form of social behavior which is spontaneous, unstructured, unpredictable, occurring most often on one occasion rather than regularly or routinely, and which is usually irrational.

Crowds and riots are the most frequently studied subjects, for not only do they make headlines and sometimes affect masses of people, but they may also result in changes of behavior of the total group. We will note later that the early stages of social change frequently have such qualities: instinctiveness, lack of structure, or lack of predictability.

Generally a *crowd* is large, temporary, and its members are anonymous. The behavior in a crowd is impersonal, and the members become highly emotional and subject to influence. What happens at an airport when a bomb is discovered? For a moment there is panic behavior, with attention focusing on the bomb-carrier. If it is learned that the bomb is not scheduled to go off at the moment and is therefore temporarily harmless, the members would probably move toward the bomb-carrier with the possibility of physical violence being directed at him. But there are definite limitations on how far any such behavior will go. The age of those waiting for the plane, their economic level, their marital status, and the degree of security each has will have something to do with restraining or increasing the possibilities of violence. It would be certain that some official of the airline would make an appearance as a leader and seek to calm the group. There are limitations, then, on crowd behavior, based on the kinds of persons involved, their customs, the emergence of leadership, and specific external controls. The nature of the crowd would undoubtedly determine the kind of limitations that would emerge.

Collective behavior is the study of all such areas of social interaction, including phases of everyday life, as well as occasional very dramatic episodes.

Social Change. As mentioned earlier, discoveries of skeletons in kneeling positions, or with pieces of jewelry on or near them, gave rise to ideas that early peoples had some primitive form of religion. We have only to look at the great cathedrals, temples, mosques, and shrines to note the enormous changes that have taken place in one area of behavior, the institution of religion. Whenever there is social interaction, and in particular collective behavior, new norms and new values occur. There will be changes in the social structure and the social relationships of the group; this is *social change*. There will be changes in the correlative parts of the culture of the group. This is *cultural change*, change in the area of the environment. Social change refers to such changes as in the age distribution within a society, the relative changes in the role of women, the economic level of the people, or the increased impersonality of living in cities, as compared with living in small towns. Cultural change refers to such changes in technology as the electronics, chemistry, and physics used in developing machines for getting man on the moon. Change in the role of women is developing into a changing set of cultural norms concerning male-female roles. There is considerable overlapping, and thus the distinction between social roles and cultural roles becomes largely a matter of theory. In practice, the two concepts are often used interchangeably.

Discovery, invention, and diffusion contribute to social change. There are certain factors that increase social change and others that slow it down. While material inventions and technological advances contribute to change, they almost invariably disrupt patterns of social living at the same time.

The inability or failure of a people to initiate social changes, to lessen the disruptions resulting from technological inventions, gives rise to what W. F. Ogburn called *cultural lag*. Cultural lag refers to the stress that occurs when interconnected behavior patterns do not change at the same rate of speed. The Industrial Revolution began about 1850 and rapidly began to exploit the labor of women and children. Workmen's compensation laws of various kinds, including child labor laws, did not begin to emerge for about half a century, and the last state to enact child labor laws finally did this about a century after children began to be exploited in labor situations. So it is with all aspects of social change. Some changes meet with ready acceptance, while others are resisted. But change is inevitable in every society in the world. Only the rate of change and the direction of change differ and are relative.

Deviant Forms of Behavior. Each society must have stability in order for it to function for the benefit of its members. Change, both social and cultural, comes to every society, with the result that methods of control are devised so that each society in turn socializes its members so that they want to conform because the norms are theirs. Occasionally the group may find it necessary to exert some form of pressure so that the individual will conform. In most instances, the primary groups to which an individual belongs are enough to extend informal controls through approval and disapproval so that the individual wishes to conform because he does not want to be different. Occasionally, force is used by secondary groups to make the individual conform. If an individual does not conform to the norms of society through these various devices, he is labeled a *deviant*. Deviant, or differing, behavior goes against social norms, and the sociology of this behavior calls attention to the role of social factors in contributing to it.

Smoking marijuana is deviant behavior. Almost everywhere in the world, society has defined this behavior as deviant, even though it would appear that some of its members, particularly the young, indulge in smoking marijuana. Since every group establishes standards of appropriate behavior, deviance becomes apparent only when this behavior violates these norms. Conforming behavior is identifiable because it satisfies group expectations and does not violate norms. A high school class was asked: "How many of you have smoked marijuana?" A number replied they had, indicating conformity to smaller-group pressures. Then the question was asked: "How many of you have had the courage not to smoke marijuana?" A larger number replied that they had, indicating conformity to still another pressure. Several significant points were thus illustrated: social pressure is the origin of social deviation, conforming to smaller-group expectations in the development of social deviation, and also conforming to smaller-group expectations in ways of handling social deviation. The members of the group decided that all of the rationalizations for smoking marijuana, such as "no worse than liquor" or "non-addictive" were irrelevant. After much in-depth searching of their thinking and values, all of those who used marijuana agreed to give it up. Their decision was based on such group values as individualism, stability of society, and law and order. They further began campaigning to "sell" others in their school on their newly found point of view. Such an isolated instance perhaps could not apply as a cure for all forms of social deviance, such as mental illness or suicide, for social deviance not only includes the violation of norms, but also implies group reactions to the violations. Group reactions to deviance include the devaluing of social worth, destruction of social identity, and sometimes sympathy. Certain types of social deviants even are rewarded by the group, as in the example of a genius. Some social deviants, furthermore, initiate social change. Every inventor has become dissatisfied with one aspect of the culture, which he thinks can be improved. He becomes a nonconformist, a social deviant to some extent. Depending on many factors, the society in turn decides whether to make him a martyr or regard him as a genius.

Social Disorganization. Every social change affects the rest of the culture. A change in one phase of the culture is bound to influence other phases of the culture. Cultural lag has already been mentioned as referring to the rates of adaptation of the various parts of the culture. If the culture is stable and organized, a change in one aspect is disruptive and disorganizing. If there is much disorganization, the security of the people becomes threatened, and there is a possibility of damage to the morale and purposes of the people. The traditional controls, the customary roles of the people, and the stability of institutional behavior become threatened and social disorganization results. It must be remembered that social change, social stability, consistency in role playing, and social normality are all relative concepts. The extent of social disorganization in a given society will depend on the nature of those and other items—such as change, stability, normality, and role expectations. To cause a disturbance in any of these would affect the other aspects of the total social situation and might therefore bring social disorganization.

Some societies are attuned to change. Children in the United States are prepared to adjust to change and appreciate change more than children in some other societies. This readiness helps American children to adapt themselves to social change. The costs and symptoms of social disorganization may therefore be offset somewhat, and personal disorganization be held at a low point as a result.

SOCIAL ORGANIZATION

It would appear that men have always been dependent on each other for survival. The fact of interdependence in society is everywhere evident, although not always observed. Ordinarily we are not aware of this interdependence in the social organization; only when something goes wrong do we become aware of it. If a war should occur, and trade between countries should be stopped, then certain lacks and needs will arise. We then become aware of the fact of international trade, which is part of the social organization involving very large social groups of nations. Likewise, in smaller groups, such as the family, the roles of the members of the groups become sorted out and a status structure arises. This, too, is part of the social organization.

Leadership. As a superior-inferior pattern develops, some individuals become more influential than others in leading the group to make certain decisions. When such a leader appears, the group begins to set up certain goals and norms. Soon, in order to enforce the behavior of the members of the group to conform to the norms of the group, controls are established. The tasks, responsibilities, and rewards attached to certain positions are determined, and *social organization* is the result.

This involves the patterns of the social relationships among the interdependent members of the group. The leader is highly important in these patterns of social interaction, since he directs the actual organization of the group. He foresees needs and trends. He develops efficient routines for completing tasks, and the followers look to him for guidance. Leadership is not a gift from the followers, nor is it certain that there is such a thing as a "born leader." The abilities needed to get jobs done are possessed by many individuals, but determination of the leader is in part made by the patterns of interaction among the members, which tend to sift out those less capable. Of great importance is the person's position in the structure of communication in the group. The specific roles that leaders play, of guiding the group to efficient accomplishment or of developing morale, are some of the interesting subjects also involved in the topic of collective behavior.

Social Levels and Mobility. In all human societies from the most primitive to the most modern, the members are sifted into different levels of prestige, esteem, power, and honor. This differential status-sorting rests on various bases, such as education, family lineage, occupation, age, sex, and race.

Social stratification is the term used to define the division of a population into layers, which determine privileges, rewards, and obligations. It is an order of rank of persons, who also behave in different ways. Most members of the various levels accept the definitions of their respective roles. Stratification tends to limit interaction between the levels of the society, for the main interaction appears to be within each level itself.

As long as the members of a particular level accept their position, a social class exists. The members of a social class think of each other as social equals. They tend to marry on the same level, live where other members of the same level live, and engage in recreational activities with their fellow members. The members of a social class almost invariably tend to think of themselves as socially superior to some and socially inferior to others. Why does each society tend to sort its members into levels of rank, which determine so much of behavior? When a society recognizes the need for some kind of order, of coordination, that is the beginning of its social classes. In every group there are always tasks of drudgery or unpleasantness to be done. Who shall do these jobs? Perhaps unconsciously, the group assigns such tasks to certain persons and keeps them at these jobs by various devices, such as rewards, punishments, and restrictions.

Social mobility is the movement from one social level to another, and includes both upward and downward movement. Each society develops its own patterns of barriers to social advancement, but eventually those barriers are broken through. Inherited wealth, discrimination, and limitations on opportunities are some of the barriers. Individual ability, ambition, sponsorship, social change, and technological improvements are some of the means of breaking through the barriers, with social mobility resulting. To the extent that the phrase "All men are created equal" is believed and accepted, there will tend to be a leveling of social classes. "From shirt-sleeves to shirt-sleeves in three generations" is another familiar phase which suggests the upward and downward mobility possible in our fluid stratification system.

Some societies are more interested and skillful than others in removing the individual and social barriers to mobility from one class to another for their members. To the extent that they are successful in accomplishing this, social stratification begins to disappear. In American society, studies indicate that members of a social class always consider themselves as occupying a higher class than that assigned them by the rest of society. This difference in role expectation may be healthy as part of the larger process in removing class barriers.

Human Ecology and Population Study. Ecology, the population explosion, and pollution are major concerns of complex societies, and increasing concerns of simpler societies, as the interdependence and interaction of these societies take place. Sociology has much to say about them.

Human ecology is the study of man's interrelationships with the physical environment. It examines the way people and their institutions affect and are affected by interaction with the environment. The distribution of people into various sizes of communities becomes part of the subject matter of human ecology. If one were to fly over all the world, he would find that men live in clusters with others. Some of these clusters are small, in desolate parts of the world, such as arctic regions and deserts; some are large, and a few are extremely large, as seen in the larger cities of the world. Urban sociology and rural sociology are subjects of vast and increasing importance. The totality of environment is an important concept here: physical, biological, and social environments. These environments provide opportunities for man to meet his needs, but also present the problems he must encounter in doing so. Man everywhere exploits the physical and biological environments, at first in order to survive, and then he exploits them even more to satisfy his social needs. The climate, topography, soils, and minerals are increasingly important in man's control of his environment. The possibilities involved in the physical environment have always been there, but it is only when man reaches a certain point in his own development that they are recognized as contributing to man's well-being.

All living systems, whether minute cells and organs, or individuals and species, face common problems of survival. Plants, animals, and man constitute the biological environment and are dependent on each other. As improvements in the skills of laborers and in technology occur, man recognizes his dominion over the physical and biological environments and becomes increasingly concerned over this fact.

Man long ago recognized the uses of natural resources, such as oil and coal. He began to exploit these resources and has now become concerned about their possible disappearance. He has also recognized the need of transporting oil and coal supplies from their source to places where man lives. He becomes concerned about the possibility of accidents resulting in oil-spills in oceans, and air pollution from releasing fumes into the atmosphere.

Sociological planning of all kinds is now being seen as a necessity for man's continuing well-being and survival. To this end of well-being and survival, the quantity and quality of the population are also being recognized as of vital concern. Birth and death rates, age distribution, sex distribution, life span, and population distribution are no longer matters for mere study. These matters have been of concern to a few for centuries, but now some of their dire predictions appear on the horizon.

The rate of population growth is approximately two per cent per year, which means that in about the year 2000 the population of the world will be doubled. Decline in death rates accounts for part of this population explosion. Development in scientific methods of food production, health measures, and increase in industrialization, with resultant decline in farming societies are also involved.

Demography is the study of human population, its distribution, composition, and change. One of its major concerns is population growth, with all that implies—birth rates, death rates, life expectancy, age and sex composition, and migrations. Demography becomes involved in predictions, such as the prediction of optimum populations, involving the potentials of the physical, biological, and social environments. It is of such vital importance today that there are national and international organizations, including the United Nations, setting up demographic planning systems of various kinds.

SOCIAL INSTITUTIONS

Structure and Functions. When one refers to a court of law, one means the person who presides, namely the judge. *Court* means a specific person. The Supreme Court of the United States is not an impersonal entity, a thing. It is nine persons. So it is with the concept "institution." *Institution*, to the sociologist, means social relationships and a system of behavior, and this means people. When people behave in specific ways about a central core of meanings, it is because there is an institution that disciplines them to do so.

Institutions are ways of doing things, and they develop largely in an unplanned fashion when individuals, through trial-and-error procedures, find the best ways of meeting social needs. There are elements of prediction in an institution, and this creates security for some, excitement for others, and perhaps even a sense of boredom for still others. Mothers act like mothers because their roles are predetermined for them even before they become mothers.

When many norms of behavior center around major aspects of human life, institutions develop. It is important to remember that the major aspects of human life are universal, existing wherever societies are. Thus, as man everywhere tries to find means of survival in providing food, he develops certain norms of behavior, which limit what one may do in meeting that particular need. The basic tool used by sociologists to analyze man's behavior in this one particular area is the "economic institution."

Most of one's behavior is spent in one way or another in six clustered areas, which are the institutions of family, education, religion, the economic order, the political order, and recreation. All societies have these six institutions involved in the behavior of their members, and it is quite possible for all six of them to differ in the specific patterns of the behavior norms.

Institutions in each society determine the roles to be played, the codes of behavior that are acceptable, the beliefs involved, the attitudes of the people, and the culture traits. Institutions, then, have stated specific functions to perform and, most of the time, the members of the societies carry out these functions. In so doing, occasional by-products may also result. As an example, in Bali, dances developed as part of the special form of the Hindu religion. These dances are performed in front of the temple with music and costumes. The obvious function, namely the religious symbolism, is there, but also sheltered stands have been erected in some locations to house sight-seers. Attendance fees exist, and the performers, both dancers and musicians, are now paid. The by-products in this instance might be considered part of the economic order and also of recreation. Hence, interrelationships of institutions become common. The observable functions are still there for the specific institution, but also behavior laps over into other institutions as a by-product.

The Family. In every society on earth, some form of family institution exists. In most societies, there are differences in the expected behavior norms of the family institution, to which the members of that society must conform. The sociologist, realizing that these differences exist and thus are part of the culture in which they are found, has developed a basic idea called *cultural relativism*, which is an attempt to judge behavior according to its own cultural background. This is important, for it helps to understand differing patterns of behavior in every one of the institutions. In the family institution, cultural relativism is important, for there are many sociologists who feel that the social, physical, economic, and mental requirements of the human species are met in different ways according to the particular society in which they are found. Thus, in remote sections of India and, until recently, in Tibet, the pattern of marriage has been polyandry, or several husbands and one wife, while in the United States, the pattern of marriage is monogamy, or one husband and one wife. The important point is that in both cultures there is a prescribed behavior norm among a cluster of related norms controlling one aspect of the family institution. A sociologist does not conclude therefore that monogamy is the best form of marriage but, using the concept of cultural relativism, he would conclude that family makeup is highly variable, and includes polygyny (several wives and one husband), polyandry, and group marriage, as well as monogamy. Furthermore, each form is "right" for the particular culture in which it is found.

We can now generalize somewhat about the functions and the structure of the activities of the family in society. The function of the family is to produce and raise children and to adapt them to society so that they in turn may be helped to meet the demands of life with more balance. The major roles in the family are father, mother, and child. But those roles may be expanded to include others, as in the American family, which is essentially a two-generation family, and the Asian family, which includes the "extended" family, consisting of other relations in addition to fathers, mothers, and children. The structure of the family includes practical and useful traits, such as a house and its furnishings, and symbolic traits, such as the ring, a wedding, and a will. The family, like all other institutions, changes. The norms of family life change as well, but the rates and direction of these changes vary with the culture involved.

Education. Every society wishes to ease the hardships of its young in reaching maturity, at the same time that it wishes to mold the child to conform to its norms. Every society sees this as necessary for its own survival. In its broadest sense, education means the socialization of the person. In most societies, these purposes are assigned to a separate group of their members, called educators, and the institution of education is the result. Its function is to teach the young to accept the culture of the society, mainly by formal patterns in specific places and for specific goals. In every society, each person is conditioned to behave in harmony with similarly conditioned people. Education is this conditioning process, including both informal and formal aspects.

Each person learns certain role expectations from the model roles to which he is exposed. When these models are consistent with the norms of the society, or normal, the child learns informally what is expected of him at various points of his life. If these models are absent, either physically or psychologically, then the child has no role model to follow. He behaves at variance with the role expectations of the group, for he has never learned them. Deviance may appear in his behavior as a result. These are some of the patterns of informal education.

Formal education is easier to note, and we can generalize about the functions and the structure of education as an institution. Its main function is to teach the young the basic values and norms of the society. This is achieved informally, as indicated above, and formally through the institution of education, in which the major roles are those of teacher and student. The practical and useful traits are the school building and books, and the symbolic traits are the diploma and degrees.

The institution of education also changes. Even though, traditionally, the institution of education conditions its members to the existing status of the society, yet to the extent that it encourages a member to analyze, make choices, be critical and to evaluate; it not only produces change in the very society to which it is supposed to condition its members, but it also eventually changes itself. The interaction of the institution of education with every other institution and with the total society is a fact, and this interaction may cause change in all aspects of the society at the same time that it acts as a preserving and leveling influence.

Religion. The institution of religion exists in every culture, although the form and content of religion may vary. It is generally agreed that religion includes three things: a belief in the supernatural, the feelings this belief in the supernatural evokes in the individual, and man's efforts to control the supernatural to act in man's behalf.

Formerly in American society religion was part of the family socializing process. But increasingly throughout the world, religion appears to be assigned to a separate group of persons who help the individual in the three areas mentioned above. In American society there is now a trend to make religion worldly, or to "humanize" religion. To the extent that this is accomplished, the singular function of religion is lost, and the religious institution becomes a welfare organization. The belief in the supernatural (whatever it may be called—Allah, God, the Almighty, Yahweh) becomes secondary to certain human behavior traits that are easily recognized, such as getting along with one's neighbor, cooperative attitudes, and helping one's fellow man.

The unique function of the institution of religion, which no other institution can manage, is that of "spiritualizing" the individual's thought to communicate with the Almighty. Religion functions to make the individual person better and at the same time to make man able to commune with the supernatural. The roles are those of the religious official, priest, rabbi, pastor, or minister. The practical and useful traits are the mosque, church, synagogue, temple, shrine, and the symbolic traits are the star, cross, and sacred books, such as Bible and the Koran.

There is more interrelationship of the institution of religion with the other institutions in some societies than in others. In American society, there is separation of church and state and, at the same time, the institution of religion generally supports the idea of the good citizen, the policies of the government, and the support of the nation in time of war. In America, notable exceptions tolerated by the majority society would be the Quakers and the Mennonites, who advocate pacifism.

The institution of religion, as all other institutions, changes. The rate and the direction of change vary. New institutional norms replace old norms, but it is highly unlikely that the institution of religion will ever disappear in any society, even though occasionally efforts are made in certain state-controlled societies to accomplish just that.

Economic Order. The family and those activities involved in the economic institution are closely interrelated, as all institutions are. In simpler societies the family serves as both the producing unit and the consuming unit, but in more complex societies the family is only the consuming unit. This means that the production and distribution of goods to meet meeds, both physiological and social, for survival and for "keeping up with the Joneses," must be done by others. This is the economic institution, which deals with such problems as production and distribution, because man's needs are relatively limited.

The determination of what is to be produced, who is to produce it, how much is to be available and for whom it is to be available, and whether any quantities should be withdrawn and held for future distribution, makes up the economic institution.

The sociologist has something to contribute to the well-established social science of economics in that he is concerned with the wider social effects of economic matters, as well as with the possible hidden effects. When we realize that people have widely different concepts of what constitutes property, of what constitutes wealth, of how economic attitudes are created and changed, and of what makes men work (or in some societies women and not men), then we can understand some of the areas of interest to the sociologist. The economic institution provides food, clothing, and shelter, but it does more than meet these basic needs.

The major roles are played by the employer, employee, the consumer and the producer. The practical and useful traits are the factory, office, and store, and the symbolic traits are patents, trademarks, consumer ratings, and product labels. The economic institutions change, as all other institutions change. For example, the mail system in America, a small part of the economic order, was at one time a private business; then it became a government function, with the Postmaster-General appointed by the President.

The institution of economics is functionally related to other institutions of the society, the occupational system being closely related to the family, and the type and amount of control permitted being related to the political institution of the government. The analyses of large-scale organizations, including industry, are becoming of interest and value to specialists in business and marketing.

Political Order. When sociology discovers, in its analyses of the economic institution in America, that there is more poverty among the non-whites and more poverty in the South than in the North, these conclusions become of interest in establishing a national policy. Government is involved at this point and the political institution emerges. It becomes involved in making and enforcing laws and rules and standards, and these functions normally are carried out by the roles of ruler and subject.

The useful and practical traits are usually observable in the government buildings and also in the public works carried out by the government in behalf of the people. The symbolic traits are important—the flag, the constitution, the charter, the legal codes—all of which become involved in the behavior of all citizens in a particular society.

There are very close interrelationships and interaction with other institutions. In the United States, the government says who may marry and when. In Communist countries, the government has strong powers of control over who may be educated and for how long. In Greece and in the Arab world, there is a very close connection between the government and the religion. The political order is closely related to the institutions of the family, education, religion, and the economic order. This was true for all the other institutions as well, it will be remembered.

The political order changes, as all institutions change. When the Supreme Court of the United States in 1954 declared the concept of "separate but equal" to be unconstitutional, this awakened both the blacks and the whites to inequalities in education, in marriage laws in various states, and in job opportunities. This in turn brought changes in legislation in regard to almost every phase of life, for the political order, or government, in every society is unique in that it is the final source of power. The effects of these changes on the economic order, education, and the family are being recognized.

The government, as the political institution, is evident in the behavior of the people involved in it and served by it, and at the same time it influences all the other social institutions. This institution exists to carry out certain functions, and in so doing it develops certain disordered functions as well. This is also true of every other institution. In the governmental institution, however, it becomes highly visible, for it finds itself unable to carry out its own functions at the same time that it is developing its malfunctions; for example, the difficulty in maintaining law and order in periods of general unrest, as in the worldwide unrest today.

Recreation. All institutions thus far discussed began to make their appearance shortly after man began to live in groups. When man found that he had spare time after the pressing needs for survival had been met, he became active in painting the walls of his cave, or carving the wood or bone handles of his tools. Recreation is the name of this phase of man's behavior. It refers to any activity, willingly undertaken for its own sake, which is thought to freshen physical and mental faculties. It is anything done "for fun."

Recreation exists in all societies and has been said to be a fair test of a people's character. There are active and passive forms of recreation. One conservative estimate states that the amount spent on active recreation in the United States is $40 billion a year. Passive recreation has given rise to a term called "spectator-itis." One aspect of this is illustrated by George Gallup's statement that 50 million American adults read comic strips. Another extimate is that more time is spent watching television than is spent at work, almost 3 billion hours per week of TV compared with 2 billion hours at work.

Vast amounts of time, energy, and money are spent in recreation, and it is understandable that such activity is bound to have concerned individuals attempting to police it. There are as a result municipal, state, and federal regulations controlling various forms of recreation, both active and passive, such as gambling, football, baseball, and motion pictures. There is expressed concern about the significance of movies and TV on juvenile delinquency. There are rating devices and published criticisms of various forms of recreation, attempting to limit participation in them.

All of this indicates the interrelationship of recreation with all other aspects of life, and of the connection between institutions. Consider the relationship of recreation with the family, giving rise to the phrase "the family that plays together stays together"; with the political and economic order; and with religion, wherein some religions specifically control or prohibit certain forms of recreation and encourage others. The role-playing in the institution of recreation is varied, for some people are participants, spectators, and regulators—as the occasion may demand. Bars, movie theaters, skating rinks, and football stadiums are some of the places for recreation and are useful and practical traits; while the "rules of the game," medals, and trophies are some of the symbolic traits. Just as all institutions change, so does recreation. And as in all other institutions, the changes do not imply the eventual disappearance of the institution concerned.

ACTION, PLANNING, AND NEW FIELDS

The Sociologist in the Field and in Social Planning. It has long been an issue whether sociology is and should be a "pure" science or an applied science. The early sociologists were social reformers: they saw their role as that of social investigators and social planners for what they considered to be the benefit of society. This idealism is now being shared by masses of others who are proceeding, often blindly, to improve society. The sociologist, in his studies of why people behave as they do in all the behavioral situations composing group life, often feels urged to share his knowledge with others. He becomes involved in social action at that point.

The term *social action* implies undisciplined and even disorderly action to some. Applied sociology appears to be a more neutral term without emotional overtones. It means social planning based on the findings of the science of sociology in specific areas. It implies the designing of both cultural and social change. Goals are always implicit in social planning, and goals always involve values. When goals, values, and social welfare become issues, there is always bound to be disagreement. Sociologists are also citizens and members of the community, and as such become concerned with the issues of concern to all society. Thus, some sociologists become social planners, become involved in applied sociology, and teach students how to use the findings of the study in action programs. It has been predicted that within ten years, all courses in sociology will have an "action component," that is, will have some kind of field experience, in which the students learn by doing.

Society is becoming increasingly concerned about the vast number of problems it faces and is seeking direction and guidance from all sources. As the sociologist is called upon to help in these matters, he is also called upon to become even more accurate in his scientific studies and in his predictions. Sociology is becoming more in demand by students, as indicated by the sharp increase in numbers of sociology students, and by society in general, as sociologists are called upon to serve as consultants and as members of committees concerned with social issues.

The fields of interest in sociology are increasing, as more knowledge of society results. In this section, attention has been given to the vast concerns of sociology and to the special point of view of the study. In meetings and conferences around the world, there are always groups devoted to these concerns. As new fields of interest develop, they in turn become the focus of attention at these meetings and conferences as well. As there is continuing development in the science of sociology, so there will continue to be new fields of interest. Three such new fields of interest will now be described.

Social Events and Their Background. The study of the "background expectancies" and methods and interpretive schemes to produce and understand ordinary social life are important to sociology. It would appear that any occasion whatsoever, including social research, can be examined for the reasonable properties of the practical actions by which members of society produce and understand social events. It is important that these practices and occasions should be studied by those persons who are actually involved, rather than by outsiders. There are specific methods used for obtaining this information from the persons involved, including the study of language. New topics for sociological research and theory include the study of social research itself.

Mathematical Sociology. It is held that all sciences consist of two parts: theory and experiment to test theory. Mathematics is important in each part—statistics for the analysis of experimental data, and mathematical theories (such as calculus and analytic geometry) for the development of theory. It is the use of mathematics in the development of social theory which is new and is now called mathematical sociology.

It is a recognized observation that groups break up into smaller groups. Mathematical sociology now states that groups *must* break up into smaller groups, or cliques. When certain persons state that cliques in American high schools are unfortunate, they perhaps do not recognize that such cliques are a direct consequence of something of which they do approve, namely loyalty to one's friends. This new specialization of sociology says that it doesn't just happen sometimes; it happens all the time—with mathematical regularity.

People have generally held that man can understand his world and solve his problems through the use of reason. Mathematical sociologists are beginning to develop the logic, which is to say the mathematics, underlying social events. To refer to the cliques mentioned above, consider the relationships of friendship between people that exists within a social group. If two people have a friend in common, they will be likely to be friends themselves. If we assume that every three people in a group of any size has this element, if two of three people are friends of the third, resulting in their becoming friends of one another, then the mathematical sociologist has proved (in the same way that a theorem is proved in plane geometry) that the group must be divided into cliques, so that everyone else in that clique are friends and that two people in different cliques are never friends.

BIBLIOGRAPHY

GENERAL

American Sociological Review (bimonthly). *American Sociological Association*

Bates, Alan P.—The Sociological Enterprise. *Houghton Mifflin* '67

Inkeles, Alex—What Is Sociology? *Prentice-Hall* '65

Merton, Robert K., and others—Sociology Today. Basic Books '59

THE FIELD AND METHODS OF SOCIOLOGY

Faris, Robert L., ed.—Handbook of Modern Sociology . . . . *Rand McNally* '64

McCormick, Thomas C. and Francis, Roy G.—Methods of Research in the Behavioral Sciences. *Harper and Bros.* '58

THE GROUP STRUCTURE OF SOCIETY

Chinoy; Ely—Sociological Perspective. *Random* '68

Goffman, Irving—Presentation of Self in Everyday Life . . . . *Doubleday* (*Anchor*) '59

SOCIAL INTERACTION

Becker, Howard S. K., ed.—Social Problems. *Wiley* '66

Lang, Kurt and Lang, Gladys Engel—Collective Dynamics . . . . *T. Y. Crowell* '61

Moore, Wilbert E.—Social Change. *Prentice-Hall* '63

Rubington, Earl and Weinberg, Martin S.—Deviance . . . . *Macmillan* '68

Shostak, Arthur B., ed.—Sociology in Action. *Dorsey Press* '66

Williams, Robin M.—Strangers Next Door. *Prentice-Hall* '64

SOCIAL ORGANIZATION

Hauser, Philip M.—Population Perspectives. *Rutgers Univ. Press* '60

Hawley, Amos—Human Ecology: A Theory of Community Structure . . . . *Ronald Press* '50

Tumin, Melvin M.—Social Stratification: The Forms and Functions of Inequality. *Prentice-Hall* '66

SOCIAL INSTITUTIONS

Christenson, Reo and McWilliams, Robert, eds.—Voice of the People . . . . . *McGraw Hill* '62

Eulau, Heinz; Eldersveld, Samuel; and Janowitz, Morris—Political Behavior: A Reader in Theory and Research . . . . *Free Press* '56

Gordon, C. Wayne—The Social System of the High School . . . . *Free Press* '57

Smelser, Neil J.—The Sociology of Economic Life. *Prentice-Hall* '63

Sussman, Marvin B., ed.—Sourcebook in Marriage and the Family . . . . . *Houghton Mifflin* '68

Williams, Robin—American Society . *Knopf* '60

Yinger, J. Milton—Sociology Looks at Religion. *Macmillan* '61

PLANNING AND NEW FIELDS

Coleman, James—Introduction to Mathematical Sociology . . . . *Free Press* '64

Coleman, James; Katz, Elihu; and Menzel, Herbert—Medical Innovation: A diffusion Study. *Bobbs-Merrill* '66

Garfinkel, Harold—Studies in Ethnomethodology. *Prentice-Hall* '67

Gouldner, Alvin W. and Miller, S. M. eds.—Applied Sociology . . . . *Free Press* '65

Lazarsfeld, Paul; Sewell, William; and Wilensky, Harolds, eds.—The Uses of Sociology. *Basic Books* '67

RECOMMENDED

Barton, Allen H.—Communities in Disaster: A Sociological Analysis of Collective Stress Situations. *Doubleday* '69

Braden, William—The Age of Aquarius: Technology and the Cultural Revolution . . *Quadrangle* '70

Brophy, W. H. and Abele, S. eds.—The Indian: America's Unfinished Business . *U. of Okla.* '69

Cavan, Ruth—The American Family. *T. Y. Crowell* '69

Deloria, Vine—We Talk, You Listen: New Tribes, New Turns . . . . *Macmillan* '70

Ferkiss, Victor C.—Technological Man: The Myth and the Reality . . . . *Braziller* '69

Fink, Arthur—The Field of Social Work. *Holt* '68

Gordon, George N.—The Language of Communication . . . . *Hastings House* '69

Gouldner, Alvin W.—The Coming Crisis of Western Sociology . . . . *Basic Books* '70

Gunther, John—Twelve Cities . . . *Harper* '69

Irvine, Keith—The Rise of the Colored Races. *Norton* '70

Jacobs, Jane—The Economy of Cities. *Random* '68

Kaufman, Carl B.—Man Incorporate: The Individual and his work in Organized Society. *Doubleday* '67

Levitas, G. B. ed.—Cultures and Consciousness: Perspectives in the Social Sciences. *Braziller* '67

Linder, S. B.—The Harried Leisure Class *Columbia* '70

Lineberry, W. P. ed.—Mass Communication. *Wilson* '69

Lipset, Seymour M. Hoftstadter, Richard, eds.—Sociology and History: Methods. *Basic Books* '68

MacKenzie, Norman, ed.—A Guide to the Social Sciences . . . . . *New American Library* '66

Mann, Peter H.—Methods of Sociological Inquiry. *Schocken Books* '68

Mead, Margaret—Culture and Commitment: A Study of the Generation Gap . . *Doubleday* '70

Nisbet, Robert A.—The Sociological Tradition. *Basic Books* '68

——Social Change and History: Aspects of the Western Theory of Development . *Oxford* '69

Packard, Vance—The Status Seekers: An Exploration of Class Behavior in America and the Hidden Barriers that Affect You, Your Community, Your Future . . . . *McKay* '59

Pettit, George A.—Prisoners of Culture. *Scribner* '70

Reich, Charles A.—The Greening of America: The Coming of a New Consciousness and the Rebirth of the Future . . . . *Random* '70

Riesman, David—The Lonely Crowd: A Study of the Changing American Character. *Yale U. Press* '50

Shoenfeld, Oscar and MacLean, Helen, eds.—City Life . . . . *Grossman* '69

Sills, David L. ed.—International Encyclopedia of the Social Sciences . . . . *Macmillan* '67

Slater, Philip E.—The Pursuit of Loneliness: American Culture at the Breaking Point . *Beacon* '70

Steiner, Stan—The New Indians . . . *Harper* '68

Still, Henry—Man: The Next 30 Years. *Hawthorn* '68

CIVILIZATION: PROBLEMS AND PROGRESS

If civilization is considered to be success in overcoming the obstacles to survival, such as hunger, disease, and destruction by natural or human enemies, the world may be said to have attained in the 20th century an unprecedented degree of civilization. The key to this advance was science. The fruits of science multiplied the productivity of the earth, tapped boundless sources of energy to perform work, and all but eliminated space as a bar to transportation and communication. Thanks to it also, diseases that once decimated the human race came under control. The enlargement of scientific knowledge became a focal point of human effort, promising still more revolutionary progress in the exploration of the universe and the understanding of the nature of life itself.

Yet with almost startling suddenness, those whose business it is to look ahead became conscious of a new set of problems that posed an ominous threat to future progress. There was first the problem of population, or how to avoid overcrowding the habitable portions of the earth. Another was the conflict problem, or how to avoid mass destruction by weapons newly available. Finally, there was the food and welfare problem, which grew ever more pressing as the human race was multiplying at a rate which, if unchecked, would cause its numbers to double in little more than a generation.

The Population Problem. In the first million years or so of mankind's existence, population is believed to have grown very slowly, often declining and then rising again. Its growth was restrained by starvation since the obtaining of food was an extremely uncertain process, at least until the invention of agriculture some 10,000 years ago. It was restrained also by almost constant warfare, first among tribes and later between nations and empires. Finally, it was kept in check by disease since nothing was known until recently about the microorganisms which constantly attack the higher forms of life.

It is estimated that the population of the world attained one billion for the first time about 1800 A. D. It took little more than a century thereafter to reach two billion. A United Nations study estimated that, by 1970, the world's population would pass three billion and that, at the rate of increase prevailing then, would be six billion by 2000 A. D.

The basic reason for the increase was three-fold. First, food and other necessities of life became easier to obtain. Second, the toll of organized warfare, although greater in the aggregate than in earlier ages, was far less in proportion to the total population. Finally, and most decisively, medical knowledge of how to combat disease and organized means of doing so cut the death rate drastically while having no effect on the birth rate. This knowledge, carried with missionary zeal to the less advanced peoples, frequently had the effect of adding hungry mouths much more rapidly than the production of the wherewithal to feed them.

The crux of the problem is that there is a limit to the area of the world where human beings can live —about 52,000,000 square miles, of which about one-third is arable. Moreover, on the most optimistic calculations, there is a limit to the world's usable resources, multiplied though they may be by the application of science.

Furthermore, overcrowding compresses the area of human freedom and leads to maddening frustrations. Witness traffic jams and the growing difficulty in getting to and from work as cities enlarge and merge into megalopolises, each covering thousands of square miles. Studies of animal societies which have suffered over-population show that such a situation with them cures itself by starvation and other processes no less cruel. An example may be seen in the lemmings of Scandinavia, which periodically overproduce their kind and then appear to be affected by a species of madness and commit mass suicide by drowning.

Solution of the problem in a rational way obviously requires limitation of births before nature steps in with the crueler methods.

Avoidance of Mass Destruction. By penetrating the secret of the atom, mankind in the 20th century made it possible to wipe out rapidly most of the human race. To prevent the use of the new weapon became a second problem of civilization. Its solution was recognized as one to be obtained, if at all, by political means. Such was the principal motivating force behind the organization of the United Nations, of plans to assist underdeveloped countries to raise their standard of living, and of other moves to lessen the likelihood of war.

Provision of Food and Welfare. While this problem has been basic throughout recorded history and before, the population problem makes it much more critical for civilization today, since advancement must be rapid if the threat of overpopulation is to be forestalled.

Plan of This Section. In this section appear articles which have a bearing on the above problems of civilization. First comes a subsection containing articles on population growth, public health, vital statistics, and medical advances, notably antibiotics, which have played a star role in prolonging human life. It is concluded with an article on population control.

The next subsection deals with mass destruction and its avoidance, containing such articles as hydrogen bomb, fallout, and guided missiles, followed by an account of the United Nations, foreign aid, and disarmament.

A third subsection, on welfare advancement, brings together articles on fertilizers, water, conservation, air contamination, urban renewal, computers, fuel cells, and other devices to assure a viable future for mankind if the population and conflict problems are solved in time.

THE POPULATION PROBLEM

Population Growth. Systematic and reasonably accurate population counts are a development of the 19th century. Partial counts, for military or tax purposes, go back at least to early Biblical times. The United States census of 1790 was the first to be taken for a political purpose—to determine representation in Congress. Leading European nations soon followed with periodic population counts. More detailed information was incorporated as the purpose widened to commercial and sociological ends. Today nearly all nations of the world take censuses, although some are sporadic and of dubious quality. The United Nations makes periodic estimates of the world's population, using censuses where available supplemented by estimates based on special studies.

The following are results for selected years as published by the Population Reference Bureau, Inc.:

6000 B.C.—5 million
14 A.D.—250 million
1000 A.D.—275 million
1600 A.D.—486 million
1830 A.D.—906 million
1920 A.D.—1810 million
1960 A.D.—2972 million
1969 A.D.—3551 million

U. N. figures for 1970 show 3706 million and it is estimated that this will double by 2006 A.D.

The increase shown from 5 to 250 million in the pre-Christian era reflects the effect of the agricultural revolution, when hunting gave way to controlled production and the rise of cities. The small increase in the millennium to 1000 A.D. mirrors the chaos of the Dark Ages. By 1600, discovery of new lands, growing wealth from commerce, and the rise once again of cities permitted doubling of mankind's numbers. From 1600 to 1920, the world's population quadrupled, due partly to the industrial revolution in some countries and particularly to medical discoveries which had the effect of drastically reducing the ravages of disease. The death rate fell; the birth rate fell much more slowly.

The United Nations estimate of 7.4 billion inhabitants in 2006 A.D. is based on the assumption of continued population growth at the rate prevailing in the 1960's. This assumption ignores the example of Europe's drop in birth rate after the massive population growth in the late 19th century or the example of Japan, whose growth rate was reduced sharply in the 1960's under the influence of government policy and private prudence.

War on Disease. In the matter of lowering the human death rate, it is difficult to exaggerate the importance of the work of Pasteur, who laid the foundations of bacteriology in 1864. Following his work, identification was established of bacteria which cause the following endemic diseases: tuberculosis and cholera by Koch in 1882 and 1884; diphtheria by Krebs in 1883; malaria by Laveran in 1884; sleeping sickness by Bruce in 1903, germs being carried by the tsetse fly; yellow fever about 1903, germs being transmitted by mosquitoes; typhus by Pickets and Wilder in 1910, the carrier being body lice; and polio by Salk in 1954.

Causes having been discovered, methods were devised which largely eliminated these diseases as important causes of death. The methods included control of carriers and development of serums and vaccines to produce immunity through inocculation into the blood stream. Even before Pasteur's discoveries, a vaccine was developed in the 1790's by Jenner which tamed the scourge of smallpox. Antiseptic surgery introduced by Lister in 1867 cut the toll of infections. Diabetes yielded to treatment by insulin, as discovered by Banting in 1922.

Antibiotics. These are chemical substances produced by various species of microorganisms which suppress the growth of, and even destroy, other microorganisms. A small number of them have been used in the treatment of infections for which previously there had been no known specific. The first to be employed (1941) in the treatment of human disease was penicillin, which Dr. Alexander Fleming in 1928 extracted from the fungus penicillium. In several varieties it is used in the treatment of syphilis, gonorrhea, and pneumococcal and streptococcal infections.

In use of penicillin against staphylococcal infections, however, it was found that resistant organisms developed. To overcome their effect, a newer form (methicillin, or staphcillin) is used.

Streptomycin was the second important antibiotic to be discovered. It was isolated in 1944 by Dr. Selman A. Waksman and associates. With it also bacterial resistance develops, and its prolonged use may cause dizziness and deafness. Its chief use is in the treatment of tuberculosis.

Then came the discovery of so-called broad spectrum antibiotics, effective against a wide range of microorganisms. Aureomycin was the first of these. Others include achromycin, chloromycetin, and erythromycin, which have been effective in the treatment of pneumonia, brucellosis, tularemia, the rickettsial diseases, psittacosis, and typhoid and paratyphoid fever. Erythromycin is an adjunct in the treatment of patients who have developed a sensitivity of penicillin.

Virus and Fungus Diseases. Antibiotics fail to control fungus and virus diseases. Other types of antimicrobal agents have been developed for this purpose. These include amphotericin B for systemic fungus infections; isoniazid, useful in the management of tuberculosis; and griseofulvin for superficial fungus infections, such as "athlete's foot."

Some virus diseases have been controlled by immunization, but the first drug found capable of killing a virus was an anti-cancer agent IDU (5-iodo-2'-deoxyuridine), used first by Dr. Herbert E. Kaufman.

Corticosteroid Hormones. These include cortisone, hydrocortisone, and ACTH (adrenocorticotrophic hormone). They produce results by some unknown alteration of the body's glandular balance. Cortisone was first used at the Mayo Clinic by Dr. Philip S. Hench for rheumatoid arthritis. ACTH, which is extracted from animal pituitary glands, stimulates the adrenal cortex of the patient to produce its own cortisone or cortisone-like substance. Cortisone and hydrocortisone particularly have proved valuable in the treatment of rheumatoid arthritis, rheumatic fever, bronchial asthma, and other inflammatory and allergic disorders.

Population Control. Methods of controlling human population go back thousands of years. Cruder forms include infanticide and, in subarctic regions, abandoning the aged to freeze to death. Use of herbs and mechanical means to produce abortion has a very ancient history. Aristotle reported that the government of ancient Crete encouraged homosexuality to restrain the birth rate.

In the 19th and early 20th century, more or less refined mechanical methods became known and widely practiced among the developed nations under the terms contraception, birth control, and family planning, despite considerable disapproval on religious grounds. Abortion, though illegal, was widespread.

By the middle of the 20th century, research began to be channeled toward discovering simple, cheap, and effective methods of avoiding conception. The most widely publicized include the contraceptive pill and the cervical ring. Reasons which contributed to this interest, both private and governmental, grew out of two developments in the United States and some other countries, namely "foreign aid" and "relief" for the needy.

The American policy of foreign aid was premised originally on enabling underdeveloped nations to raise their standard of living so as to combat a feared drift toward Communism. But it soon became apparent that, in many such countries, population was increasing faster than food production. For example, in India and South America per capita food production was less in the 1960's than in the 1930's; the standard of living was falling despite aid from abroad. In 1966, President Johnson, in his state of the union message, called for a new direction in the foreign aid program to help those nations that are trying to control their population growth. India had already called for, and received from the United Nations, assistance in a program for population control. Japan instituted such a program itself after World War II and achieved a 50 per cent drop in the birth rate to the level prevailing in the most advanced nations of Europe and well below that of the United States.

In the United States, the Office of Economic Opportunity, in its "war on poverty," took cognizance of the population problem. In 1965, it made the first grant of funds to assist a community (Corpus Christi, Tex.) in a birth-control program. Such programs were adopted in many other communities as a means of reducing relief payments to the indigent, particularly after the Supreme Court, in 1965, had held unconstitutional a law of 1779 forbidding the use of contraceptive devices.

MASS DESTRUCTION AND ITS AVOIDANCE

July 16, 1945, was a landmark in human history. That was the date of the first explosion of an atomic bomb. Its destructive power, vastly increased by subsequent research, for the first time brought within man's reach the possibility of wiping out a large part of the human race. The United States was the first country to develop the atomic bomb, followed by the hydrogen bomb, but Russia, Britain, France, and China were not far behind. Its production, becoming cheaper, was soon within the capabilities of a dozen more nations.

This new and terrible weapon, besides the secret and untried potentialities of germ warfare, drove home to the world's leaders the urgency of finding means to avoid warfare. Organization of the United Nations was an immediate response. But over and above specific devices, the objective gradually became a fixed motive in responsible national leadership.

This subsection brings together articles explaining details of the menace and of concrete efforts to avoid it.

Atomic Bomb. The Lincoln Library Encyclopedia in the Department of Science explains how, in atomic reactors, the self-reaction is controlled. If the rate of reaction is not carefully controlled, it is possible that the reaction can "run away," i.e. the rate at which energy is liberated becomes so great that an explosion results. Since in building an atomic bomb one actually desires to obtain an explosion, very highly enriched or pure U235 is used in such a device. In order for a self-sustained reaction to be established in U235 however, it is essential that its volume exceed a certain critical size. If the amount of U235 is small, neutrons released in one fission event would be likely to escape from the material before being captured by another nucleus. If, however, the amount of U235 is increased to such a size that the chance of capture by the neutrons exceeds the chance of their escape, the reaction will be self-perpetuating. Once such a reaction is started, the time between the emission of a neutron in one fission event and its capture by another nucleus is only about 1/100,000th of a second; thus an enormous number of fissions can occur within a time as short as 1/1000th of a second with the simultaneous release of a tremendous amount of energy, which of course constitutes an explosion.

The problems faced in building an atomic bomb are the separation of U235 from normal uranium and keeping the pieces of U235 at less than critical size, and then, at the desired time, suddenly uniting these pieces into one of greater than critical size and holding them together long enough to permit the reaction products to build up to high pressure before the casing splits open. The bombs dropped on Japan resulted in temperatures of some 10 million degrees, and the blast produced was equal to that from 20,000 tons of TNT.

Blasts are measured in terms of the explosive power of a ton of TNT. A kiloton is equivalent to 1000 tons of TNT; a megaton, of 1,000,000 tons of TNT. The bombs dropped on Japan in 1945 produced blasts in the order of 20 kilotons. Russia in 1961 exploded a hydrogen bomb of some 100 megatons. Blasts are accompanied by a flash of heat radiation and by the emission of gamma rays and neutrons.

Hydrogen Bomb. The hydrogen bomb differs from the so-called atomic bomb by reason of a difference in the process resulting in the explosion. The atomic bomb uses the fission process, whereby very heavy nuclei break down into lighter ones with a consequent loss of mass and increase of energy. The hydrogen bomb uses the fusion process, in which similar loss of mass and increase of energy accompany the building up of heavier nuclei from lighter ones. It is believed that the fusion process is the source of energy from the sun, in the interior of which temperatures and pressures are very great.

Fusion reactions occur only where there is very high temperature and pressure. The only known means of producing them on the earth is the explosion of an atomic bomb. Even there it appears that the temperature is not high enough to initiate the fusion reaction with the most abundant hydrogen isotope, but the process can work with the heavier hydrogen isotopes, *deuterium* and *tritium*. These isotopes are rare, but means are available to produce them in quantity.

The so-called hydrogen bomb has certain advantages over the fission bomb, in that the materials are less dangerous to handle and store and can be made in any desired size.

Guided Missiles. These are missiles which are self-propelled by means of jet engines. They are guided by electronic impulses, which are usually sent from a control station and act on gyroscopes within the missile to alter the direction. More highly sophisticated ones receive their directional impulses from heat or light waves emanating from the target. The "ancestor" of the guided missile was the V-I robot bomb developed by the Germans near the close of World War II. The missile may be equipped with conventional or atomic explosives.

Guided missiles may be divided into four main groups:

Surface-to-surface. These missiles can be fired from the sea or from the land against targets on land or sea at relatively close or extremely long range.

Surface-to-air. These are anti-aircraft weapons for defense against enemy atom bombers and guided missiles.

Air-to-surface. These are launched from aircraft, and are actually guided aerial bombs which can seek out a target on land or sea, no matter how obscured it may be by atmospheric conditions.

Air-to-air. These guided missiles are for bomber defense against speedy fighting planes, and also for use by interceptors in breaking up enemy bombing attacks.

Some of the successes achieved with American missiles include the shooting down of supersonic missiles by both Bomarc-B and Nike-Hercules surface-to-air missiles, successful firing of Polaris missiles from a submerged submarine, and successful firings of Atlas Intercontinental Ballistic Missiles with ranges up to 9000 miles.

Fallout. One of the consequences of exploding an atomic bomb is the generation of large quantities of radioactive material consisting principally of the fission fragments. When the bomb is exploded, this radioactive material is carried to great heights by the powerful updraft caused by the heat of the explosion. Once carried to such heights, this radioactive material slowly settles back to earth spreading its radioactivity over an extensive area. Depending on the altitude at which the bomb is exploded and the atmospheric conditions during the days following the explosion, the fallout may occur over an area of a few hundred square miles or may fall slowly over a large fraction of the entire earth's surface.

This radioactivity spread over large areas constitutes one of the serious hazards of Atomic Warfare. Long after an atomic bomb has exploded and the immediate effects of the blast and the associated instantaneous radiation are over, the fallout from the explosion continues to generate lethal radiation. Protection against this radiation until such time as its intensity has decayed to a safe level is afforded by underground shelters whose walls and top covering are thick enough to absorb most of the radiation coming from the fallout.

Geiger Counters (*Geiger-Mueller Counters*). A Geiger counter is a device used for the detection of ionizing particles such as those emitted by radioactive materials. Basically the Geiger counter consists of a hollow conducting cylinder along the axis of which, and insulated from it, is mounted a fine wire. This structure is enclosed in a glass envelope which can be evacuated of air and filled to any desired pressure with other gases. A mixture of argon and alcohol vapor at a pressure of from one-tenth to one-fifth of an atmosphere is commonly used. The insulation between the cylinder and the wire is such that a high electric potential (800 to 1200 volts) can be applied between them without producing appreciable flow of charge from cylinder to wire. However, any ionizing particle traversing the counter will initiate an electrical discharge causing a surge of current lasting for about one one hundred thousandth of a second. This current surge can, by the use of the proper electronic circuits, be made to produce a click in a headphone or operate a recording device.

The credit for making the first counters of this type is given to Hans Geiger and Walther Mueller, who produced such counters in 1928. As early as 1908, however, E. Rutherford and Geiger produced a counter similar to the present-day counters.

Chemical Warfare. It is known that incendiary chemicals were used in Greece as early as 1200 B.C. So-called Greek fire was invented about 600 B.C. and was used chiefly in naval warfare and sieges. The poisoning of wells likewise is of great antiquity. Use of poisonous gas (sulphur oxides) is attributed to the Spartans in their siege of Athens in 425 B.C.

In modern times, the Hague Congress of 1907 forbade the use of poisons or poisonous weapons. In World War I, however, at the battle of Ypres in April 1915, chlorine gas was used by the Germans against the French and British. Later in the war, phosgene and mustard gas were used. In the course of the war, about 9 million shells were fired containing mustard gas, producing 400,000 casualties, despite the development and use of gas masks. This was five times as effective in number of casualties as explosive shells, but only two deaths in 100 casualties resulted.

Poison gas was not used in World War II, probably because governments on both sides were known to have large stocks ready to use, but neither side was sure of the nature of the opponents' gases.

While gases used in World War I were confined mainly to blistering gas (mustard), tear gas (chloropicrin), and vomiting gas (chloroarsine), newer types were later developed, known as psychochemicals and nerve gas.

Psychochemicals are derivatives of lysergic acid. One group causes temporary disability, such as blindness, paralysis, or deafness. Another affects the mind by such bizarre effects as producing fear.

Nerve gases are certain organic phosphates which stop the action of the enzyme cholinesterase, this enzyme being essential to the functioning of nerves. The result is accumulation in the body of acetylcholine, causing symptoms similar to those of severe nicotine and curare poisoning.

These highly poisonous substances, almost colorless and odorless, would be released as liquids which immediately vaporize with highest concentration near the ground. The gas may be absorbed into the body by breathing or by entering the skin, particularly through the eyes. Highly concentrated gas, if breathed, results in death in a few seconds. Exposure to even traces causes marked contraction of the eye pupils and of the bronchial tubes. Severe exposure causes irrational behavior; milder cases may show giddiness, tension, anxiety, insomnia, and excessive dreaming. Treatment consists of injection of atropine.

Biological Warfare. Biological warfare has little history although it is recorded that the Tatars in the 14th century took a fortress in Crimea by throwing into it the bodies of victims of the bubonic plague.

Numerous diseases have been studied as to their probable effectiveness in biological warfare by producing maximum losses on the enemy while leaving the user safe. These requirements are difficult to meet. Investigators have concentrated on finding diseases having the following characteristics:

1. The disease must be virulent, easily spread by air but not by insects, and have a short incubation period, the latter to prevent detection of the source by enemy scientists.
2. The causative agent must be such that a small quantity in the laboratory can be multiplied quickly by cultures.
3. The germs to be used must retain their virulence for years, as by refrigeration or dehydration, and, in use, not resist disinfectants and explosions in battle.
4. It must be possible to protect the user by distance or vaccination; the germ should be that of a new disease or a new variant of an old disease so that a vaccine can be developed in advance, while none is available to the enemy.

Prevention of War. Opinion is sharply divided on whether war can be prevented, but there is little disagreement on the point that, unless unlimited war is prevented, the outlook for mankind is bleak.

Those holding that warfare cannot be prevented point to man's biological inheritance of aggressive behavior, which has been an indispensable element in the survival and advancement of the race.

Others, however, call attention to man's biological inheritance of other drives which inhibit such aggression as threatens survival of the group or species. They point to animal habits leading to protection of families, to tolerance or seeming affection toward others in the same social group, and finally to human cultures wherein aggression can be channeled into less destructive courses. A striking example of the latter, it is said, is the competition between the United States and Russia for primacy in space exploration.

Both world wars in the 20th century were followed by efforts to substitute what was felt to be the rule of reason or justice for the rule of force. The outcome after World War I was the League of Nations. After World War II, the United Nations was organized.

United Nations. This international organization was framed at the San Francisco Conference June 26, 1945. It came into being October 24, 1945, when Russia deposited the 29th instrument of ratification.

The highest organs of the UN are the General Assembly and the Security Council. There are four other organs—the Economic and Social Council, the Trusteeship Council, the International Court of Justice, and the Secretariat, headed by the secretary-general. In addition there are many agencies which are associated with the UN and operate under its aegis.

The General Assembly is made up of delegates from all the member nations. Each nation may send five delegates but has only one vote. Important questions require a two-thirds majority of those present and voting. It meets annually, and special sessions my be called by the secretary-general.

The Security Council is made up of five permanent members: The United States, Great Britain, Russia, China, and France; and ten non-permanent members, to be chosen for two years by the General Assembly. With the Security Council rests primary responsibility for action. Decisions require a vote of seven members, including all the permanent members. Herein lies the so-called veto, as any one of these may block action by a negative vote. The Council may intervene in any dispute, or any situation which may endanger international peace. It did intervene in 1950 when Communist North Korea invaded South Korea but was able to do so only because Russia had boycotted the Council and hence was not present to veto the move.

The Economic and Social Council supervises statistics, human rights trade in narcotics, population studies, international trade studies, and the children's fund (UNICEF, or United Nations International Children's Emergency Funds).

The Trusteeship Council supervises territories which may be placed under its protection by agreement with individual countries.

The International Court of Justice, consisting of 15 judges elected by the Security Council and the General Assembly sitting separately. It has jurisdiction over all cases referred to it by governments. There is no enforcement machinery.

The Secretariat is the executive organ of the UN. The secretary-general is elected by the General Assembly. The first incumbent, Norway's Trygve Lie, established precedents for leadership in applying the UN's policing powers for the peaceful settlement of disputes. He served from 1946 to 1953. His successor, Dag Hammarskjold, of Sweden, strengthened still further the role of the secretary-general. He secured a UN military force to act in the Israeli-Egyptian dispute in 1956 and the Congo crisis in 1960. He was killed in a plane accident in 1961.

The next secretary-general was Burmese diplomat U Thant. Thant has been praised for calming tensions in the 1962 Cuban missile confrontation and his handling of the 1964 UN financial crisis, when France and the Communist nations refused their peacekeeping assessments. Thant has been criticized for haste in complying with Egypt's demand for withdrawal of UN forces in the 1967 Sinai conflict with Israel. Also noted is his criticism of U.S. policy in Vietnam, but marked restraint at the Soviet invasion of Czechoslovakia in 1968. On January 1, 1972 Thant's term of office expired, and he was succeeded by Kurt Waldheim of Austria.

Among the numberous international agencies of the UN are the United Nations Educational, Scientific, and Cultural Organization; the International Labor Organization; the World Health Organization; the International Monetary Fund; and the International Bank for Reconstruction and Development with its affiliated International Finance Corporation.

The UN found itself unable to act if the great powers were not in agreement. Its membership grew rapidly with the increase of independent states, many of them too weak to be viable without assistance but each with one vote in the Assembly. Meaningful action became difficult as voting power had little relation to political-military power.

The first part of the first session of the United Nations was held in London, Jan. 9–Feb. 14, 1946. The second part of the session, held at New York, October 23–December 16, 1946, accepted from John D. Rockefeller, Jr., the gift of a site in New York City for its permanent headquarters.

The Security Council was completed at the first session. A Peace Conference in Paris (July 29–Oct. 15) meanwhile approved treaties of peace with Italy, Bulgaria, Rumania, Hungary, and Finland. These were revised by the Council of Foreign Ministers, and signed Feb. 10-15, 1947. The UN grew from the original charter members to a total of 148 by 1976.

NATO. The North Atlantic Treaty Organization grew out of the North Atlantic Treaty, signed in 1949 by Belgium, Canada, Denmark, France, Iceland, Italy, Luxembourg, Netherlands, Norway, Portugal, United Kingdom, and the United States. Greece and Turkey were added in 1951, and West Germany was admitted in 1954. The treaty provided

UNITED NATIONS ROSTER

Nation	Year Admitted	% of UN Budget	Nation	Year Admitted	% of UN Budget	Nation	Year Admitted	% of UN Budget
Afghanistan	1946	0.02	Ghana	1957	0.04	Oman	1971	0.02
Albania	1955	0.02	*Greece	1945	0.32	Pakistan	1947	0.14
Algeria	1962	0.08	Grenada	1974	0.02	*Panama	1945	0.02
Angola	1976	0.02	*Guatemala	1945	0.03	Papua New Guinea	1975	. . .
*Argentina	1945	0.83	Guinea	1958	0.02	*Paraguay	1945	0.02
*Australia	1945	1.44	Guinea-Bissau	1974	0.02	*Peru	1945	0.07
Austria	1955	0.56	Guyana	1966	0.02	*Philippines	1945	0.18
Bahamas	1973	0.02	*Haiti	1945	0.02	*Poland	1945	1.26
Bahrain	1971	0.02	*Honduras	1945	0.02	Portugal	1955	0.15
Bangladesh	1971	0.02	Hungary	1955	0.33	Qatar	1971	0.02
Barbados	1966	0.02	Iceland	1946	0.02	Rumania	1955	0.30
*Belgium	1945	1.05	*India	1945	1.20	Rwanda	1962	0.02
Benin (Dahomey)	1960	0.02	Indonesia[2]	1950	0.19	Sao Tome and		
Bhutan	1971	0.02	*Iran	1945	0.20	Principe	1975	. . .
*Bolivia	1945	0.02	*Iraq	1945	0.05	*Saudi Arabia	1945	0.06
Botswana	1966	0.02	Irish Republic (Eire)	1955	0.15	Senegal	1960	0.02
*Brazil	1945	0.77	Israel	1949	0.21	Seychelles	1976	0.02
Bulgaria	1955	0.14	Italy	1955	3.60	Sierra Leone	1961	0.02
Burma	1948	0.02	Ivory Coast	1960	0.02	Singapore	1965	0.04
Burundi	1962	0.02	Jamaica	1962	0.02	Somali Rep.		
*Byelorussia	1945	0.50	Japan	1956	7.15	(Somalia)	1960	0.02
Cambodia†			Jordan	1955	0.02	*South Africa	1945	0.50
(Khmer Rep.)	1955	0.02	Kenya	1963	0.02	Spain	1955	0.99
Cameroon	1960	0.02	Kuwait	1963	0.09	Sri Lanka (Ceylon)	1955	0.03
*Canada	1945	3.18	Laos	1955	0.02	Sudan	1956	0.02
Cape Verde	1975	. . .	*Lebanon	1945	0.03	Surinam	1975	. . .
Central African Emp.	1960	0.02	Lesotho	1966	0.02	Swaziland	1968	0.02
Chad	1960	0.02	*Liberia	1945	0.02	Sweden	1946	1.30
*Chile	1945	0.14	Libya	1955	0.11	*Syria	1945	0.02
China, Mainland[1]	1971	5.50	*Luxembourg	1945	0.04	Tanzania	1961	0.02
*Colombia	1945	0.16	Malagasy Rep.			Thailand	1946	0.11
Comoro Islands	1975	. . .	(Madagascar)	1960	0.02	Togo	1960	0.02
Congo Republic	1960	0.02	Malawi	1964	0.02	Trinidad and Tobago	1962	0.02
*Costa Rica	1945	0.02	Malaysia	1957	0.07	Tunisia	1956	0.02
*Cuba	1945	0.11	Maldives,			*Turkey	1945	0.29
Cyprus	1960	0.02	Republic of	1965	0.02	Uganda	1962	0.02
*Czechoslovakia	1945	0.89	Mali	1960	0.02	*Ukraine	1945	1.71
*Denmark	1945	0.63	Malta	1964	0.02	*USSR	1945	12.97
*Dominican Republic	1945	0.02	Mauritania	1961	0.02	United Arab		
*Ecuador	1945	0.02	Mauritius	1968		Emirates	1971	0.02
*Egypt	1945	0.12	*Mexico	1945	0.86	*United Kingdom	1945	5.31
*El Salvador	1945	0.02	Mongolia	1961	0.02	*United States	1945	25.00
Equatorial Guinea	1968	0.02	Morocco	1956	0.06	Upper Volta	1960	0.02
*Ethiopia	1945	0.02	Mozambique	1975	0.02	*Uruguay	1945	0.06
Fiji	1970	0.02	Nepal	1955	0.02	*Venezuela	1945	0.32
Finland	1955	0.42	*Netherlands	1945	1.24	Western Samoa	1976	0.02
*France	1945	5.86	*New Zealand	1945	0.28	Yemen	1947	0.02
Gabon	1960	0.02	*Nicaragua	1945	0.02	Yemen (Southern)	1967	0.02
Gambia	1965	0.02	Niger	1960	0.02	*Yugoslavia	1945	0.34
Germany, East	1973	1.22	Nigeria	1960	0.10	Zaire	1960	0.02
Germany, West	1973	7.10	*Norway	1945	0.43	Zambia	1964	0.02

* Charter members. [1] National China voted out, 1971. [2] Indonesia resigned, 1965; readmitted, 1966. Other political units, though not members, take part in some UN functions, including the International Court of Justice, regional economic commissions, and international control of narcotics traffic; they are the Holy See, Liechtenstein, Monaco, Korea, San Marino, Switzerland. † Cambodia closed its UN mission Apr. 29, 1975.

for forming the organization, which evolved by 1954. Its purpose was to combat Communist expansion by military, economic, and political means.

The heart of the agreement is the "trigger clause" which provides that an armed attack against one or more members is to be considered an attack against all and that all members will take action to restore and maintain the security of the Atlantic area. The agreement, however, envisioned more than a defensive alliance; it provided for a military force to which each member was obligated to contribute.

The head of NATO is the North Atlantic Council, meeting in continuous session, with a secretary-general and his secretariat of civil servants. To the Council is responsible the military committee, which oversees regional commands, the most important of which is the supreme allied command in Europe.

Although each member was under obligation to supply certain military forces, the total actually contributed was short of an adequate defense against Russian military power. NATO, therefore, in practice depended in large part on the power of the U.S. to use the atomic bomb as at least a deterrent against Communist aggression. NATO ground forces meanwhile were supplied with tactical atomic weapons.

The military forces at NATO's disposal were far below the levels which members were under obligation to supply. France at first excused itself on the plea of the need for troops in its wars in Indo-China and Algeria, and Great Britain also withdrew troops for use in Southeastern Asia. France later withdrew its fleet and troops, objecting in principle to permitting NATO to exercise authority over them. Finally, in 1966, France required NATO to withdraw troops from its territory, although claiming protection of NATO in the event of need. NATO's headquarters were withdrawn and relocated in Belgium. The other members regarded France as having withdrawn, while declaring that it might in the future resume its membership.

OAS. The Organization of American States is an international protective body consisting of the 21 republics in the Western Hemisphere. Its origin may be traced to a treaty of reciprocal assistance signed at Rio de Janeiro in 1947, which amounted to the continentalization of the Monroe Doctrine.

The Organization's charter was signed in Bogota, Colombia, on April 30, 1948, and was ratified December 31, 1951. It replaced the former Union of American Republics. Its supreme organ is the Inter-American Conference, with equal representation for each member. It meets every five years. Equal in authority is the meeting of consultations of foreign ministers to consider problems of common interest to members. These include armed attacks or acts of aggression within the territory of an American republic. It was this body which supported American action against Cuba when Russia was installing rocket pads in 1962 and which voted sanctions against Cuba for subversion in neighboring states in 1964. The third organ is the council, which acts as an executive committee.

Armament Limitation. The objective of preventing or restricting wars through limitation of armaments possibly had its seeds in early Christianity. War was considered sinful. The Jews, in their early wars with the Romans, refused to fight on the Sabbath. By the medieval "truce of God," the Church attempted to persuade combatants to desist from warfare on week ends and during Lent. The Dutch jurist Hugo Grotius in 1625 first formulated the idea of a law of nations created by international agreement. The Quakers in the 17th century returned to the Christian idea of the sinfulness of war. More practical peace lovers sought to mitigate the horrors of war, as exemplified by the Geneva conventions of 1864 and 1868, which laid down rules for the status of the Red Cross, ambulances, and treatment of wounded soldiers. The rules were eventually signed and ratified by over 50 nations.

Hague conferences in 1899 and 1907 extended these rules and for the first time took up the question of disarmament by agreement. In 1912, Great Britain tried to negotiate a "naval holiday" with Germany. The attempt failed. World War I soon followed. Armament limitation was imposed on Germany by treaty. In 1921, the U. S. called a conference on naval limitation. The Washington conference secured agreement on limiting capital ships by the U. S., Great Britain, Japan, France, and Italy. This agreement was broadened by a London conference in 1930. Shortly thereafter Japan withdrew and began a policy of aggrandizement in Asia. Germany tore up the treaty for limiting its armament. World War II was on the way.

Postwar Moves. When the United Nations was organized in San Francisco in 1945, it set up a permanent committee on disarmament. There was then a new urgency for limiting arms since arms now included the atomic bomb. The committee on disarmament met repeatedly, and the United States appointed some of its ablest citizens to negotiate limitation of armament and particularly control of atomic weapons. It was nearly 20 years before the first modest concrete results were evident—a treaty in 1963 for partial limitation in testing atomic weapons. Of the five countries with atomic weapons, the United States, Russia, and Great Britain signed, while France and China refused.

Main disagreement on which Russian-American negotiations stalled related to the matter of inspection and enforcement. A measure of inspection became possible without agreement by the development of so-called spy satellites. But little progress was made in respect of enforcement.

Despite these difficulties, a certain stability was achieved in the postwar years by what Winston Churchill called the balance of terror. When two or more powers are able to destroy each other in a few hours, each backs away from the brink.

Foreign Aid. The U. S. in 1946 adopted a policy of extending economic and military aid to other countries with the primary objective of maintaining world peace. This policy was begun at the beginning of the so-called cold war when Russia was proclaiming a program for spreading Communism throughout the world. It was believed that economic aid would combat the appeal of the new gospel of revolution by relieving poverty and misery.

The policy was successful in Western Europe, which had the world's largest skilled and politically mature population and the largest concentration of capital. There Communism's appeal diminished almost to the vanishing point, and early threats of aggression died in their tracks. Its success was less obvious in countries emerging from tribal organization with little capital and no political experience. The growth of economic well-being in such countries was undercut by rapid growth of population.

The success of foreign aid was attested by the fact that Russia and Communist China imitated it for a while in wooing underdeveloped countries in Africa and Asia, and even Latin America. Other countries followed, partly to advance their influence and prestige, partly to reduce poverty and dissatisfaction as a cause of war, and partly for humanitarian purposes. Participants included Canada, West Germany, Japan, Israel, Czechoslovakia, and East Germany. France and Great Britain contributed aid on a large scale to make viable nations of their former colonies. Of great significance also were the credit organs of the United Nations, notably the Bank for Reconstruction and Development.

Over the 18-year period from World War II to the beginning of 1964, the United States contributed outright in military and economic aid a total of nearly $104 billion. One unplanned benefit was making available to many nations dollar currency as a reserve against which local currency was issued. The dollar thus, like the British pound, supplemented gold as a basis for support of international trade.

ENVIRONMENTAL ACTION

Assuming that civilization solves the problem of intolerable overcrowding by reaching and holding to a stable population plateau and that it avoids atomic war, its most pressing problem is maintaining a tolerable condition of life for its teeming billions.

This means, as a minimum, avoiding starvation by a vast increase in food supply, provision of water for consumption and other uses, and avoiding contamination of the air. Over and above this minimum, welfare advancement entails meeting the other needs and demands of a much larger population—housing, power and fuel, transportation, communication, education, and, above all, interests which make life worth living. All this must be provided in an environment fixed by the habitable portion of the earth and from resources limited to what the earth and sea provide. Furthermore, it must be provided soon. The promise of success lies partly in science and its applications but depends also on adaptation of customs and outlook. Above all, it depends on government. The optimists point out that the processes of evaluation have produced successful adaptations that not even the wildest imagination could have foreseen. Pessimists point out that many species have failed to adapt to new conditions and have disappeared. This subsection confines itself in part to articles showing the magnitude of the various problems involved and steps which have been taken to solve them.

Water Supply and Pollution Control. Water (H_2O) is absolutely essential to all life as we know it. Without water, the entire vegetable and animal kingdoms would quickly perish, and the teeming earth would soon become as lifeless as the moon. To avoid an impending water crisis, governments and scientists turned their attention to four kinds of solutions (see *Water*, in Chemistry section). Since the 1960's, research efforts have been primarily on pollution control and saline (salt) water conversion.

Pollution Control. Despite the vast quantity of water on earth, nowhere does it occur as pure H_2O. It always contains dissolved substances. The definition of "pollution" is, therefore, difficult. However, for practical purposes, it is useful to think of polluted water as that containing substances in solution, or suspension, in quantities which make the water unfit for the use desired.

Pollution of fresh water comes chiefly from untreated or inadequately treated sewage and from industrial wastes. The pollution may be so intense that resultant biological and chemical reactions deplete the dissolved oxygen in the water to the point where aquatic life is killed in the vicinity of the discharge. Between the point of discharge and the zone of recovery, pollution exacts its esthetic and economic toll and imposes a threat to the public health. Recovery occurs as the result of dilution of the wastes, aeration of the water by stream flow or wind action, and, primarily, through the assimilation of the wastes by microorganisms.

Sewage Treatment. Almost all sewage treatment processes take advantage of this ability of microorganisms to convert wastes into relatively innocuous products. Thus sewage treatment plants may be thought of as "condensed rivers," in which the microorganisms are cultured and given engineering and scientific support to exert a vigorous attack upon the wastes. In most such processes, large quantities of air must be pumped into the sewage to supply the dissolved oxygen required by the microorganisms. Excess quantities of the microorganisms and solid materials settled from the sewage are usually taken to a digester where anaerobic microorganisms convert them to inert, solid wastes for disposal as land fill. The treated liquid wastes are sometimes disinfected with chlorine prior to discharge to surface waters. A modern complete sewage treatment plant removes between 85 and 95 per cent of the organic wastes present in domestic sewage.

As cities have grown in population, it has been necessary to increase the degree of sewage treatment provided in order to protect the surface waters. The improved treatment more completely reduces the sewage to inorganic minerals. Among these minerals are dissolved nitrate and phosphate, which are excellent plant nutrients, or fertilizers. Additional large quantities of phosphate are added to sewage through the constantly increasing use of phosphate-rich detergents in homes and industry.

However, these fertilizing substances have created a new type of pollution. Because of the more intensive sewage treatment, the receiving waters are clearer. Sunlight more easily penetrates, and photosynthetic organisms, mostly algae, use the substances to proliferate. Undesirable, explosive growths of these organisms occur. They soon die, imposing a heavy oxygen demand on the stream and, except for the public health aspect, can create conditions just as objectionable as if the sewage had not been treated. The problem has become acute in many of the world's famous lakes and rivers, including Lake Geneva, Lake Erie, Lake Tahoe, and the Potomac River.

Industrial Waste. Industrial wastes constitute the other large source of contamination in bodies of fresh water. Oil, sulfite from paper mills, acid mine wastes, steel mill wastes, organic and inorganic compounds from chemical plants, slaughterhouse wastes, brewery wastes, and many other types of industrial wastes, including heat, are not easily removed or treated. Some of these wastes contain newly developed chemicals for which little or no information on treatment exists. Others, even after extensive research, defy treatment. Control of industrial wastes at the source, pretreatment before discharge to municipal sewers, and special, complete treatment at the industrial site are the three principal methods used in combating this problem.

Governmental Action. While scientific studies may discover successful waste treatment processes and practices, their effectiveness is dependent on governmental action restraining abuses by municipalities and industrial firms. Congress passed the Water Pollution Control Act in 1948 which authorized matching Federal grants for construction of municipal facilities for waste treatment by virtue of the Federal government's jurisdiction over interstate waterways. Subsequent acts of Congress, in 1956, 1961, and 1965, made the program permanent, expanded it in the enforcement, research, and construction grant areas, and provided a mechanism for establishing water quality standards. As of the middle of 1966, 39 enforcement actions against municipalities and industries had been initiated. The moral effect was much wider, leading to policies adopted by numerous municipalities and industrial corporations to find feasible means of avoiding pollution of public waters. As a further intensification of the water pollution program, in 1966, at the specific request of the President, a new Federal Water Pollution Control Administration was established within the Department of the Interior. Water pollution control activities and personnel, previously centered within the Department of Health, Education and Welfare, were transferred to the new agency which was charged with instituting a program to clean up the Nation's rivers, lakes, and estuaries.

Desalination. The Office of Saline Water was created by Congress in 1952 to focus attention and support research on this potential method for increasing the world's fresh water supply. Countries with desert areas near the sea, like Israel and Saudi Arabia, have already established desalination plants, of which some 200 small installations were in operation throughout the world by 1966. A dramatic example is the plant which the United States Navy set up in Guantanamo, Cuba, to make the naval base independent of the Cuban water supply.

The United States took the lead in research on saline water conversion chiefly because of the water needs of its highly developed industry. American industry requires many times as much water as the population uses for personal requirements. Moreover, the water thus used must frequently be purer than water tolerable for drinking.

With the aid of government subsidies, a dozen or more firms developed pilot plants for desalination with a view toward improving the economics of the various processes used. The following are the principal methods found to be feasible technically:

1. *Distillation.* This is the oldest method, described for shipboard use by Thomas Jefferson. A number of different distillation methods are in use and under development. Simplest is the solar still. Such an installation is operated in Smyrna, Syria, where the sun's rays, passing through a plastic curtain covering a shallow basin, evaporate the water, which condenses on the under side of the curtain and runs into storage tanks.

In another distillation process, salt water is passed through evaporator units connected in series so that the condensed steam from each unit heats the water in the next. Another variation, known as flash distillation, heats saline water to a point just below boiling and then introduces it into a compartment at lower pressure. Part of the water immediately vaporizes; the rest runs into a chamber at still lower pressure, and additional water is vaporized.

2. *Freezing.* The salt water is chilled until ice crystals are formed. As water freezes, it tends to exclude impurities. Thus, the ice is free of salt and, when collected and melted, produces fresh water.

3. *Electrodialysis.* In this process, salt water is placed in a vat divided into a number of compartments by special plastic membranes. An electric current is passed through the water, causing the positive- and negative-charged ions of the dissolved salts to move toward their respective opposite poles. Some of the membranes permit passage of positive ions only and others permit only negative ions to pass. The membranes are alternately spaced. In moving toward their respective poles, ions of both charges are trapped in alternate compartments. Thus, the water in every other compartment gradually becomes fresh, while that in the others becomes very salty. The fresh water is then collected.

4. *Reverse Osmosis.* If a membrane permeable to water, but not to dissolved salts, is placed between sea water and fresh water, the latter will penetrate the membrane and diffuse into the sea water. The osmotic pressure exerted by the sea water is approximately 350 pounds per square inch and is the force driving the fresh water through the membrane. The exertion of a pressure on the sea water exceeding the osmotic pressure will cause the fresh water flow to reverse. That is, fresh water will be forced through the membrane from the sea water compartment into the fresh water compartment where it will accumulate.

Common to all the processes is a requirement for large amounts of energy. Hence the economic feasibility of conversion in competition with other sources of fresh water depends largely on the cost of power. One disadvantage of saline water conversion which places an additional power requirement on all conversion systems is that sea water, of course, occurs at sea level. Thus, the water must be pumped to its point of use. Stream water, on the other hand, is generally trapped in a reservoir at an altitude high enough to take considerable advantage of gravity for distribution.

Air Pollution. This may be defined as the excessive concentration of foreign matter in the air which adversely affects the well-being of the individual or causes damage to property. This definition, formulated by the American Medical Association in 1949, is significant by its timing. It was not until far into the 20th century that the complex nature of air pollution was recognized.

The occasions for its recognition were dramatic. In such widely separated industrial cities as Liége (Belgium), Donora (Pa.), and London (England), the atmosphere suddenly became and remained for several days irritating to breathe; a number of deaths were attributed to it. Los Angeles, Calif., whose encircling mountains screen it from winds to an unusual degree, was periodically afflicted by air contamination irritating to eyes and throat. Popularly supposed to be caused by smoke and fog, the condition was described by the newly coined word smog. But the condition was not confined to Los Angeles. It was soon reported in many other industrial centers.

Smoke Nuisance. Smoke nuisance has a respectable antiquity, as such things go. At the turn of the century, the French engineer Maximilian Ringelmann constructed a chart of smoke density, and this was made the basis of smoke evaluation in many ordinances in the United States. By 1955, it was estimated that there were 9500 communities in the country which had local air-pollution problems and that 2050 had specific legislation on the subject.

The definition given above, which includes as pollution factors any foreign matter in the air adversely affecting the individual, is very broad. Besides clearly toxic substances, it includes also a large number which are unpleasant and annoying but not toxic, such as dust and pollen, and others which may produce harmful effects after long exposure to concentrations above a certain point.

The following table lists the seven chief classes of air contaminants with important examples of each:

Air Contaminants

Group	Examples
Solids	Carbon, fly ash, ZnO, $PbCl_2$
Sulfur compounds	SO_2, H_2SO_4, H_2S, mercaptans
Organic Compounds	Aldehydes, hydrocarbons, tars
Nitrogen compounds	NO, NO_2, NH_3
Oxygen compounds	O_3, CO, CO_2
Halogen compounds	HF, HCl
Radioactive compounds	Radioactive gases, aerosols

Even these substances, if present in extremely small quantities, would not constitute contaminants since they would not, as far as known, adversely affect the individual. For some of them, tentative standards have been arrived at for determining the maximum allowable concentration in the air before the substances would have such effect. For each class, three different stages of concentration are set under the heads of warning, alert, and danger, the concentrations being expressed in parts per million. The table below gives such standards set for Los Angeles.

Maximum Allowable Concentration in Parts per Million

Pollutant	Warning	Alert	Danger
Oxides of nitrogen	3.0	5.0	10.0
Ozone	0.5	1.0	1.5
Sulfur dioxide	3.0	5.0	10.0
Carbon monoxide	100.0	200.0	300.0

Property Damage. It should be emphasized that these and similar standards are purely tentative and apply to human beings. The effect of air contaminants in damaging property is more easily assessed. Certain ones cause harm to fabrics, metals, and buildings, and are observable in every metropolitan area. There is concern also over the effect of air pollution on the operation of airplanes and ground transportation. Effects on plants and animals also may be observed and measured.

AIR POLLUTION—NATIONAL AIR SAMPLING LEVELS, SELECTED CITIES: 1968

[**In micrograms per cubic meter.** Air pollution is defined as the presence in the air of substances put there by the activities of man, in concentrations sufficient to interfere with comfort, safety, or health or with use and enjoyment of property. Data represent values of samples taken nationally on a biweekly basis by the National Air Pollution Control Administration.]

STATION		SUSPENDED PARTICULATE MATTER [1]			BENZENE-SOLUBLE ORGANIC MATTER [2]				
		Min.	Max.	Arith. avg.	1st qtr.	2d qtr.	3d qtr.	4th qtr.	Arith. avg.
Arizona	Phoenix	68	284	150	13.8	6.4	6.9	20.5	11.9
California	Los Angeles	63	272	135	17.6	8.6	9.9	23.7	15.0
	Oakland	42	248	92	11.5	3.8	4.8	7.6	6.9
	San Diego	27	161	69	4.3	2.1	3.4	14.0	6.0
	San Francisco	30	163	92	10.6	4.6	5.0	10.6	7.7
Colorado	Denver	36	471	131	19.5	6.8	9.4	15.3	13.1
Connecticut	Hartford	28	165	67	6.2	3.2	4.0	4.5	4.5
	New Haven	32	145	74	4.9	4.3	4.7	5.9	5.0
Delaware	Wilmington	79	261	125	11.9	7.3	7.3	8.7	8.8
Dist. of Columbia	Washington	27	176	92	7.6	6.3	6.4	7.8	7.0
Florida	Miami	22	94	49	(NA)	(NA)	(NA)	(NA)	(NA)
Georgia	Atlanta	23	181	90	7.2	5.6	5.6	33.5	13.0
Hawaii	Honolulu	24	83	45	2.7	2.3	2.2	3.8	2.8
Idaho	Boise	25	154	67	7.9	3.1	4.5	5.7	5.3
Illinois	Chicago	44	257	124	9.1	7.1	6.4	7.0	7.4
Indiana	Indianapolis	65	252	128	7.8	8.0	10.5	8.6	8.7
Iowa	Des Moines	43	240	100	5.1	3.8	4.6	4.0	4.4
Kansas	Wichita	25	96	60	3.2	2.5	3.2	4.6	3.4
Kentucky	Louisville	74	415	176	8.9	6.9	6.5	9.1	7.9
Louisiana	New Orleans	51	150	87	9.0	8.5	9.1	8.2	8.7
Maryland	Baltimore	36	276	110	9.6	4.5	7.9	8.1	7.5
Michigan	Detroit	42	300	154	10.7	4.9	5.5	8.3	7.4
Minnesota	Minneapolis	28	361	84	4.1	4.3	3.6	4.6	4.2
	St. Paul	31	307	104	6.9	5.4	4.8	4.9	5.5
Mississippi	Jackson	28	154	80	6.4	5.5	4.6	7.8	6.1
Missouri	Kansas City	25	242	105	6.1	4.0	6.9	9.0	6.5
	St. Louis	45	378	148	(NA)	NA)	(NA)	(NA)	(NA)
Montana	Helena	12	202	52	5.0	1.3	2.8	2.5	2.9
Nebraska	Omaha	57	353	151	7.6	9.9	6.8	5.0	7.3
Nevada	Las Vegas	51	190	108	8.5	4.9	3.5	12.3	7.3
New Hampshire	Concord	12	88	39	5.6	2.6	2.2	2.3	3.2
New Jersey	Newark	32	200	93	9.5	6.8	5.8	6.1	7.1
New York	New York	49	241	127	8.9	10.3	9.8	8.5	9.3
	Rochester	38	275	116	8.9	9.8	6.9	5.1	7.5
North Carolina	Charlotte	42	492	130	17.1	4.4	5.1	7.2	8.5
North Dakota	Bismarck	27	256	84	3.8	3.1	2.6	4.0	3.4
Ohio	Cincinnati	31	227	110	12.4	5.9	4.9	4.9	7.0
	Cleveland	50	233	139	9.4	7.0	8.1	6.1	7.7
	Columbus	38	147	96	6.1	5.1	3.7	6.2	5.3
Oklahoma	Oklahoma City	21	105	53	3.7	2.8	2.9	4.7	3.5
Oregon	Portland	16	327	79	8.8	3.9	5.1	7.2	6.3
Pennsylvania	Philadelphia	24	331	125	11.8	7.2	7.8	7.0	8.5
	Pittsburgh	69	385	180	11.9	9.8	7.1	8.2	9.3
Rhode Island	Providence	47	167	92	8.9	6.6	6.1	6.1	6.9
South Dakota	Sioux Falls	23	392	69	5.9	3.3	2.3	2.8	3.6
Tennessee	Memphis	22	187	81	6.9	4.2	4.5	3.7	4.8
	Nashville	43	306	116	11.6	8.8	7.1	11.2	9.7
Texas	Dallas	27	152	76	6.4	3.6	4.6	7.1	5.4
	Houston	49	194	79	4.5	2.7	4.0	8.6	5.0
	San Antonio	28	196	63	4.2	3.0	2.9	7.6	4.4
Utah	Salt Lake City	23	206	76	5.9	1.9	2.4	4.5	3.7
Vermont	Burlington [3]	19	77	44	3.5	1.9	2.4	2.4	2.6
Virginia	Norfolk	46	172	101	8.2	4.6	3.9	5.8	5.6
Washington	Seattle	30	210	73	9.3	2.9	5.5	8.0	6.4
West Virginia	Charleston	43	977	306	8.7	5.1	4.3	6.2	6.1
Wisconsin	Milwaukee	49	433	162	7.4	6.0	4.8	8.6	6.7
Wyoming	Cheyenne	12	99	32	2.3	2.1	1.6	2.6	2.2

NA Not available.
[1] Particles of smoke, dust, and fumes and droplets of viscous liquid remaining in the air for varying periods of time and ranging from less than 1 micron (1/25,000 inch) to 100 microns.
[2] Particulate matter soluble in benzene.
[3] 1967 data.
Source: Department of Health, Education, and Welfare, Public Health Service; annual report, *Air Quality Data*.

Sometimes much lower concentrations than with human beings may be deleterious to plants. For example, about 1946, a smelter in the Columbia River Valley set up an operating regime to prevent damage to crops in the region. It operated on the basis that plants sensitive to sulfur dioxide could stand prolonged exposure of 0.2 to 0.3 parts per million without apparent ill effect. A limit of 0.5 part per million, generally considered as allowable during the growing season, is 80 percent smaller than the limit of concentration at which human beings should be warned.

Besides sulfur dioxide, the most common air contaminants affecting plants are hydrogen fluoride and oxidizing smogs that contain ozone and organic peroxides. Several other compounds, particularly mercury, ammonia, chlorine, hydrogen sulfide, carbon monoxide, and the growth regulating substances which are used as herbicides may cause injury to plants when present in the atmosphere. When toxic concentrations are present, the more highly sensitive plants may be useful in monitoring the pollution.

Cattle are susceptible to fluorosis in regions where the air is contaminated by fluorides released in the reduction of phosphate fertilizers and aluminum, the smelting of some ores, and the manufacture of clay products. Fluorosis is caused when the cattle eat food affected by the fluorides. Its symptoms include overgrowth of the bones, and it is fatal unless the affected food is removed when the first symptoms appear in the teeth.

As in the case of fluorides, most toxic pollutants of the air are industrial by-products. Besides smoke, they include gases, fumes, acids, and other substances listed in the tables above. In addition, however, automobile exhausts contribute. Some investigators consider these as a contributing cause of lung cancer, for which cigarette smoke has been widely blamed.

Radioactive Substance. Another pollutant which has obtained wide publicity is radioactive substances resulting chiefly from atomic explosions in the air and exhaust from reactors. The radioactive material may be taken in by breathing or by eating contaminated food. The task of setting standards and applying them in regulations is extremely complex since the scores of radioactive isotopes differ widely in their effects, have different rates of decay, and affect different plants, animals, and individual organs at different thresholds. Discernible harmful effects may be long delayed or appear only in a succeeding generation. The Atomic Energy Commission is charged with monitoring this potentially dangerous pollutant. Concentration is measured in units of exposure expressed as microcuries per cubic centimeter of air averaged over a period of a year.

Difficulties in Prevention. Prevention of air pollution is an extremely difficult task for a number of reasons, chief of which are:

1. Determination of the immediate effects on individuals. Dramatic episodes are usually past before the offending pollutants (often several in number) can be identified and the sufferers can be examined.
2. Difficulties in determining delayed effects on individuals since these cannot be kept under continuing observation.
3. Difficulty in measuring nuisance and discomfort. These vary with custom. Conditions giving rise to smells that are tolerated in cities without plumbing and sewage disposal would be intolerable in cities long accustomed to these improvements.
4. Difficulty in determining local meteorological conditions which affect concentration of pollutants. Frequently in the winter months a dense layer of colder air at ground level is overlain with lighter, warmer air, thus inverting buoyancy conditions and keeping the lower polluted air unchanged. This is particularly serious where, as in Los Angeles, the topography inhibits winds which would otherwise correct the situation.

Means of Control. While means are known and equipment can be made to control emission of most pollutants from industrial plants, the application of control is less simple. This is partly due to the lack of precise knowledge of the degree of protection required in a given situation and partly also to the problems of legislation and enforcement, particularly as air pollution does not respect boundaries of legal jurisdiction. Since control may be very expensive, it is often a matter of balancing the risk of harm against the cost of safety.

Legal control may be punitive or regulatory or both. An example of the punitive type is an ordinance which forbids, under penalties, the burning of fuels that do not conform to specific standards. Nearly all states have legislation to control air pollution. The emphasis is usually placed on regulations requiring establishments to use equipment which prevents the emission of solids, gases, liquids, and vapors known to be harmful.

The United States Congress passed in 1954 a Pollution Control Act authorizing co-operation of the Public Health Service with other agencies. In 1963, the Clean Air Act extended enforcement powers to the Service. The Environmental Protection Agency was established in 1970, and several major environmental agencies were transferred to EPA. Even so, voluntary efforts by industry play a major role in avoiding air contamination.

Food Supply. Procurement of food is the major occupation of all animals in the wild state. Special techniques devised by man, however, such as agriculture and husbandry, not only removed most of the hazards in the food procurement but left him a larger portion of time for other pursuits; particularly it made possible the multiplication of the human population.

It is estimated that, taking the world as a whole, one half of human labor goes into the production of food. But this statement conceals striking contrasts between different peoples and nations. Against an estimate of 80 per cent of labor for producing of food in China or Africa, there is set about 5 per cent in the better developed countries. This proportion, in fact, may be considered one of the indexes of a developed country.

Malthus (1766–1834), looking at mankind as a whole, predicted that the human race was headed for disaster since population tends to increase at a geometric rate (like 2, 4, 8), while food production could be increased only at an arithmetic rate (like 2, 3, 4). He foresaw famine ahead. What he did not foresee was the harnessing of science to human needs in the more advanced countries: that efficient methods would supplant primitive culture; that machine power in agriculture would replace food-consuming animal power and lighten the demands on man power; that greatly superior plants and food animals would be produced by genetic research; and that chemistry would address itself to making food from substances that were not food. In the developed countries, food surpluses appeared, and the Malthusian prophecies of doom were forgotten.

NeoMalthusianism. A new factor entered the picture by the middle of the 20th century when medical science had cut the death rate drastically in both developed and undeveloped countries but the birth rate was little affected. Population mounted rapidly. The facts were widely publicized and the ideas of Malthus were disinterred.

A study in 1964 by the U. S. department of agriculture (*The World Food Budget*, 1970) pointed out that, over wide regions, food production was not keeping pace with population growth. In Latin America, for example, the food production per capita had fallen three per cent in the 1950's. The world's two largest countries, Communist China and India, were forced to import record quantities of grain to avoid famine in the mid-1960's. These are parts of the world in which the techniques of food production which had brought surpluses in the developed countries were not yet applied. The application was retarded in part by social customs and conservatism, in part by lack of capital to procure machinery and fertilizers, and in part, perhaps, by a lack of energy due to an already inadequate supply of food.

This last point has two aspects. In the matter of quality of food, the study quoted above points out that two-thirds of the world's population subsists on a diet lacking in high quality proteins. Such proteins come chiefly from farm animals and fish. Farm animals require much cultivated land which can be used to grow food directly consumed by human beings. In terms of calories, they are expensive. In China, for example, cultivated land is used almost exclusively for raising starchy foods that feed more mouths at the expense of a balanced diet.

In the matter of quantity also, the less developed countries suffer by comparison with those more advanced. It was found that the intake of calories varied from less than 2000 per capita in India and Peru to more than 3000 in the United States, Canada, Great Britain, Switzerland, Denmark, Australia, and New Zealand.

If the present is compared with earlier ages, it may be said that failure of the food supply so as to result in famine has largely disappeared. This is due chiefly to ease of transportation today since surpluses in some areas can be readily shipped to areas of crop failures. The question mark of the future, as stated by the Food and Agriculture Organization of the United Nations, is whether the total food resources could be enlarged rapidly enough to keep pace with demand of rapidly rising populations so as to avoid world-wide shortages and resulting famine.

Meanwhile public and private research was pushed in such areas as pest control, plant breeding, fertilizers, food synthesis, and farming of the sea's food resources. The key factor, however, in adequacy of food supply remained the control of population.

Fertilizers. The use of fertilizers probably goes back to the earliest stages of agriculture. The Romans were familiar with crop rotation, the use of manure, adding lime to acid soil, and growing legumes to fix nitrogen in the soil. The Chinese from time immemorial have used human as well as animal waste to increase crop yields. In the early 19th century, plant physiologists of Switzerland and Germany had shown that "artificial manures" could be made. The first fertilizer factory was established in 1843 at Rothamsted, Eng. From this beginning, inorganic fertilizers found an increasingly important place beside the "natural," or organic, fertilizers; in many parts of the world they are relied on almost exclusively because of greater availability, economy, and ease in handling. It is estimated that 20 per cent of the food production in the United States is due to the use of fertilizers.

Essential Elements. The three most essential elements in plant growth required in fertilizers are nitrogen, phosphorus, and potassium. Minor requirements are calcium, magnesium, sulphur, and about ten other so-called trace elements. Organic sources of nitrogen are chiefly waste and sewage; inorganic sources are saltpeter and ammonia compounds made from nitrogen drawn from the air. Phosphorus fertilizers come from animal bones and are manufactured from phosphate rocks, the principal supplies being in Morocco, Florida, and Russia. Organic sources of potassium fertilizers are manure and wood ashes; the inorganic sources are potassium oxide (K_2O) obtained from soluble salt deposits, which are found most abundantly in Germany, Russia, Israel, the United States, and France.

Inorganic fertilizers are usually marketed as mixtures in which the proportions of the elements are indicated by numbers arranged in the order of nitrogen, phosphorus, and potash. Thus 5–10–5 means a mixture in which, for each five pounds of nitrogen content, there are 10 pounds of phosphorus content and five pounds of potash content. Some mixtures also contain other elements in addition.

It is difficult to exaggerate the importance of fertilizers in the world's agriculture. Theoretically, their use could make production independent of the natural fertility of the soil. In those countries where they are applied plentifully and scientifically, agriculture is highly efficient and only a small proportion of the working population is required to raise the crops.

Conservation. This term is applied to a movement espoused by President Theodore Roosevelt to prevent waste of natural resources and spoliation of scenic beauty. Its early apostle was Gifford Pinchot (1865-1946). Initially it took the form of public acquisition of land for national forests and parks and reservation of rights to develop hydroelectric power. Actually the first forest reserve was acquired as early as 1891. Theodore Roosevelt increased it from 43 to 194 million acres. By 1967, the federal government owned over 500 million acres of forest and wild-life reserves—nearly one-fourth of the entire area of the United States.

Governmental policy was not only a response to private concern for husbanding natural resources, it led the way to private practices for minimizing waste. Among the varied forms which the long-range program took were contour plowing to reduce erosion of farm lands; reforestation; development of more productive strains of crop plants so that the same land area could produce a greater harvest; chemical weed control; reclamation of dry land through irrigation and of swamps by drainage; extraction of more oil and gas from wells by means of applying pressure; devising of means to utilize economically ores of lower grade; and utilization of new sources of power, such as atomic and solar energy, to lessen reliance on the exhaustible sources of coal, oil, and gas.

Some of these methods, such as irrigation, have been used for thousands of years. Others are new, their urgency having become more apparent from the rapid increase in the world's population and its higher standards of living.

Petro-chemicals. Included under the term "Petro-chemicals" is a large and growing list of products made from hydro-carbon raw materials derived from petroleum or natural gas sources. Some of these basic petro-chemicals are directly useful and are valued for their own sake. In general, however, they are important as "building blocks" for derivative products which creative chemistry has been turning out in almost incredible variety.

Pioneer research in petro-chemicals dates from the 1920's and 1930's, when methanol, formaldehyde, and ammonia made from natural gas were produced in commercial quantities. At this time *butadiene* was also produced from hydro-carbon raw materials.

In somewhat the same way that England and later Germany developed dyes and other by-products from coal in the nineteenth century, petroleum and chemical companies have recently developed innumerable useful products related to and growing out of the basic petroleum industry. Among the additions having commercial importance which are indebted at least in part to petro-chemical research are, to mention a few, plastics, high octane fuels, ethylene glycol anti-freeze solutions, aniline dyes, and, of course, synthetic rubber.

Urbanization. This term means, strictly speaking, increasing the proportion of a nation's population which lives in cities or other urban places. Mere increase in the urban population at the same rate as the total population grows is excluded from the term. Popularly, however, the term is understood as the growth of big cities.

Cities first arose about 3500 B.C. after the agricultural revolution had made possible the storage of food, the concentration of wealth, the specialization in mechanical skills, and the exercise of political and military power. There was a temporary set-back in Europe after the fall of the Roman Empire. Then with the growth of trade and the industrial revolution came the rapid rise of giant cities. Their growth accelerated as mechanization lessened the need for workers on the farm and as the cities drew more and more people to participate in their expanding opportunities for work and their other attractions. The attractions, of course, were not merely economic. The quickened pace of social and intellectual life acted as a magnet to the more gifted individuals. Hence it was the cities which were the growing points of art, science, politics, and literature.

Such was the process by which cities in Europe and America grew, drawing people from the farms as agriculture became more efficient and needed fewer workers. A different picture is presented in many countries, such as India, where agriculture continued to absorb the activities of most workers. Growth of cities came from natural increase of population and from the destitute whom farms could no longer support. Many newcomers learned to exist in the cities literally without shelter or in huts built on public property, sometimes blocking the streets and complicating the problems of sanitation and transportation.

In the 19th century, the distinction between city and rural area was usually sharp. Farms extended up to the city limits. But with the coming of the automobile, city dwellers spread into suburbs or the open country, where they lived while working in the city. It became common for a city or town to expand until it established contact with a neighbor settlement; as far as the traveler could tell, the two then formed a continuous urban place. This gave rise to the term metropolis applied to a city and its adjoining suburbs, which were often cities in their own right. Continuation of the process promised to lead to supercities, to which the name megalopolis has been applied. One such megalopolis envisaged in the future would stretch from Washington, D.C., to Boston, taking in Baltimore, Philadelphia, and many other cities along the eastern seaboard.

Decay of Cities. The rapid growth of cities into metropolises in the 20th century frequently brought about the decay of the central city. Families better able to move their places of residence into more open territory did so; stores and other business establishments soon followed. Many central cities lost population, those remaining tending to be in lower economic levels. Thus slum areas enlarged, and buildings fell into disrepair. At the same time, transportation problems became more acute since suburbanites commuted to and from the city usually in their own cars, thus creating dense traffic that could be accommodated only by better and more expensive highways. All this was accompanied by a declining tax base, so that education and other services often suffered. One result in the United States was a tendency for the central city to have a predominantly Negro population—a result which complicated the national policy of racial integration and led to extensive racial riots.

Urban Renewal. The earliest systematic attack on the problem of city decay took the form of slum clearance, which was emphasized in the Federal Housing Act of 1949. Under this and later legislation, financial assistance by the government was provided to promote rehabilitation of older residential properties and to encourage the expansion of commercial and industrial enterprises. A community renewal program was provided for in 1959, under which assistance was granted in the construction of new buildings in blighted areas. Displaced businesses were assisted in relocation. For relocating displaced slum dwellers in quarters which they could afford, rent subsidies were proposed. To further these and like measures, a cabinet post of housing and urban development was created in 1965.

Some cities did not wait for government assistance in their reconstruction plans. In Pittsburgh, for example, an association of private citizens reconstructed the dingy center of their city into the so-called Golden Triangle, where 28 major buildings were erected with an investment of $259 million. Going forward at the same time were major improvements throughout the city, including new highways, tunnels, bridges, parks, and a huge auditorium and sports arena. San Francisco began construction of a mass transportation system on an unprecedented scale. Washington, D.C., advanced plans first for a cultural center and then for a vast national square designed to transform the city's center into a scene of novel grandeur. There were few large American cities in the 1960's which did not have, in process or in planning, changes not only to combat decay but to approximate new ideals of beauty and utility.

Leading cities abroad showed the same spirit of adaptation. Some, like Rotterdam, took advantage of wide-spread destruction in World War II to replan the city. Others, like Paris, rethought their problems, chiefly in transportation, and proceeded with modern solutions despite the cost. Stockholm, with a 300-year history of city planning, continued its improvements, enlarging them into new suburbs. Toronto and Montreal rebuilt central areas in forms to challenge comparison. Venezuela began construction of an entirely new city; Guyana, ambitiously designed to establish the economy of the country on a base wider than its dominant oil industry.

The United States government in 1966 instituted a program of making funds available to the states for construction of model cities. Therein it followed a lead already made with the backing of industrial and financial institutions. A typical real estate development of this kind envisages the construction, over a period of years, of a balanced independent community zoned for industry, trade, residential and park areas, with provision for education, recreation, church and other community activities, and maximum convenience in transportation. Some of them also provide for neighborhood control of grounds owned in common.

Transistors. The transistor (**tran**sfer re**sistor**) was introduced to the public by a patent filed June 17, 1948. Its development over more than 20 years resulted from the efforts of many scientists, including not only William Schockley, John Bardeen, and Walter H. Brattain, whose names are associated with the invention, but also Seymour Benzer and others. Contributory studies were made at such research centers as Purdue University and the Bell Telephone Laboratories. Some of the more significant findings could have been released as early as 1942, but were withheld as a matter of wartime secrecy.

The core of a transistor is a tiny block of semi-conducting material, usually germanium. A semi-conductor is a material that conducts electricity better than an insulator (such as glass), but not as well as a conductor (such as copper). In ordinary copper wire, the copper atoms have electrons that are "free" to move from atom to atom. Such an electron flow forms a current. In an ideal state, semi-conductors would be insulators because they would have no free electrons. However, when small amounts of impurities such as phosphorus or arsenic are present, a few free electrons are produced and can move and form a current. These are called *n-type* semi-conductors; the *n* meaning *negative* for the negative charge of the electrons in n-type materials.

Another kind, *p-type* semi-conductors, are formed by the addition of tiny quantities of other impurities, such as boron or aluminum. These impurities take electrons away from a few atoms of the semi-conductor, and this lack of an electron is called a "hole." A hole can pass from one atom to another and a flow of such holes from atom to atom also forms an electric current. The letter *p* means *positive*, referring to the positive charge associated with holes in p-type materials. Current moving through a thin wire contact in either type emerges amplified as much as 200 times through another contact only 2/1000 of an inch away.

In its application to commercial and scientific products, the transistor has shown surprising versatility. As a tiny amplifier and rectifier, it has been employed in telephone communication made possible by a small battery fed by solar energy. Whether it is used in radio, in hearing aids, in electronic computers, or in lightweight instruments carried by earth satellites, the transistor can do the work of bulky vacuum tubes and can operate more reliably in the process. Among the advantages claimed foı it in addition to its small size are these points in its favor: it needs no light voltage power but operates "cold;" it is unbreakable; and it has a long life. An early and limited use of semi-conductors, which are essential to its construction, is recalled from the 1920's. Older persons looking back to that period, when they first became acquainted with radio, are familiar with the so-called "cat's whisker" receiver in a "crystal" set which utilized a detector crystal, or semi-conductor, to produce audible reception. From this primitive use of the semi-conductor (half conductor and half insulator) to the fully developed era of transistors is an amazing chapter of scientific and inventive progress.

Thermoelectric Effect. If two dissimilar conductors are connected together so as to form a closed loop, an electric current is observed to flow in the loop when one of the junctions where the two conductors are joined is maintained at a different temperature than the other junction. This effect was first observed by Johann Thomas Seebeck in 1821. While the current that flows in such a circuit is dependent on the resistance of the circuit, it is found that, for any given pair of conducting materials, the electromotive force developed in the circuit depends only on the temperature difference between the two junctions. It is this property of such a circuit that renders it a very practical devise for the measurement of temperature. This type of circuit when used for the measurement of temperature is referred to as a *thermocouple.*

As usually employed, one junction of the thermocouple is maintained at a fixed known temperature while the other junction is exposed to the temperature to be measured, e.g. placed in a furnace or fastened directly to a body whose temperature is to be determined. Since the electromotive force developed in the circuit depends only on the temperature difference between the junctions, and the temperature of one junction is known, a simple measurement of the electromotive force in the circuit gives a direct measure of the temperature of the other junction.

Another possible application of Seebeck's discovery is the generation of electric power by the direct conversion of heat to electrical energy. Until quite recently the use of such a thermoelectric generator was not considered practical because of the low efficiency of such a device constructed from available conducting materials. However, with the recent advances in the field of solid state physics and the availability of semi-conductor materials having thermoelectric efficiencies many times greater than that of previously available materials, considerable effort has been directed toward the development of practical thermoelectric generators and such generators are now available.

What is essentially the inverse of the Seebeck effect was observed in 1834 by Jean Charles Athanase Peltier. Peltier found that, if a battery were placed in a circuit loop made up of two dissimilar conductors such as Seebeck had used, so that an electric current was made to flow through the circuit, heat was generated at one of the circuit junctions while at the other junction heat was absorbed, that is, it was cooled. The practical application of this effect, like that of Seebeck's effect, had to await the developments of modern solid state physics. However, today thermoelectric cooling is finding extensive use.

Miniaturization. An important trend in modern manufacturing is toward producing smaller and more compact units of equipment for a great variety of uses. Typical of this development is the reduction in size of radio receiving sets. With equal or greater range and clarity of reception, the sets have become small, compact, and conveniently portable—in many instances even pocket-size. The perfecting of transistors has made possible almost unlimited reduction in the bulk and weight of these products. Similarly, in space exploration, where weight is a vital factor, and in various types of industrial operations, battery-operated units and other small automatic equipment have proved effective in accomplishing results that could not possibly be achieved by so-called "standard-size" units. A related "anti-bulk" development is the microfilm copying of documents, records, and even books, for convenience of storage, with facilities for reading in magnified form when desired.

Computer. This is a mechanical or electrical device which carries out mathematical and logical operations in accordance with a program of instructions. There are two broad types: the digital computer, in which the data to be processed are supplied in unit form, such as figures, letters of the alphabet, or other distinct symbols; and the analogue computer, in which the data are fed to the computer in a continuous stream, as in wave forms or graphs.

The earliest known form of digital computer is the abacus, which was in use in China thousands of years ago. The calculating machine was invented in the 17th century by Leibniz and Pascal, and a series of developments and adaptations led, in the 20th century, to the electric accounting machine, so-called punch card equipment, which was the precursor of the electronic computer. Analogue computers constructed of bronze by the ancient Greeks have been found in underwater explorations in the Ægean Sea. Planimeters and the differential analyzer developed by Vanevar Bush are examples of other such devices of a mechanical character.

Today it is the electronic computer which the man on the street is talking about when he refers to the "giant brain." In 1950 the first commercial computer, UNIVAC, invented by Messrs. Eckert and Mauchly, appeared on the market. From 10 to 15 machines in 1950, the number is estimated to have grown to 35,200 in the United States alone by 1966 with an expectation of 85,000 computers by 1975. In 1966, 200,000 people were engaged as programmers, preparing instructions for computers. Estimates for the five years following were as high as 500,000.

The computer has input and output devices. The input devices feed data into its central processor, where logic and memory units are located. The central processor operates with basic units of information, which are called "bits," a contraction of the words "binary digits." Hence it is into this form that the input devices convert the punched cards, punched paper tape, and direct input from magnetic tape, drums, or discs which are fed to them. Conversely, the central processor transmits data in "bit" form to various output devices, such as printers, typewriters, card punches or TV screens for the human user.

An electrical device, such as a transistor which can be in either of two states, is the basis of the computer. The two states—"magnetized" and "demagnetized"—are treated as two digits (0 and 1) in the binary scale (scale of 2), by which all numbers can be expressed. By combining these devices into registers, bit combinations are added. Usually, a seven bit code is sufficient to indicate any required symbol. For example, electrical pulses 0110001 could represent the figure 1 and pulses 1000001, the letter A.

The central processor is composed of logic elements (which control the paths to be followed by the "bits" of data) and memory elements (which store data until they are needed for subsequent processing). Here again the binary system is used. Within the memory elements are included arithmetic and control registers. Memory also provides areas for storage of program instructions, results of computations, and other general information for look-up purposes.

Since each computer has its own "machine language," this means there is not much compatibility between the computers produced by different manufacturers. All computers operate under the direction of programs, consisting of instructions prepared by "programmers." These programs are usually written in languages designed to facilitate the job for humans, such as the pattern of holes punched in cards, and the machine then translates these languages into their own "machine language." COBOL (Common Business Orientated Language) and FORTRAN (Formula Translation Language) are examples of languages used by programmers.

The speeds at which computers operate are limited only by the speed of light. This is the reason why every improvement in circuitry has improved computer performance. It is now possible for switching elements to change state in a few billionths of a second. With miniaturization of circuits, additional speed is gained. Problems which took an hour to solve on the 1950 computers could be completed in two or three seconds on the computer of 1966.

Among the uses to which computers can be put are:

1. Data processing in business, including accounting, customer billing, inventory control, and payroll preparation.

2. Process control in industry. Some plants, such as oil refineries, are run by computers from the moment crude oil is received until distillates are released.

3. Calculations in science. Calculations which are now possible would be ruled out by the time factor with only human operators. These include those on which space travel depends.

4. Teaching machines. These make possible programmed learning designed to permit each student to "converse" with a computer on an individual basis while his fellow student pursues his own studies at a different pace.

5. Monitoring patients in hospitals. The machines can take over many housekeeping functions from nurses.

6. Information retrieval. It is possible to obtain in an instant information previously organized under key words and fed into a machine.

It is known that the brain operates on the same principle as the computer in performing like operations. The brain, however, has an immensely greater number of the "electrical devices." The complex thoughts of the brain, as required for example in translating, strain or exceed the capacity of computers.

Within 20 years the computer brought to the daily activities of industry and science a revolutionary increase in capability. Its more sanguine spokesmen foresee the use of the "home computer" by which a person can push a selected button and obtain almost any desired item of information through a telephone circuit to central libraries, banks, stores, and warehouses of goods and knowledge.

Fuel Cell. The fuel cell is essentially a battery which, similar to the more familiar batteries (e.g. dry cells or storage batteries), generates electrical energy from chemical energy through the mechanism of an oxidation reaction taking place at one electrode and a reduction reaction taking place at a second electrode within the battery. The fuel cell however differs from the conventional batteries in that both the fuel that is oxidized and the oxidant are not constituents of the electrodes, but are continually supplied to the electrodes from a source external to the cell.

Thus in the operation of the fuel cell no part of the cell is consumed in the operation and the cell will function indefinitely as long as fuel and an oxidant are supplied to it. One of the attractive features of the fuel cell is that it can operate on a large variety of fuels that are both readily available and relatively inexpensive. Fuel cells using either air or oxygen gas for the oxidant have been successfully operated using such fuels as hydrogen, gaseous hydrocarbons, and alcohol. By operating the fuel cell at high temperatures it is even possible to use such fuels as ordinary coal.

Laser (*lā'zẽr*). (light amplification by stimulated emission of radiation). The laser is a device with which it is possible to obtain the amplification of light by utilizing the phenomenon of stimulated emission of radiation. This phenomenon is best described on the basis of Bohr's Theory of the atom. When the electrons in the atoms of certain elements are excited, that is, raised from their normal energy levels to higher energy levels, the electrons do not immediately jump back down to the lower energy levels, but linger for a while in the higher levels. In a volume containing a large number of such excited atoms of a particular element, the spontaneous return of the electrons to their lower energy levels, which act is accompanied by the emission of a quantum of radiation, is a completely random process and the quanta of radiation emitted, while they will all have the same energy (and frequency), since they originate from the same kind of atom, will be emitted at different times and in different directions yielding what is referred to as incoherent radiation.

It is, however, a property of an excited atom that the return of the electron to its lower energy state can be stimulated by an encounter with a quantum of radiation whose energy is exactly equal to the energy of the quantum the electron itself will emit when it jumps to its lower energy level. Furthermore, the quantum emitted by the electron will be in phase (that is, time-wise) identical with the stimulating quanta and will travel in the same direction. Thus in a volume containing a large number of identical excited atoms the spontaneous jump of an electron to its lower orbit in one of the atoms will emit a quantum of radiation. If before this quantum escapes from the volume it encounters another excited atom, it will stimulate that atom to emit a quantum, the result being two quanta traveling together. Continuing on, every excited atom encountered will be stimulated to add its quantum to the others, the net effect being a continual build-up of the number of quanta in the beam of radiation.

Unfortunately in any reasonable volume of material most of the quanta emitted will escape from the volume before encountering very many if any excited atoms. Thus there is normally little build-up of radiation in this fashion. This difficulty, however, is overcome in the laser.

In a laser the active volume of excited atoms is in the shape of a long cylinder. At each end of the cylinder there is a mirror set perpendicular to the axis of the cylinder. Thus when an atom emits a quantum parallel to the axis of the cylinder, the quantum cannot escape on hitting the end of the cylinder, but will be reflected back along the length of the cylinder. As a consequence, the quantum will travel back and forth along the length of the cylinder stimulating the emission of quanta by other excited atoms resulting in the build-up of a very great number of quanta all moving together and forming a very intense beam of radiation. Of course unless this beam can get out of the laser, it will be of little value. For this reason the mirror at one end of the laser volume is made only partially reflecting so it will be partially transparent allowing a portion of the laser beam to escape out of the laser volume. It is this radiation that escapes that constitutes the output beam of the laser. Not only is this output beam extremely intense, but it has the property of being coherent. This means that, although the beam is made up of quanta emitted by a very great number of atoms randomly distributed throughout the laser volume, the beam acts as though it were emitted by a single source.

The same principle can be applied to the amplification of microwave radiation, and the resulting device is called the *maser*. Historically, the invention of the maser preceded that of the laser, and masers are presently being used to amplify the faint radiation received from remote parts of the universe by radio telescopes.

Year	Name	Dates	Nationality	Representative Achievements
Chemistry				
1901	Van't Hoff, J. H. . . .	1852-1911	Dutch	Founded science of stereochemistry; osmotic pressure.
1902	Fischer, Emil	1852-1919	Ger.	Synthetic production of sugar.
1903	Arrhenius, Svante A. . .	1859-1927	Swed.	Theory of ionization in electrolysis of liquids.
1904	Ramsay, William . . .	1852-1916	Eng.	Discovery of neon and argon.
1905	Baeyer, Adolf von . . .	1835-1917	Ger.	Analysis of indigo; preparation of synthetic dyes.
1906	Moissan, Henri	1852-1907	Fr.	Electric furnace; artificial diamond; isolation of fluorine.
1907	Buchner, Eduard . . .	1860-1917	Ger.	Discovery of cell-less fermentation.
1908	Rutherford, Ernest . . .	1871-1937	Eng.	Proof that atom consists of proton and electrons.
1909	Ostwald, Wilhelm . . .	1853-1932	Ger.	Production of nitrogen explosives from ammonia.
1910	Wallach, Otto	1847-1931	Ger.	Synthesis of essential oils, perfumes, gums.
1911	Curie, Marie S.	1867-1934	Fr.	Discovery of polonium and radium.
1912	Grignard, F. A. Victor .	1871-1935	Fr.	Synthesis of hydrocarbons, alcohols, aldehydes.
	Sabatier, Paul	1854-1941	Fr.	Hydrogenation by catalytic agents.
1913	Werner, Alfred	1866-1919	Swiss	Co-ordination theory of valency.
1914	Richards, Theodore . .	1868-1928	Amer.	Precise determination of atomic weights.
1915	Willstätter, Richard M. .	1872-1942	Ger.	Investigations on coloring substances of plants.
1918	Haber, Fritz	1868-1934	Ger.	Synthetic production of ammonia using nitrogen of air.
1920	Nernst, Walther	1864-1941	Ger.	Invention of electric lamp and reversible galvanic cells.
1921	Soddy, Frederick . . .	1877-1956	Eng.	Formulated theory of isotopes.
1922	Aston, Francis W. . . .	1877-1945	Eng.	Investigation of isotopes by mass spectrograph.
1923	Pregl, Fritz	1869-1930	Austr.	Micro-chemical analysis; antiseptic iodine solution.
1925	Zsigmondy, Richard . .	1865-1929	Ger.	Ultra-microscope; discovery thereby of nature of colloids.
1926	Svedberg, Theodor . . .	1884-1971	Swed.	Investigation of colloids.
1927	Wieland, Heinrich . . .	1877-1957	Ger.	Study of fermentation in digestive processes.
1928	Windaus, Adolf	1876-1959	Ger.	Discovery of vitamin D; isolation of same.
1929	Harden, Sir Arthur . . .	1865-1940	Eng.	Investigation of enzyme action in sugar fermentation.
	Euler-Chelpin, H. von .	1873-1964	Swed.	Investigation of enzyme action in sugar fermentation.
1930	Fischer, Hans	1881-1945	Ger	Synthesis of hemin, blood constituent.
1931	Bergius, Friedrich . . .	1884-1949	Ger.	Liquefaction of coal to produce gasoline.
	Bosch, Karl	1874-1940	Ger.	Commercial production of ammonia from nitrogen of air.
1932	Langmuir, Irving . . .	1881-1957	Amer.	Gas-filled tungsten lamp; atomic hydrogen produced.
1934	Urey, Harold C.	1893-	Amer.	Discovery of heavy water.
1935	Joliot-Curie, Frédéric . .	1900-1958	Fr.	Method of transmuting elements by displacement or
	Joliot-Curie, Irène . . .	1897-1956	Fr.	addition of component parts of atoms.
1936	Debye, Peter J. W. . .	1884-1966	Dutch	Studies in atomic architecture of molecules.
1937	Haworth, Walter Norman	1883-1950	Eng.	Researches on vitamin C.
	Karrer, Paul	1889-1971	Swiss	Studies of vitamins A and G, and vegetable coloring.
1938	Kuhn, Richard*	1900-1967	Ger.	Isolation of vitamin G (lactoflavin).
1939	Butenandt, Adolph F. J.*	1903-	Ger.	Isolation of male sex hormone (androsterone).
	Ruzicka, Leopold . . .	1887-1976	Swiss	Synthesis of androsterone from sheep-wool fat.
1943	Hevesy, Georg von . . .	1885-1966	Hung.	Isotopes used as indicators in studying chemical processes.
1944	Hahn, Otto.	1879-1968	Ger.	Work on splitting uranium atom.
1945	Virtanen, Artturi I . . .	1895-1973	Finn.	Agricultural biochemistry.
1946	Sumner, James B. . . .	1887-1955	Amer.	Enzyme research.
	Northrop, John H. . . .	1891-	Amer.	Virus research.
	Stanley, Wendell M. . .	1904 1971	Amer.	Virus research.
1947	Robinson, Sir Robert . .	1886-1975	Eng.	Investigation of biologically important plant products.
1948	Tiselius, Arne	1902-1971	Swed.	Biochemical study of proteins, enzymes.
1949	Giauque, William . . .	1895-	Can.	Research in thermodynamics, especially on substances at low temperatures.
1950	Diels, Otto	1876-1954	Ger.	Discovery of diene synthesis, by which odors and com-
	Alder, Kurt	1902-1958	Ger.	plex chemical compounds can be reproduced artificially.
1951	Seaborg, Glenn T. . . .	1912-	Amer.	Discovery of plutonium.
	McMillan, Edwin M. . .	1907-	Amer.	
1952	Martin, Archer	1910-	Eng.	Developing method of identifying and separating chem-
	Synge, Richard	1914-	Eng.	ical elements by chromatographic analysis.
1953	Staudinger, Hermann . .	1881-1965	Ger.	Research in giant molecules.
1954	Pauling, Linus C. . . .	1901-	Amer.	Discoveries of forces which hold molecules together.
1955	Vigneaud, Vincent du .	1901-	Amer.	First synthesis of a polypeptide hormone.
1956	Hinshelwood, Cyril N. .	1897-1967	Eng.	Work on chemical reaction kinetics to improve the
	Semenov, Nikolai N. . .	1896-	USSR	internal combustion engine and plastics.
1957	Todd, Sir Alexander . .	1907-	Eng.	Work in proteins—nucleotides and nucleotic enzymes.
1958	Sanger, Frederick . . .	1918-	Eng.	Work on structure of proteins, especially insulin.
1959	Heyrovsky, Jaroslav . .	1890-1967	Czech.	Discovery and development of polarographic analysis.
1960	Libby, Willard F. . . .	1908-	Amer.	For carbon 14 dating in archaeology, geology, etc.
1961	Calvin, Melvin	1911-	Amer.	Sequence of chemical reactions in photosynthesis.
1962	Perutz, Max F.	1914-	Eng.	For mapping protein molecules with the use of X-rays.
	Kendrew, John C. . . .	1917-	Eng.	
1963	Ziegler, Karl	1898-1973	Ger.	For their work in uniting simple hydrocarbons into large
	Natta, Giulio	1903-	Ital.	molecule substances with important commercial uses.
1964	Hodgkin, Dorothy C. . .	1910-	Eng.	Determined the structure of biochemical compounds essential in combating pernicious anemia.
1965	Woodward, Robert B. .	1917-	Amer.	Contributions to the art of organic synthesis.
1966	Mullikan, Robert S. . .	1896-	Amer.	Work on the electronic structure of molecules.
1967	Eigen, Manfred	1927-	Germ.	Made it possible to study chemical reactions occurring at speeds as fast as a billionth of a second.
	Norrish, Ronald G. W. .	1897-	Eng.	
	Porter, George	1920-	Eng.	
1968	Onsager, Lars	1903-1976	Amer.	For his findings regarded as the fourth law of thermodynamics, or the science dealing with relations of heat.
1969	Barton, Derek H. R. . .	1918-	Eng.	Work concerning the shape, or conformation of organic
	Hassel, Odd	1897-	Nor.	molecules.
1970	Leloir, Luis F.	1906-	Argen.	Discovery of sugar nucleotides.
1971	Herzberg, Gerhard . . .	1904-	Can.	Research in molecular structure.

***Prize declined because of disapproval by German government**

Year	Name	Dates	Nationality	Representative Achievements
Chemistry—Con.				
1972	Anfinsen, Christian B.	1916-	Amer.	Explanation of structure of enzymes, particularly the enzyme ribonuclease, a catalyst in the digestive process.
	Moore, Stanford	1913-	Amer.	
	Stein, William H.	1911-	Amer.	
1973	Fischer, Ernst	1918-	Ger.	For independent studies on control of auto exhaust pollution.
	Wilkinson, Geoffrey	1921-	Eng.	
1974	Flory, Paul	1910-	Amer.	For achievements in the physical chemistry of polymers—long-chained molecules—developing new industrial products.
1975	Cornforth, John	1917-	Austral.	For their work in defining the three-dimensional structure of organic molecules. Cornforth's work was concentrated on enzymes; Prelog's focused on other organic molecules, including antibiotics.
	Prelog, Vladimir	1906-	Yug.	
1976	Lipscomb, William N.	1919-	Amer.	"For his studies on the structure of boranes illuminating problems of chemical bonding."

Literature *Italics* indicate titles of books.

Year	Name	Dates	Nationality	Representative Achievements
1901	Sully-Prudhomme, René	1839-1907	Fr.	Poet; *La justice, Le bonheur.*
1902	Mommsen, Theodor	1817-1903	Ger.	Historian; *History of Rome.*
1903	Björnson, Björnstjerne	1832-1910	Nor.	Novels, dramas, poems: *The Newly Married.*
1904	Mistral, Frédéric	1830-1914	Fr.	Poet of Provence; *Mirèio.*
	Echegaray, José	1832-1916	Span.	Dramatist; *The Great Galeota.*
1905	Sienkiewicz, Henryk	1846-1916	Pol.	Novelist; *Quo Vadis?*
1906	Carducci, Giosuè	1836-1907	Ital.	Poet; *Decennali, Odi barbare.*
1907	Kipling, Rudyard	1865-1936	Eng.	Poems, novels; *Puck of Pook's Hill.*
1908	Eucken, Rudolf	1846-1926	Ger.	Philosophical writer; *Religion and Life.*
1909	Lagerlöf, Selma	1858-1940	Swed.	Poems, novels; *Gösta Berling's Saga.*
1910	Heyse, Paul	1830-1914	Ger.	Short stories; *Book of Friendship.*
1911	Maeterlinck, Maurice	1862-1949	Belg.	Dramas, essays; *The Bluebird, The Life of the Bee.*
1912	Hauptmann, Gerhart	1862-1946	Ger.	Dramatist; *The Sunken Bell.*
1913	Tagore, Rabindranath	1861-1941	Ind.	Poet: *Lover's Gift, The Fugitive.*
1915	Rolland, Romain	1866-1944	Fr.	Novelist; *Jean-Christophe.*
1916	Heidenstam, Verner von	1859-1940	Swed.	Poet, novelist; *Charles XII and his Wars.*
1917	Gjellerup, Karl	1857-1919	Dan.	Novelist; *The Pilgrim Carmenita.*
	Pontoppidan, Henrik	1857-1943	Dan.	Novelist: *The Promised Land.*
1919	Spitteler, Karl	1845-1924	Swiss	Poet, essayist; *Olympic Spring, Truths Spoken in Jest*
1920	Hamsun, Knut	1859-1952	Nor.	Novelist; *Growth of the Soil.*
1921	France, Anatole	1844-1924	Fr.	Novelist; *The Human Tragedy.*
1922	Benavente y Martinez, J.	1866-1954	Span.	Dramatist; *La Malquerida.*
1923	Yeats, William Butler	1865-1939	Irish	Poet, dramatist; *The Hourglass.*
1924	Reymont, Wladislaw	1868-1925	Pol.	Novelist; *The Peasants.*
1925	Shaw, George Bernard	1856-1950	Eng.	Dramatist; *Man and Superman.*
1926	Deledda, Grazia	1875-1936	Ital.	Novels of Sardinian life; *The Mother, Ashes.*
1927	Bergson, Henri	1859-1941	Fr.	Philosophical works; *Creative Evolution.*
1928	Undset, Sigrid	1882-1949	Nor.	Novelist; *Kristin Lavransdätter.*
1929	Mann, Thomas	1875-1955	Ger.	Novelist; *Die Buddenbrooks.*
1930	Lewis, Sinclair	1885-1951	Amer.	Novelist; *Main Street, Babbitt, Arrowsmith.*
1931	Karlfeldt, Erik A.	1864-1931	Swed.	Poet; *Songs of the Wilderness and of Love.*
1932	Galsworthy, John	1867-1933	Eng.	Novelist, dramatist; *The Forsyte Saga, Strife.*
1933	Bunin Ivan	1870-1953	USSR	Novelist, short story writer; *The Village.*
1934	Pirandello, Luigi	1867-1936	Ital.	Novelist, dramatist; *As You Desire Me.*
1936	O'Neill, Eugene	1888-1953	Amer.	Dramatist; *Strange Interlude, Anna Christie*
1937	Martin du Gard, Roger	1881-1958	Fr.	Novelist; *Les Thibaults.*
1938	Buck, Pearl S.	1892-1973	Amer.	Novelist; *The Good Earth.*
1939	Sillanpää, Frans Eemil	1888-1964	Finn.	Novelist; *The Maid Silja.*
1944	Jensen, Johannes V.	1873-1950	Dane	Poet, novelist; *The Long Journey.*
1945	Mistral, Gabriela	1889-1957	Chilean	Poet; *Sonetos de La Muerte, Desolacion.*
1946	Hesse, Hermann	1877-1962	Swiss	Poet and novelist; *Unterm Rad.*
1947	Gide, André	1869-1951	Fr.	Critic and essayist; his whole literary work
1948	Eliot, T. S.	1888-1965	Eng.	Poet; pioneer work in modern poetry.
1949	Faulkner, William	1897-1962	Amer.	Novelist, short story writer. *Sanctuary.*
1950	Russell, Bertrand	1872-1970	Eng.	Philosopher, writer. *Principia Mathematica.*
1951	Lagerkvist, Pär	1891-1974	Swed.	Poet, essayist, novelist, philosopher; *Barabbas.*
1952	Mauriac, François	1885-1970	Fr.	Novelist, poet, playwright, essayist.
1953	Churchill, Winston	1874-1965	Eng.	Statesman, orator, historian, biographer.
1954	Hemingway, Ernest	1899-1961	Amer.	Novelist; *A Farewell to Arms, For Whom the Bell Tolls.*
1955	Laxness, Halldor Kiljan	1902-	Iceland	For epic power, renewing the great narrative of Iceland.
1956	Jiménez, Juan Ramón	1881-1958	Span.	For his lyrical poetry.
1957	Camus, Albert	1913-1960	Fr.	For his novel, *The Fall,* and plays.
1958	Pasternak, Boris†	1890-1960	USSR	Lyrics, works in the Russian epic tradition.

† Prize declined.

Year	Name	Dates	Nationality	Representative Achievements
Literature—Con.				
1959	Quasimodo, Salvatore . .	1901-1968	Ital.	Lyrics with classical fire, expressing the tragic experience of life in our own times.
1960	St. John Perse (Leger, Alexis)	1887-1975	Fr.	Award made under his pen name St. John Perse for poems, lyrical and philosophical in modern spirit.
1961	Andric, Ivo	1892-1975	Yugoslav	For his principal work, *Bridge on the Drina.*
1962	Steinbeck, John	1902-1968	Amer.	Principally for *The Winter of Our Discontent.*
1963	Seferis, Giorgos . . . . (Seferiades, Giorgos) . .	1900-1971	Greek	For becoming a symbol of all that is indestructible in the Hellenic acceptance of life.
1964	Sartre, Jean-Paul† . . .	1905-	Fr.	Exponent of existentialism.
1965	Sholokhov, Mikhail . .	1905-	USSR	For artistic power and integrity given creative expression in the history of the Russian people.
1966	Agnon, S. Y.	1888-1970	Isr.	Works on life of the Jewish people.
	Sachs, Nelly	1891-1970	Swed.	Writings interpret Israel's destiny with touching strength.
1967	Asturias, Miguel Angel .	1899-1974	Guat.	Especially noted for *Mr. President,* a novel about Latin American dictatorship.
1968	Kawabata, Yasunari . .	1899-1972	Jap.	For his narrative mastership in expressing the essence of the Japanese mind.
1969	Beckett, Samuel	1906-	Ireland	For his writing, which acquires its elevation in the destitution of modern man; *Waiting for Godot.*
1970	Solzhenitsyn, Aleksandr I.	1918-	USSR	For the ethical force with which he has pursued the indispensable traditions of Russian literature.
1971	Neruda, Pablo	1904-1973	Chile	Published more than 300 works, translated into 81 languages.
1972	Böll, Heinrich	1917-	Ger.	Contribution to "a renewal of German literature."
1973	White, Patrick	1912-	Austral.	Novels on pioneer life which introduced a new continent into literature.
1974	Johnson, Eyvind	1901-	Swed.	For his "narrative art . . . in the service of freedom."
	Martinsson, Henry . . .	1904-	Swed.	For writings that "reflect the cosmos."
1975	Montale, Eugenio . . .	1896-	Ital.	For his poetry that has "interpreted human values under the sign of an outlook on life with no illusions."
1976	Bellow, Saul	1915-	Amer.	For his novels; *The Adventures of Augie March.*

†Prize declined.

Year	Name	Dates	Nationality	Representative Achievements
Medicine and Physiology				
1901	Behring, Emil A. von .	1854-1917	Ger.	Discovered diphtheria antitoxin.
1902	Ross, Ronald	1857-1932	Eng.	Discovered life history of malaria parasite.
1903	Finsen, Niels R.	1860-1904	Dan.	Discovered curative effect of ultra-violet rays.
1904	Pavlov, Ivan P.	1849-1936	Russ.	Study of animal behavior—conditioned reflex.
1905	Koch, Robert	1843-1910	Ger.	Discovered bacilli of tuberculosis and cholera.
1906	Golgi, Camillo	1844-1926	Ital.	Discovered that nerves form interlacement, not network.
	Ramón y Cajal, Santiago	1852-1934	Span.	Investigations into structure of brain and nerves.
1907	Laveran, Charles L. A. .	1845-1922	Fr.	Discovered blood parasite causing malaria.
1908	Ehrlich, Paul	1854-1915	Ger.	Discovered salvarsan, specific for syphilis.
	Mechnikov, Elie	1845-1916	Russ	Study of immunity in infectious diseases.
1909	Kocher, E. Theodor . .	1841-1917	Swiss	Surgery of the thyroid gland.
1910	Kossel, Albrecht	1853-1927	Ger.	Elucidation of chemical composition of body cells.
1911	Gullstrand, Allvar . . .	1862-1930	Swed.	Investigations into the mechanism of vision.
1912	Carrel, Alexis	1873-1944	Amer.	Transplanting of living tissue.

Year	Name	Dates	Nationality	Representative Achievements
Medicine and Physiology—Con.				
1913	Richet, Charles	1850-1935	Fr.	Studies in anaphylaxis and serum therapy.
1914	Bárány, Robert	1876-1936	Austr.	Methods of diagnosis for disorders of inner ear.
1919	Bordet, Jules	1870-1961	Belg.	Elucidation of antitoxic action; serum for whooping cough.
1920	Krogh, August	1874-1949	Dan.	Discovered element regulating action of blood capillaries.
1922	Hill, Archibald V. . . .	1886-	Eng.	Study of heat produced by muscular activity.
	Meyerhof, Otto	1884-1951	Ger.	Study of chemical changes accompanying muscular contraction.
1923	Banting, Frederick G.. .	1891-1941	Can.	Insulin method for treatment of diabetes.
	MacLeod, John J. R. . .	1876-1935	Can.	Insulin method for treatment of diabetes.
1924	Einthoven, Willem . . .	1860-1927	Dutch	Invented cardiometer for measuring action of heart.
1926	Fibiger, Johannes . . .	1867-1928	Dan.	Experimental production of cancer.
1927	Wagner-Jauregg, Julius .	1857-1940	Austr.	Malarial cure for general paralysis.
1928	Nicolle, Charles	1866-1936	Fr.	Discovered typhus vaccine.
1929	Eijkman, Christiaan . .	1858-1930	Dutch	Discovered vitamin B.
	Hopkins, Frederick G. .	1861-1947	Eng.	Discovered vitamin A.
1930	Landsteiner, Karl . . .	1868-1943	Amer.	Classification of individuals by blood groups.
1931	Warburg, Otto H. . . .	1883-1970	Ger.	Cancer research.
1932	Sherrington, Charles S. .	1857-1952	Eng.	Elucidation of process by which nervous system integrates bodily functions.
	Adrian, Edgar D. . . .	1889-	Eng.	Explanation of physiological basis of sensation.
1933	Morgan, Thomas H. . .	1866-1945	Amer.	Discovered gene, physiological unit of inheritance.
1934	Minot, George R. . . .	1885-1950	Amer.	Discovery of the liver treatment for the cure of pernicious anemia.
	Murphy, William P. . .	1892-	Amer.	
	Whipple, George H. . .	1878-1976	Amer.	
1935	Spemann, Hans	1869-1941	Ger.	Discoveries in connection with embryonic evolution.
1936	Dale, Henry H.	1875-1968	Eng.	Discovery and proof of chemical origin of nervous impulses.
	Loewi, Otto	1873-1961	Austr.	
1937	Szent-Györgyi, Albert von	1893-	Hung.	Study of metabolism and effects of vitamins A and C.
1938	Heymans, Corneille. . .	1892-1968	Belg.	Showed neutral link between blood changes and breathing
1939	Domagk, Gerhard*. . .	1895-1964	Ger.	Discovery of prontosil, forerunner of sulphanilimide.
1943	Dam, Henrik	1895-1975	Amer.	Discovery of vitamin K.
	Doisy, Edward A. . . .	1893-	Amer.	Discovery of the chemical nature of vitamin K.
1944	Erlanger, Joseph	1874-1965	Amer.	Discoveries concerning the highly differentiated functions of single nerve fibers.
	Gasser, Herbert S. . . .	1888-1963	Amer.	
1945	Fleming, Sir Alexander	1881-1955	Eng.	Discovery of penicillin.
	Florey, Sir Howard W.	1898-1968	Austr.	
	Chain, Ernst B.	1906-	Eng.	
1946	Muller, Hermann J. . .	1890-1967	Amer.	Genetics: influence of X-rays.
1947	Cori, Carl F.	1896-	Amer.	Disclosing the mechanism of enzymatic synthesis of glycogen or animal starch.
	Cori, Gerty T.	1896-1957	Amer.	
	Houssay, Bernardo Alberto	1887-1971	Arg.	Discovery of the significance of the hormone produced by the frontal lobe of the hypophasis (pituitary gland).
1948	Müller, Paul	1899-1965	Swiss	Development of insect-killing DDT.
1949	Hess, Walter Rudolph. .	1881-1973	Swiss	Discoveries in brain function.
	Moniz, Antonio	1874-1955	Port.	Brain operations—prefrontal lobotomy.
1950	Kendall, Edward C. . .	1886-1972	Amer.	Research in hormones, including discovery of cortisone.
	Hench, Phillip S. . . .	1896-1965	Amer.	
	Reichstein, Tadeus . . .	1897-	Swiss	
1951	Theiler, Max	1899-1972	Amer.	Discovery of yellow fever vaccine.
1952	Waksman, Selman A. . .	1888-1973	Amer.	Work in discovery of streptomycin.
1953	Lipmann, Fritz A. . .	1899-	Amer.	Discoveries concerning living human cells.
	Krebs, Hans A.	1900-	Eng.	
1954	Enders, John F.	1897-	Amer.	Discovery that poliomyelitis virus is capable of growing in cultures of different tissues.
	Weller, Thomas H. . . .	1915-	Amer.	
	Robbins, Frederick C. .	1916-	Amer.	
1955	Theorell, Hugo	1903-	Swed.	Discoveries concerning oxidation enzymes.
1956	Richards,Jr.,DickinsonW.	1895-1973	Amer.	Forssmann's technique (1929) of working catheter in heart chamber from vein used by Richards and Cournand to test heart functioning.
	Cournand, Andre F. . .	1895-	Amer.	
	Forssmann, Werner . .	1904-	Ger.	
1957	Bovet, Daniel	1907-	It.	For drugs that relieve allergies.
1958	Beadle, George Wells . .	1903-	Amer.	One-half awarded jointly for discovery that genes regulate definite chemical events.
	Tatum, Edward Lawrie .	1909-1975	Amer.	
	Lederberg, Joshua . . .	1925-	Amer.	Genetic recombinations, genetic material of bacteria.
1959	Ochoa, Severo	1905-	Amer.	Discovery of mechanisms in biological synthesis of ribonucleic and deoxyribonucleic acids.
	Kornberg, Arthur . . .	1918-	Amer.	
1960	Medawar, Peter Brian .	1915-	Eng.	Joint discovery of acquired immunological tolerance.
	Burnet, Sir Macfarlane .	1899-	Australian	
1961	Bekesey, Georg von . .	1899-1972	Hung.	For pioneering discoveries in mechanism of the inner ear.
1962	Watson, James Dewey .	1928-	Amer.	"Discoveries concerning molecular structure of nucleic acids" which dictates growth and development of cells of the body.
	Crick, Francis H. C. . .	1916-	Eng.	
	Wilkins, Maurice H. F. .	1916-	Eng.	
1963	Hodgkin, Alan L. . . .	1914-	Eng.	For their research on nerve cells.
	Huxley, Andrew F. . .	1917-	Eng.	
	Eccles, Sir John C. . . .	1903-	Australian	
1964	Bloch, Konrad E. . . .	1912-	Amer.	Discoveries concerning mechanism and regulation of cholesterol and fatty acid metabolism.
	Lynen, Feodor	1911-	Ger.	
1965	Jacob, Francois	1920-	Fr.	Discoveries concerning genetic control of enzyme and virus synthesis.
	Lwoff, Andre	1902-	Fr.	
	Monod, Jaques	1910-1976	Fr.	
1966	Huggins, Charles B. . .	1901-	Amer.	For their pioneer lines of attack on cancer.
	Rous, Francis Peyton .	1879-1970	Amer.	
1967	Hartline, Haldan Keffer .	1903-	Amer.	Discoveries concerning physiological and chemical processes involved as the eye passes messages to the brain.
	Wald, George	1906-	Amer.	
	Granit, Ragnar	1901-	Swed.	
1968	Holley, Robert W . . .	1922-	Amer.	Deciphering the genetic code—key to the way genes determine the function of cells. Working independently, each man solved different parts to the puzzle.
	Khorana, Hargobind . .	1922-	Amer.	
	Nirenberg, Marshall W. .	1927-	Amer.	

***Prize declined because of disapproval by German government.**

Year	Name	Dates	Nationality	Representative Achievements
Medicine and Physiology—Con.				
1969	Delbruck, Max	1906-	Amer.	Study of mechanism of virus infection in living cells.
	Hershey, Alfred D.	1908-	Amer.	
	Luria, Salvador E.	1912-	Amer.	
1970	Axelrod, Julius	1912-	Amer.	Research in the chemistry of nerve transmission.
	Katz, Sir Bernard	1911-	Eng.b.Ger.	
	Von Euler, Ulf	1905-	Swed.	
1971	Sutherland, Earl W.	1915-1974	Amer.	For his work with hormones in metabolic activities.
1972	Edelman, Gerald M.	1929-	Amer.	Investigating the basic structure of antibodies. This spurred research in immunology.
	Porter, Rodney	1917-	Eng.	
1973	Lorenz, Konrad	1903-	Austrian	Behavior study helped explain sexual and aggressive drives in animals and humans.
	Tinbergen, Nikolaas	1907-	Dutch	
	Von Frisch, Karl	1886-	Austrian	
1974	Claude, Albert	1899-	Amer.	Pioneer use of electron microscope in cell studies.
	De Duve, Christian	1917-	Belg.	Discovery of lysosomes, like "stomachs of the cell."
	Palade, George	1912-	Amer.	Discovery of ribosomes, synthesizing proteins inside cells.
1975	Dulbecco, Renato	1914-	Ital.	For their work in viral and cancer research, which could lead to eventual control of cancer.
	Temin, Howard	1934-	Amer.	
	Baltimore, David	1938-	Amer.	
1976	Gajdusek, Daniel Carleton	1923-	Amer.	For study of relation between blood serum and disease.
	Blumberg, Baruch S.	1925-	Amer.	

Year	Name	Dates	Nationality	Representative Achievements
Peace				
1901	Dunant, Jean Henri	1828-1910	Swiss	Founded Red Cross society.
	Passy, Frédéric	1822-1912	Fr.	Founded first French peace society.
1902	Ducommun, Elie	1833-1906	Swiss	An organizer of International Bureau of Peace.
	Gobat, Charles A.	1843-1914	Swiss	Activities in International Bureau of Peace.
1903	Cremer, William R.	1838-1908	Eng.	Founded International Arbitration League.
1904	Inst. International Law		Belg.	Organized at Ghent, Belgium, 1873.
1905	Suttner, Bertha von	1843-1914	Austr.	Pacifist; *Lay Down Your Arms*.
1906	Roosevelt, Theodore	1858-1919	Amer.	Secured peace by mediation in Russo-Japanese war.
1907	Moneta, Ernesto	1833-1918	Ital.	Activities in Lombard League of Peace.
	Renault, Louis	1843-1918	Fr.	Judge on Hague Tribunal.
1908	Arnoldson, Klas P.	1844-1916	Swed.	Pacifist lecturer and author.
	Bajer, Fredrik	1837-1922	Dan.	An organizer of International Bureau of Peace.
1909	Beernaert, A. M. F.	1829-1912	Belg.	Activities in international peace conferences.
	D'Estournelles de Constant, Paul H. B.	1852-1924	Fr.	Member of Hague Permanent Court of Arbitration.
1910	Internatl. Peace Bureau	1891-	Swiss	Founded at Bern, Switzerland, in 1891.
1911	Asser, Tobias M.	1838-1913	Dutch	Studies in international law.
	Fried, Alfred H.	1864-1921	Ger.	Founded German Peace Society.
1912	Root, Elihu	1845-1937	Amer.	Promoted Pan-American unity; plan for World Court.
1913	La Fontaine, Henri	1854-1943	Belg.	Activities in International Bureau of Peace.
1917	International Red Cross		Swiss	Founded at Geneva, Switzerland, in 1863.
1919	Wilson, Woodrow	1856-1924	Amer.	Founder of League of Nations.
1920	Bourgeois, Leon	1851-1925	Fr.	Activities in League of Nations.
1921	Branting, Hjalmar	1860-1925	Swed.	Peaceful separation of Norway and Sweden.
	Lange, Christian	1869-1938	Nor.	Activity in Inter-Parliamentary Union.
1922	Nansen, Fridtjof	1861-1930	Nor.	Pacifist; repatriation of World War prisoners.
1925	Chamberlain, Austen	1863-1937	Eng.	Negotiation of Locarno treaties.
	Dawes, Charles G.	1865-1951	Amer.	Dawes Plan for payment of German reparations.
1926	Briand, Aristide	1862-1932	Fr.	Negotiation of Locarno treaties.
	Stresemann, Gustav	1878-1929	Ger.	Negotiation of Locarno treaties.
1927	Buisson, Ferdinand	1841-1932	Fr.	Early advocate of a league of nations.
	Quidde, Ludwig	1858-1941	Ger.	Pacifist; attacked German imperialism; *Caligula*
1929	Kellogg, Frank B.	1856-1937	Amer.	Negotiation of Paris Pact for outlawry of war
1930	Soederblom, Nathan	1866-1931	Swed.	Religious historian and peace advocate.
1931	Addams, Jane	1860-1935	Amer.	Pacifist lecturer; *Peace and Bread in Time of War*.
	Butler, Nicholas Murray	1862-1947	Amer.	Publicist; advocate of international understanding.
1933	Angell, Sir Norman	1874-1967	Eng.	Author, lecturer; *The Great Illusion*.
1934	Henderson, Arthur	1863-1935	Eng.	President of World Disarmament Conference.
1935	Ossietsky, Carl von	1889-1938	Ger.	Journalist; fearless attacks on militarism.

Year	Name	Dates	Nationality	Representative Achievements
Peace—Con.				
1936	Saavedra Lamas, Carlos	1880-1959	Arg.	Exponent of Pan-American peace pacts.
1937	Cecil of Chelwood, Viscount	1864-1958	Eng.	Active in behalf of League of Nations.
1938	Nansen International Office for Refugees	1921-1938	Swiss	Organ of League of Nations; succeeded 1939 by High Commissioner for Refugees.
1944	International Red Cross	1863-	Swiss	Founded at Geneva, Switzerland, in 1863.
1945	Hull, Cordell	1871-1955	Amer.	Services in promoting United Nations.
1946	Mott, John R.	1865-1955	Amer.	Missionary activities.
	Balch, Emily G.	1867-1961	Amer.	Activities in peace societies.
1947	American Service Comm.	1917-	Amer.	Non-combatant services to soldiers and relief for civilians during and after the World Wars.
	Friends' Service Council .	1915-	Eng.	
1949	Boyd-Orr, Baron	1880-1971	Eng.	Crusader against world food shortage.
1950	Bunche, Ralph J. . . .	1904-1971	Amer.	Work as mediator in Palestine war.
1951	Jouhaux, Léon	1879-1954	Fr.	Anti-Communist labor leader.
1952	Schweitzer, Albert . . .	1875-1965	Fr.	Philosopher, theologian, and medical missionary in Africa.
1953	Marshall, George C. . .	1880-1959	Amer.	Soldier and statesman.
1954	Office UN High Commissioner for Refugees			Founded by UN, 1951.
1955	None awarded			
1956	None awarded			
1957	Pearson, Lester B. . . .	1897-1972	Can.	For aid in settling Suez dispute.
1958	Pire, Dominique Georges	1910-1969	Belg.	Dominican Father, organized relief for refugees.
1959	Noel-Baker, Philip . . .	1889-	Eng.	Promoter of general disarmament. Member of Parliament.
1960	Luthuli, Albert J. . . .	1900-1967	S. Afr.	For amelioration of race relations in South Africa.
1961	Hammarskjold, Dag . .	1905-1961	Swed.	For his diplomatic work for peace.
1962	Pauling, Linus C. . . .	1901-	Amer.	For his campaign against nuclear testing.
1963	International Red Cross	1863-	Swiss	Founded at Geneva, Switzerland, in 1863.
	Red Cross Societies . .	1863-	Swiss	
1964	King, Martin Luther, Jr. .	1929-1968	Amer.	For his leadership of the American Negro cause.
1965	UNICEF . .		UN	United Nations Children's Fund, founded 1946.
	Reserved, 1966, 1967 . .			
1968	Cassin, René	1887-1976	Fr.	For his life work toward the extension of human rights.
1969	International Labor Org.	1919-		Past activities for world peace, and recently in world unemployment and population explosion.
1970	Borlaug, Norman E. . .	1914-	Amer.	For his efforts to ease world hunger through research.
1971	Brandt, Willy	1913-	Ger.	Promotion of East-West peace initiatives.
1972	None awarded			
1973	Kissinger, Henry . . .	1923-	Amer.	For their efforts in resolving the Vietnamese War. (Le Duc Tho refused the award.)
	Le Duc Tho	1911/12-	N. Viet.	
1974	Eisaku Sato	1901-1975	Jap.	For his work toward halting spread of nuclear arms.
	MacBride, Sean	1904-	Irish	For his work for human rights and for the independence of South-West Africa.
1975	Sakharov, Andrei	1921-	Russ.	For his struggle for human rights in the USSR, and for his efforts toward thermonuclear disarmament.
1976	None awarded			

Physics

Year	Name	Dates	Nationality	Representative Achievements
1901	Roentgen, Wilhelm K. .	1845-1923	Ger.	Discovery of X rays.
1902	Lorentz, Hendrik A. . .	1853-1928	Dutch	Investigated effects of magnetism on radiation.
	Zeeman, Pieter	1865-1943	Dutch	Displacement of spectrum lines by magnetic field.
1903	Becquerel, Antoine Henri	1852-1908	Fr.	Discovery of radioactivity.
	Curie, Marie S.	1867-1934	Fr.	Research in radioactivity.
	Curie, Pierre	1859-1906	Fr.	Research in radioactivity
1904	Rayleigh, Lord	1842-1919	Eng.	Discovery of argon.
1905	Lenard, Philipp	1862-1947	Hung.	Discovered penetrating power of cathode rays.
1906	Thomson, Joseph J. . . .	1856-1940	Eng.	Investigation of electrical properties of gases.
1907	Michelson, Albert A . .	1852-1931	Amer.	Determination of the velocity of light.
1908	Lippman, Gabriel . . .	1845-1921	Fr.	Method for color photography; capillary electrometer.
1909	Marconi, Guglielmo . .	1874-1937	Ital	Invention of radiotelegraphy.
	Braun, Ferdinand . . .	1850-1918	Ger.	Improvements in radio transmission.
1910	Waals, Johannes van der	1837-1923	Dutch	Law of continuity of liquid and gaseous states.
1911	Wien, Wilhelm	1864-1928	Ger.	Study of black body radiation.
1912	Dalen, Nils Gustav . . .	1869-1937	Swed.	Invention of automatic regulator for gas lamps.
1913	Kamerlingh-Onnes, Heike	1853-1926	Dutch	Liquefaction of helium at temp. near absolute zero.
1914	Laue, Max von	1879-1960	Ger.	Proof of regular arrangement of atoms in crystals.

Year	Name	Dates	Nationality	Representative Achievements
Physics—Con.				
1915	Bragg, William H.	1862-1942	Eng.	Elucidation of atomic structure of crystals.
	Bragg, William L.	1890-1971	Eng.	Elucidation of atomic structure of crystals.
1917	Barkla, Charles G.	1877-1944	Eng.	Discovery of characteristic radiations of elements.
1918	Planck, Max	1858-1947	Ger.	Formulation of quantum theory.
1919	Stark, Johannes	1874-1957	Ger.	Decomposition of spectrum lines by electric field.
1920	Guillaume, Charles E.	1861-1938	Swiss	Production of invar, showing minimum expansion by heat.
1921	Einstein, Albert	1879-1955	Ger. Am.	Theory of relativity; discovered law of photoelectric effect.
1922	Bohr, Niels H. D.	1885-1962	Dane	Theory of atomic structure—electrons moving in orbits.
1923	Millikan, Robert A.	1868-1953	Amer.	Proof of electrical nature of electrons.
1924	Siegbahn, Karl M. G.	1886-	Swed.	Established unit for measuring short-wave radiations.
1925	Franck, James	1882-1964	Ger.	Laws governing impact of electron upon atom.
	Hertz, Gustav	1887-1975	Ger.	Laws governing impact of electron upon atom.
1926	Perrin, Jean	1870-1942	Fr.	Explained Brownian movement in liquids.
1927	Compton, Arthur H.	1892-1962	Amer.	Proof of wave-length alteration in X-rays striking object.
	Wilson, Charles T. R.	1869-1959	Eng.	"Cloud chamber," for showing path of ionized atoms.
1928	Richardson, Owen W.	1879-1959	Eng.	Study of emission of electricity from hot bodies.
1929	De Broglie, Louis Victor	1892-	Fr.	Research on quantum theory and the wave character of electrons.
1930	Raman, C. V.	1888-1970	Ind.	Study of infra-red transparent substances.
1932	Heisenberg, Werner	1901-1976	Ger.	Set forth principle of uncertainty for electrons.
1933	Schröedinger, Erwin	1887-1961	Ger.	Established belief that the atom is a positive nucleus.
	Dirac, Paul A. M.	1902-	Eng.	Theory of one kind of fundamental particle in nature.
1935	Chadwick, Sir James	1891-1974	Eng.	Discovery of neutron.
1936	Anderson, Carl D.	1905-	Amer.	Discovery of positive electron, or positron.
	Hess, Victor F.	1883-1964	Austr.	Study on origin of cosmic radiation.
1937	Davisson, Clinton J.	1881-1958	Amer.	Interference in electronic bombardment of crystals.
	Thomson, George P.	1892-1975	Eng.	Studies in nature of thin metallic surfaces.
1938	Fermi, Enrico	1901-1954	Ital.	Transmutation of atoms by adding neutrons to nucleus.
1939	Lawrence, Ernest O.	1901-1958	Amer.	Discovery of cyclotron.
1943	Stern, Otto	1888-1969	Amer.	Discovery of magnetic moment of the proton.
1944	Rabi, Isidor I.	1898-	Amer.	For resonance method of recording the magnetic properties of atomic nuclei.
1945	Pauli, Wolfgang	1900-1958	Amer.	Atomic research; "Pauli's exclusion principle."
1946	Bridgman, Percy W.	1882-1961	Amer.	Research in atmospheric pressure.
1947	Appleton, Sir Edward V.	1892-1965	Eng.	Discovery of Appleton layer, reflecting radio short waves.
1948	Blackett, Patrick M. S.	1897-1974	Eng.	Development of Wilson method of studying courses of radioactive particles, and discoveries in cosmic radiation.
1949	Yukawa, Hideki	1907-	Jap.	Mathematical prediction of the meson.
1950	Powell, Cecil F.	1903-1970	Eng.	Work on cosmic rays.
1951	Cockcroft, Sir John D.	1897-1967	Eng.	Pioneer work on transmutation of atomic nuclei by artificially accelerated atomic particles.
	Walton, Ernest T. S.	1903-	Irish	
1952	Bloch, Felix	1905-	Amer.	Development of new method of measuring magnetic fields in atomic nuclei.
	Purcell, Edward Mills	1912-	Amer.	
1953	Zernike, Frits	1888-1966	Dutch	Development of special microscope.
1954	Born, Max	1882-1970	Ger.	Studies in connection with foundation of modern nuclear physics.
	Bothe, Walter	1891-1957	Ger.	
1955	Lamb, Willis E.	1913-	Amer.	Discoveries concerning the hydrogen spectrum.
	Kusch, Polykarp	1911-	Amer.	Determination of the magnetic moment of the electron.
1956	Bardeen, John	1908-	Amer.	Work on an electric transistor.
	Brattain, Walter H.	1902-	Amer.	
	Shockley, William B.	1910-	Amer.	
1957	Lee Tsung-Dao	1926-	Chinese	Contribution to physics, proving conservation of parity does not apply in the case of smashed atoms.
	Yang Chen Ning	1922-	in U. S.	
1958	Cerenkov, Pavel A.	1904-	USSR	Joint discovery and interpretation of Cerenkov effect.
	Frank, Ilja Michajlovic	1908-	USSR	
	Tamm, Igor Evgenevic	1895-1971	USSR	
1959	Segre, Emilio	1905-	Amer.	Awarded jointly for discovery of antiproton.
	Chamberlain, Owen	1920-	Amer.	
1960	Glaser, Donald A.	1926-	Amer.	Inv. "bubble chamber" to photograph atom smashing.
1961	Hofstadter, Robert	1915-1970	Amer.	For work on the atomic nucleus, including proton and neutron.
	Mossbauer, Rudolf L.	1929-	Ger.	
1962	Landau, Lev D.	1908-1968	USSR	Pioneering theories for condensed matter.
1963	Wigner, Eugene P.	1902-	Amer.	For his work in atomic theory.
	Goeppert-Mayer, Maria	1906-1972	Amer.	For discoveries concerning nuclear shell structure.
	Jensen, J. Hans D.	1907-1973	Ger.	
1964	Townes, Charles Hard	1915-	Amer.	Fundamental work in field of quantum electronics which led to construction of oscillators and amplifiers based on maser-laser principle.
	Prochorov, Aleksandre M.	1916-	USSR	
	Basov, Nikolai G.	1922-	USSR	
1965	Tomonaga, Sin-Itiro	1906-	Jap.	Fundamental work in quantum electrodynamics.
	Schwinger, Julian	1918-	Amer.	
	Feynman, Richard P.	1918-	Amer.	
1966	Kastler, Alfred	1902-	Fr.	Laid foundation leading to discovery of the laser.
1967	Bethe, Hans Albrecht	1906-	Ger.	Explained how stars and sun emit heat and light.
1968	Alvarez, Luis W.	1911-	Amer.	Contributions to the physics of subatomic particles.
1969	Gell-Mann, Murray	1929-	Amer.	Study of subatomic particles and their interactions.
1970	Alfvén, Hannes	1908-	Swed.	Pioneering and imaginative theories in plasma physics.
	Néel, Louis E. F.	1904-	Fr.	Discoveries concerning antiferromagnetism and ferrimagnetism, with major applications in solid-state physics.
1971	Gabor, Dennis	1900-	Eng.	Inventing holography, three-dimensional photography.
1972	Bardeen, John	1908-	Amer.	Developed a theory of superconductivity, a property of certain metals to lose all resistance to electric current at very low temperatures.
	Cooper, Leon N.	1930-	Amer.	
	Schreiffer, John R.	1931-	Amer.	
1973	Esaki, Leo	1925-	Jap.-Amer.	Expanded research into miniature electronics and superconductivity.
	Giaever, Ivar	1929-	Nor.-Amer.	
	Josephson, Brian D.	1940-	Eng.	

Year	Name	Dates	Nationality	Representative Achievement
Physics—Con.				
1974	Ryle, Sir Martin	1918-	Eng.	For work enabling radio astronomers to map the skies in detail.
	Hewish, Antony	1924-	Eng.	For role in discovery of pulsars—small, collapsed stars that emit radio-wave pulses.
1975	Bohr, Aage	1922-	Dan.	For research on the inner structure of the atom.
	Mottelson, Benjamin	1926-	Am.-Dan.	
	Rainwater, James	1917-	Amer.	
1976	Richter, Burton	1931-	Amer.	For discovery of a new subatomic particle.
	Ting, Samuel C. C.	1936-	Amer.	
Memorial Awards				
1969	Frisch, Ragnar	1895-1973	Nor.	Work in econometrics; mathematical expression of economic theory.
	Tinbergen, Jan	1903-	Neth.	
1970	Samuelson, Paul A.	1915-	Amer.	For developing scientific analysis in economic theory.
1971	Kuznets, Simon	1901-	Amer.	Gross National Product as measuring economic output.
1972	Arrow, Kenneth J.	1921-	Amer.	Pioneering contributions to general economic equilibrium theory and welfare theory.
	Hicks, John R.	1904-	Eng.	
1973	Leontief, Wassily	1906-	Amer.	"Input-output" method of economic analysis.
1974	Myrdal, Gunnar	1898-	Swed.	For work in theory of money and economic fluctuations, and for analysis of interdependence of economic, social, and institutional factors.
	Hayek, Friedrich von	1899-	Swed.	
1975	Koopmans, Tjalling	1910-	Dutch-Am.	For developing "linear programming" in economics, enabling more efficient use of workers, machines, and raw materials in production growth.
	Kantorovich, Leonid	1912-	USSR	
1976	Friedman, Milton	1912-	Amer.	For his work in international currency policy.

PROBLEMS AND PROGRESS: SELECTED CURRENT READINGS

Aron, Raymond—Industrial Society . *Praeger '67*
—Progress and Disillusion . . . . *Praeger '68*
Ball, George—The Discipline of Power . *Little '68*
Beasley, W. G.—Modern History of Japan *Praeger '74*
Bell, Daniel ed.—Toward the Year 2000 *Houghton '68*
Ben-Gurion, David—Israel: A Personal History *Funk '71*
Berger, R.—Executive Privilege: A Constitutional Myth . . . . *Harvard '74*
Bernstein, Carl & Woodward, Bob—All the President's Men . . . . *Simon & Schuster '74*
Bettelheim, Bruno—The Informed Heart: Autonomy in a Mass Age . . . . *Free Press '60*
Bhata, K.—Indira: A Biography of Prime Minister Gandhi . . . . *Praeger '74*
Carson, Rachel—Silent Spring . . . *Houghton '62*
Chomsky, Noam—American Power and the New Mandarins . . . . *Pantheon '69*
Clark, Kenneth B. & Parsons, Talcott eds.—The Negro American . . . . *Houghton '66*
Erickson, Erik—Childhood and Society *Norton '68*
Fall, Bernard—The Two Viet-Nams . *Praeger '67*
Ferkiss, Victor—Technological Man . *Braziller '69*
Forsythe, D.—United Nations Peacemaking: The Conciliation Commission for Palestine *Hopkins '73*
Frankl, Viktor—Man's Search for Meaning *Beacon '70*
Galbraith, J. K. —The New Industrial State *Houghton '67*
—Money: Whence It Came, Where It Went *Houghton '75*
Gardner, John—No Easy Victories . . *Harper '68*
Green, Mark—The Monopoly Makers *Grossman '73*
Hauser, Philip—The Population Dilemma *Prentice '70*
Heilbroner, Robert—The Limits of American Capitalism . . . . *Harper '66*
Hinton, H. C.—Introduction to Chinese Politics *Abbot '73*
Hodges, M.—Multinational Corporations and National Government . . . . . *Lexington '74*
Houn, F. W.—A Short History of Chinese Communism . . . . *Prentice '73*
Huxley, Julian—The Human Crisis *U. of Wash. '68*
Illich, Ivan—Deschooling Society . . *Harper '71*
Kahler, Erich—The Jews Among the Nations *Ungar '67*
Mead, Margaret—Culture and Commitment: A Study of the Generation Gap . *Doubleday '70*
Mills, C. Wright—The Power Elite . *Oxford '68*
Mintz, Morton & Cohen, J. S.—America, Inc. *Dell '71*
Myrdal, Gunnar—An American Dilemma: The Negro Problem and Modern Democracy *Harper '62*
—Asian Drama: An Inquiry into the Poverty of Nations . . . . . . *Twentieth Century '68*
Nuttall, Jeff—Bomb Culture . . . *Delacorte '68*
Ogley, R.—The U.N. and East-West Relations *Sussex '72*
Padover, S.—Meaning of Democracy . *Praeger '63*
Pfeffer, R. M. ed.—No More Vietnams? *Harper '68*
Rather, Dan & Gates, G.—The Palace Guard *Harper '74*
Reich, Charles—The Greening of American: The Coming of a New Consciousness . . *Random '70*
Reischauer, E. O. ed.—Japan . . . . . *Arno '74*
Richardson, B. M.—The Political Culture of Japan . . . . *U. of California '74*
Rodinson, Maxime—Israel and the Arabs *Pantheon '68*
Roszak, Theodore—The Making of a Counter Culture . . . . *Doubleday '69*
Ryder, A. J.—Twentieth-Century Germany: From Bismarck to Brandt . . . . *Columbia '73*
Sakharov, A. D.—Progress, Coexistence and Intellectual Freedom . . . *New York Times '68*
Salisbury, Harrison—Orbit of China . *Harper '67*
Samuelson, Paul—Economics: An Introductory Analysis . . . . *McGraw '70*
Schlesinger, A. M.—The Bitter Heritage: Vietnam and American Democracy . . *Fawcett '68*
—The Crisis of Confidence: Ideas, Power and Violence in America . . . . . . *Houghton '69*
—The Imperial Presidency . . . *Houghton '73*
Schwab, R. & Friedlander, H.—Detente in Historical Perspective . . . . *Cyrco '75*
Solzhenitsyn, Alexander—The Gulag Archipelago: 1918–1956 . . . . *Association '74*
—The Gulag Archipelago II . . . *Harper '75*
Steiner, Stan—The New Indians . . . *Harper '68*
Still, Henry—Man: The Next Thirty Years *Hawthorn '68*
Taylor, Gordon R.—The Doomsday Book *Holt '70*
—The Biological Time Bomb . . . . *World '68*
Toffler, Alvin—Future Shock . . . . *Random '70*
Udall, Stewart—1976: Agenda for Tomorrow *Harcourt '68*

MASTER INDEX

Letters a, b, c, d following page numbers indicate first, second, third, fourth quarters of page— [a c / b d]

E

G

H

M

Q

R